VIDEOHOUND'S
GUIDE TO
THREE- AND
FOUR-STAR
MOVIES
1998

VIDEOHOUND'S

GUIDE TO

Three- and
Four-Star

MOVIES

1998

A Stonesong Press Book

Broadway Books
New York

A Stonesong Press Book

SECOND EDITION

ISBN 0-7679-0047-2

97 98 99 00 10 9 8 7 6 5 4 3 2 1

CONTENTS

CONTENTS

INTRODUCTION

Welcome to the second year of *VideoHound's Guide to Three- and Four-Star Movies*.

For those of you familiar with *VideoHound's Golden Movie Retriever* and *VideoHound's Guide to Three- and Four-Star Movies 1997*, our advice is to skip the intro and go ahead and choose a film. For newcomers to the world of VideoHound, you're probably asking yourselves, "What kind of film guide is this?!" (*We'll explain.*) "Does the Golden Retriever actually review the films?" (*Duh.*) "Are all of my favorites in here, like *The Princess and the Swineherd*?" (*Sorry, that gem was bypassed here—only three- and four-star movies allowed.*) Well, without any further ado, we'll do our job and give you a proper introduction.

VideoHound's Guide to Three- and Four-Star Movies 1998 is a collection of the 3,200 films that come closest to meeting the tough Video-Hound criteria for film excellence—compelling watchability, strong appeal, and superior craftsmanship. It represents what we consider the best of all American and foreign films available on videocassette, laserdisc, and CD, the picks of the *Golden Movie Retriever* litter. Regrettably, space does not allow us to include all the three-star movies listed in the *Golden Movie Retriever*. If we did not include a film here, it was because its availability on video, its general appeal, and its importance to film history were not as great as other three-star films. In the end, fewer than 20 percent of the films in the *Retriever* made it into this book, an acceptance rate stiffer than some colleges.

The aim of such selectivity is your pleasure and ease of use. We hope this book can help ensure an evening of viewing enjoyment, not a return to the video store before half of the film has been watched. If a title is included in this book, you can be sure it is, in the *VideoHound*'s words, at least a "decent entertainment return on video investment"; some may even reach heights of "masterful cinematic expression." In *VideoHound's Guide to Three- and Four-Star Movies*, you will find only the original 1933 *Dinner at Eight*, not its limp 1989 TV remake. The first title listed under the word "Sunset" will be Billy Wilder's 1950 classic *Sunset Boulevard*, not the weak Blake Edwards 1988 farce *Sunset*. But under the word "Terminator" you will find both the original 1984 science fiction thriller and its even more spectacular 1991 follow-up *Terminator 2: Judgment Day*. In short, if you want a good movie, you will find it here.

Following its predecessor's lead, the selections and reviews in *VideoHound's Guide to Three- and Four-Star Movies* embody the idiosyncratic taste of the VideoHound himself. Among the thousands of films in the book, not only will you find Hollywood classics like *The Godfather* and *Citizen Kane*, but also the VideoHound trademark broad selection of independent and foreign films, and an especially healthy dose of film *noir*, silents, and horror that moves far beyond *Laura*, *Intolerance*, and *The Bride of Frankenstein*.

Like the *Golden Movie Retriever*, *VideoHound's Guide to Three- and Four-Star Movies* features some exceptional indexes that distinguish it from other, less useful video guides. You will still be able to search for films according to such subject areas as Director, Cast, and—especially—category. This category index includes some traditional categories, such as "Romantic Comedy" as well as some unorthodox groupings, such as "Flower Children."

The purpose of *VideoHound's Guide to Three- and Four-Star Movies* is simple. It offers the widest variety of high quality films available in the handiest package. Think of it as an annuity. Or a security blanket. It offers constant, reliable comfort and payment. It will make your life easier.

VIDEOHOUND RATING SCALE

Although we can pretty much guarantee satisfaction on all of the movies in our *Guide to Three- and Four-Star Movies*, the following scale will help you to distinguish between the best and the very best.

★★★ Good story, fine acting provide decent entertainment return on video investment. Would recommend to family members, even distant cousins.

★★★1/2 Memorable cinematic fare with flair, verve, polish, sheen, and panache. Easily able to recommend to friends.

★★★★ Masterful cinematic expression. Flawless or nearly so. Will want to recommend to strangers on the street.

HOW TO USE THIS BOOK

Finding Movies

VideoHound's Guide to Three- and Four-Star Movies is organized alphabetically by the first word in each title. Leading articles *(the, an, a)* are disregarded, except if the title is in a foreign language. When the first word in a title is a number or an abbreviation, it is usually alphabetized as it appears spelled out. Acronyms appear as if they were regular words.

Indexes

Category Index

Topics ranging from "Adoption and Orphans" to "Zombies," plus some other more standard classifications—like "Action Adventure" and "Docudrama"—will help you to choose the perfect video to suit your mood. Arranged alphabetically, you will quickly find three- and four-star video titles on your favorite subjects.

Cast Index

This index contains the three- and four-star movies that feature your favorite celluloid heroes, plus the years of the movies' releases. Included in this index are actors and actresses that appeared in at least three of the three- or four-star films in this book, alphabetized by actors' last names.

Director Index

Alphabetized by last names, this helpful index lists your favorite directors' most well-known *and* most esoteric three- and four-star cinematic creations. The directors mentioned have created at least three three- or four-star films.

Using Reviews

We hope you'll find *VideoHound's* reviews very easy to follow. Some reviews contain more features than others, but all include the information most crucial to the finicky video viewer. Every listing mentions the length of the movie, the year of release, cast members, whether it is shot in black and white or color, format and—of course—a brief critical review. Entries may also include songs, directors, writers, lyricists and composers, alternate titles, and the country where the movie was produced.

Movie review components appear as follows:

- Title
- Brief, descriptive critical review
- Songs ♪ (not included in every entry)
- Alternate title (not included in every entry)
- Year of release
- MPAA rating (not included in every entry)
- Length
- Black and white (B) or color (C)
- Country of production (if not American)
- Cast (includes cameos; V: indicates voiceovers)
- Direction (D) (not included in every entry)
- Writer (W) (not included in every entry)
- Composer/Lyricist (M) (not included in every entry)
- Awards (includes Academy Award nominations)
- Format (Beta, VHS, and/or LV-laserdisc)
- Three- or four-star rating

VIDEOHOUND'S
GUIDE TO
THREE- AND
FOUR-STAR
MOVIES
1998

A Nous la Liberté Two tramps encounter industrialization and automation, making one into a wealthy leader, the other into a nature-loving iconoclast. A poignant, fantastical masterpiece by Clair, made before he migrated to Hollywood. Though the view of automation may be dated, it influenced such films as Chaplin's "Modern Times." In French with English subtitles.
1931 87m/B *FR* Henri Marchand, Raymond Cordy, Rolla France, Paul Olivier, Jacques Shelly, Andre Michaud; *D:* Rene Clair; *W:* Rene Clair. National Board of Review Awards '32: 5 Best Foreign Films of the Year; Nominations: Academy Awards '32: Best Interior Decoration. **VHS, Beta, 8mm ★★★★**

Abbott and Costello Meet Frankenstein Big-budget A&C classic is one of their best efforts and was rewarded handsomely at the box office. Two unsuspecting baggage clerks deliver a crate containing the last but not quite dead remains of Dracula and Dr. Frankenstein's monster to a wax museum. The fiends are revived, wreaking havoc with the clerks. Chaney makes a special appearance to warn the boys that trouble looms. Last film to use the Universal creature pioneered by Karloff in 1931. *AKA:* Abbott and Costello Meet the Ghosts.
1948 83m/B Bud Abbott, Lou Costello, Lon Chaney Jr., Bela Lugosi, Glenn Strange, Lenore Aubert, Jane Randolph; *D:* Charles T. Barton; *V:* Vincent Price. **VHS, Beta, LV ★★★**

Abe Lincoln in Illinois Massey considered this not only his finest film but a part he was "born to play." Correct on both counts, this Hollywood biography follows Lincoln from his log cabin days to his departure for the White House. The Lincoln-Douglass debate scene and Massey's post-presidential election farewell to the citizens of Illinois are nothing short of brilliant. Written by Sherwood from his Pulitzer Prize-winning play. Contrasted with the well-known "Young Mr. Lincoln" (Henry Fonda), its relative anonymity is perplexing. *AKA:* Spirit of the People.
1940 110m/B Raymond Massey, Gene Lockhart, Ruth Gordon, Mary Howard, Dorothy Tree, Harvey Stephens, Minor Watson, Alan Baxter, Howard da Silva, Maurice Murphy, Clem Bevans, Herbert Rudley; *D:* John Cromwell; *W:* Robert Sherwood. Nominations: Academy Awards '40: Best Actor (Massey), Best Black and White Cinematography. **VHS, Beta ★★★★**

The Abominable Dr. Phibes After being disfigured in a freak car accident that killed his wife, an evil genius decides that the members of a surgical team let his wife die and shall each perish by a different biblical plague. High camp with the veteran cast in top form.
1971 (PG) 90m/C *GB* Vincent Price, Joseph Cotten, Hugh Griffith, Terry-Thomas, Virginia North, Susan Travers, Alex Scott, Caroline Munro; *D:* Robert Fuest. **VHS, Beta, LV ★★★**

Above and Beyond Good performance by Taylor as Col. Paul Tibbets, the man who piloted the Enola Gay, which dropped the atomic bomb on Hiroshima. Focuses on the secrecy of the mission and the strain this puts on Tibbets's marriage. Exciting action sequences of the mission itself.
1953 122m/B Robert Taylor, Eleanor Parker, James Whitmore, Larry Keating, Larry Gates, Robert Burton, Jim Backus; *D:* Melvin Frank, Norman Panama; *W:* Melvin Frank, Norman Panama, Beirne Lay Jr. **VHS ★★★**

Above Suspicion MacMurray and Crawford are American honeymooners (poor Fred!) asked to assist an international intelligence organization. They engage the Nazis in a tense battle of wits. Well-made and engaging.
1943 91m/B Joan Crawford, Fred MacMurray, Conrad Veidt, Basil Rathbone, Reginald Owen; *D:* Richard Thorpe. **VHS ★★★**

The Absent-Minded Professor Classic dumb Disney fantasy of the era. A professor accidentally invents an anti-gravity substance called flubber, causing inanimate objects and people to become airborne. Great sequence of the losing school basketball team taking advantage of flubber during a game. MacMurray is convincing as the absent-minded genius in this newly colored version. Followed by "Son of Flubber."
1961 97m/C Fred MacMurray, Nancy Olson, Keenan Wynn, Tommy Kirk, Leon Ames, Ed Wynn, Edward Colman. *D:* Robert Stevenson; *M:* George Bruns, Edward Colman. Nominations: Academy Awards '61: Best Art Direction/Set Decoration (B & W), Best Black and White Cinematography. **VHS, Beta, LV ★★★★**

Accatone! Accatone (Citti), a failure as a pimp, tries his luck as a thief. Hailed as a return to Italian neo-realism, this is a gritty, despairing, and dark look at the lives of the street people of Rome. Pasolini's first outing, adapted by the director from his novel, "A Violent Life." Pasolini

served as mentor to Bernardo Bertolucci, listed in the credits as an assistant director.
1961 116m/B *IT* Franco Citti, Franca Pasut, Roberto Scaringelli, Adele Cambria, Paolo Guidi, Silvana Corsini; *D:* Pier Paolo Pasolini, Tonino Delli Coli. **VHS** ★★★

The Accidental Tourist A bittersweet and subtle story, adapted faithfully from Anne Tyler's novel, of an introverted, grieving man who learns to love again after meeting an unconventional woman. After his son's death and subsequent separation from wife Turner, Macon Leary (Hurt) avoids emotional confrontation, burying himself in routines with the aid of his obsessive-compulsive siblings. Kooky dog-trainer Muriel Pritchett (an exuberant Davis) wins his attention, but not without struggle. Hurt effectively uses small gestures to describe Macon's emotional journey, while Davis grabs hearts with her open performance. Outstanding supporting cast.
1988 (PG) 121m/C William Hurt, Geena Davis, Kathleen Turner, Ed Begley Jr., David Ogden Stiers, Bill Pullman, Amy Wright; *D:* Lawrence Kasdan; *W:* Lawrence Kasdan; *M:* John Williams, John Bailey. Academy Awards '88: Best Supporting Actress (Davis); New York Film Critics Awards '88: Best Film; Nominations: Academy Awards '88: Best Adapted Screenplay, Best Picture, Best Original Score. **VHS, Beta, LV, 8mm** ★★★★

The Accused Provocative treatment of a true story involving a young woman gang raped in a bar while onlookers cheer. McGillis is the assistant district attorney who takes on the case and must contend with the victim's questionable past and a powerful lawyer hired by a wealthy defendant's parents. As the victim with a past, Foster gives an Oscar-winning performance that won raves for its strength and complexity.
1988 (R) 110m/C Jodie Foster, Kelly McGillis, Bernie Coulson, Leo Rossi, Ann Hearn, Carmen Argenziano, Steve Antin, Tom O'Brien, Peter Van Norden, Woody Brown; *D:* Jonathan Kaplan; *W:* Tom Topor; *M:* Brad Fiedel, Ralf Bode. Academy Awards '88: Best Actress (Foster); Golden Globe Awards '89: Best Actress—Drama (Foster); National Board of Review Awards '88: Best Actress (Foster). **VHS, Beta, LV, 8mm** ★★★

Across the Pacific Classic Bogie/ Huston vehicle made on the heels of "The Maltese Falcon." Bogie is an American Army officer booted out of the service on false charges of trea-

son. When no other military will accept him, he sails to China (via the Panama Canal) to offer his services to Chiang Kai-Shek. On board, he meets a variety of seedy characters who plan to blow up the canal. Huston again capitalizes on the counterpoint between the rotundly acerbic Greenstreet, who plays a spy, and stiff-lipped Bogart, who's wooing Astor. Great Bogie moments and fine direction make this an adventure classic. When he departed for the service just prior to filming the final scenes, Huston turned over direction to Vincent Sherman. Also available colorized.
1942 97m/B Humphrey Bogart, Mary Astor, Sydney Greenstreet, Charles Halton, Victor Sen Yung, Roland Got, Keye Luke, Richard Loo; *D:* John Huston. **VHS** ★★★1/2

Adam Television docudrama based on a tragic, true story. John and Reve Williams (Travanti and Williams) desperately search for their six-year-old son abducted during an outing. During their long search and struggle, they lobby Congress for use of the FBI's crime computer. Eventually their efforts led to the creation of the Missing Children's Bureau. Sensitive, compelling performances by Travanti and Williams as the agonized, courageous parents.
1983 100m/C Daniel J. Travanti, JoBeth Williams, Martha Scott, Richard Masur, Paul Regina, Mason Adams; *D:* Michael Tuchner. **VHS, Beta** ★★★1/2

Adam's Rib Classic war between the sexes cast Tracy and Hepburn as married attorneys on opposite sides of the courtroom in the trial of blonde bombshell Holliday, charged with the attempted murder of the lover of her philandering husband. The battle in the courtroom soon takes its toll at home as the couple is increasingly unable to leave their work at the office. Sharp, snappy dialogue by Gordon and Kanin with superb direction by Cukor. Perhaps the best of the nine movies pairing Tracy and Hepburn. Also available colorized.
1950 101m/B Spencer Tracy, Katharine Hepburn, Judy Holliday, Tom Ewell, David Wayne, Jean Hagen, Hope Emerson, Polly Moran, Marvin Kaplan, Paula Raymond, Tommy Noonan; *D:* George Cukor; *W:* Garson Kanin, Ruth Gordon; *M:* Miklos Rozsa. Nominations: Academy Awards '50: Best Story & Screenplay. **VHS, Beta, LV** ★★★★

The Adventures of Baron Munchausen From the director of "Time Bandits," "Brazil," and "The Fisher

King" comes an ambitious, imaginative, chaotic, and underappreciated marvel based on the tall (and often confused) tales of the Baron. Munchausen encounters the King of the Moon, Venus, and other odd and fascinating characters during what might be described as an circular narrative in which flashbacks dovetail into the present and place is never quite what it seems. Wonderful special effects and visually stunning sets occasionally dwarf the actors and prove what Gilliam can do with a big budget.
1989 (PG) 126m/C John Neville, Eric Idle, Sarah Polley, Valentina Cortese, Oliver Reed, Uma Thurman, Sting, Jonathan Pryce, Bill Paterson, Peter Jeffrey, Alison Steadman, Charles McKeown, Dennis Winston, Jack Purvis; *Cameos:* Robin Williams; *D:* Terry Gilliam; *W:* Terry Gilliam; *M:* Michael Kamen, Giuseppe Rotunno. Nominations: Academy Awards '89: Best Costume Design, Best Makeup. **VHS, Beta, LV, 8mm ★★★1/2**

Adventures of Don Juan Flynn's last spectacular epic features elegant costuming and loads of action. Don Juan saves Queen Margaret from her evil first minister. He then swashbuckles his way across Spain and England in an effort to win her heart. Grand, large-scale fun and adventure with Flynn at his self-mocking best. Special laserdisc edition includes the original trailer. *AKA:* The New Adventures of Don Juan.
1949 111m/C Errol Flynn, Viveca Lindfors, Robert Douglas, Romney Brent, Alan Hale, Raymond Burr, Aubrey Mather, Ann Rutherford; *D:* Vincent Sherman; *M:* Max Steiner. Academy Awards '49: Best Costume Design (Color); Nominations: Academy Awards '49: Best Art Direction/Set Decoration (Color). **VHS, Beta, LV ★★★1/2**

The Adventures of Huckleberry Finn Mark Twain's classic story about a boy who runs away and travels down the Mississippi on a raft, accompanied by a runaway slave, is done over in MGM-style. Rooney is understated as Huck (quite a feat), while the production occasionally floats aimlessly down the Mississippi. An entertaining follow-up to "The Adventures of Tom Sawyer."
1939 89m/B Mickey Rooney, Lynne Carver, Rex Ingram, William Frawley, Walter Connolly; *D:* Richard Thorpe. **VHS, Beta ★★★**

The Adventures of Ichabod and Mr. Toad Disney's wonderfully animated versions of Kenneth Grahame's "The Wind in the Willows" and "The Legend of Sleepy Hollow" by Washington Irving. Rathbone narrates the story of Mr. Toad, who suffers from arrogance and eventually must defend himself in court after being charged with driving a stolen vehicle (Disney did take liberties with the story). Crosby provides all the voices for "Ichabod," which features one of the all-time great animated sequences—Ichabod riding in a frenzy through the forest while being pursued by the headless horseman. A treat for all ages.
1949 68m/C *D:* Clyde Geronomi, James Algar; *V:* Jack Kinney, Bing Crosby. **VHS, LV ★★★1/2**

The Adventures of Mark Twain March stars as Mark Twain, the nom de plume of Samuel Clemens, the beloved humorist and writer. His travels and adventures along the Mississippi and on to the California gold rush would later result in the books and stories which would make him so well-known. March attains a quiet nobility as he goes from young man to old sage, along with Smith, who plays Olivia, Twain's beloved wife.
1944 130m/B Fredric March, Alexis Smith, Donald Crisp, Alan Hale, Sir C. Aubrey Smith, John Carradine, William Henry, Robert Barrat, Walter Hampden, Percy Kilbride; *D:* Irving Rapper; *W:* Alan LeMay, Harry Chandlee; *M:* Max Steiner. Nominations: Academy Awards '44: Best Interior Decoration, Best Special Effects, Best Score. **VHS, Beta ★★★**

The Adventures of Milo & Otis Delightful Japanese children's film about a farm-dwelling dog and cat and their odyssey after the cat is accidentally swept away on a river. Notable since no humans appear in the film. A record-breaking success in its homeland. Well received by U.S. children. Narrated by Dudley Moore. *AKA:* Koneko Monogatari; The Adventures of Chatran.
1989 (G) 89m/C *JP D:* Masanori Hata; *W:* Mark Saltzman; *M:* Michael Boddicker. **VHS, Beta, LV ★★★**

The Adventures of Priscilla, Queen of the Desert Quirky down-under musical comedy follows two drag queens and a transsexual across the Australian Outback on their way to a gig in a small resort town. They make the drive in a pink bus nicknamed Priscilla. Along the way they encounter, and perform for, the usual unusual assortment of local characters. Scenes depicting homophobic natives play out as expected. Finest moments occur on the bus or onstage (all hail ABBA). Strong performances, especially by usually macho Stamp as the widowed Bernadette, rise above the cliches in what is basically a bitchy, cross-dressing road movie, celebrating drag as art and the non-conformity of its heroes. Costumes (by Lizzy Gardner and Tim Chappel) are a lark, the photography's surreal, and the soundtrack fittingly campy. **1994 (R) 102m/C** *AU* Terence Stamp, Hugo Weaving, Guy Pearce, Bill Hunter, Sarah Chadwick, Mark Holmes, Julia Cortez; *D:* Stephan Elliott; *W:* Stephan Elliott; *M:* Guy Gross, Brian J. Breheny. Academy Awards '94: Best Costume Design; Australian Film Institute '94: Best Costume Design; Nominations: Australian Film Institute '94: Best Actor (Stamp), Best Actor (Weaving), Best Cinematography, Best Director (Elliott), Best Film, Best Screenplay; Golden Globe Awards '95: Best Actor—Musical/Comedy (Stamp), Best Film—Musical/Comedy. **VHS, LV** ★★★

The Adventures of Robin Hood Rollicking Technicolor tale of the legendary outlaw, regarded as the swashbuckler standard-bearer. The justice-minded Saxon knight battles the Normans, outwits evil Prince John, and gallantly romances Maid Marian. Grand castle sets and lush forest photography display ample evidence of the huge (in 1938) budget of $2 million plus. **1938 102m/C** Errol Flynn, Olivia de Havilland, Basil Rathbone, Alan Hale, Una O'Connor, Claude Rains, Patric Knowles, Eugene Pallette, Herbert Mundin, Melville Cooper, Ian Hunter, Montagu Love; *D:* Michael Curtiz; *W:* Norman Reilly Raine, Seton I. Miller; *M:* Erich Wolfgang Korngold. Academy Awards '38: Best Film Editing, Best Interior Decoration, Best Original Score; Nominations: Academy Awards '38: Best Picture. **VHS, Beta, LV** ★★★★

The Adventures of Sherlock Holmes' Smarter Brother The unknown brother of the famous Sherlock Holmes takes on some of his brother's more disposable excess cases and makes some hilarious moves. Moments of engaging farce borrowed from the Mel Brooks school of parody (and parts of the Brooks ensemble as well). **1978 (PG) 91m/C** Gene Wilder, Madeline Kahn, Marty Feldman, Dom DeLuise, Leo McKern, Roy Kinnear, John Le Mesurier, Douglas Wilmer, Thorley Walters; *D:* Gene Wilder; *W:* Gene Wilder. **VHS, Beta** ★★★

The Adventures of Tom Sawyer The vintage Hollywood adaptation of the Mark Twain classic, with art direction by William Cameron Menzies. Not a major effort from the Selznick studio, but quite detailed and the best Tom so far. **1938 91m/C** Tommy Kelly, Walter Brennan, Victor Jory, May Robson, Victor Kilian, Jackie Moran, Donald Meek, Ann Gillis, Marcia Mae Jones, Clara Blandick, Margaret Hamilton; *D:* Norman Taurog; *M:* Max Steiner. Nominations: Academy Awards '38: Best Interior Decoration. **VHS, Beta, LV** ★★★

Advise and Consent An interesting political melodrama with a fascinating cast, based upon Allen Drury's novel. The President chooses a candidate for the Secretary of State position which divides the Senate and causes the suicide of a senator. Controversial in its time, though somewhat turgid today. Laughton's last film. **1962 139m/B** Don Murray, Charles Laughton, Henry Fonda, Walter Pidgeon, Lew Ayres, Burgess Meredith, Gene Tierney, Franchot Tone, Paul Ford, George Grizzard, Betty White, Peter Lawford, Edward Andrews; *D:* Otto Preminger; *W:* Wendell Mayes. National Board of Review Awards '62: Best Supporting Actor (Meredith). **VHS, Beta** ★★★

The African Queen After Bible-thumping spinster Hepburn's missionary brother is killed in WWI Africa, hard-drinking, dissolute steamer captain Bogart offers her safe passage. Not satisfied with sanctuary, she persuades him to destroy a German gunboat blocking the British advance. The two spend most of their time battling aquatic obstacles and each other, rather than the Germans. Time alone on a African river turns mistrust and aversion to love, a transition effectively counterpointed by the continuing suspense of their daring mission. Classic war of the sexes script adapted from C.S. Forester's novel makes wonderful use of natural dialogue and humor. Shot on location in Africa. **1951 105m/C** Humphrey Bogart, Katharine Hepburn, Robert Morley, Theodore Bikel, Peter Bull, Walter Gotell; *D:* John Huston; *W:* John Huston, James Agee, Jack Cardiff. Academy Awards '51: Best Actor (Bogart); Nominations: Academy Awards '51: Best Actress (Hepburn), Best Director (Huston), Best Screenplay. **VHS, Beta, LV** ★★★★

After Hours An absurd, edgy black comedy that's filled with novel twists and turns and often more disturbing than funny. An isolated uptown New York yuppie (Dunne) takes a late night stroll downtown and meets a sexy woman in an all-night coffee shop. From there he wanders through a series of threatening and surreal misadventures, leading to his pursuit by a vigilante mob stirred by ice cream dealer O'Hara. Something like "Blue Velvet" with more Catholicism and farce. Or similar to "Something Wild" without the high school reunion. Great cameos from the large supporting cast, including Cheech and Chong as burglars. A dark view of a small hell-hole in the Big Apple. **1985 (R) 97m/C** Griffin Dunne, Rosanna Arquette, John Heard, Teri Garr, Catherine O'Hara, Verna Bloom, Linda Fiorentino, Dick Miller, Bronson Pinchot; *Cameos:* Richard "Cheech" Marin, Thomas Chong; *D:* Martin Scorsese; *M:* Howard Shore, Michael Ballhaus. Cannes Film Festival '86: Best Director (Scorsese); Independent Spirit Awards '86: Best Director (Scorsese), Best Film. **VHS, Beta, LV** ★★★1/2

After the Rehearsal Two actresses, one young, the other at the end of her career, challenge their director with love and abuse. Each questions his right to use them on stage and off. A thoughtful discussion of the meaning and reason for art originally made for Swedish television. Swedish with English subtitles. **1984 (R) 72m/C** *SW* Erland Josephson, Ingrid Thulin, Lena Olin; *D:* Ingmar Bergman; *W:* Ingmar Bergman. **VHS, Beta** ★★★

After the Thin Man Second in a series of six "Thin Man" films, this one finds Nick, Nora and Asta, the lovable terrier, seeking out a murderer from Nora's own blue-blooded relatives. Fast-paced mystery with a witty script and the popular Powell/Loy charm. Sequel to "The Thin Man," followed by "Another Thin Man." **1936 113m/B** William Powell, Myrna Loy, James Stewart, Elissa Landi, Joseph Calleia, Jessie Ralph, Alan Marshal; *D:* Woodbridge S. Van Dyke. Nominations: Academy Awards '36: Best Screenplay. **VHS, Beta** ★★★

The Age of Innocence Magnificently lavish adaptation of Edith Wharton's novel of passion thwarted by convention is visually stunning, but don't expect action since these people kill with a word or gesture. Lead performances are strong though perhaps miscast, with Ryder an exception. Outwardly docile and conventional, she nevertheless holds on to her husband with steely manipulation. Woodward's narration of Wharton's observations helps sort out what goes on behind the proper facades. Although

slow, see this one for the beautiful period authenticity, thanks to Scorsese, who obviously labored over the small details. He shows up as a photographer; his parents appear in a scene on a train. **1993 (PG) 138m/C** Daniel Day-Lewis, Michelle Pfeiffer, Winona Ryder, Richard E. Grant, Alec McCowen, Miriam Margolyes, Sian Phillips, Geraldine Chaplin, Stuart Wilson, Mary Beth Hurt, Michael Gough, Alexis Smith, Jonathan Pryce, Robert Sean Leonard, Michael Ballhaus; *Cameos:* Martin Scorsese; *D:* Martin Scorsese; *W:* Jay Cocks, Martin Scorsese; *M:* Elmer Bernstein. Academy Awards '93: Best Costume Design; British Academy Awards '93: Best Supporting Actress (Margolyes); Golden Globe Awards '94: Best Supporting Actress (Ryder); National Board of Review Awards '93: Best Director (Scorsese), Best Supporting Actress (Ryder); Nominations: Academy Awards '93: Best Adapted Screenplay, Best Art Direction/Set Decoration, Best Supporting Actress (Ryder); Directors Guild of America Awards '93: Best Director (Scorsese); Golden Globe Awards '94: Best Actress—Drama (Pfeiffer), Best Director (Scorsese), Best Film—Drama. **VHS, LV, 8mm** ★★★

Aguirre, the Wrath of God Herzog at his best, combining brilliant poetic images and an intense narrative dealing with power, irony, and death. Spanish conquistadors in 1590 search for the mythical city of gold in Peru. Instead, they descend into the hell of the jungle. Kinski is fabulous as Aguirre, succumbing to insanity while leading a continually diminishing crew in this compelling, extraordinary drama shot in the jungles of South America. Both English- and German-language versions available. **1972 94m/C** *GE* Klaus Kinski, Ruy Guerra, Del Negro, Helena Rojo, Cecilia Rivera, Peter Berling, Danny Ades; *D:* Werner Herzog; *W:* Werner Herzog. National Society of Film Critics Awards '77: Best Cinematography. **VHS** ★★★1/2

Ah, Wilderness! Delightful tale of a teen boy coming of age in small town America. Watch for the hilarious high school graduation scene. Based on the play by Eugene O'Neill. Remade in 1948 as "Summer Holiday," a musical with Mickey Rooney in the lead. **1935 101m/B** Wallace Beery, Lionel Barrymore, Aline MacMahon, Eric Linden, Cecilia Parker, Spring Byington, Mickey Rooney, Charley Grapewin, Frank Albertson; *D:* Clarence Brown. **VHS** ★★★1/2

Air Force One of the finest of the WWII movies, Hawks' exciting classic

has worn well through the years, in spite of the Japanese propaganda. It follows the hazardous exploits of a Boeing B-17 bomber crew who fight over Pearl Harbor, Manila, and the Coral Sea. Extremely realistic dog-fight sequences and powerful, intro-spective real guy interfacing by the ensemble cast are masterfully com-bined by Hawks.
1943 124m/B John Garfield, John Ridgely, Gig Young, Arthur Kennedy, Charles Drake, Harry Carey Sr., George Tobias; **D:** Howard Hawks. Academy Awards '43: Best Film Editing; Nominations: Academy Awards '43: Best Black and White Cinematography, Best Original Screenplay. **VHS ★★★1/2**

Airplane! Classic lampoon of disas-ter flicks is stupid but funny and launched a bevy of wanna-be spoofs. A former pilot who's lost both his girl (she's the attendant) and his nerve takes over the controls of a jet when the crew is hit with food poisoning. The passengers become increasingly crazed and ground support more sur-real as our hero struggles to land the plane. Clever, fast-paced, and very funny parody mangles every Holly-wood cliche within reach. The gags are so furiously paced that when one bombs it's hardly noticeable. Launched Nielsen's second career as a comic actor. And it ain't over till it's over: don't miss the amusing final credits. Followed by "Airplane 2: The Sequel."
1980 (PG) 88m/C Robert Hays, Julie Hagerty, Lloyd Bridges, Peter Graves, Robert Stack, Kareem Abdul-Jabbar, Leslie Nielsen, Stephen Stucker; **Cameos:** Ethel Merman, Barbara Billingsley; **D:** Jerry Zucker, Jim Abrahams, David Zucker; **W:** Jerry Zucker, Jim Abrahams, David Zucker; **M:** Elmer Bernstein. Writers Guild of America '80: Best Adapted Screenplay. **VHS, Beta, LV, 8mm ★★★1/2**

Airport Old-fashioned disaster thriller built around an all-star cast, fairly mo-ronic script, and an unavoidable acci-dent during the flight of a passenger airliner. A box-office hit that paved the way for many lesser disaster flicks (including its many sequels) detailing the reactions of the passengers and crew as they cope with impending doom. Considered to be the best of the "Airport" series; adapted from the Arthur Hailey novel.
1970 (G) 137m/C Dean Martin, Burt Lancaster, Jean Seberg, Jacqueline Bisset, George Kennedy, Helen Hayes, Van Heflin, Maureen Stapleton, Barry Nelson, Lloyd Nolan; **D:** George Seaton; **W:** George Seaton. Academy Awards '70: Best Supporting Actress (Hayes); Golden Globe Awards '71: Best Supporting Actress (Stapleton); Nominations: Academy Awards '70: Best Adapted Screenplay, Best Art Direction/Set Decoration, Best Cinematography, Best Costume Design, Best Film Editing, Best Picture, Best Sound, Best Supporting Actress (Stapleton), Best Original Score. **VHS, Beta, LV ★★★**

Akermania, Vol. 1 This compilation of director Akerman's shorter works includes "I'm Hungry, I'm Cold," the story of two Belgian girls on the loose in Paris, and "Saute Ma Ville," Aker-man's first film. Both are in French with English subtitles. Also included is "Hotel Monterey," a silent experi-mental film.
1992 89m/C FR Maria De Medeiros, Pascale Salkin, Chantal Akerman; **D:** Chantal Akerman. **VHS ★★★**

Aladdin Boy meets princess, loses her, finds her, wins her from evil vizier and nasty parrot. Superb animation triumphs over average songs and storyline by capitalizing on Williams' talent for ad-lib with lightning speed genie changes, lots of celebrity spoofs, and even a few pokes at Dis-ney itself. Adults will enjoy the 1,001 impersonations while kids will get a kick out of the big blue genie and the songs, three of which are the late Ashman's legacy. Kane and Salonga are responsible for the singing voices of Aladdin and Jasmine; Gottfried is a riot as the obnoxious parrot sidekick. Be forewarned: small children may be frightened by some of the scarier se-quences. ♪ A Whole New World; Prince Ali; Friend Like Me; One Jump Ahead; Arabian Nights.
1992 (G) 90m/C D: Ron Clements, John Musker; **W:** Ron Clements, John Musker, Ted Elliot, Terry Rossio; **M:** Alan Menken, Howard Ashman, Tim Rice; **V:** Robin Williams, Scott Weinger, Linda Larkin, Jonathan Freeman, Frank Welker, Gilbert Gottfried, Douglas Seale, Brad Kane, Lea Salonga. Academy Awards '92: Best Song ("A Whole New World"), Best Original Score; Golden Globe Awards '93: Best Song ("A Whole New World"), Best Score; MTV Movie Awards '93: Best Comedic Performance (Williams); Nominations: Academy Awards '92: Best Song ("Friend Like Me"), Best Sound, Best Sound Effects Editing. **VHS, Beta, LV ★★★1/2**

The Alamo Old-fashioned patriotic battle epic recounts the real events of the 1836 fight for independence in Texas. The usual band of diverse and contentious personalities, including Wayne as a coonskin-capped Davy

Crockett, defend a small fort against a very big Mexican raiding party outside of San Antonio. Before meeting mythic death, they fight with each other, learn the meaning of life, and ultimately come to respect each other. Just to make it more entertaining, Avalon sings. Big-budget production features an impeccable musical score by Tiomkin and an impressive 7,000 extras for the Mexican army alone. Wayne reportedly received directorial assistance from John Ford, particularly during the big massacre finale.
1960 161m/C John Wayne, Richard Widmark, Laurence Harvey, Frankie Avalon, Richard Boone, Carlos Arruza, Chill Wills, Veda Ann Borg; **D:** John Wayne; **M:** Dimitri Tiomkin. Academy Awards '60: Best Sound; Golden Globe Awards '61: Best Score; Nominations: Academy Awards '60: Best Color Cinematography, Best Film Editing, Best Picture, Best Song ("The Green Leaves of Summer"), Best Supporting Actor (Wills), Best Original Score. **VHS, Beta, LV** ★★★

Alexander Nevsky A story of the invasion of Russia in 1241 by the Teutonic Knights of Germany and the defense of the region by good old Prince Nevsky. Eisenstein's first completed project in nearly 10 years, it was widely regarded as an artistic disappointment upon release and as pro-war propaganda for the looming conflict with the Nazis. Fabulous Prokofiev score illuminates the classic battle scenes, which used thousands of Russian army regulars. Russian with subtitles.
1938 110m/B *RU* Nikolai Cherkassov, N.P. Okholopkov, Al Abrikossov; **D:** Sergei Eisenstein; **M:** Sergei Prokofiev. National Board of Review Awards '39: 5 Best Foreign Films of the Year. **VHS, LV** ★★★½

Alexander's Ragtime Band Energetic musical that spans 1915 to 1938 and has Power and Ameche battling for Faye's affections. Power is a society nabob who takes up ragtime. He puts together a band, naming the group after a piece of music (hence the title), and finds a singer (Faye). Ameche is a struggling composer who brings a Broadway producer to listen to their performance. Faye gets an offer to star in a show and becomes an overnight success. Over the years the trio win and lose success, marry and divorce, and finally end up happy. Corny but charming. ♪ Alexander's Ragtime Band; All Alone; Blue Skies; Easter Parade; Everybody's Doin' It; Everybody Step; For Your Country and My Country; Heat Wave; I Can Always Find a Little Sunshine at the YMCA. *AKA:* Irving Berlin's Alexander's Ragtime Band.
1938 105m/B Tyrone Power, Alice Faye, Don Ameche, Ethel Merman, Jack Haley, Jean Hersholt, Helen Westley, John Carradine, Paul Hurst, Joe King, Ruth Terry; **D:** Henry King; **W:** Kathryn Scola, Lamar Trotti; **M:** Irving Berlin. Academy Awards '38: Best Score; Nominations: Academy Awards '38: Best Film Editing, Best Interior Decoration, Best Picture, Best Song ("Now It Can Be Told"), Best Writing. **VHS** ★★★

Alfie What's it all about, Alfie? Caine, in his first starring role, plays the British playboy out of control in mod London. Alfie is a despicable, unscrupulous and vile sort of guy who uses woman after woman to fulfill his basic needs and then casts them aside until . . . tragedy strikes. Though this box office hit was seen as a sophisticated take on current sexual mores upon release, it now seems a dated but engaging comedy, notable chiefly for its performances. From the play by Bill Naughton. The title song "Alfie," sung by Dionne Warwick, was a top ten hit.
1966 (PG) 113m/C *GB* Michael Caine, Shelley Winters, Millicent Martin, Vivien Merchant, Julia Asher; **D:** Lewis Gilbert. Cannes Film Festival '67: Grand Jury Prize; Golden Globe Awards '67: Best Foreign Film; National Board of Review Awards '66: 10 Best Films of the Year, Best Supporting Actress (Merchant); Nominations: Academy Awards '66: Best Actor (Caine), Best Adapted Screenplay, Best Picture, Best Song ("Alfie"), Best Supporting Actress (Merchant). **VHS, Beta** ★★★

Algiers Nearly a scene-for-scene Americanized remake of the 1937 French "Pepe Le Moko" about a beautiful rich girl (Lamarr) who meets and falls in love with a notorious thief (Boyer, then a leading sex symbol). Pursued by French police and hiding in the underworld-controlled Casbah, Boyer meets up with Lamarr in a tragically fated romance done in the best tradition of Hollywood. Boyer provides a measured performance as Le Moko, while Lamarr is appropriately sultry in her American film debut (which made her a star). Later remade as the semi-musical "Casbah."
1938 96m/B Charles Boyer, Hedy Lamarr, Sigrid Gurie, Joseph Calleia, Alan Hale; **D:** John Cromwell. Nominations: Academy Awards '38: Best Actor (Boyer), Best Cinematography, Best Interior Decoration, Best Supporting Actor (Lockhart). **VHS, Beta** ★★★

Ali: Fear Eats the Soul A widow cleaning woman in her sixties has a love affair with a Moroccan man 30 years her junior. To no one's surprise, both encounter racism and moral hypocrisy in West Germany. Serious melodrama from Fassbinder, who wrote it and appears as the squirmy son-in-law. In German with English subtitles. *AKA:* Fear Eats the Soul. 1974 68m/C Brigitte Mira, El Hedi Ben Salem, Irm Hermann; *D:* Rainer Werner Fassbinder. Nominations: Cannes Film Festival '74: Best Film. **VHS** ★★★

Alice Farrow is "Alice," a woman plagued with doubts about her lifestyle, her religion, and her happiness. Her perfect children, husband, and apartment don't prevent her backaches, and she turns to an Oriental "herbalist" for aid. She finds his methods unusual and the results of the treatments surprising. Lightweight fairy-tale of yuppiedom gone awry. Fine performances, but superficial and pointed story that may leave the viewer looking for more. (Perhaps that's Allen's point.) Farewell performance from charactor actor Luke, unbilled cameo from Judith Ivey, and first time out for Dylan O'Sullivan Farrow, adopted daughter of Allen and Farrow, as Kate. 1990 (PG-13) 106m/C Mia Farrow, William Hurt, Joe Mantegna, Keye Luke, Alec Baldwin, Cybill Shepherd, Blythe Danner, Gwen Verdon, Bernadette Peters, Judy Davis, Patrick O'Neal, Julie Kavner, Caroline Aaron, Holland Taylor, Robin Bartlett, David Spielberg, Bob Balaban, Dylan O'Sullivan Farrow, Elle Macpherson; *D:* Woody Allen; *W:* Woody Allen. National Board of Review Awards '90: Best Actress (Farrow); Nominations: Academy Awards '90: Best Original Screenplay. **VHS, Beta, LV** ★★★

Alice in the Cities American and German culture are compared and contrasted in this early Wenders work about a German journalist in the USA on assignment who suddenly finds himself custodian to a worldly nine-year-old girl abandoned by her mother. Together they return to Germany and search for the girl's grandmother. Along the way they learn about each other, with many distinctive and graceful Wenders moments. 1974 110m/B Ruediger Vogler, Yella Rottlaender, Elisabeth Kreuzer, Edda Kochi; *D:* Wim Wenders; *W:* Wim Wenders. **VHS, Beta** ★★★1/2

Alice in Wonderland Classic Disney dream version of Lewis Carroll's famous children's story about a girl who falls down a rabbit hole into a magical world populated by strange creatures. Beautifully animated with some startling images, but served with a strange dispassion warmed by a fine batch of songs. Wynn's Mad Hatter and Holloway's Cheshire Cat are among the treats in store. ♪ Alice in Wonderland; I'm Late; A Very Merry Un-Birthday. 1951 (G) 75m/C *D:* Clyde Geronimi; *V:* Kathryn Beaumont, Ed Wynn, Sterling Holloway, Jerry Colonna, Hamilton Luske, Wilfred Jackson. Nominations: Academy Awards '51: Best Original Score. **VHS, Beta, LV** ★★★

Alien Terse direction, stunning sets and special effects, and a well-seasoned cast save this from being another "Slimy monster from Outerspace" story. Instead it's a grisly roller coaster of suspense and fear (and a huge box office hit). Intergalactic freighter's crew is invaded by an unstoppable carnivorous alien intent on picking off the crew one by one. While the cast mostly bitches and banters while awaiting the horror of their imminent departure, Weaver is exceptional as Ripley, a self-reliant survivor who goes toe to toe with the Big Ugly. Futuristic, in the belly of the beast visual design creates a vivid sense of claustrophobic doom enhanced further by the ominous score. Oscar-winning special effects include the classic baby alien busting out of the crew guy's chest routine, a rib-splitting ten on the gore meter. Successfully followed by "Aliens" and "Alien 3." 1979 (R) 116m/C Tom Skerritt, Sigourney Weaver, Veronica Cartwright, Yaphet Kotto, Harry Dean Stanton, Ian Holm, John Hurt; *D:* Ridley Scott; *W:* Dan O'Bannon; *M:* Jerry Goldsmith. Academy Awards '79: Best Visual Effects; Nominations: Academy Awards '79: Best Art Direction/Set Decoration. **VHS, Beta, LV** ★★★1/2

Aliens The bitch is back, some 50 years later. Popular sequel to "Alien" amounts to non-stop, ravaging combat in space. Contact with a colony on another planet has mysteriously stopped. Fresh from deep space sleep, Ripley and a slew of pulsar-equipped Marines return to confront the mother alien at her nest, which is also inhabited by a whole bunch of the nasty critters spewing for a fight. Something's gotta give, and the Oscar-winning special effects are especially inventive (and messy) in the alien demise department. Dimension (acting biz talk) is given to our hero Ripley, as she discovers maternal in-

stincts lurking within her space suit while looking after a young girl, the lone survivor of the colony. Tension-filled gore blaster. Followed by "Aliens 3."
1986 (R) 138m/C Sigourney Weaver, Michael Biehn, Lance Henriksen, Bill Paxton, Paul Reiser, Carrie Henn, Jenette Goldstein; *D:* James Cameron; *W:* James Cameron, Walter Hill; *M:* James Horner. Academy Awards '86: Best Sound Effects Editing, Best Visual Effects; Nominations: Academy Awards '86: Best Actress (Weaver), Best Art Direction/Set Decoration, Best Film Editing, Best Sound, Best Original Score. **VHS, Beta, LV ★★★1/2**

All About Eve One of the wittiest (and most cynical) flicks of all time follows aspiring young actress Baxter as she ingratiates herself with a prominent group of theater people so she can become a Broadway star without the usual years of work. The not-so-in-nocent babe becomes secretary to aging star Davis and ruthlessly uses everyone in her climb to the top, much to Davis' initial disbelief and eventual displeasure. Satirical, darkly funny view of the theater world features exceptional work by Davis, Sanders, and Ritter. Based on "The Wisdom of Eve" by Mary Orr. Later staged as the musical "Applause."
1950 138m/B Bette Davis, Anne Baxter, George Sanders, Celeste Holm, Gary Merrill, Thelma Ritter, Marilyn Monroe, Hugh Marlowe, Gregory Ratoff, Eddie Fisher; *D:* Joseph L. Mankiewicz; *W:* Joseph L. Mankiewicz. Academy Awards '50: Best Director (Mankiewicz), Best Picture, Best Screenplay, Best Sound, Best Supporting Actor (Sanders); Cannes Film Festival '51: Best Actress (Davis), Grand Jury Prize; Directors Guild of America Awards '50: Best Director (Mankiewicz); Golden Globe Awards '51: Best Screenplay; National Board of Review Awards '50: 10 Best Films of the Year; New York Film Critics Awards '50: Best Actress (Davis), Best Director (Mankiewicz), Best Film; Nominations: Academy Awards '50: Best Film Editing; Best Actress (Baxter), Best Actress (Davis), Best Art Direction/Set Decoration (B & W), Best Black and White Cinematography, Best Supporting Actress (Holm, Ritter), Best Original Score. **VHS, Beta, LV ★★★★**

All My Sons A wealthy family is dis-traught when their eldest son is listed as missing-in-action during WWII. They must cope with guilt, as well as grief, because the father's business reaped profits from the war. Adapted for television from the acclaimed Arthur Miller play.
1986 122m/C James Whitmore, Aidan Quinn, Joan Allen, Michael Learned; *D:* John Power. **VHS, Beta ★★★**

All Night Long Offbeat middle-age crisis comedy about a burned-out and recently demoted drugstore ex-ecutive in L.A. who leaves his wife, takes up with his fourth cousin by marriage, and begins a humorous re-bellion, becoming an extremely free-lance inventor while joining the drifters, weirdos, and thieves of the night. An obscure, sometimes uneven little gem with Hackman in top form and an appealing supporting perfor-mance by Streisand. Highlighted by delightful malapropisms and satiric inversion of the usual cliches.
1981 (R) 100m/C Gene Hackman, Barbra Streisand, Diane Ladd, Dennis Quaid, Kevin Dobson, William Griffith; *D:* Jean-Claude Tramont; *W:* W.D. Richter; *M:* Ira Newborn. **VHS, Beta ★★★**

All Quiet on the Western Front Ex-traordinary and realistic anti-war epic based on the novel by Erich Maria Remarque. Seven patriotic German youths go together from school to the battlefields of WWI. They experience the horrors of war first-hand, stuck in the trenches and facing gradual ex-termination. Centers on experiences of one of the young men, Paul Baumer, who changes from enthusi-astic war endorser to battle-weary veteran in an emotionally exact per-formance by Ayres. Boasts a gigantic budget (for the time) of $1.25 million, and features more than 2,000 extras swarming about battlefields set up on ranchland in California. Relentless anti-war message is emotionally draining and startling with both graphic shots and haunting visual po-etry. Extremely controversial in the U.S. and Germany upon release, the original version was 140 minutes long (some versions are available with re-stored footage) and featured ZaSu Pitts as Ayres mother (later reshot with Mercer replacing her). Remar-que, who had fought and been wounded on the Western Front, was eventually forced to leave Germany for the U.S. due to the film's ongoing controversy.
1930 103m/B Lew Ayres, Louis Wolheim, John Wray, Slim Summerville, Russell Gleason, Raymond Griffith, Ben Alexander, Beryl Mercer; *D:* Lewis Milestone. Academy Awards '30: Best Director (Milestone), Best Picture; National Board of Review Awards '30: 10 Best Films of the Year; Nominations: Academy Awards '30: Best Cinematography, Best Writing. **VHS, Beta, LV ★★★★**

All Screwed Up A group of young immigrants come to Milan and try to adjust to city life; they soon find that everything is in its place, but nothing is in order. Wertmuller in a lighter vein than usual. *AKA:* All in Place; Nothing in Order.
1974 104m/C *IT* Luigi Diberti, Lina Polito; *D:* Lina Wertmuller; *W:* Lina Wertmuller. **VHS, Beta** ★★★

All That Jazz Fosse's autobiographical portrait with Scheider fully occupying his best role as the obsessed, pill-popping, chain-smoking choreographer/director dancing simultaneously with love and death. But even while dying, he creates some great dancing. Vivid and imaginative with exact editing, and an eerie footnote to Fosse's similar death almost ten years later. Egocentric and self-indulgent for sure, but that's entertainment. ♪ On Broadway; Everything Old is New Again; After You've Gone; There'll Be Some Changes Made; Some of These Days; Bye Bye Love.
1979 (R) 120m/C Roy Scheider, Jessica Lange, Ann Reinking, Leland Palmer, Cliff Gorman, Ben Vereen, Erzebet Foldi, John Lithgow, Wallace Shawn, Sandahl Bergman, Nicole Fosse, Keith Gordon, Ben Masters, Theresa Merritt; *D:* Bob Fosse; *M:* Ralph Burns, Giuseppe Rotunno. Academy Awards '79: Best Art Direction/Set Decoration, Best Costume Design, Best Film Editing, Best Original Score; Cannes Film Festival '80: Best Film; Nominations: Academy Awards '79: Best Actor (Scheider), Best Cinematography, Best Director (Fosse), Best Original Screenplay, Best Picture. **VHS, Beta, LV** ★★★1/2

All the King's Men Grim and graphic classic set in the Depression follows the rise of a Louisiana farm-boy from angry and honest political hopeful to powerful but corrupt governor. Loosely based on the life (and death) of Huey Long and told by a newsman who's followed his career (Ireland). Willy Stark (Crawford, in his breakthrough role) is the politician who, while appearing to improve the state, rules dictatorially, betraying friends and constituents and proving once again that power corrupts. In her first major role, McCambridge delivers a powerful performance as the cunning political aide. Potent morality play based on the Robert Penn Warren book.
1949 109m/B Broderick Crawford, Mercedes McCambridge, John Ireland, Joanne Dru, John Derek, Anne Seymour, Shepperd Strudwick; *D:* Robert Rossen; *W:* Robert Rossen. Academy Awards '49: Best Actor (Crawford), Best Picture, Best Supporting Actress (McCambridge); New York Film Critics Awards '49: Best Actor (Crawford), Best Film; Nominations: Academy Awards '49: Best Director (Rossen), Best Film Editing, Best Screenplay, Best Supporting Actor (Ireland). **VHS, Beta, LV** ★★★★

All the President's Men True story of the Watergate break-in that led to the political scandal of the decade, based on the best-selling book by Washington Post reporters Bob Woodward and Carl Bernstein. Intriguing, terse thriller is a nail-biter even though the ending is no secret. Expertly paced by Pakula with standout performances by Hoffman and Redford as the reporters who slowly uncover and connect the seemingly isolated facts that ultimately lead to criminal indictments of the Nixon Administration. Deep Throat Holbrook and Robards as executive editor Ben Bradlee lend authenticity to the endeavor, a realistic portrayal of the stop and go of journalistic investigations.
1976 (PG) 135m/C Robert Redford, Dustin Hoffman, Jason Robards Jr., Martin Balsam, Jane Alexander, Hal Holbrook, F. Murray Abraham, Stephen Collins, Lindsay Crouse; *D:* Alan J. Pakula; *W:* William Goldman; *M:* David Shire, Gordon Willis. Academy Awards '76: Best Adapted Screenplay, Best Art Direction/Set Decoration, Best Sound, Best Supporting Actor (Robards); New York Film Critics Awards '76: Best Director (Pakula), Best Film, Best Supporting Actor (Robards); Writers Guild of America '76: Best Adapted Screenplay; Nominations: Academy Awards '76: Best Director (Pakula), Best Film Editing, Best Picture, Best Supporting Actress (Alexander). **VHS, Beta, LV** ★★★1/2

All This and Heaven Too When a governess arrives at a Parisian aristocrat's home in the 1840s, she causes jealous tension between the husband and his wife. The wife is soon found murdered. Based on Rachel Field's best-seller.
1940 141m/B Charles Boyer, Bette Davis, Barbara O'Neil, Virginia Weidler, Jeffrey Lynn, Helen Westley, Henry Daniell, Harry Davenport; *D:* Anatole Litvak; *M:* Max Steiner. Nominations: Academy Awards '40: Best Black and White Cinematography, Best Picture, Best Supporting Actress (O'Neil). **VHS, Beta** ★★★

All Through the Night A very funny spy spoof as well as a thrilling crime story with Bogart playing a gambler who takes on a Nazi spy ring. Fea-

tures memorable double-talk and a great auction scene that inspired the one with Cary Grant in "North by Northwest." Suspense builds throughout the film as Lorre appears in a sinister role as Pepi and Veidt gives a fine performance as the spymaster.
1942 107m/B Humphrey Bogart, Conrad Veidt, Karen Verne, Jane Darwell, Frank McHugh, Peter Lorre, Judith Anderson, William Demarest, Jackie Gleason, Phil Silvers, Barton MacLane, Martin Kosleck; **D:** Vincent Sherman. **VHS** ★★★

Allegro Non Troppo An energetic and bold collection of animated skits set to classical music in this Italian version of Disney's "Fantasia." Watch for the evolution of life set to Ravel's Bolero, or better yet, watch the whole darn movie. Features Nichetti (often referred to as the Italian Woody Allen, particularly by people in Italy) in the non-animated segments, who went on to write, direct, and star (he may have sold concessions in the lobby as well) in "The Icicle Thief."
1976 (PG) 75m/C *IT* Maurizio Nichetti; **D:** Bruno Bozzetto. **VHS, LV** ★★★

Alphaville Engaging and inimitable Godard attempt at science fiction mystery. P.I. Lemmy Caution searches for a scientist in a city (Paris as you've never seen it before) run by robots and overseen by a dictator. The futuristic techno-conformist society must be upended so that Caution may save the scientist as well as non-conformists everywhere. In French with subtitles. **AKA:** Alphaville, a Strange Case of Lenny Caution; Alphaville, Une Etrange Aventure de Lenny Caution.
1965 100m/B *FR* Eddie Constantine, Anna Karina, Akim Tamiroff; **D:** Jean-Luc Godard; **W:** Jean-Luc Godard. Berlin International Film Festival '65: Golden Berlin Bear. **VHS, Beta** ★★★

Altered States Obsessed with the task of discovering the inner man, Hurt's ambitious researcher ignores his family while consuming hallucinogenic drugs and floating in an immersion tank. He gets too deep inside, slipping way back through the evolutionary order and becoming a menace in the process. Confusing script based upon Chayefsky's (alias Sidney Aaron) confusing novel is supported by great special effects and the usual self-indulgent and provocative Russell direction. Chayefsky eventually washed his hands of the project after artistic differences with the producers. Others who departed from the film include initial director William Penn and special effects genius John Dykstra (relieved ably by Bran Ferren). Hurt's a solemn hoot in his first starring role.
1980 (R) 103m/C William Hurt, Blair Brown, Bob Balaban, Charles Haid, Dori Brenner, Drew Barrymore; **D:** Ken Russell; **W:** Paddy Chayefsky. Nominations: Academy Awards '80: Best Art Direction/Set Decoration, Best Original Score. **VHS, Beta, LV** ★★★

Amadeus Entertaining adaptation by Shaffer of his play about the intense rivalry between 18th-century composers Antonio Salieri and Wolfgang Amadeus Mozart. Abraham's Salieri is a man who desires greatness but is tortured by envy and sorrow. His worst attacks of angst occur when he comes into contact with Hulce's Mozart, an immature, boorish genius who, despite his gifts, remains unaffected and delighted by the beauty he creates while irking the hell out of everyone around him. Terrific period piece filmed on location in Prague; excellent musical score, beautiful sets, nifty billowy costumes, and realistic American accents for the 18th-century Europeans. ♪ Concerto No. 27 for Pianoforte and Orchestra in B Flat Major; Ave Verum Corpus; A Quintet for Strings in E Flat; A Concerto for Clarinet and Orchestra in A Major; Concerto Nos. 39 in E Flat Major; 40 in G Minor; 41 in C Major.
1984 (PG) 158m/C F. Murray Abraham, Tom Hulce, Elizabeth Berridge, Simon Callow, Roy Dotrice, Christine Ebersole, Jeffrey Jones, Kenny Baker, Cynthia Nixon, Vincent Schiavelli; **D:** Milos Forman; **W:** Peter Shaffer. Academy Awards '84: Best Actor (Abraham), Best Adapted Screenplay, Best Art Direction/Set Decoration, Best Costume Design, Best Director (Forman), Best Makeup, Best Picture, Best Sound; Cesar Awards '85: Best Foreign Film; Directors Guild of America Awards '84: Best Director (Forman); Golden Globe Awards '85: Best Actor—Drama (Abraham), Best Director (Forman), Best Film—Drama, Best Screenplay; Los Angeles Film Critics Association Awards '84: Best Director (Forman), Best Film, Best Screenplay; Nominations: Academy Awards '84: Best Actor (Hulce), Best Cinematography, Best Film Editing; Los Angeles Film Critics Association Awards '84: Best Actor (Abraham), Best Director (Forman), Best Screenplay. **VHS, Beta, LV** ★★★1/2

Amarcord Semi-autobiographical Fellini fantasy which takes place in the village of Rimini, his birthplace. Focusing on the young Zanin's impres-

sions of his town's colorful slices of life, Fellini takes aim at facism, family life, and religion in 1930s Italy. Visually ripe, delivering a generous, occasionally uneven mix of satire, burlesque, drama, and tragicomedic lyricism. Considered by people in the know as one of Fellini's best films and the topic of meaningful discussions among art film students everywhere.
1974 (R) 124m/C *IT* Magali Noel, Bruno Zanin, Pupella Maggio, Armando Brancia; **D:** Federico Fellini; **W:** Federico Fellini, Tonino Guerra; **M:** Nino Rota. Academy Awards '74: Best Foreign Language Film; National Board of Review Awards '74: 5 Best Foreign Films of the Year; New York Film Critics Awards '74: Best Director (Fellini), Best Film; Nominations: Academy Awards '75: Best Director (Fellini), Best Original Screenplay. **VHS** ★★★1/2

Amateur Former nun Huppert, trying to make a living writing pornography, hooks up with an amnesiac (Donovan) who turns out to have a criminal past and a porno actress wife (Lowensohn) who wants him dead. Blackmail plot has oddball characters racing through dark and evocative settings while unfolding a tale loaded with offbeat oppositions and an irresistibly bizarre romantic triangle. Lively and playful without becoming pretentious, Hartley's self-described "action thriller . . . with one flat tire" evokes his typical deadpan subtle style.
1994 (R) 105m/C Isabelle Huppert, Martin Donovan, Elina Lowensohn, Damian Young, Chuck Montgomery, David Simonds, Pamela Stewart; **D:** Hal Hartley; **W:** Hal Hartley; **M:** Jeff Taylor, Ned Rifle. **VHS, LV** ★★★

America's Dream Trilogy of short stories covering black life from 1938 to 1958. In "Long Black Song," based on a short story by Richard Wright, Alabama farmer Silas (Glover) lives with lonely wife Sarah (Lifford), who succumbs to the charms of white traveling salesman, David (Donovan). "The Boy Who Painted Christ Black" is young Aaron (Golden), who gives the drawing to his teacher, Miss Williams (Calloway). But the portrait causes a great deal of controversy in Aaron's 1948 Georgia school, especially for ambitious principal George Du Vaul (Snipes). Based on a story by John Henrich Clarke. The last story is Maya Angelou's "The Reunion," about Chicago jazz pianist Philomena (Toussaint), who encounters her childhood nemesis, Beth Ann (Thompson), the daughter of the white family who employed her parents as servants.
1995 (PG-13) 87m/C Danny Glover, Tina Lifford, Tate Donovan, Dan Kamin, Wesley Snipes, Jasmine Guy, Vanessa Bell Calloway, Norman D. Golden, II, Timothy Carhart, Yolanda King, Rae'ven Kelly, Lorraine Toussaint, Susanna Thompson, Carl Lumbly, Phyllis Cicero; **D:** Bill Duke, Kevin Rodney Sullivan, Paris Barclay; **W:** Ron Stacker Thompson, Ashley Tyler; **M:** Patrice Rushen. **VHS** ★★★

The American Friend Tribute to the American gangster film helped introduce Wenders to American moviegoers. Young Hamburg picture framer thinks he has a terminal disease and is set up by American expatriate Hopper to become a hired assassin in West Germany. The lure is a promise of quick money that the supposedly dying man can then leave his wife and child. After the first assasination, the two bond. Hopper is the typical Wenders protagonist, a strange man in a strange land looking for a connection. Great, creepy thriller adapted from Patricia Highsmith's novel "Ripley's Game." Fuller and Ray (better known as directors) appear briefly as gangsters.
1977 127m/C *FR GE* Bruno Ganz, Dennis Hopper, Elisabeth Kreuzer, Gerard Blain, Jean Eustache, Samuel Fuller, Nicholas Ray, Wim Wenders; **D:** Wim Wenders; **W:** Wim Wenders. National Board of Review Awards '77: 5 Best Foreign Films of the Year; Nominations: Cannes Film Festival '77: Best Film. **VHS, Beta, LV** ★★★1/2

American Graffiti Atmospheric, episodic look at growing up in the innocence of America before the Kennedy assassination and the Vietnam War. It all takes place on one hectic but typical night in the life of a group of recent California high school grads unsure of what the next big step in life is. So they spend their time cruising, listening to Wolfman Jack, and meeting at the drive-in. Slice of '60s life boasts a prudent script, great set design, authentic soundtrack, and consistently fine performances by the young cast. Catapulted Dreyfuss, Ford, and Somers to stardom, branded Lucas a hot directorial commodity with enough leverage to launch "Star Wars," and steered Howard and Williams towards continued age-of-innocence nirvana on "Happy Days."
1973 (PG) 112m/C Richard Dreyfuss, Ron Howard, Cindy Williams, MacKenzie Phillips, Paul LeMat, Charles Martin Smith, Suzanne Somers, Candy Clark, Harrison Ford, Bo Hopkins, Joe Spano, Kathleen Quinlan, Wolfman Jack; **D:** George Lucas; **W:** George Lucas, Gloria Katz, Willard

Huyck. Golden Globe Awards '74: Best Film—Musical/Comedy; New York Film Critics Awards '73: Best Screenplay; National Society of Film Critics Awards '73: Best Screenplay; Nominations: Academy Awards '73: Best Director (Lucas), Best Film Editing, Best Picture, Best Story & Screenplay, Best Supporting Actress (Clark). **VHS, Beta, LV** ★★★1/2

American Heart Jack (Bridges) is a suspicious ex-con, newly released from prison, with few prospects and little hope. He also has a teenage son, Nick (Furlong), he barely remembers but who desperately wants to have his father back in his life. Jack is reluctantly persuaded to let Nick stay with him in his cheap hotel where Nick befriends fellow resident, Molly, a teenage hooker, and other castoff street kids. Superb performances by both male leads—Furlong, both yearning and frustrated as he pursues his dream of having a family, and Bridges as the tough parolee, unwilling to open his heart. Hardboiled, poignant, and powerful.
1992 (R) 114m/C Jeff Bridges, Edward Furlong, Lucinda Jenney, Tracey Kapisky, Don Harvey, Margaret Welsh; **D:** Martin Bell; **W:** Peter Silverman; **M:** James Newton Howard. Independent Spirit Awards '94: Best Actor (Bridges); Nominations: Independent Spirit Awards '94: Best Cinematography, Best First Feature, Best Supporting Actor (Furlong), Best Supporting Actress (Jenney). **VHS, LV** ★★★1/2

An American in Paris Lavish, imaginative musical features a sweeping score, and knockout choreography by Kelly. Ex-G.I. Kelly stays on in Paris after the war to study painting, supported in his efforts by rich American Foch, who hopes to acquire a little extra attention. But Kelly loves the lovely Caron, unfortunately engaged to an older gent. Highlight is an astonishing 17-minute ballet which holds the record for longest movie dance number—and one of the most expensive, pegged at over half a million for a month of filming. For his efforts, the dance king won a special Oscar citation. While it sure looks like Paris, most of it was filmed in MGM studios. ♪ 'SWonderful; I Got Rhythm; Embraceable You; Love Is Here To Stay; Tra-La-La; I'll Build a Stairway to Paradise; Nice Work If You Can Get It; By Strauss; Concerto in F (3rd Movement).
1951 113m/C Gene Kelly, Leslie Caron, Oscar Levant, Nina Foch, Georges Guetary; **D:** Vincente Minnelli; **W:** Alan Jay Lerner; **M:** George Gershwin, Ira Gershwin,

John Alton. Academy Awards '51: Best Art Direction/Set Decoration (Color), Best Color Cinematography, Best Costume Design (Color), Best Picture, Best Story & Screenplay, Best Score; Golden Globe Awards '52: Best Film—Musical/Comedy; National Board of Review Awards '51: 10 Best Films of the Year; Nominations: Academy Awards '51: Best Director (Minnelli), Best Film Editing. **VHS, Beta, LV, 8mm** ★★★★

The American President Widower president Andrew Shepherd (Douglas) decides its time to get back into the dating game. But just what woman wants to find her romance in the public eye? Well, it turns out to be feisty environmental lobbyist Sydney Wade (the ever-charming Bening). But the Prez also has to put up with a nasty political opponent (Dreyfuss), approval ratings, and a noisy press.
1995 (PG-13) 114m/C Michael Douglas, Annette Bening, Martin Sheen, Michael J. Fox, David Paymer, Samantha Mathis, John Mahoney, Anna Deavere Smith, Nina Siemaszko, Wendie Malick, Shawna Waldron, Richard Dreyfuss, John Seale; **D:** Rob Reiner; **W:** Aaron Sorkin; **M:** Marc Shaiman. Nominations: Academy Awards '95: Best Score; Golden Globe Awards '96: Best Actor—Musical/Comedy (Douglas), Best Actress—Musical/Comedy (Bening), Best Director (Reiner), Best Film—Musical/Comedy, Best Screenplay; Writers Guild of America '95: Best Original Screenplay. **VHS, LV** ★★★

An American Werewolf in London Strange, darkly humorous version of the classic man-into-wolf horror tale became a cult hit, but never clicked with most American critics. Two American college students (Naughton and Dunne) backpacking through England are viciously attacked by a werewolf one foggy night. Dunne is killed, but keeps appearing (in progressively decomposed form) before the seriously wounded Naughton, warning him of impending werewolfdom when the moon is full; Dunne advises suicide. Seat-jumping horror and gore, highlighted by intensive metamorphosis sequences orchestrated by Rick Baker, are offset by wry humor, though the shifts in tone don't always work. Great moon songs permeate the soundtrack, including CCR's "Bad Moon Rising" and Van Morrison's "Moondance."
1981 (R) 97m/C David Naughton, Griffin Dunne, Jenny Agutter, Frank Oz, Brian Glover, David Schofield; **D:** John Landis; **W:** John Landis; **M:** Elmer Bernstein. Academy Awards '81: Best Makeup. **VHS, Beta, LV** ★★★

The Americanization of Emily A happy-go-lucky American naval officer (Garner) with no appetite for war discovers to his horror that he may be slated to become the first casualty of the Normandy invasion as part of a military PR effort in this black comedy-romance. Meanwhile, he spreads the charisma in an effort to woo and uplift Emily (Andrews), a depressed English woman who has suffered the loss of her husband, father, and brother during the war. A cynical, often funny look at military maneuvers and cultural drift that was adapted by Paddy Chayefsky from William Bradford Huie's novel. Also available colorized.
1964 117m/B James Garner, Julie Andrews, Melvyn Douglas, James Coburn, Joyce Grenfell, Keenan Wynn, Judy Carne, Liz Fraser, Edward Binns; **D:** Arthur Hiller; **W:** Paddy Chayefsky. Nominations: Academy Awards '64: Best Art Direction/Set Decoration (B & W), Best Black and White Cinematography. **VHS, LV** ★★★

Anastasia Bergman won her second Oscar, and deservedly so, for her classic portrayal of the amnesia victim chosen by Russian expatriate Brynner to impersonate Anastasia, the last surviving member of the Romanoff dynasty. As such, she becomes part of a scam to collect millions of rubles deposited in a foreign bank by her supposed father, the now-dead Czar. But is she just impersonating the princess? Brynner as the scheming White General and Hayes as the Grand Duchess who needs to be convinced turn in fine performances as well. Based on Marcelle Maurette's play.
1956 105m/C Ingrid Bergman, Yul Brynner, Helen Hayes, Akim Tamiroff; **D:** Anatole Litvak; **W:** Arthur Laurents. Academy Awards '56: Best Actress (Bergman); Golden Globe Awards '57: Best Actress—Drama (Bergman); New York Film Critics Awards '56: Best Actress (Bergman); Nominations: Academy Awards '56: Best Original Score. **VHS, LV** ★★★1/2

Anatomy of a Murder Considered by many to be the best courtroom drama ever made. Small-town lawyer in northern Michigan faces an explosive case as he defends an army officer who has killed a man he suspects was his philandering wife's rapist. Realistic, cynical portrayal of the court system isn't especially concerned with guilt or innocence, focusing instead on the interplay between the various courtroom characters. Classic performance by Stewart as the down home but brilliant defense lawyer who matches wits with Scott, the sophisticated prosecutor; terse and clever direction by Preminger. Though tame by today's standards, the language used in the courtroom was controversial. Filmed in upper Michigan; based on the best-seller by Judge Robert Traver.
1959 161m/B James Stewart, George C. Scott, Arthur O'Connell, Ben Gazzara, Lee Remick, Eve Arden, Orson Bean, Kathryn Grant, Murray Hamilton, Joseph Welch; **Cameos:** Duke Ellington; **D:** Otto Preminger; **W:** Wendell Mayes; **M:** Duke Ellington. National Board of Review Awards '59: 10 Best Films of the Year; New York Film Critics Awards '59: Best Actor (Stewart), Best Screenplay; Nominations: Academy Awards '59: Best Actor (Stewart), Best Adapted Screenplay, Best Black and White Cinematography, Best Film Editing, Best Picture, Best Supporting Actor (O'Connell, Scott). **VHS, Beta, LV** ★★★★

Anchors Aweigh Snappy big-budget (for then) musical about two horny sailors, one a girl-happy dancer and the other a shy singer. While on leave in Hollywood they return a lost urchin to his sister. The four of them try to infiltrate a movie studio to win an audition for the girl from maestro Iturbi. Kelly's famous dance with Jerry the cartoon Mouse (of "Tom and Jerry" fame) is the second instance of combining live action and animation. The young and handsome Sinatra's easy crooning and Grayson's near operatic soprano are blessed with music and lyrics by Styne and Cahn. Lots of fun, with conductor-pianist Iturbi contributing and Hollywood-style Little Mexico also in the brew. ♪ We Hate to Leave; I Fall in Love Too Easily; The Charm of You; The Worry Song; Jalousie; All of a Sudden My Heart Sings; I Begged Her; What Makes the Sun Set?; Waltz Serenade.
1945 139m/C Frank Sinatra, Gene Kelly, Kathryn Grayson, Jose Iturbi, Sharon McManus, Dean Stockwell, Carlos Ramirez, Pamela Britton; **D:** George Sidney; **M:** Jule Styne, Sammy Cahn. Academy Awards '45: Best Score; Nominations: Academy Awards '45: Best Actor (Kelly), Best Color Cinematography, Best Picture, Best Song ("I Fall in Love Too Easily"). **VHS, Beta, LV** ★★★

And Now for Something Completely Different A compilation of skits from BBC-television's "Monty Python's Flying Circus" featuring Monty Python's own weird, hilarious brand of humor. Sketches include "The Upper Class Twit of the Year Race," "Hell's Grannies" and "The

Townswomen's Guild Reconstruction of Pearl Harbour." A great introduction to Python for the uninitiated, or a chance for the converted to see their favorite sketches again.
1972 (PG) 89m/C *GB* John Cleese, Michael Palin, Eric Idle, Graham Chapman, Terry Gilliam, Terry Jones; *D:* Ian McNaughton; *W:* John Cleese, Michael Palin, Graham Chapman, Terry Gilliam, Terry Jones. **VHS, Beta, LV** ★★★

And the Band Played On Randy Shilts' monumental, and controversial, 1987 book on the AIDS epidemic comes to television in an equally controversial made for cable movie. Details the intricate medical research undertaken by doctors in France and the U.S. who fought to isolate and identify the mystery virus despite governmental neglect, red tape, clashing egos, and lack of funding. Various aspects of gay life are shown objectively, without sensationalizing. Celebrity cameos are somewhat distracting though most acquit themselves well. The script went through numerous rewrites; director Spottiswoode reportedly objected to the HBO interference at the editing stage.
1993 (PG-13) 140m/C Matthew Modine, Alan Alda, Ian McKellen, Lily Tomlin, Glenne Headly, Richard Masur, Saul Rubinek, Charles Martin Smith, Patrick Bauchau, Nathalie Baye, Christian Clemenson; *Cameos:* Richard Gere, David Clennon, Phil Collins, Alex Courtney, David Dukes, David Marshall Grant, Ronald Guttman, Anjelica Huston, Ken Jenkins, Richard Jenkins, Tcheky Karyo, Swoosie Kurtz, Jack Laufer, Steve Martin, Dakin Matthews, Peter McRobbie, Lawrence Monoson, B.D. Wong, Donal Logue, Jeffrey Nordling, Stephen Spinella; *D:* Roger Spottiswoode; *W:* Arnold Schulman, Paul Elliott; *M:* Carter Burwell. **VHS, LV** ★★★

And the Ship Sails On On the eve of WWI, a group of devoted opera lovers take a luxury cruise to pay their respects to a recently deceased opera diva. Also on board is a group of fleeing Serbo-Croation freedom fighters. A charming and absurd autumnal homage-to-life by Fellini shot entirely in the studio. *AKA:* El la Nave Va.
1983 (PG) 130m/C *IT* Freddie Jones, Barbara Jefford, Janet Suzman, Peter Cellier; *D:* Federico Fellini; *W:* Federico Fellini, Tonino Guerra. **VHS, Beta, LV** ★★★

And Then There Were None An all-star cast makes up the 10 colorful guests invited to a secluded estate in England by a mysterious host. What the invitations do not say, however, is the reason they have been specifi-

cally chosen to visit—to be murdered, one by one. Cat and mouse classic based on Agatha Christie's book with an entertaining mix of suspense and black comedy. Remade in 1966 and again in 1975 as "Ten Little Indians," but lacking the force and gloss of the original.
1945 97m/C Louis Hayward, Barry Fitzgerald, Walter Huston, Roland Young, Sir C. Aubrey Smith, Judith Anderson, Mischa Auer, June Duprez; *D:* Rene Clair. **VHS, Beta, LV** ★★★1/2

Andersonville Andersonville was an infamous Confederate prison camp in Georgia, which by August 1864 contained more than 32,000 Union POWs—and was planned to hold 8,000 men. One in four soldiers died in the camp. The story is told through the eyes of Massachusetts Corporal Josiah Day (Emick), who is captured in 1864 and struggles to survive the hellish conditions. The commander of the Andersonville was a deranged German-Swiss captain named Wirz (Triska)—who became the only Civil War soldier to be hanged for war crimes (depicted in "The Andersonville Trial"). The TV miniseries was filmed some 150 miles from the original site.
1995 168m/C Jarrod Emick, Frederic Forrest, Ted Marcoux, Jan Triska, Cliff DeYoung, Tom Aldredge, Frederick Coffin, Justin Henry, Kris Kamm, William H. Macy, Gabriel Olds, William Sanderson, Bud Davis, Carmen Argenziano, Peter Murnik; *D:* John Frankenheimer; *W:* David W. Rintels; *M:* Gary Chang. **VHS** ★★★

The Andersonville Trial Details the atrocities experienced by captured Union soldiers who were held in the Confederacy's notorious Andersonville prison during the American Civil War. Provides an interesting account of the war-crimes trial of the Georgia camp's officials, under whom more than 14,000 prisoners died. Moving, remarkable television drama based on the Pulitzer-honored book by MacKinlay Kantor.
1970 150m/C Martin Sheen, William Shatner, Buddy Ebsen, Jack Cassidy, Richard Basehart, Cameron Mitchell; *D:* George C. Scott. **VHS, Beta, LV** ★★★1/2

Andrei Rublev A 15th-century Russian icon painter must decide whether to record history or participate in it as Tartar invaders make life miserable. During the black and white portion, he becomes involved in a peasant uprising, killing a man in the process. After a bout of pessimism and a vow of silence, he goes forth to create

artistic beauty as the screen correspondingly blazes with color. A brilliant historical drama censored by Soviet authorities until 1971. In Russian with English subtitles.
1966 185m/C *RU* Anatoli Solonitzin, Ivan Lapikov, Nikolai Grinko, Nikolai Sergueiev; *D:* Andrei Tarkovsky; *W:* Andrei Tarkovsky, Andrei Konchalovsky. **VHS, LV** ★★★★

Andy Warhol's Bad In the John Waters' school of "crime is beauty," a Queens housewife struggles to make appointments for both her home electrolysis clinic and her all-female murder-for-hire operation, which specializes in children and pets (who are thrown out of windows and knived, respectively). Her life is further complicated by a boarder (King) who's awaiting the go-ahead for his own assignment, an autistic child unwanted by his mother. One of Warhol's more professional-appearing films, and very funny if your tastes run to the tasteless.
1977 (R) 100m/C Perry King, Carroll Baker, Susan Tyrrell, Stefania Cassini; *D:* Jed Johnson. **VHS, Beta, LV** ★★★

Angel and the Badman When notorious gunslinger Wayne is wounded during a shoot-out, a pacifist family takes him in and nurses him back to health. While he's recuperating, the daughter in the family (Russell) falls for him. She begs him not to return to his previous life. But Wayne, though smitten, thinks that a Duke's gotta do what a Duke's gotta do. And that means finding the dirty outlaw (Cabot) who killed his pa. Predictable but nicely done, with a good cast and script. Wayne provides one of his better performances (and also produced).
1947 100m/B John Wayne, Gail Russell, Irene Rich, Harry Carey Sr., Bruce Cabot; *D:* James Edward Grant; *W:* James Edward Grant. **VHS, LV** ★★★

An Angel at My Table New Zealand television mini-series chronicling the life of Janet Frame, New Zealand's premiere writer/poet. At once whimsical and tragic, the film tells of how a mischievous, free-spirited young girl was wrongly placed in a mental institution for eight years, yet was ultimately able to cultivate her incredible storytelling gifts, achieving success, fame and happiness. Adapted from three of Frame's novels: "To the Is-land," "An Angel at My Table," and "The Envoy From Mirror City." Highly acclaimed the world over, winner of over 20 major international awards.

1989 (R) 157m/C *NZ* Kerry Fox, Alexia Keogh, Karen Fergusson, Iris Churn, K.J. Wilson, Martyn Sanderson; *D:* Jane Campion; *W:* Laura Jones, Stuart Dryburgh. Chicago Film Critics Awards '91: Best Foreign Film; Independent Spirit Awards '92: Best Foreign Film. **VHS** ★★★★

Angel Baby Psychiatric outpatients Kate (McKenzie) and Harry (Lynch) fall in love and move in together despite some misgivings from family and the medical bureaucracy. When Kate becomes pregnant, they decide to stop taking their medication so the baby has a better chance of being born healthy. Kate's doctors believe she's not capable of dealing with a child, although she is equally determined to have her baby, while Harry struggles to make a life for all of them. Strong performances and an assured debut by writer/director Rymer. Film won all seven of the Australian Film Institute Awards for which it was nominated.
1995 104m/C *AU* John Lynch, Jacqueline McKenzie, Colin Friels, Deborra-Lee Furness, Robyn Nevin, Ellery Ryan; *D:* Michael Rymer; *W:* Michael Rymer; *M:* John Clifford Ryan. Australian Film Institute '95: Best Actor (Lynch), Best Actress (McKenzie), Best Cinematography, Best Director (Rymer), Best Film, Best Film Editing, Best Original Screenplay. **VHS** ★★★

Angel on My Shoulder A murdered convict makes a deal with the Devil (Rains) and returns to earth for revenge as a respected judge who's been thinning Hell's waiting list. Occupying the good judge, the murderous Muni has significant problems adjusting. Amusing fantasy with Muni in a rare and successful comic role. Co-written by Segall, who scripted "Here Comes Mr. Jordan," in which Rains played an angel. Remade in 1980.
1946 101m/B Paul Muni, Claude Rains, Anne Baxter, Onslow Stevens; *D:* Archie Mayo; *W:* Harry Segall. **VHS, Beta** ★★★

Angels and Insects Very strange Victorian-era romantic drama is definitely an acquired taste. The mysteries of nature are nothing compared to the mysteries of human life, as naturalist William Adamson (Rylance) comes to discover when he takes up a position at the home of amateur insect collector, Sir Harold Alabaster (Kemp). He falls in love and quickly marries blondly beautiful Eugenia (Kensit), whose outward propriety hides a sensual nature and some

decadent family secrets. Based on A. S. Byatt's novella "Morpho Eugenia." Take particular note of the costumes by Paul Brown, which mimic the exoticness of insects.
1995 (R) 116m/C Mark Rylance, Patsy Kensit, Kristin Scott Thomas, Jeremy Kemp, Anna Massey, Chris Larkin, Douglas Henshall, Annette Badland, Saskia Wickham; *D:* Phillip Haas; *W:* Belinda Haas, Phillip Haas; *M:* Alexander Balanescu. **VHS** ★★★

Angels with Dirty Faces Rousing classic with memorable Cagney twitches and the famous long walk from the cell to the chair. Two young hoods grow up on NYC's Lower East Side with diverse results—one enters the priesthood and the other opts for crime and prison. Upon release from the pen, famed gangster Cagney sets up shop in the old neighborhood, where Father O'Brien tries to keep a group of young toughs (the Dead End Kids) from following in his footsteps. Bogart's his unscrupulous lawyer and Bancroft a crime boss intent on double-crossing Cagney. Reportedly they were blasting real bullets during the big shoot-out, no doubt helping Cagney's intensity. Adapted from a story by Rowland Brown.
1938 97m/B James Cagney, Pat O'Brien, Humphrey Bogart, Ann Sheridan, George Bancroft, Billy Halop, Leo Gorcey, Huntz Hall, Bobby Jordan, Dan Jesse, Gabriel Dell, J. Frank Burke, William Tracy, Bernard Punsley; *D:* Michael Curtiz; *W:* John Wexley, Warren Duff; *M:* Max Steiner. New York Film Critics Awards '38: Best Actor (Cagney); Nominations: Academy Awards '38: Best Actor (Cagney), Best Director (Curtiz), Best Story. **VHS, Beta, LV** ★★★★

Angry Harvest During the WWII German occupation of Poland, a gentile farmer shelters a young Jewish woman on the run, and a serious, ultimately interdependent relationship forms. Holland's first film since her native Poland's martial law imposition made her an exile to Sweden. In German with English subtitles. Contains nudity and violence. *AKA:* Bittere Ernte.
1985 102m/C *GE* Armin Mueller-Stahl, Elisabeth Trissenaar, Wojciech Pszoniak, Margit Carstensen, Kurt Raab, Kathe Jaenicke, Hans Beerhenke, Isa Haller; *D:* Agnieszka Holland; *W:* Agnieszka Holland. Montreal World Film Festival '85: Best Actor (Mueller-Stahl); Nominations: Academy Awards '85: Best Foreign Language Film. **VHS, Beta** ★★★

Animal Crackers The second and possibly the funniest of the 13 Marx Brothers films, "Animal Crackers" is a screen classic. Groucho is a guest at the house of wealthy matron Dumont and he, along with Zeppo, Chico, and Harpo, destroy the tranquility of the estate. Complete with the Harry Ruby music score—including Groucho's "Hooray for Captain Spaulding" with more quotable lines than any other Marx Brothers film: "One morning I shot an elephant in my pajamas. How he got into my pajamas, I'll never know." Based on a play by George S. Kaufman.
1930 (G) 98m/B Groucho Marx, Chico Marx, Harpo Marx, Zeppo Marx, Lillian Roth, Margaret Dumont, Louis Sorin, Hal Thompson, Robert Greig; *D:* Victor Heerman; *W:* Morrie Ryskind. **VHS, Beta, LV** ★★★★

Anna Age, envy, and the theatrical world receive their due in an uneven but engrossing drama about aging Czech film star Anna, making a sad living in New York doing commercials and trying for off-Broadway roles. She takes in Krystyna, a young Czech peasant girl who eventually rockets to model stardom. Modern, strongly acted "All About Eve" with a story partially based on a real Polish actress. Kirkland drew quite a bit of flak for shamelessly self-promoting for the Oscar. She still lost.
1987 (PG-13) 101m/C Sally Kirkland, Paulina Porizkova, Robert Fields, Stefan Schnabel, Larry Pine, Ruth Maleczech; *D:* Yurek Bogayevicz; *W:* Yurek Bogayevicz, Agnieszka Holland; *M:* Greg Hawkes. Golden Globe Awards '88: Best Actress—Drama (Kirkland); Independent Spirit Awards '88: Best Actress (Kirkland); Los Angeles Film Critics Association Awards '87: Best Actress (Kirkland); Nominations: Academy Awards '87: Best Actress (Kirkland). **VHS, Beta, LV** ★★★

Anna and the King of Siam Splendid adaptation, from the book by Margaret Landon, about the true life adventures of 33-year-old English widow Anna Leonowens. In 1862 Anna and her son travelled to the exotic kingdom of Siam to educate the harem and children of the king. Dunne is splendid as the strong-willed governess as is Harrison (in his first American film) as the authoritarian eastern ruler. Remade as the musical "The King and I."
1946 128m/B Irene Dunne, Rex Harrison, Linda Darnell, Lee J. Cobb, Gale Sondergaard, Mikhail Rasumny, Dennis Hoey, Richard Lyon, John Abbott; *D:* John Cromwell; *W:* Sally Benson, Talbot Jennings; *M:* Bernard Herrmann. Academy Awards '46: Best Art Direction/Set

Decoration, Best Black and White Cinematography. **VHS** ★★★1/2

Anna Christie Silent production of Eugene O'Neill's play that even he liked. A young girl is sent away by her father, a seaman, and finds her way to Chicago, where she becomes a prostitute. Later she visits her father's barge and falls for a sailor. She shares her past life story, hoping they will understand. This film was acclaimed when it was released, and still remains a touching work of art. Remade in 1930.
1923 75m/B Blanche Sweet, George F. Marion Sr., William Russell, Eugenie Besserer, Chester Conklin, George Siegmann, Victor Potel, Fred Kohler Sr.; **D:** John Wray. **VHS, Beta** ★★★1/2

Anna Karenina Cinematic Tolstoy with Garbo as the sad, moody Anna willing to give up everything to be near Vronsky (March), the cavalry officer she's obsessed with. A classic Garbo vehicle with March and Rathbone providing excellent support. Interestingly, a remake of the Garbo and John Gilbert silent, "Love."
1935 85m/B Greta Garbo, Fredric March, Freddie Bartholomew, Maureen O'Sullivan, May Robson, Basil Rathbone, Reginald Owen, Reginald Denny; **D:** Clarence Brown. New York Film Critics Awards '35: Best Actress (Garbo). **VHS, Beta** ★★★1/2

Anne of Avonlea Equally excellent mini-series sequel to "Anne of Green Gables" in which the romantic heroine grows up and discovers romance. The same cast returns and Sullivan continues his tradition of lavish filming on Prince Edward Island and beautiful costumes. Based on the characters from L.M. Montgomery's classic novels "Anne of Avonlea," "Anne of the Island," and "Anne of Windy Poplars." CBC, PBS, and Disney worked together on this WonderWorks production. On two tapes.
AKA: Anne of Green Gables: The Sequel.
1987 224m/C CA Megan Follows, Colleen Dewhurst, Wendy Hiller, Frank Converse, Patricia Hamilton, Schuyler Grant, Jonathan Crombie, Rosemary Dunsmore; **D:** Kevin Sullivan; **W:** Kevin Sullivan; **M:** Hagood Hardy. **VHS, Beta, LV** ★★★1/2

Anne of Green Gables Splendid production of the famous Lucy Maud Montgomery classic about a young orphan girl growing to young adulthood with the help of a crusty brother and sister duo. The characters come to life under Sullivan's direction, and the movie is enhanced by the beautiful Prince Edward Island scenery and wonderful costumes. One of the few instances where an adaptation lives up to (if not exceeds) the quality of the original novel. A WonderWorks presentation that was made with the cooperation of the Disney channel, CBC, and PBS. Followed by "Anne of Avonlea." On two tapes.
1985 197m/C CA Megan Follows, Colleen Dewhurst, Richard Farnsworth, Patricia Hamilton, Schuyler Grant, Jonathan Crombie, Marilyn Lightstone, Charmion King, Rosemary Radcliffe, Jackie Burroughs; **D:** Kevin Sullivan; **W:** Kevin Sullivan, Joe Weisenfeld; **M:** Hagood Hardy. **VHS, Beta, LV** ★★★1/2

Anne of the Thousand Days Lavish re-telling of the life and loves of Henry the VIII. Henry tosses aside his current wife for the young and devastatingly beautiful Anne Boleyn. Burton's performance of the amoral king garnered him an Oscar nomination. Watch for Elizabeth Taylor as a masked courtesan at the costume ball.
1969 (PG) 145m/C Richard Burton, Genevieve Bujold, Irene Papas, Anthony Quayle, John Colicos, Michael Hordern; **D:** Hal B. Wallis; **M:** Georges Delerue. Academy Awards '69: Best Costume Design; Directors Guild of America Awards '70: Best Director (Jarrott); Golden Globe Awards '70: Best Actress—Drama (Bujold), Best Director (Jarrott), Best Film—Drama, Best Screenplay; Nominations: Academy Awards '69: Best Actor (Burton), Best Actress (Bujold), Best Adapted Screenplay, Best Art Direction/Set Decoration, Best Cinematography, Best Picture, Best Sound, Best Supporting Actor (Quayle), Best Original Score. **VHS** ★★★1/2

Annie Hall Acclaimed coming-of-cinematic-age film for Allen is based in part on his own life. His love affair with Hall/Keaton is chronicled as an episodic, wistful comedy commenting on family, love, loneliness, communicating, maturity, driving, city life, careers, and various other topics. Abounds with classic scenes, including future star Goldblum and his mantra at a cocktail party; Allen and the lobster pot; and Allen, Keaton, a bathroom, a tennis racket, and a spider. The film operates on many levels, as does Keaton's wardrobe, which started a major fashion trend. Don't blink or you'll miss several future stars in bit parts. Expertly shot by Gordon Willis.
1977 (PG) 94m/C Woody Allen, Diane Keaton, Tony Roberts, Paul Simon, Shelley Duvall, Carol Kane, Colleen Dewhurst, Christopher Walken, Janet Margolin, John Glover, Jeff Goldblum, Sigourney Weaver,

Marshall McLuhan, Beverly D'Angelo, Shelley Hack, Gordon Willis; **D:** Woody Allen; **W:** Woody Allen, Marshall Brickman. Academy Awards '77: Best Actress (Keaton), Best Director (Allen), Best Original Screenplay, Best Picture; British Academy Awards '77: Best Actress (Keaton), Best Director (Allen), Best Film, Best Screenplay; Directors Guild of America Awards '77: Best Director (Allen); Golden Globe Awards '78: Best Actress—Musical/Comedy (Keaton); Los Angeles Film Critics Association Awards '77: Best Screenplay; National Board of Review Awards '77: 10 Best Films of the Year, Best Supporting Actress (Keaton); National Society of Film Critics Awards '77: Best Actress (Keaton), Best Film, Best Screenplay; Writers Guild of America '77: Best Original Screenplay; Nominations: Academy Awards '77: Best Actor (Allen). **VHS, Beta, LV ★★★★**

Annie Oakley Energetic biographical drama based on the life and legend of sharpshooter Annie Oakley and her on-off relationship with Wild Bill Hickok. Stanwyck makes a great Oakley. Later musicalized as "Annie Get Your Gun."
1935 90m/B Barbara Stanwyck, Preston Foster, Melvyn Douglas, Pert Kelton, Andy Clyde; **D:** George Stevens. **VHS, Beta ★★★**

Another Woman The study of an intellectual woman whose life is changed when she begins to eavesdrop. What she hears provokes her to examine every relationship in her life, finding things quite different than she had believed. Heavy going, with Rowlands effective as a woman coping with an entirely new vision of herself. Farrow plays the catalyst. Although Allen's comedies are more popular than his dramas, this one deserves a look.
1988 (PG) 81m/C Gena Rowlands, Gene Hackman, Mia Farrow, Ian Holm, Betty Buckley, Martha Plimpton, Blythe Danner, Harris Yulin, Sandy Dennis, David Ogden Stiers, John Houseman, Philip Bosco, Frances Conroy, Kenneth Welsh, Michael Kirby, Sven Nykvist; **D:** Woody Allen; **W:** Woody Allen. **VHS, Beta, LV ★★★**

Antonia and Jane Enjoyable film tells the story of a longstanding, heavily tested friendship between two women. From the very beginning, they are a study in contrasts—Jane as rather plain, frumpy, and insecure; Antonia as glamorous, elegant, and successful. Both believe that each other's lives are more interesting and exciting than their own. Kidron, who directed this smart witty comedy for British television, offers an honest look into the often complex world of adult friendships.
1991 (R) 75m/C *GB* Imelda Staunton, Saskia Reeves, Patricia Leventon, Alfred Hoffman, Maria Charles, John Bennett, Richard Hope, Alfred Marks, Lila Kaye, Bill Nighy, Brenda Bruce; **D:** Beeban Kidron; **W:** Marcy Kahan; **M:** Rachel Portman. **VHS, Beta ★★★**

Aparajito The second of the Apu trilogy, about a boy growing up in India, after "Pather Panchali," and before "The World of Apu." Apu is brought to Benares and his education seriously begins. The work of a master; in Bengali with English subtitles. **AKA:** The Unvanquished.
1958 108m/B *IN* Pinaki Sen Gupta, Karuna Banerjee, Kanu Banerjee, Ramani Sen Gupta; **D:** Satyajit Ray. National Board of Review Awards '59: 5 Best Foreign Films of the Year; Venice Film Festival '57: Best Film. **VHS, Beta ★★★1/2**

The Apartment A lowly insurance clerk tries to climb the corporate ladder by "loaning" his apartment out to executives having affairs. Problems arise, however, when he unwittingly falls for the most recent girlfriend of the boss. Highly acclaimed social satire.
1960 125m/B Jack Lemmon, Shirley MacLaine, Fred MacMurray, Ray Walston, Jack Kruschen, Joan Shawlee, Edie Adams, Hope Holiday, David Lewis; **D:** Billy Wilder; **W:** I.A.L. Diamond, Billy Wilder. Academy Awards '60: Best Art Direction/Set Decoration (B & W), Best Director (Wilder), Best Film Editing, Best Picture, Best Story & Screenplay; British Academy Awards '60: Best Actor (Lemmon), Best Actress (MacLaine), Best Film; Directors Guild of America Awards '60: Best Director (Wilder); Golden Globe Awards '61: Best Actor—Musical/Comedy (Lemmon), Best Actress—Musical/Comedy (MacLaine), Best Film—Musical/Comedy; National Board of Review Awards '60: 10 Best Films of the Year; New York Film Critics Awards '60: Best Director (Wilder), Best Film, Best Screenplay; Nominations: Academy Awards '60: Best Actor (Lemmon), Best Actress (MacLaine), Best Black and White Cinematography, Best Sound, Best Supporting Actor (Kruschen). **VHS, Beta, LV ★★★1/2**

Apartment Zero A decidedly weird, deranged psychological drama about the parasite/host-type relationship between two roommates in downtown Buenos Aires: one, an obsessive British movie nut, the other, a sexually mesmerizing stud who turns out to be a cold-blooded psycho.

1988 (R) 124m/C *GB* Hart Bochner, Colin Firth, Fabrizio Bentivoglio, Liz Smith; *D:* Martin Donovan; *W:* Martin Donovan, David Koepp. **VHS, Beta, LV ★★★★**

Apocalypse Now Coppola's $40 million epic vision of the Vietnam War was inspired by Joseph Conrad's novella "Heart of Darkness," and continues to be the subject of debate. Disillusioned Army captain Sheen travels upriver into Cambodia to assassinate overweight renegade colonel Brando. His trip is punctuated by surrealistic battles and a terrifying descent into a land where human rationality seems to have slipped away. Considered by some to be the definitive picture of war in its overall depiction of chaos and primal bloodletting; by others, overwrought and unrealistic. May not translate as well to the small screen, yet worth seeing if for nothing more than Duvall's 10 minutes of scenery chewing as a battle-obsessed major ("I love the smell of napalm in the morning!"), a study in manic machismo. Stunning photography by Vittorio Storaro, awe-inspiring battle scenes, and effective soundtrack montage. Both Sheen and Coppola suffered emotional breakdowns during the prolonged filming, and that's a very young Fishburne in his major film debut. Available in widescreen format on laserdisc and in a remastered version in letterbox on VHS with a remixed soundtrack that features Dolby Surround stereo. In 1991 a documentary detailing the making of the film, "Hearts of Darkness: A Filmmaker's Apocalypse," was released.
1979 (R) 153m/C Marlon Brando, Martin Sheen, Robert Duvall, Frederic Forrest, Sam Bottoms, Scott Glenn, Albert Hall, Laurence "Larry" Fishburne, Harrison Ford, G.D. Spradlin, Dennis Hopper, Colleen Camp, Tom Mason; *D:* Francis Ford Coppola; *W:* Francis Ford Coppola, John Milius; *M:* Carmine Coppola. Academy Awards '79: Best Cinematography, Best Sound; British Academy Awards '79: Best Director (Coppola), Best Supporting Actor (Duvall); Golden Globe Awards '80: Best Director (Coppola), Best Supporting Actor (Duvall), Best Score; National Board of Review Awards '79: 10 Best Films of the Year; National Society of Film Critics Awards '79: Best Supporting Actor (Forrest); Nominations: Academy Awards '79: Best Adapted Screenplay, Best Art Direction/Set Decoration, Best Director (Coppola), Best Film Editing, Best Picture, Best Supporting Actor (Duvall). **VHS, Beta, LV, CD-I ★★★★**

Apollo 13 Realistic big-budget reenactment of the 1970 Apollo lunar mission that ran into a "problem" 205,000 miles from home reunites Hanks and Sinise from "F. Gump" and Howard and Hanks from "Splash." And an enjoyable reunion it is. Explosion in one of two oxygen tanks helping power the spacecraft leaves the three astronauts (led by Hanks) tumbling through space. With the electrical system kaput and oxygen running low, the men seek refuge in the Lunar Excursion Module. Since it's based on the real event and the outcome is known, director Howard concentrates on the personalities and the details of the seven-day adventure at Mission Control and in space, in the process delivering the dramatic payload. Weightless shots are the real deal as crew filmed for 10 days and made 600 parabolic loops in a KC-135 jet, NASA's "Vomit Comet," the long plunge creating 25 seconds of weightlessness. Special effects (by James Cameron's Digital Domain) and set design do the rest; no NASA footage is used, though original TV footage is used to dramatic effect. Script, with an uncredited rewrite by John Sayles, is based on the 1994 book, "Lost Moon," written by 13's Jim Lovell (who has a cameo as the Navy captain welcoming the astronauts aboard the recovery ship), while Apollo 15 commander David Scott served as a consultant.
1995 (PG) 140m/C Tom Hanks, Kevin Bacon, Bill Paxton, Gary Sinise, Ed Harris, Kathleen Quinlan, Brett Cullen, Emily Ann Lloyd, Miko Hughes, Max Elliott Slade, Jean Speegle Howard, Tracy Reiner, Michelle Little, David Andrews, Mary Kate Schellhardt; *D:* Ron Howard; *W:* William Broyles Jr., Al Reinert; *M:* James Horner, Dean Cundey. Directors Guild of America Awards '96: Best Director (Howard); Screen Actors Guild Award '95: Best Supporting Actor (Harris), Cast; Blockbuster Entertainment Awards '96: Drama Actor, Theatrical (Hanks); Nominations: Academy Awards '95: Best Adapted Screenplay, Best Art Direction/Set Decoration, Best Film Editing, Best Picture, Best Sound, Best Supporting Actor (Harris), Best Supporting Actress (Quinlan), Best Score; British Academy Awards '95: Best Cinematography; Golden Globe Awards '96: Best Director (Howard), Best Film—Drama, Best Supporting Actor (Harris), Best Supporting Actress (Quinlan). **VHS, LV ★★★1/2**

The Apprenticeship of Duddy Kravitz Young Jewish man in Montreal circa 1948 is driven by an insatiable need to be the "somebody" everyone has always told him he will be. A series of get-rich-quick schemes backfires in different ways, and he becomes most successful by driving people away. Young Dreyfuss is at his best. Made in Canada with thoughtful detail, and great cameo performances. Script by Richler, from his novel.

1974 (PG) 121m/C *CA* Richard Dreyfuss, Randy Quaid, Denholm Elliott, Jack Warden, Micheline Lanctot, Joe Silver; *D:* Ted Kotcheff; *W:* Mordecai Richler, Lionel Chetwynd. Berlin International Film Festival '74: Golden Berlin Bear; Writers Guild of America '74: Best Adapted Screenplay; Nominations: Academy Awards '74: Best Adapted Screenplay. **VHS, Beta** ★★★½

The Aristocats Typically entertaining Disney animated story about pampered pussy Duchess (Gabor) and her three kittens, who are left a fortune in their mistress' will. The fortune goes to the butler if the cats don't survive, so he dumps them in the country hoping they won't find their way home. The cats are aided by tough alley denizen O'Malley (Harris)—it's kind of the feline version of "Lady and the Tramp." Maurice Chevalier sings the title tune.

1970 78m/C *D:* Wolfgang Reitherman; *M:* George Bruns; *V:* Eva Gabor, Phil Harris, Sterling Holloway, Roddy Maude-Roxby, Bill Thompson, Hermione Baddeley, Carol Shelley, Pat Buttram, Nancy Kulp, Paul Winchell. **VHS** ★★★

Around the World in 80 Days Niven is the unflappable Victorian Englishman who wagers that he can circumnavigate the earth in four-score days. With his faithful manservant Cantinflas they set off on a spectacular journey. A perpetual favorite providing ample entertainment. Star-gazers will particularly enjoy the more than 40 cameo appearances by many of Hollywood's biggest names. Adapted from the novel by Jules Verne.

1956 (G) 178m/C David Niven, Shirley MacLaine, Cantinflas, Robert Newton, Charles Boyer, Joe E. Brown, Martine Carol, John Carradine, Charles Coburn, Ronald Colman; *Cameos:* Melville Cooper, Noel Coward, Andy Devine, Reginald Denny, Fernandel, Marlene Dietrich, Hermione Gingold, Cedric Hardwicke, Trevor Howard, Glynis Johns, Buster Keaton, Evelyn Keyes, Peter Lorre, Mike Mazurki, Victor McLaglen, John Mills, Robert Morley, Jack Oakie, George Raft, Cesar Romero, Gilbert Roland, Red Skelton, Frank Sinatra, Ava Gardner; *D:* Michael Anderson Sr.; *W:* James Poe, John Farrow, S.J. Perelman; *M:* Victor Young.

Academy Awards '56: Best Adapted Screenplay, Best Color Cinematography, Best Film Editing, Best Picture, Best Original Score; Golden Globe Awards '57: Best Actor—Musical/Comedy (Cantinflas), Best Film—Drama; National Board of Review Awards '56: 10 Best Films of the Year; New York Film Critics Awards '56: Best Film, Best Screenplay; Nominations: Academy Awards '56: Best Art Direction/Set Decoration (Color), Best Costume Design (Color), Best Director (Anderson). **VHS, Beta, LV** ★★★

Arsenic and Old Lace Set-bound but energetic adaptation of the classic Joseph Kesselring play. Easygoing drama critic Grant is caught in a sticky situation when he learns of his aunts' favorite pastime. Apparently the kind, sweet, lonely spinsters lure gentlemen to the house and serve them elderberry wine with a touch of arsenic, then they bury the bodies in the cellar—a cellar which also serves as the Panama Canal for Grant's cousin (who thinks he's Theodore Roosevelt). Massey and Lorre excel in their sinister roles. One of the best madcap black comedies of all time—a must-see. Shot in 1941 and released a wee bit later. Available colorized.

1944 158m/B Cary Grant, Josephine Hull, Jean Adair, Raymond Massey, Jack Carson, Priscilla Lane, John Alexander, Edward Everett Horton, John Ridgely, James Gleason, Peter Lorre; *D:* Frank Capra; *W:* Julius J. Epstein, Philip C. Epstein; *M:* Max Steiner. **VHS, Beta, LV** ★★★½

Arthur Spoiled, alcoholic billionaire Moore stands to lose everything he owns when he falls in love with a waitress. He must choose between wealth and a planned marriage, or poverty and love. Surprisingly funny, with an Oscar for Gielgud as Moore's valet, and great performance from Minnelli. Arguably the best role Moore's ever had, and he makes the most of it, taking the one-joke premise to a nomination for Oscar actor. ♪ Arthur's Theme; Blue Moon; If You Knew Susie; Santa Claus is Coming to Town.

1981 (PG) 97m/C Dudley Moore, Liza Minnelli, John Gielgud, Geraldine Fitzgerald, Stephen Elliott, Jill Eikenberry, Lou Jacobi; *D:* Steve Gordon; *M:* Burt Bacharach. Academy Awards '81: Best Song ("Arthur's Theme"), Best Supporting Actor (Gielgud); Los Angeles Film Critics Association Awards '81: Best Supporting Actor (Gielgud); New York Film Critics Awards '81: Best Supporting Actor (Gielgud); Writers Guild of America '81:

Best Original Screenplay; Nominations: Academy Awards '81: Best Actor (Moore), Best Original Screenplay. **VHS, Beta, LV, 8mm** ★★★

As You Desire Me Garbo plays an amnesia victim who returns to a husband she doesn't even remember after an abusive relationship with a novelist. An interesting, if not down-right bizarre movie, due to the pairing of the great Garbo and the intriguing von Stroheim. An adaption of Luigi Pirandello's play.
1932 71m/B Greta Garbo, Melvyn Douglas, Erich von Stroheim, Owen Moore, Hedda Hopper; **D:** George Fitzmaurice. **VHS, Beta** ★★★

Ashes and Diamonds In the closing days of WWII, a Polish resistance fighter assassinates the wrong man, tries to find love with the right women, and questions the meaning of struggle. A seminal Eastern European masterpiece that defined a generation of pre-solidarity Poles. Available in Polish with English subtitles or dubbed into English. The last installment of the trilogy that includes "A Generation" and "Kanal" and based on a novel by Jerzy Andrzewski. **AKA:** Popiol i Diament.
1958 105m/B PL Zbigniew Cybulski, Eva Krzyzewska, Adam Pawlikowski, Bogumil Kobiela, Waclaw Zastrzezynski; **D:** Andrzej Wajda. Venice Film Festival '59: International Critics Award. **VHS, Beta, LV** ★★★½

The Asphalt Jungle An aging criminal emerges from his forced retirement (prison) and assembles the old gang for one final heist. A very realistic storyline and a superb cast make this one of the best crime films ever made. Highly acclaimed; based on the work of W.R. Burnett.
1950 112m/B Sterling Hayden, Louis Calhern, Jean Hagen, James Whitmore, Sam Jaffe, John McIntire, Marc Lawrence, Barry Kelley, Anthony Caruso, Teresa Celli, Marilyn Monroe; **D:** John Huston; **W:** Ben Maddow; **M:** Miklos Rozsa. Edgar Allan Poe Awards '50: Best Screenplay; National Board of Review Awards '50: 10 Best Films of the Year, Best Director (Huston); Nominations: Academy Awards '50: Best Black and White Cinematography, Best Director (Huston), Best Screenplay, Best Supporting Actor (Jaffe). **VHS, Beta, LV** ★★★★

The Assault Powerful and disturbing drama about a Dutch boy who witnesses the arbitrary murder of his family by Nazis. The memory tortures him and leaves him empty as he matures. Years later he meets other vic-

tims and also the perpetrators of the incident, each of them changed forever by it. Thought-provoking consideration of WWII and the horrors of living in Nazi Germany from many points of view. Based on a novel by Harry Mulisch. Dutch language dubbed into English. **AKA:** De Aanslag.
1986 (PG) 149m/C NL Derek De Lint, Marc Van Uchelen, Monique Van De Ven; **D:** Fons Rademakers. Academy Awards '86: Best Foreign Language Film; Golden Globe Awards '87: Best Foreign Film. **VHS, Beta** ★★★½

Assault on Precinct 13 Urban horror invades LA. A sleepy police station in Los Angeles is suddenly under siege from a violent youth gang. Paranoia abounds as the police are attacked from all sides and can see no way out. Carpenter's musical score adds much to the setting of this unique police exploitation story that somehow stands as Carpenter's adaptation of Howard Hawks' "Rio Bravo." Semi-acclaimed and very gripping.
1976 91m/C Austin Stoker, Darwin Joston, Martin West, Tony Burton, Nancy Loomis, Kim Richards, Henry Brandon; **D:** John Carpenter; **W:** John Carpenter; **M:** John Carpenter. **VHS, Beta, LV** ★★★

At Close Range Based on the true story of Bruce Johnston Sr. and Jr. in Brandywine River Valley, Pennsylvania. Father, Walken, tempts his teenaged son, Penn, into pursuing criminal activities with talk of excitement and high living. Penn soon learns that his father is extremely dangerous and a bit unstable, but he's still fascinated by his wealth and power. Sometimes overbearing and depressing, but good acting and fancy camera work. A young cast of stars includes Masterson as the girl Penn tries to impress. Features Madonna's "Live to Tell."
1986 (R) 115m/C Sean Penn, Christopher Walken, Christopher Penn, Mary Stuart Masterson, Crispin Glover, Kiefer Sutherland, Candy Clark, Tracey Walter, Millie Perkins, Alan Autry, David Strathairn, Eileen Ryan; **D:** James Foley; **W:** Nicholas Kazan; **M:** Patrick Leonard, Juan Ruiz-Anchia. **VHS, Beta, LV** ★★★

Atlantic City A small-time, aging Mafia hood falls in love with a young clam bar waitress, and they share the spoils of a big score against the backdrop of Atlantic City. Wonderful character study that becomes something more, a piercing declaration about a city's transformation and the effect on the people who live there. Lancaster, in a sterling performance,

personifies the city, both of them fading with time. **AKA:** Atlantic City U.S.A.
1981 (R) 104m/C *FR CA* Burt Lancaster, Susan Sarandon, Kate Reid, Michel Piccoli, Hollis McLaren; **D:** Louis Malle. British Academy Awards '81: Best Actor (Lancaster), Best Director (Malle); Los Angeles Film Critics Association Awards '81: Best Actor (Lancaster), Best Film, Best Screenplay; New York Film Critics Awards '81: Best Actor (Lancaster), Best Screenplay; National Society of Film Critics Awards '81: Best Actor (Lancaster), Best Director (Malle), Best Film, Best Screenplay; Nominations: Academy Awards '81: Best Actor (Lancaster), Best Actress (Sarandon), Best Director (Malle), Best Original Screenplay, Best Picture. **VHS, Beta, LV** ★★★1/2

The Atomic Cafe A chillingly humorous compilation of newsreels and government films of the 1940s and 1950s that show America's preoccupation with the A-Bomb. Some sequences are in black and white. Includes the infamous training film "Duck and Cover," which tells us what to do in the event of an actual bombing.
1982 92m/C D: Kevin Rafferty. **VHS, Beta** ★★★

Attica Tense made-for-television depiction of the infamous Attica prison takeover in 1971 and the subsequent bloodbath as state troops were called in. Although edited due to the searing commentary by Nelson Rockefeller, it remains powerful and thought-provoking. Adapted from the Tom Wicker best-seller "A Time to Die."
1980 97m/C George Grizzard, Charles Durning, Anthony Zerbe, Roger E. Mosley; **D:** Marvin J. Chomsky. **VHS, Beta** ★★★

Au Revoir Les Enfants During the Nazi occupation of France in the 1940s, the headmaster of a Catholic boarding school hides three Jewish boys among the other students by altering their names and identities. Two of the students, Julien (Manesse) and Jean (Fejto), form a friendship that ends tragically when Jean and the other boys are discovered and taken away by the Gestapo. Compelling and emotionally wrenching coming of age tale based on an incident from director Malle's childhood is considered to be his best film. In French with English subtitles. Other 1987 movies with similar themes are "Hope and Glory" and "Empire of the Sun." **AKA:** Goodbye, Children.
1987 (PG) 104m/C *FR* Gaspard Manesse, Raphael Fejto, Francine Racette, Stanislas Carre de Malberg, Philippe Morier-Genoud, Francois Berleand, Peter Fitz, Francois Negret, Irene Jacob; **D:** Louis Malle; **W:** Louis Malle; **M:** Franz Schubert, Camille Saint-Saens. British Academy Awards '88: Best Director (Malle); Cesar Awards '88: Best Art Direction/Set Decoration, Best Cinematography, Best Director (Malle), Best Film, Best Sound, Best Writing; Los Angeles Film Critics Association Awards '87: Best Foreign Film; Venice Film Festival '87: Best Film; Nominations: Academy Awards '87: Best Foreign Language Film, Best Original Screenplay. **VHS, Beta, LV** ★★★★

Auntie Mame A young boy is brought up by his only surviving relative—flamboyant and eccentric Auntie Mame. Mame is positive that "life is a banquet and most poor suckers are starving to death." Based on the Patrick Dennis novel about his life with "Auntie Mame." Part of the "A Night at the Movies" series, this tape simulates a 1958 movie evening, with a Road Runner cartoon, "Hook, Line and Stinker," a newsreel and coming attractions for "No Time for Sergeants" and "Chase a Crooked Shadow."
1958 161m/C Rosalind Russell, Patric Knowles, Roger Smith, Peggy Cass, Forrest Tucker, Coral Browne; **D:** Morton DaCosta; **W:** Betty Comden, Adolph Green. Golden Globe Awards '59: Best Actress—Musical/Comedy (Russell); Nominations: Academy Awards '58: Best Actress (Russell), Best Art Direction/Set Decoration, Best Color Cinematography, Best Film Editing, Best Picture, Best Supporting Actress (Cass). **VHS, Beta, LV** ★★★

The Autobiography of Miss Jane Pittman The history of blacks in the South is seen through the eyes of a 110-year-old former slave. From the Civil War through the Civil Rights movement, Miss Pittman relates every piece of black history, allowing the viewer to experience the injustices. Tyson is spectacular in moving, highly acclaimed television drama. Received nine Emmy awards; adapted by Tracy Keenan Wynn from the novel by Ernest J. Gaines.
1974 110m/C Cicely Tyson, Odetta, Joseph Tremice, Richard Dysart, Michael Murphy, Katherine Helmond; **D:** John Korty. **VHS, Beta** ★★★1/2

An Autumn Afternoon Ozu's final film is a beautiful expression of his talent. In postwar Tokyo, an aging widower loses his only daughter to marriage and begins a life of loneliness. A heart-wrenching tale of rela-

tionships and loss. In Japanese with English subtitles.
1962 112m/C *JP* Chishu Ryu, Shima Iwashita, Shin-Ichiro Mikami, Mariko Okada, Keiji Sada; *D:* Yasujiro Ozu; *W:* Yasujiro Ozu. **VHS ★★★1/2**

Autumn Sonata Nordic family strife as famed concert pianist Bergman is reunited with a daughter she has not seen in years. Bergman's other daughter suffers from a degenerative nerve disease and had been institutionalized until her sister brought her home. Now the three women settle old scores, and balance the needs of their family. Excellent performance by Bergman in her last feature film.
1978 97m/C *SW* Ingrid Bergman, Liv Ullmann, Halvar Bjork, Lena Nyman, Gunnar Bjornstrand; *D:* Ingmar Bergman; *W:* Ingmar Bergman, Sven Nykvist. Golden Globe Awards '79: Best Foreign Film; National Board of Review Awards '78: 5 Best Foreign Films of the Year, Best Actress (Bergman), Best Director (Bergman); National Society of Film Critics Awards '78: Best Actress (Bergman); Nominations: Academy Awards '78: Best Actress (Bergman), Best Original Screenplay. **VHS, Beta, LV ★★★**

Avalon Powerful but quiet portrait of the break-up of the family unit as seen from the perspective of a Russian family settled in Baltimore at the close of WWII. Initally, the family is unified in their goals, ideologies and social lives. Gradually, all of this disintegrates; members move to the suburbs and television replaces conversation at holiday gatherings. Levinson based his film on experiences within his own family of Russian Jewish immigrants.
1990 (PG) 126m/C Armin Mueller-Stahl, Aidan Quinn, Elizabeth Perkins, Joan Plowright, Lou Jacobi, Leo Fuchs, Eve Gordon, Kevin Pollak, Israel Rubinek, Elijah Wood, Grant Gelt, Bernard Hiller, Allen Daviau; *D:* Barry Levinson; *W:* Barry Levinson; *M:* Randy Newman. Writers Guild of America '90: Best Original Screenplay; Nominations: Academy Awards '90: Best Cinematography, Best Costume Design, Best Original Screenplay, Best Original Score. **VHS, Beta, LV, 8mm ★★★**

Awakenings Marshall's first dramatic effort is based on the true story of Dr. Oliver Sacks, from his book of the same title. It details his experimentation with the drug L-dopa which inspired the "awakening" of a number of catatonic patients, some of whom had been "sleeping" for as long as 30 years. Occasionally over-sentimental,

but still providing a poignant look at both the patients—who find themselves confronted with lost opportunities and faded youth—and at Sacks, who must watch their exquisite suffering as they slip away. De Niro's performance as the youngest of the group is heart-rending, while Williams offers a subdued, moving performance as the doctor.
1990 (PG-13) 120m/C Robin Williams, Robert De Niro, John Heard, Julie Kavner, Penelope Ann Miller, Max von Sydow, Anne Meara; *D:* Penny Marshall; *W:* Steven Zaillian; *M:* Randy Newman. National Board of Review Awards '90: Best Actor (De Niro), Best Actor (Williams); Nominations: Academy Awards '90: Best Actor (De Niro), Best Adapted Screenplay, Best Picture. **VHS, Beta, LV, 8mm ★★★1/2**

The Awful Truth Classic screwball comedy. Young couple discards their marriage made in heaven and go their separate ways in search of happiness. Meticulously sabotaging each others' new relationships, they discover they really were made for each other. First on-screen pairing for Grant and Dunne: Grant is at his most charming with dead-on comic timing while Dunne is brilliant as his needling ex. The scene where Dunne poses as Grant's prodigal fan-dancing sister who pays a surprise cocktail-hour visit to the family of his stuffy, upper-class bride-to-be is among the most memorable screwball vignettes of all time. And don't miss the custody battle they have over the family dog (Asta of "The Thin Man" fame). Based on Arthur Richman's play. Preceded by 1925 and 1929 versions; remade in 1953 as "Let's Do it Again."
1937 92m/B Irene Dunne, Cary Grant, Ralph Bellamy, Alexander D'Arcy, Cecil Cunningham, Molly Lamont, Esther Dale, Joyce Compton, Robert Allen, Robert Warwick, Mary Forbes; *D:* Leo McCarey; *W:* Vina Delmar. Academy Awards '37: Best Director (McCarey); Nominations: Academy Awards '37: Best Actress (Dunne), Best Film Editing, Best Picture, Best Screenplay, Best Supporting Actor (Bellamy). **VHS, Beta, LV ★★★★**

Ay, Carmela! During the Spanish Civil War, two vaudevillians with strong anti-Franco views are captured by Franco forces and sentenced to execution. They are reprieved when a theater-loving Lieutenant offers to spare their lives if they will entertain the troops. Clever and entertaining farce, with poignant undertones.
1990 105m/C *SP IT* Carmen Maura,

Andres Pajares, Gabino Diego, Maurizio De Razza, Miguel Rellan, Edward Zentara, Jose Sancho, Antonio Fuentes; **D:** Carlos Saura; **W:** Rafael Azcona. **VHS** ★★★

Babe! A fine television movie about the life of one of America's most famous woman athletes, Babe Didrickson. Adapted by Joanna Lee from Didrickson's autobiography, "The Life I've Led." The movie was nominated for Outstanding Special of 1975-76 and Clark won an Emmy for her work. **1975** 120m/C Susan Clark, Alex Karras, Slim Pickens, Jeanette Nolan, Ellen Geer, Ford Rainey; **D:** Buzz Kulik; **M:** Jerry Goldsmith. **VHS** ★★★1/2

Babe Totally charming fable has intelligent piglet Babe being raised by matriarch sheepdog Fly, and learning the art of sheep herding along with his new canine brothers. Farmer Hoggett (Cromwell), Babe's owner by virtue of a winning raffle ticket, sees that he's more than just a ham, and enters them in the world sheepdog herding championship. Whimsy that never crosses the line into treacle. Four different special effects houses were used to make the barnyard animals talk and walk. Filmed on location in Australia; based on Dick King-Smith's book "The Sheep-Pig." **AKA:** Babe, the Gallant Pig. **1995** (G) 91m/C AU James Cromwell, Magna Szubanski; **D:** Chris Noonan; **W:** Chris Noonan, George Miller; **M:** Nigel Westlake; **V:** Christine Cavanaugh, Miriam Margolyes, Danny Mann, Hugo Weaving, Andrew Lesnie. Golden Globe Awards '96: Best Film—Musical/Comedy; National Society of Film Critics Awards '95: Best Film; Nominations: Academy Awards '95: Best Adapted Screenplay, Best Art Direction/Set Decoration, Best Director (Noonan), Best Film Editing, Best Picture, Best Supporting Actor (Cromwell); Writers Guild of America '95: Best Adapted Screenplay. **VHS, LV** ★★★1/2

Babette's Feast A simple, moving pageant-of-life fable. A group of religiously zealous villagers are taught love and forgiveness through a lavish banquet prepared by one of their housemaids, who turns out to be a world-class chef. Adapted from a tale by Isak Dinesen. In French and Danish with English subtitles. **1987** 102m/C DK FR Stephane Audran, Bibi Andersson, Bodil Kjer, Birgitte Federspiel, Jean-Philippe LaFont, Ebbe Rode, Jarl Kulle; **D:** Gabriel Axel; **W:** Gabriel Axel. Academy Awards '87: Best Foreign Language Film; British Academy Awards '88: Best Foreign Film. **VHS, Beta, LV** ★★★1/2

Baby Doll Suggestive sex at its best, revolving around the love of cotton in Mississippi. Nubile Baker is married to slow-witted Malden, who runs a cotton gin. His torching of Wallach's cotton gin begins a cycle of sexual innuendo and tension, brought to exhilarating life on screen, without a single filmed kiss. Performers and sets ooze during the steamy exhibition, which was considered highly erotic when released. Excellent performances from entire cast, with expert pacing by director Kazan. Screenplay is based on Tennessee Williams' "27 Wagons Full of Cotton." **1956** 115m/B Eli Wallach, Carroll Baker, Karl Malden, Mildred Dunnock, Rip Torn; **D:** Elia Kazan; **W:** Tennessee Williams. Golden Globe Awards '57: Best Director (Kazan); Nominations: Academy Awards '56: Best Actress (Baker), Best Adapted Screenplay, Best Black and White Cinematography, Best Supporting Actress (Dunnock). **VHS, Beta** ★★★

Baby It's You In New Jersey in the '60s, the relationship between a smart, attractive Jewish girl who yearns to be an actress and a street-smart Catholic Italian boy puzzles their family and friends. It all works due to Arquette's strong acting and Sayles' script, which explores adolescent dreams, the transition to adulthood, class differences, and the late 1960s with insight and humor. Interesting period soundtrack (Woolly Bully and, for some reason, Bruce Springsteen) help propel the film, a commercial job which helped finance Sayles' more independent ventures. **1982** (R) 105m/C Rosanna Arquette, Vincent Spano, Jack Davidson, Joanna Merlin, Nick Ferrari, Leora Dana, Robert Downey Jr., Tracy Pollan, Matthew Modine; **D:** John Sayles; **W:** John Sayles, Michael Ballhaus. **VHS, Beta, LV** ★★★

The Bachelor and the Bobby-Soxer Playboy Grant is brought before Judge Loy for disturbing the peace and sentenced to court her teen-age sister Temple. Cruel and unusual punishment? Maybe, but the wise Judge hopes that the dates will help Temple over her crush on handsome Grant. Instead, Loy and Grant fall for each other. **AKA:** Bachelor Knight. **1947** 95m/B Cary Grant, Myrna Loy, Shirley Temple, Rudy Vallee, Harry Davenport, Ray Collins, Veda Ann Borg; **D:** Irving Reis; **W:** Sidney Sheldon. Academy Awards '47: Best Original Screenplay. **VHS, Beta, LV** ★★★

Bachelor Mother A single salesgirl causes a scandal when she finds an

abandoned baby and is convinced by her boss to adopt the child. Smart, witty comedy with nice performance by Rogers.
1939 82m/B Ginger Rogers, David Niven, Charles Coburn; **D:** Garson Kanin. Nominations: Academy Awards '39: Best Story. **VHS, Beta, LV** ★★★

Back Door to Heaven Traces the path of a young boy who is born into a poor family and the reasons for his turning to a life of crime. A grim and powerful drama with many convincing performances.
1939 85m/B Wallace Ford, Aline MacMahon, Stuart Erwin, Patricia Ellis, Kent Smith, Van Heflin, Jimmy Lydon; **D:** William K. Howard. **VHS** ★★★1/2

Back to the Future When neighborhood mad scientist Doc Brown constructs a time machine from a DeLorean, his youthful companion Marty accidentally transports himself to 1955. There, Marty must do everything he can to bring his parents together, elude the local bully, and get back . . . to the future. Solid fast-paced entertainment is even better due to Lloyd's inspired performance as the loony Doc while Fox is perfect as the boy completely out of his element. Soundtrack features Huey Lewis and the News. Followed by two sequels.
1985 (PG) 116m/C Michael J. Fox, Christopher Lloyd, Lea Thompson, Crispin Glover, Wendie Jo Sperber, Marc McClure, Thomas F. Wilson, James Tolkan, Casey Siemaszko, Billy Zane, George DiCenzo, Courtney Gains, Claudia Wells, Jason Hervey, Harry Waters Jr., Maia Brewton, J.J. Cohen, Dean Cundey; **Cameos:** Huey Lewis; **D:** Robert Zemeckis; **W:** Robert Zemeckis, Bob Gale; **M:** Alan Silvestri. People's Choice Awards '86: Best Film; Nominations: Academy Awards '85: Best Original Screenplay, Best Song ("The Power of Love"), Best Sound. **VHS, Beta, LV** ★★★

Back to the Future, Part 3 Picks up where Part 2 climaxed a la cliffhanger. Stuck in 1955, time-traveling hero Marty frantically searches for Doc Part 1 so he can return to 1985. Instead, he finds himself in the Wild West circa 1885, trying to save Doc's life. Plot is related to earlier BTTFs, so first time viewers might be confused. For those who've seen previous incarnations, the clever interconnections are really nifty. Nearly matches the original for excitement and offers some snazzy new special effects. Supposedly the last installment, though don't be surprised if another

sequel follows. The complete trilogy is available as a boxed set.
1990 (PG) 118m/C Michael J. Fox, Christopher Lloyd, Mary Steenburgen, Thomas F. Wilson, Lea Thompson, Elisabeth Shue, Matt Clark, Richard Dysart, Pat Buttram, Harry Carey Jr., Dub Taylor, James Tolkan, Marc McClure, Wendie Jo Sperber, J.J. Cohen, Ricky Dean Logan, Jeffrey Weissman, Dean Cundey; **D:** Robert Zemeckis; **W:** Robert Zemeckis, Bob Gale; **M:** Alan Silvestri. **VHS, Beta, LV** ★★★

Backbeat Backed by the beat of early Beatle tunes as rendered by some of today's top alternative musicians, the debut for director Softley explores the Fab Four's beginnings in Hamburg's underground music scene. Storyline is driven by the complications of a romantic triangle between John Lennon, Astrid Kirchherr (the photographer who came up with the band's signature look) and Stu Sutcliffe, Lennon's best friend and the original bass player for the Beatles. Hart's dead-on as Lennon, playing him a second time (check out "The Hours and Times"). Energetic and enjoyable, particularly when the Was-produced music takes center stage.
1994 (R) 100m/C *GB* Stephen Dorff, Sheryl Lee, Ian Hart, Gary Bakewell, Chris O'Neill, Scot Williams, Kai Wiesinger, Jennifer Ehle; **D:** Iain Softley; **W:** Michael Thomas, Stephen Ward, Iain Softley; **M:** Don Was. **VHS, LV** ★★★

The Bad and the Beautiful The story of a Hollywood producer, told from the eyes of an actress, a writer, and a director. Featuring what some consider Turner's best performance ever. Winner of five Oscars, a splendid drama.
1952 118m/B Kirk Douglas, Lana Turner, Dick Powell, Gloria Grahame, Barry Sullivan, Walter Pidgeon, Gilbert Roland; **D:** Vincente Minnelli. Academy Awards '52: Best Art Direction/Set Decoration (B & W), Best Black and White Cinematography, Best Costume Design (B & W), Best Screenplay, Best Supporting Actress (Grahame); Nominations: Academy Awards '52: Best Actor (Douglas). **VHS, LV** ★★★1/2

Bad Boys When a gang member's little brother is killed in a rumble, the teen responsible (Penn, who else?) goes to a reformatory, where he quickly (though somewhat reluctantly) takes charge. Meanwhile, on the outside, his rival attacks Penn's girlfriend (Sheedy, in her feature film debut) in retaliation, is incarcerated, and ends up vying with Penn for control of the cell block. Backed into a corner by their mutual hatred and escalating peer pressure, the two are pushed over the brink into a final and shattering confrontation. Not as violent as it could be, to its credit; attempts to communicate a message. **1983 (R) 104m/C** Sean Penn, Esai Morales, Reni Santoni, Jim Moody, Eric Gurry, Ally Sheedy, Clancy Brown; **D:** Rick Rosenthal; **M:** Bill Conti, Donald E. Thorin. **VHS, Beta, LV** ★★★

Bad Company Thoughtful study of two very different Civil War draft dodgers roaming the Western frontier and eventually turning to a fruitless life of crime. Both the cast and script are wonderful in an entertaining film that hasn't been given the attention it's due. **1972 (PG) 94m/C** Jeff Bridges, Barry Brown, Jim Davis, John Savage; **D:** Robert Benton; **W:** Robert Benton, David Newman, Gordon Willis. **VHS, Beta, LV** ★★★½

Bad Day at Black Rock Story of a one-armed man uncovering a secret in a Western town. Wonderful performances from all concerned, especially Borgnine. Fine photography, shot using the new Cinemascope technique. Based on the novel by Howard Breslin. **1954 81m/C** Spencer Tracy, Robert Ryan, Anne Francis, Dean Jagger, Walter Brennan, John Ericson, Ernest Borgnine, Lee Marvin; **D:** John Sturges; **M:** Andre Previn. Cannes Film Festival '55: Best Actor (Tracy); Nominations: Academy Awards '54: Best Actor (Tracy), Best Director (Sturges). **VHS, LV** ★★★½

Bad Lieutenant Social chaos and degeneration characterize story as well as nameless loner lieutenant Keitel, who is as corrupt as they come. Assigned to a case involving a raped nun, he's confronted by his own lagging Catholic beliefs and the need for saving grace. From cult filmmaker Ferrara ("Ms. 45") and filled with violence, drugs, and grotesque sexual situations. Tense, over-the-top, urban drama is not intended for seekers of the subtle. Rent it with "Reservoir Dogs" and prepare yourself for a long tense evening of top-rated Keitel and screen-splitting violence. "R" rated version is also available at 91 minutes. **1992 (NC-17) 98m/C** Harvey Keitel, Brian McElroy, Frankie Acciario, Peggy Gormley, Stella Keitel, Victor Argo, Paul Calderone, Leonard Thomas, Frankie Thorn; **D:** Abel Ferrara; **W:** Zoe Tamerlaine Lund, Abel Ferrara; **M:** Joe Delia. Independent Spirit

Awards '93: Best Actor (Keitel). **VHS, LV** ★★★

The Bad News Bears Family comedy about a misfit Little League team that gets whipped into shape by a cranky, sloppy, beer-drinking coach who recruits a female pitcher. O'Neal and Matthau are top-notch. The kids' language is rather adult, and very titillating for younger viewers. Spawned two sequels and a television series. **1976 (PG) 102m/C** Walter Matthau, Tatum O'Neal, Vic Morrow, Joyce Van Patten, Jackie Earle Haley; **D:** Michael Ritchie, John A. Alonzo. Writers Guild of America '76: Best Original Screenplay. **VHS, Beta, LV, 8mm** ★★★

The Bad Sleep Well Japanese variation of the 1940 Warner Brothers crime dramas. A tale about corruption in the corporate world as seen through the eyes of a rising executive. **1960 135m/B** *JP* Toshiro Mifune, Masayuki Kato, Masayuki Mori, Takashi Shimura, Akira Nishimura; **D:** Akira Kurosawa. **VHS, Beta** ★★★½

Bad Taste A definite pleaser for the person who enjoys watching starving aliens devour the average, everyday human being. Alien fast-food manufacturers come to earth in hopes of harvesting all of mankind. The earth's fate lies in the hands of the government who must stop these rampaging creatures before the whole human race is gobbled up. Terrific make-up jobs on the aliens add the final touch to this gory, yet humorous cult horror flick. **1988 90m/C** *NZ* Peter Jackson, Pete O'Herne, Mike Minett, Terry Potter, Craig Smith, Doug Wren, Dean Lawrie; **D:** Peter Jackson. **VHS, LV** ★★★

Badlands Based loosely on the Charlie Starkweather murders of the 1950s, this impressive debut by director Malick recounts a slow-thinking, unhinged misfit's killing spree across the midwestern plains, accompanied by a starry-eyed 15-year-old schoolgirl. Sheen and Spacek are a disturbingly numb, apathetic, and icy duo. **1974 (PG) 94m/C** Martin Sheen, Sissy Spacek, Warren Oates; **D:** Terence Malick; **W:** Terence Malick. **VHS, Beta, LV** ★★★½

Bagdad Cafe A large German woman, played by Sagebrecht, finds herself stranded in the Mojave desert after her husband dumps her on the side of the highway. She encounters a rundown cafe where she becomes involved with the offbeat residents. A

hilarious story in which the strange people and the absurdity of their situations are treated kindly and not made to seem ridiculous. Spawned a short-lived TV series with Whoopi Goldberg. *AKA:* Out of Rosenheim.
1988 (PG) 91m/C *GE* Marianne Sagebrecht, CCH Pounder, Jack Palance, Christine Kaufmann, Monica Calhoun, Darron Flagg; *D:* Percy Adlon; *W:* Percy Adlon, Eleonore Adlon; *M:* Bob Telson. Cesar Awards '89: Best Foreign Film; Nominations: Academy Awards '88: Best Song ("Calling You"). VHS, Beta ★★★

The Baker's Wife There's a new baker in town, and he brings with him to the small French village an array of tantalizing breads, as well as a discontented wife. When she runs off with a shepherd, her loyal and naive husband refuses to acknowledge her infidelity; however, in his loneliness, the baker can't bake, so the townspeople scheme to bring his wife back. Panned as overly cute Marcel Pagnol peasant glorification, and hailed as a visual poem full of wit; you decide. In French with subtitles. Also available for French students without subtitles; a French script booklet is also available. *AKA:* La Femme du Boulanger.
1933 101m/B *FR* Raimu, Ginette LeClerc, Charles Moulton, Charpin, Robert Vattier; *D:* Marcel Pagnol. National Board of Review Awards '40: 5 Best Foreign Films of the Year; New York Film Critics Awards '40: Best Foreign Film. VHS, Beta ★★★1/2

Ball of Fire A gang moll hides out with a group of mundane professors, trying to avoid her loathsome boyfriend. The professors are busy compiling an encyclopedia and Stanwyck helps them with their section on slang in the English language. Cooper has his hands full when he falls for this damsel in distress and must fight the gangsters to keep her. Stanwyck takes a personal liking to naive Cooper and resolves to teach him more than just slang.
1941 111m/B Gary Cooper, Barbara Stanwyck, Dana Andrews, Gene Krupa, Oscar Homolka, Dan Duryea, S.Z. Sakall, Henry Travers; *D:* Howard Hawks; *W:* Billy Wilder, Charles Brackett. Nominations: Academy Awards '41: Best Actress (Stanwyck), Best Sound, Best Story, Best Original Score. VHS, Beta, LV ★★★

Ballad of a Soldier As a reward for demolishing two German tanks, a 19-year-old Russian soldier receives a six-day pass so that he can see his mother; however, he meets another woman. Well directed and photographed, while avoiding propaganda.
1960 88m/B *RU* Vladimir Ivashov, Shanna Prokhorenko; *D:* Grigori Chukrai. British Academy Awards '61: Best Film; Nominations: Academy Awards '61: Best Story & Screenplay. VHS, Beta ★★★1/2

Ballad of Cable Hogue A prospector, who had been left to die in the desert by his double-crossing partners, finds a waterhole. A surprise awaits his former friends when they visit the remote well. Not the usual violent Peckinpah horse drama, but a tongue-in-cheek comedy romance mixed with tragedy. Obviously offbeat and worth a peek.
1970 (R) 122m/C Jason Robards Jr., Stella Stevens, David Warner, L.Q. Jones, Strother Martin, Slim Pickens; *D:* Sam Peckinpah; *M:* Jerry Goldsmith. VHS, Beta, LV ★★★

The Ballad of Narayama Director Imamura's subtle and vastly moving story takes place a vague century ago. In compliance with village law designed to control population among the poverty-stricken peasants, a healthy 70-year-old woman must submit to solitary starvation atop a nearby mountain. We follow her as she sets into motion the final influence she will have in the lives of her children and her grandchildren, a situation described with detachment and without imposing a tragic perspective. In Japanese with English subtitles. *AKA:* Narayama-Bushi-Ko.
1983 129m/C *JP* Ken Ogata, Sumiko Sakamota, Takejo Aki, Tonpei Hidari, Shoichi Ozawa; *D:* Shohei Imamura; *W:* Shohei Imamura. Cannes Film Festival '83: Best Film. VHS ★★★★

Baltic Deputy An early forerunner of Soviet historic realism, where an aging intellectual deals with post-revolution Soviet life. In Russian with subtitles.
1937 95m/B *RU* Nikolai Cherkassov; *D:* Yosif Heifitz. National Board of Review Awards '37: 10 Best Films of the Year. VHS, Beta ★★★1/2

Bambi A true Disney classic, detailing the often harsh education of a newborn deer and his friends in the forest. Proves that Disney animation was—and still is—the best to be found. Thumper still steals the show and the music is delightful, including "Let's Sing a Gay Little Spring Song," "Love is a Song," "Little April Shower," "The Thumper Song," and "Twitterpated." Stands as one of the greatest children's films of all time; a

genuine perennial from generation to generation. Based very loosely on the book by Felix Salten.
1942 (G) 69m/C D: David Hand; **W:** Larry Morey; **M:** Frank Churchill, Edward Plumb; **V:** Bobby Stewart, Peter Behn, Stan Alexander, Cammie King, Donnie Dunagan, Hardie Albright, John Sutherland, Tim Davis, Sam Edwards, Sterling Holloway, Ann Gillis, Perce Pearce. Nominations: Academy Awards '42: Best Song ("Love Is a Song"), Best Sound, Best Original Score. **VHS, Beta, LV ★★★★**

Bananas Intermittently hilarious pre-"Annie Hall" Allen fare is full of the director's signature angst-ridden philosophical comedy. A frustrated product tester from New York runs off to South America, where he volunteers his support to the revolutionary force of a shaky Latin-American dictatorship and winds up the leader. Don't miss cameos by Stallone and Garfield. Witty score contributes much.
1971 (PG) 82m/C Woody Allen, Louise Lasser, Carlos Montalban, Howard Cosell, Charlotte Rae, Conrad Bain; **Cameos:** Sylvester Stallone, Allen (Goorwitz) Garfield; **D:** Woody Allen; **W:** Woody Allen; **M:** Marvin Hamlisch. **VHS, Beta, LV ★★★**

Band of Gold Unflinching British miniseries follows the lives of Yorkshire prostitutes Rosie (James), Carol (Tyson), and Gina (Gemmell). They try to survive the streets of Bradford while a serial killer is targeting the local hookers. On six cassettes.
1995 312m/C Geraldine James, Cathy Tyson, Ruth Gemmell, Barbara Dickson, David Schofield, Richard Moore, Rachel Davies, Samantha Morton; **D:** Richard Standeven, Richard Laxton; **W:** Kay Mellor; **M:** Hal Lindes. **VHS ★★★**

The Band Wagon A Hollywood song-and-dance man finds trouble when he is persuaded to star in a Broadway musical. Charisse has been called Astaire's most perfect partner, perhaps by those who haven't seen Rogers. ♪ That's Entertainment; Dancing in the Dark; By Myself; A Shine On Your Shoes; Something to Remember You By; High and Low; I Love Louisa; New Sun in the Sky; I Guess I'll Have to Change My Plan.
1953 112m/C Fred Astaire, Cyd Charisse, Oscar Levant, Nanette Fabray, Jack Buchanan, Bobby Watson; **D:** Vincente Minnelli; **W:** Betty Comden, Howard Dietz; **M:** Arthur Schwartz, Howard Dietz. Nominations: Academy Awards '53: Best Costume Design (Color), Best Story & Screenplay, Best Original Score, Best Original Score. **VHS, Beta, LV ★★★**

Bang the Drum Slowly The touching story of a major league catcher who discovers that he is dying of Hodgkins disease and wants to play just one more season. De Niro is the weakening baseball player and Moriarty is the friend who helps him see it through. Based on a novel by Mark Harris.
1973 (PG) 97m/C Robert De Niro, Michael Moriarty, Vincent Gardenia, Heather MacRae, Selma Diamond, Danny Aiello; **D:** John Hancock. National Board of Review Awards '73: 10 Best Films of the Year; New York Film Critics Awards '73: Best Supporting Actor (De Niro); Nominations: Academy Awards '73: Best Supporting Actor (Gardenia). **VHS, Beta, LV ★★★**

The Bank Dick Fields wrote the screenplay (using an alias) and stars in this zany comedy about a man who accidentally trips a bank robber and winds up as a guard. Fields' last major role is a classic, a worthy end to his great career. Side two of the laserdisc is in CAV format, which allows single frame access to the frenetic cops and robbers chase sequence. **AKA:** The Bank Detective.
1940 73m/B W.C. Fields, Cora Witherspoon, Una Merkel, Evelyn Del Rio, Jack Norton, Jessie Ralph, Franklin Pangborn, Shemp Howard, Grady Sutton, Russell Hicks, Richard Purcell, Reed Hadley; **D:** Eddie Cline; **W:** W.C. Fields. **VHS, Beta, LV ★★★★**

Barbarians at the Gate In the "greed is good" financial climate of the '80s, this made-for-cable movie chronicles the $25 billion dollar battle in 1988 for RJR Nabisco, which at the time was working on developing a "smokeless cigarette." Garner is CEO F. Ross Johnson, who is confident that their "smokeless cigarette" will boost the stock's value—until he gets the test-marketing results. Unwilling to risk the product's failure, Johnson decides to buy the company and is challenged by master dealer Kravis (Pryce). Fascinating social commentary on the nastiest mega-deal in history. Based on the book by Bryan Burrough and John Helyar.
1993 (R) 107m/C James Garner, Jonathan Pryce, Peter Riegert, Joanna Cassidy, Fred Dalton Thompson, Leilani Sarelle Ferrer, Matt Clark, Jeffrey DeMunn; **D:** Glenn Jordan; **W:** Larry Gelbart; **M:** Richard Gibbs. Golden Globe Awards '94: Best Movie/Miniseries. **VHS ★★★1/2**

Barbary Coast A ruthless club owner tries to win the love of a young girl by building her into a star attraction during San Francisco's gold rush days. **1935 90m/B** Edward G. Robinson, Walter Brennan, Brian Donlevy, Joel McCrea, Donald Meek, David Niven, Miriam Hopkins; **D:** Howard Hawks. Nominations: Academy Awards '35: Best Cinematography. **VHS, Beta, LV** ★★★

Barcelona Old-fashioned talkfest about two neurotic Americans experiencing sibling rivalry in Spain. Serious Ted (Nichols) is an American sales rep, posted to Barcelona, who can't quite get into the city's pleasure-loving rhythm. This is not a problem for Ted's cousin Fred (Eigeman), an obnoxious naval officer, with whom Ted has had a rivalry dating back to their boyhood. Set in the 1980s, the two must also deal with anti-Americanism, which leads both to violence and romantic developments. Tart dialogue, thoughtful performances, and exotic locales prove enticing in low-budget sleeper that effectively mixes drama and dry comedy. Watch for Eigeman in Tom Cruise's uniform from "A Few Good Men." **1994 (PG-13) 102m/C** Taylor Nichols, Christopher Eigeman, Tushka Bergen, Mira Sorvino, Pep Munne, Francis Creighton, Thomas Gibson, Jack Gilpin, Nuria Badia, Hellena Schmied; **D:** Whit Stillman; **W:** Whit Stillman; **M:** Tom Judson, Mark Suozzo. Independent Spirit Awards '95: Best Cinematography. **VHS, LV** ★★★

The Barefoot Contessa The story, told in flashback, of a Spanish dancer's rise to Hollywood stardom, as witnessed by a cynical director. Shallow Hollywood self-examination. **1954 128m/C** Ava Gardner, Humphrey Bogart, Edmond O'Brien, Valentina Cortese, Rossano Brazzi; **D:** Joseph L. Mankiewicz; **W:** Joseph L. Mankiewicz, Jack Cardiff. Academy Awards '54: Best Supporting Actor (O'Brien); Golden Globe Awards '55: Best Supporting Actor (O'Brien); Nominations: Academy Awards '54: Best Story & Screenplay. **VHS, Beta** ★★★

Barefoot in the Park Neil Simon's Broadway hit translates well to screen. A newly wedded bride (Fonda) tries to get her husband (Redford, reprising his Broadway role) to loosen up and be as free-spirited as she is. **1967 106m/C** Robert Redford, Jane Fonda, Charles Boyer, Mildred Natwick; **D:** Gene Saks; **W:** Neil Simon. Nominations: Academy Awards '67: Best Supporting Actress (Natwick). **VHS, Beta, LV** ★★★

Barfly Bukowski's semi-autobiographical screenplay is the story of a talented writer who chooses to spend his time as a lonely barfly, hiding his literary abilities behind glasses of liquor. Dunaway's character is right on target as the fellow alcoholic. **1987 (R) 100m/C** Mickey Rourke, Faye Dunaway, Alice Krige, Frank Stallone, J.C. Quinn, Jack Nance; **D:** Barbet Schroeder; **W:** Charles Bukowski. **VHS, Beta, LV, 8mm** ★★★

The Barkleys of Broadway The famous dancing team's last film together; they play a quarreling husband/wife showbiz team. ♫ They Can't Take That Away From Me; The Sabre Dance; Swing Trot; Manhattan Downbeat; A Weekend in the Country; My One and Only Highland Fling; You'd Be Hard to Replace; Bouncin' the Blues; Shoes With Wings On. **1949 109m/C** Fred Astaire, Ginger Rogers, Gale Robbins, Oscar Levant, Jacques Francois, Billie Burke; **D:** Charles Walters; **W:** Adolph Green, Betty Comden; **M:** Harry Warren, Ira Gershwin. Nominations: Academy Awards '49: Best Color Cinematography. **VHS, Beta, LV** ★★★

The Barretts of Wimpole Street The moving, almost disturbing, account of poetess Elizabeth Barrett, an invalid confined to her bed, with only her poetry and her dog to keep her company. She is wooed by poet Robert Browning, in whose arms she finds true happiness and a miraculous recovery. Multi-faceted drama expertly played by all. **AKA:** Forbidden Alliance. **1934 110m/B** Fredric March, Norma Shearer, Charles Laughton, Maureen O'Sullivan, Katherine Alexander, Una O'Connor, Ian Wolfe; **D:** Sidney Franklin, Frederick A. (Freddie) Young. Nominations: Academy Awards '34: Best Actress (Shearer), Best Picture. **VHS, LV** ★★★

Barry Lyndon Ravishing adaptation of the classic Thackeray novel about the adventures of an Irish gambler moving from innocence to self-destructive arrogance in the aristocracy of 18th-century England. Visually opulent. Kubrick received excellent performances from all his actors, and a stunning display of history, but the end result still overwhelms. O'Neal has seldom been better. **1975 (PG) 185m/C** Ryan O'Neal, Marisa Berenson, Patrick Magee, Hardy Kruger, Guy Hamilton; **D:** Stanley Kubrick. Academy Awards '75: Best Art Direction/Set Decoration, Best Cinematography, Best Costume Design, Best Original Score; British Academy Awards '75: Best Director (Kubrick); Los Angeles Film Critics Association Awards

'75: Best Cinematography; National Board of Review Awards '75: 10 Best Films of the Year, Best Director (Kubrick); Nominations: Academy Awards '75: Best Adapted Screenplay, Best Director (Kubrick), Best Picture. **VHS, Beta, LV** ★★★1/2

Barton Fink This eerie comic nightmare comes laden with awards (including the Palme D'Or from Cannes) but only really works if you care about the time and place. Fink is a trendy New York playwright staying in a seedy Hollywood hotel in the 1940s, straining to write a simple B-movie script. Macabre events, both real and imagined, compound his writer's block. Superb set design from Dennis Gassner complements an unforgettable cast of grotesques.
1991 (R) 116m/C John Turturro, John Goodman, Judy Davis, Michael Lerner, John Mahoney, Tony Shalhoub, Jon Polito, Steve Buscemi, David Warrilow, Richard Portnow, Christopher Murney, Roger Deakins; **D:** Joel Coen; **W:** Joel Coen, Ethan Coen; **M:** Carter Burwell. Cannes Film Festival '91: Best Actor (Turturro), Best Director (Coen), Best Film; Los Angeles Film Critics Association Awards '91: Best Cinematography, Best Supporting Actor (Lerner); National Society of Film Critics Awards '91: Best Cinematography; Nominations: Academy Awards '91: Best Art Direction/Set Decoration, Best Costume Design, Best Supporting Actor (Lerner). **VHS** ★★★

Basquiat First-time writer/director and renowned '80s pop artist Schnabel paints a celluloid portrait of African-American artist Jean Michel Basquiat, who went from graffiti artist to overnight sensation in the mid-1980s before dying from a drug overdose at 27. Schnabel's firsthand knowledge provides details of the painters, the dealers, and the patrons of the whirlwind New York art scene of the time using an all-star cast (no mean feat on a $3 million budget). Making the move from stage to screen, Wright is an aptly deep and elusive Basquiat, and Bowie stands out in a marvelously conceived portrayal of Basquiat's pseudo-mentor, the equally sensational Warhol. Features authentic works of the artists portrayed and some very convincing Basquiat reproductions done by Schnabel. **AKA:** Build a Fort Set It on Fire.
1996 104m/C David Bowie, Dennis Hopper, Gary Oldman, Jeffrey Wright, Christopher Walken, Michael Wincott, Benicio Del Toro, Parker Posey, Elina Lowensohn, Courtney Love; **D:** Julian Schnabel; **W:** Julian Schnabel; **M:** John Cale. Nominations:

Independent Spirit Awards '97: Best Supporting Actor (Del Toro), Debut Performance (Wright). **VHS** ★★★

Batman The blockbuster fantasy epic that renewed Hollywood's faith in media blitzing. The Caped Crusader is back in Gotham City, where even the criminals are afraid to walk the streets alone. There's a new breed of criminal in Gotham, led by the infamous Joker. Their random attacks via acid-based make-up are just the beginning. Keaton is surprisingly good as the dual personality hero though Nicholson steals the show. Marvelously designed and shot. Much better on the big screen. Followed in 1992 by "Batman Returns."
1989 (PG-13) 126m/C Michael Keaton, Jack Nicholson, Kim Basinger, Robert Wuhl, Tracey Walter, Billy Dee Williams, Pat Hingle, Michael Gough, Jack Palance, Jerry Hall; **D:** Tim Burton; **W:** Sam Hamm, Warren Skaaren; **M:** Danny Elfman, Prince. Academy Awards '89: Best Art Direction/Set Decoration; People's Choice Awards '90: Best Film—Drama. **VHS, Beta, LV, 8mm** ★★★1/2

Batman Forever Holy franchise, Batman! Third-time actioner considerably lightens up Tim Burton's dark vision for a more family-oriented Caped Crusader (now played by Kilmer, who fills out lip requirement nicely). The Boy Wonder also makes a first-time appearance in the bulked-up form of O'Donnell, a street-smart Robin with revenge on his mind. Naturally, the villains still steal the show in the personas of maniacal Carrey (the Riddler) and the sartorially splendid Jones as Harvey "Two-Face" Dent. Rounding out this charismatic cast is Kidman's slinky psychologist Chase Meridian, who's eager to find the man inside the bat (and who can blame her). Lots of splashy toys for the boys and awe-inspiring sets to show you where the money went. A Gotham City gas that did $53 million at its opening weekend box office—breaking the Jurassic Park record, testimony to the power of aggressive marketing.
1995 (PG-13) 121m/C Val Kilmer, Tommy Lee Jones, Jim Carrey, Chris O'Donnell, Nicole Kidman, Drew Barrymore, Debi Mazar, Michael Gough, Pat Hingle; **D:** Joel Schumacher; **W:** Janet Scott Batchler, Akiva Goldman, Lee Batchler; **M:** Elliot Goldenthal. Blockbuster Entertainment Awards '96: Action Actress, Theatrical (Kidman); Nominations: Academy Awards '95: Best Cinematography, Best Sound; Golden Globe Awards '96: Best Song

("Hold Me, Thrill Me, Kiss Me, Kill Me"); MTV Movie Awards '96: Most Desirable Male (Kilmer), Best Villain (Carrey, Jones), Best Song ("Kiss from a Rose," "Hold Me, Thrill Me, Kiss Me, Kill Me") **VHS, LV** ★★★

Battle Cry A group of U.S. Marines train, romance, and enter battle in WWII. Based on the novel by Leon Uris. Part of the "A Night at the Movies" series, this tape simulates a 1955 movie evening, with a cartoon, "Speedy Gonzales," a newsreel, and coming attractions for "Mr. Roberts" and "East of Eden."
1955 169m/C Van Heflin, Aldo Ray, Mona Freeman, Tab Hunter, Dorothy Malone, Anne Francis, James Whitmore, Raymond Massey; *D:* Raoul Walsh. Nominations: Academy Awards '55: Best Original Score. **VHS, Beta, LV** ★★★

The Battle of Algiers Famous, powerful, award-winning film depicting the uprisings against French Colonial rule in 1954 Algiers. A seminal documentary-style film which makes most political films seem ineffectual by comparison in its use of non-professional actors, gritty photography, realistic violence, and a boldly propagandistic sense of social outrage.
1966 123m/B *AL IT* Yacef Saadi, Jean Martin, Brahim Haggiag, Tommaso Neri, Samia Kerbash, Fawzia el Kader, Michele Kerbash, Mohamed Ben Kassen; *D:* Gillo Pontecorvo; *W:* Franco Solinas; *M:* Ennio Morricone. Venice Film Festival '66: Best Film; Nominations: Academy Awards '66: Best Foreign Language Film; Academy Awards '68: Best Director (Pontecorvo), Best Story & Screenplay. **VHS, Beta, LV** ★★★1/2

Battleground A tightly-conceived post-WWII character drama, following a platoon of American soldiers through the Battle of the Bulge. Available in a colorized version.
1949 118m/B Van Johnson, John Hodiak, James Whitmore, George Murphy, Ricardo Montalban, Marshall Thompson, Jerome Courtland, Don Taylor, Bruce Cowling, Leon Ames, Douglas Fowley, Richard Jaeckel, Scotty Beckett; *D:* William A. Wellman; *W:* Robert Pirosh. Academy Awards '49: Best Black and White Cinematography, Best Story & Screenplay; Golden Globe Awards '50: Best Screenplay, Best Supporting Actor (Whitmore); Nominations: Academy Awards '49: Best Director (Wellman), Best Film Editing, Best Picture, Best Supporting Actor (Whitmore). **VHS, Beta, LV** ★★★

The Battleship Potemkin Eisenstein's best work documents mutiny aboard the Russian battleship Potemkin in 1905 which led to a civilian uprising against the Czar in Odessa, and the resulting crackdown by troops loyal to the Czar. Beautiful cinematography, especially the use of montage sequences, changed filmmaking. In particular, a horrifying sequence depicting the slaughter of civilians on an Odessa beach by soldiers coming down the stairs leading to it is exceptional; many movies pay homage to this scene including "The Untouchables" and "Love and Death." Viewers should overlook obvious Marxist overtones and see this film for what it is: a masterpiece. *AKA:* Potemkin; Bronenosets Potemkin.
1925 71m/B *RU* Alexander Antonov, Vladimir Barsky, Grigori Alexandrov, Mikhail Gomorov, Sergei Eisenstein; *D:* Sergei Eisenstein; *M:* Eric Allaman. **VHS, Beta, LV** ★★★★

Beach Blanket Bingo Fifth entry in the "Beach Party" series (after "Pajama Party") is by far the best and has achieved near-cult status. Both Funicello and Avalon are back, but this time a very young Evans catches Avalon's eye. Throw in a mermaid, some moon-doggies, skydiving, sizzling beach parties, and plenty of nostalgic golly-gee-whiz fun and you have the classic '60s beach movie. Totally implausible, but that's half the fun when the sun-worshipping teens become involved in a kidnapping and occasionally break into song. Followed by "How to Stuff a Wild Bikini." ♪ Beach Blanket Bingo; The Cycle Set; Fly Boy; The Good Times; I Am My Ideal; I Think You Think; It Only Hurts When I Cry; New Love; You'll Never Change Him.
1965 96m/C Frankie Avalon, Annette Funicello, Linda Evans, Don Rickles, Buster Keaton, Paul Lynde, Harvey Lembeck, Deborah Walley, John Ashley, Jody McCrea, Marta Kristen, Timothy Carey, Earl Wilson, Bobbi Shaw; *D:* William Asher; *W:* William Asher, Sher Townsend, Leo Townsend; *M:* Les Baxter. **VHS, Beta, LV** ★★★

Beaches Based on the novel by Iris Rainer Dart about two girls whose friendship survived the test of time. The friendship is renewed once more when one of the now middle-aged women learns that she is dying slowly of a fatal disease.
1988 (PG-13) 123m/C Bette Midler, Barbara Hershey, John Heard, Spalding Gray, Lainie Kazan, James Read, Mayim Bialik, Dante Spinotti; *D:* Garry Marshall; *W:* Mary Agnes Donoghue; *M:* Georges Delerue. Nominations: Academy Awards '88: Best Art Direction/Set Decoration. **VHS, Beta, LV, 8mm** ★★★1/2

The Bear Breathtaking, effortlessly entertaining family film about an orphaned bear cub tagging after a grown male and dealing with hunters. The narrative is essentially from the cub's point of view, with very little dialogue. A huge money-maker in Europe. Based on a novel by James Oliver Curwood.
1989 (PG) 92m/C FR Jack Wallace, Tcheky Karyo, Andre Lacombe; *D:* Jean-Jacques Annaud; *W:* Gerard Brach, Michael Kane, Philippe Rousselot; *M:* Bill Conti. Nominations: Academy Awards '89: Best Film Editing. **VHS, Beta, LV ★★★**

Beat the Devil Each person on a slow boat to Africa has a scheme to beat the other passengers to the uranium-rich land that they all hope to claim. An unusual black comedy which didn't fare well when released, but over the years has come to be the epitome of spy-spoofs.
1953 89m/C Humphrey Bogart, Gina Lollobrigida, Peter Lorre, Robert Morley, Jennifer Jones; *D:* John Huston. **VHS, Beta, LV ★★★**

Beatrice In France during the Middle Ages, a barbaric soldier of the Hundred Years' War returns to his estate that his daughter has maintained, only to brutalize and abuse her. In French with English subtitles. *AKA:* La Passion Beatrice.
1988 (R) 132m/C FR Julie Delpy, Barnard Pierre Donnadieu, Nils Tavernier; *D:* Bertrand Tavernier; *W:* Colo Tavernier O'Hagan; *M:* Lili Boulanger. Cesar Awards '88: Best Costume Design. **VHS, Beta, LV ★★★1/2**

Beau Geste The classic Hollywood adventure film based on the Percival Christopher Wren story about three brothers who join the Foreign Legion after nobly claiming responsibility for a jewel theft they didn't commit. Once enlisted, they must face desert wars and the most despicable commanding officer ever, before clearing their family name. A rousing, much-copied epic.
1939 114m/B Gary Cooper, Ray Milland, Robert Preston, Brian Donlevy, Donald O'Connor, J. Carrol Naish, Susan Hayward, James Stephenson; *D:* William A. Wellman. Nominations: Academy Awards '39: Best Interior Decoration, Best Supporting Actor (Donlevy). **VHS, Beta ★★★1/2**

Beau Revel Critically acclaimed romantic drama of the silent era. A passionate dancing girl played by Vidor, one of the twenties' more prolific romantic leads (and erstwhile wife of director King Vidor), is the object of romantic interest of a father and son,

which leaves the threesome lovelorn, suicidal, and emotionally scarred. You might recognize Stone from his later role as Judge Hardy in the MGM "Hardy Family" series.
1921 70m/B Lewis Stone, Florence Vidor, Lloyd Hughes, Katherine Kirkham, William Conklin; *D:* John Wray. **VHS, Beta ★★★1/2**

Beautiful Thing Sweet, fairytale-ish, gay coming-of-age story set in a working-class southeast London housing estate. Shy teenager Jamie (Berry) lives with his barmaid mum, Sandra (Henry), and her lover, Tony (Daniels). Next door is his best mate, the stoic Ste (Neal), who's regularly abused by his father and brother. But when things get too bad, he sleeps over with Jamie. And one night, nature hesitantly takes its course. Their tart-tongued, Mama Cass fanatic, friend Leah (Empson) starts rumors about the twosome that lead to some uneasy (but ultimately conciliatory) confrontations. Fine performances; Harvey adapted from his play
1995 89m/C GB Glen Berry, Scott Neal, Linda Henry, Tameka Empson, Ben Daniels; *D:* Hettie Macdonald; *W:* Jonathan Harvey. **VHS ★★★**

Beauty and the Beast The classic medieval fairy-tale is brought to life on the big screen for the first time. Beauty takes the place of her father after he is sentenced to die by the horrible Beast and falls in love with him. Cocteau uses the story's themes and famous set-pieces to create a cohesive and captivating surreal hymn to romantic love that is still the definitive version of B&B. In French with subtitles. *AKA:* La Belle et Laete.
1946 90m/B FR Jean Marais, Josette Day, Marcel Andre, Mila Parely, Nane Germon, Michel Auclair, Georges Auric; *D:* Jean Cocteau. **VHS, Beta, LV ★★★★**

Beauty and the Beast Wonderful Disney musical combines superb animation, splendid characters, and lively songs about a beautiful girl, Belle, and the fearsome and disagreeable Beast. Supporting cast includes the castle servants (a delightful bunch of household objects). Notable as the first animated feature to be nominated for the Best Picture Oscar. Destined to become a classic. The deluxe video version features a work-in-progress rough film cut, a compact disc of the soundtrack, a lithograph depicting a scene from the film, and an illustrated book. ♪ Beauty and the Beast; Belle; Something There; Be Our Guest.

1991 (G) 84m/C D: Kirk Wise, Gary Trousdale; **M:** Alan Menken, Howard Ashman; **V:** Paige O'Hara, Robby Benson, Rex Everhart, Richard White, Jesse Corti, Angela Lansbury, Jerry Orbach, David Ogden Stiers, Bradley Michael Pierce, Jo Anne Worley, Kimmy Robertson. Academy Awards '91: Best Song ("Beauty and the Beast"), Best Score; Golden Globe Awards '92: Best Film—Musical/Comedy; Nominations: Academy Awards '91: Best Picture, Best Song ("Belle", "Be Our Guest"), Best Sound. **VHS, LV ★★★★**

Becket Adaptation of Jean Anouilh's play about the tumultuous friendship between Henry II of England and the Archbishop of Canterbury Thomas Becket. Becket views his position in the church of little relation to the sexual and emotional needs of a man, until he becomes archbishop. His growing concern for religion and his shrinking need of Henry as friend and confidant eventually cause the demise of the friendship and the resulting tragedy. Flawless acting from every cast member, and finely detailed artistic direction make up for the occasional slow moment.
1964 148m/C Richard Burton, Peter O'Toole, John Gielgud, Donald Wolfit; **D:** Peter Glenville; **W:** Edward Anhalt. Academy Awards '64: Best Adapted Screenplay; Golden Globe Awards '65: Best Actor—Drama (O'Toole), Best Film—Drama; National Board of Review Awards '64: 10 Best Films of the Year; Nominations: Academy Awards '64: Best Actor (Burton), Best Actor (O'Toole), Best Art Direction/Set Decoration (Color), Best Color Cinematography, Best Costume Design (Color), Best Director (Glenville), Best Film Editing, Best Picture, Best Sound, Best Supporting Actor (Gielgud), Best Original Score. **VHS, Beta, LV ★★★**

Bed and Sofa Adultery, abortion, and women's rights are brought about by a housing shortage which forces a man to move in with a married friend. Famous, ground-breaking Russian silent.
1927 73m/B RU Nikolai Batalov, Vladimir Fogel; **D:** Abram Room. **VHS, Beta ★★★1/2**

Bedazzled In the process of hanging himself, Stanley, a short-order cook is approached by the devil with an offer: seven wishes in exchange for his soul. Each of Stanley's wishes is granted with surprising consequences. Cult comedy is a sometimes uneven, but thoroughly entertaining and funny retelling of the Faustian story.

1968 (PG) 107m/C GB Dudley Moore, Peter Cook, Eleanor Bron, Michael Bates, Raquel Welch; **D:** Stanley Donen; **W:** Dudley Moore, Peter Cook; **M:** Dudley Moore. **VHS, Beta, LV ★★★**

Bedlam Creeper set in the famed asylum in 18th-century London. A woman, wrongfully committed, tries to stop the evil doings of the chief (Karloff) of Bedlam, and endangers herself. Fine horror film co-written by producer Lewton.
1945 79m/B Jason Robards Sr., Ian Wolfe, Glenn Vernon, Boris Karloff, Anna Lee, Billy House, Richard Fraser; **D:** Mark Robson. **VHS, Beta, LV ★★★**

Beetlejuice The after-life is confusing for a pair of ultra-nice novice ghosts who are faced with chasing an obnoxious family of postmodern art lovers who move into their house. Then they hear of a poltergeist who promises to rid the house of all trespassers for a price. Things go from bad to impossible when the maniacal Keaton (as the demonic "Betelgeuse") works his magic. The calypso scene is priceless. A cheesy, funny, surreal farce of life after death with inventive set designs popping continual surprises. Ryder is striking as the misunderstood teen with a death complex, while O'Hara is hilarious as the yuppie art poseur.
1988 (PG) 92m/C Michael Keaton, Geena Davis, Alec Baldwin, Sylvia Sidney, Catherine O'Hara, Winona Ryder, Jeffrey Jones, Dick Cavett; **D:** Tim Burton; **W:** Michael McDowell, Warren Skaaren; **M:** Danny Elfman. Academy Awards '88: Best Makeup; National Society of Film Critics Awards '88: Best Actor (Keaton). **VHS, Beta, LV, 8mm ★★★1/2**

The Beguiled During the Civil War a wounded Union soldier is taken in by the women at a girl's school in the South. He manages to seduce both a student and a teacher, and jealousy and revenge ensue. Decidedly weird psychological melodrama from action vets Siegel and Eastwood.
1970 (R) 109m/C Clint Eastwood, Geraldine Page, Elizabeth Hartman; **D:** Donald Siegel; **M:** Lalo Schifrin. **VHS, Beta, LV ★★★**

Being There A feeble-minded gardener, whose entire knowledge of life comes from watching television, is sent out into the real world when his employer dies. Equipped with his prize possession, his remote control unit, the gardener unwittingly enters the world of politics and is welcomed as a mysterious sage. Sellers is won-

derful in this satiric treat adapted by Jerzy Kosinski from his novel.
1979 (PG) 130m/C Peter Sellers, Shirley MacLaine, Melvyn Douglas, Jack Warden, Richard Dysart, Richard Basehart; *D:* Hal Ashby, Caleb Deschanel. Academy Awards '79: Best Supporting Actor (Douglas); British Academy Awards '80: Best Screenplay; Golden Globe Awards '80: Best Actor—Musical/Comedy (Sellers), Best Supporting Actor (Douglas); National Board of Review Awards '79: 10 Best Films of the Year, Best Actor (Sellers); National Society of Film Critics Awards '79: Best Cinematography; Writers Guild of America '79: Best Adapted Screenplay; Nominations: Academy Awards '79: Best Actor (Sellers); Cannes Film Festival '80: Best Film. **VHS, Beta, LV ★★★1/2**

Belle de Jour Based on Joseph Kessel's novel, one of director Bunuel's best movies has all his characteristic nuances: the hypocrisy of our society; eroticism; anti-religion. Deneuve plays Severine, a chic, frigid Parisian newlywed, who decides to become a daytime prostitute, unbeknownst to her husband. Bunuel blends reality with fantasy, and the viewer is never sure which is which in this finely crafted movie. French with subtitles.
1967 (R) 100m/C *FR* Catherine Deneuve, Jean Sorel, Genevieve Page, Michel Piccoli, Francesco Rabal, Pierre Clementi, Georges Marchal, Francoise Fabian; *D:* Luis Bunuel; *W:* Luis Bunuel, Jean-Claude Carriere. Venice Film Festival '67: CINE Golden Eagle. **VHS, LV ★★★★**

Belle Epoque Army deserter Fernando (Sanz) embarks on a personal voyage of discovery when he meets Manolo (Gomez), an eccentric old man, and father to four beautiful daughters. Fernando can't believe his luck—and the sisters share his interest, resulting in an amusing round of musical beds. Lighthearted romp set in 1930s Spain with a terrific screenplay that tastefully handles the material without stooping to the obvious leering possibilities. In addition to Oscar, won nine Spanish Goyas, including best picture, director, actress (Gil), and screenplay. Spanish with English subtitles or dubbed. *AKA:* The Age of Beauty.
1992 (R) 108m/C *SP* Jorge Sanz, Fernando Gomez, Ariadna Gil, Maribel Verdu, Penelope Cruz, Miriam Diaz-Aroca, Mary Carmen Ramirez, Michel Galabru, Gabino Diego; *D:* Fernando Trueba; *W:* Rafael Azcona. Academy Awards '93: Best Foreign Language Film. **VHS, LV ★★★**

The Belles of St. Trinian's Sim is priceless in a dual role as the eccen-tric headmistress of a chaotic, bankrupt girls' school and her bookie twin brother who scheme the school into financial security. The first in a series of movies based on a popular British cartoon by Ronald Searles about a girls' school and its mischievous students. Followed by "Blue Murder at St. Trinian's," "The Pure Hell of St. Trinian's," and "The Great St. Trinian's Train Robbery."
1953 86m/B *GB* Alastair Sim, Joyce Grenfell, Hermione Baddeley, George Cole, Eric Pohlmann, Renee Houston, Beryl Reid; *D:* Frank Launder; *M:* Malcolm Arnold. **VHS, Beta ★★★**

Bells Are Ringing A girl who works for a telephone answering service can't help but take an interest in the lives of the clients, especially a playwright with an inferiority complex. Based on Adolph Green and Betty Comden's Broadway musical. Special letterboxed edition along with the original trailer available on laserdisc format. ♪ Just in Time; The Party's Over; It's a Perfect Relationship; Do It Yourself; It's a Simple Little System; Better Than a Dream; I Met a Girl; Drop That Name; I'm Going Back.
1960 126m/C Judy Holliday, Dean Martin, Fred Clark, Eddie Foy Jr., Jean Stapleton; *D:* Vincente Minnelli; *W:* Betty Comden, Adolph Green; *M:* Andre Previn. Nominations: Academy Awards '60: Best Original Score. **VHS, Beta, LV ★★★**

The Bells of St. Mary's An easygoing priest finds himself in a subtle battle of wits with the Mother Superior over how the children of St. Mary's school should be raised. It's the sequel to "Going My Way." Songs include the title tune and "Aren't You Glad You're You?" Also available in a colorized version.
1945 126m/B Bing Crosby, Ingrid Bergman, Henry Travers; *D:* Leo McCarey. Academy Awards '45: Best Sound; Golden Globe Awards '46: Best Actress—Drama (Bergman); New York Film Critics Awards '45: Best Actress (Bergman); Nominations: Academy Awards '44: Best Actress (Bergman); Academy Awards '45: Best Actor (Crosby), Best Director (McCarey), Best Film Editing, Best Picture, Best Song ("Aren't You Glad You're You"), Best Original Score. **VHS, Beta, LV ★★★1/2**

The Belly of an Architect A thespian feast for the larger-than-life Dennehy as blustering American architect whose personal life and health both crumble as he obsesssively readies an exhibition in Rome. A multi-tiered, carefully composed tragicomedy from the ideosyncratic filmmaker

Greenaway, probably his most accessible work for general audiences.
1991 (R) 119m/C *GB IT* Brian Dennehy, Chloe Webb, Lambert Wilson; *D:* Peter Greenaway; *W:* Peter Greenaway. **VHS, LV** ★★★1/2

Ben-Hur Second film version of the renowned story of Jewish and Christian divisiveness in the time of Jesus. Battle scenes and chariot races still look good, in spite of age. Problems lingered on the set and at a cost of over $4,000,000 it was the most expensive film of its time and took years to finish. A hit at the box office, it still stands as the all-time silent classic. In 1931, a shortened version was released. Based on the novel by Lewis Wallace.
1926 148m/B Ramon Novarro, Francis X. Bushman, May McAvoy, Betty Bronson, Claire McDowell, Carmel Myers, Nigel de Brulier, Ferdinand P. Earle; *D:* Fred Niblo. **VHS, Beta, LV** ★★★★

Ben-Hur The third film version of the Lew Wallace classic stars Heston in the role of a Palestinian Jew battling the Roman empire at the time of Christ. Won a record 11 Oscars. The breathtaking chariot race is still one of the best screen races today. Perhaps one of the greatest pictures of all time. Also available in letterbox format.
1959 212m/C Charlton Heston, Jack Hawkins, Stephen Boyd, Haya Harareet, Hugh Griffith, Martha Scott, Sam Jaffe, Cathy O'Donnell, Finlay Currie; *D:* William Wyler; *M:* Karl Tunberg; *M:* Miklos Rozsa. Academy Awards '59: Best Actor (Heston), Best Art Direction/Set Decoration (Color), Best Color Cinematography, Best Costume Design (Color), Best Director (Wyler), Best Film Editing, Best Picture, Best Sound, Best Special Effects, Best Supporting Actor (Griffith), Best Original Score; British Academy Awards '59: Best Film; Directors Guild of America Awards '59: Best Director (Wyler); Golden Globe Awards '60: Best Director (Wyler), Best Film—Drama, Best Supporting Actor (Boyd); Nominations: Academy Awards '59: Best Adapted Screenplay. **VHS, Beta, LV** ★★★★

Bend of the River A haunted, hardened guide leads a wagon train through Oregon territory, pitting himself against Indians, the wilderness and a former comrade-turned-hijacker. *AKA:* Where the River Bends.
1952 91m/C James Stewart, Arthur Kennedy, Rock Hudson, Harry (Henry) Morgan, Royal Dano; *D:* Anthony Mann. **VHS, Beta** ★★★

Benji In the lovable mutt's first feature-length movie, he falls in love with a female named Tiffany, and saves two young children from kidnappers. Kiddie classic that was a box office hit when first released. Followed by "For the Love of Benji."
1974 (G) 87m/C Benji, Peter Breck, Christopher Connelly, Patsy Garrett, Deborah Walley, Cynthia Smith; *D:* Joe Camp; *W:* Joe Camp; *M:* Euel Box. Golden Globe Awards '75: Best Song ("I Feel Love"); Nominations: Academy Awards '74: Best Song ("Benji's Theme (I Feel Love)"). **VHS, Beta** ★★★

Berlin Alexanderplatz Fassbinder's 15 1/2-hour epic follows the life, death, and resurrection of Franz Biberkof, a former transit worker who has just finished a lengthy prison term and must learn to adjust in the harsh social atmosphere of Berlin in the 1920s. Melodramatic parable with Biblical overtones considered by some to be a masterpiece. Based on the novel by Alfred Doblin; originally aired as a miniseries on German television. On eight tapes.
1980 930m/C *GE* Gunter Lamprecht, Hanna Schygulla, Barbara Sukowa, Gottfried John, Elisabeth Trissenaar, Brigitte Mira, Karin Baal, Ivan Desny; *D:* Rainer Werner Fassbinder. **VHS, Beta** ★★★1/2

Berlin Express Battle of wits ensues between the Allies and the Nazis who are seeking to keep Germans divided in post-WWII Germany. Espionage and intrigue factor heavily.
1948 86m/B Robert Ryan, Merle Oberon, Paul Lukas, Charles Korvin; *D:* Jacques Tourneur. **VHS, Beta, LV** ★★★1/2

The Best Intentions Ingmar Bergman wrote the screenplay chronicling the early years of the stormy relationship of his parents. Set in Sweden at the turn of the century, the film focuses on the class differences that divide his mother and father, while portrayal of little Bergy is limited to a bundle under his mother's maternity dress. Inspired performances and directing illuminates the emotionally complex relationship, revealing truths about the universal human condition along the way. Six-hour version was shot for television in Europe and Japan. Director August and actress August met and married during filming. In Swedish with English subtitles.
1992 182m/C *SW* Samuel Froler, Pernilla August, Max von Sydow, Ghita Norby, Mona Malm, Lena Endre, Bjorn Kjellman; *D:* Bille August; *W:* Ingmar Bergman. Cannes Film Festival '92: Best Actress (August), Best Film. **VHS** ★★★1/2

The Best Little Girl in the World Exceptional made-for-TV tale of an apparently perfect teenager suffering from anorexia. Slow starvation is her only cry for help. Fine performances from Durning and Saint.
1981 96m/C Charles Durning, Eva Marie Saint, Jennifer Jason Leigh, Melanie Mayron, Viveca Lindfors, Jason Miller, David Spielberg, Lisa Pelikan, Ally Sheedy; **D:** Sam O'Steen; **M:** Billy Goldenberg. **VHS, Beta** ★★★

The Best Man An incisive, darkly satiric political tract, based on Gore Vidal's play, about two presidential contenders who vie for the endorsement of the aging ex-president, and trample political ethics in the process.
1964 104m/B Henry Fonda, Cliff Robertson, Lee Tracy, Margaret Leighton, Edie Adams, Kevin McCarthy, Ann Sothern, Gene Raymond, Shelley Berman, Mahalia Jackson; **D:** Franklin J. Schaffner, Haskell Wexler; **W:** Gore Vidal. Nominations: Academy Awards '64: Best Supporting Actor (Tracy). **VHS, Beta** ★★★½

The Best of Everything Trashy sexist soap opera about women seeking success and love in the publishing world of N.Y.C. Several stories take place, the best being Crawford's hard-nosed editor who's having an affair with a married man. Look for Evans as a philandering playboy (he went on to become the producer of "Chinatown," among others.) Based on the novel by Rona Jaffe.
1959 121m/C Hope Lange, Stephen Boyd, Suzy Parker, Diane Baker, Martha Hyer, Joan Crawford, Brian Aherne, Robert Evans, Louis Jourdan; **D:** Jean Negulesco; **W:** Edith Sommer, Mann Rubin; **M:** Alfred Newman. **VHS** ★★★

Best Seller Interesting, subtext-laden thriller about a cop/best-selling author with writer's block, and the strange symbiotic relationship he forms with a slick hired killer, who wants his own story written. Dennehy is convincing as the jaded cop, and is paired well with the psychotic Woods.
1987 (R) 112m/C James Woods, Brian Dennehy, Victoria Tennant, Paul Shenar, Seymour Cassel, Allison Balson, George Coe, Anne Pitoniak; **D:** John Flynn; **W:** Larry Cohen; **M:** Jay Michael Ferguson. **VHS, Beta, LV** ★★★

The Best Years of Our Lives Three WWII vets return home to try to pick up the threads of their lives. A film that represented a large chunk of American society and helped it readjust to the modern postwar ambience is now considered an American classic. Supporting actor Russell, an actual veteran, holds a record for winning two Oscars for a single role. In addition to his Best Supporting Actor award, Russell was given a special Oscar for bringing hope and courage to fellow veterans. Based on the novella by MacKinlay Kantor. Remade for television as "Returning Home" in 1975.
1946 170m/B Fredric March, Myrna Loy, Teresa Wright, Dana Andrews, Virginia Mayo, Harold Russell, Hoagy Carmichael, Gladys George, Roman Bohnen, Steve Cochran, Charles Halton; **D:** William Wyler; **W:** Robert Sherwood; **M:** Hugo Friedhofer. Academy Awards '46: Best Actor (March), Best Director (Wyler), Best Film Editing, Best Picture, Best Screenplay, Best Supporting Actor (Russell), Best Original Score; British Academy Awards '47: Best Film; Golden Globe Awards '47: Best Film—Drama; National Board of Review Awards '46: 10 Best Films of the Year, Best Director (Wyler); Nominations: Academy Awards '46: Best Sound. **VHS, Beta, LV** ★★★★

Betty Blue A vivid, intensely erotic film about two young French lovers and how their inordinately strong passion for each others destroys them, leading to poverty, violence, and insanity. English subtitles. From the director of "Diva." Based on the novel "37.2 Le Matin" by Philippe Djian.
1986 (R) 121m/C *FR* Beatrice Dalle, Jean-Hugues Anglade, Gerard Darmon, Consuelo de Haviland, Clementine Celarie, Jacques Mathou, Vincent Lindon; **D:** Jean-Jacques Beineix; **W:** Jean-Jacques Beineix; **M:** Gabriel Yared. Nominations: Academy Awards '86: Best Foreign Language Film; Cesar Awards '86: Best Actor (Anglade). **VHS, Beta, LV** ★★★

Between the Lines A witty, wonderfully realized ensemble comedy about the staff of a radical post-'60s newspaper always on the brink of folding, and its eventual sell-out.
1977 (R) 101m/C John Heard, Lindsay Crouse, Jeff Goldblum, Jill Eikenberry, Stephen Collins, Lewis J. Stadlen, Michael J. Pollard, Marilu Henner, Bruno Kirby; **D:** Joan Micklin Silver; **W:** Fred Barron; **M:** Michael Kamen. **VHS, Beta** ★★★½

The Bicycle Thief A world classic and indisputable masterpiece about an Italian workman who finds a job, only to have the bike he needs for work stolen; he and his son search Rome for it. A simple story that seems to contain the whole of human experience, and the masterpiece of

Italian neo-realism. Based on the book by Luigi Bartolini. In Italian with English subtitles. *AKA:* Ladri di Biciclette.

1948 90m/B *IT* Lamberto Maggiorani, Lianella Carell, Enzo Staiola, Elena Altieri, Vittorio Antonucci, Gino Saltamerenda, Fausto Guerzoni; *D:* Vittorio De Sica; *W:* Cesare Zavattini. Academy Awards '49: Best Foreign Language Film; British Academy Awards '49: Best Film; Golden Globe Awards '50: Best Foreign Film; National Board of Review Awards '49: 5 Best Foreign Films of the Year, Best Director (De Sica); Nominations: Academy Awards '49: Best Screenplay. **VHS, Beta, LV** ★★★★

Big A 13-year-old boy makes a wish at a carnival fortune-teller to be "big." When he wakes up the next morning he finds that he suddenly won't fit into his clothes and his mother doesn't recognize him. Until he finds a cure, he must learn to live in the adult world—complete with job, apartment, and romance. Perkins is wonderful as a warming cynic while Hanks is totally believable as the little boy inside a man's body. Marshall directs with authority and the whole thing clicks from the beginning.

1988 (PG) 98m/C Tom Hanks, Elizabeth Perkins, John Heard, Robert Loggia, Jared Rushton, David Moscow, Jon Lovitz, Mercedes Ruehl; *D:* Penny Marshall; *W:* Gary Ross; *M:* Howard Shore. Golden Globe Awards '89: Best Actor—Musical/Comedy (Hanks); Los Angeles Film Critics Association Awards '88: Best Actor (Hanks); People's Choice Awards '89: Best Film—Musical/Comedy; Nominations: Academy Awards '88: Best Actor (Hanks), Best Original Screenplay. **VHS, Beta, LV** ★★★1/2

The Big Chill Seven former '60s radicals, now coming upon middle age and middle class affluence, reunite on the occasion of an eighth friend's suicide and use the occasion to re-examine their past relationships and commitments. A beautifully acted, immensely enjoyable ballad to both the counter-culture and its yuppie descendants. Great period music. Kevin Costner is the dead man whose scenes never made it to the big screen.

1983 (R) 108m/C Tom Berenger, Glenn Close, Jeff Goldblum, William Hurt, Kevin Kline, Mary Kay Place, Meg Tilly, JoBeth Williams; *D:* Lawrence Kasdan; *W:* Lawrence Kasdan, Barbara Benedek, John Bailey. Writers Guild of America '83: Best Original Screenplay; Nominations: Academy Awards '83: Best Original

Screenplay, Best Picture, Best Supporting Actress (Close). **VHS, Beta, LV, 8mm** ★★★1/2

Big Combo A gangster's ex-girlfriend helps a cop to smash a crime syndicate. Focuses on the relationship between Wilde's cop and the gangster Conte in an effective film noir, with some scenes of torture that were ahead of their time.

1955 87m/B Cornel Wilde, Richard Conte, Jean Wallace, Brian Donlevy, Earl Holliman, Lee Van Cleef, Helen Walker; *D:* Joseph H. Lewis; *W:* Philip Yordan, John Alton. **VHS, Beta** ★★★

Big Deal on Madonna Street A band of inept crooks plan to make themselves very rich when they attempt to rob a jewelry store. Their elaborate plans cause numerous (and hilarious) disasters. In Italian with English subtitles. Remade as "Crackers." *AKA:* The Usual Unidentified Thieves.

1958 90m/B *IT* Marcello Mastroianni, Vittorio Gassman, Claudia Cardinale; *D:* Mario Monicelli. Nominations: Academy Awards '58: Best Foreign Language Film. **VHS, Beta** ★★★1/2

The Big Easy A terrific thriller. A slick New Orleans detective uncovers a heroin-based mob war while romancing the uptight assistant DA who's investigating corruption on the police force. An easy, Cajun-flavored mystery, a fast-moving action-comedy, a very sexy romance, and a serious exploration of the dynamics of corruption.

1987 (R) 101m/C Dennis Quaid, Ellen Barkin, Ned Beatty, John Goodman, Ebbe Roe Smith, Charles Ludlam, Lisa Jane Persky, Tom O'Brien, Grace Zabriskie; *D:* Jim McBride; *W:* Dan Petrie Jr.; *M:* Brad Fiedel. Independent Spirit Awards '88: Best Actor (Quaid). **VHS, Beta, LV** ★★★1/2

The Big Heat When detective Ford's wife (played by Jocelyn Brando, sister of Marlon) is killed in an explosion meant for him, he pursues the gangsters behind it and uncovers a police scandal. His appetite is whetted after this discovery and he pursues the criminals even more vigorously with the help of gangster moll Gloria Grahame. Definitive film noir.

1953 90m/B Glenn Ford, Lee Marvin, Gloria Grahame, Jocelyn Brando, Alexander Scourby, Carolyn Jones; *D:* Fritz Lang. Edgar Allan Poe Awards '53: Best Screenplay. **VHS, Beta, LV** ★★★1/2

The Big House Prison melodrama at its best follows top con Beery as he plans a big breakout—and is betrayed. Life in the pen is depicted as

brutal and futile, with sadistic guards and a hapless warden. Spawned numerous imitators.
1930 80m/B Wallace Beery, Chester Morris, Robert Montgomery, Lewis Stone, Leila Hyams, George F. Marion Sr., Karl Dane, DeWitt Jennings; **D:** George Hill; **W:** Frances Marion. VHS ★★★

The Big Knife Palance plays a Hollywood superstar who refuses to renew his studio contract, which enrages studio boss Steiger. It seems Steiger knows a very damaging secret about the star and is willing to go to any lengths to have Palance re-sign or wind up destroying himself. A ruthless, emotional look at fame and power, with excellent performances by all. Based on the play by Clifford Odets.
1955 113m/B Jack Palance, Rod Steiger, Ida Lupino, Shelley Winters, Wendell Corey, Jean Hagen, Ilka Chase, Everett Sloane, Wesley Addy, Paul Langton; **D:** Robert Aldrich. LV ★★★

The Big Parade Wonderful WWI silent, considered to be one of the best war flicks of all time. Gilbert and Adoree are exceptional as lovers torn apart by the conflict. Interesting and thoughtful picture of the trauma and trouble brought to men and their loved ones in wartime. Battle scenes are compelling and intense; Vidor's masterpiece.
1925 141m/B John Gilbert, Renee Adoree, Hobart Bosworth, Claire McDowell, Claire Adams, Karl Dane, Tom O'Brien; **D:** King Vidor. VHS, LV ★★★★

The Big Red One Fuller's harrowing, intense semi-autobiographical account of the U.S. Army's famous First Infantry Division in WWII, the "Big Red One." A rifle squad composed of four very young men, led by the grizzled Marvin, cut a fiery path of conquest from the landing in North Africa to the liberation of the concentration camp at Falkenau, Czechoslovakia. In part a tale of lost innocence, the film scores highest by bringing the raw terror of war down to the individual level.
1980 (PG) 113m/C Lee Marvin, Robert Carradine, Mark Hamill, Stephane Audran; **D:** Samuel Fuller; **W:** Samuel Fuller. Nominations: Cannes Film Festival '80: Best Film. VHS, Beta, LV ★★★1/2

The Big Sky It's 1830, and a rowdy band of fur trappers embark upon a back breaking expedition up the uncharted Missouri River. Based on the A.B. Guthrie Jr. novel, it's an effortlessly enjoyable and level-headed Hawksian American myth, with a streak of gentle gallows humor. Also available colorized.
1952 122m/C Kirk Douglas, Dewey Martin, Arthur Hunnicutt, Elizabeth Threatt, Buddy Baer, Steve Geray, Jim Davis; **D:** Howard Hawks. Nominations: Academy Awards '52: Best Black and White Cinematography, Best Supporting Actor (Hunnicutt). VHS, Beta ★★★

The Big Sleep Private eye Philip Marlowe, hired to protect a young woman from her own indiscretions, falls in love with her older sister while uncovering murders galore. A dense, chaotic thriller that succeeded in defining and setting a standard for its genre. The very best Raymond Chandler on film combining a witty script with great performances, especially from Bogart and Bacall.
1946 114m/B Humphrey Bogart, Lauren Bacall, John Ridgely, Martha Vickers, Louis Jean Heydt, Regis Toomey, Peggy Knudsen, Dorothy Malone, Bob Steele, Elisha Cook Jr.; **D:** Howard Hawks; **W:** William Faulkner, Jules Furthman, Leigh Brackett; **M:** Max Steiner. VHS, Beta, LV ★★★★

Big Trail This pioneering effort in wide-screen cinematography was Wayne's first feature film. A wagon train on the Oregon trail encounters Indians, buffalo, tough terrain, and romantic problems.
1930 110m/B John Wayne, Marguerite Churchill, El Brendel, Tully Marshall, Tyrone Power Sr., Ward Bond, Helen Parrish; **D:** Raoul Walsh. VHS, Beta ★★★

Bill A made-for-television movie based on a true story about a mentally retarded man who sets out to live independently after 44 years in an institution. Rooney gives an affecting performance as Bill and Quaid is strong as the filmmaker who befriends him. Awarded Emmys for Rooney's performance and the well written script. Followed by "Bill: On His Own."
1981 97m/C Mickey Rooney, Dennis Quaid, Largo Woodruff, Harry Goz; **D:** Anthony Page. VHS, Beta ★★★

Bill: On His Own Rooney is again exceptional in this sequel to the Emmy-winning TV movie "Bill." After 44 years in an institution, a mentally retarded man copes more and more successfully with the outside world. Fine supporting cast and direction control the melodramatic potential.
1983 100m/C Mickey Rooney, Helen Hunt, Teresa Wright, Dennis Quaid, Largo Woodruff, Paul Leiber, Harry Goz; **D:** Anthony Page. VHS ★★★

Billy Budd The classic Melville good-evil allegory adapted to film, dealing with a British warship in the late 1700s, and its struggle between evil master-at-arms and innocent shipmate. Stamp's screen debut as the naive Billy who is tried for the murder of the sadistic first mate. Well directed and acted.
1962 123m/B GB Terence Stamp, Peter Ustinov, Robert Ryan, Melvyn Douglas, Paul Rogers, John Neville, Ronald Lewis, David McCallum, John Meillon; **D:** Peter Ustinov; **W:** Peter Ustinov, Robert Rossen. Nominations: Academy Awards '62: Best Supporting Actor (Stamp). **VHS, Beta, LV** ★★★

Billy Rose's Jumbo Better-than-average update of the circus picture. Durante and Raye are terrific, as are the Rodgers and Hart songs. Fun, with lively production numbers in the inimitable Berkeley style. ♩ Over and Over Again; Circus on Parade; Why Can't I?; This Can't Be Love; The Most Beautiful Girl in the World; My Romance; Little Girl Blue; What is a Circus; Sawdust, Spangles and Dreams. **AKA:** Jumbo.
1962 125m/C Doris Day, Stephen Boyd, Jimmy Durante, Martha Raye, Dean Jagger; **D:** Charles Walters; **W:** Sidney Sheldon. Nominations: Academy Awards '62: Best Original Score. **VHS, LV** ★★★

Bingo Long Traveling All-Stars & Motor Kings Set in 1939, this film follows the comedic adventures of a lively group of black ball players who have defected from the old Negro National League. The All-Stars travel the country challenging local white teams.
1976 (PG) 111m/C Billy Dee Williams, James Earl Jones, Richard Pryor, Stan Shaw; **D:** John Badham; **W:** Matthew Robbins, Hal Barwood; **M:** William Goldstein. **VHS, Beta** ★★★

Bird The richly-textured, though sadly one-sided biography of jazz sax great Charlie Parker, from his rise to stardom to his premature death via extended heroin use. A remarkably assured, deeply imagined film from Eastwood that never really shows the Bird's genius of creation. The soundtrack features Parker's own solos remastered from original recordings.
1988 (R) 160m/C Forest Whitaker, Diane Venora, Michael Zelniker, Samuel E. Wright, Keith David, Michael McGuire, James Handy, Damon Whitaker, Morgan Nagler; **D:** Clint Eastwood; **W:** Joel Oliansky; **M:** Lennie Niehaus, Jack N. Green. Academy Awards '88: Best Sound; Cannes Film Festival '88: Best Actor (Whitaker); Golden Globe Awards '89: Best Director (Eastwood); New York Film Critics Awards '88: Best Supporting Actress (Venora). **VHS, Beta, LV** ★★★

The Birdcage Somewhat overlong but well-played remake of "La Cage aux Folles" features Williams suppressing his usual manic schtick to portray Armand, the subdued half of a longtime gay couple living in Miami. His partner is the ever-hysterical-but-loving drag queen Albert (Lane), whose presence provides a distinct challenge when Armand's son Val (Futterman) announces his engagement to the daughter of family values, right-wing senator Kevin Keeley (Hackman). When the Senator and family arrive for dinner, Armand tries to play it straight while Albert opts for a matronly mom impersonation (think Barbara Bush). Highlights include Armand's initial attempts to teach Albert to be butch (walk like John Wayne) and Hackman congoing in drag. **AKA:** Birds of a Feather.
1995 (R) 118m/C Robin Williams, Nathan Lane, Gene Hackman, Dianne Wiest, Hank Azaria, Dan Futterman, Christine Baranski, Calista Flockhart, Tom McGowan; Emmanuel Lubezki; **D:** Mike Nichols; **W:** Elaine May. **VHS** ★★★

Birdman of Alcatraz Robert Stroud, convicted of two murders and sentenced to life imprisonment on the Island, becomes an internationally accepted authority on birds. Lovingly told, with stunning performance from Lancaster, and exceptionally fine work from the supporting cast. The confinement of Stroud's prison cell makes the film seem claustrophobic and tedious at times, just as the imprisonment must have been. Ritter played Stroud's mother, who never stops trying to get him out of prison.
1962 143m/B Burt Lancaster, Karl Malden, Thelma Ritter, Betty Field, Neville Brand, Edmond O'Brien, Hugh Marlowe, Telly Savalas; **D:** John Frankenheimer; **M:** Elmer Bernstein. British Academy Awards '62: Best Actor (Lancaster); Nominations: Academy Awards '62: Best Actor (Lancaster), Best Black and White Cinematography, Best Supporting Actor (Savalas), Best Supporting Actress (Ritter). **VHS** ★★★

The Birds Hitchcock attempted to top the success of "Psycho" with this terrifying tale of Man versus Nature, in which Nature alights, one by one, on the trees of Bodega Bay to stage a bloody act of revenge upon the civilized world. Only Hitchcock can twist the harmless into the horrific while

avoiding the ridiculous; this is perhaps his most brutal film, and one of the cinema's purest, horrifying portraits of apocalypse. Based on a short story by Daphne Du Maurier; screenplay by novelist Evan Hunter (aka Ed McBain).
1963 120m/C Rod Taylor, Tippi Hedren, Jessica Tandy, Veronica Cartwright, Suzanne Pleshette; *D:* Alfred Hitchcock. **VHS, Beta, LV** ★★★1/2

Birdy An adaptation of the William Wharton novel about two Philadelphia youths, one with normal interests, the other obsessed with birds, and their eventual involvement in the Vietnam War, wrecking one physically and the other mentally. A hypnotic, evocative film, with a compelling Peter Gabriel soundtrack.
1984 (R) 120m/C Matthew Modine, Nicolas Cage, John Harkins, Sandy Baron, Karen Young, Bruno Kirby; *D:* Alan Parker; *W:* Jack Behr, Sandy Kroopf; *M:* Peter Gabriel. Cannes Film Festival '85: Grand Jury Prize. **VHS, Beta, LV** ★★★1/2

The Birth of a Nation Lavish Civil War epic in which Griffith virtually invented the basics of film grammar. Gish and Walthall have some of the most moving scenes ever filmed and the masterful battle choreography brought the art of cinematography to new heights. Griffith's positive attitude toward the KKK notwithstanding, this was the first feature length silent, and it brought credibility to an entire industry. Based on the play "The Clansman" and the book "The Leopard's Spots" by Thomas Dixon, it is still a rouser, and of great historical interest. Silent with music score. Also available in a 124 minute version. *AKA:* The Clansman.
1915 175m/B Lillian Gish, Mae Marsh, Henry B. Walthall, Robert "Bobbie" Harron, Wallace Reid, Joseph Henabery, Donald Crisp, Raoul Walsh, Erich von Stroheim, Eugene Pallette; *D:* D.W. Griffith. **VHS, LV** ★★★★

The Bishop's Wife An angel comes down to earth at Christmas to help a young bishop, his wife and his parishioners. Excellent performances by the cast make this an entertaining outing.
1947 109m/B Cary Grant, Loretta Young, David Niven, Monty Woolley, Elsa Lanchester, James Gleason, Gladys Cooper, Regis Toomey; *D:* Henry Koster. Academy Awards '47: Best Sound; Nominations: Academy Awards '47: Best Director (Koster), Best Film Editing, Best Picture, Best Original Score. **VHS, Beta, LV** ★★★

Bite the Bullet Moralistic western tells of a grueling 600-mile horse race where the participants reluctantly develop respect for one another. Unheralded upon release and shot in convincing epic style by Harry Stradling, Jr. Excellent cast.
1975 (PG) 131m/C Gene Hackman, James Coburn, Candice Bergen, Dabney Coleman, Jan-Michael Vincent, Ben Johnson, Ian Bannen, Paul Stewart, Sally Kirkland; *D:* Richard Brooks; *W:* Richard Brooks; *M:* Alex North. Nominations: Academy Awards '75: Best Sound, Best Original Score. **VHS, Beta, LV** ★★★1/2

The Bitter Tea of General Yen Stanwyck arrives in Shanghai to marry a missionary (Gordon) during the threatening days of China's civil war. Unexpectedly swept into the arms of an infamous warlord (Asher), she becomes fascinated, although his attempts to seduce her fail. She even remains with him while his enemies close in. Exotic and poetic, if melodramatic by today's standards. The interracial aspects were considered very daring for their time. Adapted from the book by Grace Zaring Stone.
1933 89m/B Barbara Stanwyck, Nils Asther, Gavin Gordon, Walter Connolly, Lucien Littlefield, Toschia Mori, Richard Loo, Clara Blandick; *D:* Frank Capra; *W:* Edward Paramore. **VHS** ★★★

Bizarre Bizarre A mystery writer is accused of murder and disappears, only to return in disguise to try to clear his name. Along the way, a number of French comedians are introduced with a revue of comedy-farce sketches that include slapstick, burlesque, black humor, and comedy of the absurd. In French with English subtitles. *AKA:* Drole de Drama.
1939 90m/B *FR* Louis Jouvet, Michel Simon, Francoise Rosay; *D:* Marcel Carne. **VHS, Beta** ★★★

Black and White in Color An award-winning satire about a French soldier at an African outpost, who, upon hearing the news of the beginning of WWI, takes it upon himself to attack a neighboring German fort. Calamity ensues. In French, with English subtitles. *AKA:* La Victoire en Chantant.
1976 (PG) 100m/C *FR* Jean Carmet, Jacques Dufilho, Catherine Rouvel, Jacques Spiesser, Dora Doll, Jacques Perrin; *D:* Jean-Jacques Annaud; *W:* George Conchon, Jean-Jacques Annaud; *M:* Pierre Bachelet. Academy Awards '76: Best Foreign Language Film. **VHS, Beta, LV** ★★★

The Black Cat The first of the Boris and Bela pairings stands up well years after release. Polished and taut, with fine sets and interesting acting. Confrontation between architect and devil worshipper acts as plot, with strange twists. Worth a look. Also available with "The Raven" (1935) on laserdisc. *AKA:* House of Doom.
1934 65m/B Boris Karloff, Bela Lugosi, David Manners, Jacqueline Wells, Lucille Lund, Henry Armetta; *D:* Edgar G. Ulmer. **VHS, LV ★★★1/2**

Black Fury A coal miner's efforts to protest working conditions earn him a beating by the company goons who also kill his friend. He draws national attention to this brutal plight of the workers when he barricades himself inside the mine. Muni's carefully detailed performance adds authenticity to this powerful drama, but it proved too depressing to command a big box office.
1935 95m/B Paul Muni, Barton MacLane, Henry O'Neill, John Qualen, J. Carrol Naish; *D:* Michael Curtiz. **VHS, Beta ★★★**

Black Narcissus A group of Anglican nuns attempting to found a hospital and school in the Himalayas confront native distrust and human frailties amid beautiful scenery. Adapted from the novel by Rumer Godden. Stunning cinematography. Crucial scenes were cut from the American release by censors.
1947 101m/C *GB* Deborah Kerr, David Farrar, Sabu, Jean Simmons, Kathleen Byron, Flora Robson, Esmond Knight; *D:* Michael Powell, Emeric Pressburger, Jack Cardiff. Academy Awards '47: Best Art Direction/Set Decoration (Color), Best Color Cinematography; New York Film Critics Awards '47: Best Actress (Kerr). **VHS, Beta, LV ★★★1/2**

Black Orpheus The legend of Orpheus and Eurydice unfolds against the colorful background of the carnival in Rio de Janeiro. In the black section of the city, Orpheus is a street-car conductor and Eurydice, a country girl fleeing from a man sworn to kill her. Dancing, incredible music, and black magic add to the beauty of this film. Based on the play "Orfeu da Conceica." In Portuguese with English subtitles or dubbed. *AKA:* Orfeu Negro.
1958 103m/C *BR FR PT* Breno Mello, Marpessa Dawn, Lea Garcia, Fausto Guerzoni, Lourdes De Oliveira; *D:* Marcel Camus; *M:* Antonio Carlos Jobim, Luis Bonfa. Academy Awards '59: Best Foreign Language Film; Cannes Film Festival '59: Best Film; Golden Globe Awards '60: Best Foreign Film. **VHS, Beta, LV ★★★1/2**

Black Rain Erstwhile Ozu assistant Imamura directs this powerful portrait of a post-Hiroshima family five years after the bombing. Tanaka plays a young woman who, having been caught in a shower of black rain (radioactive fallout) on an ill-timed visit to Hiroshima, returns to her village to find herself ostracized by her peers and no longer considered marriageworthy. Winner of numerous awards (including five Japanese Academy Awards). In Japanese with English subtitles. *AKA:* Kuroi Ame.
1988 123m/B *JP* Kazuo Kitamura, Yoshiko Tanaka, Etsuko Ichihara, Shoichi Ozawa, Norihei Miki; *D:* Shohei Imamura. **VHS ★★★**

Black Robe In 1634 a young Jesuit priest journeys across the North American wilderness to bring the word of God to Canada's Huron Indians. The winter journey is brutal and perilous and he begins to question his mission after seeing the strength of the Indian's native ways. Stunning cinematography, a good script, and fine acting combine to make this superb. Portrays the Indians in a realistic manner, the only flaw being that Beresford portrays the white culture with very few redeeming qualities and as the only reason for the Indian's downfall. Moore adapted his own novel for the screen. Winner of six Canadian Genie awards in 1991.
1991 (R) 101m/C *AU CA* Lothaire Bluteau, Aden Young, Sandrine Holt, August Schellenberg, Tantoo Cardinal, Billy Two Rivers, Lawrence Bayne, Harrison Liu; *D:* Bruce Beresford; *W:* Brian Moore; *M:* Georges Delerue. Australian Film Institute '92: Best Cinematography. **VHS, LV ★★★1/2**

The Black Room As an evil count lures victims into his castle of terror, the count's twin brother returns to fulfill an ancient prophecy. Karloff is wonderful in his dual role as the twin brothers.
1935 70m/B Boris Karloff, Marian Marsh, Robert Allen, Katherine DeMille, John Buckler, Thurston Hall; *D:* Roy William Neill. **Beta, LV ★★★**

The Black Stallion A young boy and a wild Arabian Stallion are the only survivors of a shipwreck, and they develop a deep affection for each other. When rescued, they begin training for an important race. Exceptionally beautiful first half. Rooney plays a horse trainer, again. Great for adults and kids.
1979 (PG) 120m/C Kelly Reno, Mickey Rooney, Teri Garr, Clarence Muse; *D:*

Carroll Ballard; **W:** William D. Wittliff, Melissa Mathison, Jeanne Rosenberg, Caleb Deschanel; **M:** Carmine Coppola. Academy Awards '79: Best Sound Effects Editing; Los Angeles Film Critics Association Awards '79: Best Cinematography; National Society of Film Critics Awards '79: Best Cinematography; Nominations: Academy Awards '79: Best Film Editing, Best Supporting Actor (Rooney). **VHS, Beta, LV** ★★★

The Black Swan Swashbuckling pirate film, based on the novel by Rafael Sabatini, stars Power as James Waring, compatriot of notorious buccanneer Henry Morgan (Cregar). Morgan is pardoned and sent to Jamaica as its new governor—if he can prevent his former associates from continuing their criminal ways. He enlists Waring to help him fight the renegades; meanwhile Waring falls in love with former governor's daughter Margaret (O'Hara). Lots of derring do. **1942 85m/C** Tyrone Power, Maureen O'Hara, Laird Cregar, Thomas Mitchell, George Sanders, Anthony Quinn, George Zucco, Edward Ashley, Fortunio Bonanova; **D:** Henry King; **W:** Ben Hecht, Seton I. Miller; **M:** Alfred Newman, Leon Shamroy. Academy Awards '42: Best Color Cinematography; Nominations: Academy Awards '42: Best Original Score. **VHS** ★★★

Black Widow A federal agent pursues a beautiful murderess who marries rich men and then kills them, making the deaths look natural. The agent herself becomes involved in the final seduction. The two women are enticing and the locations picturesque. **1987 (R) 101m/C** Debra Winger, Theresa Russell, Sami Frey, Nicol Williamson, Terry O'Quinn, Dennis Hopper, D.W. Moffett, Lois Smith, Mary Woronov, Rutanya Alda, James Hong, Diane Ladd; **Cameos:** David Mamet; **D:** Bob Rafelson; **W:** Ronald Bass; **M:** Michael Small, Conrad Hall. **VHS, Beta, LV** ★★★

Blackboard Jungle Well-remembered urban drama about an idealistic teacher in a slum area who fights doggedly to connect with his unruly students. Bill Hailey's "Rock Around the Clock" over the opening credits was the first use of rock music in a mainstream feature film. Based on Evan Hunter novel. **1955 101m/B** Glenn Ford, Anne Francis, Louis Calhern, Sidney Poitier, Vic Morrow, Richard Kiley, Margaret Hayes, John Hoyt, Warner Anderson; **D:** Richard Brooks; **W:** Richard Brooks. Nominations: Academy Awards '55: Best Art Direction/Set

Decoration (B & W), Best Black and White Cinematography, Best Film Editing, Best Screenplay. **VHS, Beta** ★★★½

Blackmail This first sound film for Great Britain and director Hitchcock features an early visualization of some typical Hitchcockian themes. The story follows the police investigation of a murder, and a detective's attempts to keep his girlfriend from being involved. Look for Hitchcock's screen cameo. Made as a silent, this was reworked to become a talkie. **1929 86m/B** *GB* Anny Ondra, John Longden, Sara Allgood, Charles Paton, Cyril Ritchard; **Cameos:** Alfred Hitchcock; **D:** Alfred Hitchcock; **W:** Charles Bennett, Alfred Hitchcock. **VHS, Beta, LV** ★★★

Blade Runner Los Angeles, the 21st century. World-weary cop tracks down a handful of renegade "replicants" (synthetically produced human slaves who, with only days left of life, search madly for some way to extend their prescribed lifetimes). Moody, beautifully photographed, dark thriller with sets from an architect's dream. Based on "Do Androids Dream of Electric Sheep" by Philip K. Dick. Laser edition features restored footage, information about special effects, and production sketches. Director's cut, released at 117 minutes, removes Ford's narration and the last scene of the film, which Scott considered too "up," and inserts several short scenes, including a dream sequence. **1982 (R) 122m/C** Harrison Ford, Rutger Hauer, Sean Young, Daryl Hannah, M. Emmet Walsh, Edward James Olmos, Joe Turkel, Brion James, Joanna Cassidy; **D:** Ridley Scott; **W:** Hampton Fancher, David Peoples; **M:** Vangelis. Los Angeles Film Critics Association Awards '82: Best Cinematography; Nominations: Academy Awards '82: Best Art Direction/Set Decoration. **VHS, Beta, LV, 8mm** ★★★½

Blazing Saddles Wild, wacky spoof by Brooks of every cliche in the western film genre. Little is Black Bart, a convict offered a reprieve if he will become a sheriff and clean up a nasty frontier town; the previous recipients of this honor have all swiftly ended up in shallow graves. A crazy, silly film with a cast full of lovable loonies including comedy greats Wilder, Kahn, and Korman. Watch for the Count Basie Orchestra. A group writing effort, based on an original story by Bergman. Was the most-viewed movie in its first year of release on HBO cable. **1974 (R) 90m/C** Cleavon Little, Harvey

Korman, Madeline Kahn, Gene Wilder, Mel Brooks, John Hillerman, Alex Karras, Dom DeLuise, Liam Dunn; **D:** Mel Brooks; **W:** Mel Brooks, Norman Steinberg, Andrew Bergman, Richard Pryor; **M:** John Morris. Writers Guild of America '74: Best Original Screenplay; Nominations: Academy Awards '74: Best Film Editing, Best Song ("Blazing Saddles"), Best Supporting Actress (Kahn). **VHS, Beta, LV** ★★★1/2

Blind Husbands An Austrian officer is attracted to the pretty wife of a dull surgeon. Controversial in its day, this lurid, sumptuous melodrama instigated many stubborn Hollywood myths, including the stereotype of the brusque, jodhpur-clad Prussian officer. This was von Stroheim's first outing as director.
1919 98m/B Erich von Stroheim, Fay Wray; **D:** Erich von Stroheim. **VHS, Beta** ★★★1/2

Bliss A savage, surreal Australian comedy about an advertising executive who dies suddenly for a few minutes, and upon his awakening he finds the world maniacally, bizarrely changed. Based on the Peter Carey novel, and one of the most inspired absurdist films of the decade.
1985 (R) 112m/C *AU* Barry Otto, Lynette Curran, Helen Jones; **D:** Ray Lawrence; **W:** Peter Carey. Australian Film Institute '85: Best Film. **VHS, Beta, LV** ★★★1/2

The Bliss of Mrs. Blossom Three's a crowd in this lighthearted romp through the machinations of a brassiere manufacturer (Attenborough) and his neglected wife (MacLaine). Mrs. Blossom finds sewing machine repairman Booth so appetizing that she hides him in the attic of the Blossom home. He reads books and redecorates, until, several plot twists later, Attenborough discovers the truth. Witty and wise, with fine supporting cast and excellent pacing.
1968 93m/C *GB* Shirley MacLaine, Richard Attenborough, James Booth, Freddie Jones, John Cleese; **D:** Joseph McGrath. **LV** ★★★

Blithe Spirit Charming and funny adaptation of Coward's famed stage play. A man re-marries and finds his long-dead wife is unhappy enough about it to come back and haunt him. Clever supporting cast, with Rutherford exceptional as the medium. Received Oscar for its special effects.
1945 96m/C *GB* Rex Harrison, Constance Cummings, Kay Hammond, Margaret Rutherford, Hugh Wakefield, Joyce Carey; **D:** David Lean. Academy Awards '46: Best Special Effects. **VHS** ★★★1/2

The Blob A hi-tech remake of the 1958 camp classic about a small town beset by a fast-growing, man-eating mound of glop shot into space by scientists, irradiated into an unnatural being, and then returned to earth. Well-developed characters make this an excellent tribute to the first film.
1988 (R) 92m/C Kevin Dillon, Candy Clark, Joe Seneca, Shawnee Smith, Donovan Leitch, Jeffrey DeMunn, Ricky Paull Goldin; **D:** Chuck Russell; **W:** Frank Darabont, Chuck Russell. **VHS, Beta, LV** ★★★

Block-heads Twenty years after the end of WWI, soldier Stan is found, still in his foxhole, and brought back to America, where he moves in with old pal Ollie. Also includes a 1934 Charley Chase short "I'll Take Vanilla."
1938 75m/B Stan Laurel, Oliver Hardy, Billy Gilbert, Patricia Ellis, James Finlayson, Charley Chase; **D:** John Blystone. **VHS, Beta** ★★★

Blonde Venus A German cafe singer marries an Englishman, but their marriage hits the skids when he contracts radiation poisoning and she gets a nightclub job to pay the bills. Sternberg's and Dietrich's fourth film together, and characteristically beautiful, though terribly strange. Dietrich's cabaret number "Hot Voodoo," in a gorilla suit and blonde afro, attains new heights in early Hollywood surrealism.
1932 94m/B Marlene Dietrich, Herbert Marshall, Cary Grant, Dickie Moore, Hattie McDaniel, Sidney Toler; **D:** Josef von Sternberg. **VHS, Beta** ★★★1/2

Blood and Sand Director Mamoulian "painted" this picture in the new technicolor technique, which makes it a veritable explosion of color and spectacle. Power is the matador who becomes famous and then falls when he is torn between two women, forsaking his first love, bullfighting. Based on the novel "Sangre y Arena" by Vicente Blasco Ibanez. This movie catapulted Hayworth to stardom, primarily for her dancing, but also for her sexiness and seductiveness (and of course, her acting). Remake of the 1922 silent classic; remade again in 1989.
1941 123m/C Tyrone Power, Linda Darnell, Rita Hayworth, Alla Nazimova, Anthony Quinn, J. Carrol Naish, John Carradine, George Reeves; **D:** Rouben Mamoulian; **W:** Jo Swerling; **M:** Alfred Newman. Academy Awards '41: Best Color Cinematography; Nominations: Academy Awards '41: Best Interior Decoration. **VHS, Beta, LV** ★★★

Blood Simple A jealous husband hires a sleazy private eye to murder his adulterous wife and her lover. A dark, intricate, morbid morality tale that deviates imaginatively from the standard murder mystery thriller. First film scripted by the Coen brothers.
1985 (R) 96m/C John Getz, M. Emmet Walsh, Dan Hedaya, Frances McDormand; **D:** Joel Coen; **W:** Ethan Coen, Joel Coen; **M:** Carter Burwell. Independent Spirit Awards '86: Best Actor (Walsh), Best Director (Coen). **VHS, Beta, LV** ★★★★

Blood Wedding A wonderfully passionate dance film from Saura and choreographed by Gades, based on the play by famed author Federico Garcia Lorca. A young bride runs off with her married lover on her wedding day and her jilted husband comes after them. If you like flamenco, there are two more: "Carmen" and "El Amor Brujo." In Spanish with English subtitles. **AKA:** Bodas de Sangre.
1981 71m/C SP Antonio Gades, Christina Hoyos, Marisol, Carmen Villena; **D:** Carlos Saura. **VHS, Beta** ★★★

Blow-Up A young London photographer takes some pictures of a couple in the park and finds out he may have recorded evidence of a murder. Though marred by badly dated 1960s modishness, this is Antonioni's most accessible film, a sophisticated treatise on perception and the film-consumer-as-voyeur, brilliantly assembled and wrought.
1966 111m/C GB IT David Hemmings, Vanessa Redgrave, Sarah Miles, Jane Birkin, Veruschka; **D:** Michelangelo Antonioni; **W:** Tonino Guerra, Michelangelo Antonioni; **M:** Herbie Hancock, Carlo DiPalma. Cannes Film Festival '67: Best Film; National Society of Film Critics Awards '66: Best Director (Antonioni), Best Film; Nominations: Academy Awards '66: Best Director (Antonioni), Best Story & Screenplay. **VHS, Beta, LV** ★★★★

The Blue Angel Tale of a man stripped of his dignity. A film classic filled with sensuality and decay, which made Dietrich a European star and led to her discovery in Hollywood. When a repressed professor (Jannings) goes to a nightclub hoping to catch some of his students in the wrong, he's taken by Lola, the sultry singer portrayed by Dietrich. After spending the night with her, losing his job, and then marrying her, he goes on tour with the troupe, peddling indiscreet photos of his wife. Versions were shot in both German and English, with the German version sporting English subtitles. ♪ Falling in Love Again; They Call Me Wicked Lola. **AKA:** Der Blaue Engel.
1930 90m/B GE Marlene Dietrich, Emil Jannings, Kurt Gerron, Rosa Valetti, Hans Albers; **D:** Josef von Sternberg; **W:** Karl Vollmoller, Robert Liebmann, Carl Zuckmayer; **M:** Friedrich Hollander. **VHS, Beta, 8mm** ★★★★

The Blue Bird A weird, dark fantasy about two children who search for the blue bird of happiness in various fantasy lands, but find it eventually at home. Overlooked and impressively fatalistic.
1940 (G) 98m/C Shirley Temple, Gale Sondergaard, John Russell, Eddie Collins, Nigel Bruce, Jessie Ralph, Spring Byington, Sybil Jason; **D:** Walter Lang. Nominations: Academy Awards '40: Best Color Cinematography. **VHS, Beta** ★★★

Blue Collar An auto assembly line worker, tired of the poverty of his life, hatches a plan to rob his own union. A study of the working class and the robbing of the human spirit.
1978 (R) 114m/C Richard Pryor, Harvey Keitel, Yaphet Kotto, Ed Begley Jr.; **D:** Paul Schrader; **W:** Paul Schrader, Leonard Schrader; **M:** Jack Nitzsche. **VHS, Beta, LV** ★★★

The Blue Dahlia Classic film noir finds Navy vet Johnny Morrison (Ladd) returning home to discover his wife Helen (Dowling) has been keeping the home fires burning—with Eddie Harwood (Da Silva), owner of the Blue Dahlia nightclub. After a nasty fight, Johnny takes off and is picked up by sultry blonde Joyce (Lake). The next day Johnny discovers he's wanted by the cops for the murder of his wife and decides to hide out until he can find the real killer, with Joyce's help. Very stylish and fast-paced with excellent performances; Chandler's first original screenplay.
1946 100m/B Alan Ladd, Veronica Lake, William Bendix, Howard da Silva, Doris Dowling, Tom Powers, Hugh Beaumont, Howard Freeman, Don Costello; **D:** George Marshall; **W:** Raymond Chandler; **M:** Victor Young, Lionel Lindon. **VHS** ★★★1/2

The Blue Kite Fifteen years of political and cultural upheaval in China is shown through the eyes of young troublemaker Tietou, who certainly earns his nickname of "Iron Head" after his 1954 birth. Soon his father is sent to a labor reform camp and his mother remarries—only to be faced with more struggles as the years go by. The kite is Tietou's cherished toy, which keeps getting lost or destroyed but is always being rebuilt, offering one token of hope. In Chinese with English subtitles.

1993 138m/C *CH* Lu Liping, Zhang Wenyao, Pu Quanxin; **D:** Tian Zhuangzhuang; **W:** Xiao Mao. Nominations: Independent Spirit Awards '95: Best Foreign Language Film. **VHS** ★★★

The Blue Lamp Action-adventure fans familiar with the hoary plot where a cop must avenge the wrongful death of his partner will appreciate this suspenseful British detective effort. It's one of the very first in the genre to explore buddy cop revenge in a very British sort of way. Also sports a concluding chase scene which has stood the test of time. Led to the long-running British TV series "Dixon of Dock Green."

1949 84m/B *GB* Dirk Bogarde, Jimmy Hanley, Jack Warner, Bernard Lee, Robert Flemyng, Patric Doonan, Bruce Seton, Frederick Piper, Betty Ann Davies, Peggy Evans; **D:** Basil Dearden. British Academy Awards '50: Best Film. **VHS** ★★★

Blue Skies Former dancer turned radio personality Astaire flashes back to his friendship with singer Crosby and the gal (Caulfield) that came between them. Flimsy plot is just an excuse for some 20 Irving Berlin songs and Astaire's split-screen dance number, "Puttin' on the Ritz." ♪ All By Myself; Always; Any Bonds Today?; Blue Skies; A Couple of Song and Dance Men; Everybody Step; Getting Nowhere; Heat Wave; I'll See You in C-U-B-A.

1946 104m/C Fred Astaire, Bing Crosby, Joan Caulfield, Billy DeWolfe, Olga San Juan, Frank Faylen; **D:** Stuart Heisler; **W:** Arthur Sheekman. **VHS, LV** ★★★

Blue Sky Carly Marshall (Lange) is an irrepressible beauty, long married to adoring but uptight military scientist Hank (Jones). Things are barely in control when they're stationed in Hawaii but after Hank's transfer to a backwater base in Alabama, Carly's emotional mood swings go wildly out of control. Hell truly breaks loose when Carly attracts the attention of the camp's commander (Boothe), who's only too willing to take advantage. Set in 1962, a nuclear radiation subplot (Hank's new project) proves a minor distraction. Exceptional performance by Lange with Jones providing a quiet counterpoint as a man still deeply in love with his disturbed wife. Director Richardson's final film. Release date was delayed to 1994 due to Orion's financial problems.

1991 (PG-13) 101m/C Jessica Lange, Tommy Lee Jones, Powers Boothe, Carrie Snodgress, Amy Locane, Chris O'Donnell, Mitchell Ryan, Dale Dye; **D:** Tony Richardson; **W:** Jerry Leichtling, Arlene Sarner, Rama Laurie Stagner; **M:** Jack Nitzsche. Academy Awards '94: Best Actress (Lange); Golden Globe Awards '95: Best Actress—Drama (Lange); Los Angeles Film Critics Association Awards '94: Best Actress (Lange); Nominations: Screen Actors Guild Award '94: Best Actress (Lange). **VHS, LV** ★★★

Blue Velvet Disturbing, unique exploration of the dark side of American suburbia, involving an innocent college youth who discovers a severed ear in an empty lot, and is thrust into a turmoil of depravity, murder, and sexual deviance. Brutal, grotesque, and unmistakably Lynch; an immaculately made, fiercely imagined film that is unlike any other. Mood is enhanced by the Badalamenti soundtrack. Graced by splashes of Lynchian humor, most notably the movie's lumber theme. Hopper is riveting as the chief sadistic nutcase and Twin Peaks' MacLachlan is a study in loss of innocence. Cinematography by Frederick Elmes.

1986 (R) 121m/C Kyle MacLachlan, Isabella Rossellini, Dennis Hopper, Laura Dern, Hope Lange, Jack Nance, Dean Stockwell, George Dickerson, Brad Dourif; **D:** David Lynch; **W:** David Lynch; **M:** Angelo Badalamenti. Independent Spirit Awards '87: Best Actress (Rossellini); Los Angeles Film Critics Association Awards '86: Best Director (Lynch), Best Supporting Actor (Hopper); National Society of Film Critics Awards '86: Best Cinematography, Best Director (Lynch), Best Film, Best Supporting Actor (Hopper); Nominations: Academy Awards '86: Best Director (Lynch). **VHS, Beta, LV** ★★★

Blume in Love An ironic comedy/drama about a man who falls hopelessly in love with his ex-wife who divorced him for cheating on her while they were married.

1973 (R) 115m/C George Segal, Susan Anspach, Kris Kristofferson, Shelley Winters, Marsha Mason; **D:** Paul Mazursky; **W:** Paul Mazursky; **M:** Bill Conti. **VHS, Beta** ★★★

Bob Dylan: Don't Look Back A famous documentary about Bob Dylan at the beginning of his career: on the road, in performance and during private moments. From the director of "Monterey Pop."

1991 95m/B Bob Dylan, Joan Baez, Donovan; **D:** D.A. Pennebaker. **VHS, Beta, LV** ★★★

Bob le Flambeur Wonderful film noir of a compulsive gambler who de-

cides to take a final fling by robbing the casino at Deauville. In French, subtitled in English. English title is "Bob the Gambler."
1955 106m/B FR Roger Duchesne, Isabel Corey, Daniel Cauchy; *D:* Jean-Pierre Melville. **VHS, Beta, LV** ★★★

Bob Roberts Pseudo-documentary satire about a 1990 Pennsylvania senatorial race between Robbins' right-wing folk singer/entrepreneur versus Vidal's aging liberal incumbent. Roberts seems like a gee-whiz kinda guy but he'll stop at nothing to get elected and he knows a lot about political dirty tricks and, even more important, manipulating the media to get what he wants. Robbins directorial debut turned out to be very timely in view of the 1992 presidential campaign. Features a number of cameos. Line to remember: "Vote first. Ask questions later."
1992 (R) 105m/C Tim Robbins, Giancarlo Esposito, Ray Wise, Rebecca Jenkins, Harry J. Lennix, John Ottavino, Robert Stanton, Alan Rickman, Gore Vidal, Brian Doyle-Murray, Anita Gillette, David Strathairn; *Cameos:* Susan Sarandon, James Spader, John Cusack, Fred Ward, Pamela Reed; *D:* Tim Robbins; *W:* Tim Robbins; *M:* David Robbins. **VHS, LV** ★★★

Body and Soul A young boxer fights his way unscrupulously to the top. Vintage '40s boxing film that defines the genre. Remade in 1981. *AKA:* An Affair of the Heart.
1947 104m/B John Garfield, Lilli Palmer, Hazel Brooks, Anne Revere, William Conrad, Canada Lee; *D:* Robert Rossen; *W:* Abraham Polonsky. Academy Awards '47: Best Film Editing; Nominations: Academy Awards '47: Best Actor (Garfield), Best Original Screenplay. **VHS, LV** ★★★1/2

Body Double A voyeuristic unemployed actor peeps on a neighbor's nightly disrobing and sees more than he wants to. A grisly murder leads him into an obsessive quest through the world of pornographic films.
1984 (R) 114m/C Craig Wasson, Melanie Griffith, Greg Henry, Deborah Shelton, Guy Boyd, Dennis Franz, David Haskell, Rebecca Stanley, Barbara Crampton; *D:* Brian DePalma; *W:* Brian DePalma, Robert J. Avrech, Stephen Burum; *M:* Pino Donaggio. National Society of Film Critics Awards '84: Best Supporting Actress (Griffith). **VHS, Beta, LV** ★★★

Body Heat During a Florida heat wave, a none-too-bright lawyer becomes involved in a steamy love affair with a mysterious woman and then in a plot to kill her husband. Hurt and Turner (in her film debut) became stars under Kasdan's direction (the three would reunite for "The Accidental Tourist"). Hot love scenes supplement a twisting mystery with a suprise ending. Rourke's arsonist and Danson's soft shoe shouldn't be missed.
1981 (R) 113m/C William Hurt, Kathleen Turner, Richard Crenna, Ted Danson, Mickey Rourke; *D:* Lawrence Kasdan; *W:* Lawrence Kasdan; *M:* John Barry. **VHS, Beta, LV** ★★★1/2

The Body Snatcher Based on Robert Louis Stevenson's story about a grave robber who supplies corpses to research scientists. Set in Edinburgh in the 19th century, this Lewton production is superior. One of Karloff's best vehicles.
1945 77m/B Edith Atwater, Russell Wade, Rita (Paula) Corday, Boris Karloff, Bela Lugosi, Henry Daniell; *D:* Robert Wise. **VHS, Beta, LV** ★★★1/2

Bohemian Girl The last of Laurel and Hardy's comic operettas finds them as guardians of a young orphan (Hood, famous for her roles in the Our Gang comedies), whom no one realizes is actually a kidnapped princess.
1936 74m/B Stan Laurel, Oliver Hardy, Mae Busch, Darla Hood, Jacqueline Wells, Thelma Todd, James Finlayson; *D:* James W. Horne. **VHS, Beta** ★★★

Bombshell Wry insightful comedy into the Hollywood of the 1930s. Harlow plays a naive young actress manipulated by her adoring press agent. He thwarts her plans until she finally notices and begins to fall in love with him. Brilliant satire with Harlow turning in perhaps the best performance of her short career. *AKA:* Blonde Bombshell.
1933 96m/B Jean Harlow, Lee Tracy, Pat O'Brien, Una Merkel, Sir C. Aubrey Smith, Franchot Tone; *D:* Victor Fleming. **VHS, Beta** ★★★

Bon Voyage, Charlie Brown The "Peanuts" comic strip group becomes exchange students in Europe, led by Charlie Brown, Linus, Peppermint Patty, Marcie, and the irrepressible beagle, Snoopy.
1980 (G) 76m/C *D:* Bill Melendez, Lee Mendelson; *W:* Charles M. Schulz; *M:* Ed Bogas; *V:* Arrin Skelley, Laura Planting, Casey Carlson, David Anderson, Annalisa Bartolin, Scott Beads. **VHS, Beta, LV** ★★★

Bonjour Tristesse An amoral French girl conspires to break up her playboy father's upcoming marriage to her stuffy godmother in order to maintain her decadent freedom. Preminger attempted, unsuccessfully, to use this soaper to catapult Seberg to stardom. Based on the novel by Francoise Sagan.

1957 94m/C *FR* Deborah Kerr, David Niven, Jean Seberg, Mylene Demongeot, Geoffrey Horne, Walter Chiari, Jean Kent; **D:** Otto Preminger; **W:** Arthur Laurents. **VHS, Beta ★★★**

Bonnie & Clyde Based on the biographies of the violent careers of Bonnie Parker and Clyde Barrow, who roamed the Southwest robbing banks. In the Depression era, when any job, even an illegal one, was cherished, money, greed, and power created an unending cycle of violence and fury. Highly controversial and influential, with pronounced bloodshed that spurred mainstream cinematic proliferation. Established Dunaway as a star; produced by Beatty in one of his best performances.

1967 111m/C Warren Beatty, Faye Dunaway, Michael J. Pollard, Gene Hackman, Estelle Parsons, Denver Pyle, Gene Wilder, Dub Taylor; **D:** Arthur Penn; **W:** David Newman, Robert Benton. Academy Awards '67: Best Cinematography, Best Supporting Actress (Parsons); National Society of Film Critics Awards '67: Best Screenplay, Best Supporting Actor (Hackman); Nominations: Academy Awards '66: Best Actor (Beatty), Best Supporting Actor (Hackman, Pollard), Best Actress (Dunaway), Best Director (Penn), Best Picture, Best Story & Screenplay; Academy Awards '67: Best Costume Design. **VHS, Beta, LV ★★★1/2**

The Border A border guard faces corruption and violence within his department and tests his own sense of decency when the infant of a poor Mexican girl is kidnapped. Excellent cast, fine cinematography, unusual Nicholson performance.

1982 (R) 107m/C Jack Nicholson, Harvey Keitel, Valerie Perrine, Warren Oates, Elpidia Carrillo; **D:** Tony Richardson; **W:** Deric Washburn, Walon Green; **M:** Ry Cooder. **VHS, Beta, LV ★★★**

Born Free The touching story of a game warden in Kenya and his wife raising Elsa the orphaned lion cub. When the cub reaches maturity, they work to return her to life in the wild. Great family entertainment based on Joy Adamson's book. Theme song became a hit. ♪ Born Free.

1966 95m/C Virginia McKenna, Bill Travers; **D:** James Hill; **M:** John Barry. Academy Awards '66: Best Song ("Born Free"), Best Original Score; National Board of Review Awards '66: 10 Best Films of the Year. **VHS, Beta, LV ★★★**

Born on the Fourth of July A riveting meditation on American life affected by the Vietnam War, based on the real-life, best-selling experiences of Ron Kovic, though some facts are subtly changed. The film follows him as he develops from a naive recruit to an angry, wheelchair-bound paraplegic to an active anti-war protestor. Well-acted and generally lauded; Kovic co-wrote the screenplay and appears as a war veteran in the opening parade sequence.

1989 (R) 145m/C Tom Cruise, Kyra Sedgwick, Raymond J. Barry, Jerry Levine, Tom Berenger, Willem Dafoe, Frank Whaley, John Getz, Caroline Kava, Bryan Larkin, Abbie Hoffman, Stephen Baldwin, Josh Evans; **D:** Oliver Stone; **W:** Oliver Stone; **M:** John Williams, Robert Richardson. Academy Awards '89: Best Director (Stone), Best Film Editing; Directors Guild of America Awards '89: Best Director (Stone); Golden Globe Awards '90: Best Actor—Drama (Cruise), Best Director (Stone), Best Film—Drama, Best Screenplay; Nominations: Academy Awards '89: Best Actor (Cruise), Best Adapted Screenplay, Best Cinematography, Best Picture, Best Sound, Best Original Score. **VHS, Beta, LV, 8mm ★★★1/2**

Born Yesterday Ambitious junk dealer Harry Brock is in love with smart but uneducated Billie Dawn. He hires newspaperman Paul Verrall to teach her the finer points of etiquette. During their sessions, they fall in love and Billie realizes how she has been used by Brock. She retaliates against him and gets to deliver that now-famous line: "Do me a favor, drop dead." Based on the Broadway play.

1950 103m/B Judy Holliday, Broderick Crawford, William Holden; **D:** George Cukor. Academy Awards '50: Best Actress (Holliday); Golden Globe Awards '51: Best Actress—Musical/Comedy (Holliday); Nominations: Academy Awards '50: Best Costume Design (B & W), Best Director (Cukor), Best Picture, Best Screenplay. **VHS, Beta, LV ★★★1/2**

The Borrowers Excellent made-for-television adaptation of the May Norton childrens classics "The Borrowers" and "The Borrowers Afield." This miniature family (about mouse-size) live beneath the floorboards of an English house and borrow what they need to survive from the normal-sized human inhabitants. Problems come when the teeny family are discovered and must make their way to a new home. Sweet and humorous. On two cassettes.

1993 199m/C *GB* Ian Holm, Penelope Wilton, Rebecca Callard; **D:** John Henderson; **W:** Richard Carpenter. **VHS** ★★★

Borsalino Delon and Belmondo are partners in crime in this seriocomic film about gang warfare in 1930s Marseilles. The costumes, settings, and music perfectly capture the mood of the period. Followed by a sequel "Borsalino and Co." Based on "The Bandits of Marseilles" by Eugene Saccomano.
1970 (R) 124m/C *FR* Jean-Paul Belmondo, Alain Delon, Michel Bouquet, Catherine Rouvel, Francoise Christophe, Corinne Marchand; **D:** Jacques Deray; **W:** Jacques Deray, Claude Sautet, Jean-Claude Carriere; **M:** Claude Bolling. **VHS** ★★★

Boudu Saved from Drowning A suicidal tramp completely disrupts the wealthy household of the man that saves him from drowning. A gentle but sardonic farce from the master filmmaker. Remade in 1986 as "Down and Out In Beverly Hills." *AKA:* Boudu Sauve des Eaux.
1932 87m/B *FR* Michel Simon, Charles Granval, Jean Daste; **D:** Jean Renoir. **VHS, Beta** ★★★1/2

Bound for Glory The award-winning biography of American folk singer Woody Guthrie set against the backdrop of the Depression. Superb portrayal of the spirit and feelings of the period featuring many of his songs encased in the incidents that inspired them. Haskell Wexler's award-winning camera work is superbly expressive.
1976 (PG) 149m/C David Carradine, Ronny Cox, Melinda Dillon, Randy Quaid; **D:** Hal Ashby; **W:** Robert Getchell, Haskell Wexler. Academy Awards '76: Best Adapted Score, Best Cinematography; Los Angeles Film Critics Association Awards '76: Best Cinematography; National Board of Review Awards '76: Best Actor (Carradine); National Society of Film Critics Awards '76: Best Cinematography; Nominations: Academy Awards '76: Best Adapted Screenplay, Best Costume Design, Best Film Editing, Best Picture; Cannes Film Festival '77: Best Film. **VHS, Beta, LV** ★★★★

The Boy Friend Russell pays tribute to the Busby Berkeley Hollywood musical. Lots of charming dance numbers and clever parody of plot lines in this adaptation of Sandy Wilson's stage play. Fun! ♪ The Boy Friend; I Could Be Happy; Won't You Charleston With Me?; Fancy Forgetting; Sur La Plage; A Room in Bloomsbury; Safety in Numbers; It's Never Too Late to Fall in Love; Poor Little Pierette.
1971 (G) 135m/C *GB* Twiggy, Christopher Gable, Moyra Fraser, Max Adrian, Vladek Sheybal, Georgina Hale, Tommy Tune; **D:** Ken Russell; **W:** Ken Russell. Golden Globe Awards '72: Best Actress—Musical/Comedy (Twiggy). **VHS** ★★★

Boy Meets Girl Cagney and O'Brien play screenwriters whose every film is a variation on the boy meets girl theme. Trouble is they're running out of ideas and their scripts get increasingly outlandish. A fading cowboy actor is supposed to star in the duo's next film—if they can ever settle down to work. Then they get the idea to feature their friend Wilson's baby in the movie—and guess who becomes a new star. Good satire on moviemaking and movie moguls, which made fine use of the Warner studio back lots, sound stages, and offices. Based on the play by Bella and Samuel Spewack who also wrote the screenplay.
1938 86m/B James Cagney, Pat O'Brien, Ralph Bellamy, Dick Foran, Marie Wilson, Frank McHugh, Bruce Lester, Ronald Reagan, Penny Singleton, James Stephenson; **D:** Lloyd Bacon; **W:** Bella Spewack, Samuel Spewack. **VHS** ★★★

Boy Meets Girl A French Holden Caulfield type character cruises the seamier side of Paris in this acclaimed film. Carax's directoral debut at age 22. In French with English subtitles.
1984 100m/B *FR* Denis Lavant, Mireille Perrier; **D:** Leos Carax; **W:** Jim Brady. **VHS** ★★★

A Boy Named Charlie Brown Charlie Brown enters the National Spelling Bee in New York and makes the final rounds with one other contestant. Based on Charles Schultz's popular comic strip characters from "Peanuts." Music by the Vince Guaraldi Trio is, as always, a treat.
1970 86m/C **D:** Bill Melendez; **W:** Charles M. Schulz; **M:** Vince Guaraldi, Rod McKuen. Nominations: Academy Awards '70: Best Original Score. **VHS, Beta, LV** ★★★

The Boy Who Could Fly After a plane crash kills his parents, a boy withdraws into a fantasy land where he can fly. The young daughter of a troubled family makes friends with him and the fantasy becomes real. A sweet film for children, charming though melancholy for adults, too. Fine cast, including Savage, Dewhurst, and Bedelia keep this from becoming sappy.

1986 (PG) 120m/C Lucy Deakins, Jay Underwood, Bonnie Bedelia, Colleen Dewhurst, Fred Savage, Fred Gwynne, Louise Fletcher, Jason Priestley; *D:* Nick Castle; *W:* Nick Castle; *M:* Bruce Broughton, Steven Poster. **VHS, Beta, LV** ★★★

The Boy with the Green Hair When he hears that his parents were killed in an air raid, a boy's hair turns green. The narrow-minded members of his community suddenly want nothing to do with him and he becomes an outcast. Thought-provoking social commentary.
1948 82m/C Pat O'Brien, Robert Ryan, Barbara Hale, Dean Stockwell; *D:* Joseph Losey. **VHS, Beta, LV** ★★★

The Boys of St. Vincent Outstanding, and heartbreaking, story of sexual abuse by Catholic clergy that was inspired by actual events. Divided into two segments, the drama begins in 1975 with 10-year-old Kevin Reevey (Morina) living at the St. Vincent orphanage in an eastern Canadian town. The orphanage is run by charismatic and terrifying Brother Lavin (Czerny), who it turns out has a special fondness for "his boy" Kevin. Nor is Brother Lavin alone—a fact eventually revealed by a police investigation, although the matter is hushed up by both the church and the government. Until 15 years later. In 1990, the case is reopened and Lavin, having married and fathered two sons, is returned to face charges. Now the young men must open wounds that have never truly healed and confront their tormentors in a court of law, amidst a blaze of publicity. Czerny gives a truly inspired performance as the self-loathing monster. The emotional agony is excruciating to watch and be forwarned that the depiction of the sexual abuse is unflinching. Made for Canadian TV.
1993 186m/C CA Henry Czerny, Johnny Morina, Sebastian Spence, Brian Dodd, David Hewlett, Jonathan Lewis, Jeremy Keefe, Phillip Dinn, Brian Dooley, Greg Thomey, Michael Wade, Lise Roy, Timothy Webber, Kristine Demers, Ashley Billard, Sam Grana; *D:* John N. Smith; *W:* Sam Grana, John N. Smith, Des Walsh; *M:* Neil Smolar, Pierre Letarte. Nominations: Independent Spirit Awards '95: Best Foreign Language Film. **VHS** ★★★★

Boys Town Righteous portrayal of Father Flanagan and the creation of Boys Town, home for juvenile soon-to-be-ex-delinquents.
1938 93m/B Spencer Tracy, Mickey Rooney, Henry Hull, Gene Reynolds, Sidney Miller, Frankie Thomas Jr.; *D:* Norman Taurog. Academy Awards '38: Best Actor (Tracy), Best Original Screenplay; Nominations: Academy Awards '38: Best Director (Taurog), Best Picture, Best Screenplay. **VHS, Beta, LV** ★★★1/2

Boyz N the Hood Singleton's debut as a writer and director is an astonishing picture of young black men, four high school students with different backgrounds, aims, and abilities trying to survive Los Angeles gangs and bigotry. Excellent acting throughout, with special nods to Fishburne and Gooding Jr. Violent outbreaks outside theaters where this ran only proves the urgency of its passionately nonviolent, pro-family message. Hopefully those viewers scared off at the time will give this a chance in the safety of their VCRs. Singleton was the youngest director ever nominated for an Oscar. The laserdisc version includes two extra scenes and an interview with Singleton.
1991 (R) 112m/C Laurence "Larry" Fishburne, Ice Cube, Cuba Gooding Jr., Nia Long, Morris Chestnut, Tyra Ferrell, Angela Bassett; *D:* John Singleton; *W:* John Singleton; *M:* Stanley Clarke. Chicago Film Critics Awards '91: Most Promising Actor (Ice Cube); MTV Movie Awards '92: Best New Filmmaker Award (Singleton); National Board of Review Awards '91: 10 Best Films of the Year; Nominations: Academy Awards '91: Best Director (Singleton), Best Original Screenplay. **VHS, Beta, LV, 8mm** ★★★1/2

The Brady Bunch Movie Grunge and CDs may be the norm in the '90s, but the Bradys still live in the eight-track world of the '70s, where Davy Jones rocks and every day is a sunshine day. Then greedy developer McKean schemes to cash in on Mike and Carol's financial woes. (Hawaii! The Grand Canyon! What were they thinking?) Great ensemble cast capably fills the white platform shoes of the originals—Cole sounds just like Mr. Brady, Cox hilariously channels Jan's tormented middle child angst, and Taylor's self-absorbed Marcia, Marcia, Marcia is dead-on, right down to the frosty pursed lips. Look for neat-o cameos from some original Bradys and most of the Monkees.
1995 (PG-13) 88m/C Shelley Long, Gary Cole, Michael McKean, Jean Smart, Henriette Mantel, Christopher Daniel Barnes, Christine Taylor, Paul Sutera, Jennifer Elise Cox, Jesse Lee, Olivia Hack, David Graf, Jack Noseworthy, Shane Conrad, RuPaul; *Cameos:* Ann B. Davis,

Florence Henderson, Davy Jones, Barry Williams, Christopher Knight, Michael Lookinland, Mickey Dolenz, Peter Tork; *D:* Betty Thomas; *W:* Bonnie Turner, Terry Turner, Laurice Elehwany, Rick Copp; *M:* Guy Moon. Nominations: MTV Movie Awards '95: Best Dance Sequence (The Brady Kids). **VHS, Beta** ★★★

Brain Dead Low-budget but brilliantly assembled puzzle-film about a brain surgeon who agrees to perform experimental surgery on a psychotic to retrieve some corporately valuable data—his first mistake, which begins a seemingly endless cycle of nightmares and identity alterations. A mind-blowing sci-fi feast from ex-"Twilight Zone" writer Charles Beaumont.
1989 (R) 85m/C Bill Pullman, Bill Paxton, Bud Cort, Patricia Charbonneau, Nicholas Pryor, George Kennedy; *D:* Adam Simon.
VHS, Beta ★★★1/2

The Brave One A love story between a Spanish boy and the bull who saves his life. The animal is later carted off to the bullring. Award-winning screenplay by the then-blacklisted Trumbo, as "Robert Rich."
1956 100m/C Michel Ray, Rodolfo Moyos, Joi Lansing; *D:* Irving Rapper; *W:* Dalton Trumbo, Jack Cardiff. Academy Awards '56: Best Original Screenplay; Nominations: Academy Awards '56: Best Film Editing. **VHS, Beta, LV** ★★★

Braveheart Producer-director-star Gibson does it all in this bold, ferocious, reasonably accurate epic about the passion and cost of freedom. Charismatic 13th-century Scottish folk hero William Wallace leads his desperate and outnumbered clansmen in revolt against British oppression. Sweeping, meticulous battle scenes fit suprisingly well with moments of stirring romance and snappy wit. Among the mostly unknown (in the States, anyway) cast, Marceau and McCormack are elegant as Wallace's lady loves, and McGoohan is positively hateful as King Edward I. Gory and excessively violent (as medieval warfare tends to be) and a bit too long (as historical epics tend to be), but rewarding entertainment for those who stick it out—where else can you see the king's army get mooned en masse? Script was based on 300 pages of rhyming verse attributed to a blind poet known as Blind Hally. Gibson put up $15 million of his own money to complete the film.
1995 (R) 178m/C Mel Gibson, Sophie Marceau, Patrick McGoohan, Catherine McCormack, Brendan Gleeson, James Cosmo, David O'Hara, Angus McFadyen, Peter Hanly; *D:* Mel Gibson; *W:* Randall Wallace, John Toll; *M:* James Horner. Golden Globe Awards '96: Best Director (Gibson); Nominations: Academy Awards '95: Best Cinematography, Best Costume Design, Best Director (Gibson), Best Film Editing, Best Makeup, Best Picture, Best Screenplay, Best Sound, Best Score; British Academy Awards '95: Best Cinematography, Best Director (Gibson), Best Score; Directors Guild of America Awards '95: Best Director (Gibson); Golden Globe Awards '96: Best Film—Drama, Best Screenplay, Best Score; Writers Guild of America '95: Best Original Screenplay.
VHS, Beta ★★★1/2

Brazil The acclaimed nightmare comedy about an Everyman trying to survive in a surreal paper-choked bureaucratic society. There are copious references to "1984" and "The Trial," fantastic mergings of glorious fantasy and stark reality, and astounding visual design.
1985 (R) 131m/C *GB* Jonathan Pryce, Robert De Niro, Michael Palin, Katherine Helmond, Kim Greist, Bob Hoskins, Ian Holm, Peter Vaughan, Ian Richardson; *D:* Terry Gilliam; *W:* Terry Gilliam, Tom Stoppard; *M:* Michael Kamen. Los Angeles Film Critics Association Awards '85: Best Director (Gilliam), Best Film, Best Screenplay; Nominations: Academy Awards '85: Best Art Direction/Set Decoration, Best Original Screenplay. **VHS, Beta, LV** ★★★1/2

Bread and Chocolate Uneducated Italian immigrant Manfredi works a series of odd jobs in complacently bourgeois Switzerland and tries desperately to fit in and better himself (which he fails utterly to do). Culture clash satire, with an engaging everyman lead. In Italian with English subtitles. *AKA:* Pane e Cioccolata.
1974 109m/C *IT* Nino Manfredi, Anna Karina, Johnny Dorelli, Paolo Turco; *D:* Franco Brusati; *W:* Nino Manfredi, Franco Brusati, Iaia Fiastri, Luciano Tovoli; *M:* Daniele Patrucchi. New York Film Critics Awards '78: Best Foreign Film. **VHS** ★★★

Breaker Morant In 1901 South Africa, three Australian soldiers are put on trial for avenging the murder of several prisoners. Based on a true story which was then turned into a play by Kenneth Ross, this riveting, popular anti-war statement and courtroom drama heralded Australia's film renaissance. Rich performances by Woodward and Waters.
1980 (PG) 107m/C *AU* Edward Woodward, Jack Thompson, John Waters, Bryan

Brown; **D:** Bruce Beresford; **W:** Jonathon Hardy, David Stevens, Bruce Beresford. Australian Film Institute '80: Best Actor (Thompson), Best Film; Nominations: Academy Awards '80: Best Adapted Screenplay; Cannes Film Festival '80: Best Film. **VHS, Beta, LV, 8mm** ★★★1/2

Breakfast at Tiffany's Truman Capote's amusing story of an endearingly eccentric New York City playgirl and her shaky romance with a young writer. Hepburn lends Holly Golightly just the right combination of naivete and worldly wisdom with a dash of melancholy. A wonderfully offbeat romance. ♪ Moon River.
1961 114m/C Audrey Hepburn, George Peppard, Patricia Neal, Buddy Ebsen, Mickey Rooney, Martin Balsam, John McGiver; **D:** Blake Edwards; **W:** George Axelrod; **M:** Henry Mancini. Academy Awards '61: Best Song ("Moon River"), Best Original Score; Nominations: Academy Awards '61: Best Actress (Hepburn), Best Adapted Screenplay, Best Art Direction/Set Decoration (Color). **VHS, Beta, LV, 8mm** ★★★1/2

The Breakfast Club Five students from different cliques at a Chicago suburban high school spend a day together in detention. Rather well done teenage culture study; these characters delve a little deeper than the standard adult view of adolescent stereotypes. One of John Hughes' best movies. Soundtrack features Simple Minds and Wang Chung.
1985 (R) 97m/C Ally Sheedy, Molly Ringwald, Judd Nelson, Emilio Estevez, Anthony Michael Hall, Paul Gleason, John Kapelos; **D:** John Hughes; **W:** John Hughes; **M:** Gary Chang, Keith Forsey. **VHS, Beta, LV** ★★★

Breaking Away A lighthearted coming-of-age drama about a high school graduate's addiction to bicycle racing, whose dreams are tested against the realities of a crucial race. An honest, open look at present Americana with tremendous insight into the minds of average youth; shot on location at Indiana University. Great bike-racing photography. Quaid, Barrie, and Christopher give exceptional performances. Basis for television series.
1979 (PG) 100m/C Dennis Christopher, Dennis Quaid, Daniel Stern, Jackie Earle Haley, Barbara Barrie, Paul Dooley, Amy Wright; **D:** Peter Yates; **W:** Steve Tesich. Academy Awards '79: Best Original Screenplay; Golden Globe Awards '80: Best Film—Musical/Comedy; National Board of Review Awards '79: 10 Best Films of the Year, Best Supporting Actor (Dooley); National Society of Film Critics

Awards '79: Best Film, Best Screenplay; Writers Guild of America '79: Best Original Screenplay; Nominations: Academy Awards '79: Best Director (Yates), Best Picture, Best Supporting Actress (Barrie), Best Original Score. **VHS, Beta, LV** ★★★1/2

Breaking the Waves Sacrificial journey of shy, religious Beth (Watson), who's living in an austere northern Scotland coastal village in the '70s. Beth, who regularly talks to God, marries Jan (Skarsgard), an adventurer working on a North Sea oil rig. It must be a case of opposites attracting, but the couple are happy until Jan is paralyzed from the neck down in a rig accident. Beth, who blames herself, begins sleeping around, believing her actions can somehow help Jan, and slides ever deeper into mental instability. Powerful story is divided into seven chapters and an epilogue.
1995 159m/C Emily Watson, Stellan Skarsgard, Katrin Cartlidge, Adrian Rawlins, Jean-Marc Barr, Sandra Voe, Udo Kier, Mikkel Gaup; **D:** Lars von Trier; **W:** Lars von Trier; **M:** Joachim Holbek. Cannes Film Festival '96: Grand Jury Prize; National Society of Film Critics Awards '96: Best Film, Best Director (von Trier), Best Actress (Watson), Best Cinematography; New York Film Critics Award '96: Best Cinematography, Best Actress (Watson), Best Director (von Trier); Nominations: Golden Globe Awards '97: Best Film—Drama, Best Actress—Drama (Watson); Independent Spirit Awards '97: Best Foreign Film. **VHS** ★★★

Breathing Lessons Sweet look at a long-term marriage that renews itself on a road trip. Flighty Maggie and pragmatic Ira have been married for 28 squabbling but loving years. They're driving from their Baltimore home to a funeral in Pennsylvania and the road stops provide some small adventures and a great deal of conversation. Drama rests easily on the capable shoulders of the veteran performers. Based on the novel by Anne Tyler. Made for TV.
1994 (PG) 98m/C James Garner, Joanne Woodward, Paul Winfield, Kathryn Erbe, Joyce Van Patten, Eileen Heckart, Tim Guinee, Henry Jones, Stephi Lineburg, Jean Louisa Kelly, John Considine; **D:** John Erman; **W:** Robert W. Lenski. **VHS** ★★★

Breathless Godard's first feature catapulted him to the vanguard of French filmmakers. A carefree Parisian crook, who emulates Humphrey Bogart, falls in love with an American girl with tragic results. Wonderful

scenes of Parisian life. Established Godard's Brechtian, experimental style. Belmondo's film debut. Mistitled "Breathless" for American release, the film's French title actually means "Out of Breath"; however, the fast-paced, erratic musical score leaves you breathless. French with English subtitles. Remade with Richard Gere in 1983 with far less intensity. *AKA:* A Bout de Souffle.
1959 90m/B *FR* Jean-Paul Belmondo, Jean Seberg, Daniel Boulanger, Jean-Pierre Melville, Liliane Robin; *D:* Jean-Luc Godard; *W:* Jean-Luc Godard. Berlin International Film Festival '60: Best Director (Godard). **VHS, Beta ★★★★**

Brewster McCloud Altman's first picture after M*A*S*H reunites much of the cast and combines fantasy, black comedy, and satire in the story of a young man whose head is in the clouds or at least in the upper reaches of the Houston Astrodome. Brewster (Cort) lives covertly in the Dome and dreams of flying. He also has a guardian angel (Kellerman) who watches over him and may actually be killing people who give him a hard time. Murphy is a cop obsessed with catching the killer. And there's a circus allegory as well. Hard to figure what it all means and offbeat as they come, but for certain tastes, exquisite.
1970 (R) 101m/C Bud Cort, Sally Kellerman, Shelley Duvall, Michael Murphy, William Windom, Rene Auberjonois, Stacy Keach, John Schuck, Margaret Hamilton; *D:* Robert Altman; *W:* Doran William Cannon. **VHS, Beta, LV ★★★1/2**

Brian's Song The story of the unique relationship between Gale Sayers, the Chicago Bears' star running back, and his teammate Brian Piccolo. The friendship between the Bears' first interracial roommates ended suddenly when Brian Piccolo lost his life to cancer. Made for television. Incredibly well-received in its time.
1971 (G) 74m/C James Caan, Billy Dee Williams, Jack Warden, Shelley Fabares, Judy Pace; *D:* Buzz Kulik. **VHS, Beta, LV ★★★★**

The Bride of Frankenstein The classic sequel to the classic original in which Dr. F. seeks to build a mate for his monster. More humor than the first, but also more pathos, including the monster's famous but short-lived friendship with a blind hermit. Lanchester plays both the bride and Mary Shelley in the opening sequence.
1935 75m/B Boris Karloff, Elsa Lanchester, Ernest Thesiger, Colin Clive, Una O'Connor, Valerie Hobson, Dwight Frye, John Carradine, E.E. Clive, O.P. Heggie, Gavin Gordon, Douglas Walton; *D:* James Whale. Nominations: Academy Awards '35: Best Sound. **VHS, Beta, LV ★★★★**

The Bride Wore Black Truffaut's homage to Hitchcock, complete with Bernard Herrmann score. A young woman exacts brutal revenge on the five men who accidentally killed her husband. Adapted from a novel by Cornell Woolrich. Excellent cinematography from Raoul Coutard. *AKA:* La Mariee Etait en Noir.
1968 107m/C *FR* Jeanne Moreau, Claude Rich, Jean-Claude Brialy, Michel Bouquet, Michael Lonsdale; *D:* Francois Truffaut; *M:* Bernard Herrmann. **VHS, LV ★★★**

Brideshead Revisited The acclaimed British miniseries based on the Evelyn Waugh classic about an Edwardian young man who falls under the spell of a wealthy aristocratic family and struggles to retain his integrity and values. On six tapes.
1981 540m/C *GB* Jeremy Irons, Anthony Andrews, Diana Quick, Laurence Olivier, John Gielgud, Claire Bloom, Stephane Audran, Mona Washbourne, John Le Mesurier, Charles Keating; *D:* Charles Sturridge, Michael Lindsay-Hogg; *M:* Geoffrey Burgon. **VHS, Beta ★★★**

The Bridge of San Luis Rey A priest investigates the famous bridge collapse in Lima, Peru, that left five people dead. Based upon the novel by Thornton Wilder.
1944 89m/B Lynn Bari, Francis Lederer, Louis Calhern, Akim Tamiroff, Donald Woods, Alla Nazimova, Blanche Yurka; *D:* Rowland V. Lee. Nominations: Academy Awards '44: Best Original Score. **VHS, Beta, LV ★★★**

The Bridge on the River Kwai Award-winning adaptation of the Pierre Bouelle novel about the battle of wills between a Japanese POW camp commander and a British colonel over the construction of a rail bridge, and the parallel efforts by escaped prisoner Holden to destroy it. Holden's role was originally cast for Cary Grant. Memorable too for whistling "Colonel Bogey March." Because the writers were blacklisted, Bouelle (who spoke no English) was credited as screenwriter.
1957 161m/C *GB* William Holden, Alec Guinness, Jack Hawkins, Sessue Hayakawa, James Donald, Geoffrey Horne, Andre Morell, Ann Sears; *D:* David Lean; *W:* Michael Wilson, Carl Foreman; *M:* Malcolm Arnold. Academy Awards '57: Best Actor (Guinness), Best Adapted

Screenplay, Best Color Cinematography, Best Director (Lean), Best Film Editing, Best Picture, Best Original Score; British Academy Awards '57: Best Actor (Guinness), Best Film, Best Screenplay; Directors Guild of America Awards '57: Best Director (Lean); Golden Globe Awards '58: Best Actor—Drama (Guinness), Best Director (Lean), Best Film—Drama; National Board of Review Awards '57: 10 Best Films of the Year, Best Actor (Guinness), Best Director (Lean), Best Supporting Actor (Hayakawa); Nominations: Academy Awards '57: Best Supporting Actor (Hayakawa). **VHS, Beta, LV** ★★★★

The Bridges at Toko-Ri Based on the James A. Michener novel, the rousing war-epic about a lawyer being summoned by the Navy to fly bombing missions during the Korean War. A powerful anti-war statement.
1955 103m/C William Holden, Grace Kelly, Fredric March, Mickey Rooney, Robert Strauss, Earl Holliman, Keiko Awaji, Charles McGraw; **D:** Mark Robson; **W:** Valentine Davies. Academy Awards '55: Best Special Effects; Nominations: Academy Awards '55: Best Film Editing. **VHS, Beta, LV** ★★★½

The Bridges of Madison County Robert Kincaid (Eastwood) is on assignment in 1965 Iowa to photograph Madison County's scenic covered bridges. Only problem is he gets lost and stops for directions at Francesca Johnson's (Streep) farmhouse. There's an immediate attraction between the repressed Italian war-bride-turned-farmwife and the charismatic world traveler, which they act on in four short days. Much of the treacle from Robert James Waller's novel has been fortunately abandoned but the mature romance remains. 64-year-old Eastwood exudes low-key sexiness while Streep (with a light Italian accent) is all earthy warmth. Fans of both book and stars should be pleased, though the leisurely paced film takes too long to get started.
1995 (PG-13) 135m/C Clint Eastwood, Meryl Streep, Victor Slezak, Annie Corley, Jim Haynie; **D:** Clint Eastwood; **W:** Richard LaGravenese; **M:** Lennie Niehaus, Jack N. Green. Nominations: Academy Awards '95: Best Actress (Streep); Golden Globe Awards '96: Best Actress—Drama (Streep), Best Film—Drama; Screen Actors Guild Award '95: Best Actress (Streep). **VHS, LV** ★★★

Brief Encounter Based on Noel Coward's "Still Life" from "Tonight at 8:30," two middle-aged, middle-class people become involved in a short and bittersweet romance in WWII England. Intensely romantic, underscored with Rachmaninoff's Second Piano Concerto.
1946 86m/B GB Celia Johnson, Trevor Howard, Stanley Holloway, Cyril Raymond, Joyce Carey; **D:** David Lean; **W:** Noel Coward. National Board of Review Awards '46: 10 Best Films of the Year; New York Film Critics Awards '46: Best Actress (Johnson); Nominations: Academy Awards '46: Best Actress (Johnson), Best Director (Lean), Best Screenplay. **VHS, Beta** ★★★★

A Brief History of Time A stunning documentary about physicist Stephen Hawking, the author of the popular book "Brief History of Time." Crippled by Lou Gehrig's Disease, Hawking narrates the film in the computer-synthesized voice he uses to speak. Interviews with family, friends, and colleagues bring Hawking's scientific theories to light.
1992 (G) 85m/C Stephen Hawking; **D:** Errol Morris; **W:** Stephen Hawking, John Bailey; **M:** Philip Glass. Sundance Film Festival '92: Filmmakers Trophy. **VHS, Beta** ★★★

Brigadoon The story of a magical, 18th-century Scottish village which awakens once every 100 years and the two modern-day vacationers who stumble upon it. Main highlight is the Lerner and Loewe score. ♪ Brigadoon; Almost Like Being in Love; I'll Go Home With Bonnie Jean; Wedding Dance; From This Day On; Heather on the Hill; Waitin' For My Dearie; Once in the Highlands.
1954 108m/C Gene Kelly, Van Johnson, Cyd Charisse; **D:** Vincente Minnelli; **M:** Frederick Loewe, Alan Jay Lerner. Nominations: Academy Awards '54: Best Art Direction/Set Decoration (Color), Best Costume Design (Color), Best Sound. **VHS, Beta, LV, 8mm** ★★★

Brighton Rock Sterling performances highlight this seamy look at the British underworld. Attenborough is Pinkie Brown, a small-time hood who ends up committing murder. He manipulates a waitress to get himself off the hook, but things don't go exactly as he plans. Based on the novel by Graham Greene. **AKA:** Young Scarface.
1947 92m/B GB Richard Attenborough, Hermione Baddeley, William Hartnell, Carol Marsh, Nigel Stock, Wylie Watson, Alan Wheatley, George Carney, Reginald Purdell; **D:** John Boulting. **VHS** ★★★

Bringing Up Baby The quintessential screwball comedy, featuring Hepburn as a giddy socialite with a "baby"

leopard, and Grant as the unwitting object of her affections. One ridiculous situation after another adds up to high speed fun. Hepburn looks lovely, the supporting actors are in fine form, and director Hawks manages the perfect balance of control and mayhem. From a story by Hagar Wilde, who helped Nichols with the screenplay. Also available in a colorized version.
1938 103m/B Katharine Hepburn, Cary Grant, May Robson, Charlie Ruggles, Walter Catlett, Fritz Feld, Jonathan Hale, Barry Fitzgerald, Ward Bond; **D:** Howard Hawks; **W:** Dudley Nichols. **VHS, Beta, LV** ★★★★

Broadcast News The acclaimed, witty analysis of network news shows, dealing with the three-way romance between a driven career-woman producer, an ace nebbish reporter and a brainless, popular on-screen anchorman. Incisive and funny, though often simply idealistic.
1987 (R) 132m/C William Hurt, Albert Brooks, Holly Hunter, Jack Nicholson, Joan Cusack, Robert Prosky, Lois Chiles, Gennie James; **Cameos:** John Cusack; **D:** James L. Brooks; **W:** James L. Brooks; **M:** Bill Conti, Michael Gore, Michael Ballhaus. Los Angeles Film Critics Association Awards '87: Best Actress (Hunter); National Board of Review Awards '87: 10 Best Films of the Year, Best Actress (Hunter); Nominations: Academy Awards '87: Best Actor (Hurt), Best Actress (Hunter), Best Cinematography, Best Film Editing, Best Original Screenplay, Best Picture, Best Supporting Actor (Brooks). **VHS, Beta, LV** ★★★1/2

Broadway Bill A man decides to abandon his nagging wife and his job in her family's business for the questionable pleasures of owning a racehorse known as Broadway Bill. This racetrack comedy was also remade by Frank Capra in 1951 as "Riding High." **AKA:** Strictly Confidential.
1934 90m/C Warner Baxter, Myrna Loy, Walter Connolly, Helen Vinson, Margaret Hamilton, Frankie Darro; **D:** Frank Capra. **VHS, Beta, LV** ★★★

Broadway Danny Rose One of Woody Allen's best films, a hilarious, heart-rending anecdotal comedy about a third-rate talent agent involved in one of his client's infidelities. The film magically unfolds as show business veterans swap Danny Rose stories at a delicatessen. Allen's Danny Rose is pathetically lovable.
1984 (PG) 85m/B Woody Allen, Mia Farrow, Nick Apollo Forte, Sandy Baron, Milton Berle, Howard Cosell, Gordon Willis;

D: Woody Allen; **W:** Woody Allen. British Academy Awards '84: Best Original Screenplay; Writers Guild of America '84: Best Original Screenplay; Nominations: Academy Awards '84: Best Director (Allen), Best Original Screenplay. **VHS, Beta, LV** ★★★★

Broadway Melody of 1936 Exceptional musical comedy with delightful performances from Taylor and Powell. Benny is a headline-hungry columnist who tries to entrap Taylor by using Powell. ♪ Broadway Melody; Broadway Rhythm; You Are My Lucky Star; I've Got a Feeling You're Fooling; All I Do Is Dream of You; Sing Before Breakfast; On a Sunday Afternoon.
1935 110m/B Jack Benny, Eleanor Powell, Robert Taylor, Una Merkel, Sid Silvers, Buddy Ebsen; **D:** Roy Del Ruth; **M:** Nacio Herb Brown, Arthur Freed. Nominations: Academy Awards '35: Best Original Screenplay, Best Picture. **VHS, Beta** ★★★

Broken Blossoms One of Griffith's most widely acclaimed films, photographed by Billy Bitzer, about a young Chinaman in London's squalid Limehouse district hoping to spread the peaceful philosophy of his Eastern religion. He befriends a pitiful street waif who is mistreated by her brutal father, resulting in tragedy. Silent. Revised edition contains introduction from Gish and a newly-recorded score.
1919 102m/B Lillian Gish, Richard Barthelmess, Donald Crisp; **D:** D.W. Griffith. **VHS, Beta, LV** ★★★★

Broken Lance Western remake of "House of Strangers" that details the dissolution of a despotic cattle baron's family. Beautifully photographed.
1954 96m/C Spencer Tracy, Richard Widmark, Robert Wagner, Jean Peters, Katy Jurado, Earl Holliman, Hugh O'Brian, E.G. Marshall; **D:** Edward Dmytryk; **W:** Philip Yordan. Academy Awards '54: Best Story; Nominations: Academy Awards '54: Best Supporting Actress (Jurado). **VHS, Beta, LV** ★★★1/2

A Bronx Tale Snapshot of a young Italian-American boy growing up in the '60s among neighborhood small-time wiseguys. As a nine-year-old Calogero witnesses mobster Sonny kill a man but doesn't rat to the police, so Sonny takes the kid under his wing. His upright bus-driving father Lorenzo doesn't approve but the kid is drawn to Sonny's apparent glamor and power. At 17, he's gotten both an education in school and on the streets but he needs to make a

choice. Good period detail and excellent performances. Palminteri shows both Sonny's charisma and violence and De Niro handles the less-showy father role with finesse. Based on Palminteri's one-man play; De Niro's directorial debut.
1993 (R) 122m/C Robert De Niro, Chazz Palminteri, Lillo Brancato, Frank Capra, Taral Hicks, Kathrine Narducci, Clem Caserta, Alfred Sauchelli Jr., Frank Pietrangolare; *Cameos:* Joe Pesci; *D:* Robert De Niro; *W:* Chazz Palminteri. **VHS, LV ★★★**

The Brother from Another Planet A black alien escapes from his home planet and winds up in Harlem, where he's pursued by two alien bounty hunters. Independently made morality fable by John Sayles before he hit the big time; features Sayles in a cameo as an alien bounty hunter.
1984 109m/C Joe Morton, Dee Dee Bridgewater, Ren Woods, Steve James, Maggie Renzi, David Strathairn; *Cameos:* John Sayles; *D:* John Sayles; *W:* John Sayles; *M:* Mason Daring. **VHS, Beta ★★★**

Brother John An early look at racial tensions and labor problems. An angel goes back to his hometown in Alabama to see how things are going.
1970 (PG) 94m/C Sidney Poitier, Will Geer, Bradford Dillman, Beverly Todd, Paul Winfield; *D:* James Goldstone; *M:* Quincy Jones. **VHS, Beta ★★★**

Brother of Sleep Elias (Eisermann), the illegitimate son of the local priest, is discovered to have perfect pitch, a beautiful voice, and a special symbiosis with nature. Which does nothing to endear him to the superstitious inhabitants of his 19th-century Austrian mountain village. Elias doesn't know whether his gift is a blessing or a curse, but he'd give it up if he could win the love of his cousin Elspeth (Vavrova). Schneider scripted from his 1992 novel, which has previously been adapted as a ballet and opera. German with subtitles. *AKA:* Schlafes Bruder
1995 127m/C GE Andre Eisermann, Dana Vavrova, Ben Becker; *D:* Joseph Vilsmaier; *W:* Robert Schneider; *M:* Norbert J. Schneider. Nominations: Golden Globe Awards '96: Best Foreign Language Film. **VHS ★★★**

Brother Orchid Mobster puts a henchman in charge of his gang while he vacations in Europe. Upon his return, he is deposed and wounded in an assassination attempt. Hiding out in a monastary, he plots to regain control of the gang, leading to fish outta water episodes and a change in his outlook on life. Fine cast fans through farce intelligently.
1940 87m/B Edward G. Robinson, Humphrey Bogart, Ann Sothern, Donald Crisp, Ralph Bellamy, Allen Jenkins, Charles D. Brown, Cecil Kellaway; *D:* Lloyd Bacon. **VHS, Beta ★★★**

The Brothers Karamazov Hollywood adaptation of the classic novel by Dostoyevsky, in which four 19th-century Russian brothers struggle with their desires for the same beautiful woman and with the father who brutalizes them. Incredible performances from every cast member, especially Cobb. Long and extremely intense, with fine direction from Brooks. Marilyn Monroe tried desperately to get Schell's part. *AKA:* Karamazov; The Murderer Dmitri Karamazov; Der Morder Dimitri Karamasoff.
1958 147m/C Yul Brynner, Claire Bloom, Lee J. Cobb, William Shatner, Maria Schell, Richard Basehart; *D:* Richard Brooks; *W:* Richard Brooks, John Alton. Nominations: Academy Awards '58: Best Supporting Actor (Cobb). **VHS, Beta ★★★**

Brother's Keeper Filmmakers Berlinger and Sinofsky document the story of the eccentric and reclusive Ward brothers, four bachelor dairy farmers who shared the same two-room shack for more than 60 years in rural New York. When Bill Ward dies, brother Delbert is accused of murder and goes to trial. The film covers a year's span in preparation for the trial and how the media attention changed the Ward's lives.
1992 104m/C *D:* Joe Berlinger, Bruce Sinofsky. National Board of Review Awards '92: Best Feature Documentary; New York Film Critics Awards '92: Best Feature Documentary; Sundance Film Festival '92: Audience Award. **VHS, LV ★★★**

The Brothers McMullen Slice of life drama finds three Irish-American brothers suddenly living under the same Long Island roof for the first time since childhood. Eldest brother Jack (Mulcahy) is a stolid high-school basketball coach married to teacher Molly (Britton) who's pressing him to have children. Cynical middle brother Barry (Burns), a writer, has just broken up with free-spirited Ann (McKay), and earnest young Patrick (McGlone) is engaged to Jewish girlfriend Susan (Albert). All three find their romantic relationships, as well as their belief in each other, tested. Generally good performances and dialogue, with Burns proving himself a triple threat as actor/writer/director.
1994 (R) 98m/C Edward Burns, Jack

Mulcahy, Mike McGlone, Connie Britton, Shari Albert, Elizabeth P. McKay, Maxine Bahns, Jennifer Jostyn; **D:** Edward Burns; **W:** Edward Burns; **M:** Seamus Egan. Sundance Film Festival '95: Grand Jury Prize; Nominations: Independent Spirit Awards '96: Best First Feature. **VHS** ★★★

The Browning Version A lonely, un-emotional classics instructor at a British boarding school realizes his failure as a teacher and as a husband. From the play by Terrence Rattigan. **1951 89m/B** *GB* Michael Redgrave, Jean Kent, Nigel Patrick, Wilfrid Hyde-White, Bill Travers; **D:** Anthony Asquith. Cannes Film Festival '51: Best Actor (Redgrave); National Board of Review Awards '51: 5 Best Foreign Films of the Year. **VHS, Beta** ★★★1/2

Bruce Lee: Curse of the Dragon A behind the scenes look at the continuing mystery surrounding the life and untimely death of the martial arts superstar who died in 1973 at the age of 32. Highlights the spectacular fight sequences from Lee's movies as well as footage from his funeral and an interview with his son Brandon Lee, whose own death in 1993 raised further comment about a Lee family curse. **AKA:** The Curse of the Dragon. **1993 90m/C VHS, Beta, LV** ★★★

The Buccaneers Lavish adaptation of the Edith Wharton novel follows the adventures of four American girls in 1870s society. Nouveaux riche, the young ladies are unable to crack New York snobbery and, after vivacious Brazilian Conchita (Sorvino) manages to snag Lord Richard (Vibert), the others are encouraged by English governess Laura Testvalley (Lunghi) to try their luck in London. There, Virginia (Elliott), sister Nan (Gugino), their friend Lizzy (Kihlstedt), and Conchita all find hope and heartbreak among the English aristocracy. Wharton's novel was unfinished at her death and, though she left story notes, scripter Wadey concedes to changes. Made for TV. **1995 288m/C** Carla Gugino, Mira Sorvino, Alison Elliott, Rya Kihlstedt, Cherie Lunghi, Connie Booth, Mark Tandy, Ronan Vibert, Jenny Agutter, Richard Huw, Greg Wise, James Frain, Michael Kitchen, Sheila Hancock, Rosemary Leach, Elizabeth Ashley, Conchata Ferrell, Peter Michael Goetz, James Rebhorn, E. Katherine Kerr; **D:** Philip Saville; **W:** Maggie Wadey; **M:** Colin Towns. **VHS** ★★★

A Bucket of Blood Cult favorite Dick Miller stars as a sculptor with a peculiar "talent" for lifelike artwork. Corman fans will see thematic similarities to his subsequent work, "Little Shop of Horrors" (1960). "Bucket of Blood" was made in just five days, while "Little Shop of Horrors" was made in a record breaking two days. Corman horror/spoof noted for its excellent beatnik atmosphere. **1959 66m/B** Dick Miller, Barboura Morris, Antony Carbone, Julian Burton, Ed Nelson, Bert Convy; **D:** Roger Corman. **VHS, Beta** ★★★

The Buddy Holly Story An acclaimed biography of the famed 1950s pop star, spanning the years from his meteoric career's beginnings in Lubbock to his tragic early death in the now famous plane crash. Busey performs Holly's hits himself. ♪ Rock Around the Ollie Vee; That'll Be the Day; Oh, Boy; It's So Easy; Well All Right; Chantilly Lace; Peggy Sue. **1978 (PG) 113m/C** Gary Busey, Don Stroud, Charles Martin Smith, Conrad Janis, William Jordan; **D:** Steve Rash; **M:** Joe Renzetti. Academy Awards '78: Best Adapted Score; National Society of Film Critics Awards '78: Best Actor (Busey); Nominations: Academy Awards '78: Best Actor (Busey), Best Sound. **VHS, Beta, LV** ★★★1/2

Buffalo Bill & the Indians A perennially underrated Robert Altman historical pastiche, portraying the famous Wild West character as a charlatan and shameless exemplar of encroaching imperialism. Great all-star cast amid Altman's signature mise-en-scene chaos. **AKA:** Sitting Bull's History Lesson. **1976 (PG) 135m/C** Paul Newman, Geraldine Chaplin, Joel Grey, Will Sampson, Harvey Keitel, Burt Lancaster, Kevin McCarthy; **D:** Robert Altman; **W:** Robert Altman, Alan Rudolph; **M:** Richard Baskin. **VHS, Beta** ★★★

Buffet Froid Surreal black comedy about a group of bungling murderers. First rate acting and directing makes this film a hilarious treat. From the director of "Menage." In French with English subtitles. **1979 95m/C** *FR* Gerard Depardieu, Bernard Blier, Jean Carmet, Genevieve Page, Denise Gence, Carole Bouquet, Jean Benguigui, Michel Serrault; **D:** Bertrand Blier; **W:** Bertrand Blier. Cesar Awards '80: Best Writing. **VHS, LV** ★★★1/2

Bugsy Beatty is Benjamin "Bugsy" Siegel, the '40s gangster who built the Flamingo Hotel in Las Vegas when it was still a virtual desert, before it became a gambling mecca. Bening is perfect as Bugsy's moll, Virginia Hill, who inspired him to carry out his dream of building the Flamingo (which was her nickname). Beatty and Bening heat up the screen and their off-screen relationship was no different. Fans anticipated their seemingly imminent marriage almost as much as the release of this movie. Almost nothing mars this film which Toback adapted from a novel by Dean Jennings, "We Only Kill Each Other: The Life and Bad Times of Bugsy Siegel."

1991 (R) 135m/C Warren Beatty, Annette Bening, Harvey Keitel, Ben Kingsley, Elliott Gould, Joe Mantegna, Richard Sarafian, Bebe Neuwirth, Wendy Phillips, Robert Beltran, Bill Graham, Lewis Van Bergen, Debrah Farentino, Allen Daviau; *D:* Barry Levinson; *W:* James Toback; *M:* Ennio Morricone. Academy Awards '91: Best Art Direction/Set Decoration, Best Costume Design; Chicago Film Critics Awards '91: Best Supporting Actor (Keitel); Golden Globe Awards '92: Best Film—Drama; Los Angeles Film Critics Association Awards '91: Best Director (Levinson), Best Film, Best Screenplay; National Board of Review Awards '91: 10 Best Films of the Year, Best Actor (Beatty); Nominations: Academy Awards '91: Best Actor (Beatty), Best Cinematography, Best Director (Levinson), Best Original Screenplay, Best Picture, Best Supporting Actor (Keitel, Kingsley), Best Original Score. **VHS, Beta, LV, 8mm** ★★★½

Bull Durham Lovable American romantic comedy, dealing with a very minor minor-league team and three of its current constituents: an aging baseball groupie that beds one player each season; a cocky, foolish new pitcher; and the older, weary catcher brought in to wise the rookie up. The scene in which Sarandon tries poetry out on the banal rookie is a hoot. Highly acclaimed, the film sears with Sarandon and Costner's love scenes.

1988 (R) 107m/C Kevin Costner, Susan Sarandon, Tim Robbins, Trey Wilson, Robert Wuhl, Jenny Robertson; *D:* Ron Shelton; *W:* Ron Shelton; *M:* Michael Convertino. Los Angeles Film Critics Association Awards '88: Best Screenplay; New York Film Critics Awards '88: Best Screenplay; National Society of Film Critics Awards '88: Best Screenplay; Writers Guild of America '88: Best Original Screenplay; Nominations: Academy Awards '88: Best Original Screenplay. **VHS, Beta, LV** ★★★½

A Bullet in the Head Violent (no surprise there) tale of friendship finds Frank (Cheung), Ben (Leung), and Paul (Lee) heading out of 1967 Hong Kong for Saigon, where they hope to make money selling contraband goods in the city. They wind up on the wrong side of the Vietnamese Army, steal a fortune in gold from a local crime lord, and end up the prisoners of the Viet Cong. There's betrayal and death and a final moral reckoning and—did we mention lots and lots of (over-the-top) violence? Chinese with subtitles.

1990 85m/C *HK* Tony Leung, Jacky Cheung, Waise Lee; *D:* John Woo. **VHS** ★★★

Bulletproof Heart Mick (LaPaglia), a hit man with a severe case of burnout, is assigned to kill Fiona (Rogers), a beautiful socialite who, conveniently, wants to die. Despite being warned by his boss (Boyle) that Fiona has a habit of making men weak, he falls in love and can't bring himself to kill her. First-time director Malone takes great care to establish the noir look and feel, capitalizing on the all-in-one-night timeframe to raise the tension level. LaPaglia and Rogers turn in riveting performances, but can't stop the film from losing momentum when it becomes self-consciously melodramatic near the end. *AKA:* Killer.

1995 (R) 95m/C Anthony LaPaglia, Mimi Rogers, Peter Boyle, Matt Craven, Monika Schnarre, Joseph Maher; *D:* Mark Malone; *W:* Gordon Melbourne, Tobias Schliessler, Mark Malone; *M:* Graeme Coleman. **VHS, LV** ★★★

Bullets or Ballots Tough New York cop goes undercover to join the mob in order to get the goods on them. Old-fashioned danger and intrigue follow, making for some action-packed thrills.

1938 82m/B Edward G. Robinson, Humphrey Bogart, Barton MacLane, Joan Blondell, Frank McHugh, Louise Beavers; *D:* William Keighley. **VHS, Beta** ★★★

Bullets Over Broadway Mediocre playwright David Shayne (Cusack, in the Allen role) talks up the virtues of artistic integrity to his pretentious hothouse contemporaries, then sells out to a gangster who agrees to finance his latest play provided his no-talent, brassy moll (Tilly) gets a part. And it's her hit-man bodyguard's (Palminteri) unexpected artistic touches that redeem Shayne's otherwise lousy work. Wiest as the eccentric diva, Ullman as the aging ingenue, Reiner as the Greenwich Village sage, and Broadbent as the increasingly plump matinee idol lead a collection of delicious, over-the-top performances in this smart and howlingly funny tribute to Jazz Age New

York City that showcases Woody at his self-conscious best.

1994 (R) 106m/C Dianne Wiest, John Cusack, Jennifer Tilly, Rob Reiner, Chazz Palminteri, Tracey Ullman, Mary-Louise Parker, Joe Viterelli, Jack Warden, Jim Broadbent, Harvey Fierstein, Annie-Joe Edwards, Carlo DiPalma; **D:** Woody Allen; **W:** Woody Allen, Douglas McGrath. Academy Awards '94: Best Supporting Actress (Wiest); Chicago Film Critics Awards '94: Best Supporting Actress (Wiest); Golden Globe Awards '95: Best Supporting Actress (Wiest); Independent Spirit Awards '95: Best Supporting Actor (Palminteri), Best Supporting Actress (Wiest); New York Film Critics Awards '94: Best Supporting Actress (Wiest); National Society of Film Critics Awards '94: Best Supporting Actress (Wiest); Screen Actors Guild Award '94: Best Supporting Actress (Wiest); Nominations: Academy Awards '94: Best Art Direction/Set Decoration, Best Costume Design, Best Director (Allen), Best Original Screenplay, Best Supporting Actor (Palminteri), Best Supporting Actress (Tilly); Independent Spirit Awards '95: Best Film, Best Screenplay. **VHS, LV ★★★1/2**

Bullitt A detective assigned to protect a star witness for 48 hours senses danger; his worst fears are confirmed when his charge is murdered. Based on the novel, "Mute Witness" by Robert L. Pike, and featuring one of filmdom's most famous car chases.

1968 (PG) 105m/C Steve McQueen, Robert Vaughn, Jacqueline Bisset, Don Gordon, Robert Duvall, Norman Fell, Simon Oakland; **D:** Peter Yates; **W:** Alan R. Trustman; **M:** Lalo Schifrin, William A. Fraker. Academy Awards '68: Best Film Editing; Edgar Allan Poe Awards '68: Best Screenplay; National Society of Film Critics Awards '68: Best Cinematography; Nominations: Academy Awards '68: Best Sound. **VHS, Beta, LV ★★★**

The Burmese Harp At the end of WWII, a Japanese soldier is spiritually traumatized and becomes obsessed with burying the masses of war casualties. A searing, acclaimed anti-war statement, in Japanese with English subtitles. Remade by Ichikawa in 1985. **AKA:** Harp of Burma; Birumano Tategoto.

1956 115m/B *JP* Shoji Yasui, Rentaro Mikuni, Tatsuya Mihashi, Tanie Kitabayashi, Yunosuke Ito; **D:** Kon Ichikawa. **VHS, Beta, LV ★★★★**

Burn! An Italian-made indictment of imperialist control by guerrilla-filmmaker Pontecorvo, depicting the efforts of a 19th-century British ambassador to put down a slave revolt on a Portuguese-run Caribbean island. Great Brando performance. **AKA:** Quemimada!.

1970 (PG) 112m/C *IT* Marlon Brando, Evarist Marquez, Renato Salvatori; **D:** Gillo Pontecorvo; **M:** Ennio Morricone. **VHS, Beta, LV ★★★1/2**

The Burning Bed A made for television dramatic expose (based on a true story) about wife-beating. Fawcett garnered accolades for her performance as the battered wife who couldn't take it anymore. Highly acclaimed and Emmy-nominated.

1985 95m/C Farrah Fawcett, Paul LeMat, Penelope Milford, Richard Masur; **D:** Robert Greenwald. **VHS, Beta ★★★1/2**

The Burning Season In one of his last performances, Julia inspires as Chico Mendes, a socialist union leader who fought to protect the homes and land of Brazilian peasants in the western Amazon rain forest. With Mendes' help the peasants form a union and struggle to prevent the building of a road that will provide easy access to forest land for speculators and cattlemen. Naturally, they are violently opposed by corruption-ridden capitalist powers in the government. Julia provides a haunting portrayal of the heroic figure who was assassinated in 1990. Based in part on the book by Andrew Revkin. Filmed on location in Mexico.

1994 123m/C Raul Julia, Edward James Olmos, Sonia Braga, Luis Guzman, Nigel Havers, Kamala Dawson, Tomas Milian, Esai Morales, Tony Plana, Carmen Argenziano; **D:** John Frankenheimer; **W:** William Mastrosimone, Michael Tolkin, Ron Hutchinson; **M:** Gary Chang. **VHS ★★★**

Burnt by the Sun Masterful evocation of '30s Stalinist Russia, covering a day in the life of Soviet revolutionary hero Serguei (Mikhalkov) and his family, far from the purges and gulags. Enjoying a country existence with wife Moroussia (Dapkounaite) and daughter Nadia (played by Mikhalkov's daughter), his idyll is disturbed by mystery man Dimitri (Menchikov), and Serguei realizes their fates are bound by the difference between their Communist dreams and reality. Symbolism is a little heavy but film delivers emotionally. Russian with subtitles. **AKA:** Outomlionnye Solntsem.

1994 (R) 134m/C *RU FR* Nikita Mikhalkov, Ingeborga Dapkounaite, Oleg Menchikov, Nadia Mikhalkov, Andre Oumansky, Viatcheslav Tikhonov, Svetlana Krioutchkova, Vladimir Ilyine; **D:** Nikita

Mikhalkov; **W:** Nikita Mikhalkov, Rustam Ibragimbekov; **M:** Eduard Artemyev. Academy Awards '94: Best Foreign Language Film; Cannes Film Festival '94: Grand Jury Prize; Nominations: British Academy Awards '95: Best Foreign Film. **VHS, LV** ★★★

Bus Stop Murray plays a naive cowboy who falls in love with Monroe, a barroom singer, and decides to marry her without her permission. Considered by many to be the finest performance by Marilyn Monroe; she sings "That Old Black Magic" in this one. Very funny with good performances by all. Based on the William Inge play. **AKA:** The Wrong Kind of Girl.
1956 96m/C Marilyn Monroe, Arthur O'Connell, Hope Lange, Don Murray, Betty Field, Casey Adams, Hans Conried, Eileen Heckart; **D:** Joshua Logan; **W:** George Axelrod. National Board of Review Awards '56: 10 Best Films of the Year; Nominations: Academy Awards '56: Best Supporting Actor (Murray). **VHS, Beta, LV** ★★★

Butch Cassidy and the Sundance Kid Two legendary outlaws at the turn of the century take it on the lam with a beautiful, willing ex-school teacher. With a clever script, humanly forcible characters, and warm, witty dialogue, this film was destined to become a box-office classic. Featured the hit song, "Raindrops Keep Falling on My Head" and renewed the buddy film industry, as Newman and Redford trade insult for insult. Look for the great scene where Newman takes on giant Ted Cassidy in a fist fight. ♪ Raindrops Keep Fallin' on My Head; On a Bicycle Built for Joy.
1969 (PG) 110m/C Paul Newman, Robert Redford, Katharine Ross, Jeff Corey, Strother Martin, Cloris Leachman, Kenneth Mars, Ted Cassidy, Henry Jones, George Furth, Sam Elliott, Conrad Hall; **D:** George Roy Hill; **W:** William Goldman; **M:** Burt Bacharach. Academy Awards '69: Best Cinematography, Best Song ("Raindrops Keep Fallin' on My Head"), Best Story & Screenplay, Best Original Score; British Academy Awards '70: Best Actor (Redford), Best Actress (Ross), Best Director (Hill), Best Film, Best Screenplay; Golden Globe Awards '70: Best Score; Writers Guild of America '69: Best Adapted Screenplay; Nominations: Academy Awards '69: Best Director (Hill), Best Picture, Best Sound. **VHS, Beta, LV** ★★★★

Butterfield 8 A seedy film of the John O'Hara novel about a prostitute that wants to go straight and settle down. Taylor won an Oscar, perhaps because she was ill and had lost in the two previous years in more deserving roles.
1960 108m/C Elizabeth Taylor, Laurence Harvey, Eddie Fisher, Dina Merrill, Mildred Dunnock, Betty Field, Susan Oliver, Kay Medford; **D:** Daniel Mann; **W:** John Michael Hayes, Charles Schnee. Academy Awards '60: Best Actress (Taylor); Nominations: Academy Awards '60: Best Color Cinematography. **VHS, Beta, LV** ★★★

Butterflies Are Free Fast-paced humor surrounds the Broadway play brought to the big screen. Blind youth Albert is determined to be self-sufficient. A next-door-neighbor actress helps him gain independence from his over-protective mother (Heckart).
1972 (PG) 109m/C Goldie Hawn, Edward Albert, Eileen Heckart, Michael Glaser; **D:** Milton Katselas; **M:** Robert Alcivar. Academy Awards '72: Best Supporting Actress (Heckart); Nominations: Academy Awards '72: Best Cinematography, Best Sound. **VHS, Beta** ★★★

Bye, Bye, Birdie Energized and sweet film version of the Broadway musical about a teen rock and roll idol (Pearson doing Elvis) coming to a small town to see one of his fans before he leaves for the army. The film that made Ann-Margret a star. ♪ Bye Bye Birdie; The Telephone Hour; How Lovely to be a Woman; Honestly Sincere; One Boy; Put on a Happy Face; Kids; One Last Kiss; A Lot of Livin' to Do.
1963 112m/C Dick Van Dyke, Janet Leigh, Ann-Margret, Paul Lynde, Jesse Pearson, Bobby Rydell, Maureen Stapleton, Ed Sullivan, Trudi Ames; **D:** George Sidney; **W:** Irving Brecher. Nominations: Academy Awards '63: Best Sound, Best Original Score. **VHS, Beta, LV** ★★★

Cabaret Hitler is rising to power, racism and anti-Semitism are growing, and the best place to hide from it all is the cabaret. With dancing girls, androgynous master of ceremonies Grey and American expatriate and singer Minnelli, you can laugh and drink and pretend tomorrow will never come. Minnelli does just that. Face to face with the increasing horrors of Nazism, she persists in the belief that the "show must go on." Based on the John Kander hit Broadway musical (taken from the Christopher Isherwood stories), the film is impressive, with excellent direction and cinematography. ♪ Cabaret; Wilkommen; Mein Herr; Maybe This Time; Two Ladies; Money, Money; Hi-eraten; Tomorrow Belongs to Me; If You Could See Her.

1972 (PG) 119m/C Liza Minnelli, Joel Grey, Michael York, Marisa Berenson; **D:** Bob Fosse; **W:** Jay Presson Allen; **M:** Ralph Burns. Academy Awards '72: Best Actress (Minnelli), Best Art Direction/Set Decoration, Best Cinematography, Best Director (Fosse), Best Film Editing, Best Sound, Best Supporting Actor (Grey), Best Score; British Academy Awards '72: Best Actress (Minnelli), Best Director (Fosse), Best Film; Golden Globe Awards '73: Best Actress—Musical/Comedy (Minnelli), Best Film—Musical/Comedy, Best Supporting Actor (Grey); National Society of Film Critics Awards '72: Best Supporting Actor (Grey); Writers Guild of America '72: Best Adapted Screenplay; Nominations: Academy Awards '72: Best Adapted Screenplay, Best Picture. **VHS, Beta, LV** ★★★1/2

Cabin in the Sky A poor woman fights to keep her husband's soul out of the devil's clutches. Based on a Broadway show and featuring an all-Black cast. Lively dance numbers and a musical score with contributions from Duke Ellington. Minnelli's first feature film. ♪ Cabin in the Sky; Happiness Is Just a Thing Called Joe; Taking a Chance on Love; Life's Full of Consequence; Li'l Black Sheep; Shine; Honey in the Honeycomb.
1943 99m/C Ethel Waters, Eddie Anderson, Lena Horne, Rex Ingram, Louis Armstrong, Duke Ellington; **D:** Vincente Minnelli; **M:** Duke Ellington, Harold Arlen, E.Y. Harburg, George Bassman. Nominations: Academy Awards '43: Best Song ("Happiness Is a Thing Called Joe"). **VHS, Beta, LV** ★★★

The Cabinet of Dr. Caligari A pioneering film in the most extreme expressionistic style about a hypnotist in a carnival and a girl-snatching somnambulist. Highly influential in its approach to lighting, composition, design and acting. Much imitated. Silent.
1919 92m/B *GE* Conrad Veidt, Werner Krauss, Lil Dagover; **D:** Robert Wiene. **VHS, Beta, LV** ★★★★

Caddyshack Inspired performances by Murray and Dangerfield drive this sublimely moronic comedy onto the green. The action takes place at Bushwood Country Club, where caddy O'Keefe is bucking to win the club's college scholarship. Characters involved in various sophomoric set pieces include obnoxious club president Knight, a playboy who is too laid back to keep his score (Chase), a loud, vulgar, and extremely rich golfer (Dangerfield), and Murray as a filthy gopher-hunting grounds-keeper. Occasional dry moments are followed by scenes of pure (and tasteless) anarchy, so watch with someone immature. Does for golf what "Major League" tried to do for baseball.
1980 (R) 99m/C Chevy Chase, Rodney Dangerfield, Ted Knight, Michael O'Keefe, Bill Murray, Sarah Holcomb, Brian Doyle-Murray; **D:** Harold Ramis; **W:** Brian Doyle-Murray, Doug Kenney, Harold Ramis. **VHS, Beta, LV** ★★★1/2

The Caine Mutiny A group of naval officers revolt against a captain they consider mentally unfit. Bogart is masterful as Captain Queeg, obsessed with cleanliness while onboard and later a study in mental meltdown during the court-martial of a crew member who participated in the mutiny. Based on the Pulitzer-winning novel by Herman Wouk, the drama takes a close look at the pressure-filled life aboard ship during WWII.
1954 125m/C Humphrey Bogart, Jose Ferrer, Van Johnson, Fred MacMurray, Lee Marvin, Claude Akins, E.G. Marshall, Robert Francis, May Wynn, Tom Tully; **D:** Edward Dmytryk; **W:** Stanley Roberts; **M:** Max Steiner. Nominations: Academy Awards '53: Best Actor (Tully); Academy Awards '54: Best Actor (Bogart), Best Film Editing, Best Picture, Best Screenplay, Best Sound, Best Original Score. **VHS, Beta, LV, 8mm** ★★★★

Cal A young Catholic man is recruited into the Irish Republican Army. He falls in love with an older Protestant widow, whose husband, a policeman, he helped kill, acting as the getaway driver for his fellow Republicans. Thoughtful and tragic, with excellent performances; set in Northern Ireland.
1984 (R) 104m/C *IR* Helen Mirren, John Lynch, Donal McCann, Kitty Gibson, Ray McAnally, John Kavanagh; **D:** Pat O'Connor; **W:** Bernard MacLaverty; **M:** Mark Knopfler. Cannes Film Festival '84: Best Actress (Mirren); Nominations: Cannes Film Festival '84: Best Film. **VHS, Beta** ★★★

Calamity Jane In one of her best Warner musicals, Day stars as the rip-snortin', gun-totin' Calamity Jane of Western lore, in an on-again, off-again romance with Wild Bill Hickok. ♪ Secret Love; Just Blew in From the Windy City; The Black Hills of Dakota; The Deadwood Stage (Whip-Crack-Away!).
1953 101m/C Doris Day, Howard Keel, Allyn Ann McLerie; **D:** David Butler; **M:** Sammy Fain, Paul Francis Webster.

Academy Awards '53: Best Song ("Secret Love"); Nominations: Academy Awards '53: Best Sound, Best Original Score. **VHS, Beta, LV** ★★★

Calendar A Canadian photographer (Egoyan) is hired to take pictures of ancient Armenian churches for a calendar. His wife (Egoyan's real-life spouse Khanjian) accompanies him, serving as a translator, and they hire a driver (Adamian) who turns out to be an architectural expert. Told in flashback, the film gradually reveals a romantic triangle—with the photographer becoming so caught up in his work that he fails to realize his wife, increasingly drawn to her ethnic heritage, and their driver are having an affair. This romantic puzzle also includes the photographer, having returned to Canada wifeless and apparently seeking a replacement, having dinner with a series of women he'd meet through the personals. In English and Armenian.
1993 78m/C CA Atom Egoyan, Arsinee Khanjian, Ashot Adamian, Norayr Kasper; **D:** Atom Egoyan; **W:** Atom Egoyan. **VHS** ★★★

California Suite The posh Beverly Hills Hotel is the setting for four unrelated Neil Simon skits, ranging from a battling husband and wife to feuding friends. Simonized dialogue is crisp and funny.
1978 (PG) 103m/C Alan Alda, Michael Caine, Bill Cosby, Jane Fonda, Walter Matthau, Richard Pryor, Maggie Smith, Elaine May; **D:** Herbert Ross; **W:** Neil Simon; **M:** Claude Bolling. Academy Awards '78: Best Supporting Actress (Smith); Golden Globe Awards '79: Best Actress—Musical/Comedy (Smith); Nominations: Academy Awards '78: Best Adapted Screenplay, Best Art Direction/Set Decoration. **VHS, Beta, LV** ★★★

Call Northside 777 Chicago reporter Stewart finds himself in the crux of a decade-old murder investigation when he follows up a newspaper ad offering $5,000 for any information leading to the arrest and conviction of a police killer. The cunning reporter discovers police coverups and missing evidence pointing to an imprisoned man's innocence. Powerful performance from Stewart directs this docudrama based on the real-life story of Chicago's Joe Majczek, unjustly imprisoned for 11 years, and the Pulitzer Prize-winning reporter Jim McGuire who, through a clever investigation, found enough evidence to have the case re-opened. **AKA:** Calling Northside 777.

1948 111m/B James Stewart, Richard Conte, Lee J. Cobb, Helen Walker, Betty Garde, Moroni Olsen, E.G. Marshall, Howard Smith, John McIntire, Paul Harvey, George Tyne, Michael Chapin, Addison Richards, Richard Rober, Eddie Dunn, Charles Lane, Walter Greaza, William Post Jr., George Melford, Charles Miller, Lionel Stander, Jonathan Hale; **D:** Henry Hathaway; **M:** Alfred Newman. **VHS** ★★★1/2

The Cameraman After moving to MGM, Keaton made his first feature with a major studio, giving up the artistic control he had enjoyed in his previous films. Spared from the vilification of studio politics (not the case with later Keaton films), "The Cameraman" enjoyed both critical and popular success. Keaton's inept tintype portrait-maker has a heart that pitter-patters for an MGM office girl. He hopes to impress her by joining the ranks of the newsreel photographers. Fortuitously poised to grab a photo scoop on a Chinese tong war, he is forced to return empty-handed when an organ-grinder's monkey absconds with his firsthand footage. Silent with a musical score.
1928 78m/B Buster Keaton, Marceline Day, Harold Goodwin, Harry Gribbon, Sidney Bracy, Edward Brophy, Vernon Dent, William Irving; **D:** Edward Sedgwick. **VHS, LV** ★★★1/2

Camille The classic Alexandre Dumas story about a dying French courtesan falling in love with a shallow young nobleman. A clean, romantic adaptation that somehow escapes the cliches and stands as one of the most telling monuments to Garbo's unique magic and presence on film.
1936 108m/B Greta Garbo, Robert Taylor, Lionel Barrymore, Henry Daniell, Elizabeth Allan, Rex O'Malley, Lenore Ulric, Laura Hope Crews; **D:** George Cukor. National Board of Review Awards '37: 10 Best Films of the Year; New York Film Critics Awards '37: Best Actress (Garbo); Nominations: Academy Awards '37: Best Actress (Garbo). **VHS, Beta** ★★★★

Camille Claudel A lushly romantic version of the art world at the turn of the century, when art was exploding in new forms and independence for women was unheard of. Sculptor Claudel's tragic love for art, Auguste Rodin (for whom she modeled), and independence clash, costing her sanity. Very long, it requires an attentive and thoughtful viewing. In French with English subtitles.
1989 (R) 149m/C FR Isabelle Adjani, Gerard Depardieu, Laurent Grevill, Alain

Cuny, Madeleine Robinson, Katrine Boorman; **D:** Bruno Nuytten; **W:** Bruno Nuytten, Marilyn Goldin; **M:** Gabriel Yared. Cesar Awards '89: Best Actress (Adjani), Best Art Direction/Set Decoration, Best Cinematography, Best Costume Design, Best Film; Nominations: Academy Awards '89: Best Actress (Adjani), Best Foreign Language Film. **VHS, Beta, LV** ★★★

The Candidate Realistic, satirical look at politics and political campaigning. A young, idealistic lawyer is talked into trying for the Senate seat and learns the truth about running for office. Ritchie's other efforts include "Downhill Racer" and "Bad News Bears."
1972 (PG) 105m/C Robert Redford, Peter Boyle, Don Porter, Allen (Goorwitz) Garfield, Karen Carlson, Melvyn Douglas, Michael Lerner; **D:** Michael Ritchie; **W:** Jeremy Larner. Academy Awards '72: Best Story & Screenplay; National Board of Review Awards '72: 10 Best Films of the Year; Writers Guild of America '72: Best Original Screenplay; Nominations: Academy Awards '72: Best Sound. **VHS, Beta, LV** ★★★

A Canterbury Tale Writer-director team Powell and Pressburger have loosely modeled a retelling of Chaucer's famous tale of a pilgrimage to the cathedral in Canterbury. Set in Nazi-threatened Britain in 1944, the story follows the pilgrimage of three Brits and an American GI to the eponymous cathedral. Strange, effective, worth looking at. The 95-minute American version, with added footage of Kim Hunter, is inferior to the 124-minute original.
1944 124m/B *GB* Eric Portman, Sheila Sim, Dennis Price, Esmond Knight, Charles Hawtrey, Hay Petrie; **D:** Michael Powell, Emeric Pressburger. **VHS** ★★★1/2

Cape Fear Former prosecutor turned small-town lawyer Peck and his family are plagued by the sadistic attentions of criminal Mitchum, who just finished a six year sabbatical at the state pen courtesy of prosecutor Peck. Taut and creepy; Mitchum's a consummate psychopath. Based on (and far superior to) John MacDonald's "The Executioners." Don't pass this one up in favor of the Scorsese remake.
1961 106m/B Gregory Peck, Robert Mitchum, Polly Bergen, Martin Balsam, Telly Savalas, Jack Kruschen; **D:** J. Lee Thompson. **VHS, Beta** ★★★★

Cape Fear Scorsese takes on this terrifying tale of brutality and manipulation (previously filmed in 1961) and cranks it up a notch as a paroled convict haunts the lawyer who put him away. Great cast, a rollercoaster of suspense. Note the cameos by Mitchum, Peck, and Balsam, stars of the first version. Original source material was "The Executioners" by John D. MacDonald. Breathtaking rollercoaster of a film. Elmer Bernstein adapted the original score by Bernard Herrmann.
1991 (R) 128m/C Robert De Niro, Nick Nolte, Jessica Lange, Juliette Lewis, Joe Don Baker, Illeana Douglas, Fred Dalton Thompson; **Cameos:** Robert Mitchum, Gregory Peck, Martin Balsam; **D:** Martin Scorsese; **W:** Wesley Strick; **M:** Bernard Herrmann, Elmer Bernstein. Chicago Film Critics Awards '91: Most Promising Actress (Lewis); Nominations: Academy Awards '91: Best Actor (De Niro), Best Supporting Actress (Lewis). **VHS, LV** ★★★

Captain Blood Sabatini adventure story launched then unknown 26-year-old Flynn and 19-year-old de Havilland to fame in perhaps the best pirate story ever. Exiled into slavery by a tyrannical governor, Irish physician Peter Blood is forced into piracy but ultimately earns a pardon for his swashbuckling ways. Love interest de Havilland would go on to appear in seven more features with Flynn, who took the part Robert Donat declined for health reasons. Cleverly budgeted using ship shots from silents, and miniature sets when possible. First original film score by composer Korngold. Also available colorized.
1935 120m/B Errol Flynn, Olivia de Havilland, Basil Rathbone, J. Carrol Naish, Guy Kibbee, Lionel Atwill; **D:** Michael Curtiz. Nominations: Academy Awards '35: Best Picture, Best Sound. **VHS, Beta** ★★★1/2

Captain Horatio Hornblower A colorful drama about the life and loves of the British sea captain during the Napoleonic wars. Peck is rather out of his element as the courageous, swashbuckling hero (Errol Flynn was originally cast) but there's enough fast-paced derring-do to make this a satisfying saga. Based on the novel by C.S. Forester.
1951 117m/C *GB* Gregory Peck, Virginia Mayo, Robert Beatty, Denis O'Dea, Christopher Lee; **D:** Raoul Walsh; **W:** Ivan Goff. **VHS, Beta, LV** ★★★

Captain Kronos: Vampire Hunter Captain Kronos fences thirsty foes in Hammer horror hybrid. Artsy, atmospheric and atypical, it's written and directed with tongue firmly in cheek by Clemens, who penned many an "Avengers" episode. **AKA:** Kronos.

1974 (R) 91m/C *GB* Horst Janson, John Carson, Caroline Munro, Ian Hendry, Shane Briant, Wanda Ventham; *D:* Brian Clemens; *W:* Brian Clemens. **VHS, Beta** ★★★

Captains Courageous Rich brat Bartholomew takes a dip sans life jacket while leaning over an ocean liner railing to relieve himself of the half dozen ice cream sodas imprudently consumed at sea. Picked up by a Portugese fishing boat, he at first treats his mandatory three month voyage as an unscheduled cab ride, but eventually, through a deepening friendship with crewman Tracy, develops a hitherto unheralded work ethic. The boy's filial bond with Tracy, of course, requires that the seaman meet with watery disaster. Based on the Rudyard Kipling novel. Director Fleming went on to "Gone With the Wind" and "The Wizard of Oz."
1937 116m/B Spencer Tracy, Lionel Barrymore, Freddie Bartholomew, Mickey Rooney, Melvyn Douglas, Charley Grapewin, John Carradine, Bobby Watson, Jack LaRue; *D:* Victor Fleming. Academy Awards '37: Best Actor (Tracy); National Board of Review Awards '37: 10 Best Films of the Year; Nominations: Academy Awards '37: Best Film Editing, Best Picture, Best Screenplay. **VHS, Beta** ★★★

Caravaggio Controversial biography of the late Renaissance painter famous for his bisexuality, fondness for prostitute models, violence and depravity. Photography by Gabriel Beristain reproduces the artist's visual style.
1986 97m/C *GB* Nigel Terry, Sean Bean, Tilda Swinton; *D:* Derek Jarman; *W:* Derek Jarman. **VHS, Beta, LV** ★★★

Carefree Dizzy radio singer Rogers can't make up her mind about beau Bellamy, so he sends her to analyst Astaire. Seems she can't even dream a little dream until shrink Astaire prescribes that she ingest some funny food, which causes her to dream she's in love with the Fredman. Au contraire, says he, it's a Freudian thing, and he hypnotically suggests that she really loves Bellamy. The two line up to march down the aisle together, and Fred stops dancing just long enough to realize he's in love with Ginger. A screwball comedy with music. ♪ I Used to be Colorblind; The Night is Filled With Music; Change Partners; The Yam.
1938 83m/B Fred Astaire, Ginger Rogers, Ralph Bellamy, Jack Carson, Franklin Pangborn, Hattie McDaniel; *D:* Mark Sandrich; *M:* Irving Berlin. Nominations: Academy Awards '38: Best Interior Decoration, Best Song ("Change Partners and Dance with Me"), Best Score. **VHS, Beta, LV** ★★★

Careful, He Might Hear You Abandoned by his father, six-year-old P.S. becomes a pawn between his dead mother's two sisters, one working class and the other wealthy, and his worldview is further overturned by the sudden reappearance of his prodigal father. Set in Depression-era Australia, Schultz's vision is touching and keenly observed, and manages a sort of child's eye sense of proportion. Based on a novel by Sumner Locke Elliott.
1984 (PG) 113m/C *AU* Nicholas Gledhill, Wendy Hughes, Robyn Nevin, John Hargreaves; *D:* Carl Schultz. Australian Film Institute '83: Best Actress (Hughes), Best Film. **VHS, Beta** ★★★

Carlito's Way Puerto Rican crime czar Carlito Brigante (Pacino) has just gotten out of jail and wants to go straight. But his drug underworld cohorts don't believe he can do it. Penn (barely recognizable) is great as a sleazy coked-out lawyer who's way out of his league. Remarkably subdued violence given DePalma's previous rep—it's effective without being gratuitous, especially the final shootout set in Grand Central Station. Pacino's performance is equally subdued, with controlled tension and lots of eye contact rather than grandiose emotions. Based on the novels "Carlito's Way" and "After Hours" by Edwin Torres. Pacino and DePalma previously teamed for "Scarface."
1993 (R) 145m/C Al Pacino, Sean Penn, Penelope Ann Miller, Luis Guzman, John Leguizamo, Ingrid Rogers, James Rebhorn, Viggo Mortensen, Jorge Porcel, Joseph Siravo, Adrian Pasdar; *D:* Brian DePalma; *W:* David Koepp; *M:* Patrick Doyle, Stephen Burum. Nominations: Golden Globe Awards '94: Best Supporting Actor (Penn), Best Supporting Actress (Miller). **VHS, LV** ★★★

Carmen Choreographer casts Carmen and finds life imitates art when he falls under the spell of the hot-blooded Latin siren. Bizet's opera lends itself to erotically charged flamenco context. Well acted, impressive scenes including cigarette girls' dance fight and romance between Carmen and Don Jose. In Spanish with English subtitles.
1983 (R) 99m/C *SP* Antonio Gades, Laura Del Sol, Paco DeLucia, Christina Hoyos; *D:* Carlos Saura. British Academy Awards '84: Best Foreign Film; Nominations: Academy Awards '83: Best Foreign Language Film;

Cannes Film Festival '83: Best Film. **VHS, Beta** ★★★

Carmen Jones Bizet's tale of fickle femme fatale Carmen heads South with an all black cast and new lyrics by Hammerstein II. Soldier Belafonte falls big time for factory working belle Dandridge during the war, and runs off with miss thang after he kills his C.O. and quits the army. Tired of pretty-boy Belafonte, Dandridge's eye wanders upon prize pugilist Escamillo, inspiring ex-soldier beau to wring her throaty little neck. Film debuts of Carroll and Peters. More than a little racist undertone to the direction. Actors' singing is dubbed. ♪ Dat's Love; Dere's a Cafe on de Corner; Beat Out Dat Rhythm on a Drum; You Talk Just Like My Maw; Stand Up and Fight; Dis Flower; My Joe.
1954 105m/C Dorothy Dandridge, Harry Belafonte, Pearl Bailey, Roy Glenn, Diahann Carroll, Brock Peters; **D:** Otto Preminger. Golden Globe Awards '55: Best Film—Musical/Comedy; Nominations: Academy Awards '54: Best Actress (Dandridge), Best Original Score. **VHS, LV** ★★★

Carnal Knowledge Carnal knowledge of the me generation. Three decades in the sex-saturated lives of college buddies Nicholson and Garfunkel, chronicled through girlfriends, affairs and marriages. Controversial upon release, it's not a flattering anatomy of Y chromosome carriers. Originally written as a play. Kane's debut.
1971 (R) 96m/C Jack Nicholson, Candice Bergen, Art Garfunkel, Ann-Margret, Rita Moreno, Carol Kane; **D:** Mike Nichols, Giuseppe Rotunno; **W:** Jules Feiffer. Golden Globe Awards '72: Best Supporting Actress (Ann-Margret); Nominations: Academy Awards '71: Best Supporting Actress (Ann-Margret). **VHS, Beta, LV, 8mm** ★★★

Carnival in Flanders When Spanish invaders enter a small 17th-century Flemish village they discover all the men have diappeared. So it's up to the women to save the town from destruction—and they decide to do it by seducing the invaders. Classic French costume farce with a witty script and fine performances. In French with English subtitles. **AKA:** La Kermesse Heroique.
1935 90m/B *FR* Francoise Rosay, Louis Jouvet, Jean Murat, Andre Aleme, Micheline Cheirel; **D:** Jacques Feyder. National Board of Review Awards '36: 5 Best Foreign Films of the Year; New York Film Critics Awards '36: Best Foreign Film;

Venice Film Festival '36: Best Director (Feyder). **VHS, Beta** ★★★1/2

Carousel Much-loved Rodgers & Hammerstein musical based on Ferenc Molnar's play "Liliom" (filmed by Fritz Lang in 1935) about a swaggering carnival barker (MacRae) who tries to change his life after he falls in love with a good woman. Killed while attempting to foil a robbery he was supposed to help commit, he begs his heavenly hosts for the chance to return to the mortal realm just long enough to set things straight with his teenage daughter. Now indisputably a classic, the film lost $2 million when it was released. ♪ If I Loved You; Soliloquy; You'll Never Walk Alone; What's the Use of Wond'rin; When I Marry Mister Snow; When the Children Are Asleep; A Real Nice Clambake; Carousel Ballet; Carousel Waltz.
1956 128m/C Gordon MacRae, Shirley Jones, Cameron Mitchell, Gene Lockhart, Barbara Ruick, Robert Rounseville, Richard Deacon, Tor Johnson; **D:** Henry King; **M:** Richard Rodgers, Oscar Hammerstein. **VHS, Beta, LV** ★★★

Carrie In a part turned down by Cary Grant, Olivier plays a married American who self destructs as the woman he loves scales the heights to fame and fortune. The manager of a posh epicurean mecca, Olivier deserts wife Hopkins and steals big bucks from his boss to head east with paramour Jones, a country bumpkin transplanted to Chicago. Once en route to thespian fame in the Big Apple, Jones abandons her erstwhile beau, who crumbles pathetically. Adapted from Theodore Dreiser's "Sister Carrie," it's mega melodrama, but the performances are above reproach.
1952 118m/B Laurence Olivier, Jennifer Jones, Miriam Hopkins, Eddie Albert, Basil Ruysdael, Ray Teal, Barry Kelley, Sara Berner, William Reynolds, Mary Murphy, Charles Halton; **D:** William Wyler. Nominations: Academy Awards '52: Best Art Direction/Set Decoration (B & W), Best Costume Design (B & W). **VHS, Beta, LV** ★★★

Carrie Overprotected by religious fanatic mother Laurie and mocked by the in-crowd, shy, withdrawn high school girl Carrie White is asked to the prom. Realizing she's been made the butt of a joke, she unleashes her considerable telekinetic talents. Travolta, Allen, and Irving are teenagers who get what they deserve. Based on the Stephen King novel. Laserdisc version features the original movie trailer, an interview with screenwriter Lawrence D. Cohen, publicity shots, a study of De Palma's film-making techniques, and commentary by film expert Laurent Bouzereau.

1976 (R) 98m/C Sissy Spacek, Piper Laurie, John Travolta, William Katt, Amy Irving, Nancy Allen, Edie McClurg, Betty Buckley; *D:* Brian DePalma; *W:* Lawrence D. Cohen; *M:* Pino Donaggio. National Society of Film Critics Awards '76: Best Actress (Spacek); Nominations: Academy Awards '76: Best Actress (Spacek), Best Supporting Actress (Laurie). **VHS, Beta, LV** ★★★

Carrington, V.C. British army major Niven is brought up for a court-martial on embezzlement charges because he arranges, without official permission, to be reimbursed for money owed to him. A former war hero, he decides to defend himself in court, and, once an affair comes to light, his vindictive wife joins the opposition. Good cast, superlative Niven performance. *AKA:* Court Martial.

1954 100m/B *GB* David Niven, Margaret Leighton, Noelle Middleton, Laurence Naismith; *D:* Anthony Asquith. **VHS, Beta** ★★★

Carry On Doctor British series continues as characters of questionable competence join the medical profession. Hospital staff gets caught in battle over secret weight loss formula.

1968 95m/C *GB* Frankie Howerd, Kenneth Williams, Jim Dale, Barbara Windsor; *D:* Gerald Thomas. **VHS** ★★★

The Cars That Ate Paris Parasitic town in the Parisian (Australia) outback preys on car and body parts generated by deliberate accidents inflicted by wreck-driving wreckless youths. Weir's first film released internationally, about a small Australian town that survives economically via deliberately contriving car accidents and selling the wrecks' scrap parts. A broad, bitter black comedy with some horror touches. *AKA:* The Cars That Eat People.

1974 (PG) 91m/C *AU* Terry Camillieri, Kevin Miles, John Meillon, Melissa Jaffe; *D:* Peter Weir; *W:* Peter Weir. **VHS, Beta** ★★★

Cartouche A swashbuckling action-comedy set in 18th-century France. Belmondo plays a charming thief who takes over a Paris gang, aided by the lovely Cardinale. When he is captured, she sacrifices her life to save him and Belmondo and his cohorts vow to have their revenge. Based on a French legend and a well-acted combination of tragedy, action, and farce. In French with English subtitles. *AKA:* Swords of Blood.

1962 115m/C *FR IT* Jean-Paul Belmondo, Claudia Cardinale, Odile Versois, Philippe Lemaire; *D:* Philippe de Broca; *W:* Philippe de Broca; *M:* Georges Delerue. **VHS** ★★★

Casablanca Can you see George Raft as Rick? Jack Warner did, but producer Hal Wallis wanted Bogart. Considered by many to be the best film ever made and one of the most quoted movies of all time, it rocketed Bogart from gangster roles to romantic leads as he and Bergman (who never looked lovelier) sizzle on screen. Bogart runs a gin joint in Morocco during the Nazi occupation, and meets up with Bergman, an old flame, but romance and politics do not mix, especially in Nazi-occupied French Morocco. Greenstreet, Lorre, and Rains all create memorable characters, as does Wilson, the piano player to whom Bergman says the oft-misquoted, "Play it, Sam." Without a doubt, the best closing scene ever written; it was scripted on the fly during the end of shooting, and actually shot several ways. Written from an unproduced play. See it in the original black and white. Laserdisc edition features restored imaging and sound and commentary by film historian Ronald Haver about the production, the play it was based on, and the famed evolution of the screenplay on audio track two. Fiftieth Anniversary Edition contains a restored and remastered print, the original 1942 theatrical trailer, a film documentary narrated by Lauren Bacall, and a booklet.

1942 (PG) 102m/B Humphrey Bogart, Ingrid Bergman, Paul Henreid, Claude Rains, Peter Lorre, Sydney Greenstreet, Conrad Veidt, S.Z. Sakall, Dooley Wilson, Marcel Dalio, John Qualen, Helmut Dantine; *D:* Michael Curtiz; *W:* Julius J. Epstein, Philip C. Epstein, Howard Koch; *M:* Max Steiner. Academy Awards '43: Best Director (Curtiz), Best Picture, Best Screenplay; National Board of Review Awards '43: 10 Best Films of the Year; Nominations: Academy Awards '43: Best Actor (Bogart), Best Black and White Cinematography, Best Film Editing, Best Supporting Actor (Rains), Best Original Score. **VHS, Beta, LV, 8mm** ★★★★

Casino Final part of the Scorsese underworld crime trilogy that began with "Mean Streets" and continued in "GoodFellas." Casino boss Sam "Ace" Rothstein (De Niro), his ex-hustler wife Ginger (Stone), and his loose-cannon enforcer pal Nicky

(Pesci) are the principals in this lengthy, fictionalized account of how the mob lost Las Vegas in a haze of drugs, sex, coincidence and betrayal. Flashy, intricate, and unflinchingly violent account of mob-run '70s Vegas clicks when exploring the inner workings of a major casino and its hierarchy. Although Stone shines as a hedonistic money chaser, visuals are great and the soundtrack is a killer, story line suffers from deja vu. Pileggi again adapted the screenplay from his own book. **1995 (R) 177m/C** Robert De Niro, Joe Pesci, Sharon Stone, James Woods, Don Rickles, Alan King, Kevin Pollak, L.Q. Jones, Dick Smothers, John Bloom; *Cameos:* Frankie Avalon, Steve Allen, Jayne Meadows, Jerry Vale, Robert Richardson; *D:* Martin Scorsese; *W:* Nicholas Pileggi, Martin Scorsese. Golden Globe Awards '96: Best Actress—Drama (Stone); Nominations: Academy Awards '95: Best Actress (Stone); Golden Globe Awards '96: Best Director (Scorsese). VHS ★★★

Casper World's friendliest ghost appears on the big screen with outstanding visual trickery (from Industrial Light and Magic) and a lively, if hokey, story. Evilish Carrigan Crittenden (Moriarty) inherits ghost-infested Whiplash Manor and hires scatterbrained "ghost therapist" Dr. Harvey (Pullman) to get rid of its unwanted occupants. His daughter Kat (Ricci) is soon the object of Casper's friendly attention while the good doc must contend with Casper's mischievous uncles—Stinkie, Fatso, and Stretch. Exec producer Spielberg shows his influence with numerous topical gags and screen references that help amuse the adults while the ghosts work their magic on the kiddies. Silberling's directorial debut; based on the comic-book and television cartoon character created more than 30 years ago. **1995 (PG) 95m/C** Christina Ricci, Bill Pullman, Cathy Moriarty, Amy Brenneman; *Cameos:* Don Novello, Rodney Dangerfield, Clint Eastwood, Mel Gibson, Dan Aykroyd; *D:* Dean Cundey, Brad Silberling; *W:* Sherri Stoner, Deanna Oliver; *M:* James Horner; *V:* Malachi Pearson, Joe Nipote, Joe Alaskey, Brad Garrett. VHS, LV ★★★

Casualties of War A Vietnam war morality play about army private Fox in the bush who refuses to let his fellow soldiers and commanding sergeant (Penn) skirt responsibility for the rape and murder of a native woman. Fox achieves his dramatic breakthrough. Based on the true story by Daniel Lang. **1989 (R) 120m/C** Sean Penn, Michael J. Fox, Don Harvey, Thuy Thu Le, John Leguizamo, Sam Robards, John C. Reilly, Erik King, Stephen Burum; *D:* Brian DePalma; *W:* David Rabe; *M:* Ennio Morricone. VHS, Beta, LV, 8mm ★★★

Cat and Mouse A very unorthodox police inspector is assigned to investigate a millionaire's mysterious death. Who done it? French dialogue with English subtitles. **1978 (PG) 107m/C** *FR* Michele Morgan, Serge Reggiani, Jean-Pierre Aumont; *D:* Claude Lelouch. VHS, Beta ★★★1/2

The Cat and the Fiddle Lovely Jerome Kern-Oscar Hammerstein operetta in which Novarro plays a struggling composer who forces his affections on MacDonald. She sings in response to his romantic proposals. The final sequence is in color. ♪ The Night Was Made for Love; She Didn't Say "Yes"; A New Love is Old; Try to Forget; One Moment Alone; Don't Ask Us Not To Sing; I Watch the Love Parade; The Breeze Kissed Your Hair; Impressions in a Harlem Flat. **1934 90m/B** Ramon Novarro, Jeanette MacDonald, Frank Morgan, Charles Butterworth. VHS ★★★

Cat Ballou At the turn of the century, a schoolmarm turns outlaw with the help of a drunken gunman. Marvin played Kid Shelleen and his silver-nosed evil twin Tim Strawn in this cheery spoof of westerns. Cole and Kaye sing the narration in a one of a kind Greek chorus. **1965 96m/C** Jane Fonda, Lee Marvin, Michael Callan, Dwayne Hickman, Reginald Denny, Nat King Cole, Stubby Kaye; *D:* Elliot Silverstein; *W:* Frank Pierson. Academy Awards '65: Best Actor (Marvin); Berlin International Film Festival '65: Best Actor (Marvin); British Academy Awards '65: Best Actor (Marvin); Golden Globe Awards '66: Best Actor—Musical/Comedy (Marvin); National Board of Review Awards '65: 10 Best Films of the Year, Best Actor (Marvin); Nominations: Academy Awards '65: Best Adapted Screenplay, Best Film Editing, Best Song ("The Ballad of Cat Ballou"), Best Original Score. VHS, Beta ★★★1/2

Cat on a Hot Tin Roof Tennessee Williams' powerful play about greed and deception in a patriarchal Southern family. Big Daddy (Ives) is dying. Members of the family greedily attempt to capture his inheritance, tearing the family apart. Taylor is a sensual wonder as Maggie the Cat, though the more controversial elements of the play were toned down for the film version. Intense, believable performances from Ives and Newman.

1958 108m/C Paul Newman, Burl Ives, Elizabeth Taylor, Jack Carson, Judith Anderson; **D:** Richard Brooks; **W:** Richard Brooks, James Poe. National Board of Review Awards '58: 10 Best Films of the Year; Nominations: Academy Awards '58: Best Director (Brooks), Best Actor (Newman), Best Actress (Taylor), Best Adapted Screenplay, Best Color Cinematography, Best Picture. **VHS, Beta, LV** ★★★1/2

Cat People A young dress designer is the victim of a curse that changes her into a deadly panther who must kill to survive. A classic among the horror genre with unrelenting terror from beginning to end. First horror film from producer Val Lewton.

1942 73m/B Jane Randolph, Elizabeth Russell, Jack Holt, Alan Napier, Simone Simon, Kent Smith, Tom Conway; **D:** Jacques Tourneur. **VHS, Beta, LV** ★★★

Catch-22 Buck Henry's adaptation of Joseph Heller's black comedy about a group of fliers in the Mediterranean during WWII. A biting anti-war satire portraying the insanity of the situation in both a humorous and disturbing manner. Perhaps too literal to the book's masterfully chaotic structure, causing occasional problems in the "are you following along department?" Arkin heads a fine and colorful cast.

1970 (R) 121m/C Alan Arkin, Martin Balsam, Art Garfunkel, Jon Voight, Richard Benjamin, Buck Henry, Bob Newhart, Paula Prentiss, Martin Sheen, Charles Grodin, Anthony Perkins, Orson Welles, Jack Gilford; **D:** Mike Nichols; **W:** Buck Henry. **VHS, Beta, LV** ★★★

The Catered Affair Davis, anti-type-cast as a Bronx housewife, and Borgnine, as her taxi-driving husband, play the determined parents of soon-to-be-wed Reynolds set on giving her away in a style to which she is not accustomed. Based on Paddy Chayefsky's teleplay, the catered affair turns into a familial trial, sharing the true-to-life poignancy that marked "Marty," the Oscar-winning Chayefsky drama of the previous year. **AKA:** Wedding Breakfast.

1956 92m/B Bette Davis, Ernest Borgnine, Debbie Reynolds, Barry Fitzgerald, Rod Taylor, Robert Simon; **D:** Richard Brooks; **W:** Gore Vidal; **M:** Andre Previn, John Alton. **VHS** ★★★

Catholics A sensitive exploration of contemporary mores and changing attitudes within the Roman Catholic church. Sheen is sent by the Pope to Ireland to reform some priests. Based on Brian Moore's short novel and made for television. **AKA:** The Conflict.

1973 86m/C Martin Sheen, Trevor Howard; **D:** Jack Gold; **M:** Carl Davis. **VHS, Beta** ★★★

Caught A woman marries for wealth and security and is desperately unhappy. She runs away and takes a job with a struggling physician, and falls in love with him. Her husband finds her, forcing her to decide between a life of security or love.

1949 90m/B James Mason, Barbara Bel Geddes, Robert Ryan, Curt Bois, Natalie Schafer, Art Smith; **D:** Max Ophuls. **VHS** ★★★

Caught in the Draft Hope's funniest role has him as a Hollywood star trying to evade the draft in WW II, but he ends up accidentally enlisting himself. Lamour plays the daughter of a colonel in the Army whom Hope plans to marry, thinking it will get him out of the service. Very funny military comedy and one of Hope's best. Based on a story by Harry Tugend.

1941 82m/B Bob Hope, Dorothy Lamour, Lynne Overman, Eddie Bracken, Clarence Kolb, Paul Hurst, Ferike Boros, Irving Bacon; **D:** David Butler; **W:** Harry Tugend. **VHS** ★★★

Cavalcade Traces the lives of the British Marryot family from the death of Queen Victoria, through WWI, the Jazz Age, and the Depression. A wistful adaptation of the hit play by Noel Coward with its touching portrayal of one family trying to weather good times and bad together.

1933 110m/B Diana Wynyard, Clive Brook, Herbert Mundin, Una O'Connor, Ursula Jeans, Beryl Mercer, Merle Tottenham, Frank Lawton, John Warburton, Margaret Lindsay, Billy Bevan; **D:** Frank Lloyd. Academy Awards '33: Best Director (Lloyd), Best Interior Decoration, Best Picture; Nominations: Academy Awards '33: Best Actress (Wynyard). **VHS** ★★★

Ceiling Zero Cagney is an irrepressible pilot who does as he pleases and loves to aggravate his soft-hearted boss O'Brien. He falls for aviatrix Travis and neglects his duties to woo her, which leads to tragedy. Naturally, this sobers Cagney up and he volunteers for a dangerous test flight. Lots of fast-paced action and Cagney is at his swaggering best. Based on a play by Frank Wead, who also wrote the screenplay. Remade in 1941 as "International Squadron."

1935 95m/B James Cagney, Pat O'Brien, June Travis, Stuart Erwin, Henry Wadsworth, Isabel Jewell, Barton MacLane; *D:* Howard Hawks; *W:* Frank Wead. **VHS ★★★**

The Celluloid Closet Terrific documentary on how Hollywood films have depicted homosexual characters, subliminally and otherwise. Working chronologically and in a historical context, beginning with silent films, there are clips from more than 100 films, along with interviews from writers and actors. (Notable is writer Gore Vidal's comments on the gay subtext in 1959's "Ben-Hur.") Based on Vito Russo's 1981 book.
1995 (R) 102m/C *D:* Robert Epstein, Jeffrey Friedman; *W:* Armistead Maupin; *M:* Carter Burwell. **VHS, LV ★★★1/2**

Cesar This is the third and most bittersweet part of Pagnol's famed trilogy based on his play depicting the lives and loves of the people of Provence, France. Marius returns after a 20-year absence to his beloved Fanny and his now-grown son, Cesariot. The first two parts of the trilogy are "Marius" and "Fanny" and were directed by Alexander Korda and Marc Allegret respectively. In French with English subtitles.
1936 117m/B *FR* Raimu, Pierre Fresnay, Orane Demazis, Charpin, Andre Fouche, Alida Rauffe; *D:* Marcel Pagnol; *W:* Marcel Pagnol; *M:* Vincent Scotto. **VHS, Beta, LV ★★★★**

The Chalk Garden A woman with a mysterious past takes on the job of governess for an unruly 14-year-old girl, with unforseen consequences. An excellent adaptation of the Enid Bagnold play, although not as suspenseful as the stage production.
1964 106m/C *GB* Deborah Kerr, Hayley Mills, Edith Evans, John Mills, Elizabeth Sellars, Felix Aylmer; *D:* Ronald Neame; *W:* John Michael Hayes; *M:* Malcolm Arnold. National Board of Review Awards '64: 10 Best Films of the Year, Best Supporting Actress (Evans); Nominations: Academy Awards '64: Best Supporting Actress (Evans). **VHS, Beta ★★★**

Chameleon Street Entertaining fact-based account of William Douglas Street, a Detroit man who successfully impersonated, among others, a Time magazine reporter and a surgeon until he was caught and sent to prison. He escaped and went to Yale, faked his identity as a student, and then returned to Michigan to impersonate a lawyer for the Detroit Human Rights Commission. Harris wrote and directed this insightful look into the man who fooled many people, including the mayor of Detroit, Coleman A. Young, who appears briefly as himself.
1989 (R) 95m/C Wendell B. Harris Jr., Angela Leslie, Amina Fakir, Paula McGee, Mano Breckenridge, Richard Kiley, Anthony Ennis; *D:* Wendell B. Harris Jr.; *W:* Wendell B. Harris Jr. Sundance Film Festival '90: Grand Jury Prize. **VHS, LV ★★★**

The Champ A washed up boxer dreams of making a comeback and receives support from no one but his devoted son. Minor classic most notorious for jerking the tears and soiling the hankies, this was the first of three Beery/Cooper screen teamings.
1931 87m/B Wallace Beery, Jackie Cooper, Irene Rich, Roscoe Ates, Edward Brophy, Hale Hamilton, Jesse Scott, Marcia Mae Jones; *D:* King Vidor; *W:* Frances Marion. Academy Awards '32: Best Actor (Beery), Best Original Screenplay; Nominations: Academy Awards '32: Best Director (Vidor), Best Picture. **VHS, Beta, LV ★★★**

Champagne for Caesar The laughs keep coming in this comedy about a self-proclaimed genius-on-every-subject who goes on a television quiz show and proceeds to win everything in sight. The program's sponsor, in desperation, hires a femme fatale to distract the contestant before the final program. Wonderful spoof of the game-show industry.
1950 90m/B Ronald Colman, Celeste Holm, Vincent Price, Art Linkletter, Barbara Britton; *D:* Richard Whorf. **VHS, Beta, LV ★★★**

Champion An ambitious prizefighter alienates the people around him as he desperately fights his way to the top. When he finally reaches his goal, he is forced to question the cost of his success. From a story by Ring Lardner. Certainly one of the best films ever made about boxing, with less sentiment than "Rocky" but concerned with sociological correctness.
1949 99m/B Kirk Douglas, Arthur Kennedy, Marilyn Maxwell, Ruth Roman, Lola Albright; *D:* Mark Robson. Academy Awards '49: Best Film Editing; Nominations: Academy Awards '49: Best Actor (Douglas), Best Black and White Cinematography, Best Screenplay, Best Supporting Actor (Kennedy), Best Original Score. **VHS ★★★1/2**

The Champion/His New Job Two classic silent shorts by Chaplin, with music; the first is alternately entitled "Champion Charlie."
1915 53m/B Charlie Chaplin, Edna Purviance, Ben Turpin, Gloria Swanson,

Mack Swain, "Broncho" Billy Anderson; **D:** Charlie Chaplin. **VHS, Beta, 8mm ★★★**

Chan Is Missing Two cab drivers try to find the man who stole their life savings. Wry, low-budget comedy filmed in San Francisco's Chinatown was an art-house smash. The first full-length American film produced exclusively by an Asian-American cast and crew.
1982 80m/B Wood Moy, Marc Hayashi, Laureen Chew, Judy Mihei, Peter Wang, Presco Tabios; **D:** Wayne Wang; **W:** Terrel Seltzer, Isaac Cronin. **VHS ★★★**

Chaplin The life and career of "The Little Tramp" is chronicled by director Attenborough and brilliantly portrayed by Downey Jr. as Chaplin. A flashback format traces his life from its poverty-stricken Dickensian origins in the London slums through his directing and acting career, to his honorary Oscar in 1972. Slow-moving at parts, but captures Chaplin's devotion to his art and also his penchant towards jailbait. In a clever casting choice, Chaplin's own daughter from his fourth marriage to Oona O'Neill, Geraldine Chaplin, plays her own grandmother who goes mad.
1992 (PG-13) 135m/C Robert Downey Jr., Dan Aykroyd, Geraldine Chaplin, Kevin Dunn, Anthony Hopkins, Milla Jovovich, Moira Kelly, Kevin Kline, Diane Lane, Penelope Ann Miller, Paul Rhys, John Thaw, Marisa Tomei, Nancy Travis, James Woods, David Duchovny, Deborah Maria Moore, Bill Paterson, John Standing, Robert Stephens; **D:** Richard Attenborough, Sven Nykvist; **W:** Bryan Forbes, William Boyd, William Goldman; **M:** John Barry. British Academy Awards '92: Best Actor (Downey); Nominations: Academy Awards '92: Best Actor (Downey), Best Art Direction/Set Decoration, Best Original Score. **VHS, LV ★★★**

Charade After her husband is murdered, a young woman finds herself on the run from crooks and double agents who want the $250,000 her husband stole during WWII. Hepburn and Grant are charming and sophisticated as usual in this stylish intrigue filmed in Paris. Based on the story "The Unsuspecting Wife" by Marc Behm and Peter Stone.
1963 113m/C Cary Grant, Audrey Hepburn, Walter Matthau, James Coburn, George Kennedy; **D:** Stanley Donen; **W:** Peter Stone; **M:** Henry Mancini. British Academy Awards '64: Best Actress (Hepburn); Edgar Allan Poe Awards '63: Best Screenplay; Nominations: Academy

Awards '63: Best Song ("Charade"). **VHS, Beta ★★★1/2**

The Charge of the Light Brigade A British army officer stationed in India deliberately starts the Balaclava charge to even an old score with Surat Khan, who's on the other side. Still an exciting film, though it's hardly historically accurate. De Havilland is along to provide the requisite romance with Flynn. Also available colorized.
1936 (PG-13) 115m/B Olivia de Havilland, Errol Flynn, David Niven, Nigel Bruce, Patric Knowles, Donald Crisp, Sir C. Aubrey Smith, J. Carrol Naish, Henry Stephenson, E.E. Clive, Scotty Beckett; **D:** Michael Curtiz; **M:** Max Steiner. Nominations: Academy Awards '36: Best Sound, Best Original Score. **VHS, Beta, LV ★★★**

Chariots of Fire A lush telling of the parallel stories of Harold Abraham and Eric Liddell, English runners who competed in the 1924 Paris Olympics. One was compelled by a hatred of anti-Semitism, the other by the love of God. Outstanding performances by the entire cast.
1981 (PG) 123m/C *GB* Ben Cross, Ian Charleson, Nigel Havers, Ian Holm, Alice Krige, Brad Davis, Dennis Christopher, Patrick Magee, Cheryl Campbell, John Gielgud, Lindsay Anderson, Nigel Davenport; **D:** Hugh Hudson; **W:** Colin Welland; **M:** Vangelis. Academy Awards '81: Best Costume Design, Best Original Screenplay, Best Picture, Best Score; British Academy Awards '81: Best Film, Best Supporting Actor (Holm); New York Film Critics Awards '81: Best Cinematography; Nominations: Academy Awards '81: Best Director (Hudson), Best Supporting Actor (Holm). **VHS, Beta, LV ★★★1/2**

Charley Varrick Matthau, a small-town hood, robs a bank only to find out that one of its depositors is the Mob. Baker's the vicious hit-man assigned the job of getting the loot back. A well-paced, on-the-mark thriller.
1973 (PG) 111m/C Walter Matthau, Joe Don Baker, Felicia Farr, John Vernon, Sheree North, Norman Fell, Andrew (Andy) Robinson; **D:** Donald Siegel; **M:** Lalo Schifrin. **VHS, Beta ★★★**

Charlie Chan at the Opera The great detective investigates an amnesiac opera star (Karloff) who may have committed murder. Considered one of the best of the series. Interesting even to those not familiar with Charlie Chan.
1936 66m/B Warner Oland, Boris Karloff,

Keye Luke, Charlotte Henry, Thomas Beck, Nedda Harrigan, William Demarest; **D:** H. Bruce Humberstone. **VHS, LV ★★★**

Charlie Chaplin: Night at the Show Chaplin plays two different mugs, both out for a night on the town. Mr. Pest, a sharp-dressed upper-cruster, clings to his disgusting habits, and Mr. Rowdy is his working-class doppleganger. Both obnoxious Chaplins-in-disguise collaborate to wreak havoc on a local theater. Contains original organ score.
1915 ?m/B Charlie Chaplin, Edna Purviance; **D:** Charlie Chaplin; **W:** Charlie Chaplin. **VHS, Beta ★★★**

Charly A retarded man becomes intelligent after brain surgery, then romances a kindly caseworker before slipping back into retardation. Moving account is well served by leads Robertson and Bloom. Adapted from the Daniel Keyes novel "Flowers for Algernon."
1968 103m/C Cliff Robertson, Claire Bloom, Lilia Skala, Leon Janney, Dick Van Patten, William Dwyer; **D:** Ralph Nelson; **W:** Stirling Silliphant. Academy Awards '68: Best Actor (Robertson); Golden Globe Awards '69: Best Screenplay; National Board of Review Awards '68: 10 Best Films of the Year, Best Actor (Robertson). **VHS, Beta, LV ★★★**

The Cheat Ward plays a frivolous socialite heavily indebted to Hayakawa as the Japanese money lender. Hayakawa makes Ward pay with her honor and her flesh by branding her. A dark and captivating drama. Silent with piano score.
1915 55m/B Fannie Ward, Sessue Hayakawa; **D:** Cecil B. DeMille. **VHS, Beta ★★★**

A Child Is Waiting Poignant and provocative story of teachers in an institution for the mentally retarded. Fine performances include Lancaster as the institution's administrator and Garland as a teacher who cares too much for everyone's good. Cassavetes incorporates footage using handicapped children as extras—not entirely seamlessly—providing a sensitive and candid edge.
1963 105m/B Burt Lancaster, Judy Garland, Gena Rowlands, Steven Hill, Bruce Ritchey; **D:** John Cassavetes; **W:** Abby Mann; **M:** Ernest Gold. **VHS, Beta ★★★**

The Children Are Watching Us Sobering drama of a family dissolution as seen by a child. Worthy example of Italian neo-realism marks the first collaboration between Zavattini

and De Sica. In Italian with subtitles. **AKA:** The Little Martyr; I Bambini Ci Guardano.
1944 92m/B *IT* Luciano de Ambrosis, Isa Pola, Emilio Cigoli; **D:** Vittorio De Sica; **W:** Cesare Zavattini, Vittorio De Sica. **VHS, Beta ★★★**

Children of a Lesser God Based upon the play by Mark Medoff, this sensitive, intelligent film deals with an unorthodox speech teacher at a school for the deaf, who falls in love with a beautiful and rebellious ex-student. Inarguably romantic; the original stage production won the Best Play Tony in 1980. Hurt and Matlin reportedly continued their romance off-screen as well.
1986 (R) 119m/C William Hurt, Marlee Matlin, Piper Laurie, Philip Bosco, E. Katherine Kerr; **D:** Randa Haines; **W:** Hesper Anderson, Mark Medoff; **M:** Michael Convertino, John Seale. Academy Awards '86: Best Actress (Matlin); Golden Globe Awards '87: Best Actress—Drama (Matlin); Nominations: Academy Awards '86: Best Actor (Hurt), Best Adapted Screenplay, Best Picture, Best Supporting Actress (Laurie). **VHS, Beta, LV, 8mm ★★★1/2**

Children of Paradise Considered by many to be the greatest film ever made, certainly one of the most beautiful. In the Parisian theatre district of the 1800s an actor falls in love with a seemingly unattainable woman. Although circumstances keep them apart, their love never dies. Produced in France during WWII right under the noses of Nazi occupiers; many of the talent (including the writer, poet Jacques Prevert) were active resistance fighters. Laserdisc version features: interview with director Marcel Carne, production photos, analysis of influences of French painting on the film, and audio essay by film authority Brian Stonehill. In French with English subtitles. **AKA:** Les Enfants du Paradise.
1944 188m/B *FR* Jean-Louis Barrault, Arletty, Pierre Brasseur, Maria Casares, Albert Remy, Leon Larive, Marcel Herrand, Pierre Renoir; **D:** Marcel Carne; **W:** Jacques Prevert; **M:** Maurice Thiriet, Joseph Kosma. **VHS, LV ★★★★**

Chimes at Midnight Classic tragedy—derived by Welles from five Shakespeare plays—about a corpulent blowhard and his friendship with a prince. Crammed with classic sequences, including a battle that is both realistic and funny. The love scene between massive Welles and a nonetheless willing Moreau also manages to be both sad and amusing. Great performances all around, but Welles understandably dominates. The film's few flaws (due to budget problems) are inconsequential before considerable strengths. This one ranks among Welles', and thus the entire cinema's, very best. **AKA:** Falstaff; Campanadas a Medianoche.

1967 115m/B *SP SI* Orson Welles, Jeanne Moreau, Margaret Rutherford, John Gielgud, Marina Vlady, Keith Baxter, Fernando Rey, Norman Rodway; **D:** Orson Welles; **W:** Orson Welles; **M:** Angelo Francesco Lavagnino. **VHS, Beta ★★★★**

China Beach TV movie/pilot launched the acclaimed series about American military women behind the lines during the chaos of the Vietnam War. Nurse McMurphy has only seven days left on her first tour of duty, and in spite of her hate of the brutality of the war, she has mixed feelings about leaving her friends and her work. A USO singer on a one week tour finds her search for men brings the war too close for comfort. Cherry, a new Red Cross volunteer, shows up at the Beach. Skillfully introduces the viewer to all the characters, their problems and joys, without melodrama or redundancy.

1988 95m/C Dana Delany, Chloe Webb, Robert Picardo, Nan Woods, Michael Boatman, Marg Helgenberger, Tim Ryan, Concetta Tomei, Jeff Kober, Brian Wimmer; **D:** Rod Holcomb; **W:** John Sacret Young. **VHS, Beta ★★★**

China Gate A band of multinational troops follows a French officer against a communist stronghold in Indochina. Conventional fare bolstered considerably by director Fuller's flair for action. Weak male leads, but Dickinson shines.

1957 97m/B Gene Barry, Angie Dickinson, Nat King Cole, Paul Dubov, Lee Van Cleef, George Givot, Marcel Dalio; **D:** Samuel Fuller; **W:** Samuel Fuller; **M:** Max Steiner. **VHS ★★★**

China Seas The captain of a commercial steamship on the China route has to fight off murderous Malay pirates, a spurned woman, and a raging typhoon to reach port safely. Fast-moving romantic action taken from Crosbie Garstin's novel.

1935 89m/B Clark Gable, Jean Harlow, Wallace Beery, Rosalind Russell, Lewis Stone, Sir C. Aubrey Smith, Dudley Digges, Robert Benchley; **D:** Tay Garnett. **VHS, Beta ★★★**

The China Syndrome A somewhat unstable executive at a nuclear plant uncovers evidence of a concealed accident, takes drastic steps to publicize the incident. Lemmon is excellent as the anxious exec, while Fonda and Douglas are scarcely less distinguished as a sympathetic TV journalist and camera operator, respectively. Tense, prophetic thriller that ironically preceded the Three Mile Island accident by just a few months. Produced by Douglas.

1979 (PG) 123m/C Jane Fonda, Jack Lemmon, Michael Douglas, Scott Brady, James Hampton, Peter Donat, Wilford Brimley, James Karen; **D:** James Bridges; **W:** Mike Gray, T.S. Cook, James Bridges. British Academy Awards '79: Best Actor (Lemmon), Best Actress (Fonda); National Board of Review Awards '79: 10 Best Films of the Year; Writers Guild of America '79: Best Original Screenplay; Nominations: Academy Awards '78: Best Actress (Fonda), Best Original Screenplay; Academy Awards '79: Best Actor (Lemmon), Best Art Direction/Set Decoration; Cannes Film Festival '79: Best Film. **VHS, Beta, LV ★★★1/2**

Chinatown Private detective finds himself overwhelmed in a scandalous case involving the rich and powerful of Los Angeles. Gripping, atmospheric mystery excels in virtually every aspect, with strong narrative drive and outstanding performances from Nicholson, Dunaway, and Huston. Director Polanski also appears in a suitable unsettling cameo. Fabulous. A sneaky, snaking delight filled with seedy characters and plots-within-plots. Followed more than 15 years later by "The Two Jakes."

1974 (R) 131m/C Jack Nicholson, Faye Dunaway, John Huston, Diane Ladd, John Hillerman, Burt Young, Perry Lopez, Darrell Zwerling; **Cameos:** Roman Polanski; **D:** Roman Polanski; **W:** Robert Towne; **M:** Jerry Goldsmith, John A. Alonzo. Academy Awards '74: Best Original Screenplay; British Academy Awards '74: Best Actor (Nicholson), Best Director (Polanski), Best Screenplay; Edgar Allan Poe Awards '74: Best Screenplay; Golden Globe Awards '75: Best Actor—Drama (Nicholson), Best Director (Polanski), Best Film—Drama, Best Screenplay; National Board of Review Awards '74: 10 Best Films of the Year; New York Film Critics Awards '74: Best Actor (Nicholson); National Society of Film Critics Awards '74: Best Actor (Nicholson); Writers Guild of America '74: Best Original Screenplay; Nominations: Academy Awards '74: Best Actor (Nicholson), Best Actress (Dunaway), Best Art Direction/Set Decoration, Best Cinematography, Best Costume Design, Best Director (Polanski), Best Film Editing, Best Picture, Best

Original Score. **VHS, Beta, LV, 8mm**
★★★★

Chloe in the Afternoon A married man finds himself inexplicably drawn to an ungainly young woman. Sixth of the "Moral Tales" series is typical of director Rohmer's talky approach. Not for all tastes, but rewarding for those who are drawn to this sort of thing. In French with English subtitles.
1972 (R) 97m/C *FR* Bernard Verley, Zouzou, Francoise Verley, Daniel Ceccaldi, Malvina Penne, Babette Ferrier, Suze Randall, Marie-Christine Barrault; *D:* Eric Rohmer; *W:* Eric Rohmer. National Board of Review Awards '72: 5 Best Foreign Films of the Year. **VHS, Beta** ★★★

Chocolat A woman recalls her childhood spent in French West Africa and the unfulfilled sexual tension between her mother and black servant. Vivid film provides a host of intriguing characters and offers splendid panoramas of rugged desert landscapes. Profound, if somewhat personal filmmaking from novice director Denis. In French with English subtitles.
1988 (PG-13) 105m/C Mireille Perrier, Emmet Judson Williamson, Cecile Ducasse, Giulia Boschi, Francois Cluzet, Isaach de Bankole, Kenneth Cranham; *D:* Claire Denis; *W:* Claire Denis, Jean-Pol Fargeau. **VHS, Beta, LV** ★★★½

The Chocolate War An idealistic student and a hardline headmaster butt heads at a Catholic boys' school over an unofficial candy business in this tense, unsettling drama. Glover is notable in his familiar villain role, and Gordon is effective in his first effort as director. Based on the Robert Cormier novel.
1988 (R) 95m/C John Glover, Jenny Wright, Wally Ward, Bud Cort, Ilan Mitchell-Smith, Adam Baldwin; *D:* Keith Gordon; *W:* Keith Gordon. **VHS, Beta, LV** ★★★

Choose Me Comedy-drama about sad, lonely, and often quirky characters linked to an unlikely L.A. radio sex therapist. Moody, memorable fare features especially strong playing from Bujold as a sexually inexperienced sex therapist and Warren as one of her regular listeners. Typically eccentric fare from director Rudolph.
1984 (R) 106m/C Keith Carradine, Genevieve Bujold, Lesley Ann Warren, Rae Dawn Chong, John Larroquette, John Considine; *D:* Alan Rudolph; *W:* Alan Rudolph. **VHS, Beta, LV** ★★★½

The Chosen Set in 1940s Brooklyn about the friendship between two teenagers—Benson, the Hassidic son of a rabbi and Miller, whose father is a Zionist professor. Based on the novel by Chaim Potok.
1981 108m/C Robby Benson, Barry Miller, Maximilian Schell, Rod Steiger, Hildy Brooks, Ron Rifkin, Val Avery; *D:* Jeremy Paul Kagan; *M:* Elmer Bernstein. **VHS**
★★★

Christ Stopped at Eboli Subdued work about an anti-Fascist writer exiled to rural Italy in the 1930s. Excellent performances from the lead Volonte and supporting players Papas and Cuny. Slow, contemplative film is probably director Rosi's masterpiece. Adapted from Carlo Levi's book. In Italian with English subtitles. *AKA:* Eboli.
1979 118m/C *IT FR* Gian Marie Volonte, Irene Papas, Paolo Bonacelli, Francois Simon, Alain Cuny, Lea Massari; *D:* Francesco Rosi; *W:* Francesco Rosi. British Academy Awards '80: Best Foreign Film; National Board of Review Awards '80: 5 Best Foreign Films of the Year. **VHS, Beta**
★★★★

Christiane F. Gripping, visually impressive story of a bored German girl's decline into drug use and prostitution. Based on a West German magazine article. Sobering and dismal look at a milieu in which innocence and youth have run amok. The film's impact is only somewhat undermined by poor dubbing. Bowie appears in a concert sequence.
1982 (R) 120m/C *GE* Natja Brunkhorst, Thomas Haustein, David Bowie; *D:* Uli Edel; *M:* David Bowie. **VHS, Beta** ★★★

A Christmas Carol A fine retelling of the classic tale about a penny-pinching holiday hater who learns appreciation of Christmas following a frightful, revealing evening with supernatural visitors. Perhaps the best rendering of the Dickens classic. "And God bless Tiny Tim!" *AKA:* Scrooge.
1951 86m/B *GB* Alastair Sim, Kathleen Harrison, Jack Warner, Michael Hordern, Patrick Macnee, Mervyn Johns, Hermione Baddeley, Clifford Mollison, George Cole, Carol Marsh, Miles Malleson, Ernest Thesiger, Hattie Jacques, Peter Bull, Hugh Dempster; *D:* Brian Desmond Hurst; *W:* Noel Langley; *M:* Richard Addinsell. **VHS, Beta, LV** ★★★★

A Christmas Carol Excellent TV adaptation of the Dickens Christmas classic features a memorable Scott as miserly misanthrope Ebenezer Scrooge, who gets a scary look at his life thanks to a Christmas Eve visit from the ghosts of Christmas Past, Present, and Future. Terrific support-

ing cast; filmed on location in Shrewsbury, England.
1984 (PG) 100m/C VHS ★★★

Christmas in Connecticut Lightweight comedy about a housekeeping magazine's successful columnist who isn't quite the expert homemaker she presents herself to be. When a war veteran is invited to her home as part of a publicity gimmick, she must master the ways of housekeeping or reveal her incompetence. Stanwyck is winning in the lead role. Also available in a colorized version. **AKA:** Indiscretion.
1945 101m/B Barbara Stanwyck, Reginald Gardiner, Sydney Greenstreet, Dennis (Stanley Morner) Morgan, S.Z. Sakall, Una O'Connor, Robert Shayne, Joyce Compton; **D:** Peter Godfrey. **VHS, Beta, LV** ★★★

Christmas in July A young man goes on a spending spree when he thinks he's won a sweepstakes. Things take a turn for the worse when he finds out that it was all a practical joke. Powell provides a winning performance in this second film from comic master Sturges.
1940 67m/B Dick Powell, Ellen Drew, Raymond Walburn, William Demarest, Franklin Pangborn; **D:** Preston Sturges. **VHS, Beta, LV** ★★★★

A Christmas Story Unlikely but winning comedy of a boy's single-minded obsession to acquire a Red Ryder BB-gun for Christmas. Particularly great sequence involving an impatient department-store Santa. Fun for everyone. Based on "In God We Trust, All Others Pay Cash," an autobiographical story by Shepherd.
1983 (PG) 95m/C Peter Billingsley, Darren McGavin, Melinda Dillon, Ian Petrella; **D:** Bob (Benjamin) Clark; **W:** Bob (Benjamin) Clark, Leigh Brown, Jean Shepherd. Genie Awards '84: Best Director (Clark). **VHS, Beta, LV** ★★★

Chuck Berry: Hail! Hail! Rock 'n' Roll Engaging, energetic portrait of one of rock's founding fathers, via interviews, behind-the-scenes footage, and performance clips of Berry at 60. Songs featured: "Johnny B. Goode," "Roll Over Beethoven," "Maybelline," and more. Appearances by Eric Clapton, Etta James, John and Julian Lennon, Roy Orbison, Linda Ronstadt, Bo Diddley, and Bruce Springsteen among others.
1987 (PG) 121m/C Chuck Berry, Eric Clapton, Etta James, Robert Cray, Julian Lennon, Keith Richards, Linda Ronstadt, John Lennon, Roy Orbison, Bo Diddley, Jerry Lee Lewis, Bruce Springsteen,

Kareem Abdul-Jabbar; **D:** Taylor Hackford. **VHS, Beta** ★★★★

Chungking Express Director Kar-Wai presents two quirky tales of loneliness and love loosely linked by a snack bar in the tourist section of Hong Kong. Cops and drugs are still a part of the storyline, but this is no chop-socky action movie. Both male protagonists are cops, identified only by their badge numbers, who have recently been dumped by their girlfriends. One has a fixation for canned pineapple and expiration dates, the other talks to the inanimate objects in his apartment. The women they eventually fall for are a blonde-wigged heroin dealer and a shy counter girl who bops to "California Dreaming" after breaking in and cleaning the cop's apartment without his knowledge. Shot commando-style in 23 days during the hiatus of Wong's "Ashes of Time" without permits or professional lighting. The high energy is reflected in the pacing and acting performances. Chosen by Quentin Tarantino as the first release of his Miramax-backed Rolling Thunder imprint.
1995 (PG-13) 102m/C **CH** Bridget Lin, Takeshi Kaneshiro, Tony Leung, Faye Wong, Valerie Chow, Piggy Chan; **D:** Wong Kar-Wai; **W:** Wong Kar-Wai; **M:** Frankie Chan, Roel A. Garcia. Nominations: Independent Spirit Awards '97: Best Foreign Film. **VHS, LV** ★★★

Cinderella Classic Disney animated fairy-tale about the slighted beauty who outshines her evil stepsisters at a royal ball, then returns to her grim existence before the handsome prince finds her again. Engaging film, with a wicked stepmother, kindly fairy godmother, and singing mice. ♪ Cinderella; Bibbidy-Bobbidi-Boo; So This Is Love; A Dream Is a Wish Your Heart Makes; The Work Song; Oh Sing, Sweet Nightingale.
1950 76m/C **D:** Wilfred Jackson; **V:** Ilene Woods, William Phipps, Verna Felton, James MacDonald. Venice Film Festival '50: Special Jury Prize; Nominations: Academy Awards '50: Best Song ("Bibbidy-Bobbidi-Boo"), Best Sound, Best Original Score. **VHS, Beta** ★★★★

Cinderella Liberty Bittersweet romance in which a kindly sailor falls for a brash hooker with a son. Sometimes funny, sometimes moving, with sometimes crude direction overcome by truly compelling performances from Caan and Mason. Story written by Darryl Ponicsan from his novel.
1973 (R) 117m/C James Caan, Marsha

Mason, Eli Wallach, Kirk Calloway, Burt Young, Bruce Kirby, Dabney Coleman, Sally Kirkland; **D:** Mark Rydell; **W:** Darryl Ponicsan, Vilmos Zsigmond; **M:** John Williams. Golden Globe Awards '74: Best Actress—Drama (Mason); Nominations: Academy Awards '73: Best Actress (Mason), Best Song ("You're So Nice to Be Around"), Best Original Score. **VHS, Beta** ★★★

Cinema Paradiso Memoir of a boy's life working at a movie theatre in small-town Italy after WWII. Film aspires to both majestic sweep and stirring poignancy, but only occasionaly hits its target. Still manages to move the viewer, and it features a suitably low-key performance by the masterful Noiret. Autobiographically inspired script written by Tornatore. The version shown in America is approximately a half-hour shorter than the original Italian form. *AKA:* Nuovo Cinema Paradiso.
1988 123m/C *IT* Philippe Noiret, Jacques Perrin, Salvatore Cascio, Marco Leonardi, Agnes Nano, Leopoldo Trieste; **D:** Giuseppe Tornatore; **W:** Giuseppe Tornatore; **M:** Ennio Morricone. Academy Awards '89: Best Foreign Language Film; British Academy Awards '90: Best Actor (Noiret), Best Foreign Film, Best Original Screenplay, Best Supporting Actor (Cascio); Golden Globe Awards '90: Best Foreign Film. **VHS, LV, 8mm** ★★★

The Circus Classic comedy silent details the tramp's exploits as a member of a traveling circus, including a romance with the bareback rider. Hilarious, less sentimental than most of Chaplin's feature films. Chaplin won a special Academy Award for "versatility and genius in writing, acting, directing and producing" for this one. Outrageous final scenes.
1919 105m/B Charlie Chaplin, Merna Kennedy; **D:** Charlie Chaplin. Nominations: Academy Awards '28: Best Actor (Chaplin), Best Director (Chaplin). **VHS** ★★★1/2

The Citadel From the A.J. Cronin novel, the intelligent and honest Hollywood drama about a young British doctor who is morally corrupted by his move from a poor mining village to a well-off practice treating wealthy hypochondriacs. Somewhat hokey but still consistently entertaining, with Donat fine in the lead.
1938 114m/C *GB* Robert Donat, Rosalind Russell, Rex Harrison, Ralph Richardson, Emlyn Williams, Penelope Dudley Ward; **D:** King Vidor. National Board of Review Awards '38: 10 Best Films of the Year; New York Film Critics Awards '38: Best Film; Nominations: Academy Awards '38: Best

Actor (Donat), Best Director (Vidor), Best Picture, Best Screenplay. **VHS, Beta** ★★★

Citizen Kane Extraordinary film is an American tragedy of a newspaper tycoon (based loosely on William Randolph Hearst) from his humble beginnings to the solitude of his final years. One of the greatest films ever made —a stunning tour-de-force in virtually every aspect, from the fragmented narration to breathtaking, deep-focus cinematography; from a vivid soundtrack to fabulous ensemble acting. Welles was only 25 when he co-wrote, directed, and starred in this masterpiece. A three disc laser edition was reproduced from a superior negative and features liner notes and running commentary from film historian Robert J. Carringer. Watch for Ladd and O'Connell as reporters.
1941 119m/B Orson Welles, Joseph Cotten, Everett Sloane, Dorothy Comingore, Ruth Warrick, George Coulouris, Ray Collins, William Alland, Paul Stewart, Erskine Sanford, Agnes Moorehead, Alan Ladd, Gus Schilling, Philip Van Zandt, Harry Shannon, Sonny Bupp, Arthur O'Connell; **D:** Orson Welles; **W:** Orson Welles, Herman J. Mankiewicz; **M:** Bernard Herrmann. Academy Awards '41: Best Original Screenplay; National Board of Review Awards '41: 10 Best Films of the Year; New York Film Critics Awards '41: Best Film; Nominations: Academy Awards '41: Best Actor (Welles), Best Black and White Cinematography, Best Director (Welles), Best Film Editing, Best Interior Decoration, Best Picture, Best Sound, Best Original Score. **VHS, Beta, LV, 8mm** ★★★★

Citizen X Based on the true story of '80s Russian serial killer Andrei Chikatilo (DeMunn) and his 52 victims. Viktor Burakov (Rea) is a beleaguered rural forensics expert who is blatantly told by party officials that the Soviet state does not have serial killers—in spite of a rising body count: His only ally is Col. Fetisov (Sutherland), who's adept at political maneuvering, but it takes the duo eight frustrating years to bring the grisly killer to justice. Fine performances highlight a literate script from Robert Cullen's book "The Killer Department." Filmed on location in Budapest, Hungary. Made for cable television.
1995 (R) 100m/C Stephen Rea, Donald Sutherland, Jeffrey DeMunn, John Wood, Joss Ackland, Max von Sydow, Ralph Nossek, Imelda Staunton; **D:** Chris Gerolmo; **W:** Chris Gerolmo; **M:** Randy Edelman. **VHS** ★★★

Citizens Band Episodic, low-key comedy about people united by their CB use in a midwestern community. Notable performance from Clark as a soft-voiced guide for truckers passing through. Demme's first comedy is characteristically idiosyncratic. **AKA:** Handle With Care.
1977 (PG) 98m/C Paul LeMat, Candy Clark, Ann Wedgeworth, Roberts Blossom, Charles Napier, Marcia Rodd, Bruce McGill, Ed Begley Jr., Alix Elias; **D:** Jonathan Demme; **W:** Paul Brickman; **M:** Bill Conti. National Society of Film Critics Awards '77: Best Supporting Actress (Wedgeworth). **VHS, Beta** ★★★

City for Conquest Two lovers go their separate ways to pursue individual careers. He attempts to become a boxing champ, but is blinded in the ring and ends up selling newspapers. She takes a shot at a dancing career but hooks up with an unscrupulous partner. Will the ill-fated pair find happiness again?
1940 101m/B James Cagney, Ann Sheridan, Frank Craven, Donald Crisp, Arthur Kennedy, Frank McHugh, George Tobias, Anthony Quinn, Blanche Yurka, Elia Kazan, Bob Steele; **D:** Anatole Litvak; **M:** Max Steiner. **VHS, Beta** ★★★

City Hall Investigating the deaths of a heroic cop, a drug dealer, and a six-year-old boy in a shoot-out, idealistic deputy mayor Cusack uncovers a web of corruption and deceit in the Big Apple. Pacino excels as charismatic mayor John Pappas by showing the crafty string-puller behind the glossy image of the modern politico. Supporting cast is also strong, including Aiello as a Rodgers and Hammerstein-loving Brooklyn boss, and Fonda as the police union lawyer and standard issue love interest. Screenplay was conceived by Ken Lipper, who was once deputy mayor under Ed Koch, but the involvement of three other scripters causes confusion over what type of picture it's aiming to be. Cash-strapped New York rented its actual City Hall out for filming at a price of $50,000.
1995 (R) 111m/C Al Pacino, John Cusack, Bridget Fonda, Danny Aiello, David Paymer, Martin Landau, Paul Schrader, Anthony (Tony) Franciosa, Lindsay Duncan, Nestor Serrano, Mel Winkler, Richard Schiff; **D:** Harold Becker; **W:** Harold Becker, Nicholas Pileggi, Bo Goldman, Ken Lipper; **M:** Jerry Goldsmith. **VHS, LV** ★★★

City Lights Masterpiece that was Chaplin's last silent film. The "Little Tramp" falls in love with a blind flower seller. A series of lucky accidents permits him to get the money she needs for a sight-restoring surgery. One of the most eloquent movies ever filmed, due to Chaplin's keen balance between comedy and tragedy.
1931 86m/B Charlie Chaplin, Virginia Cherrill, Florence Lee, Hank Mann, Harry Myers, Henry Bergman, Jean Harlow; **D:** Charlie Chaplin. National Board of Review Awards '31: 10 Best Films of the Year.
VHS, Beta, LV ★★★★

City of Hope The picture that "Bonfire of the Vanities" wanted to be, an eventful few days in the fictional metropolis of Hudson: an ugly racial incident threatens to snowball, the corrupt mayor pushes a shady real-estate deal, and a botched robbery has profound implications. Some of the subplots resolve too easily, but this cynical, crazy-quilt of urban life is worthy of comparison with "American Graffiti" and "Nashville" as pure Americana.
1991 (R) 132m/C Vincent Spano, Tony LoBianco, Joe Morton, Todd Graff, David Strathairn, Anthony John Denison, Barbara Williams, Angela Bassett, Gloria Foster, Lawrence Tierney, John Sayles, Maggie Renzi, Kevin Tighe, Chris Cooper, Jace Alexander, Frankie Faison, Tom Wright, Michael Mantell, Josh Mostel, Joe Grifasi, Louis Zorich, Gina Gershon, Rose Gregorio, Bill Raymond, Maeve Kinkead, Ray Aranha; **D:** John Sayles; **W:** John Sayles; **M:** Mason Daring, Robert Richardson. Independent Spirit Awards '92: Best Supporting Actor (Strathairn).
VHS, LV, 8mm ★★★

The City of Lost Children Weird not-for-the-kiddies fairytale finds crazed inventor Krank (Emilfork) getting his evil one-eyed minions, the appropriately named Cyclops, to kidnap local children so that he can steal their dreams (because Krank himself is incapable of dreaming). The latest victim is young Denree (Lucien), the adopted brother of sideshow strongman One (Perlman), who single-mindedly pursues a way to get Denree back—aided by nine-year-old feral child Miette (Vittet) and a band of orphan thieves. Freaks galore with avant-garde designer Jean-Paul Gaultier in charge of costumes. French with subtitles or dubbed. **AKA:** La Cite des Enfants Perdus.
1995 (R) 114m/C FR Ron Perlman, Daniel Emilfork, Joseph Lucien, Judith Vittet, Dominique Pinon, Jean Claude Dreyfus, Odile Mallet, Genevieve Brunet, Mireille Mosse, Jean-Louis Trintignant; **D:** Jean-Marie Jeunet, Marc Caro; **W:** Jean-Marie Jeunet, Marc Caro, Gilles Adrien; **M:** Angelo Badalamenti. Cesar Awards '96:

Best Art Direction/Set Decoration; Nominations: Cesar Awards '96: Best Cinematography, Best Costume Design, Best Score; Independent Spirit Awards '96: Best Foreign Language Film. **VHS, LV** ★★★

City Slickers Three men with mid-life crises leave New York City for a cattle-ranch vacation that turns into an arduous, character-building stint. Many funny moments supplied by leads Crystal, Stern, and Kirby, but Palance steals the film as a salty, wise cowpoke. Slater is fetching as the lone gal vacationer on the cattle drive. Box office winner notable for a realistic calf birthing scene, one of few in cinema history. From an idea by Crystal, who also produced. Palance stole the show from Oscar ceremonies host Crystal a second time when he accepted his award and suddenly started doing one-arm pushups, startling the audience into laughter.
1991 (PG-13) 114m/C Billy Crystal, Daniel Stern, Bruno Kirby, Patricia Wettig, Helen Slater, Jack Palance, Noble Willingham, Tracey Walter, Josh Mostel, David Paymer, Bill Henderson, Jeffrey Tambor, Phill Lewis, Kyle Secor, Yeardley Smith, Jayne Meadows, Dean Semler; **D:** Ron Underwood; **W:** Lowell Ganz, Babaloo Mandel; **M:** Marc Shaiman. Academy Awards '91: Best Supporting Actor (Palance); Golden Globe Awards '92: Best Supporting Actor (Palance); MTV Movie Awards '92: Best Comedic Performance (Crystal); People's Choice Awards '92: Best Film—Musical/Comedy. **VHS, Beta, LV, 8mm** ★★★

The Civil War, Episode 1: The Cause—1861 The blowout PBS hit mini-series, five years in the making by author and filmmaker Ken Burns, is a staggering historical achievement. Episode 1 focuses on the causes of the Civil War from the schism created by Lincoln's election, John Brown's assault on Harper's Ferry, and the firing on Fort Sumpter.
1990 99m/C D: Ken Burns; **W:** Ken Burns. **VHS** ★★★★

The Civil War, Episode 2: A Very Bloody Affair—1862 Second in the enormously popular PBS series looks at the unexpectedly extreme costs in human life of the War Between the States.
1990 69m/C D: Ken Burns; **W:** Ken Burns. **VHS** ★★★★

The Civil War, Episode 3: Forever Free—1862 Third volume in the PBS Emmy-nominated mini-series covers Antietam, Robert E. Lee and Stonewall Jackson planning Confederate strategy, and Lincoln's decision to free the slaves.
1990 76m/C D: Ken Burns; **W:** Ken Burns. **VHS** ★★★★

The Civil War, Episode 4: Simply Murder—1863 Union forces meet disaster at Fredericksburg, and Gen. Lee wins a victory but loses Stonewall Jackson in the fourth episode of the Emmy-nominated PBS mini-series.
1990 62m/C D: Ken Burns; **W:** Ken Burns. **VHS** ★★★★

The Civil War, Episode 5: The Universe of Battle—1863 Gettysburg, the battleground which claimed 150,000 American lives, is examined in the 5th episode of the Emmy-nominated PBS mini-series.
1990 95m/C D: Ken Burns; **W:** Ken Burns. **VHS** ★★★★

The Civil War, Episode 6: Valley of the Shadow of Death—1864 Profiles of Grant and Lee are offered, plus Sherman's assault on Atlanta, in this volume from the Emmy-nominated PBS mini-series.
1990 70m/C D: Ken Burns; **W:** Ken Burns. **VHS** ★★★★

The Civil War, Episode 7: Most Hallowed Ground—1864 The nation re-elects Abraham Lincoln, and the North turns General Lee's mansion into Arlington National Cemetery in this episode of the Emmy-nominated PBS mini-series.
1990 72m/C D: Ken Burns; **W:** Ken Burns. **VHS** ★★★★

The Civil War, Episode 8: War is All Hell—1865 Sherman marches to the sea and Lee surrenders to Grant in this episode from the Emmy-nominated PBS mini-series.
1990 69m/C D: Ken Burns; **W:** Ken Burns. **VHS** ★★★★

The Civil War, Episode 9: The Better Angels of Our Nature—1865 In this final episode of the Emmy-nominated PBS mini-series, Lincoln's assasination is examined, and the central characters of the war are summarized.
1990 68m/C D: Ken Burns; **W:** Ken Burns. **VHS** ★★★★

Civilization A silent epic about the horrors and immorality of war as envisioned by the ground-breaking film pioneer Ince, who was later murdered. Famous scene involves Christ walking through body-ridden battlefields.
1916 80m/B Howard Hickman, Enid

Markey, Lola May; **D:** Thomas Ince, Reginald Barker, Raymond B. West. **VHS, Beta ★★★**

Claire's Knee A grown man about to be married goes on a holiday and develops a fixation on a young girl's knee. Another of Rohmer's Moral Tales exploring sexual and erotic obsessions. Lots of talk, little else. You'll either find it fascinating or fail to watch more than 10 minutes. Most, however, consider it a classic. Sophisticated dialogue, lovely visions of summer on Lake Geneva. In French with English subtitles.
1971 105m/C *FR* Jean-Claude Brialy, Aurora Cornu, Beatrice Romand; **D:** Eric Rohmer; **W:** Eric Rohmer. National Board of Review Awards '71: 5 Best Foreign Films of the Year; National Society of Film Critics Awards '71: Best Film. **VHS, Beta, LV ★★★1/2**

Clarence, the Cross-eyed Lion Follows the many adventures of a cross-eyed lion and his human compatriots. Great family viewing from the creator of "Flipper."
1965 98m/C Marshall Thompson, Betsy Drake, Richard Haydn, Cheryl Miller, Rockne Tarkington, Maurice Marsac; **D:** Andrew Marton; **W:** Alan Cailou. **VHS ★★★**

Clash by Night A wayward woman marries a fisherman, then beds his best friend. Seamy storyline is exploited to the hilt by master filmmaker Lang. An utterly unflinching melodrama. Early Monroe shines in a supporting role too. Based on the Clifford Odets play.
1952 105m/B Barbara Stanwyck, Paul Douglas, Marilyn Monroe, Robert Ryan, J. Carrol Naish; **D:** Fritz Lang. **VHS, Beta, LV ★★★1/2**

Clean and Sober A drug addict hides out at a rehabilitation clinic and actually undergoes treatment. A serious, subtle, and realistic look at the physical/emotional detoxification of an obnoxious, substance-abusing real estate broker; unpredictable and powerful without moralizing. Keaton is fine in unsympathetic lead, with both Baker and Freeman excelling in lesser roles. Not for all tastes, but it's certainly a worthwhile work. Caron, creator of TV's "Moonlighting," debuts here as director.
1988 (R) 124m/C Michael Keaton, Kathy Baker, Morgan Freeman, M. Emmet Walsh, Claudia Christian, Pat Quinn, Ben Piazza, Brian Benben, Luca Bercovici, Tate Donovan, Henry Judd Baker, Mary Catherine Martin; **D:** Glenn Gordon Caron; **W:** Tod Carroll, Jan Kiesser. National Society of Film Critics Awards '88: Best

Actor (Keaton). **VHS, Beta, LV, 8mm ★★★1/2**

Cleo from 5 to 7 A singer strolls through Paris for 90 minutes, and reconsiders her life while awaiting the results of medical tests for cancer. Typical documentary-like effort from innovative filmmaker Varda, who constructed the film in real time. Look for a brief appearance of master director Jean-Luc Godard. In French with English subtitles. **AKA:** Cleo de 5 a 7.
1961 90m/B *FR* Corinne Marchand, Antoine Bourseillor, Dorothee Blanck, Michel Legrand, Jean-Claude Brialy, Jean-Luc Godard, Anna Karina, Eddie Constantine, Sami Frey; **D:** Agnes Varda; **W:** Agnes Varda. **VHS, Beta ★★★1/2**

Clerks "What kind of convenience store do you run here?" Day in the life of a convenience store clerk is an often hilarious lesson in the profane from first time writer/director Smith (who has a cameo as Silent Bob). Twenty-two-year-old Dante Hicks (O'Halloran) is a disaffected New Jersey Quick Stop employee who spends most of his time bored and dealing with borderline crazies. The next-door video store is clerked by his best friend Randal (Anderson), who derives equal delight from tormenting his customers and debating absolutely anything (especially anything sexual). Nothing much actually happens but the very low-budget ($27,575) production has a decidedly scuzzy charm and a cult following. Based on the director's four years of clerking at the Quick Stop and shot on location.
1994 (R) 91m/B Brian O'Halloran, Jeff Anderson, Marilyn Ghigliotti, Lisa Spoonhauer, Jason Mewes; *Cameos:* Kevin Smith; **D:** Kevin Smith; **W:** Kevin Smith; **M:** Scott Angley. Sundance Film Festival '94: Filmmakers Trophy; Nominations: Independent Spirit Awards '95: Best First Feature, Debut Performance (Anderson), First Screenplay. **VHS, LV ★★★**

Cliffhanger Action-packed thriller. Expert climber Gabe Walker (Stallone) faces his greatest challenge when criminal mastermind Lithgow and his henchman appear on the scene. Turner plays fellow climber and love interest. Lithgow makes a particularly convincing, if not downright chilling, murderous thief. Filmed in the Italian Alps with a budget of $70 million-plus; boasts stunning cinematography and breathtaking footage of the Dolomite mountain range. Harlin's expert pacing and direction combine to produce maximum thrills and suspense. The hit Stallone's been waiting for, placing eighth on the list of top 1993 box office grossers.

1993 (R) 113m/C Sylvester Stallone, John Lithgow, Michael Rooker, Janine Turner, Rex Linn, Caroline Goodall, Leon, Paul Winfield, Ralph Waite, Craig Fairbrass, Michelle Joyner, Max Perlich, Alex Thomson; **D:** Renny Harlin; **W:** Sylvester Stallone, Michael France; **M:** Trevor Jones. Nominations: Academy Awards '93: Best Sound, Best Sound Effects Editing, Best Visual Effects; MTV Movie Awards '94: Best Action Sequence. **VHS, Beta, LV, 8mm** ★★★

The Clock Appealing romance about an office worker who meets and falls in love with a soldier on two-day leave in New York City. Charismatic Walker and likeable Garland make a fine screen couple, and Wynn is memorable as the drunk. The original theatrical trailer is included on the laserdisc format. *AKA:* Under the Clock.

1945 91m/B Judy Garland, Robert Walker, James Gleason, Marshall Thompson, Keenan Wynn; **D:** Vincente Minnelli; **M:** George Bassman. **VHS, LV** ★★★

Clockers Poignant and compelling street drama has Strike (Phifer), leader of a group of bottom-feeding drug dealers ("clockers"), get in a power struggle with his boss (Lindo), his do-the-right-thing brother Victor (Washington), and his own conscience. Oh yeah, and he's suspected of murder by relentless narcotics cop Rocco Klein (Keitel). First-timer Phifer rises to the level demanded by the excellent narrative and surrounding talent. Lindo, in particular, stands out as the paternally evil Rodney. Critically lauded cinematography marred by the occasional boom shot. Based on the Richard Price novel. Lee took over after Scorsese and De Niro dropped out to make "Casino."

1995 (R) 128m/C Mekhi Phifer, Harvey Keitel, Delroy Lindo, Isaiah Washington, John Turturro, Keith David; **D:** Spike Lee; **W:** Richard Price, Spike Lee; **M:** Terence Blanchard, Malik Hassan Sayeed. **VHS, LV** ★★★1/2

The Clockmaker Contemplative drama about a clockmaker whose life is shattered when his son is arrested as a political assassin. Tavernier regular Noiret excels in the lead. In French with English subtitles.

1976 105m/C FR Philippe Noiret, Jean Rochefort, Jacques Denis, William Sabatier, Christine Pascal; **D:** Bertrand Tavernier. National Board of Review Awards '76: 5 Best Foreign Films of the Year. **VHS, Beta, LV** ★★★1/2

A Clockwork Orange In the Britain of the near future, a sadistic punk leads a gang on nightly rape and murder sprees, then is captured and becomes the subject of a grim experiment to eradicate his violent tendencies in this extraordinary adaptation of Anthony Burgess's controversial novel. The film is an exhilarating experience, with an outstanding performance by McDowell as the funny, fierce psychopath. Many memorable, disturbing sequences, including a rape conducted while assailant McDowell belts "Singing in the Rain." Truly outstanding, provocative work from master filmmaker Kubrick.

1971 (R) 137m/C GB Malcolm McDowell, Patrick Magee, Adrienne Corri, Michael Bates, Warren Clarke, Aubrey Morris, James Marcus, Steven Berkoff, David Prowse; **D:** Stanley Kubrick; **W:** Stanley Kubrick. New York Film Critics Awards '71: Best Director (Kubrick), Best Film; Nominations: Academy Awards '71: Best Adapted Screenplay, Best Director (Kubrick), Best Film Editing, Best Picture. **VHS, Beta, LV** ★★★★

Close Encounters of the Third Kind Middle-American strangers become involved in the attempts of benevolent aliens to contact earthlings. Despite the sometimes mundane nature of the characters, this Spielberg epic is a stirring achievement. Studded with classic sequences; the ending is an exhilarating experience of special effects and peace-on-earth feelings. Dreyfuss and Dillon excel as friends who are at once bewildered and obsessed by the alien presence, and French filmmaker Truffaut is also strong as the stern, ultimately kind scientist. Laserdisc includes formerly edited scenes, live interviews with Spielberg, special effects man Douglas Trumbull, and composer Williams, publicity materials, and over 1,000 production photos.

1977 (PG) 152m/C Richard Dreyfuss, Teri Garr, Melinda Dillon, Francois Truffaut, Bob Balaban, Cary Guffey, Vilmos Zsigmond; **D:** Steven Spielberg; **W:** Steven Spielberg; **M:** John Williams. Academy Awards '77: Best Cinematography, Best Sound Effects Editing; National Board of Review Awards '77: 10 Best Films of the Year; Nominations: Academy Awards '77: Best Art Direction/Set Decoration, Best Director (Spielberg), Best Film Editing, Best Sound, Best Supporting Actress (Dillon), Best Original Score. **VHS, Beta, LV** ★★★★

Closely Watched Trains A novice train dispatcher attempts to gain sexual experience in German-occupied Czechoslovakia during WWII. Many funny scenes in this film regarded by some as a classic. Based upon the Czech novel by Bohumil Hrabal. In Czech with English subtitles.
1966 89m/B *CZ* Vaclav Neckar, Jitka Bendova, Vladimir Valenta, Josef Somr; **D:** Jiri Menzel; **W:** Jiri Menzel. Academy Awards '67: Best Foreign Language Film. **VHS, Beta, LV ★★★1/2**

The Clowns An idiosyncratic documentary about circus clowns. Director Fellini has fashioned an homage that is sincere, entertaining, and personal. Contains some truly poignant sequences. Made for Italian television with English subtitles.
1971 (G) 90m/C *IT* **D:** Federico Fellini; **W:** Federico Fellini; **M:** Nino Rota. National Board of Review Awards '71: 5 Best Foreign Films of the Year. **VHS, Beta ★★★1/2**

Clueless Watch out "Beverly Hills 90210," here comes Cher. No, not the singer Cher, but ultra-filthy-rich brat Cher, who's out to make over her classmates and teachers, specifically flannel-shirted transfer student Tai (Murphy). Aerosmith vamp Silverstone stars as the teenage manipulator who knows all too well how to spend her trust fund. The only person who can match her wits is disapproving stepbrother Josh (Rudd). (Ah, love.) Loosely based on Jane Austen's "Emma," Heckerling, of "Fast Times at Ridgemont High" fame, knows this territory and directs a bright, surprisingly satirical romp. **AKA:** I Was a Teenage Teenager; No Worries.
1995 (PG-13) 113m/C Alicia Silverstone, Stacey Dash, Paul Rudd, Brittany Murphy, Donald A. Faison, Julie Brown, Jeremy Sisto, Dan Hedaya, Wallace Shawn, Breckin Meyer, Elisa Donovan, Aida Linares; **D:** Amy Heckerling; **W:** Amy Heckerling; **M:** David Kitay, Bill Pope. National Society of Film Critics Awards '95: Best Screenplay; Blockbuster Entertainment Awards '96: Female Newcomer, Theatrical (Silverstone); Nominations: Writers Guild of America '95: Best Original Screenplay. **VHS ★★★**

Coal Miner's Daughter A strong bio of country singer Loretta Lynn, who rose from Appalachian poverty to Nashville riches. Spacek is perfect in the lead, and she even provides acceptable renderings of Lynn's tunes. Band drummer Helm shines as Lynn's father, and Jones is strong as Lynn's downhome husband. Uneven melodrama toward the end, but the film is still a good one. ♪ Coal Miner's Daughter; Sweet Dreams of You; I'm a Honky-Tonk Girl; You're Lookin' at Country; One's On the Way; You Ain't Woman Enough to Take My Man; Back in My Baby's Arms.
1980 (PG) 125m/C Sissy Spacek, Tommy Lee Jones, Levon Helm, Beverly D'Angelo; **D:** Michael Apted, Ralf Bode. Academy Awards '80: Best Actress (Spacek); Golden Globe Awards '81: Best Actress—Musical/Comedy (Spacek), Best Film—Musical/Comedy; Los Angeles Film Critics Association Awards '80: Best Actress (Spacek); National Board of Review Awards '80: 10 Best Films of the Year, Best Actress (Spacek); National Society of Film Critics Awards '80: Best Actress (Spacek); Nominations: Academy Awards '80: Best Adapted Screenplay, Best Art Direction/Set Decoration, Best Cinematography, Best Film Editing, Best Picture. **VHS, Beta, LV ★★★**

The Coca-Cola Kid A smug sales executive treks to Australia to improve regional sales and becomes embroiled in sexual and professional shenanigans. Roberts is strong in the difficult lead role, and Scacchi is compelling in an awkwardly constructed part. Ambitious satire is somewhat scattershot, with more storylines than it needs. Still, filmmaker Makavejev is usually capable of juggling the entire enterprise.
1984 (R) 94m/C *AU* Eric Roberts, Greta Scacchi, Bill Kerr; **D:** Dusan Makavejev. **VHS, Beta, LV ★★★1/2**

Cocoon Humanist fantasy in which senior citizens discover their fountain of youth is actually a breeding ground for aliens. Heartwarming, one-of-a kind drama showcases elderly greats Ameche, Brimley, Gilford, Cronyn, and Tandy. A commendable, recommendable venture. Based on David Saperstein's novel and followed by "Cocoon: The Return."
1985 (PG-13) 117m/C Wilford Brimley, Brian Dennehy, Steve Guttenberg, Don Ameche, Tahnee Welch, Jack Gilford, Hume Cronyn, Jessica Tandy, Gwen Verdon, Maureen Stapleton, Tyrone Power Jr., Barret Oliver, Linda Harrison, Herta Ware, Clint Howard; **D:** Ron Howard; **W:** Tom Benedek; **M:** James Horner. Academy Awards '85: Best Supporting Actor (Ameche), Best Visual Effects. **VHS, Beta, LV ★★★**

Cold Sassy Tree Endearing romance of a scandalous May-December marriage as perceived by the younger woman's teenage son. Dunaway and

Widmark shine, and small town pettiness is vividly rendered. Adapted from the books by Olive Ann Burns. A superior made-for-cable production. **1989 95m/C** Faye Dunaway, Richard Widmark, Neil Patrick Harris, Frances Fisher, Lee Garlington, John M. Jackson; **D:** Joan Tewkesbury; **W:** Joan Tewkesbury; **M:** Brad Fiedel. **VHS ★★★1/2**

Cold Turkey Often witty satire about what happens when an entire town tries to stop smoking for a contest. Van Dyke is fine as the anti-smoking minister; newscasters Bob and Ray are riotous; oldtimer Horton's swansong. Wholesome, somewhat tame fare.
1971 (PG) 99m/C Dick Van Dyke, Pippa Scott, Tom Poston, Bob Newhart, Vincent Gardenia, Barnard Hughes, Jean Stapleton, Graham Jarvis, Edward Everett Horton; **D:** Norman Lear; **W:** Norman Lear; **M:** Randy Newman. **VHS, Beta, LV ★★★**

The Collector Compelling adaptation of the John Fowles novel about a withdrawn butterfly collector who decides to add to his collection by kidnapping a beautiful girl he admires. He locks her in his cellar hoping she will fall in love with him. Chilling, unsettling drama with Stamp unnerving, yet sympathetic in lead.
1965 119m/C GB Terence Stamp, Samantha Eggar, Maurice Dallimore, Mona Washbourne; **D:** William Wyler; **M:** Maurice Jarre. Cannes Film Festival '65: Best Actor (Stamp), Best Actress (Eggar); Nominations: Academy Awards '65: Best Actress (Eggar), Best Adapted Screenplay, Best Director (Wyler). **VHS, Beta, LV ★★★1/2**

College A high school valedictorian tries out for every sport in college, hoping to win the girl. Vintage Keaton antics, including disaster as a soda jerk, an attempt to be a track star, and the pole vault through a window to rescue the damsel in distress.
1927 60m/B Buster Keaton, A. Cornwall, Harold Goodwin; **D:** James W. Horne; **M:** John Muri. **VHS, Beta, LV ★★★1/2**

Colonel Redl Absorbing, intricately rendered psychological study of an ambitious officer's rise and fall in pre-WWI Austria. Brandauer is excellent as the vain, insecure homosexual ultimately undone by his own ambition and his superior officer's smug loathing. Muller-Stahl and Landgrebe are particularly distinguished among the supporting players. The second in the Szabo/Brandauer trilogy, after "Mephisto" and before "Hanussen." In German with English subtitles.
1984 (R) 114m/C GE HU Klaus Maria Brandauer, Armin Mueller-Stahl, Gudrun Landgrebe, Jan Niklas, Hans-Christian Blech, Laszlo Mensaros, Andras Balint; **D:** Laszlo Szabo, Lajos Koltai. British Academy Awards '85: Best Foreign Film; Cannes Film Festival '85: Special Jury Prize; Nominations: Academy Awards '85: Best Foreign Language Film. **VHS, Beta, LV ★★★★**

The Color of Money Flashy, gripping drama about former pool hustler Fast Eddie Felsen (Newman) who, after years off the circuit, takes a brilliant but immature pool shark (Cruise) under his wing. Strong performances by Newman as the grizzled veteran, Cruise as the showboating youth, and Mastrantonio and Shaver as the men's worldly girlfriends. Worthy sequel to 1961 classic "The Hustler."
1986 (R) 119m/C Paul Newman, Tom Cruise, Mary Elizabeth Mastrantonio, Helen Shaver, John Turturro, Forest Whitaker; **D:** Martin Scorsese; **W:** Richard Price, Michael Ballhaus. Academy Awards '86: Best Actor (Newman); National Board of Review Awards '86: Best Actor (Newman); Nominations: Academy Awards '86: Best Adapted Screenplay, Best Art Direction/Set Decoration, Best Supporting Actress (Mastrantonio). **VHS, Beta, LV ★★★★**

The Color Purple Celie is a poor black girl who fights for her self-esteem when she is separated from her sister and forced into a brutal marriage. Spanning 1909 to 1947 in a small Georgia town, the movie chronicles the joys, pains, and people in her life. Adaptation of Alice Walker's acclaimed book features strong lead from Goldberg (her screen debut), Glover, Avery, and talk-show host Winfrey (also her film debut). It's hard to see director Spielberg as the most suited for this one, but he acquits himself nicely, avoiding the facileness that sometimes flaws his pics. Brilliant photography by Allen Daviau and musical score by Jones (who co-produced) compliment this strong film.
1985 (PG-13) 154m/C Whoopi Goldberg, Danny Glover, Oprah Winfrey, Margaret Avery, Adolph Caesar, Rae Dawn Chong, Willard Pugh, Akosua Busia; **D:** Steven Spielberg; **M:** Chris Boardman, Quincy Jones, Allen Daviau. Directors Guild of America Awards '85: Best Director (Spielberg); Golden Globe Awards '86: Best Actress—Drama (Goldberg); National Board of Review Awards '85: 10 Best Films of the Year, Best Actress (Goldberg); Nominations: Academy Awards '85: Best Actress (Goldberg), Best Adapted Screenplay, Best Art Direction/Set Decoration, Best Cinematography, Best

Costume Design, Best Makeup, Best Picture, Best Song ("Miss Celie's Blues (Sister)"), Best Supporting Actress (Avery, Winfrey), Best Original Score. **VHS, Beta, LV** ★★★1/2

Colors Vivid, realistic cop drama pairs sympathetic veteran Duvall and trigger-tempered rookie Penn on the gang-infested streets of East Los Angeles. Fine play from leads is one of the many assets in this controversial, unsettling depiction of deadly street-life. Colorful, freewheeling direction from the underrated Hopper. Rattling rap soundtrack too. Additional footage has been added for video release.
1988 (R) 120m/C Sean Penn, Robert Duvall, Maria Conchita Alonso, Trinidad Silva, Randi Brooks, Grand Bush, Don Cheadle, Rudy Ramos; **D:** Dennis Hopper; **W:** Michael Schiffer; **M:** Herbie Hancock, Haskell Wexler. **VHS, Beta, LV** ★★★1/2

Colossus: The Forbin Project A computer designed to manage U.S. defense systems teams instead with its Soviet equal and they attempt world domination. Wire-tight, suspenseful film seems at once dated yet timely. Based on the novel by D.F. Jones. **AKA:** The Forbin Project.
1970 100m/C Eric (Hans Gudegast) Braeden, Susan Clark, Gordon Pinsent; **D:** Joseph Sargent; **W:** James Bridges; **M:** Michel Colombier. **VHS, Beta** ★★★

The Comancheros Texas Ranger Wayne and his prisoner fight with the Comancheros, an outlaw gang who is supplying guns and liquor to the dreaded Comanche Indians. Musical score adds flavor. Last film by Curtiz.
1961 108m/C John Wayne, Ina Balin, Stuart Whitman, Nehemiah Persoff, Lee Marvin, Bruce Cabot; **D:** Michael Curtiz; **M:** Elmer Bernstein. **VHS, Beta, LV** ★★★

Come and Get It A classic adaptation of the Edna Ferber novel about a lumber king battling against his son for the love of a woman. Farmer's most important Hollywood role. **AKA:** Roaring Timber.
1936 99m/B Frances Farmer, Edward Arnold, Joel McCrea, Walter Brennan, Andrea Leeds, Charles Halton; **D:** William Wyler, Howard Hawks. Academy Awards '36: Best Supporting Actor (Brennan); Nominations: Academy Awards '36: Best Film Editing. **VHS, Beta** ★★★

Come and See Harrowing, unnerving epic which depicts the horrors of war as a boy soldier roams the Russian countryside during the Nazi invasion. Some overwhelming sequences, including tracer-bullets flashing across an open field. War has rarely been rendered in such a vivid, utterly grim manner. Outstanding achievement from Soviet director Klimov. In Russian with English subtitles. **AKA:** Idi i Smotri; Go and See.
1985 142m/C *RU* Alexei Kravchenko, Olga Mironova, Lubomiras Lauciavicus; **D:** Elem Klimov. **VHS** ★★★★

Come Back, Little Sheba Unsettling drama about a worn-out housewife, her abusive, alcoholic husband and a comely boarder who causes further marital tension. The title refers to the housewife's despairing search for her lost dog. Booth, Lancaster, and Moore are all excellent. Based on the play by William Inge, this film still packs an emotional wallop.
1952 99m/B Burt Lancaster, Shirley Booth, Terry Moore, Richard Jaeckel, Philip Ober, Lisa Golm, Walter Kelley; **D:** Daniel Mann. Academy Awards '52: Best Actress (Booth); Cannes Film Festival '53: Best Actress (Booth); Golden Globe Awards '53: Best Actress—Drama (Booth); New York Film Critics Awards '52: Best Actress (Booth); Nominations: Academy Awards '52: Best Film Editing, Best Supporting Actress (Moore). **VHS, Beta, LV** ★★★1/2

Come Back to the Five & Dime Jimmy Dean, Jimmy Dean Five women convene at a run-down Texas drugstore for a 20-year reunion of a local James Dean fan club. The women recall earlier times and make some stunning revelations. Altman's filming of Ed Graczyk's sometimes funny, sometimes wrenching play proves fine vehicle for the actresses. Cher is probably the most impressive, but Dennis and Black are also memorable.
1982 (PG) 109m/C Sandy Dennis, Cher, Karen Black, Kathy Bates, Sudie Bond, Marta Heflin; **D:** Robert Altman. **VHS, Beta, LV** ★★★

Come Blow Your Horn Neil Simon's first major Broadway success is a little less successful in its celluloid wrapper, suffering a bit from a familiar script. Sinatra's a playboy who blows his horn all over town, causing his close-knit New York Jewish family to warp a bit. Dad's not keen on his son's pledge of allegiance to the good life, and kid brother Bill would like to be his sibling's understudy in playboyhood.
1963 115m/C Frank Sinatra, Lee J. Cobb, Tony Bill, Molly Picon, Barbara Rush, Jill St. John; **D:** Bud Yorkin; **W:** Norman Lear. Nominations: Academy Awards '63: Best Art Direction/Set Decoration (Color). **VHS, Beta** ★★★

C

Come to the Stable Warm, delightful story about two French nuns, Young and Holm, who arrive in New England and set about building a children's hospital. Although Catholic in intent, pic demonstrates that faith and tenacity can move mountains. (This film must have been Fox's response to Paramount's "Going My Way" and "The Bells of Saint Mary's.") Based on a story by Clare Boothe Luce.
1949 94m/B Loretta Young, Celeste Holm, Hugh Marlowe, Elsa Lanchester, Regis Toomey, Mike Mazurki; **D:** Henry Koster; **W:** Oscar Millard, Sally Benson; **M:** Cyril Mockridge. Nominations: Academy Awards '49: Best Actress (Young), Best Adapted Screenplay, Best Art Direction/Set Decoration (B & W), Best Black and White Cinematography, Best Supporting Actress (Holm, Lanchester). **VHS** ★★★

The Comedy of Terrors Comedy in which some deranged undertakers take a hands-on approach to insuring their continued employment. Much fun is supplied by the quartet of Price, Lorre, Karloff, and Rathbone, all veterans of the horror genre.
1964 84m/C Vincent Price, Peter Lorre, Boris Karloff, Basil Rathbone, Joe E. Brown, Joyce Jameson; **D:** Jacques Tourneur; **W:** Richard Matheson; **M:** Les Baxter. **VHS, LV** ★★★

Comfort and Joy After his kleptomaniac girlfriend deserts him, a Scottish disc jockey is forced to reevaluate his life. He becomes involved in an underworld battle between two mob-owned local ice cream companies. Another odd comedy gem from Forsyth, who did "Gregory's Girl" and "Local Hero." Music by Dire Straits guitarist Knopfler.
1984 (PG) 93m/C *GB* Bill Paterson, Eleanor David, C.P. Grogan, Alex Norton, Patrick Malahide, Rikki Fulton, Roberto Berrardi; **D:** Bill Forsyth; **M:** Mark Knopfler, Chris Menges. National Society of Film Critics Awards '84: Best Cinematography. **VHS, Beta** ★★★½

The Comfort of Strangers Atmospheric psychological thriller. Mary and Colin (Richardson and Everett), a handsome young British couple, take a Venetian holiday to rediscover the passion in their relationship. Lost in the city, they chance, it seems, upon Robert (Walken), a sort of Virgil in an Italian suit. He later reappears, and, abetted by his wife Caroline (Mirren), gradually leads the couple on an eerie tour of urbane decadence that hints at danger. Psychologically tantalizing and horrifyingly erotic, the movie's based on Ian McEwan's novel.

1991 (R) 102m/C Christopher Walken, Natasha Richardson, Rupert Everett, Helen Mirren; **D:** Paul Schrader; **W:** Harold Pinter; **M:** Angelo Badalamenti, Dante Spinotti. **VHS, Beta** ★★★

Coming Home Looks at the effect of the Vietnam War on home front. The wife of a gung-ho Marine officer volunteers as an aide in a Veteran's Hospital, befriends and eventually falls in love with a Vietnam vet, paralyzed from war injuries. His attitudes, pain, and first-hand knowledge of the war force her to re-examine her previously automatic responses. Honest look at the everyday life of disabled veterans, unusual vision of the possibilities of simple friendship between men and women. Fonda and Voight are great; Dern's character suffers from weak scriptwriting late in the film. Critically acclaimed. Compelling score from late '60s music.
1978 (R) 130m/C Jane Fonda, Jon Voight, Bruce Dern, Penelope Milford, Robert Carradine, Robert Ginty; **D:** Hal Ashby; **W:** Robert C. Jones, Haskell Wexler. Academy Awards '78: Best Actor (Voight), Best Actress (Fonda), Best Screenplay; Cannes Film Festival '78: Best Actor (Voight); Golden Globe Awards '79: Best Actor—Drama (Voight), Best Actress—Drama (Fonda); New York Film Critics Awards '78: Best Actor (Voight); Writers Guild of America '78: Best Original Screenplay; Nominations: Academy Awards '78: Best Director (Ashby), Best Film Editing, Best Picture, Best Supporting Actor (Dern), Best Supporting Actress (Milford). **VHS, Beta, LV** ★★★½

Coming to America An African prince (Murphy) decides to come to America in search of a suitable bride. He lands in Queens, and quickly finds American women to be more confusing than he imagined. Sometimes overly-cute entertainment relieved by clever costume cameos by Murphy and Hall. Later lawsuit resulted in columnist Art Buchwald being given credit for story.
1988 (R) 116m/C Eddie Murphy, Arsenio Hall, James Earl Jones, John Amos, Madge Sinclair, Shari Headley, Don Ameche, Louie Anderson, Paul Bates, Allison Dean, Eriq La Salle, Calvin Lockhart, Samuel L. Jackson, Cuba Gooding Jr., Vanessa Bell, Frankie Faison, Vondie Curtis-Hall; **D:** John Landis; **W:** David Sheffield, Barry W. Blaustein; **M:** Nile Rodgers. Nominations: Academy Awards '88: Best Costume Design. **VHS, Beta, LV, 8mm** ★★★

Commissar Before the Soviet Union ended up in the ashcan of history, this

film was labeled as "treason" and shelved in Red Russia. Now, even Americans can view the story of a female Soviet soldier who becomes pregnant during the civil war of 1922. The Soviet military has no policy regarding pregnancy, so the woman is dumped on a family of outcast Jews to complete her pregnancy. This film makes the strong statement that women were just as discriminated against in the U.S.S.R. as were many races or creeds, especially Jews. In Russian with English subtitles. Released in the U.S. in 1988. *AKA:* Komissar.
1968 105m/B *RU* Nonna Mordyukova, Rolan Bykov; *D:* Alexander Askoldov. **VHS** ★★★★

The Commitments Convinced that they can bring soul music to Dublin, a group of working-class youth form a band. High-energy production paints an interesting, unromanticized picture of modern Ireland and refuses to follow standard showbiz cliches, even though its lack of resolution hurts. Honest, whimsical dialog laced with poetic obscenities, delivered by a cast of mostly unknowns. Very successful soundtrack features the music of Wilson Pickett, James Brown, Otis Redding, Aretha Franklin, Percy Sledge, and others, and received a Grammy nomination. Based on the book "The Commitments" by Roddy Doyle, part of a trilogy which includes "The Snapper" and "The Van."
1991 (R) 116m/C *IR* Andrew Strong, Bronagh Gallagher, Glen Hansard, Michael Aberne, Dick Massey, Ken McCluskey, Robert Arkins, Dave Finnegan, Johnny Murphy, Angeline Ball, Felim Gormley, Maria Doyle, Colm Meaney; *D:* Alan Parker; *W:* Dick Clement, Roddy Doyle, Ian LaFrenais. British Academy Awards '91: Best Adapted Screenplay, Best Director (Parker), Best Film; Nominations: Academy Awards '91: Best Film Editing. **VHS, Beta, LV** ★★★

The Company of Wolves A young girl on the threshold of womanhood listens to her grandmother tell fairytales and dreams of a medieval fantasy world inhabited by wolves and werewolves. An adult "Little Red Riding Hood" type comedy heavy on Freudian symbolism. Not really for kids.
1985 (R) 95m/C Angela Lansbury, David Warner, Stephen Rea, Tusse Silberg, Sarah Patterson, Brian Glover, Danielle Dax, Graham Crowden, Micha Bergese; *D:* Neil Jordan; *W:* Neil Jordan, Angela Carter; *M:* George Fenton. **VHS, Beta, LV** ★★★

Compulsion Artie Strauss (Dillman) is a mother-dominated sadist who, along with submissive friend Judd Steiner (Stockwell), plan and execute a cold-blooded murder. Flamboyant lawyer Jonathan Wilk (brilliantly portrayed by Welles) knows he has no defense so he attacks the system and establishment, seeking to at least save his clients from death. A suspenseful shocker with taut direction and a tight script. Based on the notorious 1924 Leopold and Loeb murder trial, also filmed as "Rope" and "Swoon."
1959 103m/B Orson Welles, Bradford Dillman, Dean Stockwell, Diane Varsi, E.G. Marshall, Martin Milner, Richard Anderson, Robert Simon, Edward Binns, Robert Burton, Wilton Graff, Gavin MacLeod; *D:* Richard Fleischer; *W:* Richard Murphy. **VHS** ★★★1/2

Conan the Barbarian A fine sword and sorcery tale featuring brutality, excellent production values, and a rousing score. Conan's parents are killed and he's enslaved. But hardship makes him strong, so when he is set free he can avenge their murder and retrieve the sword bequeathed him by his father. Sandahl Bergman is great as The Queen of Thieves, and Schwarzenegger maintains an admirable sense of humor throughout. Jones is dandy, as always. Based on the character created by Robert E. Howard. Sequel: "Conan the Destroyer."
1982 (R) 115m/C Arnold Schwarzenegger, James Earl Jones, Max von Sydow, Sandahl Bergman, Mako, Ben Davidson, Valerie Quennessen, Cassandra Gaviola, William Smith; *D:* John Milius; *W:* John Milius, Oliver Stone; *M:* Basil Poledouris. **VHS, Beta, LV** ★★★

Confidentially Yours Truffaut's homage to Hitchcock, based on Charles Williams' "The Long Saturday Night." A hapless small-town real estate agent is framed for a rash of murders and his secretary, who is secretly in love with him, tries to clear his name. Truffaut's last film is stylish and entertaining. In French with English subtitles. *AKA:* Vivement Dimanche!; Finally, Sunday.
1983 (PG) 110m/B *FR* Fanny Ardant, Jean-Louis Trintignant, Philippe Morier-Genoud, Philippe Laudenbach, Caroline Sihol; *D:* Francois Truffaut; *W:* Suzanne Schiffman; *M:* Georges Delerue. **VHS, Beta, LV** ★★★

Conflict Bogart falls for his sister-in-law and asks his wife for a divorce. She refuses, he plots her murder, and thinks up the alibi. When the police fail to notify him of her death, Bogart is forced to report his wife missing. But is she dead? Her guilty husband smells her perfume, sees her walking down the street, and discovers the body is missing from the scene of the crime. Suspenseful thriller also features Greenstreet as a psychologist/family friend who suspects Bogart knows more than he's telling.

1945 86m/B Humphrey Bogart, Alexis Smith, Sydney Greenstreet, Rose Hobart, Charles Drake, Grant Mitchell; *D:* Curtis Bernhardt. **VHS** ★★★

The Conformist Character study of young Italian fascist, plagued by homosexual feelings, who must prove his loyalty by killing his old professor. Decadent and engrossing story is brilliantly acted. Based on the novel by Alberto Moravia. *AKA:* Il Conformist.

1971 (R) 108m/C *IT FR GE* Jean-Louis Trintignant, Stefania Sandrelli, Dominique Sanda, Pierre Clementi, Gastone Moschin, Pasquale Fortunato, Vittorio Storaro; *D:* Bernardo Bertolucci; *W:* Bernardo Bertolucci; *M:* Georges Delerue. National Board of Review Awards '71: 5 Best Foreign Films of the Year; National Society of Film Critics Awards '71: Best Cinematography, Best Director (Bertolucci); Nominations: Academy Awards '71: Best Adapted Screenplay. **VHS, Beta, LV** ★★★★

A Connecticut Yankee A charming, if somewhat dated, version of the popular Mark Twain story, "A Connecticut Yankee in King Arthur's Court." Rogers is a radio shop owner who dreams his way back to the Knights of the Round Table. Story rewritten to fit Rogers' amiable style and to make then-current wisecracks. Great cast overcomes weak points in the script.

1931 96m/B Will Rogers, Myrna Loy, Maureen O'Sullivan, William Farnum; *D:* David Butler. **VHS** ★★★

The Connection The Living Theatre's ground-breaking performance of Jack Gelber's play about heroin addicts waiting for their connection to arrive, while a documentary filmmaker hovers nearby with his camera.

1961 105m/B Warren Finnerty, Carl Lee, William Redfield, Roscoe Lee Browne, Garry Goodrow, James Anderson, Jackie McLean; *D:* Shirley Clarke. **VHS, Beta** ★★★1/2

The Conqueror Worm Price turns in a fine performance portraying the sinister Matthew Hopkins, a real-life 17th-century witchhunter. No "ham" in this low-budget, underrated thriller. The last of three films from director Reeves, who died from an accidental overdose in 1969. Also available with "Tomb of Ligeia" on laserdisc. *AKA:* Witchfinder General; Edgar Allan Poe's Conqueror Worm.

1968 95m/C *GB* Vincent Price, Ian Ogilvy, Hilary Dwyer, Rupert Davies, Robert Russell, Patrick Wymark, Wilfrid Brambell; *D:* Michael Reeves. **VHS** ★★★

Conquest Garbo, as the Polish countess Marie Walewska, tries to persuade Napoleon (Boyer) to free her native Poland from the Russian Tsar. Garbo, Boyer, and Ouspenskaya are outstanding, while the beautiful costumes and lavish production help, but the script is occasionally weak. A box office flop in the U.S., which ended up costing MGM more than any movie it had made up until that time. *AKA:* Marie Walewska.

1937 115m/B Greta Garbo, Charles Boyer, Reginald Owen, Alan Marshal, Henry Stephenson, Leif Erickson, May Whitty, Maria Ouspenskaya, Vladimir Sokoloff, Scotty Beckett; *D:* Clarence Brown. **VHS, Beta** ★★★

Conspiracy: The Trial of the Chicago Eight Courtroom drama focuses on the rambunctious trial of the Chicago Eight radicals, charged with inciting a riot at the Democratic National Convention of 1968. Dramatized footage mixed with interviews with the defendants. Imaginative reconstruction of history.

1987 118m/C Peter Boyle, Elliott Gould, Robert Carradine, Martin Sheen, David Clennon, David Kagen, Michael Lembeck, Robert Loggia; *D:* Jeremy Paul Kagan. **VHS, Beta** ★★★

The Conversation Hackman plays a surveillance expert increasingly uneasy about his job as he begins to suspect he is an accomplice to murder. Powerful statement about privacy, responsibility and guilt. One of the best movies of the '70s.

1974 (PG) 113m/C Gene Hackman, John Cazale, Frederic Forrest, Allen (Goorwitz) Garfield, Cindy Williams, Robert Duvall, Teri Garr, Michael Higgins, Elizabeth McRae, Harrison Ford; *D:* Francis Ford Coppola; *W:* Francis Ford Coppola; *M:* David Shire. Cannes Film Festival '74: Best Film; National Board of Review Awards '74: 10 Best Films of the Year, Best Actor (Hackman), Best Director (Coppola); Nominations: Academy Awards '74: Best Original Screenplay, Best Picture, Best Sound. **VHS, Beta, LV** ★★★1/2

Conversation Piece An aging art historian's life is turned upside down when a Countess and her daughters rent out the penthouse in his estate. Sometimes-talky examination of scholarly pretensions. *AKA:* Violence et Passion; Gruppo di Famiglia in un Interno.
1975 (R) 112m/C *IT FR* Burt Lancaster, Silvana Mangano, Helmut Berger, Claudia Cardinale; *D:* Luchino Visconti. **VHS, Beta** ★★★

Coogan's Bluff An Arizona deputy sheriff (Eastwood) travels to New York in order to track down a killer on the loose. First Eastwood/Siegel teaming is tense actioner. The television series "McCloud" was based on this film.
1968 (PG) 100m/C Clint Eastwood, Lee J. Cobb, Tisha Sterling, Don Stroud, Betty Field, Susan Clark, Tom Tully; *D:* Donald Siegel; *M:* Lalo Schifrin. **VHS, Beta, LV** ★★★

The Cook, the Thief, His Wife & Her Lover An exclusive restaurant houses four disturbing characters. Greenaway's powerful vision of greed, love, and violence may be too strong for some tastes. Available in several different versions: the standard unrated theatrical release, the unrated version in a letterboxed format, an R-rated cut which runs half an hour shorter, and a Spanish-subtitled version.
1990 (R) 123m/C *GB* Richard Bohringer, Michael Gambon, Helen Mirren, Alan Howard, Tim Roth; *D:* Peter Greenaway; *W:* Peter Greenaway; *M:* Michael Nyman. **VHS** ★★★1/2

Cool Hand Luke One of the last great men-in-chains films. A man (Newman) sentenced to sweat out a term on a prison farm refuses to compromise with authority. Martin shines in his supporting role as the oily warden, uttering that now-famous phrase, "What we have here is a failure to communicate." Kennedy's performance as leader of the chain gang won him an Oscar. Based on the novel by Donn Pearce.
1967 126m/C Paul Newman, George Kennedy, J.D. Cannon, Strother Martin, Dennis Hopper, Anthony Zerbe, Lou Antonio, Wayne Rogers, Harry Dean Stanton, Ralph Waite, Joe Don Baker, Richard Davalos, Jo Van Fleet; *D:* Stuart Rosenberg; *W:* Frank Pierson; *M:* Lalo Schifrin, Conrad Hall. Academy Awards '67: Best Supporting Actor (Kennedy); Nominations: Academy Awards '66: Best Adapted Screenplay, Best Original Score; Academy Awards '67: Best Actor (Newman). **VHS, Beta, LV** ★★★1/2

Cooley High Black high school students in Chicago go through the rites of passage in their senior year during the '60s. Film is funny, smart and much acclaimed. Great soundtrack featuring Motown hits of the era is a highlight. Sequel to the TV series "What's Happening."
1975 (PG) 107m/C Glynn Turman, Lawrence-Hilton Jacobs, Garrett Morris, Cynthia Davis; *D:* Michael A. Schultz; *W:* Eric Monte. **VHS, LV** ★★★

The Corn Is Green Touching story of a school teacher in a poor Welsh village who eventually sends her pet student to Oxford. Davis makes a fine teacher, though a little young, while the on-site photography provides atmosphere. Based on the play by Emlyn Williams. Remade in 1979.
1945 115m/B Bette Davis, John Dall, Nigel Bruce, Joan Lorring, Arthur Shields, Mildred Dunnock, Rhys Williams, Rosalind Ivan; *D:* Irving Rapper; *M:* Max Steiner. Nominations: Academy Awards '45: Best Supporting Actor (Dall), Best Supporting Actress (Lorring). **VHS, Beta** ★★★

Cosi Amiable Lewis (Mendelsohn) is hired to help with drama therapy at the local Sydney mental institution. Pressured by long-term patient Roy (Otto), Lewis finds himself agreeing to stage a production of Mozart's opera "Cosi Fan Tutte," though none of the patients can speak Italian or sing. Rehearsals prove a challenge, there are numerous setbacks, and then it's show time. Fine ensemble cast delivers; adapted from Nowra's play. Friels stepped into the role of security guard Errol when Bruno Lawrence died before filming was completed; pic is dedicated to Lawrence.
1995 100m/C *AU* Ben Mendelsohn, Barry Otto, Aden Young, Toni Collette, Rachel Griffiths, Colin Friels, Paul Chubb, Pamela Rabe, Jacki Weaver, David Wenham, Colin Hay, Tony Llewellyn-Jones; Cameos: Greta Scacchi, Paul Mercurio; *D:* Mark Joffel; *W:* Louis Nowra; *M:* Stephen Endelman. Australian Film Institute '95: Best Adapted Screenplay; Nominations: Australian Film Institute '95: Best Supporting Actor (Otto), Best Supporting Actress (Collette). **VHS,** ★★★

The Cotton Club With $50 million in his pocket, Francis reaches for an epic and delivers: handsome production, lots of dance, bit of singing, confused plot, uneven performances, tad too long. A musician playing at The Cotton Club falls in love with gangster Dutch Schultz's girlfriend. A black tap dancer falls in love with a member of the chorus line who can pass for white. These two love stories are told against a background of mob violence and music. Excellent performances by Hoskins and Gwynne. ♪ Minnie the Moocher; Ill Wind; The Mooch; Ring Dem Bells; Drop Me Off in Harlem; Cotton Club Stomp; Truckin; Mood Indigo; Copper Colored Gal.

1984 (R) 121m/C Diane Lane, Richard Gere, Gregory Hines, Lonette McKee, Bob Hoskins, Fred Gwynne, James Remar, Nicolas Cage, Lisa Jane Persky, Allen (Goorwitz) Garfield, Gwen Verdon, Joe Dallesandro, Jennifer Grey, Tom Waits, Diane Venora; **D:** Francis Ford Coppola; **W:** Francis Ford Coppola, William Kennedy, Mario Puzo; **M:** John Barry. Nominations: Academy Awards '84: Best Art Direction/Set Decoration, Best Film Editing. **VHS, Beta, LV, 8mm** ★★★

Cotton Comes to Harlem Cambridge and St. Jacques star as Harlem plainclothes detectives Grave Digger Jones and Coffin Ed Johnson in this successful mix of crime and comedy. They're investigating a suspicious preacher's back-to-Africa scheme which they suspect is a swindle. Directorial debut of Davis. Filmed on location in Harlem, New York. Based on the novel by Chester Himes. Followed by a weak sequel, "Come Back, Charleston Blue."

1970 (R) 97m/C Godfrey Cambridge, Raymond St. Jacques, Calvin Lockhart, Judy Pace, Redd Foxx, John Anderson, Emily Yancy, J.D. Cannon, Teddy Wilson, Eugene Roche, Cleavon Little, Lou Jacobi; **D:** Ossie Davis; **W:** Ossie Davis. **VHS** ★★★

The Count of Monte Cristo A true swashbuckling revenge tale about Edmond Dantes, who unjustly spends years in prison. After escaping, he gains ever so sweet and served quite cold revenge. Adaptation of the Alexandre Dumas classic.

1934 114m/B Robert Donat, Elissa Landi, Louis Calhern, Sidney Blackmer, Irene Hervey, Raymond Walburn, O.P. Heggie; **D:** Rowland V. Lee. **VHS, Beta** ★★★

Country Girl In the role that completely de-glamorized her (and won her an Oscar), Kelly plays the wife of alcoholic singer Crosby who tries to make a comeback with the help of director Holden. One of Crosby's four dramatic parts, undoubtedly one of his best. Seaton won an Oscar for his adaptation of the Clifford Odets play. Remade in 1982. ♪ The Search is Through; Dissertation on the State of Bliss; It's Mine, It's Yours; The Land Around Us.

1954 104m/B Bing Crosby, Grace Kelly,

William Holden, Gene Reynolds, Anthony Ross; **D:** George Seaton; **W:** George Seaton. Academy Awards '54: Best Actress (Kelly), Best Screenplay; Golden Globe Awards '55: Best Actress—Drama (Kelly); National Board of Review Awards '54: 10 Best Films of the Year, Best Actress (Kelly); Nominations: Academy Awards '54: Best Actor (Crosby), Best Black and White Cinematography, Best Director (Seaton), Best Picture, Best Art Direction/Set Decoration (B & W). **VHS, Beta** ★★★1/2

Coup de Torchon Set in 1938 French West Africa, Noiret plays corrupt police chief Lucien Cordier who is consistently harrassed by his community, particularly by the town pimp. He usually overlooks the pimp's crimes, but when Cordier catches him and a friend shooting at plague victims' bodies floating down the river he decides to murder them in cold blood. Based on the novel "POP 1280" by Jim Thompson. In French with English subtitles. **AKA:** Clean Slate.

1981 128m/C *FR* Philippe Noiret, Isabelle Huppert, Guy Marchand, Stephane Audran, Eddy Mitchell, Jean-Pierre Marielle; **D:** Bertrand Tavernier; **W:** Bertrand Tavernier. Nominations: Academy Awards '81: Best Foreign Language Film. **VHS** ★★★

Courage under Fire Army Col. Nat Serling (Washington) is unexpectedly assigned to review the candidacy of Capt. Karen Emma Walden (Ryan, seen only in flashbacks) to receive the posthumous Medal of Honor for bravery in combat. A Gulf War Medevac pilot, Walden would be the first woman awarded the honor if Serling can figure out the truth from her surviving crew's wildly conflicting reports. Ironically, Serling's dealing with a guilt complex since four members of his tank unit died in the war under friendly fire. Stellar performances, including a frightening one by Phillips. Based on the novel by Duncan, who also did the screenplay; Washington and director Zwick previously worked together on "Glory."

1996 (R) 120m/C Denzel Washington, Meg Ryan, Matt Damon, Lou Diamond Phillips, Scott Glenn, Michael Moriarty, Regina Taylor, Bronson Pinchot, Sean Astin, Seth Gilliam, Tim Guinee, Ken Jenkins, Kathleen Widdoes; **D:** Edward Zwick; **W:** Patrick Sheane Duncan; **M:** James Horner. **VHS,** ★★★

Court Jester Swashbuckling comedy stars Danny Kaye as a former circus clown who teams up with a band of outlaws trying to dethrone a tyrant king. Kaye poses as the court jester so he can learn of the evil king's intentions. Filled with more color, more song, and more truly funny lines than any three comedies put together, this is Kaye's best performance. ♪ They'll Never Outfox the Fox; Baby, Let Me Take You Dreaming; My Heart Knows a Lovely Song; The Maladjusted Jester.

1956 101m/C Danny Kaye, Glynis Johns, Basil Rathbone, Angela Lansbury, Cecil Parker, John Carradine, Mildred Natwick, Robert Middleton; **D:** Norman Panama, Melvin Frank; **W:** Norman Panama. **VHS, Beta, LV** ★★★1/2

The Court Martial of Billy Mitchell Terrific courtroom drama depicts the secret trial of Billy Mitchell, head of the Army Air Service in the 1920s, who predicted the role of airpower in subsequent warfare and the danger of war with Japan. Mitchell incurred the wrath of the military by publicly faulting the lack of U.S. preparedness for invasion. Steiger is outstanding as the attorney; Cooper is great as Mitchell. Debut for Montgomery. **AKA:** One-Man Mutiny.

1955 100m/C Gary Cooper, Charles Bickford, Ralph Bellamy, Rod Steiger, Elizabeth Montgomery, Fred Clark, James Daly, Jack Lord, Peter Graves, Darren McGavin, Robert Simon, Jack Perrin, Charles Dingle; **D:** Otto Preminger. Nominations: Academy Awards '55: Best Story & Screenplay. **VHS, LV** ★★★

The Court Martial of Jackie Robinson True story of a little known chapter in the life of the famous athlete. During his stint in the Army, Robinson refused to take a back seat on a bus and subsequently faced the possibility of court martial. Originally made for cable television.

1990 (R) 94m/C Andre Braugher, Daniel Stern, Ruby Dee, Stan Shaw, Paul Dooley, Bruce Dern; **D:** Larry Peerce; **W:** Dennis Lynton Clark. **VHS, Beta** ★★★1/2

The Courtship of Eddie's Father A clever nine-year-old boy plays matchmaker for his widowed dad in this rewarding family comedy-drama (the inspiration for the TV series). Some plot elements are outdated, but young Howard's performance is terrific; he would later excel at direction. Based on the novel by Mark Toby.

1962 117m/C Glenn Ford, Shirley Jones, Stella Stevens, Dina Merrill, Ron Howard, Jerry Van Dyke; **D:** Vincente Minnelli; **W:** John Gay. **VHS** ★★★

Cousin, Cousine Pleasant French comedy about distant cousins who meet at a round of family parties, funerals, and weddings and become

friends, but their relationship soon becomes more than platonic. Remade in the U.S. in 1989 as "Cousins." In French with English subtitles.

1976 (R) 95m/C FR Marie-Christine Barrault, Marie-France Pisier, Victor Lanoux, Guy Marchand, Ginette Garcin, Sybil Maas; **D:** Jean-Charles Tacchella; **M:** Gerard Anfosso. Cesar Awards '76: Best Supporting Actress (Pisier); National Board of Review Awards '76: 5 Best Foreign Films of the Year; Nominations: Academy Awards '76: Best Actress (Barrault), Best Foreign Language Film, Best Original Screenplay. **VHS, Beta, LV** ★★★1/2

The Cousins Set against the backdrop of Parisian student life, two very different cousins (one twisted, the other saintly) vie for the hand of Mayniel. This country mouse, city mouse adult fable ultimately depicts the survival of the fittest. Chabrol's lovely but sad second directorial effort. **AKA:** Les Cousins.

1959 112m/B FR Jean-Claude Brialy, Gerard Blain, Juliette Mayniel, Claude Cerval, Genevieve Cluny; **D:** Claude Chabrol; **W:** Claude Chabrol. **VHS** ★★★

Cover Girl A vintage wartime musical about a girl who must decide between a nightclub career and a future as a cover model. Hayworth is beautiful, Kelly dances like a dream, and Silvers and Arden are hilarious. Cinematography by Rudolph Mate. ♪ Cover Girl; Sure Thing; Make Way For Tomorrow; Put Me to the Test; Long Ago and Far Away; That's the Best of All; The Show Must Go On; Who's Complaining?; Poor John.

1944 107m/C Rita Hayworth, Gene Kelly, Phil Silvers, Otto Kruger, Lee Bowman, Jinx Falkenberg, Eve Arden, Edward Brophy, Anita Colby; **D:** Charles Vidor; **M:** Ira Gershwin, Jerome Kern. Academy Awards '44: Best Score; Nominations: Academy Awards '44: Best Color Cinematography, Best Interior Decoration, Best Song ("Long Ago and Far Away"), Best Sound. **VHS, Beta, LV** ★★★

The Cowboys Wayne stars as a cattle rancher who is forced to hire eleven schoolboys to help him drive his cattle 400 miles to market. Clever script makes this one of Wayne's better Westerns. Carradine's film debut. Inspired the television series. Laserdisc available in widescreen letterbox edition.

1972 (PG) 128m/C John Wayne, Roscoe Lee Browne, A. Martinez, Bruce Dern, Colleen Dewhurst, Slim Pickens, Robert Carradine, Clay O'Brien; **D:** Mark Rydell; **W:** Harriet Frank Jr., Irving Ravetch; **M:** John Williams. **VHS, Beta, LV** ★★★

Craig's Wife A classic soap opera about a pitiful woman driven to total ruin by her desire for social acceptance and material wealth. Russell makes her surprisingly sympathetic. Based on a Pulitzer Prize-winning George Kelly play. Remake of a silent film, was also remade as "Harriet Craig."
1936 75m/B Rosalind Russell, John Boles, Alma Kruger, Jane Darwell, Billie Burke; *D:* Dorothy Arzner. **VHS, Beta ★★★**

The Cranes Are Flying When her lover goes off to fight during WWII, a girl is seduced by his cousin. Touching love story is free of politics. Filmed in Russia; English subtitles. *AKA:* Letyat Zhuravit.
1957 91m/B *RU* Tatyana Samoilova, Alexei Batalov, Vasily Merkuryev, A. Shvorin; *D:* Mikhail Kalatozov. Cannes Film Festival '58: Best Film. **VHS, Beta, LV ★★★1/2**

Crazy from the Heart Sweet made-for-cable TV tale of a high school principal in a small south Texas town who discovers the romance of her life one weekend with a Mexican janitor. Strong, nuanced performances from Lahti and Blades make this chestnut of a story work beautifully, with able help from supporting actors.
1991 104m/C Christine Lahti, Ruben Blades, Mary Kay Place, Brent Spiner, William Russ, Louise Latham, Tommy Muntz, Robin Lively, Bibi Besch, Kamala Lopez; *D:* Thomas Schlamme. **VHS, Beta, LV ★★★**

Crazy Horse TV bio of the Oglala Sioux warrior (Greyeyes) whose home in the Black Hills of South Dakota was threatened by western expansion and the constant breaking of government treaties. As war chief, Crazy Horse, along with Teton Sioux leader Sitting Bull (Schellenberg), lead the Cheyenne and Sioux against Custer (Horton) at the battle of Little Bighorn. They elude capture but constant harassment by troops lead to Crazy Horse's surrender and death in 1877, betrayed by both the whites and some of his own people. Gripping story with a fine cast.
1996 120m/C Michael Greyeyes, Jimmy Herman, Wes Studi, Irene Bedard, Peter Horton, John Finn, Steve Reevis, Gordon Tootoosis, August Schellenberg, Sheldon Peters Wolfchild, Ned Beatty; *D:* John Irvin; *W:* Robert Schenkkan; *M:* Lennie Niehaus. **VHS ★★★**

The Crazy Ray The classic silent fantasy about a mad scientist who endeavors to put the whole population of Paris in a trance. Vintage Clair nonsense. *AKA:* Paris Qui Dort.
1922 60m/B *FR* Henri Rollan, Albert Prejean, Marcel Vallee, Madeleine Rodrigue; *D:* Rene Clair. **VHS, Beta ★★★**

Creature from the Black Lagoon An anthropological expedition in the Amazon stumbles upon the Gill-Man, a prehistoric humanoid fish monster who takes a fancy to fetching Adams, a coed majoring in "science," but the humans will have none of it. Originally filmed in 3-D, this was one of the first movies to sport top-of-the-line underwater photography and remains one of the most enjoyable monster movies ever made. Gershenson's score became a "Creature Features" standard. Based on a story by Maurice Zimm. Sequels: "Revenge of the Creature" and "The Creature Walks Among Us."
1954 79m/B Richard Carlson, Julie Adams, Richard Denning, Antonio Moreno, Whit Bissell, Nestor Paiva, Ricou Browning; *D:* Jack Arnold; *W:* Arthur Ross; *M:* Hans J. Salter. **VHS, Beta, LV ★★★**

Cria The award-winning story of a nine-year-old girl's struggle for maturity in a hostile adult world. In Spanish with English subtitles. *AKA:* Cria Cuervos; Raise Ravens.
1976 (PG) 115m/C *SP* Geraldine Chaplin, Ana Torrent, Conchita Perez; *D:* Carlos Saura. Cannes Film Festival '76: Grand Jury Prize; National Board of Review Awards '77: 5 Best Foreign Films of the Year; Nominations: Cannes Film Festival '76: Best Film. **VHS, Beta, LV ★★★**

Cries and Whispers As a woman dies slowly of tuberculosis, three women care for her: her two sisters, one sexually repressed, the other promiscuous, and her servant. The sisters remember family love and closeness, but are too afraid to see death in the face to aid their sister. Only the servant can touch her in her dying and only the servant believes in God and his will. Beautiful imagery, focused through a nervous camera, which lingers on the meaningless and whisks away from the meaningful. Absolute mastery of cinematic art by Bergman. *AKA:* Viskingar Och Rop.
1972 (R) 91m/C *SW* Harriet Andersson, Ingrid Thulin, Liv Ullmann, Kary Sylway, Erland Josephson, Henning Moritzen, Sven Nykvist; *D:* Ingmar Bergman; *W:* Ingmar Bergman. Academy Awards '73: Best Cinematography; National Board of Review Awards '73: 5 Best Foreign Films of the Year, Best Director (Bergman); National Society of Film Critics Awards '72: Best Cinematography, Best Screenplay; Nominations: Academy Awards '73: Best Costume Design, Best Director (Bergman),

Best Picture, Best Story & Screenplay.
VHS, Beta, LV ★★★

Crime and Punishment Pared down but well-executed version of the Dostoyevski novel. Lorre is superb as Raskolnikov, who robs and murders an elderly pawnbroker. Believing he has committed the perfect murder, he accepts the invitation of police inspector Porfiry (Arnold) to observe the investigation. Gradually Raskolnikov's conscience begins to overwhelm him as Porfiry slowly works to wring a confession from the killer. Von Sternberg's subdued directorial approach worked well to explore the psychological aspects of guilt, although the melodramatic French film version (released at the same time) scored better with the critics.
1935 88m/B Peter Lorre, Edward Arnold, Marian Marsh, Tala Birell, Elisabeth Risdon, Robert Allen, Douglass Dumbrille, Gene Lockhart; **D:** Josef von Sternberg; **W:** S.K. Lauren, Joseph Anthony. **VHS ★★★**

The Crime of Monsieur Lange Charming French socialist fantasy where workers at a publishing company turn the business into a thriving cooperative while their evil boss is gone. When he returns, worker Lefevre plots to kill him. Rather talky, but humorous. In French with subtitles. French script booklet also available. **AKA:** Le Crime de Monsieur Lange.
1936 90m/B *FR* Rene Lefevre, Jules Berry, Florelle, Sylvia Bataille, Jean Daste, Nadia Sibirskaia; **D:** Jean Renoir; **W:** Jacques Prevert. **VHS, Beta ★★★**

Crimes & Misdemeanors One of Allen's most mature films, exploring a whole range of moral ambiguities through the parallel and eventually interlocking stories of a nebbish filmmaker—who agrees to make a profile of a smug Hollywood television comic and then sabotages it—and an esteemed ophthalmologist who is being threatened with exposure by his neurotic mistress. Intriguing mix of drama and comedy few directors could pull off. Look for Daryl Hannah in an unbilled cameo.
1989 (PG-13) 104m/C Martin Landau, Woody Allen, Alan Alda, Mia Farrow, Joanna Gleason, Anjelica Huston, Jerry Orbach, Sam Waterston, Claire Bloom, Jenny Nichols, Caroline Aaron; **Cameos:** Daryl Hannah, Nora Ephron, Jerry Zaks, Sven Nykvist; **D:** Woody Allen; **W:** Woody Allen. National Board of Review Awards '89: Best Supporting Actor (Alda); New York Film Critics Awards '89: Best Supporting Actor (Alda); Writers Guild of America '89: Best Original Screenplay; Nominations: Academy Awards '89: Best Director (Allen), Best Original Screenplay, Best Supporting Actor (Landau). **VHS, Beta, LV ★★★**

Crimes of Dr. Mabuse Supernatural horror classic about the evil Dr. Mabuse controlling an underworld empire while confined to an insane asylum. One of the best "mad doctor" movies ever made. Also known as "The Testament of Dr. Mabuse" or "The Last Will of Dr. Mabuse."
1932 120m/B *GE* Rudolf Klein-Rogge, Otto Wernicke, Gustav Diesl, Karl Meixner; **D:** Fritz Lang. **VHS ★★★1/2**

Crimes of Passion Vintage whacked-out Russell, not intended for the kiddies. A business-like fashion designer becomes a kinky prostitute at night. A disturbed street preacher makes her the heroine of his erotic fantasies. A dark terrifying vision of the underground sex world and moral hypocrisy. Sexually explicit and violent, with an extremely black comedic center. Turner's portrayal is honest and believable, Perkins overacts until he nearly gets a nosebleed, but it's all for good effect. Cut for "R" rating to get it in the theatres; this version restores some excised footage. Also available in rated version.
1984 101m/C Kathleen Turner, Anthony Perkins, Annie Potts, John Laughlin, Bruce Davison, Norman Burton; **D:** Ken Russell; **W:** Barry Sandler; **M:** Rick Wakeman. Los Angeles Film Critics Association Awards '84: Best Actress (Turner). **VHS, Beta, LV ★★★**

The Criminal Life of Archibaldo de la Cruz Seeing the death of his governess has a lasting effect on a boy. He grows up to be a demented cretin whose failure with women leads him to conspire to kill every one he meets, a task at which he also fails. Hilarious, bitter Bunuelian diatribe. In Spanish with English subtitles. **AKA:** Ensayo de un Crimen; Rehearsal for a Crime.
1955 95m/B *MX SP* Ernesto Alonso, Ariadne Welter, Rita Macedo, Rodolfo Landa, Andrea Palma, Miroslava Stern; **D:** Luis Bunuel. **VHS, Beta ★★★**

Crimson Pirate An 18th-century buccaneer pits his wits and brawn against the might of a ruthless Spanish nobleman. Considered by many to be one of the best swashbucklers, laced with humor and enthusiastically paced. Showcase for Lancaster and Cravat's acrobatic talents.
1952 104m/C *GB* Burt Lancaster, Eva Bartok, Torin Thatcher, Christopher Lee,

Nick Cravat; **D:** Robert Siodmak. **VHS, Beta, LV** ★★★½

Crimson Tide Mutiny erupts aboard the submarine USS Alabama as Captain Ramsey (Hackman) and his Executive Officer Hunter (Washington) clash over the validity of orders to launch the sub's missiles. Ramsey, who wants to fire the missiles, and Hunter, who refuses to comply until the message is verified, battle for control of the sub. Suspenseful and well-paced thriller lets Hackman and Washington show off their considerable screen presence, while Bruckheimer, Simpson, and Scott show that they haven't lost any of their trademark big-budget, testosterone-laden flash. Original screenplay went under the knife of a number of script doctors, most notably Quentin Tarantino.
1995 (R) 116m/C Gene Hackman, Denzel Washington, George Dzundza, Viggo Mortensen, James Gandolfini, Matt Craven, Lillo Brancato, Danny Nucci, Steve Zahn, Rick Schroder, Vanessa Bell Calloway, Rocky Carroll; **Cameos:** Jason Robards Jr.; **D:** Tony Scott; **W:** Michael Schiffer, Richard P. Henrick, Dariusz Wolski; **M:** Hans Zimmer. Nominations: Academy Awards '95: Best Film Editing, Best Sound. **VHS, LV** ★★★

Crisis at Central High A dramatic television re-creation of the events leading up to the 1957 integration of Central High in Little Rock, Arkansas. Based on teacher Elizabeth Huckaby's journal. Emmy-nominated performance by Woodward as Huckaby.
1980 120m/C Joanne Woodward, Charles Durning, William Ross, Henderson Forsythe; **D:** Lamont Johnson; **M:** Billy Goldenberg. **VHS, Beta** ★★★

Criss Cross A classic grade-B film noir, in which an armored car driver is suckered into a burglary by his ex-wife and her hoodlum husband. Multiple back-stabbings and double-crossings ensue.
1948 98m/B Burt Lancaster, Yvonne De Carlo, Dan Duryea, Stephen McNally, Richard Long, Tony Curtis; **D:** Robert Siodmak; **W:** Daniel Fuchs; **M:** Miklos Rozsa. **VHS, Beta** ★★★

Crocodile Dundee New York reporter Sue Charlton is assigned to the Outback to interview living legend Mike Dundee. When she finally locates the man, she is so taken with him that she brings him back to New York with her. There, the naive Aussie wanders about, amazed at the wonders of the city and unwittingly charming everyone he comes in contact with, from high-society transves-

tites to street hookers. One of the surprise hits of 1986.
1986 (PG-13) 98m/C AU Paul Hogan, Linda Kozlowski, John Meillon, David Gulpilil, Mark Blum; **D:** Peter Faiman; **W:** Paul Hogan, John Cornell; **M:** Peter Best. Golden Globe Awards '87: Best Actor—Musical/Comedy (Hogan); Nominations: Academy Awards '86: Best Original Screenplay. **VHS, Beta, LV, 8mm** ★★★½

Crossfire A Jewish hotel guest is murdered and three soldiers just back from Europe are suspected of the crime. The first Hollywood film that explored racial bigotry. Due to the radical nature of its plot, the director and the producer were eventually black-listed for promoting "un-American" themes. Loosely based on Richard Brooks' "The Brick Foxhole."
1947 86m/B Robert Young, Robert Mitchum, Robert Ryan, Gloria Grahame, Paul Kelly; **D:** Edward Dmytryk. Edgar Allan Poe Awards '47: Best Screenplay; National Board of Review Awards '47: 10 Best Films of the Year; Nominations: Academy Awards '46: Best Picture; Academy Awards '47: Best Director (Dmytryk), Best Screenplay, Best Supporting Actor (Ryan), Best Supporting Actress (Grahame). **VHS, Beta** ★★★½

Crossing Delancey Jewish woman (Bozyk), in old world style, plays matchmaker to her independent thirtysomething granddaughter. Charming modern-day New York City fairytale deftly manipulates cliches and stereotypes. Lovely performance from Irving as the woman whose heart surprises her. Riegert is swell playing the gentle but never wimpy suitor. Perfectly cast Bozyk was a star on the Yiddish vaudeville stage, this is her film debut. Appealing music by the Roches, with Suzzy Roche giving a credible performance as Irving's friend. Adapted for the big screen by Sandler from her play of the same name.
1988 (PG) 97m/C Amy Irving, Reizl Bozyk, Peter Riegert, Jeroen Krabbe, Sylvia Miles, Suzzy Roche, George Martin, John Bedford Lloyd, Rosemary Harris, Amy Wright, Claudia Silver; **D:** Joan Micklin Silver; **W:** Susan Sandler. **VHS, Beta, LV, 8mm** ★★★

The Crowd A look at the day-to-day trials of a working-class family set against the backdrop of wealthy society. True-to-life, it's peppered with some happy moments, too. One of the best silent films. Available on laserdisc as a double feature with another '20s classic, "The Wind."
1928 104m/B Eleanor Boardman, James Murray, Bert Roach, Daniel G. Tomlinson,

C

▲

Dell Henderson, Lucy Beaumont; *D:* King Vidor. Nominations: Academy Awards '28: Best Director (Vidor). **VHS, Beta, LV**
★★★★

The Crucified Lovers A shy scroll-maker falls in love with his master's wife. Excellent Japanese tragedy with fine performances all around. *AKA:* Chikamatsu Monogatari.
1954 100m/B *JP* Kazuo Hasegawa, Kyoko Kagawa, Yoko Minamida, Eitaro Shindo, Sakae Ozawa; *D:* Kenji Mizoguchi. **VHS**
★★★1/2

Crumb Countercultural documentary looking at the life of underground cartoonist Robert Crumb—'60s satirist and social misfit who created such drug and sex characters as Fritz the Cat and Mr. Natural. Crumb's extraordinarily dysfunctional family play a significant role, with his mother and two brothers, elder brother Charles and younger brother Max, also interviewed as well as Crumb's friends and current and former wives. The dead abusive father also plays a part. Director Zwigoff spent six years filming his material, and gained wider distribution for his work after taking the Grand Jury prize at Sundance.
1994 (R) 119m/C *D:* Terry Zwigoff. National Society of Film Critics Awards '95: Best Documentary; Sundance Film Festival '95: Best Cinematography, Grand Jury Prize. **VHS, LV** ★★★1/2

Cry-Baby An homage and spoof of '50s teen-rock melodramas by the doyen of cinematic Bad Taste, involving a terminal bad-boy high schooler who goes with a square blond and starts an inter-class rumble. Musical numbers, throwaway gags and plenty of knee-bending odes to Elvis, with a weak story supported by offbeat celeb appearances.
1990 (PG-13) 85m/C Johnny Depp, Amy Locane, Polly Bergen, Traci Lords, Ricki Lake, Iggy Pop, Susan Tyrrell, Patty Hearst, Kim McGuire, Darren E. Burrows, Troy Donahue, Willem Dafoe, David Nelson, Mink Stole, Joe Dallesandro, Joey Heatherton, Robert Walsh; *D:* John Waters; *W:* John Waters; *M:* Patrick Williams. **VHS, Beta, LV** ★★★

A Cry in the Dark Tight film story of the infamous Australian murder trial of Lindy Chamberlain, who was accused of killing her own baby, mostly because of the intensely adverse public opinion, aroused by vicious press, that surrounded the case. Chamberlain blamed the death on a wild dingo dog. Near-documentary style, with Streep excellent as the religious, unknowable mother. Based on the book "Evil Angels" by John Bryson. This case was also detailed in the film "Who Killed Baby Azaria?" *AKA:* Evil Angels.
1988 (PG-13) 120m/C *AU* Meryl Streep, Sam Neill, Bruce Myles, Charles Tingwell, Nick Tate, Neil Fitzpatrick, Maurice Fields, Lewis Fitz-gerald; *D:* Fred Schepisi; *W:* Fred Schepisi, Robert Caswell; *M:* Bruce Smeaton. Australian Film Institute '89: Best Actor (Neill), Best Actress (Streep), Best Film; Cannes Film Festival '89: Best Actress (Streep); New York Film Critics Awards '88: Best Actress (Streep); Nominations: Academy Awards '88: Best Actress (Streep). **VHS, Beta, LV, 8mm** ★★★1/2

Cry, the Beloved Country A black country minister travels to Johannesberg to be with his son after the youth is accused of killing a white man. Through the events of the trial, the horror, oppression, and destruction of South Africa's apartheid system are exposed. Startling and moving, the first entertainment feature set against the backdrop of apartheid. Still trenchant; based on the novel by Alan Paton. *AKA:* African Fury.
1951 111m/B *GB* Canada Lee, Charles Carson, Sidney Poitier, Joyce Carey, Geoffrey Keen; *D:* Zoltan Korda. **VHS** ★★★1/2

Cry, the Beloved Country Alan Paton's classic South African apartheid novel (first filmed in 1951) depicts a Zulu Christian pastor and a wealthy white farmer finding common ground through personal loss—both of their sons were killed in regional violence. Rural black minister Stephen Kumalo (Jones) travels to Johannesburg only to discover his sister (Kente) is a prostitute, his younger brother John (Dutton) no longer believes in Christianity, and his son is in prison for the murder of a white man. That man turns out to be the son of rich farmer James Jarvis (Harris), from Kumalo's own village. Both Jones and Harris turn in wonderfully understated performances in this hopeful tale of potential racial harmony.
1995 (PG-13) 120m/C James Earl Jones, Richard Harris, Charles S. Dutton, Leleti Khumalo, Dambisa Kente, Vusi Kunene, Eric Miyeni, Ian Robers, *D:* Darrell Roodt; *W:* Ronald Atwood; *M:* John Barry. Nominations: Screen Actors Guild Award '95: Best Actor (Jones). **VHS, LV** ★★★

The Crying Game PR lesson in how to launch a small movie into the hypersphere and ensure critical silence on salient characterization. Jordan's gritty drama is on par with his best, a

C

complex blend of violence, love, betrayal, guilt, and redemption and is not about what it seems to be about much of the time. Wonderful performances by all, including Rea as the appealing, conscience-stricken Fergus; Richardson as the cold, violent IRA moll Jude; and Davidson, in a film debut, as the needy, charismatic Dil. Whitaker is terrific in his 15 minutes of intense screen time. Filled with definite surprises and unexpected pleasures. Title is taken from a top-5 British hit of 1964, three versions of which are heard.

1992 (R) 112m/C *IR* Stephen Rea, Jaye Davidson, Miranda Richardson, Forest Whitaker, Adrian Dunbar, Jim Broadbent, Ralph Brown, Breffini McKenna, Joe Savino, Birdie Sweeney, Andre Bernard; *D:* Neil Jordan; *W:* Neil Jordan; *M:* Anne Dudley. Academy Awards '92: Best Original Screenplay; Australian Film Institute '93: Best Foreign Film; Chicago Film Critics Awards '92: Best Foreign Film; Independent Spirit Awards '93: Best Foreign Film; Los Angeles Film Critics Association Awards '92: Best Foreign Film; New York Film Critics Awards '92: Best Screenplay, Best Supporting Actress (Richardson); Writers Guild of America '92: Best Original Screenplay; Nominations: Academy Awards '92: Best Actor (Rea), Best Director (Jordan), Best Film Editing, Best Picture, Best Supporting Actor (Davidson). **VHS, LV ★★★1/2**

Cul de Sac A macabre, psychological thriller set in a dreary castle on a small island off the British coast. Pleasence is an eccentric, middle-aged hermit living acrimoniously with his young, nympho wife (Dorleac) when their home is invaded by two wounded gangsters (Stander and MacGowran), who proceed to hold the couple hostage. MacGowran soon dies of his wounds, leaving Stander and Pleasence to fight it out, encouraged by the luscious Dorleac, who finds her fun where she can. A bleak, sinister film considered one of Polanski's best.

1966 111m/C *GB* Donald Pleasence, Francoise Dorleac, Lionel Stander, Jack MacGowran, Jacqueline Bisset; *D:* Roman Polanski; *W:* Roman Polanski, Gerard Brach. **VHS ★★★**

Curse of the Demon A famous psychologist investigates a colleague's mysterious death and enters a world of demonology and the occult, climaxing in a confrontation with a cult's patron demon. Superb thriller based upon the story "Casting the Runes" by M.R. James. *AKA:* Night of the Demon.

1957 81m/B *GB* Dana Andrews, Peggy Cummins, Niall MacGinnis, Maurice Denham; *D:* Jacques Tourneur; *W:* Charles Bennett. **VHS, Beta, LV ★★★1/2**

Cyrano de Bergerac Edmund Rostand's famous story of a large nosed yet poetic cavalier, who finds himself too ugly to be loved. He bears the pain of his devotion to Roxanne from afar, and helps the handsome but tongue-tied Christian to romance her. Ferrer became famous for this role, which won him an Oscar. Based on Brian Hooke's translation of the play. Also available colorized.

1950 112m/B Jose Ferrer, Mala Powers, William Prince, Elena Verdugo, Morris Carnovsky; *D:* Michael Gordon; *W:* Carl Foreman; *M:* Dimitri Tiomkin. Academy Awards '50: Best Actor (Ferrer); Golden Globe Awards '51: Best Actor—Drama (Ferrer); National Board of Review Awards '50: 10 Best Films of the Year. **VHS, LV ★★★★**

Cyrano de Bergerac Depardieu brings to exhilarating life Rostand's well-loved play about the brilliant but grotesque-looking swordsman/poet, afraid of nothing—except declaring his love to the beautiful Roxanne. One of France's costliest modern productions, a multi-award winner for its cast, costumes, music and sets. English subtitles (by Anthony Burgess) are designed to capture the intricate rhymes of the original French dialogue.

1990 (PG) 135m/C *FR* Gerard Depardieu, Jacques Weber, Anne Brochet, Vincent Perez, Roland Bertin, Josiane Stoleru, Phillipe Volter, Philippe Morier-Genoud, Pierre Maguelon; *D:* Jean-Paul Rappeneau; *W:* Jean-Claude Carriere, Jean-Paul Rappeneau. Academy Awards '90: Best Costume Design; Cannes Film Festival '90: Best Actor (Depardieu); Cesar Awards '91: Best Actor (Depardieu), Best Art Direction/Set Decoration, Best Cinematography, Best Costume Design, Best Director (Rappeneau), Best Film, Best Sound, Best Supporting Actor (Weber), Best Score; Golden Globe Awards '91: Best Foreign Film; Nominations: Academy Awards '90: Best Actor (Depardieu), Best Art Direction/Set Decoration, Best Foreign Language Film, Best Makeup. **VHS, LV ★★★★**

D-Day, the Sixth of June An American soldier has an affair with a Englishwoman weeks before D-Day, where he unhappily finds himself fighting side by side with her husband. Based on the novel by Lionel Shapiro. *AKA:* The Sixth of June.

1956 106m/C Richard Todd, Dana Wynter,

Robert Taylor, Edmond O'Brien, John Williams, Jerry Paris, Richard Stapley; **D:** Henry Koster. **VHS, Beta** ★★★

Daddy Long Legs Far from the great musicals, but enjoyable. An eccentric millionaire glimpses a French orphan and becomes her anonymous benefactor. Her musing over his identity spawns some surreal (often inexplicable) dance numbers, but love conquers all, even lesser Johnny Mercer songs. From a story by Jean Webster, also done in 1919 with Mary Pickford, 1931 with Janet Gaynor and 1935 with Shirley Temple as "Curly Top." ♪ Daddy Long Legs; Something's Got To Give; Sluefoot; Dream; History of the Beat; C-A-T Spells Cat; Welcome Egghead.
1955 126m/C Fred Astaire, Leslie Caron, Terry Moore, Thelma Ritter, Fred Clark, Charlotte Austin, Larry Keating; **D:** Jean Negulesco; **M:** Alex North. Nominations: Academy Awards '55: Best Art Direction/Set Decoration (Color), Best Song ("Something's Gotta Give"), Best Original Score. **VHS, LV** ★★★

Daddy Nostalgia Birkin plays the estranged daughter of Bogarde, who rushes from her home in England to France to be with her seriously ill father. She must come to terms with her feelings for him just as Bogarde must deal with his own mortality. Wonderful performances, with Bogarde a charming and dominating presence. In French with English subtitles. **AKA:** These Foolish Things.
1990 105m/C FR Dirk Bogarde, Jane Birkin, Odette Laure; **D:** Bertrand Tavernier; **W:** Colo Tavernier O'Hagan; **M:** Antoine Duhamel. **VHS** ★★★

Damage The elegant Irons portrays Stephen, a middle-aged, married British politician who has always been completely in control of his life, especially where his feelings are concerned. Then he meets Anna (Binoche), his son's less-than-innocent fiance, and immediately begins an obsessive, wildly sexual affair with her. Stephen should have listened to Anna's warning about herself, "Damaged people are dangerous, they know they can survive," because their passion leads to betrayal and tragedy. Binoche is more icon than human being but the film still hypnotizes as an exploration of passion. Based on the novel by Josephine Hart. An unrated version is also available.
1992 (R) 111m/C FR GB Jeremy Irons, Juliette Binoche, Rupert Graves, Miranda Richardson, Ian Bannen, Leslie Caron, Peter Stormare, Gemma Clark, Julian

Fellowes; **D:** Louis Malle; **W:** David Hare; **M:** Zbigniew Preisner. British Academy Awards '92: Best Supporting Actress (Richardson); Los Angeles Film Critics Association Awards '92: Best Score; Nominations: Academy Awards '92: Best Supporting Actress (Richardson). **VHS, LV** ★★★

Dames A millionaire with fanatically religious beliefs tries to stop the opening of a Broadway show. In the last of the grand budget-breaking spectacles before the "production code" came into being, distinguished choreographer Busby Berkeley took his imagination to the limit: watch for the dancing clothes on an ironing board and dancing girls with puzzle pieces on their backs which form the real Keeler. ♪ Dames; I Only Have Eyes For You; When You Were a Smile on Your Mother's Lips and a Twinkle in Your Father's Eye; Try To See It My Way; The Girl at the Ironing Board.
1934 95m/B Dick Powell, Joan Blondell, Ruby Keeler, ZaSu Pitts, Guy Kibbee, Busby Berkeley; **D:** Ray Enright; **W:** Delmer Daves. **VHS, Beta, LV** ★★★

Damn the Defiant Adventure abounds when Guinness, as captain of the HMS Defiant during the Napoleonic wars, finds himself up against not only the French but his cruel second-in-command (Bogarde) and a mutinous crew as well. In the end, both a fleet-wide mutiny and a French invasion of England are avoided. Much attention is paid to period detail in this well-crafted film. **AKA:** HMS Defiant.
1962 101m/C GB Alec Guinness, Dirk Bogarde, Maurice Denham, Anthony Quayle; **D:** Lewis Gilbert. **VHS, Beta, LV** ★★★

Damn Yankees Musical feature adapted from the Broadway hit. A baseball fan frustrated by his team's lack of success makes a pact with the devil to become the team's new star. Verdon is dynamite as the devil's accomplice. Great Bob Fosse choreography. ♪ Whatever Lola Wants; (You Gotta Have) Heart; Shoeless Joe From Hannibal Mo; Goodbye, Old Girl; A Little Brains, a Little Talent; Who's Got the Pain; Two Lost Souls; There's Something About an Empty Chair; Those Were the Good Old Days. **AKA:** What Lola Wants.
1958 110m/C Gwen Verdon, Ray Walston, Tab Hunter, Jean Stapleton, Russ Brown; **D:** George Abbott, Stanley Donen. Nominations: Academy Awards '58: Best Original Score. **VHS, Beta, LV** ★★★

A Damsel in Distress Astaire falls for an upper-class British girl, whose family wants her to have nothing to do with him. Features memorable songs from the Gershwins. ♪ A Foggy Day in Londontown; Nice Work If You Can Get It; Stiff Upper Lip; Put Me to the Test; I Can't Be Bothered Now; The Jolly Tar and the Milkmaid; Things Are Looking Up; Sing of Spring; Ah Che a Voi Perdoni Iddio.
1937 101m/B Fred Astaire, Joan Fontaine, George Burns, Gracie Allen, Ray Noble, Montagu Love, Reginald Gardiner; **D:** George Stevens; **M:** George Gershwin, George Bassman, Ira Gershwin.
Nominations: Academy Awards '37: Best Interior Decoration. **VHS, Beta, LV ★★★**

Dance Fools Dance Fast-paced drama has Crawford and Bakewell as a pair of spoiled rich kids who are forced to face poverty when the stock market crashes. He meets up with Gable, who's producing liquor illegally, while she gets a job at a newspaper. When Gable arranges something akin to the St. Valentine's Day Massacre, Bakewell's investigative reporting of the situation produces fatal results. The Hays Office had a problem with Crawford and friends appearing in their underwear. Cast notes: Gable was just starting out at MGM, which is why he was billed sixth; the William Holden here is not THE William Holden, and Edwards went on to provide the voice of Jiminy Cricket in "Pinocchio."
1931 82m/B Joan Crawford, Lester Vail, Cliff Edwards, William "Billy" Bakewell, Clark Gable; **D:** Harry Beaumont. **VHS, Beta ★★★**

Dance with a Stranger The engrossing and factual story of Ruth Ellis, who gained notoriety as the last woman hanged in Great Britain. This emotional and sometimes violent film mirrors the sensationalism produced in the 1950s. The film follows Ellis's pre-trial life and her perpetual struggle to maintain her independence. Newcomer Richardson portrays the Marilyn Monroe look-alike barmaid.
1985 (R) 101m/C *GB* Miranda Richardson, Rupert Everett, Ian Holm, Joanne Whalley-Kilmer; **D:** Mike Newell; **W:** Shelagh Delaney. Cannes Film Festival '85: Best Film. **VHS, Beta, LV ★★★1/2**

Dances with Wolves The story of a U.S. Army soldier, circa 1870, whose heroism in battle allows him his pick of posts. His choice, to see the West before it disappears, changes his life. He meets, understands and eventually becomes a member of a Lakota Sioux tribe in the Dakotas. Costner's first directorial attempt proves him a talent of vision and intelligence. This sometimes too objective movie lacks a sense of definitive character, undermining its gorgeous scenery and interesting perspective on the plight of Native Americans. Lovely music and epic proportions. Adapted by Blake from his novel.
1990 (PG-13) 181m/C Kevin Costner, Mary McDonnell, Graham Greene, Rodney Grant, Floyd "Red Crow" Westerman, Tantoo Cardinal, Robert Pastorelli, Charles Rocket, Maury Chaykin, Jimmy Herman, Nathan Lee Chasing His Horse, Wes Studi, Dean Semler; **D:** Kevin Costner; **W:** Michael Blake; **M:** John Barry. Academy Awards '90: Best Adapted Screenplay, Best Cinematography, Best Director (Costner), Best Film Editing, Best Picture, Best Sound, Best Score; Directors Guild of America Awards '90: Best Director (Costner); Golden Globe Awards '91: Best Director (Costner), Best Film—Drama, Best Screenplay; National Board of Review Awards '90: 10 Best Films of the Year, Best Director (Costner); Nominations: Academy Awards '90: Best Actor (Costner), Best Art Direction/Set Decoration, Best Costume Design, Best Supporting Actor (Greene), Best Supporting Actress (McDonnell), Best Original Score. **VHS, Beta, LV ★★★1/2**

Dangerous Liaisons Stylish and absorbing, this adaptation of the Laclos novel and the Christopher Hampton play centers around the relationship of two decadent members of 18th-century French nobility. The two, Close and Malkovich, spend their time testing and manipulating the loves of others. They find love often has a will of its own. Possibly the best of the several versions available. Interesting to comparison-view with director Milos Forman's version of this story, 1989's "Valmont."
1988 (R) 120m/C John Malkovich, Glenn Close, Michelle Pfeiffer, Uma Thurman, Keanu Reeves, Swoosie Kurtz, Mildred Natwick, Peter Capaldi; **D:** Stephen Frears; **W:** Christopher Hampton; **M:** George Fenton, Philippe Rousselot. Academy Awards '88: Best Adapted Screenplay, Best Art Direction/Set Decoration, Best Costume Design; British Academy Awards '89: Best Adapted Screenplay, Best Supporting Actress (Pfeiffer); Writers Guild of America '88: Best Adapted Screenplay; Nominations: Academy Awards '88: Best Actress (Close), Best Picture, Best Supporting Actress (Pfeiffer), Best Original Score. **VHS, Beta, LV, 8mm ★★★**

Dangerous Moves A drama built around the World Chess championship competition between a re-

nowned Russian master and a young, rebellious dissident. The chess game serves as both metaphor and background for the social and political tensions it produces. With English subtitles. *AKA:* La Diagonale du Fou.
1984 (PG) 96m/C *SI* Liv Ullmann, Michel Piccoli, Leslie Caron, Alexandre Arbatt; *D:* Richard Dembo; *W:* Richard Dembo. Academy Awards '84: Best Foreign Language Film. **VHS, Beta, LV** ★★★

Danny Boy Takes place in Ireland where a young saxaphonist witnesses a murder and, in an effort to understand it, sets out to find the killer. Thought-provoking film is meant to highlight the continuing struggles in Ireland.
1984 (R) 92m/C *IR* Stephen Rea, Veronica Quilligan, Honor Heffernan, Marie Kean, Donal McCann, Ray McAnally; *D:* Neil Jordan; *W:* Neil Jordan. **VHS, Beta** ★★★

Danton A sweeping account of the reign of terror following the French Revolution. Focuses on the title character (wonderfully portrayed by Depardieu) and is directed with searching parallels to modern-day Poland by that country's premier filmmaker, Andrzej Wajda. Well-done period sets round out a memorable film. In French with English subtitles.
1982 (PG) 136m/C *PL FR* Gerard Depardieu, Wojciech Pszoniak, Patrice Chereau, Angela Winkler, Boguslaw Linda; *D:* Andrzej Wajda; *W:* Jean-Claude Carriere, Agnieszka Holland, Boleslaw Michalek, Jacek Gasiorowski, Andrzej Wajda. British Academy Awards '83: Best Foreign Film; Cesar Awards '83: Best Director (Wajda); Montreal World Film Festival '83: Best Actor (Depardieu). **VHS, Beta, LV** ★★★★

Darby O'Gill & the Little People Set in Ireland, a roguish old story teller tumbles into a well and visits the land of leprechauns who give him three wishes in order to rearrange his life. When he tries to tell his friends what happened, they think that it is only another one of his stories. A wonderful Disney production (despite its disappointing box-office performance) with wit, charm and an ounce or two of terror.
1959 (G) 93m/C Albert Sharpe, Janet Munro, Sean Connery, Estelle Winwood; *D:* Robert Stevenson. **VHS, Beta, LV** ★★★1/2

Dark Command The story of Quantrell's Raiders who terrorized the Kansas territory during the Civil War until one man came along to put a stop to it. Colorful and talented cast

add depth to the script. Also available colorized.
1940 95m/B John Wayne, Walter Pidgeon, Claire Trevor, Roy Rogers, Marjorie Main, George "Gabby" Hayes; *D:* Raoul Walsh. Nominations: Academy Awards '40: Best Interior Decoration, Best Original Score. **VHS, Beta** ★★★

Dark Eyes An acclaimed Italian film based on a several short stories by Anton Chekov. Mastroianni is a weak-willed Italian, trapped in a marriage of convenience, who falls in love with a mysterious, also married, Russian beauty he meets in a health spa. He embarks on a journey to find her and, perhaps, his lost ideals. Hailed as Mastroianni's consummate performance. In Italian with English subtitles. *AKA:* Les Yeux Noirs; Oci Ciornie.
1987 118m/C *IT* Marcello Mastroianni, Silvana Mangano, Elena Sofonova, Marthe Keller; *D:* Nikita Mikhalkov. Cannes Film Festival '87: Best Actor (Mastroianni); Nominations: Academy Awards '87: Best Actor (Mastroianni). **VHS, Beta** ★★★1/2

Dark Mirror A psychologist and a detective struggle to determine which twin sister murdered a prominent physician. Good and evil siblings finely acted by de Havilland.
1946 85m/B Olivia de Havilland, Lew Ayres, Thomas Mitchell, Garry Owen; *D:* Robert Siodmak. Nominations: Academy Awards '46: Best Story. **VHS** ★★★

Dark Star John Carpenter's directorial debut is a low-budget, sci-fi satire which focuses on a group of scientists whose mission is to destroy unstable planets. During their journey, they battle their alien mascot (who closely resembles a walking beach ball), as well as a "sensitive" and intelligent bombing device which starts to question the meaning of its existence. Enjoyable early feature from John "Halloween" Carpenter and Dan "Aliens" O'Bannon. Fun, weird, and unpredictable.
1974 (G) 95m/C Dan O'Bannon, Brian Narelle; *D:* John Carpenter; *W:* Dan O'Bannon, John Carpenter; *M:* John Carpenter. **VHS, Beta, LV** ★★★

Dark Victory A spoiled young heiress discovers she is dying from a brain tumor. She attempts to pack a lifetime of parties into a few months, but is rescued by her doctor, with whom she falls in love. Classic final scene with Davis at the top of her form. Bogart plays an Irish stable hand, but not especially well. Also available in a colorized version.
1939 106m/B Bette Davis, George Brent,

Geraldine Fitzgerald, Humphrey Bogart, Ronald Reagan, Henry Travers; **D:** Edmund Goulding; **M:** Max Steiner. Nominations: Academy Awards '39: Best Actress (Davis), Best Picture, Best Original Score. **VHS, Beta, LV** ★★★1/2

Darkman Raimi's disfigured-man-seeks-revenge suspenser is comic-book kitsch cross-pollinated with a strain of gothic horror. Neeson plays a scientist who's on the verge of discovering the key to cloning body parts; brutally attacked by the henchmen of a crooked politico, his lab is destroyed and he's left for dead. Turns out he's not dead—just horribly disfigured and a wee bit chafed—and he stalks his deserving victims from the shadows, using his lab know-how to disguise his rugged bad looks. Exquisitely violent. Montage by Pablo Ferro.
1990 (R) 96m/C Liam Neeson, Frances McDormand, Larry Drake, Colin Friels, Nelson Mashita, Jenny Agutter, Rafael H. Robledo; **D:** Sam Raimi; **W:** Sam Raimi, Ivan Raimi; **M:** Danny Elfman. **VHS, Beta, LV** ★★★

Darling Young amoral model tries to hold boredom at bay by having a number of love affairs. She joins the international jet set and manages to reach the top of European society by marrying a prince. She then learns what an empty life she has. Christie won an Oscar for her portrayal of the disillusioned, cynical young woman.
1965 122m/B GB Julie Christie, Dirk Bogarde, Laurence Harvey; **D:** John Schlesinger; **W:** Frederic Raphael. Academy Awards '65: Best Actress (Christie), Best Costume Design (B & W), Best Story; British Academy Awards '65: Best Actor (Bogarde), Best Actress (Christie), Best Screenplay; Golden Globe Awards '66: Best Foreign Film; National Board of Review Awards '65: 10 Best Films of the Year, Best Actress (Christie), Best Director (Schlesinger); Nominations: Academy Awards '65: Best Director (Schlesinger), Best Picture. **VHS, Beta, LV** ★★★1/2

Das Boot Superb detailing of life in a German U-boat during WWII. Intense, claustrophobic atmosphere complemented by nail-biting action provides a realistic portrait of the stressful conditions that were endured on these submarines. Excellent performances, especially from Prochnow. With English subtitles. Originally a six-hour special made for German television. Also available in a dubbed version. From the novel by Lothar-Guenther Buccheim. **AKA:** The Boat.

1981 (R) 150m/C GE Juergen Prochnow, Herbert Gronemeyer, Klaus Wennemann, Hubertus Bengsch, Martin Semmelrogge, Bernd Tauber, Erwin Leder, Martin May; **D:** Wolfgang Petersen; **W:** Wolfgang Petersen; **M:** Klaus Doldinger. Nominations: Academy Awards '82: Best Adapted Screenplay, Best Cinematography, Best Director (Petersen), Best Film Editing, Best Sound. **VHS, Beta, LV** ★★★★

Das Testament des Dr. Mabuse The third, and only sound, Mabuse film by Lang. The infamous crime lord/megalomaniac plots the world's destruction from the confines of an asylum cell. In German, with English subtitles. Released as "The Last Will of Dr. Mabuse" in the U.S. in 1943. **AKA:** The Testament of Dr. Mabuse.
1933 122m/B GE Rudolf Klein-Rogge, Otto Wernicke, Gustav Diesl, Karl Meixner; **D:** Fritz Lang. **VHS, Beta** ★★★1/2

Dave Regular guy Dave Kovic (Kline) is a dead ringer for the President, launching him into the White House after the prez suffers a stroke in embarrassing circumstances. Seamless comedy prompts lots of hearty laughs and the feel-good faith that despite the overwhelming odds, everything will turn out just fine. Political cameos abound: look for real-life Senators Alan Simpson, Paul Simon, Howard Metzenbaum, Tom Harkin, and Christopher Dodd as well as the commentators from TV's "The McLaughlin Group," and Stone, poking fun at himself on "Larry King Live," as he tries to convince the public there's a conspiracy going on.
1993 (PG-13) 110m/C Kevin Kline, Sigourney Weaver, Frank Langella, Kevin Dunn, Ving Rhames, Ben Kingsley, Charles Grodin, Faith Prince, Laura Linney, Bonnie Hunt, Parley Baer, Stefan Gierasch, Anna Deavere Smith, Bonnie Bartlett; **Cameos:** Oliver Stone, Arnold Schwarzenegger, Jay Leno, Larry King; **D:** Ivan Reitman; **W:** Gary Ross; **M:** James Newton Howard. Nominations: Academy Awards '93: Best Original Screenplay; Golden Globe Awards '94: Best Actor—Musical/Comedy (Kline), Best Film—Musical/Comedy. **VHS, Beta, LV** ★★★

David and Bathsheba The Bible story comes alive in this lush and colorful Fox production. Peck and Hayward are great together and Peck is properly concerned about the wrath of God over his transgressions. Terrific costumes and special effects, lovely music and a fine supporting cast keep this a notch above other Biblical epics.
1951 116m/C Gregory Peck, Susan

Hayward, Raymond Massey, Kieron Moore, James Robertson Justice, Jayne Meadows, John Sutton, Dennis Hoey, Francis X. Bushman, George Zucco; *D:* Henry King; *W:* Philip Dunne. Nominations: Academy Awards '51: Best Art Direction/Set Decoration (Color), Best Color Cinematography, Best Costume Design (Color), Best Story & Screenplay, Best Original Score. **VHS, LV ★★★**

David and Lisa Director Perry was given an Oscar for this sensitive independently produced film. Adapted from Theodore Isaac Rubin's true case history novel concerning a young man and woman who fall in love while institutionalized for mental illness. Dullea and Margolin are excellent in the title roles of this sleeper. **1962 94m/B** Keir Dullea, Janet Margolin, Howard da Silva, Neva Patterson, Clifton James; *D:* Frank Perry. Nominations: Academy Awards '62: Best Adapted Screenplay, Best Director (Perry). **VHS, Beta, LV ★★★**

David Copperfield Superior adaptation of Charles Dickens' great novel. An orphan grows to manhood in Victorian England with a wide variety of help and harm. Terrific acting by Bartholomew, Fields, Rathbone, and all the rest. Lavish production, lovingly filmed. **1935 132m/B** Lionel Barrymore, W.C. Fields, Freddie Bartholomew, Maureen O'Sullivan, Basil Rathbone, Lewis Stone, Frank Lawton, Madge Evans, Roland Young, Edna May Oliver, Lennox Pawle, Elsa Lanchester, Una O'Connor, Arthur Treacher; *D:* George Cukor; *W:* Howard Estabrook, Hugh Walpole; *M:* Herbert Stothart. National Board of Review Awards '35: 10 Best Films of the Year; Nominations: Academy Awards '35: Best Film Editing, Academy Awards '36: Best Picture. **VHS, Beta, LV ★★★★**

Davy Crockett, King of the Wild Frontier Three episodes of the popular Disney television series are blended together here to present the life and some of the adventures of Davy Crockett. These include his days as an Indian fighter and his gallant stand in defense of the Alamo. Well-done by a splendid cast, the film helped to spread Davy-mania among the children of the 1950s. **1955 (PG) 93m/C** Fess Parker, Buddy Ebsen, Hans Conried, Ray Whiteside, Pat Hogan, William "Billy" Bakewell, Basil Ruysdael, Kenneth Tobey; *D:* Norman Foster; *M:* George Bruns. **VHS, Beta ★★★**

Dawn of the Dead Romero's gruesome sequel to his "Night of the Living Dead." A mysterious plague causes the recently dead to rise from their graves and scour the countryside for living flesh. Very violent, gory, graphic, and shocking, yet not without humor. Gives interesting consideration to the violence created by the living humans in their efforts to save themselves. **1978 126m/C** David Emge, Ken Foree, Gaylen Ross; *D:* George A. Romero; *W:* George A. Romero. **VHS, Beta, LV ★★★1/2**

Dawn Patrol Flynn plays a flight commander whose nerves are shot in this story of the British Royal Flying Corps during WWI. The focus is on the effects that the pressures and deaths have on all those concerned. Fine performances from all in this well-done remake of the 1930 film. **1938 103m/B** Errol Flynn, David Niven, Basil Rathbone, Donald Crisp, Barry Fitzgerald, Melville Cooper; *D:* Edmund Goulding; *M:* Max Steiner. **VHS, Beta ★★★**

The Day After Powerful drama graphically depicts the nuclear bombing of a midwestern city and its after-effects on the survivors. Made for television, and very controversial when first shown, gathering huge ratings and vast media coverage. **1983 122m/C** Jason Robards Jr., JoBeth Williams, John Lithgow, Steve Guttenberg; *D:* Nicholas Meyer. **VHS, Beta, LV ★★★**

A Day at the Races Though it seems labored at times, the brilliance of the brothers Marx still comes through in this rather weak tale of a patient in a sanitorium who convinces horse doctor Groucho to take on running the place. ♪ A Message from the Man in the Moon; On Blue Venetian Waters; Tomorrow is Another Day; All God's Chillun Got Rhythm. **1937 111m/B** Groucho Marx, Harpo Marx, Chico Marx, Sig Rumann, Douglass Dumbrille, Margaret Dumont, Allan Jones, Maureen O'Sullivan; *D:* Sam Wood; *M:* George Bassman. **VHS, Beta, LV ★★★1/2**

Day for Night A wryly affectionate look at the profession of moviemaking—its craft, character, and the personalities that interact against the performances commanded by the camera. In French with English subtitles. *AKA:* La Nuit Americaine. **1973 (PG) 116m/C** *FR* Jean-Pierre Leaud, Jacqueline Bisset, Jean-Pierre Aumont, Valentina Cortese, Alexandra Stewart, Dani, Nathalie Baye, Francois Truffaut; *D:* Francois Truffaut; *W:* Suzanne Schiffman, Jean-Louis Richard, Francois Truffaut; *M:* Georges Delerue. Academy Awards '73: Best Foreign Language Film; British

Academy Awards '73: Best Director (Truffaut), Best Film, Best Supporting Actress (Cortese); National Society of Film Critics Awards '73: Best Director (Truffaut), Best Film, Best Supporting Actress (Cortese); Nominations: Academy Awards '74: Best Director (Truffaut), Best Original Screenplay, Best Supporting Actress (Cortese). **VHS, Beta ★★★★**

A Day in the Country The son of the famed painter gives us the moving tale of a young woman's sudden and intense love for a man she meets while on a picnic with her family. Beautifully adapted from a story by Guy de Maupassant. Renowned photographer Henri Cartier-Bresson contributed to the wonderful cinematography. In French with English subtitles. *AKA:* Une Partie de Campagne.
1946 40m/B *FR* Sylvia Bataille, Georges Darnoux, Jane Marken, Paul Temps; *D:* Jean Renoir. **VHS, Beta ★★★1/2**

The Day of the Jackal Frederick Forsyth's best-selling novel of political intrigue is splendidly brought to the screen by Zinnemann. A brilliant and ruthless assassin hired to kill Charles de Gaulle skirts the international intelligence pool, while intuitive police work to stop him. Tense, suspenseful, beautiful location photography. Excellent acting by Fox, Cusack and Britton.
1973 (PG) 142m/C Edward Fox, Alan Badel, Tony Britton, Derek Jacobi, Cyril Cusack, Olga Georges-Picot; *D:* Fred Zinneman; *M:* Georges Delerue. Nominations: Academy Awards '73: Best Film Editing. **VHS, Beta, LV ★★★1/2**

The Day of the Locust Compelling adaptation of Nathaniel West's novel concerning the dark side of 1930s Hollywood. A no-talent amoral actress's affair with a meek accountant leads to tragedy and destruction. Told from the view of a cynical art director wise to the ways of Hollywood.
1975 (R) 140m/C Donald Sutherland, Karen Black, Burgess Meredith, William Atherton, Billy Barty, Bo Hopkins, Richard Dysart, Geraldine Page; *D:* John Schlesinger; *M:* John Barry, Conrad Hall. National Board of Review Awards '75: 10 Best Films of the Year; Nominations: Academy Awards '75: Best Cinematography, Best Supporting Actor (Meredith). **VHS, Beta, LV ★★★1/2**

Day of the Triffids The majority of Earth's population is blinded by a meteor shower which also causes plant spores to mutate into giant carnivores. Well-done adaptation of John Wyndham's science fiction classic.
1963 94m/C Howard Keel, Janet Scott, Nicole Maurey, Kieron Moore, Mervyn Johns; *D:* Steve Sekely; *W:* Philip Yordan. **VHS, Beta, LV ★★★**

Day of Wrath An involving psychological thriller based on records of witch trials from the early 1600s. An old woman, burned at the stake as a witch, puts a curse on the local parson and his family. Grim and unrelentingly pessimistic, moving from one horrific scene to another, director Dreyer creates a masterpiece of terror. Based on a play by Hans Wiers Jenssen. In Danish with English subtitles. *AKA:* Vredens Dag.
1943 110m/B *DK* Thorkild Roose, Sigrid Neiiendam, Lisbeth Movin, Preben Lerdorff, Anna Svierker; *D:* Carl Theodor Dreyer; *W:* Carl Theodor Dreyer; *M:* Poul Schierbeck. National Board of Review Awards '43: 10 Best Films of the Year. **VHS ★★★★**

The Day the Earth Caught Fire The earth is knocked out of orbit and sent hurtling toward the sun when nuclear testing is done simultaneously at both the North and South Poles. Realistic and suspenseful, this is one of the best of the sci-fi genre.
1961 95m/B Janet Munro, Edward Judd, Leo McKern; *D:* Val Guest; *W:* Val Guest, Wolf Mankowitz. British Academy Awards '61: Best Screenplay. **VHS, Beta ★★★1/2**

The Day the Earth Stood Still A gentle alien lands on Earth to deliver a message of peace and a warning against experimenting with nuclear power. He finds his views echoed by a majority of the population, but not the ones who are in control. In this account based loosely on the story of Christ, Rennie is the visitor backed by the mighty robot Gort. One of the greatest science fiction films of all time.
1951 92m/B Michael Rennie, Patricia Neal, Hugh Marlowe, Sam Jaffe, Frances Bavier, Lock Martin, Bobby Gray; *D:* Robert Wise; *M:* Bernard Herrmann. **VHS, Beta, LV ★★★1/2**

Days of Heaven Drifter Gere, his younger sister, and a woman he claims is his sister become involved with a Texas farmer. Told through the eyes of the younger girl, this is a sweeping vision of the U.S. before WWI. Loss and loneliness, deception, frustration, and anger haunt these people as they struggle to make the land their own. Deservedly awarded an Oscar for breathtaking cinematography.
1978 (PG) 95m/C Richard Gere, Brooke Adams, Sam Shepard, Linda Manz, Stuart Margolin; *D:* Terence Malick; *W:* Terence

Malick; **M:** Ennio Morricone. Academy Awards '78: Best Cinematography; Cannes Film Festival '79: Best Director (Malick); Los Angeles Film Critics Association Awards '78: Best Cinematography; National Board of Review Awards '78: 10 Best Films of the Year; New York Film Critics Awards '78: Best Director (Malick); National Society of Film Critics Awards '78: Best Cinematography, Best Director (Malick), Best Film; Nominations: Academy Awards '78: Best Costume Design, Best Sound, Best Original Score; Cannes Film Festival '79: Best Film. **VHS, Beta, LV ★★★1/2**

Days of Thrills and Laughter Delightful compilation of clips from the era of silent films, showcasing the talents of the great comics as well as daring stuntmen.
1961 93m/B Buster Keaton, Charlie Chaplin, Harold Lloyd, Stan Laurel, Oliver Hardy, Douglas Fairbanks Sr.; **D:** Robert Youngson. **VHS, Beta ★★★1/2**

Days of Wine and Roses A harrowing tale of an alcoholic advertising man who gradually drags his wife down with him into a life of booze. Part of the "A Night at the Movies" series, this tape simulates a 1962 movie evening with a Bugs Bunny cartoon, "Martian Through Georgia," a newsreel, and coming attractions for "Gypsy" and "Rome Adventure." Big screen adaptation of the play originally shown on television. ♩ Days of Wine and Roses.
1962 138m/B Jack Lemmon, Lee Remick, Charles Bickford, Jack Klugman, Jack Albertson; **D:** Blake Edwards; **M:** Henry Mancini, Johnny Mercer. Academy Awards '62: Best Song ("Days of Wine and Roses"); Nominations: Academy Awards '62: Best Actor (Lemmon), Best Actress (Remick), Best Art Direction/Set Decoration (B & W), Best Costume Design (B & W). **VHS, Beta, LV ★★★1/2**

Dazed and Confused A day in the life of a bunch of high schoolers should prove to be a trip back in time for those coming of age in the '70s. Eight seniors facing life after high school have one last year-long hurrah, as they search for Aerosmith tickets and haze the incoming freshmen. Keen characterization by writer/director Linklater captures the spirit of a generation shaped by Watergate, the Vietnam War, feminism, and marijuana. Groovy soundtrack features Alice Cooper, Deep Purple, KISS, and Foghat.
1993 (R) 97m/C Jason London, Rory Cochrane, Sasha Jensen, Wiley Wiggins, Michelle Burke, Adam Goldberg, Anthony Rapp, Marissa Ribisi, Parker Posey; **D:** Richard Linklater; **W:** Richard Linklater. **VHS, LV ★★★**

The Dead The poignant final film by Huston, based on James Joyce's short story. At a Christmas dinner party in turn-of-the-century Dublin, a man discovers how little he knows about his wife when a song reminds her of a cherished lost love. Beautifully captures the spirit of the story while providing Huston an opportunity to create a last lament on the fickle nature of time and life.
1987 (PG) 82m/C *GB* Anjelica Huston, Donal McCann, Marie Kean, Donal Donnelly, Dan O'Herlihy, Helen Carroll, Frank Patterson; **D:** John Huston; **M:** Alex North, Fred Murphy. Independent Spirit Awards '88: Best Director (Huston), Best Supporting Actress (Huston); National Society of Film Critics Awards '87: Best Film; Nominations: Academy Awards '87: Best Adapted Screenplay, Best Costume Design. **VHS, Beta, LV ★★★1/2**

Dead Again Branagh's first film since his brilliant debut as the director/star of "Henry V" again proves him a visionary force on and off camera. As the smart L.A. detective hired to discover the identity of a beautiful, but mute woman, he's realistic, clever, tender and cynical. He finds that he's apparently trapped in a nightmarish cycle of murder begun years before. Literate, lovely to look at, suspenseful, with a sense of humor to match its high style.
1991 (R) 107m/C Kenneth Branagh, Emma Thompson, Andy Garcia, Lois Hall, Richard Easton, Derek Jacobi, Hanna Schygulla, Campbell Scott, Wayne Knight, Christine Ebersole; **Cameos:** Robin Williams; **D:** Kenneth Branagh; **W:** Scott Frank; **M:** Patrick Doyle. National Board of Review Awards '91: 10 Best Films of the Year. **VHS, LV ★★★1/2**

Dead End Sidney Kingsley play, adapted for the big screen by Lillian Hellman, traces the lives of various inhabitants of the slums on New York's Lower East Side as they try to overcome their surroundings. Gritty drama saved from melodrama status by some genuinely funny moments. Film launched the Dead End Kids. ***AKA:*** Cradle of Crime.
1937 92m/B Sylvia Sidney, Joel McCrea, Humphrey Bogart, Wendy Barrie, Claire Trevor, Allen Jenkins, Marjorie Main, Leo Gorcey, Charles Halton; **D:** William Wyler. Nominations: Academy Awards '37: Best Cinematography, Best Interior Decoration, Best Picture, Best Supporting Actress (Trevor). **VHS, Beta, LV ★★★1/2**

Dead Heat on a Merry-Go-Round
Coburn turns in a great performance
as the ex-con who masterminds the
heist of an airport safe. Intricately wo-
ven plot provides suspense and surprises. The film is also notable for the
debut of Ford in a bit part (he has one
line as a hotel messenger).
1966 (R) 108m/C James Coburn, Camilla
Sparv, Aldo Ray, Nina Wayne, Robert
Webber, Rose Marie, Todd Armstrong,
Marian Moses, Severn Darden, Harrison
Ford; **D:** Bernard Girard. **VHS, Beta ★★★**

Dead Man Walking True story of a
nun whose anti-death penalty beliefs
put her in moral crisis with grieving
victims when she becomes the spiritual advisor to a death-row murderer.
Based on the book by Sister Helen
Prejean, Sarandon stars as the nun
who develops a relationship of understanding with inmate Poncelet (Penn),
unwavering in her Christian beliefs
even though Penn's character shows
little or no remorse for the two young
lovers he was accused of murdering.
Penn offers one of the best performances (but worst hair-dos) of his career, while writer/director Robbins
presents both sides of the death-
penalty issue mingled with simple hu-
man compassion.
1995 (R) 122m/C Susan Sarandon, Sean
Penn, Robert Prosky, Raymond J. Barry, R.
Lee Ermey, Celia Weston, Lois Smith; **D:**
Tim Robbins; **W:** Tim Robbins; **M:** David
Robbins. Academy Awards '95: Best
Actress (Sarandon); Independent Spirit
Awards '96: Best Actor (Penn); Screen
Actors Guild Award '95: Best Actress
(Sarandon); Nominations: Academy Awards
'95: Best Actor (Penn), Best Director
(Robbins), Best Song ("Dead Man
Walking"); Australian Film Institute '96:
Best Foreign Film; Golden Globe Awards
'96: Best Actor—Drama (Penn), Best
Actress—Drama (Sarandon), Best
Screenplay; Independent Spirit Awards '96:
Best Supporting Actress (Weston); MTV
Movie Awards '96: Best Female
Performance (Sarandon); Screen Actors
Guild Award '95: Best Actor (Penn). **VHS,
LV ★★★1/2**

Dead of Night The template for
episodic horror films, this suspense
classic, set in a remote country
house, follows the individual nightmares of five houseguests. Redgrave
turns in a chillingly convincing performance as a ventriloquist terrorized
by a demonic dummy. Not recommended for light sleepers. Truly
spine-tingling.
1945 102m/B *GB* Michael Redgrave, Sally
Ann Howes, Basil Radford, Naunton
Wayne, Mervyn Johns, Roland Culver,

Googie Withers, Frederick Valk, Antony
Baird, Judy Kelly, Miles Malleson, Ralph
Michael; **D:** Alberto Cavalcanti, Charles
Crichton, Basil Dearden, Robert Hamer; **W:**
T.E.B. Clarke, John Baines, Angus
MacPhail; **M:** Georges Auric. **VHS, Beta
★★★★**

Dead Poets Society An idealistic
English teacher inspires a group of
boys in a 1950s prep school to pursue individuality and creative endeavor, resulting in clashes with
school and parental authorities. Williams shows he can master the serious roles as well as the comic with
his portrayal of the unorthodox educator. Big box office hit occasionally
scripted with a heavy hand in order to
elevate the message. The ensemble
cast is excellent.
1989 (PG) 128m/C Robin Williams, Ethan
Hawke, Robert Sean Leonard, Josh
Charles, Gale Hansen, Kurtwood Smith,
James Waterson, Dylan Kussman, Lara
Flynn Boyle, Melora Hardin; **D:** Peter Weir;
W: Tom Schulman; **M:** Maurice Jarre, John
Seale. Academy Awards '89: Best Original
Screenplay; British Academy Awards '89:
Best Film; Cesar Awards '91: Best Foreign
Film; Nominations: Academy Awards '89:
Best Actor (Williams), Best Director (Weir),
Best Picture. **VHS, Beta, LV, 8mm
★★★1/2**

Dead Ringers A stunning, unsettling
chiller, based loosely on a real case
and the best-seller by Bari Wood and
Jack Geasland. Irons, in an excellent
dual role, is effectively disturbing as
the twin gynecologists who descend
into madness when they can no
longer handle the fame, fortune,
drugs, and women in their lives.
Acutely upsetting film made all the
more so due to its graphic images
and basis in fact.
1988 (R) 117m/C *CA* Jeremy Irons,
Genevieve Bujold, Heidi von Palleske,
Shirley Douglas, Stephen Lack; **D:** David
Cronenberg; **W:** Norman Snider, David
Cronenberg; **M:** Howard Shore. Genie
Awards '89: Best Actor (Irons), Best
Director (Cronenberg), Best Film; Los
Angeles Film Critics Association Awards
'88: Best Director (Cronenberg), Best
Supporting Actress (Bujold). **VHS, Beta, LV
★★★**

Dead Zone A man gains extraordinary
psychic powers following a near-fatal
accident. He is forced to decide between seeking absolute seclusion in
order to escape his frightening visions, or using his "gift" to save
mankind from impending evil. A good
adaptation of the Stephen King thriller.
1983 (R) 104m/C Christopher Walken,

Brooke Adams, Tom Skerritt, Martin Sheen, Herbert Lom, Anthony Zerbe, Colleen Dewhurst; **D:** David Cronenberg; **W:** Jeffrey Boam; **M:** Michael Kamen. **VHS, Beta, LV** ★★★

Dear America: Letters Home from Vietnam Acclaimed documentary featuring pictures and film of the war with voice-overs by dozens of Hollywood stars reading the words of American GIs. Initially made for cable television.
1988 (PG) 84m/C D: Bill Couture; **W:** Bill Couture; **M:** Todd Boekelheide. **VHS, Beta** ★★★½

Death and the Maiden Former political prisoner and torture victim (Weaver) turns the tables on the man she believes was her tormentor 15 years before. Pressing her civil rights lawyer husband (Wilson) into duty as defense attorney, she becomes prosecutor, judge, and jury. The accused (Kingsley) learns the dangers of picking up stranded motorists, as he is bound, gagged, and roughed up by the now empowered and vengeful Paulina. Tense, claustrophobic political thriller features a talented ensemble both on screen and behind the scenes. From the Ariel Dorfman play.
1994 (R) 102m/C Sigourney Weaver, Ben Kingsley, Stuart Wilson; **D:** Roman Polanski; **W:** Rafael Yglesias, Ariel Dorfman, Tonino Delli Colli; **M:** Wojciech Kilar. Nominations: Independent Spirit Awards '95: Best Director (Polanski). **VHS, LV** ★★★

Death Be Not Proud Based on the book by John Gunther detailing the valiant battle fought by his son against the brain tumor that took his life at the age of 17. Wonderfully acted by the three principals, especially Alexander, this film leaves us feeling hopeful despite its subject. Made for television.
1975 74m/C Arthur Hill, Robby Benson, Jane Alexander, Linden Chiles, Wendy Phillips; **D:** Donald Wrye. **VHS, Beta** ★★★

Death Becomes Her Aging actress Streep will do anything to stay young and beautiful, especially when childhood rival Hawn shows up, 200 pounds lighter and out to revenge the loss of her fiance, Streep's henpecked hubby. Doing anything arrives in the form of a potion that stops the aging process (and keeps her alive forever). Watch for the hilarious party filled with dead celebrities who all look as good as the day they died. Great special effects and fun performances by Streep and Hawn playing their glamour-girl roles to the hilt add

merit to this biting commentary on Hollywood's obsession with beauty and youth.
1992 (PG-13) 105m/C Meryl Streep, Bruce Willis, Goldie Hawn, Isabella Rossellini, Sydney Pollack, Michael Caine, Ian Ogilvy, Adam Storke, Nancy Fish, Alaina Reed Hall, Michelle Johnson, Mimi Kennedy, Jonathan Silverman, Dean Cundey; **Cameos:** Fabio Lanzoni; **D:** Robert Zemeckis; **W:** Martin Donovan, David Koepp; **M:** Alan Silvestri. Academy Awards '92: Best Visual Effects. **VHS, Beta, LV** ★★★

Death in Venice A lush, decadent adaptation of the Thomas Mann novella about an aging and jaded composer, here suggested to be Gustav Mahler, tragically obsessed with ideal beauty as personified in a young boy. **AKA:** Morte a Venezia.
1971 (PG) 124m/C IT Dirk Bogarde, Mark Burns, Bjorn Andresen, Marisa Berenson, Silvana Mangano; **D:** Luchino Visconti; **M:** Gustav Mahler. Nominations: Academy Awards '71: Best Costume Design; Cannes Film Festival '71: Best Film. **VHS, Beta** ★★★½

Death Is Called Engelchen An influential, important work of the Czech new wave. A survivor of WWII remembers his experiences with the SS leader Engelchen in a series of flashbacks. In Czech with subtitles. **AKA:** For We Too Do Not Forgive.
1963 111m/B CZ **D:** Jan Kadar, Elmar Klos. **VHS, Beta** ★★★½

Death of a Salesman A powerful made-for-television adaptation of the famous Arthur Miller play. Hoffman won an Emmy (as did Malkovich) for his stirring portrayal of Willy Loman, the aging salesman who realizes he's past his prime and tries to come to grips with the life he's wasted and the family he's neglected. Reid also turns in a fine performance as his long-suffering wife.
1986 135m/C Dustin Hoffman, John Malkovich, Charles Durning, Stephen Lang, Kate Reid, Louis Zorich; **D:** Volker Schlondorff; **M:** Alex North, Michael Ballhaus. **VHS, Beta, LV** ★★★½

The Decameron Pasolini's first epic pageant in his "Trilogy of Life" series. An acclaimed, sexually explicit adaptation of a handful of the Boccaccio tales. In Italian with English subtitles.
1970 (R) 111m/C FR IT GE Franco Citti, Ninetto Davoli, Angela Luce, Patrizia Capparelli, Jovan Jovanovich, Silvana Mangano, Pier Paolo Pasolini; **D:** Pier Paolo Pasolini; **M:** Ennio Morricone, Tonino Delli Colli. Berlin International Film Festival '71: Silver Prize. **VHS, Beta, LV** ★★★½

Deception Davis is a pianist torn between two loves: her intensely jealous sponsor (Rains) and her cellist boyfriend (Henreid). Plot in danger of going over the melodramatic edge is saved by the very effective performances of the stars.
1946 112m/B Bette Davis, Paul Henreid, Claude Rains, John Abbott, Benson Fong; **D:** Irving Rapper. **VHS, Beta ★★★**

The Decline of the American Empire The critically acclaimed French-Canadian film about eight academic intellectuals who spend a weekend shedding their sophistication and engaging in intertwining sexual affairs. Examines the differing attitudes of men and women in regards to sex and sexuality. In French with English subtitles. **AKA:** Le Declin De L'Empire Americain.
1986 (R) 102m/C *CA* Dominique Michel, Dorothee Berryman, Louise Portal, Genevieve Rioux; **D:** Denys Arcand; **W:** Denys Arcand. Genie Awards '87: Best Director (Arcand), Best Film, Best Supporting Actor (Arcand), Best Supporting Actress (Portal); Toronto-City Award '86: Best Canadian Feature Film; Nominations: Academy Awards '86: Best Foreign Language Film. **VHS, Beta ★★★1/2**

Decoration Day Garner plays a retired Southern judge who aids an angry childhood friend who has refused to accept his long-overdue Medal of Honor. Investigating the past leads to a decades-old mystery and a tragic secret that has repercussions for everyone involved. Based on the novel by John William Corrington. A Hallmark Hall of Fame presentation.
1990 (PG) 99m/C James Garner, Bill Cobbs, Judith Ivey, Ruby Dee, Laurence "Larry" Fishburne, Jo Anderson; **D:** Robert Markowitz. **VHS, LV ★★★**

The Deer Hunter A powerful and vivid portrait of Middle America with three steel-working friends who leave home to face the Vietnam War. Controversial, brutal sequences in Vietnam are among the most wrenching ever filmed; the rhythms and rituals of home are just as purely captured. Neither pro- nor anti-war, but rather the perfect evocation of how totally and forever altered these people are by the war. Emotionally shattering; not to be missed.
1978 (R) 183m/C Robert De Niro, Christopher Walken, Meryl Streep, John Savage, George Dzundza, John Cazale, Chuck Aspegren, Rutanya Alda, Shirley Stoler, Amy Wright; **D:** Michael Cimino; **W:** Deric Washburn, Michael Cimino, Vilmos

Zsigmond; **M:** John Williams. Academy Awards '78: Best Director (Cimino), Best Film Editing, Best Picture, Best Sound, Best Supporting Actor (Walken); Golden Globe Awards '79: Best Director (Cimino); Los Angeles Film Critics Association Awards '78: Best Director (Cimino); New York Film Critics Awards '78: Best Film, Best Supporting Actor (Walken); Nominations: Academy Awards '78: Best Actor (De Niro), Best Cinematography, Best Original Screenplay, Best Supporting Actress (Streep). **VHS, Beta, LV ★★★★**

Defending Your Life Brooks' cock-eyed way of looking at the world travels to the afterlife in this uneven comedy/romance. In Judgement City, where everyone goes after death, past lives are examined and judged. If you were a good enough person you get to stay in heaven (where you wear funny robes and eat all you want without getting fat). If not, it's back to earth for another go-round. Brooks plays an L.A. advertising executive who crashes his new BMW and finds himself defending his life. When he meets and falls in love with Streep, his interest in staying in heaven multiplies. Occasionally charming, seldom out-right hilarious.
1991 (PG) 112m/C Albert Brooks, Meryl Streep, Rip Torn, Lee Grant, Buck Henry, George Wallace, Lillian Lehman, Peter Schuck; **D:** Albert Brooks; **W:** Albert Brooks; **M:** Michael Gore. **VHS, LV, 8mm ★★★**

Defense of the Realm A British politician is accused of selling secrets to the KGB through his mistress and only a pair of dedicated newspapermen believe he is innocent. In the course of finding the answers they discover a national cover-up conspiracy. An acclaimed, taut thriller.
1985 (PG) 96m/C *GB* Gabriel Byrne, Greta Scacchi, Denholm Elliott, Ian Bannen, Bill Paterson, Fulton Mackay, Robbie Coltrane; **D:** David Drury. British Academy Awards '85: Best Supporting Actor (Elliott). **VHS, Beta, LV ★★★1/2**

The Defiant Ones Thought-provoking story about racism revolves around two escaped prisoners (one black, one white) from a chain gang in the rural South. Their societal conditioning to hate each other dissolves as they face constant peril together. Critically acclaimed.
1958 97m/B Tony Curtis, Sidney Poitier, Theodore Bikel, Lon Chaney Jr., Charles McGraw, Cara Williams; **D:** Stanley Kramer; **W:** Nathan E. Douglas, Harold Jacob Smith; **M:** Stephen Dorff. Academy Awards '58: Best Black and White

Cinematography, Best Original Screenplay; British Academy Awards '58: Best Actor (Poitier); Edgar Allan Poe Awards '58: Best Screenplay; Golden Globe Awards '59: Best Film—Drama; New York Film Critics Awards '58: Best Director (Kramer), Best Film, Best Screenplay; Nominations: Academy Awards '58: Best Actor (Curtis), Best Actor (Poitier), Best Director (Kramer), Best Film Editing, Best Picture, Best Supporting Actor (Bikel), Best Supporting Actress (Williams). **VHS, Beta** ★★★1/2

The Deliberate Stranger Harmon is engrossing as charismatic serial killer Ted Bundy, sentenced to death for several Florida murders and suspected in the killings of a least 25 women in several states. After eluding police for five years Bundy was finally arrested in Florida in 1979. His case became a cause celebre on capital punishment as it dragged on for nine years. Bundy was finally executed in 1989. Based on the book "Bundy: The Deliberate Stranger" by Richard W. Larsen. Made for television.
1986 188m/C Mark Harmon, M. Emmet Walsh, Frederic Forrest, John Ashton, George Grizzard, Ben Masters, Glynnis O'Connor, Bonnie Bartlett, Billy Green Bush, Lawrence Pressman; **D:** Marvin J. Chomsky. **VHS, Beta** ★★★

Deliverance Terrifying exploration of the primal nature of man and his alienation from nature, based on the novel by James Dickey, which he adapted for the film (he also makes an appearance as a sheriff). Four urban professionals, hoping to get away from it all for the weekend, canoe down a southern river, encounter crazed backwoodsmen, and end up battling for survival. Excellent performances all around, especially by Voight. Debuts for Beatty and Cox. Watch for O'Neill as a sheriff, and director Boorman's son Charley as Voight's son. "Dueling Banjos" scene and tune are memorable as is scene where the backwoods boys promise to make the fellows squeal like pigs.
1972 (R) 109m/C Jon Voight, Burt Reynolds, Ronny Cox, Ned Beatty, James Dickey, Bill McKinney, Ed O'Neill, Charley Boorman; **D:** John Boorman, Vilmos Zsigmond; **W:** James Dickey; **M:** Eric Weissburg. National Board of Review Awards '72: 10 Best Films of the Year; Nominations: Academy Awards '72: Best Director (Boorman), Best Film Editing, Best Picture. **VHS, Beta, LV** ★★★★

Demon Seed When a scientist and his wife separate so he can work on his computer, the computer takes over the house and impregnates the wife. Bizarre and taut.
1977 (R) 97m/C Julie Christie, Fritz Weaver, Gerrit Graham, Berry Kroeger, Ron Hays; **D:** Donald Cammell; **V:** Robert Vaughn. **VHS, Beta, LV** ★★★

The Dentist Fields treats several oddball patients in his office. After watching the infamous tooth-pulling scene, viewers will be sure to brush regularly.
1932 22m/B W.C. Fields, Elise Cavanna, Babe Kane, Bud Jamison, Zedna Farley. **VHS, Beta** ★★★1/2

Deranged Of the numerous movies based on the cannibalistic exploits of Ed Gein ("Psycho," "Texas Chainsaw Massacre," etc.), this is the most accurate. A dead-on performance by Blossom and a twisted sense of humor help move things along nicely. The two directors, Gillen and Ormsby, previously worked together on the classic "Children Shouldn't Play with Dead Things." An added attraction is the early special effect work of gore wizard Tom Savini.
1974 (R) 82m/C CA Roberts Blossom, Cosette Lee, Robert Warner, Marcia Diamond, Brian Sneagle; **D:** Jeff Gillen, Alan Ormsby. **VHS** ★★★

Dersu Uzala An acclaimed, photographically breathtaking film about a Russian surveyor in Siberia who befriends a crusty, resourceful Mongolian. They begin to teach each other about their respective worlds. Produced in Russia; one of Kurosawa's stranger films.
1975 124m/C JP RU Yuri Solomin, Maxim Munzuk; **D:** Akira Kurosawa. Academy Awards '75: Best Foreign Language Film. **VHS, Beta** ★★★1/2

Desert Bloom On the eve of a nearby nuclear bomb test, a beleaguered alcoholic veteran and his family struggle through tensions brought on by a promiscuous visiting aunt and the chaotic, rapidly changing world. Gish shines as the teenage daughter through whose eyes the story unfolds. From a story by Corr and Linda Ramy.
1986 (PG) 103m/C Jon Voight, JoBeth Williams, Ellen Barkin, Annabeth Gish, Allen (Goorwitz) Garfield, Jay Underwood; **D:** Eugene Corr; **W:** Eugene Corr; **M:** Brad Fiedel, Reynaldo Villalobos. **VHS, Beta, LV** ★★★

Desert Hearts An upstanding professional woman travels to Reno, Nevada in 1959 to obtain a quick divorce, and slowly becomes involved in a lesbian relationship with a free-spirited casino waitress.

1986 (R) 93m/C Helen Shaver, Audra Lindley, Patricia Charbonneau, Andra Akers, Dean Butler, Jeffrey Tambor, Denise Crosby, Gwen Welles; *D:* Donna Deitch; *W:* Natalie Cooper. VHS, Beta, LV ★★★

The Desert Rats A crusty British captain (Burton) takes charge of an Australian division during WWII. Thinking they are inferior to his own British troops, he is stiff and uncaring to the Aussies until a kind-hearted drunk and the courage of the division win him over. Crack direction from Wise and Newton's performance (as the wag) simply steal the movie. Mason reprises his role as German Army Field Marshal Rommel from "The Desert Fox."
1953 88m/B Richard Burton, Robert Newton, Robert Douglas, Torin Thatcher, Chips Rafferty, Charles Tingwell, James Mason; *D:* Robert Wise. Nominations: Academy Awards '53: Best Story & Screenplay. VHS, Beta ★★★

Designing Woman Bacall and Peck star in this mismatched tale of romance. She's a chic high-fashion designer, he's a rumpled sports writer. The fun begins when they try to adjust to married life together. Neither likes the other's friends or lifestyle. Things get even crazier when Bacall has to work with her ex-lover Helmore on a fashion show and Peck's former love Gray shows up as well. And as if that wasn't enough, Peck is being hunted by the mob because of a boxing story he's written. It's a fun, quick, witty tale that is all entertainment and no message. Bacall's performance is of note because Bogart was dying of cancer at the time.
1957 118m/C Gregory Peck, Lauren Bacall, Dolores Gray, Sam Levene, Tom Helmore, Mickey Shaughnessy, Jesse White, Chuck Connors, Edward Platt, Alvy Moore, Jack Cole; *D:* Vincente Minnelli; *W:* George Wells; *M:* Andre Previn, John Alton. Academy Awards '57: Best Story & Screenplay. VHS, Beta, LV ★★★

Desire Jewel thief Madeleine (Dietrich) manages to involve innocent tourist Tom (Cooper) into carrying her ill-gotten goods across the Spanish border. Then she entices him into joining her at the country estate of her partner-in-crime. By this time Tom is in love—and so is Madeleine but she doesn't think she's good enough for him. Lots of lying until the twosome can figure out what to do. Cooper manages to hold his own with the sophisticated Dietrich in their second film together (after "Morocco").
1936 96m/B Marlene Dietrich, Gary Cooper, John Halliday, William Frawley, Ernest Cossart, Akim Tamiroff, Alan Mowbray; *D:* Frank Borzage; *W:* Edwin Justus Mayer, Waldemar Young; *M:* Friedrich Hollander. VHS ★★★

Desk Set One of the later and less dynamic Tracy/Hepburn comedies, about an efficiency expert who installs a giant computer in an effort to update a television network's female-run reference department. Still, the duo sparkle as they bicker, battle, and give in to love. Based on William Marchant's play. *AKA:* His Other Woman.
1957 103m/C Spencer Tracy, Katharine Hepburn, Joan Blondell, Gig Young, Dina Merrill, Neva Patterson; *D:* Walter Lang. VHS, Beta, LV ★★★

Despair A chilling and comic study of a victimized chocolate factory owner's descent into madness, set against the backdrop of the Nazi rise to power in the 1930s. Adapted from the Nabokov novel by Tom Stoppard.
1978 120m/C GE Dirk Bogarde, Andrea Ferreol, Volker Spengler, Klaus Lowitsch; *D:* Rainer Werner Fassbinder; *W:* Tom Stoppard; *M:* Peer Raben, Michael Ballhaus. Nominations: Cannes Film Festival '78: Best Film. VHS, Beta ★★★

Desperado Rodriguez's nameless guitar player-turned-gunman returns —this time in the persona of heart-throb Banderas. The director also has a studio budget to play with (a sizable increase over the $7,000 for "El Mariachi"), so the action's on a bigger, more violent scale (you'll quickly lose count of flying bodies and bullets) as El Mariachi tracks infamous drug lord Bucho (de Almeida). Gringo Buscemi provides assistance, beautiful bookstore owner Carolina (Hayek) offers solace, and Tarantino meets his well-deserved cameo demise. You'll also find original Mariachi, Gallardo, in a cameo role as a musician/gunslinger amigo of the hero. Filmed in Mexico. *AKA:* El Mariachi 2.
1995 (R) 103m/C Antonio Banderas, Salma Hayek, Joaquim de Almeida, Steve Buscemi, Richard "Cheech" Marin, Carlos Gomez; Cameos: Quentin Tarantino, Carlos Gallardo; *D:* Robert Rodriguez; *W:* Robert Rodriguez. Nominations: MTV Movie Awards '96: Most Desirable Male (Banderas), Best Kiss (Antonio Banderas/Salma Hayek). VHS, LV, 8mm ★★★

Desperate Characters A slice-of-city-life story about a middle-class couple living in a once-fashionable section of Brooklyn, New York, who watch their neighborhood disinte-

grate around them. Their marriage on remote control, the two find their lives a series of small disappointments, routine work, uncertain friendships, and pervasive violence. Excellent performances, especially by MacLaine as the harried wife, but the film's depressing nature made it a complete box office flop.
1971 (R) 87m/C Shirley MacLaine, Kenneth Mars, Gerald S. O'Loughlin, Sada Thompson, Michael Higgins, Rose Gregorio, Jack Somack, Chris Gampel, Mary Alan Hokanson, Patrick McVey, Carol Kane; **D:** Frank D. Gilroy; **W:** Frank D. Gilroy. **VHS** ★★★

Desperate Hours A tough, gritty thriller about three escaped convicts taking over a suburban home and holding the family hostage. Plenty of suspense and fine acting. Based on the novel and play by Joseph Hayes.
1955 112m/B Humphrey Bogart, Fredric March, Martha Scott, Arthur Kennedy, Gig Young, Dewey Martin, Mary Murphy, Robert Middleton, Richard Eyer; **D:** William Wyler. Edgar Allan Poe Awards '55: Best Screenplay; National Board of Review Awards '55: Best Director (Wyler). **VHS, Beta** ★★★

Destry Rides Again An uncontrollably lawless western town is whipped into shape by a peaceful, unarmed sheriff. A vintage Hollywood potpourri with Dietrich's finest post-Sternberg moment; standing on the bar singing "See What the Boys in the Back Room Will Have." The second of three versions of this Max Brand story. First was released in 1932; the third in 1954. **AKA:** Justice Rides Again.
1939 94m/B James Stewart, Marlene Dietrich, Brian Donlevy, Charles Winninger, Mischa Auer, Irene Hervey, Una Merkel, Billy Gilbert, Jack Carson, Samuel S. Hinds, Allen Jenkins; **D:** George Marshall; **W:** Gertrude Purcell, Felix Jackson, Henry Myers; **M:** Frank Skinner. **VHS, Beta, LV** ★★★★

The Detective A New York detective investigating the mutilation murder of a homosexual finds political and police department corruption. Fine, gritty performances prevail in this suspense thriller. Based on the novel by Roderick Thorpe.
1968 114m/C Frank Sinatra, Lee Remick, Ralph Meeker, Jacqueline Bisset, William Windom, Robert Duvall, Tony Musante, Jack Klugman, Al Freeman Jr.; **D:** Gordon Douglas; **W:** Abby Mann. **VHS, Beta, LV** ★★★

The Detective Story Intense drama about a New York City police precinct with a wide array of characters led by a disillusioned and bitter detective (Douglas). Excellent casting is the strong point, as the film can be a bit dated. Based on Sydney Kingsley's Broadway play.
1951 103m/B Kirk Douglas, Eleanor Parker, Lee Grant, Horace McMahon, William Bendix, Craig Hill, Cathy O'Donnell, Bert Freed, George Macready, Joseph Wiseman, Gladys George, Frank Faylen, Warner Anderson, Gerald Mohr; **D:** William Wyler; **W:** Philip Yordan, Robert Wyler. Cannes Film Festival '52: Best Actress (Grant); Edgar Allan Poe Awards '51: Best Screenplay; Nominations: Academy Awards '51: Best Actress (Parker), Best Director (Wyler), Best Screenplay, Best Supporting Actress (Grant). **VHS** ★★★1/2

Detour Considered to be the creme de la creme of "B" movies, a largely unacknowledged but cult-followed noir downer. Well-designed, stylish, and compelling, if a bit contrived and sometimes annoyingly shrill. Shot in only six days with six indoor sets. Down-on-his-luck pianist Neal hitches cross-country to rejoin his fiancee. His first wrong turn involves the accidental death of the man who picked him up, then he's en route to Destiny with a capital "D" when he picks up fatal femme Savage, as vicious a vixen as ever ruined a good man. Told in flashback, it's also been called the most despairing of all "B"-pictures. As noir as they get.
1946 67m/B Tom Neal, Ann Savage, Claudia Drake, Edmund MacDonald; **D:** Edgar G. Ulmer. **VHS, Beta, LV** ★★★

Deutschland im Jahre Null The acclaimed, unsettling vision of post-war Germany as seen through the eyes of a disturbed boy who eventually kills himself. Lyrical and grim, in German with subtitles.
1947 75m/B *GE* Franz Gruber; **D:** Roberto Rossellini. **VHS, Beta** ★★★1/2

Devi A minor film in the Ray canon, it is, nonetheless, a strange and compelling tale of religious superstition. An Indian farmer becomes convinced that his beautiful daughter-in-law is the reincarnation of the goddess Kali. The girl is then pressured into accepting a worship that eventually drives her mad. In Bengali with English subtitles.
1960 96m/B *IN* Chhabi Biswas, Sharmila Tagore, Soumitra Chatterjee; **D:** Satyajit Ray. **VHS, Beta** ★★★1/2

The Devil & Daniel Webster In 1840s New Hampshire, a young farmer, who sells his soul to the devil, is saved

from a trip to Hell when Daniel Webster steps in to defend him. This classic fantasy is visually striking and contains wonderful performances. Adapted from the story by Stephen Vincent Benet, who based it on Goethe's Faust. **AKA:** All That Money Can Buy; Here Is a Man; A Certain Mr. Scratch.
1941 106m/B James Craig, Edward Arnold, Walter Huston, Simone Simon, Gene Lockhart, Jane Darwell, Anne Shirley, John Qualen, H.B. Warner; **D:** William Dieterle. Nominations: Academy Awards '41: Best Actor (Huston). **VHS, Beta, LV** ★★★1/2

The Devil & Miss Jones Engaging romantic comedy finds a big business boss posing as an ordinary salesclerk to weed out union organizers. He doesn't expect to encounter the wicked management or his beautiful co-worker, however.
1941 90m/B Jean Arthur, Robert Cummings, Charles Coburn, Edmund Gwenn, Spring Byington, William Demarest, S.Z. Sakall; **D:** Sam Wood. Nominations: Academy Awards '41: Best Original Screenplay, Best Supporting Actor (Coburn). **VHS** ★★★1/2

Devil in a Blue Dress Down-on-his-luck Easy Rawlins (Washington) is an out of work aircraft worker in 1948 L.A. He's hired to find mystery woman Daphne (Beals) by a shady businessman (Sizemore). What he finds are the usual noir staples: government corruption backed by thugs who want him to mind his own business. Easy and Daphne's torrid romance featured in the Walter Mosley novel is missing, but the racism and violence are intact. Realism and accuracy in period detail enhance solid performance by Washington, though the deliberate, literary pace is at times lulling. Cheadle takes over whenever he shows up as Mouse, Rawlins's loyal friend and muscle.
1995 (R) 102m/C Denzel Washington, Jennifer Beals, Don Cheadle, Tom Sizemore, Maury Chaykin, Terry Kinney, Mel Winkler, Albert Hall; **D:** Carl Franklin; **W:** Carl Franklin; **M:** Elmer Bernstein. Los Angeles Film Critics Association Awards '95: Best Supporting Actor (Cheadle); National Society of Film Critics Awards '95: Best Cinematography, Best Supporting Actor (Cheadle); Nominations: Screen Actors Guild Award '95: Best Supporting Actor (Cheadle). **VHS, LV** ★★★

The Devils In 1631 France, a priest is accused of commerce with the devil and sexual misconduct with nuns. Since he is also a political threat, the accusation is used to denounce and eventually execute him. Based on Aldous Huxley's "The Devils of Loudun," the movie features masturbating nuns and other excesses—shocking scenes typical of film director Russell. Supposedly this was Russell's attempt to wake the public to their desensitization of modern horrors of war. Controversial and flamboyant.
1971 (R) 109m/C GB Vanessa Redgrave, Oliver Reed, Dudley Sutton, Max Adrian, Gemma Jones, Murray Melvin; **D:** Ken Russell; **W:** Ken Russell. National Board of Review Awards '71: Best Director (Russell). **VHS, Beta** ★★★

The Devil's Playground Sexual tension rises in a Catholic seminary, distracting the boys from their theological studies. The attentions of the priests only further their sexual confusion. Winner of many Australian film awards.
1976 107m/C AU Arthur Dignam, Nick Tate, Simon Burke, Charles Frawley, Jonathon Hardy, Gerry Dugan, Thomas Keneally; **D:** Fred Schepisi; **W:** Fred Schepisi; **M:** Bruce Smeaton. Australian Film Institute '76: Best Actor (Tate), Best Actor (Burke), Best Film. **Beta** ★★★

Diabolique The mistress and the wife of a sadistic schoolmaster conspire to murder the man, carry it out, and then begin to wonder if they have covered their tracks effectively. Plot twists and double-crosses abound. In French with English subtitles. Remade for television as "Reflections of Murder." **AKA:** Les Diabolique.
1955 107m/B FR Simone Signoret, Vera Clouzot, Paul Meurisse, Charles Vanel, Michel Serrault; **D:** Henri-Georges Clouzot. National Board of Review Awards '55: 5 Best Foreign Films of the Year; New York Film Critics Awards '55: Best Foreign Film. **VHS, Beta, LV, 8mm** ★★★1/2

Dial "M" for Murder An unfaithful husband devises an elaborate plan to murder his wife for her money, but when she accidentally stabs the killer-to-be, with scissors no less, he alters his methods. Part of the "A Night at the Movies" series, this tape simulates a 1954 movie evening with a Daffy Duck cartoon, "My Little Duckaroo," a newsreel, and coming attractions for "Them" and "A Star Is Born." Filmed in 3-D. Based on the play by Frederick Knotts.
1954 123m/C Ray Milland, Grace Kelly, Robert Cummings, John Williams, Anthony Dawson; **D:** Alfred Hitchcock; **M:** Dimitri Tiomkin. **VHS, Beta, LV** ★★★

Diamonds Are Forever 007 once again battles his nemesis Blofeld, this time in Las Vegas. Bond must prevent the implementation of a plot to destroy Washington through the use of a space-orbiting laser. Fabulous stunts include Bond's wild drive through the streets of Vegas in a '71 Mach 1. Connery returned to play Bond in this film after being offered the then record-setting salary of one million dollars.
1971 (PG) 120m/C GB Sean Connery, Jill St. John, Charles Gray, Bruce Cabot, Jimmy Dean, Lana Wood, Bruce Glover, Putter Smith, Norman Burton, Joseph Furst, Bernard Lee, Desmond Llewelyn, Laurence Naismith, Leonard Barr, Lois Maxwell, Margaret Lacey, Joe Robinson, Donna Garrat, Trina Parks; D: Guy Hamilton; W: Tom Mankiewicz; M: John Barry. Nominations: Academy Awards '71: Best Sound. VHS, Beta, LV ★★★1/2

Diamonds of the Night A breakthrough masterpiece of the Czech new wave, about two young men escaping from a transport train to Auschwitz and scrambling for survival in the countryside. Surreal, powerfully expressionistic film, one of the most important of its time. In Czech with English subtitles. Accompanied by Nemec's short "A Loaf of Bread." **AKA:** Demanty Noci.
1964 71m/B CZ Ladislav Jansky, Antonin Kumbera, Ilse Bischofova; D: Jan Nemec; W: Arnost Lustig, Jan Nemec. VHS, Beta ★★★★

Diary of a Chambermaid A chambermaid wants to marry a rich man and finds herself the object of desire of a poor servant willing to commit murder for her. Excellent comic drama, but very stylized in direction and set design. Produced during Renoir's years in Hollywood. Adapted from a story by Octave Mirbeau, later turned into a play. Remade in 1964 by Luis Bunuel.
1946 86m/B Paulette Goddard, Burgess Meredith, Hurd Hatfield, Francis Lederer, Judith Anderson, Florence Bates, Almira Sessions, Reginald Owen; D: Jean Renoir. VHS ★★★

Diary of a Chambermaid Vintage Bunuelian social satire about a young girl taking a servant's job in a provincial French family, and easing into an atmosphere of sexual hypocrisy and decadence. In French with English subtitles. Remake of the 1946 Jean Renoir film. **AKA:** Le Journal d'une Femme de Chambre; Il Diario di una Cameriera.
1964 97m/C FR Jeanne Moreau, Michel Piccoli, Georges Geret, Francoise Lugagne, Daniel Ivernel; D: Luis Bunuel; W: Luis Bunuel, Jean-Claude Carriere. VHS, Beta, LV ★★★1/2

Diary of a Country Priest With "Balthazar" and "Mouchette," this is one of Bresson's greatest, subtlest films, treating the story of an alienated, unrewarded young priest with his characteristic austerity and Catholic humanism. In French with English subtitles. **AKA:** Le Journal d'un Cure de Campagne.
1950 120m/B FR Claude Layou, Jean Riveyre, Nicole Ladmiral; D: Robert Bresson; W: Robert Bresson. VHS, Beta ★★★1/2

Diary of a Lost Girl The second Louise Brooks/G.W. Pabst collaboration (after "Pandora's Box") in which a frail but mesmerizing German girl plummets into a life of hopeless degradation. Dark and gloomy, the film chronicles the difficulties she faces, from rape to an unwanted pregnancy and prostitution. Based on the popular book by Margarete Boehme. Silent. Made after flapper Brooks left Hollywood to pursue greater opportunities and more challenging roles under Pabst's guidance.
1929 99m/B GE Louise Brooks, Fritz Rasp, Josef Rovensky, Sybille Schmitz; D: G.W. Pabst. VHS, Beta, LV ★★★1/2

Diary of a Mad Housewife Despairing of her miserable family life, a housewife has an affair with a writer only to find him to be even more selfish and egotistical than her no-good husband. Snodgress plays her character perfectly, hearing the insensitive absurdity of her husband and her lover over and over again, enjoying her martyrdom even as it drives her crazy.
1970 (R) 94m/C Carrie Snodgress, Richard Benjamin, Frank Langella; D: Frank Perry. Golden Globe Awards '71: Best Actress—Musical/Comedy (Snodgress); National Board of Review Awards '70: 10 Best Films of the Year, Best Supporting Actor (Langella); Nominations: Academy Awards '70: Best Actress (Snodgress). VHS, Beta ★★★

The Diary of Anne Frank In June 1945, a liberated Jewish refugee returns to the hidden third floor of an Amsterdam factory where he finds the diary kept by his youngest daughter, Anne. The document recounts their years in hiding from the Nazis. Based on the actual diary of 13-year-old Anne Frank, killed in a death camp during WWII.
1959 150m/B Millie Perkins, Joseph

Schildkraut, Shelley Winters, Richard Beymer, Gusti Huber, Ed Wynn, Lou Jacobi, Diane Baker; **D:** George Stevens. Academy Awards '59: Best Art Direction/Set Decoration (B & W), Best Black and White Cinematography, Best Supporting Actress (Winters); Nominations: Academy Awards '59: Best Costume Design (B & W), Best Director (Stevens), Best Picture, Best Supporting Actor (Wynn), Best Original Score. **VHS, Beta, LV** ★★★1/2

Dick Tracy Beatty wears the caps of producer, director, and star, performing admirably on all fronts. One minor complaint: his Tracy is somewhat flat in comparison to the outstanding performances and makeup of the unique villains, especially Pacino. Stylistically superior, shot in only seven colors, the timeless sets capture the essence rather than the reality of the city, successfully bringing the comic strip to life. Madonna is fine as the seductive Breathless Mahoney, belting out Stephen Sondheim like she was born to do it. People expecting the gothic technology of "Batman" may be disappointed, but moviegoers searching for a memory made real will be thrilled. ♪ Sooner or Later.
1990 (PG) 105m/C Warren Beatty, Madonna, Charlie Korsmo, Glenne Headly, Al Pacino, Dustin Hoffman, James Caan, Mandy Patinkin, Paul Sorvino, Charles Durning, Dick Van Dyke, R.G. Armstrong, Catherine O'Hara, Estelle Parsons, Seymour Cassel, Michael J. Pollard, William Forsythe, Kathy Bates, James Tolkan; **D:** Warren Beatty; **W:** Jim Cash, Jack Epps Jr.; **M:** Danny Elfman, Stephen Sondheim. Academy Awards '90: Best Art Direction/Set Decoration, Best Makeup, Best Song ("Sooner or Later"); Nominations: Academy Awards '90: Best Cinematography, Best Costume Design, Best Sound, Best Supporting Actor (Pacino). **VHS, Beta, LV** ★★★1/2

Dick Tracy: The Original Serial, Vol. 1 The first seven parts of the original popular serial. The comic strip character comes to life and tries to stop the Spider, a dangerous criminal.
1937 150m/B Ralph Byrd, Smiley Burnette, Kay Hughes, Francis X. Bushman, Lee Van Atta; **D:** Ray Taylor; **W:** Alan James. **VHS, Beta** ★★★

Die Hard High-voltage action thriller pits a lone New York cop against a band of ruthless high-stakes terrorists who attack and hold hostage the employees of a large corporation as they celebrate Christmas in a new L.A. high rise. It's just as unbelievable as it sounds, but you'll love it anyway.

Rickman, who later charmed audiences as the villain in "Robin Hood: Prince of Thieves," turns in a marvelous performance as the chief bad guy. Based on the novel "Nothing Lasts Forever" by Roderick Thorp.
1988 (R) 114m/C Bruce Willis, Bonnie Bedelia, Alan Rickman, Alexander Godunov, Paul Gleason, William Atherton, Reginald Vel Johnson, Hart Bochner, James Shigeta, Mary Ellen Trainor, De'voreaux White, Robert Davi, Rick Ducommun, Jan De Bont; **D:** John McTiernan; **W:** Jeb Stuart, Steven E. de Souza; **M:** Michael Kamen. Nominations: Academy Awards '88: Best Film Editing, Best Sound. **VHS, Beta, LV** ★★★

Die Hard 2: Die Harder Fast, well-done sequel brings another impossible situation before the wise-cracking, tough-cookie cop. Our hero tangles with a group of terrorists at an airport under siege, while his wife remains in a plane circling above as its fuel dwindles. Obviously a repeat of the plot and action of the first "Die Hard," with references to the former in the script. While the bad guys lack the fiendishness of their predecessors, this installment features energetic and finely acted performances. Fairly gory, especially the icicle-in-the-eyeball scene. Adapted from the novel "58 Minutes" by Walter Wager and characters created by Roderick Thorp.
1990 (R) 124m/C Bruce Willis, William Atherton, Franco Nero, Bonnie Bedelia, John Amos, Reginald Vel Johnson, Dennis Franz, Art Evans, Fred Dalton Thompson, William Sadler, Sheila McCarthy, Robert Patrick, John Leguizamo, Robert Costanzo, Tom Verica; **D:** Renny Harlin; **W:** Doug Richardson, Steven E. de Souza; **M:** Michael Kamen. **VHS, LV** ★★★

Different for Girls Boyish motorcycle dispatch rider Paul Prentice (Graves) nearly gets run over by a London taxi whose passenger Kim Foyle (Mackintosh) seems strangely familiar. Then Paul discovers Kim used to be his boyhood school chum Karl. After a shaky start, the duo discover a genuine attraction, but when they get into an argument that leads to a police call and Paul gets thrown in jail, Kim's first instincts are to retreat to her sister's (Reeves) family and back into her quiet life. Director Spence refrains from camping up the situation, and some fine performances, especially from the engaging Graves, make this quirky film well worth a watch.
1995 92m/C *GB* Rupert Graves, Steven Mackintosh, Miriam Margolyes, Saskia Reeves, Neil Dudgeon, Charlotte Coleman;

D: Richard Spence; **W:** Tony Merchant; **M:** Stephen Warbeck. Montreal World Film Festival '95: Best Film. **VHS ★★★**

Dim Sum: A Little Bit of Heart The second independent film from the director of "Chan Is Missing." A Chinese-American mother and daughter living in San Francisco's Chinatown confront the conflict between traditional Eastern ways and modern American life. Gentle, fragile picture made with humor and care. In English and Chinese with subtitles.
1985 (PG) 88m/C Laureen Chew, Kim Chew, Victor Wong, Ida F.O. Chong, Cora Miao, John Nishio, Joan Chen; **D:** Wayne Wang; **W:** Terrel Seltzer; **M:** Todd Boekelheide. **VHS, Beta, LV ★★★**

Diner A group of old high school friends meet at "their" Baltimore diner to find that more has changed than the menu. A bittersweet look at the experiences of a group of Baltimore post-teenagers growing up, circa 1959. Particularly notable was Levinson's casting of "unknowns" who have since become household names. Features many humorous moments and fine performances.
1982 (R) 110m/C Steve Guttenberg, Daniel Stern, Mickey Rourke, Kevin Bacon, Ellen Barkin, Timothy Daly, Paul Reiser, Michael Tucker; **D:** Barry Levinson; Peter Sova. National Society of Film Critics Awards '82: Best Supporting Actor (Rourke); Nominations: Academy Awards '82: Best Original Screenplay. **VHS, Beta, LV ★★★1/2**

Dinner at Eight A social-climbing woman and her husband throw a dinner party for various members of the New York elite. During the course of the evening, all of the guests reveal something about themselves. Special performances all around, especially Barrymore, Dressler, and Harlow. Superb comedic direction by Cukor. Adapted from the play by Edna Ferber and George Kaufman.
1933 110m/C John Barrymore, Lionel Barrymore, Wallace Beery, Madge Evans, Jean Harlow, Billie Burke, Marie Dressler, Phillips Holmes, Jean Hersholt, Lee Tracy, Edmund Lowe, Karen Morley, May Robson; **D:** George Cukor; **W:** Herman J. Mankiewicz, Frances Marion, Donald Ogden Stewart. **VHS, Beta, LV, 8mm ★★★★**

Dirty Dancing An innocent 17-year-old (Grey) is vacationing with her parents in the Catskills in 1963. Bored with the program at the hotel, she finds the real fun at the staff dances. Falling for the sexy dance instructor (Swayze), she discovers love, sex, and rock and roll dancing. An old story, with little to save it, but Grey and Swayze are appealing, the dance sequences fun, and the music great. Swayze, classically trained in ballet, also performs one of the sound-track songs. ♩ (I've Had) the Time of My Life; Be My Baby; Big Girls Don't Cry; Cry to Me; Do You Love Me?; Hey Baby; Hungry Eyes; In the Still of the Night; Love is Strange.
1987 (PG-13) 97m/C Patrick Swayze, Jennifer Grey, Cynthia Rhodes, Jerry Orbach, Jack Weston, Jane Brucker, Kelly Bishop, Lonny Price, Charles "Honi" Coles, Bruce Morrow; **D:** Emile Ardolino; **W:** Eleanor Bergstein; **M:** John Morris. Academy Awards '87: Best Song ("(I've Had) the Time of My Life"); Golden Globe Awards '88: Best Song ("(I've Had) the Time of My Life"); Independent Spirit Awards '88: Best First Feature. **VHS, Beta, LV ★★★**

The Dirty Dozen A tough Army major is assigned to train and command twelve hardened convicts offered absolution if they participate in a suicidal mission into Nazi Germany in 1944. Well-made movie is a standout in its genre. Rough and gruff Marvin is good as the group leader. Three made-for-television sequels followed in the '80s.
1967 (PG) 149m/C Lee Marvin, Ernest Borgnine, Charles Bronson, Jim Brown, George Kennedy, John Cassavetes, Clint Walker, Donald Sutherland, Telly Savalas, Robert Ryan, Ralph Meeker, Richard Jaeckel, Trini Lopez; **D:** Robert Aldrich. Academy Awards '67: Best Sound Effects Editing; Nominations: Academy Awards '67: Best Film Editing, Best Sound, Best Supporting Actor (Cassavetes). **VHS, Beta, LV ★★★**

Dirty Harry Rock-hard cop Harry Callahan attempts to track down a psychopathic rooftop killer before a kidnapped girl dies. Harry abuses the murderer's civil rights, however, forcing the police to return the criminal to the streets, where he hijacks a school bus and Harry is called on once again. The only answer to stop this vicious killer seems to be death in cold blood, and Harry is just the man to do it. Taut, suspenseful direction by Siegel, who thoroughly understands Eastwood's on-screen character. Features Callahan's famous "Do you feel lucky?" line, the precursor to his "Go ahead, make my day."
1971 (R) 103m/C Clint Eastwood, Harry Guardino, John Larch, Andrew (Andy) Robinson, Reni Santoni, John Vernon; **D:** Donald Siegel; **M:** Lalo Schifrin. **VHS, Beta, LV, 8mm ★★★1/2**

Dirty Rotten Scoundrels A remake of the 1964 "Bedtime Story," in which two confidence tricksters on the Riviera endeavor to rip off a suddenly rich American woman, and each other. Caine and Martin are terrific, Martin has some of his best physical comedy ever, and Headly is charming as the prey who's always one step ahead of them. Fine direction from Oz, the man who brought us the voice of Yoda in "The Empire Strikes Back."
1988 (PG) 112m/C Steve Martin, Michael Caine, Glenne Headly, Anton Rodgers, Barbara Harris, Dana Ivey; **D:** Frank Oz; **W:** Dale Launer, Stanley Shapiro; **M:** Miles Goodman, Michael Ballhaus. **VHS, Beta, LV** ★★★

The Discreet Charm of the Bourgeoisie Bunuel in top form, satirizing modern society. These six characters are forever sitting down to dinner, yet they never eat. Dreams and reality, actual or contrived, prevent their feast. **AKA:** Le Charme Discret de la Bourgeoisie.
1972 (R) 100m/C FR Fernando Rey, Delphine Seyrig, Jean-Pierre Cassel, Bulle Ogier, Michel Piccoli, Stephane Audran, Luis Bunuel; **D:** Luis Bunuel; **W:** Luis Bunuel, Jean-Claude Carriere. Academy Awards '72: Best Foreign Language Film; British Academy Awards '73: Best Actress (Seyrig), Best Screenplay; National Board of Review Awards '72: 5 Best Foreign Films of the Year; National Society of Film Critics Awards '72: Best Director (Bunuel), Best Film; Nominations: Academy Awards '72: Best Story & Screenplay. **VHS, Beta, LV** ★★★★

Disraeli Arliss deservedly won the Best Actor Oscar for his title role as the famed British prime minister to Queen Victoria. This particular slice of the cunning statesman's life depicts his efforts to secure the Suez Canal for England against the Russians. Arliss' wife also played his screen spouse. One of Warner's earliest and best biographical pictures. Based on a play by Louis Napoleon Parker.
1929 87m/B George Arliss, Joan Bennett, Florence Arliss, Anthony Bushell, David Torrence, Doris Lloyd, Ivan Simpson, Gwendolyn Logan; **D:** Alfred E. Green. Academy Awards '30: Best Actor (Arliss); Nominations: Academy Awards '30: Best Picture, Best Writing. **VHS** ★★★

Distant Thunder A bitter, unrelenting portrait of a small Bengali neighborhood as the severe famines of 1942, brought about by the "distant thunder" of WWII, take their toll. A mature achievement from Ray; in Bengali with English subtitles.
1973 92m/C IN Soumitra Chatterjee, Sandhya Roy, Babita, Gobinda Chakravarty, Romesh Mukerji; **D:** Satyajit Ray. Berlin International Film Festival '73: Golden Berlin Bear. **VHS, Beta** ★★★1/2

Distant Voices, Still Lives A profoundly executed, disturbing film chronicling a British middle-class family through the maturation of the three children, under the dark shadow of their abusive, malevolent father. An evocative, heartbreaking portrait of British life from WWII on, and of the rhythms of dysfunctional families. A film festival favorite.
1988 87m/C GB Freda Dowie, Peter Postlethwaite, Angela Walsh, Dean Williams, Lorraine Ashbourne; **D:** Terence Davies; **W:** Terence Davies. Los Angeles Film Critics Association Awards '89: Best Foreign Film. **VHS, Beta, LV** ★★★

Diva While at a concert given by his favorite star, a young French courier secretly tapes a soprano who has refused to record. The film follows the young man through Paris as he flees from two Japanese recording pirates, and a couple of crooked undercover police who are trying to cover-up for the chief who not only has a mistress, but runs a prostitution ring. Brilliant and dazzling photography compliment the eclectic soundtrack.
1982 (R) 123m/C FR Frederic Andrei, Roland Bertin, Richard Bohringer, Gerard Darmon, Jacques Fabbri, Wilhelmenia Wiggins Fernandez, Dominique Pinon; **D:** Jean-Jacques Beineix; **W:** Jean-Jacques Beineix; **M:** Vladimir Cosma, Philippe Rousselot. Cesar Awards '82: Best Cinematography, Best Sound, Best Score; National Society of Film Critics Awards '82: Best Cinematography. **VHS, Beta, LV** ★★★1/2

Dive Bomber Exciting aviation film that focuses on medical problems related to flying. Flynn stars as an aviator-doctor who conducts experiments to eliminate pilot-blackout. MacMurray, Toomey, and Heydt perform well as three flyboys stationed in Hawaii. Great flying sequences filmed at San Diego's naval base with extra scenes shot at Pensacola. Warner Bros. released this film just months before the Japanese attacked Pearl Harbor. Based on the story "Beyond the Blue Sky" by Frank Wead.
1941 130m/B Errol Flynn, Fred MacMurray, Ralph Bellamy, Alexis Smith, Regis Toomey, Robert Armstrong, Allen Jenkins, Craig Stevens; **D:** Michael Curtiz; **W:** Frank Wead, Robert Buckner; **M:** Max Steiner. Nominations: Academy Awards

'41: Best Color Cinematography. **VHS**
★★★

Divorce—Italian Style A middle-aged baron bored with his wife begins directing his amorous attentions to a teenage cousin. Since divorce in Italy is impossible, the only way out of his marriage is murder—and the baron finds a little-known law that excuses a man from murdering his wife if she is having an affair (since he would merely be defending his honor). A hilarious comedy with a twist ending. Available in Italian with English subtitles or dubbed in English. *AKA:* Divorzio All'Italiana.
1962 104m/B *IT* Marcello Mastroianni, Daniela Rocca, Leopoldo Trieste; **D:** Pietro Germi; **W:** Pietro Germi, Ennio de Concini, Alfredo Giannetti. Academy Awards '62: Best Screenplay; British Academy Awards '63: Best Actor (Mastroianni); Golden Globe Awards '63: Best Actor—Musical/Comedy (Mastroianni), Best Foreign Film; Nominations: Academy Awards '62: Best Actor (Mastroianni), Best Director (Germi). **VHS** ★★★1/2

Do the Right Thing An uncompromising, brutal comedy about the racial tensions surrounding a white-owned pizzeria in the Bed-Stuy section of Brooklyn on the hottest day of the summer, and the violence that eventually erupts. Ambivalent and, for the most part, hilarious; Lee's coming-of-age.
1989 (R) 120m/C Spike Lee, Danny Aiello, Richard Edson, Ruby Dee, Ossie Davis, Giancarlo Esposito, Bill Nunn, John Turturro, John Savage, Rosie Perez, Frankie Faison; **D:** Spike Lee; **W:** Spike Lee. Los Angeles Film Critics Association Awards '89: Best Director (Lee), Best Film, Best Supporting Actor (Aiello); Nominations: Academy Awards '89: Best Original Screenplay, Best Supporting Actor (Aiello). **VHS, Beta, LV** ★★★1/2

D.O.A. A man is given a lethal, slow-acting poison. As his time runs out, he frantically seeks to learn who is responsible and why he was targeted for death. Dark film noir remade in 1969 as "Color Me Dead" and in 1988 with Dennis Quaid and Meg Ryan. Also available colorized.
1949 83m/B Edmond O'Brien, Pamela Britton, Luther Adler, Neville Brand, Beverly Garland; **D:** Rudolph Mate; **M:** Dimitri Tiomkin. **VHS, Beta** ★★★1/2

Docks of New York Von Sternberg made his mark in Hollywood with this silent drama about two dockside losers finding love amid the squalor. A rarely seen, early masterpiece.
1928 60m/B George Bancroft, Betty Compson, Olga Baclanova; **D:** Josef von Sternberg; **M:** Gaylord Carter. **VHS, Beta** ★★★

Dr. Jekyll and Mr. Hyde The hallucinatory, feverish classic version of the Robert Louis Stevenson story, in which the good doctor becomes addicted to the formula that turns him into a sadistic beast. Possibly Mamoulian's and March's best work, and a masterpiece of subversive, pseudo-Freudian creepiness. Eighteen minutes from the original version, lost until recently, have been restored, including the infamous whipping scene.
1931 96m/B Fredric March, Miriam Hopkins, Halliwell Hobbes, Rose Hobart, Holmes Herbert, Edgar Norton; **D:** Rouben Mamoulian. Academy Awards '32: Best Actor (March); Venice Film Festival '31: Best Actor (March); Nominations: Academy Awards '32: Best Adapted Screenplay, Best Cinematography. **VHS, Beta, LV** ★★★

Dr. Jekyll and Mr. Hyde Strangely cast adaptation of the Robert Louis Stevenson story about a doctor's experiment on himself to separate good and evil.
1941 113m/B Spencer Tracy, Ingrid Bergman, Lana Turner, Donald Crisp; **D:** Victor Fleming. Nominations: Academy Awards '41: Best Black and White Cinematography, Best Film Editing, Best Original Score. **VHS, Beta, LV** ★★★

Dr. Mabuse, Parts 1 & 2 The massive, two-part crime melodrama, introducing the raving mastermind/extortionist/villain to the world. The film follows Dr. Mabuse through his life of crime until he finally goes mad. Highly influential and inventive. Lang meant this to be a criticism of morally bankrupt post-WWI Germany. Followed some time later by "Testament of Doctor Mabuse" and "The Thousand Eyes of Dr. Mabuse." Silent. *AKA:* Doktor Mabuse der Spieler.
1922 242m/B *GE* Rudolf Klein-Rogge, Aud Egede Nissen, Alfred Abel, Gertrude Welcker, Lil Dagover, Paul Richter; **D:** Fritz Lang. **VHS, Beta** ★★★1/2

Dr. No The world is introduced to British secret agent 007, James Bond, when it is discovered that a mad scientist is sabotaging rocket launchings from his hideout in Jamaica. The first 007 film is far less glitzy than any of its successors but boasts the sexiest "Bond girl" of them all in Andress, and promptly made stars of her and Connery. On laserdisc, the film is in wide-screen transfer and includes movie bills, publicity photos, location pictures, and the British and American trailers. The sound effects and musical score can be separated from the dialogue. Audio interviews with the director, writer, and editor are included as part of the disc.

1962 (PG) 111m/C **GB** Sean Connery, Ursula Andress, Joseph Wiseman, Jack Lord, Zena Marshall, Eunice Gayson, Margaret LeWars, John Kitzmiller, Lois Maxwell, Bernard Lee, Anthony Dawson; **D:** Terence Young; **M:** John Barry. **VHS, Beta, LV** ★★★

Dr. Strangelove, or: How I Learned to Stop Worrying and Love the Bomb Sellers plays a tour-de-force triple role in Kubrick's classic black anti-war comedy. While a U.S. President (Sellers) deals with the Russian situation, a crazed general (Hayden) implements a plan to drop the A-bomb on the Soviets. Famous for Pickens' wild ride on the bomb, Hayden's character's "purity of essence" philosophy, Scott's gumchewing militarist, a soft-drink vending machine dispute, and countless other scenes. Based on the novel "Red Alert" by Peter George.

1964 93m/B **GB** Peter Sellers, George C. Scott, Sterling Hayden, Keenan Wynn, Slim Pickens, James Earl Jones, Peter Bull; **D:** Stanley Kubrick; **W:** Terry Southern, Peter George, Stanley Kubrick; **M:** Laurie Johnson. British Academy Awards '64: Best Film; New York Film Critics Awards '64: Best Director (Kubrick); Nominations: Academy Awards '64: Best Actor (Sellers), Best Adapted Screenplay, Best Director (Kubrick), Best Picture. **VHS, Beta, LV, 8mm** ★★★★

Doctor Zhivago Sweeping adaptation of the Nobel Prize-winning Boris Pasternak novel. An innocent Russian poet-intellectual is caught in the furor and chaos of the Bolshevik Revolution. Essentially a poignant love story filmed as a historical epic. Panoramic film popularized the song "Lara's Theme." Overlong, with often disappointing performances, but gorgeous scenery. Lean was more successful in "Lawrence of Arabia," where there was less need for ensemble acting.

1965 (PG-13) 197m/C Omar Sharif, Julie Christie, Geraldine Chaplin, Rod Steiger, Alec Guinness, Klaus Kinski, Ralph Richardson, Rita Tushingham, Siobhan McKenna, Tom Courtenay; **D:** David Lean; **W:** Robert Bolt; **M:** Maurice Jarre, Frederick A. (Freddie) Young. Academy Awards '65: Best Adapted Screenplay, Best Art Direction/Set Decoration (Color), Best Color Cinematography, Best Costume Design (Color), Best Original Score; Golden Globe Awards '66: Best Actor—Drama (Sharif), Best Director (Lean), Best Film—Drama, Best Screenplay, Best Score; National Board of Review Awards '65: 10 Best Films of the Year, Best Actress (Christie); Nominations: Academy Awards '65: Best Director (Lean), Best Film Editing, Best Picture, Best Sound, Best Supporting Actor (Courtenay). **VHS, Beta, LV** ★★★

Dodes 'ka-den In this departure from his samurai-genre films, Kurosawa depicts a throng of fringe-dwelling Tokyo slum inhabitants in a semi-surreal manner. Fascinating presentation and content. **AKA:** Clickety Clack.

1970 140m/C **JP** Yoshitaka Zushi, Junzaburo Ban, Kiyoko Tange; **D:** Akira Kurosawa. Nominations: Academy Awards '71: Best Foreign Language Film. **VHS, Beta** ★★★1/2

Dodge City Flynn stars as Wade Hutton, a roving cattleman who becomes the sheriff of Dodge City. His job: to run a ruthless outlaw and his gang out of town. De Havilland serves as Flynn's love interest, as she did in many previous films. A broad and colorful shoot-em-up!

1939 104m/C Errol Flynn, Olivia de Havilland, Bruce Cabot, Ann Sheridan, Alan Hale, Frank McHugh, Victor Jory, Henry Travers, Charles Halton; **D:** Michael Curtiz; **M:** Max Steiner. **VHS, Beta, LV** ★★★

Dodsworth The lives of a self-made American tycoon and his wife are drastically changed when they take a tour of Europe. The success of their marriage seems questionable as they re-evaluate their lives. Huston excels as does the rest of the cast in this film, based upon the Sinclair Lewis novel.

1936 101m/B Walter Huston, David Niven, Paul Lukas, John Payne, Mary Astor, Ruth Chatterton, Maria Ouspenskaya, Charles Halton; **D:** William Wyler. Academy Awards '36: Best Interior Decoration; New York Film Critics Awards '36: Best Actor (Huston); Nominations: Academy Awards '36: Best Actor (Huston), Best Adapted Screenplay, Best Director (Wyler), Best Picture, Best Sound, Best Supporting Actress (Ouspenskaya). **VHS, Beta, LV** ★★★1/2

Dog Day Afternoon Based on a true story, this taut, yet fantastic thriller centers on a bi-sexual and his slow-witted buddy who rob a bank to obtain money to fund a sex change operation for the ringleader's lover. Pacino is breathtaking in his role as the frustrated robber, caught in a trap of his own devising. Very controversial for its language and subject matter when released, it nevertheless became a huge success. Director Lumet keeps up the pace, fills the screen with pathos without gross sentiment. **1975 (R) 124m/C** Al Pacino, John Cazale, Charles Durning, James Broderick, Chris Sarandon, Carol Kane, Lance Henriksen, Dick Williams; *D:* Sidney Lumet; *W:* Frank Pierson. Academy Awards '75: Best Original Screenplay; British Academy Awards '75: Best Actor (Pacino); National Board of Review Awards '75: 10 Best Films of the Year, Best Supporting Actor (Durning); Nominations: Academy Awards '75: Best Actor (Pacino), Best Director (Lumet), Best Film Editing, Best Picture, Best Supporting Actor (Sarandon). **VHS, Beta, LV ★★★1/2**

Dog Star Man The silent epic by the dean of experimental American film depicts man's spiritual and physical conflicts through Brakhage's characteristically freeform collage techniques.
1964 78m/C *D:* Stan Brakhage. **VHS, Beta ★★★**

Dolores Claiborne Stephen King gets the Hollywood treatment again (the check cleared, King approved), with better results than previous outings (remember "Needful Things"?). Successful but neurotic New York journalist Selena (Leigh) confronts her troubled past when coarse, hard-talking mom Dolores (Bates) is accused of murdering her wealthy employer (Parfitt). Plummer is vengeful detective John Mackey who, like everyone else on the fictitious Maine island, believes Dolores murdered her husband 15 years before. Topnotch performances by Bates and Leigh highlight this sometimes manipulative tale. Straithairn is wonderfully despicable as the stereotypically deadbeat dad.
1994 (R) 132m/C Kathy Bates, Jennifer Jason Leigh, Christopher Plummer, Judy Parfitt, David Strathairn, John C. Reilly; *D:* Taylor Hackford; *W:* Tony Gilroy; *M:* Danny Elfman. **VHS, LV ★★★**

Dominick & Eugene Dominick is a little slow, but he makes a fair living as a garbageman—good enough to put his brother through medical school. Both men struggle with the other's faults and weaknesses, as they learn the meaning of family and friendship. Well-acted, especially by Hulce, never melodramatic or weak.
1988 (PG-13) 96m/C Ray Liotta, Tom Hulce, Jamie Lee Curtis, Todd Graff, Bill Cobbs, David Strathairn; *D:* Robert M.

Young; *W:* Alvin Sargent, Corey Blechman; *M:* Trevor Jones. **VHS, Beta, LV ★★★**

Don Juan Barrymore stars as the swashbuckling Italian duke with Spanish blood who seduces a castleful of women in the 1500s. Many exciting action sequences, including classic sword fights in which Barrymore eschewed a stunt double. Great attention is also paid to the detail of the costumes and settings of the Spanish-Moor period. Noted for employing fledgling movie sound effects and music-dubbing technology, which, ironically, were responsible for eclipsing the movie's reputation. Watch for Loy as an Asian vamp and Oland as a pre-Charlie Chan Cesare Borgia.
1926 90m/B John Barrymore, Mary Astor, Willard Louis, Estelle Taylor, Helene Costello, Myrna Loy, June Marlowe, Warner Oland, Montagu Love, Hedda Hopper, Gustav von Seyffertitz; *D:* Alan Crosland. **VHS, LV ★★★1/2**

Don Quixote Miguel de Cervantes' tale of the romantic who would rather be a knight in shining armor than shining armor at night. Chaliapin stars as the knight-errant on his nightly errands, tilting at windmills and charging flocks of sheep. Certain scenes were adapted to fit the pre-WWII atmosphere, as it was filmed during the same time that the Nazis were burning books.
1935 73m/B Feodor Chaliapin, George Robey, Sidney Fox, Miles Mander, Oscar Asche, Emily Fitzroy, Wally Patch; *D:* G.W. Pabst; *W:* Paul Morand, Alexandre Arnoux; *M:* Jacques Ibert. **VHS ★★★★**

Don Quixote The lauded, visually ravishing adaptation of the Cervantes classic, with a formal integrity inherited from Eisenstein and Dovshenko. In Russian with English subtitles.
1957 110m/B *SP RU* Nikolai Cherkassov, Yuri Tobubeyev; *D:* Grigori Kosintsev. **VHS, Beta ★★★1/2**

Dona Flor and Her Two Husbands A woman becomes a widow when her philandering husband finally expires from drink, gambling, and ladies. She remarries, but her new husband is so boring and proper that she begins fantasizing spouse number one's return. But is he only in her imagination? Based on the novel by Jorge Amado. In Portuguese with English subtitles. Remade as "Kiss Me Goodbye." *AKA:* Dona Flor e Seus Dois Maridos.
1978 106m/C *BR* Sonia Braga, Jose Wilker, Mauro Mendonca; *D:* Bruno Barreto; *W:* Bruno Barreto; *M:* Chico Buarque. **VHS, Beta, LV ★★★**

Donovan's Brain A scientist maintains the still-living brain of a dead millionaire and begins to be controlled by its powerful force. Based on Curt Siodmak's novel.
1953 85m/B Lew Ayres, Gene Evans, Nancy Davis, Steve Brodie; **D:** Felix Feist. **VHS, Beta, LV** ★★★

Donovan's Reef Two WWII buddies meet every year on a Pacific atoll to engage in a perpetual bar-brawl, until a stuck-up Bostonian maiden appears to find her dad, a man who has fathered a brood of lovable half-casts. A rollicking, good-natured film from Ford.
1963 109m/C John Wayne, Lee Marvin, Jack Warden, Elizabeth Allen, Dorothy Lamour, Mike Mazurki, Cesar Romero; **D:** John Ford. **VHS, Beta, LV** ★★★

Don't Look Back Musician and heroin addict Jesse Parish (Stoltz) stumbles across a suitcase full of cash after witnessing a drug deal gone wrong. He heads back to family and friends in Texas so he can kick his habit but is marked for death by the drug dealers who want their money back. Strong script and performances; made for cable TV.
1996 91m/C Eric Stoltz, John Corbett, Josh Hamilton, Annabeth Gish, Dwight Yoakam, Amanda Plummer; **W:** Billy Bob Thornton, Tom Epperson; **D:** Geoff Murphy. **VHS** ★★★

Don't Look Now A psychological thriller about a couple's trip to Venice after their child drowns. Notable for a steamy love scene and a chilling climax. Based on the novel by Daphne Du Maurier.
1973 (R) 110m/C Donald Sutherland, Julie Christie, Hilary Mason; **D:** Nicolas Roeg; **W:** Chris Bryant, Allan Scott; **M:** Pino Donaggio. **VHS, Beta, LV** ★★★

The Doom Generation Alienated trio on the road trip to hell (doubling as L.A.). Beautiful 17-year-old druggie Amy Blue (McGowan), her sweetly dim boyfriend Jordan White (Duval), and hot-tempered stud/drifter Xavier Red (Schaech) flee after Red kills a store clerk. They're basically from nowhere, going nowhere, and finding sex and (lots of gruesomely depicted) violence along the way. The subtitle, "A Heterosexual Movie by Gregg Araki," may be technically accurate, but the homoerotic subtext is very clear. Terrific performances. Second film in Araki's teen trilogy, following "Totally F***ked Up," and preceding "Nowhere." An unrated version is also available.
1995 (R) 84m/C Rose McGowan, James Duval, Johnathon Schaech; **Cameos:** Parker Posey; **D:** Gregg Araki; **W:** Gregg Araki. Nominations: Independent Spirit Awards '96: Debut Performance (McGowan). **VHS** ★★★

Double Indemnity The classic seedy story of an insurance agent seduced by a deadly woman into killing her husband so they can collect together from his company. Terrific, influential film noir, the best of its kind. Based on the James M. Cain novel.
1944 107m/B Fred MacMurray, Barbara Stanwyck, Edward G. Robinson, Tom Powers, Porter Hall, Jean Heather, Byron Barr, Fortunio Bonanova; **D:** Billy Wilder; **W:** Raymond Chandler, Billy Wilder; **M:** Miklos Rozsa. Nominations: Academy Awards '44: Best Actress (Stanwyck), Best Black and White Cinematography, Best Director (Wilder), Best Picture, Best Screenplay, Best Sound, Best Original Score. **VHS, Beta, LV** ★★★★

A Double Life Colman plays a Shakespearean actor in trouble when the characters he plays begin to seep into his personal life and take over. Things begin to look really bad when he is cast in the role of the cursed Othello. Colman won an Oscar for this difficult role, and the moody musical score garnered another for Rozsa.
1947 107m/B Ronald Colman, Shelley Winters, Signe Hasso, Edmond O'Brien, Ray Collins, Millard Mitchell; **D:** George Cukor; **W:** Ruth Gordon, Garson Kanin; **M:** Miklos Rozsa. Academy Awards '47: Best Actor (Colman), Best Score; Golden Globe Awards '48: Best Actor—Drama (Colman); Nominations: Academy Awards '47: Best Director (Cukor), Best Original Screenplay. **VHS** ★★★

Double Wedding Madcap comedy starring Powell as a wacky painter who doesn't believe in working and Loy as a workaholic dress designer. Loy has chosen a fiance for her younger sister, Irene, to marry, but Irene has plans of her own. When Irene and her beau meet bohemian Powell, the fun really begins. Script suffers slightly from too much slapstick and not enough wit, although the stars (in their seventh outing as a duo) play it well. Based on the play "Great Love" by Ferenc Molnar.
1937 86m/B William Powell, Myrna Loy, Florence Rice, John Beal, Jessie Ralph, Edgar Kennedy, Sidney Toler, Mary Gordon; **D:** Richard Thorpe; **W:** Jo Swerling. **VHS** ★★★

Down & Dirty A scathing Italian satire about a modern Roman family steeped in petty crime, incest, murder, adultery, drugs, and arson. In Italian with English subtitles. *AKA:* Brutti, Sporchi, e Cattivi.

1976 115m/C *IT* Nino Manfredi, Francesco Anniballi, Maria Bosco; *D:* Ettore Scola; *W:* Ettore Scola. Cannes Film Festival '76: Best Director (Scola). **VHS, Beta ★★★**

Down Argentine Way A lovely young woman falls in love with a suave argentinian horse breeder. First-rate Fox musical made a star of Grable and was Miranda's first American film. ♪ South American Way; Down Argentina Way; Two Dreams Met; Mama Yo Quiero; Sing to Your Senorita.

1940 90m/C Don Ameche, Betty Grable, Carmen Miranda, Charlotte Greenwood, J. Carrol Naish, Henry Stephenson, Leonid Kinskey; *D:* Irving Cummings. Nominations: Academy Awards '40: Best Color Cinematography, Best Interior Decoration, Best Song ("Down Argentine Way"). **VHS, Beta, LV ★★★**

Down by Law In Jarmusch's follow-up to his successful "Stranger than Paradise," he introduces us to three men: a pimp, an out-of-work disc jockey, and an Italian tourist. When the three break out of prison, they wander through the Louisiana swampland with some regrets about their new-found freedom. Slow-moving at times, beautifully shot throughout. Poignant and hilarious, the film is true to Jarmusch form: some will love the film's offbeat flair, and others will find it bothersome.

1986 (R) 107m/C John Lurie, Tom Waits, Roberto Benigni, Ellen Barkin, Billie Neal, Rockets Redglare, Vernel Bagneris, Nicoletta Braschi; *D:* Jim Jarmusch; *W:* Jim Jarmusch; *M:* John Lurie, Tom Waits. **VHS, Beta ★★★**

Dracula, Lugosi, in his most famous role, plays a vampire who terrorizes the countryside in his search for human blood. From Bram Stoker's novel. Although short of a masterpiece due to slow second half, deservedly rated a film classic. What would Halloween be like without this movie? Sequelled by "Dracula's Daughter."

1931 75m/B Bela Lugosi, David Manners, Dwight Frye, Helen Chandler, Edward Van Sloan; *D:* Tod Browning. **VHS, Beta, LV ★★★**

Dragon: The Bruce Lee Story Entertaining, inspiring account of the life of Chinese-American martial-arts legend Bruce Lee. Jason Scott Lee (no relation) is great as the talented spirit, exuding his joy of life and gentle spirit, before his mysterious brain disorder death at the age of 32. Ironi-

cally, this release coincided with son Brandon's accidental death on a movie set. The martial arts sequences in "Dragon" are extraordinary, but there's also romance as Lee meets and marries his wife (Holly, who acquits herself well). Based on the book "Bruce Lee: The Man Only I Knew" by his widow, Linda Lee Caldwell.

1993 (PG-13) 121m/C Jason Scott Lee, Lauren Holly, Robert Wagner, Michael Learned, Nancy Kwan, Kay Tong Lim, Sterling Macer, Ric Young, Sven Ole-Thorsen; *D:* Rob Cohen; *W:* Edward Khmara, John Raffo, Rob Cohen; *M:* Randy Edelman. Nominations: MTV Movie Awards '94: Breakthrough Performance (Lee). **VHS, LV ★★★**

The Draughtsman's Contract A beguiling mystery begins when a wealthy woman hires an artist to make drawings of her home. Their contract is quite unusual, as is their relationship. Everything is going along at an even pace until murder is suspected, and things spiral down to darker levels. A simple story turned into a bizarre puzzle. Intense enough for any thriller fan.

1982 (R) 103m/C *GB* Anthony Higgins, Janet Suzman, Anne Louise Lambert, Hugh Fraser; *D:* Peter Greenaway; *W:* Peter Greenaway; *M:* Michael Nyman. **VHS ★★★**

The Dresser Film adaptation of Harwood's play (he also wrote the screen version) about an aging English actor/manager (Finney), his dresser (Courtenay), and their theater company touring England during WWII. Marvelous showbiz tale is lovingly told, superbly acted.

1983 (PG) 119m/C Albert Finney, Tom Courtenay, Edward Fox, Michael Gough, Zena Walker, Eileen Atkins, Cathryn Harrison; *D:* Peter Yates; *W:* Ronald Harwood; *M:* James Horner. Golden Globe Awards '84: Best Actor—Drama (Courtenay); Nominations: Academy Awards '83: Best Actor (Courtenay), Best Actor (Finney), Best Adapted Screenplay, Best Director (Yates), Best Picture. **VHS, Beta, LV ★★★★**

Drifting Weeds A remake by Ozu of his 1934 silent film about a troupe of traveling actors whose leader visits his illegitimate son and his lover after years of separation. Classic Ozu in his first color film. In Japanese with English subtitles. *AKA:* Floating Weeds; The Duckweed Story; Ukigusa.

1959 128m/B *JP* Ganjiro Nakamura, Machiko Kyo, Haruko Sugimura, Ayako

Wakao; **D:** Yasujiro Ozu. **VHS, Beta, LV**
★★★1/2

Driving Miss Daisy Tender and sincere portrayal of a 25-year friendship between an aging Jewish woman and the black chauffeur forced upon her by her son. Humorous and thought-provoking, skillfully acted and directed, it subtly explores the effects of prejudice in the South. The development of Aykroyd as a top-notch character actor is further evidenced here. Part of the fun is watching the changes in fashion and auto design. Adapted from the play by Alfred Uhry.
1989 (PG) 99m/C Jessica Tandy, Morgan Freeman, Dan Aykroyd, Esther Rolle, Patti LuPone; **D:** Bruce Beresford; **W:** Alfred Uhry; **M:** Hans Zimmer. Academy Awards '89: Best Actress (Tandy), Best Adapted Screenplay, Best Makeup, Best Picture; British Academy Awards '90: Best Actress (Tandy); Golden Globe Awards '90: Best Actor—Musical/Comedy (Freeman), Best Actress—Musical/Comedy (Tandy), Best Film—Musical/Comedy; National Board of Review Awards '89: 10 Best Films of the Year, Best Actor (Freeman); Writers Guild of America '89: Best Adapted Screenplay; Nominations: Academy Awards '89: Best Actor (Freeman), Best Costume Design, Best Film Editing, Best Supporting Actor (Aykroyd). **VHS, Beta, LV, 8mm** ★★★1/2

Drowning by Numbers Three generations of women, each named Cissie Colpitts, solve their marital problems by drowning their husbands and making deals with a bizarre coroner. Further strange visions from director Greenaway, complemented by stunning cinematography courtesy of Sacha Vierny. A treat for those who appreciate Greenaway's uniquely curious cinematic statements.
1987 (R) 121m/C GB Bernard Hill, Joan Plowright, Juliet Stevenson, Joely Richardson; **D:** Peter Greenaway; **W:** Peter Greenaway; **M:** Michael Nyman. **VHS, LV** ★★★1/2

Drugstore Cowboy A gritty, uncompromising depiction of a pack of early 1970s drugstore-robbing junkies as they travel around looking to score. Brushes with the law and tragedy encourage them to examine other lifestyles, but the trap seems impossible to leave. A perfectly crafted piece that reflects the "me generation" era, though it tends to glamorize addiction. Dillon's best work to date. Based on a novel by prison inmate James Fogle.
1989 (R) 100m/C Matt Dillon, Kelly Lynch, James Remar, James LeGros, Heather Graham, William S. Burroughs, Beah Richards, Grace Zabriskie, Max Perlich; **D:** Gus Van Sant; **W:** Gus Van Sant, Daniel Yost; **M:** Elliot Goldenthal. Independent Spirit Awards '90: Best Actor (Dillon), Best Cinematography, Best Screenplay, Best Supporting Actor (Perlich); New York Film Critics Awards '89: Best Screenplay; National Society of Film Critics Awards '89: Best Director (Van Sant), Best Film, Best Screenplay. **VHS, Beta, LV** ★★★1/2

Drums Along the Mohawk Grand, action-filled saga about pre-Revolutionary America, detailing the trials of a colonial newlywed couple as their village in Mohawk Valley is besieged by Indians. Based on the Walter Edmonds novel, and vintage Ford.
1939 104m/C Henry Fonda, Claudette Colbert, Edna May Oliver, Eddie Collins, John Carradine, Dorris Bowdon, Arthur Shields, Ward Bond, Jessie Ralph, Robert Lowery; **D:** John Ford. Nominations: Academy Awards '39: Best Color Cinematography, Best Supporting Actress (Oliver). **VHS, Beta, LV** ★★★1/2

Drunken Angel Alcoholic doctor gets mixed up with local gangster. Kurosawa's first major film aided by strong performances. With English subtitles.
1948 108m/B JP Toshiro Mifune, Takashi Shimura, Choko Iida; **D:** Akira Kurosawa. **VHS, Beta** ★★★

A Dry White Season A white Afrikaner living resignedly with apartheid confronts the system when his black gardener, an old friend, is persecuted and murdered. A well-meaning expose that, like many others, focuses on white people.
1989 (R) 105m/C Donald Sutherland, Marlon Brando, Susan Sarandon, Zakes Mokae, Janet Suzman, Juergen Prochnow, Winston Ntshona, Susannah Harker, Thoko Ntshinga, Rowan Elmes; **D:** Euzhan Palcy; **W:** Colin Welland, Euzhan Palcy; **M:** Dave Grusin. Nominations: Academy Awards '89: Best Supporting Actor (Brando). **VHS, Beta, LV** ★★★

Duck Soup The Marx Brothers satiric masterpiece (which failed at the box office). Groucho becomes the dictator of Freedonia, and hires Chico and Harpo as spies. Jam-packed with the classic anarchic and irreverent Marx shtick; watch for the mirror scene. Zeppo plays a love-sick tenor, in this, his last film with the brothers.
1933 70m/B Groucho Marx, Chico Marx, Harpo Marx, Zeppo Marx, Louis Calhern, Margaret Dumont, Edgar Kennedy, Raquel Torres, Leonid Kinskey, Charles Middleton; **D:** Leo McCarey; **W:** Harry Ruby, Nat Perrin, Bert Kalmar, Arthur Sheekman; **M:** Harry Ruby, Bert Kalmar. **VHS, Beta, LV** ★★★★

Duel Spielberg's first notable film, a made-for-television exercise in paranoia. A docile traveling salesman is repeatedly attacked and threatened by a huge, malevolent tractor-trailer on an open desert highway. Released theatrically in Europe.
1971 (PG) 90m/C Dennis Weaver, Lucille Benson, Eddie Firestone, Cary Loftin; **D:** Steven Spielberg; **W:** Richard Matheson; **M:** Billy Goldenberg. **VHS, Beta** ★★★

Duel at Diablo An exceptionally violent film that deals with racism in the Old West. Good casting; western fans will enjoy the action.
1966 103m/C James Garner, Sidney Poitier, Bibi Andersson, Dennis Weaver, Bill Travers; **D:** Ralph Nelson. **VHS** ★★★

Duel in the Sun A lavish, lusty David O. Selznick production of a minor western novel about a vivacious half-breed Indian girl, living on a powerful dynastic ranch, who incites two brothers to conflict. Selznick's last effort at outdoing his epic success with "Gone With the Wind."
1946 130m/C Gregory Peck, Jennifer Jones, Joseph Cotten, Lionel Barrymore, Lillian Gish, Butterfly McQueen, Harry Carey Sr., Walter Huston, Charles Bickford, Herbert Marshall; **D:** King Vidor. Nominations: Academy Awards '46: Best Actress (Jones), Best Supporting Actress (Gish). **VHS, Beta** ★★★

The Duellists A beautifully photographed picture about the long-running feud between two French officers during the Napoleonic wars. Based on "The Duel" by Joseph Conrad.
1977 (PG) 101m/C *GB* Keith Carradine, Harvey Keitel, Albert Finney, Edward Fox, Tom Conti, Christina Raines, Diana Quick; **D:** Ridley Scott. Nominations: Cannes Film Festival '77: Best Film. **VHS, Beta, LV** ★★★

Dumbo Animated Disney classic about a baby elephant growing up in the circus who is ridiculed for his large ears, until he discovers he can fly. The little elephant who could fly then becomes a circus star. Expressively and imaginatively animated, highlighted by the hallucinatory dancing pink elephants sequence. Endearing songs by Frank Churchill, Oliver Wallace, and Ned Washington, including "Baby Mine," "Pink Elephants on Parade," and "I See an Elephant Fly."
1941 63m/C **D:** Ben Sharpsteen; **W:** Joe Grant, Dick Huemer; **M:** Frank Churchill, Oliver Wallace; **V:** Sterling Holloway, Edward Brophy, Verna Felton, Herman Bing, Cliff Edwards. Academy Awards '41:

Best Score; National Board of Review Awards '41: 10 Best Films of the Year; Nominations: Academy Awards '41: Best Song ("Baby Mine"). **VHS, Beta, LV** ★★★★

The Dybbuk A man's bride is possessed by a restless spirit. Set in the Polish-Jewish community before WWI and based on the play by Sholom Anski. Considered a classic for its portrayal of Jewish religious and cultural mores. In Yiddish with English subtitles.
1937 123m/B *PL* Abraham Morewski, Isaac Samberg, Moshe Lipman, Lili Liliana, Dina Halpern; **D:** Michal Waszynski. **VHS, Beta** ★★★½

The Eagle In this tale of a young Cossack "Robin Hood," Valentino assumes the persona of the Eagle to avenge his father's murder. The romantic rogue encounters trouble when he falls for the beautiful Banky much to the chagrin of the scorned Czarina Dresser. Fine performances from Valentino and Dresser. Silent, based on a Alexander Pushkin story. Released on video with a new score by Davis.
1925 77m/B Rudolph Valentino, Vilma Banky, Louise Dresser, George Nicholls Jr., James Marcus; **D:** Clarence Brown; **M:** Carl Davis. **VHS, Beta, LV** ★★★

An Early Frost Highly praised, surprisingly intelligent made-for-television drama following the anguish of a successful lawyer who tells his closed-minded family that he is gay and dying of AIDS. Sensitive performance by Quinn in one of the first TV films to focus on the devastating effects of HIV. Rowlands adeptly displays her acting talents as the despairing mother.
1985 97m/C Aidan Quinn, Gena Rowlands, Ben Gazzara, John Glover, D.W. Moffett, Sylvia Sidney; **D:** John Erman. **VHS, Beta, LV** ★★★½

Early Summer A classic from renowned Japanese director Ozu, this film chronicles family tensions in post-WWII Japan caused by newly-independent women rebelling against the social conventions they are expected to fulfill. Perhaps the best example of this director's work. Winner of Japan's Film of the Year Award. In Japanese with English subtitles. **AKA:** Bakushu.
1951 150m/B *JP* Ichiro Sugai, Chishu Ryu, Setsuko Hara, Chikage Awashima, Chieko Higashiyama, Haruko Sugimura, Kuniko Miyake, Kan Nihon-yanagi, Shuji Sano, Toyoko Takahashi, Seiji Miyaguchi; **D:** Yasujiro Ozu. **VHS, Beta** ★★★

The Earrings of Madame De . . . A simple story about a society woman who sells a pair of diamond earrings that her husband gave her, then lies about it. Transformed by Ophuls into his most opulent, overwrought masterpiece, the film displays a triumph of form over content. In French with English subtitles. *AKA:* Diamond Earrings; Madame De.
1954 105m/C *FR* Charles Boyer, Danielle Darrieux, Vittorio De Sica, Lea di Lea, Jean Debucourt; *D:* Max Ophuls. Nominations: Academy Awards '54: Best Costume Design (B & W). **VHS, Beta ★★★★**

Earth Classic Russian silent film with English subtitles. Problems begin in a Ukrainian village when a collective farm landowner resists handing over his land. Outstanding camera work. Kino release runs 70 minutes. *AKA:* Zemlya; Soul.
1930 57m/B *RU* Semyon Svashenko, Mikola Nademsy, Stephan Shkurat, Yelena Maximova; *D:* Alexander Dovzhenko. **VHS, Beta ★★★★**

East of Eden Steinbeck's contemporary retelling of the biblical Cain and Abel story receives superior treatment from Kazan and his excellent cast. Dean, in his first starring role, gives a reading of a young man's search for love and acceptance that defines adolescent pain. Though filmed in the 1950s, this story still rivets today's viewers with its emotional message.
1954 115m/C James Dean, Julie Harris, Richard Davalos, Raymond Massey, Jo Van Fleet, Burl Ives, Albert Dekker; *D:* Elia Kazan; *W:* Paul Osborn; *M:* Leonard Rosenman. Academy Awards '55: Best Supporting Actress (Van Fleet); Golden Globe Awards '56: Best Film—Drama; National Board of Review Awards '55: 10 Best Films of the Year; Nominations: Academy Awards '55: Best Actor (Dean), Best Director (Kazan), Best Screenplay. **VHS, Beta, LV ★★★★**

Easter Parade A big musical star (Astaire) splits with his partner (Miller) claiming that he could mold any girl to replace her in the act. He tries and finally succeeds after much difficulty. Astaire and Garland in peak form, aided by a classic Irving Berlin score. ♪ Happy Easter; Drum Crazy; It Only Happens When I Dance With You; Everybody's Doin' It; I Want to Go Back to Michigan; Beautiful Faces Need Beautiful Clothes; A Fella With an Umbrella; I Love a Piano; Snookey Ookums.
1948 103m/C Fred Astaire, Judy Garland, Peter Lawford, Ann Miller, Jules Munshin, Joi Lansing; *D:* Charles Walters; *W:* Sidney Sheldon; *M:* Irving Berlin. Academy Awards '48: Best Score. **VHS, Beta, LV ★★★1/2**

Easy Rider Slim-budget, generation-defining movie. Two young men in late 1960s undertake a motorcycle trek throughout the Southwest in search of the real essence of America. Along the way they encounter hippies, rednecks, prostitutes, drugs, Nicholson, and tragedy. One of the highest-grossing pictures of the decade, undoubtedly an influence on two generations of "youth-oriented dramas," which all tried unsuccessfully to duplicate the original accomplishment. Psychedelic scenes and a great role for Nicholson are added bonuses. Look for the graveyard dancing scene in New Orleans. Features one of the best '60s rock scores around, including "Mean Streets" and "The Wanderers."
1969 (R) 94m/C Peter Fonda, Dennis Hopper, Jack Nicholson, Karen Black, Toni Basil, Robert Walker Jr.; *D:* Dennis Hopper; *W:* Terry Southern. New York Film Critics Awards '69: Best Supporting Actor (Nicholson); National Society of Film Critics Awards '69: Best Supporting Actor (Nicholson); Nominations: Academy Awards '69: Best Story & Screenplay, Best Supporting Actor (Nicholson). **VHS, Beta, LV, 8mm ★★★1/2**

Easy Street Chaplin portrays a derelict who, using some hilarious methods, reforms the residents of Easy Street. Chaplin's row with the town bully is particularly amusing. Silent with musical soundtrack added.
1916 20m/B Charlie Chaplin; *D:* Charlie Chaplin. **VHS, Beta ★★★**

Eat a Bowl of Tea Endearing light drama-comedy concerning a multigenerational Chinese family. They must learn to deal with the problems of life in America and in particular, marriage, when Chinese women are finally allowed to immigrate with their husbands to the United States following WWII. Adaptation of Louis Chu's story, directed by the man who brought us "Dim Sum." A PBS "American Playhouse" presentation.
1989 (PG-13) 102m/C Cora Miao, Russell Wong, Lau Siu Ming, Eric Tsiang Chi Wai, Victor Wong, Jessica Harper, Lee Sau Kee; *D:* Wayne Wang; *W:* Judith Rascoe; *M:* Mark Adler. **VHS, Beta, LV ★★★**

Eat Drink Man Woman In Taipei, widowed master chef serves weekly feast of elaborate food and familial guilt to his three grown daughters, all of whom still live at home. They spend their time sorting out professional and romantic difficulties, searching for independence, and fulfilling traditional family obligations. Each character has a lot going on, but no one's story gets lost in the mix. Lee uses irony to great effect, introducing us to the culinary artist who has lost his sense of taste and has a daughter who works at a Wendy's. Food preparation scenes (more than 100 recipes are served up) illustrate a careful attention to detail (and are guaranteed to make you hungry). Lee's follow-up to "The Wedding Banquet" is a finely observed, comic tale of generational drift, the richness of tradition, and the power of love to redeem or improve. In Chinese with subtitles or dubbed.

1994 (R) 123m/C *TW* Sihung Lung, Kuei-Mei Yang, Yu-Wen Wang, Chien-Lien Wu, Sylvia Chang, Winston Chao; **D:** Ang Lee; **W:** Hui-Ling Wang, James Schamus, Ang Lee, Jong Lin. National Board of Review Awards '94: Best Foreign Film; Nominations: Academy Awards '94: Best Foreign Language Film; Golden Globe Awards '95: Best Foreign Language Film; Independent Spirit Awards '95: Best Actor (Lung), Best Actress (Wu), Best Cinematography, Best Director (Lee), Best Film, Best Screenplay. **VHS, LV** ★★★1/2

Eating Raoul The Blands are a happily married couple who share many interests: good food and wine, entrepreneurial dreams, and an aversion to sex. The problem is, they're flat broke. So, when the tasty swinger from upstairs makes a pass at Mary and Paul accidentally kills him, they discover he's got loads of money; Raoul takes a cut in the deal by disposing of—or rather recycling—the body. This may just be the way to finance that restaurant they've been wanting to open. Wonderful, offbeat, hilariously dark comedy.

1982 (R) 83m/C Mary Woronov, Paul Bartel, Buck Henry, Ed Begley Jr., Edie McClurg, Robert Beltran, John Paragon; **D:** Mary Woronov, Paul Bartel; **W:** Paul Bartel, Richard Blackburn. **VHS, Beta** ★★★1/2

The Eclipse The last of Antonioni's trilogy (after "L'Avventura" and "La Notte"), wherein another fashionable and alienated Italian woman passes from one lover to another searching unsuccessfully for truth and love. Highly acclaimed. In Italian with subtitles. **AKA:** L'eclisse.

1966 123m/B *IT* Monica Vitti, Alain Delon, Francesco Rabal, Louis Seigner; **D:** Michelangelo Antonioni; **W:** Michelangelo Antonioni, Carlo DiPalma. **VHS, Beta** ★★★1/2

Ed Wood Leave it to Burton to bring to the screen the story of a director many consider to be the worst of all time (he's at least in the top three) and who now occupies a lofty position as a cult icon. In this hilarious and touching tribute to a Hollywood maverick with grade-Z vision, detailed homage is paid to Wood's single-mindedness and optimism in the face of repeated failure and lack of financing, even down to the black and white photography. Depp is convincing (and engaging) as Ed Wood, Jr., the cross-dressing, angora-sweater-wearing, low-budget auteur of such notoriously "bad" cult films as "Glen or Glenda" and "Plan 9 From Outer Space." Depp is supported by terrific portrayals of the motley Wood crew, led by Landau's morphine-addicted, down-on-his-luck Bela Lugosi. Burton focuses on Wood's relationship with Lugosi, whose career is over by the time Wood befriends him. Based on Rudolph Grey's book, "Nightmare of Ecstasy: The Life and Art of Edward D. Wood, Jr."

1994 (R) 127m/B Johnny Depp, Sarah Jessica Parker, Martin Landau, Bill Murray, Jim Myers, Patricia Arquette, Jeffrey Jones, Lisa Marie, Vincent D'Onofrio; **D:** Tim Burton; **W:** Scott Alexander, Larry Karaszewski. Academy Awards '94: Best Makeup, Best Supporting Actor (Landau); Golden Globe Awards '95: Best Supporting Actor (Landau); Los Angeles Film Critics Association Awards '94: Best Cinematography, Best Original Score; New York Film Critics Awards '94: Best Cinematography, Best Supporting Actor (Landau); Screen Actors Guild Award '94: Best Supporting Actor (Landau); Nominations: British Academy Awards '95: Best Supporting Actor (Landau); Golden Globe Awards '95: Best Actor—Musical/Comedy (Depp), Best Film—Musical/Comedy. **VHS, LV** ★★★1/2

Edge of Darkness Compelling war-drama about the underground movement in Norway during Nazi takeover of WWII. Flynn plays a Norwegian fisherman who leads the local underground movement and Sheridan is his loyal fiancee. Although several problems occurred throughout filming, this picture earned high marks for its superb performances and excellent camerawork. Based on the novel by William Woods.

1943 120m/B Errol Flynn, Ann Sheridan, Walter Huston, Nancy Coleman, Helmut Dantine, Judith Anderson, Ruth Gordon, John Beal; **D:** Lewis Milestone; **W:** Robert Rossen. **VHS** ★★★1/2

Edge of the World Moody, stark British drama of a mini-society in its death throes, expertly photographed on a six-square-mile island in the Shetlands. A dwindling fishing community of fewer than 100 souls agonize over whether to migrate to the mainland; meanwhile the romance of a local girl with an off-islander takes a tragic course. Choral effects were provided by the Glasgow Orpheus Choir.

1937 80m/B *GB* Finlay Currie, Niall MacGinnis, Grant Sutherland, John Laurie, Michael Powell; **D:** Michael Powell; **W:** Michael Powell. **VHS** ★★★

Educating Rita Walters and Caine team beautifully in this adaptation of the successful Willy Russell play which finds an uneducated hairdresser determined to improve her knowledge of literature. In so doing, she enlists the aid of a tutor: a disillusioned alcoholic, adeptly played by Caine. Together, the two find inspiration in one another's differences and experiences. Ultimately, the teacher receives a lesson in how to again appreciate his work and the classics as he observes his pupil's unique approach to her studies. Some deem this a "Pygmalion" for the '80s.

1983 (PG) 110m/C *GB* Michael Caine, Julie Walters, Michael Williams, Maureen Lipman; **D:** Lewis Gilbert; **W:** Willy Russell. British Academy Awards '83: Best Actor (Caine), Best Actress (Walters), Best Film; Golden Globe Awards '84: Best Actor—Musical/Comedy (Caine), Best Actress—Musical/Comedy (Walters); Nominations: Academy Awards '83: Best Actor (Caine), Best Actress (Walters), Best Adapted Screenplay. **VHS, Beta, LV, 8mm** ★★★1/2

Edward Scissorhands Depp's a young man created by loony scientist Price, who dies before he can attach hands to his boy-creature. Then the boy is rescued from his lonely existence outside of suburbia by an ingratiating Avon lady. With scissors in place of hands, he has more trouble fitting into suburbia than would most new kids on the block, and he struggles with being different and lonely in a cardboard-cutout world. Visually captivating fairy-tale full of splash and color, however predictable the Hollywood-prefab denouement.

1990 (PG-13) 100m/C Johnny Depp, Winona Ryder, Dianne Wiest, Vincent Price, Anthony Michael Hall, Alan Arkin, Kathy Baker, Conchata Ferrell, Caroline Aaron, Dick Anthony Williams, Robert Oliveri, John Davidson; **D:** Tim Burton; **W:** Caroline Thompson, Tim Burton; **M:** Danny Elfman.

Nominations: Academy Awards '90: Best Makeup. **VHS, Beta, LV** ★★★

The Effect of Gamma Rays on Man-in-the-Moon Marigolds A wonderful drama based on the Pulitzer Prize-winning play by Paul Zindel. The story centers around eccentric young Matilda and her depressed family. Matilda is preparing her experiment for the school science fair, determined to beat her competition. Her exhibit shows how radiation sometimes kills the helpless marigolds, but sometimes causes them to grow into even more beautiful mutations. This mirrors Matilda, who flowers even amidst the drunkenness of her mother and the dullness of her sister.

1973 (PG) 100m/C Joanne Woodward, Nell Potts, Roberta Wallach, Judith Lowry, Richard Venture; **D:** Paul Newman. Cannes Film Festival '73: Best Actress (Woodward); Nominations: Cannes Film Festival '73: Best Film. **VHS** ★★★

Effi Briest A 19th-century tragedy well-played by Schygulla and empowered with Fassbinder's directorial skills. Effi (Schygulla) is a 17-year-old beauty, unhappily married to a much older man. She drifts into a brief affair, which is not discovered for several years. When her husband does discover her past infidelity, the Prussian legal code permits him a chilling revenge. Based on a popular 19th-century novel by Theodor Fontane. In German with English subtitles. ***AKA:*** Fontane Effi Briest.

1974 135m/B *GE* Hanna Schygulla, Wolfgang Schenck, Lilo Pempeit, Ulli Lommel; **D:** Rainer Werner Fassbinder; **W:** Rainer Werner Fassbinder. **VHS** ★★★1/2

Egg and I Based on the true-life adventures of best-selling humorist Betty MacDonald. A young urban bride agrees to help her new husband realize his life-long dream of owning a chicken farm. A dilapidated house, temperamental stove, and suicidal chickens test the bride's perseverance, as do the zany antics of her country-bumpkin neighbors, Ma and Pa Kettle, who make their screen debut. Plenty of old-fashioned laughs.

1947 104m/B Claudette Colbert, Fred MacMurray, Marjorie Main, Percy Kilbride, Louise Allbritton, Richard Long, Billy House, Donald MacBride; **D:** Chester Erskine. Nominations: Academy Awards '47: Best Supporting Actress (Main). **VHS, Beta, LV** ★★★

8 1/2 The acclaimed Fellini self-portrait of a revered Italian film director struggling with a fated film project wanders through his intermixed life,

childhood memories, and hallucinatory fantasies. Subtitled in English. **AKA:** Otto E Mezzo; Federico Fellini's 8 1/2.
1963 135m/B *IT* Marcello Mastroianni, Claudia Cardinale, Anouk Aimee, Sandra Milo, Barbara Steele, Rossella Falk, Eddra Gale, Mark Herron, Madeleine LeBeau, Caterina Boratto; **D:** Federico Fellini; **W:** Tullio Pinelli, Ennio Flaiano, Brunello Rondi, Federico Fellini; **M:** Nino Rota. Academy Awards '63: Best Costume Design (B & W), Best Foreign Language Film; National Board of Review Awards '63: 5 Best Foreign Films of the Year; New York Film Critics Awards '63: Best Foreign Film; Nominations: Academy Awards '63: Best Art Direction/Set Decoration (B & W), Best Director (Fellini), Best Story & Screenplay. **VHS, Beta, LV ★★★★**

Eight Men Out Taken from Eliot Asinof's book, a moving, full-blooded account of the infamous 1919 "Black Sox" scandal, in which members of the Chicago White Sox teamed to throw the World Series for $80,000. A dirge of lost innocence, this is among Sayles' best films. Provides an interesting look at the "conspiracy" that ended "shoeless" Joe Jackson's major-league career. The actual baseball scenes are first-rate, and Straithairn, Sweeney, and Cusack give exceptional performances. Sayles makes an appearance as Ring Lardner. Enjoyable viewing for even the non-sports fan.
1988 (PG) 121m/C John Cusack, D.B. Sweeney, Perry Lang, Jace Alexander, Bill Irwin, Clifton James, Michael Rooker, Michael Lerner, Christopher Lloyd, Studs Terkel, David Strathairn, Charlie Sheen, Kevin Tighe, John Mahoney, John Sayles, Gordon Clapp, Richard Edson, James Reed, Don Harvey, John Anderson, Maggie Renzi; **D:** John Sayles; **W:** John Sayles; **M:** Mason Daring, Robert Richardson. **VHS, Beta, LV ★★★1/2**

84 Charing Cross Road A lonely woman in New York and a book-seller in London begin corresponding for business reasons. Over a 20-year period, their relationship grows into a friendship, and then into a romance, though they communicate only by mail. Based on a true story.
1986 (PG) 100m/C Anne Bancroft, Anthony Hopkins, Judi Dench, Jean De Baer, Maurice Denham, Eleanor David, Mercedes Ruehl, Daniel Gerroll, Hugh Whitemore; **D:** David Jones; **M:** George Fenton. British Academy Awards '87: Best Actress (Bancroft). **VHS, Beta, LV ★★★**

84 Charlie Mopic A widely acclaimed drama about the horrors of Vietnam seen through the eyes of a cameraman assigned to a special front-line unit. Filled with a cast of unknowns, this is an unsettling film that sheds new light on the subject of the Vietnam war. Powerful and energetic; music by Donovan.
1989 (R) 89m/C Richard Brooks, Christopher Burgard, Nicholas Cascone, Jonathon Emerson, Glen Morshower, Jason Tomlins, Byron Thames; **D:** Patrick Duncan; **W:** Patrick Duncan; **M:** Donovan. **VHS, Beta, LV ★★★**

Eijanaika A gripping story of a poor Japanese man who returns to his country after a visit to America in the 1860s. Memorable performances make this an above-average film. In Japanese with English subtitles. **AKA:** Why Not?.
1981 151m/C *JP* Ken Ogata, Shigeru Izumiya; **D:** Shohei Imamura. **VHS, LV ★★★1/2**

El Cid Charts the life of Rodrigo Diaz de Bivar, known as El Cid, who was the legendary 11th-century Christian hero who freed Spain from Moorish invaders. Noted for its insanely lavish budget, this epic tale is true to its setting and features elaborate battle scenes.
1961 184m/C Charlton Heston, Sophia Loren, Raf Vallone, Hurd Hatfield, Genevieve Page; **D:** Anthony Mann; **W:** Philip Yordan; **M:** Miklos Rozsa. Nominations: Academy Awards '61: Best Art Direction/Set Decoration (Color), Best Song ("Love Theme (The Falcon and the Dove)"), Best Original Score. **VHS, Beta, LV ★★★**

El Dorado A gunfighter rides into the frontier town of El Dorado to aid a reckless cattle baron in his war with farmers over land rights. Once in town, the hired gun meets up with an old friend—the sheriff—who also happens to be the town drunkard. Switching allegiances, the gunslinger helps the lawman sober up and defend the farmers. This Hawks western displays a number of similarities to the director's earlier "Rio Bravo" (1959), starring Wayne, Dean Martin, and Ricky Nelson—who charms viewers as the young sidekick "Colorado" much like Caan does as "Mississippi" in "El Dorado."
1967 126m/C John Wayne, Robert Mitchum, James Caan, Charlene Holt, Ed Asner, Arthur Hunnicutt, Christopher George, R.G. Armstrong, Jim Davis, Paul Fix, Johnny Crawford, Michele Carey; **D:** Howard Hawks. **VHS, Beta, LV ★★★**

El Mariachi Extremely low-budget but clever mixture of humor and violence in a tale of mistaken identity set in a small Mexican border town. 24-year-old director Rodriguez makes his feature film debut with this $7000 feature, originally intended only for the Spanish-language market. Film festival awards and critical attention brought the work to wider release. In Spanish with English subtitles or dubbed. The laserdisc version includes director's commentary and Rodriguez's 8-minute film "Bedhead." **1993 (R) 81m/C** *MX* Carlos Gallardo, Consuelo Gomez, Peter Marquardt, Jaime de Hoyos, Reinol Martinez, Ramiro Gomez; *D:* Robert Rodriguez; *W:* Carlos Gallardo, Robert Rodriguez. Independent Spirit Awards '94: Best First Feature; Sundance Film Festival '93: Audience Award; Nominations: Independent Spirit Awards '94: Best Director (Rodriguez). **VHS, Beta, LV, 8mm ★★★**

El Norte Gripping account of a Guatemalan brother and sister, persecuted in their homeland, who make an arduous journey north ("El Norte") to America. Their difficult saga continues as they struggle against overwhelming odds in an attempt to realize their dreams. Passionate, sobering, and powerful. In English and Spanish with English subtitles. Produced in association with the "American Playhouse" series for PBS. Produced by Anna Thomas who also co-wrote the story with Nava. **1983 (R) 139m/C** *SP* David Villalpando, Zaide Silvia Gutierrez, Ernesto Cruz, Eracio Zepeda, Stella Quan, Alicia del Lugo, Lupe Ontiveros; *D:* Gregory Nava; *W:* Anna Thomas, Gregory Nava. Nominations: Academy Awards '84: Best Original Screenplay. **VHS, Beta ★★★★**

El: This Strange Passion Disturbing drama in which a man, convinced he is cuckolded, slowly descends into madness. Bunuel's surreal, almost Freudian look at the Spanish male's obsession with female fidelity. In Spanish with English subtitles. **1952 82m/B** *SP* Arturo de Cordova, Delia Garces, Luis Beristain, Aurora Walker; *D:* Luis Bunuel. **VHS ★★★**

Eleanor & Franklin An exceptional television dramatization of the personal lives of President Franklin D. Roosevelt and his wife Eleanor. Based on Joseph Lash's book, this Emmy award-winning film features stunning performances by Alexander and Herrmann in the title roles. **1976 208m/C** Jane Alexander, Edward Herrmann, Ed Flanders, Rosemary Murphy, MacKenzie Phillips, Pamela Franklin, Anna Lee, Linda Purl, Linda Kelsey, Lindsay Crouse; *D:* Daniel Petrie; *M:* John Barry. **VHS, Beta ★★★1/2**

Elena and Her Men The romantic entanglements and intrigues of a poor Polish princess are explored in this enjoyable French film. Beautiful cinematography by Claude Renoir. In French with subtitles. *AKA:* Paris Does Strange Things; Elena et les Hommes. **1956 98m/C** *FR* Ingrid Bergman, Jean Marais, Mel Ferrer, Jean Richard, Magali Noel, Pierre Bertin, Juliette Greco; *D:* Jean Renoir. **VHS, Beta, LV ★★★**

Elephant Boy An Indian boy helps government conservationists locate a herd of elephants in the jungle. Sabu's first film. Available in digitally remastered stereo. **1937 80m/B** *GB* Sabu, Walter Hudd, W.E. Holloway; *D:* Robert Flaherty, Zoltan Korda. Venice Film Festival '37: Best Director (Flaherty). **VHS, Beta, LV ★★★**

The Elephant Man A biography of John Merrick, a severely deformed man who, with the help of a sympathetic doctor, moved from freak shows into posh London society. Lynch's first mainstream film, shot in black and white, it presents a startlingly vivid picture of the hypocrisies evident in the social mores of the Victorian era. Moving performance from Hurt in title role. **1980 (PG) 125m/B** Anthony Hopkins, John Hurt, Anne Bancroft, John Gielgud, Wendy Hiller, Freddie Jones, Kenny Baker; *D:* David Lynch; *W:* Eric Bergren, Christopher DeVore, David Lynch; *M:* John Morris, Samuel Barber. British Academy Awards '80: Best Actor (Hurt), Best Film; Cesar Awards '82: Best Foreign Film; National Board of Review Awards '80: 10 Best Films of the Year; Nominations: Academy Awards '80: Best Actor (Hurt), Best Art Direction/Set Decoration, Best Costume Design, Best Director (Lynch), Best Film Editing, Best Picture, Best Original Score. **VHS, Beta, LV ★★★★**

11 Harrowhouse The Consolidated Selling System at 11 Harrowhouse, London, controls much of the world's diamond trade. Four adventurous thieves plot a daring heist relying on a very clever cockroach. A rather successful stab at spoofing detailed "heist" films. *AKA:* Anything for Love; Fast Fortune. **1974 (PG) 95m/C** *GB* Charles Grodin, Candice Bergen, James Mason, Trevor Howard, John Gielgud; *D:* Aram Avakian; *W:* Jeffrey Bloom. **VHS, Beta ★★★**

Elizabeth R Jackson is outstanding in the title role of this TV drama focusing on the life of Elizabeth I, from 17 to 70. Constantly besieged by court intrigue and political machinations, the Virgin Queen managed to restore England to glory and power amidst private and public turmoil. Six 90-minute cassettes.

1972 540m/C *GB* Glenda Jackson, Rosalie Crutchley, Robin Ellis, Robert Hardy, Peter Jeffrey, Stephen Murray, Vivian Pickles, Sarah Frampton, Ronald Hines; *D:* Claude Whatham, Herbert Wise, Roderick Graham, Richard Martin, Donald Whatham; *W:* Hugh Whitemore, John Hale, Julian Mitchell, John Prebble, Ian Rodger, Rosemary Anne Sisson. **VHS ★★★**

Elmer Gantry The classic multi-Oscar-winning adaptation of the Sinclair Lewis novel written to expose and denounce the flamboyant, small-town evangelists spreading through America at the time. In the film, Lancaster is the amoral Southern preacher who exacts wealth and power from his congregation, and takes a nun as a mistress. Jones stars as his ex-girlfriend who resorts to a life of prostitution.

1960 146m/C Burt Lancaster, Shirley Jones, Jean Simmons, Dean Jagger, Arthur Kennedy, Patti Page, Edward Andrews, John McIntire, Hugh Marlowe, Rex Ingram; *D:* Richard Brooks; *W:* Richard Brooks; *M:* Andre Previn, John Alton. Academy Awards '60: Best Actor (Lancaster), Best Adapted Screenplay, Best Supporting Actress (Jones); National Board of Review Awards '60: 10 Best Films of the Year, Best Supporting Actress (Jones); Nominations: Academy Awards '60: Best Picture, Best Original Score. **VHS, Beta, LV ★★★1/2**

The Elusive Corporal Set in a P.O.W. camp on the day France surrendered to Germany, this is the story of the French and Germans, complete with memories of a France that is no more. *AKA:* Le Caporal Epingle.

1962 108m/B Jean-Pierre Cassel, Claude Brasseur, O.E. Hasse, Claude Rich; *D:* Jean Renoir. **VHS, Beta, LV ★★★1/2**

Elvira Madigan Chronicles the 19th-century Swedish romance between a young officer and a beautiful circus tight-rope walker. Based on a true incident. Exceptional direction and photography. In Swedish with English subtitles.

1967 (PG) 90m/C *SW* Pia Degermark, Thommy Berggren, Lennart Malmer, Nina Widerberg, Cleo Jensen; *D:* Bo Widerberg; *W:* Bo Widerberg. Cannes Film Festival '67: Best Actress (Degermark); National Board of Review Awards '67: 5 Best Foreign Films of the Year. **VHS, Beta, LV ★★★**

The Emerald Forest Captivating adventure about a young boy who is kidnapped by a primitive tribe of Amazons while his family is traveling through the Brazilian jungle. Boothe is the father who searches 10 years for him. An engrossing look at tribal life in the vanishing jungle. Beautifully photographed and based upon a true story. Features the director's son as the kidnapped youth.

1985 (R) 113m/C Powers Boothe, Meg Foster, Charley Boorman, Dira Pass, Rui Polonah; *D:* John Boorman; *W:* Rospo Pallenberg, Philippe Rousselot. **VHS, Beta, LV, 8mm ★★★**

The Emigrants Farmer von Sydow decides to gather his wife (Ullmann) and family together and leave 19th-century Sweden for the promise of a new life in America. Film is divided into their leaving, the voyage over, and the journey to a settlement in Minnesota. Pacing is somewhat slow; notable cinematography (by director Troell). Adapted from the novels by Vilhelm Moberg. Dubbed into English. Followed by "The New Land." Also edited into the sequel for TV as "The Emigrant Saga." *AKA:* Utvandrarna.

1972 (PG) 151m/C *SW* Max von Sydow, Liv Ullmann, Allan Edwall, Eddie Axberg, Svenolof Bern, Aina Alfredsson, Monica Zetterlund, Pierre Lindstedt; *D:* Jan Troell; *W:* Jan Troell, Bengt Forslund; *M:* Erik Nordgren. New York Film Critics Awards '72: Best Actress (Ullmann); Nominations: Academy Awards '72: Best Actress (Ullmann), Best Adapted Screenplay, Best Director (Troell), Best Picture. **VHS ★★★**

Emma Jane Austen's 1816 novel about wealthy, 21-year-old Emma Woodhouse (Paltrow), who makes it her goal to "fix" the lives of all her friends while ignoring her own problems (the modern adaptation was "Clueless"). Emma focuses much of her attention on Harriet Smith (Collette), a simple young woman who Emma believes is in need of the perfect mate. Meanwhile, Emma neglects to notice the attractive and exasperated Mr. Knightley (Northam). After the success of "Sense and Sensibility," Austen's name is making it in the movies in the footsteps of the likes of John Grisham.

1996 111m/C Gwyneth Paltrow, Jeremy Northam, Greta Scacchi, Toni Collette, Alan Cumming, Juliet Stevenson, Polly Walker, Ewan McGregor, James Cosmo, Sophie Thompson, Phyllida Law; *D:* Douglas McGrath; *W:* Douglas McGrath; *M:* Rachel Portman. **VHS ★★★**

Emma British TV adaptation of the Jane Austen novel featuring young, matchmaking Emma (Beckinsale) wrecking havoc amongst her friends and neighbors with her would-be romantic alliances. Can the level-headed Mr. Knightley (Strong) show Emma the errors of her ways? Excellent cast easily matches the talents of the 1996 big-screen version. *AKA:* Jane Austen's Emma.
1997 107m/C *GB* Kate Beckinsale, Mark Strong, Samantha Bond, Prunella Scales, Bernard Hepton, James Hazeldine, Samantha Morton; *D:* Diarmuid Lawrence; *W:* Andrew Davis. **VHS** ★★★

Emma's Shadow In the 1930s, a young girl fakes her own kidnapping to get away from her inattentive family and comes to befriend an ex-convict sewer worker. In Danish with English subtitles. Winner of the Prix de la Jeunesse at Cannes, it was voted 1988's Best Danish Film. *AKA:* Skyggen Af Emma.
1988 93m/C *DK* Bjorje Ahistedt, Line Kruse; *D:* Soeren Kragh-Jacobsen. **VHS** ★★★

The Empire of Passion A peasant woman and her low-life lover kill the woman's husband, but find the future they planned with each other is not to be. The husband's ghost returns to haunt them, and destroy the passionate bond which led to the murder. Oshima's follow-up to "In the Realm of the Senses." In Japanese with English subtitles.
1976 110m/C *JP* Nagisa Oshima, Kazuko Yoshiyuki, Tatsuya Fuji, Takahiro Tamura, Takuzo Kawatani; *D:* Nagisa Oshima. Cannes Film Festival '78: Best Director (Oshima); Nominations: Cannes Film Festival '78: Best Film. **VHS** ★★★

Empire of the Sun Spielberg's mature, extraordinarily vivid return to real storytelling, from the best-selling J.G. Ballard novel. Yearns to be a great film, but occasional flat spots keep it slightly out of contention. Young, wealthy British Bale lives in Shanghai, but is thrust into a life of poverty and discomfort when China is invaded by Japan at the onset of WWII and he's separated from his family and interred in a prison camp. A mysterious, breathtaking work, in which Spielberg's heightened juvenile romanticism has a real, heartbreaking context. Two other 1987 releases explore the WWII memories of young boys: "Au Revoir Les Enfants" and "Hope and Glory."
1987 (PG) 153m/C Christian Bale, John Malkovich, Miranda Richardson, Nigel Havers, Joe Pantoliano, Leslie Phillips, Rupert Frazer, Ben Stiller, Robert Stephens, Burt Kwouk, Masato Ibu, Emily Richard, Allen Daviau; *Cameos:* J.G. Ballard; *D:* Steven Spielberg; *W:* Tom Stoppard; *M:* John Williams. National Board of Review Awards '87: 10 Best Films of the Year, Best Director (Spielberg); Nominations: Academy Awards '87: Best Art Direction/Set Decoration, Best Cinematography, Best Costume Design, Best Film Editing, Best Sound, Best Original Score. **VHS, Beta, LV, 8mm** ★★★

The Empire Strikes Back Second film in the epic "Star Wars" trilogy finds young Luke Skywalker and the Rebel Alliance plotting new strategies as they prepare to battle the evil Darth Vader and the forces of the Dark Side. Luke learns the ways of a Jedi knight from master Yoda, while Han and Leia find time for romance and a few adventures of their own. Introduces the charismatic Lando Calrissian, vulgar and drooling Jabba the Hut, and a mind-numbing secret from Vadar. Offers the same superb special effects and hearty plot as set by 1977's excellent "Star Wars." Followed by "Return of the Jedi" in 1983. Also available on Laserdisc with "The Making of 'Star Wars'."
1980 (PG) 124m/C Mark Hamill, Carrie Fisher, Harrison Ford, Billy Dee Williams, Alec Guinness, David Prowse, Kenny Baker, Frank Oz, Anthony Daniels, Peter Mayhew, Clive Revill, Julian Glover, John Ratzenberger; *D:* Irvin Kershner; *W:* Leigh Brackett, Lawrence Kasdan; *M:* John Williams; *V:* James Earl Jones. Academy Awards '80: Best Sound, Best Visual Effects; People's Choice Awards '81: Best Film; Nominations: Academy Awards '80: Best Art Direction/Set Decoration, Best Original Score. **VHS, Beta, LV** ★★★★

The End of St. Petersburg A Russian peasant becomes a scab during a workers' strike in 1914. He is then forced to enlist in the army prior to the 1917 October Revolution. Fascinating, although propagandistic film commissioned by the then-new Soviet government. Silent.
1927 75m/B Ivan Chuvelov; *D:* Vsevolod Pudovkin. **VHS, Beta** ★★★1/2

The Endless Summer Classic surfing documentary about the freedom and sense of adventure that surfing symbolizes. Director Brown follows two young surfers around the world in search of the perfect wave. (They finally find it at a then-unknown break off Cape Saint Francis in South America.) Besides the excellent surfing photography, Big Kahuna Brown provides the amusing tongue-in-cheek narrative. Considered by many to be the best surf movie ever.

1966 90m/C Mike Hynson, Robert August; *D:* Bruce Brown; *W:* Bruce Brown. **VHS, Beta, LV** ★★★

Enemies, a Love Story A wonderfully resonant, subtle tragedy based on the novel by Isaac Bashevis Singer. A post-Holocaust Jew, living in Coney Island, can't choose between three women—his current wife (who hid him during the war), his tempestuous lover, and his reappearing pre-war wife he presumed dead. A hilarious, confident tale told with grace and patience.

1989 (R) 119m/C Ron Silver, Lena Olin, Anjelica Huston, Margaret Sophie Stein, Paul Mazursky, Alan King, Judith Malina, Rita Karin, Phil Leeds, Elya Baskin, Marie-Adele Lemieux; *D:* Paul Mazursky; *W:* Paul Mazursky; *M:* Maurice Jarre, Fred Murphy. New York Film Critics Awards '89: Best Director (Mazursky), Best Supporting Actress (Olin); Nominations: Academy Awards '89: Best Adapted Screenplay, Best Supporting Actress (Huston, Olin). **VHS, Beta, LV** ★★★1/2

Enemy Below Suspenseful WWII sea epic, in which an American destroyer and a German U-Boat chase one another and square off in the South Atlantic.

1957 98m/C Robert Mitchum, Curt Jurgens, David Hedison, Theodore Bikel, Doug McClure, Russell Collins; *D:* Dick Powell. Academy Awards '57: Best Special Effects; National Board of Review Awards '57: 10 Best Films of the Year. **VHS, Beta** ★★★

The English Patient Filled with flashbacks and moral ambiguities, this adult romance is a complicated WWII saga that finds fragile French-Canadian nurse Hana (Binoche) caring for an enigmatic, dying burn patient, Almasy (Fiennes), in an abandoned monastery in Tuscany. Hana's joined by thief-turned-spy Caravaggio (Dafoe), who has a private score to settle with Almasy, and two British bomb disposal experts, Kip (Andrews), a Sikh who falls in love with Hana, and Sgt. Hardy (Whately). Almasy spends his days recalling his illicit love affair with Katharine Clifton (Scott Thomas), the wife of fellow cartographer, Geoffrey (Firth), as they map the North African desert. Exquisitely photographed in a golden glow by Seale with wonderful performances by the entire cast. Based on the novel by Michael Ondaatje.

1996 162m/C Ralph Fiennes, Kristin Scott Thomas, Juliette Binoche, Willem Dafoe, Naveen Andrews, Colin Firth, Julian Wadham, Juergen Prochnow, Kevin Whately, Clive Merrison, Nino Castelnuovo; *D:* Anthony Minghella; *W:* Anthony Minghella; *M:* Gabriel Yared. Golden Globe Awards '97: Best Film—Drama, Best Original Score; Los Angeles Film Critics Association Awards '96: Best Cinematography; National Board of Review Awards '96: Best Supporting Actress (Binoche), Best Supporting Actress (Thomas); Nominations: Directors Guild of America Awards '96: Best Director (Minghella); Golden Globe Awards '97: Best Actress—Drama (Scott Thomas), Best Actor—Drama (Fiennes), Best Supporting Actress (Binoche), Best Director (Minghella); Nominations: Golden Globe Awards '97: Best Screenplay; Screen Actors Guild Award '96: Best Actor (Fiennes), Best Actress (Scott Thomas), Best Supporting Actress (Binoche), Cast. **VHS** ★★★★

An Englishman Abroad During the Cold War, a British actress visits Moscow and chances to meet a notorious English defector. Behind their gossip and small talk is a tragicomic portrait of the exiled traitor/spy. He was the infamous Guy Burgess; the actress was Coral Browne, here playing herself in a pointed re-creation. Made for British TV; nuances may be lost on yank viewers. Winner of several British awards.

1983 63m/C *GB* Alan Bates, Coral Browne, Charles Gray; *D:* John Schlesinger; *W:* Alan Bennett; *M:* George Fenton. **VHS** ★★★

The Englishman Who Went Up a Hill but Came Down a Mountain Charming if slight tale of town pride based on writer/director Monger's family stories. In 1917 two English cartographers—pompous George (McNeice) and naive Reginald (Grant)—travel into Wales to measure the height of Ffynnon Garw (a running gag has the surveyors struggling with the Welsh language). To the proud locals it is the first mountain in Wales, and without that designation they might as well redraw the maps and be part of England—God forbid. But in order to be designated a mountain Ffynnon Garw must be 1,000 feet high, and she measures only 984. Grant stammers boyishly as the Englishman who is not only captivated by the village, but also by spirited local lass Betty (Fitzgerald, with whom he starred in "Sirens"). Meaney slyly shines as innkeeper Morgan the Goat, leading the townful of color characters. Wales is shown to great advantage by cinematographer Layton.

1995 (PG) 96m/C Hugh Grant, Tara Fitzgerald, Colm Meaney, Ian McNeice, Ian Hart, Kenneth Griffith; **D:** Christopher Monger; **W:** Christopher Monger; **M:** Stephen Endelman. **VHS, LV** ★★★

Enter the Dragon The American film that broke Bruce Lee worldwide combines Oriental conventions with 007 thrills. Spectacular fighting sequences including Karate, Judo, Tae Kwon Do, and Tai Chi Chuan are featured as Lee is recruited by the British to search for opium smugglers in Hong Kong. **AKA:** The Deadly Three.

1973 (R) 98m/C Bruce Lee, John Saxon, Jim Kelly; **D:** Robert Clouse; **M:** Lalo Schifrin. **VHS, Beta, LV** ★★★

The Entertainer Splendid drama of a down and out vaudevillian who tries vainly to gain the fame his dying father once possessed. His blatant disregard for his alcoholic wife and his superficial sons brings his world crashing down around him, and he discovers how self-destructive his life has been. Remade in 1975 for television. Adapted from the play by John Osborne.

1960 97m/B *GB* Laurence Olivier, Brenda de Banzie, Roger Livesey, Joan Plowright, Daniel Massey, Alan Bates, Shirley Anne Field, Albert Finney, Thora Hird; **D:** Tony Richardson; **W:** John Osborne; **M:** John Addison. Nominations: Academy Awards '60: Best Actor (Olivier). **VHS** ★★★1/2

Entre-Nous Two attractive, young French mothers find in each other the fulfillment their husbands cannot provide. One of the women was confined in a concentration camp during WWII; the other is a disaffected artist. In French with English subtitles. **AKA:** Between Us; Coup de Foudre.

1983 (PG) 112m/C *FR* Isabelle Huppert, Miou-Miou, Guy Marchand; **D:** Diane Kurys; **W:** Diane Kurys; **M:** Luis Bacalov. Nominations: Academy Awards '83: Best Foreign Language Film. **VHS, Beta** ★★★1/2

Era Notte a Roma An American, Russian, and British soldier each escape from a concentration camp in the waning days of WWII and find refuge in the home of a young woman.

1960 145m/C *IT* **D:** Roberto Rossellini; **W:** Roberto Rossellini. **VHS** ★★★

Eraserhead The infamous cult classic about a numb-brained everyman wandering through what amounts to a sick, ironic parody of the modern urban landscape, innocently impregnating his girlfriend and fathering a pestilent embryonic mutant. Surreal and bizarre, the film has an inner, completely unpredictable logic all its own. Lynch's first feature-length film stars Nance, who later achieved fame in Lynch's "Twin Peaks" as Pete the Logger.

1978 90m/B Jack Nance, Charlotte Stewart, Jack Fisk, Jeanne Bates; **D:** David Lynch; **W:** David Lynch. **VHS, Beta, LV** ★★★

Escape from Alcatraz A fascinating account of the one and only successful escape from the maximum security prison at Alcatraz in 1962. The three men were never heard from again.

1979 (PG) 112m/C Clint Eastwood, Patrick McGoohan, Roberts Blossom, Fred Ward, Danny Glover; **D:** Donald Siegel. **VHS, Beta, LV** ★★★

Escape from the Planet of the Apes Reprising their roles as intelligent, English-speaking apes, McDowall and Hunter flee their world before it's destroyed, and travel back in time to present-day America. In L.A. they become the subjects of a relentless search by the fearful population, much like humans Charlton Heston and James Franciscus were targeted for experimentation and destruction in simian society in the earlier "Planet of the Apes" and "Beneath the Planet of the Apes." Sequelled by "Conquest of the Planet of the Apes" and a television series.

1971 (G) 98m/C Roddy McDowall, Kim Hunter, Sal Mineo, Ricardo Montalban, William Windom, Bradford Dillman, Natalie Trundy, Eric (Hans Gudegast) Braeden; **D:** Don Taylor; **M:** Jerry Goldsmith. **VHS, Beta, LV** ★★★

E.T.: The Extra-Terrestrial Spielberg's famous fantasy, one of the most popular films in history, portrays a limpid-eyed alien stranded on earth and his special bonding relationship with a young boy. A modern fairy-tale providing warmth, humor and sheer wonder. Held the first place spot as the highest grossing movie of all time for years until a new Spielberg hit replaced it—"Jurassic Park." Debra Winger contributed to the voice of E.T.

1982 (PG) 115m/C Henry Thomas, Dee Wallace Stone, Drew Barrymore, Robert MacNaughton, Peter Coyote, C. Thomas Howell, Sean Frye, K.C. Martel; **D:** Steven Spielberg; **W:** Melissa Mathison, Allen Daviau; **M:** John Williams. Academy Awards '82: Best Sound, Best Visual Effects, Best Original Score; Golden Globe Awards '83: Best Film—Drama, Best

Score; Los Angeles Film Critics Association Awards '82: Best Director (Spielberg), Best Film; National Society of Film Critics Awards '82: Best Director (Spielberg); People's Choice Awards '83: Best Film; Writers Guild of America '82: Best Original Screenplay; Nominations: Academy Awards '81: Best Film Editing; Academy Awards '82: Best Cinematography, Best Director (Spielberg), Best Picture, Best Sound. **VHS, Beta, LV** ★★★★

Europa, Europa The incredible, harrowing and borderline-absurdist true story of Solomon Perel, a young Jew who escaped the Holocaust by passing for German at an elite, Nazi-run academy. Such a sharp evocation of the era that the modern German establishment wouldn't submit it for the Academy Awards. In German and Russian with English subtitles.
1991 (R) 115m/C *GE* Marco Hofschneider, Klaus Abramowsky, Michele Gleizer, Rene Hofschneider, Nathalie Schmidt, Delphine Forest, Julie Delpy; *D:* Agnieszka Holland; *W:* Agnieszka Holland. Golden Globe Awards '92: Best Foreign Film; National Board of Review Awards '91: Best Foreign Film; New York Film Critics Awards '91: Best Foreign Film; Nominations: Academy Awards '91: Best Adapted Screenplay. **VHS** ★★★1/2

The Europeans Fine adaptation of Henry James's satiric novel. British brother and sister visit their staid American cousins in 19th-century New England in an effort to improve their prospects through fortuitous marriages.
1979 90m/C Lee Remick, Lisa Eichhorn, Robin Ellis, Wesley Addy, Tim Woodward; *D:* James Ivory; *W:* Ruth Prawer Jhabvala. National Board of Review Awards '79: 10 Best Films of the Year; Nominations: Academy Awards '79: Best Costume Design; Cannes Film Festival '79: Best Film. **VHS, Beta** ★★★

Every Man for Himself & God Against All Kaspar Hauser is a young man who mysteriously appears in the town square of Nuremberg, early in the 19th century. He cannot speak or stand upright and is found to have been kept in a dungeon for the first 18 years of his life. He becomes an attraction in society with his alternate vision of the world and attempts to reconcile with reality. A lovely, though demanding film which is based on a true story. In German with English subtitles. **AKA:** The Mystery of Kaspar Hauser; Jeder Fur Sich Und Gott Gegen Alle; The Enigma of Kaspar Hauser.

1975 110m/C *GE* Bruno S, Brigitte Mira, Walter Ladengast, Hans Musaus, Willy Semmelrogge, Michael Kroecher, Henry van Lyck; *D:* Werner Herzog; *W:* Werner Herzog; *M:* Albinoni Pachelbel, Orlando Di Lasso. Nominations: Cannes Film Festival '75: Best Film. **VHS, Beta** ★★★★

Everything You Always Wanted to Know about Sex (But Were Afraid to Ask) Satiric comical sketches about sex includes a timid sperm cell, an oversexed court jester, a sheep folly, and a giant disembodied breast. Quite entertaining in its own jolly way. Based on the book by Dr. David Reuben.
1972 (R) 88m/C Woody Allen, John Carradine, Lou Jacobi, Louise Lasser, Anthony Quayle, Geoffrey Holder, Lynn Redgrave, Tony Randall, Burt Reynolds, Gene Wilder, Robert Walden, Jay Robinson; *D:* Woody Allen; *W:* Woody Allen. **VHS, Beta, LV** ★★★

Excalibur A sweeping, visionary retelling of the life of King Arthur, from his conception, to the sword in the stone, to the search for the Holy Grail and the final battle with Mordred. An imperfect, sensationalized version, but still the best yet filmed.
1981 (R) 140m/C Nigel Terry, Nicol Williamson, Nicholas Clay, Helen Mirren, Cherie Lunghi, Paul Geoffrey, Gabriel Byrne, Liam Neeson, Patrick Stewart, Charley Boorman, Corin Redgrave; *D:* John Boorman; *W:* John Boorman, Rospo Pallenberg; *M:* Trevor Jones. Nominations: Academy Awards '81: Best Cinematography; Cannes Film Festival '81: Best Film. **VHS, Beta, LV** ★★★1/2

The Execution of Private Slovik This quiet powerhouse of a TV movie recounts in straightforward terms the case of Eddie Slovik, a WWII misfit who became the only American soldier executed for desertion since the Civil War. The Levinson/Link screenplay (based on the book by William Bradford Huie) ends up deifying Slovik, which some might find hard to take. But there's no arguing the impact of the drama, or of Sheen's unaffected lead performance.
1974 122m/C Martin Sheen, Mariclare Costello, Ned Beatty, Gary Busey, Matt Clark, Ben Hammer, Warren Kemmerling; *D:* Lamont Johnson; *W:* Richard Levinson, William Link. **VHS** ★★★1/2

Executive Suite One of the first dog-eat-dog dramas about high finance and big business. The plot centers on the question of a replacement for the freshly buried owner of a gigantic furniture company.
1954 104m/B William Holden, June

Allyson, Barbara Stanwyck, Fredric March, Walter Pidgeon, Louis Calhern, Shelley Winters, Paul Douglas, Nina Foch, Dean Jagger; *D:* Robert Wise; *W:* Ernest Lehman. Nominations: Academy Awards '54: Best Art Direction/Set Decoration (B & W), Best Black and White Cinematography, Best Costume Design (B & W), Best Supporting Actress (Foch). **VHS, Beta** ★★★

Exodus Chronicles the post-WWII partition of Palestine into a homeland for Jews; the anguish of refugees from Nazi concentration camps held on ships in the Mediterranean; the struggle of the tiny nation with forces dividing it from within and destroying it from the outside; and the heroic men and women who saw a job to be done and did it. Based on the novel by Leon Uris; filmed in Cyprus and Israel. Preminger battled the Israeli government, the studio, and the novel's author to complete this epic. Cost more than $4 million, a phenomenal amount at the time.
1960 208m/C Paul Newman, Eva Marie Saint, Lee J. Cobb, Sal Mineo, Ralph Richardson, Hugh Griffith, Gregory Ratoff, Felix Aylmer, Peter Lawford, Jill Haworth, John Derek, David Opatoshu, Marius Goring, Alexandra Stewart, Michael Wager, Martin Benson, Paul Stevens, George Maharis; *D:* Otto Preminger; *W:* Dalton Trumbo; *M:* Ernest Gold. Academy Awards '60: Best Original Score; Golden Globe Awards '61: Best Supporting Actor (Mineo); Nominations: Academy Awards '60: Best Color Cinematography, Best Supporting Actor (Mineo). **VHS, Beta, LV** ★★★

The Exorcist Truly terrifying story of a young girl who is possessed by a malevolent spirit. Brilliantly directed by Friedkin, with underlying themes of the workings and nature of fate. Impeccable casting and unforgettable, thought-provoking performances. A rare film that remains startling and engrossing with every viewing, it spawned countless imitations and changed the way horror films were made. Based on the best-seller by Blatty, who also wrote the screenplay. Not for the squeamish. When first released, the film created mass hysteria in theaters, with people fainting and paramedics on the scene.
1973 (R) 120m/C Ellen Burstyn, Linda Blair, Jason Miller, Max von Sydow, Jack MacGowran, Lee J. Cobb, Kitty Winn; *D:* William Friedkin; *W:* William Peter Blatty; *M:* Jack Nitzsche, Owen Roizman. Academy Awards '73: Best Adapted Screenplay, Best Sound; Golden Globe Awards '74: Best Director (Friedkin), Best Film—Drama, Best Screenplay, Best

Supporting Actress (Blair); Nominations: Academy Awards '73: Best Actress (Burstyn), Best Art Direction/Set Decoration, Best Cinematography, Best Director (Friedkin), Best Film Editing, Best Picture, Best Supporting Actor (Miller), Best Supporting Actress (Blair). **VHS, Beta, LV** ★★★1/2

Exotica Daunting look at eroticism, secrecy, and despair. Christina (Kirshner) is at the center of some complicated relationships. She dresses as a schoolgirl while working at the Exotica strip club in Toronto, where her former lover Eric (Koteas) is the creepily suggestive DJ. Christina's also the obsession of seemingly mild-mannered tax man Francis (Greenwood), who has turned her table dancing into a strange private ritual. Lest this seem to make sense be assured that director Egoyan has much, much more going on—not all of it clear and most of it disturbing.
1994 (R) 104m/C *CA* Mia Kirshner, Elias Koteas, Bruce Greenwood, Don McKellar, Victor Garber, Arsinee Khanjian, Sarah Polley; *D:* Atom Egoyan; *W:* Atom Egoyan; *M:* Mychael Danna. Genie Awards '94: Best Art Direction/Set Decoration, Best Cinematography, Best Costume Design, Best Director (Egoyan), Best Film, Best Screenplay, Best Supporting Actor (McKellar), Best Original Score; Toronto-City Award '94: Best Canadian Feature Film; Nominations: Genie Awards '94: Best Actor (Greenwood), Best Actor (Koteas). **VHS, LV** ★★★

The Exterminating Angel A fierce, funny, surreal nightmare, wherein dinner guests find they cannot, for any definable reason, leave the dining room; full of dream imagery and characteristically scatological satire. One of Bunuel's best. In Spanish with English subtitles.
1962 95m/B *MX SP* Silvia Pinal, Enrique Rambal, Jacqueline Andere, Jose Baviera, Augusto Benedico, Luis Beristain; *D:* Luis Bunuel. **VHS, Beta** ★★★1/2

F/X A Hollywood special effects expert is contracted by the government to fake an assassination to protect a mob informer. After completing the assignment, he learns that he's become involved in a real crime and is forced to reach into his bag of F/X tricks to survive. Twists and turns abound in this fast-paced story that was the sleeper hit of the year. Followed by a sequel.
1986 (R) 109m/C Bryan Brown, Cliff DeYoung, Diane Venora, Brian Dennehy, Jerry Orbach, Mason Adams, Joe Grifasi, Martha Gehman; *D:* Robert Mandel; *W:*

Robert T. Megginson, Gregory Fleeman; **M:** Bill Conti. **VHS, Beta, LV ★★★**

Fabiola The first of the big Italian spectacle movies, this one opened the door for a flood of low-budget imitators. Fabiola, the daughter of a Roman senator, becomes a Christian when her father's Christian servants are accused of murdering him. In the meantime, the Emperor Constantine speeds toward Rome to convert it to Christian status. You can bet plenty of Christians will lose their heads, be thrown to the lions and generally burn at the stake before he does.
1948 96m/C *IT* Michel Simon, Henri Vidal, Gino Cervi; **D:** Alessandro Blasetti. **VHS ★★★**

The Fabulous Baker Boys Two brothers have been performing a tired act as nightclub pianists for 15 years. When they hire a sultry vocalist to revitalize the routine, she inadvertently triggers long-suppressed hostility between the "boys." The story may be a bit uneven at times, but fine performances by the three leading actors, the steamy 1940s atmosphere, and Pfeiffer's classic rendition of "Makin' Whoopee," are worth the price of the rental.
1989 (R) 116m/C Michelle Pfeiffer, Jeff Bridges, Beau Bridges, Elie Raab, Jennifer Tilly; **D:** Steven Kloves; **W:** Steven Kloves; **M:** Dave Grusin, Michael Ballhaus. Golden Globe Awards '90: Best Actress—Drama (Pfeiffer); Los Angeles Film Critics Association Awards '89: Best Actress (Pfeiffer), Best Cinematography; National Board of Review Awards '89: Best Actress (Pfeiffer); New York Film Critics Awards '89: Best Actress (Pfeiffer); National Society of Film Critics Awards '89: Best Actress (Pfeiffer), Best Cinematography, Best Supporting Actor (Beau Bridges); Nominations: Academy Awards '89: Best Actress (Pfeiffer), Best Cinematography, Best Film Editing, Best Original Score. **VHS, Beta, LV, 8mm ★★★**

A Face in the Crowd Journalist (Neal) discovers a down-home philosopher (Griffith) and puts him on her television show. His aw-shucks personality soon wins him a large following and increasing influence—even political clout. Off the air he reveals his true nature to be insulting, vengeful, and power-hungry—all of which Neal decides to expose. Marks Griffith's spectacular film debut as a thoroughly despicable character and debut of Remick as the pretty cheerleader in whom he takes an interest. Schulburg wrote the screenplay from his short story "The Arkansas Trav-

eler." He and director Kazan collaborated equally well in "On the Waterfront."
1957 126m/B Andy Griffith, Patricia Neal, Lee Remick, Walter Matthau, Anthony (Tony) Franciosa; **D:** Elia Kazan; **W:** Budd Schulberg. **VHS, Beta ★★★1/2**

Face to Face Bergman's harrowing tale of a mental breakdown. Ullmann has a bravura role as a psychiatrist deciding to vacation at her grandparent's house in the country. Once there she begins to experience depression and hallucinations tied to her past with both her mother and grandmother. Her deeply repressed feelings eventually lead to a suicide attempt, which brings some much needed help. Originally a four-hour series made for Swedish television. In Swedish with English subtitles.
1976 136m/C *SW* Liv Ullmann, Erland Josephson, Gunnar Bjornstrand, Aino Taube-Henrikson, Sven Lindberg; **D:** Ingmar Bergman; **W:** Ingmar Bergman, Sven Nykvist. Golden Globe Awards '77: Best Foreign Film; Los Angeles Film Critics Association Awards '76: Best Actress (Ullmann), Best Foreign Film; National Board of Review Awards '76: Best Actress (Ullmann); New York Film Critics Awards '76: Best Actress (Ullmann); Nominations: Academy Awards '76: Best Actress (Ullmann), Best Director (Bergman). **VHS ★★★**

Faces Cassavetes's first independent film to find mainstream success portrays the breakup of the 14-year marriage of middle-aged Richard (Marley) and Maria (Carlin) Forst. Both seek at least momentary comfort with others—Richard with prostitute Jeannie (Rowlands) and Maria with aging hippie Chet (Cassel). The director's usual improvisational and documentary style can either be viewed as compelling or tedious but the performances are first-rate.
1968 (R) 129m/B John Marley, Lynn Carlin, Gena Rowlands, Seymour Cassel, Val Avery, Dorothy Gulliver, Joanne Moore Jordan, Fred Draper, Darlene Conley; **D:** John Cassavetes, Al Ruban; **W:** John Cassavetes; **M:** Jack Ackerman. National Society of Film Critics Awards '68: Best Screenplay, Best Supporting Actor (Cassel); Nominations: Academy Awards '68: Best Screenplay, Best Supporting Actor (Carlin), Best Supporting Actress (Cassel). **VHS ★★★1/2**

Fahrenheit 451 Chilling adaptation of the Ray Bradbury novel about a futuristic society that has banned all reading material and the firemen whose job it is to keep the fires at 451 degrees: the temperature at which paper burns. Werner is a fireman who begins to question the rightness of his actions when he meets the book-loving Christie—who also plays the dual role of Werner's TV-absorbed wife. Truffaut's first color and English-language film. **1966 112m/C** *FR* Oskar Werner, Julie Christie, Cyril Cusack, Anton Diffring; *D:* Francois Truffaut. **VHS, Beta, LV** ★★★

Fail-Safe A nail-biting nuclear age nightmare, in which American planes have been erroneously sent to bomb the USSR, with no way to recall them. An all-star cast impels this bitterly serious thriller, the straight-faced flip-side of "Dr. Strangelove." **1964 111m/B** Henry Fonda, Dan O'Herlihy, Walter Matthau, Larry Hagman, Fritz Weaver, Dom DeLuise; *D:* Sidney Lumet; *W:* Walter Bernstein. **VHS, Beta, LV** ★★★¹/₂

The Falcon and the Snowman True story of Daulton Lee and Christopher Boyce, two childhood friends who, almost accidentally, sell American intelligence secrets to the KGB in 1977. Hutton and Penn are excellent, creating a relationship we care about and strong characterizations. **1985 (R) 110m/C** Sean Penn, Timothy Hutton, Lori Singer, Pat Hingle, Dorian Harewood, Richard Dysart, David Suchet, Jennifer Runyon, Priscilla Pointer, Nicholas Pryor, Joyce Van Patten, Mady Kaplan, Michael Ironside; *D:* John Schlesinger; *W:* Steven Zaillian; *M:* Lyle Mays, Pat Metheny. **VHS, Beta, LV** ★★★

The Fall of the House of Usher The moody Roger Corman/Vincent Price interpretation, the first of their eight Poe adaptations, depicting the collapse of the famous estate due to madness and revenge. Terrific sets and solid direction as well as Price's inimitable presence. *AKA:* House of Usher. **1960 85m/C** Vincent Price, Myrna Fahey, Mark Damon; *D:* Roger Corman; *W:* Richard Matheson; *M:* Les Baxter. **VHS, Beta** ★★★

The Fall of the Roman Empire An all-star, big budget extravaganza set in ancient Rome praised for its action sequences. The licentious son of Marcus Aurelius arranges for his father's murder and takes over as emperor while Barbarians gather at the gate. Great sets, fine acting, and thundering battle scenes. **1964 187m/C** Sophia Loren, Alec Guinness, James Mason, Stephen Boyd, Christopher Plummer, John Ireland, Anthony Quayle, Eric Porter, Mel Ferrer, Omar Sharif; *D:* Anthony Mann; *W:* Philip Yordan. Golden Globe Awards '65: Best Score; Nominations: Academy Awards '64: Best Original Score. **VHS, Beta, LV** ★★★

Fallen Angels 1 Trilogy of hard-boiled, film noirish tales set in Los Angeles. "The Frightening Frammis" concerns a grifter (Gallagher) who meets his match in a mystery woman (Rossellini) in this adaptation of a Jim Thompson story. Cruise's directorial debut. "Murder, Obliquely" finds a plain Jane (Dern) falling for a heel (Rickman) who may have murdered his previous girl in a Cornell Woolrich tale. "Since I Don't Have You" has Buzz Meeks (Busey) hired to find a dame sought by both Howard Hughes (Matheson) and gangster Mickey Cohen (Woods). From a story by James Elroy. Made for cable television. **1993 90m/C** Peter Gallagher, Isabella Rossellini, Nancy Travis, John C. Reilly, Bill Erwin, Laura Dern, Alan Rickman, Diane Lane, Robin Bartlett, Gary Busey, Tim Matheson, James Woods, Aimee Graham, Dick Miller, Ken Lerner; *D:* Tom Cruise, Alfonso Cuaron, Jonathan Kaplan; *W:* Jon Robin Baitz, Howard A. Rodman, Amanda Silver, Steven Katz; *M:* Elmer Bernstein. **VHS** ★★★

Fallen Champ: The Untold Story of Mike Tyson Director Kopple's provocative documentary on the boxing champ, from his roots in a Brooklyn ghetto to his conviction for rape in 1991. Tyson is shown as pathetic, vulnerable, and violent—psychologically unprepared for both acclaim and responsibility, as well as easily manipulated by promoters and opportunists. A mixture of ring footage and interviews with sportswriters, promoters, trainers, and others as well as media coverage of Tyson. Made for television. **1993 93m/C** *D:* Barbara Kopple. **VHS** ★★★

The Fallen Idol A young boy wrongly believes that a servant he admires is guilty of murdering his wife. Unwittingly, the child influences the police investigation of the crime so that the servant becomes the prime suspect. Richardson as the accused and Henrey as the boy are notable. Screenplay adapted by Greene from his short story, "The Basement Room." *AKA:* The Lost Illusion. **1948 92m/B** *GB* Ralph Richardson, Bobby Henrey, Michele Morgan, Sonia Dresdel, Jack Hawkins, Bernard Lee; *D:* Carol Reed; *W:* Graham Greene. British Academy Awards '48: Best Film; National Board of Review Awards '49: 10 Best Films of the

Year, Best Actor (Richardson); Nominations: Academy Awards '49: Best Director (Reed), Best Screenplay. **VHS, Beta, LV ★★★**

Fame Follows eight talented teenagers from their freshmen year through graduation from New York's High School of Performing Arts. Insightful and absorbing, director Parker allows the kids to mature on screen, revealing the pressures of constantly trying to prove themselves. A faultless parallel is drawn between these "special" kids and the pressures felt by high schoolers everywhere. Great dance and music sequences. The basis for the television series. ♪ Fame; Red Light; I Sing the Body Electric; Dogs in the Yard; Hot Lunch Jam; Out Here On My Own; Is It OK If I Call You Mine?.
1980 (R) 133m/C Irene Cara, Barry Miller, Paul McCrane, Anne Meara, Joanna Merlin, Richard Belzer, Maureen Teefy; **D:** Alan Parker; **M:** Michael Gore. Academy Awards '80: Best Song ("Fame"), Best Original Score; Golden Globe Awards '81: Best Song ("Fame"); Nominations: Academy Awards '80: Best Film Editing, Best Film Editing, Best Original Screenplay, Best Song ("Out Here on My Own"), Best Sound. **VHS, Beta, LV ★★★**

The Family An 80-year-old patriarch prepares for his birthday celebration reminiscing about his family's past triumphs, tragedies and enduring love. The charming flashbacks, convincingly played, all take place in the family's grand old Roman apartment. In Italian with English subtitles or dubbed. **AKA:** La Famiglia.
1987 128m/C *IT* Vittorio Gassman, Fanny Ardant, Philippe Noiret, Stefania Sandrelli, Andrea Occhipinti, Jo Ciampa; **D:** Ettore Scola; **W:** Ettore Scola, Ruggero Maccari, Furio Scarpelli; **M:** Armando Trovajoli. Nominations: Academy Awards '87: Best Foreign Language Film. **VHS, Beta, LV ★★★**

A Family Thing Racial issues are addressed in this character-driven story of two brothers. Southerner Earl Pilcher (Duvall) learns his biological mother was black and that she died during his birth. In a letter written by the recently deceased woman who raised him, Earl discovers he also has a half brother, Ray (Jones), who is black and living in Chicago. He drives to Chicago and seeks out Ray, who, to Earl's surprise, knows about him already and is not exactly thrilled about the family ties either. As the two brothers, expertly played by Duvall and Jones, slowly find common ground, Hall steals the show as the irascible Aunt T.
1996 (PG-13) 109m/C Robert Duvall, James Earl Jones, Michael Beach, Grace Zabriskie, Regina Taylor, Mary Jackson, Paula Marshall, Jim Harrell, Irma P. Hall; **D:** Richard Pearce; **W:** Billy Bob Thornton, Tom Epperson. **VHS, LV ★★★**

Family Upside Down An aging couple fight their separation after the husband has a heart attack and is put into a nursing home. The fine cast received several Emmy nominations, with Astaire the winner. Made for television.
1978 100m/C Helen Hayes, Fred Astaire, Efrem Zimbalist Jr., Patty Duke; **D:** David Lowell Rich; **M:** Henry Mancini. **VHS, Beta ★★★**

Fanny Second part of Marcel Pagnol's trilogy depicting the lives of the people of Provence, France. The poignant tale of Fanny, a young woman who marries an older man when Marius, her young lover, leaves her pregnant when he goes to sea. Remade several times but the original holds its own very well. "Marius" was first in the trilogy; "Cesar" was third.
1932 128m/B *FR* Raimu, Charpin, Orane Demazis, Pierre Fresnay, Alida Rauffe; **D:** Marc Allegret; **W:** Marcel Pagnol; **M:** Vincent Scotto. **VHS, Beta, LV ★★★★**

Fanny Young girl falls in love with an adventurous sailor, and finds herself pregnant after he returns to the sea. With the help of the sailor's parents, she finds, marries, and eventually grows to love a much older man, who in turn cares for her and adores her son as if he were his own. When the sailor returns, all involved must confront their pasts and define their futures. Beautifully made, with fine performances and a plot which defies age or nationality. Part of the "A Night at the Movies" series, this tape simulates a 1961 movie evening, with a Tweety Pie cartoon, a newsreel and coming attractions for "Splendor in the Grass" and "The Roman Spring of Mrs. Stone."
1961 148m/C *FR* Leslie Caron, Maurice Chevalier, Charles Boyer, Horst Buchholz, Lionel Jeffries; **D:** Joshua Logan; **W:** Julius J. Epstein, Philip C. Epstein, Jack Cardiff. National Board of Review Awards '61: 10 Best Films of the Year; Nominations: Academy Awards '60: Best Color Cinematography; Academy Awards '61: Best Actor (Boyer), Best Film Editing, Best Picture, Best Original Score. **VHS, Beta ★★★**

Fanny and Alexander The culmination of Bergman's career, this autobiographical film is set in a rural Swedish town in 1907. It tells the story of one year in the lives of the Ekdahl family, as seen by the young children, Fanny and Alexander. Magic and religion, love and death, reconciliation and estrangement are skillfully captured in this carefully detailed, lovingly photographed film. In Swedish with English subtitles or dubbed. *AKA:* Fanny Och Alexander. **1983 (R) 197m/C** *SW* Pernilla Allwin, Bertil Guve, Gunn Walgren, Allan Edwall, Ewa Froling, Erland Josephson, Harriet Andersson, Jarl Kulle, Jan Malmsjo; *D:* Ingmar Bergman; *W:* Ingmar Bergman; *M:* Daniel Bell, Sven Nykvist. Academy Awards '83: Best Art Direction/Set Decoration, Best Cinematography, Best Costume Design, Best Foreign Language Film; Cesar Awards '84: Best Foreign Film; Golden Globe Awards '84: Best Foreign Film; Los Angeles Film Critics Association Awards '83: Best Cinematography, Best Foreign Film; New York Film Critics Awards '83: Best Director (Bergman), Best Foreign Film; Nominations: Academy Awards '83: Best Director (Bergman), Best Original Screenplay. **VHS, Beta, LV ★★★★**

Fantasia Disney's most personal animation feature first bombed at the box office and irked purists who couldn't take the plotless, experimental mix of classical music and cartoons. It became a cult movie, embraced by more liberal generations of moviegoers. Reissue of the original version, painstakingly restored, ceased because of a planned remake. ♪ Toccata & Fugue in D; The Nutcracker Suite; The Sorcerer's Apprentice; The Rite of Spring; Pastoral Symphony; Dance of the Hours; Night on Bald Mountain; Ave Maria; The Cossack Dance. **1940 116m/C VHS, LV ★★★★**

Fantastic Voyage An important scientist, rescued from behind the Iron Curtain, is so severely wounded by enemy agents that traditional surgery is impossible. After being shrunk to microscopic size, a medical team journeys inside his body where they find themselves threatened by the patient's natural defenses. Great action, award-winning special effects. *AKA:* Microscopia; Strange Journey. **1966 100m/C** Stephen Boyd, Edmond O'Brien, Raquel Welch, Arthur Kennedy, Donald Pleasence, Arthur O'Connell, William Redfield, James Brolin; *D:* Richard Fleischer. Academy Awards '66: Best Art Direction/Set Decoration (Color), Best Visual Effects; Nominations: Academy Awards '66: Best Color Cinematography, Best Film Editing. **VHS, Beta, LV ★★★**

Far Country Cattlemen must battle the elements and frontier lawlessness in this classic. Stewart leads his herd to the Yukon in hopes of large profits, but ends up having to kidnap it back from the crooked sheriff and avenging the deaths of his friends. Entertaining and the Yukon setting takes it out of the usual Western arena. **1955 97m/C** James Stewart, Ruth Roman, Walter Brennan, Harry (Henry) Morgan, Corinne Calvet, Jay C. Flippen, John McIntire; *D:* Anthony Mann; *M:* Henry Mancini. **VHS, Beta ★★★**

Far from the Madding Crowd A lavish, long adaptation of Thomas Hardy's 19th-century classic about the beautiful Bathsheba and the three very different men who love her. Her first love is a handsome and wayward soldier (Stamp), her second the local noble lord (Finch), and her third the ever-loving and long-patient farmer (Bates). Christie is well cast as the much-desired beauty. The gorgeous cinematography is by Nicolas Roeg. **1967 (PG) 165m/C** *GB* Julie Christie, Terence Stamp, Peter Finch, Alan Bates, Prunella Ransome; *D:* John Schlesinger; *W:* Frederic Raphael; *M:* Richard Rodney Bennett. National Board of Review Awards '67: 10 Best Films of the Year, Best Actor (Finch); Nominations: Academy Awards '67: Best Original Score. **VHS, Beta, LV ★★★**

Farewell, My Lovely A remake of the 1944 Raymond Chandler mystery, "Murder, My Sweet," featuring private eye Phillip Marlowe hunting for an ex-convict's lost sweetheart in 1941 Los Angeles. Perhaps the most accurate of Chandler adaptations, but far from the best, this film offers a nicely detailed production. Mitchum is a bit too world-weary as the seen-it-all detective. **1975 (R) 95m/C** *GB* Robert Mitchum, Charlotte Rampling, Sylvia Miles, John Ireland, Anthony Zerbe, Jack O'Halloran, Harry Dean Stanton, Sylvester Stallone, Cheryl "Rainbeaux" Smith; *D:* Dick Richards; *W:* David Zelag Goodman; *M:* David Shire, John A. Alonzo. National Board of Review Awards '75: 10 Best Films of the Year; Nominations: Academy Awards '75: Best Supporting Actress (Miles). **VHS, Beta ★★★**

A Farewell to Arms The original film version of Ernest Hemingway's novel about the tragic love affair between an American ambulance driver and an English nurse during the Italian campaign of WWI. The novelist disavowed the ambiguous ending, but

the public loved the film. Fine performances and cinematography.
1932 85m/B Helen Hayes, Gary Cooper, Adolphe Menjou, Mary Philips, Jack LaRue, Blanche Frederici; **D:** Frank Borzage. Academy Awards '33: Best Cinematography, Best Sound; National Board of Review Awards '32: 10 Best Films of the Year; Nominations: Academy Awards '33: Best Interior Decoration, Best Picture. **VHS, Beta, LV** ★★★

Fargo Another malicious comedy from the Coen brothers. Car salesman Jerry Lundegaard (Macy) hires a couple of losers to kidnap his wife so he can swindle the ransom money out of his father-in-law. Naturally, the scheme begins to unravel, and the very pregnant police chief Marge Gunderson (McDormand) treks through the frozen tundra of Minnesota to put the pieces of the puzzle together. McDormand's performance as the chatty competent chief is first rate. Needling the flat-accented Midwesterners of their youth, the Coens have also returned to their filmmaking roots after the disappointing big-budget "Hudsucker Proxy." Because Minneapolis was having its warmest, driest winter in 100 years, the Coens were forced to shoot most of the exteriors in wintery North Dakota.
1996 (R) 97m/C William H. Macy, Frances McDormand, Steve Buscemi, Peter Stormare, Harve Presnell, Steve Reevis, John Carroll Lynch, Kristin Rudrud, Steve Park; Cameos: Jose Feliciano; **D:** Joel Coen; **W:** Joel Coen, Ethan Coen; **M:** Carter Burwell. Australian Film Institute '95: Best Foreign Film; Cannes Film Festival '96: Best Director (Coen); National Board of Review Awards '96: Best Director (Coen), Best Actress (McDormand); New York Film Critics Awards '96: Best Film; Nominations: Directors Guild of America Awards '96: Best Director (Coen); Golden Globe Awards '97: Best Film—Musical/Comedy, Best Actress—Musical/Comedy (McDormand), Best Director (Coen), Best Screenplay; Independent Spirit Awards '97: Best Film, Best Director (Coen), Best Actress (McDormand), Best Actor (Macy), Best Screenplay, Best Cinematography; Screen Actors Guild Award '96: Best Actress (McDormand), Best Supporting Actor (Macy). **VHS, LV** ★★★

The Farmer's Daughter Young portrays Katrin Holmstrom, a Swedish farm girl who becomes a maid to Congressman Cotten and winds up running for office herself (not neglecting to find romance as well). The outspoken and multi-talented character charmed audiences and was the basis of a television series in the 1960s.
1947 97m/B Loretta Young, Joseph Cotten, Ethel Barrymore, Charles Bickford, Harry Davenport, Lex Barker, James Arness, Rose Hobart; **D:** H.C. Potter. Academy Awards '47: Best Actress (Young); Nominations: Academy Awards '47: Best Supporting Actor (Bickford). **VHS, Beta** ★★★

Fast Times at Ridgemont High Teens at a Southern California high school revel in sex, drugs, and rock 'n' roll. A full complement of student types meet at the Mall—that great suburban microcosm percolating with angst-ridden teen trials—to contemplate losing their virginity, plot skipping homeroom, and move inexorably closer to the end of their adolescence. The talented young cast became household names: Sean Penn is most excellent as the California surfer dude who antagonizes teacher, Walston, aka "Aloha Mr. Hand." Based on the best-selling book by Cameron Crowe, it's one of the best of this genre.
1982 (R) 91m/C Sean Penn, Jennifer Jason Leigh, Judge Reinhold, Robert Romanus, Brian Backer, Phoebe Cates, Ray Walston, Scott Thomson, Vincent Schiavelli, Amanda Wyss, Forest Whitaker, Kelli Maroney, Eric Stoltz, Pamela Springsteen, James Russo, Martin Brest, Anthony Edwards; **D:** Amy Heckerling; **W:** Cameron Crowe. **VHS, Beta, LV** ★★★

Fat City One of Huston's later triumphs, a seedy, street-level drama based on the Leonard Gardner novel about an aging alcoholic boxer trying to make a comeback and his young worshipful protege. Highly acclaimed. Tyrrell earned an Oscar nomination as the boxer's world-weary lover.
1972 (PG) 93m/C Stacy Keach, Jeff Bridges, Susan Tyrrell, Candy Clark, Nicholas Colasanto; **D:** John Huston; **M:** Marvin Hamlisch, Conrad Hall. Nominations: Academy Awards '72: Best Supporting Actress (Tyrrell). **VHS, Beta** ★★★1/2

Fatal Attraction When a very married New York lawyer is seduced by a beautiful blonde associate, the one-night stand leads to terror as she continues to pursue the relationship. She begins to threaten his family and home with possessive, violent acts. An expertly made, manipulative thriller; one of the most hotly discussed films of the 1980s. A successful change of role for Close as the sexy, scorned, and deadly other woman. Also available in a special "director's series" edition, featuring Lyne's original, controversial ending.

1987 (R) 120m/C Michael Douglas, Glenn Close, Anne Archer, Stuart Pankin, Ellen Hamilton-Latzen, Ellen Foley, Fred Gwynne, Meg Mundy, J.J. Johnston; **D:** Adrian Lyne; **W:** James Dearden; **M:** Maurice Jarre. People's Choice Awards '88: Best Film—Drama; Nominations: Academy Awards '87: Best Actress (Close), Best Adapted Screenplay, Best Director (Lyne), Best Film Editing, Best Picture, Best Supporting Actress (Archer). **VHS, Beta, LV, 8mm, CD-I** ★★★

Father of the Bride A classic, quietly hilarious comedy about the tribulations of a father preparing for his only daughter's wedding. Tracy is suitably overwhelmed as the loving father and Taylor radiant as the bride. A warm vision of American family life, accompanied by the 1940 MGM short "Wedding Bills." Also available in a colorized version. Followed by "Father's Little Dividend" and later a television series. Remade in 1991.
1950 106m/C Spencer Tracy, Elizabeth Taylor, Joan Bennett, Billie Burke, Leo G. Carroll, Russ Tamblyn, Don Taylor, Moroni Olsen, John Alton; **D:** Vincente Minnelli; **W:** Frances Goodrich, Albert Hackett. Nominations: Academy Awards '50: Best Actor (Tracy), Best Picture, Best Screenplay. **VHS, Beta, LV** ★★★1/2

Father's Little Dividend Tracy expects a little peace and quiet now that he's successfully married off Taylor in this charming sequel to "Father of the Bride." However, he's quickly disillusioned by the news he'll soon be a grandfather—a prospect that causes nothing but dismay. Reunited the stars, director, writers, and producer from the successful first film.
1951 82m/B Spencer Tracy, Joan Bennett, Elizabeth Taylor, Don Taylor, Billie Burke, Russ Tamblyn, Moroni Olsen; **D:** Vincente Minnelli; **W:** Frances Goodrich, Albert Hackett. **VHS, Beta, LV** ★★★

Faust The classic German silent based upon the legend of Faust, who sells his soul to the devil in exchange for youth. Based on Goethe's poem, and directed by Murnau as a classic example of Germanic expressionism. Remade as "All That Money Can Buy" in 1941.
1926 117m/B *GE* Emil Jannings, Warner Fuetterer, Gosta Ekman, Camilla Horn; **D:** F.W. Murnau. **VHS, Beta** ★★★1/2

The FBI Story Mr. Stewart goes to Washington in this anatomy of the Federal Bureau of Investigation. If you're a fan of the gangster genre (LeRoy earlier directed "Little Caesar"), and not especially persnickety about fidelity to the facts, this ac-tioner offers a pseudo-factual (read fictional) glimpse—based on actual cases from the 1920s through the 1950s—into the life of a fictitious agent-family man.
1959 149m/C James Stewart, Vera Miles, Nick Adams, Murray Hamilton, Larry Pennell; **D:** Mervyn LeRoy; **M:** Max Steiner. **VHS, LV** ★★★

Fear Strikes Out Perkins plays Jimmy Piersall, star outfielder for the Boston Red Sox, and Malden, his demanding father, in the true story of the baseball star's battle for sanity. One of Perkins' best screen performances.
1957 100m/B Anthony Perkins, Karl Malden, Norma Moore, Adam Williams, Perry Wilson; **D:** Robert Mulligan; **M:** Elmer Bernstein. **VHS, Beta, LV** ★★★

Fearless Two plane crash survivors reach out to each other as they try and cope with everday life. Bridges is riveting as the transformed Max, and Perez compelling as the sorrowful Carla. Hulce provides dead-on amusement as a casualty lawyer who knows he's slime but can't help himself. Opening sequences of smoke in the corn fields are haunting as are flashbacks of the crash itself. Weir provides an engrossing look at facing death, both psychological and spiritual, but the ending is something of a letdown in its sappiness. Based on the novel by Yglesias.
1993 (R) 122m/C Jeff Bridges, Isabella Rossellini, Rosie Perez, Tom Hulce, John Turturro, Benicio Del Toro, Deidre O'Connell, John de Lancie, Allen Daviau; **D:** Peter Weir; **W:** Rafael Yglesias; **M:** Maurice Jarre. Los Angeles Film Critics Association Awards '93: Best Supporting Actress (Perez); Nominations: Academy Awards '94: Best Supporting Actress (Perez); Golden Globe Awards '94: Best Supporting Actress (Perez). **VHS, Beta, LV** ★★★

Fellini Satyricon Fellini's famous, garish, indulgent pastiche vision of ancient Rome, based on the novel "Satyricon" by Petronius, follows the adventures of two young men through the decadences of Nero's reign. Actually an exposition on the excesses of the 1960s, with the actors having little to do other than look good and react to any number of sexual situations. Crammed with excesses of every variety. In Italian with English subtitles. Also available on laserdisc with additional footage and letterboxing. **AKA:** Satyricon.
1969 (R) 129m/C *IT* Martin Potter, Capucine, Hiram Keller, Salvo Randone,

F

Max Born; **D:** Federico Fellini; **W:** Federico Fellini; **M:** Nino Rota, Giuseppe Rotunno. Nominations: Academy Awards '70: Best Director (Fellini). **VHS, Beta, LV** ★★★

Ferris Bueller's Day Off It's almost graduation and if Ferris can get away with just one more sick day—it had better be a good one. He sweet talks his best friend into borrowing his dad's antique Ferrari and sneaks his girlfriend out of school to spend a day in Chicago. Their escapades lead to fun, adventure, and almost getting caught. Broderick is charismatic as the notorious Bueller with Grey amusing as his tattle-tale sister doing everything she can to see him get caught. Early Sheen appearance as a juvenile delinquent who pesters Grey. Led to TV series. One of Hughes' more solid efforts.
1986 (PG-13) 103m/C Matthew Broderick, Mia Sara, Alan Ruck, Jeffrey Jones, Jennifer Grey, Cindy Pickett, Edie McClurg, Charlie Sheen, Del Close, Virginia Capers, Max Perlich, Louis Anderson, Tak Fujimoto; **D:** John Hughes; **W:** John Hughes; **M:** Ira Newborn. **VHS, Beta, LV, 8mm** ★★★

Fever Controversial Polish film based on Andrzej Strug's novel "The Story of One Bomb." Focusing on a period in Polish history marked by anarchy, violence, resistance, and revolution, it was banned before it won eventual acclaim at the Gdansk Film Festival. In Polish with English subtitles.
1981 115m/C PL **D:** Agnieszka Holland. **VHS** ★★★

A Few Good Men Strong performances by Cruise and Nicholson carry this story of a peacetime military coverup. Cruise is a smart aleck Navy lawyer sleepwalking through his comfortable career in DC. He's ready to write off two soldiers pinned for the murder of their cohort until he interviews their commanding officer, Nicholson. Cruise smells a rat, but Nicholson practically dares him to prove it. Moore is another military lawyer assigned to the case, though her function seems to be holding Kaffee's hand (there's no actual romance between the two). Incredible fireworks between Cruise and Nicholson in the courtroom. Based on the play by Sorkin, who also wrote the screenplay.
1992 (R) 138m/C Tom Cruise, Jack Nicholson, Demi Moore, Kevin Bacon, Kevin Pollak, Kiefer Sutherland, James Marshall, J.T. Walsh, Christopher Guest, J.A. Preston, Matt Craven, Wolfgang Bodison, Xander Berkeley, Cuba Gooding Jr., Robert Richardson; **D:** Rob Reiner; **W:** Aaron Sorkin; **M:** Marc Shaiman. Chicago Film Critics Awards '93: Best Supporting Actor (Nicholson); MTV Movie Awards '93: Best Film; National Board of Review Awards '92: Best Supporting Actor (Nicholson); People's Choice Awards '93: Best Film, Best Film—Drama; Nominations: Academy Awards '92: Best Film Editing, Best Picture, Best Sound, Best Supporting Actor (Nicholson). **VHS, Beta, LV, 8mm** ★★★1/2

Fiddler on the Roof Based on the long-running Broadway musical. The poignant story of Tevye, a poor Jewish milkman at the turn of the century in a small Ukrainian village, and his five dowry-less daughters, his lame horse, his wife, and his companionable relationship with God. Topol, an Israeli who played the role in London, is charming, if not quite as wonderful as Zero Mostel, the Broadway star. Finely detailed set decoration and choreography, strong performances from the entire cast create a sense of intimacy in spite of near epic proportions of the production. Play was based on the Yiddish stories of Tevye the Dairyman, written by Sholem Aleichem. ♪ Tradition; Matchmaker, Matchmaker; If I Were a Rich Man; Sabbath Prayer; To Life; Miracle of Miracles; Tevye's Dream; Sunrise, Sunset; Wedding Celebration.
1971 (G) 184m/C Chaim Topol, Norma Crane, Leonard Frey, Molly Picon; **D:** Norman Jewison; **M:** John Williams. Academy Awards '71: Best Cinematography, Best Sound, Best Score; Golden Globe Awards '72: Best Actor—Musical/Comedy (Topol), Best Film—Musical/Comedy; Nominations: Academy Awards '71: Best Actor (Topol), Best Art Direction/Set Decoration, Best Director (Jewison), Best Picture, Best Supporting Actor (Frey). **VHS, Beta, LV** ★★★1/2

The Field After an absence from the big screen, intense and nearly over the top Harris won acclaim as an iron-willed peasant fighting to retain a patch of Irish land he's tended all his life, now offered for sale to a wealthy American. His uncompromising stand divides the community in this glowing adaptation of John B. Keane's classic play, an allegory of Ireland's internal conflicts.
1990 (PG-13) 113m/C GB Richard Harris, Tom Berenger, John Hurt, Sean Bean, Brenda Fricker, Frances Tomelty, Sean McGinley, Jenny Conroy; **D:** Jim Sheridan; **W:** Jim Sheridan. Nominations: Academy Awards '90: Best Actor (Harris). **VHS, LV** ★★★1/2

Field of Dreams Uplifting mythic fantasy based on W.P. Kinsella's novel "Shoeless Joe." Iowa corn farmer heeds a mysterious voice that instructs "If you build it, he will come" and cuts a baseball diamond in his corn field. Soon the ball field is inhabited by the spirit of Joe Jackson and others who were disgraced in the notorious 1919 "Black Sox" baseball scandal. Jones, as a character based on reclusive author J.D. Salinger, is reluctantly pulled into the mystery. It's all about chasing a dream, maintaining innocence, finding redemption, reconciling the child with the adult, and celebrating the mythic lure of baseball. Costner and Madigan are strong, believable characters.

1989 (PG) 106m/C Kevin Costner, Amy Madigan, James Earl Jones, Burt Lancaster, Ray Liotta, Timothy Busfield, Frank Whaley, Gaby Hoffman; *D:* Phil Alden Robinson; *W:* Phil Alden Robinson; *M:* James Horner. Nominations: Academy Awards '89: Best Adapted Screenplay, Best Picture, Best Original Score. **VHS, Beta, LV** ★★★1/2

55 Days at Peking A costume epic depicting the Chinese Boxer Rebellion and the fate of military Britishers caught in the midst of the chaos. Standard fare superbly handled by director Ray and an all-star cast.

1963 150m/C Charlton Heston, Ava Gardner, David Niven, John Ireland, Flora Robson, Paul Lukas, Jacques Sernas; *D:* Nicholas Ray; *W:* Philip Yordan. Nominations: Academy Awards '63: Best Song ("So Little Time"), Best Original Score. **VHS, Beta, LV** ★★★

The Fighting 69th Cornball but entertaining WWI drama with lots of action. Cagney is a Brooklyn street tough who joins the all-Irish 69th New York regiment but could care less about its famed military history. He promptly defies his superiors and barely scrapes through his training. Sent to France, the swaggering Cagney turns coward when confronted by the horrors of war but eventually redeems himself. O'Brien is the famed regimental chaplain Father Duffy, while Brent is commander "Wild Bill" Donovan, who would later found the OSS in WWII. Lots of heart-tugging emotion backed with a fine supporting cast.

1940 90m/B James Cagney, Pat O'Brien, George Brent, Jeffrey Lynn, Alan Hale, Frank McHugh, Dennis (Stanley Morner) Morgan, William Lundigan, Dick Foran, Guinn "Big Boy" Williams, Henry O'Neill, John Litel, George Reeves; *D:* William Keighley; *W:* Fred Niblo, Norman Reilly Raine, Dean Franklin. **VHS** ★★★

The Fighting Sullivans The true story of five brothers killed on the Battleship Juneau at Guadalcanal during WWII. The tale tells of the fury felt by the siblings after Pearl Harbor, their enlistment to fight for their country, and their tragic fate in the heat of battle. Truly a stirring tribute to all lives lost in combat. *AKA:* The Sullivans.

1942 110m/B Anne Baxter, Thomas Mitchell, Selena Royle, Eddie Ryan, Trudy Marshall, James B. Cardwell, Roy Roberts, Ward Bond, Mary McCarty, Bobby Driscoll, Addison Richards, Selmer Jackson, Mae Marsh, Harry Strang, Barbara Brown; *D:* Lloyd Bacon. **VHS** ★★★1/2

The Final Cut Follows "House of Cards" and "To Play the King" in portraying the political adventures of Francis Urquardt (Richardson), Prime Minister. At 65, Urquardt has two goals: he wants to beat Margaret Thatcher's 11-year reign, and he wants to establish a secret retirement fund (the plot involves Cyprus and could—finally—lead to Urquardt's downfall). Author Michael Dobbs objected to the adaptation and insisted his name be removed from the script. On two cassettes.

1995 200m/C Ian Richardson, Diane Fletcher, Paul Freeman, Isla Blair, Nick Brimble, Erika Hoffman, Nickolas Grace, Julian Fellowes; *D:* Mike Vardy; *W:* Andrew Davies; *M:* Jim Parker. **VHS** ★★★

A Fine Madness A near-classic comedy about a lusty, rebellious poet thrashing against the pressures of the modern world, and fending off a bevy of lobotomy-happy psychiatrists. Shot on location in New York City, based on Elliot Baker's novel.

1966 104m/C Sean Connery, Joanne Woodward, Jean Seberg, Patrick O'Neal, Colleen Dewhurst, Clive Revill, John Fiedler; *D:* Irvin Kershner; *M:* John Addison. **VHS, Beta** ★★★

Finian's Rainbow A leprechaun comes to America to steal back a pot of gold taken by an Irishman and his daughter in this fanciful musical comedy based on a 1947 Broadway hit. Both the sprite and the girl find romance; the share-cropping locals are saved by the cash; a bigot learns the error of his ways; and Finian (Astaire) dances off to new adventures. The fine production and talented cast are not used to their best advantage by the director who proved much better suited for "The Godfather." Entertaining, nonetheless. ♪ How Are Things in Glocca Morra?; Look To the Rainbow; That Old Devil Moon; If This Isn't Love; Something Sort of Grandish; The Be-Gat; This Time of Year; The Great Come and Get It Day; When I'm Not Near the Girl I Love. **1968 (G) 141m/C** Fred Astaire, Petula Clark, Tommy Steele, Keenan Wynn, Al Freeman Jr., Don Francks, Susan Hancock, Dolph Sweet; *D:* Francis Ford Coppola. Nominations: Academy Awards '68: Best Sound, Best Original Score. **VHS, Beta, LV** ★★★

Fiorile Covers several generations of a Tuscan clan living under a family curse which dates back to Napoleon's invasion of Italy. At that time Jean, a handsome French lieutenant, falls in love with Tuscan peasant girl Elisabetta, nicknamed Fiorile. When Jean is executed for a theft committed by her brother, the pregnant Fiorile vows revenge. Throughout sucessive generations, haunted by the past, the family's personal bad luck persists. Several of the actors play their character's ancestors, lending continuity. Attractive cast does well with the Taviani brothers' visual style and romantic narrative. In Italian with English subtitles. *AKA:* Wild Flower. **1993 (PG-13) 118m/C** *IT* Michael Vartan, Galatea Ranzi, Claudio Bigagli, Lino Capolicchio, Constanze Engelbrecht, Athina Cenci, Giovanni Guidelli, Chiara Caselli; *D:* Paolo Taviani, Vittorio Taviani; *W:* Paolo Taviani, Vittorio Taviani, Sandro Petraglia; *M:* Nicola Piovani. **VHS, LV** ★★★

Fire Over England Young naval officer volunteers to spy at the Spanish court to learn the plans for the invasion of his native England and to identify the traitors among the English nobility. He arouses the romantic interest of his queen, Elizabeth I, one of her ladies, and a Spanish noblewoman who helps with his missions, and later leads the fleet to victory over the huge Spanish Armada. The first on-screen pairing of Olivier and Leigh is just one of the many virtues of this entertaining drama. **1937 81m/B** *GB* Flora Robson, Raymond Massey, Laurence Olivier, Vivien Leigh, Leslie Banks, James Mason; *D:* William K. Howard. **VHS, Beta** ★★★

The Firemen's Ball A critically acclaimed comedy about a small-town ball held for a retiring fire chief. Plans go amusingly awry as beauty contestants refuse to show themselves, raffle prizes and other items—including the gift for the guest of honor—are stolen, and the firemen are unable to prevent an old man's house from burning down. Forman's second film is sometimes interpreted as political allegory. In Czech with English subtitles.

1968 73m/C *CZ* Vaclav Stockel, Josef Svet; *D:* Milos Forman. Nominations: Academy Awards '68: Best Foreign Language Film. **VHS, Beta** ★★★

The Firm Top-flight cast promises a good time—the script based on the top-selling 1991 novel by John Grisham nearly guarantees it. Ambitious, idealistic Ivy League law school grad Cruise accepts a great offer from a small but wealthy Memphis law firm. As with anything that seems too good to be true, he discovers too late that nothing in life is free. Good performances by nearly everyone involved makes up for predictability. Sorvino has an uncredited cameo as a mob boss. Book fans beware: the script is fairly faithful until the end. The movie rights were snapped up before the book was published. Placed third in the 1993 race for top box office gross. **1993 (R) 154m/C** Tom Cruise, Jeanne Tripplehorn, Gene Hackman, Hal Holbrook, Terry Kinney, Wilford Brimley, Ed Harris, Holly Hunter, David Strathairn, Gary Busey, Steven Hill, Tobin Bell, Barbara Garrick, Jerry Hardin, Karina Lombard, John Beal; *Cameos:* Paul Sorvino, John Seale; *D:* Sydney Pollack; *W:* Robert Towne, David Rayfiel; *M:* Dave Grusin. Nominations: Academy Awards '93: Best Original Screenplay, Best Supporting Actress (Hunter); MTV Movie Awards '94: Best Actor (Cruise), Most Desirable Male (Cruise). **VHS, Beta, LV, CD-I** ★★★

A Fish Called Wanda Absurd, high-speed farce about four criminals trying to retrieve $20 million they've stolen from a safety deposit box—and each other. Meanwhile, barrister Cleese falls in love with the female thief (Curtis). Some sick, but tastelessly funny, humor involves Palin's problem with stuttering and some very dead doggies. Written by Monty Python alum Cleese and director Crichton, who understand that silence is sometimes funnier than speech, and that timing is everything. Wickedly funny. **1988 (R) 98m/C** John Cleese, Kevin Kline, Jamie Lee Curtis, Michael Palin, Tom Georgeson, Maria Aitken, Patricia Hayes, Geoffrey Palmer; *D:* Charles Crichton; *W:* John Cleese, Charles Crichton; *M:* John Du Prez. Academy Awards '88: Best Supporting Actor (Kline); British Academy Awards '88: Best Actor (Cleese), Best Supporting Actor (Palin); Nominations: Academy Awards '88: Best Director (Crichton), Best Original Screenplay. **VHS, Beta, LV** ★★★

The Fisher King In derelict-infested Manhattan a down-and-out radio DJ meets a crazed vagabond (Williams) obsessed with medieval history and in search of the Holy Grail. At first the whimsical mix of Arthurian myth and modern urban hell seems amazingly wrongheaded. In retrospect it still does. But while this picture runs it weaves a spell that pulls you in, especially in its quiet moments. Your reaction to the silly ending depends entirely on how well you're bamboozled by a script that equates madness with enlightment and the homeless with holy fools. Filmed on the streets of New York, with many street people playing themselves. **1991 (R) 138m/C** Robin Williams, Jeff Bridges, Amanda Plummer, Mercedes Ruehl, Michael Jeter, Harry Shearer, John de Lancie, Kathy Najimy, David Hyde Pierce; **D:** Terry Gilliam; **W:** Richard LaGravenese. Academy Awards '91: Best Supporting Actress (Ruehl); Chicago Film Critics Awards '91: Best Supporting Actress (Ruehl); Golden Globe Awards '92: Best Actor—Musical/Comedy (Williams), Best Supporting Actress (Ruehl); Nominations: Academy Awards '91: Best Actor (Williams), Best Art Direction/Set Decoration, Best Original Screenplay, Best Original Score. **VHS, Beta, LV, 8mm** ★★★

A Fistful of Dollars The epitome of the "spaghetti western" pits Eastwood as "the man with no name" against two families who are feuding over land. A remake of Kurosawa's "Yojimbo," and followed by Leone's "For a Few Dollars More" and "The Good, The Bad, and The Ugly." **1964 (R) 101m/C** *IT* Clint Eastwood, Gian Marie Volonte, Marianne Koch; **D:** Sergio Leone; **M:** Ennio Morricone. **VHS, Beta, LV** ★★★

A Fistful of Dynamite A spaghetti western, with Leone's trademark humor and a striking score by Morricone. An Irish demolitions expert and a Mexican peasant team up to rob a bank during a revolution in Mexico. **AKA:** Duck, You Sucker; Giu la Testa. **1972 (PG) 138m/C** *IT* James Coburn, Rod Steiger, Romolo Valli; **D:** Sergio Leone; **M:** Ennio Morricone. **VHS, Beta, LV** ★★★

Fists of Fury Bruce Lee stars in this violent but charming Kung Fu action adventure in which he must break a solemn vow to avoid fighting in order to avenge the murder of his teacher by drug smugglers. **AKA:** The Big Boss. **1973 (R) 102m/C** Bruce Lee, Maria Yi; **D:** Lo Wei. **VHS, Beta** ★★★

Fitzcarraldo Although he failed to build a railroad across South America, Fitzcarraldo is determined to build an opera house in the middle of the Amazon jungles and have Enrico Caruso sing there. Based on a true story of a charismatic Irishman's impossible quest at the turn of the century. Of note: No special effects were used in this movie—everything you see actually occurred during filming, including hauling a large boat over a mountain. **1982 (PG) 157m/C** *GE* Klaus Kinski, Claudia Cardinale, Jose Lewgoy, Miguel Angel Fuentes, Paul Hittscher; **D:** Werner Herzog; **W:** Werner Herzog; **M:** Popul Vuh. Cannes Film Festival '82: Best Director (Herzog); Nominations: Cannes Film Festival '82: Best Film. **VHS, Beta** ★★★★

Five Corners A quixotic, dramatic comedy about the inhabitants of the 5 Corners section of the Bronx in 1964, centering around a girl being wooed by a psychotic rapist, her crippled boyfriend, and the hero-turned-racial-pacifist who cannot rescue her out of principle. **1988 (R) 92m/C** Jodie Foster, John Turturro, Todd Graff, Tim Robbins, Elizabeth Berridge, Rose Gregorio, Gregory Rozakis, Rodney Harvey, John Seitz; **D:** Tony Bill; **W:** John Patrick Shanley; **M:** James Newton Howard, Fred Murphy. Independent Spirit Awards '89: Best Actress (Foster). **VHS, Beta** ★★★

Five Easy Pieces Nicholson's superb acting brings to life this character study of a talented musician who has given up a promising career and now works on the oil rigs. After twenty years he returns home to attempt one last communication with his dying father and perhaps, reconcile himself with his fear of failure and desire for greatness. Black, Anspach, and Bush create especially memorable characters. Nicholson ordering toast via a chicken salad sandwich is a classic. **1970 (R) 98m/C** Jack Nicholson, Karen Black, Susan Anspach, Lois Smith, Billy Green Bush, Fannie Flagg, Ralph Waite, Sally Struthers, Helena Kallianiotes; **D:** Bob Rafelson; **W:** Adrien (Carole Eastman) Joyce, Bob Rafelson. Golden Globe Awards '71: Best Supporting Actress (Black); National Board of Review Awards '70: Best Supporting Actress (Black); New York Film Critics Awards '70: Best Director (Rafelson), Best Film, Best Supporting Actress (Black); Nominations: Academy Awards '70: Best Actor (Nicholson), Best Picture, Best Story & Screenplay, Best Supporting Actress (Black). **VHS, Beta, LV, 8mm** ★★★★

Five Fingers Under the alias "Cicero," Albanian valet Mason joins the

F

espionage ring, selling highly confidential British war papers to the Germans during WWII. True story with odd real-life ending—unconvinced of document authenticity, the Nazis never acted on the information, even when they had the time and date of the European invasion! Fast-paced and absorbing. Adapted from the book "Operation Cicero" by L.C. Moyzisch. *AKA:* Operation Cicero.
1952 108m/B James Mason, Danielle Darrieux, Michael Rennie, Walter Hampden, Oscar Karlweis, Herbert Berghof, John Wengraf, Michael Pate, Ivan Triesault, Hanne Axman, David Wolfe, Nestor Paiva, Richard Loo, Keith McConnell; *D:* Joseph L. Mankiewicz; *W:* Michael Wilson; *M:* Bernard Herrmann. Golden Globe Awards '53: Best Screenplay. **VHS ★★★1/2**

The 5000 Fingers of Dr. T In Dr. Seuss's only non-animated movie, a boy tries to evade piano lessons and runs right into the castle of the evil Dr. Terwilliger, where hundreds of boys are held captive for piano lessons. Worse yet, they're forced to wear silly beanies with "happy fingers" waving on top. Luckily, the trusted family plumber is on hand to save the day through means of an atomic bomb. Wonderful satire, horrible music, mesmerizing Seussian sets. The skating brothers (who are joined at their beards) are a treat.
1953 88m/C Peter Lind Hayes, Mary Healy, Tommy Rettig, Hans Conried; *D:* Roy Rowland; *W:* Theodore "Dr. Seuss" Geisel, Allan Scott. Nominations: Academy Awards '53: Best Original Score. **VHS, Beta, LV ★★★**

The Flame & the Arrow Dardo the Arrow, a Robin Hood-like outlaw in medieval Italy, leads his band of mountain fighters against a mercenary warlord who has seduced his wife and kidnapped his son. Spectacular acrobatics, with Lancaster performing his own stunts, add interest to the usual swashbuckling.
1950 88m/C Burt Lancaster, Virginia Mayo, Aline MacMahon, Nick Cravat, Robert Douglas, Frank Allenby; *D:* Jacques Tourneur; *M:* Max Steiner. Nominations: Academy Awards '50: Best Color Cinematography, Best Original Score. **VHS, Beta, LV ★★★**

Flaming Star In 1870s Texas, a family with a white father and an Indian mother is caught in the midst of an Indian uprising. The mixed-blood youth, excellently played by Presley, must choose a side with tragic results for all. A stirring, well-written drama

of frontier prejudice and one of Presley's best films.
1960 101m/C Elvis Presley, Dolores Del Rio, Barbara Eden, Steve Forrest, John McIntire, Richard Jaeckel, L.Q. Jones; *D:* Donald Siegel. **VHS, Beta ★★★**

The Flamingo Kid Brooklyn teen Dillon gets a summer job at a fancy beach club on Long Island. His father, a plumber, remembers how to dream but is also aware of how rough the world is on dreamers. Suddenly making lots of money at a mostly easy job, the kid's attracted to the high style of the local sports car dealer, and finds his father's solid life a bore. By the end of the summer, he's learned the true value of both men, and the kind of man he wants to be. Excellent performances all around, nice ensemble acting among the young men who play Dillon's buddies. Great sound track. Film debut of Jones, who seems a little old for her part as a California college sophomore.
1984 (PG-13) 100m/C Matt Dillon, Hector Elizondo, Molly McCarthy, Martha Gehman, Richard Crenna, Jessica Walter, Carole Davis, Janet Jones, Fisher Stevens, Bronson Pinchot; *D:* Garry Marshall. **VHS, Beta, LV ★★★**

Flamingo Road A scandalously entertaining melodrama in which Crawford portrays a carnival dancer who intrigues Scott and Brian in a small Southern town where the carnival stops. Crawford shines in a role that demands her to be both tough and sensitive in a corrupt world full of political backstabbing and sleazy characters. Remade as a TV movie and television soap-opera series in 1980.
1949 94m/B Joan Crawford, Zachary Scott, David Brian, Sydney Greenstreet, Gertrude Michael, Gladys George, Virginia Huston, Fred Clark, Alice White; *D:* Michael Curtiz; *W:* Edmund H. North, Robert Wilder; *M:* Max Steiner. **VHS, LV ★★★**

Flesh An Andy Warhol-produced seedy urban farce about a bisexual street hustler who meets a variety of drug-addicted, deformed, and sexually deviant people. Dallesandro fans will enjoy his extensive exposure (literally).
1968 90m/C Joe Dallesandro, Geraldine Smith, Patti D'Arbanville; *D:* Paul Morrissey. **VHS, Beta ★★★**

The Flesh and the Devil Classic Garbo at her seductive best as a woman who causes a feud between two friends. Gilbert is an Austrian officer, falls for the married Garbo and winds up killing her husband in a

duel. Banished to the African Corps he asks his best friend (Hanson) to look after his lady love. But Hanson takes his job too seriously, falling for the lady himself. Great silent movie with surprise ending to match. The first Gilbert and Garbo pairing.
1927 112m/B John Gilbert, Greta Garbo, Lars Hanson, Barbara Kent, George Fawcett, Eugenie Besserer; *D:* Clarence Brown. **VHS** ★★★1/2

The Flight of the Phoenix A group of men stranded in the Arabian desert after a plane crash attempt to rebuild their plane in order to escape before succumbing to the elements. Big budget, all-star survival drama based on the novel by Elleston Trevor.
1965 147m/C James Stewart, Richard Attenborough, Peter Finch, Hardy Kruger, Dan Duryea, George Kennedy, Ernest Borgnine, Ian Bannen; *D:* Robert Aldrich. Nominations: Academy Awards '65: Best Film Editing, Best Supporting Actor (Bannen). **VHS, Beta, LV** ★★★

Flipper They still call him Flipper! Flipper, who in some scenes is played by a robot dolphin, reappears in a feature film for the first time since 1966. Sullen 14-year-old city boy Sandy Ricks (Wood) must spend the summer with crusty bachelor uncle Porter (Hogan), who would rather fish than look after his troublesome nephew. The duo witness the heartless killing of Flipper's family and are adopted by him. In addition to causing their seafood bill to skyrocket, the dolphin helps them uncover an illegal toxic waste dumper, who happens to be the same guy who made Flipper's mama sleep with the fishes. Updated along with the story is the soundtrack, which features a version of the famous theme song by Matthew Sweet.
1996 (PG) 97m/C Elijah Wood, Paul Hogan, Chelsea Field, Isaac Hayes, Jonathan Banks, Luke Halpin; *D:* Alan Shapiro; *W:* Alan Shapiro; *M:* Joel McNeely. **VHS, LV** ★★★

Flirting with Disaster Mel Coplin (Stiller) is your average neurotic New York entomologist searching for his birth parents so he can finally name his four-month-old child and make love to his wife. Tagging along on his bumpy ride are his wife Nancy (Arquette), a beautiful quirky adoption agency shrink (Leoni), and a pair of bisexual FBI agents. The excellent cast also features Moore as Mel's bra-baring adoptive mother, Segal as his weirdly paranoid adoptive father, and Alda and Tomlin as hilarious send-ups of ex-hippie mentality. As events spin madly out of control, every type of relationship is satirized, and every character is left in his or her underwear. This is director Russell's first big-budget movie and is as close to a vintage screwball comedy as you'll see in the '90s.
1995 (R) 92m/C Ben Stiller, Patricia Arquette, Téa Leoni, Alan Alda, Mary Tyler Moore, George Segal, Lily Tomlin, Josh Brolin, Richard Jenkins, Celia Weston, David Patrick Kelly, John Ford Noonan, Glenn Fitzgerald, Beth Ostrosky, Cynthia Lamontagne, Charlet Oberly; *D:* David O. Russell; *W:* David O. Russell; *M:* Stephen Endelman. Nominations: Independent Spirit Awards '97: Best Screenplay, Best Director (Russell), Best Supporting Actress (Tomlin), Best Supporting Actor (Jenkins). **VHS** ★★★

Flirting with Fate Early Fairbanks-cum-acrobat vehicle. Having hired a hitman to rub himself out, a young man decides he doesn't want to die, after all. Seems there's a girl involved . . .
1916 51m/B Douglas Fairbanks Sr., Jewel Carmen, Howard Gaye, William E. Lawrence, George Beranger, Dorothy Hadel, Lillian Langdon; *D:* Christy Cabanne. **VHS, Beta** ★★★

The Floorwalker/By the Sea Two early Chaplin short comedies, featuring a hilarious scene on an escalator in the first film. Silent.
1915 51m/B Charlie Chaplin, Edna Purviance, Eric Campbell; *D:* Charlie Chaplin. **VHS, Beta, 8mm** ★★★

The Flower of My Secret Emotional yet restrained story about middle-aged Leo (Paredes), whose longtime marriage is fast ending (and it's not her idea). Leo writes hugely popular romance novels under a pseudonym, but her current work is so bleak it's unpublishable. So, Leo gets a job at a newspaper, where editor Angel (Echanove) immediately falls for her, and indeed, lives up to his name as her guardian. Willfully myopic about her own life, Leo undergoes further trials until she slowly realizes the mess she's in and becomes willing to change. Surprisingly subdued given Almodovar's usual flamboyance but, it's a welcome change of pace. Spanish with subtitles. *AKA:* La Flor de Mi Secreto.
1995 (R) 107m/C *SP* Marisa Paredes, Juan Echanove, Imanol Arias, Carmen Elias, Rossy de Palma, Chus Lampreave, Joaquin Cortes, Manuela Vargas; *D:* Pedro Almodovar; *W:* Pedro Almodovar; *M:* Alberto Inglesias. **VHS, LV** ★★★

The Fly The historic, chillingly original '50s sci-fi tale about a hapless scientist experimenting with teleportation who accidentally gets anatomically confused with a housefly. Campy required viewing; two sequels followed, and a 1986 remake which itself has spawned one sequel.
1958 94m/C Vincent Price, David Hedison, Herbert Marshall, Patricia Owens; *D:* Kurt Neumann; *W:* James Clavell. **VHS, Beta, LV** ★★★

The Fly A sensitive, humanistic remake of the 1958 horror film about a scientist whose flesh is genetically intermixed with a housefly via his experimental transportation device. A thoughtful, shocking horror film, with fine performances from Goldblum and Davis and a brutally emotional conclusion. Followed by "The Fly II" in 1989.
1986 (R) 96m/C Jeff Goldblum, Geena Davis, John Getz, Joy Boushel; *D:* David Cronenberg; *W:* David Cronenberg, Charles Edward Pogue; *M:* Howard Shore. Academy Awards '86: Best Makeup. **VHS, Beta, LV** ★★★

The Flying Deuces Ollie's broken heart lands Laurel and Hardy in the Foreign Legion. The comic pair escape a firing squad only to suffer a plane crash that results in Hardy's reincarnation as a horse. A musical interlude with a Laurel soft shoe while Hardy sings "Shine On, Harvest Moon" is one of the film's highlights. *AKA:* Flying Aces.
1939 65m/B Stan Laurel, Oliver Hardy, Jean Parker, Reginald Gardiner, James Finlayson; *D:* Edward Sutherland. **VHS, Beta, LV** ★★★

Flying Leathernecks Tough squadron leader Wayne fights with his fellow officer Ryan in Guadalcanal when their leadership styles clash. But when the real fighting begins all is forgotten as Wayne leads his men into victorious battle, winning the admiration and devotion of his fliers. Memorable WWII film deals with war in human terms.
1951 102m/C John Wayne, Robert Ryan, Janis Carter; *D:* Nicholas Ray. **VHS, Beta, LV** ★★★

Follow the Boys Vaudeville performer Tony West (Raft) heads out to California to try his luck and gets a double break when he's noticed by leading lady Gloria Vance (Zorina). Not only does he become a star but he marries Gloria as well. When WWII breaks out Tony's turned down for military service, so he organizes camp shows for the soldiers. They're a big success but misunderstandings have put his marriage in jeopardy. Plot's merely an excuse to have haute Hollywood (including Marlene Dietrich, Orson Welles, Jeanette MacDonald, and W.C. Fields) sing, dance, and tell jokes. ♪ Beyond the Blue Horizon; I'll See You In My Dreams; The Bigger the Army and the Navy; Some of These Days; I'll Get By; I'll Walk Alone; Mad About Him Blues; The House I Live In.
1944 111m/B George Raft, Vera Zorina, Grace McDonald, Charles Butterworth, Martha O'Driscoll, Charley Grapewin, Elizabeth Patterson; *D:* Edward Sutherland; *W:* Lou Breslow, Gertrude Purcell. **VHS** ★★★

Follow the Fleet A song-and-dance man joins the Navy and meets two sisters in need of help in this Rogers/Astaire bon-bon featuring a classic Berlin score. Look for Betty Grable, Lucille Ball, and Tony Martin in minor roles. Hilliard went on to be best known as the wife of Ozzie Nelson in TV's "The Adventures of Ozzie and Harriet." ♪ Let's Face the Music and Dance; We Saw the Sea; I'm Putting All My Eggs In One Basket; Get Thee Behind Me, Satan; But Where Are You?; I'd Rather Lead a Band; Let Yourself Go.
1936 110m/B Fred Astaire, Ginger Rogers, Randolph Scott, Harriet Hilliard Nelson, Betty Grable, Lucille Ball; *D:* Mark Sandrich; *M:* Irving Berlin, Max Steiner. **VHS, Beta, LV** ★★★

Foolish Wives A remake of Von Stroheim's classic depicting the confused milieu of post-war Europe as reflected through the actions of a bogus count and his seductive, corrupt ways. Comes as close as possible to the original film.
1922 107m/B Erich von Stroheim, Mae Busch, Maude George, Cesare Gravina, Harrison Ford; *D:* Erich von Stroheim. **VHS, Beta, LV** ★★★½

Footlight Parade Broadway producer Cagney is out of work. Sound films have scared off his backers until his idea for staging live musical numbers before the cinema features lures them back. Lots of authentic backstage action precedes three spectacular Busby Berkeley-choreographed numbers that climax the film, including the giant water ballet featuring more than 100 performers. ♪ Ah, the Moon is Here; Sittin' on a Backyard Fence; Honeymoon Hotel; By A Waterfall; Shanghai Lil.
1933 104m/B James Cagney, Joan Blondell, Dick Powell, Ruby Keeler, Guy

Kibbee, Ruth Donnelly; **D:** Lloyd Bacon. Beta, LV ★★★

For Heaven's Sake Lloyd's first film for Paramount has him making an accidental donation to a skid row mission, then marrying the preacher's daughter and converting all the neighborhood tough guys.
1926 60m/B Harold Lloyd, Jobyna Ralston, Noah Young, James Mason, Paul Weigel; **D:** Sam Taylor. **VHS** ★★★

For Whom the Bell Tolls Hemingway novel, gorgeously translated to the big screen, features a star-crossed romantic tale of derring-do. American schoolteacher Robert Jordan (Cooper) decides to join the Spanish Civil War and fight the fascists. He's ordered to rendezvous with peasant guerillas, to aid in blowing up a bridge, and in the rebel camp Jordan meets the beautiful Maria (Bergman). Lots of heroics (and some romance under the stars). Both leads were personally selected by the author. Originally released at 170 minutes.
1943 130m/C Gary Cooper, Ingrid Bergman, Akim Tamiroff, Katina Paxinou, Arturo de Cordova, Vladimir Sokoloff, Mikhail Rasumny, Fortunio Bonanova, Victor Varconi; **D:** Sam Wood; **W:** Dudley Nichols; **M:** Victor Young, Ray Rennahan. Academy Awards '43: Best Supporting Actress (Paxinou); Nominations: Academy Awards '43: Best Actor (Cooper), Best Actress (Bergman), Best Art Direction/Set Decoration (Color), Best Color Cinematography, Best Film Editing, Best Picture, Best Supporting Actor (Tamiroff), Best Score. **VHS** ★★★1/2

For Your Eyes Only In this James Bond adventure, 007 must keep the Soviets from getting hold of a valuable instrument aboard a sunken British spy ship. Sheds the gadgetry of its more recent predecessors in the series in favor of some spectacular stunt work and the usual beautiful girl and exotic locale. Glen's first outing as director, though he handled second units on previous Bond films. Sheena Easton sang the hit title tune.
1981 (PG) 136m/C *GB* Roger Moore, Carole Bouquet, Chaim Topol, Lynn-Holly Johnson, Julian Glover, Cassandra Harris, Jill Bennett, Michael Gothard, John Wyman, Jack Hedley, Lois Maxwell, Desmond Llewelyn, Geoffrey Keen, Walter Gotell, Charles Dance; **D:** John Glen; **W:** Michael G. Wilson; **M:** Bill Conti. Nominations: Academy Awards '81: Best Song ("For Your Eyes Only"). **VHS, Beta, LV** ★★★

Forbidden Games Famous anti-war drama about two French children play-acting the dramas of war amid the carnage of WWII. Young refugee Fossey sees her parents and dog killed. She meets a slightly older boy whose family takes the girl in. The children decide to bury the animals they have seen killed in the same way that people are buried—even stealing crosses from the cemetery to use over the animal graves. Eventually they are discovered and Fossey is again separated from her newfound home. Acclaimed; available in both dubbed and English-subtitled versions. *AKA:* Les Jeux Interdits.
1952 90m/B *FR* Brigitte Fossey, Georges Poujouly, Amedee, Louis Herbert; **D:** Rene Clement. Academy Awards '52: Best Foreign Language Film; British Academy Awards '53: Best Film; National Board of Review Awards '52: 5 Best Foreign Films of the Year; New York Film Critics Awards '52: Best Foreign Film; Venice Film Festival '52: Best Film; Nominations: Academy Awards '54: Best Story. **VHS, Beta, LV** ★★★★

Forbidden Planet In 2200 A.D., a space cruiser visits the planet Altair-4 to uncover the fate of a previous mission of space colonists. They are greeted by Robby the Robot and discover the only survivor of the Earth colony which has been preyed upon by a terrible space monster. A classic science fiction version of the Shakespearean classic "The Tempest." Laserdisc features formerly "cut" scenes, production and publicity photos, the original screen treatment, and special effects outtakes.
1956 98m/C Walter Pidgeon, Anne Francis, Leslie Nielsen, Warren Stevens, Jack Kelly, Richard Anderson, Earl Holliman, George Wallace; **D:** Fred M. Wilcox; **M:** Bebe Barron, Louis Barron. **VHS, Beta, LV** ★★★1/2

Force of Evil A cynical attorney who works for a mob boss and for Wall Street tries to save his brother from the gangster's takeover of the numbers operation. The honorable, though criminal, brother refuses the help of the amoral lawyer, and he is finally forced to confront his conscience. Garfield's sizzling performance and the atmospheric photography have made this a film noir classic.
1949 82m/B John Garfield, Thomas Gomez, Marie Windsor, Sheldon Leonard, Roy Roberts; **D:** Abraham Polonsky; **W:** Abraham Polonsky. **VHS, LV** ★★★

Foreign Affairs Vinnie Miller (Woodward) is a prim New England college teacher off to London on a research sabbatical. On the flight Vinnie's seatmate is boisterous good-ole-boy Chuck Mumpson (Dennehy), with whom she appears to have nothing in common. Naturally the two middle-aged romantics find a funny, though bittersweet, love together. A rather distracting subplot find's Vinnie's young colleague Fred (Stolz) involved in an affair with an older, eccentric British actress (Beacham). Based on the novel by Alison Lurie. Made for cable television.

1993 100m/C Joanne Woodward, Brian Dennehy, Eric Stoltz, Stephanie Beacham, Ian Richardson, Robert Hands; **D:** Jim O'Brien; **W:** Chris Bryant. National Academy of Cable Programming ACE Awards '93: Best Actor (Dennehy). **VHS, LV** ★★★

Foreign Correspondent A classic Hitchcock tale of espionage and der-ring-do. A reporter is sent to Europe during WWII to cover a pacifist con-ference in London, where he be-comes romantically involved with the daughter of the group's founder and befriends an elderly diplomat. When the diplomat is kidnapped, the re-porter uncovers a Nazi spy-ring headed by his future father-in-law.

1940 120m/B Joel McCrea, Laraine Day, Herbert Marshall, George Sanders, Robert Benchley, Albert Basserman, Edmund Gwenn, Eduardo Ciannelli, Harry Davenport, Martin Kosleck, Charles Halton; **D:** Alfred Hitchcock; **W:** Robert Benchley, Charles Bennett, Joan Harrison, James Hilton; **M:** Alfred Newman. National Board of Review Awards '40: 10 Best Films of the Year; Nominations: Academy Awards '40: Best Black and White Cinematography, Best Interior Decoration, Best Original Screenplay, Best Picture, Best Supporting Actor (Basserman). **VHS, Beta, LV** ★★★★

Forever and a Day Tremendous salute to British history centers around a London manor originally built by an English admiral during the Napoleonic era and the exploits of succeeding generations. The house even manages to survive the blitz of WWII showing English courage dur-ing wartime. Once-in-a-lifetime cast-ing and directing.

1943 104m/B Brian Aherne, Robert Cummings, Ida Lupino, Charles Laughton, Herbert Marshall, Ray Milland, Anna Neagle, Merle Oberon, Claude Rains, Victor McLaglen, Buster Keaton, Jessie Matthews, Roland Young, Sir C. Aubrey Smith, Edward Everett Horton, Elsa Lanchester, Edmund Gwenn; **D:** Rene Clair, Edmund Goulding, Cedric Hardwicke, Frank Lloyd, Victor Saville, Robert Stevenson, Herbert Wilcox, Kent Smith; **W:** Charles Bennett, Michael Hogan, Peter Godfrey, Christopher Isherwood, Gene Lockhart, Donald Ogden Stewart. **VHS** ★★★★

Forrest Gump Grandly ambitious and slightly flawed, amounting to a wonderful bit of movie magic. As the intelligence-impaired Gump with a heart of gold and more than enough character and dignity, Hanks supplies another career highlight. Field con-tributes a nice turn as his dedicated mama (they were last together in "Punchline"), while Sinise is particu-larly effective as a handicapped Viet-nam veteran with a bad attitude. In-credible special effects put Gump in the middle of historic events over a four decade period, but the real story is the life-affirming, non-judgmental power of Gump to transform the lives of those around him. From the novel by Winston Groom.

1994 (PG-13) 142m/C Tom Hanks, Robin Wright, Sally Field, Gary Sinise, Mykelti Williamson, Don Burgess; **D:** Robert Zemeckis; **W:** Eric Roth. Academy Awards '94: Best Actor (Hanks), Best Adapted Screenplay, Best Director (Zemeckis), Best Film Editing, Best Picture, Best Visual Effects; Chicago Film Critics Awards '94: Best Actor (Hanks); Directors Guild of America Awards '94: Best Director (Zemeckis); Golden Globe Awards '95: Best Actor—Drama (Hanks), Best Director (Zemeckis), Best Film—Drama; National Board of Review Awards '94: Best Actor (Hanks), Best Film, Best Supporting Actor (Sinise); Writers Guild of America '94: Best Adapted Screenplay; Blockbuster Entertainment Awards '95: Movie, Theatrical, Drama Actor, Theatrical (Hanks); Nominations: Academy Awards '94: Best Art Direction/Set Decoration, Best Cinematography, Best Makeup, Best Sound, Best Supporting Actor (Sinise), Best Original Score; Golden Globe Awards '95: Best Screenplay, Best Supporting Actor (Sinise), Best Supporting Actress (Wright), Best Original Score; MTV Movie Awards '95: Best Film, Best Male Performance (Hanks), Breakthrough Performance (Williamson). **VHS, Beta** ★★★★

Fort Apache The first of director Ford's celebrated cavalry trilogy, in which a fanatical colonel (Fonda) leads his reluctant men to an eventual slaughter, recalling George Custer at Little Big Horn. In residence: Ford hallmarks of spectacular landscapes and stirring action, as well as many vignettes of life at a remote outpost. Don't forget to catch "She Wore a Yellow Ribbon" and "Rio Grande," the next films in the series. Also available in a colorized version.

1948 125m/B John Wayne, Henry Fonda, Shirley Temple, John Agar, Pedro Armendariz Sr., Victor McLaglen, Ward Bond, Anna Lee; **D:** John Ford. **VHS, Beta, LV** ★★★1/2

Fort Apache, the Bronx A police drama set in the beleaguered South Bronx of New York City, based on the real-life experiences of two former New York cops who served there. Newman is a decent cop who goes against every kind of criminal and crazy and against his superiors in trying to bring law and justice to a downtrodden community.
1981 (R) 123m/C Paul Newman, Ed Asner, Ken Wahl, Danny Aiello, Rachel Ticotin, Pam Grier, Kathleen Beller; **D:** Daniel Petrie; **W:** Heywood Gould. **VHS, Beta, LV** ★★★

The Fortune Cookie After receiving a minor injury during a football game, a TV cameraman is convinced by his seedy lawyer brother-in-law to exaggerate his injury and start an expensive lawsuit. A classic, biting comedy by Wilder. First of several Lemmon-Matthau comedies. The letterbox laserdisc version contains the original theatrical trailer. **AKA:** Meet Whiplash Willie.
1966 125m/B Jack Lemmon, Walter Matthau, Ron Rich, Cliff Osmond, Judi West, Lurene Tuttle; **D:** Billy Wilder; **W:** Billy Wilder, I.A.L. Diamond; **M:** Andre Previn. Academy Awards '66: Best Supporting Actor (Matthau); Nominations: Academy Awards '66: Best Art Direction/Set Decoration (B & W), Best Black and White Cinematography, Best Story & Screenplay. **VHS, Beta, LV** ★★★

The Forty-Ninth Parallel Six Nazi servicemen, seeking to reach neutral American land, are trapped and their U-boat sunk by Royal Canadian Air Force bombers, forcing them into Canada on foot, where they run into an array of stalwart patriots. Dated wartime propaganda made prior to the U.S. entering the war; riddled with entertaining star turns. **AKA:** The Invaders.
1941 90m/B *GB* Laurence Olivier, Leslie Howard, Eric Portman, Raymond Massey, Glynis Johns, Finlay Currie, Anton Walbrook; **D:** Michael Powell; **W:** Emeric Pressburger, Rodney Ackland. **VHS, Beta, LV** ★★★

42nd Street A Broadway musical producer faces numerous problems in his efforts to reach a successful opening night. Choreography by Busby Berkeley. A colorized version of the film is also available. ♪ You're Getting to Be a Habit With Me; Shuffle Off to Buffalo; Young and Healthy; Forty-Second Street; It Must Be June.
1933 89m/B Warner Baxter, Ruby Keeler, Bebe Daniels, George Brent, Dick Powell, Guy Kibbee, Ginger Rogers, Una Merkel, Busby Berkeley, Ned Sparks, George E. Stone; **D:** Lloyd Bacon; **W:** Rian James, James Seymour; **M:** Harry Warren, Al Dubin. Nominations: Academy Awards '33: Best Picture, Best Sound. **VHS, Beta, LV** ★★★★

47 Ronin, Part 1 Turn of the 18th-century epic chronicling the samurai legend. The warriors of Lord Asano set out to avenge their leader, tricked into committing a forced seppuku, or hara-kiri. The photography is generously laden with views of 18th-century gardens as well as panoramic vistas. This is the largest and most popular film of the Kabuki version of the story by Seika Mayama. In Japanese with English subtitles. **AKA:** The Loyal 47 Ronin; 47 Samurai.
1942 111m/C *JP* **D:** Kenji Mizoguchi. **VHS** ★★★

47 Ronin, Part 2 Second half of the film in which the famous Japanese folklore tale of Lord Asano and his warriors is told. The film follows Asano's samurai as they commit themselves to avenging their leader in 1703. In Japanese with English subtitles.
1942 108m/C *JP* **D:** Kenji Mizoguchi. **VHS** ★★★

48 Hrs. An experienced San Francisco cop (Nolte) springs a convict (Murphy) from jail for 48 hours to find a vicious murdering drug lord. Murphy's film debut is great and Nolte is perfect as his gruff foil.
1982 (R) 97m/C Nick Nolte, Eddie Murphy, James Remar, Annette O'Toole, David Patrick Kelly, Sonny Landham, Brion James, Denise Crosby; **D:** Walter Hill; **W:** Walter Hill, Larry Gross, Steven E. de Souza, Roger Spottiswoode; **M:** James Horner. **VHS, Beta, LV** ★★★

The Fountainhead Cooper is an idealistic, uncompromising architect who refuses to change his designs. When he finds out his plans for a public housing project have been radically altered he blows up the building and winds up in court defending his actions. Neal is the subplot love interest. Based on the novel by Ayn Rand.
1949 113m/C Gary Cooper, Patricia Neal, Raymond Massey, Ray Collins, Henry Hull; **D:** King Vidor; **M:** Max Steiner. **VHS, Beta** ★★★

Four Daughters Classic, three-hankie outing in which four talented daughters of music professor Rains fall in love and marry. Garfield shines, in a role tailor-made for him, as the world-weary suitor driven to extremes in the name of love. Great performances from all. Based on the novel "Sister Act" by Fannie Hurst.

1938 90m/B Claude Rains, John Garfield, May Robson, Priscilla Lane, Lola Lane, Rosemary Lane, Gale Page, Dick Foran, Jeffrey Lynn; **D:** Michael Curtiz; **M:** Max Steiner. Nominations: Academy Awards '38: Best Director (Curtiz), Best Picture, Best Screenplay, Best Sound, Best Supporting Actor (Garfield). **VHS** ★★★

The Four Feathers A grand adventure from a story by A.E.W. Mason. After resigning from the British Army a young man is branded a coward and given four white feathers as symbols by three of his friends and his lady love. Determined to prove them wrong he joins the Sudan campaign of 1898 and rescues each of the men from certain death. They then take back their feathers as does his girl upon learning of his true courage. Excellent performances by Smith and Richardson.

1939 99m/C *GB* John Clements, Ralph Richardson, Sir C. Aubrey Smith, June Duprez, Donald Gray, Jack Allen, Clive Barker, Allan Jeayes; **D:** Zoltan Korda; **W:** R.C. Sherriff; **M:** Miklos Rozsa. Nominations: Academy Awards '39: Best Color Cinematography. **VHS, Beta, LV** ★★★★

The Four Horsemen of the Apocalypse Silent classic and star maker for Valentino concerning an Argentine family torn apart by the outbreak of WWI. Valentino is a painter who moves from his native Argentina to France and is persuaded to enlist by a recruiter who invokes the image of the Biblical riders. His excellence as a soldier, however, proves to be his undoing. The 1962 remake can't hold a candle to original, adapted from a novel by Vicente Blasco-Ibanez.

1921 110m/B Rudolph Valentino, Alice Terry, Pomeroy Cannon, Josef Swickard, Alan Hale, Mabel van Buren, Nigel de Brulier, Bowditch Turner, Wallace Beery; **D:** Rex Ingram. **VHS** ★★★1/2

The 400 Blows The classic, groundbreaking semiautobiography that initiated Truffaut's career and catapulted him to international acclaim, about the trials and rebellions of a 12-year-old French schoolboy. One of the greatest and most influential of films, and the first of Truffaut's career-long Antoine Doinel series. In French with English subtitles. **AKA:** Les Quartre Cents Coups.

1959 97m/B *FR* Jean-Pierre Leaud, Claire Maurier, Albert Remy, Guy Decomble, Georges Flament, Patrick Auffay, Jeanne Moreau, Jean-Claude Brialy, Jacques Demy, Francois Truffaut; **D:** Francois Truffaut; **W:** Marcel Moussey, Francois Truffaut; **M:** Jean Constantin. Cannes Film Festival '59: Best Director (Truffaut); New York Film Critics Awards '59: Best Foreign Film; Nominations: Academy Awards '59: Best Story & Screenplay. **VHS, Beta, LV** ★★★★

The Four Musketeers A fun-loving continuation of "The Three Musketeers," reportedly filmed simultaneously. Lavish swashbuckler jaunts between France, England, and Italy, in following the adventures of D'Artagnan and his cohorts. Pictures give an amusing depiction of Lester-interpreted 17th-century Europe, with fine performances especially by Dunaway as an evil countess seeking revenge on our heroes and Welch as the scatterbrained object of York's affections. Followed, in 1989, by "The Return of the Musketeers." **AKA:** The Revenge of Milady.

1975 (PG) 108m/C Michael York, Oliver Reed, Richard Chamberlain, Frank Finlay, Raquel Welch, Christopher Lee, Faye Dunaway, Jean-Pierre Cassel, Geraldine Chaplin, Simon Ward, Charlton Heston, Roy Kinnear, Nicole Calfan; **D:** Richard Lester; **M:** Lalo Schifrin. Nominations: Academy Awards '75: Best Costume Design. **VHS, Beta** ★★★

Four Weddings and a Funeral Refreshing, intelligent adult comedy brimming with stiff upper-lip wit and sophistication. Thirtyish Brit bachelor Charles (Grant) spends his time attending the weddings of his friends, but manages to avoid taking the plunge himself. Then he falls for Carrie (MacDowell), who's about to wed another. Great beginning offers loads of laughs as the first two weddings unfold, then becomes decidedly bittersweet. While Grant makes this a star turn as the romantic bumbler, MacDowell charms without seeming particularly needed. Supporting characters are superb, especially Coleman as the "flirty" Scarlett and Atkinson as a new minister. Surprising box office hit found a broad audience.

1994 (R) 118m/C *GB* Hugh Grant, Andie MacDowell, Simon Callow, Kristin Scott Thomas, James Fleet, John Hannah, Charlotte Coleman, David Bower, Corin Redgrave, Rowan Atkinson; **D:** Mike Newell; **W:** Richard Curtis; **M:** Richard

Rodney Bennett. Australian Film Institute '94: Best Foreign Film; British Academy Awards '94: Best Actor (Grant), Best Director (Newell), Best Film, Best Supporting Actress (Scott Thomas); Golden Globe Awards '95: Best Actor—Musical/Comedy (Grant); Writers Guild of America '94: Best Original Screenplay; Nominations: Academy Awards '94: Best Original Screenplay, Best Picture; Directors Guild of America Awards '94: Best Director (Newell); Golden Globe Awards '95: Best Actress—Musical/Comedy (MacDowell), Best Film—Musical/Comedy, Best Screenplay; MTV Movie Awards '95: Breakthrough Performance (Grant). **VHS, LV** ★★★

Fox and His Friends Fassbinder's breakthrough tragidrama, about a lowly gay carnival barker who wins the lottery, thus attracting a devious, exploiting lover, who takes him for everything he has. In German with English subtitles. *AKA:* Faustrecht der Freiheit; Fist Right of Freedom. **1975** 123m/C *GE* Rainer Werner Fassbinder, Peter Chatel, Karl-Heinz Boehm, Adrian Hoven, Harry Baer, Ulla Jacobsson, Kurt Raab, Michael Ballhaus; *D:* Rainer Werner Fassbinder. **VHS, Beta** ★★★1/2

Foxfire In the role that won her Tony and Emmy awards, Tandy stars as Annie Nations, a woman who has lived her entire life in the Blue Ridge Mountains. Widowed, all she has left are the memories of her beloved husband, with whom she regularly communes. Her son tries to convince her to move, and it becomes a clash of the wills as Annie tries to decide to stay in her past or change her future. Made for television. **1987** (PG) 118m/C Jessica Tandy, Hume Cronyn, John Denver, Gary Grubbs, Harriet Hall; *D:* Jud Taylor. National Media Owl Awards '88: Second Prize. **VHS** ★★★

Frances The tragic story of Frances Farmer, the beautiful and talented screen actress of the '30s and early '40s, who was driven to a mental breakdown by bad luck, drug and alcohol abuse, a neurotic, domineering mother, despicable mental health care, and her own stubbornness. After being in and out of mental hospitals, she is finally reduced to a shadow by a lobotomy. Not nearly as bleak as it sounds, this film works because Lange understands this character from the inside out, and never lets her become melodramatic or weak. **1982** 134m/C Jessica Lange, Kim Stanley, Sam Shepard; *D:* Graeme Clifford; *W:*

Christopher DeVore, Nicholas Kazan, Eric Bergren; *M:* John Barry. Nominations: Academy Awards '82: Best Actress (Lange), Best Supporting Actress (Stanley). **VHS, Beta, LV** ★★★

Francis the Talking Mule The first of the silly but funny series about, what else, a talking mule. Peter Stirling (O'Connor) is the dim-bulb G.I. who hooks up with Francis while fighting in Burma. Francis helps Peter become a war hero but of course everyone thinks he's crazy when Peter insists the mule can talk. The joke is that Francis is smarter than any of the humans. O'Connor starred in six of the films, with Mickey Rooney taking over the final adventure. Director Lubin went on to create the television series "Mr. Ed," about a talking horse. *AKA:* Francis. **1949** 91m/B Donald O'Connor, Patricia Medina, ZaSu Pitts, Ray Collins, John McIntire, Eduard Franz, Howland Chamberlin, Frank Faylen, Tony Curtis; *D:* Arthur Lubin; *M:* Frank Skinner; *V:* Chill Wills. **VHS, LV** ★★★

Frank and Ollie If you have children, chances are you have a collection of Disney classics, including "Cinderella," "Snow White and the Seven Dwarfs," or "Bambi." Look closely at any of the opening credits and you'll see that two of those names, part of Disney's famed "Nine Old Men," are 80-something animators Frank Thomas and Ollie Johnston. Documentary, from Thomas's son Theodore, highlights the 60-plus year friendship and storied careers of these two pioneers, who are still well-known thanks to the recent animation craze. Seven years from conception to release, the film has many great pencil drawings and scenes from the movies, but focuses as much on the men's longtime friendship. **1995** (PG) 89m/C *D:* Theodore Thomas; *W:* Theodore Thomas; *M:* James Stemple. **VHS** ★★★

Frankenstein The definitive expressionistic Gothic horror classic that set the mold. Adapted from the Mary Shelley novel about Dr. Henry Frankenstein, the scientist who creates a terrifying, yet strangely sympathetic monster. Great performance by Karloff as the creation, which made him a monster star. Several powerful scenes, excised from the original version, have been restored. Side two of the laserdisc version contains the original theatrical trailer, plus a collection of photos and scenes replayed for study purposes.

1931 71m/B Boris Karloff, Colin Clive, Mae Clarke, John Boles, Dwight Frye, Edward Van Sloan, Frederick Kerr, Lionel Belman; *D:* James Whale; *W:* Francis Edwards Faragoh, Garrett Fort, John Balderston, Robert Florey; *M:* David Broeckman. **VHS, Beta, LV** ★★★★

Frankenstein Unbound Corman returns after nearly 20 years with a better than ever B movie. Hurt plays a nuclear physicist time traveler who goes back to the 1800s and runs into Lord Byron, Percy and Mary Shelley and their neighbor Dr. Frankenstein and his monster. Great acting, fun special effects, intelligent and subtle message, with a little sex to keep things going. *AKA:* Roger Corman's Frankenstein Unbound.
1990 (R) 86m/C John Hurt, Raul Julia, Bridget Fonda, Jason Patric, Michael Hutchence, Catherine Rabett, Nick Brimble, Catherine Corman, Mickey Knox; *D:* Roger Corman; *W:* Roger Corman, F.X. Feeney; *M:* Carl Davis; *V:* Terri Treas. **VHS, Beta, LV** ★★★

Frankie and Johnny Ex-con gets a job as a short-order cook and falls for a world-weary waitress. She doesn't believe in romance, but finally gives into his pleas for a chance and finds out he may not be such a bad guy after all. Nothing can make Pfeiffer dowdy enough for this role, but she and Pacino are charming together. In a change of pace role, Nelligan has fun as a fellow waitress who loves men. Based on the play "Frankie and Johnny in the Clair de Lune" by McNally, who also wrote the screenplay.
1991 (R) 117m/C Al Pacino, Michelle Pfeiffer, Hector Elizondo, Nathan Lane, Kate Nelligan, Jane Morris, Greg Lewis, Al Fann, K. Callan, Phil Leeds, Tracy Reiner, Dey Young; *D:* Garry Marshall; *W:* Terrance McNally; *M:* Marvin Hamlisch, Dante Spinotti. British Academy Awards '91: Best Supporting Actress (Nelligan); National Board of Review Awards '91: 10 Best Films of the Year, Best Supporting Actress (Nelligan). **VHS, LV** ★★★

Frantic From Louis Malle comes one of the first French New Wave film noir dramas. A man kills his boss with the connivance of the employer's wife, his lover, and makes it look like suicide. Meanwhile, teenagers have used his car and gun in the murder of a tourist couple and he is indicted for that crime. Their perfectly planned murder begins to unravel into a panic-stricken nightmare. A suspenseful and captivating drama. Director Malle's first feature film. Musical score by jazz legend Miles Davis.

AKA: Elevator to the Gallows; Ascenseur Pour L'Echafaud.
1958 92m/B *FR* Maurice Ronet, Jeanne Moreau, Georges Poujouly; *D:* Louis Malle; *M:* Miles Davis. **VHS, Beta, 8mm** ★★★

Freaks The infamous, controversial, cult-horror classic about a band of circus freaks that exacts revenge upon a beautiful aerialist and her strongman lover after enduring humiliation and exploitation. Based on Ted Robbins's story "Spurs." It was meant to out-horror "Frankenstein" but was so successful that it was repeatedly banned. Browning's film may be a shocker but it is never intended to be exploitative since the "Freaks" are the only compassionate, loyal, and loving people around. *AKA:* Nature's Mistakes; Forbidden Love; The Monster Show.
1932 66m/B Wallace Ford, Olga Baclanova, Leila Hyams, Roscoe Ates, Harry Earles; *D:* Tod Browning. **VHS, Beta, LV** ★★★1/2

Freeze-Die-Come to Life First feature film from Kanevski, who spent eight years in a labor camp before glasnost. The story of two children who overcome the crushing poverty and bleakness of life in a remote mining community with friendship and humor. Beautifully filmed images, fine acting, touching but never overly sentimental story. The title comes from a children's game of tag. In Russian with English subtitles. *AKA:* Zamri Oumi Voskresni.
1990 105m/B *RU* Pavel Nazarov, Dinara Drukarova; *D:* Vitaly Kanevski. **VHS** ★★★1/2

French Can-Can Dramatically sparse but visually stunning depiction of the can-can's revival in Parisian nightclubs. Gabin plays the theater impressario who discovers laundress Arnoul and decides to turn her into the dancing star of his new revue at the Moulin Rouge. In French with English subtitles. *AKA:* Only the French Can!.
1955 93m/C *FR* Jean Gabin, Francoise Arnoul, Maria Felix, Jean-Roger Caussimon, Edith Piaf, Patachou; *D:* Jean Renoir. **VHS, Beta, LV** ★★★

The French Connection Two NY hard-nosed narcotics detectives stumble onto what turns out to be one of the biggest narcotics rings of all time. Cat-and-mouse thriller will keep you on the edge of your seat; contains one of the most exciting chase scenes ever filmed. Hackman's portrayal of Popeye Doyle is exact and the teamwork with Scheider special. Won multiple awards. Based on a true story from the book by Robin Moore. Followed in 1975 by "French Connection 2."

1971 (R) 102m/C Gene Hackman, Roy Scheider, Fernando Rey, Tony LoBianco, Eddie Egan, Sonny Grosso, Marcel Bozzuffi; *D:* William Friedkin, Owen Roizman. Academy Awards '71: Best Actor (Hackman), Best Adapted Screenplay, Best Director (Friedkin), Best Film Editing, Best Picture; British Academy Awards '72: Best Actor (Hackman); Directors Guild of America Awards '71: Best Director (Friedkin); Edgar Allan Poe Awards '71: Best Screenplay; Golden Globe Awards '72: Best Actor—Drama (Hackman), Best Director (Friedkin), Best Film—Drama; National Board of Review Awards '71: 10 Best Films of the Year, Best Actor (Hackman); Writers Guild of America '71: Best Adapted Screenplay; Nominations: Academy Awards '71: Best Cinematography, Best Sound, Best Supporting Actor (Scheider). **VHS, Beta, LV** ★★★1/2

French Connection 2 New York policeman "Popeye" Doyle goes to Marseilles to crack a heroin ring headed by his arch nemesis, Frog One, who he failed to stop in the United States. Dour, super-gritty sequel to the 1971 blockbuster, and featuring one of Hackman's most uncompromising performances.

1975 (R) 118m/C Gene Hackman, Fernando Rey, Bernard Fresson; *D:* John Frankenheimer; *W:* Robert Dillon. **VHS, Beta, LV** ★★★

The French Lieutenant's Woman Romantic love and tragedy in the form of two parallel stories, that of an 19th-century woman who keeps her mysterious past from the scientist who loves her, and the lead actor and actress in the film of the same story managing an illicit affair on the set. Extraordinary performances and beautifully shot. Based on the John Fowles novel.

1981 (R) 124m/C Meryl Streep, Jeremy Irons, Leo McKern, Lynsey Baxter; *D:* Karel Reisz; *W:* Harold Pinter; *M:* Carl Davis. British Academy Awards '81: Best Actress (Streep); Golden Globe Awards '82: Best Actress—Drama (Streep); Los Angeles Film Critics Association Awards '81: Best Actress (Streep); Nominations: Academy Awards '81: Best Actress (Streep), Best Adapted Screenplay, Best Art Direction/Set Decoration, Best Costume Design, Best Film Editing. **VHS, Beta, LV** ★★★1/2

Frenzy The only film in which Hitchcock was allowed to totally vent the violence and perverse sexuality of his distinctive vision, in a story about a strangler stalking London women in the late '60s. Finch plays the convicted killer-only he's innocent and must escape prison to find the real killer. McGowen is wonderful as the put-upon police inspector. A bit dated, but still ferociously hostile and cunningly executed.

1972 (R) 116m/C *GB* Jon Finch, Barry Foster, Barbara Leigh-Hunt, Anna Massey, Alec McCowen, Vivien Merchant, Billie Whitelaw, Jean Marsh; *D:* Alfred Hitchcock; *W:* Anthony Shaffer. National Board of Review Awards '72: 10 Best Films of the Year. **VHS, Beta, LV** ★★★

The Freshman Country boy Lloyd goes to college and, after many comic tribulations, saves the day with the winning touchdown at the big game and wins the girl of his dreams. This was one of the comedian's most popular films.

1925 75m/B Harold Lloyd, Jobyna Ralston, Brooks Benedict, James Anderson, Hazel Keener; *D:* Fred Newmeyer, Sam Taylor; *W:* Sam Taylor. **VHS, Beta** ★★★★

Fried Green Tomatoes Two stories about four women, love, friendship, Southern charm, and eccentricity are untidily held together by wonderful performances. Unhappy, middle-aged Evelyn (Bates) meets the talkative 83-year-old Ninny Threadgoode (Tandy). Ninny reminisces about her Depression-era life in the town of Whistle Stop, Alabama and the two women, Idgie (Masterson) and Ruth (Parker), who ran the local cafe. Back-and-forth narrative as it tracks multiple storylines is occasionally confusing, though strong character development holds interest. Surprising box office hit adapted by Fannie Flagg from her novel "Fried Green Tomatoes at the Whistle Stop Cafe."

1991 (PG-13) 130m/C Kathy Bates, Jessica Tandy, Mary Stuart Masterson, Mary-Louise Parker, Cicely Tyson, Chris O'Donnell, Stan Shaw, Gailard Sartain, Timothy Scott, Gary Basaraba, Lois Smith, Grace Zabriskie; *D:* Jon Avnet; *W:* Fannie Flagg, Carol Sobieski; *M:* Thomas Newman. National Media Owl Awards '92: First Prize; Nominations: Academy Awards '91: Best Adapted Screenplay, Best Supporting Actress (Tandy). **VHS, Beta, LV** ★★★

Friendly Fire Based on a true story of an American family in 1970 whose soldier son is killed by "friendly fire" in Vietnam, and their efforts to uncover the circumstances of the tragedy.

Touching and powerful, with an excellent dramatic performance by Burnett. Made for television.
1979 146m/C Carol Burnett, Ned Beatty, Sam Waterston, Timothy Hutton; *D:* David Greene. **VHS, Beta** ★★★

Friendly Persuasion Earnest, solidly acted tale about a peaceful Quaker family struggling to remain true to its ideals in spite of the Civil War which touches their farm life in southern Indiana. Cooper and McGuire are excellent as the parents with Perkins fine as the son worried he's using his religion to hide his cowardice. Based on a novel by Jessamyn West. *AKA:* Except For Me and Thee.
1956 140m/C Gary Cooper, Dorothy McGuire, Anthony Perkins, Marjorie Main, Charles Halton; *D:* William Wyler; *M:* Dimitri Tiomkin, Ellsworth Fredericks. Cannes Film Festival '57: Best Film; Nominations: Academy Awards '56: Best Adapted Screenplay, Best Director (Wyler), Best Picture, Best Song ("Friendly Persuasion (Thee I Love)"), Best Sound, Best Supporting Actor (Perkins). **VHS, Beta, LV** ★★★

Fritz the Cat Ralph Bakshi's animated tale for adults about a cat's adventures as he gets into group sex, college radicalism, and other hazards of life in the '60s. Loosely based on the underground comics character by Robert Crumb. Originally X-rated.
1972 77m/C *D:* Ralph Bakshi; *W:* Ralph Bakshi; *M:* Ed Bogas. **VHS, Beta** ★★★

From Here to Eternity Complex, hard-hitting look at the on- and off-duty life of soldiers at the Army base in Honolulu in the days before the Pearl Harbor attack. There's sensitive Pvt. Pruitt (Clift), his always in trouble best friend Maggio (Sinatra), and their good-guy top sergeant (Lancaster) who just happens to be having a torrid affair with the commander's wife (Kerr). Pruitt, meanwhile, is introduced to a club "hostess" (Reed) who is a lot more vulnerable than she's willing to admit. A movie filled with great performances. Still has the best waves-on-the-beach love scene in filmdom. Based on the novel by James Jones, which was toned down by the censors.
1953 118m/B Burt Lancaster, Montgomery Clift, Frank Sinatra, Deborah Kerr, Donna Reed, Ernest Borgnine, Philip Ober, Jack Warden, Mickey Shaughnessy, George Reeves, Claude Akins; *D:* Fred Zinneman; *W:* Daniel Taradash; *M:* George Duning. Academy Awards '53: Best Black and White Cinematography, Best Director (Zinneman), Best Film Editing, Best Picture, Best Screenplay, Best Sound, Best Supporting Actor (Sinatra), Best Supporting Actress (Reed); Golden Globe Awards '54: Best Supporting Actor (Sinatra); National Board of Review Awards '53: 10 Best Films of the Year; New York Film Critics Awards '53: Best Actor (Lancaster), Best Director (Zinneman), Best Film; Nominations: Academy Awards '53: Best Actor (Clift), Best Actor (Lancaster), Best Actress (Kerr), Best Costume Design (B & W); Golden Globe Awards '54: Best Director (Zinneman). **VHS, Beta, LV, 8mm** ★★★★

From Russia with Love Bond is back and on the loose in exotic Istanbul looking for a super-secret coding machine. He's involved with a beautiful Russian spy and has the SPECTRE organization after him, including villainess Rosa Klebb (she of the killer shoe). Lots of exciting escapes but not an over-reliance on the gadgetry of the later films. The second Bond feature, thought by many to be the best. The laserdisc edition includes interviews with director Terence Young and others on the creative staff. The musical score and special effects can be separated from the actors' dialogue. Also features publicity shots, American and British trailers, on-location photos, and movie posters.
1963 (PG) 125m/C *GB* Sean Connery, Daniela Bianchi, Pedro Armendariz Sr., Lotte Lenya, Robert Shaw, Eunice Gayson, Walter Gotell, Lois Maxwell, Bernard Lee, Desmond Llewelyn, Nadja Regin, Alizia Gur, Martine Beswick, Leila; *D:* Terence Young; *M:* John Barry. **VHS, Beta, LV** ★★★½

From the Life of the Marionettes A repressed man in a crumbling marriage rapes and kills a young prostitute. Another look at the powers behind individual motivations from Bergman, who uses black and white and color to relate details of the incident.
1980 (R) 104m/C *SW* Robert Atzorn, Christine Buchegger, Martin Benrath, Rita Russek, Lola Muethel, Walter Schmidinger, Heinz Bennent; *D:* Ingmar Bergman; *W:* Ingmar Bergman, Sven Nykvist. **VHS, Beta, LV** ★★★

The Front Woody is the bookmaker who becomes a "front" for blacklisted writers during the communist witch hunts of the 1950s in this satire comedy. The scriptwriter and several of the performers suffered blacklisting themselves during the Cold War. Based more or less on a true story.
1976 (PG) 95m/C Woody Allen, Zero

Mostel, Herschel Bernardi, Michael Murphy, Danny Aiello, Andrea Marcovicci; **D:** Martin Ritt; **W:** Walter Bernstein, Michael Chapman; **M:** Dave Grusin. National Board of Review Awards '76: 10 Best Films of the Year; Nominations: Academy Awards '76: Best Original Screenplay. **VHS, Beta, LV ★★★**

The Front Page The original screen version of the Hecht-MacArthur play about the shenanigans of a battling newspaper reporter and his editor in Chicago. O'Brien's film debut here is one of several hilarious performances in this breathless pursuit of an exclusive with an escaped death row inmate.
1931 101m/B Adolphe Menjou, Pat O'Brien, Edward Everett Horton, Mae Clarke, Walter Catlett; **D:** Lewis Milestone. National Board of Review Awards '31: 10 Best Films of the Year; Nominations: Academy Awards '31: Best Actor (Menjou), Best Director (Milestone), Best Picture. **VHS, Beta ★★★1/2**

The Fugitive Fonda is a priest devoted to God and the peasants under his care when he finds himself on the run after religion is outlawed in this nameless South-of-the-border dictatorship. Despite the danger of capture, he continues to minister to his flock. His eventual martyrdom unites the villagers in prayer. Considered Fonda's best performance; Ford's favorite film. Shot on location in Mexico. Excellent supporting performances. Based on the Graham Greene novel "The Power and the Glory" although considerably cleaned up for the big screen—Greene's priest had lost virtually all of his faith and moral code. Here the priest is a genuine Ford hero. A gem.
1948 99m/B Henry Fonda, Dolores Del Rio, Pedro Armendariz Sr., J. Carrol Naish, Leo Carrillo, Ward Bond, Robert Armstrong, John Qualen; **D:** John Ford; **W:** Dudley Nichols. **VHS, Beta, LV ★★★★**

The Fugitive Exciting big-screen version of the '60s TV series with the same basic storyline: Dr. Richard Kimble's wife is murdered and he's implicated, so he goes on the lam to find the real killer, the mysterious one-armed man. Lots of mystery and action, particularly a spectacular train/bus crash sequence, keeps the tension high. Due to illness, Richard Jordan was replaced by Krabbe after production had begun. Alec Baldwin was originally slated to star as Kimble, but backed out and Ford was cast. Sound familiar? Ford also replaced Baldwin as Jack Ryan in "Pa-

triot Games." The second highest grossing movie of 1993.
1993 (PG-13) 127m/C Harrison Ford, Tommy Lee Jones, Jeroen Krabbe, Julianne Moore, Sela Ward, Joe Pantoliano, Andreas Katsulas, Daniel Roebuck, Michael Chapman; **D:** Andrew Davis; **W:** David N. Twohy, Jeb Stuart; **M:** James Newton Howard. Academy Awards '93: Best Supporting Actor (Jones); Golden Globe Awards '94: Best Supporting Actor (Jones); Los Angeles Film Critics Association Awards '93: Best Supporting Actor (Jones); MTV Movie Awards '94: Best On-Screen Duo (Harrison Ford/Tommy Lee Jones), Best Action Sequence; Blockbuster Entertainment Awards '95: Action Actor, Video (Ford); Nominations: Academy Awards '93: Best Cinematography, Best Film Editing, Best Original Screenplay, Best Picture, Best Sound, Best Sound Effects Editing; British Academy Awards '93: Best Supporting Actor (Jones); Directors Guild of America Awards '93: Best Director (Davis); Golden Globe Awards '94: Best Actor—Drama (Ford), Best Director (Davis). **VHS, LV ★★★1/2**

Full Metal Jacket A three-act Vietnam War epic, about a single Everyman impetuously passing through basic training then working in the field as an Army photojournalist and fighting at the onset of the Tet offensive. First half of the film is the most realistic bootcamp sequence ever done. Unfocused but powerful. Based on the novel by Hasford, who also co-scripted.
1987 (R) 116m/C Matthew Modine, R. Lee Ermey, Vincent D'Onofrio, Adam Baldwin, Dorian Harewood, Arliss Howard, Kevyn Major Howard; **D:** Stanley Kubrick; **W:** Michael Herr, Gustav Hasford, Stanley Kubrick. Nominations: Academy Awards '87: Best Adapted Screenplay. **VHS, Beta, LV, 8mm ★★★1/2**

The Funeral A sharp satire of the clash of modern Japanese culture with the old. The hypocrisies, rivalries, and corruption in an average family are displayed at the funeral of its patriarch who also happened to own a house of ill repute. Itami's breakthrough film. In Japanese with English subtitles.
1984 112m/C *JP* Tsutomu Yamazaki, Nobuko Miyamoto, Kin Sugai, Ichiro Zaitsu, Nekohachi Edoya, Shoji Otake; **D:** Juzo Itami. **VHS ★★★1/2**

The Funeral Ferrara fuels fantastic performances from his famous thesps in this fatalistic tale of a family of gangsters in 1930s New York. Flashbacks from the opening funeral scene show a complex and troubled family of Italian brothers (Walken, Penn, and Gallo), from their formative years through their quest for justice after youngest brother Johnny is murdered. Not just another mob movie; characters are multidimensional with interesting quirks, and Penn, especially, sprints into his role. More subtle than "Bad Lieutenant" and less pretentious than "The Addiction," this Ferrara flick is the one to see.

1996 96m/C Christopher Walken, Benicio Del Toro, Vincent Gallo, Christopher Penn, Isabella Rossellini, Annabella Sciorra, John Ventimiglia, Paul Hipp, Gretchen Mol; **D:** Abel Ferrara; **W:** Nicholas St. John; **M:** Joe Delia. Nominations: Independent Spirit Awards '97: Best Film, Best Director (Ferrara), Best Actor (Penn), Best Screenplay, Best Cinematography. **VHS** ★★★

Funny Face A musical satire on beatniks and the fashion scene also features the May-December romance between Astaire and the ever-lovely Hepburn. He is a high-fashion photographer (based on Richard Avedon); she is a Greenwich Village bookseller fond of shapeless, drab clothing. He decides to take her to Paris and show her what modeling's all about. The elegant musical score features classic Gershwin. The laserdisc includes the original theatrical trailer and is available in widescreen. ♪ Let's Kiss and Make Up; He Loves and She Loves; Funny Face; How Long Has This Been Going On?; Clap Yo' Hands; 'SWonderful; Bonjour Paris; On How To Be Lovely; Marche Funebre.

1957 103m/C Fred Astaire, Audrey Hepburn, Kay Thompson, Suzy Parker; **D:** Stanley Donen; **M:** George Gershwin, Ira Gershwin. Nominations: Academy Awards '57: Best Art Direction/Set Decoration, Best Cinematography, Best Costume Design, Best Story & Screenplay. **VHS, Beta, LV, 8mm** ★★★

Funny Girl Follows the early career of comedian Fanny Brice, her rise to stardom with the Ziegfeld Follies and her stormy romance with gambler Nick Arnstein in a fun and funny look at back stage music hall life in the early 1900s. Streisand's film debut followed her auspicious performance of the role on Broadway. Score was augmented by several tunes sung by Brice during her performances. Excellent performances from everyone, captured beautifully by Wyler in his musical film debut. ♪ My Man; Second Hand Rose; I'd Rather Be Blue Over

You; People; Don't Rain On My Parade; I'm The Greatest Star; Sadie, Sadie; His Love Makes Me Beautiful; You Are Woman, I Am Man.

1968 (G) 151m/C Barbra Streisand, Omar Sharif, Walter Pidgeon, Kay Medford, Anne Francis; **D:** William Wyler. Academy Awards '68: Best Actress (Streisand); Golden Globe Awards '69: Best Actress—Musical/Comedy (Streisand); Nominations: Academy Awards '68: Best Cinematography, Best Film Editing, Best Picture, Best Song ("Funny Girl"), Best Sound, Best Supporting Actress (Medford), Best Original Score. **VHS, Beta, LV** ★★★

A Funny Thing Happened on the Way to the Forum A bawdy Broadway farce set in ancient Rome where a conniving slave plots his way to freedom by aiding in the romantic escapades of his master's inept son. Terrific performances by Mostel and Gilford. Keaton's second-to-last film role. The Oscar-winning score includes such highlights as "Comedy Tonight," "Lovely," and "Everybody Ought to Have a Maid."

1966 100m/C Zero Mostel, Phil Silvers, Jack Gilford, Buster Keaton, Michael Hordern, Michael Crawford, Annette Andre; **D:** Richard Lester; **M:** Ken Thorne. Academy Awards '66: Best Score. **VHS, Beta, LV** ★★★

Fury Tracy gives an excellent performance as an innocent young man framed for kidnapping and then nearly murdered by a lynch mob. His plans for revenge are thwarted by his girlfriend, who fears that he will turn into the murderer he has been accused of being. Powerful anti-violence message is well-made, with strong ensemble acting. Lang's favorite of his American-made films.

1936 96m/B Spencer Tracy, Sylvia Sidney, Walter Abel, Bruce Cabot, Edward Ellis, Walter Brennan, Frank Albertson; **D:** Fritz Lang. Nominations: Academy Awards '36: Best Story. **VHS, Beta** ★★★1/2

"G" Men Powerful story based loosely on actual events that occurred during FBI operations in the early 1930s, with Cagney on the right side of the law, though still given to unreasonable fits of anger. Raised and educated by a well-known crime kingpin, a young man becomes an attorney. When his friend the FBI agent is killed in the line of duty, he joins the FBI to seek vengeance on the mob. But his mob history haunts him, forcing him to constantly prove to his superiors that he is not under its influence. Tense and thrilling classic.

1935 86m/B James Cagney, Barton

G

▲

MacLane, Ann Dvorak, Margaret Lindsay, Robert Armstrong, Lloyd Nolan, William Harrigan, Regis Toomey; **D:** William Keighley. **VHS, Beta ★★★1/2**

The Gallant Hours Biography of Admiral "Bull" Halsey (Cagney) covers five weeks, October 18 through December 1, 1942, in the WWII battle of Guadalcanal in the South Pacific. Director Montgomery forgoes battle scenes to focus on the human elements in a war and what makes a great leader. Fine performance by Cagney.
1960 115m/B James Cagney, Dennis Weaver, Ward Costello, Richard Jaeckel, Les Tremayne, Robert Burton, Raymond Bailey, Karl Swenson, Harry Landers, James T. Goto; **D:** Robert Montgomery; **W:** Frank D. Gilroy. **VHS ★★★**

Gallipoli History blends with the destiny of two friends as they become part of the legendary WWI confrontation between Australia and the German-allied Turks. A superbly filmed, gripping commentary on the wastes of war. Haunting score; excellent performances by Lee and a then-unknown Gibson. Remake of a lesser 1931 effort "Battle of Gallipoli."
1981 (PG) 111m/C *AU* Mel Gibson, Mark Lee, Bill Kerr, David Argue, Tim McKenzie, Robert Grubb; **D:** Peter Weir; **W:** David Williamson, Peter Weir, John Seale. Australian Film Institute '81: Best Actor (Gibson), Best Film. **VHS, Beta, LV ★★★★**

Gallowglass A "gallowglass" is an ancient Gaelic term for a servant willing to sacrifice his life for his master. In this moody TV mystery, Joe (Sheen), whose life was saved by manipulative, handsome Sandor (Rhys), who now demands his absolute loyalty. Sandor needs his help in kidnapping Nina (Whitely), an unhappy ex-model who was the victim of a kidnapping years before in Italy and now lives with her husband in wealthy seclusion in the country. There, Nina is under the protection of bodyguard/chauffeur Paul (McArdle), and their mutual attraction leads to unexpected complications. Based on the thriller by Ruth Rendell (writing as Barbara Vine).
1995 150m/C Paul Rhys, Michael Sheen, Arkie Whiteley, John McArdle, Claire Hackett, Gary Waldhorn; **D:** Tim Fywell. **VHS ★★★**

The Gambler College professor Axel Freed has a gambling problem so vast that it nearly gets him killed by his bookies. He goes to Las Vegas to recoup his losses and wins big, only to blow the money on stupid sports bets that get him deeper into trouble. Excellent character study of a compulsive loser on a downward spiral.
1974 (R) 111m/C James Caan, Lauren Hutton, Paul Sorvino, Burt Young, James Woods; **D:** Karel Reisz; **W:** James Toback. **VHS, Beta, LV ★★★**

Gandhi The biography of Mahatma Gandhi from the prejudice he encounters as a young attorney in South Africa, to his role as spiritual leader to the people of India and his use of passive resistance against the country's British rulers, and his eventual assassination. Kingsley is a marvel in his Academy Award-winning role and the picture is a generally riveting epic worthy of its eight Oscars.
1982 (PG) 188m/C *GB* Ben Kingsley, Candice Bergen, Edward Fox, John Gielgud, John Mills, Saeed Jaffrey, Trevor Howard, Ian Charleson, Roshan Seth, Athol Fugard, Martin Sheen, Daniel Day-Lewis, Rohini Hattangady; **D:** Richard Attenborough; **W:** John Briley; **M:** George Fenton. Academy Awards '82: Best Actor (Kingsley), Best Art Direction/Set Decoration, Best Cinematography, Best Costume Design, Best Director (Attenborough), Best Film Editing, Best Original Screenplay, Best Picture; British Academy Awards '82: Best Actor (Kingsley), Best Director (Attenborough), Best Film, Best Supporting Actress (Hattangady); Golden Globe Awards '83: Best Actor—Drama (Kingsley), Best Director (Attenborough), Best Foreign Film, Best Screenplay; Los Angeles Film Critics Association Awards '82: Best Actor (Kingsley); National Board of Review Awards '82: Best Actor (Kingsley); New York Film Critics Awards '82: Best Actor (Kingsley), Best Film; Nominations: Academy Awards '82: Best Makeup, Best Original Score. **VHS, Beta, LV ★★★1/2**

The Garden of Allah Dietrich finds hyper-romantic encounters in the Algerian desert with Boyer, but his terrible secret may doom them both. This early Technicolor production, though flawed, is an absolute must for Dietrich fans. Yuma, Arizona, substituted for the exotic locale.
1936 85m/C Marlene Dietrich, Charles Boyer, Basil Rathbone, Sir C. Aubrey Smith, Tilly Losch, Joseph Schildkraut, Henry Kleinbach (Brandon), John Carradine; **D:** Richard Boleslawski; **M:** Max Steiner. Nominations: Academy Awards '36: Best Original Score. **VHS, LV ★★★**

The Garden of the Finzi-Continis Acclaimed film by De Sica about an aristocratic Jewish family living in Italy under increasing Fascist oppression on the eve of WWII. The garden wall symbolizes the distance between the Finzi-Continis and the Nazi reality about to engulf them. Flawless acting and well-defined direction. Based on the novel by Giorgio Bassani, who collaborated on the script but later repudiated the film. Music by De Sica's son, Manuel. In Italian with English subtitles or dubbed. *AKA:* Il Giardino Del Finzi-Contini.

1971 (R) 90m/C *IT* Dominique Sanda, Helmut Berger, Lino Capolicchio, Fabio Testi, Romolo Valli; *D:* Vittorio De Sica; *W:* Cesare Zavattini; *M:* Manuel De Sica. Academy Awards '71: Best Foreign Language Film; Berlin International Film Festival '71: Golden Berlin Bear; National Board of Review Awards '71: 5 Best Foreign Films of the Year; Nominations: Academy Awards '71: Best Adapted Screenplay. **VHS, Beta, LV** ★★★★

Gas Food Lodging Saga casts Adams as Nora, a weary waitress in Laramie, New Mexico, trying her best to raise two teenaged daughters on her own. The daughters, Skye and Balk, are disillusioned about love and family. Balk's special friend is Darius, an eccentric window dresser, played by Leitch, Skye's brother. Nothing works out quite as intended but multi-dimensional characters, poignant situtations, and enormous emotional appeal highlight the directorial debut of Anders. Based on the Richard Peck novel "Don't Look and It Won't Hurt."

1992 (R) 100m/C Brooke Adams, Ione Skye, Fairuza Balk, James Brolin, Rob Knepper, Donovan Leitch, David Lansbury, Jacob Vargas, Chris Mulkey, Tiffany Anders; *D:* Allison Anders; *W:* Allison Anders; *M:* J. Mascis, Barry Adamson. Independent Spirit Awards '93: Best Actress (Balk). **VHS, LV** ★★★

Gaslight A forgotten British classic that fell victim to the American production of the same title and theme that was filmed only five years later. Set in late Victorian London, Wynyard is the rich innocent married to the calculating Walbrook, who slowly tries driving his bride insane in order to discover some hidden family jewels. She comes under the protection of a Scotland Yard detective (Pettingell) who suspects Walbrook has already murdered once. An outstandingly eerie psychological thriller. Based on the play "Angel Street" by Patrick Hamilton. *AKA:* Angel Street.

1939 84m/C *GB* Anton Walbrook, Diana Wynyard, Frank Pettingell, Cathleen Cordell; *D:* Thorold Dickinson. **VHS** ★★★1/2

Gaslight Lavish remake of the 1939 film, based on the Patrick Hamilton play "Angel Street." A man tries to drive his beautiful wife insane while searching for priceless jewels. Her only clue to his evil acts is the frequent dimming of their gaslights. A suspenseful Victorian era mystery. Lansbury's film debut, as the tarty maid. *AKA:* The Murder in Thorton Square.

1944 114m/B Charles Boyer, Ingrid Bergman, Joseph Cotten, Angela Lansbury, Terry Moore, May Whitty, Barbara Everest, Emil Rameau, Edmund Breon, Halliwell Hobbes, Tom Stevenson; *D:* George Cukor. Academy Awards '44: Best Actress (Bergman), Best Interior Decoration; Golden Globe Awards '45: Best Actress—Drama (Bergman); Nominations: Academy Awards '44: Best Actor (Boyer), Best Black and White Cinematography, Best Picture, Best Screenplay, Best Supporting Actress (Lansbury). **VHS, Beta, LV** ★★★1/2

Gate of Hell Set in 12th-century Japan. A warlord desires a beautiful married woman and seeks to kill her husband to have her. However, he accidentally kills her instead. Filled with shame and remorse, the warlord abandons his life to seek solace as a monk. Heavily awarded and critically acclaimed; the first Japanese film to use color photography. In Japanese with English subtitles. *AKA:* Jigokumen.

1954 89m/C *JP* Kazuo Hasegawa, Machiko Kyo; *D:* Teinosuke Kinugasa. Academy Awards '54: Best Costume Design (Color), Best Foreign Language Film; Cannes Film Festival '54: Best Film; National Board of Review Awards '54: 10 Best Films of the Year. **VHS, Beta, 8mm** ★★★1/2

The Gay Divorcee Astaire pursues Rogers to an English seaside resort, where she mistakes him for the hired correspondent in her divorce case. Based on the musical play "The Gay Divorce" by Dwight Taylor and Cole Porter. The title was slightly changed for the movie because of protests from the Hays Office. ♪ Don't Let It Bother You; A Needle in a Haystack; Let's K-nock K-nees; Night and Day; The Continental. *AKA:* The Gay Divorce.

1934 107m/B Fred Astaire, Ginger Rogers, Edward Everett Horton, Eric Blore, Alice Brady, Erik Rhodes, Betty Grable; *D:* Mark Sandrich; *M:* Max Steiner. Academy Awards '34: Best Song ("The Continental"); Nominations: Academy Awards '34: Best Interior Decoration, Best Picture, Best Sound, Best Score. **VHS, Beta, LV** ★★★

The General Keaton's masterpiece and arguably the most formally perfect and funniest of silent comedies. Concerns a plucky Confederate soldier who single-handedly retrieves a pivotal train from Northern territory. Full of eloquent man-vs-machinery images and outrageous sight gags. Remade as "The Great Locomotive Chase" in 1956 with Fess Parker.
1927 78m/B Buster Keaton, Marion Mack, Glen Cavender, Jim Farley, Joe Keaton; **D:** Buster Keaton, Clyde Bruckman. **VHS, Beta, LV, 8mm ★★★★**

The General Died at Dawn A clever, atmospheric suspense film about an American mercenary in Shanghai falling in love with a beautiful spy as he battles a fierce Chinese warlord who wants to take over the country. Playwright-to-be Odets' first screenplay; he, O'Hara and '30s gossip hound Skolsky have cameos as reporters.
1936 93m/B Gary Cooper, Madeleine Carroll, Akim Tamiroff, Dudley Digges, Porter Hall, William Frawley, Philip Ahn; **Cameos:** John O'Hara, Clifford Odets, Sidney Skolsky; **D:** Lewis Milestone; **W:** Clifford Odets. Nominations: Academy Awards '36: Best Cinematography, Best Supporting Actor (Tamiroff), Best Original Score. **VHS, Beta ★★★**

The General Line Eisenstein's classic pro-Soviet semi-documentary about a poor farm woman who persuades her village to form a cooperative. Transgresses its party-line instructional purpose by vivid filmmaking. The director's last silent film. **AKA:** The Old and the New.
1929 90m/B *RU* Marfa Lapkina; **D:** Sergei Eisenstein. National Board of Review Awards '30: 5 Best Foreign Films of the Year. **VHS, Beta ★★★★**

Generale Della Rovere A WWII black marketeer is forced by the Nazis to go undercover in a local prison. To find out who the resistance leaders are, he poses as a general. But when prisoners begin to look to him for guidance, he finds the line between his assumed role and real identity diminished, leading to a tragic conclusion. Acclaimed film featuring a bravura lead performance by veteran director De Sica. In Italian with English subtitles. **AKA:** Il Generale Della-Rovere.
1960 139m/B *IT* Vittorio De Sica, Otto Messmer, Sandra Milo; **D:** Roberto Rossellini. **VHS, Beta ★★★1/2**

A Generation During WWII, a young man escapes from the Warsaw Ghetto and finds his way to the Polish Resistance. He falls in love with the leader of the local group and finds the courage to fight for his freedom. Strong directorial debut from Wajda. Part 1 of his "War Trilogy," followed by "Kanal" and "Ashes and Diamonds." Scripted by Czeszko from his novel "Pokolenie." In Polish with English subtitles.
1954 90m/B *PL* Tadeusz Lomnicki, Ursula Modrzynska, Zbigniew Cybulski, Roman Polanski; **D:** Andrzej Wajda; **W:** Bohdan Czeszko. **VHS ★★★**

Genevieve A 1904 Darracq roadster is the title star of this picture which spoofs "classic car" owners and their annual rally from London to Brighton. Two married couples challenge each other to a friendly race which becomes increasingly intense as they near the finish line.
1953 86m/C *GB* John Gregson, Dinah Sheridan, Kenneth More, Kay Kendall; **D:** Henry Cornelius; **M:** Larry Adler. British Academy Awards '53: Best Film; Golden Globe Awards '55: Best Foreign Film; Nominations: Academy Awards '54: Best Story & Screenplay, Best Original Score. **VHS, Beta ★★★**

Gentleman Jim A colorful version of the life of old-time heavyweight boxing great Jim Corbett, transformed from a typical Warner Bros. bio-pic by director Walsh into a fun-loving, anything-for-laughs donnybrook. Climaxes with Corbett's fight for the championship against the great John L. Sullivan. One of Flynn's most riotous performances.
1942 104m/B Errol Flynn, Alan Hale, Alexis Smith, Jack Carson, Ward Bond, Arthur Shields, William Frawley; **D:** Raoul Walsh. **VHS, Beta, LV ★★★1/2**

Gentleman's Agreement A magazine writer (Peck) looks for a new angle for an article on anti-Semitism by pretending to be Jewish. His new identity pervades his life in unexpected ways, almost destroys his relationships, but contributes to the success of his magazine series. This movie was Hollywood's first major attack on anti-Semitism. Controversial in its day, yet still timely.
1947 118m/B Gregory Peck, Dorothy McGuire, John Garfield, Celeste Holm, Anne Revere, June Havoc, Albert Dekker, Jane Wyatt, Dean Stockwell, Nicholas Joy; **D:** Elia Kazan; **W:** Moss Hart. Academy Awards '47: Best Director (Kazan), Best Picture, Best Supporting Actress (Holm); New York Film Critics Awards '47: Best Director (Kazan), Best Film; Nominations: Academy Awards '47: Best Actress (McGuire); Academy Awards '47: Best

Actor (Peck), Best Film Editing, Best Screenplay, Best Supporting Actress (Revere). **VHS, LV** ★★★

Gentlemen Prefer Blondes Amusing satire involving two show-business girls from Little Rock trying to make it big in Paris. Seeking rich husbands or diamonds, their capers land them in police court. Monroe plays Lorelei Lee, Russell is her sidekick. Despite an occasionally slow plot, the music, comedy, and performances are great fun. Film version of a Broadway adaption of a story by Anita Loos. Followed by (but without Monroe) "Gentlemen Marry Brunettes." ♪ A (Two) Little Girl(s) From Little Rock; Bye, Bye Baby; Ain't There Anyone Here For Love?; When Love Goes Wrong; Diamonds Are A Girl's Best Friend.
1953 91m/C Marilyn Monroe, Jane Russell, Charles Coburn, Elliott Reid, Tommy Noonan, George Winslow; *D:* Howard Hawks. **VHS, Beta, LV** ★★★

George Washington Slept Here Hilarious side-splitter about a couple who moves from their Manhattan apartment to an old, broken-down country home in Connecticut. It's one catastrophe after another as the couple tries to renovate their home and deal with a greedy neighbor. Based on the play by George S. Kaufman and Moss Hart.
1942 93m/B Jack Benny, Ann Sheridan, Charles Coburn, Percy Kilbride, Hattie McDaniel, William Tracy; *D:* William Keighley. Nominations: Academy Awards '42: Best Interior Decoration. **VHS** ★★★

Georgia Character study about sibling rivalry, self-destruction, and the Seattle music scene. Struggling rock singer Sadie (Leigh), who relies on booze, drugs, and men to help her make it through the night, returns to Seattle to crash with big sister Georgia (Winningham). Settled, with loving husband and kids, the much more talented Georgia is also a popular folk icon and has the type of personal/career success angry and ambitious Sadie can only dream about. Fine performances—particularly from the chameleonlike Leigh; both leads do their own singing. Screenwriter Turner is Leigh's mother.
1995 (R) 117m/C Jennifer Jason Leigh, Mare Winningham, Ted Levine, Max Perlich, John Doe, John C. Reilly, Jimmy Witherspoon; *D:* Ulu Grosbard; *W:* Barbara Turner. Independent Spirit Awards '96: Best Supporting Actress (Winningham), Best Actress (Leigh), Best Director (Grosbard); Montreal World Film Festival

'95: Best Film, Best Actress (Leigh); New York Film Critics Awards '95: Best Actress (Leigh); Nominations: Academy Awards '95: Best Supporting Actress (Winningham); Independent Spirit Awards '96: Best Supporting Actor (Perlich); Screen Actors Guild Award '95: Best Supporting Actress (Winningham). **VHS, LV** ★★★

Georgy Girl Redgrave finely plays the overweight ugly-duckling Georgy who shares a flat with the beautiful and promiscuous Meredith (Rampling). Georgy is, however, desired by the wealthy and aging Mason and soon by Meredith's lover (Bates), who recognizes her good heart. When Meredith becomes pregnant, Georgy persuades her to let her raise the baby, leaving Georgy with the dilemma of marrying the irresponsible Bates (the baby's father) or the settled Mason. The film and title song (sung by the Seekers) were both huge hits. Based on the novel by Margaret Foster who also co-wrote the screenplay.
1966 100m/B *GB* Lynn Redgrave, James Mason, Charlotte Rampling, Alan Bates, Bill Owen, Claire Kelly, Rachel Kempson; *D:* Silvio Narizzano. Golden Globe Awards '67: Best Actress—Musical/Comedy (Redgrave); National Board of Review Awards '66: 10 Best Films of the Year; New York Film Critics Awards '66: Best Actress (Redgrave); Nominations: Academy Awards '66: Best Actress (Redgrave), Best Black and White Cinematography, Best Song ("Georgy Girl"), Best Supporting Actor (Mason). **VHS, Beta, LV** ★★★

Gertrud The simple story of an independent Danish woman rejecting her husband and lovers in favor of isolation. Cold, dry, minimalistic techniques make up Dreyer's final film. In Danish with English subtitles.
1964 116m/B *DK* Nina Pens Rode, Bendt Rothe, Ebbe Rode; *D:* Carl Theodor Dreyer; *W:* Carl Theodor Dreyer. National Board of Review Awards '65: 5 Best Foreign Films of the Year. **VHS, Beta** ★★★½

Get Out Your Handkerchiefs Unconventional comedy about a husband desperately attempting to make his sexually frustrated wife happy. Determined to go to any lengths, he asks a Mozart-loving teacher to become her lover. She is now, however, bored by both men. Only when she meets a 13-year-old genius at the summer camp where the three adults are counselors does she come out of her funk and find her sexual happiness. Laure is a beautiful character,

but Depardieu and Dewaere are wonderful as the bewildered would-be lovers. Academy Award winner for best foreign film. In French with English subtitles. *AKA:* Preparez Vous Mouchoirs.
1978 (R) 109m/C *FR* Gerard Depardieu, Patrick Dewaere, Carole Laure; *D:* Bertrand Blier; *W:* Bertrand Blier; *M:* Georges Delerue. Academy Awards '78: Best Foreign Language Film; Cesar Awards '79: Best Score; National Society of Film Critics Awards '78: Best Film. **VHS, Beta, LV** ★★★1/2

Get Shorty Low-level Miami loan shark and film buff Chili Palmer (Travolta) heads to Hollywood via Las Vegas, looking for a deadbeat dry-cleaner (Paymer) and a grade-Z movie producer (Hackman) who owes Vegas $150,000. Aided by B-movie scream-queen (Russo), Palmer is pitted against a variety of shady Hollywood-types, including egomaniacal star (DeVito), while trying to get into showbiz himself. Snappy scripting and performances finally do screen justice to an Elmore Leonard crime novel. DeVito, with the smaller title role, was originally cast as Chili Palmer, a role Travolta twice turned down until the ubiquitous Quentin Tarantino advised him to take it.
1995 (R) 105m/C John Travolta, Gene Hackman, Danny DeVito, Rene Russo, Dennis Farina, Delroy Lindo, David Paymer, James Gandolfini, Don Peterman; *Cameos:* Bette Midler, Harvey Keitel, Penny Marshall; *D:* Barry Sonnenfeld; *W:* Scott Frank; *M:* John Lurie. Golden Globe Awards '96: Best Actor—Musical/Comedy (Travolta); Nominations: Golden Globe Awards '96: Best Film—Musical/Comedy, Best Screenplay; Screen Actors Guild Award '95: Cast; Writers Guild of America '95: Best Adapted Screenplay. **VHS** ★★★

Gettysburg Civil War buff Ted Turner (who has a cameo as a Confederate soldier) originally intended Michael Shaara's Pulitzer Prize-winning novel "The Killer Angels" to be adapted as a three-part miniseries for his "TNT" network, but the lure of the big screen prevailed, marking the first time the battle has been committed to film and the first time a film crew has been allowed to film battle scenes on the Gettysburg National Military Park battlefield. The greatest battle of the war and the bloodiest in U.S. history is realistically staged by more than 5,000 Civil War re-enactors. The all-male cast concentrates on presenting the human cost of the war, with Daniels particularly noteworthy as the scholarly Colonel Chamberlain, deter-

mined to hold Little Big Top for the Union. Last film role for Jordan, to whom the movie is co-dedicated. The full scale re-creation of Pickett's Charge is believed to be the largest period scale motion-picture sequence filmed in North America since D.W. Griffith's "Birth of a Nation."
1993 (PG) 254m/C Jeff Daniels, Martin Sheen, Tom Berenger, Sam Elliott, Richard Jordan, Stephen Lang, Kevin Conway, C. Thomas Howell, Maxwell Caulfield, Andrew Prine, James Lancaster, Royce D. Applegate, Brian Mallon; *Cameos:* Ken Burns, Ted Turner; *D:* Ronald F. Maxwell; *W:* Ronald F. Maxwell; *M:* Randy Edelman. **VHS** ★★★1/2

Ghost Zucker, known for overboard comedies like "Airplane!" and "Ruthless People," changed tack and directed this undemanding romantic thriller, which was the surprising top grosser of 1990. Swayze is a murdered investment consultant attempting (from somewhere near the hereafter) to protect his lover, Moore, from imminent danger when he learns he was the victim of a hit gone afoul. Goldberg is the medium who suddenly discovers that the powers she's been faking are real. A winning blend of action, special effects (from Industrial Light and Magic), and romance.
1990 (PG-13) 127m/C Patrick Swayze, Demi Moore, Whoopi Goldberg, Tony Goldwyn, Rick Aviles, Vincent Schiavelli, Gail Boggs, Armelia McQueen, Phil Leeds; *D:* Jerry Zucker; *W:* Bruce Joel Rubin; *M:* Maurice Jarre. Academy Awards '90: Best Original Screenplay, Best Supporting Actress (Goldberg); Golden Globe Awards '91: Best Supporting Actress (Goldberg); People's Choice Awards '91: Best Film—Drama; Nominations: Academy Awards '90: Best Film Editing, Best Picture, Best Original Score. **VHS, Beta, LV, 8mm** ★★★

The Ghost and Mrs. Muir A charming, beautifully orchestrated fantasy about a feisty widow who, with her young daughter, buys a seaside house and refuses to be intimidated by the crabby ghost of its former sea captain owner. When the widow falls into debt, the captain dictates his sea adventures, which she adapts into a successful novel. The ghost also falls in love with the beautiful lady. Tierney is exquisite and Harrison is sharp-tongued and manly. Based on R. A. Dick's novel.
1947 104m/B Gene Tierney, Rex Harrison, George Sanders, Edna Best, Anna Lee, Vanessa Brown, Robert Coote, Natalie Wood, Isobel Elsom; *D:* Joseph L. Mankiewicz; *W:* Philip Dunne; *M:* Bernard Herrmann. Nominations: Academy Awards

'47: Best Black and White Cinematography. **VHS, Beta, LV** ★★★

The Ghost Breakers As a follow-up to the Hope/Goddard 1939 comedy thriller "The Cat and the Canary," this spooky comedy was even better. Lots of laughs and real chills as Hope and Goddard investigate a haunted mansion that she's inherited in Cuba. Effective horror scenes are expertly handled by director Marshall. Remade in 1953 as "Scared Stiff" with Dean Martin and Jerry Lewis. Based on the play by Paul Dickey and Charles Goddard.
1940 83m/B Bob Hope, Paulette Goddard, Richard Carlson, Paul Lukas, Willie Best, Pedro de Cordoba, Noble Johnson, Anthony Quinn; **D:** George Marshall. **VHS, LV** ★★★

Ghostbusters After losing their scholastic funding, a group of "paranormal" investigators decide to go into business for themselves, aiding New York citizens in the removal of ghosts, goblins, and other annoying spirits. This comedy-thriller about Manhattan being overrun by ghosts contains great special effects, zany characters, and some of the best laughs of the decade. Also available in a laserdisc version with letterboxing, analysis of all special effects, complete screenplay, and original trailer. Followed by a sequel.
1984 (PG) 103m/C Bill Murray, Dan Aykroyd, Harold Ramis, Rick Moranis, Sigourney Weaver, Annie Potts, Ernie Hudson, William Atherton; **D:** Ivan Reitman; **W:** Dan Aykroyd, Harold Ramis; **M:** Elmer Bernstein. Nominations: Academy Awards '84: Best Song ("Ghostbusters"). **VHS, Beta, LV, 8mm** ★★★

Giant Based on the Edna Ferber novel, this epic saga covers two generations of a wealthy Texas cattle baron (Hudson) who marries a strong-willed Virginia woman (Taylor) and takes her to live on his vast ranch. It explores the problems they have adjusting to life together, as well as the politics and prejudice of the time. Dean plays the resentful ranch hand (who secretly loves Taylor) who winds up striking oil and beginning a fortune to rival that of his former boss. Dean's last movie—he died in a car crash shortly before filming was completed.
1956 201m/C Elizabeth Taylor, Rock Hudson, James Dean, Carroll Baker, Chill Wills, Dennis Hopper, Rod Taylor, Earl Holliman, Jane Withers, Sal Mineo, Mercedes McCambridge; **D:** George Stevens. Academy Awards '56: Best Director (Stevens); Directors Guild of America Awards '56: Best Director (Stevens); Nominations: Academy Awards '56: Best Actor (Dean), Best Actor (Hudson), Best Adapted Screenplay, Best Art Direction/Set Decoration (Color), Best Costume Design (Color), Best Film Editing, Best Picture, Best Supporting Actress (McCambridge), Best Original Score. **VHS, Beta, LV** ★★★1/2

Gigi Based on Colette's story of a young Parisian girl (Caron) trained to become a courtesan to the wealthy Gaston (Jourdan). But he finds out he prefers her to be his wife rather than his mistress. Chevalier is Gaston's roguish father who casts an always admiring eye on the ladies; Gingold is Gigi's grandmother and former Chevalier flame, and Gabor amuses as Gaston's current, and vapid, mistress. One of the first MGM movies to be shot on location, this extravaganza features some of the best tributes to the French lifestyle ever filmed. Score includes memorable classics. ♪ Gigi; Ah Yes, I Remember It Well; Thank Heaven For Little Girls; The Night They Invented Champagne; She's Not Thinking of Me; It's a Bore; Gossip; I'm Glad I'm Not Young Anymore; The Parisians.
1958 119m/C Leslie Caron, Louis Jourdan, Maurice Chevalier, Hermione Gingold, Eva Gabor, Isabel Jeans, Jacques Bergerac; **D:** Vincente Minnelli; **W:** Alan Jay Lerner; **M:** Frederick Loewe. Academy Awards '58: Best Adapted Screenplay, Best Art Direction/Set Decoration, Best Color Cinematography, Best Costume Design, Best Director (Minnelli), Best Film Editing, Best Picture, Best Song ("Gigi"), Best Score; Directors Guild of America Awards '58: Best Director (Minnelli); Golden Globe Awards '59: Best Director (Minnelli), Best Film—Musical/Comedy, Best Supporting Actress (Gingold). **VHS, Beta, LV, 8mm** ★★★★

Gilda An evil South American gambling casino owner hires young American Ford as his trusted aide, unaware that Ford and his sultry wife Hayworth have engaged in a steamy affair. Hayworth does a striptease to "Put the Blame on Mame" in this prominently sexual film. This is the film that made Hayworth into a Hollywood sex goddess.
1946 110m/B Rita Hayworth, Glenn Ford, George Macready, Joseph Calleia; **D:** Charles Vidor. **VHS, Beta, LV** ★★★1/2

Gin Game Taped London performance of the Broadway play about an aging couple who find romance in an old age home. Two-character per-

formance won awards; touching and insightful.
1984 82m/C Jessica Tandy, Hume Cronyn; **D:** Mike Nichols. VHS, Beta ★★★

Ginger & Fred An acclaimed story of Fellini-esque poignancy about an aging dance team. Years before they had gained success by reverently impersonating the famous dancing duo of Astaire and Rogers. Now, after thirty years, they reunite under the gaudy lights of a high-tech television special. Wonderful performances by the aging Mastroianni and the still sweet Masina. In Italian with English subtitles.
1986 (PG-13) 126m/C *IT* Marcello Mastroianni, Giulietta Masina, Franco Fabrizi, Frederick Von Ledenberg, Martin Blau, Toto Mignone; **D:** Federico Fellini; **W:** Federico Fellini, Tonino Guerra, Tullio Pinelli, Tonino Delli Colli; **M:** Nicola Piovani. VHS, Beta ★★★

The Girl The first of Meszaros' trilogy, dealing with a young girl who leaves an orphanage to be reunited with her mother, a traditional country peasant. In Hungarian with English subtitles. Meszaros' first film. Followed by "Riddance" (1973) and "Adoption" (1975).
1968 86m/B *HU* **D:** Marta Meszaros. VHS, Beta ★★★

Girl Crazy A wealthy young playboy is sent to an all-boy school in Arizona to get his mind off girls. Once there, he still manages to fall for a local girl who can't stand the sight of him. The eighth film pairing for Rooney and Garland. ♪ Sam and Delilah; Embraceable You; I Got Rhythm; Fascinating Rhythm; Treat Me Rough; Bronco Busters; Bidin' My Time; But Not For Me; Do. **AKA:** When the Girls Meet the Boys.
1943 99m/B Mickey Rooney, Judy Garland, Nancy Walker, June Allyson; **D:** Norman Taurog; **M:** George Gershwin, Ira Gershwin. VHS, Beta, LV ★★★

The Girl from Missouri Cute comedy in which Harlow tries to snag a millionaire without sacrificing her virtues. Lots of laughs and hilarious action, especially the scene where Harlow arrives at the yacht in Florida. Kelly is great as Harlow's wise-cracking girlfriend. Witty dialogue by Emerson and Loos, who also wrote "Gentleman Prefer Blondes." **AKA:** One Hundred Percent Pure.
1934 75m/B Jean Harlow, Lionel Barrymore, Franchot Tone, Lewis Stone, Patsy Kelly, Alan Mowbray, Clara Blandick, Russell Hopton; **D:** Jack Conway; **W:** Anita Loos, John Emerson. VHS ★★★

Girl Shy Harold is a shy tailor's apprentice who is trying to get a collection of his romantic fantasies published. Finale features Lloyd chasing wildly after girl of his dreams.
1924 65m/B Harold Lloyd, Jobyna Ralston, Richard Daniels; **D:** Fred Newmeyer; **W:** Sam Taylor. VHS, Beta ★★★

Girlfriends Bittersweet story of a young Jewish photographer learning to make it on her own. Directorial debut of Weill reflects her background in documentaries as the true-to-life episodes unfold.
1978 (PG) 87m/C Melanie Mayron, Anita Skinner, Eli Wallach, Christopher Guest, Amy Wright, Viveca Lindfors, Bob Balaban; **D:** Claudia Weill; **W:** Vicki Polon. Sundance Film Festival '78: Grand Jury Prize. VHS, Beta ★★★

The Glass Key The second version of Dashiell Hammet's novel, a vintage mystery movie concerning a nominally corrupt politician (Donlevy) being framed for murder, and his assistant sleuthing out the real culprit. One of Ladd's first starring vehicles; Lake is the mystery woman who loves him, and Bendix a particularly vicious thug.
1942 85m/B Alan Ladd, Veronica Lake, Brian Donlevy, William Bendix, Bonita Granville, Richard Denning, Joseph Calleia, Moroni Olsen, Dane Clark; **D:** Stuart Heisler. VHS, Beta, LV ★★★

The Glass Menagerie An aging Southern belle deals with her crippled daughter Laura, whose one great love is her collection of glass animals. The third film adaptation of the Tennessee Williams classic, which preserves the performances of the Broadway revival cast, is a solid-but-not-stellar adaptation of the play. All-star acting ensemble.
1987 (PG) 134m/C Joanne Woodward, Karen Allen, John Malkovich, James Naughton; **D:** Paul Newman; **W:** Tennessee Williams; **M:** Henry Mancini, Max Steiner, Michael Ballhaus. VHS, Beta, LV ★★★

Glengarry Glen Ross A seven-character study chronicling 48 hours in the lives of some sleazy real estate men in danger of getting the ax from their hard-driving bosses. A standout cast includes Pacino as the glad-handing sales leader, Lemmon as the hustler fallen on dim prospects, and Baldwin, briefly venomous, as the company hatchet-man. Brutal and hard-edged with very strong language. Mamet scripted from his Tony Award-winning Broadway play.
1992 (R) 100m/C Al Pacino, Jack

Lemmon, Ed Harris, Alec Baldwin, Alan Arkin, Kevin Spacey, Jonathan Pryce, Bruce Altman, Jude Ciccolella; **D:** James Foley, Juan Ruiz-Anchia; **W:** David Mamet; **M:** James Newton Howard. National Board of Review Awards '92: Best Actor (Lemmon); Venice Film Festival '93: Best Actor (Lemmon); Nominations: Academy Awards '92: Best Supporting Actor (Pacino). **VHS, LV ★★★**

The Glenn Miller Story The music of the Big Band Era lives again in this warm biography of the legendary Glenn Miller, following his life from the late '20s to his untimely death in a WWII plane crash. Stewart's likably convincing and even fakes the trombone playing well. ♪ Moonlight Serenade; In the Mood; Tuxedo Junction; Little Brown Jug; Adios; String of Pearls; Pennsylvania 6-5000; Stairway to the Stars; American Patrol. **1954 (G) 113m/C** James Stewart, June Allyson, Harry (Henry) Morgan, Gene Krupa, Louis Armstrong, Ben Pollack; **D:** Anthony Mann; **W:** Oscar Brodney; **M:** Henry Mancini. Academy Awards '54: Best Sound; Nominations: Academy Awards '54: Best Story & Screenplay, Best Original Score. **VHS, Beta, LV ★★★**

Glory A rich, historical spectacle chronicling the 54th Massachusetts, the first black volunteer infantry unit in the Civil War. The film manages to artfully focus on both the 54th and their white commander, Robert Gould Shaw. Based on Shaw's letters, the film uses thousands of accurately costumed "living historians" (re-enactors) as extras in this panoramic production. A haunting, bittersweet musical score pervades what finally becomes an anti-war statement. Stunning performances throughout, with exceptional work from Freeman and Washington. **1989 (R) 122m/C** Matthew Broderick, Morgan Freeman, Denzel Washington, Cary Elwes, Jihmi Kennedy, Andre Braugher, John Finn, Donovan Leitch, John Cullum, Bob Gunton, Jane Alexander, Raymond St. Jacques; **D:** Edward Zwick; **W:** Kevin Jarre; **M:** James Horner, Freddie Francis. Academy Awards '89: Best Cinematography, Best Sound, Best Supporting Actor (Washington); Nominations: Academy Awards '89: Best Film Editing. **VHS, Beta, LV, 8mm ★★★1/2**

The Go-Between Wonderful tale of hidden love. Young boy Guard acts as a messenger between the aristocratic Christie and her former lover Bates. But tragedy befalls them all when the lovers are discovered. The story is told as the elderly messenger (now played by Redgrave) recalls his younger days as the go-between and builds to a climax when he is once again asked to be a messenger for the lady he loved long ago. Based on a story by L.P. Hartley. **1971 (PG) 116m/C** GB Julie Christie, Alan Bates, Dominic Guard, Margaret Leighton, Michael Redgrave, Michael Gough, Edward Fox; **D:** Joseph Losey; **W:** Harold Pinter. British Academy Awards '71: Best Screenplay, Best Supporting Actor (Fox), Best Supporting Actress (Leighton); Nominations: Academy Awards '71: Best Supporting Actress (Leighton). **VHS ★★★1/2**

Go Tell the Spartans In Vietnam, 1964, a hard-boiled major is ordered to establish a garrison at Muc Wa with a platoon of burned out Americans and Vietnamese mercenaries. Blundering but politically interesting war epic pre-dating the flood of 1980s American-Vietnam apologetics. Based on Daniel Ford's novel. **1978 (R) 114m/C** Burt Lancaster, Craig Wasson, David Clennon, Marc Singer; **D:** Ted Post; **W:** Wendell Mayes. **VHS, Beta, LV ★★★**

The Goalie's Anxiety at the Penalty Kick A chilling landmark film that established Wenders as one of the chief film voices to emerge from post-war Germany. The story deals with a soccer player who wanders around Vienna after being suspended, commits a random murder, and slowly passes over the brink of sanity and morality. A suspenseful, existential adaptation of the Peter Handke novel. In German with English subtitles. **1971 101m/C** GE Arthur Brauss, Erika Pluhar, Kai Fischer; **D:** Wim Wenders. **VHS, Beta ★★★1/2**

The Goddess Sordid story of a girl who rises to fame as a celluloid star by making her body available to anyone who can help her career. When the spotlight dims, she keeps going with drugs and alcohol to a bitter end. **1958 105m/B** Kim Stanley, Lloyd Bridges, Patty Duke; **D:** John Cromwell; **W:** Paddy Chayefsky. Nominations: Academy Awards '58: Best Story & Screenplay. **VHS, Beta, LV ★★★**

The Godfather Coppola's award-winning adaptation of Mario Puzo's novel about a fictional Mafia family in the late 1940s. Revenge, envy, and parent-child conflict mix with the rituals of Italian mob life in America. Minutely detailed, with excellent performances by Pacino, Brando, and Caan as the violence-prone Sonny.

Film debut of Coppola's daughter Sophia, the infant in the baptism scene, who returns in "Godfather III." The horrific horse scene is an instant chiller. Indisputably an instant piece of American culture. Followed by two sequels.

1972 (R) 171m/C Marlon Brando, Al Pacino, Robert Duvall, James Caan, Diane Keaton, John Cazale, Talia Shire, Richard Conte, Richard Castellano, Abe Vigoda, Alex Rocco, Sterling Hayden, John Marley, Al Lettieri, Sofia Coppola, Al Martino, Morgana King; *D:* Francis Ford Coppola; *W:* Mario Puzo, Francis Ford Coppola, Gordon Willis; *M:* Nino Rota. Academy Awards '72: Best Actor (Brando), Best Adapted Screenplay, Best Picture; Directors Guild of America Awards '72: Best Director (Coppola); Golden Globe Awards '73: Best Actor—Drama (Brando), Best Director (Coppola), Best Film—Drama, Best Screenplay, Best Score; National Board of Review Awards '72: 10 Best Films of the Year, Best Supporting Actor (Pacino); National Society of Film Critics Awards '72: Best Actor (Pacino); Writers Guild of America '72: Best Adapted Screenplay; Nominations: Academy Awards '72: Best Costume Design, Best Director (Coppola), Best Film Editing, Best Sound, Best Supporting Actor (Caan, Duvall, Pacino). **VHS, Beta, LV, 8mm** ★★★★

The Godfather 1902-1959: The Complete Epic Coppola's epic work concerning the lives of a New York crime family. Comprises the first two "Godfather" films, reedited into a chronological framework of the Corleone family history, with much previously discarded footage restored.

1981 386m/C Marlon Brando, Al Pacino, Robert Duvall, James Caan, Richard Castellano, Diane Keaton, Robert De Niro, John Cazale, Lee Strasberg, Talia Shire, Michael V. Gazzo, Troy Donahue, Joe Spinell, Abe Vigoda, Alex Rocco, Sterling Hayden, John Marley, Richard Conte, G.D. Spradlin, Bruno Kirby, Harry Dean Stanton, Roger Corman, Al Lettieri; *D:* Francis Ford Coppola; *W:* Mario Puzo, Francis Ford Coppola; *M:* Nino Rota. **VHS, Beta** ★★★★

The Godfather, Part 2 A continuation and retracing of the first film, interpolating the maintenance of the Corleone family by the aging Michael, and its founding by the young Vito (De Niro, in a terrific performance) 60 years before in New York City's Little Italy. Often considered the second half of one film, the two films stand as one of American film's greatest efforts, and as a 1970s high-water mark. Combined into one work for television presentation. Followed by a sequel.

1974 (R) 200m/C Al Pacino, Robert De Niro, Diane Keaton, Robert Duvall, James Caan, Danny Aiello, John Cazale, Lee Strasberg, Talia Shire, Michael V. Gazzo, Troy Donahue, Joe Spinell, Abe Vigoda, Marianna Hill, Fay Spain, G.D. Spradlin, Bruno Kirby, Harry Dean Stanton, Roger Corman, Kathleen Beller, John Aprea, Morgana King; *D:* Francis Ford Coppola; *W:* Mario Puzo, Francis Ford Coppola; *M:* Nino Rota, Carmine Coppola, Gordon Willis. Academy Awards '74: Best Adapted Screenplay, Best Art Direction/Set Decoration, Best Director (Coppola), Best Picture, Best Supporting Actor (De Niro), Best Original Score; Directors Guild of America Awards '74: Best Director (Coppola); National Society of Film Critics Awards '74: Best Director (Coppola); Writers Guild of America '74: Best Adapted Screenplay; Nominations: Academy Awards '74: Best Actor (Pacino), Best Costume Design, Best Supporting Actor (Gazzo, Strasberg), Best Supporting Actress (Shire). **VHS, Beta, LV, 8mm** ★★★★

The Godfather, Part 3 Don Corleone (Pacino), now aging and guilt-ridden, determines to buy his salvation by investing in the Catholic Church, which he finds to be a more corrupt brotherhood than his own. Meanwhile, back on the homefront, his young daughter discovers her sexuality as she falls in love with her first cousin. Weakest entry of the trilogy is still a stunning and inevitable conclusion to the story; Pacino adds exquisite finishing touches to his time-worn character. Beautifully photographed in Italy by Gordon Willis. Video release contains the final director's cut featuring nine minutes of footage not included in the theatrical release.

1990 (R) 170m/C Al Pacino, Diane Keaton, Andy Garcia, Joe Mantegna, George Hamilton, Talia Shire, Sofia Coppola, Eli Wallach, Don Novello, Bridget Fonda, John Savage, Al Martino, Raf Vallone, Franc D'Ambrosio, Donal Donnelly, Richard Bright, Helmut Berger; *D:* Francis Ford Coppola; *W:* Mario Puzo, Francis Ford Coppola, Gordon Willis; *M:* Nino Rota, Carmine Coppola. Golden Raspberry Awards '90: Worst Supporting Actress (Coppola), Worst New Star (Coppola); Nominations: Academy Awards '90: Best Art Direction/Set Decoration, Best Cinematography, Best Director (Coppola), Best Film Editing, Best Picture, Best Song ("Promise Me You'll Remember"), Best Supporting Actor (Garcia). **VHS, Beta, LV, 8mm** ★★★

God's Little Acre Delves into the unexpectedly passionate lives of Georgia farmers. One man, convinced

there's buried treasure on his land, nearly brings himself and his family to ruin trying to find it. Based on the novel by Erskine Caldwell.
1958 110m/B Robert Ryan, Tina Louise, Michael Landon, Buddy Hackett, Vic Morrow, Jack Lord, Aldo Ray, Fay Spain; **D:** Anthony Mann; **W:** Philip Yordan; **M:** Elmer Bernstein. **VHS, Beta ★★★**

The Gods Must Be Crazy An innocent and charming film. A peaceful Bushman travels into the civilized world to return a Coke bottle "to the gods." Along the way he meets a transplanted schoolteacher, an oafishly clumsy microbiologist and a gang of fanatical terrorists. A very popular film, disarmingly crammed with slapstick and broad humor of every sort. Followed by a weak sequel.
1984 (PG) 109m/C N!xau, Marius Weyers, Sandra Prinsloo, Louw Verwey, Jamie Uys, Michael Thys, Nic de Jager; **D:** Jamie Uys; **M:** Johnny Bishop, John Boshoff. **VHS, Beta, LV ★★★1/2**

Going Hollywood Amusing musical/romantic fluff about a French teacher (Davies) who falls in love with a radio crooner (Crosby in his first MGM film). He's got the movie bug and heads for Hollywood, where he becomes an overnight sensation with a sultry costar (d'Orsay). Davies follows and proceeds to get Crosby out of d'Orsay's clutches and winds up replacing her rival in the film, promptly becoming a star herself. The underrated Davies was a fine light comedienne and supplied glamour to the production as well. Kelly, in her film debut, supplied the slapstick. The last Hearst-Cosmopolitan production made with MGM. ♪ Temptation; We'll Make Hay While the Sun Shines; Going Hollywood; Our Big Love Scene; After Sundown; Cinderella's Fella; Beautiful Girl; Just an Echo in the Valley.
1933 78m/B Marion Davies, Bing Crosby, Fifi d'Orsay, Stuart Erwin, Patsy Kelly, Ned Sparks; **D:** Raoul Walsh; **W:** Donald Ogden Stewart. **VHS ★★★**

Going in Style Three elderly gentlemen, tired of doing nothing, decide to liven up their lives by pulling a daylight bank stick-up. They don't care about the consequences because anything is better than sitting on a park bench all day long. The real fun begins when they get away with the robbery. Great cast makes this a winner.
1979 (PG) 91m/C George Burns, Art Carney, Lee Strasberg; **D:** Martin Brest; **W:** Martin Brest. **VHS, Beta ★★★1/2**

Going My Way A musical-comedy about a progressive young priest assigned to a downtrodden parish who works to get the parish out of debt, but clashes with his elderly curate, who's set in his ways. Followed by "The Bells of St. Mary's." Fitzgerald's Oscar-winning Supporting Actor performance was also nominated in the Best Actor category. ♪ The Day After Forever; Swinging on a Star; Too-ra-loo-ra-loo-ra; Going My Way; Silent Night; Habanera; Ave Maria.
1944 126m/B Bing Crosby, Barry Fitzgerald, Rise Stevens, Frank McHugh, Gene Lockhart, Porter Hall; **D:** Leo McCarey; **W:** Frank Butler, Frank Cavett, Leo McCarey. Academy Awards '44: Best Actor (Crosby), Best Director (McCarey), Best Picture, Best Song ("Swinging on a Star"), Best Story & Screenplay, Best Supporting Actor (Fitzgerald); National Board of Review Awards '44: 10 Best Films of the Year; New York Film Critics Awards '44: Best Actor (Fitzgerald), Best Director (McCarey), Best Film; Nominations: Academy Awards '44: Best Actor (Fitzgerald), Best Black and White Cinematography, Best Film Editing. **VHS, Beta, LV ★★★1/2**

Gold Diggers of 1933 In this famous period musical, showgirls help a songwriter save his Busby Berkeley-choreographed show. Followed by two sequels. ♪ We're in the Money; Shadow Waltz; I've Got to Sing a Torch Song; Pettin' in the Park; Remember My Forgotten Man.
1933 96m/B Joan Blondell, Ruby Keeler, Aline MacMahon, Dick Powell, Guy Kibbee, Warren William, Ned Sparks, Ginger Rogers; **D:** Mervyn LeRoy. Nominations: Academy Awards '33: Best Sound. **VHS, Beta, LV ★★★1/2**

Gold Diggers of 1935 The second Gold Diggers film, having something to do with a New England resort, romance, and a charity show put on at the hotel. Plenty of Berkeleian large-scale drama, especially the bizarre, mock-tragic "Lullaby of Broadway" number, which details the last days of a Broadway baby. ♪ I'm Going Shopping With You; The Words Are in My Heart; Lullaby of Broadway.
1935 95m/B Dick Powell, Adolphe Menjou, Gloria Stuart, Alice Brady, Frank McHugh, Glenda Farrell, Grant Mitchell, Hugh Herbert, Wini Shaw; **D:** Busby Berkeley. **VHS, Beta, LV ★★★**

The Gold Rush Chaplin's most critically acclaimed film. The best definition of his simple approach to film form; adept maneuvering of visual pathos. The "Little Tramp" searches

C

for gold and romance in the Klondike in the mid-1800s. Includes the dance of the rolls, pantomime sequence of eating the shoe, and Chaplin's lovely music.
1925 85m/B Charlie Chaplin, Mack Swain, Tom Murray, Georgia Hale; **D:** Charlie Chaplin. **VHS, Beta, LV, 8mm** ★★★★

Golden Boy Holden plays a young and gifted violinist who earns money for his musical education by working as a part-time prizefighter. Fight promoter Menjou has Stanwyck cozy up to the impressionable young man to convince him to make the fight game his prime concern. She's successful but it leads to tragedy. Holden's screen debut, with Cobb as his immigrant father and Stanwyck successfully slinky as the corrupting love interest. Classic pugilistic drama with well-staged fight scenes. Based on Clifford Odets' play with toned down finale.
1939 99m/B William Holden, Adolphe Menjou, Barbara Stanwyck, Lee J. Cobb, Joseph Calleia, Sam Levene, Don Beddoe, Charles Halton; **D:** Rouben Mamoulian; **W:** Daniel Taradash, Victor Heerman, Sarah Y. Mason. Nominations: Academy Awards '39: Best Original Score. **VHS, Beta, LV** ★★★

The Golden Coach Based on a play by Prosper Merimee, the tale of an 18th-century actress in Spanish South America who takes on all comers, including the local viceroy who creates a scandal by presenting her with his official coach. Rare cinematography by Claude Renoir. *AKA:* Le Carrosse D'Or.
1952 101m/C *FR* Anna Magnani, Odoardo Spadaro, Nada Fiorelli, Dante Rino, Duncan Lamont; **D:** Jean Renoir. **VHS, Beta, LV** ★★★

Goldeneye Bond is back, in the long-awaited (eight years) debut of Brosnan as legendary Brit agent 007. Since we're through the Cold War, Bond has to make do with the villainy of the Russian Mafia, who are planning to sabotage global financial markets utilizing the "Goldeneye" satellite weapon. There's a spectacularly impossible stunt to start things out in familiar territory and lots more noisy (if prolonged) action pieces. Brosnan (who looks great in a tux) is slyly self-aware that his character is more myth than man and Janssen does a suitably over-the-top job as bad Bond girl Xenia Onatopp. Tina Turner sings the dreary title track.
1995 (PG-13) 130m/C Pierce Brosnan, Famke Janssen, Sean Bean, Izabela Scorupco, Joe Don Baker, Robbie Coltrane, Judi Dench, Tcheky Karyo, Gottfried John, Alan Cumming, Desmond Llewelyn, Michael Kitchen, Serena Gordon, Samantha Bond; *Cameos:* Minnie Driver; **D:** Martin Campbell; **W:** Michael France, Jeffrey Caine; **M:** Eric Serra, Phil Meheux. Blockbuster Entertainment Awards '96: Action Actor, Theatrical (Brosnan). **VHS** ★★★

Goldfinger Ian Fleming's James Bond, Agent 007, attempts to prevent international gold smuggler Goldfinger and his pilot Pussy Galore from robbing Fort Knox. Features villainous assistant Oddjob and his deadly bowler hat. The third in the series is perhaps the most popular. Shirley Bassey sings the theme song. The laserdisc edition includes audio interviews with the director, the writer, the editor, and the production designer; music and sound effects/ dialogue separation; publicity stills, movie posters, trailers, and on-location photos. A treat for Bond fans.
1964 (PG) 117m/C *GB* Sean Connery, Honor Blackman, Gert Frobe, Shirley Eaton, Tania Mallet, Harold Sakata, Cec Linder, Bernard Lee, Lois Maxwell, Desmond Llewelyn, Nadja Regin; **D:** Guy Hamilton; **M:** John Barry. Academy Awards '64: Best Sound Effects Editing. **VHS, Beta, LV** ★★★

The Golem A huge clay figure is given life by a rabbi in hopes of saving the Jews in the ghetto of medieval Prague. Rarely seen Wegener expressionist myth-opus that heavily influenced the "Frankenstein" films of the sound era.
1920 80m/B *GE* Paul Wegener, Albert Steinruck, Ernst Deutsch, Syda Salmonava; **D:** Paul Wegener. **VHS, Beta** ★★★1/2

Gone with the Wind Epic Civil War drama focuses on the life of petulant southern belle Scarlett O'Hara. Starting with her idyllic lifestyle on a sprawling plantation, the film traces her survival through the tragic history of the South during the Civil War and Reconstruction, and her tangled love affairs with Ashley Wilkes and Rhett Butler. Classic Hollywood doesn't get any better than this; one great scene after another, equally effective in intimate drama and sweeping spectacle. The train depot scene, one of the more technically adroit shots in movie history, involved hundreds of extras and dummies, and much of the MGM lot was razed to simulate the burning of Atlanta. Based on Margaret Mitchell's novel, screenwriter Howard

was assisted by producer Selznick and novelist F. Scott Fitzgerald. For its 50th anniversary, a 231-minute restored version was released that included the trailer for "The Making of a Legend: GWTW." The laserdisc is available in a limited, numbered edition, fully restored to Technicolor from the original negative, with an enhanced soundtrack and seven minutes of rare footage, including the original trailer.
1939 231m/C Clark Gable, Vivien Leigh, Olivia de Havilland, Leslie Howard, Thomas Mitchell, Hattie McDaniel, Butterfly McQueen, Evelyn Keyes, Harry Davenport, Jane Darwell, Ona Munson, Barbara O'Neil, William "Billy" Bakewell, Rand Brooks, Ward Bond, Laura Hope Crews, Yakima Canutt, George Reeves, Marjorie Reynolds, Ann Rutherford, Victor Jory, Carroll Nye, Paul Hurst, Isabel Jewell, Cliff Edwards, Eddie Anderson, Oscar Polk, Eric Linden, Violet Kemble-Cooper; *D:* Victor Fleming; *W:* Sidney Howard; *M:* Max Steiner. Academy Awards '39: Best Actress (Leigh), Best Color Cinematography, Best Director (Fleming), Best Film Editing, Best Interior Decoration, Best Picture, Best Screenplay, Best Supporting Actress (McDaniel); New York Film Critics Awards '39: Best Actress (Leigh); Nominations: Academy Awards '39: Best Actor (Gable), Best Sound, Best Special Effects, Best Supporting Actress (de Havilland), Best Original Score. **VHS, Beta, LV ★★★★**

The Good Earth Pearl S. Buck's classic re-creation of the story of a simple Chinese farm couple beset by greed and poverty. Outstanding special effects. MGM's last film produced by master Irving Thalberg and dedicated to his memory. Rainer won the second of her back-to-back Best Actress Oscars for her portrayal of the self-sacrificing O-Lan.
1937 138m/B Paul Muni, Luise Rainer, Charley Grapewin, Keye Luke, Walter Connolly; *D:* Sidney Franklin. Academy Awards '37: Best Actress (Rainer), Best Cinematography; Nominations: Academy Awards '37: Best Director (Franklin), Best Film Editing, Best Picture. **VHS, Beta ★★★1/2**

Good Morning, Vietnam Based on the story of Saigon DJ Adrian Cronauer, although Williams' portrayal is reportedly a bit more extroverted than the personality of Cronauer. Williams spins great comic moments that may have been scripted but likely were not as a man with no history and for whom everything is manic radio material. The character ad libs, swoops, and swerves, finally accepting adult responsibility. Engaging all the way

with an outstanding period soundtrack.
1987 (R) 121m/C Robin Williams, Forest Whitaker, Bruno Kirby, Richard Edson, Robert Wuhl, J.T. Walsh, Noble Willingham, Floyd Vivino, Tung Thanh Tran, Chintara Sukapatana; *D:* Barry Levinson; *W:* Mitch Markowitz; *M:* Alex North, Peter Sova. Golden Globe Awards '88: Best Actor—Musical/Comedy (Williams); Nominations: Academy Awards '87: Best Actor (Williams). **VHS, Beta, LV, 8mm ★★★**

The Good, the Bad and the Ugly Leone's grandiloquent, shambling tribute to the American Western. Set during the Civil War, it follows the seemingly endless adventures of three dirtbags in search of a cache of Confederate gold buried in a nameless grave. Violent, exaggerated, beautifully crafted, it is the final and finest installment of the "Dollars" trilogy: a spaghetti Western chef d'oeuvre.
1967 161m/C *IT* Clint Eastwood, Eli Wallach, Lee Van Cleef, Chelo Alonso, Luigi Pistilli, Tonino Delli Colli; *D:* Sergio Leone; *W:* Sergio Leone; *M:* Ennio Morricone. **VHS, Beta, LV ★★★1/2**

Goodbye Columbus Philip Roth's novel about a young Jewish librarian who has an affair with the spoiled daughter of a nouveau riche family is brought to late-'60s life, and vindicated by superb performances all around. Benjamin and McGraw's first starring roles.
1969 (PG) 105m/C Richard Benjamin, Ali MacGraw, Jack Klugman, Nan Martin, Jaclyn Smith; *D:* Larry Peerce; *M:* Charles Fox. Writers Guild of America '69: Best Adapted Screenplay; Nominations: Academy Awards '69: Best Adapted Screenplay. **VHS, Beta, LV ★★★**

The Goodbye Girl Neil Simon's story of a former actress, her precocious nine-year-old daughter, and the aspiring actor who moves in with them. The daughter serves as catalyst for the other two to fall in love. While Mason's character is fairly unsympathetic, Dreyfuss is great and Simon's dialogue witty.
1977 (PG) 110m/C Richard Dreyfuss, Marsha Mason, Quinn Cummings, Barbara Rhoades, Marilyn Sokol; *D:* Herbert Ross; *W:* Neil Simon; *M:* Dave Grusin. Academy Awards '77: Best Actor (Dreyfuss); British Academy Awards '78: Best Actor (Dreyfuss); Golden Globe Awards '78: Best Actor—Musical/Comedy (Dreyfuss), Best Actress—Musical/Comedy (Mason), Best Film—Musical/Comedy, Best Screenplay; Los Angeles Film Critics Association Awards '77: Best Actor (Dreyfuss);

Nominations: Academy Awards '77: Best Picture, Best Actress (Mason), Best Original Screenplay, Best Supporting Actress (Cummings). **VHS, Beta, LV** ★★★

Goodbye, Mr. Chips An MGM classic, the sentimental rendering of the James Hilton novel about a shy Latin professor in an English school who marries the vivacious Garson only to tragically lose her. He spends the rest of his life devoting himself to his students and becoming a school legend. Multi-award-winning soaper featuring Garson's first screen appearance, which was Oscar nominated. Special two-disc letterboxed laserdisc edition includes the original trailer and an extra-special production featurette. Remade in 1969 as a fairly awful musical starring Peter O'Toole.
1939 115m/B Robert Donat, Greer Garson, Paul Henreid, John Mills; **D:** Sam Wood, Frederick A. (Freddie) Young. Academy Awards '39: Best Actor (Donat); National Board of Review Awards '39: 10 Best Films of the Year; Nominations: Academy Awards '39: Best Actress (Garson), Best Director (Wood), Best Film Editing, Best Picture, Best Screenplay, Best Sound. **VHS, Beta, LV** ★★★1/2

Goodfellas Quintessential picture about "wiseguys," at turns both violent and funny. A young man grows up in the mob, works hard to advance himself through the ranks, and enjoys the life of the rich and violent, oblivious to the horror of which he is a part. Cocaine addiction and many wiseguy missteps ultimately unravel his climb to the top. Excellent performances (particularly Liotta and Pesci, with De Niro pitching in around the corners), with visionary cinematography and careful pacing. Watch for Scorsese's mom as Pesci's mom. Based on the life of Henry Hill, ex-mobster now in the Witness Protection Program. Adapted from the book by Nicholas Pileggi.
1990 (R) 146m/C Robert De Niro, Ray Liotta, Joe Pesci, Paul Sorvino, Lorraine Bracco, Frank Sivero, Mike Starr, Frank Vincent, Samuel L. Jackson, Henny Youngman, Tony Darrow, Chuck Low, Frank DiLeo, Christopher Serrone, Jerry Vale, Michael Ballhaus; **D:** Martin Scorsese; **W:** Nicholas Pileggi, Martin Scorsese. Academy Awards '90: Best Supporting Actor (Pesci); British Academy Awards '90: Best Adapted Screenplay, Best Director (Scorsese), Best Film; Los Angeles Film Critics Association Awards '90: Best Cinematography, Best Director (Scorsese), Best Film, Best Supporting Actor (Pesci), Best Supporting Actress (Bracco); New York Film Critics Awards

'90: Best Actor (De Niro), Best Director (Scorsese), Best Film; National Society of Film Critics Awards '90: Best Director (Scorsese), Best Film; Nominations: Academy Awards '90: Best Adapted Screenplay, Best Director (Scorsese), Best Film Editing, Best Picture, Best Supporting Actress (Bracco). **VHS, Beta, LV, 8mm** ★★★★

Gorillas in the Mist The life of Dian Fossey, animal rights activist and world-renowned expert on the African gorilla, from her pioneering contact with mountain gorillas to her murder at the hands of poachers. Weaver is totally appropriate as the increasingly obsessed Fossey, but the character moves away from us, just as we need to see and understand more about her. Excellent special effects.
1988 (PG-13) 117m/C Sigourney Weaver, Bryan Brown, Julie Harris, Iain Cuthbertson, John Omirah Miluwi, Constantin Alexandrov, Waigwa Wachira, John Seale; **D:** Michael Apted; **W:** Anna Hamilton Phelan; **M:** Maurice Jarre. Golden Globe Awards '88: Best Actress—Drama (Weaver); Golden Globe Awards '89: Best Score; Nominations: Academy Awards '88: Best Actress (Weaver), Best Adapted Screenplay, Best Film Editing, Best Sound, Best Original Score. **VHS, Beta, LV** ★★★

The Gospel According to St. Matthew Perhaps Pasolini's greatest film, retelling the story of Christ in gritty, neo-realistic tones and portraying the man less as a divine presence than as a political revolutionary. The yardstick by which all Jesus-films are to be measured. In Italian with English subtitles or dubbed. **AKA:** Il Vangelo Secondo Matteo; L'Evangile Selon Saint-Matthieu.
1964 142m/B *IT* Enrique Irazoqui, Susanna Pasolini, Margherita Caruso, Marcello Morante, Mario Socrate; **D:** Pier Paolo Pasolini; **W:** Pier Paolo Pasolini; **M:** Luis Bacalov, Tonino Delli Colli. National Board of Review Awards '66: 5 Best Foreign Films of the Year; Nominations: Academy Awards '66: Best Art Direction/Set Decoration (B & W), Best Costume Design (B & W), Best Original Score. **VHS, Beta, LV, 8mm** ★★★★

The Graduate Famous, influential slice of comic Americana stars Hoffman as Benjamin Braddock, a shy, aimless college graduate who, without any idea of responsibility or ambition, wanders from a sexual liaison with a married woman (the infamous Mrs. Robinson) to pursuit of her engaged daughter. His pursuit of Elaine right to her wedding has become a film classic. Extremely popular and almost solely responsible for establishing both Hoffman and director Nichols. The career advice given to Benjamin, "plastics," became a catchword for the era. Watch for Dreyfuss in the Berkeley rooming house, Farrell in the hotel lobby, and screenwriter Henry as the desk clerk. Based on the novel by Charles Webb. Laserdisc edition includes screen tests, promotional stills, and a look at the creative process involved in making a novel into a movie. A 25th Anniversary Limited Edition is also available, presented in a wide-screen format and including the original movie trailer and interviews with the cast and crew.

1967 (PG) 106m/C Dustin Hoffman, Anne Bancroft, Katharine Ross, Murray Hamilton, Brian Avery, Marion Lorne, Alice Ghostley, William Daniels, Elizabeth Wilson, Norman Fell, Buck Henry, Richard Dreyfuss, Mike Farrell; **D:** Mike Nichols; **W:** Buck Henry, Calder Willingham; **M:** Paul Simon, Art Garfunkel, Dave Grusin. Academy Awards '67: Best Director (Nichols); British Academy Awards '68: Best Director (Nichols), Best Film, Best Screenplay; Directors Guild of America Awards '67: Best Director (Nichols); Golden Globe Awards '68: Best Actress—Musical/Comedy (Bancroft), Best Director (Nichols), Best Film—Musical/Comedy; National Board of Review Awards '67: 10 Best Films of the Year; New York Film Critics Awards '67: Best Director (Nichols); Nominations: Academy Awards '66: Best Adapted Screenplay, Best Cinematography, Best Supporting Actress (Ross). **VHS, Beta, LV, 8mm ★★★★**

Grand Hotel A star-filled cast is brought together by unusual circumstances at Berlin's Grand Hotel and their lives become hopelessly intertwined over a 24-hour period. Adapted (and given the red-carpet treatment) from a Vicki Baum novel; notable mostly for Garbo's world-weary ballerina. Time has taken its toll on the concept and treatment, but still an interesting star vehicle.

1932 112m/B Greta Garbo, John Barrymore, Joan Crawford, Lewis Stone, Wallace Beery, Jean Hersholt, Lionel Barrymore; **D:** Edmund Goulding. Academy Awards '32: Best Picture. **VHS, Beta, LV ★★★1/2**

Grand Illusion Unshakably classic anti-war film by Renoir, in which French prisoners of war attempt to escape from their German captors during WWI. An indictment of the way Old World, aristocratic nobility was brought to modern bloodshed in the Great War. Renoir's optimism remains relentless, but was easier to believe in before WWII. In French, with English subtitles. The laserdisc version includes an audio essay by Peter Crowe.

1937 111m/B *FR* Jean Gabin, Erich von Stroheim, Pierre Fresnay, Marcel Dalio, Julien Carette, Gaston Modot, Jean Daste, Dita Parlo; **D:** Jean Renoir. National Board of Review Awards '38: 5 Best Foreign Films of the Year; New York Film Critics Awards '38: Best Foreign Film; Nominations: Academy Awards '38: Best Picture. **VHS, Beta, LV, 8mm ★★★★**

The Grapes of Wrath John Steinbeck's classic American novel about the Great Depression. We follow the impoverished Joad family as they migrate from the dust bowl of Oklahoma to find work in the orchards of California and as they struggle to maintain at least a little of their dignity and pride. A sentimental but dignified, uncharacteristic Hollywood epic.

1940 129m/B Henry Fonda, Jane Darwell, John Carradine, Charley Grapewin, Zeffie Tilbury, Dorris Bowdon, Russell Simpson, John Qualen, Eddie Quillan, O.Z. Whitehead, Grant Mitchell; **D:** John Ford; **W:** Nunnally Johnson. Academy Awards '40: Best Director (Ford), Best Supporting Actress (Darwell); New York Film Critics Awards '40: Best Director (Ford), Best Film; Nominations: Academy Awards '40: Best Actor (Fonda), Best Adapted Screenplay, Best Picture, Best Sound, Best Original Score. **VHS, Beta, LV ★★★1/2**

Grease Film version of the hit Broadway musical about summer love. Set in the 1950s, this spirited musical follows a group of high-schoolers throughout their senior year. The story offers a responsible moral: act like a tart and you'll get your guy; but, hey, it's all in fun anyway. Followed by a weak sequel. ♪ Grease; Summer Nights; Hopelessly Devoted To You; You're the One That I Want; Sandy; Beauty School Dropout; Look at Me, I'm Sandra Dee; Greased Lightnin'; It's Raining on Prom Night.

1978 (PG) 110m/C John Travolta, Olivia Newton-John, Jeff Conaway, Stockard Channing, Eve Arden, Frankie Avalon, Sid Caesar; **D:** Randal Kleiser. People's Choice Awards '79: Best Film; Nominations: Academy Awards '78: Best Song ("Hopelessly Devoted to You"). **VHS, Beta, LV ★★★**

The Great Dictator Chaplin's first all-dialogue film, a searing satire on Nazism in which he has dual roles as a Jewish barber with amnesia who is mistaken for a Hitlerian dictator, Ade-

noid Hynkel. A classic scene involves Hynkel playing with a gigantic balloon of the world. Hitler banned the film's release to the German public due to its highly offensive portrait of him. The film also marked Chaplin's last wearing of the Little Tramp's (and Hitler's equally little) mustache.
1940 126m/B Charlie Chaplin, Paulette Goddard, Jack Oakie, Billy Gilbert, Reginald Gardiner, Henry Daniell, Maurice Moscovich; *D:* Charlie Chaplin; *W:* Charlie Chaplin. National Board of Review Awards '40: 10 Best Films of the Year; New York Film Critics Awards '40: Best Actor (Chaplin); Nominations: Academy Awards '40: Best Actor (Chaplin), Best Original Screenplay, Best Picture, Best Supporting Actor (Oakie), Best Original Score. **VHS, Beta, LV ★★★★**

The Great Escape During WWII, troublesome allied POW's are thrown by the Nazis into an escape-proof camp, where they join forces in a single mass break for freedom. One of the great war movies, with a superb ensemble cast and lots of excitement. The story was true, based on the novel by Paul Brickhill. McQueen performed most of the stunts himself, against the wishes of director Sturges. Laserdisc features an analysis of the true story that inspired the movie, actual photos of the camp, prisoners, and guards, commentary by director Sturges, composer Bernstein, and stuntman Bud Ekins, excerpts from the script by novelist/screenwriter Clavell, over 250 production photos, and the original movie trailer. Followed by a made-for-TV movie 25 years later.
1963 170m/C Steve McQueen, James Garner, Richard Attenborough, Charles Bronson, James Coburn, Donald Pleasence, David McCallum, James Donald, Gordon Jackson; *D:* John Sturges; *W:* James Clavell, W.R. Burnett; *M:* Elmer Bernstein. National Board of Review Awards '63: 10 Best Films of the Year. **VHS, Beta, LV ★★★1/2**

Great Expectations Lean's magisterial adaptation of the Dickens tome, in which a young English orphan is graced by a mysterious benefactor and becomes a well-heeled gentleman. Hailed and revered over the years; possibly the best Dickens on film. Well-acted by all, but especially notable is Hunt's slightly mad and pathetic Miss Havisham. Remake of the 1934 film.
1946 118m/B *GB* John Mills, Valerie Hobson, Anthony Wager, Alec Guinness, Finlay Currie, Jean Simmons, Bernard Miles, Francis L. Sullivan, Martita Hunt, Ivan Barnard, Freda Jackson, Torin Thatcher, Eileen Erskine, Hay Petrie; *D:* David Lean; *W:* David Lean. Academy Awards '47: Best Art Direction/Set Decoration (B & W), Best Black and White Cinematography; National Board of Review Awards '47: 10 Best Films of the Year; Nominations: Academy Awards '47: Best Director (Lean), Best Picture, Best Screenplay. **VHS, Beta, LV ★★★★**

The Great Lie A great soaper with Davis and Astor as rivals for the affections of Brent, an irresponsible flyer. Astor is the concert pianist who marries Brent and then finds out she's pregnant after he's presumed dead in a crash. The wealthy Davis offers to raise the baby so Astor can continue her career. But when Brent does return, who will it be to? Sparkling, catty fun. Astor's very short, mannish haircut became a popular trend.
1941 107m/B Bette Davis, Mary Astor, George Brent, Lucile Watson, Hattie McDaniel, Grant Mitchell, Jerome Cowan; *D:* Edmund Goulding; *M:* Max Steiner. Academy Awards '41: Best Supporting Actress (Astor). **VHS, Beta, LV ★★★**

The Great McGinty Sturges' directorial debut, about the rise and fall of a small-time, bribe-happy politician is an acerbic, ultra-cynical indictment of modern politics that stands, like much of his other work, as bracingly courageous as anything that's ever snuck past the Hollywood censors. Political party boss Tamiroff chews the scenery with gusto while Donlevy, in his first starring role, is more than his equal as the not-so-dumb political hack. *AKA:* Down Went McGinty.
1940 82m/B Brian Donlevy, Muriel Angelus, Akim Tamiroff, Louis Jean Heydt, Arthur Hoyt, William Demarest; *D:* Preston Sturges; *W:* Preston Sturges. Academy Awards '40: Best Original Screenplay. **VHS, Beta, LV ★★★1/2**

The Great Muppet Caper A group of hapless reporters (Kermit, Fozzie Bear, and Gonzo) travel to London to follow up on a major jewel robbery.
1981 (G) 95m/C Jim Henson's Muppets, Charles Grodin, Diana Rigg; *Cameos:* John Cleese, Robert Morley, Peter Ustinov, Peter Falk, Jack Warden; *D:* Jim Henson; *W:* Jack Rose; *V:* Frank Oz. Nominations: Academy Awards '81: Best Song ("The First Time It Happens"). **VHS, Beta, LV ★★★**

The Great Santini Lt. Col. Bull Meechum, the "Great Santini," a Marine pilot stationed stateside, fights a war involving his frustrated career goals, repressed emotions, and family. His family becomes his company

of marines, as he abuses them in the name of discipline, because he doesn't allow himself any other way to show his affection. With a standout performance by Duvall, the film successfully blends warm humor and tenderness with the harsh cruelties inherent with dysfunctional families and racism. Based on Pat Conroy's autobiographical novel, the movie was virtually undistributed when first released, but re-released due to critical acclaim. *AKA:* Ace.
1980 (PG) 118m/C Robert Duvall, Blythe Danner, Michael O'Keefe, Julie Ann Haddock, Lisa Jane Persky, David Keith; *D:* Lewis John Carlino; *W:* Lewis John Carlino; *M:* Elmer Bernstein. Montreal World Film Festival '80: Best Actor (Duvall); National Board of Review Awards '80: 10 Best Films of the Year; Nominations: Academy Awards '80: Best Actor (Duvall), Best Supporting Actor (O'Keefe). **VHS, Beta, 8mm** ★★★

The Great Train Robbery A dapper thief arranges to heist the Folkstone bullion express in 1855, the first moving train robbery. Well-designed, fast-moving costume piece based on Crichton's best-selling novel. *AKA:* The First Great Train Robbery.
1979 (PG) 111m/C *GB* Sean Connery, Donald Sutherland, Lesley-Anne Down, Alan Webb; *D:* Michael Crichton; *W:* Michael Crichton; *M:* Jerry Goldsmith. **VHS, Beta, LV** ★★★

A Great Wall A Chinese-American family travels to mainland China to discover the country of their ancestry and to visit relatives. They experience radical culture shock. Wang's first independent feature. In English and Chinese with subtitles. *AKA:* The Great Wall is a Great Wall.
1986 (PG) 103m/C Peter Wang, Sharon Iwai, Kelvin Han Yee, Lin Qinqin, Hy Xiaoguang; *D:* Peter Wang; *W:* Peter Wang, Shirley Sun; *M:* David Liang, Ge Ganru. **VHS, Beta, LV** ★★★

The Great Ziegfeld Big bio-pic of the famous showman; acclaimed in its time as the best musical biography ever done, still considered the textbook for how to make a musical. Look for cameo roles by many famous stars, as well as a walk-on role by future First Lady Pat Nixon. The movie would have stood up as a first-rate biography of Ziegfeld, even without the drop-dead wonderful songs. ♪ Won't You Come Play With Me?; It's Delightful to be Married; If You Knew Susie; Shine On Harvest Moon; A Pretty Girl is Like a Melody; You Gotta Pull Strings; She's a Fol-

lies Girl; You; You Never Looked So Beautiful.
1936 179m/B William Powell, Luise Rainer, Myrna Loy, Frank Morgan, Reginald Owen, Nat Pendleton, Ray Bolger, Virginia Bruce, Harriet Hocter, Ernest Cossart, Robert Greig, Gilda Gray, Leon Errol, Dennis (Stanley Morner) Morgan, Mickey Daniels, William Demarest; *Cameos:* Fanny Brice; *D:* Robert Z. Leonard; *W:* William Anthony McGuire. Academy Awards '36: Best Actress (Rainer), Best Picture; New York Film Critics Awards '36: Best Actress (Rainer); Nominations: Academy Awards '36: Best Director (Leonard), Best Film Editing, Best Interior Decoration, Best Story. **VHS, Beta, LV** ★★★1/2

The Greatest Show on Earth DeMille is in all his epic glory here in a tale of a traveling circus wrought with glamour, romance, mysterious clowns, a tough ringmaster, and a train wreck.
1952 149m/C Betty Hutton, Cornel Wilde, James Stewart, Charlton Heston, Dorothy Lamour, Lawrence Tierney; *D:* Cecil B. DeMille. Academy Awards '52: Best Picture, Best Story; Golden Globe Awards '53: Best Director (DeMille), Best Film—Drama; Nominations: Academy Awards '52: Best Costume Design (Color), Best Director (DeMille), Best Film Editing. **VHS, Beta, LV** ★★★

Greed A wife's obsession with money drives her husband to murder. Although the original version's length (eight hours) was trimmed to 140 minutes, it remains one of the greatest and most highly acclaimed silent films ever made. Effective use of Death Valley locations. Adapted from the Frank Norris novel "McTeague."
1924 140m/B Dale Fuller, Gibson Gowland, ZaSu Pitts, Jean Hersholt, Chester Conklin; *D:* Erich von Stroheim. **VHS, LV** ★★★★

Green Eyes Winfield, an ex-GI, returns to postwar Vietnam to search for his illegitimate son, who he believes will have green eyes. A highly acclaimed, made-for-television drama featuring moving performances from Winfield and Jonathan Lippe.
1976 100m/C Paul Winfield, Rita Tushingham, Jonathon Lippe, Victoria Racimo, Royce Wallace, Claudia Bryar; *D:* John Erman. **VHS** ★★★1/2

Green Pastures An adaptation of Marc Connelly's 1930 Pulitzer Prize-winning play which attempts to retell Biblical stories in Black English Vernacular of the '30s. Southern theater owners boycotted the controversial film which has an all-Black cast.
1936 93m/C Rex Ingram, Oscar Polk,

Eddie Anderson, George Reed, Abraham Graves, Myrtle Anderson, Frank Wilson; **D:** William Keighley, Marc Connelly. National Board of Review Awards '36: 10 Best Films of the Year. **VHS, Beta** ★★★

Gregory's Girl Sweet, disarming comedy established Forsyth. An awkward young Scottish schoolboy falls in love with the female goalie of his soccer team. He turns to his 10-year-old sister for advice, but she's more interested in ice cream than love. His best friend is no help, either, since he has yet to fall in love. Perfect mirror of teenagers and their instantaneous, raw, and all-consuming loves. Very sweet scene with Gregory and his girl lying on their backs in an open space illustrates the simultaneous simplicity and complexity of young love.
1980 91m/C GB Gordon John Sinclair, Dee Hepburn, Jake D'Arcy, Chic Murray, Alex Norton, John Bett, Clare Grogan; **D:** Bill Forsyth; **W:** Bill Forsyth. British Academy Awards '81: Best Screenplay. **VHS, Beta** ★★★1/2

Gremlins Comedy horror with deft satiric edge. Produced by Spielberg. Fumbling gadget salesman Rand Peltzer is looking for something really special to get his son Billy. He finds it in a small store in Chinatown. The wise shopkeeper is reluctant to sell him the adorable "mogwai" but relents after fully warning him "Don't expose him to bright light, don't ever get him wet, and don't ever, ever feed him after midnight." Naturally, this all happens and the result is a gang of nasty gremlins who decide to tear up the town on Christmas Eve. Followed by "Gremlins 2, the New Batch" which is less black comedy, more parody, and perhaps more inventive.
1984 (PG) 106m/C Zach Galligan, Phoebe Cates, Hoyt Axton, Polly Holliday, Frances Lee McCain, Keye Luke, Dick Miller, Corey Feldman, Judge Reinhold; **D:** Joe Dante; **W:** Chris Columbus; **M:** Jerry Goldsmith. **VHS, Beta, LV, 8mm** ★★★

Gremlins 2: The New Batch The sequel to "Gremlins" is superior to the original, which was quite good. Set in a futuristic skyscraper in the Big Apple, director Dante presents a less violent but far more campy vision, paying myriad surreal tributes to scores of movies, including "The Wizard of Oz" and musical extravaganzas of the past. Also incorporates a Donald Trump parody, takes on television news, and body slams modern urban living. Great fun.
1990 (PG-13) 107m/C Phoebe Cates, Christopher Lee, John Glover, Zach

Galligan; **Cameos:** Jerry Goldsmith; **D:** Joe Dante; **M:** Jerry Goldsmith. **VHS, Beta, LV, 8mm** ★★★1/2

The Grey Fox A gentlemanly old stagecoach robber tries to pick up his life after 30 years in prison. Unable to resist another heist, he tries train robbery, and winds up hiding out in British Columbia where he meets an attractive photographer, come to document the changing West. Farnsworth is perfect as the man who suddenly finds himself in the 20th century trying to work at the only craft he knows. Based on the true story of Canada's most colorful and celebrated outlaw, Bill Miner.
1983 (PG) 92m/C CA Richard Farnsworth, Jackie Burroughs, Wayne Robson, Timothy Webber, Ken Pogue; **D:** Phillip Borsos; **M:** Michael Conway Baker. Genie Awards '83: Best Director (Borsos), Best Film, Best Supporting Actress (Burroughs). **VHS, Beta, LV** ★★★★

The Grifters Evocative rendering of a terrifying sub-culture. Huston, Cusak, and Bening are con artists, struggling to stay on top in a world where violence, money, and lust are the prizes. Bening and Huston fight for Cusak's soul, while he's determined to decide for himself. Seamless performances and dazzling atmosphere, along with superb pacing, make for a provocative film. Based on a novel by Jim Thompson.
1990 (R) 114m/C Anjelica Huston, John Cusack, Annette Bening, Pat Hingle, J.T. Walsh, Charles Napier, Henry Jones, Gailard Sartain; **D:** Stephen Frears; **W:** Donald E. Westlake; **M:** Elmer Bernstein. Independent Spirit Awards '91: Best Actress (Huston), Best Film; Los Angeles Film Critics Association Awards '90: Best Actress (Huston); National Society of Film Critics Awards '90: Best Actress (Huston), Best Supporting Actress (Bening); Nominations: Academy Awards '90: Best Actress (Huston), Best Adapted Screenplay, Best Director (Frears), Best Supporting Actress (Bening). **VHS, Beta, LV** ★★★1/2

The Grissom Gang Remake of the 1948 British film "No Orchids for Miss Blandish." Darby is a wealthy heiress kidnapped by a family of grotesques, led by a sadistic mother. The ransom gets lost in a series of bizarre events, and the heiress appears to be falling for one of her moronic captors. Director Robert Aldrich skillfully blends extreme violence with dark humor. Superb camera work, editing, and 1920s period sets.
1971 (R) 127m/C Kim Darby, Scott Wilson,

Tony Musante, Ralph Waite, Connie Stevens, Robert Lansing, Wesley Addy; **D:** Robert Aldrich. **VHS ★★★**

Groundhog Day Phil (Murray), an obnoxious weatherman, is in Punxatawney, Pennsylvania, to cover the annual emergence of the famous rodent from its hole. After he's caught in a blizzard that he didn't predict, he finds himself trapped in a time warp, doomed to relive the same day over and over again until he gets it right. Lighthearted romantic comedy takes a funny premise and manages to carry it through to the end. Murray has fun with the role, although he did get bitten by the groundhog during the scene when they're driving. Elliott, who has been missed since his days as the man under the seats on "Late Night with David Letterman" is perfectly cast as a smart-mouthed cameraman.
1993 (PG) 103m/C Bill Murray, Andie MacDowell, Chris Elliott, Stephen Tobolowsky, Brian Doyle-Murray, Marita Geraghty, Angela Paton; **D:** Harold Ramis; **W:** Harold Ramis, Daniel F. Rubin; **M:** George Fenton. British Academy Awards '93: Best Original Screenplay. **VHS, LV ★★★**

Grumpy Old Men Lemmon and Matthau team for their seventh movie, in parts that seem written just for them. Boyhood friends and retired neighbors, they have been feuding for so long that neither of them can remember why. Doesn't matter much, when it provides a reason for them to spout off at each other every morning and play nasty practical jokes every night. This, and ice-fishing, is life as they know it, until feisty younger woman Ann-Margret moves into the neighborhood and lights some long dormant fires. Eighty-three-year old Meredith is a special treat playing Lemmon's ninetysomething father. Filmed in Wabasha, Minnesota, and grumpy, in the most pleasant way.
1993 (PG-13) 104m/C Jack Lemmon, Walter Matthau, Ann-Margret, Burgess Meredith, Daryl Hannah, Kevin Pollak, Ossie Davis, Buck Henry, Christopher McDonald; **D:** Donald Petrie; **W:** Mark Steven Johnson; **M:** Alan Silvestri. **VHS, LV, 8mm ★★★**

The Guardsman Broadway's illustrious couple Lunt and Fontanne shine in this adaptation of the clever marital comedy by French playwright Molnar in which they also starred. This sophisticated comedy was their only starring film, although they were offered large sums of money to appear in other movies—they just couldn't tear themselves away from the stage. Remade as "The Chocolate Soldier" and "Lily in Love."
1931 89m/B Alfred Lunt, Lynn Fontanne, Roland Young, ZaSu Pitts, Maude Eburne, Herman Bing, Ann Dvorak; **D:** Sidney Franklin. Nominations: Academy Awards '32: Best Actor (Lunt), Best Actress (Fontanne). **VHS ★★★**

Guess Who's Coming to Dinner Controversial in its time. A young white woman brings her black fiance home to meet her parents. The situation truly tests their open-mindedness and understanding. Hepburn and Tracy (in his last film appearance) are wonderful and serve as the anchors in what would otherwise have been a rather sugary film. Houghton, who portrays the independent daughter, is the real-life niece of Hepburn.
1967 108m/C Katharine Hepburn, Spencer Tracy, Sidney Poitier, Katharine Houghton, Cecil Kellaway; **D:** Stanley Kramer; **W:** William Rose. Academy Awards '67: Best Actress (Hepburn), Best Original Screenplay; British Academy Awards '68: Best Actor (Tracy), Best Actress (Hepburn); Nominations: Academy Awards '67: Best Actor (Tracy), Best Picture, Best Supporting Actor (Kellaway). **VHS, Beta, LV ★★★**

Gun Crazy Annie Laurie Starr—Annie Oakley in a Wild West show—meets gun-lovin' Bart Tare, who says a gun makes him feel good inside, "like I'm somebody." Sparks fly, and the two get married and live happily ever after—until the money runs out and fatal femme Laurie's craving for excitement and violence starts to flare up. The two become lovebirds-on-the-lam. Now a cult fave, it's based on a MacKinlay Kantor story. Ex-stuntman Russell Harlan's photography is daring; the realism of the impressive robbery scenes is owed in part to the technical consultation of former train robber Al Jennings. And watch for a young Tamblyn as the 14-year-old Bart. **AKA:** Deadly is the Female.
1949 87m/B Peggy Cummins, John Dall, Berry Kroeger, Morris Carnovsky, Anabel Shaw, Nedrick Young, Trevor Bardette, Russ Tamblyn; **D:** Joseph H. Lewis; **W:** Dalton Trumbo. **VHS ★★★**

Gunfight at the O.K. Corral The story of Wyatt Earp and Doc Holliday joining forces in Dodge City to rid the town of the criminal Clanton gang. Filmed in typical Hollywood style, but redeemed by its great stars.
1957 122m/C Burt Lancaster, Kirk

Douglas, Rhonda Fleming, Jo Van Fleet, John Ireland, Kenneth Tobey, Lee Van Cleef, Frank Faylen, DeForest Kelley, Earl Holliman; **D:** John Sturges; **W:** Leon Uris. Nominations: Academy Awards '57: Best Sound. **VHS, Beta, LV ★★★**

The Gunfighter A mature, serious, Hollywood-western character study about an aging gunfighter searching for peace and quiet but unable to avoid his reputation and the duel-challenges it invites. One of King's best films. **1950 85m/B** Gregory Peck, Helen Westcott, Millard Mitchell, Jean Parker, Karl Malden, Skip Homeier, Mae Marsh; **D:** Henry King. Nominations: Academy Awards '50: Best Story. **VHS, Beta, LV ★★★1/2**

Gunga Din The prototypical "buddy" film. Three veteran British sergeants in India try to suppress a native uprising, but it's their water boy, the intrepid Gunga Din, who saves the day. Friendship, loyalty, and some of the best action scenes ever filmed. Based loosely on Rudyard Kipling's famous poem, the story is credited to Ben Hecht, Charles MacArthur and William Faulkner (who is uncredited). Also available colorized. **1939 117m/B** Cary Grant, Victor McLaglen, Douglas Fairbanks Jr., Sam Jaffe, Eduardo Ciannelli, Montagu Love, Joan Fontaine, Abner Biberman, Robert Coote, Lumsden Hare, Cecil Kellaway; **D:** George Stevens; **W:** Fred Guiol, Joel Sayre; **M:** Alfred Newman. Nominations: Academy Awards '39: Best Black and White Cinematography. **VHS, Beta, LV ★★★★**

The Guns of Navarone During WWII, British Intelligence in the Middle East sends six men to the Aegean island of Navarone to destroy guns manned by the Germans. Consistently interesting war epic based on the Alistair MacLean novel, with a vivid cast. **1961 159m/C** Gregory Peck, David Niven, Anthony Quinn, Richard Harris, Stanley Baker, Anthony Quayle, James Darren, Irene Papas; **D:** J. Lee Thompson. Academy Awards '61: Best Special Effects; Golden Globe Awards '62: Best Film—Drama, Best Score; Nominations: Academy Awards '61: Best Adapted Screenplay, Best Director (Thompson). **VHS, Beta, LV ★★★1/2**

Guys and Dolls New York gambler Sky Masterson takes a bet that he can romance a Salvation Army lady. Based on the stories of Damon Runyon with Blaine, Kaye, Pully, and Silver re-creating their roles from the Broadway hit. Brando's not-always-convincing musical debut. ♪ More I

Cannot Wish You; My Time of Day; Guys and Dolls; Fugue for Tinhorns; Follow the Fold; Sue Me; Take Back Your Mink; If I Were a Bell; Luck Be a Lady. **1955 150m/C** Marlon Brando, Jean Simmons, Frank Sinatra, Vivian Blaine, Stubby Kaye, Sheldon Leonard, Veda Ann Borg; **D:** Joseph L. Mankiewicz; **W:** Joseph L. Mankiewicz; **M:** Frank Loesser. Golden Globe Awards '56: Best Actress—Musical/Comedy (Simmons), Best Film—Musical/Comedy; Nominations: Academy Awards '55: Best Art Direction/Set Decoration (Color), Best Color Cinematography, Best Costume Design (Color), Best Original Score. **VHS, Beta, LV ★★★**

Gypsy The life story of America's most famous striptease queen, Gypsy Rose Lee. Russell gives a memorable performance as the infamous Mama Rose, Gypsy's stage mother. Based on both Gypsy Rose Lee's memoirs and the hit Broadway play by Arthur Laurents. ♪ Small World; All I Need is the Girl; You'll Never Get Away From Me; Let Me Entertain You; Some People; Everything's Coming Up Roses; You Gotta Have a Gimmick; Baby Jane and the Newsboys; Mr. Goldstone, I Love You. **1962 144m/C** Rosalind Russell, Natalie Wood, Karl Malden, Ann Jillian, Parley Baer, Paul Wallace, Betty Bruce; **D:** Mervyn LeRoy. Golden Globe Awards '63: Best Actress—Musical/Comedy (Russell); Nominations: Academy Awards '62: Best Color Cinematography, Best Costume Design (Color), Best Original Score. **VHS, Beta, LV ★★★**

Hail the Conquering Hero A slight young man is rejected by the Army. Upon returning home, he is surprised to find out they think he's a hero. Biting satire with Demarest's performance stealing the show. **1944 101m/B** Eddie Bracken, Ella Raines, William Demarest, Franklin Pangborn, Raymond Walburn; **D:** Preston Sturges. Nominations: Academy Awards '44: Best Original Screenplay. **VHS ★★★1/2**

Hair Film version of the explosive 1960s Broadway musical about the carefree life of the flower children and the shadow of the Vietnam War that hangs over them. Great music, as well as wonderful choreography by Twyla Tharp, help portray the surprisingly sensitive evocation of the period so long after the fact. Forman has an uncanny knack for understanding the textures of American life. Watch for a thinner Nell Carter.

1979 (PG) 122m/C Treat Williams, John Savage, Beverly D'Angelo, Annie Golden, Nicholas Ray; **D:** Milos Forman; **W:** Michael Weller. **VHS, Beta, LV** ★★★½

Hairspray Waters' first truly mainstream film, if that's even possible, and his funniest. Details the struggle among teenagers in 1962 Baltimore for the top spot in a local TV dance show. Deals with racism and stereotypes, as well as typical "teen" problems (hair-do's and don'ts). Filled with refreshingly tasteful, subtle social satire (although not without typical Waters touches that will please diehard fans). Lake is lovable and appealing as Divine's daughter; Divine, in his last film, is likeable as an irontoting mom. Look for Waters in a cameo and Divine as a man. Great '60s music, which Waters refers to as "the only known remedy to today's Hit Parade of Hell."
1988 (PG) 94m/C Ricki Lake, Divine, Jerry Stiller, Colleen Fitzpatrick, Sonny Bono, Deborah Harry, Ruth Brown, Pia Zadora, Ric Ocasek, Michael St. Gerard, Leslie Ann Powers, Shawn Thompson; **Cameos:** John Waters; **D:** John Waters; **W:** John Waters. **VHS, Beta, LV** ★★★

Hallelujah! Haynes plays an innocent young man who turns to religion and becomes a charismatic preacher after a family tragedy. He retains all his human weaknesses, however, including falling for the lovely but deceitful McKinney. Great music included traditional spirituals and songs by Berlin, such as "At the End of the Road" and "Swanee Shuffle." Shot on location in Tennessee. The first all-black feature film and the first talkie for director Vidor was given the go-ahead by MGM production chief Irving Thalberg, though he knew the film would be both controversial and get minimal release in the deep South.
1929 90m/B Daniel L. Haynes, Nina Mae McKinney, William Fontaine, Harry Gray, Fannie Belle DeKnight, Everett McGarrity; **D:** King Vidor; **M:** Irving Berlin. Nominations: Academy Awards '30: Best Director (Vidor). **VHS** ★★★½

Halloween John Carpenter's horror classic has been acclaimed "the most successful independent motion picture of all time." A deranged youth returns to his hometown with murderous intent after 15 years in an asylum. Very, very scary—you feel this movie more than see it.
1978 (R) 90m/C Jamie Lee Curtis, Donald Pleasence, Nancy Loomis, P.J. Soles; **D:** John Carpenter; **W:** John Carpenter, Debra

Hill, Dean Cundey; **M:** John Carpenter. **VHS, Beta, LV** ★★★½

Hamlet Splendid adaptation of Shakespeare's dramatic play. Hamlet vows vengeance on the murderer of his father in this tight version of the four hour stage play. Some scenes were cut out, including all of Rosencrantz and Guildenstern. Beautifully photographed in Denmark. An Olivier triumph. Remade several times.
1948 153m/B GB Laurence Olivier, Basil Sydney, Felix Aylmer, Jean Simmons, Stanley Holloway, Peter Cushing, Christopher Lee, Eileen Herlie, John Laurie, Esmond Knight, Anthony Quayle; **D:** Laurence Olivier; **W:** Alan Dent; **M:** William Walton; **V:** John Gielgud. Academy Awards '48: Best Actor (Olivier), Best Art Direction/Set Decoration (B & W), Best Costume Design (B & W), Best Picture; British Academy Awards '48: Best Film; Golden Globe Awards '49: Best Actor—Drama (Olivier); New York Film Critics Awards '48: Best Actor (Olivier); Nominations: Academy Awards '48: Best Director (Olivier), Best Supporting Actress (Simmons), Best Original Score. **VHS** ★★★★

Hamlet Zeffirelli—in his fourth attempt at Shakespeare—creates a surprisingly energetic and accessible interpretation of the Bard's moody play. Gibson brings charm, humor and a carefully calculated sense of violence, not to mention a good deal of solid flesh, to the eponymous role, and handles the language skillfully (although if you seek a poetic Dane, stick with Olivier). Exceptional work from Scofield and Bates; Close seems a tad hysterical (not to mention too young to play Gibson's mother), but brings insight and nuance to her role. Purists beware: this isn't a completely faithful adaptation. Beautifully costumed; shot on location in Northern Scotland.
1990 (PG) 135m/C Mel Gibson, Glenn Close, Alan Bates, Paul Scofield, Ian Holm, Helena Bonham Carter, Nathaniel Parker, Peter Postlethwaite; **D:** Franco Zeffirelli; **W:** Franco Zeffirelli, Christopher DeVore. Nominations: Academy Awards '90: Best Art Direction/Set Decoration, Best Costume Design. **VHS, Beta, LV, 8mm** ★★★½

Hangin' with the Homeboys One night in the lives of four young men. Although the Bronx doesn't offer much for any of them, they have little interest in escaping its confines, and they are more than willing to complain. Characters are insightfully written and well portrayed, with strongest

work from Serrano as a Puerto Rican who is trying to pass himself off as Italian. Lack of plot may frustrate some viewers.
1991 (R) 89m/C Mario Joyner, Doug E. Doug, John Leguizamo, Nestor Serrano, Kimberly Russell, Mary B. Ward; *D:* Joseph B. Vasquez; *W:* Joseph B. Vasquez. Sundance Film Festival '91: Best Screenplay. **VHS, LV ★★★**

The Hanging Tree Cooper plays a frontier doctor who rescues a thief (Piazza) from a lynch mob and nurses a temporarily blind girl (Schell). Malden is the bad guy who tries to attack Schell and Cooper shoots him. The townspeople take Cooper out to "The Hanging Tree" but this time it's Schell and Piazza who come to his rescue. Slow-paced western with good performances. Scott's screen debut.
1959 108m/B Gary Cooper, Maria Schell, Ben Piazza, Karl Malden, George C. Scott, Karl Swenson, Virginia Gregg, King Donovan; *D:* Delmer Daves; *W:* Wendell Mayes, Halsted Welles; *M:* Max Steiner. Nominations: Academy Awards '59: Best Song ("The Hanging Tree"). **VHS ★★★**

Hank Aaron: Chasing the Dream Docudrama combines archival footage, interviews, and reenactments to tell the story of the life and career of Henry Aaron. Follows Aaron's development as a Hall of Fame outfielder for the Milwaukee and Atlanta Braves and as a leader in the civil rights movement. Emphasis on personal and societal issues, as well as on-the-field accomplishments, raises this one above most sports biography documentaries.
1995 120m/C VHS ★★★

Hannah and Her Sisters Allen's grand epic about a New York showbiz family, its three adult sisters and their various complex romantic entanglements. Excellent performances by the entire cast, especially Caine and Hershey. Classic Allen themes of life, love, death, and desire are explored in an assured and sensitive manner. Witty, ironic, and heartwarming.
1986 (PG) 103m/C Mia Farrow, Barbara Hershey, Dianne Wiest, Michael Caine, Woody Allen, Maureen O'Sullivan, Lloyd Nolan, Sam Waterston, Carrie Fisher, Max von Sydow, Julie Kavner, Daniel Stern, Tony Roberts, John Turturro, Carlo DiPalma; *D:* Woody Allen; *W:* Woody Allen. Academy Awards '86: Best Original Screenplay, Best Supporting Actor (Caine), Best Supporting Actress (Wiest); Golden Globe Awards '87: Best Film—Musical/Comedy; Los Angeles Film Critics Association Awards '86: Best Film, Best Screenplay, Best Supporting Actress (Wiest); New York Film Critics Awards '86: Best Director (Allen), Best Film, Best Supporting Actress (Wiest); Writers Guild of America '86: Best Original Screenplay; Nominations: Academy Awards '85: Best Art Direction/Set Decoration; Academy Awards '86: Best Director (Allen), Best Film Editing, Best Picture. **VHS, Beta, LV ★★★¹/₂**

Hanussen The third of Szabo and Brandauer's price-of-power trilogy (after "Mephisto" and "Colonel Redl"), in which a talented German magician and clairvoyant (based on a true-life figure) collaborates with the Nazis during their rise to power in the 1930s, although he can foresee the outcome of their reign. In German with English subtitles.
1988 (R) 110m/C *GE HU* Klaus Maria Brandauer, Erland Josephson, Walter Schmidinger; *D:* Istvan Szabo, Lajos Koltai. Nominations: Academy Awards '88: Best Foreign Language Film. **VHS, Beta, LV ★★★¹/₂**

Happy New Year Charming romantic comedy in which two thieves plan a robbery but get sidetracked by the distracting woman who lives next door to the jewelry store. Available in both subtitled and dubbed versions. Remade in 1987. *AKA:* The Happy New Year Caper.
1974 114m/C *FR IT* Francoise Fabian, Lino Ventura, Andre Falcon; *D:* Claude Lelouch; *W:* Claude Lelouch. **VHS, Beta ★★★**

A Hard Day's Night The Beatles' first film is a joyous romp through an average "day in the life" of the Fab Four, shot in a pseudo-documentary style with great flair by Lester and noted as the first music video. Laser version includes original trailer and an interview with Lester. ♪ A Hard Day's Night; Tell Me Why; I Should Have Known Better; She Loves You; I'm Happy Just To Dance With You; If I Fell; And I Love Her; This Boy; Can't Buy Me Love.
1964 90m/B *GB* John Lennon, Paul McCartney, George Harrison, Ringo Starr; *D:* Richard Lester. Nominations: Academy Awards '64: Best Story & Screenplay, Best Original Score. **VHS, Beta, LV, CD-I ★★★¹/₂**

The Harder They Fall A cold-eyed appraisal of the scum-infested boxing world. An unemployed reporter (Bogart in his last role) promotes a fighter for the syndicate, while doing an expose on the fight racket. Bogart became increasingly debilitated dur-

ing filming and died soon afterward. Based on Budd Schulberg's novel.
1956 109m/B Humphrey Bogart, Rod Steiger, Jan Sterling, Mike Lane, Max Baer Sr.; **D:** Mark Robson; **W:** Philip Yordan. Nominations: Academy Awards '56: Best Black and White Cinematography. **VHS, Beta** ★★★

Harold and Maude Cult classic pairs Cort as a dead-pan disillusioned 20-year-old obsessed with suicide (his staged attempts are a highlight) and a lovable Gordon as a fun-loving 80-year-old eccentric. They meet at a funeral (a mutual hobby), and develop a taboo romantic relationship, in which they explore the tired theme of the meaning of life with a fresh perspective. The script was originally the 20-minute long graduate thesis of UCLA student Higgins, who showed it to his landlady, wife of film producer Lewis. Features music by the pre-Islamic Cat Stevens.
1971 (PG) 92m/C Ruth Gordon, Bud Cort, Cyril Cusack, Vivian Pickles, Charles Tyner, Ellen Geer; **D:** Hal Ashby; **W:** Colin Higgins; **M:** Cat Stevens, John A. Alonzo. **VHS, Beta, LV, 8mm** ★★★★

Harper A tight, fast-moving genre piece about cynical LA private eye Newman investigating the disappearance of Bacall's wealthy husband. From a Ross McDonald novel, adapted by William Golding. Later sequelled in "The Drowning Pool." **AKA:** The Moving Target.
1966 121m/C Paul Newman, Shelley Winters, Lauren Bacall, Julie Harris, Robert Wagner, Janet Leigh, Arthur Hill, Conrad Hall; **D:** Jack Smight. Edgar Allan Poe Awards '66: Best Screenplay. **VHS, Beta, LV** ★★★

Harry and Tonto A gentle comedy about an energetic septuagenarian who takes a cross-country trip with his cat, Tonto. Never in a hurry, still capable of feeling surprise and joy, he makes new friends and visits old lovers. Carney deserved his Oscar. Mazursky has seldom been better.
1974 115m/C Art Carney, Ellen Burstyn, Larry Hagman, Geraldine Fitzgerald, Chief Dan George, Arthur Hunnicutt, Josh Mostel; **D:** Paul Mazursky; **W:** Paul Mazursky; **M:** Bill Conti. Academy Awards '74: Best Actor (Carney); Golden Globe Awards '75: Best Actor—Musical/Comedy (Carney); National Board of Review Awards '74: 10 Best Films of the Year; Nominations: Academy Awards '74: Best Original Screenplay. **VHS, Beta** ★★★

Harvest A classically Pagnolian rural pageant-of-life melodrama, wherein a pair of loners link up together in an abandoned French town and completely revitalize it and the land around it. From the novel by Jean Giono. In French with English subtitles.
1937 128m/B *FR* Fernandel, Gabriel Gabrio, Orane Demazis, Edouard Delmont, Henri Poupon; **D:** Marcel Pagnol; **W:** Marcel Pagnol; **M:** Arthur Honegger. National Board of Review Awards '39: 5 Best Foreign Films of the Year; New York Film Critics Awards '39: Best Foreign Film. **VHS, Beta** ★★★★

Harvey Straightforward version of the Mary Chase play about a friendly drunk with an imaginary six-foot rabbit friend named Harvey, and a sister who tries to have him committed. A fondly remembered, charming comedy. Hull is a standout, well deserving her Oscar.
1950 104m/B James Stewart, Josephine Hull, Victoria Horne, Peggy Dow, Cecil Kellaway, Charles Drake, Jesse White, Wallace Ford, Nana Bryant; **D:** Henry Koster; **W:** Oscar Brodney. Academy Awards '50: Best Supporting Actress (Hull); Golden Globe Awards '51: Best Supporting Actress (Hull); Nominations: Academy Awards '50: Best Actor (Stewart). **VHS, Beta, LV** ★★★1/2

The Harvey Girls Lightweight musical about a restaurant chain that sends its waitresses to work in the Old West. ♪ In the Valley Where the Evening Sun Goes Down; Wait and See; On the Atchison, Topeka and Santa Fe; It's a Great Big World; The Wild Wild West.
1946 102m/C Judy Garland, Ray Bolger, John Hodiak, Preston Foster, Angela Lansbury, Virginia O'Brien, Marjorie Main, Chill Wills, Kenny L. Baker, Selena Royle, Cyd Charisse; **D:** George Sidney; **M:** Harry Warren, Johnny Mercer. Academy Awards '46: Best Song ("On the Atchison, Topeka and Santa Fe"); Best Original Score. **VHS, Beta, LV** ★★★

Hate Twenty hours in the lives of young, disenfranchised Said (Taghmaoui), Vinz (Cassel), and Hubert (Kounde), who are living in a housing project outside Paris. A riot breaks out, thanks to police brutality of an Arab resident, and Vinz finds a gun the cops lost. A Paris sojourn leads to a police interrogation of Hubert and Said, a fight with some skinheads, a return to their home turf, and an unexpected conclusion. Intelligent look at the idiocy engendered by societal oppression and a buildup of hatred. In French with English subtitles. **AKA:** La Haine; Hatred.
1995 97m/B *FR* Vincent Cassel, Hubert

Kounde, Said Taghmaoui, Francois Levantal; **D:** Mathieu Kassovitz, Pierre Aim, Georges Diane; **W:** Mathieu Kassovitz. Cannes Film Festival '95: Best Director (Kassovitz); Cesar Awards '96: Best Film, Best Film Editing; Nominations: Cesar Awards '96: Best Actor (Cassel), Best Cinematography, Best Director (Kassovitz), Best Screenplay, Best Sound. **VHS** ★★★

The Haunted Castle One of Murnau's first films, and a vintage, if crusty, example of German expressionism. A nobleman entertains guests at his country mansion when strange things start to occur. Silent, with English titles. **AKA:** Schloss Vogelod.
1921 56m/B Arnold Korff, Lulu Keyser-Korff; **D:** F.W. Murnau. **VHS, Beta** ★★★

The Haunting A subtle, bloodless horror film about a weekend spent in a monstrously haunted mansion by a parapsychologist, the mansion's skeptic heir, and two mediums. A chilling adaptation of Shirley Jackson's "The Haunting of Hill House," in which the psychology of the heroine is forever in question.
1963 113m/B Julie Harris, Claire Bloom, Russ Tamblyn, Richard Johnson; **D:** Robert Wise. **VHS, Beta, LV** ★★★1/2

He Walked by Night Los Angeles homicide investigators track down a cop killer in this excellent drama. Based on a true story from the files of the Los Angeles police, this first rate production reportedly inspired Webb to create "Dragnet."
1948 80m/B Richard Basehart, Scott Brady, Roy Roberts, Jack Webb, Whit Bissell; **D:** Alfred Werker, Anthony Mann, John Alton. **VHS, Beta** ★★★1/2

He Who Gets Slapped Chaney portrays a brilliant scientist whose personal and professional humiliations cause him to join a travelling French circus as a masochistic clown (hence the title). There he falls in love with a beautiful circus performer and plans a spectacular revenge. Brilliant use of lighting and Expressionist devices by director Sjostrom (who used the Americanized version of his name-Seastrom-in the credits). Adapted from the Russian play "He, The One Who Gets Slapped" by Leonid Andreyev.
1924 85m/B Lon Chaney Sr., Norma Shearer, John Gilbert, Tully Marshall, Ford Sterling, Marc McDermott; **D:** Victor Sjostrom; **W:** Carey Wilson, Victor Sjostrom. **VHS** ★★★

Hear My Song Mickey O'Neill (Dunbar) is an unscrupulous club promoter, who books singers with names like Franc Cinatra, while trying to revive his failing nightclub in this charming, hilarious comedy. He hires the mysterious Mr. X, who claims he is really the legendary exiled singer Josef Locke, only to find out he is an imposter. To redeem himself with his fiancee and her mother, he goes to Ireland to find the real Locke (Beatty) and bring him to Liverpool to sing. Dunbar is appealing in his role, and Beatty is magnificent as the legendary Locke—so much so that he was nominated for a Golden Globe for Best Supporting Actor.
1991 (R) 104m/C *GB* Ned Beatty, Adrian Dunbar, Shirley Anne Field, Tara Fitzgerald, William Hootkins, David McCallum; **D:** Peter Chelsom; **W:** Peter Chelsom; **M:** John Altman. **VHS, Beta** ★★★★

The Heart Is a Lonely Hunter Set in the South, Carson McCuller's tale of angst and ignorance, loneliness and beauty comes to the screen with the film debuts of Keach and Locke. Arkin gives an instinctive, gentle performance as the deaf mute.
1968 (G) 124m/C Alan Arkin, Cicely Tyson, Sondra Locke, Stacy Keach, Chuck McCann, Laurinda Barrett; **D:** Robert Ellis Miller; **M:** Dave Grusin. New York Film Critics Awards '68: Best Actor (Arkin); Nominations: Academy Awards '68: Best Actor (Arkin), Best Supporting Actress (Locke). **VHS, Beta** ★★★

Heart of Glass A pre-industrial Bavarian village becomes deeply troubled when their glassblower dies without imparting the secret of making his unique Ruby glass. The townspeople go to extremes, from madness to murder to magic, to discover the ingredients. From German director Herzog (who hypnotized his cast daily), this somewhat apocalyptic tale is based on legend. The colors are incredible in their intensity. In German with English subtitles.
1974 93m/C *GE* Josef Bierbichler, Stefan Autter, Scheitz Clemens, Volker Prechtel, Sonia Skiba; **D:** Werner Herzog. **VHS** ★★★

The Heartbreak Kid Director May's comic examination of love and hypocrisy. Grodin embroils himself in a triangle with his new bride and a woman he can't have, an absolutely gorgeous and totally unloving woman he shouldn't want. Walks the fence between tragedy and comedy, with an exceptional performance from Berlin. Based on Bruce Jay Friedman's story.
1972 (PG) 106m/C Charles Grodin, Cybill Shepherd, Eddie Albert, Jeannie Berlin,

Audra Lindley, Art Metrano; **D:** Elaine May; **W:** Neil Simon, Owen Roizman. New York Film Critics Awards '72: Best Supporting Actress (Berlin); National Society of Film Critics Awards '72: Best Supporting Actor (Albert), Best Supporting Actress (Berlin); Nominations: Academy Awards '72: Best Supporting Actor (Albert), Best Supporting Actress (Berlin). **VHS, Beta, LV** ★★★

Heartbreak Ridge An aging Marine recon sergeant is put in command of a young platoon to whip them into shape to prepare for combat in the invasion of Grenada. Eastwood whips this old story into shape too, with a fine performance of a man who's given everything to the Marines. The invasion of Grenada, though, is not epic material. (Also available in English with Spanish subtitles.)
1986 (R) 130m/C Clint Eastwood, Marsha Mason, Everett McGill, Arlen Dean Snyder, Bo Svenson, Moses Gunn, Eileen Heckart, Boyd Gaines, Mario Van Peebles; **D:** Clint Eastwood; **W:** Jim Carabatsos; **M:** Lennie Niehaus, Jack N. Green. Nominations: Academy Awards '86: Best Sound. **VHS, Beta, LV, 8mm** ★★★

Heartland Set in 1910, this film chronicles the story of one woman's life on the Wyoming Frontier, the hazards she faces, and her courage and spirit. Stunningly realistic and without cliche. Based on the diaries of Elinore Randall Stewart.
1981 (PG) 95m/C Conchata Ferrell, Rip Torn, Barry Primus, Lilia Skala, Megan Folson; **D:** Richard Pearce. Sundance Film Festival '81: Grand Jury Prize. **VHS, Beta** ★★★1/2

Hearts of Darkness: A Filmmaker's Apocalypse This riveting, critically acclaimed documentary about the making of Francis Ford Coppola's masterpiece "Apocalypse Now" is based largely on original footage shot and directed by his wife Eleanor. Also included are recent interviews with cast and crew members including Coppola, Martin Sheen, Robert Duvall, Frederic Forrest and Dennis Hopper.
1991 (R) 96m/C Sam Bottoms, Eleanor Coppola, Francis Ford Coppola, Robert Duvall, Laurence "Larry" Fishburne, Frederic Forrest, Albert Hall, Dennis Hopper, George Lucas, John Milius, Martin Sheen; **D:** Fax Bahr, George Hickenlooper; **W:** Fax Bahr, George Hickenlooper; **M:** Todd Boekelheide. National Board of Review Awards '91: Best Feature Documentary. **VHS, Beta** ★★★★

Hearts of the West A fantasy-filled farm boy travels to Hollywood in the 1930s and seeks a writing career. Instead, he finds himself an ill-suited western movie star in this small offbeat comedy-drama that's sure to charm. **AKA:** Hollywood Cowboy.
1975 (PG) 103m/C Jeff Bridges, Andy Griffith, Donald Pleasence, Alan Arkin, Blythe Danner; **D:** Howard Zieff; **W:** Rob Thompson. National Board of Review Awards '75: 10 Best Films of the Year; New York Film Critics Awards '75: Best Supporting Actor (Arkin). **VHS, Beta** ★★★1/2

Hearts of the World A vintage Griffith epic about a young boy who goes off to WWI and the tribulations endured by both him and his family on the homefront. Overly sentimental but powerfully made melodrama, from Griffith's waning years. Silent with music score.
1918 152m/B Lillian Gish, Robert "Bobbie" Harron, Dorothy Gish, Erich von Stroheim, Ben Alexander, Josephine Crowell, Noel Coward, Mary Gish; **D:** D.W. Griffith. **VHS, Beta, LV, 8mm** ★★★

Heat Another Andy Warhol-produced journey into drug-addled urban seediness. Features a former child actor/ junkie and a has-been movie star barely surviving in a run-down motel. This is one of Warhol's better film productions; even non-fans may enjoy it.
1972 102m/C Joe Dallesandro, Sylvia Miles, Pat Ast; **D:** Paul Morrissey. **VHS, Beta** ★★★

Heat Pacino and De Niro in the same scene. Together. Finally. Obsessive master thief McCauley (De Niro) leads a crack crew on various military-style heists across L.A. while equally obsessive detective Hanna (Pacino) tracks him. Each man recognizes and respects the other's ability and dedication, even as they express the willingness to kill each other, if necessary. Excellent script with all the fireworks you'd expect, as well as a surprising look into emotional and personal sacrifice. Beautiful cinematography shows industrial landscape to great effect. Writer-director Mann held onto the screenplay for twelve years.
1995 (R) 172m/C Robert De Niro, Al Pacino, Val Kilmer, Jon Voight, Diane Venora, Ashley Judd, Wes Studi, Tom Sizemore, Mykelti Williamson, Amy Brenneman, Ted Levine, Dennis Haysbert, William Fichtner, Natalie Portman, Hank Azaria, Henry Rollins, Kevin Gage; **Cameos:** Tone Loc, Bud Cort, Jeremy Piven, Dante Spinotti; **D:** Michael Mann; **W:** Michael Mann; **M:** Elliot Goldenthal. **VHS** ★★★1/2

Heathers Clique of stuck-up girls named Heather rule the high school social scene until the newest member (not a Heather) decides that enough is enough. She and her outlaw boyfriend embark (accidentally on her part, intentionally on his) on a murder spree disguised as a rash of teen suicides. Dense, take-no-prisoners black comedy with buckets of potent slang, satire and unforgiving hostility. Humor this dark is rare; sharply observed and acted, though the end is out of place. Slater does his best Nicholson impression.
1989 (R) 102m/C Winona Ryder, Christian Slater, Kim Walker, Shannen Doherty, Lisanne Falk, Penelope Milford, Glenn Shadix, Lance Fenton, Patrick Laborteaux; **D:** Michael Lehmann; **M:** David Newman. Edgar Allan Poe Awards '89: Best Screenplay; Independent Spirit Awards '90: Best First Feature. **VHS, Beta, LV ★★★1/2**

Heaven Can Wait Social satire in which a rogue tries to convince the Devil to admit him into Hell by relating the story of his philandering life and discovers that he was a more valuable human being than he thought. A witty Lubitsch treat based on the play "Birthdays."
1943 112m/C Don Ameche, Gene Tierney, Laird Cregar, Charles Coburn, Marjorie Main, Eugene Pallette, Allyn Joslyn, Spring Byington, Signe Hasso, Louis Calhern, Dickie Moore, Florence Bates, Scotty Beckett, Charles Halton; **D:** Ernst Lubitsch. Nominations: Academy Awards '43: Best Color Cinematography, Best Director (Lubitsch), Best Picture. **VHS, Beta, LV ★★★**

Heaven Can Wait A remake of 1941's "Here Comes Mr. Jordan," about a football player who is mistakenly summoned to heaven before his time. When the mistake is realized, he is returned to Earth in the body of a corrupt executive about to be murdered by his wife. Not to be confused with the 1943 film of the same name.
1978 (PG) 101m/C Warren Beatty, Julie Christie, Charles Grodin, Dyan Cannon, James Mason, Jack Warden; **D:** Warren Beatty, Buck Henry; **W:** Warren Beatty, Elaine May; **M:** Dave Grusin, William A. Fraker. Academy Awards '78: Best Art Direction/Set Decoration; Golden Globe Awards '79: Best Actor—Musical/Comedy (Beatty), Best Film—Musical/Comedy, Best Supporting Actress (Cannon); Nominations: Academy Awards '78: Best Actor (Beatty), Best Adapted Screenplay, Best Director (Beatty, Henry), Best Picture, Best Supporting Actor (Warden), Best Original Score. **VHS, Beta, LV ★★★**

Heavenly Creatures Haunting and surreal drama chronicles the true-life case of two young schoolgirls, Pauline and Juliet, who were charged with clubbing to death Pauline's mother in Christchurch, New Zealand in 1954. Opens two years before the murder, and follows the friendship as the two teens become obsessed with each other, retreating into a rich fantasy life. They create an elaborate, medieval kingdom where they escape to their dream lovers and romantic alter egos. Elaborate morphing and animation effects vividly express the shared inner fantasy world, while innovative camerawork creates the sensations of hysteria and excitement that the girls experience as their infatuation becomes uncontrollable. Leads Lynskey and Winslet are convincing as the awkward, quiet Pauline and the pretty, intelligent, upper class Juliet. Bizarre crime story is stylish and eerily compelling, and made more so by real life events: after the film was released, mystery writer Anne Perry was revealed as Juliet Hulme.
1994 (R) 110m/C *NZ* Melanie Lynskey, Kate Winslet, Sarah Pierse, Diana Kent, Clive Merrison, Simon O'Connor; **D:** Peter Jackson; **W:** Peter Jackson, Frances Walsh. Nominations: Academy Awards '94: Best Original Screenplay; Australian Film Institute '95: Best Foreign Film. **VHS, LV ★★★1/2**

The Heiress Based on the Henry James novel "Washington Square," about a wealthy plain Jane, her tyrannical father, and the handsome fortune-seeking scoundrel who seeks to marry her.
1949 115m/B Olivia de Havilland, Montgomery Clift, Ralph Richardson, Miriam Hopkins; **D:** William Wyler; **M:** Aaron Copland. Academy Awards '49: Best Actress (de Havilland), Best Art Direction/Set Decoration (B & W), Best Costume Design (B & W), Best Original Score; Golden Globe Awards '50: Best Actress—Drama (de Havilland); National Board of Review Awards '49: 10 Best Films of the Year, Best Actor (Richardson); Nominations: Academy Awards '49: Best Black and White Cinematography, Best Director (Wyler), Best Picture, Best Supporting Actor (Richardson). **VHS, Beta, LV ★★★1/2**

Hell Is for Heroes McQueen stars as the bitter leader of a small infantry squad outmanned by the Germans in this tight WWII drama. A strong cast and riveting climax make this a must for action fans.
1962 90m/B Steve McQueen, Bobby Darin, Fess Parker, Harry Guardino, James

H

Coburn, Mike Kellin, Nick Adams, Bob Newhart; **D:** Donald Siegel; **W:** Robert Pirosh, Richard Carr. **VHS, Beta, LV** ★★★1/2

Hell's Angels Classic WWI aviation movie is sappy and a bit lumbering, but still an extravagant spectacle with awesome air scenes. Studio owner Hughes fired directors Howard Hawks and Luther Reed, spent an unprecedented $3.8 million, and was ultimately credited as director (although Whale also spent some time in the director's chair). Three years in the making, the venture cost three pilots their lives and lost a bundle. Harlow replaced Swedish Greta Nissen when sound was added and was catapulted into blond bombshelldom as a two-timing dame. And the tinted and two-color scenes—restored in 1989—came well before Ted Turner ever wielded a Crayola.
1930 135m/B Jean Harlow, Ben Lyon, James Hall, John Darrow, Lucien Prival; **D:** Howard Hughes; **W:** Harry Behn, Howard Estabrook, Joseph Moncure March. Nominations: Academy Awards '30: Best Cinematography. **VHS** ★★★

The Hellstrom Chronicle A powerful quasi-documentary about insects, their formidable capacity for survival, and the conjectured battle man will have with them in the future.
1971 (G) 90m/C Lawrence Pressman; **D:** Walon Green; **W:** David Seltzer. Academy Awards '71: Best Feature Documentary. **VHS, Beta** ★★★

Help! Ringo's ruby ring is the object of a search by a cult who chase the Fab Four all over the globe in order to acquire the bauble. The laserdisc version includes a wealth of Beatles memorabilia, rare footage behind the scenes and at the film's premiere, and extensive publicity material. ♪ Help!; You're Gonna Lose That Girl; You've Got To Hide Your Love Away; The Night Before; Another Girl; Ticket To Ride; I Need You.
1965 (G) 90m/C John Lennon, Paul McCartney, Ringo Starr, George Harrison, Leo McKern, Eleanor Bron; **D:** Richard Lester; **W:** Charles Wood, Marc Behm. **VHS, Beta, LV** ★★★

Henry V Classic, epic adaptation of the Shakespeare play, and Olivier's first and most successful directorial effort, dealing with the medieval British monarch that defeated the French at Agincourt. Distinguished by Olivier's brilliant formal experiment of beginning the drama as a 16th-century performance of the play in the Globe Theatre, and having the stage eventually transform into realistic historical settings of storybook color. Filmed at the height of WWII suffering in Britain (and meant as a parallel to the British fighting the Nazis), the film was not released in the U.S. until 1946.
1944 136m/C GB Laurence Olivier, Robert Newton, Leslie Banks, Esmond Knight, Renee Asherson, Leo Genn, George Robey, Ernest Thesiger, Felix Aylmer, Ralph Truman; **D:** Laurence Olivier, Reginald Beck; **W:** Laurence Olivier, Alan Dent; **M:** William Walton. National Board of Review Awards '46: 10 Best Films of the Year, Best Actor (Olivier); Nominations: Academy Awards '46: Best Actor (Olivier), Best Interior Decoration, Best Picture, Best Original Score. **VHS, Beta** ★★★★

Henry V Stirring, expansive retelling of Shakespeare's drama about the warrior-king of England. Branagh stars as Henry, leading his troops and uniting his kingdom against France. Very impressive production rivals Olivier's 1944 rendering but differs by stressing the high cost of war—showing the egomania, doubts, and subterfuge that underlie conflicts. Marvelous film-directorial debut for Branagh (who also adapted the screenplay). Wonderful supporting cast includes some of Britain's finest actors.
1989 138m/C GB Kenneth Branagh, Derek Jacobi, Brian Blessed, Alec McCowen, Ian Holm, Brian Briers, Robert Stephens, Robbie Coltrane, Christian Bale, Judi Dench, Paul Scofield, Michael Maloney, Emma Thompson; **D:** Kenneth Branagh; **W:** Kenneth Branagh; **M:** Patrick Doyle. Academy Awards '89: Best Costume Design; British Academy Awards '89: Best Director (Branagh); National Board of Review Awards '89: Best Director (Branagh); Nominations: Academy Awards '89: Best Actor (Branagh), Best Director (Branagh). **VHS, LV** ★★★★

Henry & June Based on the diaries of writer Anais Nin, which chronicled her triangular relationship with author Henry Miller and his wife June, a relationship that provided the erotic backdrop to Miller's "Tropic of Capricorn." Set in Paris in the early '30s, the setting moves between the impecunious expatriate's cheap room on the Left bank—filled with artists, circus performers, prostitutes, and gypsies—to the conservative, well-appointed home of Nin and her husband. Captures the heady atmosphere of Miller's gay Paris; no one plays an American better than Ward (who replaced Alec Baldwin). Notable for having prompted the creation of an NC-17 rating because of its adult theme.

1990 (NC-17) 136m/C Fred Ward, Uma Thurman, Maria De Medeiros, Richard E. Grant, Kevin Spacey; **D:** Philip Kaufman, Philippe Rousselot; **W:** Philip Kaufman. Nominations: Academy Awards '90: Best Cinematography. **VHS, LV** ★★★1/2

Henry: Portrait of a Serial Killer Based on the horrific life and times of serial killer Henry Lee Lucas, this film has received wide praise for its straight-forward and uncompromising look into the minds of madmen. The film follows Henry and his room-mate Otis as they set out on mindless murder sprees (one of which they videotape. Extremely disturbing and graphic film. Unwary viewers should be aware of the grisly scenes and use their own discretion when viewing this otherwise genuinely moving film.

1990 (X) 90m/C Michael Rooker, Tom Towles, Tracy Arnold; **D:** John McNaughton; **W:** Richard Fire, John McNaughton. **VHS, Beta, LV** ★★★★

Here Come the Waves Easygoing wartime musical finds Der Bingle as a singing idol drafted into the Navy, assigned to direct WAVE shows. The crooner meets identical twins (both played by Hutton) and falls hard. Only problem is he can't tell the gals apart—and one twin can't stand him. Amusing romantic complications mix well with some spoofing of a star's life. ♪ Ac-cent-tchu-ate the Positive; I Promise You; Let's Take the Long Way Home; That Old Black Magic; There's a Fellow Waiting in Pough-keepsie; Here Come the Waves; My Mama Thinks I'm a Star; Join the Navy.

1944 99m/B Bing Crosby, Betty Hutton, Sonny Tufts, Ann Doran, Noel Neill, Mae Clarke, Gwen Crawford, Catherine Craig; **D:** Mark Sandrich; **W:** Zion Myers. **VHS** ★★★

Here Comes Mr. Jordan Montgomery is the young prizefighter killed in a plane crash because of a mix-up in heaven. He returns to life in the body of a soon-to-be murdered millionaire. Rains is the indulgent and advising guardian angel. A lovely fantasy/romance remade in 1978 as "Heaven Can Wait." Laserdisc edition includes actress Elizabeth Montgomery talking about her father Robert Montgomery as well as her television show "Bewitched."

1941 94m/B Robert Montgomery, Claude Rains, James Gleason, Evelyn Keyes, Edward Everett Horton, Rita Johnson, John Emery; **D:** Alexander Hall; **W:** Sidney Buchman, Seton I. Miller; **M:** Friedrich Hollander. Academy Awards '41: Best Story & Screenplay; National Board of Review Awards '41: 10 Best Films of the Year. **VHS, Beta, LV** ★★★★

Hester Street Set at the turn of the century, the film tells the story of a young Jewish immigrant who ventures to New York City to be with her husband. As she re-acquaints herself with her husband, she finds that he has abandoned his Old World ideals. The film speaks not only to preserving the heritage of the Jews, but to cherishing all heritages and cultures. Highly regarded upon release, unfortunately forgotten today.

1975 89m/C Carol Kane, Doris Roberts, Steven Keats, Mel Howard; **D:** Joan Micklin Silver; **M:** William Bolcom. Nominations: Academy Awards '75: Best Actress (Kane). **VHS, Beta** ★★★1/2

Hi, Mom! De Palma's follow-up to "Greetings" finds amateur pornographer/movie maker De Niro being advised by a professional in the field (Garfield) of sleazy filmmaking. De Niro films the residents of his apartment building and eventually marries one of his starlets. One of De Palma's earlier and better efforts with De Niro playing a crazy as only he can. **AKA:** Confessions of A Peeping John; Blue Manhattan.

1970 (R) 87m/C Robert De Niro, Charles Durnham, Allen (Goorwitz) Garfield, Lara Parker, Jennifer Salt, Gerrit Graham; **D:** Brian De Palma; **W:** Brian De Palma. **VHS** ★★★

The Hidden Fortress Kurosawa's tale of a warrior who protects a princess from warring feudal lords. An inspiration for George Lucas' "Star Wars" series and deserving of its excellent reputation. In Japanese with English subtitles. The laserdisc edition is letterboxed to retain the film's original integrity. **AKA:** Kakushi Toride No San Akunin; Three Rascals in the Hidden Fortress; Three Bad Men in the Hidden Fortress.

1958 139m/B JP Toshiro Mifune, Misa Vehara, Minoru Chiaki; **D:** Akira Kurosawa. Berlin International Film Festival '59: Best Director (Kurosawa). **VHS, Beta, LV** ★★★1/2

Hide in Plain Sight A distraught blue-collar worker searches for his children who disappeared when his ex-wife and her mobster husband are given new identities by federal agents. Caan's fine directorial debut is based on a true story.

1980 (PG) 96m/C James Caan, Jill Eikenberry, Robert Viharo, Kenneth

McMillan, Josef Sommer, Danny Aiello; **D:** James Caan. **VHS, Beta ★★★**

High & Low Fine Japanese film noir about a wealthy businessman who is being blackmailed by kidnappers who claim to have his son. When he discovers that they have mistakenly taken his chauffeur's son he must decide whether to face financial ruin or risk the life of a young boy. Based on an Ed McBain novel. In Japanese with English subtitles. **AKA:** Tengoku To Jigoku.
1962 (R) 143m/B *JP* Toshiro Mifune, Tatsuya Mihashi, Tatsuya Nakadai; **D:** Akira Kurosawa. **VHS, Beta, LV ★★★1/2**

High Heels An outrageous combination murder-melodrama-comedy from Almodovar. Rebecca is a TV anchorwoman in Madrid whose flamboyant singer/actress mother has returned to the city for a concert. Rebecca happens to be married to one of her mother's not-so-ex-flames. When her husband winds up dead, Rebecca confesses to his murder during her newscast—but is she telling the truth or just covering up for mom? Mix in a drag queen/judge, a dancing chorus of women prison inmates, and a peculiar police detective, and see if the plot convolutions make sense. In Spanish with English subtitles. **AKA:** Tacones Lejanos.
1991 (R) 113m/C *SP* Victoria Abril, Marisa Paredes, Miguel Bose, Feodor Atkine, Bibi Andersen, Rocio Munoz; **D:** Pedro Almodovar; **W:** Pedro Almodovar; **M:** Ryuichi Sakamoto. Cesar Awards '93: Best Foreign Film. **VHS, Beta ★★★**

High Hopes A moving yet nasty satiric comedy about a pair of ex-hippies maintaining their counterculture lifestyle in Margaret Thatcher's England, as they watch the signs of conservative "progress" overtake them and their geriatric, embittered Mum. Hilarious and mature.
1988 110m/C *GB* Philip Davis, Ruth Sheen, Edna Dore, Philip Jackson, Heather Tobias, Leslie Manville, David Bamber; **D:** Mike Leigh; **W:** Mike Leigh; **M:** Andrew Dixon. **VHS, Beta ★★★**

High Noon Landmark Western about Hadleyville town marshal Will Kane (Cooper) who faces four professional killers alone, after being abandoned to his fate by the gutless townspeople who profess to admire him. Cooper is the ultimate hero figure, his sheer presence overwhelming. Note the continuing use of the ballad written by Dimitri Tiomkin, "Do Not Forsake Me, Oh My Darlin'" (sung by Tex Ritter) to heighten the tension and ac-

tion. Laserdisc includes the original trailer, an essay by Howard Suber on audio 2, a photo essay of production stills, Carl Foreman's original notes of the film and the complete text of "The Tin Star," the story on which the film is based. ♪ High Noon (Do Not Forsake Me, Oh My Darlin').
1952 85m/B Gary Cooper, Grace Kelly, Lloyd Bridges, Lon Chaney Jr., Thomas Mitchell, Otto Kruger, Katy Jurado, Lee Van Cleef, Harry (Henry) Morgan, Robert J. Wilke, Sheb Wooley; **D:** Fred Zinnemann; **W:** Carl Foreman; **M:** Dimitri Tiomkin. Academy Awards '52: Best Actor (Cooper), Best Film Editing, Best Song ("High Noon (Do Not Forsake Me, Oh My Darlin')"), Best Score; Golden Globe Awards '53: Best Actor—Drama (Cooper), Best Supporting Actress (Jurado), Best Score; National Board of Review Awards '52: 10 Best Films of the Year; New York Film Critics Awards '52: Best Director (Zinneman), Best Film; Nominations: Academy Awards '52: Best Director (Zinneman), Best Picture, Best Screenplay. **VHS, LV ★★★★**

High Sierra Bogart is Roy "Mad Dog" Earle, an aging gangster whose last job backfires, so he's hiding out from the police in the High Sierras. Bogart's first starring role. Based on the novel by W.R. Burnett. Remade in 1955 as "I Died A Thousand Times." Also available colorized.
1941 96m/B Humphrey Bogart, Ida Lupino, Arthur Kennedy, Joan Leslie, Cornel Wilde, Henry Travers, Henry Hull; **D:** Raoul Walsh; **W:** John Huston, W.R. Burnett. National Board of Review Awards '41: 10 Best Films of the Year. **VHS, Beta, LV ★★★**

High Society A wealthy man attempts to win back his ex-wife who's about to be remarried in this enjoyable remake of "The Philadelphia Story." Letterboxed laserdisc format also includes the original movie trailer. ♪ High Society Calypso; Little One; Who Wants to Be a Millionaire?; True Love; You're Sensational; I Love You, Samantha; Now You Has Jazz; Well, Did You Evah?; Mind if I Make Love to You?.
1956 107m/C Frank Sinatra, Bing Crosby, Grace Kelly, Louis Armstrong, Celeste Holm, Sidney Blackmer, Louis Calhern; **D:** Charles Walters; **M:** Cole Porter. Nominations: Academy Awards '56: Best Song ("True Love"), Best Story, Best Original Score. **VHS, Beta, LV, 8mm ★★★**

High Tide A strong and strange drama once again coupling the star and director of "My Brilliant Career." A small-time rock 'n' roll singer who is stranded in a small beach town fortuitously meets up with her previously-abandoned teenage daughter. Acclaimed.

1987 (PG-13) 120m/C AU Judy Davis, Jan Adele, Claudia Karvan, Colin Friels, John Clayton, Mark Hembrow, Frankie J. Holden, Monica Trapaga; **D:** Gillian Armstrong; **W:** Laura Jones; **M:** Peter Best, Ricky Fataar, Mark Moffiatt. Australian Film Institute '87: Best Actress (Davis); National Society of Film Critics Awards '88: Best Actress (Davis). **VHS, Beta, LV, 8mm ★★★**

Hiroshima Haunting depiction recreates the circumstances surrounding the dropping of the first atomic bomb in 1945. Juxtaposes scenes between the U.S., Japan, and their leaders—President Truman (Welsh) and Emperor Hirohito (Umewaka)—with the development of the Manhattan Project, the bombing itself, and its consequences. Filmed primarily in B&W, with newsreel and contemporary witness interviews in color; Japanese sequences are subtitled in English. Filmed on location in Montreal, PQ, and Tokyo, Japan; made for cable TV.

1995 (PG) 180m/C JP CA Kenneth Welsh, Naohiko Umewaka, Wesley Addy, Richard Masur, Hisashi Igawa, Ken Jenkins, Jeffrey DeMunn, Leon Pownall, Saul Rubinek, Timothy West, Koji Takahashi, Kazuo Kato; **D:** Roger Spottiswoode, Koreyoshi Kurahara, Pierre Mignot; **W:** John Hopkins, Toshiro Ishido, Shohei Ando. **VHS ★★★**

Hiroshima, Mon Amour A profoundly moving drama exploring the shadow of history over the personal lives of a lonely French actress living in Tokyo and a Japanese architect with whom she's having an affair. Presented in a complex network of flashbacks. Highly influential; adapted by Marguerite Duras from her book. In Japanese with English subtitles.

1959 88m/B JP FR Emmanuelle Riva, Eiji Okada, Bernard Fresson, Stella Dassas, Pierre Barbaud; **D:** Alain Resnais; **W:** Marguerite Duras; **M:** Georges Delerue, Giovanni Fusco. National Board of Review Awards '60: 5 Best Foreign Films of the Year; New York Film Critics Awards '60: Best Foreign Film; Nominations: Academy Awards '60: Best Story & Screenplay. **VHS, Beta, 8mm ★★★★**

Hiroshima: Out of the Ashes The terrible aftermath of the bombing of Hiroshima, August, 1945, as seen through the eyes of American and Japanese soldiers, the Japanese people, and a priest. Carefully detailed and realistic, creates an amazing emotional response. Don't miss the scene in which Nelson and his

buddy find themselves surrounded by Japanese—the enemy—only to realize that their "captors" have been blinded by the blast. Created as an homage for the 45th anniversary of the bombing.

1990 (PG) 98m/C Max von Sydow, Judd Nelson, Mako, Tamlyn Tomita, Stan Egi, Sab Shimono, Noriyuki "Pat" Morita, Kim Miyori; **D:** Peter Werner. **VHS ★★★**

His First Flame A classic Langdon silent romantic comedy.

1926 62m/B Harry Langdon, Vernon Dent, Natalie Kingston; **W:** Frank Capra. **VHS, Beta ★★★**

His Girl Friday Classic, unrelentingly hilarious war-between-the-sexes comedy in which a reporter and her ex-husband editor help a condemned man escape the law—while at the same time furthering their own ends as they try to get the big scoop on political corruption in the town. One of Hawks' most furious and inventive screen combats in which women are given uniquely equal (for Hollywood) footing, with staccato dialogue and wonderful performances. Based on the Hecht-MacArthur play "The Front Page," which was originally filmed in 1931. Remade again in 1974 as "The Front Page," and in 1988 as "Switching Channels." Also available colorized.

1940 92m/B Cary Grant, Rosalind Russell, Ralph Bellamy, Gene Lockhart, John Qualen, Porter Hall, Roscoe Karns, Abner Biberman, Cliff Edwards, Billy Gilbert, Helen Mack, Ernest Truex, Clarence Kolb, Frank Jenks; **D:** Howard Hawks; **W:** Charles Lederer; **M:** Morris Stoloff. **VHS, Beta ★★★★**

History Is Made at Night A wife seeks a divorce from a jealous husband while on an Atlantic cruise; she ends up finding both true love and heartbreak in this story of a love triangle at sea.

1937 98m/B Charles Boyer, Jean Arthur, Leo Carrillo, Colin Clive; **D:** Frank Borzage. **VHS, Beta, LV ★★★**

The Hitch-Hiker Two young men off on the vacation of their dreams pick up a psychopathic hitchhiker with a right eye that never closes, even when he sleeps. Taut suspense makes this flick worth seeing.

1953 71m/B Edmond O'Brien, Frank Lovejoy, William Talman, Jose Torvay; **D:** Ida Lupino. **VHS ★★★**

Hitler's Children Two young people, a German boy and an American girl, are caught in the horror of Nazi Germany. He's attracted to Hitler's rant,

she's repelled. Exploitative yet engrossing.
1943 83m/B Tim Holt, Bonita Granville, Otto Kruger, H.B. Warner, Irving Reis, Hans Conried, Lloyd Corrigan; **D:** Edward Dmytryk. **VHS, Beta ★★★**

Hoffa The story of union organizer James R. Hoffa, who oversaw the rise of the Teamsters, a labor union composed mostly of truck drivers, from its fledgling infancy during the Great Depression to a membership of 2 million by the 1970s. Powerful performances by Nicholson in the title role and DeVito, who plays a union aide, a fictitious composite of several men who actually served Hoffa. This almost affectionate biographical treatment stands out in contrast from a career bristling with tension and violence. Proceeds through a series of flashbacks from the day Hoffa disappeared, July 30, 1975.
1992 (R) 140m/C Jack Nicholson, Danny DeVito, Armand Assante, J.T. Walsh, Frank Whaley, Kevin Anderson, John P. Ryan, Robert Prosky, Natalija Nogulich, Nicholas Pryor, John C. Reilly, Karen Young, Cliff Gorman; **D:** Danny DeVito; **W:** David Mamet; **M:** David Newman, Stephen Burum. Nominations: Academy Awards '92: Best Cinematography, Best Makeup. **VHS, LV ★★★**

Hold That Ghost Abbott and Costello inherit an abandoned roadhouse where the illicit loot of its former owner, a "rubbed out" mobster, is supposedly hidden. **AKA:** Oh, Charlie.
1941 86m/B Bud Abbott, Lou Costello, Joan Davis, Richard Carlson, Mischa Auer, The Andrews Sisters; **D:** Arthur Lubin. **VHS, Beta ★★★**

Hold Your Man Great star vehicle that turns from comedy to drama with Harlow falling for hustler Gable. Harlow and Gable are at their best in this unlikely story of a crooked couple. Direction drags at times, but snappy dialogue and the stars' personalities more than make up for it.
1933 86m/B Jean Harlow, Clark Gable, Stuart Erwin, Dorothy Burgess, Garry Owen, Paul Hurst, Elizabeth Patterson, Laura La Plante; **D:** Sam Wood; **W:** Anita Loos, Howard Emmett Rogers. **VHS ★★★**

Holiday The classically genteel screwball comedy about a rich girl who steals her sister's fiance. A yardstick in years to come for sophisticated, urbane Hollywood romanticism. Based on the play by Philip Barry, who later wrote "The Philadelphia Story." **AKA:** Free to Live; Unconventional Linda.

1938 93m/B Cary Grant, Katharine Hepburn, Doris Nolan, Edward Everett Horton, Ruth Donnelly, Lew Ayres, Binnie Barnes; **D:** George Cukor; **W:** Donald Ogden Stewart, Sidney Buchman. Nominations: Academy Awards '38: Best Interior Decoration. **VHS, Beta, LV ★★★1/2**

Holiday Inn Fred Astaire and Bing Crosby are rival song-and-dance men who decide to work together to turn a Connecticut farm into an inn, open only on holidays. Remade in 1954 as "White Christmas." ♪ White Christmas; Be Careful, It's My Heart; Plenty to Be Thankful For; Abraham, Abraham; Let's Say It With Firecrackers; I Gotta Say I Love You Cause I Can't Tell A Lie; Let's Start the New Year Right; Happy Holidays; Song of Freedom.
1942 101m/B Bing Crosby, Fred Astaire, Marjorie Reynolds, Walter Abel, Virginia Dale; **D:** Mark Sandrich. Academy Awards '42: Best Song ("White Christmas"); Nominations: Academy Awards '42: Best Story, Best Original Score. **VHS, Beta, LV ★★★**

Hollywood Canteen Star-studded extravaganza with just about every Warner Bros. lot actor in this tribute to love and nationalism. Lovesick G.I. Hutton falls for Leslie, wins a date with her in a phony raffle set up at the Hollywood Canteen, and the sparks fly right away. But he thinks she tricked him as he boards his train and she's not there to see him off. Lame story is redeemed by the talented cast and wonderful musical numbers which make this picture fly with charm and style. Before production began there were arguments over "unpatriotic" actors—labeled as such due to their lack of participation in this, and other similar movies produced at the time. ♪ Don't Fence Me In; Sweet Dreams, Sweetheart; You Can Always Tell A Yank; We're Having a Baby; What Are You Doin' the Rest of Your Life; The General Jumped At Dawn; Gettin' Corns For My Country; Voodoo Moon; Tumblin' Tumbleweeds.
1944 124m/B Robert Hutton, Dane Clark, Janis Paige, Jonathan Hale, Barbara Brown, James Flavin, Eddie Marr, Ray Teal, Bette Davis, Joan Leslie, Jack Benny, Jimmy Dorsey, Joan Crawford, John Garfield, Barbara Stanwyck, Ida Lupino, Eddie Cantor, Jack Carson, Eleanor Parker, Alexis Smith, S.Z. Sakall, Peter Lorre, Sydney Greenstreet, Helmut Dantine; **D:** Delmer Daves; **W:** Delmer Daves. Nominations: Academy Awards '44: Best Song ("Sweet Dreams Sweetheart"), Best Sound, Best Original Score. **VHS ★★★★**

Holocaust The war years of 1935 to 1945 are relived in this account of the Nazi atrocities, focusing on the Jewish Weiss family, destroyed by the monstrous crimes, and the Dorf family, Germans who thrived under the Nazi regime. Highly acclaimed riveting made-for-television mini-series with an exceptional cast. Won eight Emmys.
1978 475m/C Michael Moriarty, Fritz Weaver, Meryl Streep, James Woods, Joseph Bottoms, Tovah Feldshuh, David Warner, Ian Holm, Michael Beck, Marius Goring; **D:** Marvin J. Chomsky. **VHS, Beta** ★★★1/2

Hombre A white man in the 1880s, raised by a band of Arizona Apaches, is forced into a showdown. In helping a stagecoach full of settlers across treacherous country, he not only faces traditional bad guys, but prejudice as well. Based on a story by Elmore Leonard.
1967 111m/C Paul Newman, Fredric March, Richard Boone, Diane Cilento, Cameron Mitchell, Barbara Rush, Martin Balsam; **D:** Martin Ritt; **W:** Harriet Frank Jr., Irving Ravetch. **VHS, Beta, LV** ★★★

Home Alone Eight-year-old Kevin is accidentally left behind when his entire (and large) family makes a frantic rush for the airport. That's the plausible part. Alone and besieged by burglars, Culkin turns into a pint-sized Rambo defending his suburban castle with the resources of a boy genius with perfect timing and unlimited wherewithal. That's the implausible part. Pesci and Stern, the targets of Macauley's wrath, enact painful slapstick with considerable vigor, while Candy has a small but funny part as the leader of a polka band traveling cross-country with mom O'Hara. The highest-grossing picture of 1990, surpassing "Ghost" and "Jaws."
1990 (PG) 105m/C Macaulay Culkin, Catherine O'Hara, Joe Pesci, Daniel Stern, John Heard, Roberts Blossom, John Candy, Billie Bird, Angela Goethals, Devin Ratray, Kieran Culkin; **D:** Chris Columbus; **W:** John Hughes; **M:** John Williams. Nominations: Academy Awards '90: Best Song ("Somewhere in My Memory"), Best Original Score. **VHS, Beta, LV** ★★★

The Home and the World Another masterpiece from India's Ray, this film deals with a sheltered Indian woman who falls in love with her husband's friend and becomes politically committed in the turmoil of 1907–1908. Based on Rabindranath Tagore's novel. In Bengali with English subtitles. **AKA:** Ghare Baire.

1984 130m/C IN Victor Banerjee, Soumitra Chatterjee; **D:** Satyajit Ray. **VHS, Beta** ★★★1/2

Home from the Hill A solemn, brooding drama about a southern landowner and his troubled sons, one of whom is illegitimate. This one triumphs because of casting. Cinematography by Milton Krasner.
1960 150m/C Robert Mitchum, George Peppard, George Hamilton, Eleanor Parker, Everett Sloane, Luana Parker, Constance Ford; **D:** Vincente Minnelli; **W:** Harriet Frank Jr., Irving Ravetch. National Board of Review Awards '60: Best Actor (Mitchum). **VHS, Beta, LV** ★★★

Home of the Brave A black soldier is sent on a top secret mission in the South Pacific, but finds that he must battle with his white comrades as he is subjected to subordinate treatment and constant racial slurs. Hollywood's first outstanding statement against racial prejudice.
1949 86m/B Lloyd Bridges, James Edwards, Frank Lovejoy, Jeff Corey; **D:** Mark Robson. National Board of Review Awards '49: 10 Best Films of the Year. **VHS, Beta, LV** ★★★

Homeward Bound: The Incredible Journey Successful remake of the 1963 Disney release "The Incredible Journey." Two dogs and a cat once again try to find their way home after their family relocates, armed with greater depth of character than the original. Hard not to shed a tear for the brave animal trio who develop a trusting bond through assorted misadventures. Based on the novel by Sheila Burnford. Superior family fare.
1993 (G) 85m/C Robert Hays, Kim Greist, Jean Smart, Benj Thall, Veronica Lauren, Kevin Timothy Chevalia; **D:** Duwayne Dunham; **W:** Linda Woolverton, Carolyn Thompson; **M:** Bruce Broughton; **V:** Don Ameche, Michael J. Fox, Sally Field. **VHS, LV** ★★★

Homicide Terrific police thriller with as much thought as action; a driven detective faces his submerged Jewish identity while probing an anti-Semitic murder and a secret society. Playwright/filmmaker Mamet creates nail-biting suspense and shattering epiphanies without resorting to Hollywood glitz. Rich (often profane) dialogue includes a classic soliloquy mystically comparing a lawman's badge with a Star of David.
1991 (R) 100m/C Joe Mantegna, William H. Macy, Natalija Nogulich, Ving Rhames, Rebecca Pidgeon; **D:** David Mamet; **W:** David Mamet, Roger Deakins. National

Board of Review Awards '91: 10 Best Films of the Year. **VHS, LV, 8mm ★★★¹/₂**

Hondo In 1874, whites have broken their treaty with the Apache nation who are now preparing for war. Calvary dispatch rider Hondo Lane (Wayne) encounters Angie (Page) and her young son at an isolated ranch and warns her of the danger but she refuses to leave. After various Indian attacks, Hondo persuades Angie (they've fallen in love) to leave for California with him. Based on the story "The Gift of Cochise" by Louis L'Amour.
1953 84m/C John Wayne, Geraldine Page, Ward Bond, Michael Pate, James Arness, Rodolfo Acosta, Leo Gordon, Lee Aaker, Paul Fix; **D:** John Farrow; **W:** James Edward Grant. **VHS ★★★**

Honky Tonk A western soap opera in which ne'er-do-well Clark marries Lana and tries to live a respectable life. In this, the first of several MGM teamings between Gable and Turner, the chemistry between the two is evident. So much so in fact that Gable's then wife Carole Lombard let studio head Louis B. Mayer know that she was not at all thrilled. The public was pleased however, and made the film a hit.
1941 106m/B Clark Gable, Lana Turner, Frank Morgan, Claire Trevor, Marjorie Main, Albert Dekker, Chill Wills, Henry O'Neill, John Maxwell, Morgan Wallace, Betty Blythe, Francis X. Bushman, Veda Ann Borg; **D:** Jack Conway. **VHS, Beta ★★★**

The Hoodlum Priest Biography of the Rev. Charles Dismas Clark (Murray), a Jesuit priest who dedicated his life to working with juvenile delinquents and ex-cons in St. Louis. Dullea made his screen debut as Billy Lee Jackson, a thief who finds the straight and narrow is a hard road with more detours than he can handle. Fine performances with Murray co-scripting under the pseudonym Don Deer.
1961 101m/B Don Murray, Keir Dullea, Larry Gates, Logan Ramsey, Cindi Wood; **D:** Irvin Kershner; **W:** Don Murray, Joseph Landon, Haskell Wexler. **VHS, Beta ★★★**

Hoop Dreams Exceptional documentary follows two inner-city basketball phenoms' lives through high school as they chase their dreams of playing in the NBA. We meet Arthur Agee and William Gates as they prepare to enter St. Joseph, a predominantly white Catholic school that has offered them partial athletic scholarships. The coach tabs Gates as the "next Isaiah Thomas," alluding to the school's most famous alum. There's plenty of game footage, but the more telling and fascinating parts of the film deal with the kids' families and home life. Both players encounter dramatic reversals of fortune on and off the court, demonstrating the incredibly long odds they face.
1994 (PG-13) 169m/C Arthur Agee, William Gates; **D:** Steve James. Chicago Film Critics Awards '94: Best Film; Los Angeles Film Critics Association Awards '94: Best Feature Documentary; MTV Movie Awards '95: Best New Filmmaker Award (James); National Board of Review Awards '94: Best Feature Documentary; New York Film Critics Awards '94: Best Feature Documentary; National Society of Film Critics Awards '94: Best Feature Documentary; Sundance Film Festival '94: Audience Award; Nominations: Academy Awards '94: Best Film Editing. **VHS, LV ★★★★**

Hoosiers In Indiana, where basketball is the sport of the gods, a small town high school basketball team gets a new, but surprisingly experienced coach. He makes the team, and each person in it, better than they thought possible. Classic plot rings true because of Hackman's complex and sensitive performance coupled with Hopper's touching portrait of an alcoholic basketball fanatic.
1986 (PG) 115m/C Gene Hackman, Barbara Hershey, Dennis Hopper, David Neidorf, Sheb Wooley, Fern Parsons, Brad Boyle, Steve Hollar, Brad Long, Fred Murphy; **D:** David Anspaugh; **W:** Angelo Pizzo; **M:** Jerry Goldsmith. Los Angeles Film Critics Association Awards '86: Best Supporting Actor (Hopper); Nominations: Academy Awards '86: Best Supporting Actor (Hopper), Best Original Score. **VHS, Beta, LV ★★★**

Hopalong Cassidy In this first of a long series of "Hopalong Cassidy" films, Hoppy and his pals intervene in a brewing range war. A gang of rustlers is helped by a two-timing foreman who's playing both sides off each other. After a career in silent films, Boyd was pretty much washed up before taking on the role of Cassidy. He was originally asked to play the villain and declined, but agreed to be the good guy if the character was cleaned up. "Gabby" Hayes's stock character was killed off in this episode, but was brought back for later installments. *AKA:* Hopalong Cassidy Enters.
1935 60m/B William Boyd, James Ellison, Paula Stone, Robert Warwick, Charles Middleton, Frank McGlynn, Kenneth Thomson, George "Gabby" Hayes, James

Mason, Franklyn Farnum; **D:** Howard Bretherton. **VHS** ★★★

Hope and Glory Boorman turns his memories of WWII London into a complex and sensitive film. Father volunteers, and mother must deal with the awakening sexuality of her teen-age daughter, keep her son in line, balance the ration books, and try to make it to the bomb shelter in the middle of the night. Seen through the boy's eyes, war creates a playground of shrapnel to collect and wild imaginings come true. Nice companion film to "Empire of the Sun" and "Au Revoir Les Enfants," two more 1987 releases that explore WWII from the recollections of young boys.
1987 (PG-13) 97m/C *GB* Sebastian Rice Edwards, Geraldine Muir, Sarah Miles, Sammi Davis, David Hayman, Derrick O'Connor, Susan Wooldridge, Jean-Marc Barr, Ian Bannen, Jill Baker, Charley Boorman, Annie Leon, Katrine Boorman, Gerald James; **D:** John Boorman; **W:** John Boorman, Philippe Rousselot. British Academy Awards '87: Best Film, Best Supporting Actress (Wooldridge); Los Angeles Film Critics Association Awards '87: Best Director (Boorman), Best Film, Best Screenplay; National Board of Review Awards '87: 10 Best Films of the Year; National Society of Film Critics Awards '87: Best Cinematography, Best Director (Boorman), Best Film, Best Screenplay; Nominations: Academy Awards '87: Best Art Direction/Set Decoration, Best Cinematography, Best Director (Boorman), Best Original Screenplay, Best Picture. **VHS, Beta, LV, 8mm** ★★★½

The Horn Blows at Midnight A band trumpeter falls asleep and dreams he's a bumbling archangel, on Earth to blow the note bringing the end of the world. But a pretty girl distracts him, and . . . A wild, high-gloss, well-cast fantasy farce, uniquely subversive in its lighthearted approach to biblical Doomsday. Benny made the film notorious by acting ashamed of it in his later broadcast routines.
1945 78m/B Jack Benny, Alexis Smith, Dolores Moran, Allyn Joslyn, Reginald Gardiner, Guy Kibbee, John Alexander, Margaret Dumont; **D:** Raoul Walsh. **VHS** ★★★

The Horror Chamber of Dr. Faustus A wickedly intelligent, inventive piece of Grand Guignol about a mad doctor who kills young girls so he may graft their skin onto the face of his accidentally mutilated daughter. In French with English subtitles. *AKA:* Eyes Without a Face; Les Yeux Sans Visage; Occhi Senza Volto.
1959 84m/B *FR* Alida Valli, Pierre Brasseur, Edith Scob, Francois Guerin; **D:** Georges Franju; **M:** Maurice Jarre. **VHS, Beta, LV** ★★★★

The Horror of Dracula The first Hammer Dracula film, in which the infamous vampire is given a new, elegant and ruthless persona, as he battles Prof. Van Helsing after coming to England. Possibly the finest, most inspired version of Bram Stoker's macabre chestnut, and one that singlehandedly revived the horror genre. *AKA:* Dracula.
1958 82m/C *GB* Peter Cushing, Christopher Lee, Michael Gough, Melissa Stribling, Carol Marsh, John Van Eyssen, Valerie Gaunt; **D:** Terence Fisher; **W:** Jimmy Sangster; **M:** James Bernard. **VHS, Beta, LV** ★★★½

The Horse A moving, mature Turkish film about a father and son trying to overcome socioeconomic obstacles and their own frailties in order to make enough money to send the boy to school. In Turkish with English subtitles. *AKA:* Horse, My Horse.
1982 116m/C *TU* **D:** Ali Ozgenturk. **VHS, Beta** ★★★½

Horse Feathers Huxley College has to beef up its football team to win the championship game, and the corrupt new college president knows just how to do it. Features some of the brothers' classic routines, and the songs "Whatever It Is, I'm Against It" and "Everyone Says I Love You."
1932 67m/B Groucho Marx, Chico Marx, Harpo Marx, Zeppo Marx, Thelma Todd, David Landau, Nat Pendleton; **D:** Norman Z. McLeod. **VHS, Beta, LV** ★★★½

The Horse Thief Noted as the first movie from the People's Republic of China to be released on video, this epic tells the tale of Norbu, a man who, exiled from his people for horse thievery, is forced to wander the Tibetan countryside with his family in search of work. His son dies while he is in exile, and he, a devout Buddhist, is ultimately forced to accept tribal work in a ritual exorcism, after which he pleads to be accepted back into his clan. Beautiful and image-driven, offering a rare glimpse into the Tibet you won't see in travel brochures. Filmed on location with locals as actors. In Mandarin with English subtitles. *AKA:* Daoma Zei.
1987 88m/C *CH* **D:** Tian Zhuangzhuang. **VHS** ★★★

The Horse's Mouth An obsessive painter discovers that he must rely upon his wits to survive in London. A hilarious adaptation of the Joyce Cary novel. The laserdisc version is accompanied by an episode of the British documentary series "The Art of Film" profiling Guinness and his screen career. *AKA:* The Oracle.

1958 93m/C *GB* Alec Guinness, Kay Walsh, Robert Coote, Renee Houston, Michael Gough; *D:* Ronald Neame. National Board of Review Awards '58: 5 Best Foreign Films of the Year, Best Supporting Actress (Walsh); Nominations: Academy Awards '58: Best Adapted Screenplay. **VHS, Beta, LV ★★★**

The Hospital Cult favorite providing savage, unrelentingly sarcastic look at the workings of a chaotic metropolitan hospital beset by murders, witchdoctors, madness, and plain ineptitude.

1971 (PG) 101m/C George C. Scott, Diana Rigg, Barnard Hughes, Stockard Channing, Nancy Marchand, Richard Dysart; *D:* Arthur Hiller; *W:* Paddy Chayefsky. Academy Awards '71: Best Story & Screenplay; Berlin International Film Festival '72: Silver Prize; British Academy Awards '72: Best Screenplay; Golden Globe Awards '72: Best Screenplay; Writers Guild of America '71: Best Original Screenplay; Nominations: Academy Awards '71: Best Actor (Scott). **VHS, Beta ★★★1/2**

Hot Shots! Another entry from "The Naked Gun" team of master movie parodists, this has lots of clever sight gags but the verbal humor often plummets to the ground. Spoofs "Top Gun" and similar gung-ho air corps adventures but doesn't forget other popular films including "Dances with Wolves" and "The Fabulous Baker Boys." Sheen is very funny as ace fighter pilot Sean "Topper" Harley who's to avenge the family honor. Great when you're in the mood for laughs that don't require thought.

1991 (PG-13) 83m/C Charlie Sheen, Cary Elwes, Valeria Golino, Lloyd Bridges, Kevin Dunn, Jon Cryer, William O'Leary, Kristy Swanson, Efrem Zimbalist Jr., Bill Irwin, Heidi Swedberg, Judith Kahan, Pat Proft; *Cameos:* Charles Barkley, Bill Laimbeer; *D:* Jim Abrahams; *W:* Pat Proft, Jim Abrahams; *M:* Sylvester Levay. **VHS ★★★**

The Hound of the Baskervilles The curse of a demonic hound threatens descendants of an English noble family until Holmes and Watson solve the mystery. Also available with "Sherlock Holmes Faces Death" on laserdisc.

1939 80m/B *GB* Basil Rathbone, Nigel Bruce, Richard Greene, John Carradine, Wendy Barrie, Lionel Atwill, E.E. Clive; *D:* Sidney Lanfield. **VHS, Beta ★★★**

The Hour of the Star The poignant, highly acclaimed feature debut by Amaral, about an innocent young woman moving to the city of Sao Paulo from the impoverished countryside of Brazil, and finding happiness despite her socioeconomic failures. Based on Clarice Lispector's novel. In Portuguese with English subtitles. *AKA:* A Hora Da Estrela.

1985 96m/C *BR* Marcelia Cartaxo; *D:* Suzana Amaral. Berlin International Film Festival '85: Best Actress (Cartaxo). **VHS, Beta ★★★1/2**

Hour of the Wolf An acclaimed, surreal view into the tormented inner life of a painter as he and his wife are isolated on a small northern island. Cinematography by Sven Nykvist. In Swedish with English subtitles.

1968 89m/B *SW* Max von Sydow, Liv Ullmann, Ingrid Thulin, Erland Josephson, Gertrud Fridh, Gudrun Brost; *D:* Ingmar Bergman; *W:* Ingmar Bergman. National Board of Review Awards '68: Best Actress (Ullmann); National Society of Film Critics Awards '68: Best Director (Bergman). **VHS, Beta ★★★1/2**

House of Strangers Conte, in a superb performance, swears vengeance on his brothers, whom he blames for his father's death. Robinson, in a smaller part than you'd expect from his billing, is nevertheless excellent as the ruthless banker father who sadly reaps a reward he didn't count on. Based on Philip Yordan's "I'll Never Go There Again."

1949 101m/B Edward G. Robinson, Susan Hayward, Richard Conte, Luther Adler, Efrem Zimbalist Jr., Debra Paget; *D:* Joseph L. Mankiewicz; *W:* Philip Yordan. Cannes Film Festival '49: Best Actor (Robinson). **VHS ★★★1/2**

House of Wax A deranged sculptor (Price, who else?) builds a sinister wax museum which showcases creations that were once alive. A remake of the early horror flick "Mystery of the Wax Museum," and one of the 50s' most popular 3-D films. This one still has the power to give the viewer the creeps, thanks to another chilling performance by Price. Look for a very young Charles Bronson, as well as Carolyn "Morticia Addams" Jones as a victim.

1953 (PG) 88m/C Vincent Price, Frank Lovejoy, Carolyn Jones, Phyllis Kirk, Paul Cavanagh, Charles Bronson; *D:* Andre de Toth. **VHS, Beta, LV ★★★**

House on 92nd Street Documentary-style thriller finds federal investigator George Briggs (Nolan) contacted by German-American student

Bill Dietrich (Eythe), who's been sought out by Nazi spies. Briggs encourages Dietrich to play along and report their nefarious activities to the feds. What Dietrich discovers is that a scientist, working on the atomic bomb project, is actually a Nazi agent. Lots of atmosphere and action, with director Hathaway incorporating newsreel footage to highlight the true-to-life feel. Title refers the the house where the head of the Nazi spies resides.

1945 89m/B William Eythe, Lloyd Nolan, Signe Hasso, Gene Lockhart, Leo G. Carroll, William Post Jr., Harry Bellaver; *D:* Henry Hathaway; *W:* Barre Lyndon, John Monks Jr., Charles G. Booth; *M:* David Buttolph, Norbert Brodine. Academy Awards '45: Best Story. **VHS ★★★**

Household Saints Chronicling one family from post-WWII Little Italy through the 1970s, this is a quirky little story about sausage, religion, women, and families (not necessarily in that order). Joseph (D'Onofrio) wins his bride (Ullman) in a pinochle game, much to his superstitious Catholic mother's (Malina) chagrin. The product of that union is a slightly obsessive girl (Taylor), who sees visions and wants to be a saint. Interesting study of Italian-American families, and the roles religion and food play in the culture of Little Italy.

1993 (R) 124m/C Tracey Ullman, Vincent D'Onofrio, Lili Taylor, Judith Malina, Michael Rispoli, Victor Argo, Michael Imperioli, Rachael Bella, Illeana Douglas, Joe Grifasi; *D:* Nancy Savoca; *W:* Richard Guay, Nancy Savoca. Independent Spirit Awards '94: Best Supporting Actress (Taylor); Nominations: Independent Spirit Awards '94: Best Actor (D'Onofrio), Best Screenplay. **VHS ★★★**

Housekeeping A quiet but bizarre comedy by Forsyth (his first American film). A pair of orphaned sisters are cared for by their newly arrived eccentric, free-spirited aunt in a small and small-minded community in Oregon in the 1950s. Conventional townspeople attempt to intervene, but the sisters' relationship with their offbeat aunt has become strong enough to withstand the coercion of the townspeople. May move too slowly for some viewers. Based on novel by Marilynne Robinson.

1987 (PG) 117m/C Christine Lahti, Sarah Walker, Andrea Burchill; *D:* Bill Forsyth; *W:* Bill Forsyth; *M:* Michael Gibbs. **VHS, Beta ★★★**

How Green Was My Valley Compelling story of the trials and tribulations of a Welsh mining family, from the youthful perspective of the youngest child (played by a 13-year-old McDowall). Spans 50 years, from the turn of the century, when coal mining was a difficult but fair-paying way of life, and ends, after unionization, strikes, deaths, and child abuse, with the demise of a town and its culture. Considered by many to be director Ford's finest work. When WWII prevented shooting on location, producer Zanuck built a facsimile Welsh valley in California (although Ford, born Sean Aloysius O'Fearna, was said to have been thinking of his story as taking place in Ireland rather than Wales). Based on the novel by Richard Llewellyn.

1941 118m/C Walter Pidgeon, Maureen O'Hara, Donald Crisp, Anna Lee, Roddy McDowall, John Loder, Sara Allgood, Barry Fitzgerald, Patric Knowles, Rhys Williams, Arthur Shields, Ann Todd, Mae Marsh; *D:* John Ford; *W:* Philip Dunne; *M:* Alfred Newman. Academy Awards '41: Best Black and White Cinematography, Best Director (Ford), Best Interior Decoration, Best Picture, Best Supporting Actor (Crisp); Nominations: Academy Awards '41: Best Film Editing, Best Screenplay, Best Sound, Best Supporting Actress (Allgood), Best Original Score. **VHS, Beta ★★★★**

How the Grinch Stole Christmas Classic television Christmas special from the Dr. Seuss book about a Christmas-hating grinch who steals Christmas from the town of Whoville. Fun for the whole family.

1965 26m/C V: Boris Karloff. **VHS, Beta ★★★**

How the West Was Won A panoramic view of the American West, focusing on the trials, tribulations and travels of three generations of one family, set against the background of wars and historical events. Particularly notable for its impressive cast list and expansive western settings.

1963 (G) 165m/C John Wayne, Carroll Baker, Lee J. Cobb, Spencer Tracy, Gregory Peck, Karl Malden, Robert Preston, Eli Wallach, Henry Fonda, George Peppard, Debbie Reynolds, Carolyn Jones, Richard Widmark, James Stewart, Walter Brennan, Andy Devine, Raymond Massey, Agnes Moorehead, Harry (Henry) Morgan, Thelma Ritter, Russ Tamblyn; *D:* John Ford, Henry Hathaway, George Marshall; *W:* James R. Webb. Academy Awards '63: Best Film Editing, Best Sound, Best Story & Screenplay; National Board of Review Awards '63: 10 Best Films of the Year; Nominations: Academy Awards '63: Best Art Direction/Set Decoration (Color), Best Color Cinematography, Best Costume

Design (Color), Best Picture, Best Original Score. **VHS, Beta, LV** ★★★

How to Steal a Million Sophisticated comedy-crime caper involving a million-dollar heist of a sculpture in a Paris art museum. Hepburn and O'Toole are perfectly cast as partners in crime and Griffith gives a good performance as Hepburn's art-forging father. A charming, lightweight script and various Parisian locales combine for fun, above-average fluff. Original title was "How to Steal a Million Dollars and Live Happily Ever After." Based on the story "Venus Rising" by George Bradshaw.
1966 127m/C Audrey Hepburn, Peter O'Toole, Eli Wallach, Hugh Griffith, Charles Boyer, Fernand Gravet, Marcel Dalio, Jacques Marin; **D:** William Wyler; **W:** Harry Kurnitz; **M:** John Williams. **VHS** ★★★

How to Succeed in Business without Really Trying Classic musical comedy about a window-washer who charms his way to the top of a major company. Robert Morse repeats his Tony-winning Broadway role. Loosely based on a non-fiction book of the same title by Shepherd Mead, whose book Morse purchases on his first day of work. Excellent transfer of stage to film, with choreography by Moreda expanding Bob Fosse's original plan. Dynamite from start to finish. ♫ I Believe In You; The Company Way; Coffee Break; The Brotherhood of Man; A Secretary Is Not A Toy; Grand Old Ivy; Been A Long Day; Rosemary; Finch's Frolic.
1967 121m/C Robert Morse, Michele Lee, Rudy Vallee, Anthony Teague, George Fenneman, Maureen Arthur; **D:** David Swift; **W:** David Swift, Abe Burrows; **M:** Frank Loesser. **VHS, LV** ★★★1/2

Howard's End E.M. Forster's 1910 novel about property, privilege, class differences, and Edwardian society is brought to enchanting life by the Merchant Ivory team. A tragic series of events occurs after two impulsive sisters become involved with a working class couple and a wealthy family. Tragedy aside, this is a visually beautiful effort with subtle performances where a glance or a gesture says as much as any dialog. The winner of numerous awards and wide critical acclaim. Thompson is especially notable as the compassionate Margaret, while Hopkins plays the repressed English gentleman brilliantly.
1992 (PG) 143m/C *GB* Anthony Hopkins, Emma Thompson, Helena Bonham Carter, Vanessa Redgrave, James Wilby, Sam West, Jemma Redgrave, Nicola Duffett, Prunella Scales, Joseph Bennett; *Cameos:* Simon Callow, Tony Pierce-Roberts; **D:** James Ivory; **W:** Ruth Prawer Jhabvala. Academy Awards '92: Best Actress (Thompson), Best Adapted Screenplay, Best Art Direction/Set Decoration; British Academy Awards '92: Best Actress (Thompson); Chicago Film Critics Awards '92: Best Actress (Thompson); Golden Globe Awards '93: Best Actress—Drama (Thompson); Los Angeles Film Critics Association Awards '92: Best Actress (Thompson); National Board of Review Awards '92: Best Actress (Thompson), Best Director (Ivory), Best Film; New York Film Critics Awards '92: Best Actress (Thompson); National Society of Film Critics Awards '92: Best Actress (Thompson); Nominations: Academy Awards '92: Best Cinematography, Best Costume Design, Best Director (Ivory), Best Picture, Best Supporting Actress (Redgrave), Best Original Score; Cannes Film Festival '92: Best Film. **VHS, LV, 8mm** ★★★★

Hud Newman is a hard-driving, hard-drinking, woman-chasing young man whose life is a revolt against the principles of stern father Douglas. Neal is outstanding as the family housekeeper. Excellent photography.
1963 112m/B Paul Newman, Melvyn Douglas, Patricia Neal, Brandon de Wilde, John Ashley; **D:** Martin Ritt; **W:** Irving Ravetch, Harriet Frank Jr.; **M:** Elmer Bernstein. Academy Awards '63: Best Actress (Neal), Best Black and White Cinematography, Best Supporting Actor (Douglas); National Board of Review Awards '63: 10 Best Films of the Year, Best Actress (Neal), Best Supporting Actor (Douglas); Nominations: Academy Awards '63: Best Actor (Newman), Best Adapted Screenplay, Best Art Direction/Set Decoration (B & W), Best Director (Ritt). **VHS, Beta, LV** ★★★★

The Human Comedy A small-town boy experiences love and loss and learns the meaning of true faith during WWII. Straight, unapologetically sentimental version of the William Saroyan novel.
1943 117m/B Mickey Rooney, Frank Morgan, James Craig, Fay Bainter, Ray Collins, Donna Reed, Van Johnson, Barry Nelson, Robert Mitchum, Jackie "Butch" Jenkins; **D:** Clarence Brown; **W:** William Saroyan. Academy Awards '43: Best Story; Nominations: Academy Awards '43: Best Actor (Rooney), Best Black and White Cinematography, Best Director (Brown), Best Picture. **VHS, Beta, LV** ★★★1/2

Humoresque A talented but struggling young musician finds a patron in the married, wealthy, and older Crawford. His appreciation is not as romantic as she hoped. Stunning performance from Crawford, with excellent supporting cast, including a young Robert Blake. Fine music sequences (Isaac Stern dubbed the violin), and lush production values. Laserdisc version features the original movie trailer.

1946 123m/B Joan Crawford, John Garfield, Oscar Levant, J. Carrol Naish, Joan Chandler, Tom D'Andrea, Peggy Knudsen, Ruth Nelson, Craig Stevens, Paul Cavanagh, Richard Gaines, John Abbott, Robert (Bobby) Blake; **D:** Jean Negulesco. Nominations: Academy Awards '46: Best Original Score. **VHS, LV** ★★★1/2

The Hunchback of Notre Dame The first film version of Victor Hugo's novel about the tortured hunchback bellringer of Notre Dame Cathedral, famous for the contortions of Lon Chaney's self-transformations via improvised makeup. Also available at 68 minutes.

1923 100m/B Lon Chaney Sr., Patsy Ruth Miller, Norman Kerry, Ernest Torrence; **D:** Wallace Worsley. **VHS, LV** ★★★

The Hunchback of Notre Dame Best Hollywood version of the Victor Hugo classic, infused with sweep, sadness and an attempt at capturing a degree of spirited, Hugoesque detail. Laughton is Quasimodo, a deformed Parisian bellringer, who provides sanctuary to a young gypsy woman accused by church officials of being a witch. The final scene of the townspeople storming the cathedral remains a Hollywood classic. Great performances all around; the huge facade of the Notre Dame cathedral was constructed on a Hollywood set for this film. Remake of several earlier films, including 1923's Lon Chaney silent. Remade in 1957 and later for television.

1939 117m/B Charles Laughton, Maureen O'Hara, Edmond O'Brien, Cedric Hardwicke, Thomas Mitchell, George Zucco, Alan Marshal, Walter Hampden, Harry Davenport, Curt Bois, George Tobias, Rod La Rocque; **D:** William Dieterle; **W:** Sonya Levien, Bruno Frank; **M:** Alfred Newman. Nominations: Academy Awards '39: Best Sound, Best Score. **VHS, Beta, LV** ★★★★

The Hunchback of Notre Dame Animated/musical version of Victor Hugo's story about deformed bellringer Quasimodo (Hulce) and his love for the beautiful gypsy Esmerelda (Moore). The original isn't exactly fun fare, but you can expect Disney to find a way to leave everybody

humming (and happy). The sweeping music was provided by "Pocahontas" tunesmiths Menken and Schwartz. Comic relief is supplied by three gargoyles, companions to Quasimodo, who are voiced wonderfully by Alexander, Kimbrough, and Wickes. Wickes, 85, died six weeks after voicing her role. Looks like another boatload of box office, merchandising, and video sale cash is making its way into old Walt's vaults.

1996 (G) 86m/C V: Tom Hulce, Demi Moore, Kevin Kline, Charles Kimbrough, Jason Alexander, Mary Wickes, David Ogden Stiers, Tony Jay; **D:** Kirk Wise, Gary Trousdale; **M:** Alan Menken, Stephen Schwartz. Nominations: Golden Globe Awards '97: Best Score. **VHS** ★★★

The Hunt for Red October Based on Tom Clancy's blockbuster novel, a high-tech Cold War yarn about a Soviet nuclear sub turning rogue and heading straight for U.S. waters, as both the U.S. and the U.S.S.R. try to stop it. Complicated, ill-plotted potboiler that succeeds breathlessly due to the cast and McTiernan's tommy-gun direction. Introduces the character of CIA analyst Jack Ryan, who returns in "Patriot Games," though in the guise of Harrison Ford.

1990 (PG) 137m/C Sean Connery, Alec Baldwin, Richard Jordan, Scott Glenn, Joss Ackland, Sam Neill, James Earl Jones, Peter Firth, Tim Curry, Courtney B. Vance, Jeffrey Jones, Fred Dalton Thompson; **D:** John McTiernan; **W:** Larry Ferguson, Donald Stewart, Jan De Bont; **M:** Basil Poledouris. Academy Awards '90: Best Sound Effects Editing; Nominations: Academy Awards '90: Best Film Editing, Best Sound. **VHS, Beta, LV, 8mm, CD-I** ★★★

Hurricane A couple on the run from the law are aided by a hurricane and are able to build a new life for themselves on an idyllic island. Filmed two years before the Academy's "special effects" award came into being, but displaying some of the best effects of the decade. Boringly remade in 1979.

1937 102m/B Jon Hall, Dorothy Lamour, Mary Astor, Sir C. Aubrey Smith, Raymond Massey; **D:** John Ford. Academy Awards '37: Best Sound; Nominations: Academy Awards '37: Best Supporting Actor (Mitchell), Best Original Score. **VHS, Beta, LV** ★★★

Husbands and Wives Art imitates life as Allen/Farrow relationship dissolves onscreen (and off) and Woody becomes involved with young student. Mature, penetrating look at modern pair bonding and loneliness offers more painful honesty and sadness than outright laughs, though still retains essential Allen charm. Stylistically burdened by experiment with pseudo-documentary telling of tale and spasmodic hand-held cameras that annoy more than entertain. Excellent, intriguing cast, notably Davis as the overwhelming, overbearing wife/friend. Trailers became unintentionally funny in light of the highly publicized personal problems of Allen and Farrow. **1992 (R) 107m/C** Woody Allen, Mia Farrow, Judy Davis, Sydney Pollack, Liam Neeson, Juliette Lewis, Lysette Anthony, Blythe Danner, Carlo DiPalma; *D:* Woody Allen; *W:* Woody Allen. British Academy Awards '92: Best Original Screenplay; Chicago Film Critics Awards '93: Best Supporting Actress (Davis); Los Angeles Film Critics Association Awards '92: Best Supporting Actress (Davis); National Board of Review Awards '92: Best Supporting Actress (Davis); National Society of Film Critics Awards '92: Best Supporting Actress (Davis); Nominations: Academy Awards '92: Best Original Screenplay, Best Supporting Actress (Davis). **VHS, LV** ★★★½

Hush, Hush, Sweet Charlotte A fading southern belle finds out the truth about her fiance's murder when the case is reopened 37 years later by her cousin in an elaborate plot to drive her crazy. Grisly and superbly entertaining Southern Gothic horror tale, with vivid performances from the aging leads. **1964 134m/B** Bette Davis, Olivia de Havilland, Joseph Cotten, Agnes Moorehead, Mary Astor, Bruce Dern; *D:* Robert Aldrich. Edgar Allan Poe Awards '64: Best Screenplay; Golden Globe Awards '65: Best Supporting Actress (Moorehead); Nominations: Academy Awards '64: Best Art Direction/Set Decoration (B & W), Best Black and White Cinematography, Best Costume Design (B & W), Best Film Editing, Best Song ("Hush, Hush, Sweet Charlotte"), Best Supporting Actress (Moorehead), Best Original Score. **VHS, Beta, LV** ★★★

The Hustler The original story of Fast Eddie Felsen and his adventures in the seedy world of professional pool. Newman plays the naive, talented and self-destructive Felsen perfectly, Laurie is oustanding as his lover, and Gleason epitomizes the pool great Minnesota Fats. Rivetingly atmospheric and exquisitely photographed. Parent to the reprise "The Color of Money," made 25 years later. **1961 134m/B** Paul Newman, Jackie Gleason, Piper Laurie, George C. Scott, Myron McCormick, Murray Hamilton, Michael Constantine, Jake La Motta, Vincent Gardenia; *D:* Robert Rossen; *W:* Robert Rossen. Academy Awards '61: Best Art Direction/Set Decoration (B & W), Best Black and White Cinematography; British Academy Awards '61: Best Actor (Newman), Best Film; National Board of Review Awards '61: 10 Best Films of the Year, Best Supporting Actor (Gleason); Nominations: Academy Awards '61: Best Actor (Newman), Best Actress (Laurie), Best Adapted Screenplay, Best Director (Rossen), Best Picture, Best Supporting Actor (Gleason, Scott). **VHS, Beta, LV** ★★★★

Hustling A reporter writing a series of articles on prostitution in New York City takes an incisive look at their unusual and sometimes brutal world. Notable performance by Remick as the reporter and Clayburgh as a victimized hooker. Made for TV and based on a novel by Gail Sheehy. **1975 96m/C** Jill Clayburgh, Lee Remick, Alex Rocco, Monte Markham; *D:* Joseph Sargent. **VHS, Beta** ★★★

I Am a Camera A young English writer develops a relationship with a reckless young English girl in Berlin during the 1930s. Based on the Berlin stories by Christopher Isherwood, later musicalized as "Cabaret." **1955 99m/B** *GB* Julie Harris, Shelley Winters, Laurence Harvey, Patrick McGoohan; *D:* Henry Cornelius; *M:* Malcolm Arnold. **VHS, Beta** ★★★

I Am a Fugitive from a Chain Gang WWI veteran Muni returns home with dreams of traveling across America. After a brief stint as a clerk, he strikes out on his own. Near penniless, Muni meets up with a tramp who takes him to get a hamburger. He becomes an unwilling accomplice when the bum suddenly robs the place. Convicted and sentenced to a Georgia chain gang, he's brutalized and degraded, though he eventually escapes and lives the life of a criminal on the run. Based on the autobiography by Robert E. Burns. Brutal docu-details combine with powerhouse performances to create a classic. Timeless and thought-provoking. *AKA:* I Am a Fugitive From the Chain Gang. **1932 93m/B** Paul Muni, Glenda Farrell, Helen Vinson, Preston Foster, Edward Ellis, Allen Jenkins; *D:* Mervyn LeRoy; *W:* Howard J. Green. National Board of Review Awards '32: 10 Best Films of the Year; Nominations: Academy Awards '33: Best Actor (Muni), Best Picture, Best Sound. **VHS, Beta** ★★★★

I Know Where I'm Going A young woman (Hiller), who believes that money brings happiness, is on the verge of marrying a rich old man, until she meets a handsome naval officer (Livesey) and finds a happy, simple life. Early on the female lead appears in a dream sequence filmed in the mode of surrealist painter Salvador Dali and avant garde director Luis Bunuel. Scottish setting and folk songs give a unique flavor. Brown provides a fine performance as a native Scot.

1945 91m/B *GB* Roger Livesey, Wendy Hiller, Finlay Currie, Pamela Brown; *D:* Michael Powell. **VHS, Beta, LV** ★★★

I Know Why the Caged Bird Sings A black writer's memories of growing up in the rural South during the 1930s. Strong performances from Rolle and Good. Made-for-television film is based on the book by Maya Angelou.

1979 100m/C Diahann Carroll, Ruby Dee, Esther Rolle, Roger E. Mosley, Paul Benjamin, Constance Good; *D:* Fielder Cook. **VHS, Beta** ★★★

I Live in Fear Nakajima, an elderly, wealthy owner of a foundry, becomes increasingly fearful of atomic war and the threats to his family's safety. He tries to persuade them to leave Japan and move with him to Brazil but they fear the family will be ruined financially. Nakajima then burns down his foundry to force his children to move but instead they go to court and have him declared mentally incompetent. He is placed in an institution where he finds peace in the delusion that he has escaped to another planet and that the Earth has indeed suffered a nuclear holocaust. Provocative look at the fear of atomic warfare and radiation. In Japanese with English subtitles. *AKA:* Record of a Living Being; Kimono No Kiroku.

1955 105m/C *JP* Toshiro Mifune, Takashi Shimura, Eiko Miyoshi, Haruko Togo; *D:* Akira Kurosawa. **VHS** ★★★

I Love You Again A classic screwball comedy with Powell and Loy working together (wonderfully) in something other than their "Thin Man" series. Powell is a gloomy businessman who's about to be divorced by Loy. But after an accident it turns out Powell had been suffering from amnesia and has now regained his memory (which he keeps a secret). It seems Mr. Respectable used to be a con man and he decides to revert to his criminal ways. He also doesn't remember Loy but falls instantly in love

with her and must decide what kind of life he wants. Witty dialog, amusing situations, fine direction.

1940 97m/B William Powell, Myrna Loy, Frank McHugh, Edmund Lowe; *D:* Woodbridge S. Van Dyke. **VHS, LV** ★★★1/2

I Married a Witch A witch burned at the stake during the Salem witch trials comes back to haunt the descendants of her accusers and gets romantic with one of them. Wonderfully played fantasy/comedy.

1942 77m/B Veronica Lake, Fredric March, Susan Hayward, Broderick Crawford; *D:* Rene Clair. Nominations: Academy Awards '42: Best Original Score. **VHS, Beta, LV** ★★★

I Never Promised You a Rose Garden A disturbed 16-year-old girl spirals down into madness and despair while a hospital psychiatrist struggles to bring her back to life. Based on the Joanne Greenberg best-seller. Compelling and unyielding exploration of the clinical treatment of schizophrenia.

1977 (R) 90m/C Kathleen Quinlan, Bibi Andersson, Sylvia Sidney, Diane Varsi; *D:* Anthony Page; *W:* Gavin Lambert, Lewis John Carlino. Nominations: Academy Awards '77: Best Adapted Screenplay. **VHS, Beta** ★★★

I Never Sang for My Father A devoted son must choose between caring for his cantankerous but well-meaning father, and moving out West to marry the divorced doctor whom he loves. While his mother wants him to stay near home, his sister, who fell out of her father's favor by marrying out of the family faith, argues that he should do what he wants. An introspective, stirring story based on the Robert Anderson play.

1970 (PG) 90m/C Gene Hackman, Melvyn Douglas, Estelle Parsons, Dorothy Stickney; *D:* Gilbert Cates; *W:* Robert Anderson. National Board of Review Awards '70: 10 Best Films of the Year; Writers Guild of America '70: Best Adapted Screenplay; Nominations: Academy Awards '70: Best Actor (Douglas), Best Adapted Screenplay, Best Supporting Actor (Hackman). **VHS, Beta, LV** ★★★1/2

I Remember Mama A true Hollywood heart tugger chronicling the life of a Norwegian immigrant family living in San Francisco during the early 1900s. Dunne triumphs as the mother, with a perfect Norwegian accent, and provides her family with wisdom and inspiration. A kindly father and four children round out the nuclear family. A host of oddball characters regularly pop in on the household—three high-strung aunts and an eccentric doctor who treats a live-in uncle. Adapted from John Van Druten's stage play, based on Kathryn Forbes memoirs "Mama's Bank Account;" a TV series came later.

1948 95m/B Irene Dunne, Barbara Bel Geddes, Oscar Homolka, Ellen Corby, Cedric Hardwicke, Edgar Bergen, Rudy Vallee, Barbara O'Neil, Florence Bates; **D:** George Stevens. Golden Globe Awards '49: Best Supporting Actress (Corby); Nominations: Academy Awards '48: Best Actress (Dunne), Best Black and White Cinematography, Best Supporting Actor (Homolka), Best Supporting Actress (Corby, Bel Geddes). **VHS, Beta, LV** ★★★1/2

I Shot Andy Warhol Based on a true story, this black comedy focuses on the 15 minutes of fame achieved by Valerie Solanas, the woman who shot pop artist Andy Warhol for ignoring her in 1968. Taylor manages to re-create the more unpleasant aspects of Solanas without making her completely unsympathetic. Writer/director Mary Harron, making her feature film debut, does a wonderful job of re-creating the drugged-out world Warhol and his cohorts inhabited. Her script succeeds by attempting to understand Solanas's actions, while not excusing or sensationalizing them. Features music by former Velvet Underground member, Cale.

1996 100m/C Lili Taylor, Stephen Dorff, Jared Harris, Martha Plimpton, Donovan Leitch, Tahnee Welch, Michael Imperioli, Lothaire Bluteau, Anna Thompson, Peter Friedman, Jill Hennessey; **M:** John Cale; **D:** Mary Harron; **W:** Daniel Minahan, Mary Harron. Nominations: Independent Spirit Awards '97: Best First Feature. **VHS** ★★★

I Shot Jesse James In his first film, director Fuller breathes characteristically feverish, maddened fire into the story of Bob Ford (Ireland) after he killed the notorious outlaw. An essential moment in Fuller's unique, America-as-tabloid-nightmare canon, and one of the best anti-westerns ever made.

1949 83m/B John Ireland, Barbara Britton, Preston Foster, Reed Hadley; **D:** Samuel Fuller; **W:** Samuel Fuller. **VHS, Beta** ★★★

I Vitelloni Fellini's semi-autobiographical drama, argued by some to be his finest work. Five young men grow up in a small Italian town. As they mature, four of them remain in Romini and limit their opportunities by roping themselves off from the rest of the world. The characters are multi-dimensional, including a loafer who is supported by his sister and a young stud who impregnates a local woman. The script has some brilliant insights into youth, adulthood and what's in between. **AKA:** The Young and the Passionate; Vitelloni; Spivs.

1953 104m/B *IT* Alberto Sordi, Franco Interlenghi, Franco Fabrizi, Leopoldo Trieste; **D:** Federico Fellini; **W:** Federico Fellini, Ennio Flaiano; **M:** Nino Rota. Nominations: Academy Awards '57: Best Story & Screenplay. **VHS, LV** ★★★1/2

I Walked with a Zombie The definitive and eeriest of the famous Val Lewton/Jacques Tourneur horror films. Dee, a young American nurse, comes to Haiti to care for the catatonic matriarch of a troubled family. Local legends bring themselves to bear when the nurse takes the ill woman to a local voodoo ceremony for "healing." Superb, startling images and atmosphere create a unique context for this serious "Jane Eyre"-like story; its reputation has grown through the years.

1943 69m/B Frances Dee, Tom Conway, James Ellison, Christine Gordon, Edith Barrett, Darby Jones, Sir Lancelot; **D:** Jacques Tourneur. **VHS, Beta, LV** ★★★1/2

I Want to Live! Based on a scandalous true story, Hayward gives a riveting, Oscar-winning performance as a prostitute framed for the murder of an elderly woman and sentenced to death in the gas chamber. Producer Walter Wanger's seething indictment of capital punishment.

1958 120m/B Susan Hayward, Simon Oakland, Theodore Bikel; **D:** Robert Wise; **M:** Johnny Mandel. Academy Awards '58: Best Actress (Hayward); Golden Globe Awards '59: Best Actress—Drama (Hayward); New York Film Critics Awards '58: Best Actress (Hayward); Nominations: Academy Awards '58: Best Adapted Screenplay, Best Black and White Cinematography, Best Director (Wise), Best Sound. **VHS, Beta, LV** ★★★

I Was a Male War Bride Hilarious WWII comedy. French officer Grant falls in love with and marries WAC lieutenant Sheridan in occupied Europe. Planning to leave the continent and settle down in the U.S., the couple hits a roadblock of red tape and Grant must cross-dress in order to accompany his bride on the troop ship taking her home. Worth watching for Grant's performance alone. Based on the novel by Henri Rochard.

1949 105m/B Cary Grant, Ann Sheridan, Randy Stuart, Kenneth Tobey, William Neff, Marion Marshall; **D:** Howard Hawks; **W:**

Charles Lederer, Leonard Spigelgass, William Neff; **M:** Cyril Mockridge. **VHS** ★★★

I Will Fight No More Forever A vivid recounting of the epic true story of the legendary Chief Joseph, who led the Nez Perce tribe on a 1,600-mile trek to Canada in 1877. Disturbing and powerful. Made for television.
1975 100m/C James Whitmore, Ned Romero, Sam Elliott; **D:** Richard T. Heffron. **VHS, Beta** ★★★

The Idiot Dostoevski's Russian novel is transported by Kurosawa across two centuries to post-war Japan, where the madness and jealousy continue to rage. In Japanese with English subtitles.
1951 166m/B Toshiro Mifune, Masayuki Mori, Setsuko Hara, Yoshiko Kuga, Takashi Shimura; **D:** Akira Kurosawa. **VHS** ★★★★

Idiot's Delight At an Alpine hotel, a song and dance man meets a gorgeous Russian countess who reminds him of a former lover. Incredibly, Gable sings and dances through "Puttin' on the Ritz," the film's big highlight. Based on the Pulitzer Prize-winning play by Robert Sherwood.
1939 107m/B Clark Gable, Norma Shearer, Burgess Meredith, Edward Arnold; **D:** Clarence Brown. **VHS, Beta, LV** ★★★

If . . . Three unruly seniors at a British boarding school refuse to conform. A popular, anarchic indictment of staid British society, using the same milieu as Vigo's "Zero de Conduite," with considerably more violence. The first of Anderson and McDowell's trilogy, culminating in "O Lucky Man!" and "Britannia Hospital." In color and black and white.
1969 (R) 111m/C *GB* Malcolm McDowell, David Wood, Christine Noonan, Richard Warwick, Robert Swann, Arthur Lowe, Mona Washbourne, Graham Crowden, Simon Ward; **D:** Lindsay Anderson. Cannes Film Festival '69: Best Film. **VHS, Beta, LV** ★★★★

Ikiru When a clerk finds out he is dying of cancer, he decides to build a children's playground and give something of himself back to the world. Highly acclaimed, heartbreaking drama from the unusually restrained Kurosawa; possibly his most "eastern" film. In Japanese with English subtitles. **AKA:** To Live.
1952 134m/B *JP* Takashi Shimura, Nobuo Kaneko, Kyoko Seki, Miki Odagiri, Yunosuke Ito; **D:** Akira Kurosawa. **VHS, Beta, LV** ★★★★

I'll Cry Tomorrow Hayward brilliantly portrays actress Lillian Roth as she descends into alcoholism and then tries to overcome her addiction. Based on Roth's memoirs. ♪ Sing You Sinners; When The Red Red Robin Comes Bob Bob Bobbin' Along; Happiness Is Just a Thing Called Joe; Vagabond King Waltz.
1955 119m/B Susan Hayward, Richard Conte, Eddie Albert, Jo Van Fleet, Margo, Don Taylor, Ray Danton, Veda Ann Borg; **D:** Daniel Mann; **M:** Alex North. Academy Awards '55: Best Costume Design (B & W); Cannes Film Festival '56: Best Actress (Hayward); Nominations: Academy Awards '55: Best Actress (Hayward), Best Art Direction/Set Decoration (B & W), Best Black and White Cinematography. **VHS, Beta, LV** ★★★

The Illusion Travels by Streetcar Odd but enchanting story of two men who restore a streetcar, only to find that it will not be used by the city. In a gesture of defiance, they steal the streetcar and take it for one last ride, picking up an interesting assortment of characters along the way. In Spanish with English subtitles. Not released in the U.S. until 1977. **AKA:** La Illusion en Travnia.
1953 90m/B *MX* Lilia Prado, Carlos Navarro, Domingo Soler, Fernando Soto, Agustin Isunza, Miguel Manzano; **D:** Luis Bunuel. **VHS** ★★★

I'm All Right Jack Sellers plays a pompous communist union leader in this hilarious satire of worker-management relations. Based on Alan Hackney's novel "Private Life."
1959 101m/B Peter Sellers, Ian Carmichael, Terry-Thomas, Victor Maddern; **D:** John Boulting. British Academy Awards '59: Best Actor (Sellers), Best Screenplay; National Board of Review Awards '60: 5 Best Foreign Films of the Year. **VHS, Beta** ★★★

I'm Gonna Git You Sucka Parody of "blaxploitation" films popular during the '60s and '70s. Funny and laced with out-right bellylaughs. A number of stars who made "blaxploitation" films, including Jim Brown, take part in the gags.
1988 (R) 89m/C Keenen Ivory Wayans, Bernie Casey, Steve James, Isaac Hayes, Jim Brown, Ja'net DuBois, Anne-Marie Johnson, Antonio Fargas, Eve Plumb, John Vernon, Clu Gulager, Kadeem Hardison, Damon Wayans, Gary Owens, Clarence Williams III, David Alan Grier, Kim Wayans, Robin Harris, Chris Rock, Dawnn Lewis, Jester Hairston; **Cameos:** Robert Townsend; **D:** Keenen Ivory Wayans; **W:** Keenen Ivory Wayans; **M:** David Michael Frank. **VHS, Beta, LV** ★★★

I'm No Angel "Beulah, peel me a grape." Well, you'd be hungry too if you spent your time eyeing playboy Grant as West does. She's a circus floozy who's prone to extorting money from her men (after hashing over their shortcomings with her seen-it-all-maid, the aforementioned Beulah). However, after wooing Grant, she sues for breach of promise. This leads to a comic courtroom scene with Grant bringing in all West's ex-lovers as witnesses. Grant's second film with West, following "She Done Him Wrong."
1933 88m/B Mae West, Cary Grant, Gregory Ratoff, Edward Arnold, Ralf Harolde, Kent Taylor, Gertrude Michael, Russell Hopton, Dorothy Peterson, William B. Davidson, Gertrude Howard; **D:** Wesley Ruggles; **W:** Mae West. **VHS** ★★★

Imitation of Life Remake of the successful 1939 Claudette Colbert outing of the same title, and based on Fanny Hurst's novel, with a few plot changes. Turner is a single mother, more determined to achieve acting fame and fortune than function as a parent. Her black maid, Moore, is devoted to her own daughter (Kohner), but loses her when the girl discovers she can pass for white. When Turner discovers that she and her daughter are in love with the same man, she realizes how little she knows her daughter, and how much the two of them have missed by not having a stronger relationship. Highly successful at the box office.
1959 124m/C Lana Turner, John Gavin, Troy Donahue, Sandra Dee, Juanita Moore, Susan Kohner; **D:** Douglas Sirk. Golden Globe Awards '60: Best Supporting Actress (Kohner); Nominations: Academy Awards '59: Best Supporting Actress (Kohner), Best Supporting Actress (Moore). **VHS, Beta** ★★★

The Immigrant Chaplin portrays a newly arrived immigrant who falls in love with the first girl he meets. Silent with musical soundtrack added.
1917 20m/B Charlie Chaplin; **D:** Charlie Chaplin. **VHS, Beta** ★★★1/2

Importance of Being Earnest Fine production of classic Oscar Wilde comedy-of-manners. Cast couldn't be better or the story funnier.
1952 95m/C Michael Redgrave, Edith Evans, Margaret Rutherford, Michael Denison, Joan Greenwood; **D:** Anthony Asquith. **VHS, Beta** ★★★

In a Lonely Place Bogart is outstanding as a volatile Hollywood screenwriter who has an affair with starlet Grahame while under suspi-

cion of murder. Offbeat, yet superb film noir entry became one of the most memorable of the genre. Expertly directed by Ray. Based on the novel by Dorothy B. Hughes and an adaptation by Edmund H. North.
1950 93m/B Humphrey Bogart, Gloria Grahame, Frank Lovejoy, Carl Benton Reid, Art Smith, Jeff Donnell; **D:** Nicholas Ray; **W:** Andrew Solt. **VHS, Beta** ★★★1/2

In Cold Blood Truman Capote's supposedly factual novel provided the basis for this hard-hitting docudrama about two ex-cons who ruthlessly murder a Kansas family in 1959 in order to steal their non-existent stash of money. Blake is riveting as one of the killers.
1967 133m/B Robert (Bobby) Blake, Scott Wilson, John Forsythe; **D:** Richard Brooks; **W:** Richard Brooks; **M:** Quincy Jones, Conrad Hall. National Board of Review Awards '67: 10 Best Films of the Year, Best Director (Brooks); Nominations: Academy Awards '67: Best Adapted Screenplay, Best Cinematography, Best Director (Brooks), Best Original Score. **VHS, Beta, LV** ★★★1/2

In Old Chicago The O'Leary family travels to Chicago to seek their fortune, with mom working as a washerwoman to support her sons. Brothers Power and Ameche become power-broking rivals and when mom comes to break up a brawl between the two, she neglects to properly restrain the family cow. This leads to the great Chicago fire of 1871, supposedly started when the cow kicks over a lantern and sets the barn ablaze. The city burns down in a spectacular 20-minute sequence. Based on the story "We the O'Learys" by Niven Busch.
1938 115m/B Tyrone Power, Alice Faye, Don Ameche, Alice Brady, Andy Devine, Brian Donlevy, Phyllis Brooks, Tom Brown, Sidney Blackmer, Gene Reynolds, Berton Churchill, Bobs Watson; **D:** Henry King; **W:** Lamar Trotti, Sonya Levien. Nominations: Academy Awards '38: Best Picture. **VHS** ★★★

In the Good Old Summertime This pleasant musical version of "The Shop Around the Corner" tells the story of two bickering co-workers who are also anonymous lovelorn pen pals. Minnelli made her second screen appearance at 18 months in the final scene. ♪ I Don't Care; Meet Me Tonight In Dreamland; Play That Barbershop Chord; In the Good Old Summertime; Put Your Arms Around Me Honey; Wait Till the Sun Shines Nellie; Chicago; Merry Christmas.

1949 104m/C Judy Garland, Van Johnson, S.Z. Sakall, Buster Keaton, Spring Byington, Liza Minnelli, Clinton Sundberg; **D:** Robert Z. Leonard. **VHS, Beta, LV ★★★**

In the Heat of the Night A wealthy industrialist in a small Mississippi town is murdered. A black homicide expert is asked to help solve the murder, despite resentment on the part of the town's chief of police. Powerful script with underlying theme of racial prejudice is served well by taut direction and powerhouse performances. Poitier's memorable character Virgil Tibbs appeared in two more pictures, "They Call Me Mister Tibbs" and "The Organization."
1967 109m/C Sidney Poitier, Rod Steiger, Warren Oates, Lee Grant; **D:** Norman Jewison; **W:** Stirling Silliphant, Haskell Wexler; **M:** Quincy Jones. Academy Awards '67: Best Actor (Steiger), Best Film Editing, Best Picture, Best Sound; British Academy Awards '67: Best Actor (Steiger); Edgar Allan Poe Awards '67: Best Screenplay; Golden Globe Awards '68: Best Actor—Drama (Steiger), Best Film—Drama, Best Screenplay; New York Film Critics Awards '67: Best Actor (Steiger), Best Director (Jewison), Best Film; National Society of Film Critics Awards '67: Best Actor (Steiger), Best Cinematography; Nominations: Academy Awards '67: Best Director (Jewison). **VHS, Beta, LV ★★★1/2**

In the Line of Fire Aging Secret Service agent meets his match in a spooky caller who threatens his honor and the president in an exciting, fast paced cat and mouse game. Terrific performance by Eastwood includes lots of dry humor and an unscripted emotional moment, but is nearly overshadowed by Malkovich's menacing bad guy. Eerie special effects add to the mood. The Secret Service cooperated and most scenes are believable, with a few Hollywood exceptions; the end result clearly pays homage to the agents who protect our presidents. Intriguing trailer showed the number "6" in "1963" slowly turning to "9" to become "1993." The seventh highest grossing movie of 1993.
1993 (R) 128m/C Clint Eastwood, John Malkovich, Rene Russo, Dylan McDermott, Gary Cole, Fred Dalton Thompson, John Mahoney, Gregory Alan Williams; **D:** Wolfgang Petersen; **W:** Jeff Maguire; **M:** Ennio Morricone, John Bailey. Nominations: Academy Awards '93: Best Film Editing, Best Original Screenplay, Best Supporting Actor (Malkovich); Golden Globe Awards '94: Best Supporting Actor (Malkovich); MTV Movie Awards '94: Best Villain (Malkovich). **VHS, LV, 8mm ★★★1/2**

In the Name of the Father Compelling true story of Gerry Conlon and the Guildford Four, illegally imprisoned in 1974 by British officials after a tragic IRA bombing in Guildford, near London. The British judicial system receives a black eye, but so does the horror and cruelty of IRA terrorism. Politics and family life in a prison cell share the focus, as Sheridan captures superior performances from Day-Lewis and Postlethwaite (beware the thick Belfast brogue). Thompson was accused of pro-IRA sympathies in the British press for her role as the lawyer who believed in Conlon's innocence. Adapted from "Proved Innocent," Conlon's prison memoirs; reunites Sheridan and Day-Lewis after "My Left Foot." Includes original songs by U2's Bono, with a haunting theme sung by Sinead O'Connor.
1993 (R) 133m/C *GB IR* Daniel Day-Lewis, Peter Postlethwaite, Emma Thompson, John Lynch, Corin Redgrave, Beatie Edney, John Benfield, Paterson Joseph, Marie Jones, Gerard McSorley, Frank Harper, Mark Sheppard, Don Baker, Britta Smith, Aidan Grennell, Daniel Massey, Bosco Hogan; **D:** Jim Sheridan; **W:** Jim Sheridan, Terry George; **M:** Trevor Jones, Bono, Sinead O'Connor. Berlin International Film Festival '94: Golden Berlin Bear; Nominations: Academy Awards '93: Best Actor (Day-Lewis), Best Adapted Screenplay, Best Director (Sheridan), Best Film Editing, Best Picture, Best Supporting Actor (Postlethwaite), Best Supporting Actress (Thompson); Golden Globe Awards '94: Best Actor—Drama (Day-Lewis), Best Film—Drama, Best Song ("(You Made Me the) Thief of Your Heart"), Best Supporting Actress (Thompson). **VHS, LV ★★★1/2**

In the Realm of the Senses Taboo-breaking story of a woman and man who turn their backs on the militaristic rule of Japan in the mid-1930s by plunging into an erotic and sensual world all their own. Striking, graphic work that was seized by U.S. customs when it first entered the country. Violent with explicit sex, and considered by some critics as pretentious, while others call it Oshima's masterpiece. In Japanese with English subtitles.
1976 (NC-17) 105m/C *JP FR* Tatsuya Fuji, Eiko Matsuda, Aio Nakajima, Meika Seri; **D:** Nagisa Oshima. **VHS ★★★**

In Which We Serve Much stiff upper-lipping in this classic that captures the spirit of the British Navy during WWII. The sinking of the destroyer HMS Torrin during the Battle of Crete is told via flashbacks, with an emphasis on realism that was unusual in

wartime flag-wavers. Features the film debuts of Johnson and Attenborough, and the first Lean directorial effort. Coward received a special Oscar for his "outstanding production achievement," having scripted, scored, codirected and costarred.
1942 114m/B *GB* Noel Coward, John Mills, Bernard Miles, Celia Johnson, Kay Walsh, James Donald, Richard Attenborough; *D:* Noel Coward, David Lean; *W:* Noel Coward; *M:* Noel Coward. National Board of Review Awards '42: 10 Best Films of the Year; New York Film Critics Awards '42: Best Film; Nominations: Academy Awards '43: Best Original Screenplay, Best Picture. **VHS, Beta** ★★★1/2

The Incident Political thriller set during WWII in Lincoln Bluff, Colorado. Matthau is excellent in his TV debut as a small-town lawyer who must defend a German prisoner of war accused of murder at nearby Camp Bremen. An all-star cast lends powerful performances to this riveting made-for-TV drama.
1989 95m/C Walter Matthau, Susan Blakely, Harry (Henry) Morgan, Robert Carradine, Barnard Hughes, Peter Firth, William Schallert; *D:* Joseph Sargent. **VHS** ★★★

Incident at Oglala: The Leonard Peltier Story Offers a detailed account of the violent events leading to the murder of two FBI agents in Oglala, South Dakota in 1975. American Indian activist Leonard Peltier was convicted of the murders and is presently serving two consecutive life sentences, but he's cited as a political prisoner by Amnesty International. The documentary examines the highly controversial trial and the tensions between the government and the Oglala Nation stemming back to the Indian occupation of Wounded Knee in 1973. Director Apted is sympathetic to Peltier and offers reasons why he should be allowed a retrial; he examined similar incidents in his film "Thunderheart."
1992 90m/C *D:* Michael Apted; *M:* John Trudell, Jackson Browne. **VHS** ★★★

The Incredible Shrinking Man Adapted by Richard Matheson from his own novel, the sci-fi classic is a philosophical thriller about a man who is doused with radioactive mist and begins to slowly shrink. His new size means that everyday objects take on sinister meaning and he must fight for his life in an increasingly hostile, absurd environment. A surreal, suspenseful allegory with impressive special effects. Endowed with the tension usually reserved for Hitchcock films.
1957 81m/B Grant Williams, Randy Stuart, April Kent, Paul Langton, Raymond Bailey; *D:* Jack Arnold; *W:* Richard Matheson. **VHS, Beta, LV** ★★★1/2

Independence Day The biggest of the new wave of disaster flicks paying tribute to the Irwin Allen celebrity-fests of the '70s finds an alien armada descending on Earth to create some fireworks on the July 4th weekend. The fate of the world rests in the hands of an unlikely band of Earthlings led by President Whitmore (Pullman), a computer expert (Goldblum), and a Marine fighter pilot (Smith). Special effects, despite forgoing some of the more expensive newer technology, don't disappoint. Strong (if not A-list) cast and plenty of action. Devlin and Emmerich wrote the script while promoting "Stargate," after a reporter asked Emmerich if he believed in aliens.
1996 (PG-13) 135m/C Bill Pullman, Will Smith, Jeff Goldblum, Judd Hirsch, Brent Spiner, Randy Quaid, James Rebhorn, Mary McDonnell, Harry Connick Jr., Robert Loggia, Harvey Fierstein, James Duvall, Margaret Colin, Vivica Fox; *D:* Roland Emmerich; *W:* Dean Devlin, Roland Emmerich; *M:* David Arnold. **VHS** ★★★

The Indian Fighter Exciting actioner has Douglas as a scout hired to lead a wagon train to Oregon in 1870. The train must past through dangerous Sioux territory and Douglas tries to make peace with the Sioux leader but a secret Indian gold mine and romance cause trouble and keep things lively.
1955 88m/C Kirk Douglas, Elsa Martinelli, Walter Abel, Walter Matthau, Diana Douglas, Lon Chaney Jr., Eduard Franz, Alan Hale Jr., Elisha Cook Jr., Harry Landers; *D:* Andre de Toth; *W:* Ben Hecht. **VHS** ★★★

Indiana Jones and the Last Crusade In this, the third and last (?) Indiana Jones adventure, the fearless archaeologist is once again up against the Nazis in a race to find the Holy Grail. Connery is perfectly cast as Indy's father; opening sequence features Phoenix as a teenage Indy and explains his fear of snakes and the origins of the infamous fedora. Returns to the look and feel of the original with more adventures, exotic places, dastardly villains, and daring escapes than ever before; a must for Indy fans.
1989 (PG) 126m/C Harrison Ford, Sean

Connery, Denholm Elliott, Alison Doody, Julian Glover, John Rhys-Davies, River Phoenix, Michael Byrne, Alex Hyde-White; **D:** Steven Spielberg; **W:** Jeffrey Boam; **M:** John Williams. Nominations: Academy Awards '89: Best Sound, Best Original Score. **VHS, Beta, LV, 8mm** ★★★

Indiana Jones and the Temple of Doom Daredevil archaeologist Indiana Jones is back. This time he's on the trail of the legendary Ankara Stone and a ruthless cult that has enslaved hundreds of children. More gore and violence than the original; Capshaw's whining character is an irritant, lacking the fresh quality that Karen Allen added to the original. Enough action for ten movies, special effects galore, and the usual booming Williams score make it a cinematic roller coaster ride, but with less regard for plot and pacing than the original. Though second in the series, it's actually a prequel to "Raiders of the Lost Ark." Followed by "Indiana Jones and the Last Crusade." **1984 (PG) 118m/C** Harrison Ford, Kate Capshaw, Ke Huy Quan, Amrish Puri; **D:** Steven Spielberg; **W:** Willard Huyck, Gloria Katz; **M:** John Williams. Academy Awards '84: Best Visual Effects; Nominations: Academy Awards '84: Best Original Score. **VHS, Beta, LV, 8mm** ★★★

Indictment: The McMartin Trial Woods stars as attorney Danny Davis, who has the unenviable task of providing a defense in the notorious McMartin child molestation trial. In 1983, Manhattan Beach, California was rocked by reports that some 60 preschoolers had been abused at a day-care center. Seven defendants were accused thanks to lurid videotaped interviews with the children. The trial lasted six years (the longest and most expensive on record) and all charges were eventually dismissed. It's clear from this telepic that public hysteria and media hype lead to a grave miscarriage of justice that put the legal system on trial as well. **1995 (R) 132m/C** James Woods, Henry Thomas, Mercedes Ruehl, Shirley Knight, Sada Thompson, Mark Blum, Alison Elliott, Chelsea Field, Richard Bradford, Lolita Davidovich; **D:** Mick Jackson; **W:** Abby Mann, Myra Mann, Rodrigo Garcia; **M:** Peter Melnick. **VHS, LV** ★★★

Indiscreet A charming American diplomat in London falls in love with a stunning actress, but protects himself by saying he is married. Needless to say, she finds out. Stylish romp with Grant and Bergman at their sophisticated best. Adapted by Norman Krasna from his stage play "Kind Sir." **1958 100m/C** Cary Grant, Ingrid Bergman, Phyllis Calvert; **D:** Stanley Donen; **M:** Richard Rodney Bennett, Frederick A. (Freddie) Young. **VHS** ★★★

Indochine Soapy melodrama follows the fortunes of Eliane (Deneuve), a Frenchwoman born and reared in Indochina, from 1930 to the communist revolution 25 years later. She contends with the changes to her country as well as her adopted daughter as she grows up and becomes independent. Deneuve's controlled performance (and unchanging beauty) is eminently watchable. Filmed on location in Vietnam with breathtaking cinematography by Francois Catonne. In French with English subtitles. **1992 (PG-13) 155m/C** *FR* Catherine Deneuve, Linh Dan Pham, Vincent Perez, Jean Yanne, Dominique Blanc, Henri Marteau, Carlo Brandt, Gerard Lartigau; **D:** Regis Wargnier; **W:** Erik Orsenna, Louis Gardel, Catherine Cohen, Regis Wargnier; **M:** Patrick Doyle. Academy Awards '92: Best Foreign Language Film; Cesar Awards '93: Best Actress (Deneuve), Best Art Direction/Set Decoration, Best Cinematography, Best Sound, Best Supporting Actress (Blanc); National Board of Review Awards '92: Best Foreign Film; Nominations: Academy Awards '92: Best Actress (Deneuve); British Academy Awards '93: Best Foreign Language Film. **VHS, LV, 8mm** ★★★

The Informer Based on Liam O'Flaherty's novel about the Irish Sinn Fein Rebellion of 1922, it tells the story of a hard-drinking Dublin man (McLaglen) who informs on a friend (a member of the Irish Republican Army) in order to collect a 20-pound reward. When his "friend" is killed during capture, he goes on a drinking spree instead of using the money, as planned, for passage to America. Director Ford allowed McLaglen to improvise his lines during the trial scene in order to enhance the realism, leading to excruciating suspense. Wonderful score. **1935 91m/B** Victor McLaglen, Heather Angel, Wallace Ford, Margot Grahame, Joseph Sawyer, Preston Foster, Una O'Connor, J.M. Kerrigan, Donald Meek; **D:** John Ford; **W:** Dudley Nichols; **M:** Max Steiner. Academy Awards '35: Best Actor (McLaglen), Best Director (Ford), Best Screenplay, Best Original Score; National Board of Review Awards '35: 10 Best Films of the Year; New York Film Critics Awards '35: Best Director (Ford), Best Film; Nominations: Academy Awards '35: Best

Film Editing, Best Picture. **VHS, Beta, LV**
★★★★

Inherit the Wind Powerful courtroom drama, based on the Broadway play, is actually a fictionalized version of the infamous Scopes "Monkey Trial" of 1925. Tracy is the defense attorney for the schoolteacher on trial for teaching Darwin's Theory of Evolution to a group of students in a small town ruled by religion. March is the prosecutor seeking to put the teacher behind bars and restore religion to the schools.
1960 128m/B Spencer Tracy, Fredric March, Florence Eldridge, Gene Kelly, Dick York; **D:** Stanley Kramer; **M:** Ernest Gold. Berlin International Film Festival '60: Best Actor (March); National Board of Review Awards '60: 10 Best Films of the Year; Nominations: Academy Awards '60: Best Actor (Tracy), Best Adapted Screenplay, Best Black and White Cinematography, Best Film Editing. **VHS, Beta, LV** ★★★1/2

The Inn of the Sixth Happiness Inspiring story of Gladys Aylward, an English missionary in 1930s China, who leads a group of children through war-torn countryside. Donat's last film.
1958 158m/C Ingrid Bergman, Robert Donat, Curt Jurgens; **D:** Mark Robson; **M:** Malcolm Arnold, Frederick A. (Freddie) Young. National Board of Review Awards '58: Best Actress (Bergman); Nominations: Academy Awards '58: Best Director (Robson). **VHS, Beta** ★★★

The Inner Circle Ivan Sanshin is a meek, married man working as a movie projectionist for the KGB in 1935 Russia. Sanshin is taken by the KGB to the Kremlin to show movies, primarily Hollywood features, to leader Joseph Stalin, a job he cannot discuss with anyone, even his wife. Under the spell of Stalin's personality, Sanshin sees only what he's told and overlooks the oppression and persecution of the times. Based on the life of the projectionist who served from 1935 until Stalin's death in 1953. Filmed on location at the Kremlin.
1991 (PG-13) 122m/C Tom Hulce, Lolita Davidovich, Bob Hoskins, Alexandre Zbruev, Maria Baranova, Feodor Chaliapin Jr, Bess Meyer; **D:** Andrei Konchalovsky; **W:** Andrei Konchalovsky, Anatoli Usov; **M:** Eduard Artemyev. **VHS, LV, 8mm** ★★★

The Innocent The setting: turn of the century Rome, ablaze with atheism and free love. The story: Giannini's a Sicilian aristocrat who ignores wife Antonelli and dallies with scheming mistress O'Neill. Discovering his wife's infidelity, he's profoundly disil

lusioned, and his manly notion of self disintegrates. Visconti's last film, it was an art house fave and is considered by many to be his best. Lavishly photographed, well set and costumed, and true to Gabrielle D'Annunzio's novel. In Italian with English subtitles. **AKA:** L'Innocente.
1976 (R) 125m/C /T Laura Antonelli, Jennifer O'Neill, Giancarlo Giannini; **D:** Luchino Visconti. **VHS, Beta** ★★★1/2

Inside Harrowing anti-apartheid drama finds university professor and white Afrikaaner Peter Martin Strydom (Stoltz) being held in a Johannesburg government prison. He's being interrogated by Colonel Kruger (Hawthorne), head of the prison security force, supposedly for conspiracy against the South African regime. Tortured, Strydom's will begins to break as the drama flashes forward ten years, with Colonel Kruger now subjected to interrogation by a nameless black questioner (Gossett Jr.) investigating human rights crimes, including Strydom's fate. Made for cable.
1996 94m/C Eric Stoltz, Nigel Hawthorne, Louis Gossett Jr.; **D:** Arthur Penn; **W:** Bima Stagg; **M:** Robert Levin. **VHS** ★★★

Insignificance A film about an imaginary night spent in a New York hotel by characters who resemble Marilyn Monroe, Albert Einstein, Joe McCarthy, and Joe DiMaggio. Entertaining and often amusing as it follows the characters as they discuss theory and relativity, the Russians, and baseball among other things.
1985 110m/C GB Gary Busey, Tony Curtis, Theresa Russell, Michael Emil, Will Sampson; **D:** Nicolas Roeg; **W:** Terry Johnson; **M:** Hans Zimmer. **VHS, Beta, LV** ★★★

The Inspector General Classic Kaye craziness of mistaken identities with the master comic portraying a carnival medicine man who is mistaken by the villagers for their feared Inspector General. If you like Kaye's manic performance, you'll enjoy this one. ♪ The Gypsy Drinking Song; Onward Onward; The Medicine Show; The Inspector General; Lonely Heart; Soliloquy For Three Heads; Happy Times; Brodny. **AKA:** Happy Times.
1949 103m/C Danny Kaye, Walter Slezak, Barbara Bates, Elsa Lanchester, Gene Lockhart, Walter Catlett, Alan Hale; **D:** Henry Koster. Golden Globe Awards '50: Best Score. **VHS, Beta** ★★★

Interiors Ultra serious, Bergmanesque drama about three neurotic adult sisters, coping with the dissolution of their family. When Father de cides to leave mentally unbalanced mother for a divorcee, the daughters are shocked and bewildered. Depressing and humorless, but fine performances all the way around, supported by the elegant camera work of Gordon Willis. Original theatrical trailer available on the laserdisc format.

1978 (R) 95m/C Diane Keaton, Mary Beth Hurt, E.G. Marshall, Geraldine Page, Richard Jordan, Sam Waterston, Kristin Griffith, Maureen Stapleton; *D:* Woody Allen; *W:* Woody Allen, Gordon Willis. British Academy Awards '78: Best Supporting Actress (Page); Los Angeles Film Critics Association Awards '78: Best Supporting Actress (Stapleton); Nominations: Academy Awards '78: Best Actress (Page), Best Director (Allen), Best Original Screenplay, Best Supporting Actress (Stapleton). **VHS, Beta, LV** ★★★1/2

Intermezzo Married violinist Ekman meets pianist Bergman and they fall in love. He deserts his family to tour with Bergman, but the feelings for his wife and children become too much. When Bergman sees their love won't last, she leaves him. Shakily, he returns home and as his daughter runs to greet him, she is hit by a truck and he realizes that his family is his true love. One of the great grab-your-hanky melodramas. In Swedish with English subtitles. 1939 English remake features Bergman's American film debut. *AKA:* Interlude.

1936 88m/B *SW* Gosta Ekman, Inga Tidblad, Ingrid Bergman, Bullen Berglund; *D:* Gustaf Molander. **VHS, LV** ★★★

Intermezzo Fine, though weepy, love story of a renowned, married violinist who has an affair with his stunningly beautiful protege (Bergman), but while on concert tour realizes that his wife and children hold his heart, and he returns to them. A re-make of the 1936 Swedish film, it's best known as Bergman's American debut. Howard's violin playing was dubbed by Jascha Heifetz. *AKA:* Intermezzo: A Love Story.

1939 70m/B *IT* Ingrid Bergman, Leslie Howard, Edna Best, Ann Todd; *D:* Gregory Ratoff; *M:* Max Steiner. Nominations: Academy Awards '39: Best Black and White Cinematography, Best Score. **VHS, Beta, LV** ★★★

Interrupted Melody True story of opera diva Marjorie Lawrence's courageous battle with polio and her fight to appear once more at the Metropolitan Opera. Parker was nominated for an Oscar in her excellent portrayal of the Australian singer who continues her career despite her handicap. Vocals dubbed by opera star Eileen Farrell. Based on the book by Marjorie Lawrence.

1955 106m/C Glenn Ford, Eleanor Parker, Roger Moore, Cecil Kellaway, Evelyn Ellis, Walter Baldwin; *D:* Curtis Bernhardt; *W:* William Ludwig, Sonya Levien. Nominations: Academy Awards '55: Best Screenplay (Ludwig), Best Screenplay (Levien). **VHS** ★★★

Intolerance Griffith's largest film in every aspect. An interwoven, four-story epic about human intolerance, with segments set in Babylon, ancient Judea, and Paris. One of the cinema's grandest follies, and greatest achievements. Silent with music score. Laserdisc version contains supplemental material including cuts from other Griffith works. Black and white with some restored color footage.

1916 175m/B Lillian Gish, Mae Marsh, Constance Talmadge, Bessie Love, Elmer Clifton, Erich von Stroheim, Eugene Pallette, Seena Owen, Alfred Paget; *D:* D.W. Griffith. **VHS, LV** ★★★★

Intruder in the Dust A small southern community develops a lynch mob mentality when a black man is accused of killing a white man. Powerful but largely ignored portrait of race relations in the South. Solid performances from the whole cast; filmed in Mississippi. Adapted from a novel by William Faulkner.

1949 87m/B David Brian, Claude Jarman Jr., Juano Hernandez, Porter Hall, Elizabeth Patterson; *D:* Clarence Brown. **VHS** ★★★1/2

Invasion of the Body Snatchers The one and only post-McCarthy paranoid sci-fi epic, where a small California town is infiltrated by pods from outer space that replicate and replace humans. A chilling, genuinely frightening exercise in nightmare dislocation. Based upon a novel by Jack Finney. Remade in 1978. The laserdisc version contains commentary by Maurice Yacowar, the text of an interview with Siegel, and the original theatrical trailer. The film itself is presented in its original wide-screen format.

1956 80m/B Kevin McCarthy, Dana Wynter, Carolyn Jones, King Donovan, Donald Siegel; *D:* Donald Siegel; *W:* Sam Peckinpah, Ellsworth Fredericks. **VHS, LV** ★★★

Invasion of the Body Snatchers One of the few instances where a remake is an improvement on the origi-

nal, which was itself a classic. This time, the "pod people" are infesting San Francisco, with only a small group of people aware of the invasion. A ceaselessly inventive, creepy version of the alien-takeover paradigm, with an intense and winning performance by Sutherland.
1978 (PG) 115m/C Donald Sutherland, Brooke Adams, Veronica Cartwright, Leonard Nimoy, Jeff Goldblum, Kevin McCarthy, Donald Siegel, Art Hindle; **D:** Philip Kaufman; **W:** W.D. Richter, Michael Chapman. **VHS, Beta, LV ★★★1/2**

The Invisible Man The vintage horror-fest based on H. G. Wells' novella about a scientist whose formula for invisibility slowly drives him insane. His mind definitely wandering, he plans to use his recipe to rule the world. Rains' first role; though his body doesn't appear until the final scene, his voice characterization is magnificent. The visual detail is excellent, setting standards that are imitated because they are difficult to surpass; with special effects by John P. Fulton.
1933 71m/B Claude Rains, Gloria Stuart, Dudley Digges, William Harrigan, Una O'Connor, E.E. Clive, Dwight Frye; **D:** James Whale; **W:** R.C. Sherriff. **VHS, Beta, LV ★★★★**

The Ipcress File The first of the Harry Palmer spy mysteries that made Caine a star. Based upon the bestseller by Len Deighton, it features the flabby, nearsighted spy investigating the kidnapping of notable British scientists. Solid scenes, including a scary brainwashing session, and tongue-firmly-in-British-cheek humor. Lots of camera play to emphasize Caine's myopia. Two sequels: "Funeral in Berlin" and "Billion Dollar Brain."
1965 108m/C GB Michael Caine, Nigel Green, Guy Doleman, Sue Lloyd; **D:** Sidney J. Furie; **M:** John Barry. British Academy Awards '65: Best Film. **VHS, Beta ★★★**

Iphigenia Based on the classic Greek tragedy by Euripides, this story concerns the Greek leader Agamemnon, who plans to sacrifice his lovely daughter, Iphigenia, to please the gods. Mere mortals protest and start a save-the-babe movement, but Euripides' moral—you can't please 'em all—is devastatingly realized. Fine adaptation that becomes visually extravagant at times, with an equally fine musical score. In Greek with English subtitles.
1977 130m/C GR Irene Papas, Costa Kazakos, Tatiana Papamoskou; **D:** Michael Cacoyannis; **M:** Mikis Theodorakis. Nominations: Academy Awards '77: Best Foreign Language Film; Cannes Film Festival '77: Best Film. **VHS, Beta ★★★**

Ironweed Grim and gritty drama about bums living the hard life in Depression-era Albany. Nicholson excels as a former ballplayer turned drunk bothered by visions of the past, and Streep is his equal in the lesser role of a tubercular boozer. Waits also shines. Another grim view from "Pixote" director Babenco. Kennedy scripted based on his Pulitzer Prize-winning tragedy.
1987 (R) 135m/C Jack Nicholson, Meryl Streep, Tom Waits, Carroll Baker, Michael O'Keefe, Fred Gwynne, Diane Venora, Margaret Whitton, Jake Dengel, Nathan Lane, James Gammon, Joe Grifasi, Bethel Leslie, Ted Levine, Frank Whaley; **D:** Hector Babenco; **W:** William Kennedy; **M:** John Morris. Los Angeles Film Critics Association Awards '87: Best Actor (Nicholson); New York Film Critics Awards '87: Best Actor (Nicholson); Nominations: Academy Awards '87: Best Actor (Nicholson), Best Actress (Streep). **VHS, Beta, LV ★★★**

Is Paris Burning? A spectacularly star-studded but far too sprawling account of the liberation of Paris from Nazi occupation. The script, in which seven writers had a hand, is based on Larrry Collins and Dominique Lapierre's best-seller. **AKA:** Paris Brule-T-Il?.
1968 173m/C FR Jean-Paul Belmondo, Charles Boyer, Leslie Caron, Jean-Pierre Cassel, George Chakiris, Claude Dauphin, Alain Delon, Kirk Douglas, Glenn Ford, Gert Frobe, Daniel Gelin, E.G. Marshall, Yves Montand, Anthony Perkins, Claude Rich, Simone Signoret, Robert Stack, Jean-Louis Trintignant, Pierre Vaneck, Orson Welles, Bruno Cremer, Suzy Delair, Michael Lonsdale; **D:** Rene Clement; **W:** Gore Vidal, Francis Ford Coppola; **M:** Maurice Jarre. **VHS ★★★**

Isadora A loose, imaginative biography of Isadora Duncan, the cause celebre dancer in the 1920s who became famous for her scandalous performances, outrageous behavior, public love affairs, and bizarre, early death. Redgrave is exceptional in the lead, and Fox provides fine support. Restored from its original 131-minute print length by the director. **AKA:** The Loves of Isadora.
1968 153m/C Vanessa Redgrave, Jason Robards Jr., James Fox, Ivan Tchenko, John Fraser, Bessie Love; **D:** Karel Reisz; **W:** Melvin Bragg; **M:** Maurice Jarre. Cannes Film Festival '69: Best Actress

(Redgrave); National Board of Review Awards '69: 10 Best Films of the Year; National Society of Film Critics Awards '69: Best Actress (Redgrave); Nominations: Academy Awards '68: Best Actress (Redgrave); Cannes Film Festival '69: Best Film. **VHS, Beta** ★★★

Island of Lost Souls Horrifying adaptation of H.G. Wells's "The Island of Dr. Moreau" was initially banned in parts of the U.S. because of its disturbing contents. Laughton is a mad scientist on a remote island obsessed with making men out of jungle animals. When a shipwreck survivor gets stranded on the island, little does he know that Laughton wants to mate him with Lota, the Panther Woman, to produce the first human-animal child. As unsettling today as it was in the '30s. Burke beat out more than 60,000 young women in a nationwide search to play the Panther Woman, winning the role because of her "feline" look. Remade as "The Island of Dr. Moreau."
1932 71m/B Charles Laughton, Bela Lugosi, Richard Arlen, Leila Hyams, Kathleen Burke, Stanley Fields, Robert F. (Bob) Kortman; *Cameos:* Alan Ladd, Randolph Scott, Buster Crabbe; *D:* Erle C. Kenton; *W:* Philip Wylie, Waldemar Young. **VHS** ★★★1/2

Island of Terror First-rate science fiction chiller about an island overrun by shell-like creatures that suck the bones out of their living prey. Good performances and interesting twists make for prickles up the spine. *AKA:* Night of the Silicates; The Creepers.
1966 90m/C *GB* Peter Cushing, Edward Judd, Carole Gray, Sam Kydd, Niall MacGinnis; *D:* Terence Fisher. **VHS** ★★★

Isn't Life Wonderful Outstanding Griffith film depicts the unbearable conditions in post-WWI Germany. Filmed on location.
1924 90m/B Carol Dempster, Neil Hamilton, Lupino Lane, Hans von Schlettow; *D:* D.W. Griffith; *W:* D.W. Griffith. **VHS, Beta** ★★★★

It Came from Outer Space Aliens take on the form of local humans to repair their spacecraft in a small Arizona town. Good performances and outstanding direction add up to a fine science fiction film. Based on the story "The Meteor" by Ray Bradbury, who also wrote the script. Originally filmed in 3-D.
1953 81m/B Richard Carlson, Barbara Rush, Charles Drake, Russell Johnson; *D:* Jack Arnold; *W:* Ray Bradbury; *M:* Herman Stein. **VHS** ★★★

It Happened One Night Classic Capra comedy about an antagonistic couple determined to teach each other about life. Colbert is an unhappy heiress who runs away from her affluent home in search of contentment. On a bus she meets newspaper reporter Gable, who teaches her how "real" people live. She returns the favor in this first of the 1930s screwball comedies. The plot is a framework for an amusing examination of war between the sexes. Colbert and Gable are superb as affectionate foes. Remade as the musicals "Eve Knew Her Apples" and "You Can't Run Away From It."
1934 105m/B Clark Gable, Claudette Colbert, Roscoe Karns, Walter Connolly, Alan Hale, Ward Bond; *D:* Frank Capra; *W:* Robert Riskin. Academy Awards '34: Best Actor (Gable), Best Actress (Colbert), Best Adapted Screenplay, Best Director (Capra), Best Picture; National Board of Review Awards '34: 10 Best Films of the Year. **VHS, Beta, LV** ★★★★

It Happens Every Spring A chemistry professor, working on a bug repellant for trees, accidentally invents a potion that repels any kind of wood that it comes in contact with. Since he needs some big bucks to pop the question to his sweetie, the prof, who also loves baseball, gets a tryout as a pitcher with a major league team and uses the solution on the baseballs he pitches. Naturally, it's strikeout time and the prof becomes a pitching phenom. Now, if he can only keep his little secret. Wacky baseball footage is a highlight.
1949 87m/B Ray Milland, Jean Peters, Paul Douglas, Ed Begley Sr., Ted de Corsia, Ray Collins, Jessie Royce Landis, Alan Hale Jr., Gene Evans; *D:* Lloyd Bacon; *W:* Valentine Davies; *M:* Leigh Harline. **VHS** ★★★1/2

It Should Happen to You An aspiring model attempts to boost her career by promoting herself on a New York City billboard. The results, however, are continually surprising. Fine comedy teamwork from master thespians Holliday and Lemmon in this, the latter's first film.
1954 87m/B Judy Holliday, Jack Lemmon, Peter Lawford; *D:* George Cukor; *W:* Ruth Gordon, Garson Kanin. Nominations: Academy Awards '54: Best Costume Design (B & W). **VHS, Beta, LV** ★★★

It Started in Naples Good performances by both Gable and Loren in this comedy-drama about an American lawyer in Italy who, upon preparing his late brother's estate, finds that his brother's nephew is living with a stripper. A custody battle ensues, but love wins out in the end. Loren is incredible in nightclub scenes.

1960 100m/C Clark Gable, Sophia Loren, Marietto, Vittorio De Sica, Paolo Carlini, Claudio Ermelli, Giovanni Filidoro; **D:** Melville Shavelson; **W:** Melville Shavelson, Jack Rose. Nominations: Academy Awards '60: Best Art Direction/Set Decoration (Color). **VHS ★★★**

It Started with Eve Funny comedy about a grumpy old millionaire (Laughton) whose dying wish is to meet the young lady his son Johnny is to wed. Unfortunately, the bride-to-be is unavailable, so Johnny (Cummings) finds a replacement in hatcheck girl Durbin. Of course, Durbin steals the old man's heart and he miraculously makes a full-blown recovery, which means big trouble for Cummings. Remade in 1964 as "I'd Rather Be Rich." Based on the story "Almost An Angel" by Hans Kraly. ♪ Clavelitos; Going Home.

1941 92m/B Deanna Durbin, Charles Laughton, Robert Cummings, Guy Kibbee, Margaret Tallichet, Catherine Doucet, Walter Catlett, Charles Coleman, Clara Blandick; **D:** Henry Koster; **W:** Norman Krasna, Leo Townsend. **VHS ★★★**

Italian Straw Hat Classic silent about the chain of errors that ensues when a man's horse eats a woman's hat. His vast, unending struggle to replace the hat is the source of continual comedy. From Eugene Labiche's play. **AKA:** Un Chapeau de Paille d'Italie.

1927 72m/B *FR* Albert Prejean; **D:** Rene Clair. **VHS, Beta ★★★**

It's a Gift A grocery clerk moves his family west to manage orange groves in this classic Fields comedy. Several inspired sequences. The supporting cast shines too. A real find for the discriminating comedy buff. Remake of the silent "It's the Old Army Game."

1934 71m/B W.C. Fields, Baby LeRoy, Kathleen Howard; **D:** Norman Z. McLeod. **VHS, Beta, LV ★★★1/2**

It's a Wonderful Life American classic about a man saved from suicide by a considerate angel, who then shows the hero how important he's been to the lives of loved ones. Corny but inspirational and heartwarming, with an endearing performance by Travers as angel Clarence. Stewart and Reed are typically wholesome. Perfect film for people who want to feel good, joyfully teetering on the border between Hollywood schmaltz and genuine heartbreak. Also available colorized. The laserdisc version includes production and publicity stills, the theatrical trailer, and commentary by film professor Jeanine Basinger. Also available in a 160-minute Collector's Edition with original preview trailer, "The Making of 'It's a Wonderful Life,'" and a new digital transfer from the original negative.

1946 125m/B James Stewart, Donna Reed, Henry Travers, Thomas Mitchell, Lionel Barrymore, Samuel S. Hinds, Frank Faylen, Gloria Grahame, H.B. Warner, Ellen Corby, Sheldon Leonard, Beulah Bondi, Ward Bond, Frank Albertson, Todd Karns, Mary Treen, Charles Halton; **D:** Frank Capra; **W:** Frances Goodrich, Albert Hackett, Jo Swerling; **M:** Dimitri Tiomkin. Golden Globe Awards '47: Best Director (Capra); Nominations: Academy Awards '46: Best Actor (Stewart), Best Director (Capra), Best Film Editing, Best Picture, Best Sound. **VHS, LV ★★★★**

It's Alive Cult film about a mutated baby that is born to a normal Los Angeles couple, who escapes and goes on a bloodthirsty, murderous rampage, is a sight to behold. Fantastic score by Bernard Herrmann makes this chilling film a memorable one.

1974 (PG) 91m/C John P. Ryan, Sharon Farrell, Andrew Duggan, Guy Stockwell, James Dixon, Michael Ansara; **D:** Larry Cohen; **W:** Larry Cohen. **VHS ★★★**

Ivan the Terrible, Part 1 Contemplative epic of Russia's first czar is a classic, innovative film from cinema genius Eisenstein. Visually stunning, with a fine performance by Cherkassov. Ivan's struggles to preserve his country is the main concern of the first half of Eisenstein's masterwork (which he originally planned as a trilogy). In Russian with English subtitles.

1944 96m/B *RU* Nikolai Cherkassov, Ludmila Tselikovskaya, Serafina Birman, Piotr Kadochnikev; **D:** Sergei Eisenstein; **W:** Sergei Eisenstein; **M:** Sergei Prokofiev. **VHS, Beta, LV, 8mm ★★★★**

Ivan the Terrible, Part 2 Landed gentry conspire to dethrone the czar in this continuation of the innovative epic. More stunning imagery from master Eisenstein, who makes no false moves in this one. Slow going, but immensely rewarding. Russian dialogue with English subtitles; contains color sequences.

1946 84m/B *RU* Nikolai Cherkassov, Ludmila Tselikovskaya, Serafina Birman, Piotr Kadochnikev; **D:** Sergei Eisenstein. **VHS, Beta, LV, 8mm ★★★1/2**

Ivanhoe Knights fight each other and woo maidens in this chivalrous ro-

mance derived from the Sir Walter Scott classic. Taylor is suitably noble, while Sanders is familiarly serpentine. Remade in 1982.
1952 107m/C Robert Taylor, Elizabeth Taylor, Joan Fontaine, George Sanders, Finlay Currie, Felix Aylmer; **D:** Richard Thorpe; **M:** Miklos Rozsa, Frederick A. (Freddie) Young. Nominations: Academy Awards '52: Best Color Cinematography, Best Picture, Best Original Score. **VHS, Beta** ★★★

I've Heard the Mermaids Singing Independent Canadian semi-satiric romantic comedy details the misadventures of a klutzy woman who suddenly obtains a desirable job in an art gallery run by a lesbian on whom she develops a crush. Good-natured tone helped considerably by McCarthy's winning performance.
1987 81m/C *CA* Sheila McCarthy, Paule Baillargeon, Ann-Marie MacDonald, John Evans; **D:** Patricia Rozema; **M:** Mark Korven. Genie Awards '88: Best Actress (McCarthy), Best Supporting Actress (Baillargeon). **VHS, Beta, LV** ★★★

J'Accuse A Frenchman creates a device he believes will stop the war but it is confiscated by the government and used as part of the national defense. Subsequently, he goes mad. Gance (known for his 1927 "Napoleon"), remade his 1919 silent film, retelling the powerful anti-war message with great sensitivity. Banned in Nazi Germany. **AKA:** I Accuse; That They May Live.
1937 125m/B *FR* Victor Francen, Jean Max, Deltaire, Renee Devillers; **D:** Abel Gance. **VHS** ★★★

Jack the Ripper Another retelling of the life of the legendary serial killer. Caine is the Scotland Yard inspector who tracks down the murderer. Ending is based on recent evidence found by director/co-writer Wickes. Extremely well done made-for-television film.
1988 200m/C Michael Caine, Armand Assante, Ray McNally, Susan George, Jane Seymour, Lewis Collins, Ken Bones; **D:** David Wickes; **W:** David Wickes. **VHS** ★★★

The Jackie Robinson Story Chronicles Robinson's rise from UCLA to his breakthrough as the first black man to play baseball in the major leagues. Robinson plays himself; the film deals honestly with the racial issues of the time.
1950 76m/B Jackie Robinson, Ruby Dee, Minor Watson, Louise Beavers, Richard Lane, Harry Shannon, Joel Fluellen, Ben Lessy; **D:** Alfred E. Green. **VHS, Beta** ★★★

Jailhouse Rock While in jail for manslaughter, a teenager learns to play the guitar. After his release, he slowly develops into a top recording star. Probably the only film that captured the magnetic power of the young Elvis Presley; an absolute must for fans. Also available in a colorized version. ♪ Jailhouse Rock; Treat Me Nice; Baby, I Don't Care; Young and Beautiful; Don't Leave Me Now; I Wanna Be Free; One More Day.
1957 (G) 96m/B Elvis Presley, Judy Tyler, Vaughn Taylor, Dean Jones, Mickey Shaughnessy, William Forrest, Glenn Strange; **D:** Richard Thorpe. **VHS, Beta, LV**

James and the Giant Peach Combo of live action and stop-motion animation in this adaptation of Roald Dahl's 1961 children's book. Orphaned James is sent to live with his wicked aunts. When magic "crocodile tongues," given to James by a hobo, spill at the base of a peach tree, one fruit grows to such a tremendous size that James crawls inside, meets six insect friends, and goes on numerous adventures, all the while trying to face his fears. Dahl's books are creepy, and since the people who brought you "Nightmare Before Christmas" are also doing "James," expect the visuals to be astonishing but too scary for the little ones.
1996 (PG) 80m/C Paul Terry, Miriam Margolyes, Pete Postlethwaite, Joanna Lumley; **V:** Richard Dreyfuss, Susan Sarandon, David Thewlis, Simon Callow, Jane Leeves; **D:** Henry Selick; **M:** Randy Newman. **VHS** ★★★

Jane Eyre Excellent adaptation of the Charlotte Bronte novel about the plain governess with the noble heart and her love for the mysterious and tragic Mr. Rochester. Fontaine has the proper backbone and yearning in the title role but to accommodate Welles' emerging popularity the role of Rochester was enlarged. Excellent bleak romantic-Gothic look. Taylor, in her third film role, is seen briefly in the early orphanage scenes.
1944 97m/B Joan Fontaine, Orson Welles, Margaret O'Brien, Peggy Ann Garner, John Sutton, Sara Allgood, Henry Daniell, Agnes Moorehead, Aubrey Mather, Edith Barrett, Barbara Everest, Hillary Brooke, Elizabeth Taylor; **D:** Robert Stevenson; **W:** John Houseman, Aldous Huxley, Robert Stevenson; **M:** Bernard Herrmann. **VHS** ★★★

Jane Eyre A made-for-British-television mini-series based on the famed Charlotte Bronte novel about the

maturation of a homeless English waif, her love for the tormented Rochester, and her quest for permanent peace.
1983 239m/C *GB* Timothy Dalton, Zelah Clarke; *D:* Julian Aymes. VHS, Beta, LV ★★★

Jane Eyre Zeffirelli creates an eloquent yet spare interpretation of Charlotte Bronte's 1847 masterpiece about a meek governess and her mysterious employer, in its fourth filmic incarnation. Everything about it, from the lighting to the score, is muted and somber. Still a beautiful film, it seems to lack a certain passion that earlier versions (especially the 1944 version) brought to the screen. Strong performances all around, including Oscar-winner Paquin and French star Gainsbourg as the younger and older Jane, and Hurt as the tormented Rochester.
1996 (PG) 116m/C William Hurt, Anna Paquin, Charlotte Gainsbourg, Joan Plowright, Elle Macpherson, Geraldine Chaplin, Fiona Shaw, John Wood, Amanda Root, Marc Schneider, Josephine Serre; *D:* Franco Zeffirelli; *W:* Franco Zeffirelli, Hugh Whitemore; *M:* Alessio Vlad, Claudio Capponi. VHS, LV ★★★

Jason and the Argonauts Jason, son of the King of Thessaly, sails on the Argo to the land of Colchis, where the Golden Fleece is guarded by a seven-headed hydra. Superb special effects and multitudes of mythological creatures; fun for the whole family.
1963 (G) 104m/C *GB* Todd Armstrong, Nancy Kovack, Gary Raymond, Laurence Naismith, Nigel Green, Michael Gwynn, Honor Blackman; *D:* Don Chaffey; *W:* Jan Read, Beverley Cross. VHS, Beta, LV, 8mm ★★★

Jaws Early directorial effort by Spielberg from the Peter Benchley potboiler. A tight, very scary, and sometimes hilarious film about the struggle to kill a giant great white shark that is terrorizing an eastern beach community's waters. The characterizations by Dreyfuss, Scheider, and Shaw are much more endurable than the shock effects. Memorable score. Sequeled by "Jaws 2" in 1978, "Jaws 3" 1983, and "Jaws the Revenge" in 1987. Look for Benchley as a TV reporter.
1975 (PG) 124m/C Roy Scheider, Robert Shaw, Richard Dreyfuss, Lorraine Gary, Murray Hamilton, Carl Gottlieb; *Cameos:* Peter Benchley; *D:* Steven Spielberg; *W:* Carl Gottlieb, Peter Benchley; *M:* John Williams. Academy Awards '75: Best Film Editing, Best Sound, Best Original Score; Golden Globe Awards '76: Best Score; People's Choice Awards '76: Best Film; Nominations: Academy Awards '75: Best Picture. VHS, Beta, LV ★★★1/2

Jean de Florette The first of two films (with "Manon of the Spring") based on Marcel Pagnol's novel. A single spring in drought-ridden Provence, France is blocked by two scheming countrymen (Montand and Auteuil). They await the imminent failure of the farm nearby, inherited by a city-born hunchback, whose chances for survival fade without water for his crops. A devastating story with a heartrending performance by Depardieu as the hunchback. Lauded and awarded; in French with English subtitles.
1987 (PG) 122m/C *FR* Gerard Depardieu, Yves Montand, Daniel Auteuil, Elisabeth Depardieu, Ernestine Mazurowna; *D:* Claude Berri; *W:* Gerard Brach, Claude Berri. British Academy Awards '87: Best Adapted Screenplay, Best Film, Best Supporting Actor (Auteuil); National Board of Review Awards '87: 5 Best Foreign Films of the Year. VHS, Beta, LV ★★★1/2

Jeremiah Johnson The story of a man who turns his back on civilization, circa 1850, and learns a new code of survival in a brutal land of isolated mountains and hostile Indians. In the process, he becomes part of the mountains and their wildlife. A notable and picturesque film.
1972 (PG) 107m/C Robert Redford, Will Geer; *D:* Sydney Pollack; *W:* Edward Anhalt, John Milius. Nominations: Cannes Film Festival '72: Best Film. VHS, Beta, LV ★★★

Jesus of Montreal A vagrant young actor (stage-trained Canadian star Bluteau) is hired by a Montreal priest to produce a fresh interpretation of an Easter passion play. Taking the good book at its word, he produces a contemporized literal telling that captivates audiences, inflames the men of the cloth, and eventually wins the players' faith. Quebecois director Arcand (keep an eye out for him as the judge) tells a compelling, acerbically satirical and haunting story that never forces its Biblical parallels. In French with English subtitles. *AKA:* Jesus de Montreal.
1989 (R) 119m/C *FR CA* Gilles Pelletier, Lothaire Bluteau, Catherine Wilkening, Robert Lepage, Johanne-Marie Tremblay, Remy Girard, Marie-Christine Barrault; *D:* Denys Arcand; *W:* Denys Arcand. Cannes Film Festival '89: Special Jury Prize; Genie Awards '90: Best Actor (Girard), Best Director (Arcand), Best Film, Best Supporting Actor (Girard); Nominations:

Academy Awards '89: Best Foreign Language Film. **VHS, LV ★★★1/2**

Jesus of Nazareth An all-star cast vividly portrays the life of Christ in this made-for-television mini-series. Wonderfully directed and sensitively acted. On three cassettes.
1977 371m/C Robert Powell, Anne Bancroft, Ernest Borgnine, Claudia Cardinale, James Mason, Laurence Olivier, Anthony Quinn; *D:* Franco Zeffirelli; *M:* Maurice Jarre. **VHS, Beta ★★★**

Jezebel Davis is a willful Southern belle who loses fiance Fonda through her selfish and spiteful ways in this pre-Civil War drama. When he becomes ill, she realizes her cruelty and rushes to nurse him back to health. Davis' role won her an Oscar for Best Actress, and certainly provided Scarlett O'Hara with a rival for most memorable female character of all time.
1938 105m/B Bette Davis, George Brent, Henry Fonda, Margaret Lindsay, Fay Bainter, Donald Crisp, Spring Byington, Eddie Anderson; *D:* William Wyler; *M:* Max Steiner. Academy Awards '38: Best Actress (Davis), Best Supporting Actress (Bainter); Nominations: Academy Awards '38: Best Cinematography, Best Picture, Best Score. **VHS, Beta, LV ★★★1/2**

JFK Highly controversial examination of President John F. Kennedy's 1963 assassination, from the viewpoint of New Orleans district attorney Jim Garrison. Hotly debated because of Stone's conspiracy theory, it sparked new calls to open the sealed government records from the 1977 House Select Committee on Assassinations investigation. Outstanding performances from all-star principal and supporting casts, stunning cinematography, and excellent editing. Even Garrison himself shows up as Chief Justice Earl Warren. Considered by some to be a cinematic masterpiece, others see it as revisionist history that should be taken with a grain of salt. Extended version adds 17 minutes.
1991 (R) 189m/C Kevin Costner, Sissy Spacek, Kevin Bacon, Tommy Lee Jones, Laurie Metcalf, Gary Oldman, Michael Rooker, Jay O. Sanders, Beata Pozniak, Joe Pesci, Donald Sutherland, John Candy, Jack Lemmon, Walter Matthau, Ed Asner, Vincent D'Onofrio, Sally Kirkland, Brian Doyle-Murray, Wayne Knight, Tony Plana, Tomas Milian, Sean Stone; *Cameos:* Lolita Davidovich, Frank Whaley, Jim Garrison, Robert Richardson; *D:* Oliver Stone; *W:* Oliver Stone, Zachary Sklar; *M:* John Williams. Academy Awards '91: Best Cinematography, Best Film Editing; Golden Globe Awards '92: Best Director (Stone);

Nominations: Academy Awards '91: Best Adapted Screenplay, Best Director (Stone), Best Picture, Best Sound, Best Supporting Actor (Jones), Best Original Score. **VHS, Beta, LV ★★★1/2**

Joan of Paris A French resistance leader dies so that Allied pilots can escape from the Nazis. A well done, but obviously dated propaganda feature.
1942 91m/B Michele Morgan, Paul Henreid, Thomas Mitchell, Laird Cregar, May Robson, Alexander Granach, Alan Ladd; *D:* Robert Stevenson; *W:* Charles Bennett. Nominations: Academy Awards '42: Best Original Score. **VHS, Beta ★★★1/2**

Johnny Belinda A compassionate physician cares for a young deaf mute woman and her illegitimate child. Tension builds as the baby's father returns to claim the boy.
1948 103m/B Jane Wyman, Lew Ayres, Charles Bickford, Agnes Moorehead; *D:* Jean Negulesco; *M:* Max Steiner. Academy Awards '48: Best Actress (Wyman); Golden Globe Awards '49: Best Actress—Drama (Wyman), Best Film—Drama; Nominations: Academy Awards '48: Best Actor (Ayres), Best Art Direction/Set Decoration (B & W), Best Black and White Cinematography, Best Director (Negulesco), Best Film Editing, Best Picture, Best Screenplay, Best Sound, Best Supporting Actor (Bickford), Best Supporting Actress (Moorehead), Best Original Score. **VHS, Beta ★★★**

Johnny Eager Glossy crime melodrama starring Taylor as an unscrupulous racketeer and Turner as the daughter of D.A. Arnold who falls for him and ends up becoming a pawn in his schemes. Heflin won an Oscar for his outstanding performance as Taylor's alcoholic confidant. Excellent direction by LeRoy makes this a top-rate gangster film. Based on a story by James Edward Grant.
1942 107m/B Robert Taylor, Lana Turner, Edward Arnold, Van Heflin, Robert Sterling, Patricia Dane, Glenda Farrell, Barry Nelson, Henry O'Neill, Charles Dingle, Cy Kendall; *D:* Mervyn LeRoy; *W:* James Edward Grant, John Lee Mahin. Academy Awards '42: Best Supporting Actor (Heflin). **VHS ★★★**

Johnny Guitar Women strap on six-guns in Nicholas Ray's unintentionally hilarious, gender-bending western. A guitar-playing loner wanders into a small town feud between lovelorn saloon owner Crawford and McCambridge, the town's resident lynch-mob-leading harpy. This fascinating

cult favorite has had film theorists arguing for decades: is it a parody, a political McCarthy-era allegory, or Freudian exercise? The off-screen battles of the two female stars are equally legendary. Stick around for the end credits to hear Peggy Lee sing the title song.
1953 116m/C Joan Crawford, Ernest Borgnine, Sterling Hayden, Mercedes McCambridge, Scott Brady, Ward Bond, Royal Dano, John Carradine; *D:* Nicholas Ray; *W:* Philip Yordan. **VHS, LV ★★★¹/2**

Johnny Handsome An ugly, deformed hood, after he's been double-crossed and sent to prison, volunteers for a reconstructive surgery experiment and is released with a new face, determined to hunt down the scum that set him up. A terrific modern B-picture based on John Godey's "The Three Worlds of Johnny Handsome."
1989 (R) 96m/C Mickey Rourke, Ellen Barkin, Lance Henriksen, Elizabeth McGovern, Morgan Freeman, Forest Whitaker, Scott Wilson, Blake Clark; *D:* Walter Hill; *W:* Ken Friedman; *M:* Ry Cooder. **VHS, Beta, LV ★★★**

The Jolson Story A smash Hollywood bio of Jolson, from his childhood to super-stardom. Features dozens of vintage songs from Jolson's parade of hits. Jolson himself dubbed the vocals for Parks, rejuvenating his own career in the process. ♪ Swanee; You Made Me Love You; By the Light of the Silvery Moon; I'm Sitting On Top of the World; There's a Rainbow Round My Shoulder; My Mammy; Rock-A-Bye Your Baby With a Dixie Melody; Liza; Waiting for the Robert E. Lee.
1946 128m/C Larry Parks, Evelyn Keyes, William Demarest, Bill Goodwin, Tamara Shayne, John Alexander, Jimmy Lloyd, Ludwig Donath, Scotty Beckett; *D:* Alfred E. Green; *M:* Morris Stoloff. Academy Awards '46: Best Sound, Best Score; Nominations: Academy Awards '46: Best Actor (Parks), Best Color Cinematography, Best Film Editing, Best Supporting Actor (Demarest). **VHS, Beta, LV ★★★**

Jonah Who Will Be 25 in the Year 2000 A group of eight friends, former 60s radicals, try to adjust to growing older and coping with life in the '70s. The eccentric octet include a disillusioned journalist turned gambler, an unorthodox teacher, and a grocery store cashier who gives away food to the elderly. Wonderful performances highlight this social comedy. In French with English subtitles. *AKA:* Jonas—Qui Aura 25 Ans en l'an 2000.
1976 110m/C *SI* Jean-Luc Bideau, Myriam Meziere, Miou-Miou, Jacques Denis, Rufus, Dominique Labourier, Roger Jendly, Miriam Boyer, Raymond Bussieres, Jonah; *D:* Alain Tanner; *W:* Alain Tanner. National Society of Film Critics Awards '76: Best Screenplay. **VHS ★★★¹/2**

The Josephine Baker Story Made-for-cable bio of exotic entertainer/activist Josephine Baker, an Afro-American woman from St. Louis who found superstardom in pre-WWII Europe, but repeated racism and rejection in the U.S. At times trite treatment turns her eventful life into a standard rise-and-fall showbiz tale, but a great cast and lavish scope pull it through. Whitfield re-creates Baker's (sometimes topless) dance routines; Carol Dennis dubs her singing. Filmed on location in Budapest.
1990 (R) 129m/C Lynn Whitfield, Ruben Blades, David Dukes, Craig T. Nelson, Louis Gossett Jr., Kene Holliday, Vivian Bonnell; *D:* Brian Gibson; *M:* Ralph Burns. Emmy Awards '91: Best Actress (Whitfield), Best Director (Gibson). **VHS ★★★**

Joshua Then and Now When a Jewish-Canadian novelist (Woods) is threatened by the breakup of his marriage to his WASPy wife, compounded by a gay scandal, he re-examines his picaresque history, including his life with his gangster father (Arkin). A stirring story that is enhanced by a strong performance by Woods, as well as a picturesque Canadian backdrop. Adapted by Mordecai Richler from his own novel.
1985 (R) 102m/C *CA* James Woods, Gabrielle Lazure, Alan Arkin, Michael Sarrazin, Chuck Shamata, Linda Sorensen, Alan Scarfe, Alexander Knox, Robert Joy, Ken Campbell; *D:* Ted Kotcheff; *W:* Mordecai Richler; *M:* Philippe Sarde. Genie Awards '86: Best Supporting Actor (Arkin), Best Supporting Actress (Sorensen). **VHS, Beta ★★★**

Jour de Fete Tati's first film, dealing with a French postman's accelerated efforts at efficiency after viewing a motivational film of the American post service. Wonderful slapstick moments. In French with English subtitles. *AKA:* The Big Day; Holiday.
1948 79m/B *FR* Jacques Tati, Guy Decomble, Paul Fankeur; *D:* Jacques Tati. **VHS, Beta, LV ★★★¹/2**

Journey for Margaret Young and Day star as an expectant American couple living in London during WWII so Young can cover the war for a newspaper back home. After she loses her baby during an air raid, Day heads back to the States. Young stays in London where he meets two young orphans and takes them under his wing. He decides to take them back to the United States and adopt them, but problems arise. A real tear-jerker and a good story that shows the war through the eyes of children. O'Brien's first film. Based on the book by William L. White.

1942 81m/B Robert Young, Laraine Day, Fay Bainter, Signe Hasso, Margaret O'Brien, Nigel Bruce, G.P. Huntley Jr., William Severn, Doris Lloyd, Halliwell Hobbes, Jill Esmond; **D:** Woodbridge S. Van Dyke. **VHS** ★★★

Journey into Fear During WWII, an American armaments expert is smuggled out of Istanbul, but Axis agents are close behind. From the novel by Eric Ambler; remade for television in 1974.

1942 71m/B Joseph Cotten, Dolores Del Rio, Orson Welles, Agnes Moorehead, Norman Foster; **D:** Norman Foster. **VHS, Beta, LV** ★★★

Journey of Hope Powerful drama about Kurdish family that sells its material possessions in hopes of emigrating legally to Switzerland, where life will surely be better. During the perilous journey, smugglers take their money and the family must attempt crossing the formidable slopes of the Swiss Mountains on foot. Based on a true story. In Turkish with English subtitles.

1990 (PG) 111m/C *SI* Necmettin Cobanoglu, Nur Surer, Emin Sivas, Yaman Okay, Mathias Gnaedinger, Dietmar Schoenherr; **D:** Xavier Koller; **W:** Xavier Koller. Academy Awards '90: Best Foreign Language Film. **VHS, LV** ★★★1/2

The Journey of Natty Gann With the help of a wolf (brilliantly portrayed by a dog) and a drifter, a 14-year-old girl travels across the country in search of her father in this warm and touching film. Excellent Disney representation of life during the Great Depression.

1985 (PG) 101m/C Meredith Salenger, John Cusack, Ray Wise, Scatman Crothers, Lainie Kazan, Verna Bloom; **D:** Jeremy Paul Kagan; **W:** Jeanne Rosenberg; **M:** James Horner. Nominations: Academy Awards '85: Best Costume Design. **VHS, Beta, LV** ★★★1/2

Journey to the Center of the Earth A scientist and student undergo a hazardous journey to find the center of the earth and along the way they find the lost city of Atlantis. Based upon the Jules Verne novel.

1959 132m/C James Mason, Pat Boone, Arlene Dahl, Diane Baker, Thayer David; **D:** Henry Levin. Nominations: Academy Awards '59: Best Art Direction/Set Decoration (Color), Best Sound. **VHS, Beta, LV** ★★★

The Joy Luck Club Universal themes in mother/daughter relationships are explored in a context Hollywood first rejected as too narrow, but which proved to be a modest sleeper hit. Tan skillfully weaves the plot of her 1989 best-seller into a screenplay which centers around young June's going-away party. Slowly the stories of four Chinese women, who meet weekly to play mah-jongg, are unraveled. Each vignette reveals life in China for the four women and the tragedies they survived, before reaching into the present to capture the relationships between the mothers and their daughters. Powerful, relevant, and moving.

1993 (R) 136m/C Tsai Chin, Kieu Chinh, France Nuyen, Rosalind Chao, Tamlyn Tomita, Lisa Lu, Lauren Tom, Ming-Na Wen, Michael Paul Chan, Andrew McCarthy, Christopher Rich, Russell Wong, Victor Wong, Vivian Wu, Jack Ford, Diane Baker; **D:** Wayne Wang; **W:** Amy Tan, Ronald Bass. **VHS, LV** ★★★

Joyless Street Silent film focuses on the dismal life of the middle class in Austria during an economic crisis. Lovely piano score accompanies the film.

1925 96m/B *GE* Greta Garbo, Werner Krauss, Asta Nielson; **D:** G.W. Pabst. **VHS, Beta, LV** ★★★1/2

Ju Dou Breath-taking story of an aging factory owner in search of an heir. He takes a third wife, but she finds caring in the arms of another man when her husband's brutality proves too much. Beautiful color cinematography, excellent acting, and epic story. Oscar nominee for Best Foreign Film. In Chinese with English subtitles.

1990 (PG-13) 98m/C *CH* Gong Li, Li Bao-Tian, Li Wei, Zhang Yi, Zheng Jian; **D:** Zhang Yimou, Gu Changwei. Nominations: Academy Awards '90: Best Foreign Language Film. **VHS** ★★★★

Jud Suess Classic, scandalous Nazi anti-Semitic tract about a Jew who rises to power under the duchy of Wuerttemberg by stepping on, abusing, and raping Aryans. A film that caused riots at its screenings and tragedy for its cast and crew, and the Third Reich's most notorious fictional expression of policy. In German with English subtitles.

1940 100m/B *GE* Ferdinand Marian, Werner Krauss, Heinrich George, Kristina

Soderbaum, Eugene Klopfer; **D:** Veit Harlan. **VHS, Beta ★★★**

Jude Engrossing retelling of Thomas Hardy's depressing 1896 novel "Jude the Obscure," set in his fictional Wessex. Country stonemason Jude (Eccleston) hopes to improve his impoverished lot in life by becoming a student at Christminister University. But first he's distracted into an unwise marriage with lively Arabella (Griffiths), who soon leaves him, and then into an ill-fated romance with his capricious cousin Sue Brideshead (Winslet). Class and societal barriers prove impossible for the couple to overcome and lead to a shocking tragedy. Hardy's book was so badly received by critics that he never wrote another novel and stuck to poetry for the rest of his life. **AKA:** Jude the Obscure.
1996 123m/C Christopher Eccleston, Kate Winslet, Liam Cunningham, Rachel Griffiths; **D:** Michael Winterbottom; **W:** Hossein Amini. **VHS ★★★**

The Judge and the Assassin Intriguing courtroom drama. A prejudiced judge has his values challenged when he must decide if a child-killer is insane or not. The relationship that develops between the judge and the killer is the film's focus. Excellent direction by Tavernier. In French with English subtitles. **AKA:** Le Juge et L'assassin.
1975 130m/C *FR* Philippe Noiret, Michel Galabru, Isabelle Huppert, Jean-Claude Brialy; **D:** Bertrand Tavernier; **W:** Bertrand Tavernier. Cesar Awards '77: Best Writing, Best Score. **VHS, Beta, LV ★★★1/2**

Judge Priest Small-town judge in the old South stirs up the place with stinging humor and common-sense observances as he tangles with prejudices and civil injustices. Funny, warm slice-of-life is occasionally defeated by racist characterizations. Ford remade it later as "The Sun Shines Bright." Taken from the Irvin S. Cobb stories.
1934 80m/B Will Rogers, Stepin Fetchit, Anita Louise, Henry B. Walthall; **D:** John Ford. **VHS, Beta ★★★**

Judgment at Nuremberg It's 1948 and a group of high-level Nazis are on trial for war crimes. Chief Justice Tracy must resist political pressures as he presides over the trials. Excellent performances throughout, especially by Dietrich and Garland. Considers to what extent an individual may be held accountable for actions committed under orders of a superior officer. Consuming account of the Holocaust and WWII; deeply moving and powerful. Based on a "Playhouse 90" television program.
1961 178m/B Spencer Tracy, Burt Lancaster, Richard Widmark, Montgomery Clift, Maximilian Schell, Judy Garland, Marlene Dietrich, William Shatner; **D:** Stanley Kramer; **W:** Abby Mann; **M:** Ernest Gold. Academy Awards '61: Best Actor (Schell), Best Adapted Screenplay; Golden Globe Awards '62: Best Actor—Drama (Schell), Best Director (Kramer); New York Film Critics Awards '61: Best Actor (Schell), Best Screenplay; Nominations: Academy Awards '61: Best Actor (Tracy), Best Art Direction/Set Decoration (B & W), Best Black and White Cinematography, Best Costume Design (B & W), Best Director (Kramer), Best Film Editing, Best Picture, Best Supporting Actor (Clift), Best Supporting Actress (Garland). **VHS, Beta, LV ★★★★**

Judith of Bethulia A young widow uses her charm and wits to save her city from attack by the Assyrians. Based on the Apocrypha, this is the last film Griffith directed for Biograph. It was re-released as "Her Condoned Sin" in 1971, including two reels of Griffith's outtakes.
1914 65m/B Blanche Sweet, Henry B. Walthall, Mae Marsh, Robert "Bobbie" Harron, Lillian Gish, Dorothy Gish, Kate Bruce, Harry Carey Sr.; **D:** D.W. Griffith; **W:** D.W. Griffith. **VHS, LV ★★★**

Jules and Jim Beautiful film with perfect casting, particularly Moreau. Spanning from 1912 to 1932, it is the story of a friendship between two men and their 20-year love for the same woman. Werner is the shy German Jew and Serre the fun-loving Frenchman, who meet as students. The two men discover and woo the bohemian, destructive Moreau, although it is Werner she marries. After WWI, the friends are reunited but the marriage of Moreau and Werner is in trouble and she has an affair with Serre, which leads to tragedy for all three. Adapted from the novel by Henri-Pierre Roche. In French with English subtitles. **AKA:** Jules et Jim.
1962 104m/B *FR* Jeanne Moreau, Oskar Werner, Henri Serre, Marie DuBois, Vanna Urbino; **D:** Francois Truffaut; **W:** Jean Gruault; **M:** Georges Delerue. **VHS, Beta, LV ★★★★**

Julia The story recounted in Lillian Hellman's fictional memoir "Pentimento." Fonda plays Hellman as she risks her life smuggling money into Germany during WWII for the sake of Julia, her beloved childhood friend (Redgrave), who is working in the Resistance. All cast members shine in their performances; watch for Streep in her screen debut.

1977 (PG) 118m/C Jane Fonda, Jason Robards Jr., Vanessa Redgrave, Maximilian Schell, Hal Holbrook, Rosemary Murphy, Meryl Streep, Lisa Pelikan; **D:** Fred Zinnemann; **W:** Alvin Sargent; **M:** Georges Delerue. Academy Awards '77: Best Adapted Screenplay, Best Supporting Actor (Robards), Best Supporting Actress (Redgrave); Golden Globe Awards '78: Best Actress—Drama (Fonda), Best Supporting Actress (Redgrave); National Board of Review Awards '77: 10 Best Films of the Year; New York Film Critics Awards '77: Best Supporting Actor (Schell); Writers Guild of America '77: Best Adapted Screenplay; Nominations: Academy Awards '77: Best Actress (Fonda), Best Cinematography, Best Costume Design, Best Director (Zinneman), Best Film Editing, Best Picture, Best Supporting Actor (Schell), Best Original Score. **VHS, Beta, LV ★★★1/2**

Julia Misbehaves Charming comedy that has Garson returning to ex-husband Pidgeon and daughter Taylor after an 18-year absence. Taylor is about to be married at a chateau in France and wants Garson to be there. While traveling to France from England, Garson encounters a bunch of colorful circus characters who are taking their act to Paris. Wonderful slapstick scenes give the stars a chance to have some real fun. Based on the novel "The Nutmeg Tree" by Margery Sharp.

1948 99m/B Greer Garson, Walter Pidgeon, Peter Lawford, Cesar Romero, Elizabeth Taylor, Lucile Watson, Nigel Bruce, Mary Boland, Reginald Owen, Veda Ann Borg, Joi Lansing; **D:** Jack Conway. **VHS ★★★**

Juliet of the Spirits Fellini uses the sparse story of a woman (Fellini's real-life wife) deliberating over her husband's possible infidelity to create a wild, often senseless surrealistic film. With a highly symbolic internal logic and complex imagery, Fellini's fantasy ostensibly elucidates the inner life of a modern woman. In Italian with English subtitles. **AKA:** Giulietta Degli Spiriti.

1965 142m/C *IT* Giulietta Masina, Valentina Cortese, Sylva Koscina, Mario Pisu; **D:** Federico Fellini; **W:** Federico Fellini, Tullio Pinelli, Ennio Flaiano, Brunello Rondi; **M:** Nino Rota. National Board of Review Awards '65: 5 Best Foreign Films of the Year; New York Film Critics Awards '65: Best Foreign Film; Nominations: Academy Awards '66: Best Art Direction/Set Decoration (Color), Best

Costume Design (Color). **VHS, Beta, LV ★★★**

Julius Caesar All-star version of the Shakespearean tragedy, heavily acclaimed and deservedly so. Working directly from the original Shakespeare, director Mankiewicz produced a lifelike, yet poetic production.

1953 121m/B James Mason, Marlon Brando, John Gielgud, Greer Garson, Deborah Kerr, Louis Calhern, Edmond O'Brien, George Macready, John Hoyt, Michael Pate; **D:** Joseph L. Mankiewicz; **W:** Joseph L. Mankiewicz; **M:** Miklos Rozsa. Academy Awards '53: Best Art Direction/Set Decoration (B & W); British Academy Awards '53: Best Actor (Brando); Nominations: Academy Awards '53: Best Actor (Brando), Best Black and White Cinematography, Best Picture, Best Original Score. **VHS, Beta, LV ★★★1/2**

The Jungle Book Based on Kipling's classic, a young boy raised by wolves must choose between his jungle friends and human "civilization." Along the way he meets a variety of jungle characters including zany King Louie, kind-hearted Baloo, wise Bagherra and the evil Shere Khan. Great, classic songs including "Trust in Me," "I Wanna Be Like You," and Oscar-nominated "Bare Necessities." Last Disney feature overseen by Uncle Walt himself and a must for kids of all ages.

1967 78m/C D: Wolfgang Reitherman; **M:** George Bruns; **V:** Phil Harris, Sebastian Cabot, Louis Prima, George Sanders, Sterling Holloway, J. Pat O'Malley, Verna Felton, Darlene Carr. Nominations: Academy Awards '67: Best Song ("The Bare Necessities"). **VHS, Beta, LV ★★★**

Jungle Fever Married black architect's affair with his white secretary provides the backdrop for a cold look at interracial love. Focuses more on the discomfort of friends and families than with the intense world created by the lovers for themselves. Provides the quota of humor and fresh insight we expect from Lee, but none of the joyous sexuality experienced by the lovers in "She's Gotta Have It." In fact, Lee tells viewers that interracial love is unnatural, never more than skin deep, never more than a blind obsession with the allure of the opposite race. Very fine cast but if you don't agree with Lee, a real disappointment as well.

1991 (R) 131m/C Wesley Snipes, Annabella Sciorra, John Turturro, Samuel L. Jackson, Ossie Davis, Ruby Dee,

Lonette McKee, Anthony Quinn, Spike Lee, Halle Berry, Tyra Ferrell, Veronica Webb, Frank Vincent, Tim Robbins, Brad Dourif; **D:** Spike Lee; **W:** Spike Lee; **M:** Terence Blanchard. National Board of Review Awards '91: 10 Best Films of the Year; New York Film Critics Awards '91: Best Supporting Actor (Jackson). **VHS, Beta, LV** ★★★

Junior Bonner A rowdy modern-day western about a young drifting rodeo star who decides to raise money for his father's new ranch by challenging a formidable bull.
1972 (PG) 100m/C Steve McQueen, Robert Preston, Ida Lupino, Ben Johnson, Joe Don Baker, Barbara Leigh; **D:** Sam Peckinpah. **VHS, Beta** ★★★

Jurassic Park Crichton's spine-tingling thriller translates well (but not faithfully) due to its main attraction: realistic, rampaging dinosaurs. Genetically cloned from prehistoric DNA, all is well until they escape from their pens—smarter and less predictable than expected. Contrived plot and thin characters (except Goldblum), but who cares? The true stars are the dinos, an incredible combination of models and computer animation. Violent, suspenseful, and realistic with gory attack scenes. Not for small kids, though much of the marketing is aimed at them. Spielberg knocked his own "E.T." out of first place as "JP" became the highest grossing movie of all time. Also available in a letterbox version.
1993 (PG-13) 127m/C Sam Neill, Laura Dern, Jeff Goldblum, Richard Attenborough, Bob Peck, Martin Ferrero, B.D. Wong, Joseph Mazzello, Ariana Richards, Samuel L. Jackson, Wayne Knight; **D:** Steven Spielberg; **W:** David Koepp, Michael Crichton, Dean Cundey; **M:** John Williams; **V:** Richard Kiley. Academy Awards '93: Best Sound, Best Sound Effects Editing, Best Visual Effects; Nominations: MTV Movie Awards '94: Best Film, Best Villain (T-Rex), Best Action Sequence. **VHS, LV** ★★★½

Kagemusha A thief is rescued from the gallows because of his striking resemblance to a warlord in 16th-century Japan. When the ambitious warlord is fatally wounded, the thief is required to pose as the warlord. In Japanese with English subtitles. **AKA:** The Shadow Warrior; The Double.
1980 (PG) 160m/C *JP* Tatsuya Nakadai, Tsutomu Yamazaki, Kenichi Hagiwara; **D:** Akira Kurosawa. British Academy Awards '80: Best Director (Kurosawa); Cannes Film Festival '80: Best Film; Cesar Awards '81: Best Foreign Film; National Board of Review Awards '80: 5 Best Foreign Films of the Year; Nominations: Academy Awards '80: Best Art Direction/Set Decoration, Best Foreign Language Film. **VHS, Beta, LV** ★★★½

Kameradschaft A great, early German sound film about Germans struggling to free themselves and French miners trapped underground on the countries' border. In German and French with English subtitles.
1931 80m/B *GE* Ernst Busch, Alexander Granach, Fritz Kampers; **D:** G.W. Pabst. National Board of Review Awards '32: 10 Best Films of the Year. **VHS, Beta** ★★★½

Kanal Wajda's first major success, a grueling account of Warsaw patriots, upon the onset of the Nazis toward the end of the war, fleeing through the ruined city's sewers. Highly acclaimed. Part 2 of Wajda's "War Trilogy," preceded by "A Generation" and followed by "Ashes and Diamonds." In Polish with English subtitles or dubbed. **AKA:** They Loved Life.
1956 96m/B *PL* Teresa Izewska, Tadeusz Janczar; **D:** Andrzej Wajda. Cannes Film Festival '57: Grand Jury Prize. **VHS, Beta** ★★★½

Kansas City Altman mixes music, politics, crime, and the movies in this bittersweet homage to his hometown, set in the jazz-driven 1930s. Starstruck, tough-talking Blondie (Leigh) kidnaps Carolyn Stilton (Richardson), a self-sedating wife of a political shaker (Murphy), in a hare-brained scheme to save her husband from a local mobster (Belafonte). Styled to imitate the brilliant jazz scores played by the likes of Joshua Redman and James Carter, the action can become a bit confusing, and Leigh is beyond irritating with her derivative dame routine. Belafonte, however, is brilliant, relishing the part of the legendary Seldom Seen, a real-life K.C. gangster.
1995 110m/C Jennifer Jason Leigh, Miranda Richardson, Harry Belafonte, Michael Murphy, Dermot Mulroney, Steve Buscemi, Brooke Smith, Jane Adams; **D:** Robert Altman; **W:** Robert Altman, Frank Barhydt; **M:** Hal Willner. New York Film Critics Awards '96: Best Supporting Actor (Belafonte). **VHS, LV** ★★★

Kapo A 14-year-old Jewish girl and her family are imprisoned by the Nazis in a concentration camp. There, the girl changes identities with the help of the camp doctor, and rises to the position of camp guard. She proceeds to become taken with her

power until a friend commits suicide and jolts the girl back into harsh reality. An Academy Award nominee for Best Foreign Film (lost to "The Virgin Spring"). Primarily English dialogue, with subtitles for foreign language.
1959 116m/B IT FR YU Susan Strasberg, Laurent Terzieff, Emmanuelle Riva, Gianni "John" Garko; **D:** Gillo Pontecorvo; **W:** Gillo Pontecorvo. Nominations: Academy Awards '60: Best Foreign Language Film. **VHS ★★★**

The Karate Kid A teen-age boy finds out that Karate involves using more than your fists when a handyman agrees to teach him martial arts. The friendship that they develop is deep and sincere; the Karate is only an afterthought. From the director of the original "Rocky," this movie is easy to like.
1984 (PG) 126m/C Ralph Macchio, Noriyuki "Pat" Morita, Elisabeth Shue, Randee Heller, Martin Kove, Chad McQueen; **D:** John G. Avildsen; **W:** Robert Mark Kamen; **M:** Bill Conti. Nominations: Academy Awards '84: Best Supporting Actor (Morita). **VHS, Beta, LV, 8mm ★★★1/2**

Key Largo A gangster melodrama set in Key West, Florida, where hoods take over a hotel in the midst of a hurricane. Based on a play by Maxwell Anderson.
1948 101m/B Humphrey Bogart, Lauren Bacall, Claire Trevor, Edward G. Robinson, Lionel Barrymore; **D:** John Huston; **W:** Richard Brooks, John Huston; **M:** Max Steiner. Academy Awards '48: Best Supporting Actress (Trevor). **VHS, Beta, LV ★★★1/2**

The Keys of the Kingdom An earnest adaptation of A.J. Cronin's novel about a young Scottish missionary spreading God's word in 19th-century China.
1944 137m/B Gregory Peck, Thomas Mitchell, Edmund Gwenn, Vincent Price, Roddy McDowall, Cedric Hardwicke, Peggy Ann Garner, James Gleason, Anne Revere, Rose Stradner, Sara Allgood, Abner Biberman, Arthur Shields; **D:** John M. Stahl; **W:** Joseph L. Mankiewicz, Nunnally Johnson. Nominations: Academy Awards '45: Best Actor (Peck), Best Black and White Cinematography, Best Interior Decoration, Best Original Score. **VHS, Beta, LV ★★★**

Kicking and Screaming Baumbach's deft, though slightly self-conscious directorial debut examines the post-college grad angst of Grover (Hamilton) and his three other slacker roomies. In denial of their recently achieved nonstudent status, the four

bond together in pursuit of the inane and trivial, while their various girlfriends slip more easily into adulthood. Funny and tender flashback scenes of Grover and girlfriend Jane (D'Abo) add depth without all the dialogue, well-written though it is. Hilarious highlight occurs as roommate Otis interviews for that most popular of low-budget, Gen-X movie jobs—video store clerk.
1995 (R) 96m/C Josh Hamilton, Olivia D'Abo, Carlos Jacott, Christopher Eigeman, Eric Stoltz, Jason Wiles, Parker Posey, Cara Buono, Elliott Gould; **D:** Noah Baumbach; **W:** Noah Baumbach, Oliver Berkman; **M:** Phil Marshall. **VHS ★★★**

The Kid Sensitive and sassy film about a tramp who takes home an orphan. Chaplin's first feature. Also launched Coogan as the first child superstar.
1921 60m/B Charlie Chaplin, Jackie Coogan, Edna Purviance; **D:** Charlie Chaplin. **VHS ★★★**

The Kid Brother The shy, weak son of a tough sheriff, Harold fantasizes about being a hero like his father and big brothers, falls in love with a carnival lady, and somehow saves the day. Classic silent comedy.
1927 84m/B Harold Lloyd, Walter James, Jobyna Ralston; **D:** Ted Wilde. **VHS, Beta ★★★1/2**

Kid Galahad Well acted boxing drama with Robinson playing an honest promoter who wants to make Morris into a prize fighter. Davis plays the girl they both want. Remade as "The Wagons Roll at Night" and then made again as an Elvis Presley vehicle. Shown on television. **AKA:** The Battling Bellhop.
1937 101m/B Edward G. Robinson, Bette Davis, Humphrey Bogart, Wayne Morris, Jane Bryan, Harry Carey Sr., Veda Ann Borg; **D:** Michael Curtiz; **W:** Seton I. Miller; **M:** Max Steiner. **VHS ★★★**

The Kid/Idle Class The Little Tramp adopts a homeless orphan in "The Kid," Chaplin's first feature-length film. This tape also includes "The Idle Class," a rare Chaplin short.
1921 85m/B Charlie Chaplin, Jackie Coogan, Edna Purviance, Chuck Reisner, Lita Grey Chaplin; **D:** Charlie Chaplin. **VHS, Beta ★★★**

The Killer Jeffrey Chow is a gangster gunman who wants out. He's hired by his best friend to perform one last killing, but it doesn't go as smoothly as he wanted. He's almost caught by "Eagle" Lee, a detective who vows to hunt him down using Jennie, a singer

blinded by Chow in crossfire. Lots of action and gunfights, but also pretty corny and sentimental. Very similar to American action movies, but using Chinese and Asian cultural conventions. A good introduction to the Chinese gangster-flick genre. Available with subtitles or dubbed in English. *AKA:* Die Xue Shuang Xiong.
1990 (R) 110m/C *HK* Chow Yun-fat, Sally Yeh, Danny Lee, Kenneth Tsang, Chu Kong; *D:* John Woo; *W:* John Woo. VHS ★★★1/2

The Killing The dirty, harsh, street-level big heist epic that established Kubrick and presented its genre with a new and vivid existentialist aura, as an ex-con engineers the rip-off of a racetrack with disastrous results. Displays characteristic nonsentimental sharp-edged Kubrick vision. Cinematography by Lucien Ballard. Based on the novel "Clean Break" by Lionel White.
1956 83m/B Sterling Hayden, Marie Windsor, Elisha Cook Jr., Jay C. Flippen, Vince Edwards, Timothy Carey, Coleen Gray, Joseph Sawyer, Ted de Corsia; *D:* Stanley Kubrick. VHS, Beta, LV ★★★

The Killing Fields Based on the New York Times' Sydney Schanberg's account of his friendship with Cambodian interpreter Dith Pran. They separated during the fall of Saigon, when Western journalists fled, leaving behind countless assistants who were later accused of collusion with the enemy by the Khmer Rouge and killed or sent to re-education camps during the bloodbath known as "Year Zero." Schanberg searched for Pran through the Red Cross and U.S. government, while Pran struggled to survive, finally escaping and walking miles to freedom. Ngor's own experiences echoed those of his character Pran. Malkovich's debut is intense. Joffe's directorial debut shows a generally sure hand, with only a bit of melodrama at the end.
1984 (R) 142m/C *GB* Sam Waterston, Haing S. Ngor, John Malkovich, Athol Fugard, Craig T. Nelson, Julian Sands, Spalding Gray, Bill Paterson; *D:* Roland Joffe; *W:* Bruce Robinson. Academy Awards '84: Best Cinematography, Best Film Editing, Best Supporting Actor (Ngor); Golden Globe Awards '85: Best Supporting Actor (Ngor); Los Angeles Film Critics Association Awards '84: Best Cinematography; New York Film Critics Awards '84: Best Cinematography; National Society of Film Critics Awards '84: Best Cinematography; Writers Guild of America '84: Best Adapted Screenplay; Nominations: Academy Awards '84: Best

Actor (Waterston), Best Adapted Screenplay, Best Director (Joffe), Best Picture. VHS, Beta, LV ★★★1/2

A Killing in a Small Town Candy Morrison seems like the perfect member of her small Texas community—but appearances can be deceiving, particularly after she's charged with killing a fellow churchgoer by striking her 41 times with an axe (shades of Lizzie Borden)! Dennehy is her skeptical lawyer who isn't sure if it was self-defense or a peculiar sort of revenge. Good performances by Hershey and Dennehy lift this above the usual tawdry made-for-TV level. Based on a true story; originally a television miniseries.
1990 (R) 95m/C Barbara Hershey, Brian Dennehy, Hal Holbrook, Richard Gilliland, John Terry, Lee Garlington; *D:* Stephen Gyllenhaal; *M:* Richard Gibbs. VHS, LV ★★★

Kim A colorful Hollywood adaptation of the Rudyard Kipling classic about an English boy disguised as a native in 19th-century India, and his various adventures.
1950 113m/C Errol Flynn, Dean Stockwell, Paul Lukas, Cecil Kellaway; *D:* Victor Saville; *M:* Andre Previn. VHS, Beta ★★★

Kind Hearts and Coronets Black comedy in which an ambitious young man sets out to bump off eight relatives in an effort to claim a family title. Guinness is wonderful in his role as all eight of the fated relations. Based on Roy Horiman's novel.
1949 104m/B *GB* Alec Guinness, Dennis Price, Valerie Hobson, Joan Greenwood; *D:* Robert Hamer. National Board of Review Awards '50: 5 Best Foreign Films of the Year. VHS, Beta, LV ★★★1/2

King Docudrama with terrific cast follows the life and career of one of the greatest nonviolent civil rights leaders of all time, Martin Luther King Jr. Made for television.
1978 272m/C Paul Winfield, Cicely Tyson, Roscoe Lee Browne, Ossie Davis, Art Evans, Ernie Banks, Howard E. Rollins Jr., William Jordan, Cliff DeYoung; *D:* Abby Mann; *W:* Abby Mann; *M:* Billy Goldenberg. VHS, Beta ★★★

The King and I Wonderful adaptation of Rodgers and Hammerstein's Broadway play based on the novel "Anna and the King of Siam" by Margaret Landon. English governess Kerr is hired to teach the King of Siam's many children and bring them into the 19th century. She has more of a job than she realizes, for this is a king, a country, and a people who value tradition above all else. Features one of Rodgers and Hammerstein's best-loved scores. Brynner made this role his, playing it over 4,000 times on stage and screen before his death. Kerr's voice was dubbed when she sang; the voice you hear is Marni Nixon, who also dubbed the stars' singing voices in "West Side Story" and "My Fair Lady." ♪ Shall We Dance?; Getting To Know You; Hello, Young Lovers; We Kiss in a Shadow; I Whistle a Happy Tune; March of the Siamese Children; I Have Dreamed; A Puzzlement; Something Wonderful.

1956 133m/C Deborah Kerr, Yul Brynner, Rita Moreno, Martin Benson, Terry Saunders, Rex Thompson, Alan Mowbray, Carlos Rivas; **D:** Walter Lang; **W:** Ernest Lehman; **M:** Richard Rodgers, Oscar Hammerstein. Academy Awards '56: Best Actor (Brynner), Best Art Direction/Set Decoration (Color), Best Costume Design (Color), Best Sound, Best Score; Golden Globe Awards '57: Best Actress— Musical/Comedy (Kerr), Best Film— Musical/Comedy; Nominations: Academy Awards '56: Best Actress (Kerr), Best Color Cinematography, Best Director (Lang), Best Picture. **VHS, Beta, LV ★★★★**

King Kong The original beauty and the beast film classic tells the story of Kong, a giant ape captured in Africa and brought to New York as a sideshow attraction. Kong falls for Wray, escapes from his captors and rampages through the city, ending up on top of the newly built Empire State Building. Moody Steiner score adds color, and Willis O'Brien's stop-motion animation still holds up well. Remade numerous times with various theme derivations. Available in a colorized version. The laserdisc, produced from a superior negative, features extensive liner notes and running commentary by film historian Ronald Haver.

1933 105m/B Fay Wray, Bruce Cabot, Robert Armstrong, Frank Reicher, Noble Johnson, Sam Hardy, James Flavin; **D:** Ernest B. Schoedsack; **M:** Max Steiner. **VHS, Beta, LV, 8mm ★★★★**

King Lear Brook's version of Shakespeare tragedy. The king drives away the only decent daughter he has, and when he realizes this, it is too late. Powerful performances and interesting effort at updating the bard.

1971 137m/B *GB* Paul Scofield, Irene Worth, Jack MacGowran, Alan Webb, Cyril Cusack, Patrick Magee; **D:** Peter Brook. **VHS ★★★1/2**

King of Comedy An unhinged would-be comedian haunts and eventually kidnaps a massively popular Johnny Carson-type television personality. A cold, cynical farce devised by Scorsese seemingly in reaction to John Hinckley's obsession with his film "Taxi Driver." Controlled, hard-hitting performances, especially by De Niro and Lewis.

1982 (PG) 101m/C Robert De Niro, Jerry Lewis, Sandra Bernhard, Tony Randall, Diahnne Abbott, Shelley Hack, Liza Minnelli; **D:** Martin Scorsese. British Academy Awards '83: Best Original Screenplay; National Society of Film Critics Awards '83: Best Supporting Actress (Bernhard); Nominations: Cannes Film Festival '83: Best Film. **VHS, Beta, LV ★★★**

The King of Hearts In WWI, a Scottish soldier finds a battle-torn French town evacuated of all occupants except a colorful collection of escaped lunatics from a nearby asylum. The lunatics want to make him their king, which is not a bad alternative to the insanity of war. Bujold is cute as ballerina wannabe; look for Serrault ("La Cage aux Folles") as, not surprisingly, a would-be effeminate hairdresser. Lighthearted comedy with a serious message; definitely worthwhile. **AKA:** Le Roi de Coeur.

1966 101m/C *FR GB* Alan Bates, Genevieve Bujold, Adolfo Celi, Francoise Christophe, Micheline Presle; **D:** Philippe de Broca; **M:** Georges Delerue. **VHS, Beta, LV ★★★**

The King of Kings The life of Christ is intelligently told, with an attractive visual sense and a memorable score. Remake of Cecil B. DeMille's silent film, released in 1927. Laserdisc format features a special letterboxed edition of this film.

1961 170m/C Jeffrey Hunter, Siobhan McKenna, Hurd Hatfield, Robert Ryan, Rita Gam, Viveca Lindfors, Rip Torn; **D:** Nicholas Ray; **W:** Philip Yordan; **M:** Miklos Rozsa. **VHS, Beta, LV ★★★**

King of New York Drug czar Frank White (Walken), recently returned from a prison sabbatical, regains control of his New York drug empire with the aid of a loyal network of black dealers. How? Call it dangerous charisma, an inexplicable sympatico. Headquartered in Manhattan's chic Plaza hotel, he ruthlessly orchestrates the drug machine, while funneling the profits into a Bronx hospital for the poor. As inscrutable as White himself, Walken makes the drug czar's power tangible, believable, yet never fathomable.

1990 (R) 106m/C Christopher Walken, Laurence "Larry" Fishburne, David Caruso,

Victor Argo, Wesley Snipes, Janet Julian, Joey Chin, Giancarlo Esposito, Steve Buscemi; **D:** Abel Ferrara; **W:** Nicholas St. John; **M:** Joe Delia. VHS, LV ★★★

King of the Hill Quiet depression-era drama focuses on Aaron, a 12-year-old who lives in a seedy hotel in St. Louis. The family is barely scraping by: his mother is in a tuberculosis sanitarium, his younger brother has been sent away to live with relatives, and Aaron must fend for himself when his father gets work as a traveling salesman. Aaron excels at school and his efforts there, as well as his hotel friends, manage to provide him with some semblance of a regular life. Soderberg's third directorial effort is unsentimental but admiring of his character's resourcefulness and imagination during difficult times. Based on the book by A.E. Hochner describing his own childhood.
1993 (PG-13) 102m/C Jesse Bradford, Jeroen Krabbe, Lisa Eichhorn, Karen Allen, Spalding Gray, Elizabeth McGovern, Joseph Chrest, Adrien Brody, Cameron Boyd, Chris Samples, Katherine Heigl, Amber Benson, John McConnell, Ron Vawter, John Durbin, Lauryn Hill, David Jensen; **D:** Steven Soderbergh; **W:** Steven Soderbergh; **M:** Cliff Martinez. Nominations: Cannes Film Festival '93: Best Film. VHS, LV ★★★★

King of the Wild Horses Engaging children's story about a wild stallion that comes to the rescue. Terrific action photography of Rex going through his paces. Look for Chase in a rare dramatic role. Silent.
1924 50m/B Rex, Edna Murphy, Leon Barry, Pat Hartigan, Frank Butler, Charley Chase; **D:** Fred Jackman. VHS, Beta ★★★

King Rat Drama set in a WWII Japanese prisoner-of-war camp. Focuses on the effect of captivity on the English, Australian, and American prisoners. An American officer bribes his Japanese captors to live more comfortably than the rest. Based on James Clavell's novel.
1965 134m/B George Segal, Tom Courtenay, James Fox, James Donald, Denholm Elliott, Patrick O'Neal, John Mills; **D:** Bryan Forbes; **M:** John Barry. Nominations: Academy Awards '65: Best Art Direction/Set Decoration (B & W), Best Black and White Cinematography. VHS, Beta ★★★

King Solomon's Mines A lavish version of the classic H. Rider Haggard adventures about African explorers searching out a fabled diamond mine. Remake of the 1937 classic; remade again in 1985.

1950 102m/C Stewart Granger, Deborah Kerr, Richard Carlson, Hugo Haas, Lowell Gilmore; **D:** Compton Bennett. Academy Awards '50: Best Color Cinematography, Best Film Editing; Nominations: Academy Awards '50: Best Picture. VHS, Beta ★★★

Kings of the Road—In the Course of Time A writer and a film projectionist travel by truck across Germany. The film stands out for its simple and expressive direction, and truly captures the sense of physical and ideological freedom of being on the road. A landmark Wenders epic. In German with English subtitles.
1976 176m/B GE Ruediger Vogler, Hanns Zischler, Elisabeth Kreuzer; **D:** Wim Wenders; **W:** Wim Wenders. Nominations: Cannes Film Festival '76: Best Film. VHS, Beta ★★★1/2

Kings Row The Harry Bellamann best-selling Middle American potboiler comes to life. Childhood friends grow up with varying degrees of success, in a decidedly macabre town. All are continually dependent on and inspired by Parris (Cummings), a psychiatric doctor and genuine gentleman. Many cast members worked against type with unusual success. Warner held the film for a year after its completion, in concern for its dark subject matter, but it received wide acclaim. Shot completely within studio settings—excellent scenic design by William Cameron Menzies, and wonderful score.
1941 127m/B Ann Sheridan, Robert Cummings, Ronald Reagan, Betty Field, Charles Coburn, Claude Rains, Judith Anderson, Nancy Coleman, Karen Verne, Maria Ouspenskaya, Harry Davenport, Ernest Cossart, Pat Moriarity, Scotty Beckett; **D:** Sam Wood; **M:** Erich Wolfgang Korngold. Nominations: Academy Awards '42: Best Black and White Cinematography, Best Director (Wood), Best Picture. VHS, Beta ★★★

Kismet Original screen version of the much filmed lavish Arabian Nights saga (remade in '30, '44 and '55). A beggar is drawn into deception and intrigue among Bagdad upper-crusters. Glorious sets and costumes; silent with original organ score.
1920 98m/B Otis Skinner, Elinor Fair, Herschel Mayall; **D:** Louis Gasnier. VHS ★★★

The Kiss Garbo, the married object of earnest young Ayres' lovelorn affection, innocently kisses him nighty night since a kiss is just a kiss. Or so she thought. Utterly misconstrued, the platonic peck sets the stage for

disaster, and murder and courtroom anguish follow. French Feyder's direction is stylized and artsy. Garbo's last silent and Ayres' first film.
1929 89m/B Greta Garbo, Conrad Nagel, Holmes Herbert, Lew Ayres, Anders Randolf; *D:* Jacques Feyder. **VHS ★★★**

Kiss Me Deadly Aldrich's adaptation of Mickey Spillane's private eye tale takes pulp literature high concept. Meeker, as Mike Hammer, is a self interested rough and tumble all American dick (detective, that is). When a woman to whom he happened to give a ride is found murdered, he follows the mystery straight into a nuclear conspiracy. Aldrich, with tongue deftly in cheek, styles a message through the medium; topsy turvy camerawork and rat-a-tat-tat pacing tell volumes about Hammer, the world he orbits, and that special '50s kind of paranoia. Now a cult fave, it's considered to be the American granddaddy to French New Wave. Cinematography by Ernest Laszlo.
1955 105m/B Ralph Meeker, Albert Dekker, Paul Stewart, Wesley Addy, Cloris Leachman, Strother Martin, Marjorie Bennett, Jack Elam; *D:* Robert Aldrich. **VHS, Beta, LV ★★★1/2**

Kiss Me Kate A married couple can't separate their real lives from their stage roles in this musical-comedy screen adaptation of Shakespeare's "Taming of the Shrew," based on Cole Porter's Broadway show. Bob Fosse bursts from the screen—particularly if you see the 3-D version—when he does his dance number. ♪ Out of This World; From This Moment On; So In Love; I Hate Men; Were Thine That Special Face; I've Come To Wive It Wealthily In Padua; Where Is The Life That Late I Led?; Always True To You Darling In My Fashion.
1953 110m/C Kathryn Grayson, Howard Keel, Ann Miller, Tommy Rall, Bob Fosse, Bobby Van, Keenan Wynn, James Whitmore; *D:* George Sidney; *M:* Andre Previn. Nominations: Academy Awards '53: Best Original Score. **VHS, Beta, LV ★★★**

Kiss of Death Paroled when he turns state's evidence, Mature must now watch his back constantly. Widmark, in his film debut, seeks to destroy him. Police chief Donlevy tries to help. Filmed on location in New York, this gripping and gritty film is a vision of the most terrifying sort of existence, one where nothing is certain, and everything is dangerous. Excellent.
1947 98m/B Victor Mature, Richard Widmark, Anne Grey, Brian Donlevy, Karl Malden, Coleen Gray; *D:* Henry Hathaway. Nominations: Academy Awards '47: Best Story, Best Supporting Actor (Widmark). **VHS ★★★**

Kiss of the Spider Woman From the novel by Manuel Puig, an acclaimed drama concerning two cell mates in a South American prison, one a revolutionary, the other a homosexual. Literate, haunting, powerful.
1985 (R) 119m/C *BR* William Hurt, Raul Julia, Sonia Braga, Jose Lewgoy, Milton Goncalves, Nuno Leal Maia, Denise Dumont; *D:* Hector Babenco; *W:* Leonard Schrader; *M:* John Neschling, Wally Badarou. Academy Awards '85: Best Actor (Hurt); British Academy Awards '85: Best Actor (Hurt); Cannes Film Festival '85: Best Actor (Hurt); Independent Spirit Awards '86: Best Foreign Film; Los Angeles Film Critics Association Awards '85: Best Actor (Hurt); National Board of Review Awards '85: Best Actor (Hurt), Best Actor (Julia); Nominations: Academy Awards '85: Best Adapted Screenplay, Best Director (Babenco), Best Picture. **VHS, Beta, LV, 8mm ★★★**

Kitty Foyle From the novel by Christopher Morley, Rogers portrays the white-collar working girl whose involvement with a married man presents her with both romantic and social conflicts.
1940 108m/B Ginger Rogers, Dennis (Stanley Morner) Morgan, James Craig, Gladys Cooper, Ernest Cossart, Eduardo Ciannelli; *D:* Sam Wood. Academy Awards '40: Best Actress (Rogers); Nominations: Academy Awards '40: Best Adapted Screenplay, Best Director (Wood), Best Picture, Best Sound. **VHS, Beta ★★★**

Klute A small-town policeman (Sutherland) comes to New York in search of a missing friend and gets involved with a prostitute/would-be actress (Fonda) being stalked by a killer. Intelligent, gripping drama.
1971 (R) 114m/C Jane Fonda, Donald Sutherland, Charles Cioffi, Roy Scheider, Rita Gam, Jean Stapleton; *D:* Alan J. Pakula, Gordon Willis. Academy Awards '71: Best Actress (Fonda); Golden Globe Awards '72: Best Actress—Drama (Fonda); New York Film Critics Awards '71: Best Actress (Fonda); National Society of Film Critics Awards '71: Best Actress (Fonda); Nominations: Academy Awards '71: Best Story & Screenplay. **VHS, Beta, LV ★★★1/2**

The Knack Amusing, fast-paced adaptation of the play by Ann Jellicoe. Schoolteacher Crawford is baffled by his tenant Brooks' extreme luck with the ladies so Brooks de-

cides to teach him the "knack" of picking up women. Crawford promptly falls for the first woman (Tushingham) he meets. Swinging London at its most mod. *AKA:* The Knack . . . and How to Get It.
1965 84m/B *GB* Michael Crawford, Ray Brooks, Rita Tushingham, Donal Donnelly; *D:* Richard Lester; *W:* Charles Wood; *M:* John Barry. VHS ★★★

Knife in the Water A journalist, his wife and a hitchhiker spend a day aboard a sailboat. Sex and violence can't be far off. Tense psychological drama. Served as director Polanski's debut. In Polish with English subtitles. *AKA:* Noz w Wodzie.
1962 94m/B *PL* Leon Niemczyk, Jolanta Umecka, Zygmunt Malandowicz; *D:* Roman Polanski; *W:* Jerzy Skolimowski, Roman Polanski. Venice Film Festival '62: International Critics Award; Nominations: Academy Awards '63: Best Foreign Language Film. VHS, Beta, LV ★★★★

The Knockout/Dough and Dynamite Two Chaplin shorts: "The Knockout" (1914), in which Charlie referees a big fight; "Dough and Dynamite" (1914), in which a labor dispute at a bake shop leaves Charlie in charge when the regular baker walks out.
1914 54m/B Charlie Chaplin, Fatty Arbuckle, Mabel Normand, The Keystone Cops; *D:* Charlie Chaplin, Sydney Chaplin. VHS, Beta ★★★

Knute Rockne: All American Life story of Notre Dame football coach Knute Rockne, who inspired many victories with his powerful speeches. Reagan, as the dying George Gipp, utters that now-famous line, "Tell the boys to win one for the Gipper." *AKA:* A Modern Hero.
1940 96m/B Ronald Reagan, Pat O'Brien, Gale Page, Donald Crisp, John Qualen; *D:* Lloyd Bacon. VHS, Beta ★★★

Kojiro A sprawling epic by prolific Japanese director Inagaki about a dashing rogue's bid for power in feudal times. With English subtitles.
1967 152m/C *JP* Kikunosuke Onoe, Tatsuya Nakadai; *D:* Hiroshi Inagaki. VHS, Beta ★★★

Kolya Set in the late '80s, just before the Velvet Revolution ended Soviet domination of Czechoslovakia, womanizing Prague cellist Louka (Sverak) agrees to marry (for money) a Russian woman who wants Czech papers. She soon clears out to join her lover in Berlin, and Louka finds himself saddled with her five-year-old son, Kolya (Chalimon). Grumpy Louka isn't dad material, and they don't even speak the same language, but the kid (who's adorable without being cloying) manages to worm his way into his new life. Czech with subtitles.
1996 111m/C *CZ* Zdenek Sverak, Andre Chalimon; *D:* Zdenek Sverak; *W:* Zdenek Sverak. Golden Globe Awards '97: Best Foreign Language Film. VHS ★★★

Korczak Based on the life of Dr. Janusz Korczak, an outspoken critic of the Nazis, who ran the Jewish orphanage in Warsaw, Poland and accompanied 200 children to to the Treblinka concentration camp. Harshly poetic film quietly details Polish resistance to the Nazi terror. Criticized for end scenes of the children romping in the countryside, implying that they were somehow freed—since the director did not want to show the children actually entering the gas chambers, he used this allegory to imply that their souls were freed. In Polish with English subtitles.
1990 118m/C *PL* Wojtek Pszoniak, Ewa Dalkowska, Piotr Kozlowski, Marzena Trybala, Wojciech Klata, Adam Siemion; *D:* Andrzej Wajda; *W:* Agnieszka Holland. VHS ★★★

Kotch An elderly man resists his children's attempts to retire him. Warm detailing of old age with a splendid performance by Matthau. Lemmon's directorial debut.
1971 (PG) 113m/C Walter Matthau, Deborah Winters, Felicia Farr; *D:* Jack Lemmon; *M:* Marvin Hamlisch. Golden Globe Awards '72: Best Song ("Life Is What You Make It"); Writers Guild of America '71: Best Adapted Screenplay; Nominations: Academy Awards '71: Best Actor (Matthau), Best Film Editing, Best Song ("Life Is What You MaKe It"), Best Sound. VHS ★★★

Koyaanisqatsi A mesmerizing film that takes an intense look at modern life (the movie's title is the Hopi word for "life out of balance"). Without dialogue or narration, it brings traditional background elements, landscapes and cityscapes, up front to produce a unique view of the structure and mechanics of our daily lives. Riveting and immensely powerful. A critically acclaimed score by Glass, and Reggio's cinematography prove to be the perfect match to this brilliant film. Followed by "Powaqqatsi."
1983 87m/C *D:* Godfrey Reggio; *M:* Philip Glass. Los Angeles Film Critics Association Awards '83: Best Score. VHS, Beta, LV ★★★★

Kramer vs. Kramer Highly acclaimed family drama about an advertising executive husband and child left behind when their wife and mother leaves on a quest to find herself, and the subsequent courtroom battle for custody when she returns. Hoffman and Streep give exacting performances as does young Henry. Successfully moves you from tears to laughter and back again. Based on the novel by Avery Corman.

1979 (PG) 105m/C Dustin Hoffman, Meryl Streep, Jane Alexander, Justin Henry, Howard Duff, JoBeth Williams; *D:* Robert Benton; *W:* Robert Benton. Academy Awards '79: Best Actor (Hoffman), Best Adapted Screenplay, Best Director (Benton), Best Picture, Best Supporting Actress (Streep); Golden Globe Awards '80: Best Actor—Drama (Hoffman), Best Film—Drama, Best Screenplay, Best Supporting Actress (Streep); National Board of Review Awards '79: 10 Best Films of the Year, Best Supporting Actress (Streep); National Society of Film Critics Awards '79: Best Actor (Hoffman), Best Director (Benton), Best Supporting Actress (Streep); Nominations: Academy Awards '79: Best Cinematography, Best Film Editing, Best Supporting Actor (Henry). **VHS, Beta, LV ★★★1/2**

The Krays An account of British gangsters Reggie and Ronnie Kray, the brothers who ruled London's East End with brutality and violence, making them bizarre celebrities of the sixties. The leads are portrayed by Gary and Martin Kemp, founders of the British pop group Spandau Ballet.

1990 (R) 119m/C *GB* Gary Kemp, Martin Kemp, Billie Whitelaw, Steven Berkoff, Susan Fleetwood, Charlotte Cornwell; *D:* Peter Medak; *W:* Philip Ridley; *M:* Michael Kamen. **VHS, LV, 8mm ★★★1/2**

Kriemhilde's Revenge The second film, following "Siegfried," of Lang's "Die Nibelungen," a lavish silent version of the Teutonic legends Wagner's "Ring of the Nibelungen" was based upon. In this episode, Kriemhilde avenges Siegfried's death by her marriage to the Kings of the Huns, thus fulfilling a prophecy of destruction. *AKA:* Die Nibelungen.

1924 95m/B *GE* Paul Richter, Margareta Schoen, Theodore Loos, Hanna Ralph, Rudolf Klein-Rogge; *D:* Fritz Lang. **VHS, LV ★★★★**

Kwaidan A haunting, stylized quartet of supernatural stories, each with a surprise ending. Adapted from the stories of Lafcadio Hearn, an American author who lived in Japan just before the turn of the century. The visual effects are splendid. In Japanese with English subtitles.

1964 164m/C *JP* Michiyo Aratama, Rentaro Mikuni, Katsuo Makamura, Keiko Kishi, Tatsuya Nakadai, Takashi Shimura; *D:* Masaki Kobayashi; *M:* Toru Takemitsu. Cannes Film Festival '65: Grand Jury Prize; Nominations: Academy Awards '65: Best Foreign Language Film. **VHS, Beta, LV ★★★★**

La Balance An underworld stool pigeon is recruited by the Parisian police to blow the whistle on a murderous mob. Baye, as a prostitute in love with the pimp-stoolie, is a standout. Critically acclaimed in France; won many Cesar awards, including for Best Picture. In French with English subtitles.

1982 (R) 103m/C *FR* Philippe Leotard, Nathalie Baye, Bob Swaim; *D:* Reymond LePlont; *M:* Roland Bocquet. Cesar Awards '83: Best Actor (Leotard), Best Actress (Baye), Best Film. **VHS, Beta ★★★**

La Bamba A romantic biography of the late 1950s pop idol Ritchie Valens, concentrating on his stormy relationship with his half-brother, his love for his WASP girlfriend, and his tragic, sudden death in the famed plane crash that also took the lives of Buddy Holly and the Big Bopper. Soundtrack features Setzer, Huntsberry, Crenshaw, and Los Lobos as, respectively, Eddie Cochran, the Big Bopper, Buddy Holly, and a Mexican bordello band.

1987 (PG-13) 99m/C Lou Diamond Phillips, Esai Morales, Danielle von Zernaeck, Joe Pantoliano, Brian Setzer, Marshall Crenshaw, Howard Huntsberry, Rosana De Soto, Elizabeth Pena, Rick Dees; *D:* Luis Valdez; *W:* Luis Valdez; *M:* Carlos Santana, Miles Goodman. **VHS, Beta, LV, 8mm ★★★**

La Belle Noiseuse The connections between art and life are explored in this beautiful (and long) drama. Creatively crippled, an aging painter has left unfinished a masterpiece work, entitled "La Belle Noiseuse," for 10 years. When an admiring younger artist and his beautiful lover arrive for a visit, the painter is newly inspired by the young woman and makes her the model and muse for his masterwork. The film details every nuance of the work from the first to the last brushstroke and the battle of wills between artist and model over the symbiotic creative process. Based on a novella by Honore Balzac. In French with English subtitles. "Divertimento" is actually a recut and shortened version (126 minutes) of the original film. *AKA:* Divertimento.

1990 240m/C *FR* Michel Piccoli,

Emmanuelle Beart, Jane Birkin, David Bursztein, Marianne Denicourt; **D:** Jacques Rivette. Cannes Film Festival '91: Grand Jury Prize; Los Angeles Film Critics Association Awards '91: Best Foreign Film. **VHS ★★★1/2**

La Bete Humaine A dark, psychological melodrama about human passion and duplicity, as an unhinged trainman plots with a married woman to kill her husband. Wonderful performances and stunning photography. Based on the Emile Zola novel. In French with English subtitles. 1954 Hollywood remake, "Human Desire," was directed by Fritz Lang. **AKA:** The Human Beast.
1938 90m/B *FR* Jean Gabin, Simone Simon, Julien Carette, Fernand Ledoux; **D:** Jean Renoir. **VHS, Beta, 8mm ★★★1/2**

La Cage aux Folles Adaption of the popular French play. A gay nightclub owner and his transvestite lover play it straight when Tognazzi's son from a long-ago liaison brings his fiancee and her conservative parents home for dinner. Charming music and lots of fun. So successful, it was followed by two sequels, "La Cage Aux Folles II & III" and also a Broadway musical. In French with English subtitles.
1978 (R) 91m/C *FR* Ugo Tognazzi, Michel Serrault, Michel Galabru, Claire Maurier, Remy Laurent, Benny Luke; **D:** Edouard Molinaro; **W:** Francis Veber; **M:** Ennio Morricone. Cesar Awards '79: Best Actor (Serrault); Golden Globe Awards '80: Best Foreign Film; Nominations: Academy Awards '79: Best Adapted Screenplay, Best Costume Design, Best Director (Molinaro). **VHS, Beta, LV ★★★1/2**

La Ceremonie Sullen maid Sophie (Bonnaire) is hired by the rich Lelievre family to work at their country estate. She's befriended by independent postmistress Jeanne (Huppert), who's disliked by Sophie's employers and who encourages Sophie into small defiant actions. Something's off about the entire situation, and there's violence beneath the seemingly calm surface. Based on Ruth Rendell's chiller "Judgement in Stone." French with subtitles. **AKA:** A Judgment in Stone.
1995 111m/C *FR* Sandrine Bonnaire, Isabelle Huppert, Jacqueline Bisset, Jean-Pierre Cassel; **D:** Claude Chabrol; **W:** Claude Chabrol, Caroline Eliacheff. Cesar Awards '96: Best Actress (Huppert); Los Angeles Film Critics Association Awards '96: Best Foreign Film; National Society of Film Critics Awards '96: Best Foreign Language Film; Nominations: Cesar Awards '96: Best Film, Best Director (Chabrol), Best Actress (Bonnaire), Best

Supporting Actress (Bisset), Best Screenplay, Best Supporting Actor (Cassel). **VHS ★★★**

La Chevre A screwball French comedy about two policemen (Richard and Depardieu—picture Nick Nolte and Gene Wilder with accents) stumbling along the path of a missing heiress who suffers from chronic bad luck. Contains a hilarious scene with chairs used to test the luck of the investigative team; based on one partner's ability to sit on the only broken chair in a rather large collection, he is judged to be sufficiently jinxed to allow them to re-create the same outrageous misfortunes that befell the heiress in her plight. In French with English subtitles. **AKA:** The Goat.
1981 91m/C *FR* Gerard Depardieu, Pierre Richard, Corynne Charbit, Michel Robin, Pedro Armendariz Jr.; **D:** Francis Veber; **M:** Vladimir Cosma. **VHS, Beta ★★★★**

La Chienne Dark, troubling tale of a bedraggled husband whose only excitement is his painting hobby until he becomes consumed by the ever-tempting prostitute Lulu. Director Renoir broke ground with his use of direct sound and Paris shooting locations, and the experiment was a hit. Portrays marriage with acidity; Renoir's own marriage broke up as a result of this film's casting. Mareze died shortly after the filming was complete in a car crash. Based on the novel by Georges de la Fouchardiere. Produced in 1931, but didn't reach American theaters until 1975. In French with English subtitles. Remade in 1945 as "Scarlet Street." **AKA:** Isn't Life A Bitch?; The Bitch.
1931 93m/B *FR* Michel Simon, Janie Mareze, Georges Flament, Madeleine Berubet; **D:** Jean Renoir; **W:** Andre Girard, Jean Renoir. **VHS, Beta, LV ★★★★**

La Dolce Vita In this influential and popular work a successful, sensationalistic Italian journalist covers the show-biz life in Rome, and alternately covets and disdains its glitzy shallowness. The film follows his dealings with the "sweet life" over a pivotal week. A surreal, comic tableaux with award-winning costuming; one of Fellini's most acclaimed films. In this film Fellini called his hungry celebrity photographers the Paparazzo—and it is as the paparazzi they have been ever since. In Italian with English subtitles.
1960 174m/B *IT* Marcello Mastroianni, Anita Ekberg, Anouk Aimee, Alain Cuny, Lex Barker, Yvonne Furneaux, Barbara Steele, Nadia Gray, Magali Noel, Walter

Santesso, Jacques Sernas, Annabelle Ninchi; **D:** Federico Fellini; **W:** Tullio Pinelli, Ennio Flaiano, Brunello Rondi, Federico Fellini; **M:** Nino Rota. Academy Awards '61: Best Costume Design (B & W); Cannes Film Festival '60: Best Film; National Board of Review Awards '61: 5 Best Foreign Films of the Year; New York Film Critics Awards '61: Best Foreign Film; Nominations: Academy Awards '61: Best Art Direction/Set Decoration (B & W), Best Director (Fellini), Best Story & Screenplay. **VHS, LV ★★★★**

La Femme Nikita Stylish French noir version of Pygmalion. Having killed a cop during a drugstore theft gone awry, young French sociopath Nikita (Parillaud) is reprieved from a death sentence in order to enroll in a government finishing school, of sorts. Trained in etiquette and assassination, she's released after three years, and starts a new life with a new beau, all the while carrying out agency-mandated assassinations. Parillaud is excellent as the once-amoral street urchin transformed into a woman of depth and sensitivity—a bitterly ironic moral evolution for a contract killer. Remade as "Point of No Return." **1991 (R) 117m/C** *FR* Anne Parillaud, Jean-Hugues Anglade, Tcheky Karyo, Jeanne Moreau, Jean Reno, Jean Bouise; **D:** Luc Besson; **W:** Luc Besson; **M:** Eric Serra. Cesar Awards '91: Best Actress (Parillaud). **VHS ★★★**

La Grande Vadrouille In 1943 German-occupied France, three Allied parachutists drop in on a Paris Opera conductor and a house painter. If the pair wish to find some peace, they must help the trio get to the free zone. France's number one box office hit for almost thirty years. Also available dubbed. **AKA:** Don't Look Now, We've Been Shot At. **1966 122m/C** *FR* Louis de Funes, Bourvil, Terry-Thomas; **D:** Gerard Oury. **VHS ★★★**

L.A. Law The pilot episode of the acclaimed dramatic series, in which the staff of a Los Angeles law firm tries a variety of cases. **1986 97m/C** Michael Tucker, Jill Eikenberry, Harry Hamlin, Richard Dysart, Jimmy Smits, Alan Rachins, Susan Ruttan, Susan Dey, Corbin Bernsen; **D:** Gregory Hoblit. **VHS, Beta ★★★**

La Marseillaise Sweeping epic by Renoir made before he hit his stride with "Grand Illusion." It details the events of the French Revolution in the summer of 1789 using a cast of thousands. The opulent lifestyle of the French nobility is starkly contrasted with the peasant lifestyle of poverty

and despair. The focus is on two new recruits who have joined the Marseilles division of the revolutionary army as they begin their long march to Paris, the heart of France. As they travel, they adopt a stirring and passionate song that embodies the spirit and ideals of the revolution, known as "La Marseillaise," now France's national anthem. In French with English subtitles. **1937 130m/B** *FR* Pierre Renoir, Lisa Delamare, Louis Jouvet, Aime Clairmond, Andrex Andrisson, Paul Dullac; **D:** Jean Renoir; **W:** Jean Renoir. **VHS, Beta ★★★1/2**

La Nuit de Varennes This semi-historical romp is based on an actual chapter in French history when King Louis XVI and Marie Antoinette fled from revolutionary Paris to Varennes in 1791. On the way they meet an unlikely group of characters, including Casanova and Thomas Paine. At times witty and charming, the melange of history and fiction is full of talk, sometimes profane, punctuated by sex and nudity. Director Scola's imagination stretches to light up this night. In French with English subtitles. **1982 (R) 133m/C** *FR IT* Marcello Mastroianni, Harvey Keitel, Jean-Louis Barrault, Hanna Schygulla, Jean-Claude Brialy; **D:** Ettore Scola; **W:** Ettore Scola. Nominations: Cannes Film Festival '82: Best Film. **VHS, Beta, LV ★★★**

La Ronde A classic comedy of manners and sharply witty tour-de-farce in which a group of people in 1900 Vienna keep changing romantic partners until things wind up where they started. Ophuls' swirling direction creates a fast-paced farce of desire and regret with wicked yet subtle style. Based on Arthur Schnitzler's play and remade as "Circle of Love." In French with English subtitles. **1951 97m/B** *FR* Simone Signoret, Anton Walbrook, Simone Simon, Serge Reggiani, Daniel Gelin, Danielle Darrieux, Jean-Louis Barrault, Fernand Gravet, Odette Joyeux, Isa Miranda, Gerard Philipe; **D:** Max Ophuls. British Academy Awards '51: Best Film; Nominations: Academy Awards '51: Best Art Direction/Set Decoration (B & W), Best Screenplay. **VHS, Beta ★★★1/2**

La Scorta Slick, fact-based political thriller focuses on four carabinieri (state police officers) who struggle to maintain some semblance of their normal lives after they are assigned to protect a judge investigating government corruption and a related murder in a Sicilian town. A crackling alternative to Americanized mobster melo-

drama, marked by taut direction, meaty characters, and coolly understated performances that seamlessly portray brotherhood, heroism, suspicion, and betrayal amid the battle for power between the Italian state and the Mafia. In Italian with English subtitles. *AKA:* The Bodyguards; The Escorts.
1994 92m/C Claudio Amendola, Enrico Lo Verso, Tony Sperandeo, Ricky Memphis, Carlo Cecchi, Leo Gullotta; *D:* Ricardo Tognazzi; *W:* Graziano Diana, Simona Izzo; *M:* Ennio Morricone. VHS ★★★1/2

La Signora di Tutti An early Italian biography of Gaby Doriot, a movie star whose professional success is paired by personal misery. Prestigious director Ophuls, working in exile from his native Germany, was unable to complete many projects in the years leading up to and during WWII. This is one of the few. Watch for innovative camera work intended to underscore the film's mood. In Italian with English subtitles.
1934 92m/B *IT* Isa Miranda; *D:* Max Ophuls. VHS, Beta ★★★

L.A. Story Livin' ain't easy in the city of angels. Harris K. Telemacher (Martin), a weatherman in a city where the weather never changes, wrestles with the meaning of life and love while consorting with beautiful people, distancing from significant other Henner, cavorting with valley girl Parker, and falling for newswoman Tennant (Martin's real life wife). Written by the comedian, the story's full of keen insights into the everyday problems and ironies of living in the Big Tangerine. (It's no wonder the script's full of so much thoughtful detail: Martin is said to have worked on it intermittently for seven years.) Charming, fault forgiving but not fault ignoring portrait.
1991 (PG-13) 98m/C Steve Martin, Victoria Tennant, Richard E. Grant, Marilu Henner, Sarah Jessica Parker, Sam McMurray, Patrick Stewart, Iman, Kevin Pollak; *D:* Mick Jackson; *W:* Steve Martin; *M:* Peter Melnick. VHS, Beta, LV ★★★

La Strada Simple-minded girl, played by Fellini's wife, Masina, is sold to a brutal, coarse circus strong-man and she falls in love with him despite his abuse. They tour the countryside and eventually meet up with a gentle acrobat, played by Basehart, who alters their fate. Fellini masterwork was the director's first internationally acclaimed film, and is, by turns, somber and amusing as it demonstrates the filmmaker's sensitivity to the under-

privileged of the world and his belief in spiritual redemption. Subtitled in English. *AKA:* The Road.
1954 107m/B *IT* Giulietta Masina, Anthony Quinn, Richard Basehart, Aldo Silvani; *D:* Federico Fellini; *W:* Ennio Flaiano, Brunello Rondi, Tullio Pinelli, Federico Fellini; *M:* Nino Rota. Academy Awards '56: Best Foreign Language Film; National Board of Review Awards '56: 5 Best Foreign Films of the Year; New York Film Critics Awards '56: Best Foreign Film; Nominations: Academy Awards '56: Best Original Screenplay. VHS, Beta, LV ★★★★

La Symphonie Pastorale A Swiss pastor takes in an orphan blind girl who grows up to be beautiful. The pastor then competes for her affections with his son. Quiet drama based on the Andre Gide novel, with breathtaking mountain scenery as the backdrop for this tragedy rife with symbolism.
1946 105m/B *FR* Pierre Blanchar, Michele Morgan, Jean Desailly, Line Noro, Andree Clement; *D:* Jean Delannoy. Cannes Film Festival '46: Best Actress (Morgan). VHS ★★★1/2

La Terra Trema The classic example of Italian neo-realism, about a poor Sicilian fisherman, his family and their village. A spare, slow-moving, profound and ultimately lyrical tragedy, this semi-documentary explores the economic exploitation of Sicily's fishermen. Filmed on location with the villagers playing themselves; highly acclaimed though not commercially successful. In Sicilian with English subtitles. Some radically cut versions may be available, but are to be avoided. Franco Zefferelli was one of the assistant directors. *AKA:* Episoda Del Mare; The Earth Will Tremble.
1948 161m/B *IT* Antonio Pietrangeli; *D:* Luchino Visconti. VHS, Beta ★★★1/2

The Lacemaker Huppert's first shot at stardom, on laserdisc with digital sound and a letterboxed print. A young beautician and a university student fall in love on vacation but soon begin to realize the differences in their lives. Adapted from the novel by Pascal Laine. In French with English subtitles. *AKA:* La Dentielliere.
1977 107m/C *FR SI GE* Isabelle Huppert, Yves Beneyton, Florence Giorgetti, Anna Marie Duringer; *D:* Claude Goretta. Nominations: Cannes Film Festival '77: Best Film. LV ★★★1/2

Lady and the Tramp The animated Disney classic about two dogs who fall in love. Tramp is wild and carefree; Lady is a spoiled pedigree who runs away from home after her owners

have a baby. They just don't make dog romances like this anymore. ♪ He's a Tramp; La La Lu; Siamese Cat Song; Peace on Earth; Bella Notte.
1955 (G) 76m/C D: Hamilton Luske; **M:** Peggy Lee, Sonny Burke; **V:** Larry Roberts, Peggy Lee, Barbara Luddy, Stan Freberg, Alan Reed, Bill Thompson, Bill Baucon, Verna Felton, George Givot, Dallas McKennon, Lee Millar. **VHS, Beta, LV**
★★★★

The Lady Eve Two con artists, out to trip up wealthy beer tycoon Fonda, instead find themselves tripped up when one falls in love with the prey. Ridiculous situations, but Sturges manages to keep them believable and funny. With a train scene that's every man's nightmare. Perhaps the best Sturges ever. Based on the story "The Faithful Heart" by Monckton Hoffe. Later remade as "The Birds and the Bees."
1941 93m/B Barbara Stanwyck, Henry Fonda, Charles Coburn, Eugene Pallette, William Demarest, Eric Blore, Melville Cooper; **D:** Preston Sturges; **W:** Preston Sturges. National Board of Review Awards '41: 10 Best Films of the Year; Nominations: Academy Awards '41: Best Story. **VHS, Beta, LV** ★★★★

Lady for a Day Delightful telling of the Damon Runyon story, "Madame La Gimp," about an apple peddler (Robson) down on her luck, who is transformed into a lady by a criminal with a heart. "Lady By Choice" is the sequel.
1933 96m/B May Robson, Warren William, Guy Kibbee, Glenda Farrell, Ned Sparks, Jean Parker, Walter Connolly; **D:** Frank Capra. Nominations: Academy Awards '33: Best Actress (Robson), Best Adapted Screenplay, Best Director (Capra), Best Picture. **VHS, Beta, LV** ★★★1/2

The Lady from Shanghai An unsuspecting seaman becomes involved in a web of intrigue when a woman hires him to work on her husband's yacht. Hayworth (a one-time Mrs. Orson Welles), in her only role as a villainess, plays a manipulative, sensual schemer. Wonderful and innovative cinematic techniques from Welles, as usual, including a tense scene in a hall of mirrors. Filmed on a yacht belonging to Errol Flynn.
1948 87m/B Orson Welles, Rita Hayworth, Everett Sloane, Glenn Anders, Ted de Corsia, Erskine Sanford, Gus Schilling; **D:** Orson Welles; **W:** Orson Welles. **VHS, Beta, LV** ★★★1/2

Lady in a Cage A wealthy widow is trapped in her home elevator during a power failure and becomes desper-

ate when hoodlums break in. Shocking violence ahead of its time probably plays better than when first released. Young Caan is a standout among the star-studded cast.
1964 95m/B Olivia de Havilland, Ann Sothern, James Caan, Jennifer Billingsley, Jeff Corey, Scatman Crothers, Rafael Campos; **D:** Walter Grauman; **W:** Luther Davis. **VHS, Beta** ★★★

Lady Jane An accurate account of the life of 15-year-old Lady Jane Grey, who secured the throne of England for nine days in 1553 as a result of political maneuvering by noblemen and the Church of England. A wonderful film even for non-history buffs. Carter's first film.
1985 (PG-13) 140m/C GB Helena Bonham Carter, Cary Elwes, Sara Kestelman, Michael Hordern, Joss Ackland, Richard Johnson, Patrick Stewart; **D:** Trevor Nunn. **VHS, Beta, LV** ★★★1/2

The Lady Vanishes When a kindly old lady disappears from a fast-moving train, her young friend finds an imposter in her place and a spiraling mystery to solve. Hitchcock's first real winner, a smarmy, wit-drenched British mystery that precipitated his move to Hollywood. Along with "39 Steps," considered an early Hitchcock classic. From the novel "The Wheel Spins," by Ethel Lina White. Special edition contains short subject on Hitchcock's cameos in his films. Remade in 1979.
1938 99m/B GB Margaret Lockwood, Paul Lukas, Michael Redgrave, May Whitty, Googie Withers, Basil Radford, Naunton Wayne, Cecil Parker, Linden Travers, Catherine Lacey; **Cameos:** Alfred Hitchcock; **D:** Alfred Hitchcock; **W:** Sidney Gilliat, Frank Launder; **M:** Louis Levy. New York Film Critics Awards '38: Best Director (Hitchcock). **VHS, Beta, LV** ★★★★

Ladybird, Ladybird Loach's emotionally bruising look at working-class life and family in the '90s. Maggie (Rock) is a tough unmarried mother of four who's been battered by her lovers and has come under the overwatchful eye of Britain's social services. She meets Jorge (Vega), a gentle Paraguayan, and just when things are looking up, Jorge gets immigration heat, and her baby daughter is taken into care by child welfare. Rock has a no-nonsense manner and acerbic wit that precludes any hand-wringing for her character, even as you hope she'll win out over circumstance. Based on a true story.
1993 (R) 102m/C GB Crissy Rock,

Vladimir Vega, Ray Winstone, Sandie Lavelle, Mauricio Venegas, Clare Perkins, Jason Stracey, Luke Brown, Lily Farrell; **D:** Ken Loach; **W:** Rona Munro. Berlin International Film Festival '94: Best Actress (Rock); Nominations: Independent Spirit Awards '95: Best Foreign Language Film. **VHS ★★★**

The Ladykillers A gang of bumbling bank robbers is foiled by a little old lady. Hilarious antics follow, especially on the part of Guinness, who plays the slightly demented-looking leader of the gang. **AKA:** The Lady Killers.
1955 87m/C *GB* Alec Guinness, Cecil Parker, Katie Johnson, Herbert Lom, Peter Sellers; **D:** Alexander MacKendrick; **W:** William Rose; **M:** Tristram Cary. British Academy Awards '55: Best Actress (Johnson), Best Screenplay. **VHS, Beta ★★★1/2**

L'Age D'Or Bunuel's first full-length film and his masterpiece of sex, repression, and of course, death. A hapless man is prevented from reaching his beloved by middle-class morality, forces of the establishment, the Church, government and every bastion of modern values. Banned for years because of its anti-religious stance. Co-scripted by Dali. A mercilessly savage, surreal satire, the purest expression of Bunuel's wry misanthropy. In French with English subtitles. **AKA:** Age of Gold.
1930 62m/B *FR* Gaston Modot, Lya Lys, Max Ernst, Pierre Prevert, Marie Berthe Ernst, Paul Eluard; **D:** Luis Bunuel; **W:** Salvador Dali, Luis Bunuel. **VHS, Beta, LV ★★★★**

The Lair of the White Worm Scottish archaeologist uncovers a strange skull, and then a bizarre religion to go with it, and then a very big worm. An unusual look at the effects of Christianity and paganism on each other, colored with sexual innuendo and, of course, giant worms. A cross between a morality play and a horror film. Adapted from Bram Stoker's last writings, done while he was going mad from Bright's disease. Everything you'd expect from Russell.
1988 (R) 93m/C *GB* Amanda Donohoe, Sammi Davis, Catherine Oxenberg, Hugh Grant, Peter Capaldi, Stratford Johns, Paul Brooke, Christopher Gable; **D:** Ken Russell; **W:** Ken Russell; **M:** Stanislas Syrewicz. **VHS, Beta, LV ★★★**

Lamerica Two Italian hustlers, Fiore (Placido) and his younger partner Gino (Lo Verso), head for poverty-stricken Albania in 1991, the first year after the collapse of the Communist dictatorship. They intend to set up a phony corporation and scam money from government grants, but they need an Albanian figurehead. The duo find simple-minded, elderly Spiro (Di Mazzarelli), who's spent most of his life in prison camps and stash him in an orphanage for safe keeping. Only when Spiro gets away, Gino heads for the countryside to find him and discovers some secrets about Spiro's past and just how the wily Albanian has been surviving. Italian with subtitles.
1995 120m/C *IT* Enrico Lo Verso, Michele Placido, Carmelo Di Mazzarelli, Piro Milkani; **D:** Gianni Amelio; **W:** Gianni Amelio, Andrea Porporati, Alessandro Sermoneta; **M:** Franco Piersanti. Nominations: Independent Spirit Awards '97: Best Foreign Film. **VHS ★★★**

Land and Freedom Earnestly talky drama focusing on idealist Liverpudlian communist David Carr (Hart), who heads to Spain in 1937 to fight against Franco's fascists. What David learns is that the Republican forces, made up of independent militia, are bitterly divided, with much infighting and betrayal from the Stalinist forces within David's own party. He falls for socialist Blanca (Pastor) and learns how terrifying and haphazard war can be (with time out for ideological discussions). Sympathetic characters and sweeping action help to compensate for the political polemics.
1995 109m/C *GB* Ian Hart, Rosana Pastor, Iciar Bollain, Tom Gilroy, Frederic Pierrot, Marc Martinez; **D:** Ken Loach; **W:** Jim Allen; **M:** George Fenton. Cesar Awards '96: Best Foreign Film; Nominations: British Academy Awards '95: Best Film. **VHS ★★★**

Larks on a String Banned for 23 years, this wonderful film is Menzel's masterpiece, even better than his Oscar-winning "Closely Watched Trains." Portrays the story of life in labor camps where men and women are re-educated at the whim of the government. No matter what the hardships, these people find humor, hope, and love. Their individuality will not be lost, nor their humanity dissolved. Excellent performances, tellingly directed with a beautiful sense of composition and tone. Screenplay written by Menzel and Bohumil Hrabil, author of the short story on which it is based. In Czech with English subtitles.
1968 96m/C *CZ* Vaclav Neckar, Jitka Zelenohorska, Jaroslav Satoransky, Rudolf Hrusinsky; **D:** Jiri Menzel; **W:** Jiri Menzel. **VHS ★★★1/2**

Larry McMurtry's Streets of Laredo
Texas Ranger-turned-bounty hunter Woodrow F. Call (a splendid Garner) is hired by the railroad to track down ruthless Mexican bandit Joey Garza (Cruz), pitting an old man's skills against a young man's daring, and driving both men across Texas, deep into Mexican territory. Call's old friend Pea Eye Parker (Shepard) reluctantly comes along, with ex-prostitute Lorena (Spacek), who's Parker's wife, and Maria (Braga), Joey's tough-but-deluded mom, providing strong support. Casual cruelty and violence are the norm in the sunset days of both Call's life and that of the west itself. Third in the TV sagas, following "Return to Lonesome Dove." *AKA:* Streets of Laredo.
1995 227m/C James Garner, Alexis Cruz, Sam Shepard, Sissy Spacek, Sonia Braga, Wes Studi, Randy Quaid, Charles Martin Smith, Kevin Conway, George Carlin, Ned Beatty, James Gammon, Tristan Tait, Anjanette Comer; *D:* Joseph Sargent; *W:* Larry McMurtry, David Shire. **VHS** ★★★

The Last Angry Man An old, idealistic Brooklyn doctor attracts a television producer wanting to make a documentary about his life and career, and the two conflict. Muni was Oscar-nominated for this, his last film.
1959 100m/B Paul Muni, David Wayne, Betsy Palmer, Luther Adler, Dan Tobin; *D:* Daniel Mann. Nominations: Academy Awards '59: Best Actor (Muni), Best Art Direction/Set Decoration (B & W). **VHS, Beta** ★★★½

Last Command Famous powerful silent film by Sternberg about a expatriate Czarist general forging out a pitiful living as a silent Hollywood extra, where he is hired by his former adversary to reenact the revolution he just left. Next to "The Last Laugh," this is considered Jannings' most acclaimed performance. Deeply ironic, visually compelling film with a new score by Gaylord Carter.
1928 88m/B Emil Jannings, William Powell, Evelyn Brent, Nicholas Soussanin, Michael Visaroff, Jack Raymond, Fritz Feld; *D:* Josef von Sternberg; *W:* Warren Duff; *M:* Max Steiner, Gaylord Carter. Academy Awards '28: Best Actor (Jannings); Nominations: Academy Awards '28: Best Original Screenplay, Best Picture. **VHS, Beta** ★★★★

The Last Detail Two hard-boiled career petty officers (Nicholson and Young) are commissioned to transfer a young sailor facing an eight-year sentence for petty theft from one brig to another. In an act of compassion, they attempt to show the prisoner a final good time. Nicholson shines in both the complexity and completeness of his character. Adapted from a Daryl Ponicsan novel.
1973 (R) 104m/C Jack Nicholson, Otis Young, Randy Quaid, Clifton James, Michael Moriarty, Carol Kane, Nancy Allen; *Cameos:* Gilda Radner; *D:* Hal Ashby; *W:* Robert Towne; *M:* Johnny Mandel, Michael Chapman. British Academy Awards '74: Best Actor (Nicholson), Best Screenplay; Cannes Film Festival '74: Best Actor (Nicholson); National Board of Review Awards '74: 10 Best Films of the Year; New York Film Critics Awards '74: Best Actor (Nicholson); National Society of Film Critics Awards '74: Best Actor (Nicholson); Nominations: Academy Awards '73: Best Actor (Nicholson), Best Adapted Screenplay, Best Supporting Actor (Quaid). **VHS, Beta, LV** ★★★★

The Last Emperor Deeply ironic epic detailing life of Pu Yi, crowned at the age of three as the last emperor of China before the onset of communism. Follows Pu Yi from childhood to manhood (sequestered away in the Forbidden City) to fugitive to puppet-ruler to party proletariat. O'Toole portrays the sympathetic Scot tutor who educates the adult Pu Yi (Lone) in the ways of the western world after Pu Yi abdicates power in 1912. Shot on location inside the People's Republic of China with a cast of thousands; authentic costumes. Rich, visually stunning movie. The Talking Heads' David Byrne contributed to the score. Cinematography by Vittorio Storaro.
1987 (PG-13) 140m/C *IT* John Lone, Peter O'Toole, Joan Chen, Victor Wong, Ryuichi Sakamoto, Dennis Dun, Maggie Han, Ying Ruocheng, Ric Young, Vittorio Storaro; *D:* Bernardo Bertolucci; *W:* Mark Peploe, Bernardo Bertolucci; *M:* Ryuichi Sakamoto, David Byrne. Academy Awards '87: Best Adapted Screenplay, Best Art Direction/Set Decoration, Best Cinematography, Best Costume Design, Best Director (Bertolucci), Best Film Editing, Best Picture, Best Sound, Best Original Score; British Academy Awards '88: Best Film; Cesar Awards '88: Best Foreign Film; Directors Guild of America Awards '87: Best Director (Bertolucci); Golden Globe Awards '88: Best Director (Bertolucci), Best Film—Drama, Best Screenplay, Best Score; Los Angeles Film Critics Association Awards '87: Best Cinematography; National Board of Review Awards '87: 10 Best Films of the Year; New York Film Critics Awards '87: Best Cinematography. **VHS, Beta, LV, 8mm** ★★★★

Last Exit to Brooklyn Hubert Selby, Jr.'s shocking book comes to the screen in a vivid film. Leigh gives a stunning performance as a young Brooklyn girl caught between the Mafia, union men, and friends struggling for something better. Set in the 1950s. Fine supporting cast; excellent pacing.
1989 (R) 102m/C Jennifer Jason Leigh, Burt Young, Stephen Lang, Ricki Lake, Jerry Orbach, Maia Danzinger, Stephen Baldwin; **D:** Uli Edel. New York Film Critics Awards '89: Best Supporting Actress (Leigh). **VHS, LV ★★★1/2**

The Last Laugh An elderly man, who as the doorman of a great hotel was looked upon as a symbol of "upper class," is demoted to washroom attendant due to his age. Important due to camera technique and consuming performance by Jannings. Silent with music score. A 91-minute version is also available. **AKA:** Der Letzte Mann.
1924 77m/B GE Emil Jannings, Maly Delshaft, Max Hiller; **D:** F.W. Murnau. **VHS, Beta ★★★★**

The Last Metro Truffaut's alternately gripping and touching drama about a theater company in Nazi-occupied Paris. In 1942, Lucas Steiner (Bennent) is a successful Jewish theater director who is forced into hiding. He turns the running of the theater over to his wife, Marion (the always exquisite Deneuve), who must contend with a pro-Nazi theater critic (Richard) and her growing attraction to the company's leading man (Depardieu), who is secretly working with the Resistance. In French with English subtitles. **AKA:** Le Dernier Metro.
1980 135m/C FR Catherine Deneuve, Gerard Depardieu, Heinz Bennent, Jean-Louis Richard, Jean Poiret, Andrea Ferreol, Paulette Dubost, Sabine Haudepin; **D:** Francois Truffaut; **W:** Suzanne Schiffman; **M:** Georges Delerue. Cesar Awards '81: Best Actor (Depardieu), Best Actress (Deneuve), Best Art Direction/Set Decoration, Best Cinematography, Best Director (Truffaut), Best Film, Best Sound, Best Writing, Best Score; Nominations: Academy Awards '80: Best Foreign Language Film. **VHS, Beta, LV ★★★**

The Last of Mrs. Cheyney Remake of Norma Shearer's 1929 hit, based on the play by Frederick Lonsdale, about a sophisticated jewel thief in England. Crawford stars as the jewel thief who poses as a wealthy woman to get into parties hosted by London bluebloods. Dripping with charm, she works her way into Lord Drilling's mansion where she plans a huge heist. The film is handled well, and the cast gives solid performances throughout. This chic comedy of high society proved to be one of Crawford's most popular films of the '30s.
1937 98m/B Joan Crawford, Robert Montgomery, William Powell, Frank Morgan, Nigel Bruce, Jessie Ralph; **D:** Richard Boleslawski, George Fitzmaurice. **VHS ★★★**

The Last of the Mohicans Color tints enhance this silent version of the James Fenimore Cooper rouser. Beery is the villainous Magua, with Bedford memorable as the lovely Cora and Roscoe as the brave Uncas. Fine action sequences, including the Huron massacre at Fort Henry. Director credit was shared when Tourneur suffered an on-set injury and was off for three months.
1920 75m/B Wallace Beery, Barbara Bedford, Albert Roscoe, Lillian Hall-Davis, Henry Woodward, James Gordon, George Hackathorne, Harry Lorraine, Nelson McDowell, Theodore Lorch, Boris Karloff; **D:** Maurice Tourneur, Clarence Brown; **W:** Robert Dillon. **VHS, LV ★★★**

The Last of the Mohicans It's 1757, at the height of the French and English war in the American colonies, with various Native American tribes allied to each side. Hawkeye (Day-Lewis), a white frontiersman raised by the Mohicans, wants nothing to do with either "civilized" side, until he rescues the beautiful Cora (Stowe) from the revenge-minded Huron Magua (Studi in a powerful performance). Graphically violent battle scenes are realistic, but not gratuitous. The real pleasure in this adaptation, which draws from both the James Fenimore Cooper novel and the 1936 film, is in its lush look and attractive stars. Means is terrific in his film debut as Hawkeye's foster-father. Released in a letterbox format to preserve the original integrity of the film.
1992 (R) 114m/C Daniel Day-Lewis, Madeleine Stowe, Wes Studi, Russell Means, Eric Schweig, Jodhi May, Steven Waddington, Maurice Roeves, Colm Meaney, Patrice Chereau, Dante Spinotti; **D:** Michael Mann; **W:** Christopher Crowe, Michael Mann; **M:** Trevor Jones, Randy Edelman. Academy Awards '92: Best Sound. **VHS, LV ★★★**

The Last Picture Show Slice of life/nostalgic farewell to an innocent age, based on Larry McMurtry's novel. Set in Archer City, a backwater Texas town, most of the story plays out at the local hangout run by ex-cowboy Sam the Lion. Bridges is

hooked up with spoiled pretty girl Shepherd, while Bottoms, a sensitive guy, is having an affair with the coach's neglected wife (Leachman). Loss of innocence, disillusionment, and confusion are played out against the backdrop of a town about to close its cinema. Shepherd's and Bottoms' film debuts. Stunningly photographed in black and white (Bogdanovich claimed he didn't want to "prettify" the picture by shooting in color) by Robert Surtees. Available in a laserdisc special edition with 17 minutes restored. Followed by a weak sequel, "Texasville." A boxed set featuring both films is also available.
1971 (R) 118m/B Jeff Bridges, Timothy Bottoms, Ben Johnson, Cloris Leachman, Cybill Shepherd, Ellen Burstyn, Eileen Brennan, Clu Gulager, Sharon Taggart, Randy Quaid, Sam Bottoms, John Hillerman; **D:** Peter Bogdanovich; **W:** Larry McMurtry, Peter Bogdanovich. Academy Awards '71: Best Supporting Actor (Johnson), Best Supporting Actress (Leachman); Golden Globe Awards '72: Best Supporting Actor (Johnson); National Board of Review Awards '71: Best Supporting Actor (Johnson), Best Supporting Actress (Leachman); National Society of Film Critics Awards '71: Best Supporting Actress (Burstyn); Nominations: Academy Awards '71: Best Adapted Screenplay, Best Cinematography, Best Director (Bogdanovich), Best Picture, Best Supporting Actor (Bridges), Best Supporting Actress (Burstyn). **VHS, LV, 8mm ★★★★**

The Last Polka SCTV vets Candy and Levy are Yosh and Stan Schmenge, polka kings interviewed for a "documentary" on their years in the spotlight and on the road. Hilarious spoof on Martin Scorsese's "The Last Waltz," about The Band's last concert. Several fellow Second Cityers keep the laughs coming. If you liked SCTV or "This is Spinal Tap," you'll like this. Made for cable (HBO).
1984 54m/C John Candy, Eugene Levy, Rick Moranis, Robin Duke, Catherine O'Hara; **M:** John Blanchard. **VHS, Beta ★★★**

The Last Seduction Dahl, the master of modern noir, delivers another stylish hit exploring the darker side of urban life. Fiorentino gives the performance of her life as the most evil, rotten femme fatale to ever hit the big screen. Bridget (Fiorentino) rips off the money her husband Clay (Pullman) made in a pharmaceutical drug deal and leaves Manhattan for a small town in upstate New York. Once

there, she takes nice, naive Mike (Berg) as her lover, while Clay tries to ferret her out and get his money back. Lots of dry humor and a wickedly amusing heroine make for a devilishly entertaining film.
1994 (R) 110m/C Linda Fiorentino, Peter Berg, J.T. Walsh, Bill Nunn, Bill Pullman; **D:** John Dahl; **W:** Steve Barancik; **M:** Joseph Vitarelli. Independent Spirit Awards '95: Best Actress (Fiorentino); New York Film Critics Awards '94: Best Actress (Fiorentino). **VHS, LV ★★★★**

Last Summer in the Hamptons In her last film, Lindfors stars as Helena Mora, the matriarch of a charming three-generation theatrical clan that gets together one weekend a year at her spacious, slightly run-down estate to participate in drama workshops and perform plays. When Helena is forced to sell the estate, the family reunites for one last weekend of bickering and performing. Featuring fine performances from the entire ensemble (including Lindfors's son and Jaglom's wife), Jaglom's touching and engaging tribute to his family gives nepotism a good name.
1996 (R) 105m/C Victoria Foyt, Viveca Lindfors, Jon Robin Baitz, Kristopher Tabori, Andre Gregory, Melissa Leo, Martha Plimpton, Roddy McDowall, Henry Jaglom, Nick Gregory, Savannah Smith Boucher, Roscoe Lee Browne, Ron Rifkin, Diane Salinger, Brooke Smith, Holland Taylor; **D:** Henry Jaglom; **W:** Victoria Foyt, Henry Jaglom; **M:** Johnny Mercer, Harold Arlen. **VHS ★★★1/2**

Last Tango in Paris Brando plays a middle-aged American who meets a French girl and tries to forget his wife's suicide with a short, extremely steamy affair. Bertolucci proves to be a master; Brando gives one of his best performances. Very controversial when made, still quite explicit. Visually stunning. The X-rated version, at 130 minutes, is also available.
1973 (R) 126m/C IT FR Marlon Brando, Maria Schneider, Jean-Pierre Leaud; **D:** Bernardo Bertolucci; **W:** Bernardo Bertolucci; **M:** Gato Barbieri, Vittorio Storaro. New York Film Critics Awards '73: Best Actor (Brando); National Society of Film Critics Awards '73: Best Actor (Brando); Nominations: Academy Awards '73: Best Actor (Brando), Best Director (Bertolucci). **VHS, Beta, LV ★★★1/2**

The Last Temptation of Christ Scorsese's controversial adaptation of the Nikos Kazantzakis novel, portraying Christ in his last year as an ordinary Israelite tormented by divine doubt, human desires, and the voice of God. The controversy engulfing the film, as it was heavily protested and widely banned, tended to divert attention from what is an exceptional statement of religious and artistic vision. Excellent score by Peter Gabriel.

1988 (R) 164m/C Willem Dafoe, Harvey Keitel, Barbara Hershey, Harry Dean Stanton, Andre Gregory, David Bowie, Verna Bloom, Juliette Caton, John Lurie, Roberts Blossom, Irvin Kershner, Barry Miller, Tomas Arana, Nehemiah Persoff, Paul Herman; **D:** Martin Scorsese; **W:** Paul Schrader; **M:** Peter Gabriel, Michael Ballhaus. Nominations: Academy Awards '88: Best Director (Scorsese). **VHS, Beta, LV** ★★★1/2

The Last Wave An Australian attorney takes on a murder case involving an aborigine and he finds himself becoming distracted by apocalyptic visions concerning tidal waves and drownings that seem to foretell the future. Weir's masterful creation and communication of time and place are marred by a somewhat pat ending.

1977 (PG) 109m/C AU Richard Chamberlain, Olivia Hamnett, David Gulpilil, Frederick Parslow; **D:** Peter Weir, John Seale; **W:** Peter Weir. **VHS, Beta** ★★★

Last Year at Marienbad A young man tries to lure a mysterious woman to run away with him from a hotel in France. Once a hit on the artsy circuit, it's most interesting for its beautiful photography. In French with English subtitles. **AKA:** L'Anee Derniere a Marienbad.

1961 93m/B FR IT Delphine Seyrig, Giorgia Albertazzi, Sacha Pitoeff, Luce Garcia-Ville; **D:** Alain Resnais. Nominations: Academy Awards '62: Best Story & Screenplay. **VHS, Beta, 8mm** ★★★

L'Atalante Vigo's great masterpiece, a slight story about a husband and wife quarreling, splitting, and reuniting around which has been fashioned one of the cinema's greatest poetic films. In French with English subtitles.

1934 82m/B FR Dita Parlo, Jean Daste, Michel Simon; **D:** Jean Vigo. **VHS, Beta** ★★★1/2

The Late Show A veteran private detective finds his world turned upside down when his ex-partner comes to visit and winds up dead, and a flaky woman whose cat is missing decides to become his sidekick. Carney and Tomlin are fun to watch in this sleeper, a tribute to the classic detective film noirs.

1977 (PG) 93m/C Art Carney, Lily Tomlin,

Bill Macy, Eugene Roche, Joanna Cassidy, John Considine; **D:** Robert Benton; **W:** Robert Benton. Edgar Allan Poe Awards '77: Best Screenplay; National Board of Review Awards '77: 10 Best Films of the Year; National Society of Film Critics Awards '77: Best Actor (Carney); Nominations: Academy Awards '77: Best Original Screenplay. **VHS, Beta** ★★★

Late Spring An exquisite Ozu masterpiece. A young woman lives with her widowed father for years. He decides to remarry so that she can begin life for herself. Highly acclaimed, in Japanese with English subtitles. Reworked in 1960 as "Late Autumn."

1949 107m/B JP Setsuko Hara, Chishu Ryu, Jun Usami, Haruko Sugimura; **D:** Yasujiro Ozu. **VHS, Beta** ★★★★

Laura A detective assigned to the murder investigation of the late Laura Hunt finds himself falling in love with her painted portrait. Superb collaboration by excellent cast and fine director. Superior suspense yarn, enhanced by a love story. Based on the novel by Vera Caspary. Rouben Mamoulian was the original director, then Preminger finished the film.

1944 85m/B Gene Tierney, Dana Andrews, Clifton Webb, Lane Chandler, Vincent Price, Judith Anderson, Grant Mitchell, Dorothy Adams; **D:** Otto Preminger; **M:** David Raksin. Academy Awards '44: Best Black and White Cinematography; Nominations: Academy Awards '44: Best Director (Preminger), Best Interior Decoration, Best Screenplay, Best Supporting Actor (Webb). **VHS, Beta, LV** ★★★★

The Lavender Hill Mob A prim and prissy bank clerk schemes to melt the bank's gold down and remold it into miniature Eiffel Tower paperweights for later resale. The foolproof plan appears to succeed, but then develops a snag. An excellent comedy that is still a delight to watch. Also available with "The Man in the White Suit" on laserdisc.

1951 78m/B GB Alec Guinness, Stanley Holloway, Sidney James, Alfie Bass, Marjorie Fielding, John Gregson; **Cameos:** Audrey Hepburn; **D:** Charles Crichton; **W:** T.E.B. Clarke. Academy Awards '52: Best Story & Screenplay; British Academy Awards '51: Best Film; Nominations: Academy Awards '52: Best Actor (Guinness). **VHS, Beta, LV** ★★★1/2

L'Avventura A stark, dry, and minimalist exercise in narrative by Antonioni, dealing with the search for a girl on an Italian island by her lethargic socialite friends who eventually forget her in favor of their own preoccupations. A highly acclaimed, innovative film; somewhat less effective now, in the wake of many film treatments of angst and amorality. In Italian with English subtitles. Laserdisc edition features the original trailer, commentary, and a collection of still photographs from Antonioni's work. **AKA:** The Adventure.

1960 145m/C *IT* Monica Vitti, Gabriele Ferzetti, Lea Massari, Dominique Blanchar, James Addams; **D:** Michelangelo Antonioni; **W:** Tonino Guerra, Michelangelo Antonioni. Cannes Film Festival '60: Special Jury Prize. **VHS, Beta, LV** ★★★1/2

Law of Desire A wicked, Almodovarian attack-on-decency farce about a love-obsessed gay Madridian and his transsexual brother-sister, among others, getting hopelessly entangled in cross-gender relationships. Unlike the work of any other director; in Spanish with English subtitles. **AKA:** La Ley del Deseo.

1986 100m/C *SP* Carmen Maura, Eusebio Poncela, Antonio Banderas, Bibi Andersson; **D:** Pedro Almodovar; **W:** Pedro Almodovar. **VHS, Beta, LV** ★★★1/2

Lawrence of Arabia Exceptional biography of T.E. Lawrence, a British military "observer" who strategically aids the Bedouins battle the Turks during WWI. Lawrence, played masterfully by O'Toole in his first major film, is a hero consumed more by a need to reject British tradition than to save the Arab population. He takes on Arab costume and a larger-than-life persona. Stunning photography of the desert in all its harsh reality. Blacklisted co-writer Wilson had his screen credit restored by the Writers Guild of America in 1995. Laser edition contains 20 minutes of restored footage and a short documentary about the making of the film. Available in letterboxed format.

1962 (PG) 221m/C *GB* Peter O'Toole, Omar Sharif, Anthony Quinn, Alec Guinness, Jack Hawkins, Claude Rains, Anthony Quayle, Arthur Kennedy, Jose Ferrer; **D:** David Lean; **W:** Robert Bolt, Michael Wilson, Frederick A. (Freddie) Young; **M:** Maurice Jarre. Academy Awards '62: Best Art Direction/Set Decoration (Color), Best Color Cinematography, Best Director (Lean), Best Film Editing, Best Picture, Best Sound, Best Original Score; British Academy Awards '62: Best Actor (O'Toole), Best Film, Best Screenplay; Directors Guild of America Awards '62: Best Director (Lean); Golden Globe Awards '63: Best Director (Lean), Best Film—Drama, Best Supporting Actor (Sharif); Nominations: Academy Awards '62: Best Actor (O'Toole), Best Adapted Screenplay,

Best Supporting Actor (Sharif). **VHS, Beta, LV** ★★★★

Laws of Gravity Critically acclaimed debut film from 29-year-old writer/director Gomez is a three day slice of life set in Brooklyn. Hotheaded Jon (Trese) and married friend Jimmy (Greene) channel violent energy into their relationships and illegal activities. Camera follows "cinema verite" style and captures urban tension as it trails them through a gun heist and subsequent arrest.

1992 (R) 100m/C Peter Greene, Edie Falco, Adam Trese, Arabella Field, Paul Schulzie; **D:** Nick Gomez; **W:** Nick Gomez. **VHS** ★★★

LBJ: The Early Years The early years of President Lyndon Baines Johnson's political career are dramatized in this made-for-television movie. Winning performances hoist this above other biographies.

1988 144m/C Randy Quaid, Patti LuPone, Morgan Brittany, Pat Hingle, Kevin McCarthy, Barry Corbin, Charles Frank; **D:** Peter Werner. **VHS, Beta** ★★★

Le Bal You won't find many films with the music of Paul McCartney and Chopin in the credits, and even fewer without dialogue. With only music and dancing the film uses a French dance hall to illustrate the changes in French society over a 50-year period. Based on a French play. ♪ La Vie en Rose; In the Mood; Michelle; Top Hat White Tie and Tails; Let's Face the Music and Dance; Harlem Nocturne; Shuffle Blues; Tutti Frutti; Only You.

1982 112m/C *IT FR* **D:** Ettore Scola; **M:** Irving Berlin, Paul McCartney, John Lennon, Frederic Chopin, Vladimir Cosma. Cesar Awards '84: Best Director (Scola), Best Film, Best Score; Nominations: Academy Awards '83: Best Foreign Language Film. **VHS** ★★★

Le Beau Mariage An award-winning comedy from the great French director about a zealous woman trying to find a husband and the unsuspecting man she chooses to marry. In French with English subtitles. **AKA:** A Good Marriage; The Well-Made Marriage.

1982 (R) 97m/C *FR* Beatrice Romand, Arielle Dombasle, Andre Dussollier; **D:** Eric Rohmer; **W:** Eric Rohmer. Venice Film Festival '82: Best Actress (Romand). **VHS, Beta** ★★★

Le Beau Serge A convalescing Frenchman returns to his home village and tries to help an old friend, who's become a hopeless drunkard, change his life. Chabrol's first film, and a major forerunner of the nou-

velle vogue. In French with English subtitles. **AKA:** Handsome Serge.
1958 97m/B FR Gerard Blain, Jean-Claude Brialy, Michele Meritz, Bernadette LaFont; **D:** Claude Chabrol; **W:** Claude Chabrol. **VHS, Beta** ★★★

Le Chat A middle-aged couple's marriage dissolves into a hate-filled battle of wits, centering around the husband's love for their cat. In French with English subtitles. **AKA:** The Cat.
1971 88m/C FR Jean Gabin, Simone Signoret, Annie Cordy, Jacques Rispal; **D:** Pierre Granier-Deferre. Berlin International Film Festival '71: Best Actor (Gabin). **VHS, Beta, LV** ★★★1/2

Le Corbeau A great, notorious drama about a small French village whose everyday serenity is ruptured by a series of poison pen letters that lead to suicide and despair. The film was made within Nazi-occupied France, sponsored by the Nazis, and has been subjected to much misdirected malice because of it. In French with English subtitles. **AKA:** The Raven.
1943 92m/B FR Pierre Fresnay, Noel Roquevort, Ginette LeClerc, Pierre Larquey, Antoine Belpetre; **D:** Henri-Georges Clouzot. **VHS, Beta** ★★★

Le Crabe Tambour Rochefort plays a dying naval captain remembering his relationship with his first officer. Revealed via flashbacks, the recollections concern the adventures which transpired on a North Atlantic supply ship. Great performances from all and award-winning cinematography by Raoul Coutard. Winner of several French Cesars. A French script booklet is available.
1977 120m/C FR Jean Rochefort, Claude Rich, Jacques Dufilho, Jacques Perrin, Odile Versois, Aurore Clement; **D:** Pierre Schoendoerffer. Cesar Awards '78: Best Actor (Rochefort), Best Cinematography, Best Supporting Actor (Dufilho). **VHS, LV** ★★★

Le Dernier Combat A stark film about life after a devastating nuclear war marks the directorial debut of Besson. The characters fight to survive in a now speechless world by staking territorial claims and forming new relationships with other survivors. An original and expressive film made without dialogue. **AKA:** The Last Battle.
1984 (R) 93m/B FR Pierre Jolivet, Fritz Wepper, Jean Reno, Jean Bouise, Christiane Kruger; **D:** Luc Besson; **W:** Luc Besson. **VHS, Beta** ★★★

Le Doulos Compelling story of an ex-convict and his buddy, a man who

may be a police informant. Chronicles the efforts of the snitch (the "doulos" of the title) to bring the criminal element before the law. Melville blends in several plot twists and breathes a new French life into the cliche-ridden genre.
1961 108m/B FR Serge Reggiani, Jean-Paul Belmondo, Michel Piccoli; **D:** Jean-Pierre Melville. **VHS, Beta** ★★★

Le Grand Chemin A sweet, slice-of-life French film about a young boy's idyllic summer on a family friend's farm while his mother is having a baby. Hubert's son plays the boy Louis in this retelling of the director's own childhood. In French with English subtitles. Remade with an American setting in 1991 as "Paradise." **AKA:** The Grand Highway.
1987 107m/C FR Anemone, Richard Bohringer, Antoine Hubert, Vanessa Guedj, Christine Pascal, Raoul Billerey, Pascale Roberts; **D:** Jean-Loup Hubert; **W:** Jean-Loup Hubert; **M:** Georges Granier. Cesar Awards '88: Best Actor (Bohringer), Best Actress (Anemone). **VHS, Beta, LV** ★★★

Le Jour Se Leve The dark, expressionist film about a sordid and destined murder/love triangle that starts with a police standoff and evolves into a series of flashbacks. The film that put Carne and Gabin on the cinematic map. Highly acclaimed. In French with English subtitles. Remade in 1947 as "The Long Night." **AKA:** Daybreak.
1939 89m/B FR Jean Gabin, Jules Berry, Arletty, Jacqueline Laurent; **D:** Marcel Carne. **VHS** ★★★1/2

Le Million A comedy/musical masterpiece of the early sound era which centers on an artist's adventures in searching for a winning lottery ticket throughout Paris. Highly acclaimed member of the Clair school of subtle French farce. In French with English subtitles.
1931 89m/B FR Annabella, Rene Lefevre, Paul Olivier, Louis Allibert; **D:** Rene Clair. National Board of Review Awards '31: 5 Best Foreign Films of the Year. **VHS, Beta** ★★★1/2

Le Petit Amour A popular French comedy about the fateful romance between a 40-year-old divorced woman and a 15-year-old boy obsessed with a kung fu video game. In French with English subtitles. **AKA:** Kung Fu Master.
1987 (R) 80m/C FR Jane Birkin, Mathieu Demy, Charlotte Gainsbourg, Lou Doillon; **D:** Agnes Varda. **VHS, Beta** ★★★

The League of Gentlemen An ex-Army officer plots a daring bank rob-

bery using specially skilled military personnel and irreproachable panache. Hilarious British humor fills the screen.
1960 115m/B *GB* Jack Hawkins, Nigel Patrick, Richard Attenborough, Roger Livesey, Bryan Forbes; **D:** Basil Dearden. **VHS, Beta** ★★★1/2

A League of Their Own Charming look at sports history and the Rockford Peaches, one of the teams in the real-life All American Girls Professional Baseball League, formed in the '40s when the men were off at war. Main focus is on sibling rivalry between Davis, the beautiful, crackerjack catcher, and Petty, the younger, insecure pitcher. Boozy coach Hanks is wonderful as he reluctantly leads the team; he also gets credit for the classic "There's no crying in baseball" scene. Great cast of supporting characters, including sarcastic talent scout Lovitz, opinionated, sleazy taxi dancer Madonna, loud-mouthed O'Donnell, and shy, homely Cavanagh. Lots of baseball for the sports fan.
1992 (PG) 127m/C Tom Hanks, Geena Davis, Madonna, Lori Petty, Jon Lovitz, David Strathairn, Garry Marshall, Bill Pullman, Rosie O'Donnell, Megan Cavanagh, Tracy Reiner, Bitty Schram, Ann Cusack, Anne Elizabeth Ramsay, Freddie Simpson, Renee Coleman; **D:** Penny Marshall; **W:** Lowell Ganz, Babaloo Mandel; **M:** Hans Zimmer. **VHS, Beta, LV, 8mm** ★★★

Leave Her to Heaven Beautiful neurotic Tierney takes drastic measures to keep hubby all to herself and will do anything to get what she wants. Tierney, in a departure from her usual roles, is excellent as this pathologically possessive creature. Oscar-winner Leon Shamroy's photography (in Technicolor) is breathtaking. Based on the novel by Ben Ames Williams.
1945 110m/C Gene Tierney, Cornel Wilde, Jeanne Crain, Vincent Price, Mary Philips, Ray Collins, Darryl Hickman, Gene Lockhart; **D:** John M. Stahl; **W:** Jo Swerling; **M:** Alfred Newman. Academy Awards '45: Best Cinematography; Nominations: Academy Awards '45: Best Actress (Tierney). **VHS** ★★★

Leaving Las Vegas Ben Sanderson (Cage) is a hopeless alcoholic who goes to Vegas to drink himself to death and meets Sera (Shue), a lonely hooker who loves him enough not to stop him. Definitely as depressing as it sounds, but still manages to have both a subtle sense of humor and

compassion. Cage tops his best work, and Shue proves she deserves better than the lightweight roles she's had in the past. Not for everyone, but worth the effort for people who like to see honest emotion and hate Hollywood's insistence on happy endings. Based on the semiautobiographical novel by John O'Brien, who committed suicide shortly before preproduction began.
1995 (R) 120m/C Nicolas Cage, Elisabeth Shue, Julian Sands, Laurie Metcalf, David Brisbin, Richard Lewis, Valeria Golino, Steven Weber; **D:** Mike Figgis; **W:** Mike Figgis; **M:** Mike Figgis. Academy Awards '95: Best Actor (Cage); Golden Globe Awards '96: Best Actor—Drama (Cage); Independent Spirit Awards '96: Best Film, Best Director (Figgis), Best Actress (Shue), Best Cinematography; Los Angeles Film Critics Association Awards '95: Best Film, Best Actor (Cage), Best Director (Figgis), Best Actress (Shue); National Board of Review Awards '95: Best Actor (Cage); National Society of Film Critics Awards '95: Best Director (Figgis), Best Actor (Cage), Best Actress (Shue); New York Film Critics Awards '95: Best Film, Best Actor (Cage); Screen Actors Guild Award '95: Best Actor (Cage); Nominations: Academy Awards '95: Best Actress (Shue), Best Director (Figgis), Best Adapted Screenplay; British Academy Awards '95: Best Actor (Cage), Best Actress (Shue), Best Adapted Screenplay; Directors Guild of America Awards '95: Best Director (Figgis); Golden Globe Awards '96: Best Film—Drama, Best Actress—Drama (Shue), Best Director (Figgis); Independent Spirit Awards '96: Best Actor (Cage), Best Screenplay; Screen Actors Guild Award '95: Best Actress (Shue); Writers Guild of America '95: Best Adapted Screenplay. **VHS, LV** ★★★1/2

The Left Hand of God After an American pilot escapes from a Chinese warlord in post-WWII, he disguises himself as a Catholic priest and takes refuge in a missionary hospital. Bogie is great as the flyboy/ cleric.
1955 87m/C Humphrey Bogart, E.G. Marshall, Lee J. Cobb, Agnes Moorehead, Gene Tierney; **D:** Edward Dmytryk. **VHS, Beta** ★★★

The Left-Handed Gun An offbeat version of the exploits of Billy the Kid, which portrays him as a 19th-century Wild West juvenile delinquent. Newman's role, which he method-acted, was originally intended for James Dean. Based on a 1955 Philco teleplay by Gore Vidal.
1958 102m/B Paul Newman, Lita Milan, John Dehner; **D:** Arthur Penn. **VHS, Beta** ★★★

Lenny Smoky nightclubs, drug abuse, and obscenities abound in Hoffman's portrayal of the controversial comedian Lenny Bruce, whose use of street language led to his eventual blacklisting. Perrine is a gem as his stripper wife. Adapted from the Julian Barry play, this is a visually compelling piece that sharply divided critics upon release.
1974 (R) 111m/B Dustin Hoffman, Valerie Perrine, Jan Miner, Stanley Beck; **D:** Bob Fosse; **W:** Julian Barry; **M:** Ralph Burns. Cannes Film Festival '75: Best Actress (Perrine); National Board of Review Awards '74: 10 Best Films of the Year, Best Supporting Actress (Perrine); Nominations: Academy Awards '74: Best Actor (Hoffman), Best Actress (Perrine), Best Adapted Screenplay, Best Cinematography, Best Director (Fosse), Best Picture; Cannes Film Festival '75: Best Film. **VHS, Beta, LV** ★★★

Les Biches An exquisite film that became a landmark in film history with its theme of bisexuality and upper class decadence. A rich socialite picks up a young artist drawing on the streets of Paris, seduces her, and then takes her to St. Tropez. Conflict arises when a suave architect shows up and threatens to come between the two lovers. In French with English subtitles. **AKA:** The Heterosexuals.
1968 (R) 95m/C *FR* Stephane Audran, Jean-Louis Trintignant, Jacqueline Sassard; **D:** Claude Chabrol; **W:** Claude Chabrol. **VHS, LV** ★★★1/2

Les Carabiniers A cynical, grim anti-war tract, detailing the pathetic adventures of two young bums lured into enlisting with promises of rape, looting, torture and battle without justification. Controversial in its day, and typically elliptical and non-narrative. In French with English subtitles. **AKA:** The Soldiers.
1963 80m/B *GB IT FR* Anna Karina, Genevieva Galea, Marino Mase; **D:** Jean-Luc Godard. **VHS, Beta** ★★★

Les Enfants Terrible The classic, lyrical treatment of adolescent deviance adapted by Cocteau from his own play, wherein a brother and sister born into extreme wealth eventually enter into casual crime, self-destruction, and incest. In French with English subtitles. **AKA:** The Strange Ones.
1950 105m/B *FR* Edouard Dermithe, Nicole Stephane; **D:** Jean-Pierre Melville; **W:** Jean Cocteau, Jean-Pierre Melville. **VHS, Beta** ★★★

Les Miserables Victor Hugo's classic novel about small-time criminal Jean Valjean and 18th-century France. After facing poverty and prison, escape and torture, Valjean is redeemed by the kindness of a bishop. As he tries to mend his ways, he is continually hounded by the policeman Javert, who is determined to lock him away. The final act is set during a student uprising in the 1730s. This version is the best of many, finely detailed and well-paced with excellent cinematography by Gregg Toland.
1935 108m/B Fredric March, Charles Laughton, Cedric Hardwicke, Rochelle Hudson, John Beal, Frances Drake, Florence Eldridge, John Carradine, Jessie Ralph, Leonid Kinskey; **D:** Richard Boleslawski; **W:** W.P. Lipscomb; **M:** Alfred Newman. National Board of Review Awards '35: 10 Best Films of the Year; Nominations: Academy Awards '35: Best Cinematography, Best Picture; Academy Awards '36: Best Film Editing. **VHS, Beta, LV** ★★★★

Les Miserables An excellent made-for-television version of the Victor Hugo classic about the criminal Valjean and the policeman Javert playing cat-and-mouse in 18th-century France. Dauphin's last film role.
1978 150m/C Richard Jordan, Anthony Perkins, John Gielgud, Cyril Cusack, Flora Robson, Celia Johnson, Claude Dauphin; **D:** Glenn Jordan. **VHS, Beta, LV** ★★★1/2

Les Mistons This study of male adolescence finds five teen-age boys worshiping a beautiful girl from afar, following her everywhere, spoiling her dates, and finally reaching maturity in light of their mistakes.
1957 18m/C *FR* **D:** Francois Truffaut. **VHS, Beta** ★★★

Les Nuits Fauves Collard's semi-autobiographical film about the emotional and physical havoc an H.I.V.-positive filmmaker visits on the two objects of his violent affections—an innocent 18-year-old girl and a sado-masochistic 20-year-old boy. As Jean displays increasing desperation with his situation, the life around him shows an equally arbitrary violence and humor. In French with English subtitles. Collard died of AIDS shortly before his film won both best first film and best French film at the 1993 Cesars—a first in the ceremony's history. **AKA:** Savage Nights.
1992 129m/C *FR* Cyril Collard, Romane Bohringer, Carlos Lopez, Maria Schneider; **D:** Cyril Collard; **W:** Cyril Collard. Cesar Awards '93: Best Film. **VHS** ★★★

Les Visiteurs du Soir A beautiful, charming fairy-tale about the devil's intrepid interference with a particular

love affair in 15th-century France, which he cannot squelch. Purportedly a parable about Hitler's invasion of France. Interestingly, this was released after the Nazi occupation of France, so one assumes that the Germans didn't make the connection. In French with English subtitles. *AKA: The Devil's Envoys.*
1942 120m/B *FR* Arletty, Jules Berry, Marie Dea, Alain Cuny, Fernand Ledoux, Marcel Herrand; *D:* Marcel Carne; *W:* Jacques Prevert, Pierre Laroche. **VHS** ★★★1/2

Let Him Have It Compelling, controversial film about a miscarriage of British justice. In 1952 Christopher Craig, 16, and Derek Bentley, 19, climbed onto the roof of a warehouse in an apparent burglary attempt. The police arrived and captured Bentley; Craig shot and wounded one policeman and killed another. According to testimony Bentley shouted "Let him have it" but did he mean shoot or give the officer the gun? Bentley, whose IQ was 66, was sentenced to death by the British courts—though he didn't commit the murder. The uproar over the sentence was reignited by this release, leading to a request for a reexamination of evidence and sentencing by the British Home Office.
1991 (R) 115m/C *GB* Christopher Eccleston, Paul Reynolds, Tom Bell, Eileen Atkins, Clare Holman, Michael Elphick, Mark McGann, Tom Courtenay; *D:* Peter Medak. **VHS, LV** ★★★1/2

Lethal Weapon In Los Angeles, a cop nearing retirement (Glover) unwillingly begins work with a new partner (Gibson), a suicidal, semi-crazed risk-taker who seems determined to get the duo killed. Both Vietnam vets, the pair uncover a vicious heroin smuggling ring run by ruthless ex-Special Forces personnel. Packed with plenty of action, violence, and humorous undertones. Clapton's contributions to the musical score are an added bonus. Gibson and Glover work well together and give this movie extra punch. Followed by (so far) two sequels.
1987 (R) 110m/C Mel Gibson, Danny Glover, Gary Busey, Mitchell Ryan, Tom Atkins, Darlene Love, Traci Wolfe, Steve Kahan; *D:* Richard Donner; *W:* Shane Black; *M:* Michael Kamen, Eric Clapton. Nominations: Academy Awards '87: Best Sound. **VHS, Beta, LV, 8mm** ★★★

Lethal Weapon 2 This sequel to the popular cop adventure finds Gibson and Glover taking on a variety of blond South African "diplo-

mats" who try to use their diplomatic immunity status to thwart the duo's efforts to crack their smuggling ring. Gibson finally finds romance, and viewers learn the truth about his late wife's accident. Also features the introduction of obnoxious, fast-talking con artist Leo ("OK, OK") Getz, adeptly played by Pesci, who becomes a third wheel to the crimefighting team. Followed by a second sequel.
1989 (R) 114m/C Mel Gibson, Danny Glover, Joe Pesci, Joss Ackland, Derrick O'Connor, Patsy Kensit, Darlene Love, Traci Wolfe, Steve Kahan, Mary Ellen Trainor; *D:* Richard Donner; *W:* Jeffrey Boam; *M:* Michael Kamen, Eric Clapton, David Sanborn. **VHS, Beta, LV, 8mm** ★★★

The Letter When a man is shot and killed on a Malaysian plantation, the woman who committed the murder pleads self-defense. Her husband and his lawyer attempt to free her, but find more than they expected in this tightly-paced film noir. Based on the novel by W. Somerset Maugham. Davis emulated the originator of her role, Jeanne Eagels, in her mannerisms and line readings, although Eagels later went mad from drug abuse and overwork.
1940 96m/B Bette Davis, Herbert Marshall, James Stephenson, Gale Sondergaard, Bruce Lester, Cecil Kellaway, Victor Sen Yung, Frieda Inescort; *D:* William Wyler; *W:* Howard Koch; *M:* Max Steiner. Nominations: Academy Awards '40: Best Actor (Stephenson), Best Actress (Davis), Best Black and White Cinematography, Best Director (Wyler), Best Picture. **VHS, Beta, LV** ★★★★

Letter from an Unknown Woman A woman falls in love with a concert pianist on the eve of his departure. He promises to return but never does. The story is told in flashbacks as the pianist reads a letter from the woman. A great romantic melodrama.
1948 90m/B Joan Fontaine, Louis Jourdan, Mady Christians, Marcel Journet, Art Smith; *D:* Max Ophuls. **VHS, LV** ★★★

A Letter to Three Wives Crain, Darnell, and Sothern star as three friends who, shortly before embarking on a Hudson River boat trip, each receive a letter from Holm (who's never shown), the fourth member in their set. The letter tells them that she has run off with one of their husbands but does not specify her identity. The women spend the rest of the trip reviewing their sometimes shaky unions which provides some of the funniest and most caustic scenes, including Douglas (as Sothern's husband) ranting against the advertising business which supports his wife's radio soap opera. Sharp dialogue, moving performances. Based on the novel by John Klempner. Remade for television in 1985.

1949 103m/B Jeanne Crain, Linda Darnell, Ann Sothern, Kirk Douglas, Paul Douglas, Jeffrey Lynn, Thelma Ritter, Barbara Lawrence, Connie Gilchrist, Florence Bates; *D:* Joseph L. Mankiewicz; *W:* Joseph L. Mankiewicz; *M:* Alfred Newman; *V:* Celeste Holm. Academy Awards '49: Best Director (Mankiewicz), Best Screenplay (Mankiewicz); Nominations: Academy Awards '49: Best Picture. **VHS, Beta, LV ★★★★**

Letters from My Windmill A series of three short stories: "The Three Low Masses," "The Elixir of Father Gaucher," and "The Secret of Master Cornille" from respected director Pagnol. The unique format only enhances this film. In French with English subtitles.

1954 116m/B *FR* Henri Velbert, Yvonne Gamy, Robert Vattier, Roger Crouzet; *D:* Marcel Pagnol. **VHS ★★★1/2**

Lianna Acclaimed screenwriter/director John Sayles wrote and directed this story of a woman's romantic involvement with another woman. Chronicles an unhappy homemaker's awakening to the feelings of love that she develops for a female professor. Sayles makes an appearance as a family friend.

1983 (R) 110m/C Jon DeVries, Linda Griffiths, Jane Hallaren, Jo Henderson, Jessica Wright MacDonald; *Cameos:* John Sayles; *D:* John Sayles; *W:* John Sayles; *M:* Mason Daring. **VHS, Beta ★★★**

Libeled Lady A fast, complicated screwball masterwork, dealing with a newspaper editor's efforts to get something on a bratty heiress with the help of his own fiancee and a reporter he recently fired. One of the era's funniest Hollywood films. Remade in 1946 as "Easy to Wed."

1936 98m/B Myrna Loy, Spencer Tracy, Jean Harlow, William Powell, Walter Connolly, Charley Grapewin, Cora Witherspoon, E.E. Clive, Charles Trowbridge, Dennis O'Keefe, Hattie McDaniel; *D:* Jack Conway. Nominations: Academy Awards '36: Best Picture. **VHS, Beta, LV ★★★1/2**

License to Kill Dalton's second Bond effort, in which drug lords try to kill 007's best friend and former CIA agent. Disobeying orders for the first time and operating without his infamous "license to kill," Bond goes af-

ter the fiends. Fine outing for Dalton (and Bond, too).

1989 (PG-13) 133m/C *GB* Timothy Dalton, Carey Lowell, Robert Davi, Frank McRae, Talisa Soto, David Hedison, Anthony Zerbe, Everett McGill, Wayne Newton, Benicio Del Toro, Desmond Llewelyn, Priscilla Barnes; *D:* John Glen; *W:* Michael G. Wilson, Richard Maibaum; *M:* Michael Kamen. **VHS, Beta, LV ★★★**

Lies My Father Told Me Simple drama about growing up in the 1920s in a Jewish ghetto. The story revolves around a young boy's relationship with his immigrant grandfather. Quiet and moving.

1975 (PG) 102m/C *CA* Yossi Yadin, Len Birman, Marilyn Lightstone, Jeffery Lynas; *D:* Jan Kadar; *W:* Ted Allan. Golden Globe Awards '76: Best Foreign Film; Nominations: Academy Awards '75: Best Original Screenplay. **VHS ★★★**

The Life and Adventures of Nicholas Nickleby Nine-hour performance of the 1838 Dickens' tale by the Royal Shakespeare Company, featuring the work of 39 actors portraying 150 characters. Wonderful performances are characterized by frantic action and smoothly meshing intertwining plots, focusing on the trials and tribulations of the Nickleby family, amidst wealth, poverty, and injustice in Victorian England. Nine cassettes. *AKA:* Nicholas Nickleby.

1981 540m/C *GB* Roger Rees, David Thewlis, Emily Richard, John Woodvine; *D:* Jim Goddard; *W:* David Edgar; *M:* Stephen Oliver. **VHS ★★★1/2**

The Life and Death of Colonel Blimp Chronicles the life of a British soldier who survives three wars (Boer, WWI, and WWII), falls in love with three women (all portrayed by Kerr), and dances a fine waltz. Fine direction and performance abound. *AKA:* Colonel Blimp.

1943 115m/C *GB* Roger Livesey, Deborah Kerr, Anton Walbrook, Ursula Jeans, Albert Lieven; *D:* Michael Powell, Emeric Pressburger. **VHS, Beta, LV ★★★★**

Life and Nothing But Two young women search for their lovers at the end of WWI. They're helped by a French officer brutalized by the war and driven to find all of France's casualties. Romantic, evocative, and saddening. In French with English subtitles. *AKA:* La Vie est Rien d'Autre.

1989 (PG) 135m/C *FR* Philippe Noiret, Sabine Azema, Francoise Perrot; *D:* Bertrand Tavernier; *W:* Bertrand Tavernier. British Academy Awards '89: Best Foreign

Film; Cesar Awards '90: Best Actor (Noiret), Best Score; Los Angeles Film Critics Association Awards '90: Best Foreign Film. **VHS, Beta ★★★1/2**

Life Begins for Andy Hardy Andy gets a job in New York before entering college and finds the working world to be a sobering experience. Surprisingly downbeat and hard-hitting for an Andy Hardy film. Garland's last appearance in the series.
1941 100m/B Mickey Rooney, Judy Garland, Lewis Stone, Ann Rutherford, Fay Holden, Gene Reynolds, Ralph Byrd; **D:** George B. Seitz. **VHS, Beta ★★★**

Life Is Sweet The consuming passions of food and drink focus the lives of an oddball English working-class family beset by hopeless dreams and passions. Mother is always fixing family meals—in between helping her friend open a gourmet restaurant which features such revolting dishes as pork cyst and prune quiche. Dad is a chef who buys a snack truck and dreams of life on the road. Natalie and Nicola, the grown twins, eat their meals in front of the television but Nicola is also a bulimic who binges and purges on chocolate bars behind her bedroom door. (Note the chocolate scene between Nicola and her boyfriend.) An affectionate, if sometimes unattractive, look at a chaotic family.
1990 (R) 103m/C GB Alison Steadman, Jane Horrocks, Jim Broadbent, Claire Skinner, Timothy Spall, Stephen Rea, David Thewlis; **D:** Mike Leigh; **W:** Mike Leigh. Los Angeles Film Critics Association Awards '91: Best Supporting Actress (Horrocks); National Society of Film Critics Awards '91: Best Actress (Steadman), Best Film, Best Supporting Actress (Horrocks). **VHS, LV ★★★1/2**

The Life of Emile Zola Writer Emile Zola intervenes in the case of Alfred Dreyfus, who was sent to Devil's Island for a crime he did not commit. Well-crafted production featuring a handsome performance from Muni.
1937 117m/B Paul Muni, Gale Sondergaard, Gloria Holden, Joseph Schildkraut; **D:** William Dieterle; **M:** Max Steiner. Academy Awards '37: Best Picture, Best Screenplay, Best Supporting Actor (Schildkraut); Nominations: Academy Awards '37: Best Actor (Muni), Best Director (Dieterle), Best Interior Decoration, Best Sound, Best Story, Best Original Score. **VHS, Beta, LV ★★★1/2**

Life of Oharu A near masterpiece rivaled only by "Ugetsu" in the Mizoguchi canon, this film details the slow and agonizing moral decline of a woman in feudal Japan, from wife to concubine to prostitute. A scathing portrait of social pre-destination based on a novel by Ibara Saikaku. In Japanese with English subtitles. **AKA:** Diary of Oharu; Saikaku Ichidai Onna.
1952 136m/B JP Kinuyo Tanaka, Toshiro Mifune; **D:** Kenji Mizoguchi. **VHS, Beta ★★★1/2**

Life with Father Based on the writings of the late Clarence Day, Jr., this is the story of his childhood in New York City during the 1880s. A delightful saga about a stern but loving father and his relationship with his knowing wife and four red-headed sons.
1947 118m/C William Powell, Irene Dunne, Elizabeth Taylor, Edmund Gwenn, ZaSu Pitts, Jimmy Lydon, Martin Milner; **D:** Michael Curtiz; **M:** Max Steiner. Golden Globe Awards '48: Best Score; New York Film Critics Awards '47: Best Actor (Powell); Nominations: Academy Awards '47: Best Actor (Powell), Best Art Direction/Set Decoration (Color), Best Color Cinematography. **VHS, Beta ★★★1/2**

Lifeboat When a German U-boat sinks a freighter during WWII, the eight survivors seek refuge in a tiny lifeboat. Tension peaks after the drifting passengers take in a stranded Nazi. Hitchcock saw a great challenge in having the entire story take place in a lifeboat and pulled it off with his usual flourish. In 1989, the film "Dead Calm" replicated the technique. From a story by John Steinbeck. Bankhead shines.
1944 96m/B Tallulah Bankhead, John Hodiak, William Bendix, Canada Lee, Walter Slezak, Hume Cronyn, Henry Hull, Mary Anderson; **D:** Alfred Hitchcock. National Board of Review Awards '44: 10 Best Films of the Year; New York Film Critics Awards '44: Best Actress (Bankhead); Nominations: Academy Awards '44: Best Director (Hitchcock). **VHS, Beta, LV ★★★1/2**

Like Water for Chocolate Magical Mexican fairy-tale set in the early 1900s about family, love, and the power of food. Formidable Mama Elena is left a widow with three daughters. The youngest, Tita, grows up in the kitchen surrounded by all the magic Nacha, the housekeeper, can impart to her about food. Doomed by tradition to spend her days caring for her mother, Tita escapes by cooking, releasing her sorrows and longings into the food, infecting all who eat it. Wonderfully

sensuous and slyly exaggerated. Based on the novel by Esquivel who also wrote the screenplay and whose husband, Arau, directed. In Spanish with English subtitles; also available dubbed. *AKA:* Como Agua para Chocolate.
1993 (R) 105m/C *MX* Lumi Cavazos, Marco Leonardi, Regina Torne, Mario Ivan Martinez, Ada Carrasco, Yareli Arizmendi, Caludette Maille, Pilar Aranda; *D:* Steven Bernsein, Alfonso Arau; *W:* Laura Esquivel; *M:* Leo Brower. Nominations: British Academy Awards '93: Best Foreign Language Film; Independent Spirit Awards '94: Best Foreign Film. **VHS, LV ★★★1/2**

Lili Delightful musical romance about a 16-year-old orphan who joins a traveling carnival and falls in love with a crippled, embittered puppeteer. Heartwarming and charming, if occasionally cloying. Leslie Caron sings the film's song hit, "Hi-Lili, Hi-Lo."
1953 81m/C Leslie Caron, Jean-Pierre Aumont, Mel Ferrer, Kurt Kasznar, Zsa Zsa Gabor; *D:* Charles Walters; *M:* Bronislau Kaper. Academy Awards '53: Best Score; British Academy Awards '53: Best Actress (Caron); Golden Globe Awards '54: Best Screenplay; National Board of Review Awards '53: 10 Best Films of the Year; Nominations: Academy Awards '53: Best Actress (Caron), Best Art Direction/Set Decoration (Color), Best Color Cinematography, Best Director (Walters), Best Screenplay. **VHS, Beta ★★★**

Lilies of the Field Five East German nuns enlist the aid of a free-spirited U.S. Army veteran. They persuade him to build a chapel for them and teach them English. Poitier is excellent as the itinerant laborer, holding the saccharine to an acceptable level, bringing honesty and strength to his role. Actress Skala had been struggling to make ends meet in a variety of day jobs until this opportunity. Poitier was the first African-American man to win an Oscar, and the first African-American nominated since Hattie MacDaniel in 1939. Followed by "Christmas Lilies of the Field," (1979).
1963 94m/B Sidney Poitier, Lilia Skala, Lisa Mann, Isa Crino, Stanley Adams; *D:* Ralph Nelson; *M:* Jerry Goldsmith. Academy Awards '63: Best Actor (Poitier); Berlin International Film Festival '63: Best Actor (Poitier); Golden Globe Awards '64: Best Actor—Drama (Poitier); National Board of Review Awards '63: 10 Best Films of the Year; Nominations: Academy Awards '63: Best Adapted Screenplay, Best Black and White Cinematography, Best Picture, Best Supporting Actress (Skala). **VHS, Beta ★★★**

Liliom Boyer goes to heaven and is put on trial to see if he is deserving of his wings. Lang's first film after leaving Nazi Germany is filled with wonderful ethereal imagery, surprising coming from the man responsible for such grim visions as "Metropolis." In French only.
1935 85m/B *FR* Charles Boyer, Madeleine Ozeray, Florelle, Roland Toutain; *D:* Fritz Lang. **VHS, Beta ★★★**

Lilith Therapist-in-training Beatty falls in love with beautiful mental patient Seberg and approaches madness himself. A look at the doctor-patient relationship among the mentally ill and at the nature of madness and love. Doesn't always satisfy, but intrigues. Rossen's swan song.
1964 114m/B Warren Beatty, Jean Seberg, Peter Fonda, Gene Hackman, Kim Hunter; *D:* Robert Rossen. **VHS, Beta ★★★**

Limelight A nearly washed-up music hall comedian is stimulated by a young ballerina to a final hour of glory. A subtle if self-indulgent portrait of Chaplin's own life, featuring an historic pairing of Chaplin and Keaton.
1952 120m/B Charlie Chaplin, Claire Bloom, Buster Keaton, Nigel Bruce; *D:* Charlie Chaplin. National Board of Review Awards '52: 10 Best Films of the Year. **VHS, Beta, LV ★★★**

The Lion in Winter Medieval monarch Henry II and his wife, Eleanor of Aquitaine, match wits over the succession to the English throne and much else in this fast-paced film version of James Goldman's play. The family, including three grown sons, and visiting royalty are united for the Christmas holidays fraught with tension, rapidly shifting allegiances, and layers of psychological manipulation. Superb dialogue and perfectly realized characterizations. O'Toole and Hepburn are triumphant. Screen debuts for Hopkins and Dalton. Shot on location, this literate costume drama surprised the experts with its box-office success.
1968 (PG) 134m/C Peter O'Toole, Katharine Hepburn, Jane Merrow, Nigel Terry, Timothy Dalton, Anthony Hopkins, John Castle, Nigel Stock; *D:* Anthony Harvey; *W:* James Goldman; *M:* John Barry. Academy Awards '68: Best Actress (Hepburn), Best Adapted Screenplay, Best Score; Directors Guild of America Awards '68: Best Director (Harvey); Golden Globe Awards '69: Best Actor—Drama (O'Toole), Best Film—Drama; National Board of Review Awards '68: 10 Best Films of the Year; New York Film Critics Awards '68:

Best Film; Nominations: Academy Awards '68: Best Actor (O'Toole), Best Costume Design, Best Director (Harvey), Best Picture. **VHS, LV ★★★★**

A Lion Is in the Streets Cagney stars as a backwoods politician in a southern state who fights on the side of the sharecroppers and wins their support when he exposes the corrupt practices of a powerful businessman. On his way up the political ladder, however, Cagney betrays and exploits the very people who support him. Although this is a familiar storyline, Cagney is riveting as the corrupt politician, and Hale is wonderful as his patient wife.
1953 88m/C James Cagney, Barbara Hale, Anne Francis, Warner Anderson, John McIntire, Jeanne Cagney, Lon Chaney Jr., Frank McHugh, Larry Keating, Onslow Stevens; **D:** Raoul Walsh. **VHS ★★★**

The Lion King Highest grossing film in Disney history (likely a temporary title) is a winner for kids and their folks. Like his dad Mufasa (Jones), Lion cub Simba (Taylor) is destined to be king of the beasts, until evil uncle Scar (Irons) plots against him and makes him an outcast. Growing up in the jungles of Africa, Simba (now Broderick) learns about life and responsibility, before facing his uncle once again. Supporting characters frequently steal the show, with Sabella's Pumba the warthog and Lane's Timon the meerkat heading the procession (though Chong and Goldberg as hyenas give them a run). Disney epic features heartwarming combo of crowd-pleasing songs, a story with depth, emotion, and politically correct multiculturalism, and stunning animation. The sound quality is equally spectacular; during the 2 1/2 minute wildebeest stampede scene, you'll swear the animals are running amuck in the house. 32nd Disney animated feature is the first without human characters, the first based on an original story, and the first to use the voices of a well-known, ethnically diverse cast. Scenes of violence in the animal kingdom may be too much for younger viewers. ♪ Can You Feel the Love Tonight; The Circle of Life; I Just Can't Wait to Be King; Be Prepared; Hakuna Matata.
1994 (G) 88m/C D: Rob Minkoff, Roger Allers; **W:** Jonathan Roberts, Irene Mecchi; **M:** Elton John, Hans Zimmer, Tim Rice; **V:** Matthew Broderick, Jeremy Irons, James Earl Jones, Madge Sinclair, Robert Guillaume, Jonathan Taylor Thomas, Richard "Cheech" Marin, Whoopi Goldberg, Rowan Atkinson, Nathan Lane, Ernie Sabella, Niketa Calame, Moira Kelly, Jim Cummings. Academy Awards '94: Best Song ("Can You Feel the Love Tonight"), Best Original Score; Chicago Film Critics Awards '94: Best Score; Golden Globe Awards '95: Best Film—Musical/Comedy, Best Song ("Can You Feel the Love Tonight?"), Best Original Score; Blockbuster Entertainment Awards '95: Family Movie, Theatrical, Best Soundtrack; Nominations: Academy Awards '94: Best Song ("Circle of Life"), Best Song ("Hakuna Matata"); MTV Movie Awards '95: Best Villain (Irons), Best Song ("Can You Feel the Love Tonight"). **VHS ★★★★**

The List of Adrian Messenger A crafty murderer resorts to a variety of disguises to eliminate potential heirs to a family fortune. Solid Huston-directed thriller with a twist: you won't recognize any of the name stars.
1963 98m/B Kirk Douglas, George C. Scott, Robert Mitchum, Dana Wynter, Burt Lancaster, Frank Sinatra; **D:** John Huston; **M:** Jerry Goldsmith. **VHS, Beta ★★★**

Little Big Man Based on Thomas Berger's picaresque novel, this is the story of 121-year-old Jack Crabb and his quixotic life as gunslinger, charlatan, Indian, ally to George Custer, and the only white survivor of Little Big Horn. Told mainly through flashbacks. Hoffman provides a classic portrayal of Crabb, as fact and myth are jumbled and reshaped.
1970 (PG) 135m/C Dustin Hoffman, Faye Dunaway, Chief Dan George, Richard Mulligan, Martin Balsam, Jeff Corey, Aimee Eccles; **D:** Arthur Penn; **W:** Calder Willingham. New York Film Critics Awards '70: Best Supporting Actor (George); National Society of Film Critics Awards '70: Best Supporting Actor (George); Nominations: Academy Awards '70: Best Supporting Actor (George). **VHS, Beta, LV ★★★1/2**

Little Caesar A small-time hood rises to become a gangland czar, but his downfall is as rapid as his rise. Still thrilling. The role of Rico made Robinson a star and typecast him as a crook for all time.
1930 80m/B Edward G. Robinson, Glenda Farrell, Sidney Blackmer, Douglas Fairbanks Jr.; **D:** Mervyn LeRoy. Nominations: Academy Awards '31: Best Adapted Screenplay. **VHS, Beta ★★★**

The Little Colonel After the Civil War, an embittered Southern patriarch turns his back on his family, until his dimple-cheeked granddaughter softens his heart. Hokey and heartwarming. Shirley's first teaming with Bill "Bojangles" Robinson features the famous dance scene. Adapted by William Conselman from the Annie Fellows Johnston best-seller. **1935 (PG) 80m/B** Shirley Temple, Lionel Barrymore, Evelyn Venable, John Lodge, Hattie McDaniel, Bill Robinson, Sidney Blackmer; **D:** David Butler. **VHS, Beta** ★★★

Little Dorrit, Film 1: Nobody's Fault The mammoth version of the Dickens tome, about a father and daughter trapped interminably in the dreaded Marshalsea debtors' prison, and the good samaritan who works to free them. Told in two parts (on four tapes), "Nobody's Fault," and "Little Dorrit's Story." **1988 369m/C** *GB* Alec Guinness, Derek Jacobi, Cyril Cusack, Sarah Pickering, Joan Greenwood, Max Wall, Amelda Brown, Daniel Chatto, Miriam Margolyes, Bill Fraser, Roshan Seth, Michael Elphick, Eleanor Bron, Patricia Hayes, Robert Morley, Sophie Ward; **D:** Christine Edzard; **W:** Christine Edzard; **M:** Giuseppe Verdi. Los Angeles Film Critics Association Awards '88: Best Film, Best Supporting Actor (Guinness); Nominations: Academy Awards '88: Best Adapted Screenplay, Best Supporting Actor (Guinness). **VHS, Beta, LV** ★★★

Little Dorrit, Film 2: Little Dorrit's Story The second half of the monumental adaptation of Dickens' most popular novel during his lifetime tells of Amy Dorrit's rise from debtor's prison to happiness. **1988 369m/C** *GB* Alec Guinness, Derek Jacobi, Cyril Cusack, Sarah Pickering, Joan Greenwood, Max Wall, Amelda Brown, Daniel Chatto, Miriam Margolyes, Bill Fraser, Roshan Seth, Michael Elphick, Patricia Hayes, Robert Morley, Sophie Ward, Eleanor Bron; **D:** Christine Edzard; **W:** Christine Edzard; **M:** Giuseppe Verdi. Los Angeles Film Critics Association Awards '88: Best Film, Best Supporting Actor (Guinness); Nominations: Academy Awards '88: Best Adapted Screenplay, Best Supporting Actor (Guiness). **VHS, Beta, LV** ★★★

The Little Drummer Girl An Israeli counterintelligence agent recruits an actress sympathetic to the Palestinian cause to trap a fanatical terrorist leader. Solid performances from Keaton as the actress and Kinski as the Israeli counterintelligence officer sustain interest through a puzzling, sometimes boring and frustrating, cinematic maze of espionage. Keaton is at or near her very best. Based on the best-selling novel by John Le Carre. **1984 (R) 130m/C** Diane Keaton, Klaus

Kinski, Yorgo Voyagis, Sami Frey, Michael Cristofer, Anna Massey, Thorley Walters; **D:** George Roy Hill; **M:** Dave Grusin. **VHS, Beta, LV** ★★★

The Little Foxes A vicious southern woman will destroy everyone around her to satisfy her desire for wealth and power. Filled with corrupt characters who commit numerous revolting deeds. The vicious matriarch is a part made to fit for Davis, and she makes the most of it. Script by Lillian Hellman from her own play. **1941 116m/B** Bette Davis, Herbert Marshall, Dan Duryea, Teresa Wright, Charles Dingle, Richard Carlson, Patricia Collinge; **D:** William Wyler. Nominations: Academy Awards '41: Best Actress (Davis), Best Director (Wyler), Best Film Editing, Best Interior Decoration, Best Picture, Best Screenplay, Best Supporting Actress (Collinge, Wright), Best Original Score. **VHS, Beta, LV** ★★★1/2

Little House on the Prairie The pilot for the television series based on the life of Laura Ingalls Wilder and her family's struggles on the American plains in the 1860s. Other episodes are also available on tape, including one in which Patricia Neal guest stars as a terminally ill widow seeking a home for her children. Neal's performance earned her a best actress Emmy in 1975. **1974 98m/C** Michael Landon, Karen Grassle, Victor French, Melissa Gilbert, Melissa Sue Anderson; **D:** Michael Landon. **VHS, Beta** ★★★

Little Lord Fauntleroy The vintage Hollywood version of the Frances Hodgson Burnett story of a fatherless American boy who discovers he's heir to a British dukedom. Also available in computer-colorized version. Well cast, charming, remade for TV in 1980. Smith is lovable as the noble tyke's crusty old guardian. **1936 102m/B** Freddie Bartholomew, Sir C. Aubrey Smith, Mickey Rooney, Dolores Costello, Jessie Ralph, Guy Kibbee; **D:** John Cromwell; **M:** Max Steiner. **VHS, Beta** ★★★1/2

Little Man Tate A seven-year-old genius is the prize in a tug of war between his mother, who wants him to lead a normal life, and a domineering school director who loves him for his intellect. An acclaimed directorial debut for Foster, with overtones of her own extraordinary life as a child prodigy. **1991 (PG) 99m/C** Jodie Foster, Dianne Wiest, Harry Connick Jr., Adam Hann-Byrd, George Plimpton, Debi Mazar, Celia Weston, David Pierce, Danitra Vance, Josh

Mostel, P.J. Ochlan; **D:** Jodie Foster; **W:** Scott Frank; **M:** Mark Isham. **VHS** ★★★

The Little Mermaid Headstrong teenage mermaid falls in love with a human prince and longs to be human too. She makes a pact with the evil Sea Witch to trade her voice for a pair of legs. Sebastian the Crab nearly steals the show with his wit and showstopping number "Under the Sea." ♪ Under the Sea; Kiss the Girl; Daughters of Triton; Part of Your World; Poor Unfortunate Souls; Les Poissons.
1989 (G) 82m/C D: John Musker, Ron Clements; **W:** John Musker, Ron Clements; **M:** Alan Menken, Howard Ashman; **V:** Jodi Benson, Christopher Daniel Barnes, Pat Carroll, Rene Auberjonois, Samuel E. Wright, Buddy Hackett, Jason Marin, Edie McClurg, Kenneth Mars, Nancy Cartwright. Academy Awards '89: Best Song ("Under the Sea"), Best Original Score; Golden Globe Awards '90: Best Song ("Under the Sea"), Best Score; Nominations: Academy Awards '89: Best Song ("Kiss the Girl"). **VHS, Beta, LV, 8mm** ★★★½

Little Minister An adaptation of the James Barrie novel about a prissy Scottish pastor who falls in love with a free-spirited gypsy . . . he thinks she is, in fact, the local earl's daughter.
1934 101m/B Katharine Hepburn, John Beal, Alan Hale, Donald Crisp; **D:** Richard Wallace; **M:** Max Steiner. **VHS, Beta** ★★★

Little Miss Marker Heartwarming story starring Temple, who is the IOU for a gambling debt and steals her way into everyone's heart. Remade three times as "Sorrowful Jones," as "40 Pounds of Trouble," and in 1980 with the original title. **AKA:** Girl in Pawn.
1934 88m/B Adolphe Menjou, Shirley Temple, Dorothy Dell, Charles Bickford, Lynne Overman; **D:** Alexander Hall. **VHS** ★★★

The Little Princess Based on the Frances Hodgson Burnett children's classic; perhaps the best of the moppet's films. Shirley is a young schoolgirl in Victorian London sent to a harsh boarding school when her Army officer father is posted abroad. When her father is declared missing, the penniless girl must work as a servant at the school to pay her keep, all the while haunting the hospitals, never believing her father has died. A classic tearjerker.
1939 (G) 91m/B Shirley Temple, Richard Greene, Anita Louise, Ian Hunter, Cesar Romero, Arthur Treacher, Sybil Jason, Miles Mander, Marcia Mae Jones, E.E.

Clive; **D:** Walter Lang. **VHS, Beta, LV** ★★★½

A Little Princess Compelling fantasy, based on the children's book by Frances Hodgson Burnett, and previously best known for the 1939 Shirley Temple incarnation. Sara (Matthews) has been raised in India by her widowed father (Cunningham). When he's called up to fight in WWI, Sara is taken to New York to be educated at stern Miss Michin's (Bron) school, where her money makes her a favored boarder. However, the irrepressible Sara suffers a severe reversal of fortune when her father is reported killed and Miss Michin promptly makes her a servant to pay her way. But Sara's charm has made her some true friends who become her allies under trying circumstances. Lively script, dazzling visuals, and a welcome lack of sappiness create a classic-in-the-making.
1995 (G) 97m/C Liesl Matthews, Eleanor Bron, Liam Cunningham, Rusty Schwimmer, Arthur Malet, Vanessa Lee Chester, Errol Sitahal, Heather DeLoach, Taylor Fry; **D:** Alfonso Cuaron; **W:** Richard LaGravenese, Elizabeth Chandler, Emmanuel Lubezki; **M:** Patrick Doyle. Nominations: Academy Awards '95: Best Art Direction/Set Decoration, Best Cinematography. **VHS, LV** ★★★½

A Little Romance An American girl living in Paris falls in love with a French boy; eventually they run away, to seal their love with a kiss beneath a bridge. Olivier gives a wonderful, if not hammy, performance as the old pickpocket who encourages her. Gentle, agile comedy based on the novel by Patrick Cauvin.
1979 (PG) 110m/C Laurence Olivier, Diane Lane, Thelonious Bernard, Sally Kellerman, Broderick Crawford; **D:** George Roy Hill; **W:** Allan Burns; **M:** Georges Delerue. Academy Awards '79: Best Original Score; Nominations: Academy Awards '79: Best Adapted Screenplay. **VHS, Beta, LV** ★★★

Little Shop of Horrors The landmark cheapie classic, which Roger Corman reputedly filmed in three days, about a nebbish working in a city florist shop who unknowingly cultivates an intelligent plant that demands human meat for sustenance. Notable for then-unknown Nicholson's appearance as a masochistic dental patient. Hilarious, unpretentious farce—if you liked this one, check out Corman's "Bucket of Blood" for more of the same. Inspired a musical of the same name, remade as a movie again in 1986. Available colorized.

1960 70m/B Jackie Joseph, Jonathan Haze, Mel Welles, Jack Nicholson, Dick Miller; **D:** Roger Corman. VHS, Beta, LV ★★★1/2

Little Shop of Horrors During a solar eclipse, Seymour buys an unusual plant and takes it back to the flower shop where he works. The plant, Audrey 2, becomes a town attraction as it grows at an unusual rate, but Seymour learns that he must feed Audrey fresh human blood to keep her growing. Soon, Audrey is giving the orders ("Feed me") and timid Seymour must find "deserving" victims. Martin's performance as the masochistic dentist is alone worth the price. Song, dance, gore, and more prevail in this outrageous musical comedy. Four Tops' Levi Stubbs is the commanding voice of Audrey 2. Based on the Off-Broadway play, which was based on Roger Corman's 1960 horror spoof. ♪ Mean Green Mother From Outer Space; Some Fun Now; Your Day Begins Tonight.
1986 (PG-13) 94m/C Rick Moranis, Ellen Greene, Vincent Gardenia, Steve Martin, James Belushi, Christopher Guest, Bill Murray, John Candy; **D:** Frank Oz; **M:** Miles Goodman, Howard Ashman. Nominations: Academy Awards '86: Best Song ("Mean Green Mother from Outer Space"). VHS, Beta, LV ★★★

The Little Theatre of Jean Renoir A farewell by director Jean Renoir featuring three short films. In the first, Renoir's humanist beliefs are apparent in "The Last Christmas Dinner," a Hans Christian Andersen-inspired story. Next, "The Electric Floor Waxer" is a comic opera. The third piece is called "A Tribute to Tolerance." Slight but important late statement by a great director. In French with English subtitles.
1971 100m/C Jean Renoir, Fernand Sardou, Jean Carmet, Francoise Arnoul, Jeanne Moreau; **D:** Jean Renoir; **W:** Jean Renoir. VHS, Beta, LV ★★★

The Little Thief Touted as Francois Truffaut's final legacy, this trite minidrama is actually based on a story he co-wrote with Claude de Givray about a post-WWII adolescent girl who reacts to the world around her by stealing and petty crime. Truffaut's hand is markedly absent, but this film is a testament to his abruptly and sadly truncated career. Director Miller was Truffaut's longtime assistant. In French with English subtitles.
1989 (PG-13) 108m/C FR Charlotte Gainsbourg, Simon de la Brosse, Didier Bezace, Raoul Billerey, Nathalie Cardone;

D: Claude Miller; **W:** Annie Miller, Claude Miller; **M:** Alain Jomy. VHS, Beta, LV ★★★

Little Women Louisa May Alcott's Civil War story of the four March sisters—Jo, Beth, Amy, and Meg—who share their loves, their joys, and their sorrows. Everything about this classic film is wonderful, from the lavish period costumes to the excellent script, and particularly the captivating performances by the cast. A must-see for fans of Alcott and Hepburn, and others will find it enjoyable. Remade in 1949, again in 1978 for television, and in 1994.
1933 107m/B Katharine Hepburn, Joan Bennett, Paul Lukas, Edna May Oliver, Frances Dee, Spring Byington, Jean Parker, Douglass Montgomery; **D:** George Cukor; **W:** Victor Heerman, Sarah Y. Mason; **M:** Max Steiner. Academy Awards '33: Best Adapted Screenplay; Venice Film Festival '34: Best Actress (Hepburn); Nominations: Academy Awards '33: Best Director (Cukor), Best Picture. VHS, Beta, 8mm ★★★★

Little Women Stylized color remake of the George Cukor 1933 classic. Top-notch if too obvious cast portrays Louisa May Alcott's story of teenage girls growing up against the backdrop of the Civil War. Remade again, for television in 1978.
1949 121m/C June Allyson, Peter Lawford, Margaret O'Brien, Elizabeth Taylor, Janet Leigh, Mary Astor; **D:** Mervyn LeRoy; **W:** Andrew Solt; **M:** Adolph Deutsch. Academy Awards '49: Best Art Direction/Set Decoration (Color); Nominations: Academy Awards '49: Best Color Cinematography. VHS ★★★

Little Women Beloved story of the March women is beautifully portrayed in a solid production that blends a seamless screenplay with an excellent cast, authentic period costumes, and lovely cinematography and music. Ryder, perfectly cast as the unconventional Jo, is also the strongest of the sisters: domestically inclined Meg (Alvarado), the fragile Beth (Danes), and the youngest, mischievous Amy (the delightful Dunst) who grows up into a sedate young lady (Mathis). Charming adaptation remains faithful to the spirit of the Alcott classic while adding contemporary touches. Fittingly brought to the big screen by producer Denise Di Novi, writer/co-producer Swicord, and director Armstrong.
1994 (PG) 118m/C Winona Ryder, Gabriel Byrne, Trini Alvarado, Samantha Mathis, Kirsten Dunst, Claire Danes, Christian Bale, Eric Stoltz, John Neville, Mary Wickes,

Susan Sarandon; **D:** Gillian Armstrong; **W:** Robin Swicord; **M:** Thomas Newman, Geoffrey Simpson. Chicago Film Critics Awards '94: Most Promising Actress (Dunst); Nominations: Academy Awards '94: Best Actress (Ryder), Best Costume Design, Best Original Score. **VHS, LV, 8mm** ★★★★

The Lives of a Bengal Lancer One of Hollywood's greatest rousing adventures. Three British Lancers, of varying experience, encounter a vicious revolution against colonial rule. Rivaled only by "Gunga Din" as the ultimate 1930s swashbuckler. Swell plot, lotsa action, great comraderie. Based on the novel by Major Francis Yeats-Brown, and remade in 1939 as "Geronimo."
1935 110m/B Gary Cooper, Franchot Tone, Richard Cromwell, Guy Standing, Sir C. Aubrey Smith, Monte Blue, Kathleen Burke, Noble Johnson, Lumsden Hare, Akim Tamiroff, J. Carrol Naish, Douglass Dumbrille; **D:** Henry Hathaway; **W:** Waldemar Young, John Balderston; **M:** Milan Roder. National Board of Review Awards '35: 10 Best Films of the Year; Nominations: Academy Awards '35: Best Adapted Screenplay, Best Director (Hathaway), Best Film Editing, Best Interior Decoration, Best Picture, Best Sound. **VHS, Beta** ★★★★

The Living Daylights After being used as a pawn in a fake Russian defector plot, our intrepid spy tracks down an international arms and opium smuggling ring. Fine debut by Dalton as 007 in a rousing, refreshing cosmopolitan shoot-em-up. Let's be frank: we were all getting a little fatigued by Roger Moore.
1987 (PG) 130m/C Timothy Dalton, Maryam D'Abo, Jeroen Krabbe, John Rhys-Davies, Robert Brown, Joe Don Baker, Desmond Llewelyn, Art Malik, Geoffrey Keen, Walter Gotell, Andreas Wisniewski; **D:** John Glen; **W:** Richard Maibaum, Michael G. Wilson; **M:** John Barry. **VHS, Beta, LV** ★★★

Local Hero Riegert is a yuppie representative of a huge oil company who endeavors to buy a sleepy Scottish fishing village for excavation, and finds himself hypnotized by the place and its crusty denizens. Back in Texas at company headquarters, tycoon Lancaster deals with a psycho therapist and gazes at the stars looking for clues. A low-key, charmingly offbeat Scottish comedy with its own sense of logic and quiet humor, poetic landscapes, and unique characters, epitomizing Forsyth's original style.

1983 (PG) 112m/C GB Peter Riegert, Denis Lawson, Burt Lancaster, Fulton Mackay, Jenny Seagrove, Peter Capaldi, Norman Chancer; **D:** Bill Forsyth; **W:** Bill Forsyth; **M:** Mark Knopfler. British Academy Awards '83: Best Director (Forsyth); New York Film Critics Awards '83: Best Screenplay; National Society of Film Critics Awards '83: Best Screenplay. **VHS, Beta, LV** ★★★★

The Lodger A mysterious lodger is thought to be a rampaging mass murderer of young women. First Hitchcock film to explore the themes and ideas that would become his trademarks. Silent. Climactic chase is memorable. Remade three times. Look closely for the Master in this first cameo. **AKA:** The Case of Jonathan Drew; The Lodger: A Case of London Fog.
1926 91m/B GB Ivor Novello, Marie Ault, Arthur Chesney, Malcolm Keen; **Cameos:** Alfred Hitchcock; **D:** Alfred Hitchcock; **W:** Alfred Hitchcock. **VHS, Beta** ★★★

Lola A wonderful tale of a nightclub dancer and her amorous adventures. Innovative film that marked the beginning of French New Wave. In French with English subtitles.
1961 90m/B FR Anouk Aimee, Marc Michel, Elina Labourdette, Jacques Harden; **D:** Jacques Demy. **VHS** ★★★

Lola Montes Ophuls' final masterpiece recounts the life and sins of the famous courtesan, mistress of Franz Liszt and the King of Bavaria. Ignored upon release, but hailed later by the French as a cinematic landmark. Presented in its original wide-screen format; in French with English subtitles. Also available in a 110-minute version. Adapted from an unpublished novel by Cecil Saint-Laurent.
1955 140m/C FR Martine Carol, Peter Ustinov, Anton Walbrook, Ivan Desny, Oskar Werner; **D:** Max Ophuls; **W:** Max Ophuls; **M:** Georges Auric. **Beta, LV** ★★★★

Lolita A middle-aged professor is consumed by his lust for a teenage nymphet in this strange film considered daring in its time. Based on Vladimir Nabokov's novel. Watch for Winters' terrific portrayal as Lolita's sex-starved mother.
1962 152m/B GB James Mason, Shelley Winters, Peter Sellers, Sue Lyon; **D:** Stanley Kubrick. Nominations: Academy Awards '62: Best Adapted Screenplay. **VHS, Beta, LV** ★★★

Lone Star Terrific contemporary western set in the border town of Frontera, Texas. Sheriff Sam Deeds

(Cooper) is still dealing with the legacy of his father, legendary lawman Buddy Deeds (McConaughey) who, 40 years before, wrestled control of the town from his racist, corrupt predecessor Charlie Wade (Kristofferson) and supposedly sent him packing. But when skeletal remains and a sheriff's badge turn up on an abandoned Army rifle range, guess whose bones they turn out to be. Buddy's friends would like Sam to just leave the past lie, but he can't and learns some hard home truths. This is only one of the town's stories that Sayles gracefully tells and, as always, his ensemble cast all offer outstanding performances. **1995 (R) 134m/C** Chris Cooper, Matthew McConaughey, Kris Kristofferson, Elizabeth Pena, Joe Morton, Ron Canada, Clifton James, Miriam Colon, Frances McDormand; *D:* John Sayles; *W:* John Sayles; *M:* Mason Daring. Nominations: Golden Globe Awards '97: Best Screenplay; Independent Spirit Awards '97: Best Film, Best Actor (Cooper), Best Supporting Actress (Pena), Best Screenplay. **VHS ★★★1/2**

The Loneliness of the Long Distance Runner Courtenay, in his film debut, turns in a powerful performance as an angry young man infected by the poverty and hopelessness of the British slums. His first attempt at crime is a bust and lands him in a boys reformatory where he is recruited for the running team. While training for the big event with a rival school, Redgrave's obsession with winning the race and Courtenay's continued indifference to the outcome lock the two in an intriguing, seemingly one-sided power struggle. Though widely overlooked when first released, it has since been praised as one of the finest teenage angst films of the '60s. Riveting depiction on a boy's rite of passage into manhood. *AKA:* Rebel with a Cause. **1962 104m/B** *GB* Tom Courtenay, Michael Redgrave, Avis Bunnage, Peter Madden, James Bolam, Julia Foster, Topsy Jane, Frank Finlay; *D:* Tony Richardson; *M:* John Addison. **VHS, Beta ★★★**

Lonely Are the Brave A free-spirited cowboy out of sync with the modern age tries to rescue a buddy from a local jail, and in his eventual escape is tracked relentlessly by modern law enforcement. A compelling, sorrowful essay on civilized progress and exploitation of nature. Adapted from the novel "Brave Cowboy" by Edward Abbey. **1962 107m/B** Kirk Douglas, Walter

Matthau, Gena Rowlands, Carroll O'Connor, George Kennedy; *D:* David Miller; *M:* Jerry Goldsmith. **VHS, Beta, LV ★★★**

The Lonely Passion of Judith Hearne A self-effacing Dublin spinster meets a man who gives her his attention, but she must overcome her own self-doubt and crisis of faith. Adapted from Brian Moore's 1955 novel. Excellent performances from both Hoskins and Smith. **1987 (R) 116m/C** *GB* Maggie Smith, Bob Hoskins, Wendy Hiller, Marie Kean, Ian McNeice, Alan Devlin, Rudi Davies, Prunella Scales; *D:* Jack Clayton; *W:* Peter Nelson; *M:* Georges Delerue. British Academy Awards '88: Best Actress (Smith). **VHS ★★★**

Lonesome Dove Classic western saga with Duvall and Jones in outstanding roles as two aging ex-Texas Rangers who decide to leave their quiet lives for a last adventure—a cattle drive from Texas to Montana. Along the way they encounter a new love (Lane), a lost love (Huston), and a savage renegade Indian (well-played by Forrest). Based on Larry McMurtry's Pulitzer Prize-winning novel, this handsome television miniseries is a finely detailed evocation of the Old West, with a wonderful cast and an equally fine production. Available in a four volume boxed set. Followed by "Return to Lonesome Dove." **1989 480m/C** Robert Duvall, Frederic Forrest, Tommy Lee Jones, Anjelica Huston, Danny Glover, Diane Lane, Rick Schroder, Robert Urich, D.B. Sweeney; *D:* Simon Windsor; *W:* William D. Wittliff; *M:* Basil Poledouris. **VHS, LV ★★★1/2**

The Long Day Closes It's 1956 Liverpool and 11-year-old Bud (McCormack) is part of a working-class Catholic family who longs to escape from his humdrum life. And how? By going to the movies of course and filling his head with pop songs. Nostalgic view of family life filled with sweet, small everyday moments set in a dreary postwar England. Sequel to Davies's also autobiographical film "Distant Voices, Still Lives." **1992 (PG) 84m/C** *GB* Leigh McCormack, Marjorie Yates, Anthony Watson, Ayse Owens; *D:* Terence Davies; *W:* Terence Davies. Nominations: Cannes Film Festival '92: Best Film. **VHS ★★★**

Long Day's Journey into Night A brooding, devastating film based on Eugene O'Neill's most powerful and autobiographical play. Depicts a day in the life of a family deteriorating un-

der drug addiction, alcoholism, and imminent death. Hepburn's performance is outstanding. In 1988, the Broadway version was taped and released on video.
1962 174m/B Ralph Richardson, Katharine Hepburn, Dean Stockwell, Jeanne Barr, Jason Robards Jr.; *D:* Sidney Lumet; *W:* Eugene O'Neill; *M:* Andre Previn. Cannes Film Festival '62: Best Actress (Hepburn); National Board of Review Awards '62: 10 Best Films of the Year, Best Supporting Actor (Robards); Nominations: Academy Awards '62: Best Actress (Hepburn). **VHS, LV** ★★★★

Long Day's Journey into Night Eugene O'Neill's autobiographical play about his family is adapted from Canada's Stratford Festival production. The Tyrones are a troubled Irish-American family: bullying James (Hutt) was a once-great Shakespearean actor who has been typecast in a popular stage potboiler; wife Mary (Henry) is a morphine addict; elder son James Jr. (Donaldson) is an alcoholic; and O'Neill's alter ego is Edmund (McCamus), an overly sensitive, consumptive writer.
1996 174m/C *CA* William Hutt, Martha Henry, Tom McCamus, Peter Donaldson, Martha Burns; *D:* David Wellington; *W:* Eugene O'Neill; *M:* Ron Sures. Genie Awards '96: Best Actor (Hutt), Best Supporting Actor (Donaldson), Best Actress (Henry), Best Supporting Actress (Burns), Best Film; Toronto-City Award '96: Best Canadian Feature Film; Nominations: Genie Awards '96: Best Actor (McCamus), Best Film Editing. **VHS** ★★★

The Long Good Friday Set in London's dockland, this is a violent story of a crime boss who meets his match. Hoskin's world crumbles over an Easter weekend when his buildings are bombed and his men murdered. He thinks its the work of rival gangsters only to discover an even deadlier threat is behind his troubles. One of the best of the crime genre, with an exquisitely charismatic performance by Hoskins.
1979 109m/C *GB* Bob Hoskins, Helen Mirren, Dave King, Bryan Marshall, George Coulouris, Pierce Brosnan, Derek Thompson, Eddie Constantine; *D:* John MacKenzie, Phil Meheux. Edgar Allan Poe Awards '82: Best Screenplay. **VHS, Beta** ★★★1/2

The Long Goodbye Raymond Chandler's penultimate novel with the unmistakable Altman touch—which is to say that some of the changes to the story have pushed purist noses out of joint. Gould is cast as an insouciant anti-Marlowe, the film noir atmosphere has been transmuted into a Hollywood film neon, genre jibing abounds, and the ending has been rewritten. But the revamping serves a purpose, which is to make Marlowe a viable character in a contemporary world. Handsomely photographed by Vilmos Zsigmond. Don't miss bulky boy Arnold's cameo (his second film appearance).
1973 (R) 112m/C Elliott Gould, Nina Van Pallandt, Sterling Hayden, Henry Gibson, Mark Rydell, David Arkin, Warren Berlinger; *Cameos:* Arnold Schwarzenegger, David Carradine; *D:* Robert Altman; *W:* Leigh Brackett; *M:* John Williams, Vilmos Zsigmond. National Society of Film Critics Awards '73: Best Cinematography. **VHS, Beta, LV** ★★★

The Long Gray Line Power gives an outstanding performance as Marty Maher, a humble Irish immigrant who became an institution at West Point. This is the inspiring story of his rise from an unruly cadet to one of the academy's most beloved instructors. O'Hara does a fine job of playing his wife, who like her husband, adopts the young cadets as her own. Director Ford gracefully captures the spirit and honor associated with West Point in this affectionate drama.
1955 138m/C Tyrone Power, Maureen O'Hara, Robert Francis, Donald Crisp, Ward Bond, Betsy Palmer, Phil Carey; *D:* John Ford. **VHS** ★★★

The Long, Hot Summer A tense, well-played adaptation of the William Faulkner story about a wanderer latching himself onto a tyrannical Mississippi family. The first on-screen pairing of Newman and Woodward, and one of the best. Remade for television in 1986.
1958 117m/C Paul Newman, Orson Welles, Joanne Woodward, Lee Remick, Anthony (Tony) Franciosa, Angela Lansbury, Richard Anderson; *D:* Martin Ritt; *W:* Harriet Frank Jr., Irving Ravetch; *M:* Alex North. Cannes Film Festival '58: Best Actor (Newman). **VHS, Beta** ★★★1/2

The Long, Hot Summer A made-for-television version of the William Faulkner story, "The Hamlet," about a drifter taken under a Southern patriarch's wing. He's bribed into courting the man's unmarried daughter. Wonderful performances from the entire cast, especially Ivey and surprisingly, Johnson. Remake of the 1958 film with Paul Newman and Joanne Woodward that is on par with the original.
1986 172m/C Don Johnson, Cybill

Shepherd, Judith Ivey, Jason Robards Jr., Ava Gardner, William Russ, Wings Hauser, William Forsythe, Albert Hall; *D:* Stuart Cooper; *M:* Charles Bernstein. **VHS, Beta** ★★★1/2

The Long Riders Excellent mythic western in which the Jesse James and Cole Younger gangs raid banks, trains, and stagecoaches in post-Civil War Missouri. Stylish, meticulous and a violent look back, with one of the better slow-motion shoot-outs in Hollywood history. Notable for the portrayal of four sets of brothers by four Hollywood brother sets. Complimented by excellent Cooder score. **1980 (R) 100m/C** Stacy Keach, James Keach, Randy Quaid, Dennis Quaid, David Carradine, Keith Carradine, Robert Carradine, Christopher Guest, Nicholas Guest, Pamela Reed, Savannah Smith, James Whitmore Jr., Harry Carey Jr.; *D:* Walter Hill; *W:* Stacy Keach, James Keach, Bill Bryden; *M:* Ry Cooder. Nominations: Cannes Film Festival '80: Best Film. **VHS, Beta, LV** ★★★

The Long Voyage Home A talented cast performs this must-see screen adaptation of Eugene O'Neill's play about crew members aboard a merchant steamer in 1939. Wayne plays a young lad from Sweden who is trying to get home and stay out of trouble as he and the other seaman let shore leave. **1940 105m/B** John Wayne, Thomas Mitchell, Ian Hunter, Barry Fitzgerald, Mildred Natwick, John Qualen; *D:* John Ford. National Board of Review Awards '40: 10 Best Films of the Year; New York Film Critics Awards '40: Best Director (Ford); Nominations: Academy Awards '40: Best Black and White Cinematography, Best Film Editing, Best Picture, Best Screenplay, Best Original Score. **VHS, Beta, LV** ★★★1/2

The Long Walk Home In Montgomery Alabama, in the mid-1950s, sometime after Rosa Parks refused to sit in the black-designated back of the bus, Martin Luther King Jr. led a bus boycott. Spacek is the affluent wife of a narrow-minded businessman while Goldberg is their struggling maid. When Spacek discovers that Goldberg is supporting the boycott by walking the nine-mile trek to work, she sympathizes and tries to help, antagonizing her husband. The plot marches inevitably toward a white-on-white showdown on racism while quietly exploring gender equality between the women. Outstanding performances by Spacek and Goldberg, and a great '50s feel.

1989 (PG) 95m/C Sissy Spacek, Whoopi Goldberg, Dwight Schultz, Ving Rhames, Dylan Baker; *D:* Richard Pearce; *W:* John Cork; *M:* George Fenton. **VHS, LV** ★★★

The Longest Day The complete story of the D-Day landings at Normandy on June 6, 1944, as seen through the eyes of American, French, British, and German participants. Exhaustively accurate details and extremely talented cast make this one of the all-time great Hollywood epic productions. The first of the big budget, all-star war productions; based on the book by Cornelius Ryan. Three directors share credit. Also available in a colorized version. **1962 179m/C** John Wayne, Richard Burton, Red Buttons, Robert Mitchum, Henry Fonda, Robert Ryan, Paul Anka, Mel Ferrer, Edmond O'Brien, Fabian, Sean Connery, Roddy McDowall, Arletty, Curt Jurgens, Rod Steiger, Jean-Louis Barrault, Peter Lawford, Robert Wagner, Sal Mineo, Leo Genn, Richard Beymer, Jeffrey Hunter, Stuart Whitman, Eddie Albert, Tom Tryon, Alexander Knox, Ray Danton, Kenneth More, Richard Todd, Gert Frobe, Christopher Lee; *D:* Ken Annakin; *W:* Bernhard Wicki; *M:* Maurice Jarre. Academy Awards '62: Best Black and White Cinematography, Best Special Effects; National Board of Review Awards '62: 10 Best Films of the Year; Nominations: Academy Awards '62: Best Art Direction/Set Decoration (B & W), Best Film Editing, Best Picture. **VHS, Beta, LV** ★★★1/2

Longtime Companion Critically acclaimed film follows a group of gay men and their friends during the 1980s. The closely knit group monitors the progression of the AIDS virus from early news reports until it finally hits home and begins to take the lives of their loved ones. One of the first films to look at the situation in an intelligent and touching manner. Produced by the PBS "American Playhouse" company. **1990 (R) 100m/C** Stephen Caffrey, Patrick Cassidy, Brian Cousins, Bruce Davison, John Dossett, Mark Lamos, Dermot Mulroney, Mary-Louise Parker, Michael Schoeffling, Campbell Scott, Robert Joy; *D:* Norman Rene. Golden Globe Awards '91: Best Supporting Actor (Davison); Independent Spirit Awards '91: Best Supporting Actor (Davison); New York Film Critics Awards '90: Best Supporting Actor (Davison); National Society of Film Critics Awards '90: Best Supporting Actor (Davison); Sundance Film Festival '90: Audience Award; Nominations: Academy Awards '90: Best Supporting Actor (Davison). **VHS** ★★★1/2

Look Back in Anger Based on John Osborne's famous play, the first British "angry young man" film, in which a squalor-living lad takes out his anger on the world by seducing his friend's wife.
1958 99m/B *GB* Richard Burton, Claire Bloom, Mary Ure, Edith Evans, Gary Raymond; *D:* Tony Richardson; *W:* John Osborne; *M:* John Addison. National Board of Review Awards '59: 10 Best Films of the Year. VHS, Beta, LV ★★★1/2

Look Who's Talking When Alley bears the child of a married, and quite fickle man, she sets her sights elsewhere in search of the perfect father; Travolta is the cabbie with more on his mind than driving Alley around and babysitting. All the while, the baby gives us his views via the voice of Bruce Willis. A very light comedy with laughs for the whole family.
1989 (PG-13) 90m/C John Travolta, Kirstie Alley, Olympia Dukakis, George Segal, Abe Vigoda; *D:* Amy Heckerling; *W:* Amy Heckerling; *M:* David Kitay; *V:* Bruce Willis. People's Choice Awards '90: Best Film—Musical/Comedy. VHS, Beta, LV ★★★

Looking for Richard A Shakespearean "Vanya on 42nd Street," "Richard" is the first semidocumentary addition to the barrage of Bard redeauxs. Pacino's protracted pic dwells on a filmmaker's struggles to understand the play. Punctuated with comic relief, Pacino makes a pilgrimage to the Globe Theatre, taps Brit theater heavyweights Gielgud and Redgrave for thoughts on interpreting Shakespeare, and combs the streets of New York for candid "man in the street" impressions in a quest to bring his subject to a wider public. Four years in the making, we also witness Pacino, in various stages of facial hair growth, play the deformed usurper with a cast of worthy Americans (Spacey, Kline, Ryder, Baldwin, and Quinn) illustrating key scenes of the play.
1996 108m/C Al Pacino, Alec Baldwin, Winona Ryder, Kevin Spacey, Aidan Quinn, F. Murray Abraham, Kenneth Branagh, Kevin Conway, John Gielgud, James Earl Jones, Kevin Kline, Estelle Parsons, Vanessa Redgrave, Harris Yulin, Penelope Allen; *D:* Al Pacino; *M:* Howard Shore. VHS ★★★

Lord Jim A ship officer (O'Toole) commits an act of cowardice that results in his dismissal and disgrace, which leads him to the Far East in search of self-respect. Excellent supporting cast. Based on Joseph Conrad's novel.
1965 154m/C Peter O'Toole, James Mason, Curt Jurgens, Eli Wallach, Jack Hawkins, Paul Lukas, Akim Tamiroff, Daliah Lavi, Andrew Keir, Jack MacGowran, Walter Gotell; *D:* Richard Brooks; *W:* Richard Brooks, Frederick A. (Freddie) Young. VHS, Beta ★★★

Lord of the Flies Proper English schoolboys stranded on a desert island during a nuclear war are transformed into savages. A study in greed, power, and the innate animalistic/survivalistic instincts of human nature. Based on William Golding's novel, which he described as a journey to the darkness of the human heart. The laserdisc version contains outtakes, the film trailer, and additional material.
1963 91m/B *GB* James Aubrey, Tom Chapin, Hugh Edwards, Roger Elwin, Tom Gamen; *D:* Peter Brook; *W:* Peter Brook. National Board of Review Awards '63: 10 Best Films of the Year. VHS, Beta, LV ★★★1/2

Lorenzo's Oil Based on the true story of Augusto and Michaela Odone's efforts to find a cure for their five-year-old, Lorenzo, diagnosed with the rare and incurable disease ALD (Adrenoleukodystrophy). Confronted by a slow-moving and clinically cold medical community, the Odones embark on their own quest for a cure. Sarandon delivers an outstanding and emotionally charged performance as Lorenzo's determined mother. Nolte is his equally devoted Italian father, complete with black hair and hand gestures. They are a powerful presence in a film which could have easily degenerated into a made-for-TV movie, but is instead a tribute to what love and hope can accomplish.
1992 (PG-13) 135m/C Nick Nolte, Susan Sarandon, Zach O'Malley-Greenberg, Peter Ustinov, Kathleen Wilhoite, Gerry Bamman, Margo Martindale, James Rebhorn, Ann Hearn, John Seale; *D:* George Miller; *W:* Nick Enright, George Miller. Nominations: Academy Awards '92: Best Actress (Sarandon), Best Original Screenplay. VHS, Beta, LV ★★★

Los Olvidados From surrealist Bunuel, a powerful story of the poverty and violence of young people's lives in Mexico's slums. In Spanish with English subtitles. *AKA:* The Young and the Damned.
1950 81m/B *MX* Alfonso Mejias, Roberto Cobo; *D:* Luis Bunuel. Cannes Film Festival '51: Best Director (Bunuel), Best Film. VHS, Beta, 8mm ★★★1/2

Lost Horizon A group of strangers fleeing revolution in China are lost in

the Tibetan Himalayas and stumble across the valley of Shangri La. The inhabitants of this Utopian community have lived for hundreds of years in kindness and peace—but what will the intrusion of these strangers bring? The classic romantic role for Colman. Capra's directorial style meshed perfectly with the pacifist theme of James Hilton's classic novel, resulting in one of the most memorable films of the 1930s. This version restores more than 20 minutes of footage which had been cut from the movie through the years.
1937 132m/B Ronald Colman, Jane Wyatt, H.B. Warner, Sam Jaffe, Thomas Mitchell, Edward Everett Horton, Isabel Jewell, John Howard, Margo; **D:** Frank Capra; **W:** Robert Riskin; **M:** Dimitri Tiomkin. Academy Awards '37: Best Film Editing, Best Interior Decoration; Nominations: Academy Awards '37: Best Picture, Best Sound, Best Supporting Actor (Warner), Best Original Score. **VHS, Beta, LV ★★★★**

Lost in America After deciding that he can't "find himself" at his current job, advertising executive David Howard and his wife sell everything they own and buy a Winnebago to travel across the country. This Albert Brooks comedy is a must-see for everyone who thinks that there is more in life than pushing papers at your desk and sitting on "Mercedes leather." Available in widescreen on laserdisc.
1985 (R) 91m/C Albert Brooks, Julie Hagerty, Michael Greene, Tom Tarpey, Garry Marshall, Art Frankel; **D:** Albert Brooks; **W:** Albert Brooks, Monica Johnson; **M:** Arthur B. Rubinstein. National Society of Film Critics Awards '85: Best Screenplay. **VHS, Beta, LV ★★★**

The Lost Patrol WWI British soldiers lost in the desert are shot down one by one by Arab marauders as Karloff portrays a religious soldier convinced he's going to die. The usual spiffy Ford exteriors peopled by great characters with a stirring score. Based on the story, "Patrol" by Philip MacDonald.
1934 66m/B Victor McLaglen, Boris Karloff, Reginald Denny, Wallace Ford, Alan Hale; **D:** John Ford; **M:** Max Steiner. National Board of Review Awards '34: 10 Best Films of the Year; Nominations: Academy Awards '34: Best Score. **VHS, Beta, LV ★★★★**

The Lost Weekend The heartrending Hollywood masterpiece about alcoholism, depicting a single weekend in the life of a writer, who cannot believe he's addicted. Except for its pat ending, it is an uncompromising, startlingly harsh treatment, with Milland giving one of the industry's bravest lead performances ever. Acclaimed then and now.
1945 100m/B Ray Milland, Jane Wyman, Phillip Terry, Howard da Silva, Doris Dowling, Frank Faylen, Mary Young; **D:** Billy Wilder; **W:** Charles Brackett, Billy Wilder; **M:** Miklos Rozsa. Academy Awards '45: Best Actor (Milland), Best Director (Wilder), Best Picture, Best Screenplay; Cannes Film Festival '46: Best Actor (Milland), Best Film; Golden Globe Awards '46: Best Actor—Drama (Milland), Best Director (Wilder), Best Film—Drama; National Board of Review Awards '45: 10 Best Films of the Year, Best Actor (Milland); Nominations: Academy Awards '45: Best Black and White Cinematography, Best Film Editing, Best Original Score. **VHS, Beta, LV ★★★★**

Louisiana Story The final effort by the master filmmaker, depicting the effects of oil industrialization on the southern Bayou country as seen through the eyes of a young boy. One of Flaherty's greatest, widely considered a premiere achievement.
1948 77m/B D: Robert Flaherty; **M:** Virgil Thomson. National Board of Review Awards '48: 10 Best Films of the Year; Nominations: Academy Awards '48: Best Story. **VHS, Beta ★★★**

Loulou A woman leaves her middle-class husband for a leather-clad, un-educated jock who is more attentive. Romantic and erotic. In French with English subtitles.
1980 (R) 110m/C FR Isabelle Huppert, Gerard Depardieu, Guy Marchand; **D:** Maurice Pialat. Nominations: Cannes Film Festival '80: Best Film. **VHS, Beta ★★★1/2**

Love Torocsik, touted as Hungary's leading actress in the '70s, plays a young woman whose husband has been imprisoned for political crimes. Living in a cramped apartment with her mother-in-law, she keeps the news from the aged and dying woman (Darvas) by reading letters she's fabricated to keep alive the woman's belief that her son is a successful movie director in America. The story is punctuated by the older woman's dreamy remembrances of things past. Exceptional performances by both women, it was Darvas' final film. Based on two novellas by Tibor Dery, it won a special jury prize at the 1971 Cannes film festival. In Hungarian with English subtitles.
1971 100m/C HU Lili Darvas, Mari Torocsik, Ivan Darvas; **D:** Karoly Makk.

Nominations: Cannes Film Festival '71: Best Film. **VHS, LV ★★★1/2**

Love Affair Multi-kleenex weepie inspired countless romantic dreams of true love atop the Empire State Building. Dunn and Boyer fall in love on a ship bound for NYC, but they're both involved. They agree to meet later at, guess where, to see if their feelings hold true, but tragedy intevenes. Excellent comedy-drama is witty at first, more subdued later, with plenty of romance and melodrama. Remade in 1957 (by McCarey) as "An Affair to Remember," a lesser version whose popularity overshadows the original. Look for fleeting glimpses of Leslie, Beckett, and Mohr. Ignore the public domain video, which replaces the original music. Remade again in 1994 as "Love Affair."
1939 87m/B Irene Dunne, Charles Boyer, Maria Ouspenskaya, Lee Bowman, Astrid Allwyn, Maurice Moscovich, Scotty Beckett, Joan Leslie, Gerald Mohr, Dell Henderson, Carol Hughes; **D:** Leo McCarey; **W:** Delmer Daves, Leo McCarey, Donald Ogden Stewart. Nominations: Academy Awards '39: Best Actress (Dunne), Best Interior Decoration, Best Picture, Best Song ("Wishing"), Best Story, Best Supporting Actress (Ouspenskaya). **VHS ★★★1/2**

Love Among the Ruins A made-for-television romance about an aging, wealthy widow who, after being scandalously sued for breach of promise by her very young lover, turns for aid to an old lawyer friend who has loved her silently for more than 40 years.
1975 100m/C Laurence Olivier, Katharine Hepburn, Leigh Lawson, Colin Blakely; **D:** George Cukor; **M:** John Barry. **VHS, Beta, LV ★★★**

Love and Anarchy An oppressed peasant vows to assassinate Mussolini after a close friend is murdered. Powerful drama about the rise of Italian facism. In Italian with English subtitles. **AKA:** Film d'Amore et d'Anarchia.
1973 108m/C *IT* Giancarlo Giannini, Mariangela Melato; **D:** Lina Wertmuller; **W:** Lina Wertmuller; **M:** Nino Rota. Cannes Film Festival '73: Best Actor (Giannini); Nominations: Cannes Film Festival '73: Best Film. **VHS, Beta ★★★**

Love and Death In 1812 Russia, a condemned man reviews the follies of his life. Woody Allen's satire on "War and Peace," and every other major Russian novel.
1975 (PG) 89m/C Woody Allen, Diane Keaton, Georges Adel, Despo Diamantidou, Frank Adu, Harold Gould; **D:**

Woody Allen; **W:** Woody Allen. **VHS, Beta, LV ★★★**

Love Crazy Powell and Loy team once again for a non-"Thin Man" romp through a married-people farce. Via a nosy mother-in-law and a series of misunderstandings, Powell and Loy squabble almost to the point of divorce. Not the wry wit the team was known for, but zany, high-action comedy at its best.
1941 99m/B William Powell, Myrna Loy, Gail Patrick, Jack Carson, Florence Bates, Sidney Blackmer, Sig Rumann; **D:** Jack Conway. **VHS ★★★1/2**

Love 'Em and Leave 'Em Two sisters, with opposite personalities, are department store sales clerks. Brent is the "good" girl and Brooks the "bad" flirt who, under the influence of Perkins, bets the store's welfare benefit money on the horses and loses it all. Brent manages to make things right, while keeping boyfriend Gray from her sister's clutches. Brooks' baby vamp (the actress was 19) stole the picture. Introduced the "Black Bottom" shimmy dance to the screen. Remade in 1929 as "The Saturday Night Kid" with Clara Bow and Jean Arthur.
1926 70m/B Louise Brooks, Evelyn Brent, Lawrence Gray, Osgood Perkins; **D:** Frank Tuttle. **VHS, Beta ★★★**

Love Finds Andy Hardy Young Andy Hardy finds himself torn between three girls before returning to the girl next door. Garland's first appearance in the acclaimed Andy Hardy series features her singing "In Between" and "Meet the Best of my Heart." Also available with "Andy Hardy Meets Debutante" on laserdisc.
1938 90m/B Mickey Rooney, Judy Garland, Lana Turner, Ann Rutherford, Fay Holden, Lewis Stone, Marie Blake, Cecilia Parker, Gene Reynolds; **D:** George B. Seitz. **VHS, Beta, LV ★★★**

Love Letters A young disc jockey falls under the spell of a box of love letters that her mother left behind which detailed her double life. She, in turn, begins an affair with a married man. Thoughtful treatment of the psychology of infidelity. **AKA:** Passion Play; My Love Letters.
1983 (R) 102m/C Jamie Lee Curtis, Amy Madigan, Bud Cort, Matt Clark, Bonnie Bartlett, Sally Kirkland, James Keach; **D:** Amy Holden Jones. **VHS, Beta, LV ★★★**

Love Me or Leave Me A hard-hitting biography of '20s torch singer Ruth Etting and her rise and fall at the hand of her abusive, gangster husband, a part just made for Cagney. Day emotes and sings expressively in one of the best performances of her career. ♪ I'll Never Stop Loving You; Never Look Back; Shaking the Blues Away; Mean to Me; Love Me or Leave Me; Sam, the Old Accordian Man; At Sundown; Everybody Loves My Baby; Five Foot Two.

1955 122m/C Doris Day, James Cagney, Cameron Mitchell, Robert Keith, Tom Tully, Veda Ann Borg; **D:** Charles Vidor. Academy Awards '55: Best Story; Nominations: Academy Awards '55: Best Actor (Cagney), Best Screenplay, Best Song ("I'll Never Stop Loving You"), Best Sound, Best Original Score. **VHS, Beta, LV** ★★★

Love Story Melodrama had enormous popular appeal. O'Neal is the son of Boston's upper crust at Harvard; McGraw's the daughter of a poor Italian on scholarship to study music at Radcliffe. They find happiness, but only for a brief period. Timeless story, simply told, with artful direction from Hiller pulling exceptional performances from the young duo (who have never done as well since). The end result is perhaps better than Segal's simplistic novel, which was produced after he sold the screenplay and became a best-seller before the picture's release—great publicity for any film. Remember: "Love means never having to say you're sorry."

1970 (PG) 100m/C Ryan O'Neal, Ali MacGraw, Ray Milland, John Marley, Tommy Lee Jones; **D:** Arthur Hiller; **W:** Erich Segal. Academy Awards '70: Best Original Score; Golden Globe Awards '71: Best Actress—Drama (MacGraw), Best Director (Hiller), Best Film—Drama, Best Screenplay, Best Score; National Board of Review Awards '70: 10 Best Films of the Year; Nominations: Academy Awards '70: Best Actor (O'Neal), Best Actress (MacGraw), Best Director (Hiller), Best Picture, Best Story & Screenplay, Best Supporting Actor (Marley). **VHS, Beta, LV** ★★★

Love with the Proper Stranger A quiet, gritty romance about an itinerant musician and a young working girl in Manhattan awkwardly living through the consequences of their one night stand. Moved Wood well into the realm of adult roles, after years playing teenagers and innocents. Although the story is about an Italian neighborhood and family, an exceptional number of the cast members were Jewish, as was the screenwriter. Story does not conclude strongly, although this did not hamper the box office returns.

1963 102m/B Natalie Wood, Steve McQueen, Edie Adams, Herschel Bernardi, Tom Bosley, Harvey Lembeck, Penny Santon, Virginia Vincent, Nick Alexander, Augusta Ciolli; **D:** Robert Mulligan; **W:** Arnold Schulman; **M:** Elmer Bernstein. Nominations: Academy Awards '63: Best Actress (Wood), Best Art Direction/Set Decoration (B & W), Best Black and White Cinematography, Best Costume Design (B & W), Best Story & Screenplay. **VHS, Beta, LV** ★★★

The Loved One A famously outlandish, death-mocking farce based on Evelyn Waugh's satire about a particularly horrendous California funeral parlor/cemetery and how its denizens do business. A shrill, protracted spearing of American capitalism.

1965 118m/B Robert Morse, John Gielgud, Rod Steiger, Liberace, Anjanette Comer, Jonathan Winters, James Coburn, Dana Andrews, Milton Berle, Tab Hunter, Robert Morley, Lionel Stander, Margaret Leighton, Roddy McDowall, Bernie Kopell, Alan Napier; **D:** Tony Richardson; **W:** Terry Southern, Christopher Isherwood; **M:** John Addison, Haskell Wexler. **VHS, Beta, LV** ★★★

Lovely to Look At Three wanna-be Broadway producers (Skelton, Keel, Champion) go to gay Paree to peddle Skelton's half interest in Madame Roberta's, a chi chi dress shop. There, they meet the shop's other half interest, two sisters (Champion and Miller), and together they stage a fashion show to finance the floundering hospice of haute couture. Lavish production, light plot. Filmed in Technicolor based on Kern's 1933 Broadway hit (inspired by Alice Duer Miller's "Gowns by Roberta"). Vincente Minnelli staged the fashion show, with gowns by Adrian (watch for copbeater Zsa Zsa as a model). Laserdisc format features the original motion picture trailer. ♪ Opening Night; Smoke Gets in Your Eyes; Lovely to Look At; The Touch of Your Hand; Yesterdays; I Won't Dance; You're Devastating; The Most Exciting Night; I'll Be Hard to Handle.

1952 105m/C Kathryn Grayson, Red Skelton, Howard Keel, Gower Champion, Marge Champion, Ann Miller, Zsa Zsa Gabor, Kurt Kasznar, Marcel Dalio, Diane Cassidy; **D:** Mervyn LeRoy; **M:** Jerome Kern. **VHS, LV** ★★★

The Lovers Chic tale of French adultery with Moreau starring as a provincial wife whose shallow life changes overnight when she meets a young man. Had a controversial American debut because of the film's

tender eroticism and innocent view of adultery. In French with English subtitles.
1959 90m/B FR Jeanne Moreau, Alain Cuny, Jose-Luis De Villalonga, Jean-Mark Bory; **D:** Louis Malle; **W:** Louis Malle. Venice Film Festival '59: Special Jury Prize. **VHS ★★★**

Lovers and Other Strangers Two young people decide to marry after living together for a year and a half. Various tensions surface between them and among their families as the wedding day approaches. Good comedy features some charming performances. Keaton's first film. ♪ For All We Know.
1970 (R) 106m/C Gig Young, Beatrice Arthur, Bonnie Bedelia, Anne Jackson, Harry Guardino, Michael Brandon, Richard Castellano, Bob Dishy, Marian Hailey, Cloris Leachman, Anne Meara, Diane Keaton; **D:** Cy Howard; **W:** Renee Taylor, Joseph Bologna, David Zelag Goodman. Academy Awards '70: Best Song ("For All We Know"); Nominations: Academy Awards '70: Best Adapted Screenplay, Best Supporting Actor (Castellano). **VHS ★★★**

Loves of a Blonde A shy teenage factory girl falls in love with a visiting piano player when the reservist army comes to her small town. But when she goes to visit his family, she discovers things aren't as she imagined. Touching look at the complications of love and our expectations. In Czech with English subtitles. **AKA:** A Blonde in Love; Lasky Jedne Plavovlasky.
1965 88m/B CZ Jana Brejchova, Josef Sebanek, Vladimir Pucholt; **D:** Milos Forman. Nominations: Academy Awards '66: Best Foreign Language Film. **VHS, Beta ★★★1/2**

The Lower Depths Renoir's adaptation of the Maxim Gorky play about a thief and a financially ruined baron learning about life from one another. In French with English subtitles. **AKA:** Les Bas Fonds; Underground.
1936 92m/B FR Jean Gabin, Louis Jouvet, Vladimir Sokoloff, Jean Le Vigan, Suzy Prim; **D:** Jean Renoir. National Board of Review Awards '37: 10 Best Films of the Year. **VHS, Beta ★★★1/2**

The Lower Depths Kurosawa sets the Maxim Gorky play in Edo during the final Tokugawa period, using Noh theatre elements in depicting the lowly denizens of a low-rent hovel. In Japanese with English subtitles.
1957 125m/B JP Toshiro Mifune, Isuzu Yamada, Ganjiro Nakamura, Kyoko Kagawa, Bokuzen Hidari; **D:** Akira Kurosawa. **VHS, Beta ★★★1/2**

Lust for Life Absorbing, serious biography of Vincent Van Gogh, from his first paintings to his death. Remarkable for Douglas' furiously convincing portrayal. Featuring dozens of actual Van Gogh works from private collections. Based on an Irving Stone novel, produced by John Houseman.
1956 122m/C Kirk Douglas, Anthony Quinn, James Donald, Pamela Brown, Everett Sloane, Henry Daniell, Niall MacGinnis, Noel Purcell, Lionel Jeffries, Jill Bennett; **D:** Vincente Minnelli; **M:** Miklos Rozsa. Academy Awards '56: Best Supporting Actor (Quinn); Golden Globe Awards '57: Best Actor—Drama (Douglas); National Board of Review Awards '56: 10 Best Films of the Year; New York Film Critics Awards '56: Best Actor (Douglas); Nominations: Academy Awards '56: Best Actor (Douglas), Best Adapted Screenplay, Best Art Direction/Set Decoration (Color). **VHS, Beta, LV ★★★1/2**

Lust in the Dust When part of a treasure map is found on the derriere of none other than Divine, the hunt is on for the other half. This comedy western travels to a sleepy town called Chile Verde (green chili for those who don't speak Spanish) and the utterly ridiculous turns comically corrupt. Deliciously distasteful fun. Features Divine singing a bawdy love song in his/her break from John Waters.
1985 (R) 85m/C Tab Hunter, Divine, Lainie Kazan, Geoffrey Lewis, Henry Silva, Cesar Romero, Gina Gallego, Courtney Gains, Woody Strode, Pedro Gonzalez-Gonzalez; **D:** Paul Bartel; **W:** Philip John Taylor; **M:** Peter Matz. **VHS, Beta, LV ★★★**

The Lusty Men Two rival rodeo champions, both in love with the same woman, work the rodeo circuit until a tragic accident occurs. Mitchum turns in a fine performance as the has-been rodeo star trying to make it big again.
1952 113m/B Robert Mitchum, Susan Hayward, Arthur Kennedy, Arthur Hunnicutt; **D:** Nicholas Ray. **VHS, Beta, LV ★★★**

M The great Lang dissection of criminal deviance, following the tortured last days of a child murderer, and the efforts of both the police and the underground to bring him to justice. Poetic, compassionate, and chilling. Inspired by real-life serial killer known as "Vampire of Dusseldorf," Lang also borrowed story elements from Jack the Ripper's killing spree. Lorre's screen debut. Lang's personal favorite among his own films. In German with English subtitles. Remade in 1951.

1931 99m/B GE Peter Lorre, Ellen Widmann, Inge Landgut, Gustav Grundgens; **D:** Fritz Lang; **W:** Fritz Lang. National Board of Review Awards '33: 10 Best Films of the Year. **VHS, Beta, LV, 8mm** ★★★★

Mac It's a family affair. Immigrant carpenter's funeral is the starting point for the story of his three sons, construction workers who live in Queens, New York in the 1950s. The passionate bros battle, bitch, and build, with Turturro as the eldest summing up the prevailing philosophy: "It's the doing, that's the thing." Turturro's directorial debut is a labor of love and a tribute to his own dad. Filmed on location in New York City. Fine performances from newcomers Badalucco and Capotorto are complemented by smaller roles from Amos, Barkin, and Turturro's real-life wife Borowitz and brother Nick.
1993 (R) 118m/C John Turturro, Carl Capotorto, Michael Badalucco, Katherine Borowitz, John Amos, Olek Krupa, Ellen Barkin, Joe Paparone, Nicholas Turturro, Dennis Farina; **D:** John Turturro; **W:** John Turturro, Brandon Cole; **M:** Richard Termini, Vin Tese. Nominations: Independent Spirit Awards '94: Best Director (Turturro), Best First Feature. **VHS, LV** ★★★

Macao On the lam for a crime he didn't commit, an adventurer sails to the exotic Far East, meets a buxom cafe singer, and helps Interpol catch a notorious crime boss. A strong film noir entry. Russell sneers, Mitchum wise cracks. Director von Sternberg's last film for RKO.
1952 81m/B Robert Mitchum, Jane Russell, William Bendix, Gloria Grahame; **D:** Josef von Sternberg. **VHS, Beta, LV** ★★★

Macbeth Shakespeare's classic tragedy is performed with a celebrated lead performance by Welles, who plays the king as a demonic leader of a barbaric society. A low-budget adaptation with cheap sets, a three-week shooting schedule, lots of mood, and an attempt at Scottish accents. After making this film, Welles took a 10-year break from Hollywood.
1948 111m/B Orson Welles, Jeanette Nolan, Dan O'Herlihy, Roddy McDowall, Robert Coote; **D:** Orson Welles. **VHS, LV** ★★★½

Macbeth Polanski's notorious adaptation of the Shakespearean classic, marked by realistic design, unflinching violence, and fatalistic atmosphere. Contains stunning fight scenes and fine acting. Polanski's first film following the grisly murder of his pregnant wife, actress Sharon Tate, was torn apart by critics. It is in fact a worthy continuation of his work in the horror genre. Very well made. First film made by Playboy Enterprises. Originally rated X.
1971 (R) 139m/C Jon Finch, Nicholas Selby, Martin Shaw, Francesca Annis, Terence Baylor; **D:** Roman Polanski. National Board of Review Awards '71: 10 Best Films of the Year. **VHS, Beta, LV** ★★★

Macbeth An extraordinary version of Shakespeare's "Macbeth" in which all the fire, ambition, and doom of his text come brilliantly to life.
1976 137m/C Eric Porter, Janet Suzman. ★★★

Mad Love A brilliant surgeon (Lorre) falls madly in love with an actress, but she rebuffs him. When her pianist husband's hands are cut off in a train accident, Lorre agrees to attach new hands, using those of a recently executed murderer. Lorre then kills the man's stepfather, and to drive him crazy uses psychological terror to make the pianist think he killed him. There's also an appearance by the supposedly executed murderer who shows up to reclaim his hands. A real chiller about obsessive love and psychological fear. The only downfall to this one is the unnecessary comic relief by Healy. Lorre's first American film. **AKA:** The Hands of Orlac.
1935 70m/B Peter Lorre, Colin Clive, Frances Drake, Ted Healy, Edward Brophy, Sara Haden, Henry Kolker; **D:** Karl Freund. **VHS** ★★★

Mad Max Set on the stark highways of the post-nuclear future, an ex-cop seeks personal revenge against a rovin' band of vicious outlaw bikers who killed his wife and child. Futuristic scenery and excellent stunt work make for an exceptionally entertaining action-packed adventure. Followed by "The Road Warrior" (also known as "Mad Max 2") in 1981 and "Mad Max Beyond Thunderdome" in 1985.
1980 (R) 93m/C Mel Gibson, Joanne Samuel, Hugh Keays-Byrne, Steve Bisley, Tim Burns, Roger Ward; **D:** George Miller; **W:** George Miller. **VHS, Beta, LV** ★★★½

Madame Bovary A young adultress with delusions of romantic love finds only despair in this offbeat adaptation of Flaubert's masterpiece. In French with English subtitles.
1934 102m/B FR Pierre Renoir, Valentine Tessier, Max Dearly; **D:** Jean Renoir. **VHS, Beta** ★★★

Madame Bovary Young adultress with delusions of romantic love finds only despair, even in this Hollywood version of Flaubert's classic. Mason/Flaubert is put on trial for indecency following publication of the novel, with the story told from the witness stand. While this device occasionally slows the narrative, astute direction helps the plot along. Minnelli's handling of the celebrated ball sequence is superb.
1949 115m/B Jennifer Jones, Van Heflin, Louis Jourdan, James Mason, Gene Lockhart, Gladys Cooper, George Zucco; *D:* Vincente Minnelli; *M:* Miklos Rozsa. Nominations: Academy Awards '49: Best Art Direction/Set Decoration (B & W). **VHS, Beta** ★★★

Madame Curie The film biography of Madame Marie Curie, the woman who discovered radium. A deft portrayal by Garson, who is reteamed with her "Mrs. Miniver" co-star, Pidgeon. Certainly better than most biographies from this time period and more truthful as well.
1943 124m/B Greer Garson, Walter Pidgeon, Robert Walker, May Whitty, Henry Travers, Sir C. Aubrey Smith, Albert Basserman, Victor Francen, Reginald Owen, Van Johnson; *D:* Mervyn LeRoy. Nominations: Academy Awards '43: Best Actor (Pidgeon), Best Actress (Garson), Best Black and White Cinematography, Best Interior Decoration, Best Picture, Best Sound, Best Original Score. **VHS, LV** ★★★

Madame Rosa An aging Jewish prostitute tends prostitutes' offspring in this warmhearted work. A survivor of the Holocaust, the old woman finds her spirit revived by one of her charges—an abandoned Arab boy. In French with English subtitles. *AKA:* La Vie Devant Soi.
1977 (PG) 105m/C *FR IS* Simone Signoret, Claude Dauphin; *D:* Moshe Mizrahi. Academy Awards '77: Best Foreign Language Film; Cesar Awards '78: Best Actress (Signoret); Los Angeles Film Critics Association Awards '78: Best Foreign Film. **VHS, Beta** ★★★

Madame Sousatzka Eccentric, extroverted piano teacher helps students develop spiritually as well as musically. When she engages a teenage Indian student, however, she finds herself considerably challenged. MacLaine is perfectly cast in this powerful, winning film.
1988 (PG-13) 113m/C Shirley MacLaine, Peggy Ashcroft, Shabana Azmi, Twiggy, Leigh Lawson, Geoffrey Bayldon, Navin Chowdhry, Lee Montague; *D:* John Schlesinger; *W:* Ruth Prawer Jhabvala,

John Schlesinger; *M:* Gerald Gouriet. Golden Globe Awards '89: Best Actress—Drama (MacLaine); Venice Film Festival '88: Best Actress (MacLaine). **VHS, Beta, LV** ★★★

Made for Each Other Newlyweds must overcome meddlesome in-laws, poverty, and even serious illness in this classic melodrama. Dated but appealing.
1939 85m/B James Stewart, Carole Lombard, Charles Coburn, Lucile Watson; *D:* John Cromwell. **VHS, Beta** ★★★

Madigan Realistic and exciting and among the best of the behind-the-scenes urban police thrillers. Hardened NYC detectives (Widmark and Guardino) lose their guns to a sadistic killer and are given 72 hours to track him down. Fonda is the police chief none too pleased with their performance. Adapted by Howard Rodman, Abraham Polonsky, and Harry Kleiner from Richard Dougherty's "The Commissioner."
1968 101m/C Richard Widmark, Henry Fonda, Inger Stevens, Harry Guardino, James Whitmore, Susan Clark, Michael Dunn, Don Stroud; *D:* Donald Siegel; *W:* Abraham Polonsky. **VHS, Beta** ★★★

The Madness of King George Poor King George is a monarch with problems—his 30 years of royal authority are being usurped by Parliament, his American colonies have been lost, and, in 1788, he's begun to periodically lose his mind. So what do you do when a ruler becomes irrational? The royal physicians are baffled, his loving Queen Charlotte (Mirren) is in despair, but the noxious Prince of Wales (Everett) can barely contain his glee at finally having a chance at the throne. A last resort is offered by Dr. Willis (Holm), a former clergyman with some unusual and sadistic ideas about treating the mentally ill (even if they do have royal blood). Brilliant performance by Hawthorne (who originated the stage role in Bennett's 1991 play "The Madness of George III"). Screen note explains that King George suffered from the metabolic disorder known as porphyria. A Tony Award-winner for his Broadway productions of "Miss Saigon" and "Carousel," Hytner makes his feature-film directing debut.
1994 (R) 110m/C *GB* Nigel Hawthorne, Helen Mirren, Ian Holm, Rupert Everett, Amanda Donohoe, Rupert Graves, Julian Wadham, John Wood, Julian Rhind-Tutt; *D:* Nicholas Hytner; *W:* Alan Bennett; *M:* George Fenton. Academy Awards '94: Best Art Direction/Set Decoration; Cannes Film

Festival '95: Best Actress (Mirren); Nominations: Academy Awards '94: Best Actor (Hawthorne), Best Adapted Screenplay, Best Supporting Actress (Mirren). **VHS, LV** ★★★1/2

Maedchen in Uniform A scandalous early German talkie about a rebellious schoolgirl who falls in love with a female teacher and commits suicide when the teacher is punished for the relationship. A controversial criticism of lesbianism and militarism that impelled the Nazis, rising to power two years later, to exile its director. It was also banned in the United States. In German with English subtitles. Remade in 1965. **AKA:** Girls in Uniform.
1931 90m/B *GE* Dorothea Wieck, Ellen Schwannecke, Hertha Thiele; **D:** Leontine Sagan. National Board of Review Awards '32: 5 Best Foreign Films of the Year. **VHS, Beta** ★★★1/2

The Magic Flute Bergman's acclaimed version of Mozart's famous comic opera, universally considered one of the greatest adaptations of opera to film ever made. Staged before a live audience for Swedish television. In Swedish with English subtitles.
1973 (G) 134m/C *SW* Josef Kostlinger, Irma Urrila, Hakan Hagegard, Elisabeth Erikson; **D:** Ingmar Bergman. **VHS, Beta, LV** ★★★★

The Magician A master magician in 19th-century Sweden (von Sydow) wreaks ill in this darkly comical, supernatural parable. Dark, well photographed early Bergman effort. In Swedish with English subtitles.
1958 101m/B *SW* Max von Sydow, Ingrid Thulin, Gunnar Bjornstrand, Bibi Andersson, Naima Wifstrand; **D:** Ingmar Bergman; **W:** Ingmar Bergman. Venice Film Festival '59: Special Jury Prize. **VHS, Beta, LV** ★★★

The Magnificent Ambersons Welles' second film. A fascinating, inventive translation of the Booth Tarkington novel about a wealthy turn of the century family collapsing under the changing currents of progress. Pure Welles, except the glaringly bad tacked-on ending that the studio shot (under the direction of the great Robert Wise and Fred Fleck), after taking the film from him. It seems they wanted the proverbial happy ending. Also available on laserdisc, with interviews and the original story boards.
1942 88m/B Joseph Cotten, Anne Baxter, Tim Holt, Richard Bennett, Dolores Costello, Erskine Sanford, Ray Collins, Agnes Moorehead; **D:** Freddie Fleck,

Robert Wise, Orson Welles; **W:** Orson Welles; **M:** Bernard Herrmann, Roy Webb. New York Film Critics Awards '42: Best Actress (Moorehead); Nominations: Academy Awards '42: Best Black and White Cinematography, Best Interior Decoration, Best Picture, Best Supporting Actress (Moorehead). **VHS, Beta, LV** ★★★★

The Magnificent Seven Western remake of Akira Kurosawa's classic "The Seven Samurai." Mexican villagers hire gunmen to protect them from the bandits who are destroying their town. Most of the actors were relative unknowns, though not for long. Sequelled by "Return of the Seven" in 1966, "Guns of the Magnificent Seven" in 1969, and "The Magnificent Seven Ride" in 1972. Excellent score. Uncredited writing by Walter Newman and Walter Bernstein.
1960 126m/C Yul Brynner, Steve McQueen, Robert Vaughn, James Coburn, Charles Bronson, Horst Buchholz, Eli Wallach, Brad Dexter; **D:** John Sturges; **W:** William Roberts; **M:** Elmer Bernstein. Nominations: Academy Awards '60: Best Original Score. **VHS, Beta, LV** ★★★★

The Magnificent Yankee Adaptation of Emmet Lavery's Broadway play on the life of Supreme Court Justice Oliver Wendell Holmes, starring Calhern (who also did the stage version). America's foremost legal mind was well-served by Calhern, with Harding as his ever-patient wife. **AKA:** The Man with Thirty Sons.
1950 80m/B Louis Calhern, Ann Harding, Eduard Franz, Philip Ober, Ian Wolfe, Edith Evanson, Richard Anderson, Jimmy Lydon, Robert Sherwood, Hugh Sanders; **D:** John Sturges; **W:** Emmet Lavery. Nominations: Academy Awards '50: Best Actor (Calhern). **VHS, Beta** ★★★

Major Barbara A wealthy, idealistic girl joins the Salvation Army against her father's wishes. Based on the play by George Bernard Shaw. The excellent adaptation of the original and the cast make this film a winner. Deborah Kerr's film debut.
1941 90m/B *GB* Wendy Hiller, Rex Harrison, Robert Morley, Sybil Thorndike, Deborah Kerr; **D:** Gabriel Pascal. **VHS, Beta** ★★★1/2

Malcolm X Stirring tribute to the controversial black activist, a leader in the struggle for black liberation. Hitting bottom during his imprisonment in the '50s, he became a Black Muslim and then a leader in the Nation of Islam. His assassination in 1965 left a legacy of black nationalism, self-determination, and racial pride. Marked by strong direction from Lee and good performances (notably Freeman Jr. as Elijah Muhammad), it is Washington's convincing performance in the title role that truly brings the film alive. Based on "The Autobiography of Malcolm X" by Malcolm X and Alex Haley.

1992 (PG-13) 201m/C Denzel Washington, Angela Bassett, Albert Hall, Al Freeman Jr., Delroy Lindo, Spike Lee, Theresa Randle, Kate Vernon, Lonette McKee, Tommy Hollis, James McDaniel, Ernest Thompson, Jean LaMarre, Giancarlo Esposito, Craig Wasson, John Ottavino, David Patrick Kelly, Shirley Stoler; *Cameos:* Christopher Plummer, Karen Allen, Peter Boyle, William Kunstler, Bobby Seale, Al Sharpton; *D:* Spike Lee; *W:* Spike Lee, Arnold Perl, James Baldwin; *M:* Terence Blanchard. Chicago Film Critics Awards '93: Best Actor (Washington), Best Film; MTV Movie Awards '93: Best Male Performance (Washington); New York Film Critics Awards '92: Best Actor (Washington); Nominations: Academy Awards '92: Best Actor (Washington), Best Costume Design. **VHS, Beta, LV, 8mm** ★★★

Male and Female A group of British aristocrats is shipwrecked on an island and must allow their efficient butler (Meighan) to take command for their survival. Swanson is the spoiled rich girl who falls for her social inferior. Their rescue provides a return to the rigid British class system. Based on the play "The Admirable Crichton" by James M. Barrie.

1919 110m/B Gloria Swanson, Thomas Meighan, Lila Lee, Raymond Hatton, Bebe Daniels; *D:* Cecil B. DeMille. **VHS, Beta** ★★★★

The Maltese Falcon After the death of his partner, detective Sam Spade finds himself enmeshed in a complicated, intriguing search for a priceless statuette. "It's the stuff dreams are made of," says Bogart of the Falcon. Excellent, fast-paced film noir with outstanding performances, great dialogue, and concentrated attention to details. Director Huston's first film and Greenstreet's talky debut. First of several films by Bogart and Astor. Based on the novel by Dashiell Hammett. Also available colorized.

1941 101m/B Humphrey Bogart, Mary Astor, Peter Lorre, Sydney Greenstreet, Ward Bond, Barton MacLane, Gladys George, Lee Patrick, Elisha Cook Jr., Jerome Cowan; *Cameos:* Walter Huston; *D:* John Huston; *W:* John Huston; *M:* Adolph Deutsch. Nominations: Academy Awards '41: Best Picture, Best Screenplay, Best Supporting Actor (Greenstreet). **VHS, Beta, LV** ★★★★

Mamma Roma Pasolini's second film is a heartbreaking story of family ties, escaping the past, and dreams of the future. The title character (Magnani) is a former prostitute who attempts respectability for herself and her teenage son (Garofolo). But her ex-pimp (Citti) threatens her new life and Rome's big-city temptations prove to be a pathway to crime and tragedy for the boy. Magnani gives one of her finest performances. In Italian with English subtitles.

1962 110m/B *IT* Anna Magnani, Ettore Garofolo, Franco Citti, Silvana Corsini, Luisa Loiano, Tonino Delli Colli; *D:* Pier Paolo Pasolini; *W:* Pier Paolo Pasolini. **VHS** ★★★1/2

A Man and a Woman When a man and a woman, both widowed, meet and become interested in one another but experience difficulties in putting their past loves behind them. Intelligently handled emotional conflicts within a well-acted romantic drama, acclaimed for excellent visual detail. Remade in 1977 as "Another Man, Another Chance." Followed in 1986 with "A Man and A Woman: 20 Years Later." Dubbed. *AKA:* Un Homme et Une Femme.

1966 102m/C *FR* Anouk Aimee, Jean-Louis Trintignant, Pierre Barouh, Valerie Lagrange; *D:* Claude Lelouch; *W:* Claude Lelouch. Academy Awards '66: Best Foreign Language Film, Best Original Screenplay; British Academy Awards '67: Best Actress (Aimee); Cannes Film Festival '66: Best Film; Golden Globe Awards '67: Best Actress—Drama (Aimee), Best Foreign Film; Nominations: Academy Awards '66: Best Actress (Aimee), Best Director (Lelouch). **VHS, Beta** ★★★

A Man Called Horse After a wealthy Britisher is captured and tortured by the Sioux Indians in the Dakotas, he abandons his formal ways and discovers his own strength. As he passes their torture tests, he is embraced by the tribe. In this very realistic and gripping portrayal of American Indian life, Harris provides a strong performance. Sequelled by "Return of a Man Called Horse" (1976) and "Triumphs of a Man Called Horse" (1983).

1970 (PG) 114m/C Richard Harris, Judith Anderson, Jean Gascon, Stanford Howard, Manu Tupou, Dub Taylor; *D:* Elliot Silverstein; *W:* Jack DeWitt, Robert B. Hauser. **VHS, Beta, LV** ★★★

A Man Called Peter A biographical epic about Peter Marshall, a Scottish chaplain who served the U.S. Senate. Todd does his subject justice by sensitively showing all that was human in

Marshall, and a talented supporting cast makes for a thoroughly watchable film.

1955 119m/C Richard Todd, Jean Peters, Marjorie Rambeau, Jill Esmond, Les Tremayne, Robert Burton; *D:* Henry Koster. Nominations: Academy Awards '55: Best Color Cinematography. **VHS, Beta ★★★**

A Man Escaped There's an excruciating realism about Bresson's account of a WWII Resistance fighter's escape from a Nazi prison just before he was to be executed by the Gestapo. It's the sounds and lingering camera shots, not the wham bam variety of action, that create and sustain the film's suspense. Bresson, who had been a Nazi prisoner, solicited the supervision of Andre Devigny, whose true story the film tells. Contributing to the realistic feel was the use of nonprofessional actors. An award-winning film that fellow director Truffaut lauded as the most crucial French film of the previous ten years. In French with English subtitles. *AKA:* Un Condamne a Mort s'est Echappe; The Wind Bloweth Where it Listeth.

1957 102m/B Francois Leterrier; *D:* Robert Bresson. Cannes Film Festival '57: Best Director (Bresson); National Board of Review Awards '57: 5 Best Foreign Films of the Year. **VHS ★★★1/2**

Man Facing Southeast The acclaimed Argentinean film about the sudden appearance of a strange man in an asylum who claims to be an extraterrestrial, and a psychologist's attempts to discover his true identity. The sense of mystery intensifies when the new patient indeed seems to have some remarkable powers. Although the pace at times lags, the story intriguingly keeps one guessing about the stranger right to the end. In Spanish with English subtitles. *AKA:* Hombre Mirando Al Sudeste; Man Looking Southeast.

1986 (R) 105m/C *AR* Lorenzo Quinteros, Hugo Soto, Ines Vernengo; *D:* Eliseo Subiela; *M:* Pedro Aznar. **VHS, Beta, LV ★★★1/2**

A Man for All Seasons Sterling, heavily Oscar-honored biographical drama concerning the life and subsequent martyrdom of 16th-century Chancellor of England, Sir Thomas More (Scofield). Story revolves around his personal conflict when King Henry VIII (Shaw) seeks a divorce from his wife, Catherine of Aragon, so he can wed his mistress, Anne Boleyn—events that ultimately lead the King to bolt from the Pope and declare himself head of the Church of England. Remade for television in 1988 with Charlton Heston in the lead role.

1966 (G) 120m/C *GB* Paul Scofield, Robert Shaw, Orson Welles, Wendy Hiller, Susannah York, John Hurt, Nigel Davenport, Vanessa Redgrave; *D:* Fred Zinneman; *W:* Constance Willis, Robert Bolt; *M:* Georges Delerue. Academy Awards '66: Best Actor (Scofield), Best Adapted Screenplay, Best Color Cinematography, Best Costume Design (Color), Best Director (Zinneman), Best Picture; British Academy Awards '67: Best Actor (Scofield), Best Film, Best Screenplay; Directors Guild of America Awards '66: Best Director (Zinneman); Golden Globe Awards '67: Best Actor—Drama (Scofield), Best Director (Zinneman), Best Film—Drama, Best Screenplay; National Board of Review Awards '66: 10 Best Films of the Year, Best Actor (Scofield), Best Director (Zinneman), Best Supporting Actor (Shaw); Nominations: Academy Awards '66: Best Supporting Actor (Shaw), Best Supporting Actress (Hiller). **VHS, Beta, LV ★★★★**

The Man from Laramie A ranch baron who is going blind worries about which of his two sons he will leave the ranch to. Into this tension-filled familial atmosphere rides Stewart, a cow-herder obsessed with hunting down the men who sold guns to the Indians that killed his brother. Needless to say, the tension increases. Tough, surprisingly brutal western, the best of the classic Stewart-Mann films.

1955 104m/C James Stewart, Arthur Kennedy, Donald Crisp, Alex Nicol, Cathy O'Donnell, Aline MacMahon, Wallace Ford, Jack Elam; *D:* Anthony Mann; *W:* Philip Yordan. **VHS, Beta ★★★1/2**

Man from the Alamo A soldier sent from the Alamo during its last hours to get help is branded as a deserter, and struggles to clear his name. Well acted, this film will satisfy those with a taste for action.

1953 79m/C Glenn Ford, Julie Adams, Chill Wills, Victor Jory, Hugh O'Brian; *D:* Budd Boetticher. **VHS ★★★**

The Man I Love Slick drama about nightclub singer Lupino falling for no-good mobster Alda. Enjoyable and well-acted, although script doesn't make sense. Great selection of tunes. This film inspired Scorsese's "New York, New York." Based on the novel "Night Shift" by Maritta Wolff. ♪ Body and Soul; Why Was I Born; Bill; The Man I Love; Liza; If I Could Be With You.

1946 96m/B Ida Lupino, Robert Alda,

Andrea King, Martha Vickers, Bruce (Herman Brix) Bennett, Alan Hale, Dolores Moran, John Ridgely, Don McGuire, Warren Douglas, Craig Stevens; **D:** Raoul Walsh, John Maxwell; **W:** Catherine Turney, Jo Pagano; **M:** Max Steiner. **VHS** ★★★

The Man in the Iron Mask Swashbuckling tale about twin brothers separated at birth. One turns out to be King Louis XIV of France, and the other a carefree wanderer and friend of the Three Musketeers. Their eventual clash leads to action-packed adventure and royal revenge. Remake of the "The Iron Mask" (1929) with Douglas Fairbanks. Remade for television in 1977 with Richard Chamberlain.
1939 110m/B Louis Hayward, Alan Hale, Joan Bennett, Warren William, Joseph Schildkraut, Walter Kingsford, Marion Martin; **D:** James Whale. Nominations: Academy Awards '39: Best Original Score. **VHS, Beta** ★★★

The Man in the Moon Beautifully rendered coming-of-age tale. On a farm outside a small Louisiana town in the 1950s, 14-year-old Dani wonders if she will ever be as pretty and popular as her 17-year-old sister Maureen. This becomes especially important as Dani is beginning to notice boys, particularly Court, the 17-year-old young man she meets when swimming. Although Dani and Maureen have always been especially close, a rift develops between the sisters after Court meets Maureen. Intelligently written, excellent direction, lovely cinematography, and exceptional acting make this a particularly worthwhile and entertaining film.
1991 (PG-13) 100m/C Reese Witherspoon, Emily Warfield, Jason London, Tess Harper, Sam Waterston, Gail Strickland; **D:** Robert Mulligan. **VHS** ★★★1/2

The Man in the White Suit A humble laboratory assistant in a textile mill invents a white cloth that won't stain, tear, or wear out, and can't be dyed. The panicked garment industry sets out to destroy him and the fabric, resulting in some sublimely comic situations and a variety of inventive chases. Also available with "Lavender Hill Mob" on laserdisc.
1951 82m/B *GB* Alec Guinness, Joan Greenwood; **D:** Alexander MacKendrick. National Board of Review Awards '52: 10 Best Films of the Year; Nominations: Academy Awards '52: Best Screenplay. **VHS, Beta** ★★★1/2

Man of a Thousand Faces A tasteful and touching portrayal of Lon Chaney, from his childhood with his deaf and mute parents to his success as a screen star. Re-creates some of Chaney's most famous roles, including the Phantom of the Opera and Quasimodo in "Notre Dame." Cagney is magnificent as the long-suffering film star who was a genius with makeup and mime.
1957 122m/B James Cagney, Dorothy Malone, Jane Greer, Marjorie Rambeau, Jim Backus, Roger Smith, Robert Evans; **D:** Joseph Pevney; **W:** Ivan Goff. Nominations: Academy Awards '57: Best Story & Screenplay. **VHS, LV** ★★★1/2

Man of Aran Celebrated account of a fisherman's struggle for survival on a barren island near the west coast of Ireland, featuring amateur actors. Three years in the making, it's the last word in man against nature cinema, and a visual marvel. A former explorer, Flaherty became an influential documentarian. Having first gained fame with "Nanook of the North," he compiled an opus of documentaries made for commercial release.
1934 132m/B D: Robert Flaherty. **VHS** ★★★

Man of Iron Director Wajda's followup to "Man of Marble" deals with a reporter (Opania) who is expected to toe the government line when writing about the Gdansk shipyard strike of 1980. He meets the harassed laborer son (Radziwilowicz) of worker-hero Birkut, against whom Opania is expected to conduct a smear campaign, and finds his loyalties tested. In Polish with English subtitles. *AKA:* Czlowiek z Zelaza.
1981 (PG) 116m/C *PL* Jerzy Radziwilowicz, Marian Opania, Krystyna Janda; **D:** Andrzej Wajda; **W:** Aleksander Scibor-Rylski; **M:** Andrezej Korzynski. Cannes Film Festival '81: Best Film. **VHS** ★★★

Man of Marble A satire on life in post-WWII Poland. A young filmmaker sets out to tell the story of a bricklayer who, because of his exceptional skill, once gained popularity with other workers. He became a champion for worker rights, only to then find himself being persecuted by the government. The conclusion was censored by the Polish government. Highly acclaimed and followed by "Man of Iron" in 1981. In Polish with English subtitles.
1976 160m/C *PL* Krystyna Janda, Jerzy Radziwilowicz, Tadeusz Lomnicki, Jacek Lomnicki, Krystyna Zachwatowicz; **D:** Andrzej Wajda; **W:** Aleksander Scibor-Rylski; **M:** Andrezej Korzynski. **VHS** ★★★

The Man Who Came to Dinner
Based on the Moss Hart-George S. Kaufman play, this comedy is about a bitter radio celebrity (Woolley) on a lecture tour (a character based on Alexander Woolcott). He breaks his hip and must stay in a quiet suburban home for the winter. While there, he occupies his time by barking orders, being obnoxious and generally just driving the other residents nuts. Woolley reprises his Broadway role in this film that succeeds at every turn, loaded with plenty of satiric jabs at the Algonquin Hotel Roundtable regulars.
1941 112m/B Monty Woolley, Bette Davis, Ann Sheridan, Jimmy Durante, Reginald Gardiner, Richard Travis, Billie Burke, Grant Mitchell, Mary Wickes, George Barbier, Ruth Vivian, Elisabeth Fraser; **D:** William Keighley; **W:** Julius J. Epstein, Philip C. Epstein. **VHS, Beta, LV ★★★1/2**

The Man Who Could Work Miracles
A mild-mannered draper's assistant becomes suddenly endowed with supernatural powers to perform any feat he wishes. Great special effects (for an early film) and fine performances result in a classic piece of science fiction.
1937 82m/B Ralph Richardson, Joan Gardner, Roland Young; **D:** Lothar Mendes. **VHS, Beta, LV ★★★1/2**

The Man Who Fell to Earth Entertaining and technically adept cult classic about a man from another planet (Bowie, in a bit of typecasting) who ventures to earth in hopes of finding water to save his family and drought-stricken planet. Instead he becomes a successful inventor and businessman, along the way discovering the human vices of booze, sex, and television. Also available in a restored version at 138 minutes. Remade for television in 1987 and based on Walter Tevis' novel.
1976 (R) 118m/C GB David Bowie, Candy Clark, Rip Torn, Buck Henry, Bernie Casey; **D:** Nicolas Roeg. **VHS, Beta, LV ★★★1/2**

The Man Who Knew Too Much Hitchcock's first international success. A British family man on vacation in Switzerland is told of an assassination plot by a dying agent. His daughter is kidnapped to force his silence. In typical Hitchcock fashion, the innocent person becomes caught in a web of intrigue; the sticky situation culminates with surprising events during the famous shoot-out in the final scenes. Remade by Hitchcock in 1956.
1934 75m/B GB Leslie Banks, Edna Best,

Peter Lorre, Nova Pilbeam, Pierre Fresnay; **D:** Alfred Hitchcock; **W:** Emlyn Williams, Charles Bennett. **VHS, Beta ★★★**

The Man Who Laughs Veidt's sensitive performance highlights this silent classic. He plays a young man whose features are surgically altered into a permanent smile because his relatives are political enemies of the current ruler. The man is befriended by the owner of a sideshow who first exhibits him as a freak but later finds Veidt gaining fame as a clown. A beautiful blind girl in the show loves Veidt for who he is and the two find happiness.
1927 110m/B Conrad Veidt, Mary Philbin, Olga Baclanova, Josephine Crowell, George Siegmann, Brandon Hurst; **D:** Paul Leni. **VHS ★★★1/2**

The Man Who Loved Women An intelligent, sensitive bachelor writes his memoirs and recalls the many, many, many women he has loved. Truffaut couples sophistication and lightheartedness, the thrill of the chase and, when it leads to an accidental death, the wondering what-it's-all-about in the mourning after. In French with English subtitles. Remade in 1983. **AKA:** L'Homme Qui Aimait les Femmes.
1977 119m/C FR Charles Denner, Brigitte Fossey, Leslie Caron; **D:** Francois Truffaut; **W:** Suzanne Schiffman. National Board of Review Awards '77: 5 Best Foreign Films of the Year. **VHS, Beta, LV ★★★**

The Man Who Shot Liberty Valance Tough cowboy Wayne and idealistic lawyer Stewart join forces against dreaded gunfighter Liberty Valance, played leatherly by Marvin. While Stewart rides to Senatorial success on his reputation as the man who shot the villain, he suffers moral crises about the act, but is toughened up by Wayne. Wayne's use of the word "pilgrim" became a standard for his impersonators. Strong character acting, great Western scenes, and value judgements to ponder over make this last of Ford's black and white westerns among his best.
1962 123m/B James Stewart, John Wayne, Vera Miles, Lee Marvin, Edmond O'Brien, Andy Devine, Woody Strode, Ken Murray, Jeanette Nolan, John Qualen, Strother Martin, Lee Van Cleef, John Carradine, Carleton Young; **D:** John Ford. Nominations: Academy Awards '62: Best Costume Design (B & W). **VHS, Beta, LV ★★★1/2**

The Man Who Would Be King A grand, old-fashioned adventure based on the classic story by Rud-

yard Kipling about two mercenary soldiers who travel from India to Kafiristan in order to conquer it and set themselves up as kings. Splendid characterizations by Connery and Caine, and Huston's royal directorial treatment provides it with adventure, majestic sweep, and well-developed characters.
1975 (PG) 129m/C Sean Connery, Michael Caine, Christopher Plummer, Saeed Jaffrey, Shakira Caine; **D:** John Huston; **W:** Gladys Hill, John Huston; **M:** Maurice Jarre. Nominations: Academy Awards '75: Best Adapted Screenplay, Best Art Direction/Set Decoration, Best Costume Design, Best Film Editing. **VHS, Beta, LV** ★★★★

The Man with a Movie Camera A plotless, experimental view of Moscow through the creative eye of the cameraman Dziga Vertov, founder of the Kino Eye. The editing methods and camera techniques used in this silent film were very influential and still stand up to scrutiny today.
1929 69m/B *RU* **D:** Dziga Vertov. **VHS, Beta** ★★★1/2

The Man with the Golden Arm A gripping film version of the Nelson Algren junkie melodrama, about an ex-addict who returns to town only to get mixed up with drugs again. Considered controversial in its depiction of addiction when released. Sinatra's performance as Frankie Machine is a stand-out.
1955 119m/B Frank Sinatra, Kim Novak, Eleanor Parker, Arnold Stang, Darren McGavin, Robert Strauss, George Mathews, John Conte, Doro Merande; **D:** Otto Preminger; **M:** Elmer Bernstein. Nominations: Academy Awards '55: Best Actor (Sinatra), Best Art Direction/Set Decoration (B & W), Best Original Score. **VHS, Beta** ★★★

Man Without a Star A cowboy helps ranchers stop a ruthless cattle owner from taking over their land. The conflict between freedom in the wild west and the need for order and settlements is powerfully internalized in Douglas, whose fight for justice will tame the cowboy code he lives by. You'll shed a tear for the fading frontier.
1955 89m/B Kirk Douglas, Jeanne Crain, Claire Trevor, William Campbell; **D:** King Vidor. **VHS, Beta** ★★★

The Manchurian Candidate Political thriller about an American Korean War vet who suspects that he and his platoon may have been brainwashed during the war, with his highly decorated, heroic friend programmed by commies to be an operational assassin. Loaded with shocks, conspiracy, inventive visual imagery, and bitter political satire of naivete and machinations of the left and right. Excellent performances by an all-star cast, with Lansbury and Gregory particularly frightening. Based on the Richard Condon novel. Featuring a special interview with Sinatra and Frankenheimer in which Sinatra is deified.
1962 126m/B Frank Sinatra, Laurence Harvey, Angela Lansbury, Janet Leigh, James Gregory, Leslie Parrish, John McGiver, Henry Silva, Khigh Deigh; **D:** John Frankenheimer; **W:** George Axelrod, John Frankenheimer; **M:** David Amram. Golden Globe Awards '63: Best Supporting Actress (Lansbury); National Board of Review Awards '62: Best Supporting Actress (Lansbury); Nominations: Academy Awards '62: Best Film Editing, Best Supporting Actress (Lansbury). **VHS, Beta, LV** ★★★★

Mandela A gripping, powerful drama about human rights and dignity, tracing the real-life trials of Nelson and Winnie Mandela. The story focuses on the couple's early opposition to South African apartheid, as well as the events leading up to Nelson's life-imprisonment sentencing in 1964. Excellent, restrained performances from Glover and Woodard. Made for cable television.
1987 135m/C Danny Glover, Alfre Woodard, John Matshikiza, Warren Clarke, Allan Corduner, Julian Glover; **D:** Philip Saville. **VHS, Beta** ★★★

Manhattan Successful TV writer Allen yearns to be a serious writer. He struggles through a series of ill-fated romances, including one with high school senior Hemingway, about 25 years younger, and another with Keaton, who's also having an on-again, off-again affair with Murphy, Allen's best friend. Scathingly serious and comic view of modern relationships in urban America and of the modern intellectual neuroses. Shot in black-and-white to capture the mood of Manhattan and mated with an excellent Gershwin soundtrack, the video version preserves the wide-screen effect adding yet another impressive element to the overall production.
1979 (R) 96m/B Woody Allen, Diane Keaton, Meryl Streep, Mariel Hemingway, Michael Murphy, Wallace Shawn, Anne Byrne, Tisa Farrow, Mark Linn-Baker, David Rasche, Karen Allen; **D:** Woody Allen; **W:** Woody Allen, Marshall Brickman; **M:** George Gershwin, Gordon Willis. British Academy Awards '79: Best Film, Best

Screenplay; Cesar Awards '80: Best Foreign Film; Los Angeles Film Critics Association Awards '79: Best Supporting Actress (Streep); National Board of Review Awards '79: 10 Best Films of the Year; New York Film Critics Awards '79: Best Director (Allen), Best Supporting Actress (Streep); Nominations: Academy Awards '79: Best Original Screenplay, Best Supporting Actress (Hemingway). **VHS, Beta, LV** ★★★★

Manhattan Melodrama Powell and Gable are best friends from childhood, growing up together in an orphanage. Their adult lives take different paths, however, as Powell becomes a respected prosecuting attorney while Gable becomes a notorious gambler/racketeer. Lovely Loy is Gable's girl who comes between the two. Eventually, Powell must prosecute his life-long friend for murder in order to win the governorship. One of Gable's toughest roles; Powell's character, however, is a bit unbelievable as his ethics seem to extend beyond love and friendship. This is the first film to team Powell and Loy, who would go on to make 13 more films together, including the "Thin Man" series.
1934 93m/B Clark Gable, William Powell, Myrna Loy, Leo Carrillo, Nat Pendleton, George Sidney, Isabel Jewell, Muriel Evans, Claudelle Kaye, Frank Conroy, Jimmy Butler, Mickey Rooney, Edward Van Sloan; **D:** Woodbridge S. Van Dyke. **VHS, Beta, LV** ★★★1/2

Manhattan Murder Mystery Keaton and Allen team up again as two New Yorkers who get involved in a mystery when their neighbor dies under strange circumstances. Light, entertaining comedy steers clear of some of Allen's heavier themes and should keep audiences laughing till the end. Allen, writing with Brickman for the first time since "Annie Hall" and "Manhattan," makes viewers fall in love with the magic of NYC all over again.
1993 (PG) 105m/C Woody Allen, Diane Keaton, Anjelica Huston, Alan Alda, Jerry Adler, Ron Rifkin, Joy Behar, Lynn Cohen, Melanie Norris; **D:** Woody Allen; **W:** Woody Allen, Marshall Brickman. Nominations: Golden Globe Awards '94: Best Actress—Musical/Comedy (Keaton). **VHS, LV, 8mm** ★★★

Manhunter FBI forensic specialist— who retired after a harrowing pursuit of a serial killer—is called back to duty to find a psychotic family killer. His technique: to match the thought processes of serial killers and thus anticipate their moves. Intense thriller, based on the Thomas Harris novel "Red Dragon." Harris also wrote "The Silence of the Lambs," whose most notorious character Hannibal ("The Cannibal") Lecter, appears in this movie as well. Director Mann applies the slick techniques he introduced in the popular television series "Miami Vice," creating a quiet, moody intensity broken by sudden onslaughts of violence. Available in widescreen on laserdisc. **AKA:** Red Dragon.
1986 (R) 100m/C William L. Petersen, Kim Greist, Joan Allen, Brian Cox, Dennis Farina, Stephen Lang, Tom Noonan; **D:** Michael Mann; **W:** Michael Mann. **VHS, Beta, LV** ★★★

Manny & Lo Krueger's directorial debut features fine performances in a story about three misfits forming a unique family bond. Surly 16-year-old Lo (Palladino) and her serious 11-year-old sister Manny (Johansson) have run away from their foster homes and hit the road together. Living hand-to-mouth, it's Manny who persuades her irresponsible pregnant sister that they need a home, and they settle into an isolated cabin. When the sisters visit a baby store, eccentric clerk Elaine (Place) seems such a font of wisdom that the girls kidnap her and hold her as a hostage to help with the pregnancy. But Elaine's not trying to escape and has an agenda of her own.
1996 90m/C Mary Kay Place, Paul Guilfoyle, Scarlett Johansson, Aleksa Palladino, Glenn Fitzgerald, Cameron Boyd; **D:** Lisa Krueger; **W:** Lisa Krueger; **M:** John Lurie. Nominations: Independent Spirit Awards '97: Best First Feature, Best Actress (Johansson), Best Supporting Actress (Place). **VHS, LV** ★★★

Manon of the Spring In this excellent sequel to "Jean de Florette," the adult daughter of the dead hunchback, Jean, discovers who blocked up the spring on her father's land. She plots her revenge, which proves greater than she could ever imagine. Montand is astonishing. Based on a Marcel Pagnol novel. In French with English subtitles. **AKA:** Manon des Sources; Jean de Florette 2.
1987 (PG) 113m/C *FR* Yves Montand, Daniel Auteuil, Emmanuelle Beart, Hippolyte Girardot; **D:** Claude Berri; **W:** Gerard Brach, Claude Berri. National Board of Review Awards '87: 5 Best Foreign Films of the Year. **VHS, Beta, LV** ★★★1/2

Marat/Sade A theatrical production presented by patients at a mental institution is directed by the Marquis de

Sade. Well directed and visually effective, featuring Jackson's first film performance. Based on a play by Peter Weiss. Some theaters were forced to add extensions to the marquee when the film was first released. *AKA:* Persecution and Assassination of Jean-Paul Marat as Performed by the Inmates of the Asylum of Charenton Under the Direction of the Marquis De Sade.
1966 (R) 115m/C *GB* Patrick Magee, Clifford Rose, Glenda Jackson, Ian Richardson, Brenda Kempner, Ruth Baker, Michael Williams; *D:* Peter Brook. **VHS, LV** ★★★1/2

Marathon Man Nightmarish chase-thriller in which a graduate student becomes entangled in a plot involving a murderous Nazi fugitive. As student Hoffman is preparing for the Olympic marathon, he is reunited with his secret-agent brother, setting the intricate plot in motion. Courtesy of his brother, Hoffman becomes involved with Olivier, an old crazed Nazi seeking jewels taken from concentration camp victims. Non-stop action throughout, including a torture scene sure to set your teeth on edge. Goldman adapted the screenplay from his novel.
1976 (R) 125m/C Dustin Hoffman, Laurence Olivier, Marthe Keller, Roy Scheider, William Devane, Fritz Weaver; *D:* John Schlesinger; *W:* William Goldman, Conrad Hall. Golden Globe Awards '77: Best Supporting Actor (Olivier); Nominations: Academy Awards '76: Best Supporting Actor (Olivier). **VHS, Beta, LV** ★★★

March of the Wooden Soldiers The classic Mother Goose tale about the secret life of Christmas toys, with Laurel and Hardy as Santa's helpers who must save Toyland from the wicked Barnaby. A Yuletide "must see." Also available in a colorized version. *AKA:* Babes in Toyland.
1934 73m/B Stan Laurel, Oliver Hardy, Charlotte Henry, Henry Kleinbach (Brandon), Felix Knight, Jean Darling, Johnny Downs, Marie Wilson; *D:* Charles R. Rogers, Gus Meins. **VHS, LV** ★★★

Marianne and Juliane Powerful combination of relationships and politics in West Germany as experienced through the lives of two sisters—Juliane, a feminist editor, and Marianne, a political terrorist. Based on the lives of Gudrun and Christiane Ensslin. In German with English subtitles.
1982 106m/C *GE* Jutta Lampe, Barbara Sukowa, Ruediger Vogler, Doris Schade, Franz Rudnick; *D:* Margarethe von Trotta. **VHS** ★★★1/2

Marilyn: The Untold Story Nominated for an Emmy, Hicks elevates what could easily have been a dull made-for-TV movie with her remarkable performance as Marilyn Monroe. Based on the book by Norman Mailer.
1980 156m/C Catherine Hicks, Richard Basehart, Frank Converse, John Ireland, Sheree North, Anne Ramsey, Viveca Lindfors, Jason Miller, Bill Vint; *D:* Jack Arnold, John Flynn, Lawrence Schiller; *M:* William Goldstein. **VHS** ★★★

Marius This is the first of Marcel Pagnol's trilogy ("Fanny" and "Cesar" followed), about the lives and adventures of the people of Provence, France. Marius is a young man who dreams of going away to sea. When he acts on those dreams, he leaves behind his girlfriend, Fanny. Realistic dialogue and vivid characterizations. Adapted by Pagnol from his play. The musical play and film "Fanny" (1961) were adapted from this trilogy.
1931 125m/B *FR* Raimu, Pierre Fresnay, Charpin, Orane Demazis; *D:* Alexander Korda; *W:* Marcel Pagnol; *M:* Francis Gromon. **VHS, Beta, LV** ★★★★

The Mark Story of a convicted child molester who cannot escape his past upon his release from prison. Whitman gives a riveting performance as the convict.
1961 127m/B *GB* Stuart Whitman, Maria Schell, Rod Steiger, Brenda de Banzie, Maurice Denham, Donald Wolfit, Paul Rogers, Donald Houston; *D:* Guy Green; *M:* Richard Rodney Bennett. Nominations: Academy Awards '61: Best Actor (Whitman). **VHS, Beta** ★★★1/2

Mark of Zorro Fairbanks plays a dual role as the hapless Don Diego and his dashing counterpart, Zorro, the hero of the oppressed. Silent film.
1920 80m/B Douglas Fairbanks Sr., Marguerite de la Motte, Noah Beery Sr.; *D:* Fred Niblo. **VHS, LV** ★★★

The Mark of Zorro The dashing Power swashbuckles his way through this wonderfully acted and directed romp. He plays the foppish son of a 19th-century California aristocrat who is secretly the masked avenger of the oppressed peons. Bromberg plays the wicked governor, with the beautiful niece (Darnell) beloved by Power, and Rathbone is supremely evil as his cruel minion. Lots of swordplay with a particularly exciting duel to the death between Rathbone and Power. Based on the novel "The Curse of Capistrano" by Johnston McCulley. Remake of the 1921 silent film and followed by a number of other Zorro incarnations.

1940 93m/B Tyrone Power, Linda Darnell, Basil Rathbone, Gale Sondergaard, Eugene Pallette, J. Edward Bromberg, Montagu Love, Janet Beecher; **D:** Rouben Mamoulian; **W:** Jan Taintor Foote; **M:** Alfred Newman. **VHS** ★★★1/2

Marked Woman Gangster drama about crusading District Attorney who persuades a group of clipjoint hostesses to testify against their gangster boss. A gritty studio melodrama loosely based on a true story.
1937 97m/B Bette Davis, Humphrey Bogart, Eduardo Ciannelli, Isabel Jewell, Jane Bryan, Mayo Methot, Allen Jenkins, Lola Lane; **D:** Lloyd Bacon. Venice Film Festival '37: Best Actress (Davis). **VHS, Beta, LV** ★★★

Marnie A lovely blonde with a mysterious past robs her employers and then changes her identity. When her current boss catches her in the act and forces her to marry him, he soon learns the puzzling aspects of Marnie's background. Criticized at the time of its release, the movie has since been accepted as a Hitchcock classic.
1964 130m/C Tippi Hedren, Sean Connery, Diane Baker, Bruce Dern; **D:** Alfred Hitchcock; **W:** Jay Presson Allen. **VHS, Beta, LV** ★★★1/2

The Marriage Circle A pivotal silent comedy depicting the infidelity of several married couples in Vienna. Director Lubitsch's first American comedy. Remade as a musical, "One Hour With You," in 1932. Silent.
1924 90m/B Florence Vidor, Monte Blue, Marie Prevost, Creighton Hale, Adolphe Menjou, Harry Myers, Dale Fuller; **D:** Ernst Lubitsch. **VHS** ★★★

Marriage Italian Style When an engaged man hears that his mistress is on her death bed, he goes to her side and, in an emotional gesture, promises to marry her if she survives. She does, and holds him to his promise. When they're married, however, she gives him a big surprise—three grown sons. A silly film, but De Sica's direction keeps it from being too fluffy. Lots of fun. Based on the play "Filumena Marturano" by Eduardo De Filippo.
1964 102m/C *IT* Sophia Loren, Marcello Mastroianni, Aldo Puglisi, Tecla Scarano, Marilu Tolo; **D:** Vittorio De Sica. Golden Globe Awards '65: Best Foreign Film; Nominations: Academy Awards '64: Best Actress (Loren), Best Foreign Language Film. **VHS** ★★★

The Marriage of Maria Braun In post-WWII Germany, a young woman uses guile and sexuality to survive as the nation rebuilds itself into an industrial power. The first movie in Fassbinder's trilogy about German women in Germany during the postwar years, it is considered one of the director's finest films, and an indispensable example of the New German Cinema. In German with English subtitles. **AKA:** Die Ehe Der Maria Braun.
1979 (R) 120m/C *GE* Hanna Schygulla, Klaus Lowitsch, Ivan Desny, Gottfried John, Gisela Uhlen; **D:** Rainer Werner Fassbinder; **W:** Rainer Werner Fassbinder; **M:** Peer Raben, Michael Ballhaus. Berlin International Film Festival '79: Best Actress (Schygulla); National Board of Review Awards '79: 5 Best Foreign Films of the Year. **VHS, Beta** ★★★★

Married to the Mob After the murder of her husband, an attractive Mafia widow tries to escape "mob" life, but ends up fighting off amorous advances from the current mob boss while being wooed by an undercover cop. A snappy script and a spry performance by Pfeiffer pepper this easy-to-watch film.
1988 (R) 102m/C Michelle Pfeiffer, Dean Stockwell, Alec Baldwin, Matthew Modine, Mercedes Ruehl, Anthony J. Nici, Joan Cusack, Ellen Foley, Chris Isaak, Trey Wilson, Charles Napier, Tracey Walter, Al Lewis, Nancy Travis, David Johansen, Jonathan Demme; **D:** Jonathan Demme; **W:** Mark Burns, Barry Strugatz, Tak Fujimoto; **M:** David Byrne. New York Film Critics Awards '88: Best Supporting Actor (Stockwell); National Society of Film Critics Awards '88: Best Supporting Actor (Stockwell), Best Supporting Actress (Ruehl); Nominations: Academy Awards '88: Best Supporting Actor (Stockwell). **VHS, Beta, LV** ★★★

Marty Marty is a painfully shy bachelor who feels trapped in a pointless life of family squabbles. When he finds love, he also finds the strength to break out of what he feels is a meaningless existence. A sensitive and poignant film from the writer of "Altered States." Remake of a television version that originally aired in 1953. Notable for Borgnine's sensitive portrayal, one of his last quality jobs before sinking into the B-Movie sludge pit.
1955 91m/B Ernest Borgnine, Betsy Blair, Joe Mantelli, Joe De Santis, Esther Minciotti, Jerry Paris, Karen Steele; **D:** Delbert Mann; **W:** Paddy Chayefsky. Academy Awards '55: Best Actor (Borgnine), Best Director (Mann), Best Picture, Best Screenplay; British Academy Awards '55: Best Actor (Borgnine), Best

Actress (Blair); Golden Globe Awards '56: Best Actor—Drama (Borgnine); National Board of Review Awards '55: 10 Best Films of the Year, Best Actor (Borgnine); Nominations: Academy Awards '55: Best Art Direction/Set Decoration (B & W), Best Black and White Cinematography, Best Supporting Actor (Mantell), Best Supporting Actress (Blair). **VHS, Beta, LV** ★★★1/2

The Marx Brothers in a Nutshell A tribute to the Marx Brothers, narrated by Gene Kelly. Contains clips from "Duck Soup," "Horse Feathers," "Animal Crackers," "Cocoanuts," and "Room Service." Also contains rare outtakes and interviews with the brothers, plus guest appearances by Dick Cavett, Robert Klein, David Steinberg, and others. Indispensible. **1990 100m/B** Groucho Marx, Chico Marx, Harpo Marx, Zeppo Marx, Robert Klein, David Steinberg, George Fenneman, Dick Cavett. **VHS, LV** ★★★1/2

Mary of Scotland The historical tragedy of Mary, Queen of Scots and her cousin, Queen Elizabeth I of England is enacted in this classic film. Traces Mary's claims to the throne of England which ultimately led to her execution. Based on the Maxwell Anderson play. **1936 123m/B** Katharine Hepburn, Fredric March, Florence Eldridge, Douglas Walton, John Carradine, Robert Barrat, Gavin Muir, Ian Keith, Moroni Olsen, William Stack, Alan Mowbray; **D:** John Ford. **VHS, Beta, LV** ★★★

Mary Poppins Magical English nanny arrives one day on the East Wind and takes over the household of a very proper London banker. She introduces her two charges to her friends and family, including Bert, the chimney sweep (Van Dyke), and eccentric Uncle Albert (Wynn). She also changes the lives of everyone in the family. From her they learn that life can always be happy and joyous if you take the proper perspective. Film debut of Andrews. Based on the books by P.L. Travers. A Disney classic that hasn't lost any of its magic. Look for the wonderful sequence where Van Dyke dances with animated penguins. ♪ Chim Chim Cheree; A Spoonful of Sugar; The Perfect Nanny; Sister Suffragette; The Life I Lead; Stay Awake; Feed the Birds; Fidelity Feduciary Bank; Let's Go Fly a Kite. **1964 139m/C** Ed Wynn, Hermione Baddeley, Julie Andrews, Dick Van Dyke, David Tomlinson, Glynis Johns; **D:** Robert Stevenson, Edward Colman. Academy Awards '64: Best Actress (Andrews), Best Film Editing, Best Song ("Chim Chim Cheree"), Best Visual Effects, Best Score; Golden Globe Awards '65: Best Actress—Musical/Comedy (Andrews); Nominations: Academy Awards '64: Best Adapted Screenplay, Best Art Direction/Set Decoration (Color), Best Color Cinematography, Best Costume Design (Color), Best Director (Stevenson), Best Picture, Best Sound, Best Original Score. **VHS, Beta, LV** ★★★1/2

Masada Based on Ernest K. Gann's novel "The Antagonists," this dramatization re-creates the first-century A.D. Roman siege of the fortress Masada, headquarters for a group of Jewish freedom fighters. Abridged from the original television presentation. **1981 131m/C** Peter O'Toole, Peter Strauss, Barbara Carrera, Anthony Quayle, Giulia Pagano, David Warner; **D:** Boris Sagal; **M:** Jerry Goldsmith. **VHS, Beta** ★★★

Masculine Feminine A young Parisian just out of the Army engages in some anarchistic activities when he has an affair with a radical woman singer. Hailed as one of the best French New Wave films. In French with English subtitles. **AKA:** Masculin Feminin. **1966 103m/B** FR Jean-Pierre Leaud, Chantal Goya, Marlene Jobert; **D:** Jean-Luc Godard. Berlin International Film Festival '66: Best Actor (Leaud). **VHS, Beta** ★★★1/2

M*A*S*H Hilarious, irreverent, and well-cast black comedy about a group of surgeons and nurses at a Mobile Army Surgical Hospital in Korea. The horror of war is set in counterpoint to their need to create havoc with episodic late-night parties, practical jokes, and sexual antics. An all-out anti-war festival, highlighted by scenes that starkly uncover the chaos and irony of war, and establish Altman's influential style. Watch for real-life football players Fran Tarkenton, Ben Davidson, and Buck Buchanan in the game. Loosely adapted from the novel by the pseudonymous Richard Hooker (Dr. H. Richard Hornberger and William Heinz). Subsequent hit TV series moved even further from the source novel. **1970 (R) 116m/C** Donald Sutherland, Elliott Gould, Tom Skerritt, Sally Kellerman, JoAnn Pflug, Robert Duvall, Rene Auberjonois, Roger Bowen, Gary Burghoff, Fred Williamson, John Schuck, Bud Cort, G. Wood; **D:** Robert Altman; **W:** Ring Lardner Jr.; **M:** Johnny Mandel. Academy

Awards '70: Best Adapted Screenplay; Cannes Film Festival '70: Best Film; Golden Globe Awards '71: Best Film—Musical/Comedy; National Society of Film Critics Awards '70: Best Film; Writers Guild of America '70: Best Adapted Screenplay; Nominations: Academy Awards '70: Best Director (Altman), Best Film Editing, Best Picture, Best Supporting Actress (Kellerman). **VHS, Beta, LV** ★★★★

M*A*S*H: Goodbye, Farewell & Amen The final two-hour special episode of the television series "M*A*S*H" follows Hawkeye, B.J., Colonel Potter, Charles, Margaret, Klinger, Father Mulcahy, and the rest of the men and women of the 4077th through the last days of the Korean War, the declaration of peace, the dismantling of the camp, and the fond and tearful farewells.
1983 120m/C Alan Alda, Mike Farrell, Harry (Henry) Morgan, David Ogden Stiers, Loretta Swit, Jamie Farr, William Christopher, Allan Arbus. **VHS, Beta, LV** ★★★1/2

Mask A dramatization of the true story of a young boy afflicted with craniodiaphyseal dysplasia (elephantiasis). The boy overcomes his appearance and revels in the joys of life in the California bikers' community. Well-acted, particularly the performances of Stoltz and Cher. A touching film, well-directed by Bogdanovich, that only occasionally slips into maudlin territory.
1985 (PG-13) 120m/C Cher, Sam Elliott, Eric Stoltz, Estelle Getty, Richard Dysart, Laura Dern, Harry Carey Jr., Lawrence Monoson, Marsha Warfield, Barry Tubb, Andrew (Andy) Robinson, Alexandra Powers; **D:** Peter Bogdanovich; **W:** Anna Hamilton Phelan. Academy Awards '85: Best Makeup; Cannes Film Festival '85: Best Actress (Cher). **VHS, Beta, LV** ★★★

The Mask Adolescent supernatural comedy with lollapalooza special effects is Carrey's follow-up to "Ace Ventura." Mild-mannered bank clerk Carrey discovers an ancient mask that has supernatural powers. Upon putting on the mask, he turns into one truly animated guy. He falls for a dame mixed up with gangsters and from there on, our hero deals not only with the incredible powers of the mask, but also with hormones and bad guys as well. Based on the Dark Horse comic book series and originally conceived as a horror flick, director Russell, who gave Freddy Krueger a sense of humor, recast this one as a hellzapoppin' cartoon-action black comedy. Carrey's rubber face is an asset magnified by the breakthrough special effects courtesy of Industrial Light and Magic.
1994 (PG-13) 100m/C Jim Carrey, Cameron Diaz, Peter Greene, Peter Riegert, Amy Yasbeck, Orestes Matacena, Richard Jeni; **D:** Chuck Russell; **W:** Mike Werb; **M:** Randy Edelman. Blockbuster Entertainment Awards '95: Comedy Actor, Theatrical (Carrey), Female Newcomer, Theatrical (Diaz); Nominations: Academy Awards '94: Best Visual Effects; Golden Globe Awards '95: Best Actor—Musical/Comedy (Carrey); MTV Movie Awards '95: Breakthrough Performance (Diaz), Most Desirable Female (Diaz), Best Comedic Performance (Carrey), Best Dance Sequence (Jim Carrey/Cameron Diaz). **VHS** ★★★

Masque of the Red Death An integral selection in the famous Edgar Allan Poe/Roger Corman canon, it deals with an evil prince who traffics with the devil and playfully murders any of his subjects not already dead of the plague. Photographed by Nicholas Roeg. Remade in 1989 with Corman as producer.
1965 88m/C GB Vincent Price, Hazel Court, Jane Asher, Patrick Magee; **D:** Roger Corman. **VHS, Beta** ★★★

Mata Hari During WWI, a lovely German spy steals secrets from the French through her involvement with two military officers. Lavish production and exquisite direction truly make this one of Garbo's best. Watch for her exotic pseudo-strip tease.
1932 90m/B Greta Garbo, Ramon Novarro, Lionel Barrymore, Lewis Stone, C. Henry Gordon, Karen Morley, Alec B. Francis; **D:** George Fitzmaurice. **VHS, Beta** ★★★

The Matchmaker An adaptation of the Thornton Wilder play concerning two young men in search of romance in 1884 New York. Later adapted as "Hello Dolly." An amusing diversion.
1958 101m/B Shirley Booth, Anthony Perkins, Shirley MacLaine, Paul Ford, Robert Morse, Perry Wilson, Wallace Ford, Russell Collins, Rex Evans, Gavin Gordon, Torben Meyer; **D:** Joseph Anthony; **W:** John Michael Hayes. **VHS, Beta, LV** ★★★

Matewan An acclaimed dramatization of the famous Matewan massacre in the 1920s, in which coal miners in West Virginia, reluctantly influenced by a young union organizer, rebelled against terrible working conditions. Complex and imbued with myth, the film is a gritty, moving, powerful drama with typically superb Sayles dialogue and Haskell Wexler's beautiful and poetic cinematography. Jones delivers an economical yet intense portrayal of the black leader of the miners. The director makes his usual on-screen appearance, this time as an establishment-backed reactionary minister. Partially based on the Sayles novel "Union Dues."

1987 (PG-13) 130m/C Chris Cooper, James Earl Jones, Mary McDonnell, William Oldham, Kevin Tighe, David Strathairn; **D:** John Sayles; **W:** John Sayles; **M:** Mason Daring, Haskell Wexler. Independent Spirit Awards '88: Best Cinematography; Nominations: Academy Awards '87: Best Cinematography. **VHS, Beta, LV ★★★1/2**

Matilda Intelligent child Matilda Wormwood (Wilson) is oppressed by both her monstrous parents (DeVito and Perlman) and awful school principal, Trunchbull. However, her first grade teacher, appropriately named Miss Honey (Davidtz), believes in her, which is enough to make Matilda plot an appropriate fate for the miserable people in her life. Excellent adaptation of a typically subversive book by Roald Dahl. Director DeVito, who wanted to create the illusion of a live-action cartoon, built among other things a "Carrot-cam" to capture the flying food of a food fight.

1996 93m/C Danny DeVito, Rhea Perlman, Embeth Davidtz, Mara Wilson, Paul (Pee Wee Herman) Reubens, Tracey Walter; **D:** Danny DeVito; **W:** Robin Swicord, Nicholas Kazan; **M:** David Newman. **VHS, LV ★★★**

May Fools Malle portrays individuals collectively experiencing personal upheaval against the backdrop of unrelated social upheaval. An uppercrust family gathers at a country estate for the funeral of the clan's matriarch, while the May of '68 Parisian riots unfold. Few among the family members mourn the woman's passing, save her son Milou (Piccoli) who leads a pastoral existence tending grapes on the estate. Milou's daughter (Miou-Miou), like the others, is more concerned with her personal gain, suggesting, to her father's horror, that they divide the estate in three. Touching, slow, keenly observed. In French with English subtitles. **AKA:** Milou en Mai; Milou in May.

1990 (R) 105m/C *FR* Michel Piccoli, Miou-Miou, Michael Duchaussoy, Dominique Blanc, Harriet Walter, Francois Berleand, Paulette Dubost, Bruno Carette, Martine Gautier; **D:** Louis Malle; **W:** Jean-Claude Carriere, Louis Malle; **M:** Stephane Grappelli. Cesar Awards '91: Best Supporting Actress (Blanc). **VHS, LV ★★★**

Mayerling Considered one of the greatest films about doomed love. Story of the tragic and hopeless affair between Crown Prince Rudolf of Hapsburg and young Baroness Marie Vetsera. Heart wrenching and beautiful, with stupendous acting. Remade in 1968. In French with English subtitles.

1936 95m/B Charles Boyer, Danielle Darrieux; **D:** Anatole Litvak. New York Film Critics Awards '37: Best Foreign Film. **VHS, Beta, LV ★★★1/2**

Maytime Lovely story of an opera star (MacDonald) and penniless singer (Eddy) who fall in love in Paris, but her husband/teacher (Barrymore) interferes. One of the best films the singing duo ever made. ♪ Maytime Finale; Virginia Ham and Eggs; Vive l'Opera; Student Drinking Song; Carry Me Back to Old Virginny; Reverie; Jump Jim Crow; Road to Paradise; Page's Aria.

1937 132m/B Jeanette MacDonald, Nelson Eddy, John Barrymore, Herman Bing, Tom Brown, Lynne Carver; **D:** Robert Z. Leonard; **W:** Noel Langley. Nominations: Academy Awards '37: Best Sound, Best Original Score. **VHS, LV ★★★**

McCabe & Mrs. Miller Altman's take on the Western casts Beatty as an entrepreneur who opens a brothel in the Great North. Christie is the madame who helps stabilize the haphazard operation. Unfortunately, success comes at a high price, and when gunmen arrive to enforce a business proposition, Beatty must become the man he has merely pretended to be.

1971 (R) 121m/C Warren Beatty, Julie Christie, William Devane, Keith Carradine, John Schuck, Rene Auberjonois, Shelley Duvall, Bert Remsen, Michael Murphy, Hugh Millais, Jack Riley; **D:** Robert Altman; **W:** Robert Altman; **M:** Leonard Cohen, Vilmos Zsigmond. Nominations: Academy Awards '71: Best Actress (Christie). **VHS, Beta, LV ★★★★**

Mean Streets A grimy slice of street life in Little Italy among lower echelon Mafiosos, unbalanced punks, and petty criminals, marking the formal debut by Scorsese. Unorthodox camera movement and gritty performances by De Niro and Keitel.

1973 (R) 112m/C Harvey Keitel, Robert De Niro, David Proval, Amy Robinson, Richard Romanus, David Carradine, Robert Carradine, Cesare Danova, George Memmoli; **D:** Martin Scorsese; **W:** Mardik Martin, Martin Scorsese. National Society of Film Critics Awards '73: Best Supporting Actor (De Niro). **VHS, Beta, LV ★★★★**

Mediterraneo Comedy based on the premise that love does make the world go 'round—especially in wartime. In 1941, eight misfit Italian soldiers are stranded on a tiny Greek island and are absorbed into the life of the island, finding love and liberty in the idyllic setting. Italian with English subtitles.
1991 (R) 90m/C *IT* Diego Abatantuono, Giuseppe Cederna, Claudio Bigagli, Vanna Barba, Claudio Bisio, Luigi Alberti, Ugo Conti, Memo Dini, Vasco Mirandola, Luigi Montini, Irene Grazioli, Antonio Catania; *D:* Gabriele Salvatores. Academy Awards '91: Best Foreign Language Film. **VHS, Beta, LV** ★★★

Medium Cool Commentary focusing on a television news cameraman and his apathy with the events around him. His involvement with an Appalachian woman and her young son reawakens his conscience, leading to the three getting caught up in the turbulence of the 1968 Chicago Democratic convention.
1969 111m/C Robert Forster, Verna Bloom, Peter Bonerz, Marianna Hill, Peter Boyle; *D:* Haskell Wexler; *W:* Haskell Wexler. **VHS, Beta** ★★★1/2

Meet John Doe A social commentary about an unemployed, down-and-out man selected to be the face of a political goodwill campaign. Honest and trusting, he eventually realizes that he is being used to further the careers of corrupt politicians. Available in colorized version.
1941 123m/B Gary Cooper, Barbara Stanwyck, Edward Arnold, James Gleason, Walter Brennan, Spring Byington, Gene Lockhart, Regis Toomey, Ann Doran, Rod La Rocque; *D:* Frank Capra. Nominations: Academy Awards '41: Best Story. **VHS, LV** ★★★

Meet Me in St. Louis Wonderful music in this charming tale of the St. Louis family during the 1903 World's Fair. One of Garland's better musical performances. ♪ You and I; Skip to My Lou; Over the Bannister; Meet Me In St. Louis; Brighten the Corner; Summer In St. Louis; All Hallow's Eve; Ah, Love; The Horrible One.
1944 113m/C Judy Garland, Margaret O'Brien, Mary Astor, Lucille Bremer, Tom Drake, June Lockhart, Harry Davenport; *D:* Vincente Minnelli. National Board of Review Awards '44: 10 Best Films of the Year; Nominations: Academy Awards '44: Best Color Cinematography, Best Screenplay, Best Song ("The Trolley Song"), Best Original Score. **VHS, Beta, LV, 8mm** ★★★1/2

Melvin and Howard Story of Melvin Dummar, who once gave Howard Hughes a ride. Dummar later claimed a share of Hughes's will. Significant for Demme's direction and fine acting from Steenburgen/LeMat, and Robards in a small role as Hughes.
1980 (R) 95m/C Paul LeMat, Jason Robards Jr., Mary Steenburgen, Michael J. Pollard, Dabney Coleman, Elizabeth Cheshire, Pamela Reed, Cheryl "Rainbeaux" Smith; *D:* Jonathan Demme; *W:* Bo Goldman. Academy Awards '80: Best Original Screenplay, Best Supporting Actress (Steenburgen); Los Angeles Film Critics Association Awards '80: Best Supporting Actress (Steenburgen); National Board of Review Awards '80: 10 Best Films of the Year; New York Film Critics Awards '80: Best Director (Demme), Best Screenplay, Best Supporting Actress (Steenburgen); Writers Guild of America '80: Best Original Screenplay; Nominations: Academy Awards '80: Best Supporting Actor (Robards). **VHS, Beta, LV** ★★★1/2

The Member of the Wedding While struggling through her adolescence, a 12-year-old girl growing up in 1945 Georgia seeks solace from her family's cook. Based on Carson McCullers's play, this story of family, belonging, and growth is well acted and very touching.
1952 90m/C Ethel Waters, Julie Harris, Brandon de Wilde, Arthur Franz; *D:* Fred Zinneman; *W:* Edward Anhalt; *M:* Alex North. Nominations: Academy Awards '52: Best Actress (Harris). **VHS, Beta** ★★★

Men . . . A funny and insightful satire about a man who discovers his loving wife has been having an affair with a young artist. In a unique course of revenge, the husband ingratiates himself with the artist and gradually turns him into a carbon copy of himself. In German with English subtitles or dubbed.
1985 96m/C *GE* Heiner Lauterbach, Uwe Ochsenknecht, Ulrike Kriener, Janna Marangosoff; *D:* Doris Dorrie. **VHS** ★★★1/2

Men of the Fighting Lady Action-adventure offers plenty of exciting battle footage. Features the stories of selected pilots stationed on a U.S. aircraft carrier in the Pacific during the Korean War. The stories, told to Calhern as writer James A. Michener, center around the lead pilot Johnson. Dramatic airflights include a scene in which Johnson helps a blinded Martin land his plane safely on the carrier deck. Gene Ruggerio's editing of the war footage was so expertly done that he was questioned by the Pentagon when they had a hard time believing the scenes were achieved by skillful editing and painted backdrops. Look for "Beaver" Mathers as one of Wynn's sons.

1954 81m/C Van Johnson, Walter Pidgeon, Louis Calhern, Dewey Martin, Keenan Wynn, Frank Lovejoy, Robert Horton, Bert Freed, Jerry Mathers; **D:** Andrew Marton; **M:** Miklos Rozsa. **VHS, Beta ★★★1/2**

Menace II Society Portrayal of black teens lost in inner-city hell is realistically captured by 21-year-old twin directors, in their big-screen debut. Caine (Turner) lives with his grandparents and peddles drugs for spending money, from the eve of his high school graduation to his decision to escape south-central Los Angeles for Atlanta. Bleak and haunting, with some of the most unsettling, bloodiest violence ever shown in a commercial film. Disturbing to watch, but critically acclaimed. The Hugheses make their mark on contemporary black cinema with intensity, enhanced by an action-comics visual flair. Based on a story by the Hugheses and Tyger Williams.

1993 (R) 104m/C Tyrin Turner, Larenz Tate, Samuel L. Jackson, Glenn Plummer, Julian Roy Doster, Bill Duke, Charles S. Dutton, Jada Pinkett; **D:** Allen Hughes, Albert Hughes; **W:** Tyger Williams. Independent Spirit Awards '94: Best Cinematography; MTV Movie Awards '94: Best Film; Nominations: Independent Spirit Awards '94: Best Actor (Turner), Best First Feature. **VHS, LV ★★★1/2**

Mephisto An egomaniacal actor, compellingly played by Brandauer, sides with the Nazis to further his career, with disastrous results. The first of three brilliant films by Szabo and Brandauer exploring the price of power and personal sublimation in German history. Critically hailed. In German with English subtitles. From the novel by Klaus Mann. Followed by "Colonel Redl" and "Hanussen."

1981 144m/C *HU* Klaus Maria Brandauer, Krystyna Janda, Ildiko Bansagi, Karin Boyd, Rolf Hoppe, Christine Harbort, Gyorgy Cserhalmi, Christiane Graskoff, Peter Andorai, Ildiko Kishonti; **D:** Istvan Szabo, Lajos Koltai. Academy Awards '81: Best Foreign Language Film; Nominations: Cannes Film Festival '81: Best Film. **VHS, Beta ★★★1/2**

The Merchant of Four Seasons Story focuses on the depression and unfulfilled dreams of an average street merchant. Direction from Fass-binder is slow, deliberate, and mesmerizing. In German with English subtitles.

1971 88m/C Hans Hirschmuller, Irm Hermann, Hanna Schygulla, Andrea Schober, Gusti Kreissl; **D:** Rainer Werner Fassbinder; **W:** Rainer Werner Fassbinder. **VHS, Beta ★★★**

The Merchant of Venice Shakespeare's tragedy of prejudice, vengeance, and sacrifice stars Olivier as the persecuted money lender Shylock, who demands his payment of a pound of flesh for a defaulted loan.

1973 131m/C *GB* Laurence Olivier, Joan Plowright, Jeremy Brett. **VHS ★★★**

Merry Christmas, Mr. Lawrence An often overlooked drama about a WWII Japanese POW camp. Taut psychological drama about clashing cultures and physical and emotional survival focusing on the tensions between Bowie as a British POW and camp commander Sakamato, who also composed the outstanding score. A haunting and intense film about the horrors of war. Based on the novel by Laurens van der Post.

1983 (R) 124m/C *JP GB* David Bowie, Tom Conti, Ryuichi Sakamoto, Takeshi, Jack Thompson; **D:** Nagisa Oshima. National Board of Review Awards '83: Best Actor (Conti); Nominations: Cannes Film Festival '83: Best Film. **VHS, Beta ★★★**

The Merry Widow The first sound version of the famous Franz Lehar operetta, dealing with a playboy from a bankrupt kingdom who must woo and marry the land's wealthy widow or be tried for treason. A delightful musical comedy, with a sterling cast and patented Lubitschian gaiety. Made as a silent in 1912 and 1925; remade in color in 1952. ♪ Girls, Girls, Girls; Vilia; Tonight Will Teach Me to Forget; Melody of Laughter; Maxim's; The Girls at Maxim's; The Merry Widow Waltz; If Widows are Rich; Russian Dance. *AKA:* The Lady Dances.

1934 99m/B Maurice Chevalier, Jeanette MacDonald, Edward Everett Horton, Una Merkel, George Barbier, Minna Gombell, Ruth Channing, Sterling Holloway, Henry Armetta, Barbara Leanard, Donald Meek, Akim Tamiroff, Herman Bing; **D:** Ernst Lubitsch; **M:** Franz Lehar, Lorenz Hart. Academy Awards '34: Best Interior Decoration. **VHS, Beta, LV ★★★1/2**

Metropolis Now a classic meditation on futurist technology and mass mentality, this fantasy concerns mechanized society. Original set design and special effects made this an innovative and influential film in its

day. Is now considered one of the hippest films of the sci-fi genre. Silent, with musical score. The 1984 rerelease features some color tinting, reconstruction, and a digital score with songs by Pat Benatar, Bonnie Tyler, Giorgio Moroder, and Queen.
1926 115m/B GE Brigitte Helm, Alfred Abel, Gustav Froehlich, Rudolf Klein-Rogge, Fritz Rasp; **D:** Fritz Lang. **VHS, Beta, LV ★★★★**

Metropolitan The Izod set comes of age on Park Avenue during Christmas break. Tom Townsend (Clements), a member of the middle class, finds himself drawn into a circle of self-proclaimed urban haute bourgeoisie types. They're embarrassingly short on male escorts for the holiday season's parties so he stands in and gets an inside look at life with the brat pack. Intelligently written and carefully made, it transcends the flirting-with-adulthood genre.
1990 (PG-13) 98m/C Carolyn Farina, Edward Clements, Taylor Nichols, Christopher Eigeman, Allison Rutledge-Parisi, Dylan Hundley, Isabel Gillies, Bryan Leder, Will Kempe, Elizabeth Thompson; **D:** Whit Stillman; **W:** Whit Stillman; **M:** Mark Suozzo. Independent Spirit Awards '91: Best First Feature; New York Film Critics Awards '90: Best Director (Stillman); Nominations: Academy Awards '90: Best Original Screenplay. **VHS, LV ★★★**

Michael Collins Collins (Neeson) was a revolutionary leader with the Irish Volunteers, a guerilla force (an early version of the IRA) dedicated to freeing Ireland from British rule by any means necessary. After a number of successful moves against British intelligence, Collins is unwillingly drawn into a stateman's role as negotiations for an Anglo-Irish Treaty begin in 1921, ultimately dividing the country in two and leading to Collins's own assassination. Controversy surrounded the film as historians, politicians, and the media took potshots at director Jordan's admittedly personal look at the complexities of Irish life and one of its equally complicated heroes.
1996 117m/C Liam Neeson, Aidan Quinn, Alan Rickman, Stephen Rea, Julia Roberts, Ian Hart, Sean McGinley, Gerald McSorley, Stuart Graham, Charles Dance, Jonathan Rhys Myers; **D:** Neil Jordan; **W:** Neil Jordan; **M:** Elliot Goldenthal. Los Angeles Film Critics Association Awards '96: Best Cinematography; Venice Film Festival '96: Golden Lion, Best Actor (Neeson); Nominations: Golden Globe Awards '97: Best Actor—Drama (Neeson), Best Score. **VHS ★★★**

Midnight Struggling showgirl Colbert masquerades as Hungarian countess in sophisticated comedy of marital conflicts. Near-classic film scripted by Wilder and Brackett. Based on a story by Edwin Justus Mayer and Franz Schulz. Remade as "Masquerade in Mexico."
1939 94m/B Claudette Colbert, Don Ameche, John Barrymore, Francis Lederer, Mary Astor, Hedda Hopper, Rex O'Malley; **D:** Mitchell Leisen; **W:** Billy Wilder, Charles Brackett. **VHS ★★★1/2**

A Midnight Clear Sensitive war drama that takes place in the Ardennes Forest, near the French-German border in December 1944. It's Christmastime and six of the remaining members of a 12-member squad are sent on a dangerous mission to an abandoned house to locate the enemy. Filmed in a dreamy surreal style, the setting is somewhat reminiscent of a fairy-tale, although a sense of anguish filtrates throughout the picture. A solid script, excellent direction, and a good cast make this a worthwhile film that pits the message of peace against the stupidity of war. Adapted from the novel by William Wharton.
1992 (PG) 107m/C Peter Berg, Kevin Dillon, Arye Gross, Ethan Hawke, Gary Sinise, Frank Whaley, John C. McGinley, Larry Joshua, Curt Lowens; **D:** Keith Gordon; **W:** Keith Gordon; **M:** Mark Isham. **VHS, LV ★★★**

Midnight Cowboy Drama about the relationship between a naive Texan hustler and a seedy derelict, set in the underbelly of New York City. Graphic and emotional character study is brilliantly acted and engaging. Shocking and considered quite risque at the time of its release, this film now carries an "R" rating. It is the only film carrying an "X" rating ever to win the Best Picture Oscar. From James Leo Herlihy's novel. Laserdisc version features: audio commentary by director John Schlesinger and producer Jerome Hellman, behind the scenes production photos, and original movie trailer.
1969 (R) 113m/C Dustin Hoffman, Jon Voight, Sylvia Miles, Brenda Vaccaro, John McGiver, Bob Balaban, Barnard Hughes; **D:** John Schlesinger; **W:** Waldo Salt; **M:** John Barry, Adam Holender. Academy Awards '69: Best Adapted Screenplay, Best Director (Schlesinger), Best Picture; British Academy Awards '69: Best Actor (Hoffman), Best Director (Schlesinger), Best Film, Best Screenplay; Directors Guild of America Awards '69: Best Director (Schlesinger); New York Film Critics

Awards '69: Best Actor (Voight); National Society of Film Critics Awards '69: Best Actor (Voight); Writers Guild of America '69: Best Adapted Screenplay; Nominations: Academy Awards '69: Best Actor (Hoffman), Best Actor (Voight), Best Film Editing, Best Supporting Actress (Miles). **VHS, Beta, LV ★★★1/2**

Midnight Express Gripping and powerful film based on the true story of Billy Hayes. Davis plays Hayes as a young American in Turkey who is busted trying to smuggle hashish. He is sentenced to a brutal and nightmarish prison for life. After enduring tremendous mental and physical torture, he seeks escape along the "Midnight Express." Not always easy to watch, but the overall effect is riveting and unforgettable.
1978 (R) 120m/C John Hurt, Randy Quaid, Brad Davis, Paul Smith, Bo Hopkins, Oliver Stone; **D:** Alan Parker; **W:** Oliver Stone; **M:** Giorgio Moroder. Academy Awards '78: Best Adapted Screenplay, Best Score; British Academy Awards '78: Best Director (Parker), Best Supporting Actor (Hurt); National Board of Review Awards '78: 10 Best Films of the Year; Writers Guild of America '78: Best Adapted Screenplay; Nominations: Academy Awards '78: Best Director (Parker), Best Film Editing, Best Picture, Best Supporting Actor (Hurt). **VHS, Beta, LV, 8mm ★★★**

Midnight Run An ex-cop bounty hunter must bring in an ex-mob accountant who has embezzled big bucks from his former boss. After he catches up with the thief, the hunter finds that bringing his prisoner from New York to Los Angeles will be very trying, especially when it is apparent that the Mafia and FBI are out to stop them. The friction between the two leads—De Niro and Grodin—is fun to watch, while the action and comic moments are enjoyable.
1988 (R) 125m/C Robert De Niro, Charles Grodin, Yaphet Kotto, John Ashton, Dennis Farina, Joe Pantoliano, Richard Foronjy, Wendy Phillips, Donald E. Thorin; **D:** Martin Brest; **W:** George Gallo; **M:** Danny Elfman. **VHS, Beta, LV ★★★**

A Midsummer Night's Dream Famed Reinhardt version of the Shakespeare classic, featuring nearly every star on the Warner Brothers lot. The plot revolves around the amorous battle between the king and queen of a fairy kingdom, and the humans who are drawn into their sport. Features de Havilland's first film role. Classic credit line: Dialogue by William Shakespeare.
1935 117m/B James Cagney, Dick Powell, Joe E. Brown, Hugh Herbert, Olivia de Havilland, Ian Hunter, Mickey Rooney, Victor Jory, Arthur Treacher, Billy Barty; **D:** Max Reinhardt, William Dieterle. Academy Awards '35: Best Cinematography, Best Film Editing; Nominations: Academy Awards '35: Best Picture. **VHS, Beta ★★★**

A Midsummer Night's Sex Comedy Allen's homage to Shakespeare, Renoir, Chekhov, Bergman, and who knows who else is an engaging ensemble piece about hijinks among friends and acquaintances gathered at a country house at the turn of the century. Standouts include Ferrer as pompous professor and Steenburgen as Allen's sexually repressed wife. Mia's first for the Woodman.
1982 (PG) 88m/C Woody Allen, Mia Farrow, Mary Steenburgen, Tony Roberts, Julie Hagerty, Jose Ferrer, Gordon Willis; **D:** Woody Allen; **W:** Woody Allen. **VHS, Beta ★★★1/2**

The Migrants Adaptation of the Tennessee Williams play about the hardscrabble world of a migrant family yearning for a better life. Made for TV.
1974 83m/C Cloris Leachman, Ron Howard, Sissy Spacek, Cindy Williams, Ed Lauter, Lisa Lucas, Mills Watson, Claudia McNeil, Dolph Sweet; **D:** Tom Gries; **W:** Lanford Wilson. **VHS ★★★**

The Milagro Beanfield War Redford's endearing adaptation of John Nichols's novel about New Mexican townfolk opposing development. Seemingly simple tale provides plenty of insight into human spirit. Fine cast, with especially stellar turns from Blades, Braga, and Vennera.
1988 (R) 118m/C Chick Vennera, John Heard, Ruben Blades, Sonia Braga, Daniel Stern, Julie Carmen, Christopher Walken, Richard Bradford, Carlos Riquelme, James Gammon, Melanie Griffith, Freddy Fender, M. Emmet Walsh; **D:** Robert Redford; **W:** David S. Ward, Robbie Greenberg; **M:** Dave Grusin. Academy Awards '88: Best Original Score. **VHS, Beta, LV ★★★1/2**

Mildred Pierce Gripping melodrama features Crawford as hard-working divorcee rivaling daughter for man's love. Things, one might say, eventually get ugly. Adaptation of James M. Cain novel is classic of its kind.
1945 113m/B Joan Crawford, Jack Carson, Zachary Scott, Eve Arden, Ann Blyth, Bruce (Herman Brix) Bennett; **D:** Michael Curtiz; **W:** Ranald MacDougall; **M:** Max Steiner. Academy Awards '45: Best Actress (Crawford); Nominations: Academy Awards '45: Best Black and White Cinematography, Best Picture, Best Screenplay, Best Supporting Actress (Arden, Blyth). **VHS, Beta, LV ★★★1/2**

The Milky Way Wicked anticlerical farce. Two bums team up on a religious pilgrimage and encounter seemingly all manner of strangeness and sacrilege in this typically peculiar Bunuel work. Perhaps the only film in which Jesus is encouraged to shave. In French with English subtitles.
1968 102m/C *FR* Laurent Terzieff, Paul Frankeur, Delphine Seyrig, Alain Cuny, Bernard Verley, Michel Piccoli, Edith Scob; *D:* Luis Bunuel; *W:* Jean-Claude Carriere. **VHS, Beta, LV** ★★★

Miller's Crossing From the Coen brothers (makers of "Blood Simple" and "Raising Arizona") comes this extremely dark entry in the gangster movie sweepstakes of 1990. Jewish, Italian, and Irish mobsters spin webs of deceit, protection, and revenge over themselves and their families. Byrne is the protagonist, but no hero, being as deeply flawed as the men he battles. Harden stuns as the woman who sleeps with Byrne and his boss, Finney, in hopes of a better life and protection for her small-time crook brother. Visually exhilarating, excellently acted, and perfectly paced.
1990 (R) 115m/C Albert Finney, Gabriel Byrne, Marcia Gay Harden, John Turturro, Jon Polito, J.E. Freeman; *D:* Joel Coen; *W:* Ethan Coen, Joel Coen; *M:* Carter Burwell. **VHS, Beta, LV** ★★★1/2

The Miracle An innocent peasant woman is seduced by a shepherd and becomes convinced that her pregnancy will produce a second Christ. Controversial, compelling film derived from a story by Federico Fellini. In Italian with English subtitles. *AKA:* Ways of Love.
1948 43m/B *IT* Anna Magnani, Federico Fellini; *D:* Roberto Rossellini. **VHS, Beta** ★★★

Miracle in Milan An innocent, child-like fantasy about heavenly intervention driving capitalists out of a Milanese ghetto and helping the poor to fly to a new Utopia. Happy mixture of whimsy and neo-realism. In Italian with English subtitles. *AKA:* Miracolo a Milano.
1951 95m/B *IT* Francesco Golisano, Brunella Bova, Emma Gramatica, Paolo Stoppa; *D:* Vittorio De Sica; *W:* Cesare Zavattini. Cannes Film Festival '51: Best Film; National Board of Review Awards '51: 5 Best Foreign Films of the Year; New York Film Critics Awards '51: Best Foreign Film. **VHS, Beta, LV** ★★★

Miracle of Morgan's Creek The breakneck comedy that stands as Sturges' premier achievement. Details the misadventures of a wartime floozy who gets drunk, thinks she marries a soldier on leave, gets pregnant by him, forgets the whole thing, and then tries to evade scandal by getting a local schnook to marry her again. And she's expecting sextuplets. Hilarious, out-to-make-trouble farce that shouldn't have, by all rights, made it past the censors of the time. Sturges' most scathing assault on American values earned him an Oscar nomination for writing. Remade as "Rock-A-Bye Baby" in 1958.
1944 98m/B Eddie Bracken, Betty Hutton, Diana Lynn, Brian Donlevy, Akim Tamiroff, Porter Hall, Emory Parnell, Alan Bridge, Julius Tannen, Victor Potel, Almira Sessions, Chester Conklin, William Demarest, Jimmy Conlin; *D:* Preston Sturges; *W:* Preston Sturges; *M:* Leo Shuken, Charles Bradshaw. Nominations: Academy Awards '44: Best Original Screenplay. **VHS, Beta** ★★★★

Miracle on 34th Street The actual Kris Kringle is hired as Santa Claus for the Macy's Thanksgiving parade but finds difficulty in proving himself to the cynical parade sponsor. When the boss's daughter also refuses to acknowledge Kringle, he goes to extraordinary lengths to convince her. Holiday classic equal to "It's a Wonderful Life," with Gwenn and Wood particularly engaging. Also available colorized. *AKA:* The Big Heart.
1947 97m/B Maureen O'Hara, John Payne, Edmund Gwenn, Natalie Wood, William Frawley, Porter Hall, Gene Lockhart, Thelma Ritter, Jack Albertson; *D:* George Seaton; *W:* George Seaton; *M:* Cyril Mockridge. Academy Awards '47: Best Story & Screenplay, Best Supporting Actor (Gwenn); Nominations: Academy Awards '47: Best Picture. **VHS, Beta, LV** ★★★★

The Miracle Worker Depicts the unconventional methods that teacher Anne Sullivan used to help the deaf and blind Helen Keller adjust to the world around her and shows the relationship that built between the two courageous women. An intense, moving experience. William Gibson adapted his own play for the screen.
1962 107m/B Anne Bancroft, Patty Duke, Victor Jory, Inga Swenson, Andrew Prine, Beah Richards; *D:* Arthur Penn. Academy Awards '62: Best Actress (Bancroft), Best Supporting Actress (Duke); National Board of Review Awards '62: 10 Best Films of the Year, Best Actress (Bancroft); Nominations: Academy Awards '62: Best Adapted Screenplay, Best Costume Design (B & W), Best Director (Penn). **VHS, Beta** ★★★1/2

The Miracle Worker Remade for television story of blind, deaf and mute Helen Keller and her teacher, Annie Sullivan, whose patience and perseverance finally enable Helen to learn to communicate with the world. Duke was Keller in the 1962 original, but plays the teacher in this version.
1979 98m/C Patty Duke, Melissa Gilbert; **D:** Paul Aaron; **M:** Billy Goldenberg. **VHS, Beta** ★★★

Misery Author Caan decides to chuck his lucrative but unfulfilling pulp novels and write seriously by finishing off his most popular character, Misery Chastain. However, fate intervenes when he crashes his car near the home of Bates, his "biggest fan ever," who saves his life, but then tortures him into resurrecting her favorite character. Bates is chillingly glib and calmly brutal—watch your ankles. Based on the novel by Stephen King.
1990 (R) 107m/C James Caan, Kathy Bates, Lauren Bacall, Richard Farnsworth, Frances Sternhagen, Graham Jarvis; **D:** Rob Reiner; **W:** William Goldman; **M:** Marc Shaiman. Academy Awards '90: Best Actress (Bates); Golden Globe Awards '91: Best Actress—Drama (Bates). **VHS, Beta, LV** ★★★

The Misfits A cynical floozy befriends grim cowboys in this downbeat drama. Compelling performances from leads Clift, Monroe (screenwriter Miller's wife), and Gable. Last film for the latter two performers, and nearly the end for Clift.
1961 124m/B Clark Gable, Marilyn Monroe, Montgomery Clift, Thelma Ritter, Eli Wallach, James Barton, Estelle Winwood; **D:** John Huston; **W:** Arthur Miller; **M:** Alex North. **VHS, Beta, LV** ★★★

Mishima: A Life in Four Chapters Somewhat detached account and indulgent portrayal of the narcissistic Japanese author (and actor, filmmaker, and militarist) alternates between stylized interpretations of his books and a straightforward account of his life. Culminates in a pseudo-military operation that, in turn, resulted in Mishima's ritualistic suicide. A U.S./Japanese production. Innovative design by Eiko Ishioka. In Japanese with English subtitles.
1985 (R) 121m/C Ken Ogata, Kenji Sawada, Yasosuke Bando; **D:** Paul Schrader; **W:** Leonard Schrader, Paul Schrader, John Bailey; **M:** Philip Glass. **VHS, Beta** ★★★

Ms. 45 Rough, bristling cult favorite about a mute girl who, in response to being raped and beaten twice in one night, goes on a man-killing murder spree. Wild ending. **AKA:** Angel of Vengeance.
1981 (R) 84m/C Zoe Tamerlis, Steve Singer, Jack Thibeau, Peter Yellen, Darlene Stuto, Editta Sherman, Albert Sinkys, Jimmy Laine; **D:** Abel Ferrara. **VHS, Beta, LV** ★★★

Miss Rose White Sedgwick is Rose, a modern young career woman in post-WWII New York, as American as apple pie, who lives two very separate lives. Born Rayzel Weiss, a Polish Jew, she immigrated to the U.S. with her father as a very young girl, before the holocaust devastated her remaining family in Poland. After the war her older sister, thought dead, comes to America. The haunted Luisa causes Rose to question whether she can ever leave her past behind. Above average Hallmark Hall of Fame presentation has a good cast, particularly Plummer as Luisa. Based on the play "A Shayna Maidel" by Barbara Lebow.
1992 (PG) 95m/C Kyra Sedgwick, Amanda Plummer, Maximilian Schell, D.B. Sweeney, Penny Fuller, Milton Selzer, Maureen Stapleton; **D:** Joseph Sargent; **W:** Anna Sandor. **VHS** ★★★

Miss Sadie Thompson Based on the novel "Rain" by W. Somerset Maugham. Promiscuous tart Hayworth arrives on a Pacific island occupied by a unit of Marines and a sanctimonious preacher played by Ferrer. While Hayworth parties with the Marines and becomes involved with Ray's Sgt. O'Hara, Ferrer moralizes and insists her return to the mainland to face morals charges. Quasi-musical with a scattering of dubbed songs by Hayworth includes a memorable erotic dance scene complete with tight dress and dripping sweat. Hayworth's strong performance carries the picture with Ferrer and Ray turning in cardboard versions of their Maugham characters. Originally filmed in 3-D.
1953 91m/C Rita Hayworth, Jose Ferrer, Aldo Ray, Charles Bronson; **D:** Curtis Bernhardt. Academy Awards Nominations: Academy Awards '53: Best Song ("Sadie Thompson's Song (Blue Pacific Blues)"). **VHS, Beta, LV** ★★★

Missiles of October Telling the story of the October 1962 Cuban Missile crisis, this made-for-TV drama keeps you on the edge of your seat while unfolding the sequence of events within the U.S. government. Well written, with a strong cast including Devane, who turns in a convincing performance as—guess who—J.F.K.

1974 155m/C William Devane, Ralph Bellamy, Martin Sheen, Howard da Silva; **D:** Anthony Page. VHS, Beta ★★★

Missing At the height of a military coup in Chile (never named in the movie), a young American writer (Shea) disappears. His right-wing father Lemmon tries to get to the bottom of his disappearance while bickering with Shea's wife, played by Spacek, a bohemian who is the political opposite of her father-in-law. Outstanding performances by Spacek and Lemmon along with excellent writing and direction result in a gripping and thought-provoking thriller. Based on the book by Thomas Hauser from the true story of Charles Horman.
1982 (PG) 122m/C Jack Lemmon, Sissy Spacek, John Shea, Melanie Mayron, David Clennon, Charles Cioffi, Joe Regalbuto, Richard Venture, Janice Rule; **D:** Constantin Costa-Gavras; **W:** Constantin Costa-Gavras, Donald Stewart; **M:** Vangelis. Academy Awards '82: Best Adapted Screenplay; British Academy Awards '82: Best Screenplay; Cannes Film Festival '82: Best Actor (Lemmon), Best Film; Writers Guild of America '82: Best Adapted Screenplay; Nominations: Academy Awards '82: Best Actor (Lemmon), Best Actress (Spacek), Best Picture. VHS, Beta, LV ★★★1/2

Mission: Impossible Cruise and director DePalma did not completely succeed or fail in their mission to create a blockbuster hit based on the popular '60s TV series. Cruise (one of the film's producers) is Ethan Hunt, pointman extraordinaire of the IMF team headed by Jim Phelps (Jon Voight). Their team is sent to recover a computer disk with devastating information from a mercenary Russian spy. Smelling a double cross, Hunt confronts his conniving agency boss Kitteridge (the perfectly cast Czerny) and creates his own team of crack agents to get to the truth, mind-boggling plot twists and crazy train rides be damned. The plotline may have self-destructed two-thirds into the movie, and the absence of a truly sinister villain causes some damage, but with solid acting talent, tight pacing, alluring European locales, and tension-inducing special effects, who has time to notice? $100 million gross in the first two weeks would seem to indicate a sequel is in order.
1996 (PG-13) 110m/C Tom Cruise, Jon Voight, Emmanuelle Beart, Ving Rhames, Henry Czerny, Emilio Estevez, Vanessa Redgrave; **D:** Brian DePalma; **W:** Robert Towne, David Koepp; **M:** Danny Elfman. VHS ★★★

Mississippi Burning Hard-edged social drama centers around the civil rights movement in Mississippi in 1964. When three activists turn up missing, FBI agents Hackman and Dafoe are sent to head up the investigation. Unfortunately, this is another example of a "serious" film about racial conflict in which white characters predominate and blacks provide background.
1988 (R) 127m/C Gene Hackman, Willem Dafoe, Frances McDormand, Brad Dourif, R. Lee Ermey, Gailard Sartain, Stephen Tobolowsky, Michael Rooker, Pruitt Taylor Vince, Badja Djola, Kevin Dunn, Frankie Faison, Tom Mason, Park Overall; **D:** Alan Parker; **W:** Chris Gerolmo, Peter Biziou; **M:** Trevor Jones. Academy Awards '88: Best Cinematography; Berlin International Film Festival '88: Best Actor (Hackman); National Board of Review Awards '88: 10 Best Films of the Year, Best Actor (Hackman), Best Director (Parker), Best Supporting Actress (McDormand); Nominations: Academy Awards '88: Best Actor (Hackman), Best Director (Parker), Best Film Editing, Best Picture, Best Sound, Best Supporting Actress (McDormand). VHS, Beta, LV ★★★

Mississippi Mermaid Truffaut generally succeeds in merging his own directorial style with Hitchcockian suspense, but this is not considered one of his best. Millionaire tobacco planter Belmondo looks for a bride in the personals and finds Deneuve. Belmondo feels lucky landing this beauty until she leaves him and takes his money with her. A lookalike, also played by Deneuve, takes over his wife's role and attempts to poison Belmondo. Look for numerous references to the movies, including Bogart, Balzac and Cocteau. Based on the Cornell Woolrich novel "Waltz into Darkness." In French with English subtitles.
1969 (PG) 110m/C *FR IT* Jean-Paul Belmondo, Catherine Deneuve, Michel Bouquet, Nelly Borgeaud, Marcel Berbert, Martine Ferriere; **D:** Francois Truffaut; **W:** Francois Truffaut; **M:** Antoine Duhamel. VHS, LV ★★★

Mrs. Miniver A moving tale of a courageous, gentle middle-class British family and its struggle to survive during WWII. A classic that garnered six Academy Awards, it's recognized for contributions to the Allied effort. Contains one of the most powerful orations in film history, delivered by Wilcoxon, who portrayed the vicar.

Followed by "The Miniver Story." Adapted from Jan Struther's book. **1942 134m/B** Greer Garson, Walter Pidgeon, Teresa Wright, May Whitty, Richard Ney, Henry Travers, Reginald Owen, Henry Wilcoxon, Helmut Dantine, Aubrey Mather, Rhys Williams, Tom Conway, Peter Lawford; *D:* William Wyler; *W:* George Froeschel, James Hilton, Arthur Wimperis, Claudine West; *M:* Herbert Stothart. Academy Awards '42: Best Actress (Garson), Best Black and White Cinematography, Best Director (Wyler), Best Picture, Best Screenplay, Best Supporting Actress (Wright); Nominations: Academy Awards '42: Best Actor (Pidgeon), Best Film Editing, Best Sound, Best Supporting Actor (Travers), Best Supporting Actress (Whitty). **VHS, Beta, LV** ★★★★

Mr. & Mrs. Bridge Set in the thirties and forties in Kansas City, Ivory's adaptation of Evan S. Connell's novels painstakingly portrays an upper middle-class family struggling to survive within an emotional vacuum. Newman and Woodward, together for the first time in many years as Walter and Ivory Bridge, bring a wealth of experience and insight to their characterizations. Many consider this to be Newman's best, most subtle and nuanced performance.
1990 (PG-13) 127m/C Joanne Woodward, Paul Newman, Kyra Sedgwick, Blythe Danner, Simon Callow, Diane Kagan, Robert Sean Leonard, Saundra McClain, Margaret Welsh, Austin Pendleton, Gale Garnett, Remak Ramsay; *D:* James Ivory, Tony Pierce-Roberts; *W:* Ruth Prawer Jhabvala. New York Film Critics Awards '90: Best Actress (Woodward), Best Screenplay; Nominations: Academy Awards '90: Best Actress (Woodward). **VHS, LV** ★★★★

Mr. & Mrs. Loving Fact-based cable movie, set in the 1960s, follows the romance, marriage, and struggle of Richard Loving (Hutton) and Mildred "Bean" Jeter (Rochon). Growing up in rural Central Point, Virginia, their interracial relationship isn't considered uncommon. But when Bean gets pregnant, they won't be allowed to marry and live together because of Virginia's racial laws. Instead, the Lovings start a life in Washington, D.C., but desperately homesick and increasingly aware of the civil rights movement, Bean writes a letter to the Attorney General's office. What results is young ACLU lawyer Bernie Cohen (Parker) taking on their case—which eventually leads to a landmark Supreme Court decision about miscegenation laws.
1996 (PG-13) 95m/C Timothy Hutton, Lela Rochon, Corey Parker, Ruby Dee, Isaiah Washington, Bill Nunn, Charles Gray; *D:* Richard Friedenberg; *W:* Richard Friedenberg; *M:* Branford Marsalis. **VHS, LV** ★★★

Mr. & Mrs. Smith Hitchcock's only screwball comedy, an underrated, endearing farce about a bickering but happy modern couple who discover their marriage isn't legitimate and go through courtship all over again. Vintage of its kind, with inspired performances and crackling dialogue.
1941 95m/B Carole Lombard, Robert Montgomery, Gene Raymond, Jack Carson, Lucile Watson, Charles Halton; *D:* Alfred Hitchcock; *W:* Norman Krasna. **VHS, Beta, LV** ★★★1/2

Mr. Arkadin Screenwriter, director, star Welles, adapting from his own novel, gave this plot a dry run on radio during early 1950s. Welles examines the life of yet another ruthless millionaire, but this one can't seem to remember the sordid source of all that cash. Investigator Arden follows the intriguing and descending trail to a surprise ending. As in "Citizen Kane," oblique camera angles and layered dialogue prevail, but this time only serve to confuse the story. Shot over two years around Europe, it required seven years of post production before finding distribution in 1962. *AKA:* Confidential Report.
1955 99m/B *GB* Orson Welles, Akim Tamiroff, Michael Redgrave, Patricia Medina, Mischa Auer; *D:* Orson Welles. **VHS, Beta, LV** ★★★

Mr. Blandings Builds His Dream House Classic comedy features Grant as an adman who tires of city life and moves his family to the country, where his troubles really begin. Grant is at his funniest. Loy and Douglas provide strong backup. A must for all homeowners.
1948 93m/B Cary Grant, Myrna Loy, Melvyn Douglas, Lex Barker, Reginald Denny, Louise Beavers; *D:* H.C. Potter; *W:* Norman Panama. **VHS, Beta, LV** ★★★1/2

Mr. Deeds Goes to Town Typical Capra fare offers Cooper as philanthropic fellow who inherits $20 million and promptly donates it to the needy. He also manages to find time to fall in love with a beautiful reporter. Arthur is the hard-edged reporter determined to fathom the good guy's motivation. Superior entertainment. Based on Clarence Budington Kelland's play "Opera Hut."
1936 118m/B Gary Cooper, Jean Arthur, Raymond Walburn, Walter Catlett, Lionel

Stander, George Bancroft, H.B. Warner, Ruth Donnelly, Douglass Dumbrille, Margaret Seddon, Margaret McWade; **D:** Frank Capra; **W:** Robert Riskin. Academy Awards '36: Best Director (Capra); National Board of Review Awards '36: 10 Best Films of the Year; New York Film Critics Awards '36: Best Film; Nominations: Academy Awards '36: Best Actor (Cooper), Best Picture, Best Screenplay, Best Sound. **VHS, Beta, LV** ★★★1/2

Mr. Hobbs Takes a Vacation Good-natured comedy in which beleagured parents try to resolve family squabbles while the entire brood is on a seaside vacation. Stewart and O'Hara are especially fine and funny as the well-meaning parents. **1962 116m/C** James Stewart, Maureen O'Hara, Fabian, John Saxon, Marie Wilson, John McGiver, Reginald Gardiner; **D:** Henry Koster; **M:** Henry Mancini. Berlin International Film Festival '62: Best Actor (Stewart). **VHS, Beta** ★★★

Mr. Holland's Opus Well-done Disney tearjerker begins in 1965 as musican Glenn Holland (Dreyfuss) takes a teaching job to get himself off the wedding reception circuit and help support his wife, Iris (Headly), and their deaf son. Spanning three decades, with actual newsreel footage thrown in to highlight time passing, Holland sets aside his dream of composing a great symphony and finds his true calling—mentoring and inspiring young minds. Holland's son being deaf might have proved corny, but their rocky relationship is deeply rooted to the storyline. Dreyfuss turns in his most vibrant performance in years and, while sentimental buttons are definitely pushed, director Herek avoids falling into sappiness. **1995 (PG) 142m/C** Richard Dreyfuss, Glenne Headly, Jay Thomas, Olympia Dukakis, William H. Macy, Alicia Witt, Jean Louisa Kelly, Anthony Natale; **D:** Stephen Herek; **W:** Patrick Sheane Duncan; **M:** Michael Kamen. Nominations: Academy Awards '95: Best Actor (Dreyfuss); Golden Globe Awards '95: Best Actor—Drama (Dreyfuss), Best Screenplay. **VHS LV** ★★★

Mr. Hulot's Holiday Superior slapstick details the misadventures of a dullard's seaside holiday. Inventive French comedian Tati at his best. Lighthearted and natural, with magical mime sequences. Followed by "Mon Oncle." **AKA:** Les Vacances de Monsieur Hulot; Monsieur Hulot's Holiday. **1953 86m/B** *FR* Jacques Tati, Natalie Pascaud, Michelle Rolla; **D:** Jacques Tati.

National Board of Review Awards '54: 5 Best Foreign Films of the Year; Nominations: Academy Awards '55: Best Story & Screenplay. **VHS, Beta, LV, 8mm** ★★★1/2

Mr. Klein Cleverly plotted script and fine direction in this dark and intense film about a French-Catholic merchant who buys valuables from Jews trying to escape Nazi occupied France in 1942, paying far less than what the treasures are worth. Ironically, he is later mistaken for a Jew by the same name who has been using this man's reputation as a cover. **1975 (PG) 122m/C** Alain Delon, Jeanne Moreau; **D:** Joseph Losey. Nominations: Cannes Film Festival '76: Best Film. **VHS, Beta** ★★★

Mr. Mom A tireless auto exec loses his job and stays home with the kids while his wife becomes the breadwinner. He's forced to cope with the rigors of housework and child care, resorting to drugs, alcohol and soap operas. Keaton's hilarious as the homebound dad chased by killer appliances and poker buddy to the ladies in the neighborhood. **1983 (PG) 92m/C** Michael Keaton, Teri Garr, Christopher Lloyd, Martin Mull, Ann Jillian, Jeffrey Tambor, Edie McClurg, Valri Bromfield; **D:** Stan Dragoti; **W:** John Hughes. **VHS, Beta, LV** ★★★

Mister Roberts Crew of a Navy cargo freighter in the South Pacific during WWII relieves the boredom of duty with a series of elaborate practical jokes, mostly at the expense of their long-suffering and slightly crazy captain, who then determines that he will get even. The ship's cargo officer, Mr. Roberts, longs to be transferred to a fighting vessel and see some action. Originally a hit Broadway play (based on the novel by Thomas Heggen) which also featured Fonda in the title role. Great performance from Lemmon as Ensign Pulver. Powell's last film. Sequelled in 1964 by "Ensign Pulver," and later a short-lived TV series as well as a live TV special. Newly transferred in 1988 from a pristine stereo print. **1955 120m/C** Henry Fonda, James Cagney, Jack Lemmon, William Powell, Betsy Palmer, Ward Bond, Harry Carey Jr., Nick Adams, Phil Carey, Ken Curtis, Martin Milner, Jack Pennick, Perry Lopez, Patrick Wayne; **D:** John Ford, Mervyn LeRoy; **W:** Frank Nugent, Joshua Logan; **M:** Franz Waxman. Academy Awards '55: Best Supporting Actor (Lemmon); National Board of Review Awards '55: 10 Best Films of the Year; Nominations: Academy Awards

'55: Best Picture, Best Sound. **VHS, Beta**
★★★★

Mr. Skeffington A super-grade soap opera spanning 26 years in the life of a ravishing, spoiled New York socialite. The beauty with a fondness for bedrooms marries for convenience, abuses her husband, then enjoys a highly equitable divorce settlement. Years later when diphtheria leaves her totally deformed and no man will have her, she is saved by her former husband. Based on the novel by "Elizabeth" (Mary Annette Beauchamp Russell) and adapted by "Casablanca"s Julius and Philip Epstein.
1944 147m/B Bette Davis, Claude Rains, Walter Abel, Richard Waring, George Coulouris, John Alexander; **D:** Vincent Sherman. Nominations: Academy Awards '44: Best Actress (Davis), Best Supporting Actor (Rains). **VHS, Beta, LV** ★★★

Mr. Smith Goes to Washington Another classic from Hollywood's golden year of 1939. Jimmy Stewart is an idealistic and naive young man selected to fill in for an ailing Senator. Upon his arrival in the Capitol, he is inundated by a multitude of corrupt politicians. He takes a stand for his beliefs and tries to denounce many of those he feels are unfit for their positions, meeting with opposition from all sides. Great cast is highlighted by Stewart in one of his most endearing performances. Quintessential Capra tale sharply adapted from Lewis Foster's story. Outstanding in every regard.
1939 130m/B James Stewart, Jean Arthur, Edward Arnold, Claude Rains, Thomas Mitchell, Beulah Bondi, Eugene Pallette, Guy Kibbee, Harry Carey Sr., H.B. Warner, Porter Hall, Jack Carson, Charles Lane; **D:** Frank Capra; **W:** Sidney Buchman; **M:** Dimitri Tiomkin. Academy Awards '39: Best Story; National Board of Review Awards '39: 10 Best Films of the Year; New York Film Critics Awards '39: Best Actor (Stewart); Nominations: Academy Awards '39: Best Actor (Stewart), Best Director (Capra), Best Interior Decoration, Best Picture, Best Screenplay, Best Sound, Best Supporting Actor (Rains, Carey), Best Score. **VHS, Beta, LV** ★★★★

Mistress A classic Japanese period piece about an innocent woman who believes she's married to a ruthless industrialist, only to find he is already married and she is but his mistress. Her love for a medical student unleashes tragedy. Subtly moving in a low-key way; starkly beautiful in black and white. In Japanese, with English subtitles. **AKA:** Wild Geese.

1953 106m/B *JP* Hideko Takamine, Hiroshi Akutagawa; **D:** Shiro Toyoda. **VHS, Beta** ★★★

Moana, a Romance of the Golden Age An early look through American eyes at the society of the people of Samoa, in the Pacific Islands. Picturesque successor to Flaherty's "Nanook of the North."
1926 76m/B Ta'avale, Fa'amgase, Moana; **D:** Robert Flaherty. **VHS** ★★★1/2

Moby Dick This adaptation of Herman Melville's high seas saga features Peck as Captain Ahab. His obsession with desire for revenge upon the great white whale, Moby Dick, isn't always believable, but the moments that click, however, make the film more than worthwhile.
1956 116m/C Gregory Peck, Richard Basehart, Orson Welles, Leo Genn, Harry Andrews, Friedrich Ledebur; **D:** John Huston; **W:** Ray Bradbury, John Huston. National Board of Review Awards '56: 10 Best Films of the Year, Best Director (Huston). **VHS, Beta, LV** ★★★

Modern Times This "mostly" silent film finds Chaplin playing a factory worker who goes crazy from his repetitious job on an assembly line and his boss' demands for greater speed and efficiency. Ultimately encompassing the tyranny of machine over man, this cinematic masterpiece has more relevance today than ever. Chaplin wrote the musical score which incorporates the tune "Smile." Look for a young Gloria De Haven as one of Goddard's sisters; she's the real-life daughter of Chaplin's assistant director.
1936 87m/B Charlie Chaplin, Paulette Goddard, Henry Bergman, Stanley Sandford, Gloria De Haven, Chester Conklin; **D:** Charlie Chaplin; **W:** Charlie Chaplin; **M:** Charlie Chaplin. National Board of Review Awards '36: 10 Best Films of the Year. **VHS, Beta, LV** ★★★★

Mogambo Remake of "Red Dust," this is the steamy story of a love triangle between an African game hunter, a proper British lady, and an American showgirl in the jungles of Kenya.
1953 115m/C Clark Gable, Ava Gardner, Grace Kelly; **D:** John Ford. Golden Globe Awards '54: Best Supporting Actress (Kelly); National Board of Review Awards '53: 10 Best Films of the Year; Nominations: Academy Awards '53: Best Actress (Gardner), Best Supporting Actress (Kelly). **VHS, Beta** ★★★

Mon Oncle Tati's celebrated comedy contrasts the simple life of Monsieur

Hulot with the technologically complicated life of his family when he aids his nephew in war against his parents' ultramodern, push-button home. An easygoing, delightful comedy, this is the director's first piece in color. Sequel to "Mr. Hulot's Holiday," followed by "Playtime." In French with English subtitles. **AKA:** My Uncle; My Uncle, Mr. Hulot.

1958 110m/C *FR* Jacques Tati, Jean-Pierre Zola, Adrienne Serrantie, Alain Bacourt; *D:* Jacques Tati. Academy Awards '58: Best Foreign Language Film; Cannes Film Festival '58: Grand Jury Prize; National Board of Review Awards '58: 5 Best Foreign Films of the Year; New York Film Critics Awards '58: Best Foreign Film. **VHS, Beta, LV, 8mm ★★★★**

Mon Oncle D'Amerique Three French characters are followed as they try to find success of varying kinds in Paris, interspersed with ironic lectures about Prof. Henri Laborit about the biology that impels human behavior. Their disappointments lead them to dream of a legendary American uncle, who could make their desires come true. An acclaimed, witty comedy by former Nouvelle Vague filmmaker, dubbed into English. **AKA:** Les Somnambules.

1980 (PG) 123m/C *FR* Gerard Depardieu, Nicole Garcia, Roger-Pierre, Marie DuBois; *D:* Alain Resnais; *W:* Jean Gruault. Cannes Film Festival '80: Grand Jury Prize; New York Film Critics Awards '80: Best Foreign Film; Nominations: Academy Awards '80: Best Original Screenplay; Cannes Film Festival '80: Best Film. **VHS, Beta ★★★1/2**

Mona Lisa Jordan's wonderful, sad, sensitive story of a romantic, small-time hood who gets personally involved with the welfare and bad company of the high-priced whore he's been hired to chauffeur. Hoskins is especially touching and Caine is chilling as a suave gangster. Fine film debut for Tyson. Brilliantly filmed and critically lauded.

1986 (R) 104m/C *GB* Bob Hoskins, Cathy Tyson, Michael Caine, Clarke Peters, Kate Hardie, Robbie Coltrane, Zoe Nathenson, Sammi Davis, Rod Bedall, Joe Brown, Pauline Melville; *D:* Neil Jordan; *W:* Neil Jordan; *M:* Michael Kamen. British Academy Awards '86: Best Actor (Hoskins); Cannes Film Festival '86: Best Actor (Hoskins); Golden Globe Awards '87: Best Actor—Drama (Hoskins); Los Angeles Film Critics Association Awards '86: Best Actor (Hoskins), Best Supporting Actress (Tyson); National Society of Film Critics Awards '86: Best Actor (Hoskins);

Nominations: Academy Awards '86: Best Actor (Hoskins). **VHS, Beta, LV ★★★★**

Monkey Business Marx Brothers run amok as stowaways on ocean liner. Fast-paced comedy provides seemingly endless amount of gags, quips, and pratfalls, including the fab four imitating Maurice Chevalier at Immigration. This film, incidentally, was the group's first to be written—by noted humorist Perelman—directly for the screen.

1931 77m/B Groucho Marx, Harpo Marx, Chico Marx, Zeppo Marx, Thelma Todd, Ruth Hall, Harry Woods; *D:* Norman Z. McLeod. **VHS, Beta, LV ★★★1/2**

Monkey Business A scientist invents a fountain-of-youth potion, a lab chimpanzee mistakenly dumps it into a water cooler, and then grown-ups start turning into adolescents. Top-flight crew occasionally labors in this screwball comedy, though comic moments shine. Monroe is the secretary sans skills, while absent-minded Grant and sexy wife Rogers race hormonally as teens.

1952 97m/B Cary Grant, Ginger Rogers, Charles Coburn, Marilyn Monroe, Hugh Marlowe, Larry Keating, George Winslow; *D:* Howard Hawks; *W:* Ben Hecht, Charles Lederer, I.A.L. Diamond. **VHS, Beta, LV ★★★**

Monsieur Beaucaire Entertaining Hope vehicle that casts him as a barber impersonating a French nobleman in the court of Louis XV. He's set to wed a Spanish princess in order to prevent a full-scale war from taking place. However, he really wants to marry social-climber chambermaid Caulfield. Director Marshall was at his best here. Based on the novel by Booth Tarkington.

1946 93m/B Bob Hope, Joan Caulfield, Patric Knowles, Marjorie Reynolds, Cecil Kellaway, Joseph Schildkraut, Reginald Owen, Constance Collier; *D:* George Marshall; *W:* Melvin Frank, Norman Panama. **VHS ★★★**

Monsieur Hire The usual tale of sexual obsesssion and suspense. Mr. Hire spends much of his time trying to spy on his beautiful young female neighbor, alternately alienated and engaged by her love affairs. The voyeur soon finds his secret desires have entangled him in a vicious intrigue. Political rally set-piece is brilliant. Excellent acting, intense pace, elegant photography. Based on "Les Fiancailles de M. Hire" by Georges Simenone and adapted by Leconte and Patrick Dewolf. In French with English subtitles. **AKA:** M. Hire.

1989 (PG-13) 81m/C *FR* Michel Blanc, Sandrine Bonnaire, Luc Thuillier, Eric Berenger, Andre Wilms; **D:** Patrice Leconte; **W:** Patrice Leconte. Cesar Awards '90: Best Sound. VHS, LV ★★★1/2

Monsieur Verdoux A thorough Chaplin effort, as he produced, directed, wrote, scored and starred. A prim and proper bank cashier in Paris marries and murders rich women in order to support his real wife and family. A mild scandal in its day, though second-thought pacifism and stale humor date it. A bomb upon release (leading Chaplin to shelve it for 17 years) and a cult item today, admired for both its flaws and complexity. Raye fearlessly chews scenery and croissants. Initially based upon a suggestion from Orson Welles.
1947 123m/B Charlie Chaplin, Martha Raye, Isobel Elsom, Mady Correll, Marilyn Nash, Irving Bacon, William Frawley, Allison Roddan, Robert Lewis; **D:** Charlie Chaplin; **W:** Charlie Chaplin. National Board of Review Awards '47: 10 Best Films of the Year; Nominations: Academy Awards '47: Best Original Screenplay. VHS, Beta, LV ★★★

The Monster This silent horror film has all the elements that would become genre standards. A mad scientist (Chaney), working in an asylum filled with lunatics, abducts strangers to use in his fiendish experiments to bring the dead back to life. There's the obligatory dungeon and even a lovely heroine that needs rescuing. Great atmosphere and Chaney's usual spine-tingling performance.
1925 86m/B Lon Chaney Sr., Gertrude Olmsted, Johnny Arthur, Charles Sellon; **D:** Roland West. VHS ★★★

Monterey Pop This pre-Woodstock rock 'n' roll festival in Monterey, California features landmark performances by some of the most popular sixties rockers. Compelling for the performances, and historically important as the first significant rock concert film. Appearances by Jefferson Airplane, Janis Joplin, Jimi Hendrix, Simon and Garfunkel, The Who, and Otis Redding.
1968 72m/C VHS, Beta, LV, 8mm ★★★1/2

A Month by the Lake Redgrave takes the plunge into romantic comedy in "Lake," and glides effortlessly through this delightful adaptation of an H.E. Bates short story. Set in pre-WWII northern Italy, Miss Bentley (Redgrave) sets her spinster's eye on the somewhat wooden, but gradually warming, English Major Wilshaw

(Fox). Thurman, thoroughly petulant as an American nanny, arrives to provide an arresting diversion for Wilshaw, while Gassman proves an unwitting pawn for Miss Bentley's game of "get the major." Touching and lighthearted performances, especially by heavyweight Redgrave, are complemented by glorious cinematography.
1995 (PG) 94m/C Vanessa Redgrave, Edward Fox, Uma Thurman, Alida Valli, Alessandro Gassman, Carlo Cartier; **D:** John Irvin; **W:** Trevor Bentham; **M:** Nicola Piovani, Pasqualino de Santis. Nominations: Golden Globe Awards '96: Best Actress—Musical/Comedy (Redgrave). VHS ★★★

Monty Python and the Holy Grail Britain's famed comedy band assaults the Arthurian legend in a cult classic replete with a Trojan rabbit and an utterly dismembered, but inevitably pugnacious, knight. Fans of manic comedy—and graphic violence—should get more than their fill here.
1975 (PG) 90m/C *GB* Graham Chapman, John Cleese, Terry Gilliam, Eric Idle, Terry Jones, Michael Palin, Carol Cleveland, Connie Booth, Neil Innes, Patsy Kensit; **D:** Terry Gilliam, Terry Jones; **W:** Graham Chapman, John Cleese, Terry Gilliam, Eric Idle, Terry Jones, Michael Palin. VHS, Beta, LV, 8mm ★★★1/2

Monty Python Live at the Hollywood Bowl The revered comedy group perform many of their most celebrated routines in this uproarious performance documentary. A must-see for all Python aficionados.
1982 78m/C *GB* Eric Idle, Michael Palin, John Cleese, Terry Gilliam, Terry Jones, Graham Chapman; **D:** Terry Hughes; **W:** John Cleese, Terry Gilliam; **M:** John Du Prez. VHS, Beta, LV ★★★

Monty Python's Life of Brian Often riotous spoof of Christianity tracks hapless peasant mistaken for the messiah in 32 A.D. Film reels from routine to routine, and only the most pious will remain unmoved by a chorus of crucifixion victims. Probably the group's most daring, controversial venture. *AKA:* Life of Brian.
1979 (R) 94m/C *GB* Graham Chapman, John Cleese, Terry Gilliam, Eric Idle, Michael Palin, George Harrison, Terry Jones; **D:** Terry Jones; **W:** Graham Chapman, John Cleese, Terry Gilliam, Eric Idle, Michael Palin, Terry Jones; **M:** Geoffrey Burgon. VHS, Beta, LV ★★★1/2

The Moon and Sixpence Stockbroker turns ambitious painter in this adaptation of W. Somerset Maugham's novel that was, in turn,

inspired by the life of artist Paul Gauguin. Fine performance from Sanders. Filmed mainly in black and white, but uses color sparingly to great advantage. Compare this one to "Wolf at the Door," in which Gauguin is played by Donald Sutherland.
1943 89m/B George Sanders, Herbert Marshall, Steve Geray, Doris Dudley, Eric Blore, Elena Verdugo, Florence Bates, Albert Basserman, Heather Thatcher; **D:** Albert Lewin. Nominations: Academy Awards '43: Best Original Score. **VHS** ★★★

Moonlighting Compelling drama about Polish laborers illegally hired to renovate London flat. When their country falls under martial law, the foreman conceals the event and pushes workers to complete project. Unlikely casting of Irons as foreman is utterly successful.
1982 (PG) 97m/C *PL GB* Jeremy Irons, Eugene Lipinski, Jiri Stanislay, Eugeniusz Haczkiewicz; **D:** Jerzy Skolimowski; **M:** Hans Zimmer, Tony Pierce-Roberts. Nominations: Cannes Film Festival '82: Best Film. **VHS, Beta, LV** ★★★1/2

Moonstruck Winning romantic comedy about widow engaged to one man but falling in love with his younger brother in Little Italy. Excellent performances all around, with Cher particularly fetching as attractive, hapless widow. Unlikely casting of usually dominating Aiello, as unassuming mama's boy also works well, and Cage is at his best as a tormented one-handed opera lover/baker.
1987 (PG-13) 103m/C Cher, Nicolas Cage, Olympia Dukakis, Danny Aiello, Vincent Gardenia, Julie Bovasso, Louis Guss, Anita Gillette, Feodor Chaliapin Jr, John Mahoney; **D:** Norman Jewison; **W:** John Patrick Shanley. Academy Awards '87: Best Actress (Cher), Best Original Screenplay, Best Supporting Actress (Dukakis); Golden Globe Awards '88: Best Actress—Musical/Comedy (Cher), Best Supporting Actress (Dukakis); National Board of Review Awards '87: Best Supporting Actress (Dukakis); Writers Guild of America '87: Best Original Screenplay; Nominations: Academy Awards '87: Best Director (Jewison), Best Picture, Best Supporting Actor (Gardenia). **VHS, Beta, LV** ★★★1/2

The More the Merrier Likeable romantic comedy in which working girl must share apartment with two bachelors in Washington, D.C., during WWII. Arthur is especially endearing as a young woman in male company.
1943 104m/B Joel McCrea, Jean Arthur,

Charles Coburn, Richard Gaines, Bruce (Herman Brix) Bennett, Ann Savage, Ann Doran, Frank Tully, Grady Sutton; **D:** George Stevens. Academy Awards '43: Best Supporting Actor (Coburn); New York Film Critics Awards '43: Best Director (Stevens); Nominations: Academy Awards '43: Best Actress (Arthur), Best Director (Stevens), Best Picture, Best Story. **VHS, Beta, LV** ★★★

Morocco A foreign legion soldier falls for a world-weary chanteuse along the desert sands. Cooper has never been more earnest, and Dietrich has never been more blase and exotic. In her American film debut, Dietrich sings "What am I Bid?" A must for anyone drawn to improbable, gloriously well-done kitsch. Based on Benno Vigny's novel, "Amy Jolly."
1930 92m/B Marlene Dietrich, Gary Cooper, Adolphe Menjou, Ullrich Haupt, Francis McDonald, Eve Southern, Paul Porcasi; **D:** Josef von Sternberg. Nominations: Academy Awards '31: Best Actress (Dietrich), Best Cinematography, Best Director (von Sternberg), Best Interior Decoration. **VHS, Beta, LV** ★★★1/2

The Mortal Storm Phyllis Bottome's famous novel comes to life in this extremely well acted film about the rise of the Nazi regime. Stewart and Sullavan are young lovers who risk everything to escape the country after their families are torn apart by the Nazi takeover. Although Germany is never identified as the country, it is obvious in this story about the early days of WWII. Hitler took one look at this and promptly banned all MGM movies in Nazi Germany.
1940 100m/B Margaret Sullavan, James Stewart, Robert Young, Frank Morgan, Robert Stack, Bonita Granville, Irene Rich; **D:** Frank Borzage; **W:** Claudine West, George Froeschel, Anderson Ellis. **VHS** ★★★1/2

Moscow Does Not Believe in Tears Three Soviet women realize very different fates when they pursue their dreams in 1950s Moscow. Bittersweet, moving fare that seems a somewhat surprising production from pre-Glasnost USSR. Brief nudity and violence. In Russian with English subtitles. A 150-minute version has also been released. *AKA:* Moscow Distrusts Tears; Moskwa Sljesam Nje Jerit.
1980 115m/C *RU* Vera Alentova, Irina Muravyova, Raisa Ryazanova, Natalie Vavilova, Alexei Batalov; **D:** Vladimir Menshov. Academy Awards '80: Best Foreign Language Film. **VHS, Beta, LV** ★★★

Mother Pudovkin's innovative classic about a Russian family shattered by the uprising in 1905. A masterpiece of Russian cinema that established Pudovkin, and rivaled only Eisenstein for supremacy in montage, poetic imagery, and propagandistic ideals. Based on Maxim Gorky's great novel, it's one of cinematic history's seminal works. Striking cinematography, stunning use of montage make this one important. Silent with English subtitles.
1926 70m/B *RU* Vera Baranovskaya, Nikolai Batalov; *D:* Vsevolod Pudovkin. **VHS, Beta** ★★★1/2

Mother A Japanese family is undone after the devastation of WWII. An uncharacteristically dramatic, and thus more accessible, film from one of the Japanese cinema's greatest masters. In Japanese with English subtitles. *AKA:* Okasan.
1952 98m/B *JP* Kinuyo Tanaka, Kyoko Kagawa, Eiji Okada, Akihiko Katayama; *D:* Mikio Naruse. **VHS, Beta, LV** ★★★1/2

Mother Kusters Goes to Heaven Mrs. Kusters's husband is a frustrated factory worker who goes over the edge and kills the factory owner's son and himself. Left alone, she learns that everyone is using her husband's death to further their own needs, including her daughter, who uses the publicity to enhance her singing career. A statement that you should trust no one, not even your family and friends. This film was banned from the Berlin Film Festival because of its political overtones. In German with English subtitles. *AKA:* Mutter Kusters Fahrt Zum Himmel.
1976 108m/C *GE* Brigitte Mira, Ingrid Caven, Armin Meier, Irm Hermann, Gottfried John, Margit Carstensen, Michael Ballhaus; *D:* Rainer Werner Fassbinder; *W:* Rainer Werner Fassbinder. **VHS** ★★★

Mothra Classic Japanese monster shenanigans about an enraged giant caterpillar that invades Tokyo while searching for the Alilenas, a set of very tiny, twin princesses who've been kidnapped by an evil nightclub owner in the pursuit of big profits. After tiring of crushing buildings and wreaking incidental havoc, the enormous crawly thing zips up into a cocoon and emerges as Mothra, a moth distinguished by both its size and bad attitude. Mothra and the wee babes make appearances in later Godzilla epics.
1962 101m/C *JP* Yumi Ito, Frankie Sakai, Lee Kresel, Emi Ito; *D:* Inoshiro Honda. **VHS, Beta** ★★★

Mouchette A lonely 14-year-old French girl, daughter of a drunk father and dying mother, eventually finds spiritual release by committing suicide. Typically somber, spiritual fare from unique master filmmaker Bresson. Perhaps the most complete expression of Bresson's austere, Catholic vision. In French with English subtitles.
1960 80m/B *FR* Nadine Nortier, Maria Cardinal, Paul Hebert; *D:* Robert Bresson. **VHS, Beta** ★★★1/2

Moulin Rouge Colorful, entertaining portrait of acclaimed Impressionist painter Toulouse-Lautrec, more famous for its production stories than on-screen drama, Ferrer delivers one of his most impressive performances as the physically stunted, cynical artist who basked in the seamy Montmartre nightlife.
1952 119m/C Jose Ferrer, Zsa Zsa Gabor, Christopher Lee, Peter Cushing, Colette Marchand, Katherine Kath, Michael Balfour, Eric Pohlmann; *D:* John Huston. Academy Awards '52: Best Art Direction/Set Decoration (Color), Best Costume Design (Color); National Board of Review Awards '53: 5 Best Foreign Films of the Year; Nominations: Academy Awards '52: Best Actor (Ferrer), Best Director (Huston), Best Film Editing, Best Picture, Best Supporting Actress (Marchand). **VHS, Beta, LV** ★★★1/2

Mountains of the Moon Sprawling adventure detailing the obsessive search for the source of the Nile conducted by famed Victorian rogue/explorer Sir Richard Burton and cohort John Hanning Speke in the late 1800s. Spectacular scenery and images. Director Rafelson, better known for overtly personal films such as "Five Easy Pieces" and "The King of Marvin Gardens," shows considerable skill with this epic. Cinematography by Roger Deakins. From William Harrison's novel "Burton and Speke."
1990 (R) 140m/C Patrick Bergin, Iain Glen, Fiona Shaw, Richard E. Grant, Peter Vaughan, Roger Rees, Bernard Hill, Anna Massey, Leslie Phillips, John Savident, James Villiers, Delroy Lindo, Roshan Seth, Roger Deakins; *D:* Bob Rafelson; *W:* Bob Rafelson. **VHS, Beta, LV** ★★★1/2

The Mouse That Roared With its wine export business going down the drain, a tiny, desperate country decides to declare war on the United States in hopes that the U.S., after its inevitable triumph, will revive the conquered nation. So off to New York go 20 chain-mail clad warriors armed with bow and arrow. Featured in three roles, Sellers is great as the duchess, less effective (though still funny) as the prime minister, and a military leader. A must for Sellers' fans; maintains a sharp satiric edge throughout. Based on the novel by Leonard Wibberley.

1959 83m/C *GB* Peter Sellers, Jean Seberg, Leo McKern, David Kossoff, William Hartnell, Timothy Bateson, MacDonald Parke, Monte Landis; *D:* Jack Arnold; *W:* Roger MacDougall, Stanley Mann; *M:* Edwin Astley. **VHS, Beta ★★★**

Much Ado about Nothing Shakespeare for the masses details romance between two sets of would-be lovers—the battling Beatrice and Benedick (Thompson and Branagh) and the ingenuous Hero and Claudio (Beckinsale and Leonard). Washington is the noble warrior leader, Reeves his evil half-dressed half-brother, and Keaton serves comic relief as the officious, bumbling Dogberry. Sunlit, lusty, and revealing about all the vagaries of love, Branagh brings passion to his quest of making Shakespeare more approachable. His second attempt after "Henry V" at breaking the stuffy Shakespearean tradition. Filmed on location in Tuscany, Italy.

1993 (PG-13) 110m/C *GB* Kenneth Branagh, Emma Thompson, Robert Sean Leonard, Kate Beckinsale, Denzel Washington, Keanu Reeves, Michael Keaton, Brian Blessed, Phyllida Law, Imelda Staunton, Gerard Horan, Jimmy Yuill, Richard Clifford, Ben Elton; *D:* Kenneth Branagh; *W:* Kenneth Branagh; *M:* Patrick Doyle. Nominations: Cannes Film Festival '93: Best Film; Golden Globe Awards '94: Best Film—Musical/Comedy; Independent Spirit Awards '94: Best Actress (Thompson), Best Film. **VHS, LV ★★★1/2**

The Mummy Eerie chills mark this classic horror tale of an Egyptian priest, buried alive nearly 4,000 years earlier, who comes back to life after a 1921 archaeological dig. Eight hours of extraordinary makeup transformed Karloff into the macabre mummy, who believes the soul of his long-deceased (and probably long-decayed) lover resides in the body of a young woman. Marked the directing debut of famed German cinematographer Freund.

1932 72m/B Boris Karloff, Zita Johann, David Manners, Edward Van Sloan; *D:* Karl Freund. **VHS, Beta, LV ★★★1/2**

The Mummy A group of British archaeologists discover they have made a grave mistake when a mummy kills off those who have violated his princess' tomb. A summation of all the previous "mummy" films, this one has a more frightening mummy (6'4" Lee) who is on screen much of the time. Additionally, there is pathos in this monster, not merely murder and revenge. An effective remake of the 1932 classic.

1959 88m/C *GB* Peter Cushing, Christopher Lee, Felix Aylmer, Yvonne Furneaux; *D:* Terence Fisher; *W:* Jimmy Sangster. **VHS, Beta, LV ★★★**

The Muppet Movie Seeking fame and footlights, Kermit the Frog and his pal Fozzie Bear travel to Hollywood, and along the way are joined by sundry human and muppet characters, including the lovely Miss Piggy. A delightful cult favorite filled with entertaining cameos, memorable (though somewhat pedestrian) songs and crafty special effects—Kermit rides a bike and rows a boat! A success for the late Jim Henson. ♫ The Rainbow Connection; Frog's Legs So Fine; Movin' Right Along; Can You Picture That?; Never Before; Something Better; This Looks Familiar; I'm Going Back There Someday.

1979 (G) 94m/C *GB* Jim Henson's Muppets; *Cameos:* Edgar Bergen, Milton Berle, Mel Brooks, Madeline Kahn, Steve Martin, Carol Kane, Paul Williams, Charles Durning, Bob Hope, James Coburn, Dom DeLuise, Elliott Gould, Cloris Leachman, Telly Savalas, Orson Welles; *D:* James Frawley; *W:* Jack Burns; *M:* Paul Williams; *V:* Jim Henson, Frank Oz. Nominations: Academy Awards '79: Best Song ("The Rainbow Connection"), Best Original Score. **VHS, Beta, LV ★★★1/2**

The Muppets Take Manhattan Following a smashing success with a college musical, the Muppets take their show and talents to Broadway, only to face misfortune in the form of an unscrupulous producer. A less imaginative script than the first two Muppet movies, yet an enjoyable experience with numerous major stars making cameo appearances.

1984 (G) 94m/C Jim Henson's Muppets; *Cameos:* Dabney Coleman, James Coco, Art Carney, Joan Rivers, Gregory Hines, Linda Lavin, Liza Minnelli, Brooke Shields, John Landis; *D:* Frank Oz; *M:* Ralph Burns; *V:* Jim Henson, Frank Oz. Nominations: Academy Awards '84: Best Original Score. **VHS, Beta, LV ★★★**

Murder Believing in a young woman's innocence, one jurist begins to organize the pieces of the crime in order to save her. Fine early effort by Hitchcock based on play "Enter Sir

John," by Clemense Dane and Helen Simpson.

1930 92m/B *GB* Herbert Marshall, Nora Baring, Phyllis Konstam, Miles Mander; *D:* Alfred Hitchcock; *W:* Alfred Hitchcock. **VHS, Beta ★★★**

Murder at the Gallop Snooping Miss Marple doesn't believe a filthy rich old-timer died of natural causes, despite the dissenting police point of view. Wheedling her way into the police investigation, she discovers the secret of the Gallop club, a place where people bounce up and down on top of horses. Much mugging between Dame Margaret and Morley. Marple's assistant, Mr. Stringer, is the real life Mr. Dame Margaret. Based on Christie's Poirot mystery "After the Funeral."

1963 81m/B Margaret Rutherford, Robert Morley, Flora Robson, Charles Tingwell, Duncan Lamont; *D:* George Pollock. **VHS, Beta ★★★1/2**

Murder, My Sweet Down-on-his-luck private detective Philip Marlowe (Powell) searches for an ex-convict's missing girlfriend through a dark world of murder, mayhem and ever-twisting directions. Classic film noir screen version of Raymond Chandler's tense novel "Farewell, My Lovely," which employs flashback fashion using that crisp Chandler narrative. A breakthrough dramatically for singer Powell; Chandler's favorite version. Remade using the novel's title in 1975. *AKA:* Farewell, My Love.

1944 95m/B Dick Powell, Claire Trevor, Mike Mazurki, Otto Kruger, Anne Shirley, Miles Mander; *D:* Edward Dmytryk. Edgar Allan Poe Awards '45: Best Screenplay. **VHS, Beta, LV ★★★1/2**

The Murder of Mary Phagan Lemmon stars as John Slaton, governor of Georgia during one of America's most notorious miscarriages of justice. In 1913, timid, Jewish factory manager Leo Frank is accused of the brutal murder of a female worker. Prejudice and a power hungry prosecuting attorney conspire to seal the man's fate at the end of the hangman's noose. Sensing the injustice, Slaton re-opens the case, causing riots in Atlanta. Top notch television drama, featuring a superb re-creation of turn of the century atmosphere and a compelling, true story which was not finally resolved until the 1970s.

1987 (PG) 251m/C Jack Lemmon, Peter Gallagher, Richard Jordan, Robert Prosky, Paul Dooley, Rebecca Miller, Kathryn Walker, Charles S. Dutton, Kevin Spacey, Wendy J. Cooke; *D:* Billy Hale; *M:* Maurice Jarre. **VHS ★★★1/2**

Murder on the Orient Express An Agatha Christie mystery lavishly produced with an all-star cast. In 1934, a trainful of suspects and one murder victim make the trip from Istanbul to Calais especially interesting. Supersleuth Hercule Poirot sets out to solve the mystery. An entertaining whodunit, ably supported by the remarkable cast. Followed by "Death on the Nile."

1974 (PG) 128m/C *GB* Albert Finney, Martin Balsam, Ingrid Bergman, Lauren Bacall, Sean Connery, Richard Widmark, Anthony Perkins, John Gielgud, Jacqueline Bisset, Jean-Pierre Cassel, Wendy Hiller, Rachel Roberts, Vanessa Redgrave, Michael York, Colin Blakely, George Coulouris; *D:* Sidney Lumet; *M:* Richard Rodney Bennett. Academy Awards '74: Best Supporting Actress (Bergman); British Academy Awards '74: Best Supporting Actor (Gielgud), Best Supporting Actress (Bergman); Nominations: Academy Awards '74: Best Actor (Finney), Best Adapted Screenplay, Best Cinematography, Best Costume Design, Best Original Score. **VHS, Beta, LV ★★★**

Murderers among Us: The Simon Wiesenthal Story Powerful re-enactment of concentration camp survivor Simon Wiesenthal's search for war criminals. Kingsley's gripping performance drives this made-for-cable film. Be prepared for disturbing death camp scenes.

1989 157m/C Ben Kingsley, Renee Soutendijk, Craig T. Nelson, Paul Freeman, Louisa Haigh, Jack Shepherd; *D:* Brian Gibson; *W:* Abby Mann; *M:* Bill Conti. **VHS ★★★**

The Murders in the Rue Morgue The fifth filmed version of the Edgar Allan Poe story. Set in 19th-century Paris; actors in a mystery play find their roles coming to life. Scott is terrific, with good supporting help. Made for television.

1986 (PG) 92m/C George C. Scott, Rebecca DeMornay, Val Kilmer, Ian McShane, Neil Dickson; *D:* Jeannot Szwarc. **VHS ★★★**

Muriel A complex, mosaic drama about a middle-aged woman who meets an old lover at Boulogne, and her stepson who cannot forget the needless suffering he caused a young woman named Muriel while he was a soldier at war. Throughout, director Alain Resnais plumbs the essential meanings of memory, age, and the anxieties created from the tension between personal and public actions.

Acclaimed; in French with English subtitles. *AKA:* Muriel, Ou le Temps d'Un Retour; The Time of Return; Muriel, Or the Time of Return. **1963** 115m/C *FR IT* Delphine Seyrig, Jean-Pierre Kerien, Nita Klein, Jean-Baptiste Thierree; *D:* Alain Resnais; *M:* Georges Delerue. Venice Film Festival '63: Best Actress (Seyrig). **VHS, Beta ★★★1/2**

Muriel's Wedding Muriel (Collette) can catch a bridal bouquet, but can she catch a husband? Her blonde, bitch-goddess friends don't think so. But dowdy, pathetic, overweight Muriel dreams of a fairy-tale wedding anyway. How she fulfills her obsessive fantasy is the basis for this quirky, hilarious, and often touchingly poignant ugly duckling tale with the occasional over-the-top satiric moment. Strong cast is led by sympathetic and engaging performances from Collette (who gained 40-plus pounds for the role) and Griffiths as her best friend, Rhonda. '70s pop supergroup ABBA lends its kitschy but catchy tunes to the plot and soundtrack. Not released in the U.S. until 1995. **1994** (R) 105m/C *AU* Toni Collette, Bill Hunter, Rachel Griffiths, Jeanie Drynan, Gennie Nevinson Brice, Matt Day, Daniel Lapaine; *D:* P.J. Hogan; *W:* P.J. Hogan; *M:* Peter Best. Australian Film Institute '94: Best Actress (Collette), Best Film, Best Sound, Best Supporting Actress (Griffiths); Nominations: Australian Film Institute '94: Best Director (Hogan), Best Screenplay, Best Supporting Actor (Hunter), Best Supporting Actress (Drynan); Golden Globe Awards '96: Best Actress— Musical/Comedy (Collette); Writers Guild of America '95: Best Original Screenplay. **VHS, LV ★★★**

Murmur of the Heart Honest treatment of a 14-year-old boy's coming of age. After his older brothers take him to a prostitute for his first sexual experience, he comes down with scarlet fever. He then travels to a health spa with his mother to recover. There they find that their mother-son bond is stronger than most. Music by Charlie Parker is featured in the score. In French with English subtitles. **1971** (R) 118m/C *FR* Benoit Ferreux, Daniel Gelin, Lea Massari, Corinne Kersten, Jacqueline Chauveau, Marc Wincourt, Michael Lonsdale; *D:* Louis Malle; *W:* Louis Malle. Nominations: Academy Awards '72: Best Story & Screenplay; Cannes Film Festival '71: Best Film. **VHS, Beta, LV ★★★1/2**

The Music Man Con man in the guise of a traveling salesman gets off the train in River City, Iowa. After hearing about plans to build a pool hall, he argues it would be the gateway to hell for the young, impressionable males of the town. He then convinces the River Cityians to look toward the future of the community and finance a wholesome children's marching band. Although the huckster plans to take their money and run before the instruments arrive, his feelings for the town librarian cause him to think twice about fleeing the Heartland. This isn't just a slice of Americana; it's a whole pie. Acting and singing are terrific "with a capital 'T' and that rhymes with 'P' and that stands for" Preston, who epitomizes the charismatic pitchman. ♪ Seventy-six Trombones; Trouble; If You Don't Mind My Saying So; Till There Was You; The Wells Fargo Wagon; Being in Love; Goodnight, My Someone; Rock Island; Iowa Stubborn. **1962** (G) 151m/C Robert Preston, Shirley Jones, Buddy Hackett, Hermione Gingold, Paul Ford, Pert Kelton, Ron Howard; *D:* Morton DaCosta; *W:* Marion Hargrove. Academy Awards '62: Best Adapted Score; Golden Globe Awards '63: Best Film— Musical/Comedy; Nominations: Academy Awards '62: Best Art Direction/Set Decoration (Color), Best Costume Design (Color), Best Film Editing, Best Picture, Best Sound. **VHS, Beta, LV ★★★★**

Mutiny on the Bounty Compelling adaptation of the true story of sadistic Captain Bligh, Fletcher Christian, and their turbulent journey aboard the HMS Bounty. No gray here: Laughton's Bligh is truly a despicable character and extremely memorable in this MGM extravaganza. Remade twice, in 1962 and again in 1984 as "The Bounty." Much, much better than the 1962 remake. **1935** 132m/B Clark Gable, Franchot Tone, Charles Laughton, Donald Crisp, Dudley Digges, Spring Byington, Henry Stephenson, Eddie Quillan, Herbert Mundin, Movita, Ian Wolfe; *D:* Frank Lloyd; *W:* Talbot Jennings, Jules Furthman, Carey Wilson; *M:* Herbert Stothart. Academy Awards '35: Best Picture; National Board of Review Awards '35: 10 Best Films of the Year; New York Film Critics Awards '35: Best Actor (Laughton); Nominations: Academy Awards '35: Best Actor (Gable), Best Actor (Tone, Laughton), Best Adapted Screenplay, Best Director (Lloyd), Best Film Editing, Best Score. **VHS, Beta, LV, 8mm ★★★★**

My Beautiful Laundrette Omar (Warnecke), the nephew of a Pakistani businessman, is given the opportunity to better himself by turning his

uncle's run-down laundry into a profitable business. He reunites with Johnny (Day-Lewis), a childhood friend and a working-class street punk, and they go into the business together. They find themselves battling the prejudice of each other's families and friends in order to succeed. An intelligent look at sexuality, race relations, and economic problems of Thatcher's London. Great performances by a relatively unknown cast (for contrast, note Day-Lewis' performance in "Room with a View," released in the same year.)
1985 (R) 93m/C Gordon Warnecke, Daniel Day-Lewis, Saeed Jaffrey, Roshan Seth, Shirley Anne Field, Derrick Branche; **D:** Stephen Frears; **W:** Hanif Kureishi; **M:** Ludus Tonalis. National Board of Review Awards '86: Best Supporting Actor (Day-Lewis); New York Film Critics Awards '86: Best Screenplay, Best Supporting Actor (Day-Lewis); Nominations: Academy Awards '86: Best Original Screenplay. **VHS, Beta, LV** ★★★

My Brilliant Career A headstrong young woman spurns the social expectations of turn-of-the-century Australia and pursues opportunities to broaden her intellect and preserve her independence. Davis is wonderful as the energetic and charismatic community trendsetter. Based on an autobiographical novel by Miles Franklin which has been marvelously transferred to the screen. Armstrong deserves credit for her fine direction.
1979 (G) 101m/C *AU* Judy Davis, Sam Neill, Wendy Hughes; **D:** Gillian Armstrong. Australian Film Institute '79: Best Film; British Academy Awards '80: Best Actress (Davis); Nominations: Academy Awards '80: Best Costume Design; Cannes Film Festival '79: Best Film. **VHS, Beta** ★★★1/2

My Cousin Vinny Vinny Gambini (Pesci), a lawyer who took the bar exam six times before passing, goes to Wahzoo City, Alabama to get his cousin and a friend off the hook when they're accused of killing a store clerk. Leather jackets, gold chains, Brooklyn accents, and his fiancee Tomei's penchant for big hair and bold clothing don't go over well with conservative judge Gwynne, causing plenty of misunderstandings. Surprising hit with simplistic story reaches popular heights via entertaining performances by the entire cast. Tomei in particular steals every scene she's in and has an Oscar to prove it.
1992 (R) 120m/C Joe Pesci, Ralph Macchio, Marisa Tomei, Mitchell Whitfield, Fred Gwynne, Lane Smith, Austin

Pendleton, Bruce McGill; **D:** Jonathan Lynn; **W:** Dale Launer; **M:** Randy Edelman. Academy Awards '92: Best Supporting Actress (Tomei); MTV Movie Awards '93: Breakthrough Performance (Tomei). **VHS** ★★★

My Darling Clementine One of the best Hollywood westerns ever made, this recounts the precise events leading up to and including the gunfight at the O.K. Corral. Ford allegedly knew Wyatt Earp and used his stories to recount the details vividly, though not always accurately. Remake of 1939's "Frontier Marshal."
1946 97m/B Henry Fonda, Victor Mature, Walter Brennan, Linda Darnell, Tim Holt, Ward Bond, John Ireland; **D:** John Ford. **VHS, Beta, LV** ★★★1/2

My Dinner with Andre Two friends talk about their lives and philosophies for two hours over dinner one night. A wonderful exploration into storytelling, the conversation juxtaposes the experiences and philosophies of nerdish, bumbling Shawn and the globe-trotting spiritual pilgrimage of Gregory, in this sometimes poignant, sometimes comic little movie that starts you thinking.
1981 110m/C Andre Gregory, Wallace Shawn; **D:** Louis Malle. **VHS, Beta, LV** ★★★1/2

My Fair Lady Colorful production of Lerner and Loewe's musical version of "Pygmalion," about an ill-mannered cockney girl who is plucked from her job as a flower girl by Professor Henry Higgins. Higgins makes a bet with a colleague that he can turn this rough diamond into a "lady." Winner of eight Academy Awards. Hepburn's singing voice is dubbed by Marni Nixon, who was also responsible for the singing in "The King and I" and "West Side Story;" the dubbing may have undermined her chance at an Oscar nomination. Typecasting role for Harrison as the crusty, egocentric Higgins. A timeless classic. ♪ Why Can't the English?; Wouldn't It Be Lovely?; I'm an Ordinary Man; With a Little Bit of Luck; Just You Wait, 'Enry 'Iggins; The Servant's Chorus; The Rain in Spain; I Could Have Danced all Night; Ascot Gavotte.
1964 (G) 170m/C Audrey Hepburn, Rex Harrison, Stanley Holloway, Wilfrid Hyde-White, Theodore Bikel, Mona Washbourne, Jeremy Brett, Robert Coote, Gladys Cooper; **D:** George Cukor; **M:** Frederick Loewe, Alan Jay Lerner. Academy Awards '64: Best Actor (Harrison), Best Adapted Score, Best Art Direction/Set Decoration

(Color), Best Color Cinematography, Best Costume Design (Color), Best Director (Cukor), Best Picture, Best Sound; British Academy Awards '65: Best Film; Directors Guild of America Awards '64: Best Director (Cukor); Golden Globe Awards '65: Best Actor—Musical/Comedy (Harrison), Best Director—Film—Musical/Comedy; National Board of Review Awards '64: 10 Best Films of the Year; New York Film Critics Awards '64: Best Actor (Harrison), Best Film; Nominations: Academy Awards '64: Best Adapted Screenplay, Best Film Editing, Best Supporting Actor (Holloway), Best Supporting Actress (Cooper). **VHS, Beta, LV ★★★1/2**

My Family Patriarch Jose Sanchez (Rojas) comes to America in the early 1900s from Mexico and soon finds that the grass is not always greener on the other side. Thus begins the multigenerational saga of the Sanchez family in L.A., which chronicles their struggles and hopes over a time span of 60 years. Overlooked in the glut of Hispanic-themed movies released, featuring soulful performances from the ensemble cast, especially Smits and Morales as troubled men from separate generations. Their deep-seated need to assimilate matched by a disdain for authority provide most of the family's heartaches. English and Spanish dialogue. **1994 (R) 126m/C** Jimmy Smits, Esai Morales, Eduardo Lopez Rojas, Jenny Gago, Elpidia Carrillo, Lupe Ontiveros, Jacob Vargas, Jennifer Lopez, Scott Bakula, Edward James Olmos; **D:** Gregory Nava; **W:** Anna Thomas, Edward Lachman, Gregory Nava; **M:** Pepe Avila, Mark McKenzie. Nominations: Academy Awards '95: Best Makeup; Independent Spirit Awards '96: Best Actor (Smits), Best Supporting Actress (Lopez). **VHS, LV ★★★1/2**

My Favorite Blonde Beautiful British spy Carroll convinces Hope to aid her in carrying out a secret mission. Lots of fun as Hope and his trained penguin, along with Carroll, embark on a cross-country chase to elude the Nazis. Hope's behavior is hilarious and the pacing of the film is excellent. Based on a story by Melvin Frank and Norman Panama. **1942 78m/B** Bob Hope, Madeleine Carroll, Gale Sondergaard, George Zucco, Lionel Royce, Walter Kingsford, Victor Varconi; **Cameos:** Bing Crosby; **D:** Sidney Lanfield; **W:** Frank Butler, Don Hartman. **VHS ★★★**

My Favorite Wife Handsome widower Grant remarries only to discover that first wife Dunne, shipwrecked seven years earlier and presumed dead, has reappeared. Eventually, a judge must decide what to do in this most unusual situation, completely lacking precedent. Farcical and hilarious story filled with a clever cast. The 1963 remake "Move Over Darling" lacks the style and wit of this presentation. Also available colorized. **1940 88m/B** Irene Dunne, Cary Grant, Randolph Scott, Gail Patrick, Scotty Beckett; **D:** Garson Kanin; **W:** Samuel Spewack, Bella Spewack, Leo McCarey. Nominations: Academy Awards '40: Best Story, Best Original Score. **VHS, Beta, LV ★★★**

My Favorite Year A young writer on a popular live television show in the 1950s is asked to keep a watchful eye on the week's guest star—his favorite swashbuckling movie hero. Through a series of misadventures, he discovers his matinee idol is actually a drunkard and womanizer who has trouble living up to his cinematic standards. Sterling performance from O'Toole, with memorable portrayal from Bologna as the show's host, King Kaiser (a take-off of Sid Caesar from "Your Show of Shows"). **AKA:** My Favourite Year. **1982 (PG) 92m/C** Peter O'Toole, Mark Linn-Baker, Joseph Bologna, Jessica Harper, Lainie Kazan, Bill Macy, Anne DeSalvo, Lou Jacobi, Adolph Green, Cameron Mitchell, Gloria Stuart; **D:** Richard Benjamin; **W:** Norman Steinberg; **M:** Ralph Burns. Nominations: Academy Awards '82: Best Actor (O'Toole). **VHS, Beta, LV ★★★**

My Friend Flicka Boy makes friends with four-legged beast. Dad thinks the horse is full of wild oats, but young Roddie trains it to be the best gosh darned horse in pre-Disney family faredom. Based on Mary O'Hara book, followed by "Thunderhead, Son of Flicka," and TV series. **1943 89m/C** Roddy McDowall, Preston Foster, Rita Johnson, James Bell, Jeff Corey; **D:** Harold Schuster. **VHS, Beta ★★★**

My Left Foot A gritty, unsentimental drama based on the life and autobiography of cerebral-palsy victim Christy Brown. Considered an imbecile by everyone but his mother (Fricker, in a stunning award-winning performance) until he teaches himself to write. He survives his impoverished Irish roots to become a painter and writer using his left foot, the only appendage over which he has control. He also falls in love and finds some heartaches along the way. Day-Lewis is astounding; the supporting cast, especially Shaw and Cusack, match him measure for measure. **1989 (R) 103m/C** *IR* Daniel Day-Lewis, Brenda Fricker, Ray McAnally, Cyril Cusack, Fiona Shaw, Hugh O'Conor, Adrian Dunbar, Ruth McCabe, Alison Whelan; *D:* Jim Sheridan; *W:* Shane Connaughton, Jim Sheridan; *M:* Elmer Bernstein. Academy Awards '89: Best Actor (Day-Lewis), Best Supporting Actress (Fricker); Independent Spirit Awards '90: Best Foreign Film; Los Angeles Film Critics Association Awards '89: Best Actor (Day-Lewis), Best Supporting Actress (Fricker); New York Film Critics Awards '89: Best Actor (Day-Lewis), Best Film; National Society of Film Critics Awards '89: Best Actor (Day-Lewis); Nominations: Academy Awards '89: Best Adapted Screenplay, Best Director (Sheridan), Best Picture. **VHS, Beta, LV ★★★★**

My Life as a Dog A troublesome boy is separated from his brother and is sent to live with relatives in the country when his mother is taken ill. Unhappy and confused, he struggles to understand sexuality and love and tries to find security and acceptance. Remarkable Swedish film available with English subtitles or dubbed. *AKA:* Mitt Liv Som Hund. **1985 101m/C** *SW* Anton Glanzelius, Tomas Van Bromssen, Anki Liden, Melinda Kinnaman, Kicki Rundgren, Ing-mari Carlsson; *D:* Lasse Hallstrom. Golden Globe Awards '88: Best Foreign Film; Independent Spirit Awards '88: Best Foreign Film; New York Film Critics Awards '87: Best Foreign Film; Nominations: Academy Awards '87: Best Adapted Screenplay, Best Director (Hallstrom). **VHS, Beta, LV ★★★★**

My Life to Live A woman turns to prostitution in this probing examination of sexual, and social, relations. Idiosyncratic Godard has never been more starstruck than in this vehicle for the endearing Karina, his wife at the time. A classic. In French with English subtitles. *AKA:* Vivre Savie; It's My Life. **1962 85m/B** *FR* Anna Karina, Sady Rebbot, Andre S. Labarthe, Guylaine Schlumberger; *D:* Jean-Luc Godard; *W:* Jean-Luc Godard; *M:* Michel Legrand. Venice Film Festival '62: Special Jury Prize. **VHS, Beta ★★★★**

My Little Chickadee Classic comedy about a gambler and a fallen woman who marry for convenience so they can respectably enter an unsuspecting town. Sparks fly in their adventures together. Fields and West are both at their best playing their larger-than-life selves. **1940 91m/B** W.C. Fields, Mae West, Joseph Calleia, Dick Foran, Margaret Hamilton, Donald Meek; *D:* Eddie Cline. **VHS, Beta, LV ★★★**

My Man Godfrey A spoiled rich girl picks up someone she assumes is a bum as part of a scavenger hunt and decides to keep him on as her butler. In the process, he teaches her about life, money, and happiness. Topnotch screwball comedy defines the genre. Lombard is a stunner alongside the equally charming Powell. Watch for Jane Wyman as an extra in the party scene. Remade in 1957 with June Allyson and David Niven. From the novel by Eric Hatch, who also co-scripted. **1936 95m/B** William Powell, Carole Lombard, Gail Patrick, Alice Brady, Mischa Auer, Eugene Pallette, Alan Mowbray, Franklin Pangborn, Jane Wyman; *D:* Gregory La Cava; *W:* Morrie Ryskind, Gregory La Cava. Nominations: Academy Awards '36: Best Actor (Powell), Best Actress (Lombard), Best Director (La Cava), Best Screenplay, Best Supporting Actor (Auer), Best Supporting Actress (Brady). **VHS, Beta ★★★★**

My Name Is Ivan Tarkovsky's first feature film is a vivid, wrenching portrait of a young Soviet boy surviving as a spy behind enemy lines during WWII. Technically stunning, heralding the coming of modern cinema's greatest formalist. In Russian with English subtitles. *AKA:* Ivan's Childhood; The Youngest Spy. **1962 84m/B** *RU* Kolya Burlyayev, Valentin Zubkov, Ye Zharikov, S. Krylov; *D:* Andrei Tarkovsky. Venice Film Festival '62: Best Film. **VHS, Beta, LV ★★★1/2**

My Night at Maud's Typically subtle Rohmer entry concerns quandary of upright fellow who finds himself drawn to comparatively carefree woman. Talky, somewhat arid film is one of director's Six Moral Tales. You'll either find it fascinating or wish you were watching "Rocky XXIV" instead. Cinematography by Nestor Almendros; in French with English subtitles. *AKA:* My Night with Maud; Ma Nuit Chez Maud. **1969 111m/B** *FR* Jean-Louis Trintignant, Francoise Fabian, Marie-Christine Barrault, Antoine Vitez; *D:* Eric Rohmer; *W:* Eric Rohmer, Nestor Almendros. New York Film Critics Awards '70: Best Screenplay; National Society of Film Critics Awards '70: Best Cinematography, Best Screenplay; Nominations: Academy Awards '69: Best Foreign Language Film; Cannes Film Festival '69: Best Film. **VHS, Beta, LV ★★★**

My Own Private Idaho Director Van Sant of "Drugstore Cowboy" returns to the underworld to examine another group of outsiders, this time young, homosexual hustlers. On the streets of Seattle, narcoleptic hustler Mike meets slumming rich boy Scott, and together they begin a search for Mike's lost mother, which leads them to Idaho and Italy. Stunning visuals, an elliptical plot, and a terrific performance by Phoenix highlight this search for love, the meaning of life, and power. Van Sant couples these activities with scenes from Shakespeare's "Henry IV" for a sometimes inscrutable, but always memorable film. Look for director Richert's Falstaff role as an aging chickenhawk.
1991 (R) 105m/C River Phoenix, Keanu Reeves, James Russo, William Richert, Rodney Harvey, Michael Parker, Flea, Chiara Caselli, Udo Kier, Grace Zabriskie, Tom Troupe; *D:* Gus Van Sant; *W:* Gus Van Sant. Independent Spirit Awards '92: Best Actor (Phoenix), Best Screenplay; National Society of Film Critics Awards '91: Best Actor (Phoenix). **VHS, LV** ★★★

My Sister Eileen Ruth and Eileen are two small-town Ohio sisters who move to Manhattan seeking excitement. They live in a basement apartment in Greenwich Village with an assortment of oddball tenants as they pursue success and romance. Everyone is daffy and charming, as is the film. Fun, but unmemorable songs. However the terrific choreography is by Fosse, who also appears as one sister's suitor. Remake of a 1942 film which was based on a Broadway play, which was based on a series of autobiographical stories published in the New Yorker. The play was later turned into a Broadway musical known as "Wonderful Town," which has nothing to do with this version of the original stories. ♪ Give Me a Band and My Baby; It's Bigger Than You and Me; There's Nothing Like Love; As Soon As They See Eileen; I'm Great; Conga; Atmosphere.
1955 108m/C Janet Leigh, Betty Garrett, Jack Lemmon, Bob Fosse, Kurt Kasznar, Dick York, Lucy Marlow, Tommy Rall, Barbara Brown, Horace McMahon; *D:* Richard Quine; *W:* Blake Edwards, Richard Quine; *M:* Jule Styne. **VHS** ★★★

Mysterious Island Exhilirating sci-fi classic adapted from Jules Verne's novel about escaping Civil War soldiers who go up in Verne balloon and come down on a Pacific island populated by giant animals. They also encounter two shipwrecked English ladies, pirates, and Captain Nemo (and his sub). Top-rate special effects by master Ray Harryhausen.
1961 101m/C *GB* Michael Craig, Joan Greenwood, Michael Callan, Gary Merrill, Herbert Lom, Beth Rogan, Percy Herbert, Dan Jackson, Nigel Green; *D:* Cy Endfield; *M:* Bernard Herrmann. **VHS, Beta, LV** ★★★1/2

Mystery of the Wax Museum Rarely seen, vintage horror classic about a wax-dummy maker who, after a disfiguring fire, resorts to murder and installs the wax-covered bodies of his victims in his museum. Famous for its pioneering use of two-strip Technicolor. Remade in 1953 in 3-D as "House of Wax."
1933 77m/C Lionel Atwill, Fay Wray, Glenda Farrell; *D:* Michael Curtiz. **VHS, Beta, LV** ★★★

Mystery Train A run down hotel in Memphis is the scene for three vignettes concerning the visit of foreigners to the U.S. Themes of mythic Americana, Elvis, and life on the fringe pervade this hip and quirky film. The three vignettes all tie together in clever and funny overlaps. Waits fans should listen for his performance as a DJ.
1989 (R) 110m/C Masatoshi Nagase, Youki Kudoh, Jay Hawkins, Cinque Lee, Joe Strummer, Nicoletta Braschi, Elizabeth Bracco, Steve Buscemi, Tommy Noonan, Rockets Redglare, Rick Aviles, Rufus Thomas; *D:* Jim Jarmusch; *W:* Jim Jarmusch; *M:* John Lurie; *V:* Tom Waits. **VHS, LV** ★★★

Mystic Pizza Intelligent coming of age drama centers on two sisters and their best friend as they struggle with their hopes, loves, and family rivalries in the small town of Mystic, Connecticut. At times predictable, there are enough unexpected moments to keep interest high; definite appeal to young women, but others may not relate. The relatively unknown Roberts got most of the attention, but is the weakest of the three leads, so watch this one for the strong performances from Gish and Taylor.
1988 (R) 101m/C Annabeth Gish, Julia Roberts, Lili Taylor, Vincent D'Onofrio, William R. Moses, Adam Storke, Conchata Ferrell, Joanna Merlin; *D:* Donald Petrie; *W:* Amy Holden Jones, Perry Howze, Alfred Uhry; *M:* David McHugh. Independent Spirit Awards '89: Best First Feature. **VHS, Beta, LV** ★★★

Nadja Fresh, modern comic take on the vampire tale is about family ties and the power of home, with the required AIDS analogy and lesbian sex scenes. Tired of nightly blood-letting, the daughter of the now-deceased Count, Nadja (Lowensohn), lives in New York's East Village, hoping to change her life. She seduces and falls in love with Lucy (Craze), whose husband is the nephew of old family nemesis Van Helsing (Fonda, in a surprisingly comedic role). Manic Fonda Van Helsing sets out to save Lucy and steal the film. Meanwhile, Nadja finds her long lost twin brother (Harris, son of Richard) and Lucy discovers sex with Nadja is draining. Innovative camera work (vampire point-of-view scenes shot with a toy Pixel-vision camera and blown up to 35mm for a moody, grainy look) and a great score keep "Nadja" very watchable despite some missteps in the plot. (Director Almereyda pioneered use of the Pixel-vision camera in "Another Girl, Another Planet.") Executive producer David Lynch contributes a cameo as a guard at the morgue where Nadja claims her father's body.

1995 (R) 92m/B Elina Lowensohn, Suzy Amis, Galaxy Craze, Martin Donovan, Peter Fonda, Karl Geary, Jared Harris; **Cameos:** David Lynch; **D:** Michael Almereyda; **W:** Michael Almereyda; **M:** Simon Fisher Turner. Nominations: Independent Spirit Awards '96: Best Actress (Lowensohn), Best Director (Almereyda), Best Cinematography. **VHS ★★★**

Naked Existential angst in a '90s London filled with Leigh's usual eccentrics. The unemployed Johnny (Thewlis) comes to London and bunks with former girlfriend Louise (Sharp). After seducing her flatmate Sophie (Cartlidge), Johnny leaves to wander the streets, exchanging philosophical, if foul-mouthed, dialogues with a variety of odd characters. Thewlis gives an explosive performance as the calculatingly brutal and desolate Johnny. Chaotic shifts in mood from comedy to violence to love prove a challenge and the pervasive abuse of all the women characters is very disturbing. Critically acclaimed; see it as a reflection on the mess of modern England. **AKA:** Mike Leigh's Naked.

1993 (R) 131m/C *GB* David Thewlis, Lesley Sharp, Katrin Cartlidge, Greg Cruttwell, Claire Skinner, Peter Wight, Ewen Bremmer, Susan Vidler; **D:** Mike Leigh; **W:** Mike Leigh; **M:** Andrew Dickinson. Cannes Film Festival '93: Best Actor (Thewlis), Best Director (Leigh); National Society of Film Critics Awards '93: Best Actor (Thewlis); Nominations: British Academy Awards '93: Best Film; Cannes Film Festival '93: Best Film; Independent

Spirit Awards '94: Best Foreign Film. **VHS, LV ★★★**

The Naked City Film noir classic makes spectacular use of its NYC locations. Beautiful playgirl is murdered and police detectives Fitzgerald and Taylor are left without clues. They spend most of their time running down weak leads and interviewing various suspects and witnesses. When they finally get a break, it leads to playboy Duff. Spectacular ending on the Brooklyn Bridge between cops and killer. Producer Hellinger provided the hard-boiled narration, patterned after the tabloid newspaper stories he once wrote. Served as the impetus for the TV show of the same name, where Hellinger's film postscript also became the show's noted tagline: "There are eight million stories in the naked city, this has been one of them."

1948 96m/B Barry Fitzgerald, Don Taylor, Howard Duff, Ted de Corsia, Dorothy Hart; **D:** Jules Dassin; **M:** Miklos Rozsa. Academy Awards '48: Best Black and White Cinematography, Best Film Editing; Nominations: Academy Awards '48: Best Story. **VHS ★★★1/2**

The Naked Civil Servant Remarkable film, based on the life of flamboyant homosexual Quentin Crisp, who came out of the closet in his native England, long before his lifestyle would be tolerated by Britains. For mature audiences.

1975 80m/C John Hurt; **D:** Jack Gold; **M:** Carl Davis. **VHS, Beta ★★★1/2**

The Naked Gun: From the Files of Police Squad More hysterical satire from the creators of "Airplane!" The short-lived television cop spoof "Police Squad" moves to the big screen and has Lt. Drebin uncover a plot to assassinate Queen Elizabeth while she is visiting Los Angeles. Nearly nonstop gags and pratfalls provide lots of laughs. Nielsen is perfect as Drebin and the supporting cast is strong; cameos abound.

1988 (PG-13) 85m/C Leslie Nielsen, Ricardo Montalban, Priscilla Presley, George Kennedy, O.J. Simpson, Nancy Marchand, John Houseman; **Cameos:** Weird Al Yankovic, Reggie Jackson, Dr. Joyce Brothers; **D:** David Zucker; **W:** Jerry Zucker, Jim Abrahams, Pat Proft, David Zucker; **M:** Ira Newborn. **VHS, Beta, LV, 8mm ★★★**

Naked Lunch Whacked-out movie based on William S. Burroughs's autobiographical account of drug abuse, homosexuality, violence, and weirdness set in the drug-inspired land called Interzone. Hallucinogenic images are carried to the extreme: typewriters metamorphose into beetles, bloblike creatures with sex organs scurry about, and characters mainline insecticide. Some of the characters are clearly based on writers of the Beat generation, including Jane and Paul Bowles, Allen Ginsberg, and Jack Kerouac.

1991 (R) 117m/C Peter Weller, Judy Davis, Ian Holm, Julian Sands, Roy Scheider, Monique Mercure, Nicholas Campbell, Michael Zelniker, Robert A. Silverman, Joseph Scorsiani; **D:** David Cronenberg; **W:** David Cronenberg; **M:** Howard Shore. Genie Awards '92: Best Adapted Screenplay, Best Art Direction/Set Decoration, Best Cinematography, Best Director (Cronenberg), Best Film, Best Sound, Best Supporting Actress (Mercure); National Society of Film Critics Awards '91: Best Director (Cronenberg), Best Screenplay. **VHS ★★★**

The Naked Spur A compulsive bounty hunter tracks down a vicious outlaw and his beautiful girlfriend. An exciting film from the Mann-Stewart team and considered one of their best, infusing the traditional western with psychological confusion. Wonderful use of Rockies locations.

1953 93m/C James Stewart, Robert Ryan, Janet Leigh, Millard Mitchell; **D:** Anthony Mann. Nominations: Academy Awards '53: Best Story & Screenplay. **VHS, Beta ★★★½**

Nana French version of Emile Zola's novel about an actress-prostitute who seduces the high society of Paris in the late 1880s, and suffers a heart-breaking downfall and death. Film has three remakes of the original 1926 version.

1955 118m/C *FR* Charles Boyer, Martine Carol. **VHS, Beta ★★★**

Napoleon A vivid, near-complete restoration of Gance's epic silent masterpiece about the famed conqueror's early years, from his youth through the Italian Campaign. An innovative, spectacular achievement with its use of multiple split screens, montage, color, and triptychs. Given a gala theatrical re-release in 1981. Remade in 1955.

1927 235m/B *FR* Albert Dieudonne, Antonin Artaud, Pierre Batcheff, Gina Manes, Armand Bernard, Harry Krimer, Albert Bras, Abel Gance, Georges Cahuzac; **D:** Abel Gance; **M:** Carmine Coppola. **VHS, Beta, LV ★★★★**

The Narrow Margin Well-made, harrowing adventure about a cop who is in charge of transporting a gangster's widow to a trial where she is to testify. On the train he must try to keep her safe from the hit-men who would murder her. A real cat and mouse game—one of the best suspense movies of the '50s.

1952 71m/B Charles McGraw, Marie Windsor, Jacqueline White, Queenie Leonard, Gordon Gebert, Don Beddoe, Harry Harvey; **D:** Richard Fleischer. Nominations: Academy Awards '52: Best Story. **VHS ★★★**

Nashville Altman's stunning, brilliant film tapestry that follows the lives of 24 people during a political campaign/music festival in Nashville. Seemingly extemporaneous vignettes, actors playing themselves (Elliott Gould and Julie Christie), funny, touching, poignant character studies concerning affairs of the heart and despairs of the mind. Repeatedly blurs reality and fantasy. ♪ I'm Easy; Two Hundred Years; Keep A'Goin'; One, I Love You; Let Me Be the One; The Day I Looked Jesus in the Eye; For the Sake of the Children; I Never Get Enough; It Don't Worry Me.

1975 (R) 159m/C Keith Carradine, Lily Tomlin, Henry Gibson, Ronee Blakley, Keenan Wynn, David Arkin, Geraldine Chaplin, Lauren Hutton, Shelley Duvall, Barbara Harris, Allen (Goorwitz) Garfield, Karen Black, Christina Raines, Michael Murphy, Ned Beatty, Barbara Baxley, Scott Glenn, Jeff Goldblum, Gwen Welles, Bert Remsen, Robert DoQui; *Cameos:* Elliott Gould, Julie Christie; **D:** Robert Altman; **W:** Joan Tewkesbury; **M:** Richard Baskin. Academy Awards '75: Best Song ("I'm Easy"); Golden Globe Awards '76: Best Song ("I'm Easy"); National Board of Review Awards '75: 10 Best Films of the Year, Best Director (Altman), Best Supporting Actress (Blakley); National Society of Film Critics Awards '75: Best Director (Altman), Best Film, Best Supporting Actor (Gibson), Best Supporting Actress (Tomlin); Nominations: Academy Awards '75: Best Director (Altman), Best Picture, Best Supporting Actress (Blakley, Tomlin). **VHS, Beta, LV ★★★★**

The Nasty Girl A bright young German model plans to enter a national essay contest on the topic of her hometown's history during the Third Reich. While researching the paper, she's harassed and even brutalized, but refuses to cease her sleuthing. Excellent performances, tight direction, with comedic touches that charmingly imparts an important message. Based on a true story. In German with English subtitles.

1990 (PG-13) 93m/C *GE* Lena Stolze, Monika Baumgartner, Michael Gahr; **D:** Michael Verhoeven; **W:** Michael Verhoeven. British Academy Awards '91: Best Foreign Film; New York Film Critics Awards '90: Best Foreign Film; Nominations: Academy Awards '90: Best Foreign Language Film. **VHS ★★★1/2**

National Lampoon's Animal House Classic Belushi vehicle running amuck. Set in 1962 and responsible for launching Otis Day and the Knights and defining cinematic food fights. Every college tradition from fraternity rush week to the homecoming pageant is irreverently and relentlessly mocked in this wild comedy about Delta House, a fraternity on the edge. Climaxes with the homecoming parade from hell. Sophomoric, but very funny, with a host of young stars who went on to more serious work. Remember: "Knowledge is good." **AKA:** Animal House.
1978 (R) 109m/C John Belushi, Tim Matheson, John Vernon, Donald Sutherland, Peter Riegert, Stephen Furst, Bruce McGill, Mark Metcalf, Verna Bloom, Karen Allen, Tom Hulce, Mary Louise Weller, Kevin Bacon; **D:** John Landis; **W:** Harold Ramis; **M:** Elmer Bernstein. People's Choice Awards '79: Best Film. **VHS, Beta, LV ★★★1/2**

National Velvet A young English girl wins a horse in a raffle and is determined to train it to compete in the famed Grand National race. Taylor, only 12 at the time, is superb in her first starring role. Rooney also gives a fine performance. Filmed with a loving eye on lushly decorated sets, this is a masterpiece version of the story of affection between a girl and her pet. Based on the novel by Enid Bagnold and followed by "International Velvet" in 1978.
1944 (G) 124m/C Elizabeth Taylor, Mickey Rooney, Arthur Treacher, Donald Crisp, Anne Revere, Angela Lansbury, Reginald Owen, Norma Varden, Jackie "Butch" Jenkins, Terence Kilburn; **D:** Clarence Brown; **W:** Helen Deutsch, Theodore Reeves; **M:** Herbert Stothart. Academy Awards '45: Best Film Editing, Best Supporting Actress (Revere); Nominations: Academy Awards '45: Best Color Cinematography, Best Director (Brown). **VHS, LV ★★★★**

The Natural A beautifully filmed movie about baseball as myth. A young man, whose gift for baseball sets him apart, finds that trouble dogs him, particularly with a woman. In time, as an aging rookie, he must fight against his past to lead his team to the World Series, and win the woman who is meant for him. From the Bernard Malamud story.
1984 (PG) 134m/C Robert Redford, Glenn Close, Robert Duvall, Kim Basinger, Wilford Brimley, Barbara Hershey, Richard Farnsworth, Robert Prosky, Darren McGavin, Joe Don Baker, Michael Madsen; **D:** Barry Levinson; **M:** Randy Newman, Caleb Deschanel. Nominations: Academy Awards '84: Best Art Direction/Set Decoration, Best Cinematography, Best Supporting Actress (Close). **VHS, Beta, LV ★★★**

The Navigator Ever the quick thinker, Keaton actually bought a steamer headed for the scrap heap and used it to film an almost endless string of sight gags. Rejected by a socialite, millionaire Keaton finds himself alone with her on the abandoned boat. As he saves her from various and sundry perils, the gags and thrills abound—including one stunt that was inspired by a near-accident on the set. Too bad they don't make 'em like this anymore. Silent.
1924 60m/B Buster Keaton, Kathryn McGuire, Frederick Vroom, Noble Johnson, Clarence Burton, H. M. Clugston; **D:** Buster Keaton, Donald Crisp. **VHS ★★★**

Nazarin Bunuel's scathing indictment of Christianity finds its perfect vehicle in the adventures of a defrocked priest attempting to relive Christ's life. Gathering a group of disciples, he wanders into the Mexican desert as a cross between Christ and Don Quixote. Filmed in Mexico, this is Bunuel at his grimmest. In Spanish with English subtitles.
1958 92m/B *MX* Francesco Rabal, Rita Macedo, Margo Lopez, Rita McLedo, Ignacio Lopez Tarso, Jesus Fernandez; **D:** Luis Bunuel. **VHS, Beta, LV ★★★**

Nelly et Monsieur Arnaud Chatty adult May/December would-be romance between 25-year-old secretary Nelly (Beart) and Pierre Arnaud (Serrault), the mid-60s retired magistrate for whom she's working. The arrogant divorced Arnaud is intrigued by the independent Nelly, whom he finds he can't control, while she comes to appreciate their emotional ties (altogether different from the selfishness of the younger men she knows). Conclusion avoids a neat resolution to a situation beset by bad timing. French with subtitles. **AKA:** Nelly and Mr. Arnaud.
1995 105m/C *FR* Emmanuelle Beart, Michel Serrault, Jean-Hugues Anglade, Francoise Brion, Claire Nadeau, Michael Lonsdale, Charles Berling, Michele Laroque; **D:**

Claude Sautet; **W:** Claude Sautet, Jacques Fieschi; **M:** Philippe Sarde. Cesar Awards '96: Best Director (Sautet), Best Actor (Serrault), Best Film, Best Actress (Beart), Best Screenplay; Nominations: Cesar Awards '96: Best Supporting Actress (Nadeau), Best Supporting Actor (Anglade), Best Supporting Actor (Lonsdale), Best Film Editing, Best Score, Best Sound. **VHS** ★★★

Network As timely now as it was then; a scathing indictment of the television industry and its propensity towards self-prostitution. A television newscaster's mental breakdown turns him into a celebrity when the network tries to profit from his illness. The individual characters are startlingly realistic and the acting is excellent.
1976 (R) 121m/C Faye Dunaway, Peter Finch, William Holden, Robert Duvall, Wesley Addy, Ned Beatty, Beatrice Straight; **D:** Sidney Lumet, Owen Roizman; **W:** Paddy Chayefsky. Academy Awards '76: Best Actor (Finch), Best Actress (Dunaway), Best Original Screenplay, Best Supporting Actress (Straight); Golden Globe Awards '77: Best Actor—Drama (Finch), Best Actress—Drama (Dunaway), Best Director (Lumet), Best Screenplay; Los Angeles Film Critics Association Awards '76: Best Director (Lumet), Best Film; National Board of Review Awards '76: 10 Best Films of the Year; New York Film Critics Awards '76: Best Screenplay; Writers Guild of America '76: Best Original Screenplay; Nominations: Academy Awards '76: Best Actor (Holden), Best Cinematography, Best Director (Lumet), Best Film Editing, Best Picture, Best Supporting Actor (Beatty). **VHS, Beta, LV** ★★★1/2

Never Cry Wolf A young biologist is sent to the Arctic to study the behavior and habitation of wolves, then becomes deeply involved with their sub-society. Based on Farley Mowat's book. Beautifully photographed.
1983 (PG) 105m/C Charles Martin Smith, Brian Dennehy, Samson Jorah; **D:** Carroll Ballard; **W:** Curtis Hanson, Sam Hamm. National Society of Film Critics Awards '83: Best Cinematography; Nominations: Academy Awards '83: Best Sound. **VHS, Beta, LV** ★★★1/2

Never Give a Sucker an Even Break An almost plotless comedy, based on an idea reputedly written on a napkin by Fields (he took screenplay credit as Otis Criblecoblis), and features Fields at his most unleashed. It's something of a cult favorite, but not for all tastes. Classic chase scene ends it. Fields' last role in a feature-length film. **AKA:** What a Man.
1941 71m/B W.C. Fields, Gloria Jean, Franklin Pangborn, Leon Errol, Margaret Dumont; **D:** Eddie Cline. **VHS, Beta, LV** ★★★1/2

Never on Sunday An American intellectual tries to turn a Greek prostitute into a refined woman. Fine performances and exhilarating Greek photography. Fun all around. ♫ Never on Sunday.
1960 91m/B GR Melina Mercouri, Titos Vandis, Jules Dassin, Mitsos Liguisos; **D:** Jules Dassin; **W:** Jules Dassin; **M:** Manos Hadjidakis. Academy Awards '60: Best Song ("Never on Sunday"); Cannes Film Festival '60: Best Actress (Mercouri); Nominations: Academy Awards '60: Best Actress (Mercouri), Best Costume Design (B & W), Best Director (Dassin), Best Story & Screenplay. **VHS, Beta** ★★★

Never Weaken/Why Worry? Silent comedy shorts from Harold. In "Never Weaken" (1921), Lloyd hustles customers. In "Why Worry?" (1923), he plays a wealthy young man who journeys to South America for his health and gets caught in the middle of a revolution.
1923 78m/B Harold Lloyd. **VHS, Beta** ★★★

The NeverEnding Story A lonely young boy helps a warrior save the fantasy world in his book from destruction by the Nothing. A wonderful, intelligent family movie about imagination, with swell effects and a sweet but not overly sentimental script. Petersen's first English-language film, based on the novel by Michael Ende.
1984 (PG) 94m/C Barret Oliver, Noah Hathaway, Gerald McRaney, Moses Gunn, Tami Stronach, Patricia Hayes, Sydney Bromley; **D:** Wolfgang Petersen; **W:** Wolfgang Petersen; **M:** Klaus Doldinger, Giorgio Moroder. **VHS, Beta, LV, 8mm** ★★★1/2

New York, New York Tragic romance evolves between a saxophonist and an aspiring singer/actress in this salute to the big-band era. A love of music isn't enough to hold them together through career rivalries and life on the road. Fine performances by De Niro and Minnelli and the supporting cast. Re-released in 1981 with the "Happy Endings" number, which was cut from the original. Look for "Big Man" Clarence Clemons on sax. ♫ New York, New York; There Goes the Ball Game; Happy Endings; But the World Goes 'Round; Night in Tunisia; Opus One; Avalon; You Brought a New Kind of Love to Me; I'm Getting Sentimental Over You.

1977 (PG) 163m/C Robert De Niro, Liza Minnelli, Lionel Stander, Barry Primus, Mary Kay Place, Dick Miller, Diahnne Abbott; *D:* Martin Scorsese; *W:* Mardik Martin; *M:* Ralph Burns. **VHS, Beta, LV** ★★★

New York Stories Entertaining anthology of three separate short films by three esteemed directors, all set in New York. In "Life Lessons" by Scorsese, an impulsive artist tries to prevent his live-in girlfriend from leaving him. "Life Without Zoe" by Coppola involves a youngster's fantasy about a wealthy 12-year-old who lives mostly without her parents. Allen's "Oedipus Wrecks," generally considered the best short, is about a 50-year-old man who is tormented by the specter of his mother.
1989 (PG) 124m/C Nick Nolte, Rosanna Arquette, Woody Allen, Mia Farrow, Mae Questel, Julie Kavner, Talia Shire, Giancarlo Giannini, Don Novello, Patrick O'Neal, Peter Gabriel, Paul Herman, Deborah Harry, Steve Buscemi, Heather McComb, Chris Elliott, Carole Bouquet, Edward I. Koch; *D:* Woody Allen, Martin Scorsese, Francis Ford Coppola; *W:* Woody Allen, Francis Ford Coppola, Richard Price, Sofia Coppola; *M:* Carmine Coppola, Sven Nykvist. **VHS, Beta, LV** ★★★

Next Stop, Greenwich Village An affectionate, autobiographical look by Mazursky at a Brooklyn boy who moves to Greenwich Village in 1953. Good performances, especially by Winters as the overbearing mother.
1976 (R) 109m/C Lenny Baker, Christopher Walken, Ellen Greene, Shelley Winters, Lou Jacobi, Mike Kellin; *D:* Paul Mazursky; *W:* Paul Mazursky; *M:* Bill Conti. Nominations: Cannes Film Festival '76: Best Film. **VHS** ★★★

Next Summer A large, character-studded French family pursues power, love and beauty. Excellent performances. In French with English subtitles. *AKA:* L'Ete Prochain.
1984 120m/C *FR* Jean-Louis Trintignant, Claudia Cardinale, Fanny Ardant, Philippe Noiret, Marie Trintignant; *D:* Nadine Trintignant. **VHS, Beta** ★★★

Nico Icon Documentary probes the life of Velvet Underground sensation and Warhol superstar Nico. A pastiche showing V.U. concert footage and movie clips from Nico's most famous film appearances: Fellini's "La Dolce Vita" and Warhol's "The Chelsea Girls." Also features interviews from Warhol's Factory inhabitants, band members, and Nico's grown son Ari. Visually as interesting

as the subject herself, film manages to bring the viewer closer to the untouchable Teutonic figure without being sensational or overly flashy. Director Paul Morrissey and musician Jackson Browne make appearances. Some French and German language; subtitled.
1996 70m/C *GE D:* Susanne Ofteringer; *W:* Susanne Ofteringer. **VHS** ★★★

Night and the City Harry Fabian (De Niro), a con-artist/ambulance-chaser, concocts a scheme to make it big, and approaches an old boxing great (Warden) to come out of retirement and revive a local boxing night. Problem is, although Harry has energy and ambition, he also has a talent for making enemies out of the wrong people, like the boxer's brother (King), a neighborhood mobster. Filled with details more interesting than the plot; more about fast-living, fast-talking New Yorkers, a fine showcase for De Niro's talent. Winkler's remake of the 1950 Jules Dassin film.
1992 (R) 98m/C Robert De Niro, Jessica Lange, Cliff Gorman, Alan King, Jack Warden, Eli Wallach, Barry Primus, Gene Kirkwood, Pedro Sanchez, Tak Fujimoto; *Cameos:* Regis Philbin, Joy Philbin, Richard Price; *D:* Irwin Winkler; *W:* Richard Price; *M:* James Newton Howard. **VHS, LV** ★★★

A Night at the Opera The Marx Brothers get mixed up with grand opera in their first MGM-produced epic and their first without Zeppo. Jones, as a budding opera singer warbles "Alone" and "Cosi Cosa." One of their best films, blessed with a big budget—used to reach epic anarchic heights. Some scenes were tested on live audiences before inclusion, including the Groucho/Chico paper-tearing contract negotiation and the celebrated stateroom scene, in which the boys are joined in a small closet by two maids, the ship's engineer, his assistant, a manicurist, a young woman, a cleaning lady, and four food-laden waiters. Laserdisc includes letterboxing, digital sound, original trailers, production photos, memorabilia, and soundtrack commentary by film critic Leonard Maltin.
1935 92m/B Groucho Marx, Chico Marx, Harpo Marx, Allan Jones, Kitty Carlisle Hart, Sig Rumann, Margaret Dumont, Walter Woolf King; *D:* Sam Wood; *W:* George S. Kaufman, Morrie Ryskind, Bert Kalmar, Harry Ruby, Al Boasberg; *M:* Herbert Stothart. **VHS, Beta, LV** ★★★★

Night Gallery Serling is the tour guide through an unusual art gallery

consisting of portraits that reflect people's greed, desire and guilt. Made for television pilot for the series, which ran from 1969 to 1973. Three stories, including "Eyes," which saw novice Spielberg directing veteran Crawford.
1969 95m/C Joan Crawford, Roddy McDowall, Tom Bosley, Barry Sullivan, Ossie Davis, Sam Jaffe, Kate Greenfield; *D:* Steven Spielberg, Boris Sagal. VHS, Beta ★★★

Night Moves While tracking down a missing teenager, a Hollywood detective uncovers a bizarre smuggling ring in the Florida Keys. Hackman is realistic as the detective whose own life is unraveling and in one of her early roles, Griffith plays the teenager. The dense, disjointed plot reaches a shocking end. Underrated when released and worth a view.
1975 (R) 100m/C Gene Hackman, Susan Clark, Jennifer Warren, Melanie Griffith, Harris Yulin, Edward Binns, Kenneth Mars, James Woods, Dennis Dugan, Max Gail; *D:* Arthur Penn. VHS, Beta ★★★1/2

Night of the Generals A Nazi intelligence officer is pursuing three Nazi generals who may be involved in the brutal murder of a Warsaw prostitute. Dark and sinister, may be too slow for some tastes. Based on Hans Helmut Kirst's novel. *AKA:* La Nuit de Generaux.
1967 (R) 148m/C Peter O'Toole, Omar Sharif, Tom Courtenay, Joanna Pettet, Donald Pleasence, Christopher Plummer, Philippe Noiret, John Gregson; *D:* Anatole Litvak; *M:* Maurice Jarre. VHS, Beta, LV ★★★

The Night of the Hunter The nightmarish story of a psychotic preacher who marries a lonely widow with two children in the hopes of finding the cache of money her thieving husband had stashed. A dark, terrifying tale, completely unique in Hollywood's history. Mitchum is terrific. From novel by Davis Grubb and, sadly, Laughton's only directorial effort.
1955 93m/B Robert Mitchum, Shelley Winters, Lillian Gish, Don Beddoe, Evelyn Varden, Peter Graves, James Gleason, Billy Chapin, Sally Jane Bruce; *D:* Charles Laughton; *W:* James Agee. VHS, Beta, LV ★★★★

The Night of the Iguana An alcoholic ex-minister acts as a tour guide in Mexico, becoming involved with a spinster and a hotel owner. Based on Tennessee Williams' play. Excellent performances from Burton and Gardner.
1964 125m/B Richard Burton, Deborah Kerr, Ava Gardner, Grayson Hall, Sue Lyon; *D:* John Huston. Academy Awards '64: Best Costume Design (B & W); Nominations: Academy Awards '64: Best Art Direction/Set Decoration (B & W), Best Black and White Cinematography, Best Supporting Actress (Hall). VHS, Beta, LV ★★★

Night of the Living Dead Cult favorite is low budget but powerfully frightening. Space experiments set off a high level of radiation that makes the newly dead return to life, with a taste for human flesh. Handful of holdouts find shelter in a farmhouse. Claustrophobic, terrifying, gruesome, extreme, and yes, humorous. Followed by "Dawn of the Dead" (1979) and "Day of the Dead" (1985). Romero's directorial debut. Available in a colorized version. *AKA:* Night of the Flesh Eaters.
1968 90m/B Judith O'Dea, Duane Jones, Russell Streiner, Karl Hardman; *D:* George A. Romero. VHS, LV ★★★★

The Night of the Shooting Stars Set in an Italian village during the last days of WWII, this film highlights the schism in the village between those who support the fascists and those who sympathize with the Allies. This division comes to a head in the stunning final scene. A poignant, deeply moving film. *AKA:* The Night of San Lorenzo; La Notte di San Lorenzo.
1982 (R) 106m/C *IT* Omero Antonutti, Margarita Lozano, Claudio Bigagli, Massimo Bonetti, Norma Martel; *D:* Paolo Taviani, Vittorio Taviani; *W:* Tonino Guerra, Giuliani G. De Negri, Paolo Taviani, Vittorio Taviani; *M:* Nicola Piovani. Cannes Film Festival '82: Grand Jury Prize; National Society of Film Critics Awards '83: Best Director (Taviani), Best Film; Nominations: Cannes Film Festival '82: Best Film. VHS, Beta ★★★★

Night on Earth Jarmusch's "road" movie comprises five different stories taking place on the same night in five different cities—Los Angeles, New York, Paris, Rome, and Helsinki—between cabbies and their passengers. As with any anthology some stories work better than others but all have their moments in this ambitious film with its outstanding international cast. Subtitled in English for the three foreign segments.
1991 (R) 125m/C Winona Ryder, Gena Rowlands, Giancarlo Esposito, Armin Mueller-Stahl, Rosie Perez, Beatrice Dalle, Roberto Benigni, Paolo Bonacelli, Matti Pellonpaa, Kari Vaananen, Sakari Kuosmanen, Tomi Salmela; *D:* Jim Jarmusch; *W:* Jim Jarmusch; *M:* Tom

Waits. Independent Spirit Awards '93: Best Cinematography. **VHS, LV ★★★**

The Night They Raided Minsky's Chaotic but interesting period comedy about a young Amish girl who leaves her tyrannical father to come to New York City in the 1920s. She winds up at Minsky's Burlesque and accidentally invents the striptease. Lahr's last performance—he died during filming. ♩ The Night They Raided Minsky's; Take Ten Terrific Girls But Only 9 Costumes; How I Love Her; Perfect Gentleman; You Rat, You; Penny Arcade; Wait For Me. **AKA:** The Night They Invented Striptease.
1969 (PG) 97m/C Jason Robards Jr., Britt Ekland, Elliott Gould, Bert Lahr, Norman Wisdom, Denholm Elliott; **D:** William Friedkin; **W:** Norman Lear, Arnold Schulman. **VHS, Beta ★★★**

A Night to Remember A murder-mystery writer's wife convinces him to move to a new apartment because she thinks the change might help him finish a novel he started long ago. When they find a dead body behind their new building, they try their hands at sleuthing. A clever and witty mystery, indeed, supported by likeable performances.
1942 91m/B Loretta Young, Brian Aherne, Sidney Toler, Gale Sondergaard, William Wright, Donald MacBride, Blanche Yurka; **D:** Richard Wallace. **VHS ★★★**

A Night to Remember Gripping tale of the voyage of the Titanic with an interesting account of action in the face of danger and courage amid despair. Large cast is effectively used. Adapted by Eric Ambler from the book by Walter Lord.
1958 119m/B GB Kenneth More, David McCallum, Anthony Bushell, Honor Blackman, Michael Goodliffe, George Rose, Laurence Naismith, Frank Lawton, Alec McCowen; **D:** Roy Ward Baker; **W:** Eric Ambler. Golden Globe Awards '59: Best Foreign Film; National Board of Review Awards '58: 5 Best Foreign Films of the Year. **VHS, Beta, LV ★★★**

Nightfall Ray, accused of a crime he didn't commit, is forced to flee from both the law and the underworld. Classic example of film noir, brilliantly filmed by Tourneur.
1956 78m/B Aldo Ray, Brian Keith, Anne Bancroft, Jocelyn Brando, James Gregory, Frank Albertson; **D:** Jacques Tourneur; **W:** Stirling Silliphant. **VHS ★★★**

The Nightmare Before Christmas Back when he was an animator trainee at Disney, Burton came up with this adventurous idea but couldn't get it made; subsequent directorial success brought more clout. Relies on a painstaking stop-motion technique that took more than two years to film and is justifiably amazing. The story revolves around Jack Skellington, the Pumpkin King of the dangerously weird Halloweentown. Suffering from ennui, he accidentally discovers the wonders of Christmastown and decides to kidnap Santa and rule over this peaceable holiday. Fast pace is maintained by the equally breathless score. Not cuddly, best appreciated by those with a feel for the macabre. **AKA:** Tim Burton's The Nightmare Before Christmas.
1993 (PG) 75m/C D: Henry Selick; **W:** Caroline Thompson, Tim Burton; **M:** Danny Elfman; **V:** Danny Elfman, Chris Sarandon, Catherine O'Hara, William Hickey, Ken Page, Ed Ivory, Paul (Pee Wee Herman) Reubens, Glenn Shadix. Nominations: Academy Awards '93: Best Visual Effects; Golden Globe Awards '94: Best Original Score. **VHS, LV ★★★**

Nights of Cabiria Fellini classic which details the personal decline of a naive prostitute who thinks she's found true love. In Italian with English subtitles or dubbed. Basis for the musical "Sweet Charity." **AKA:** Le Notti de Cabiria; Cabiria.
1957 111m/B IT Giulietta Masina, Amedeo Nazzari; **D:** Federico Fellini; **W:** Federico Fellini, Tullio Pinelli, Ennio Flaiano; **M:** Nino Rota. Academy Awards '57: Best Foreign Language Film; Cannes Film Festival '57: Best Actress (Masina). **VHS, Beta ★★★1/2**

1900 Bertolucci's impassioned epic about two Italian families, one land-owning, the other, peasant. Shows the sweeping changes of the 20th century begun by the trauma of WWI and the onslaught of Italian socialism. Edited down from its original 360-minute length and dubbed in English from three other languages, the film suffers somewhat from editing and from its nebulous lack of commitment to any genre. Elegantly photographed by Vittorio Storaro. Also titled "Novecento."
1976 (R) 255m/C FR IT GE Robert De Niro, Gerard Depardieu, Burt Lancaster, Donald Sutherland, Dominique Sanda, Sterling Hayden, Laura Betti, Francesca Bertini, Werner Bruhns, Stefania Sandrelli, Anna Henkel, Alida Valli; **D:** Bernardo Bertolucci; **W:** Giuseppe Bertolucci, Bernardo Bertolucci, Vittorio Storaro. **VHS, Beta, LV ★★★**

1984 A very fine adaptation of George Orwell's infamous novel, this version differs from the overly simplistic and

cautionary 1954 film because of fine casting and production design. The illegal love affair of a government official becomes his attempt to defy the crushing inhumanity and lack of simple pleasures of an omniscient government. Filmed in London, it skillfully visualizes our time's most central prophetic nightmare.
1984 (R) 117m/C GB John Hurt, Richard Burton, Suzanna Hamilton, Cyril Cusack, Gregory Fisher, Andrew Wilde, Rupert Baderman; **D:** Michael Radford, Roger Deakins. **VHS, Beta, LV** ★★★½

Ninotchka Delightful romantic comedy. Garbo is a cold Russian agent sent to Paris to check up on her comrades, who are being seduced by capitalism. She inadvertently falls in love with a playboy, who melts her communist heart. Garbo talks and laughs. Satirical, energetic, and witty. Later a Broadway musical called "Silk Stockings."
1939 (R) 110m/B Greta Garbo, Melvyn Douglas, Ina Claire, Sig Rumann, Felix Bressart, Bela Lugosi; **D:** Ernst Lubitsch; **W:** Billy Wilder. National Board of Review Awards '39: 10 Best Films of the Year; Nominations: Academy Awards '39: Best Actress (Garbo), Best Picture, Best Screenplay, Best Story. **VHS, Beta, LV, 8mm** ★★★½

Nixon Stone again "interprets" historical events of the '60s and '70s with a sprawling, bold bio of Richard Nixon. Covering all the highlights of Nixon's public life and speculating on his private one, Hopkins convincingly portrays "Tricky Dick" as an embattled, lonely political genius. Gigantic all-star cast is led by Oscar-caliber performance of Allen as Pat Nixon. Even at over three hours, there isn't nearly enough time to explore the significance of all the events covered here. As usual, Stone has taken some creative license, which led to the Nixon daughters publicly trashing the film, and Walt Disney's daughter expressing "shame" at being affiliated with it.
1995 (R) 192m/C Anthony Hopkins, Joan Allen, Ed Harris, Bob Hoskins, David Paymer, Paul Sorvino, J. T. Walsh, James Woods, Madeline Kahn, Brian Bedford, Mary Steenburgen, Powers Boothe, E. G. Marshall, David Hyde Pierce, Kevin Dunn, Annabeth Gish, Tony Goldwyn, Larry Hagman, Edward Herrmann, Saul Rubinek, Tony LoBianco; **D:** Oliver Stone; **W:** Christopher Wilkinson, Stephen J. Rivele, Oliver Stone; **M:** John Williams. Los Angeles Film Critics Association Awards '95: Best Supporting Actress (Allen); National Society of Film Critics Awards '95: Best Supporting Actress (Allen);

Nominations: Academy Awards '95: Best Actor (Hopkins), Best Supporting Actress (Allen), Best Screenplay, Best Score; British Academy Awards '95: Best Supporting Actress (Allen); Golden Globe Awards '95: Best Actor—Drama (Hopkins); Screen Actors Guild Award '95: Best Actor (Hopkins), Best Actress (Allen), Cast. **VHS, LV** ★★★

No Regrets for Our Youth A feminist saga depicting the spiritual growth of a foolish Japanese girl during the tumultuous years of WWII. In Japanese with English subtitles.
1946 110m/B JP Setsuko Hara; **D:** Akira Kurosawa. **VHS** ★★★

No Time for Sergeants Hilarious film version of the Broadway play by Ira Levin. Young Andy Griffith is excellent as the Georgia farm boy who gets drafted into the service and creates mayhem among his superiors and colleagues. Story also told on an earlier television special and later in a series. Note Don Knotts and Benny Baker in small roles along with Jameel Farah who went on to star in TV's M*A*S*H after changing his name to Jamie Farr.
1958 119m/B Andy Griffith, Nick Adams, Murray Hamilton, Don Knotts, Jamie Farr, Myron McCormick; **D:** Mervyn LeRoy. **VHS, Beta, LV** ★★★

No Way Out Career Navy man Costner is involved with a beautiful, sexy woman who is murdered. Turns out she was also the mistress of the Secretary of Defense, Costner's boss. Assigned to investigate the murder, he suddenly finds himself the chief suspect. A tight thriller based on 1948's "The Big Clock," with a new surprise ending.
1987 (R) 114m/C Kevin Costner, Sean Young, Gene Hackman, Will Patton, Howard Duff, George Dzundza, Iman, Chris D, Marshall Bell, Jason Bernard, Fred Dalton Thompson, David Paymer; **D:** Roger Donaldson; **W:** Robert Garland; **M:** Maurice Jarre. **VHS, Beta, LV** ★★★

No Way to Treat a Lady Steiger is a psychotic master of disguise who stalks and kills various women in this suspenseful cat-and-mouse game. Segal, as the detective assigned to the case, uncovers clues, falls in love, and discovers that his new girl may be the killer's next victim.
1968 108m/C Rod Steiger, Lee Remick, George Segal, Eileen Heckart, Murray Hamilton; **D:** Jack Smight; **W:** John Gay, Jack Priestley. **VHS, Beta** ★★★

Nobody's Fool Newman shines as 60-year-old Donald "Sully" Sullivan, a construction worker who, in spite of himself, begins mending his many broken relationships over the course of the holiday season. Seemingly plotless scenario is sprinkled with enough humor, hope, and under-stated inspiration to become a delightfully modest celebration of a perfectly ordinary man. Character-driven story is blessed with commendable performances by supporting players—obviously inspired by Newman's brilliant portrayal. Based on the novel by Richard Russo.

1994 (R) 110m/C Paul Newman, Jessica Tandy, Bruce Willis, Melanie Griffith, Dylan Walsh, Pruitt Taylor Vince, Gene Saks, Josef Sommer, Philip S. Hoffman, Philip Bosco, Margo Martindale, Jay Patterson; **D:** Robert Benton; **W:** Robert Benton; **M:** John Bloom, Roger Deakins. Berlin International Film Festival '94: Best Actor (Newman); New York Film Critics Awards '94: Best Actor (Newman); National Society of Film Critics Awards '94: Best Actor (Newman); Nominations: Academy Awards '94: Best Actor (Newman), Best Adapted Screenplay; Golden Globe Awards '95: Best Actor—Drama (Newman); Screen Actors Guild Award '94: Best Actor (Newman). **VHS, Beta ★★★1/2**

None But the Lonely Heart In the days before WWII, a Cockney drifter (Grant) wanders the East End of London. When his get-rich-quick schemes fail, his dying shopkeeper-mother tries to help and lands in prison. Interesting characterization of life in the slums. Odets not only directed, but wrote the screenplay.

1944 113m/B Cary Grant, Ethel Barrymore, Barry Fitzgerald, Jane Wyatt, Dan Duryea, George Coulouris, June Duprez; **D:** Clifford Odets; **W:** Clifford Odets. Academy Awards '44: Best Supporting Actress (Barrymore); National Board of Review Awards '44: 10 Best Films of the Year; Nominations: Academy Awards '44: Best Actor (Grant), Best Film Editing, Best Original Score. **VHS, Beta ★★★**

Norma Rae A poor, uneducated textile worker joins forces with a New York labor organizer to unionize the reluctant workers at a Southern mill. Field was a surprise with her fully developed character's strength, beauty, and humor; her Oscar was well-deserved. Ritt's direction is top-notch. Jennifer Warnes sings the theme song, "It Goes Like It Goes," which also won an Oscar. ♪ It Goes Like It Goes.

1979 (PG) 114m/C Sally Field, Ron Leibman, Beau Bridges, Pat Hingle; **D:** Martin Ritt; **W:** Harriet Frank Jr., Irving Ravetch; **M:** David Shire, John A. Alonzo. Academy Awards '79: Best Actress (Field), Best Song ("It Goes Like It Goes"); Golden Globe Awards '80: Best Actress—Drama (Field); Los Angeles Film Critics Association Awards '79: Best Actress (Field); National Board of Review Awards '79: Best Actress (Field); New York Film Critics Awards '79: Best Actress (Field); National Society of Film Critics Awards '79: Best Actress (Field); Nominations: Academy Awards '79: Best Adapted Screenplay, Best Picture; Cannes Film Festival '79: Best Film. **VHS, Beta, LV ★★★**

North and South Book 1 Lavish spectacle about a friendship tested by the turbulent times leading up to Civil War. Orry Main (Swayze) is a South Carolina plantation owner while his best friend George Hazard (Read) comes from a Pennsylvania industrial family. Orry is also involved in a doomed romance with the beautiful Madeline (Down), who's forced to marry the odious Justin LaMotte (Carradine). Lots of intrigue and excitement. Based on the novel by John Jakes. Filmed on location in Charleston, South Carolina. Originally broadcast as a six-part TV miniseries. Available on six cassettes.

1985 561m/C Patrick Swayze, James Read, Lesley-Anne Down, David Carradine, Kirstie Alley, Jean Simmons, Inga Swenson, Jonathon Frakes, Genie Francis, Terri Garber, Georg Stanford Brown, Olivia Cole, David Ogden Stiers, Robert Guillaume, Hal Holbrook, Gene Kelly, Robert Mitchum, Johnny Cash, Elizabeth Taylor; **M:** Bill Conti. **VHS, Beta ★★★**

North and South Book 2 Equally dramatic sequel follows the southern Main clan and the northern Hazard family into the Civil War as friendship and romance struggle to survive the fighting. Casnoff is a notable presence as the aptly-named Bent, who will go to any length to settle old scores with both families. Based on the John Jakes novel "Love and War." Originally broadcast as a six-part TV miniseries; on six cassettes. The last of the Jakes trilogy, "Heaven and Hell," was finally filmed for TV in '94 but proved a major disappointment.

1986 570m/C Patrick Swayze, James Read, Lesley-Anne Down, Terri Garber, Genie Francis, Jean Simmons, Kirstie Alley, Philip Casnoff, Hal Holbrook, Lloyd Bridges, James Stewart, Morgan Fairchild, Nancy Marchand, Parker Stevenson, Lewis Smith; **M:** Bill Conti. **VHS ★★★**

North by Northwest Self-assured Madison Avenue ad exec Grant inadvertently gets involved with international spies when they mistake him for someone else. His problems are compounded when he's framed for murder. The movie where Grant and Saint dangle from the faces of Mount Rushmore and a plane chases Grant through farm fields. Exceptional performances, particularly Grant's. Plenty of plot twists are mixed with tongue-in-cheek humor. Considered by many to be one of Hitchcock's greatest films. Laserdisc includes letterboxing, digital soundtrack, Hitchcock interview, production and publicity photos, storyboards, and the original trailer.

1959 136m/C Cary Grant, Eva Marie Saint, James Mason, Leo G. Carroll, Martin Landau, Jessie Royce Landis, Philip Ober, Adam Williams, Josephine Hutchinson, Edward Platt; *D:* Alfred Hitchcock; *W:* Ernest Lehman; *M:* Bernard Herrmann. Edgar Allan Poe Awards '59: Best Screenplay; Nominations: Academy Awards '59: Best Art Direction/Set Decoration (Color), Best Film Editing, Best Story & Screenplay. **VHS, Beta, LV ★★★★**

North Dallas Forty Based on the novel by former Dallas Cowboy Peter Gent, the film focuses on the labor abuses in pro-football. One of the best football movies ever made, it contains searing commentary and very good acting, although the plot is sometimes dropped behind the line of scrimmage.

1979 (R) 119m/C Nick Nolte, Mac Davis, Charles Durning, Bo Svenson, Brian Dennehy, John Matuszak, Dayle Haddon, Steve Forrest, Dabney Coleman, G.D. Spradlin; *D:* Ted Kotcheff. National Board of Review Awards '79: 10 Best Films of the Year. **VHS, Beta, LV ★★★1/2**

The North Star Gripping war tale of Nazis overrunning an eastern Russian city, with courageous villagers fighting back. Colorized version available. *AKA:* Armored Attack.

1943 108m/B Dana Andrews, Walter Huston, Anne Baxter, Farley Granger, Walter Brennan, Erich von Stroheim, Jack Perrin, Dean Jagger; *D:* Lewis Milestone; *M:* Aaron Copland. Nominations: Academy Awards '43: Best Black and White Cinematography, Best Interior Decoration, Best Original Screenplay, Best Sound, Best Original Score. **VHS, Beta ★★★**

Northwest Passage The lavish first half of a projected two-film package based on Kenneth Roberts' popular novel, depicting the troop of Rogers' Rangers fighting the wilderness and hostile Indians. Beautifully produced; the second half was never made and the passage itself is never seen.

1940 126m/C Spencer Tracy, Robert Young, Ruth Hussey, Walter Brennan, Nat Pendleton, Robert Barrat, Lumsden Hare; *D:* King Vidor. Nominations: Academy Awards '40: Best Color Cinematography. **VHS, Beta ★★★**

Nosferatu The first film adaptation of Bram Stoker's "Dracula" remains one of the creepiest and most atmospheric versions. Murnau knew how to add just the right touches to make this one of the best vampire films ever made. All it lacks is the name of Dracula, which was changed due to copyright problems with Stoker's widow. Filmed in Bavaria. Silent with music and English titles. Remade by Werner Herzog in 1979. *AKA:* Nosferatu, Eine Symphonie des Grauens; Nosferatu, A Symphony of Terror; Nosferatu, A Symphony of Horror; Nosferatu, The Vampire.

1922 63m/B *GE* Max Schreck, Alexander Granach, Gustav von Wagenheim, Greta Schroeder; *D:* F.W. Murnau. **VHS, Beta, LV ★★★★**

Nothing Sacred Slick, overzealous reporter takes advantage of a small-town girl's situation. As a publicity stunt, his newspaper brings her to the Big Apple to distract her from her supposedly imminent death in order to manipulate the public's sentiment as a means to sell more copy. Innocent young Lombard, however, is far from death's door, and deftly exploits her exploitation. Scathing indictment of the mass media and bovine mentality of the masses. Both hysterically funny and bitterly cynical; boasts Lombard's finest performance as the small-town rube who orchestrates the ruse. Remade in 1954 as "Living It Up."

1937 75m/C Fredric March, Carole Lombard, Walter Connolly, Sig Rumann, Charles Winninger, Margaret Hamilton; *D:* William A. Wellman; *W:* Ben Hecht; *M:* Oscar Levant. **VHS, Beta, LV ★★★1/2**

Notorious Post-WWII story of a beautiful playgirl sent by the US government to marry a suspected spy living in Brazil. Grant is the agent assigned to watch her. Duplicity and guilt are important factors in this brooding, romantic spy thriller. Suspenseful throughout, with a surprise ending. The acting is excellent all around and Hitchcock makes certain that suspense is maintained throughout this classy and complex thriller. Laser edition contains original trailer, publicity photos, and additional footage.

1946 101m/B Cary Grant, Ingrid Bergman,

Claude Rains, Louis Calhern, Madame Konstantin, Reinhold Schunzel, Moroni Olsen; *D:* Alfred Hitchcock; *W:* Ben Hecht. Nominations: Academy Awards '46: Best Original Screenplay, Best Supporting Actor (Rains). **VHS, Beta, LV ★★★★**

Now, Voyager Davis plays a lonely spinster who is transformed into a vibrant young woman by therapy. She comes out of her shell to have a romantic affair with a suave European (who turns out to be married) but still utters the famous phrase "Oh, Jerry, we have the stars. Let's not ask for the moon." Definitely melodramatic, but an involving story nonetheless. Based on a novel by Olive Higgins Prouty.
1942 117m/B Bette Davis, Gladys Cooper, Claude Rains, Paul Henreid, Bonita Granville; *D:* Irving Rapper; *M:* Max Steiner. Academy Awards '42: Best Score; Nominations: Academy Awards '42: Best Actress (Davis), Best Supporting Actress (Cooper). **VHS, Beta, LV ★★★1/2**

The Nun's Story The melancholy tale of a young nun working in the Congo and Belgium during WWII, and struggling to reconcile her free spirit with the rigors of the order. Highly acclaimed; from the Kathryn Hulme novel.
1959 152m/C Audrey Hepburn, Peter Finch, Edith Evans, Peggy Ashcroft, Mildred Dunnock, Dean Jagger, Beatrice Straight, Colleen Dewhurst; *D:* Fred Zinnemann; *W:* Robert Anderson. British Academy Awards '59: Best Actress (Hepburn); National Board of Review Awards '59: 10 Best Films of the Year, Best Director (Zinnemann), Best Supporting Actress (Evans); Nominations: Academy Awards '59: Best Actress (Hepburn), Best Adapted Screenplay, Best Color Cinematography, Best Director (Zinnemann), Best Film Editing, Best Picture, Best Sound, Best Original Score. **VHS, Beta, LV ★★★1/2**

The Nutty Professor A mild-mannered chemistry professor creates a potion that turns him into a suave, debonair, playboy type with an irresistible attraction to women. Lewis has repeatedly denied the slick character is a Dean Martin parody, but the evidence is quite strong. Easily Lewis's best film.
1963 107m/C Jerry Lewis, Stella Stevens, Howard Morris, Kathleen Freeman; *D:* Jerry Lewis; *W:* Jerry Lewis. **VHS, Beta, LV ★★★**

The Nutty Professor In this remake of the Jerry Lewis 1963 comedy, Murphy stars as Professor Sherman Klump, a severely overweight but bright man whose heft gets in the way of his love life. He takes a swig of his own secret potion and is transformed into the slim and suave Buddy Love. Only the formula isn't perfect and seems to wear off at the worst possible times. After a string of bad movies, Murphy may have stumbled upon his own formula for a comeback by relinquishing creative control and concentrating on the comedy. Reminiscent of "Coming to America," Murphy plays eight different roles. The fat jokes and the fart jokes are plentiful and so are the laughs.
1996 (PG-13) 96m/C Eddie Murphy, Jada Pinkett, James Coburn, Dave Chappelle; *D:* Tom Shadyac; *W:* David Sheffield, Barry W. Blaustein, Steve Oedekerk, Tom Shadyac; *M:* David Newman. National Society of Film Critics Awards '96: Best Actor (Murphy); Nominations: Golden Globe Awards '97: Best Actor—Musical/Comedy (Murphy). **VHS, LV ★★★**

O Lucky Man! Surreal, black comedy following the rise and fall and eventual rebirth of a modern British coffee salesman. Several actors play multiple roles with outstanding performances throughout. Price's excellent score combines with the hilarity for an extraordinary experience.
1973 (R) 178m/C *GB* Malcolm McDowell, Ralph Richardson, Rachel Roberts, Arthur Lowe, Alan Price, Helen Mirren, Mona Washbourne, Warren Clarke; *D:* Lindsay Anderson; *M:* Alan Price. British Academy Awards '73: Best Supporting Actor (Lowe); National Board of Review Awards '73: 10 Best Films of the Year; Nominations: Cannes Film Festival '73: Best Film. **VHS, Beta ★★★★**

The Object of Beauty Two Americans, trapped in Europe by their love of pleasure and their lack of money, bicker over whether to sell their one object of value - a tiny Henry Moore sculpture. When it disappears, their relationship is challenged. Excellent acting and telling direction. Forces an examination of one's own value placement.
1991 (R) 105m/C Andie MacDowell, John Malkovich, Joss Ackland, Lolita Davidovich, Peter Riegert, Bill Paterson, Rudi Davies, Ricci Harnett; *D:* Michael Lindsay-Hogg; *W:* Michael Lindsay-Hogg; *M:* Tom Bahler. **VHS, LV ★★★**

Objective, Burma! Deemed by many to be the greatest and most moving WWII production released during the war. American paratroopers are dropped over Burma where their mission is to destroy a Japanese radar

station. The Americans led by Flynn are successful in wiping out the station, but they are spotted and descended upon by Japanese forces. Impeded from returning to Allied lines, the American soldiers must try to survive enemy encounters, exhaustion, starvation, and the elements until they are rescued. Splendid performance by Flynn and exceptional direction from Walsh; excellent performances enhanced by energetic score.
1945 142m/B Errol Flynn, James Brown, William Prince, George Tobias, Henry Hull, Warner Anderson, Richard Erdman, Mark Stevens, Anthony Caruso, Hugh Beaumont; *D:* Raoul Walsh; *W:* Ranald MacDougall, Lester Cole; *M:* Franz Waxman. Nominations: Academy Awards '45: Best Film Editing, Best Story, Best Original Score. **VHS, Beta** ★★★★

Oblomov A production of the classic Goncharov novel about a symbolically inert Russian aristocrat whose childhood friend helps him find a reason for action. Well made, with fine performances. In Russian with English subtitles. *AKA:* A Few Days in the Life of I.I. Oblomov; Neskolko Dnei iz Zhizni I.I. Oblomov.
1981 145m/C *RU* Oleg Tabakov, Elena Solovei; *D:* Nikita Mikhalkov. **VHS, Beta** ★★★1/2

The Odd Couple Two divorced men with completely opposite personalities move in together. Lemmon's obsession with neatness drives slob Matthau up the wall, and their inability to see eye-to-eye results in many hysterical escapades. A Hollywood rarity, it is actually better in some ways than Neil Simon's original Broadway version. Basis for the hit television series.
1968 (G) 106m/C Jack Lemmon, Walter Matthau, Herb Edelman, John Fiedler, Monica Evans, Carol Shelley; *D:* Gene Saks, Robert B. Hauser; *W:* Neil Simon. Nominations: Academy Awards '68: Best Adapted Screenplay, Best Film Editing. **VHS, Beta, LV** ★★★1/2

Odd Man Out An Irish revolutionary is injured during a robbery attempt. Suffering from gunshot wounds and closely pursued by the police, he must rely on the help of others who could betray him at any moment. A gripping tale of suspense and intrigue that will keep the proverbial seat's edge warm until the final credits. Adapted from F.L. Green's novel, previously filmed as "The Last Man." *AKA:* Gang War.
1947 111m/B *GB* James Mason, Robert Newton, Dan O'Herlihy, Kathleen Ryan,

Cyril Cusack; *D:* Carol Reed. British Academy Awards '47: Best Film; National Board of Review Awards '47: 10 Best Films of the Year; Nominations: Academy Awards '47: Best Film Editing. **VHS, Beta, LV** ★★★1/2

Oedipus Rex A new twist on the famous tragedy as Pasolini gives the story a modern prologue and epilogue. The classic plot has Oedipus spiraling downward into moral horror as he tries to avoid fulfilling the prophecy that he will murder his father and sleep with his mother. Cross-cultural curiosities include Japanese music and Lenin-inspired songs, some written by Pasolini, who also stars as the high priest. In Italian with English subtitles. *AKA:* Edipo Re.
1967 110m/C *IT* Franco Citti, Silvana Mangano, Alida Valli, Julian Beck, Pier Paolo Pasolini; *D:* Pier Paolo Pasolini. **VHS** ★★★

Of Human Bondage The first movie version of W. Somerset Maugham's classic novel in which a young, handicapped medical student falls in love with a crude cockney waitress, in a mutually destructive affair. Established Davis's role as the tough, domineering woman. Remade in 1946 and 1964.
1934 84m/B Bette Davis, Leslie Howard, Frances Dee, Reginald Owen, Reginald Denny, Alan Hale; *D:* John Cromwell; *M:* Max Steiner. **VHS, Beta, LV** ★★★

Of Mice and Men A powerful adaptation of the classic Steinbeck tragedy about the friendship between two itinerant Southern ranch hands during the Great Depression. Chaney is wonderful as the gentle giant and mentally retarded Lenny, cared for by migrant worker Meredith. They both get into an irreversible situation when a woman is accidentally killed.
1939 107m/C Lon Chaney Jr., Burgess Meredith, Betty Field, Bob Steele, Noah Beery Jr., Charles Bickford; *D:* Lewis Milestone; *M:* Aaron Copland. Nominations: Academy Awards '39: Best Picture, Best Sound, Best Score. **VHS, Beta** ★★★★

Of Mice and Men Set on the migratory farms of California, John Steinbeck's novel covers the friendship of the simple-minded Lenny, his protector George, and a flirtatious farm wife who doesn't know Lenny's strength. Director Sinise got permission from Steinbeck's widow to film the novel (actually the third adaptation).
1992 (PG-13) 110m/C John Malkovich, Sherilyn Fenn, Casey Siemaszko, Joe Morton, Ray Walston, Gary Sinise, John

Terry, Richard Riehle; **D:** Gary Sinise; **W:** Horton Foote. Nominations: Cannes Film Festival '92: Best Film. **VHS, LV ★★★1/2**

An Officer and a Gentleman Young drifter Gere, who enters Navy Officer Candidate School because he doesn't know what else to do with his life, becomes a better person almost despite himself. Winger is the love interest who sets her sights on marrying Gere, and Gossett is the sergeant who whips him into shape. Strong performances by the whole cast made this a must-see in 1982 that is still appealing, despite the standard Hollywood premise. ♪ Up Where We Belong; Hungry for Your Love; An Officer and a Gentleman; Treat Me Right; Tunnel of Love.
1982 (R) 126m/C Richard Gere, Louis Gossett Jr., David Keith, Lisa Eilbacher, Debra Winger, David Caruso, Robert Loggia, Lisa Blount, Donald E. Thorin; **D:** Taylor Hackford; **M:** Jack Nitzsche. Academy Awards '82: Best Song ("Up Where We Belong"), Best Supporting Actor (Gossett); Nominations: Academy Awards '82: Best Actress (Winger), Best Film Editing, Best Original Screenplay, Best Original Score. **VHS, Beta, LV, 8mm ★★★1/2**

The Official Story A devastating drama about an Argentinian woman who realizes her young adopted daughter may be a child stolen from one of the thousands of citizens victimized by the country's repressive government. A powerful, important film. In Spanish with English subtitles or dubbed. **AKA:** La Historia Oficial; The Official History; The Official Version.
1985 (R) 112m/C *AR* Norma Aleandro, Hector Alterio, Chunchuna Villafane, Patricio Contreras; **D:** Luis Puenzo; **W:** Luis Puenzo, Aida Bortnik. Academy Awards '85: Best Foreign Language Film; Cannes Film Festival '85: Best Actress (Aleandro); Golden Globe Awards '86: Best Foreign Film; Los Angeles Film Critics Association Awards '85: Best Foreign Film; New York Film Critics Awards '85: Best Actress (Aleandro); Nominations: Academy Awards '85: Best Original Screenplay. **VHS, Beta, LV ★★★1/2**

Oklahoma! Jones's film debut; a must-see for musical fans. A cowboy and country girl fall in love, but she is tormented by another unwelcomed suitor. At over two hours, cuteness wears thin for some. Actually filmed in Arizona. Adapted from Rodgers and Hammerstein's broadway hit with original score; choreography by Agnes de Mille. ♪ Oh, What a Beautiful Morning; Surrey with the Fringe on Top; I Cain't Say No; Many a New Day; People Will Say We're in Love; Poor Jud Is Dead; All 'Er Nuthin'; Everything's Up to Date in Kansas City; The Farmer and the Cowman.
1955 (G) 145m/C Gordon MacRae, Shirley Jones, Rod Steiger, Gloria Grahame, Eddie Albert, Charlotte Greenwood, James Whitmore, Gene Nelson, Barbara Lawrence, Jay C. Flippen; **D:** Fred Zinneman; **W:** Sonya Levien, William Ludwig; **M:** Richard Rodgers, Oscar Hammerstein. Academy Awards '55: Best Sound, Best Score; Nominations: Academy Awards '55: Best Color Cinematography, Best Film Editing. **VHS, Beta, LV ★★★1/2**

Oklahoma Kid Offbeat, hilarious western with Bogie as the villain and gunfighter Cagney seeking revenge for his father's wrongful death. Highlight is Cagney's rendition of "I Don't Want To Play In Your Yard," complete with six-shooter accompaniment.
1939 82m/B James Cagney, Humphrey Bogart, Rosemary Lane, Ward Bond, Donald Crisp, Charles Middleton, Harvey Stephens; **D:** Lloyd Bacon; **M:** Max Steiner. **VHS, Beta ★★★**

The Old Dark House An atmospheric horror film, with more than a touch of comedy, well-directed by Whale. In an old haunted house live the bizarre Femm family: the 102- year-old patriarch, an atheist son, a religious fanatic daughter, and a crazed pyromaniac son, all watched over by the mute, scarred, and psychotic butler (Karloff's first starring role). Into this strange group wander five unsuspecting, stranded travelers who set all sorts of dastardly plots in motion. Based on the novel "Benighted" by J.B. Priestley.
1932 71m/B Boris Karloff, Melvyn Douglas, Charles Laughton, Gloria Stuart, Ernest Thesiger, Raymond Massey, Lillian Bond, Eva Moore, Brember Wills, John Dudgeon; **D:** James Whale; **W:** Robert Dillon. **VHS ★★★**

Old Ironsides Silent, black-and-white version of the big budget/important director and features action-adventure. Merchant marines aboard the famous Old Ironsides battle 19th-century Barbary pirates in rousing action scenes. Home video version features an engaging organ score by Gaylord Carter. Based on the poem "Constitution" by Oliver Wendell Holmes.
1926 111m/B Esther Ralston, Wallace Beery, Boris Karloff, Charles Farrell, George Bancroft; **D:** James Cruze; **M:** Gaylord Carter. **VHS, Beta ★★★**

The Old Maid After her beau is killed in the Civil War, a woman allows her cousin to raise her illegitimate daughter, and therein begins a years-long struggle over the girl's affections. High grade soaper based on Zoe Adkin's stage adaptation of Edith Wharton's novel.
1939 96m/B Bette Davis, Miriam Hopkins, George Brent, Donald Crisp, Jane Bryan, Louise Fazenda, Henry Stephenson; *D:* Edmund Goulding; *M:* Max Steiner. **VHS, Beta ★★★**

Old Yeller Disney Studios' first and best boy-and-his-dog film. Fifteen-year-old Kirk is left in charge of the family farm while Parker is away. When his younger brother brings home a stray dog, Kirk is displeased but lets him stay. Yeller saves Kirk's life, but contracts rabies in the process. Kirk is forced to kill him. Keep tissue handy, especially for the kids. Stong acting, effective scenery —all good stuff. Based on the novel by Fred Gipson. Sequel "Savage Sam" released in 1963.
1957 (G) 84m/C Dorothy McGuire, Fess Parker, Tommy Kirk, Kevin Corcoran, Jeff York, Beverly Washburn, Chuck Connors; *D:* Robert Stevenson. **VHS, Beta, LV ★★★1/2**

Oldest Confederate Widow Tells All TV drama starts with the recollections of 99-year-old Lucy Marsden (Bancroft), the widow of the title, as she revisits her marriage to troubled Civil War veteran Capt. William Marsden (Sutherland, sporting an impressive set of whiskers). In 1899, the teenaged Lucy (played by Lane) marries the eccentric 50-year-old, who constantly relives battlefield horrors and the loss of his boyhood friend, while she deals with family and various domestic crises. Somewhat meandering story with fine performances and subtle details. Based on Allan Gurganus' novel.
1995 180m/C Diane Lane, Donald Sutherland, Anne Bancroft, Cicely Tyson, Blythe Danner, E.G. Marshall, Gwen Verdon, Maureen Mueller, Wil Horneff; *D:* Ken Cameron; *W:* Joyce Eliason; *M:* Mark Snow. **VHS ★★★**

Oliver! Splendid big-budget musical adaptation of Dickens' "Oliver Twist." An innocent orphan is dragged into a life of crime when he is befriended by a gang of pickpockets. ♪ Food, Glorious Food; Oliver; Boy For Sale; Where Is Love?; Consider Yourself; Pick a Pocket or Two; I'd Do Anything; Be Back Soon; As Long As He Needs Me.
1968 (G) 145m/C *GB* Mark Lester, Jack Wild, Ron Moody, Shani Wallis, Oliver Reed, Hugh Griffith; *D:* Carol Reed. Academy Awards '68: Best Art Direction/Set Decoration, Best Director (Reed), Best Picture, Best Sound, Best Score; Golden Globe Awards '69: Best Actor—Musical/Comedy (Moody), Best Film—Musical/Comedy; National Board of Review Awards '68: 10 Best Films of the Year; Nominations: Academy Awards '68: Best Actor (Moody), Best Adapted Screenplay, Best Cinematography, Best Costume Design, Best Film Editing, Best Supporting Actor (Wild). **VHS, Beta, LV ★★★1/2**

Oliver Twist Charles Dickens' immortal story of a workhouse orphan who is forced into a life of crime with a gang of pickpockets. The best of many film adaptations, with excellent portrayals by the cast.
1948 116m/C *GB* Robert Newton, John Howard Davies, Alec Guinness, Francis L. Sullivan, Anthony Newley, Kay Walsh, Diana Dors, Henry Stephenson; *D:* David Lean; *W:* David Lean. **VHS, Beta, LV ★★★★**

On Dangerous Ground A world-weary detective is sent to the countryside to investigate a murder. He encounters the victim's revenge-hungry father and the blind sister of the murderer. In the hateful father the detective sees a reflection of the person he has become, in the blind woman, he learns the redeeming qualities of humanity and compassion. A well-acted example of film noir that features the composer Herrman's favorite score.
1951 82m/B Robert Ryan, Ida Lupino, Ward Bond, Ed Begley Sr., Cleo Moore, Charles Kemper; *D:* Nicholas Ray; *M:* Bernard Herrmann. **VHS, Beta, LV ★★★**

On Golden Pond Henry Fonda won his first, and long overdue, Oscar for his role as the curmudgeonly patriarch of the Thayer family. He and his wife have grudgingly agreed to look after a young boy while at their summer home in Maine. Through his gradually affectionate relationship with the boy, Fonda learns to allay his fears of mortality. He also gains an understanding of his semi-estranged daughter. Jane Fonda plays his daughter and Hepburn is his loving wife in this often funny adaptation of Ernest Thompson's 1978 play. Predictable but deeply moving. Henry Fonda's final screen appearance.
1981 (PG) 109m/C Henry Fonda, Jane Fonda, Katharine Hepburn, Dabney

Coleman, Doug McKeon, William Lanteau; **D:** Mark Rydell; **W:** Ernest Thompson; **M:** Dave Grusin. Academy Awards '81: Best Actor (Fonda), Best Actress (Hepburn), Best Adapted Screenplay; British Academy Awards '82: Best Actress (Hepburn); Golden Globe Awards '82: Best Actor—Drama (Fonda), Best Film—Drama, Best Screenplay; National Board of Review Awards '81: Best Actor (Fonda); Writers Guild of America '81: Best Adapted Screenplay; Nominations: Academy Awards '81: Best Cinematography, Best Director (Rydell), Best Film Editing, Best Sound, Best Supporting Actress (Fonda), Best Original Score. **VHS, Beta, LV** ★★★1/2

On Her Majesty's Secret Service In the sixth 007 adventure, Bond again confronts the infamous Blofeld, who is planning a germ-warfare assault on the entire world. Australian Lazenby took a crack at playing the super spy, with mixed results. Many feel this is the best-written of the Bond films and might have been the most famous, had Sean Connery continued with the series. Includes the song "We Have All the Time In the World," sung by Louis Armstrong.
1969 (PG) 144m/C *GB* George Lazenby, Diana Rigg, Telly Savalas, Gabriele Ferzetti, Ilse Steppat, Bernard Lee, Lois Maxwell, Desmond Llewelyn, Catherine Schell, Julie Ege, Joanna Lumley, Mona Chong, Anouska Hempel, Jenny Hanley; **D:** Peter Hunt; **M:** John Barry. **VHS, Beta, LV** ★★★

On the Avenue Broadway showman Powell opens up a new musical, starring Faye as the richest girl in the world, in this musical-comedy satirizing upper-crust society. Debutante Carroll is outraged because she realizes it's mocking her actual life. Carroll tries to get Powell to change the show, they fall in love, Faye gets her nose out of joint, and after lots of fuss everything ends happily. Fine Berlin score. ♩ He Ain't Got Rhythm; You're Laughing at Me; This Year's Kisses; Slumming on Park Avenue; The Girl on the Police Gazette; I've Got My Love to Keep Me Warm.
1937 90m/B Dick Powell, Madeleine Carroll, Alice Faye, George Barbier, The Ritz Brothers, Alan Mowbray, Cora Witherspoon, Walter Catlett, Stepin Fetchit, Sig Rumann, Douglas Fowley, Joan Davis; **D:** Roy Del Ruth; **W:** Gene Markey; **M:** Irving Berlin. **VHS** ★★★

On the Beach A group of survivors attempt to live normal lives in post-apocalyptic Australia, waiting for the inevitable arrival of killer radiation. Astaire is strong in his first dramatic role. Though scientifically implausible, still a good anti-war vehicle. Based on the best-selling novel by Nevil Shute.
1959 135m/B Gregory Peck, Anthony Perkins, Donna Anderson, Ava Gardner, Fred Astaire; **D:** Stanley Kramer; **M:** Ernest Gold. Golden Globe Awards '60: Best Score; National Board of Review Awards '59: 10 Best Films of the Year; Nominations: Academy Awards '59: Best Film Editing, Best Original Score. **VHS, Beta, LV** ★★★1/2

On the Town Kelly's directorial debut features three sailors on a one day leave searching for romance in the Big Apple. Filmed on location in New York City, with uncompromisingly authentic flavor. Based on the successful Broadway musical, with a score composed by Leonard Bernstein, Betty Comden, and Adolph Green. Additional songs by Roger Edens. Available in a deluxe collector's laser-disc edition. ♩ New York, New York; I Feel Like I'm Not Out of Bed Yet; Come Up to My Place; Miss Turnstiles Ballet; Main Street; You're Awful; On the Town; You Can Count on Me; Pearl of the Persian Sea.
1949 98m/C Gene Kelly, Frank Sinatra, Vera-Ellen, Ann Miller, Betty Garrett; **D:** Gene Kelly, Stanley Donen; **W:** Betty Comden, Adolph Green. Academy Awards '49: Best Score. **VHS, Beta, LV** ★★★1/2

On the Waterfront A trend-setting, gritty portrait of New York dock workers embroiled in union violence. Cobb is the gangster union boss, Steiger his crooked lawyer, and Brando, Steiger's ex-fighter brother who "could've been a contender!" Intense performances and excellent direction stand up well today. The picture was a huge financial success.
1954 108m/B Marlon Brando, Rod Steiger, Eva Marie Saint, Lee J. Cobb, Karl Malden, Pat Henning, Leif Erickson, Tony Galento, John Hamilton, Nehemiah Persoff; **D:** Elia Kazan; **W:** Budd Schulberg; **M:** Leonard Bernstein. Academy Awards '54: Best Actor (Brando), Best Art Direction/Set Decoration (B & W), Best Black and White Cinematography, Best Director (Kazan), Best Film Editing, Best Picture, Best Story & Screenplay, Best Supporting Actress (Saint); Directors Guild of America Awards '54: Best Director (Kazan); Golden Globe Awards '55: Best Actor—Drama (Brando), Best Director (Kazan), Best Film—Drama; National Board of Review Awards '54: 10 Best Films of the Year; New York Film Critics Awards '54: Best Actor (Brando), Best Director (Kazan), Best Film; Nominations: Academy Awards '54: Best Supporting Actor (Cobb), Best Supporting

Actor (Malden, Steiger), Best Original Score. **VHS, Beta, LV** ★★★★

Once Upon a Time in America The uncut original version of director Leone's saga of five young men growing up in Brooklyn during the '20s who become powerful mob figures. Also available in a 143-minute version. Told from the perspective of De Niro's Noodles as an old man looking back at 50 years of crime, love, and death, told with a sweeping and violent elegance.
1984 (R) 225m/C Robert De Niro, James Woods, Elizabeth McGovern, Treat Williams, Tuesday Weld, Burt Young, Joe Pesci, Danny Aiello, Darlanne Fluegel, Jennifer Connelly; **D:** Sergio Leone; **M:** Ennio Morricone, Tonino Delli Colli. **VHS, Beta, LV** ★★★1/2

Once Upon a Time in the West The uncut version of Leone's sprawling epic about a band of ruthless gunmen who set out to murder a mysterious woman waiting for the railroad to come through. Filmed in John Ford's Monument Valley, it's a revisionist western with some of the longest opening credits in the history of the cinema. Fonda is cast against type as an extremely cold-blooded villain. Brilliant musical score.
1968 (PG) 165m/C *IT* Henry Fonda, Jason Robards Jr., Charles Bronson, Claudia Cardinale, Keenan Wynn, Lionel Stander, Woody Strode, Jack Elam; **D:** Sergio Leone; **W:** Sergio Leone, Bernardo Bertolucci, Dario Argento, Tonino Delli Colli; **M:** Ennio Morricone. **VHS, Beta, LV** ★★★1/2

Once Upon a Time . . . When We Were Colored Actor Reid makes a fine directorial debut with the story of a black youngster growing up parentless in 1950s Mississippi. His family faces the usual troubles of the time, including poor wages and white bigotry, but manages to provide a positive and loving home life for him. Nostalgic, sensitive, and heartwarming adaption of Clifton Taulbert's autobiographical book.
1995 (PG) 112m/C Al Freeman Jr., Paula Kelly, Phylicia Rashad, Polly Bergen, Richard Roundtree, Charles Taylor, Willie Norwood Jr., Johnny Simmons, Damon Hines, Leon; **D:** Tim Reid; **W:** Paul Cooper; **M:** Steve Tyrell. **VHS, LV** ★★★

One Arabian Night When an exotic dancer in a traveling carnival troupe is kidnapped into a harem, a dwarf acts on his unrequited love and avenges her death by murdering the sheik who killed her. Secured a place in American filmmaking for director Lubitsch. *AKA:* Sumurun.
1921 85m/B *GE* Pola Negri, Ernst Lubitsch, Paul Wegener; **D:** Ernst Lubitsch. **VHS, Beta** ★★★

One Day in the Life of Ivan Denisovich The film version of Nobel Prize-winner Alexander Solzhenitsyn's novel about a prisoner's experiences in a Soviet labor camp. A testament to human endurance. Photography by Sven Nykvist.
1971 105m/C *NO GB* Tom Courtenay, Alfred Burke, Espen Skjonberg, James Maxwell, Eric Thompson; **D:** Caspar Wrede; **W:** Ronald Harwood. **VHS, LV** ★★★

One-Eyed Jacks An often engaging, but lengthy, psychological western about an outlaw who seeks to settle the score with a former partner who became a sheriff. Great acting by all, particularly Brando, who triumphed both as star and director. Stanley Kubrick was the original director, but Brando took over mid-way through the filming. The photography is wonderful and reflects the effort that went into it.
1961 141m/C Marlon Brando, Karl Malden, Katy Jurado, Elisha Cook Jr., Slim Pickens, Ben Johnson, Pina Pellicer, Timothy Carey; **D:** Marlon Brando; **W:** Calder Willingham. Nominations: Academy Awards '61: Best Color Cinematography. **VHS, Beta, LV** ★★★1/2

One False Move Black psycho Pluto, his white-trash partner Ray, and Ray's biracial lover Fantasia are three low-level drug dealers on the streets of Los Angeles who get involved in murder. Fleeing the city for Fantasia's small hometown in Arkansas, they come up against the local sheriff and two L.A. cops sent to bring them back. Not a typical crime thriller. First-time feature director Franklin is more interested in a psychological character study of racism and smalltown mores than in your average shoot 'em up action picture. Good performances, especially by Williams as the deceptive bad girl.
1991 (R) 105m/C Bill Paxton, Cynda Williams, Michael Beach, Jim Metzler, Earl Billings, Billy Bob Thornton, Natalie Canderday, Robert Ginnaven, Robert Anthony Bell, Kevin Hunter; **D:** Carl Franklin; **W:** Billy Bob Thornton, Tom Epperson. Independent Spirit Awards '93: Best Director (Franklin); MTV Movie Awards '93: Best New Filmmaker Award (Franklin). **VHS, LV** ★★★

One Flew Over the Cuckoo's Nest Touching, hilarious, dramatic, and completely effective adaptation of Ken Kesey's novel. Nicholson is a two-bit crook, who, facing a jail sentence, feigns insanity to be sentenced to a cushy mental hospital. The hospital is anything but cushy, with a tyrannical head nurse out to squash any vestige of the patients' independence. Nicholson proves to be a crazed messiah and catalyst for these mentally troubled patients and a worthy adversary for the head nurse. Classic performs superbly on numerous levels.

1975 (R) 129m/C Jack Nicholson, Brad Dourif, Louise Fletcher, Will Sampson, William Redfield, Danny DeVito, Christopher Lloyd, Scatman Crothers, Vincent Schiavelli, Michael Berryman, Peter Brocco, Louisa Moritz; **D:** Milos Forman; **W:** Ken Kesey, Bo Goldman, Haskell Wexler; **M:** Jack Nitzsche. Academy Awards '75: Best Actor (Nicholson), Best Actress (Fletcher), Best Adapted Screenplay, Best Director (Forman), Best Picture; British Academy Awards '76: Best Actor (Nicholson), Best Actress (Fletcher), Best Director (Forman), Best Film, Best Supporting Actor (Dourif); Golden Globe Awards '76: Best Actor—Drama (Nicholson), Best Actress—Drama (Fletcher), Best Director (Forman), Best Film—Drama, Best Screenplay; National Board of Review Awards '75: 10 Best Films of the Year, Best Actor (Nicholson); National Society of Film Critics Awards '75: Best Actor (Nicholson); People's Choice Awards '75: Best Film; Writers Guild of America '75: Best Adapted Screenplay; Nominations: Academy Awards '75: Best Cinematography, Best Film Editing, Best Supporting Actor (Dourif), Best Original Score. **VHS, Beta, LV** ★★★★

100 Men and a Girl Charming musical features Durbin as the daughter of an unemployed musician, who decides she will try to persuade Leopold Stokowski to help her launch an orchestra that will employ her father and his musician friends. Beautiful mix of classical and pop music. Based on a story by Hans Kraly. ♪ Hungarian Rhapsody No. 2; Symphony No. 5; Alleluja; It's Raining Sunbeams; A Heart That's Free.
1937 85m/B Deanna Durbin, Leopold Stokowski, Adolphe Menjou, Alice Brady, Eugene Pallette, Mischa Auer, Billy Gilbert, Alma Kruger, Christian Rub, Jed Prouty, Jack Mulhall; **D:** Henry Koster. Academy Awards '37: Best Score; Nominations: Academy Awards '37: Best Film Editing, Best Picture, Best Story. **VHS** ★★★

101 Dalmatians Disney classic is one of the highest-grossing animated films in the history of Hollywood.

Dogowners Roger and Anita, and their spotted pets Pongo and Perdita, are shocked when their puppies are kidnapped by Cruella de Vil, villainess extraordinaire, to make a simply fabulous spotted coat. The aid of various animals including a dog named Colonel, a horse, a cat, and a goose is enlisted to rescue the doomed pups. Imagine their surprise when they find not only their own puppies, but 84 more as well. You can expect a happy ending and lots of spots—6,469,952 to be exact. Based on the children's book by Dodie Smith. Technically notable for the first time use of the Xerox process to transfer the animator's drawings onto celluloid, which made the film's opening sequence of dots evolving into 101 barking dogs possible. ♪ Remember When; Cruella de Vil; Dalmation Plantation; Kanine Krunchies Kommercial.
1961 (G) 79m/C D: Clyde Geronomi, Wolfgang Reitherman, Hamilton Luske; **M:** George Bruns; **V:** Rod Taylor, Betty Lou Gerson, Lisa Davis, Ben Wright, Frederick Worlock, J. Pat O'Malley. **VHS, Beta** ★★★1/2

One Night of Love Moore's best quasi-operetta, about a young American diva rebelling in response to her demanding Italian teacher. "Pygmalion"-like story has her falling in love with her maestro. Despite being nearly 60 years old, this film is still enchanting and fresh. ♪ One Night of Love; Ciri-Biri-Bin; Sempre Libera; Sextet; Indian Love Call; 'Tis the Last Rose of Summer; Habanera; Un bel di; None But the Lonely Heart.
1934 95m/B Grace Moore, Tullio Carminati, Lyle Talbot, Jane Darwell, Nydia Westman, Mona Barrie, Jessie Ralph, Luis Alberni; **D:** Victor Schertzinger. Academy Awards '34: Best Sound, Best Score; Nominations: Academy Awards '34: Best Actress (Moore), Best Director (Schertzinger), Best Film Editing, Best Picture. **VHS, Beta, LV** ★★★1/2

One of Our Aircraft Is Missing The crew of an R.A.F. bomber downed in the Netherlands struggles to escape Nazi capture. A thoughtful study of wars and the men who fight them, with an entertaining melodramatic plot. Look for the British version, which runs 106 minutes. Some of the American prints only run 82 minutes.
1941 106m/B GB Godfrey Tearle, Eric Portman, Hugh Williams, Pamela Brown, Googie Withers, Peter Ustinov; **D:** Emeric Pressburger, Michael Powell. National Board of Review Awards '42: 10 Best Films of the Year; Nominations: Academy Awards

'42: Best Original Screenplay. **VHS** ★★★½

One, Two, Three Cagney, an American Coca-Cola exec in Germany, zealously pursues any opportunity to run Coke's European operations. He does the job too well and loses his job to a Communist hippie turned slick capitalist. Fast-paced laughs, wonderful cinematography, and a fine score.
1961 110m/B James Cagney, Horst Buchholz, Arlene Francis; **D:** Billy Wilder; **W:** Billy Wilder, I.A.L. Diamond; **M:** Andre Previn. National Board of Review Awards '61: 10 Best Films of the Year; Nominations: Academy Awards '61: Best Black and White Cinematography. **VHS, Beta, LV** ★★★½

The Onion Field True story about the mental breakdown of an ex-cop who witnessed his partner's murder. Haunted by the slow process of justice and his own feelings of insecurity, he is unable to get his life together. Based on the novel by Joseph Wambaugh, who also wrote the screenplay. Compelling script and excellent acting.
1979 (R) 126m/C John Savage, James Woods, Ronny Cox, Franklyn Seales, Ted Danson; **D:** Harold Becker. **VHS, Beta, LV** ★★★½

Only Angels Have Wings Melodramatic adventure about a broken-down Peruvian air mail service. Large cast adds to the love tension between Grant, a pilot, and Arthur, a showgirl at the saloon. Nominated for special effects, a category recognized by the academy that year for the first time. William Rankin and Eleanor Griffin are uncredited writers.
1939 121m/B Cary Grant, Thomas Mitchell, Richard Barthelmess, Jean Arthur, Noah Beery Jr., Rita Hayworth, Sig Rumann, John Carroll, Allyn Joslyn; **D:** Howard Hawks; **W:** Jules Furthman; **M:** Dimitri Tiomkin. Nominations: Academy Awards '39: Best Black and White Cinematography, Best Special Effects. **VHS, Beta** ★★★★

Only Two Can Play Sellers is a hilarious Casanova librarian who puts the moves on a society lady to get a promotion. Funny, of course, and based on Kingsley Amis' novel "That Uncertain Feeling."
1962 106m/C *GB* Peter Sellers, Virginia Maskell, Mai Zetterling, Richard Attenborough; **D:** Sidney Gilliat; **M:** Richard Rodney Bennett. **VHS, Beta** ★★★

Open City A leader in the Italian underground resists Nazi control of the city. A stunning film, making Rossellini's realistic style famous. In Italian with English subtitles. **AKA:** Roma, Citta Aperta; Rome, Open City.
1945 103m/B *IT* Anna Magnani, Aldo Fabrizi, Marcel Pagliero, Maria Michi, Vito Annichiarico, Nando Bruno, Harry Feist; **D:** Roberto Rossellini; **W:** Federico Fellini, Sergio Amidei. National Board of Review Awards '46: 5 Best Foreign Films of the Year; New York Film Critics Awards '46: Best Foreign Film; Nominations: Academy Awards '46: Best Screenplay. **VHS, Beta, 8mm** ★★★★

Open Doors Bitter review of Fascist rule and justice. The Fascist regime promises security, safety, and tranquility. So, on the morning that a white collar criminal murders his former boss, murders the man who got his job, and then rapes and murders his wife, tensions rise and the societal structures are tested. The people rally for his death. A judge and a juror struggle to uphold justice rather than serve popular passions. Winner of 4 Donatello Awards, Italian Golden Globes for Best Film, Best Actor, and Best Screenplay, and many international film awards. In Italian with English subtitles. **AKA:** Porte Aperte.
1989 (R) 109m/C *IT* Gian Marie Volonte, Ennio Fantastichini, Lidia Alfonsi; **D:** Gianni Amelio; **W:** Gianni Amelio. Nominations: Academy Awards '90: Best Foreign Language Film. **VHS** ★★★½

Operation Petticoat Submarine captain Grant teams with wheeler-dealer Curtis to make his sub seaworthy. They're joined by a group of Navy women, and the gags begin. Great teamwork from Grant and Curtis keeps things rolling. Jokes may be considered sexist these days. Later remake and TV series couldn't hold a candle to the original.
1959 120m/C Cary Grant, Tony Curtis, Joan O'Brien, Dina Merrill, Gene Evans, Arthur O'Connell, Virginia Gregg; **D:** Blake Edwards. Nominations: Academy Awards '59: Best Story & Screenplay. **VHS, LV** ★★★½

Orchestra Wives A drama bursting with wonderful Glenn Miller music. A woman marries a musician and goes on the road with the band and the other wives. Trouble springs up with the sultry singer who desperately wants the woman's new husband. The commotion spreads throughout the group. ♪ People Like You and Me; At Last; Serenade in Blue; I've Got a Gal in Kalamazoo.

1942 98m/B George Montgomery, Glenn Miller, Lynn Bari, Carole Landis, Jackie Gleason, Cesar Romero, Ann Rutherford, Virginia Gilmore, Mary Beth Hughes, Harry (Henry) Morgan; **D:** Archie Mayo. Nominations: Academy Awards '42: Best Song ("I've Got a Gal in Kalamazoo"). **VHS, Beta, LV** ★★★

Ordet A man who believes he is Jesus Christ is ridiculed until he begins performing miracles, which result in the rebuilding of a broken family. A statement on the nature of religious faith vs. fanaticism by the profoundly religious Dreyer, and based on the play by Kaj Munk. In Danish with English subtitles. **AKA:** The Word.
1955 126m/B *DK* Henrik Malberg; **D:** Carl Theodor Dreyer. Golden Globe Awards '56: Best Foreign Film; National Board of Review Awards '57: 5 Best Foreign Films of the Year; Venice Film Festival '55: Best Film. **VHS, Beta** ★★★1/2

Ordinary People Powerful, well-acted story of a family's struggle to deal with one son's accidental death and the other's subsequent guilt-ridden suicide attempt. Features strong performances by all, but Moore is especially believable as the cold and rigid mother. McGovern's film debut as well as Redford's directorial debut. Based on the novel by Judith Guest.
1980 (R) 124m/C Mary Tyler Moore, Donald Sutherland, Timothy Hutton, Judd Hirsch, M. Emmet Walsh, Elizabeth McGovern, Adam Baldwin, Dinah Manoff, James B. Sikking; **D:** Robert Redford; **W:** Alvin Sargent; **M:** Marvin Hamlisch, John Bailey. Academy Awards '80: Best Adapted Screenplay, Best Director (Redford), Best Picture, Best Supporting Actor (Hutton); Golden Globe Awards '81: Best Actress—Drama (Moore), Best Director (Redford), Best Film—Drama, Best Supporting Actor (Hutton); National Board of Review Awards '80: 10 Best Films of the Year, Best Director (Redford); Writers Guild of America '80: Best Adapted Screenplay; Nominations: Academy Awards '80: Best Actress (Moore), Best Supporting Actor (Hirsch). **VHS, Beta, LV** ★★★1/2

Orlando Potter's sumptuous film adaptation of Virginia Woolf's 1928 novel, which covers 400 years in the life of an English nobleman, who not only defies death but evolves from a man to a woman in the intervening years. Orlando (Swinton) is first seen as a young man in the court of Queen Elizabeth I (Crisp) but after a deep sleep it's suddenly 40 years later. Things like this just keep happening and by 1750 he is now a she (and remains so), finding and losing love, and eventually gaining fulfillment in the 20th century. Elaborate productions never overwhelm Swinton's serene, self-assured performance.
1992 (PG-13) 93m/C *GB* Tilda Swinton, Charlotte Valandrey, Billy Zane, Lothaire Bluteau, John Wood, Quentin Crisp, Heathcote Williams, Dudley Sutton, Thom Hoffman; **D:** Sally Potter; **W:** Sally Potter. Nominations: Academy Awards '93: Best Art Direction/Set Decoration, Best Costume Design; Independent Spirit Awards '94: Best Foreign Film. **VHS, LV** ★★★

Orphans of the Storm Two sisters are separated and raised in opposite worlds—one by thieves, the other by aristocrats. Gish's poignant search for her sister is hampered by the turbulent maelstrom preceding the French Revolution. Silent. Based on the French play "The Two Orphans."
1921 190m/B Lillian Gish, Dorothy Gish, Monte Blue, Joseph Schildkraut; **D:** D.W. Griffith. **VHS, LV** ★★★1/2

Ossessione An adaptation of "The Postman Always Rings Twice," transferred to Fascist Italy, where a drifter and an innkeeper's wife murder her husband. Visconti's first feature, which initiated Italian neo-realism, was not released in the U.S. until 1975 due to a copyright dispute. In Italian with English subtitles.
1942 135m/B *IT* Massimo Girotti, Clara Calamai, Juan deLanda, Elio Marcuzzo; **D:** Luchino Visconti. **VHS, Beta** ★★★1/2

Otello An uncommon film treat for opera fans, with a stellar performance by Domingo as the troubled Moor who murders his wife in a fit of jealous rage and later finds she was never unfaithful. Be prepared, however, for changes from the Shakespeare and Verdi stories, necessitated by the film adaptation. Highly acclaimed and awarded; in Italian with English subtitles.
1986 (PG) 123m/C *IT* Placido Domingo, Katia Ricciarelli, Justino Diaz; **D:** Franco Zeffirelli. Nominations: Academy Awards '86: Best Costume Design. **VHS, Beta, LV** ★★★1/2

Othello Welles' striking adaptation of the Shakespeare tragedy casts him as the self-deluding Moor, with MacLiammoir as the despicable Iago and Cloutier as innocent victim, Desdemona. Welles filmed his epic over a four-year period due to budget difficulties, which also resulted in his filming in a number of different countries and settings. The film underwent a $1 million restoration, supervised by

Welles' daughter, prior to its limited theatrical re-release in 1992.
1952 90m/B Orson Welles, Michael MacLiammoir, Suzanne Cloutier, Robert Coote, Hilton Edwards, Michael Lawrence, Nicholas Bruce, Fay Compton, Doris Dowling, Jean Davis, Joseph Cotten, Joan Fontaine; **D:** Orson Welles. Cannes Film Festival '52: Best Film. **VHS, LV ★★★**

Our Daily Bread Vidor's sequel to the 1928 "The Crowd." A young couple inherit a farm during the Depression and succeed in managing the land. A near-classic, with several sequences highly influenced by directors Alexander Dovshenko and Sergei Eisenstein. Director Vidor also co-scripted this film, risking bankruptcy to finance it. **AKA:** Miracle of Life.
1934 80m/B Karen Morley, Tom Keene, John Qualen, Barbara Pepper, Addison Richards; **D:** King Vidor; **W:** King Vidor. **VHS, Beta, LV ★★★**

Our Hospitality One of Keaton's finest silent films, with all the elements in place. William McKay (Keaton) travels to the American South on a quaint train (a near-exact replica of the Stephenson Rocket, to claim an inheritance as the last survivor of his family. En route, a young woman traveler informs him that her family has had a long, deadly feud with his, and that they intend to kill him. McKay resolves to get the inheritance, depending on the Southern rule of hospitality to guests to save his life until he can make his escape. Watch for the river scene where, during filming, Keaton's own life was really in danger. By the way, Keaton married his leading lady in real life.
1923 74m/B Buster Keaton, Natalie Talmadge, Joe Keaton, Buster Keaton Jr., Kitty Bradbury, Joe Roberts; **D:** Buster Keaton, John Blystone. **VHS, LV ★★★★**

Our Relations Confusion reigns when Stan and Ollie meet the twin brothers they never knew they had, a pair of happy-go-lucky sailors. Laurel directs the pair through madcap encounters with their twins' wives and the local underworld. One of the pair's best efforts, though not well-remembered. Based on a story by W.W. Jacobs.
1936 94m/B Stan Laurel, Oliver Hardy, Alan Hale, Sidney Toler, James Finlayson, Daphne Pollard; **D:** Harry Lachman. **VHS, Beta ★★★1/2**

Our Town Small-town New England life in Grover's Corners in the early 1900s is celebrated in this well-performed and directed adaptation of the Pulitzer Prize-winning play by Thornton Wilder. Film debut of Scott.
1940 90m/B Martha Scott, William Holden, Thomas Mitchell, Fay Bainter, Guy Kibbee, Beulah Bondi, Frank Craven; **D:** Sam Wood; **M:** Aaron Copland. National Board of Review Awards '40: 10 Best Films of the Year; Nominations: Academy Awards '40: Best Actress (Scott), Best Interior Decoration, Best Picture, Best Sound, Best Original Score. **VHS, Beta ★★★**

Our Vines Have Tender Grapes A change of pace role for the volatile Robinson who plays a kind Norwegian widower, living in Wisconsin with his daughter, the spunky O'Brien. The film is made up of small-town moments as O'Brien learns a few of life's lessons, eased by the thoughtful compassion of Robinson. Based on the novel "For Our Vines Have Tender Grapes" by George Victor Martin.
1945 105m/B Edward G. Robinson, Margaret O'Brien, James Craig, Agnes Moorehead, Jackie "Butch" Jenkins, Morris Carnovsky, Frances Gifford, Sara Haden, Louis Jean Heydt; **D:** Roy Rowland; **W:** Dalton Trumbo. **VHS ★★★1/2**

Out of Africa An epic film of the years spent by Danish authoress Isak Dinesen (her true name is Karen Blixen) on a Kenya coffee plantation. She moved to Africa to marry, and later fell in love with Denys Finch-Hatten, a British adventurer. Based on several books, including biographies of the two lovers. Some critics loved the scenery and music; others despised the acting and the script. A definite "no" for those who love action.
1985 (PG) 161m/C Meryl Streep, Robert Redford, Klaus Maria Brandauer, Michael Kitchen, Malick Bowens, Michael Gough, Suzanna Hamilton, Rachel Kempson, Graham Crowden, Shane Rimmer, Donal McCann, Iman, Joseph Thiaka, Stephen Kinyanjui; **D:** Sydney Pollack; **W:** Kurt Luedtke; **M:** John Barry. Academy Awards '85: Best Adapted Screenplay, Best Art Direction/Set Decoration, Best Cinematography, Best Director (Pollack), Best Picture, Best Sound, Best Original Score; British Academy Awards '86: Best Adapted Screenplay; Golden Globe Awards '86: Best Film—Drama, Best Supporting Actor (Brandauer), Best Score; Los Angeles Film Critics Association Awards '85: Best Actress (Streep), Best Cinematography; National Board of Review Awards '85: Best Supporting Actor (Brandauer); New York Film Critics Awards '85: Best Cinematography, Best Supporting Actor (Brandauer); Nominations: Academy Awards '85: Best Actress (Streep), Best Costume Design,

Best Supporting Actor (Brandauer). **VHS, Beta, LV** ★★★

Out of the Past A private detective gets caught in a complex web of love, murder, and money in this film noir classic. The plot is torturous but clear thanks to fine directing. Mitchum became an overnight star after this film, which was overlooked but now considered one of the best in its genre. Based on Geoffrey Homes' novel "Build My Gallows High." Remade in 1984 as "Against All Odds." *AKA:* Build My Gallows High.
1947 97m/B Robert Mitchum, Kirk Douglas, Jane Greer, Rhonda Fleming, Steve Brodie, Dickie Moore; *D:* Jacques Tourneur; *W:* Geoffrey Homes. **VHS, Beta, LV** ★★★1/2

The Out-of-Towners A pair of Ohio rubes travels to New York City and along the way everything that could go wrong does. Lemmon's performance is excellent and Simon's script is, as usual, both wholesome and funny.
1970 (G) 98m/C Jack Lemmon, Sandy Dennis, Anne Meara, Sandy Baron, Billy Dee Williams; *D:* Arthur Hiller; *W:* Neil Simon. Writers Guild of America '70: Best Original Screenplay. **VHS, Beta, LV** ★★★

Outbreak Smuggled African monkey spits on someone who kisses someone else who sneezes on a bunch of people, thus initiating the spread of a highly infectious mystery disease in a northern California 'burb. Hoffman leads a team of scientists in a search for the anti-serum, but it's a secret government plot to exterminate the victims that literally sends Hoffman and crew into action movie cliche overdrive (add "helicopter" to the list of chase scene vehicles). Not that that's so bad—if the beat-the-clock tempo doesn't grab you, paranoia certainly will. But Hoffman's hardly a threat to Arnold or Sylvester as the next action hero, and the talented Russo remains suspiciously ravishing even with festering pustules. Based on two books: Richard Preston's "The Hot Zone" and Laurie Garrett's "The Coming Plague."
1994 (R) 128m/C Dustin Hoffman, Rene Russo, Morgan Freeman, Donald Sutherland, Cuba Gooding Jr., Kevin Spacey; *D:* Wolfgang Petersen; *W:* Laurence Dworet, Robert Roy Pool, Michael Ballhaus; *M:* James Newton Howard. New York Film Critics Awards '95: Best Supporting Actor (Spacey). **VHS, LV** ★★★

The Outer Limits: Sandkings Made-for-cable revival of the '60s sci-fi series is creepier than ever with this tale of loony scientist Simon Kress (Bridges). He discovers tiny alien eggs while doing an analysis of Martian soil samples and decides to take his research home with him when the government cuts off funding. Big mistake—the critters he successfully hatches in his barn are mean and hungry. Features both dad Lloyd and Beau's 10-year-old son, Dylan, in roles. **AKA:** Sandkings.
1995 93m/C Beau Bridges, Lloyd Bridges, Helen Shaver, Dylan Bridges; *D:* Stuart Gillard; *M:* Melinda M. Snodgrass. **VHS** ★★★

The Outlaw Josey Wales Eastwood plays a farmer with a motive for revenge—his family was killed and for years he was betrayed and hunted. His desire to play the lone killer is, however, tempered by his need for family and friends. He kills plenty, but in the end finds happiness. Considered one of the last great Westerns, with many superb performances. Eastwood took over directorial chores during filming from Kaufman, who co-scripted. Adapted from "Gone To Texas" by Forest Carter.
1976 (PG) 135m/C Clint Eastwood, Chief Dan George, Sondra Locke, Matt Clark, John Vernon, Bill McKinney, Sam Bottoms; *D:* Clint Eastwood; *W:* Philip Kaufman. Nominations: Academy Awards '76: Best Original Score. **VHS, Beta, LV** ★★★1/2

The Overcoat An adaptation of Nikolai Gogol's classic story about the dehumanizing life endured in 20th-century bureaucracy. All a menial civil servant wants is a new overcoat. When he finally gets one, this treasured article not only keeps him warm but makes him feel self-satisfied as well. In Russian with English subtitles.
1959 93m/B *RU* Rolan Bykov; *D:* Alexei Batalov. National Board of Review Awards '59: 5 Best Foreign Films of the Year. **VHS, Beta** ★★★1/2

The Owl and the Pussycat Nerdy author gets the neighborhood hooker evicted from her apartment. She returns the favor, and the pair hit the street—and the sack—in Buck Henry's hilarious adaptation of the Broadway play. Streisand's first non-singing role.
1970 (PG) 96m/C Barbra Streisand, George Segal, Robert Klein, Allen (Goorwitz) Garfield; *D:* Herbert Ross; *W:* Buck Henry. **VHS, Beta, LV** ★★★

The Ox-Bow Incident A popular rancher is murdered, and a mob of angry townspeople can't wait for the sheriff to find the killers. They hang the young man, despite the protests of Fonda, a cowboy with a conscience. Excellent study of mob mentality with strong individual characterizations. A brilliant western based on a true story by Walter Van Tilburg Clark. Also see "Twelve Angry Men"—less tragic but just as moving. **AKA:** Strange Incident.

1943 75m/B Henry Fonda, Harry (Henry) Morgan, Dana Andrews, Anthony Quinn, Frank Conroy, Harry Davenport, Jane Darwell, William Eythe, Mary Beth Hughes; **D:** William A. Wellman; **W:** Lamar Trotti; **M:** Cyril Mockridge. National Board of Review Awards '43: 10 Best Films of the Year, Best Director (Wellman); Nominations: Academy Awards '43: Best Picture. **VHS, Beta, LV ★★★★**

Pacific Heights Young San Francisco couple takes on mammoth mortgage assuming tenants will write their ticket to the American dream, but psychopathic tenant Keaton moves in downstairs and redecorates. He won't pay the rent and he won't leave. Creepy psycho-thriller has lapses but builds to effective climax. It's a treat to watch mother/daughter actresses Hedren and Griffith work together. Watch for D'Angelo as Keaton's lover.

1990 (R) 103m/C Melanie Griffith, Matthew Modine, Michael Keaton, Mako, Nobu McCarthy, Laurie Metcalf, Carl Lumbly, Dorian Harewood, Luca Bercovici, Tippi Hedren, Sheila McCarthy, Dan Hedaya, Beverly D'Angelo, Nicholas Pryor, Miriam Margolyes; **D:** John Schlesinger; **W:** Daniel Pyne; **M:** Hans Zimmer. **VHS, LV ★★★**

Padre Padrone The much acclaimed adaptation of the Gavino Ledda autobiography about his youth in agrarian Sardinia with a brutal, tyrannical father. Eventually he overcomes his handicaps, breaks the destructive emotional ties to his father and successfully attends college. Highly regarded although low budget; in an Italian dialect (Sardinian) with English subtitles. **AKA:** Father Master; My Father, My Master.

1977 113m/C *IT* Omero Antonutti, Saverio Marconi, Marcella Michelangeli, Fabrizio Forte, Salverio Marioni; **D:** Paolo Taviani, Vittorio Taviani; **W:** Paolo Taviani, Vittorio Taviani. Cannes Film Festival '77: Best Film. **VHS, Beta ★★★1/2**

Paisan Six episodic tales of life in Italy, several featuring Allied soldiers and nurses during WWII. One of the stories tells of a man who tries to develop a relationship without being able to speak Italian. Another focuses on a young street robber who is confronted by one of his victims. Strong stories that covers a wide range of emotions. In Italian with English subtitles.

1946 90m/B *IT* Maria Michi, Carmela Sazio, Gar Moore, William Tubbs, Harriet White, Robert Van Loon, Dale Edmonds, Carla Pisacane, Dots Johnson; **D:** Roberto Rossellini; **W:** Federico Fellini, Roberto Rossellini. National Board of Review Awards '48: 5 Best Foreign Films of the Year, Best Director (Fellini); Nominations: Academy Awards '49: Best Story & Screenplay. **VHS, Beta, 8mm ★★★**

The Pajama Game A spritely musical about the striking workers of a pajama factory and their plucky negotiator, who falls in love with the boss. Based on the hit Broadway musical, which was based on Richard Bissell's book "Seven and a Half Cents" and adapted for the screen by Bissell and Abbott. Bob Fosse choreographed the dance numbers. ♪ I'm Not at All in Love; Small Talk; There Once Was a Man; Steam Heat; Hernando's Highway; Hey There; Once-a-Year Day; Seven and a Half Cents; I'll Never Be Jealous Again.

1957 101m/C Doris Day, John Raitt, Eddie Foy Jr., Reta Shaw, Carol Haney; **D:** Stanley Donen, George Abbott. **VHS, Beta, LV ★★★1/2**

Pal Joey Musical comedy about an opportunistic singer who courts a wealthy socialite in hopes that she will finance his nightclub. His play results in comedic complications. Stellar choreography, fine direction, and beautiful costumes complement performances headed by Hayworth and Sinatra. Oscar overlooked his pal Joey when awards were handed out. Songs include some of Rodgers and Hart's best. Based on John O'Hara's book and play. ♪ Zip; Bewitched, Bothered and Bewildered; I Could Write a Book; That Terrific Rainbow; Whad Do I Care for a Dame?; Happy Hunting Horn; Plant You Now, Dig You Later; Do It the Hard Way; Take Him.

1957 109m/C Frank Sinatra, Rita Hayworth, Kim Novak; **D:** George Sidney; **M:** Richard Rodgers, Lorenz Hart. Golden Globe Awards '58: Best Actor—Musical/Comedy (Sinatra); Nominations: Academy Awards '57: Best Art Direction/Set Decoration, Best Costume Design, Best Film Editing, Best Sound. **VHS, Beta, LV ★★★**

Pale Rider A mysterious nameless stranger rides into a small California gold rush town to find himself in the middle of a feud between a mining syndicate and a group of indepen-

dent prospectors. Christ-like Eastwood evokes comparisons to "Shane." A classical western theme well complemented by excellent photography and a rock-solid cast.
1985 (R) 116m/C Clint Eastwood, Michael Moriarty, Carrie Snodgress, Sydney Penny, Richard Dysart, Richard Kiel, Christopher Penn, John Russell, Charles Hallahan, Douglas McGrath, Fran Ryan; **D:** Clint Eastwood; **W:** Michael Butler, Dennis Shryack; **M:** Lennie Niehaus. **VHS, Beta, LV, 8mm** ★★★

The Paleface A cowardly dentist becomes a gunslinging hero when Calamity Jane starts aiming for him. A rip-roarin' good time as the conventions of the Old West are turned upside down. Includes the Oscar-winning song "Buttons and Bows." The 1952 sequel is "Son of Paleface." Remade in 1968 as "The Shakiest Gun in the West." ♪ Buttons and Bows; Get a Man!; Meetcha 'Round the Corner.
1948 91m/C Jane Russell, Bob Hope, Robert Armstrong, Iris Adrian, Robert Watson; **D:** Norman Z. McLeod. Academy Awards '48: Best Song ("Buttons and Bows"). **VHS, Beta, LV** ★★★

The Palm Beach Story Colbert and McCrea play a married couple who have everything—except money. The wife decides to divorce her current husband, marry a rich man, and finance her former husband's ambitions. She decides the best place to husband-hunt is Palm Beach. A Sturges classic screwball comedy.
1942 88m/B Claudette Colbert, Joel McCrea, Mary Astor, Rudy Vallee, William Demarest, Franklin Pangborn; **D:** Preston Sturges. **VHS, Beta, LV** ★★★

Pandora's Box This silent classic marked the end of the German Expressionist era and established Brooks as a major screen presence. She plays the tempestuous Lulu, who destroys everyone she comes in contact with, eventually sinking to prostitution and a fateful meeting with Jack the Ripper. Silent with orchestral score. **AKA:** Die Buechse Der Pandora.
1928 110m/B *GE* Louise Brooks, Fritz Kortner, Francis Lederer, Carl Goetz; **D:** G.W. Pabst; **W:** G.W. Pabst. **VHS, Beta** ★★★★

Panic in Needle Park Drugs become an obsession for a young girl who goes to New York for an abortion. Her new boyfriend is imprisoned for robbery committed in order to support both their habits. She resorts to prostitution to continue her drug habit,
and trouble occurs when her boyfriend realizes she was instrumental in his being sent to jail. Strikes a vein in presenting an uncompromising look at drug use. May be too much of a depressant for some. Pacino's first starring role.
1971 (R) 90m/C Al Pacino, Kitty Winn, Alan Vint, Richard Bright, Kiel Martin, Warren Finnerty, Raul Julia, Paul Sorvino; **D:** Jerry Schatzberg; **W:** Joan Didion, John Gregory Dunne, Adam Holender. Cannes Film Festival '71: Best Actress (Winn); Nominations: Cannes Film Festival '71: Best Film. **VHS, LV** ★★★

Panic in the Streets The Black Death threatens New Orleans in this intense tale. When a body is found on the waterfront, a doctor (Widmark) is called upon for a diagnosis. The carrier proves to be deadly in more ways than one. Fine performances, taut direction (this was one of Kazan's favorite movies). Filmed on location in New Orleans.
1950 96m/B Richard Widmark, Jack Palance, Barbara Bel Geddes, Paul Douglas, Zero Mostel; **D:** Elia Kazan; **W:** Edward Anhalt. Academy Awards '50: Best Story. **VHS, LV** ★★★

Papa's Delicate Condition Based on the autobiographical writings of silent screen star Corinne Griffith. Gleason is Papa whose "delicate condition" is a result of his drinking. His antics provide a constant headache to his family. A paean to turn-of-the-century family life. No I.D.s required as the performances are enjoyable for the whole family. Features the Academy Award-winning song "Call Me Irresponsible." ♪ Call Me Irresponsible; Bill Bailey, Won't You Please Come Home?.
1963 98m/C Jackie Gleason, Glynis Johns, Charlie Ruggles, Laurel Goodwin, Elisha Cook Jr., Murray Hamilton; **D:** George Marshall; **W:** Jack Rose. Academy Awards '63: Best Song ("Call Me Irresponsible"). **VHS, Beta** ★★★

The Paper Chase Students at Harvard Law School suffer and struggle through their first year. A realistic, sometimes acidly humorous look at Ivy League ambitions, with Houseman stealing the show as the tough professor. Wonderful adaptation of the John Jay Osborn novel which later became the basis for the acclaimed television series.
1973 (PG) 111m/C Timothy Bottoms, Lindsay Wagner, John Houseman, Graham Beckel, Edward Herrmann, James Naughton, Craig Richard Nelson, Bob Lydiard; **D:** James Bridges; **W:** James

Bridges; *M:* John Williams, Gordon Willis. Academy Awards '73: Best Supporting Actor (Houseman); Golden Globe Awards '74: Best Supporting Actor (Houseman); National Board of Review Awards '73: Best Supporting Actor (Houseman); Nominations: Academy Awards '73: Best Adapted Screenplay, Best Sound. **VHS, Beta, LV ★★★**

Paper Moon Award-winning story set in depression-era Kansas with Ryan O'Neal as a Bible-wielding con who meets up with a nine-year-old orphan. During their travels together, he discovers that the orphan (his daughter, Tatum) is better at "his" game than he is. Irresistible chemistry between the O'Neals, leading to Tatum's Oscar win (she is the youngest actor ever to take home a statue). Cinematically picturesque and cynical enough to keep overt sentimentalism at bay. Based on Joe David Brown's novel, "Addie Pray." The director's version contains a prologue by director Bogdanovich.
1973 (PG) 102m/B Ryan O'Neal, Tatum O'Neal, Madeline Kahn, John Hillerman, Randy Quaid; *D:* Peter Bogdanovich; *W:* Alvin Sargent. Academy Awards '73: Best Supporting Actress (O'Neal); National Board of Review Awards '73: 10 Best Films of the Year; Writers Guild of America '73: Best Adapted Screenplay; Nominations: Academy Awards '73: Best Adapted Screenplay, Best Sound, Best Supporting Actress (Kahn). **VHS, Beta, LV ★★★1/2**

Papillon McQueen is a criminal sent to Devil's Island in the 1930s determined to escape from the remote prison. Hoffman is the swindler he befriends. A series of escapes and recaptures follow. Box-office winner based on the autobiographical writings of French thief Henri Charriere. Excellent portrayal of prison life and fine performances from the prisoners. Certain segments would have been better left on the cutting room floor. The film's title refers to the lead's butterfly tattoo.
1973 (PG) 150m/C Steve McQueen, Dustin Hoffman, Victor Jory, George Coulouris, Anthony Zerbe; *D:* Franklin J. Schaffner; *M:* Jerry Goldsmith. Nominations: Academy Awards '73: Best Original Score. **VHS, Beta, LV ★★★**

Parade A series of vignettes in a circus, "Parade" is actually a play within a play, meshing the action with events offstage. The laserdisc edition includes Rene Clement's 1936 "Soigne Ton Gauche," Tati's inspiration.
1974 85m/C *FR* Jacques Tati; *D:* Jacques Tati; *W:* Jacques Tati. **VHS, LV ★★★**

The Parallax View A reporter tries to disprove a report which states that a presidential candidate's assassination was not a conspiracy. As he digs deeper and deeper, he uncovers more than he bargained for and becomes a pawn in the conspirators' further plans. Beatty is excellent and the conspiracy is never less than believable. A lesser-known, compelling political thriller that deserves to be more widely seen.
1974 (R) 102m/C Warren Beatty, Hume Cronyn, William Daniels, Paula Prentiss, Kenneth Mars, Bill McKinney, Anthony Zerbe, Walter McGinn, Gordon Willis; *D:* Alan J. Pakula. National Society of Film Critics Awards '74: Best Cinematography. **VHS, Beta ★★★★**

Pardon Mon Affaire When a middle-aged civil servant gets a look at a model in a parking garage, he decides it's time to cheat on his wife. Enjoyable French farce. Re-made as in the United States "The Woman in Red" and followed by "Pardon Mon Affaire, Too!" Subtitled. *AKA:* Un Elephant a Trompe Enormement.
1976 (PG) 107m/C *FR* Jean Rochefort, Claude Brasseur, Guy Bedos, Victor Lanoux, Daniele Delorme, Martine Sarcey, Anny Duperey; *D:* Yves Robert; *M:* Vladimir Cosma. Cesar Awards '77: Best Supporting Actor (Brasseur). **VHS, Beta, LV ★★★**

Parenthood Four grown siblings and their parents struggle with various levels of parenthood. From the college drop-out, to the nervous single mother, to the yuppie couple raising an overachiever, every possibility is explored, including the perspective from the older generation, portrayed by Robards. Genuinely funny with dramatic moments that work most of the time, with an affecting performance from Martin and Wiest. Director Howard has four kids and was inspired to make this film when on a European jaunt with them.
1989 (PG-13) 124m/C Steve Martin, Mary Steenburgen, Dianne Wiest, Martha Plimpton, Keanu Reeves, Tom Hulce, Jason Robards Jr., Rick Moranis, Harley Jane Kozak, Joaquin Rafael (Leaf) Phoenix, Paul Linke, Dennis Dugan; *D:* Ron Howard; *W:* Lowell Ganz, Babaloo Mandel, Ron Howard; *M:* Randy Newman. Nominations: Academy Awards '89: Best Song ("I Love to See You Smile"), Best Supporting Actress (Wiest). **VHS, Beta, LV ★★★**

Paris Is Burning Livingston's documentary portrayal of New York City's transvestite balls where men dress up, dance, and compete in various categories. Filmed between 1985 and 1989, this is a compelling look at a subculture of primarily black and Hispanic men and the one place they can truly be themselves. Madonna noted this look and attitude (much watered down) in her song "Vogue."

1991 (R) 71m/C Dorian Corey, Pepper Labeija, Venus Xtravaganza, Octavia St. Laurant, Willi Ninja, Anji Xtravaganza, Freddie Pendavis, Junior Labeija; *D:* Jennie Livingston. National Society of Film Critics Awards '91: Best Feature Documentary; Sundance Film Festival '91: Grand Jury Prize. **VHS ★★★**

Paris, Texas After four years a drifter returns to find his son is being raised by his brother because the boy's mother has also disappeared. He tries to reconnect with the boy. Introspective script acclaimed by many film critics, but others found it to be too slow.

1983 (PG) 145m/C *FR GE* Harry Dean Stanton, Nastassia Kinski, Dean Stockwell, Hunter Carson, Aurore Clement; *D:* Wim Wenders; *W:* Sam Shepard, L.M. Kit Carson; *M:* Ry Cooder. British Academy Awards '84: Best Director (Wenders); Cannes Film Festival '84: Best Film. **VHS, Beta, LV ★★★★**

The Party Disaster-prone Indian actor wreaks considerable havoc at a posh Hollywood gathering. Laughs come quickly in this quirky Sellers vehicle.

1968 99m/C Peter Sellers, Claudine Longet, Marge Champion, Sharron Kimberly, Denny Miller, Gavin MacLeod, Carol Wayne; *D:* Blake Edwards; *W:* Blake Edwards; *M:* Henry Mancini. **VHS ★★★**

Party Girl A crime drama involving an attorney representing a 1920s crime boss and his henchmen when they run afoul of the law. The lawyer falls in love with a nightclub dancer who successfully encourages him to leave the mob, but not before he is wounded in a gang war attack, arrested, and forced to testify against the mob as a material witness. The mob then takes his girlfriend hostage to prevent his testifying, leading to an exciting climax. Must-see viewing for Charisse's steamy dance numbers.

1958 99m/C Robert Taylor, Cyd Charisse, Lee J. Cobb, John Ireland, Kent Smith, Claire Kelly, Corey Allen; *D:* Nicholas Ray. **VHS, Beta, LV ★★★★**

Pascali's Island A Turkish spy becomes involved with an adventurer's plot to steal rare artifacts, then finds himself ensnared in political and personal intrigue. Superior tragedy features excellent performances from Kingsley, Dance, and Mirren.

1988 (PG-13) 106m/C *GB* Ben Kingsley, Helen Mirren, Charles Dance, Sheila Allen, Vernon Dobtcheff; *D:* James Dearden; *W:* James Dearden; *M:* Loek Dikker. **VHS, Beta, LV ★★★1/2**

A Passage to India An ambitious adaptation of E.M. Forster's complex novel about relations between Brits and Indians in the 1920s. Drama centers on a young British woman's accusations that an Indian doctor raped her while serving as a guide in some rather ominous caves. Film occasionally flags, but is usually compelling. Features particularly strong performances from Bannerjee, Fox, and Davis.

1984 (PG) 163m/C *GB* Peggy Ashcroft, Alec Guinness, James Fox, Judy Davis, Victor Banerjee, Nigel Havers; *D:* David Lean; *M:* Maurice Jarre. Academy Awards '84: Best Supporting Actress (Ashcroft), Best Original Score; British Academy Awards '85: Best Actress (Ashcroft); Golden Globe Awards '85: Best Foreign Film, Best Supporting Actress (Ashcroft), Best Score; Los Angeles Film Critics Association Awards '84: Best Supporting Actress (Ashcroft); National Board of Review Awards '84: Best Actor (Banerjee), Best Actress (Ashcroft), Best Director (Lean); Nominations: Academy Awards '84: Best Adapted Screenplay, Best Art Direction/Set Decoration, Best Cinematography, Best Costume Design, Best Director (Lean), Best Film Editing, Best Picture, Best Sound, Best Actress (Davis). **VHS, Beta, LV ★★★**

Passage to Marseilles Hollywood propaganda in which convicts escape from Devil's Island and help French freedom fighters combat Nazis. Routine but entertaining. What else could it be with Bogart, Raines, Greenstreet, and Lorre, who later made a pretty good film set in Casablanca?

1944 110m/B Humphrey Bogart, Claude Rains, Sydney Greenstreet, Peter Lorre, Helmut Dantine, George Tobias, John Loder, Eduardo Ciannelli, Michele Morgan; *D:* Michael Curtiz; *M:* Max Steiner. **VHS, Beta ★★★**

The Passenger A dissatisfied television reporter changes identities with a dead man while on assignment in Africa, then learns that he is posing as a gunrunner. Mysterious, elliptical production from Italian master Antonioni, who co-wrote. Nicholson is fine in the low-key role, and Schneider is surprisingly winning as the woman drawn to him. The object of much de-

bate, hailed by some as quintessential cinema and by others as slow and unrewarding. *AKA:* Profession: Reporter.
1975 (PG) 119m/C *IT* Jack Nicholson, Maria Schneider, Ian Hendry, Jenny Runacre, Steven Berkoff; *D:* Michelangelo Antonioni; *W:* Mark Peploe, Michelangelo Antonioni; *M:* Claude Bolling. National Board of Review Awards '75: 10 Best Films of the Year. **VHS, Beta ★★★★**

Passion Fish McDonnell plays May-Alice, a soap opera actress who is paralyzed after a taxi accident in New York. Confined to a wheelchair, the bitter woman moves back to her Louisiana home and alienates a number of live-in nurses until Chantelle (Woodard), who has her own problems, comes along. Blunt writing and directing by Sayles overcome the story's inherent sentimentality as do the spirited performances of the leads, including Curtis-Hall as the rogue romancing Chantelle and Strathairn as the Cajun bad boy McDonnell once loved. The laserdisc is available in letterbox format.
1992 (R) 136m/C Mary McDonnell, Alfre Woodard, David Strathairn, Vondie Curtis-Hall, Nora Dunn, Sheila Kelley, Angela Bassett, Mary Portser, Maggie Renzi, Leo Burmester, Roger Deakins; *D:* John Sayles; *W:* John Sayles; *M:* Mason Daring. Independent Spirit Awards '93: Best Supporting Actress (Woodard); Nominations: Academy Awards '92: Best Actress (McDonnell), Best Original Screenplay. **VHS, LV ★★★**

The Passion of Anna A complicated psychological drama about four people on an isolated island. Von Sydow is an ex-con living a hermit's existence when he becomes involved with a crippled widow (Ullmann) and her two friends—all of whom have secrets in their pasts. Brutal and disturbing. Wonderful cinematography by Sven Nykvist. Filmed on the island of Faro. In Swedish with English subtitles.
1970 (R) 101m/C *SW* Max von Sydow, Liv Ullmann, Bibi Andersson, Erland Josephson, Erik Hell; *D:* Ingmar Bergman; *W:* Ingmar Bergman. National Society of Film Critics Awards '70: Best Director (Bergman). **VHS ★★★**

The Passion of Joan of Arc Masterful silent film relates the events of St. Joan's trial and subsequent martyrdom. Moving, eloquent work features legendary performace by Falconetti. Also rates among master Dreyer's finest efforts. A classic. Silent with music.
1928 114m/B *FR* Maria Falconetti, Eugena Sylvaw, Maurice Schultz, Antonin Artaud; *D:* Carl Theodor Dreyer. **VHS, Beta ★★★★**

Pat and Mike War of the sexes rages in this comedy about a leathery sports promoter who futilely attempts to train a woman for athletic competition. Tracy and Hepburn have fine chemistry, but supporting players contribute too. Watch for the first on-screen appearance of Bronson (then Charles Buchinski) as a crook.
1952 95m/B Spencer Tracy, Katharine Hepburn, Aldo Ray, Jim Backus, William Ching, Sammy White, Phyllis Povah, Charles Bronson, Chuck Connors, Mae Clarke, Carl "Alfalfa" Switzer; *D:* George Cukor; *W:* Ruth Gordon, Garson Kanin. Nominations: Academy Awards '52: Best Story & Screenplay. **VHS, Beta, LV ★★★**

Pat Garrett & Billy the Kid Coburn is Garrett, one-time partner of Billy the Kid (Kristofferson), turned sheriff. He tracks down and eventually kills the outlaw. The uncut director's version which was released on video is a vast improvement over the theatrically released and television versions. Dylan's soundtrack includes the now famous "Knockin' on Heaven's Door."
1973 106m/C Kris Kristofferson, James Coburn, Bob Dylan, Richard Jaeckel, Katy Jurado, Chill Wills, Charles Martin Smith, Slim Pickens, Harry Dean Stanton; *D:* Sam Peckinpah; *W:* Rudy Wurlitzer; *M:* George Duning. **VHS, Beta, LV ★★★**

Pather Panchali Somber, moving story of a young Bengali boy growing up in impoverished India. Stunning debut from India's master filmmaker Ray, who continued the story in "Aparajito" and "World of Apu." A truly great work. In Bengali with English subtitles. *AKA:* The Song of the Road; The Saga of the Road; The Lament of the Path.
1954 112m/B *IN* Kanu Banerjee, Karuna Banerjee, Uma Das Gupta, Subir Banerji, Runki Banerji, Chunibala Devi; *D:* Satyajit Ray; *W:* Satyajit Ray; *M:* Ravi Shankar. **VHS, Beta ★★★★**

Pathfinder A young boy in Lapland of 1,000 years ago comes of age prematurely after he falls in with cut-throat nomads who already slaughtered his family and now want to wipe out the rest of the village. Gripping adventure in the ice and snow features stunning scenery. In Lappish with English subtitles and based on an old Lapp fable.
1987 88m/C *NO* Mikkel Gaup, Nils Utsi, Svein Scharffenberg, Helgi Skulason, Sara Marit Gaup, Sverre Porsanger; *D:* Nils Gaup; *W:* Nils Gaup. Nominations:

Academy Awards '87: Best Foreign Language Film. **VHS** ★★★1/2

Paths of Glory Classic anti-war drama set in WWI France. A vain, ambitious officer imposes unlikely battle strategy on his hapless troops, and when it fails, he demands that three soldiers be selected for execution as cowards. Menjou is excellent as the bloodless French officer, with Douglas properly heroic as the French officer who knows about the whole disgraceful enterprise. Fabulous, wrenching fare from filmmaking great Kubrick, who co-wrote. Based on a true story from Humphrey Cobb's novel of the same name.
1957 86m/B Kirk Douglas, Adolphe Menjou, George Macready, Ralph Meeker, Richard Anderson, Wayne Morris, Timothy Carey, Susanne Christian, Bert Freed; **D:** Stanley Kubrick; **W:** Calder Willingham, Stanley Kubrick. **VHS, Beta, LV** ★★★★

Patriot Games Jack Ryan, retired CIA analyst, takes his wife and daughter to England on a holiday and ends up saving a member of the Royal Family from assassination by IRA extremists. Ryan, who has killed one of the terrorists, then becomes the target of revenge by the dead man's brother. Good action sequences but otherwise predictable adaptation of the novel from Tom Clancy. Companion to "The Hunt for Red October," with Ford taking over the role of Ryan from Alec Baldwin. Since this movie did well, we can probably expect two more from Ford, who's becoming the king of trilogies. Followed by "Clear and Present Danger."
1992 (R) 117m/C Harrison Ford, Anne Archer, Patrick Bergin, Thora Birch, Sean Bean, Richard Harris, James Earl Jones, James Fox, Samuel L. Jackson, Polly Walker; **D:** Phillip Noyce; **W:** W. Peter Iliff, Donald Stewart; **M:** James Horner. **VHS, Beta, CD-I** ★★★

Patterns Realistic depiction of big business. Heflin starts work at a huge New York office that is under the ruthless supervision of Sloane. Serling's astute screenplay (adapted from his TV play) is adept at portraying ruthless, power-struggling executives and the sundry workings of a large corporation. Film has aged slightly, but it still has some edge to it. Originally intended for television. **AKA:** Patterns of Power.
1956 83m/B Van Heflin, Everett Sloane, Ed Begley Sr., Beatrice Straight, Elizabeth Wilson; **D:** Fielder Cook; **W:** Rod Serling. **VHS** ★★★

Patton Lengthy but stellar bio of the vain, temperamental American general who masterminded significant combat triumphs during WWII. "Old Blood and Guts," who considered himself an 18th-century commander living in the wrong era, produced victory after victory in North Africa and Europe, but not without a decided impact upon his troops. Scott is truly magnificent in the title role, and Malden shines in the supporting role of General Omar Bradley. Not a subtle film, but neither is its subject. Interesting match-up with the 1986 made-for-TV movie "The Last Days of Patton," also starring Scott. **AKA:** Patton—Lust for Glory; Patton: A Salute to a Rebel.
1970 (PG) 171m/C George C. Scott, Karl Malden, Stephen Young, Michael Strong, Frank Latimore, James Edwards, Lawrence Dobkin, Michael Bates, Tim Considine; **D:** Franklin J. Schaffner; **W:** Francis Ford Coppola, Edmund H. North; **M:** Jerry Goldsmith. Academy Awards '70: Best Actor (Scott), Best Art Direction/Set Decoration, Best Director (Schaffner), Best Film Editing, Best Picture, Best Sound, Best Story & Screenplay; Directors Guild of America Awards '70: Best Director (Schaffner); Golden Globe Awards '71: Best Actor—Drama (Scott); National Board of Review Awards '70: 10 Best Films of the Year, Best Actor (Scott); National Society of Film Critics Awards '70: Best Actor (Scott); Writers Guild of America '70: Best Original Screenplay; Nominations: Academy Awards '70: Best Original Score. **VHS, Beta, LV** ★★★1/2

Pauline at the Beach A young woman accompanies her more experienced cousin to the French coast for a summer of sexual hijinks. Contemplative, not coarse, though the leads look great in—and out—of their swimsuits. Breezy, typically talky fare from small-film master Rohmer. Cinematography by Nester Almendro. In French with English subtitles. **AKA:** Pauline a la Plage.
1983 (R) 95m/C *FR* Amanda Langlet, Arielle Dombasle, Pascal Greggory, Rosette; **D:** Eric Rohmer; **W:** Eric Rohmer. **VHS, Beta, LV** ★★★1/2

The Pawnbroker A Jewish pawnbroker in Harlem is haunted by his grueling experiences in a Nazi camp during the Holocaust. Powerful and well done. Probably Steiger's best performance. Adapted from a novel by Edward Lewis Wallant.
1965 120m/B Rod Steiger, Brock Peters, Geraldine Fitzgerald, Jaime Sanchez, Thelma Oliver; **D:** Sidney Lumet; **M:** Quincy Jones. Berlin International Film Festival

'65: Best Actor (Steiger); British Academy Awards '66: Best Actor (Steiger); Nominations: Academy Awards '65: Best Actor (Steiger). **VHS, LV** ★★★★

The Pedestrian A prominent German industrialist is exposed as a Nazi officer who supervised the wholesale devastation of a Greek village during WWII. Impressive debut for director Schell, who also appears in a supporting role. **AKA:** Der Fussgaenger. 1973 (PG) 97m/C *GE SI* Maximilian Schell, Peggy Ashcroft, Lil Dagover, Francoise Rosay, Elisabeth Bergner; **D:** Maximilian Schell; **M:** Manos Hadjidakis. Golden Globe Awards '74: Best Foreign Film; National Board of Review Awards '74: 5 Best Foreign Films of the Year; Nominations: Academy Awards '73: Best Foreign Language Film. **VHS, Beta** ★★★½

Pee Wee's Big Adventure Zany, endearing comedy about an adult nerd's many adventures while attempting to recover his stolen bicycle. Chock full of classic sequences, including a barroom encounter between Pee Wee and several ornery bikers, and a tour through the Alamo. A colorful, exhilarating experience. 1985 (PG) 92m/C *Paul (Pee Wee Herman) Reubens*, Elizabeth Daily, Mark Holton, Diane Salinger, Judd Omen, Cassandra Peterson, James Brolin, Morgan Fairchild, Tony Bill, Jan Hooks; **D:** Tim Burton; **W:** Paul (Pee Wee Herman) Reubens, Phil Hartman, Michael Varhol; **M:** Danny Elfman. **VHS, Beta, LV** ★★★½

Peeping Tom Controversial, unsettling thriller in which a psychopath lures women before his film camera, then records their deaths at his hand. Unnerving subject matter is rendered impressively by British master Powell. A classic of its kind, but definitely not for everyone. This is the original uncut version of the film, released in the U.S. in 1979 with the assistance of Martin Scorsese. 1963 88m/C Karl-Heinz Boehm, Moira Shearer, Anna Massey, Maxine Audley, Esmond Knight, Shirley Anne Field, Brenda Bruce, Pamela Green, Jack Watson, Nigel Davenport, Susan Travers, Veronica Hurst; **D:** Michael Powell. **VHS, Beta, LV** ★★★½

Pelle the Conqueror Overpowering tale of a Swedish boy and his widower father who serve landowners in late 19th-century Denmark. Compassionate saga of human spirit contains numerous memorable sequences. Hvenegaard is wonderful as young Pelle, but von Sydow delivers what is probably his finest performance as a sympathetic weakling. American distributors foolishly trimmed the film by some 20 minutes (140 minute version). From the novel by Martin Anderson Nexo. In Swedish with English subtitles. 1988 160m/C *SW DK* Max von Sydow, Pelle Hvenegaard, Erik Paaske, Bjorn Granath, Axel Strobye, Astrid Villaume, Troels Asmussen, John Wittig, Anne Lise Hirsch Bjerrum, Kristina Tornqvist, Morten Jorgensen; **D:** Bille August; **W:** Bille August. Academy Awards '88: Best Foreign Language Film; Cannes Film Festival '88: Best Film; Golden Globe Awards '89: Best Foreign Film; Nominations: Academy Awards '88: Best Actor (von Sydow). **VHS, Beta, LV** ★★★★

Pennies from Heaven Underrated, one-of-a-kind musical about a horny sheet-music salesman in Chicago and his escapades during the Depression. Extraordinary musical sequences have stars lip-synching to great effect. Martin is only somewhat acceptable as the hapless salesman, but Peters and Harper deliver powerful performances as the women whose lives he ruins. Walken brings down the house in a stunning song-and-dance sequence. Adapted by Dennis Potter from his British television series. ♪ The Clouds Will Soon Roll By; Did You Ever See A Dream Walking?; Yes, Yes; Pennies From Heaven; Love Is Good for Anything That Ails You; I Want to Be Bad; Let's Misbehave; Life Is Just a Bowl of Cherries; Let's Face the Music and Dance. 1981 (R) 107m/C Steve Martin, Bernadette Peters, Christopher Walken, Jessica Harper, Vernel Bagneris; **D:** Herbert Ross; **W:** Dennis Potter; **M:** Ralph Burns, Marvin Hamlisch, Gordon Willis. Golden Globe Awards '82: Best Actress—Musical/Comedy (Peters); National Society of Film Critics Awards '81: Best Cinematography; Nominations: Academy Awards '81: Best Adapted Screenplay, Best Costume Design, Best Sound. **VHS, Beta, LV** ★★★½

Penny Serenade Newlyweds adopt a child, but tragedy awaits. Simplistic story nonetheless proves to be a moving experience. They don't make 'em like this anymore, and no one plays Grant better than Grant. Dunne is adequate. Also available colorized. 1941 120m/B Cary Grant, Irene Dunne, Beulah Bondi, Edgar Buchanan; **D:** George Stevens. Nominations: Academy Awards '41: Best Actor (Grant). **VHS, LV** ★★★

People Will Talk Grant plays Dr. Noah Praetorius, a doctor and educator who believes that the mind is a better healer than medicine. Archenemy Cronyn is the fellow instructor with a vengeance. Sickened by Grant's goodwill and the undying attention he receives, Cronyn reports Grant's unconventional medical practices to the higher-ups in hopes of ruining his reputation as doctor/ educator. Witty and satirical, this well-crafted comedy-drama is chock-full of interesting characters and finely tuned dialogue. Adapted from the play "Dr. Praetorius" by Curt Goetz. **1951 110m/B** Cary Grant, Jeanne Crain, Finlay Currie, Hume Cronyn, Walter Slezak, Sidney Blackmer, Basil Ruysdael, Katherine Locke, Margaret Hamilton, Carleton Young, Billy House, Stuart Holmes; *D:* Joseph L. Mankiewicz; *W:* Joseph L. Mankiewicz. VHS ★★★1/2

Pepe Le Moko An influential French film about a notorious gangster holed up in the Casbah, emerging at his own peril out of love for a beautiful woman. Stirring film established Gabin as a matinee idol. Cinematography is particularly fine too. Based upon the D'Ashelbe novel. The basis for both "Algiers," the popular Boyer-Lamarr melodrama, and the musical "The Casbah." In French with English subtitles. **1937 87m/B** *FR* Jean Gabin, Mireille Balin, Gabriel Gabrio, Lucas Gridoux; *D:* Julien Duvivier. National Board of Review Awards '41: 5 Best Foreign Films of the Year. VHS, Beta, 8mm ★★★

Peppermint Soda Kurys' affecting directorial debut is a semi-autobiographical tale of two teenaged sisters set in 1963 Paris. Seen through the eyes of the 13-year-old Anne, who lives with 15-year-old sister Frederique and their divorced mother, this is the year of first loves, strict teachers, dreaded family vacations, and a general awareness of growing up. Sweet look at adolescence and all its embarassing tribulations. In French with English subtitles. **1977 97m/C** *FR* Eleonore Klarwein, Odile Michel, Anouk Ferjac, Tsilla Chelton, Coralie Clement, Marie-Veronique Maurin, Puterflam, Philippe Rousselot; *D:* Diane Kurys; *W:* Diane Kurys. VHS ★★★

Performance Grim and unsettling psychological account of a criminal who hides out in a bizarre house occupied by a peculiar rock star and his two female companions. Entire cast scores high marks, with Pallenberg especially compelling as a somewhat mysterious and attractive housemate to mincing Jagger. A cult favorite,

with music by Nitzsche under the direction of Randy Newman. **1970 (R) 104m/C** *GB* James Fox, Mick Jagger, Anita Pallenberg; *D:* Donald Cammell, Nicolas Roeg; *W:* Donald Cammell; *M:* Jack Nitzsche. VHS, Beta, LV ★★★1/2

Perry Mason Returns Perry Mason returns to solve another baffling mystery. This time he must help his long-time assistant, Della Street, when she is accused of killing her new employer. **1985 95m/C** Raymond Burr, Barbara Hale, William Katt, Patrick O'Neal, Richard Anderson, Cassie Yates, Al Freeman Jr.; *D:* Ron Satlof. VHS, Beta ★★★

Persona A famous actress turns mute and is treated by a talkative nurse at a secluded cottage. As their relationship turns increasingly tense, the women's personalities begin to merge. Memorable, unnerving—and atypically avant garde—fare from cinema giant Bergman. First of several collaborations between the director and leading lady Ullman. In Swedish with English subtitles. **1966 100m/C** *SW* Bibi Andersson, Liv Ullmann, Gunnar Bjornstrand, Margareta Krook, Sven Nykvist; *D:* Ingmar Bergman; *W:* Ingmar Bergman. National Board of Review Awards '67: 5 Best Foreign Films of the Year; National Society of Film Critics Awards '67: Best Actress (Andersson), Best Director (Bergman), Best Film. VHS, Beta, 8mm ★★★★

Personal Best Lesbian lovers compete while training for the 1990 Olympics. Provocative fare often goes where few films have gone before, but overly stylized direction occasionally overwhelms characterizations. It gleefully exploits locker-room nudity, with Hemingway in her pre-implant days. Still, an ambitious, often accomplished production. Towne's directorial debut. **1982 (R) 126m/C** Mariel Hemingway, Scott Glenn, Patrice Donnelly; *D:* Robert Towne; *W:* Robert Towne; *M:* Jack Nitzsche, Michael Chapman. VHS, Beta ★★★

Persuasion Charming British costume romance, based on Jane Austen's final novel, deals with the constricted life of practical, plain, put-upon Anne Elliot (Root). Thanks to well-meaning interference, Anne refused the marriage proposal of the manly Frederick Wentworth (Hinds) and instead stuck by her snobbish and demanding family. Eight years later, Anne is given a second chance at love when the now-wealthy Wentworth happens back into her life—but

she still has her obnoxious relations to contend with. It's wonderful to see Anne blossom from mouse to lioness although the swirl of supporting players (and settings) provide some confusion.
1995 (PG) 104m/C *GB* Amanda Root, Ciaran Hinds, Susan Fleetwood, Corin Redgrave, Fiona Shaw, John Woodvine, Phoebe Nicholls, Sam West, Sophie Thompson, Judy Cornwell, Felicity Dean, Simon Russell Beale, Victoria Hamilton, Emma Roberts; *D:* Roger Mitchell; *W:* Nick Dear, Jeremy Sams, John Daly. **VHS, LV** ★★★★

Peter Pan Disney classic about a boy who never wants to grow up. Based on J.M. Barrie's book and play. Still stands head and shoulders above any recent competition in providing fun family entertainment. Terrific animation and lovely hummable music.
1953 (G) 76m/C *D:* Hamilton Luske; *V:* Bobby Driscoll, Kathryn Beaumont, Hans Conried, Heather Angel, Candy Candido. **VHS, Beta, LV** ★★★

Peter Pan A TV classic, this videotape of a performance of the 1954 Broadway musical adapted from the J.M. Barrie classic features Mary Martin in one of her most famous incarnations, as the adolescent Peter Pan. Songs include "I'm Flying," "Neverland," and "I Won't Grow Up."
1960 100m/C Mary Martin, Cyril Ritchard, Sondra Lee, Heather Halliday, Luke Halpin; *D:* Vincent J. Donehue. **VHS, Beta, LV** ★★★★

Peter the Great Dry but eye-pleasing TV mini-series follows the life of Russia's colorful, very tall ruler from childhood on. Much of the interesting cast is wasted in tiny roles.
1986 371m/C Maximilian Schell, Laurence Olivier, Omar Sharif, Vanessa Redgrave, Ursula Andress. **VHS** ★★★

Petrified Forest Patrons and employees are held captive by a run-away gangster's band in a desert diner. Often gripping, with memorable performances from Davis, Howard, and Bogart. Based on the play by Robert Sherwood with Howard and Bogart re-creating their stage roles.
1936 83m/B Bette Davis, Leslie Howard, Humphrey Bogart, Dick Foran, Charley Grapewin, Porter Hall; *D:* Archie Mayo. **VHS, Beta** ★★★

Petulia Overlooked, offbeat drama about a flighty woman who spites her husband by dallying with a sensitive, recently divorced surgeon. Classic '60s document and cult favorite offers great performance from the appealing Christie, with Scott fine as the vulnerable surgeon. On-screen performances by the Grateful Dead and Big Brother. Among idiosyncratic director Lester's best. Photographed by Nicholas Roeg. From the novel "Me and the Arch Kook Petulia" by John Haase.
1968 (R) 105m/C George C. Scott, Richard Chamberlain, Julie Christie, Shirley Knight, Arthur Hill, Joseph Cotten, Pippa Scott, Richard Dysart, Kathleen Widdoes, Austin Pendleton, Rene Auberjonois; *D:* Richard Lester; *W:* Lawrence B. Marcus; *M:* John Barry. **VHS, Beta** ★★★★

Peyton Place Passion, scandal, and deception in a small New England town set the standard for passion, scandal, and deception in soap operadom. Shot on location in Camden, Maine. Performances and themes now seem dated, but produced a blockbuster in its time. Adapted from Grace Metalious' popular novel and followed by "Return to Peyton Place."
1957 157m/C Lana Turner, Hope Lange, Lee Philips, Lloyd Nolan, Diane Varsi, Lorne Greene, Russ Tamblyn, Arthur Kennedy, Terry Moore, Barry Coe, David Nelson, Betty Field, Mildred Dunnock, Leon Ames, Alan Reed Jr.; *D:* Mark Robson; *W:* John Michael Hayes. Nominations: Academy Awards '57: Best Director (Robson), Best Supporting Actress (Lange). **VHS, LV** ★★★

Phantom of Liberty Master surrealist Bunuel's episodic film wanders from character to character and from event to event. Animals wander through a man's bedroom, soldiers conduct military exercises in an inhabited area, a missing girl stands before her parents even as they futilely attempt to determine her whereabouts, and an assassin is found guilty, then applauded and led to freedom. They don't get much more surreal than this. If you think you may like it, you'll probably love it. Bunuel, by the way, is among the firing squad victims in the film's opening enactment of Goya's May 3, 1808. In French with English subtitles. *AKA:* Le Fantome de la Liberte; The Specter of Freedom.
1974 104m/C *FR* Adrianna Asti, Jean-Claude Brialy, Michel Piccoli, Adolfo Celi, Monica Vitti; *D:* Luis Bunuel. National Board of Review Awards '74: 5 Best Foreign Films of the Year. **VHS, Beta, LV** ★★★½

The Phantom of the Opera Deranged, disfigured music lover haunts the sewers of a Parisian opera house and kills to further the career of an

unsuspecting young soprano. First of many film versions still packs a wallop, with fine playing from Chaney, Sr. Silent with two-color Technicolor "Bal Masque" sequence. Versions with different running times are also available, including 79 and 88 minutes.
1925 101m/B Lon Chaney Sr., Norman Kerry, Mary Philbin, Gibson Gowland; *D:* Rupert Julian. **VHS ★★★**

The Phantom of the Opera Second Hollywood version—the first with talking—of Gastron Leroux novel about a madman who promotes fear and mayhem at a Paris opera house. Raines is good in lead; Eddy warbles away.
1943 92m/C Claude Rains, Nelson Eddy, Susanna Foster, Edgar Barrier, Leo Carrillo, Hume Cronyn, J. Edward Bromberg; *D:* Arthur Lubin. Academy Awards '43: Best Color Cinematography, Best Interior Decoration; Nominations: Academy Awards '43: Best Sound. **VHS, Beta, LV ★★★**

Phantom Tollbooth A young boy drives his car into an animated world, where the numbers are at war with the letters and he has been chosen to save Rhyme and Reason, to bring stability back to the Land of Wisdom. Completely unique and typically Jonesian in its intellectual level and interests. Bright children will be interested, but this is really for adults who will understand the allegory. Based on Norman Justers' metaphorical novel.
1969 (G) 89m/C *D:* Chuck Jones; *V:* Mel Blanc, Hans Conried. **VHS, Beta ★★★**

Philadelphia AIDS goes Hollywood as hot-shot corporate attorney Andrew Beckett (Hanks), fired because he has the disease, hires brilliant but homophobic personal injury attorney Washington as his counsel when he sues for discrimination. Box office winner was criticized by some gay activists as too mainstream, which is the point. It doesn't probe deeply into the gay lifestyle, focusing instead on justice and compassion. Boasts a good script, make-up that transforms Hanks, sure direction, great soundtrack, and a strong supporting cast, but all would mean little without Hanks' superb performance, his best to date. ♪ Streets of Philadelphia.
1993 (PG-13) 125m/C Tom Hanks, Denzel Washington, Antonio Banderas, Jason Robards Jr., Joanne Woodward, Mary Steenburgen, Ron Vawter, Robert Ridgely, Obba Babatunde, Robert Castle, Daniel Chapman, Roger Corman, John Bedford Lloyd, Roberta Maxwell, Warren Miller, Anna Deavere Smith, Kathryn Witt, Andre B. Blake, Ann Dowd, Bradley Whitford, Chandra Wilson, Charles Glenn, Peter Jacobs, Paul Lazar, Dan Olmstead, Joey Perillo, Lauren Roselli, Bill Rowe, Lisa Talerico, Daniel von Bargen, Tracey Walter; *Cameos:* Karen Finley, David Drake, Quentin Crisp, Tak Fujimoto; *D:* Jonathan Demme; *W:* Ron Nyswaner; *M:* Howard Shore. Academy Awards '93: Best Actor (Hanks), Best Song ("Streets of Philadelphia"); Golden Globe Awards '94: Best Actor—Drama (Hanks), Best Song ("Streets of Philadelphia"); Blockbuster Entertainment Awards '95: Drama Actor, Video (Hanks); Nominations: Academy Awards '93: Best Makeup, Best Original Screenplay; MTV Movie Awards '94: Best Film, Best On-Screen Duo (Tom Hanks/Denzel Washington), Best Song ("Streets of Philadelphia"). **VHS, LV, 8mm ★★★1/2**

The Philadelphia Story A woman's plans to marry again go awry when her dashing ex-husband arrives on the scene. Matters are further complicated when a loopy reporter—assigned to spy on the nuptials—falls in love with the blushing bride. Classic comedy, with trio of Hepburn, Grant, and Stewart all serving aces. Based on the hit Broadway play by Philip Barry, and remade as the musical "High Society" in 1956 (stick to the original). Also available colorized.
1940 112m/B Katharine Hepburn, Cary Grant, James Stewart, Ruth Hussey, Roland Young, John Howard, John Halliday, Virginia Weidler, Henry Daniell, Hillary Brooke, Mary Nash; *D:* George Cukor; *W:* Donald Ogden Stewart; *M:* Franz Waxman. Academy Awards '40: Best Actor (Stewart), Best Screenplay; New York Film Critics Awards '40: Best Actress (Hepburn); Nominations: Academy Awards '40: Best Actress (Hepburn), Best Director (Cukor), Best Picture, Best Supporting Actress (Hussey). **VHS, Beta, LV ★★★★**

The Piano In the 1850s, Ada (Hunter), a mute Scottish widow with a young daughter, agrees to an arranged marriage with Stewart (Neill), a colonial landowner in New Zealand. The way she expresses her feelings is by playing her cherished piano, left behind on the beach by her new husband. Another settler, George, (Keitel) buys it, arranges for lessons with Ada, and soon the duo begin a grand passion leading to a cruelly calculated revenge. Fiercely poetic and well acted (with Keitel in a notably romantic role), though the film may be too dark and intense for some. Fine original score with Hunter doing her own piano playing.

1993 (R) 120m/C *AU* Holly Hunter, Harvey Keitel, Sam Neill, Anna Paquin, Kerry Walker, Genevieve Lemon; *D:* Jane Campion; *W:* Jane Campion; *M:* Michael Nyman, Stuart Dryburgh. Academy Awards '93: Best Actress (Hunter), Best Original Screenplay, Best Supporting Actress (Paquin); British Academy Awards '94: Best Actress (Hunter); Cannes Film Festival '93: Best Actress (Hunter), Best Film; Golden Globe Awards '94: Best Actress—Drama (Hunter); Independent Spirit Awards '94: Best Foreign Film; Los Angeles Film Critics Association Awards '93: Best Actress (Hunter), Best Cinematography, Best Director (Campion), Best Screenplay, Best Supporting Actress (Paquin); New York Film Critics Awards '93: Best Actress (Hunter), Best Director (Campion), Best Screenplay; National Society of Film Critics Awards '93: Best Actress (Hunter), Best Screenplay; Writers Guild of America '93: Best Original Screenplay; Nominations: Academy Awards '93: Best Cinematography, Best Costume Design, Best Director (Campion), Best Film Editing, Best Picture; British Academy Awards '94: Best Director (Campion), Best Film, Best Original Screenplay, Best Original Score; Directors Guild of America Awards '93: Best Director (Campion); Golden Globe Awards '94: Best Director (Campion), Best Film—Drama, Best Screenplay, Best Supporting Actress (Paquin), Best Original Score. **VHS, LV** ★★★1/2

The Piano Lesson The prized heirloom of the Charles family is an 80-year-old, ornately carved upright piano, jealously guarded by widowed Berniece (Woodard), and housed in the Pittsburgh home of Uncle Doaker (Gordon). When Berniece's brother Willie Boy (Dutton) visits from Mississippi, it's to persuade her to sell the piano in order to buy some land that their grandfather had worked as a slave. But the past, carved into the piano's panels, has a strong hold—one that Berniece refuses to give up. Set in 1936. Adaptation by Wilson of his 1990 Pulitzer Prize-winning play. **1994 (PG) 99m/C** Alfre Woodard, Charles S. Dutton, Courtney B. Vance, Carl Gordon, Tommy Hollis, Zelda Harris, Lou Myers, Rosalyn Coleman, Tommy La Fitte; *D:* Lloyd Richards; *W:* August Wilson; *M:* Stephen James Taylor, Dwight Andrews. **VHS, LV** ★★★

Pickpocket Slow moving, documentary-like account of a petty thief's existence is a moral tragedy inspired by "Crime and Punishment." Ending is particularly moving. Classic filmmaking from Bresson, France's master of austerity. In French with English subtitles. **1959 75m/B** *FR* Martin LaSalle, Marika

Green, Pierre Leymarie; *D:* Robert Bresson. **VHS, Beta** ★★★1/2

Pickup on South Street Petty thief Widmark lifts woman's wallet only to find it contains top secret Communist micro-film for which pinko agents will stop at nothing to get back. Intriguing look at the politics of the day. The creme of "B" movies. **1953 80m/B** Richard Widmark, Jean Peters, Thelma Ritter, Murvyn Vye, Richard Kiley, Milburn Stone; *D:* Samuel Fuller; *W:* Samuel Fuller. Nominations: Academy Awards '53: Best Supporting Actress (Ritter). **VHS, Beta** ★★★

Picnic A wanderer arrives in a small town and immediately wins the love of his friend's girl. The other women in town seem interested too. Strong, romantic work, with Holden excelling in the lead. Novak provides a couple of pointers too. Lavish Hollywood adaptation of the William Inge play, including the popular tune "Moonglow/Theme from Picnic." **1955 113m/C** William Holden, Kim Novak, Rosalind Russell, Susan Strasberg, Arthur O'Connell, Cliff Robertson, Betty Field, Verna Felton, Reta Shaw, Nick Adams, Phyllis Newman, Raymond Bailey; *D:* Joshua Logan; *W:* Daniel Taradash; *M:* George Duning. Academy Awards '55: Best Art Direction/Set Decoration (Color), Best Film Editing; Golden Globe Awards '56: Best Director (Logan); National Board of Review Awards '55: 10 Best Films of the Year; Nominations: Academy Awards '55: Best Picture, Best Supporting Actor (O'Connell). **VHS, Beta, LV** ★★★1/2

Picnic at Hanging Rock School outing in 1900 into a mountainous region ends tragically when three girls disappear. Eerie film is strong on atmosphere, as befits mood master Weir. Lambert is extremely photogenic—and suitable subdued—as one of the girls to disappear. Otherwise beautifully photographed on location. From the novel by Joan Lindsey. **1975 (PG) 110m/C** *AU* Margaret Nelson, Rachel Roberts, Dominic Guard, Helen Morse, Jacki Weaver; *D:* Peter Weir; *M:* Bruce Smeaton, John Seale. **VHS, Beta** ★★★

Picture of Dorian Gray Hatfield plays the rake who stays young while his portrait ages in this adaptation of Oscar Wilde's classic novel. Lansbury steals this one. **1945 110m/B** Hurd Hatfield, George Sanders, Donna Reed, Angela Lansbury, Peter Lawford, Lowell Gilmore; *D:* Albert Lewin. Academy Awards '45: Best Black and White Cinematography; Golden Globe Awards '46: Best Supporting Actress

(Lansbury); Nominations: Academy Awards '45: Best Interior Decoration, Best Supporting Actress (Lansbury). **VHS, Beta, LV** ★★★

Pierrot le Fou A woman fleeing a gangster joins a man leaving his wife in this stunning, occasionally confusing classic from iconoclast Godard. A hallmark in 1960s improvisational filmmaking, with rugged Belmondo and always-photogenic Karina effortlessly excelling in leads. In French with English subtitles.
1965 110m/C *FR IT* Samuel Fuller, Jean-Pierre Leaud, Jean-Paul Belmondo, Anna Karina, Dirk Sanders; *D:* Jean-Luc Godard; *M:* Antoine Duhamel. **VHS, LV** ★★★1/2

Pillow Talk Sex comedy in which a man woos a woman who loathes him. By the way, they share the same telephone party line. Narrative provides minimal indication of the film's strengths, which are many. Classic '50s comedy with masters Day and Hudson exhibiting considerable rapport, even when fighting. Lighthearted, constantly funny.
1959 102m/C Rock Hudson, Doris Day, Tony Randall, Thelma Ritter, Nick Adams, Lee Patrick; *D:* Michael Gordon. Academy Awards '59: Best Story & Screenplay; Nominations: Academy Awards '59: Best Actress (Day), Best Art Direction/Set Decoration (Color), Best Supporting Actress (Ritter). **VHS, Beta, LV** ★★★1/2

The Pink Panther Bumbling, disaster-prone inspector invades a Swiss ski resort and becomes obsessed with capturing a jewel thief hoping to lift the legendary "Pink Panther" diamond. Said thief is also the inspector's wife's lover, though the inspector doesn't know it. Slick slapstick succeeds on strength of Sellers' classic portrayal of Clouseau, who accidentally destroys everything in his path while speaking in a funny French accent. Followed by "A Shot in the Dark," "Inspector Clouseau" (without Sellers), "The Return of the Pink Panther," "The Pink Panther Strikes Again," "Revenge of the Pink Panther," "Trail of the Pink Panther," and "Curse of the Pink Panther." Memorable theme supplied by Mancini.
1964 113m/C *GB* Peter Sellers, David Niven, Robert Wagner, Claudia Cardinale, Capucine, Brenda de Banzie; *D:* Blake Edwards; *W:* Blake Edwards; *M:* Henry Mancini. Nominations: Academy Awards '64: Best Original Score. **VHS, Beta, LV** ★★★

The Pink Panther Strikes Again Fifth in the series has the incompetent inspector tracking his former boss, who has gone insane and has become preoccupied with destroying the entire world. A must for Sellers buffs and anyone who appreciates slapstick.
1976 (PG) 103m/C *GB* Peter Sellers, Herbert Lom, Lesley-Anne Down, Colin Blakely, Leonard Rossiter, Burt Kwouk; *D:* Blake Edwards; *W:* Edwards Waldman, Frank Waldman; *M:* Henry Mancini. Writers Guild of America '76: Best Adapted Screenplay; Nominations: Academy Awards '76: Best Song ("Come to Me"). **VHS, Beta, LV** ★★★

Pinky Early Hollywood treatment of the tragic choice made by some black Americans to pass as white in order to attain a better life for themselves and their families. The story is still relevant today. Waters and Barrymore also star, but the lead black character is portrayed by a white actress. Based on the novel "Quality" by Cyd Ricketts Sumner.
1949 102m/B Jeanne Crain, Ethel Barrymore, Ethel Waters, Nina Mae McKinney, William Lundigan; *D:* Elia Kazan; *W:* Philip Dunne, Dudley Nichols; *M:* Alfred Newman. Nominations: Academy Awards '49: Best Actress (Crain), Best Supporting Actress (Barrymore, Waters). **VHS** ★★★

Pinocchio Second Disney animated film features Pinocchio, a little wooden puppet, made with love by the old woodcarver Geppetto, and brought to life by a good fairy. Except Pinocchio isn't content to be just a puppet—he wants to become a real boy. Lured off by a sly fox, Pinocchio undergoes a number of adventures as he tries to return safely home. Has some scary scenes, including Geppetto, Pinocchio, and their friend Jiminy Cricket getting swallowed by a whale, and Pleasure Island, where naughty boys are turned into donkeys. An example of animation at its best and a Disney classic that has held up over time. ♪ When You Wish Upon a Star; Give a Little Whistle; Turn on the Old Music Box; Hi-Diddle-Dee-Dee (An Actor's Life For Me); I've Got No Strings.
1940 (G) 87m/C *D:* Ben Sharpsteen; *V:* Dick Jones, Cliff Edwards, Evelyn Venable, Walter Catlett, Frankie Darro, Charles Judels, Don Brodie, Christian Rub. Academy Awards '40: Best Song ("When You Wish Upon a Star"), Best Original Score. **VHS, Beta, LV** ★★★★

The Pirate A traveling actor poses as a legendary pirate to woo a lonely woman on a remote Caribbean island. Minnelli always scores with this type of fare, and both Garland and

Kelly make the most of the Cole Porter score. ♪ Be a Clown; Nina; Mack the Black; You Can Do No Wrong; Sweet Ices, Papayas, Berry Man; Sea Wall; Serafin; The Ring; Judy Awakens.

1948 102m/C Judy Garland, Gene Kelly, Walter Slezak, Gladys Cooper, George Zucco, Reginald Owen, Nicholas Brothers; *D:* Vincente Minnelli. Nominations: Academy Awards '48: Best Original Score. **VHS, Beta, LV ★★★**

The Pit and the Pendulum A woman and her lover plan to drive her brother mad, and he responds by locking them in his torture chamber, which was built by his loony dad, whom he now thinks he is. Standard Corman production only remotely derived from the classic Poe tale, with the cast chewing on a loopy script. A landmark in Gothic horror.

1961 80m/C Vincent Price, John Kerr, Barbara Steele, Luana Anders; *D:* Roger Corman; *W:* Richard Matheson; *M:* Les Baxter. **VHS, Beta ★★★**

Pixote Wrenching, documentary-like account of an orphan boy's life on the streets in a Brazilian metropolis. Graphic and depressing, it's not for all tastes but nonetheless masterfully done. In Portuguese with English subtitles.

1981 127m/C *BR* Fernando Ramos Da Silva, Marilia Pera, Jorge Juliao, Gilberto Moura, Jose Nilson dos Santos, Edilson Lino; *D:* Hector Babenco; *W:* Hector Babenco; *M:* John Neschling. Los Angeles Film Critics Association Awards '81: Best Foreign Film; New York Film Critics Awards '81: Best Foreign Film; National Society of Film Critics Awards '81: Best Actress (Pera). **VHS, Beta ★★★★**

A Place in the Sun Melodramatic adaptation of "An American Tragedy," Theodore Dreiser's realist classic about an ambitious laborer whose aspirations to the high life with a gorgeous debutante are threatened by his lower-class lover's pregnancy. Clift is magnificent in the lead, and Taylor and Winters also shine in support. Burr, however, grossly overdoes his role of the vehement prosecutor. Still, not a bad effort from somewhat undisciplined director Stevens.

1951 120m/B Montgomery Clift, Elizabeth Taylor, Shelley Winters, Raymond Burr, Anne Revere; *D:* George Stevens; *M:* Franz Waxman. Academy Awards '51: Best Black and White Cinematography, Best Costume Design (B & W), Best Director (Stevens), Best Film Editing, Best Screenplay, Best Score; Directors Guild of America Awards '51: Best Director (Stevens); Golden Globe Awards '52: Best Film—Drama; National Board of Review Awards '51: 10 Best Films of the Year; Nominations: Academy Awards '51: Best Actor (Clift), Best Actress (Winters), Best Picture. **VHS, Beta, LV ★★★**

A Place in the World Returning from exile to their native Argentina during a military dictatorship, Mario and Ana (Luppi and Roth) work to help the less advantaged in their society, determined to make a difference. Story is seen as a flashback from point-of-view of the couples' son Ernesto (Batyi). Well-crafted, finely acted piece exploring political, social, and interpersonal themes. 1993 Oscar bid retracted due to controversy over country of film's origin.

1995 120m/C *AR* Jose Sacristan, Federico Luppi, Cecilia Roth, Leonor Benedetto, Gaston Batyi, Lorena Del Rio; *D:* Adolfo Aristarain; *W:* Adolfo Aristarain, Alberto Lecchi; *M:* Emilio Kauderer. **VHS ★★★**

Places in the Heart A young widow determines to make the best of a bad situation on a small farm in Depression-era Texas, fighting poverty, racism, and sexism while enduring back-breaking labor. Support group includes a blind veteran and a black drifter. Hokey but nonetheless moving film is improved significantly by strong performances by virtually everyone in the cast. In his debut, Malkovich shines through this stellar group. Effective dust-bowl photography by Nestor Almendros.

1984 (PG) 113m/C Sally Field, John Malkovich, Danny Glover, Ed Harris, Lindsay Crouse, Amy Madigan, Terry O'Quinn; *D:* Robert Benton; *W:* Robert Benton; *M:* Howard Shore. Academy Awards '84: Best Actress (Field), Best Original Screenplay; Golden Globe Awards '85: Best Actress—Drama (Field); National Board of Review Awards '84: Best Supporting Actor (Malkovich); New York Film Critics Awards '84: Best Screenplay; National Society of Film Critics Awards '84: Best Supporting Actor (Malkovich); Nominations: Academy Awards '84: Best Costume Design, Best Director (Benton), Best Picture, Best Supporting Actor (Malkovich), Best Supporting Actress (Crouse). **VHS, Beta, LV ★★★**

Planet of the Apes Astronauts crash-land on a planet where apes are masters and humans are merely brute animals. Superior science fiction with sociological implications marred only by unnecessary humor. Heston delivers one of his more plausible performances. Superb ape makeup creates realistic pseudo-

simians of McDowall, Hunter, Evans, Whitmore, and Daly. Adapted from Pierre Boulle's novel "Monkey Planet." Followed by four sequels and two television series.
1968 (G) 112m/C Charlton Heston, Roddy McDowall, Kim Hunter, Maurice Evans, Linda Harrison, James Whitmore, James Daly; **D:** Franklin J. Schaffner; **W:** Rod Serling, Michael G. Wilson; **M:** Jerry Goldsmith. National Board of Review Awards '68: 10 Best Films of the Year; Nominations: Academy Awards '68: Best Costume Design, Best Original Score.
VHS, Beta, LV ★★★★

Platinum Blonde Screwball comedy in which a newspaper journalist (Williams) marries a wealthy girl (Harlow) but finds that he doesn't like the restrictions and confinement of high society. Yearning for a creative outlet, he decides to write a play and hires a reporter (Young) to collaborate with him. The results are funny and surprising when Young shows up at the mansion flanked by a group of hard-drinking, fun-loving reporters.
1931 86m/B Loretta Young, Robert Williams, Jean Harlow, Louise Closser Hale; **D:** Frank Capra; **W:** Jo Swerling, Dorothy Howell. **VHS ★★★**

Platoon A grunt's view of the Vietnam War is provided in all its horrific, inexplicable detail. Sheen is wooden in the lead, but both Dafoe and Berenger are resplendent as, respectively, good and bad soldiers. Strong, visceral filmmaking from fearless director Stone, who based the film on his own GI experiences. Highly acclaimed; considered by many to be the most realistic portrayal of the war on film.
1986 (R) 113m/C Charlie Sheen, Willem Dafoe, Tom Berenger, Francesco Quinn, Forest Whitaker, John C. McGinley, Kevin Dillon, Richard Edson, Reggie Johnson, Keith David, Johnny Depp; **D:** Oliver Stone; **W:** Oliver Stone; **M:** Georges Delerue, Robert Richardson. Academy Awards '86: Best Director (Stone), Best Film Editing, Best Picture, Best Sound; British Academy Awards '87: Best Director (Stone); Directors Guild of America Awards '86: Best Director (Stone); Golden Globe Awards '87: Best Director (Stone), Best Film—Drama, Best Supporting Actor (Berenger); National Board of Review Awards '86: 10 Best Films of the Year; Nominations: Academy Awards '86: Best Cinematography, Best Original Screenplay, Best Supporting Actor (Berenger, Dafoe).
VHS, Beta, LV ★★★½

Play It Again, Sam Allen is—no surprise—a nerd, and this time he's in love with his best friend's wife. Modest storyline provides a framework of endless gags, with Allen borrowing heavily from "Casablanca." Bogey even appears periodically to counsel Allen on the ways of wooing women. Superior comedy isn't hurt by Ross directing instead of Allen, who adapted the script from his own play.
1972 (PG) 85m/C Woody Allen, Diane Keaton, Tony Roberts, Susan Anspach, Jerry Lacy, Jennifer Salt, Joy Bang, Viva, Herbert Ross; **D:** Herbert Ross; **W:** Woody Allen; **M:** Billy Goldenberg, Owen Roizman.
VHS, Beta, LV, 8mm ★★★½

Play Misty for Me A radio deejay obliges a psychotic woman's song request and suddenly finds himself the target of her obsessive behavior, which rapidly turns from seductive to murderous. Auspicious directorial debut for Eastwood, borrowing from the Siegel playbook (look for the director's cameo as a barkeep). Based on a story by Heims.
1971 (R) 102m/C Jessica Walter, Donna Mills, John Larch, Irene Hervey, Jack Ging, Clint Eastwood; **Cameos:** Donald Siegel; **D:** Clint Eastwood; **W:** Jo Heims, Dean Riesner; **M:** Dee Barton. **VHS, Beta, LV ★★★**

The Player Clever, entertaining, and biting satire of the movie industry and the greed that controls it. Robbins is dead-on as Griffin Mill, a young studio exec who becomes the chief suspect in a murder investigation. He personifies Hollywood's ethics (or lack thereof) in a performance both cold and vulnerable, as he looks for the right buttons to push and the proper back to stab. Strong leading performances are supplemented by 65 star cameos. Some viewers may be put off by the inside-Hollywood jokes, but Altman fans will love it. The laserdisc version includes commentary by Altman, interviews with 20 screenwriters, and celebrity cameos that didn't make the final cut.
1992 (R) 123m/C Tim Robbins, Greta Scacchi, Fred Ward, Whoopi Goldberg, Peter Gallagher, Brion James, Cynthia Stevenson, Vincent D'Onofrio, Dean Stockwell, Richard E. Grant, Dina Merrill, Sydney Pollack, Lyle Lovett, Randall Batinkoff, Gina Gershon; **Cameos:** Burt Reynolds, Cher, Nick Nolte, Jack Lemmon, Lily Tomlin, Marlee Matlin, Julia Roberts, Bruce Willis, Anjelica Huston, Elliott Gould, Sally Kellerman, Steve Allen, Richard Anderson, Harry Belafonte, Shari Belafonte, Karen Black, Gary Busey, Robert Carradine, James Coburn, Cathy Lee Crosby, John Cusack, Brad Davis, Peter Falk, Teri Garr, Leeza Gibbons, Scott

Glenn, Jeff Goldblum, Joel Grey, Buck Henry, Kathy Ireland, Sally Kirkland, Andie MacDowell, Martin Mull, Mimi Rogers, Jill St. John, Susan Sarandon, Rod Steiger, Joan Tewkesbury, Robert Wagner, Michael Tolkin; *D:* Robert Altman; *W:* Michael Tolkin; *M:* Thomas Newman. British Academy Awards '92: Best Adapted Screenplay; Cannes Film Festival '92: Best Actor (Robbins), Best Director (Altman); Golden Globe Awards '93: Best Actor—Musical/Comedy (Robbins), Best Film—Musical/Comedy; Independent Spirit Awards '93: Best Film; New York Film Critics Awards '92: Best Cinematography, Best Director (Altman), Best Film; Writers Guild of America '92: Best Adapted Screenplay; Nominations: Academy Awards '92: Best Adapted Screenplay, Best Director (Altman), Best Film Editing; Cannes Film Festival '92: Best Film. **VHS, LV** ★★★1/2

Playing for Time Compelling, award-winning television drama based on actual experiences of a Holocaust prisoner who survives by leading an inmate orchestra. Strong playing from Redgrave and Mayron. Pro-Palestinian Redgrave's political beliefs made her a controversial candidate for the role of Jewish Fania Fenelon, but her stunning performance is on the mark. **1980 148m/C** Vanessa Redgrave, Jane Alexander, Maud Adams, Verna Bloom, Melanie Mayron; *D:* Daniel Mann; *M:* Brad Fiedel. **VHS, Beta** ★★★

Playtime Occasionally enterprising comedy in which the bemused Frenchman Hulot tries in vain to maintain an appointment in an urban landscape of glass and steel. The theme of cold, unfeeling civilization is hardly unique, but the film is nonetheless enjoyable. The third in the Hulot trilogy, preceded by "Mr. Hulot's Holiday" and "Mon Oncle." In French with English subtitles. **1967 108m/C** *FR* Jacques Tati, Barbara Dennek, Jacqueline Lecomte, Jack Gautier; *D:* Jacques Tati. **VHS, Beta** ★★★

Plaza Suite Three alternating skits from Neil Simon's play about different couples staying at the New York hotel. Matthau shines in all three vignettes. Some of Simon's funnier stuff, with the first sketch being the best: Matthau and Stapleton are a couple celebrating their 24th anniversary. She's sentimental, while he's yearning for his mistress. Number two has producer Matthau putting the make on old flame Harris, while the finale has father Matthau coaxing his anxious daughter out of the bathroom on her wedding day.

1971 (PG) 114m/C Walter Matthau, Maureen Stapleton, Barbara Harris, Lee Grant, Louise Sorel; *D:* Arthur Hiller; *W:* Neil Simon; *M:* Maurice Jarre. **VHS, Beta, LV** ★★★

Pocahontas It's 1607 and spirited Powhatan maiden Pocahontas and British settler Captain John Smith strike an unlikely but doomed romance in Disney's 33rd animated feature, its first based on the life of a historical figure. Lovely Poca, a virtual post-adolescent Native American superbabe, introduces the roguish captain (spoken and sung by Gibson) to the wonders of unspoiled nature and serves as peacemaker in the clash of European and Native American cultures. Disney puts its spin on history but maintains cultural sensitivity: several characters are voiced by Native American performers, including Chief Powhatan, spoken by American Indian activist Means, who led the 1973 siege at Wounded Knee, and Bedard as Pocahontas. Just don't tell the kids the real Pocahontas married someone else, moved to England, and died of smallpox at 21. Stunningly animated, but its mediocre soundtrack and decidedly somber tone leave it lacking in typical Disney majesty and charm. Premiered at New York's Central Park, for the usual theater crowd of 100,000 or so. **1995 (G) 90m/C** *D:* Mike Gabriel, Eric Goldberg; *W:* Carl Binder, Susannah Grant, Philip LaZebnik; *M:* Alan Menken, Stephen Schwartz; *V:* Irene Bedard, Judy Kuhn, Mel Gibson, Joe Baker, Christian Bale, Billy Connolly, James Apaumut Fall, Linda Hunt, John Kassir, Danny Mann, Bill Cobbs, David Ogden Stiers, Michelle St. John, Gordon Tootoosis, Frank Welker. Golden Globe Awards '96: Best Song ("Colors of the Wind"); Nominations: Academy Awards '95: Best Song ("Colors of the Wind"), Best Score; Golden Globe Awards '96: Best Score. **VHS** ★★★

Pocketful of Miracles Capra's final film, a remake of his 1933 "Lady for a Day," is just as corny and sentimental but doesn't work quite as well. Davis is delightful as Apple Annie, a down-on-her-luck street vendor who will go to any extreme to hide her poverty from the well-married daughter she adores. Ford is terrific as the man who transforms Annie into a lady in time for her daughter's visit. Touching. Maybe too touching. Also marks Ann-Margret's film debut. **1961 136m/C** Bette Davis, Glenn Ford, Peter Falk, Hope Lange, Arthur O'Connell, Ann-Margret, Thomas Mitchell, Jack Elam, Edward Everett Horton, David Brian,

Mickey Shaughnessy; **D:** Frank Capra. Golden Globe Awards '62: Best Actor— Musical/Comedy (Ford); Nominations: Academy Awards '61: Best Costume Design (Color), Best Song ("Pocketful of Miracles"), Best Supporting Actor (Falk). **VHS, Beta, LV** ★★★

Poison A controversial, compelling drama weaving the story of a seven-year-old boy's murder of his father with two other tales of obsessive, fringe behavior. From the director of the underground hit "Superstar: The Karen Carpenter Story," which was shot using only a cast of "Barbie" dolls.
1991 (R) 85m/C Edith Meeks, Larry Maxwell, Susan Norman, Scott Renderer, James Lyons; **D:** Todd Haynes; **W:** Todd Haynes; **M:** James Bennett. Sundance Film Festival '91: Grand Jury Prize. **VHS** ★★★

Poldark Tempestuous love, political intrigue, and family struggles all set in 18th-century Cornwall, then the copper-producing center of England. Heroic Ross Poldark has just returned from fighting upstart Americans in the Revolutionary War only to discover that his father has died and the family mines are about to be sold to the scheming Warleggan family. Ross struggles to pay off family debts, reclaim his heritage, resolve his feelings for an old love, and fight his attraction to the beguiling, but completely unsuitable, Demelza. Adapted from the novels by Winston Graham. Made for British television; 12 episodes on six cassettes.
1975 720m/C *GB* Robin Ellis, Angharad Rees, Jill Townsend, Judy Geeson, Ralph Bates, Richard Morant, Clive Francis, John Baskcomb, Paul Curran, Tilly Tremayne, Mary Wimbush; **D:** Paul Annett, Christopher Barry, Kenneth Ives; **W:** Paul Wheeler, Jack Russell, Peter Draper, Jack Pulman. **VHS** ★★★

Poldark 2 The further adventures of Ross Poldark, wife Demelza, and assorted family, friends, and enemies, all set in 18th-century Cornwall. Demelza's two meddlesome younger brothers come to live at Nampara, enemy George Warleggan and Ross' old love Elizabeth move too close for comfort, and the uncertainties all bring their share of trouble. Adapted from the novels by Winston Graham. Made for British TV; six cassettes.
1975 720m/C *GB* Robin Ellis, Angharad Rees, Jill Townsend, Judy Geeson, Ralph Bates, Kevin McNally, Brian Stirner, Michael Cadman, Jane Wymark, David Delve, Christopher Biggins, Trudie Styler;

D: Philip Dudley, Roger Jenkins; **W:** Alexander Baron, John Wiles, Martin Worth. **VHS** ★★★

Pollyanna Based on the Eleanor Porter story about an enchanting young girl whose contagious enthusiasm and zest for life touches the hearts of all she meets. Mills is perfect in the title role and was awarded a special Oscar for outstanding juvenile performance. A distinguished supporting cast is the icing on the cake in this delightful Disney confection. Original version was filmed in 1920 with Mary Pickford.
1960 134m/C Hayley Mills, Jane Wyman, Richard Egan, Karl Malden, Nancy Olson, Adolphe Menjou, Donald Crisp, Agnes Moorehead, Kevin Corcoran; **D:** David Swift. **VHS, Beta, LV** ★★★½

Poltergeist This production has Stephen Spielberg written all over it. A young family's home becomes a house of horrors when they are terrorized by menacing spirits who abduct their five-year-old daughter . . . through the TV screen! Rollercoaster thrills and chills, dazzling special effects, and perfectly timed humor highlight this stupendously scary ghost story.
1982 (PG) 114m/C JoBeth Williams, Craig T. Nelson, Beatrice Straight, Heather O'Rourke, Zelda Rubinstein, Dominique Dunne, Oliver Robbins, Richard Lawson, James Karen; **D:** Tobe Hooper; **W:** Steven Spielberg, Michael Grais, Mark Victor; **M:** Jerry Goldsmith. Nominations: Academy Awards '82: Best Original Score. **VHS, Beta, LV** ★★★★

A Poor Little Rich Girl Mary Pickford received raves in this film, in which she portrayed Gwendolyn, with everything money could buy, except the attention of her family. Gwendolyn has a bizarre dream in which she sees a number of horrors and is tempted by death. Elaborate sets and special effects, as well as Pickford's delicate performance, make this one special. Organ score.
1917 64m/B Mary Pickford, Madeline Traverse, Charles Wellesley, Gladys Fairbanks; **D:** Maurice Tourneur. **VHS, Beta** ★★★

Pork Chop Hill A powerful, hard-hitting account of the last hours of the Korean War. Peck is totally believable as the man ordered to hold his ground against the hopeless onslaught of Chinese Communist hordes. A chilling, stark look in the face of a no-win situation. Top notch cast and masterful directing.
1959 97m/B Gregory Peck, Harry

Guardino, Rip Torn, George Peppard, James Edwards, Bob Steele, Woody Strode, Robert (Bobby) Blake, Martin Landau, Norman Fell, Bert Remsen; **D:** Lewis Milestone. **VHS, Beta, LV** ★★★

Portrait of Jennie In this haunting, romantic fable, a struggling artist is inspired by and smitten with a strange and beautiful girl who he also suspects may be the spirit of a dead woman. A fine cast works wonders with what could have been a forgettable story. The last reel was tinted green in the original release with the last scene shot in Technicolor. Oscar-winning special effects. **AKA:** Jennie; Tidal Wave.
1948 86m/B Joseph Cotten, Jennifer Jones, Cecil Kellaway, Ethel Barrymore, David Wayne, Lillian Gish, Henry Hull, Florence Bates, Felix Bressart, Anne Francis; **D:** William Dieterle. Academy Awards '48: Best Special Effects; Venice Film Festival '49: Best Actor (Cotten); Nominations: Academy Awards '48: Best Black and White Cinematography. **VHS, Beta, LV** ★★★1/2

The Positively True Adventures of the Alleged Texas Cheerleader-Murdering Mom Satirical melodrama about Texas housewife Wanda Holloway (Hunter), accused of hiring a hit man to murder the mother of her daughter's chief cheerleading rival. She figures the girl will be so distraught that her own daughter can easily replace her. Ruthless and hilarious, this fact-based made-for-cable movie goes way over the top in satirizing suburban lifestyle excess and media overkill. Hunter, complete with whiney Texas twang, is perfect in her role as self-absorbed Wanda and Bridges is great as her loopy ex-brother-in-law and partner in planned homicide. A riot compared to the usual dramatic movies served up by the networks.
1993 (R) 99m/C Holly Hunter, Beau Bridges, Swoosie Kurtz, Greg Henry, Matt Frewer, Frankie Ingrassia, Elizabeth Ruscio, Megan Berwick; **W:** Jane Anderson; **M:** Lucy Simon. National Academy of Cable Programming ACE Awards '93: Best Movie/Miniseries, Best Actress (Hunter). **VHS** ★★★1/2

Posse There's a hidden agenda, fueled by political ambition, in a lawman's (Douglas) dauntless pursuit of an escaped bandit (Dern). An interesting contrast between the evil of corrupt politics and the honesty of traditional lawlessness. Well performed, well photographed, and almost insightful.

1975 (PG) 94m/C Kirk Douglas, Bruce Dern, James Stacy, Bo Hopkins, Luke Askew, David Canary, Alfonso Arau, Kate Woodville, Mark Roberts; **D:** Kirk Douglas; **W:** William Roberts; **M:** Maurice Jarre. **VHS, Beta, LV** ★★★

Postcards from the Edge Fisher adapted her best-selling novel, tamed and tempered, for the big screen with a tour-de-force of talent. Streep very fine as a delightfully harried actress struggling with her career, her drug dependence, and her competitive, overwhelming showbiz mother. Autobiographical script is bitingly clever and filled with refreshingly witty dialogue. Lots of cameos by Hollywood's hippest.
1990 (R) 101m/C Meryl Streep, Shirley MacLaine, Dennis Quaid, Gene Hackman, Richard Dreyfuss, Rob Reiner, Mary Wickes, Conrad Bain, Annette Bening, Michael Ontkean, Dana Ivey; **Cameos:** Robin Bartlett, Anthony Heald, Oliver Platt, CCH Pounder, Michael Ballhaus; **D:** Mike Nichols; **W:** Carrie Fisher. Nominations: Academy Awards '90: Best Actress (Streep), Best Song ("I'm Checkin' Out"). **VHS, Beta, LV, 8mm** ★★★1/2

The Postman Bittersweet, charming film about Mario (Troisi), a shy villager who winds up the personal postman of poet Pablo Neruda (Noiret), who is exiled from his beloved Chile in 1952, granted asylum by the Italian government, and who finds himself living in the tiny Italian community of Isla Negra. The tongue-tied Mario has fallen in love with barmaid Beatrice (Cucinotta) and asks the poet's help in wooing the dark-eyed beauty, striking up an unlikely friendship with the worldly Neruda. Based on the novel "Burning Patience" by Antonio Skarmeta. Troisi, a beloved comic actor in his native Italy, was gravely ill, needing a heart transplant, during the making of the film (all too apparent from his gaunt appearance) and died the day after filming was completed. In Italian with English subtitles. **AKA:** Il Postino.
1994 (PG) 115m/C *IT* Massimo Troisi, Philippe Noiret, Maria Grazia Cucinotta, Linda Moretti, Renato Scarpa, Anna Buonaiuto, Mariana Rigillo; **D:** Michael Radford; **W:** Massimo Troisi, Michael Radford, Furio Scarpelli, Anna Pavignano, Giacomo Scarpelli, Franco Di Giacomo; **M:** Luis Bacalov. Nominations: Academy Awards '95: Best Actor (Troisi), Best Adapted Screenplay, Best Director (Radford), Best Picture, Best Score; British Academy Awards '95: Best Actor (Troisi), Best Adapted Screenplay, Best Director (Radford), Best Foreign Film, Best Score;

Directors Guild of America Awards '95: Best Director (Radford); Screen Actors Guild Award '95: Best Actor (Troisi). **VHS** ★★★1/2

The Postman Always Rings Twice Even without the brutal sexuality of the James M. Cain novel, Garfield and Turner sizzle as the lust-laden lovers in this lurid tale of fatal attraction. Garfield steals the show as the streetwise drifter who blows into town and lights a fire in Turner. As their affair steams up the two conspire to do away with her husband and circumstances begin to spin out of control. Tense and compelling. A classic.
1946 113m/B Lana Turner, John Garfield, Cecil Kellaway, Hume Cronyn, Leon Ames, Audrey Totter, Alan Reed; *D:* Tay Garnett; *M:* George Bassman. **VHS, Beta, LV** ★★★1/2

The President's Analyst A superbly written, brilliantly executed satire from the mind of Theodore J. Flicker, who wrote as well as directed. Coburn steals the show as a psychiatrist who has the dubious honor of being appointed "secret shrink" to the President of the U.S. Pressures of the job steadily increase his paranoia until he suspects he is being pursued by agents and counter agents alike. Is he losing his sanity or . . . ? Vastly entertaining.
1967 104m/C James Coburn, Godfrey Cambridge, Severn Darden, Joan Delaney, Pat Harrington, Will Geer, William Daniels; *D:* Theodore J. Flicker; *W:* Theodore J. Flicker; *M:* Lalo Schifrin. **VHS** ★★★1/2

Pressure Point Poitier stars as a prison psychiatrist treating an inmate who is a racist and a member of the Nazi party. Darin gives an excellent performance as the Nazi patient in this intelligent drama based on a true case.
1962 87m/B Sidney Poitier, Bobby Darin, Peter Falk, Carl Benton Reid, Barry Gordon, Howard Caine, Mary Munday; *D:* Hubert Cornfield; *M:* Ernest Gold. **VHS** ★★★

Presumed Innocent Assistant district attorney is the prime suspect when a former lover turns up brutally murdered. Cover-ups surround him, the political climate changes, and friends and enemies switch sides. Slow-paced courtroom drama with excellent performances from Ford, Julia, and Bedelia. Skillfully adapted from the best-seller by Chicago attorney Scott Turow.
1990 (R) 127m/C Harrison Ford, Brian Dennehy, Bonnie Bedelia, Greta Scacchi, Raul Julia, Paul Winfield, John Spencer, Joe Grifasi, Anna Maria Horsford, Sab Shimono, Christine Estabrook, Michael Tolan, Tom Mardirosian, Gordon Willis; *D:* Alan J. Pakula; *W:* Frank Pierson, Alan J. Pakula; *M:* John Williams. **VHS, Beta, LV, 8mm** ★★★

Pretty Baby Shields' launching pad and Malle's first American film is a masterpiece of cinematography and style, nearly upstaged by the plodding storyline. Carradine manages to be effective but never succeeds at looking comfortable as the New Orleans photographer besotted with, and subsequently married to, an 11-year-old prostitute (Shields). Low-key, disturbingly intriguing story, beautifully photographed by Sven Nykist.
1978 (R) 109m/C Brooke Shields, Keith Carradine, Susan Sarandon, Barbara Steele, Diana Scarwid, Antonio Fargas; *D:* Louis Malle. National Board of Review Awards '78: 10 Best Films of the Year; Nominations: Academy Awards '78: Best Original Score; Cannes Film Festival '78: Best Film. **VHS, Beta, LV** ★★★

Pretty Poison You won't need an antidote for this one. Original, absorbing screenplay, top-notch acting, and on-target direction combine to raise this low-budget, black comedy above the crowd. Perkins at his eerie best as a burned-out arsonist who cooks up a crazy scheme and enlists the aid of a hot-to-trot high schooler, only to discover too late she has some burning desires of her own. Weld is riveting as the turbulent teen.
1968 89m/C Anthony Perkins, Tuesday Weld, Beverly Garland, John Randolph, Dick O'Neill; *D:* Noel Black. New York Film Critics Awards '68: Best Screenplay. **VHS** ★★★1/2

Pretty Woman An old story takes a fresh approach as a successful but stuffy businessman hires a fun-loving, energetic young hooker to be his companion for a week. The film caused some controversy over its upbeat portrayal of prostitution, but its popularity at the box office catapulted Roberts to stardom.
1990 (R) 117m/C Richard Gere, Julia Roberts, Ralph Bellamy, Jason Alexander, Laura San Giacomo, Hector Elizondo, Alex Hyde-White, Elinor Donahue, Larry Miller, Jane Morris; *D:* Garry Marshall; *W:* J.F. Lawton; *M:* James Newton Howard. Golden Globe Awards '91: Best Actress—Musical/Comedy (Roberts); People's Choice Awards '91: Best Film, Best Film—Musical/Comedy; Nominations: Academy Awards '90: Best Actress (Roberts). **VHS, Beta, LV** ★★★

Prick Up Your Ears Film biography of popular subversive playwright Joe Orton depicts his rise to fame and his eventual murder at the hands of his homosexual lover in 1967. Acclaimed for its realistic and sometimes humorous portrayal of the relationship between two men in a society that regarded homosexuality as a crime, the film unfortunately pays scant attention to Orton's theatrical success. The occasional sluggishness of the script detracts a bit from the three leads' outstanding performances.
1987 (R) 110m/C *GB* Gary Oldman, Alfred Molina, Vanessa Redgrave, Julie Walters, Lindsay Duncan, Wallace Shawn, James Grant, Frances Barber, Janet Dale, David Atkins; **D:** Stephen Frears; **W:** Alan Bennett; **M:** Stanley Myers. New York Film Critics Awards '87: Best Supporting Actress (Redgrave). **VHS, Beta, LV ★★★**

Pride and Prejudice Classic adaptation of Austen's classic novel of manners as a young marriageable woman spurns the suitor her parents choose for her. Excellent cast vividly re-creates 19th-century England, aided by the inspired set design that won the film an Oscar.
1940 114m/B Greer Garson, Laurence Olivier, Edmund Gwenn, Edna May Oliver, Mary Boland, Maureen O'Sullivan, Ann Rutherford, Frieda Inescort; **D:** Robert Z. Leonard. Academy Awards '40: Best Interior Decoration. **VHS, Beta, LV ★★★1/2**

Pride and Prejudice Lavish TV adaptation of the Jane Austen novel finds bright Elizabeth Bennet (Ehle) unwillingly smitten by the wealthy, mysterious, and arrogant Mr. Darcy (Firth). Her family, filled with unmarried daughters, is rather silly, and, of course, Elizabeth should be looking to get married (or at least not hinder her sisters' chances). Filmed on location in Derbyshire. On six cassettes.
1995 300m/C Jennifer Ehle, Colin Firth, Susannah Harker, Alison Steadman, Julia Sawalha, Benjamin Whitrow, David Bamber, Crispin Bonham Carter, Anna Chancellor, David Bark-Jones, Barbara Leigh-Hunt, Polly Maberly, Lucy Briers, Adrian Lukis; **D:** Simon Langton; **W:** Andrew Davies; **M:** Carl Davis **VHS ★★★**

The Pride of the Yankees Excellent portrait of baseball great Lou Gehrig. Beginning as he joined the Yankees in 1923, the film follows this great American through to his moving farewell speech as his career was tragically cut short by the disease that bears his name. Cooper is inspiring in the title role.
1942 128m/B Gary Cooper, Teresa Wright, Babe Ruth, Walter Brennan, Dan Duryea; **D:** Sam Wood. Academy Awards '42: Best Film Editing; Nominations: Academy Awards '42: Best Actress (Wright); Academy Awards '42: Best Actor (Cooper), Best Black and White Cinematography, Best Interior Decoration, Best Picture, Best Sound, Best Story, Best Original Score. **VHS, Beta, LV ★★★1/2**

The Prime of Miss Jean Brodie Oscar-winning performance by Smith as a forward-thinking teacher in a Scottish Girls' school during the 1920s. She captivates her impressionable young students with her fascist ideals and free-thinking attitudes in this adaptation of the play taken from Muriel Spark's novel.
1969 (PG) 116m/C *GB* Maggie Smith, Pamela Franklin, Robert Stephens, Celia Johnson, Gordon Jackson, Jane Carr; **D:** Ronald Neame; **W:** Jay Presson Allen. Academy Awards '69: Best Actress (Smith); British Academy Awards '69: Best Actress (Smith), Best Supporting Actress (Johnson); National Board of Review Awards '69: Best Supporting Actress (Franklin); Nominations: Academy Awards '69: Best Song ("Jean"); Cannes Film Festival '69: Best Film. **VHS, Beta ★★★**

Prime Suspect Mirren stars as Detective Chief Inspector Jane Tennison in this British television police procedural. When a male inspector dies of a heart attack while investigating a rape-murder, Tennison, the only women of senior police status, wants the case. But she runs into multiple obstructions, not the least being the smug male police system. Then the case really takes a turn when it appears Tennison is searching for a serial killer. But Jane is no quitter and she has both the brains and the guts to back up her orders. Adapted from the book by Lynda La Plante, who also wrote the teleplay.
1992 240m/C *GB* Helen Mirren, Tom Bell, Zoe Wanamaker, John Bowe, Tom Wilkinson, Ralph Fiennes; **D:** Christopher Menaul; **W:** Lynda La Plante. **VHS ★★★**

Prime Suspect 2 DCI Jane Tennison (Mirren) returns in another British made-for-TV police drama. Jane has been off at a police seminar where she has a brief liaison with a black police detective, Robert Oswalde (Salmon). She is recalled to investigate the decomposed body of a young woman found in one of London's Afro-Caribbean neighborhoods and must deal with their resentment of the police. When detective Oswalde is reassigned to Jane's depart-

ment, she begins having trouble separating her public and private feelings, while trying to obtain a confession from her most likely suspect. Based on a story by Lynda La Plante. **1993 240m/C** *GB* Helen Mirren, Colin Salmon, Tom Watson, Ian Fitzgibbon, Philip Wright, Jack Ellis, Craig Fairbrass; *D:* John Strickland; *W:* Allan Cubitt. **VHS**
★★★

Prime Suspect 3 The BBC returns Jane Tennison to the beat (as does her portrayer Mirren) in another intriguing police drama. Tennison has transferred from homicide to the vice squad but still can't escape murder investigations—or male chauvinists. Oh yes, Tennison has a new team of macho colleagues to contend with and she's still getting heat from her bosses about her job. Still, this is one copper who lets nothing stand in her way. Made for British TV; on three cassettes. **1993 205m/C** *GB* Helen Mirren, Tom Bell, Peter Capaldi, David Thewlis, Ciaran Hinds, Terrence Hardiman, Mark Strong, Karen Tomlin, Struan Rodger, Liza Sadovy, Andrew Woodall, Kelly Hunter; *D:* David Drury; *W:* Lynda La Plante; *M:* Stephen Warbeck. **VHS** ★★★

Prime Suspect: The Scent of Darkness Could this be curtains for the career of the irascible Jane Tennison? Not bloody likely, but she's got more than her fair share of trouble when a new wave of murders are in the same modus operandi as multiple killer George Marlow—whom Tennison put away four years before (in "Prime Suspect"). Now Marlow's conviction is called into question, as are Jane's methods, so she's placed on suspension. But that isn't going to stop her from getting to the truth. **1995 102m/C** Helen Mirren, Tim Woodward, Stuart Wilson, Richard Hawley, John Benfield, Christopher Fulford, Joyce Redman, Stephen Boxer; *D:* Paul Marcus. **VHS** ★★★

The Prince and the Pauper Satisfying adaptation of the classic Mark Twain story of a young street urchin who trades places with the young king of England. Wonderful musical score by noted composer Korngold who provided the music for many of Flynn's adventure films. Also available in a computer-colorized version. **1937 118m/B** Errol Flynn, Claude Rains, Alan Hale, Billy Mauch, Montagu Love, Henry Stephenson, Barton MacLane; *D:* William Keighley; *M:* Erich Wolfgang Korngold. **VHS, Beta, LV** ★★★

Prince Brat and the Whipping Boy Orphaned Jemmy (Munro) is living on the streets of the 18th-century German town of Brattenburg with his younger sister Annyrose (Salt). Neglected, spoiled Prince Horace (Knight) has been causing mischief in the castle but instead of being punished himself, the king's men catch Jemmy and use him as a punishment stand-in. Jemmy escapes the castle to get back to his sister, and the Prince decides to go along for the adventure. Filmed on location in North Rhine-Westphalia and Burgundy, Germany. Adventurous TV movie with spunky leads; adapted from Sid Fleischman's novella. *AKA:* The Whipping Boy. **1995 (G) 96m/C** *GE* Truan Munro, Nic Knight, Karen Salt, George C. Scott, Kevin Conway, Vincent Schiavelli, Andrew Bicknell, Jean Anderson, Mathilda May; *D:* Syd Macartney; *W:* Max Brindle; *M:* Lee Holdridge. **VHS, LV** ★★★

Prince of the City Docudrama of a police officer who becomes an informant in an effort to end corruption within his narcotics unit, but finds he must pay a heavy price. Based on the true story told in Robert Daly's book, the powerful script carries the tension through what would otherwise be an overly long film. Excellent performances make this a riveting character study. **1981 (R) 167m/C** Treat Williams, Jerry Orbach, Richard Foronjy, Don Billett, Kenny Marino, Lindsay Crouse, Lance Henriksen; *D:* Sidney Lumet; *W:* Jay Presson Allen, Sidney Lumet. New York Film Critics Awards '81: Best Director (Lumet); Nominations: Academy Awards '81: Best Adapted Screenplay. **VHS, Beta, LV** ★★★

The Prince of Tides Conroy's sprawling southern-fried saga is neatly pared down to essentials in this tale of the dysfunctional Wingo family, whose dark tragedies are gradually revealed as twins Tom and Savannah come to grips with personal demons under the ministering aid of psychiatrist Streisand. Bravura performance by Nolte in what may be his best role to date; Streisand is restrained in both her performance and direction although a subplot dealing with her bad marriage and rebellious son is a predictable distraction. The South Carolina low country, and even New York City, never looked better. Conroy adapted the screenplay from his novel of the same name with Johnston's help.

1991 (R) 132m/C Nick Nolte, Barbra Streisand, Blythe Danner, Kate Nelligan, Jeroen Krabbe, Melinda Dillon, George Carlin, Jason Gould, Brad Sullivan; *D:* Barbra Streisand; *W:* Pat Conroy, Becky Johnston; *M:* James Newton Howard. Golden Globe Awards '92: Best Actor—Drama (Nolte); Los Angeles Film Critics Association Awards '91: Best Actor (Nolte); Nominations: Academy Awards '91: Best Actor (Nolte), Best Adapted Screenplay, Best Art Direction/Set Decoration, Best Cinematography, Best Picture, Best Supporting Actress (Nelligan), Best Original Score. **VHS, Beta, LV, 8mm** ★★★1/2

The Princess and the Pirate Hope at his craziest as a vaudevillian who falls for a beautiful princess while on the run from buccaneers on the Spanish Main. Look for Crosby in a closing cameo performance. Available in digitally remastered stereo with original movie trailer.
1944 94m/C Bob Hope, Walter Slezak, Walter Brennan, Virginia Mayo, Victor McLaglen; *Cameos:* Bing Crosby; *D:* David Butler. Nominations: Academy Awards '44: Best Interior Decoration, Best Original Score. **VHS, Beta, LV** ★★★

The Princess Bride A modern update of the basic fairy-tale crammed with all the cliches, this adventurously irreverent love story centers around a beautiful maiden and her young swain as they battle the evils of the mythical kingdom of Florin to be reunited with one another. Great dueling scenes and offbeat satire of the genre make this fun for adults as well as children. Based on William Goldman's cult novel.
1987 (PG) 98m/C Cary Elwes, Mandy Patinkin, Robin Wright, Wallace Shawn, Peter Falk, Andre the Giant, Chris Sarandon, Christopher Guest, Billy Crystal, Carol Kane, Fred Savage, Peter Cook, Mel Smith; *D:* Rob Reiner; *W:* William Goldman; *M:* Mark Knopfler. Nominations: Academy Awards '87: Best Song ("Storybook Love"). **VHS, Beta, LV, 8mm** ★★★1/2

Princess Yang Kwei Fei Set in 8th-century China and based on the life of the last T'ang emperor and the beautiful servant girl he loves and makes his bride. She falls victim to court jealousies and he to his greedy family, though even death cannot end their love. Beautifully filmed and acted romantic tragedy. In Japanese with English subtitles. *AKA:* Yokihi; The Empress Yang Kwei Fei.
1955 91m/C *JP* Machiko Kyo, Masayuki Mori, Sakae Ozawa, So Yamamura; *D:* Kenji Mizoguchi. **VHS** ★★★

Prisoner of Zenda An excellent cast and splendid photography make this the definitive film adaptation of Anthony Hope's swashbuckling novel. A British commoner is forced to pose as his cousin, the kidnapped king of a small European country, to save the throne. Complications of the romantic sort ensue when he falls in love with the queen. Excellent acting, robust sword play, and beautifully designed costumes make this an enjoyable spectacle.
1937 101m/B Ronald Colman, Douglas Fairbanks Jr., Madeleine Carroll, David Niven, Raymond Massey, Mary Astor, Sir C. Aubrey Smith, Montagu Love, Byron Foulger, Alexander D'Arcy, Charles Halton; *D:* John Cromwell; *W:* Donald Ogden Stewart, John Balderston, Wells Root. Nominations: Academy Awards '37: Best Original Score, Best Interior Decoration. **VHS, Beta, LV** ★★★1/2

The Private Life of Henry VIII Lavish historical spectacle lustily portraying the life and lovers of notorious British Monarch, King Henry VIII. A tour de force for Laughton as the robust 16th-century king, with outstanding performances by the entire cast.
1933 97m/B *GB* Charles Laughton, Binnie Barnes, Elsa Lanchester, Robert Donat, Merle Oberon, Miles Mander, Wendy Barrie, John Loder; *D:* Alexander Korda; *W:* Arthur Wimperis, Lajos Biro. Academy Awards '33: Best Actor (Laughton); Nominations: Academy Awards '33: Best Picture. **VHS, Beta, LV** ★★★★

The Private Life of Sherlock Holmes A unique perspective on the life of the famous detective reveals a complex character. Beautifully photographed, with fine performances by the supporting cast, the film boasts a haunting musical score but received suprisingly little recognition despite Wilder's high caliber direction.
1970 (PG-13) 125m/C *GB* Robert Stephens, Colin Blakely, Genevieve Page, Irene Handl, Stanley Holloway, Christopher Lee, Clive Revill; *D:* Billy Wilder; *W:* I.A.L. Diamond, Billy Wilder; *M:* Miklos Rozsa. **VHS, LV** ★★★1/2

Private Lives Stylish adaptation of Noel Coward play starring Shearer and Montgomery as a couple with a tempestuous relationship. Although once married, they have since divorced and married other mates. While honeymooning at the same French hotel (Quelle coincidence!), they have trouble showing affection to their new spouses and realize they still feel passionately about one another. Excellent acting combined with

Coward's witty dialogue makes this film a treat.
1931 92m/B Norma Shearer, Robert Montgomery, Reginald Denny, Una Merkel, Jean Hersholt; *D:* Sidney Franklin. **VHS, LV** ★★★1/2

The Private Lives of Elizabeth & Essex Cast reads like a Who's Who in Hollywood in this lavishly costumed dramatization of the love affair between Queen Elizabeth I and the second Earl of Essex. Forced to choose between her kingdom and her lover, Davis' monarch is the epitome of a regal women. Fabray made her first film appearance as an adult in the adaptation of Maxwell Anderson's "Elizabeth the Queen."
1939 106m/C Bette Davis, Errol Flynn, Vincent Price, Nanette Fabray, Olivia de Havilland, Alan Hale, Donald Crisp, Leo G. Carroll; *D:* Michael Curtiz. Nominations: Academy Awards '39: Best Color Cinematography, Best Special Effects, Best Score. **VHS, Beta** ★★★

A Private Matter Based on the true story of Sherri Finkbine (hostess of TV's "Romper Room") and the controversy surrounding her decision to terminate her pregnancy in 1962. Pregnant with her fifth child, she discovered her sleeping medication contained thalidomide, known to cause severe birth defects. Although technically illegal, her doctor agreed to quietly perform an abortion. Sherri warned a local newspaper reporter about the drug's dangers and her identity was mistakenly revealed. A storm of adverse publicity forced her to Sweden for the abortion. Great performances highlight this complex and traumatic issue. Made for cable television.
1992 (PG-13) 89m/C Sissy Spacek, Aidan Quinn, Estelle Parsons, Sheila McCarthy, Leon Russom, William H. Macy; *D:* Joan Micklin Silver; *W:* William Nicholson. **VHS, LV** ★★★

The Prize Gripping spy story laced with laughs based on a novel by Irving Wallace (adapted by Lehman). In Stockholm, writer accepts the Nobel prize for dubious reasons and then finds himself in the midst of political intrigue. Newman and Sommer turn in great performances in this action drama.
1963 136m/C Paul Newman, Edward G. Robinson, Elke Sommer, Leo G. Carroll, Diane Baker, Micheline Presle, Gerard Oury, Sergio Fantoni; *D:* Mark Robson; *W:* Ernest Lehman; *M:* Jerry Goldsmith. **VHS** ★★★

The Prizefighter and the Lady In his first film role boxer Baer (who won the heavyweight boxing crown in 1934) is a natural as a fighter who falls for a beautiful nightclub singer (Loy). Baer and Loy get, but don't stay, together but she does turn out to be his lucky charm in the big fight finale. Fellow professional boxer Carnera, Baer's opponent in the climatic fight scene, refused to lose as the script indicated and the film ending was eventually rewritten. The likeable Baer later earned his living as an actor. *AKA:* Every Woman's Man.
1933 102m/B Max Baer Sr., Myrna Loy, Otto Kruger, Primo Carnera, Walter Huston, Vince Barnett, Muriel Evans; *D:* Woodbridge S. Van Dyke. Nominations: Academy Awards '33: Best Original Screenplay. **LV** ★★★

Prizzi's Honor Highly stylized, sometimes leaden black comedy about an aging and none-to-bright hit man from a New York mob family who breaks with family loyalties when he falls for an upwardly mobile tax consultant who's also a hired killer. Skirting caricature in every frame, Nicholson is excellent in his portrayal of the thick-skulled mobster, as are Anjelica Huston as the hot-to-trot Mafia daughter and Hickey as the Don. Adapted by Richard Condon and Janet Roach from Condon's novel.
1985 (R) 130m/C Jack Nicholson, Kathleen Turner, Robert Loggia, John Randolph, Anjelica Huston, Lawrence Tierney, William Hickey, Lee Richardson, Michael Lombard, Joseph Ruskin, CCH Pounder; *D:* John Huston; *W:* Richard Condon, Janet Roach; *M:* Alex North. Academy Awards '85: Best Supporting Actress (Huston); British Academy Awards '85: Best Adapted Screenplay; Golden Globe Awards '86: Best Actor— Musical/Comedy (Nicholson), Best Actress—Musical/Comedy (Turner), Best Director (Huston), Best Film— Musical/Comedy; Los Angeles Film Critics Association Awards '85: Best Supporting Actress (Huston); New York Film Critics Awards '85: Best Actor (Nicholson), Best Director (Huston), Best Film, Best Supporting Actress (Huston); Writers Guild of America '85: Best Adapted Screenplay; Nominations: Academy Awards '85: Best Actor (Nicholson), Best Adapted Screenplay, Best Costume Design, Best Director (Huston), Best Film Editing, Best Picture, Best Supporting Actor (Hickey). **VHS, Beta, LV** ★★★

The Producers Considered one of Brooks' best films, this hilarious farce follows an attempted swindle by a con artist and his accountant who attempt to stage a Broadway flop only to have it backfire. Achieving cult status, the film is known for musical interlude "Springtime for Hitler." The phony play was later actually produced by Alan Johnson.

1968 90m/C Zero Mostel, Gene Wilder, Dick Shawn, Kenneth Mars, Estelle Winwood; *D:* Mel Brooks; *W:* Mel Brooks. Academy Awards '68: Best Story & Screenplay; Writers Guild of America '68: Best Original Screenplay; Nominations: Academy Awards '68: Best Supporting Actor (Wilder). **VHS, Beta, LV, 8mm** ★★★1/2

The Professionals Action and adventure count for more than a storyline in this exciting western about four mercenaries hired by a wealthy cattle baron to rescue his young wife from Mexican kidnappers. Breathtaking photography re-creates turn-of-the-century Mexico in this adaptation of the Frank O'Rourke novel.

1966 (PG) 117m/C Burt Lancaster, Lee Marvin, Claudia Cardinale, Jack Palance, Robert Ryan, Woody Strode, Ralph Bellamy; *D:* Richard Brooks; *W:* Richard Brooks; *M:* Maurice Jarre, Conrad Hall. Nominations: Academy Awards '66: Best Color Cinematography, Best Director (Brooks), Best Story & Screenplay. **VHS, Beta, LV** ★★★1/2

Prospero's Books Greenaway's free-ranging adaptation of Shakespeare's "The Tempest" has all his usual hallmarks of the bizarre. Gielgud is the aged Propsero, exiled to a magical island with his innocent daughter Miranda, and 24 beloved books containing the magician's recipe for life, each of which becomes a separate chapter in the film. Greenaway mixes film and high-definition video to create, with cinematographer Sacha Vierny, dazzling visuals that threaten to overwhelm but don't quite, thanks to both Greenaway's skill and the astonishing performance of the then 87-year-old Gielgud.

1991 (R) 129m/C John Gielgud, Michel Blanc, Erland Josephson, Isabelle Pasco, Tom Bell, Kenneth Cranham, Michael Clark, Mark Rylance; *D:* Peter Greenaway; *W:* Peter Greenaway; *M:* Michael Nyman. **VHS, Beta, LV** ★★★

Providence An interesting score highlights this British fantasy drama of a dying writer envisioning his final novel as a fusion of the people from his past with the circumstances he encounters on a daily basis. The first English-language effort by French director Resnais.

1977 (R) 104m/C *GB* John Gielgud, Dirk Bogarde, Ellen Burstyn, David Warner, Elaine Stritch; *D:* Alain Resnais; *M:* Miklos Rozsa. Cesar Awards '78: Best Art Direction/Set Decoration, Best Director (Resnais), Best Film, Best Sound, Best Writing, Best Score; New York Film Critics Awards '77: Best Actor (Gielgud). **VHS, Beta** ★★★

Psycho Hitchcock counted on his directorial stature and broke all the rules in this story of violent murder, transvestism, and insanity. Based on Robert Bloch's novelization of an actual murder, Leigh plays a fleeing thief who stops at the secluded Bates Motel where she meets her death in Hitchcock's classic "shower scene." Shot on a limited budget in little more than a month, "Psycho" changed the Hollywood horror film forever. Followed by "Psycho II" (1983), "Psycho III" (1986), and a made-for-television movie.

1960 109m/B Anthony Perkins, Janet Leigh, Vera Miles, John Gavin, John McIntire, Martin Balsam, Simon Oakland, Ted Knight, John Anderson, Frank Albertson, Patricia Hitchcock; *D:* Alfred Hitchcock; *W:* Joseph Stefano; *M:* Bernard Herrmann. Edgar Allan Poe Awards '60: Best Screenplay; Golden Globe Awards '61: Best Supporting Actress (Leigh); Nominations: Academy Awards '60: Best Art Direction/Set Decoration (B & W), Best Black and White Cinematography, Best Director (Hitchcock), Best Supporting Actress (Leigh). **VHS, Beta, LV** ★★★★

Public Enemy Cagney's acting career was launched by this story of two Irish boys growing up in a Chicago shantytown to become hoodlums during the prohibition era. Cagney and Woods hook up with molls Clarke and Blondell on their rise to the top. Considered the most realistic "gangster" film, Wellman's movie is also the most grimly brutal due to its release prior to Hollywood censorship. The scene where Cagney smashes a grapefruit in Clarke's face was credited with starting a trend in abusing film heroines. *AKA:* Enemies of the Public.

1931 85m/B James Cagney, Edward Woods, Leslie Fenton, Joan Blondell, Mae Clarke, Jean Harlow; *D:* William A. Wellman. Nominations: Academy Awards '31: Best Original Screenplay. **VHS, Beta, LV** ★★★1/2

The Public Eye Underappreciated film noir homage casts Pesci as a crime photographer with an unsuspected romantic streak. It's 1942 in NYC and cynical freelancer Leon "Bernzy" Bernstein's always looking

for the perfect shot. Hershey's the recent widow whose nightclub-owner husband had mob ties and decides Pesci would be a likely patsy for helping her out. Hershey seems decorative and the romantic angle never quite develops, but Pesci delivers a rich, low-key performance as the visionary, hard-boiled artist. Climactic mob shoot-out is cinematic bullet ballet. Based loosely on the career of '40s photog Weegee, who defined New York and its times in his work.
1992 (R) 98m/C Joe Pesci, Barbara Hershey, Stanley Tucci, Richard Foronjy, Richard Riehle, Jared Harris, Jerry Adler, Dominic Chianese, Gerry Becker; **D:** Howard Franklin; **W:** Howard Franklin; **M:** John Barry. VHS, Beta, LV ★★★1/2

Pueblo Affair A dramatization of the capture of the American spy ship "Pueblo" by the North Koreans, during which time the crew was tortured, imprisoned, and all intelligence documents were confiscated.
1973 99m/C Hal Holbrook, Andrew Duggan, Richard Mulligan, George Grizzard, Gary Merrill, Mary Fickett; **D:** Anthony Page. VHS, Beta ★★★

Pulp Fiction Tarantino moves into the cinematic mainstream with his trademark violence and '70s pop culture mindset intact in this stylish crime trilogy. A day in the life of a criminal community unexpectedly shifts from outrageous, esoteric dialogue to violent mayhem with solid scripting that takes familiar stories to unexplored territory. Offbeat cast offers superb performances, led by Travolta, who ditches the baby talk for his best role to date as a hit man whose adventures with partner Jackson tie the seemingly unrelated stories together. Clever, almost gleeful look at everday life on the fringes of mainstream society. Inspired by "Black Mask" magazine. A special collector's edition includes never-before-seen footage and commentary by Tarantino.
1994 (R) 154m/C John Travolta, Samuel L. Jackson, Uma Thurman, Harvey Keitel, Tim Roth, Amanda Plummer, Maria De Medeiros, Ving Rhames, Eric Stoltz, Rosanna Arquette, Christopher Walken, Bruce Willis, Quentin Tarantino; **D:** Quentin Tarantino; **W:** Quentin Tarantino, Roger Roberts Avary. Academy Awards '94: Best Original Screenplay; British Academy Awards '94: Best Original Screenplay, Best Supporting Actor (Jackson); Chicago Film Critics Awards '94: Best Director (Tarantino), Best Screenplay; Golden Globe Awards '95: Best Screenplay; Independent Spirit Awards '95: Best Actor (Jackson), Best Director (Tarantino), Best Film, Best Screenplay; Los Angeles Film Critics Association Awards '94: Best Actor (Travolta), Best Director (Tarantino), Best Film, Best Screenplay; MTV Movie Awards '95: Best Film, Best Dance Sequence (John Travolta/Uma Thurman); New York Film Critics Awards '94: Best Director (Tarantino), Best Screenplay; National Society of Film Critics Awards '94: Best Director (Tarantino), Best Film, Best Screenplay; Nominations: Academy Awards '94: Best Actor (Travolta), Best Director (Tarantino), Best Film Editing, Best Picture, Best Supporting Actor (Jackson), Best Supporting Actress (Thurman); Directors Guild of America Awards '94: Best Director (Tarantino); Golden Globe Awards '95: Best Actor—Drama (Travolta), Best Director (Tarantino), Best Film—Drama, Best Supporting Actor (Jackson), Best Supporting Actress (Thurman); MTV Movie Awards '95: Best Male Performance (Travolta), Best Female Performance (Thurman), Best On-Screen Duo (John Travolta/Samuel L. Jackson), Best Song ("Girl, You'll Be A Woman Soon"). VHS, LV ★★★★

The Pumpkin Eater British housewife Jo (Bancroft) has seemingly found contentment with her third husband, famous and wealthy writer Jake (Finch), and her eight children. But as Jo struggles to face middle age she discovers Jake is chronically unfaithful and goes into an emotional tailspin. Last film for Hardwicke. Slow-paced film with fine performances; based on the novel by Penelope Mortimer.
1964 110m/C *GB* Anne Bancroft, Peter Finch, James Mason, Richard Johnson, Cedric Hardwicke, Maggie Smith, Alan Webb, Eric Porter; **D:** Jack Clayton; **W:** Harold Pinter; **M:** Georges Delerue. British Academy Awards '64: Best Screenplay; Nominations: Academy Awards '64: Best Actress (Bancroft). VHS ★★★

The Purple Rose of Cairo A diner waitress, disillusioned by the Depression and a lackluster life, escapes into a film playing at the local movie house where a blond film hero, tiring of the monotony of his role, makes a break from the celluloid to join her in the real world. The ensuing love story allows director-writer Allen to show his knowledge of old movies and provide his fans with a change of pace. Farrow's film sister is also her real-life sister Stephanie, who went on to appear in Allen's "Zelig."
1985 (PG) 82m/C Mia Farrow, Jeff Daniels, Danny Aiello, Dianne Wiest, Van Johnson, Zoe Caldwell, John Wood, Michael Tucker, Edward Herrmann, Milo O'Shea, Glenne

Headly, Karen Akers, Deborah Rush; **D:** Woody Allen; **W:** Woody Allen; **M:** Dick Hyman, Gordon Willis. British Academy Awards '85: Best Film, Best Original Screenplay; Cesar Awards '86: Best Foreign Film; Golden Globe Awards '86: Best Screenplay; New York Film Critics Awards '85: Best Screenplay; Nominations: Academy Awards '85: Best Original Screenplay. **VHS, Beta, LV ★★★**

Putney Swope Comedy about a token black ad man mistakenly elected Chairman of the Board of a Madison Avenue ad agency who turns the company upside-down. A series of riotous spoofs on commercials is the highpoint in this funny, though somewhat dated look at big business.
1969 (R) 84m/B Arnold Johnson, Laura Greene, Stanley Gottlieb, Mel Brooks; **D:** Robert Downey. **VHS, Beta ★★★**

Pygmalion Oscar-winning film adaptation of Shaw's play about a cockney flower-girl who is transformed into a "lady" under the guidance of a stuffy phonetics professor. Shaw himself aided in writing the script in this superbly acted comedy that would be adapted into the musical, "My Fair Lady," first on Broadway in 1956 and for the screen in 1964.
1938 96m/B GB Leslie Howard, Wendy Hiller, Wilfred Lawson, Marie Lohr; **D:** Leslie Howard, Anthony Asquith. Academy Awards '38: Best Adapted Screenplay; Venice Film Festival '38: Best Actor (Howard); Nominations: Academy Awards '38: Best Actor (Howard), Best Actress (Hiller), Best Picture. **VHS, Beta, LV ★★★★**

QB VII A knighted physician brings a suit for libel against a novelist for implicating him in war crimes. Hopkins as the purportedly wronged doctor and Gazzara as the writer are both superb. Ending is stunning. Adapted from the novel by Leon Uris. Over five hours long; made for TV. Available only as a three-cassette set.
1974 313m/C Anthony Hopkins, Ben Gazzara, Lee Remick, Leslie Caron, Juliet Mills, John Gielgud, Anthony Quayle; **D:** Tom Gries; **M:** Jerry Goldsmith. **VHS, Beta, LV ★★★½**

Quackser Fortune Has a Cousin in the Bronx An Irish fertilizer salesman meets an exchange student from the U.S., who finds herself attracted to this unlearned, but not unknowing, man. An original love story with drama and appeal. *AKA:* Fun Loving.
1970 (R) 88m/C IR Gene Wilder, Margot Kidder; **D:** Waris Hussein. **VHS, Beta, LV ★★★**

Quadrophenia Pete Townshend's excellent rock opera about an alienated youth looking for life's meaning in Britain's rock scene circa 1963. Music by The Who is powerful and apt. Fine performance by Sting in his acting debut.
1979 (R) 115m/C GB Phil Daniels, Mark Wingett, Philip Davis, Leslie Ash, Sting; **D:** Franc Roddam. **VHS, Beta, LV ★★★**

Quartet A young French woman is taken in by an English couple after her husband goes to prison. The husband seduces her, and she becomes trapped emotionally and socially. Superbly acted, claustrophobic drama based on a Jean Rhys novel.
1981 (R) 101m/C GB FR Isabelle Adjani, Alan Bates, Maggie Smith, Anthony Higgins; **D:** James Ivory; **W:** Ruth Prawer Jhabvala. Cannes Film Festival '81: Best Actress (Adjani); Nominations: Cannes Film Festival '81: Best Film. **VHS, Beta ★★★**

The Quatermass Experiment Excellent British production about an astronaut who returns to Earth carrying an alien infestation that causes him to turn into a horrible monster. Competent acting and tense direction. Followed by "Enemy From Space." *AKA:* The Creeping Unknown.
1956 78m/B GB Brian Donlevy, Margia Dean, Jack Warner, Richard Wordsworth; **D:** Val Guest; **M:** James Bernard. **VHS ★★★**

Queen Christina A stylish, resonant star vehicle for Garbo, portraying the 17th-century Swedish queen from her ascension to the throne to her romance with a Spanish ambassador. Alternately hilarious and moving, it holds some of Garbo's greatest and most memorable moments. Gilbert's second to last film and his only successful outing after the coming of sound.
1933 101m/B Greta Garbo, John Gilbert, Lewis Stone, Sir C. Aubrey Smith, Ian Keith, Reginald Owen, Elizabeth Young; **D:** Rouben Mamoulian. **VHS, Beta, LV ★★★½**

Queen Kelly The popularly known, slapdash version of von Stroheim's famous final film, in which an orphan goes from royal marriage to white slavery to astounding wealth. Never really finished, the film is the edited first half of the intended project, prepared for European release after von Stroheim had been fired. Even so, a campy, extravagant, and lusty melodrama. Silent.
1929 113m/B Gloria Swanson, Walter Byron, Seena Owen, Tully Marshall, Madame Sul Te Wan; **D:** Erich von Stroheim. **VHS, Beta, LV, 8mm ★★★**

Queen Margot Blood-soaked period of French history is duly rendered on-screen in a big-budget costume epic. Beautiful Catholic, Marguerite de Valois (Adjani), is the pawn of her devious mother, the widowed queen Catherine de Medici (Lisi) who skillfully manipulates unstable son Charles IX (Anglade), the nominal ruler of 1570s France, while she plots to marry Margot off to Protestant Henri de Navarre (Auteuil). Margot is contemptuous of her new husband, preferring to find her amatory amusements in the Paris streets, where she takes a handsome lover (Perez). But both Margot and Henri are united against the Queen when Catherine's minions order the murder of the rival Huguenots—a notably violent affair known as the St. Bartholomew's Day Massacre. The history's confusing, the violence graphic, the acting flamboyant, and the visuals top-notch. Based on the novel by Alexandre Dumas. In French with English subtitles; originally re-leased at 161 minutes. *AKA:* La Reine Margot.
1994 (R) 135m/C *FR* Isabelle Adjani, Daniel Auteuil, Virna Lisi, Jean-Hugues Anglade, Vincent Perez, Pascal Greggory, Miguel Bose, Dominique Blanc, Claudio Amendola, Asia Argento, Julien Rassam, Jean-Claude Brialy; *D:* Patrice Chereau; *W:* Patrice Chereau, Daniele Thompson; *M:* Goran Bregovic. Cannes Film Festival '94: Special Jury Prize, Best Actress (Lisi); Nominations: Academy Awards '94: Best Costume Design; British Academy Awards '95: Best Foreign Film; Cesar Awards '95: Best Director (Chereau), Best Film, Best Supporting Actress (Blanc). **VHS, LV ★★★1/2**

Queen of Hearts Excellent, original romantic comedy is a directorial triumph for Amiel in his first feature. An Italian couple defy both their families and marry for love. Four children later, we find them running a diner in England. Humorous, dramatic, sad—everything a movie can and should be. Fine performances.
1989 (PG) 112m/C *GB* Anita Zagaria, Joseph Long, Eileen Way, Vittorio Duse, Vittorio Amandola, Ian Hawkes; *D:* Jon Amiel; *M:* Michael Convertino. **VHS, Beta, LV ★★★★**

Queen of the Stardust Ballroom Well-made television drama about a lonely widow who goes to a local dance hall, where she meets a man and begins an unconventional late love.
1975 98m/C Maureen Stapleton, Charles Durning, Michael Strong, Charlotte Rae, Sam O'Steen; *D:* Michael Brandon; *M:* Billy Goldenberg. **Beta ★★★**

Quest for Fire An interesting story sans the usual dialogue thing. A group of men during the Ice Age must wander the land searching for fire after they lose theirs fending off an attack. During their quest, they en-counter and battle various animals and tribesmen in order to survive. The special language they speak was developed by Anthony Burgess, while the primitive movements were devel-oped by Desmond "The Naked Ape" Morris. Perlman went on to become the Beast in TV's "Beauty and the Beast"; Chong is the daughter of Tommy Chong of the comic duo Cheech and Chong.
1982 (R) 75m/C *FR* Everett McGill, Ron Perlman, Nameer El-Kadi, Rae Dawn Chong; *D:* Jean-Jacques Annaud; *W:* Gerard Brach. Academy Awards '82: Best Makeup; Genie Awards '83: Best Actress (Chong). **VHS, Beta, LV ★★★**

The Quiet Man The classic incarna-tion of Hollywood Irishness, and one of Ford's best, and funniest films. Wayne is Sean Thornton, a weary American ex-boxer who returns to the Irish hamlet of his childhood and tries to take a spirited lass as his wife, de-spite the strenuous objections of her brawling brother (McLaglen). Thorn-ton's aided by the leprechaun-like Fitzgerald and the local parish priest, Bond. A high-spirited and memorable film filled with Irish stew, wonderful banter, and shots of the lush country-side. Listen for the Scottish bagpipes at the start of the horse race, a slight geographic inaccuracy.
1952 129m/C John Wayne, Maureen O'Hara, Barry Fitzgerald, Victor McLaglen, Arthur Shields, Jack MacGowran, Ward Bond, Mildred Natwick, Ken Curtis, Mae Marsh, Sean McClory, Francis Ford; *D:* John Ford; *W:* Frank Nugent; *M:* Victor Young. Academy Awards '52: Best Color Cinematography, Best Director (Ford); National Board of Review Awards '52: 10 Best Films of the Year; Venice Film Festival '52: Best Director (Ford); Nominations: Academy Awards '52: Best Art Direction/Set Decoration (Color), Best Picture, Best Screenplay, Best Sound, Best Supporting Actor (McLaglen). **VHS, LV ★★★★**

The Quiller Memorandum An Amer-ican secret agent travels to Berlin to uncover a deadly neo-Nazi gang. Re-freshingly different from other spy tales of its era. Good screenplay adapted from Adam Hall's novel, "The Berlin Memorandum."

R

1966 103m/C George Segal, Senta Berger, Alec Guinness, Max von Sydow, George Sanders; **D:** Michael Anderson Sr.; **W:** Harold Pinter; **M:** John Barry. **VHS, Beta** ★★★

Quiz Show Redford's intelligent, entertaining, and morally complex film about the TV game show scandals of the late '50s is his most accomplished work to date. At the center of the film is Charles Van Doren (Fiennes), an intellectual golden boy who dethrones Herbert Stempel (Turturro), the reigning champion of the rigged "Twenty-One." The program's sponsor felt Stempel, a nerdy Jewish grad's everyman qualities were wearing thin and wanted a more polished image, which they found in handsome, sophisticated Van Doren. Federal investigator Goodwin (Morrow) suspects Van Doren's reign is a sham and sets out to expose him as a fraud. Acting is of the highest caliber with Fiennes, Turturro, and Morrow all giving beautiful performances. Notable among supporting cast is Scofield as Van Doren's Pulitzer prize-winning father. With strong script and gorgeous lensing, this modern Faust story is a brilliant reflection on corporate greed, class rivalry, and the powers of television. Based on the book "Remembering America: A Voice From the Sixties" by Richard N. Goodwin.
1994 (PG-13) 133m/C John Turturro, Rob Morrow, Ralph Fiennes, Paul Scofield, David Paymer, Hank Azaria, Christopher McDonald, Johann Carlo, Elizabeth Wilson, Mira Sorvino, Griffin Dunne, Martin Scorsese, Barry Levinson; **D:** Robert Redford; **W:** Paul Attanasio; **M:** Mark Isham. British Academy Awards '94: Best Adapted Screenplay; New York Film Critics Awards '94: Best Film; Nominations: Academy Awards '94: Best Adapted Screenplay, Best Director (Redford), Best Picture, Best Supporting Actor (Scofield); Golden Globe Awards '95: Best Director (Redford), Best Film—Drama, Best Screenplay, Best Supporting Actor (Turturro). **VHS, LV** ★★★★

Quo Vadis Larger-than-life production about Nero and the Christian persecution. Done on a giant scale: features exciting fighting scenes, romance, and fabulous costumes. Definitive version of the classic novel by Henryk Siekiewicz. Remade for Italian television in 1985.
1951 171m/C Robert Taylor, Deborah Kerr, Peter Ustinov, Patricia Laffan, Finlay Currie, Leo Genn, Abraham Sofaer, Marina Berti, Buddy Baer, Felix Aylmer, Nora Swinburne;

Cameos: Sophia Loren, Elizabeth Taylor; **D:** Mervyn LeRoy; **M:** Miklos Rozsa. Golden Globe Awards '52: Best Supporting Actor (Ustinov); Nominations: Academy Awards '51: Best Art Direction/Set Decoration (Color), Best Color Cinematography, Best Costume Design (Color), Best Film Editing, Best Picture, Best Supporting Actor (Genn, Ustinov), Best Original Score. **VHS, Beta** ★★★

Rachel and the Stranger A God-fearing farmer declares his love for his wife when a handsome stranger (Mitchum) nearly woos her away. Well-cast, well-paced, charming Western comedy-drama.
1948 93m/B Loretta Young, Robert Mitchum, William Holden, Gary Gray; **D:** Norman Foster. **VHS, Beta, LV** ★★★

Rachel, Rachel Rachel teaches by day, wearing simple, practical dresses and her hair up. By night she caters to her domineering mother by preparing refreshments for her parties. This sexually repressed, spinster schoolteacher, however, gets one last chance at romance in her small Connecticut town. Woodward mixes just the right amounts of loneliness and sweetness in the leading role. A surprising award-winner that was an independent production of Newman. Based on Margaret Laurence's "A Jest of God."
1968 (R) 102m/C Joanne Woodward, James Olson, Estelle Parsons, Geraldine Fitzgerald, Donald Moffat; **D:** Paul Newman; **W:** Stewart Stern. Golden Globe Awards '69: Best Actress—Drama (Woodward), Best Director (Newman); New York Film Critics Awards '68: Best Actress (Woodward), Best Director (Newman); Nominations: Academy Awards '68: Best Actress (Woodward), Best Adapted Screenplay, Best Picture, Best Supporting Actress (Parsons). **VHS, Beta** ★★★★

Racing with the Moon Sweet, nostalgic film about two buddies awaiting induction into the Marines in 1942. They have their last chance at summer romance. Benjamin makes the most of skillful young actors and conventional story. Great period detail. Keep your eyes peeled for glimpses of many rising young stars including Hannah and Carvey.
1984 (PG) 108m/C Sean Penn, Elizabeth McGovern, Nicolas Cage, John Karlen, Rutanya Alda, Max Showalter, Crispin Glover, Suzanne Adkinson, Page Hannah, Michael Madsen, Dana Carvey, Carol Kane, Michael Talbott, John Bailey; **D:** Richard Benjamin; **W:** Steven Kloves; **M:** Dave Grusin. **VHS, Beta, LV** ★★★

Radio Days A lovely, unpretentious remembrance of the pre-television radio culture. Allen tells his story in a series of vignettes centering around his youth in Brooklyn, his eccentric extended family, and the legends of radio they all followed. The ubiquitous Farrow is a young singer hoping to make it big.
1987 (PG) 96m/C Mia Farrow, Dianne Wiest, Julie Kavner, Michael Tucker, Wallace Shawn, Josh Mostel, Tony Roberts, Jeff Daniels, Kenneth Mars, Seth Green, William Magerman, Diane Keaton, Renee Lippin, Danny Aiello, Gina DeAngelis, Kitty Carlisle Hart, Mercedes Ruehl, Tito Puente; **D:** Woody Allen; **W:** Woody Allen. Nominations: Academy Awards '87: Best Art Direction/Set Decoration, Best Original Screenplay. **VHS, Beta, LV** ★★★

A Rage in Harlem The crime novels of Chester A. Himes were translated into the best movies of the early '70s blaxploitation era. Now, a Himes story gets the big budget Hollywood treatment with juice and aplomb. A voluptuous lady crook enters Harlem circa 1950 with a trunkful of stolen gold sought by competing crooks, and the chase is on, with one virtuous soul (Whitaker) who only wants the girl. Great cast and characters, much humor, but unsparing in its violence.
1991 (R) 108m/C Forest Whitaker, Gregory Hines, Robin Givens, Zakes Mokae, Danny Glover, Tyler Collins, Ron Taylor, T.K. Carter, Willard Pugh, Samm-Art Williams, Jay Hawkins, Badja Djola, John Toles-Bey, Stack Pierce, George Wallace; **D:** Bill Duke; **W:** John Toles-Bey, Bobby Crawford; **M:** Elmer Bernstein. **VHS, LV** ★★★

Raging Bull Scorsese's depressing but magnificent vision of the dying American Dream and suicidal macho codes in the form of the rise and fall of middleweight boxing champ Jake LaMotta, a brutish, dull-witted animal who can express himself only in the ring and through violence. A photographically expressive, brilliant drama, with easily the most intense and brutal boxing scenes ever filmed. De Niro provides a vintage performance, going from the young LaMotta to the aging has-been, and is ably accompanied by Moriarty as his girl and Pesci as his loyal, much beat-upon bro.
1980 (R) 128m/B Robert De Niro, Cathy Moriarty, Joe Pesci, Frank Vincent, Nicholas Colasanto, Theresa Saldana, Michael Chapman; **D:** Martin Scorsese; **W:** Paul Schrader, Mardik Martin. Academy Awards '80: Best Actor (De Niro), Best Film Editing; Golden Globe Awards '81: Best Actor—Drama (De Niro); Los Angeles Film Critics Association Awards '80: Best Actor (De Niro), Best Film; National Board of Review Awards '80: Best Actor (De Niro), Best Supporting Actor (Pesci); National Society of Film Critics Awards '80: Best Cinematography, Best Director (Scorsese), Best Supporting Actor (Pesci); Nominations: Academy Awards '80: Best Cinematography, Best Director (Scorsese), Best Picture, Best Sound, Best Supporting Actor (Pesci), Best Supporting Actress (Moriarty). **VHS, Beta, LV, 8mm** ★★★★

Ragtime The lives and passions of a middle class family weave into the scandals and events of 1906 America. A small, unthinking act represents all the racist attacks on one man, who refuses to back down this time. Wonderful period detail. From the E.L. Doctorow novel, but not nearly as complex. Features Cagney's last film performance.
1981 (PG) 156m/C Howard E. Rollins Jr., Kenneth McMillan, Brad Dourif, Mary Steenburgen, James Olson, Elizabeth McGovern, Pat O'Brien, James Cagney, Debbie Allen, Jeff Daniels, Moses Gunn, Donald O'Connor, Mandy Patinkin, Norman Mailer; **D:** Milos Forman; **W:** Michael Weller; **M:** Randy Newman. Nominations: Academy Awards '81: Best Adapted Screenplay, Best Art Direction/Set Decoration, Best Cinematography, Best Costume Design, Best Song ("One More Hour"), Best Supporting Actor (Rollins), Best Supporting Actress (McGovern), Best Original Score. **VHS, Beta, LV** ★★★

Raid on Entebbe Dramatization of the Israeli rescue of passengers held hostage by terrorists at Uganda's Entebbe Airport in 1976. A gripping actioner all the more compelling because true. Finch received an Emmy nomination in this, his last film. Made for television.
1977 (R) 113m/C Charles Bronson, Peter Finch, Horst Buchholz, John Saxon, Martin Balsam, Jack Warden, Yaphet Kotto, Sylvia Sidney; **D:** Irvin Kershner; **M:** David Shire. **VHS, Beta** ★★★

Raiders of the Lost Ark Classic '30s-style adventure reminiscent of early serials spawned two sequels and numerous rip-offs. Made Ford a household name as dashing hero and intrepid archaeologist Indiana Jones. He battles mean Nazis, decodes hieroglyphics, fights his fear of snakes, and even has time for a little romance in his quest for the Biblical Ark of the Covenant. Allen is perfectly cast as his feisty ex-flame, more than a little irritated with the smooth talker who dumped her years earlier. Asks view-

ers to suspend belief as every chase and stunt tops the last. Unrelated opening sequence does a great job of introducing the character. Followed by "Indiana Jones and the Temple of Doom."
1981 (PG) 115m/C Harrison Ford, Karen Allen, Wolf Kahler, Paul Freeman, John Rhys-Davies, Denholm Elliott, Ronald Lacey, Anthony Higgins, Alfred Molina; **D:** Steven Spielberg; **W:** George Lucas, Philip Kaufman; **M:** John Williams. Academy Awards '81: Best Art Direction/Set Decoration, Best Film Editing, Best Sound, Best Visual Effects; People's Choice Awards '82: Best Film; Nominations: Academy Awards '81: Best Cinematography, Best Director (Spielberg), Best Picture, Best Original Score. **VHS, Beta, LV, 8mm ★★★★**

The Railway Children At the turn of the century in England, the father of three children is framed and sent to prison during Christmas. The trio and their mother must survive on a poverty-stricken farm near the railroad tracks. They eventually meet a new friend who helps them prove their father's innocence. Wonderfully directed by Jeffries. From the classic Edith Nesbitt children's novel.
1970 104m/C *GB* Jenny Agutter, William Mervyn, Bernard Cribbins, Dinah Sheridan, Iain Cuthbertson; **D:** Lionel Jeffries. **VHS, Beta ★★★1/2**

Rain Man When his father dies, ambitious and self-centered Charlie Babbit finds he has an older autistic brother who's been institutionalized for years. Needing him to claim an inheritance, he liberates him from the institution and takes to the road, where both brothers undergo subtle changes. The Vegas montage is wonderful. Critically acclaimed drama and a labor of love for the entire cast. Cruise's best performance to date as he goes from cad to recognizing something wonderfully human in his brother and himself. Hoffman is exceptional.
1988 (R) 128m/C Dustin Hoffman, Tom Cruise, Valeria Golino, Jerry Molen, Jack Murdock, Michael D. Roberts, Ralph Seymour, Lucinda Jenney, Bonnie Hunt, Kim Robillard, Beth Grant; **D:** Barry Levinson; **W:** Ronald Bass, Barry Morrow, John Seale; **M:** Hans Zimmer. Academy Awards '88: Best Actor (Hoffman), Best Director (Levinson), Best Original Screenplay, Best Picture; Berlin International Film Festival '88: Golden Berlin Bear; Directors Guild of America Awards '88: Best Director (Levinson); Golden Globe Awards '89: Best Actor—Drama (Hoffman), Best Film—Drama;

People's Choice Awards '89: Best Film—Drama; Nominations: Academy Awards '88: Best Art Direction/Set Decoration, Best Cinematography, Best Film Editing, Best Original Score. **VHS, Beta, LV, 8mm ★★★1/2**

The Rain People Pregnant housewife Knight takes to the road in desperation and boredom; along the way she meets retarded ex-football player Caan. Well directed by Coppola from his original script. Pensive drama.
1969 (R) 102m/C Shirley Knight, James Caan, Robert Duvall; **D:** Francis Ford Coppola; **W:** Francis Ford Coppola. **VHS, Beta ★★★**

The Rainbow Mature, literate rendering of the classic D.H. Lawrence novel about a young woman's sexual awakening. Beautiful cinematography. Companion/prequel to director Russell's earlier Lawrence adaptation, "Women in Love" (1969).
1989 (R) 104m/C *GB* Sammi Davis, Amanda Donohoe, Paul McGann, Christopher Gable, David Hemmings, Glenda Jackson, Kenneth Colley; **D:** Ken Russell; **W:** Vivian Russell, Ken Russell; **M:** Carl Davis. **VHS, LV ★★★**

The Rainmaker Reminiscent of "Elmer Gantry" in his masterful performance, Lancaster makes it all believable as a con man who comes to a small midwestern town and works miracles not only on the weather but on spinster Hepburn, although both were a little long in the tooth for their roles. Written by Nash from his own play.
1956 121m/C Burt Lancaster, Katharine Hepburn, Wendell Corey, Lloyd Bridges, Earl Holliman, Cameron Prudhomme, Wallace Ford; **D:** Joseph Anthony; **W:** N. Richard Nash; **M:** Alex North. Golden Globe Awards '57: Best Supporting Actor (Holliman); Nominations: Academy Awards '56: Best Actress (Hepburn), Best Original Score. **VHS, LV ★★★**

Raise the Red Lantern Set in 1920s China, Zhang explores its claustrophobic world of privilege and humiliation. Songlian, an educated 19-year-old beauty, is forced into marriage as the fourth wife of a wealthy and powerful old man. She discovers that the wives have their own separate quarters and servants, and spend most of their time battling to attract their husband's attention. Over the course of a year, Songlian's fury and resentment grow until self-defeating rebellion is all she has. Gong Li is exquisite as the young woman struggling for dignity in a portrayal which is both both haunting and tragic.

1991 (PG) 125m/C *CH* Gong Li, Ma Jingwu, He Caifei, Cao Cuifeng, Jin Shuyuan, Kong Lin, Ding Weimin; *D:* Zhang Yimou. British Academy Awards '92: Best Foreign Film; Los Angeles Film Critics Association Awards '92: Best Cinematography; New York Film Critics Awards '92: Best Foreign Film; National Society of Film Critics Awards '92: Best Cinematography, Best Foreign Film; Nominations: Academy Awards '91: Best Foreign Language Film. **VHS, LV** ★★★1/2

A Raisin in the Sun Outstanding story of a black family trying to make a better life for themselves in an all-white neighborhood in Chicago. The characters are played realistically and make for a moving story. Each person struggles with doing what he must while still maintaining his dignity and sense of self. Based on the Broadway play by Hansberry, who also wrote the screenplay.
1961 128m/B Diana Sands, John Fiedler, Ivan Dixon, Louis Gossett Jr., Sidney Poitier, Claudia McNeil, Ruby Dee; *D:* Daniel Petrie; *W:* Lorraine Hansberry. National Board of Review Awards '61: 10 Best Films of the Year, Best Supporting Actress (Dee). **VHS, Beta, LV** ★★★★

Raising Arizona Hi's an ex-con and the world's worst hold-up man. Ed's a policewoman. They meet, fall in love, marry, and kidnap a baby (one of a family of quints). Why not? Ed's infertile and the family they took the baby from has "more than enough," so who will notice? But unfinished furniture tycoon Nathan Arizona wants his baby back, even if he has to hire an axe-murderer on a motorcycle to do it. A brilliant, original comedy narrated in notorious loopy deadpan style by Cage. Innovative camerawork by Barry Sonnenfeld. Wild, surreal and hilarious.
1987 (PG-13) 94m/C Nicolas Cage, Holly Hunter, John Goodman, William Forsythe, Randall "Tex" Cobb, Trey Wilson, M. Emmet Walsh, Frances McDormand; *D:* Joel Coen; *W:* Ethan Coen, Joel Coen; *M:* Carter Burwell. **VHS, Beta, LV** ★★★1/2

Rambling Rose Dern is Rose, a free-spirited, sexually liberated before her time young woman taken in by a Southern family in 1935. Rose immediately has an impact on the male members of the clan, father Duvall and son Haas, thanks to her insuppressible sexuality. This causes consternation with the strait-laced patriarch, who attempts to control his desire for the girl. Eventually Rose decides she must try to stick to one man, but this only causes further problems.

Dern gives her best performance yet in this excellent period piece, and solid support is offered from the rest of the cast, in particular Duvall and Dern's real-life mother Ladd.
1991 (R) 115m/C Laura Dern, Diane Ladd, Robert Duvall, Lukas Haas, John Heard, Kevin Conway, Robert Burke, Lisa Jakub, Evan Lockwood; *D:* Martha Coolidge; *W:* Calder Willingham; *M:* Elmer Bernstein. Independent Spirit Awards '92: Best Director (Coolidge), Best Film, Best Supporting Actress (Ladd); Nominations: Academy Awards '91: Best Actress (Dern), Best Supporting Actress (Ladd). **VHS, LV** ★★★

Ran The culmination of Kurosawa's career stands as his masterpiece. Loosely adapting Shakespeare's "King Lear," with plot elements from "Macbeth," he's fashioned an epic, heartbreaking statement about honor, ambition, and the futility of war. Aging medieval warlord Hidetora gives control of his empire to his oldest son, creating conflict with two other sons. Soon he's an outcast, as ambition and greed seize the two sons. Stunning battle scenes illuminate the full-blown tragedy of Kurosawa's vision. Superb acting with a scene-stealing Harada as the revenge-minded Lady Kaede; period costumes took three years to create. In Japanese with English subtitles.
1985 (R) 160m/C *JP FR* Tatsuya Nakadai, Akira Terao, Jinpachi Nesu, Daisuke Ryu, Meiko Harada, Hisashi Igawa; *D:* Akira Kurosawa; *W:* Akira Kurosawa, Hideo Oguni, Masato Ide; *M:* Toru Takemitsu. Academy Awards '85: Best Costume Design; British Academy Awards '86: Best Foreign Film; Los Angeles Film Critics Association Awards '85: Best Foreign Film; National Board of Review Awards '85: Best Director (Kurosawa); New York Film Critics Awards '85: Best Foreign Film; National Society of Film Critics Awards '85: Best Cinematography, Best Film; Nominations: Academy Awards '85: Best Art Direction/Set Decoration, Best Cinematography, Best Director (Kurosawa). **VHS, Beta, LV** ★★★★

Rancho Notorious Kennedy, on the trail of his girlfriend's murderer, falls for dance hall girl Dietrich. Fine acting. A "period" sample of 50s westerns, but different. A must for Dietrich fans.
1952 89m/C Marlene Dietrich, Arthur Kennedy, Mel Ferrer, William Frawley, Jack Elam, George Reeves; *D:* Fritz Lang; *W:* Daniel Taradash. **VHS, Beta, LV** ★★★

Random Harvest A masterful, tear-jerking film based on the James

Hilton novel. A shell-shocked WWI amnesiac meets and is made happy by a beautiful music hall dancer. He regains his memory and forgets about the dancer and their child. This is Garson's finest hour, and a shamelessly potent sobfest.

1942 126m/B Greer Garson, Ronald Colman, Reginald Owen, Philip Dorn, Susan Peters, Henry Travers, Margaret Wycherly, Bramwell Fletcher; **D:** Mervyn LeRoy. Nominations: Academy Awards '42: Best Actor (Colman), Best Adapted Screenplay, Best Director (LeRoy), Best Interior Decoration, Best Picture, Best Supporting Actress (Peters). **VHS, Beta** ★★★

Rashomon In 12th-century Japan, two travelers attempt to discover the truth about an ambush/rape/murder. They get four completely different versions of the incident from the three people involved in the crime and the single witness. An insightful masterpiece that established Kurosawa and Japanese cinema as major artistic forces. Fine performances, particularly Mifune as the bandit. Visually beautiful and rhythmic. Remade as a western, "The Outrage," in 1964. In Japanese with English subtitles. **AKA:** In the Woods.

1951 83m/B JP Machiko Kyo, Toshiro Mifune, Masayuki Mori, Takashi Shimura; **D:** Akira Kurosawa; **W:** Akira Kurosawa. Academy Awards '51: Best Foreign Language Film; National Board of Review Awards '51: 5 Best Foreign Films of the Year, Best Director (Kurosawa); Nominations: Academy Awards '52: Best Art Direction/Set Decoration (B & W). **VHS, Beta, LV** ★★★★

Rasputin: Dark Servant of Destiny Charismatic Russian peasant/mystic Grigori Rasputin (a mesmerizing Rickman), having received a vision of the Virgin Mary, comes to St. Petersburg in order to relieve the suffering of young hemophiliac, Prince Alexei (Findlay). Tsarina Alexandra (Scacchi) approves of anyone who can help her stricken son, while Tsar Nicholas II (McKellen) tentatively agrees to accept the self-proclaimed holy man into the Russian court. But Rasputin's growing influence begins to undermine the government and will lead to the downfall of Imperial Russia. TV movie filmed in St. Petersburg.

1996 120m/C Alan Rickman, Ian McKellen, Greta Scacchi, Freddie Findlay, David Warner, John Wood, James Frain, Diana Quick, Ian Hogg, Peter Jeffrey, Ian McDiarmid, Julian Curry; **D:** Uli Edell; **W:** Peter Bruce; **M:** Brad Fiedel. **VHS** ★★★

Rasputin and the Empress Lavish historical epic teamed the three Barrymore sibs for the first and only time, as they vied for scene-stealing honors. Ethel is Empress Alexandra of Russia, tied to the weak-willed Nicholas II (Morgan) and under the spell of Rasputin, played by Lionel. John is a nobleman who seeks to warn the Russian rulers of their perilous perch on the throne, made only worse by Rasputin's spreading power and corruption. Ethel's first talkie and Wynyard's first film role. Uncredited director Charles Brabin was replaced by Boleslawski due to his incompatability with the imperious Ethel. **AKA:** Rasputin: The Mad Monk.

1932 123m/B Ethel Barrymore, John Barrymore, Lionel Barrymore, Ralph Morgan, Diana Wynyard, Tad Alexander, C. Henry Gordon, Edward Arnold, Gustav von Seyffertitz, Anne Shirley, Jean Parker, Henry Kolker; **D:** Richard Boleslawski; **W:** Charles MacArthur. Nominations: Academy Awards '33: Best Original Screenplay. **VHS** ★★★

The Rat Race A dancer and a musician venture to Manhattan to make it big, and end up sharing an apartment. Their relationship starts pleasantly and becomes romantic. Enjoyable farce. Well photographed and scripted, with the supporting characters stealing the show.

1960 105m/C Tony Curtis, Debbie Reynolds, Jack Oakie, Kay Medford, Don Rickles, Joe Bushkin; **D:** Robert Mulligan; **M:** Elmer Bernstein. **VHS** ★★★

The Raven A lunatic surgeon (Lugosi), who has a dungeon full of torture gadgets inspired by Edgar Allan Poe's stories, is begged by a man to save his daughter's life. The surgeon does, and then falls in love with the girl. But when she rejects his love (she's already engaged), he plans revenge in his chamber of horrors. Karloff plays the criminal who winds up ruining the mad doctor's plans. Lugosi is at his prime in this role, and any inconsistencies in the somewhat shaky script can be overlooked because of his chilling performance.

1935 62m/B Boris Karloff, Bela Lugosi, Irene Ware, Lester Matthews, Samuel S. Hinds; **D:** Lew (Louis Friedlander) Landers. **VHS, LV** ★★★

The Raven This could-have-been monumental teaming of horror greats Karloff, Lorre and Price is more of a satire than a true horror film. One of the more enjoyable of the Corman/Poe adaptations, the movie takes only the title of the poem. As for the

storyline: Price and Karloff play two rival sorcerers who battle for supremacy, with Lorre as the unfortunate associate turned into the bird of the title.
1963 86m/C Vincent Price, Boris Karloff, Peter Lorre, Jack Nicholson, Hazel Court; *D:* Roger Corman; *W:* Richard Matheson; *M:* Les Baxter. **VHS, Beta, LV** ★★★

The Razor's Edge Adaptation of the W. Somerset Maugham novel. A rich young man spends his time between WWI & WWII searching for essential truth, eventually landing in India. A satisfying cinematic version of a difficult novel, supported by an excellent cast. Remade in 1984 with Bill Murray in the lead role.
1946 146m/B Tyrone Power, Gene Tierney, Anne Baxter, Clifton Webb, Herbert Marshall, John Payne, Elsa Lanchester; *D:* Edmund Goulding. Academy Awards '46: Best Supporting Actress (Baxter); Golden Globe Awards '47: Best Supporting Actor (Webb), Best Supporting Actress (Baxter); Nominations: Academy Awards '46: Best Interior Decoration, Best Picture, Best Supporting Actor (Webb). **VHS, Beta, LV** ★★★

Re-Animator Based on an H.P. Lovecraft story, this grisly film deals with a medical student who re-animates the dead. It has quickly turned into a black humor cult classic. Also available in an "R" rated version, and followed by "Bride of Re-Animator."
1984 86m/C Jeffrey Combs, Bruce Abbott, Barbara Crampton, David Gale, Robert Sampson; *D:* Stuart Gordon; *W:* Stuart Gordon, Dennis Paoli, William J. Norris; *M:* Richard Band. **VHS, Beta, LV** ★★★

Rear Window A newspaper photographer with a broken leg (Stewart) passes the time recuperating by observing his neighbors through the window. When he sees what he believes to be a murder, he decides to solve the crime himself. With help from his beautiful girlfriend and his nurse, he tries to catch the murderer without getting killed himself. Top-drawer Hitchcock blends exquisite suspense with occasional on-target laughs. Based on the story by Cornell Woolrich.
1954 112m/C James Stewart, Grace Kelly, Thelma Ritter, Wendell Corey, Raymond Burr, Judith Evelyn; *D:* Alfred Hitchcock; *W:* John Michael Hayes; *M:* Franz Waxman. Edgar Allan Poe Awards '54: Best Screenplay; Nominations: Academy Awards '54: Best Director (Hitchcock), Best Screenplay, Best Sound. **VHS, Beta, LV** ★★★★

Rebecca Based on Daphne Du Maurier's best-selling novel about a young unsophisticated girl who marries a moody and prominent country gentleman haunted by the memory of his first wife. Fontaine and Olivier turn in fine performances as the unlikely couple. Suspenseful and surprising. Hitchcock's first American film and only Best Picture Oscar. Laserdisc features: rare screen tests of Vivien Leigh, Anne Baxter, Loretta Young, and Joan Fontaine, footage from Rebecca's winning night at the Academy Awards, original radio broadcasts of film by Orson Welles and David O. Selznick, and commentary of film with interview excerpts with Hitchcock.
1940 130m/B Joan Fontaine, Laurence Olivier, Judith Anderson, George Sanders, Nigel Bruce, Florence Bates, Gladys Cooper, Reginald Denny, Leo G. Carroll, Sir C. Aubrey Smith, Melville Cooper; *D:* Alfred Hitchcock; *W:* Joan Harrison, Robert Sherwood; *M:* Franz Waxman. Academy Awards '40: Best Black and White Cinematography, Best Picture; National Board of Review Awards '40: 10 Best Films of the Year; Nominations: Academy Awards '40: Best Actor (Olivier), Best Actress (Fontaine), Best Adapted Screenplay, Best Director (Hitchcock), Best Film Editing, Best Interior Decoration, Best Supporting Actress (Anderson), Best Original Score. **VHS, Beta, LV** ★★★★

Rebel Without a Cause James Dean's most memorable screen appearance. In the second of his three films, he plays a troubled teenager from the right side of the tracks. Dean's portrayal of Jim Stark, a teen alienated from both his parents and peers, is excellent. He befriends outcasts Wood and Mineo in a police station and together they find a common ground. Superb young stars carry this in-the-gut story of adolescence. All three leads met with real-life tragic ends.
1955 111m/C James Dean, Natalie Wood, Sal Mineo, Jim Backus, Nick Adams, Dennis Hopper, Ann Doran, William Hopper, Rochelle Hudson, Corey Allen, Edward Platt; *D:* Nicholas Ray; *W:* Stewart Stern; *M:* Leonard Rosenman. Nominations: Academy Awards '55: Best Supporting Actor (Mineo), Best Story, Best Supporting Actress (Wood). **VHS, Beta, LV** ★★★★

Reckless Moment A mother commits murder to save her daughter from an unsavory older man, and finds herself blackmailed. Gripping, intense thriller.
1949 82m/B James Mason, Joan Bennett,

Geraldine Brooks; *D:* Max Ophuls. **VHS, Beta ★★★**

The Red Badge of Courage John Huston's adaptation of the Stephen Crane Civil War novel is inspired, despite cutting room hatchet job by the studio. A classic study of courage and cowardice. Sweeping battle scenes and intense personal drama. **1951 69m/B** Audie Murphy, Bill Mauldin, Douglas Dick, Royal Dano, Andy Devine; *D:* John Huston. National Board of Review Awards '51: 10 Best Films of the Year. **VHS, Beta ★★★1/2**

The Red Balloon The story of Pascal, a lonely French boy who befriends a wondrous red balloon which follows him everywhere. Lovely, finely done parable of childhood, imagination and friendship. **1956 34m/C** *FR* Pascal Lamorisse; *D:* Albert Lamorisse. Academy Awards '56: Best Original Screenplay; National Board of Review Awards '57: 5 Best Foreign Films of the Year. **VHS, Beta, LV, 8mm ★★★1/2**

Red Balloon/Occurrence at Owl Creek Bridge Two classic award-winning shorts have been combined on one tape: "The Red Balloon" (color, 1956) and "An Occurrence at Owl Creek Bridge." The former is a children's story about a balloon on the loose; the latter is a perfectly rendered adaptation of the Ambrose Bierce short story of the same title, a taut narration of a Civil War hanging. **1962 60m/C** *FR* Pascal Lamorisse, Roger Jacquet; *D:* Robert Enrico, Albert Lamorisse. **VHS, Beta ★★★★**

Red Beard An uncharacteristic drama by Kurosawa, about a young doctor in Japan awakening to life and love under the tutelage of a compassionate old physician. Highly acclaimed; in Japanese with English subtitles. *AKA:* Akahige. **1965 185m/B** *JP* Toshiro Mifune, Yuzo Kayama, Yoshio Tsuchiya, Reiko Dan; *D:* Akira Kurosawa. **VHS, Beta, LV ★★★**

The Red Desert Antonioni's first color film, depicting an alienated Italian wife who searches for meaning in the industrial lunar landscape of northern Italy, to no avail. Highly acclaimed, and a masterpiece of visual form. Cinematography by Carlo di Palma. In Italian with English subtitles. **1964 120m/C** *IT* Monica Vitti, Richard Harris, Carlos Chionetti; *D:* Michelangelo Antonioni; *W:* Michelangelo Antonioni, Tonino Guerra, Carlo DiPalma. Venice Film Festival '64: International Critics Award, Best Film. **VHS, Beta ★★★**

Red Dust The overseer of a rubber plantation in Indochina causes all kinds of trouble when he falls in love with a young engineer's wife. Filled with free-spirited humor and skillfully directed; remarkably original. Remade in 1940 as "Congo Maisie" and in 1954 as "Mogambo." **1932 83m/B** Clark Gable, Jean Harlow, Mary Astor, Gene Raymond, Donald Crisp; *D:* Victor Fleming. **VHS, Beta ★★★**

Red Headed Woman Harlow plays an unscrupulous woman who charms her way into the lives of influential men. She causes her boss to divorce his wife and marry her while she sleeps with the chauffeur (Boyer) and others. Audiences loved the scandalous material, but the Hays Office objected to the fact that the immoral woman goes unpunished. Boyer's small but important role salvaged his floundering American film career. Harlow is sultry and funny. **1932 79m/B** Jean Harlow, Chester Morris, Lewis Stone, Leila Hyams, Una Merkel, Henry Stephenson, May Robson, Charles Boyer, Harvey Clark; *D:* Jack Conway. **VHS, Beta ★★★**

The Red Pony A young boy escapes from his family's fighting through his love for a pet pony. Based on the novel by John Steinbeck. Remade for television in 1976. Timeless classic that the whole family can enjoy. **1949 89m/C** Myrna Loy, Robert Mitchum, Peter Miles, Louis Calhern, Shepperd Strudwick, Margaret Hamilton, Beau Bridges; *D:* Lewis Milestone; *M:* Aaron Copland. **VHS, LV ★★★**

The Red Pony Excellent TV remake of a classic 1949 adaptation of John Steinbeck. Fonda is superb as a troubled young fonda's difficult father. **1976 101m/C** Henry Fonda, Maureen O'Hara, Clint Howard, Jack Elam, Ben Johnson; *D:* Robert Totten. **VHS, Beta, LV ★★★**

Red River The classic Hawks epic about a gruelling cattle drive and the battle of wills between father and son. Generally regarded as one of the best westerns ever made, and Wayne's shining moment as a reprehensible, obsessive man. Featuring Clift in his first film. Restored version has eight minutes of previously edited material. Remade for television in 1988 with James Arness and Bruce Boxleitner. **1948 133m/B** John Wayne, Montgomery Clift, Walter Brennan, Joanne Dru, John Ireland, Noah Beery Jr., Paul Fix, Coleen Gray, Harry Carey Jr., Harry Carey Sr., Chief Yowlachie, Hank Worden; *D:* Howard

Hawks; **W:** Borden Chase, Charles Schnee; **M:** Dimitri Tiomkin. Nominations: Academy Awards '48: Best Film Editing, Best Story. **VHS, Beta, LV** ★★★★

Red Rock West Nothing is what it seems in this stylish and entertaining film noir set in a desolate Wyoming town. Perennial loser and nice guy Michael (Cage) is headed to a job at oil rig, but blows his chance by admitting he has a bad leg. Landing in the tiny burg of Red Rock, he's mistaken for the hit man hired by local barkeep Walsh to kill his pretty wife (Boyle). Then Boyle doubles Walsh's offer—what's a film noir boy to do? And Hopper, the real killer, strides into town. Full of twists, turns, and shades of "El Mariachi," this enjoyable, well-acted thriller is a real gem that escaped directly to cable before being rescued by a San Francisco exhibitor. **1993 (R) 98m/C** Nicolas Cage, Dennis Hopper, Lara Flynn Boyle, J.T. Walsh, Timothy Carhart, Dan Shor, Dwight Yoakam, Bobby Joe McFadden; **D:** John Dahl; **W:** John Dahl, Rick Dahl; **M:** William Olvis. Nominations: Independent Spirit Awards '95: Best Director (Dahl), Best Screenplay. **VHS, LV** ★★★1/2

The Red Shoes British classic about a young ballerina torn between love and success. Inspired by the Hans Christian Andersen fairy-tale. Noted for its lavish use of Technicolor. **1948 136m/C** *GB* Anton Walbrook, Moira Shearer, Marius Goring, Leonide Massine, Robert Helpmann, Albert Basserman, Ludmila Tcherina, Esmond Knight, Jack Cardiff; **D:** Emeric Pressburger, Michael Powell; **W:** Emeric Pressburger, Michael Powell. Academy Awards '48: Best Art Direction/Set Decoration (Color), Best Score; Golden Globe Awards '49: Best Score; National Board of Review Awards '48: 10 Best Films of the Year; Nominations: Academy Awards '48: Best Film Editing, Best Picture, Best Story. **VHS, Beta, LV** ★★★★

Red Sorghum A stunning visual achievement, this new wave Chinese film (and Yimou's directorial debut) succeeds on many levels—as an ode to the color red, as dark comedy, and as a sweeping epic with fairy-tale overtones. Set in rural China in the 1920s, during the period of the Japanese invasion. The sorghum plot nearby is a symbolic playing field in the movie's most stunning scenes. Here, people make love, murder, betray, and commit acts of bravery, all under the watchful eye of nature. In Mandarin with English subtitles. **1987 91m/C** *CH* Gong Li, Jiang Wen, Ji Cun Hua; **D:** Zhang Yimou, Gu Changwei. **VHS** ★★★1/2

Reds The re-creation of the life of author John Reed ("Ten Days that Shook the World"), his romance with Louise Bryant, his efforts to start an American Communist party, and his reporting of the Russian Revolution. A sweeping, melancholy epic using dozens of "witnesses" who reminisce about what they saw. See director Sergei Eisenstein's silent masterpiece "Ten Days that Shook the World," based on Reed's book, for the Russian view of some of the events depicted in Beatty's film. **1981 (PG) 195m/C** Warren Beatty, Diane Keaton, Jack Nicholson, Edward Herrmann, Maureen Stapleton, Gene Hackman, Jerzy Kosinski, George Plimpton, Paul Sorvino, William Daniels, M. Emmet Walsh, Dolph Sweet, Josef Sommer; **D:** Warren Beatty; **W:** Warren Beatty; **M:** Dave Grusin, Stephen Sondheim. Academy Awards '81: Best Cinematography, Best Director (Beatty), Best Supporting Actress (Stapleton); Directors Guild of America Awards '81: Best Director (Beatty); Golden Globe Awards '82: Best Director (Beatty); Los Angeles Film Critics Association Awards '81: Best Cinematography, Best Director (Beatty), Best Supporting Actress (Stapleton); New York Film Critics Awards '81: Best Film; National Society of Film Critics Awards '81: Best Supporting Actress (Stapleton); Writers Guild of America '81: Best Original Screenplay; Nominations: Academy Awards '81: Best Actor (Beatty), Best Actress (Keaton), Best Art Direction/Set Decoration, Best Costume Design, Best Film Editing, Best Original Screenplay, Best Picture, Best Sound, Best Supporting Actor (Nicholson). **VHS, Beta, LV** ★★★

Reilly: Ace of Spies Covers the exploits of the real-life superspy and womanizer Sydney Reilly who uncovers Russian secrets in 1901, allowing the Japanese to sink the Russian fleet and invade China. After a lively spying career for the British, Reilly eventually plots against the Bolsheviks and comes close to overthrowing Lenin and installing himself as the new leader of the Russian government. Eleven episodes on four cassettes. **1987 572m/C** *GB* Sam Neill, Sebastian Shaw, Jeananne Crowley; **D:** Jim Goddard. **VHS, Beta, LV** ★★★

The Reluctant Debutante Harrison and Kendall are the urbane parents of Dee who are trying to find a suitable British husband for their girl. It seems

their choices just won't do however, and Dee falls for American bad boy musician Saxon. A very lightweight yet extremely enjoyable romantic comedy thanks to Harrison and in particular his real-life wife Kendall, who unfortunately died the following year.
1958 96m/C Rex Harrison, Kay Kendall, John Saxon, Sandra Dee, Angela Lansbury, Diane Clare; **D:** Vincente Minnelli. **VHS, Beta, LV** ★★★

The Remains of the Day If repression is your cup of tea then this is the film for you. Others may want to shake British butler par excellence Stevens (Hopkins) and tell him to express an emotion. In the 1930s, Stevens is the rigidly traditional butler to Lord Darlington (Fox). When Miss Kenton (Thompson), the almost vivacious new housekeeper, expresses a quietly personal interest in Stevens, his loyalty to an unworthy master prevents him from a chance at happiness. A quiet movie, told in flashback. Hopkins's impressive performance gets by strictly on nuance with Thompson at least allowed a small amount of natural charm. Based on the novel by Kazuo Ishiguro.
1993 (PG) 135m/C *GB* Anthony Hopkins, Emma Thompson, James Fox, Christopher Reeve, Peter Vaughan, Hugh Grant, Michael Lonsdale, Tim Pigott-Smith; **D:** James Ivory; **W:** Ruth Prawer Jhabvala, Tony Pierce-Roberts; **M:** Richard Robbins. British Academy Awards '93: Best Actor (Hopkins); Los Angeles Film Critics Association Awards '93: Best Actor (Hopkins); National Board of Review Awards '93: Best Actor (Hopkins); Nominations: Academy Awards '93: Best Actor (Hopkins), Best Actress (Thompson), Best Adapted Screenplay, Best Art Direction/Set Decoration, Best Costume Design, Best Director (Ivory), Best Original Screenplay, Best Picture; British Academy Awards '93: Best Actress (Thompson), Best Adapted Screenplay, Best Director (Ivory), Best Film; Directors Guild of America Awards '93: Best Director (Ivory); Golden Globe Awards '94: Best Actor—Drama (Hopkins), Best Actress—Drama (Thompson), Best Director (Ivory), Best Film—Drama, Best Screenplay. **VHS, LV, 8mm** ★★★

Remember the Night Another Sturges-scripted winner in which assistant D.A. MacMurray falls for sophisticated shoplifter Stanwyck, who has stolen a diamond bracelet amidst the Christmas holiday bustle. On a promise that she will return for the trial MacMurray postpones the trial and offers her a ride home for the hol-

idays. Stanwyck is turned away by her mother and MacMurray brings her home for a real family Christmas, where love blooms. A sentimental, funny romance that boisters holiday cheer any time of year.
1940 94m/B Barbara Stanwyck, Fred MacMurray, Beulah Bondi, Elizabeth Patterson, Willard Robertson, Sterling Holloway; **D:** Mitchell Leisen; **W:** Preston Sturges, Ted Tetzlaff; **M:** Frederick Hollander. **VHS** ★★★

Repentance A popular, surreal satire of Soviet and Communist societies. A woman is arrested for repeatedly digging up a dead local despot, and put on trial. Wickedly funny and controversial; released under the auspices of glasnost. In Russian with English subtitles. *AKA:* Pokayaniye; Confession.
1987 (PG) 151m/C *RU* Avtandil Makharadze, Zeinab Botsvadze, Ia Ninidze, Edisher Giorgobiani, Ketevan Abuladze, Kakhi Kavsadze; **D:** Tengiz Abuladze. Cannes Film Festival '87: Grand Jury Prize. **VHS, Beta, LV** ★★★

Repo Man An inventive, perversely witty portrait of sick modern urbanity, following the adventures of a punk rocker taking a job as a car repossessor in a barren city. The landscape is filled with pointless violence, no-frills packaging, media hypnosis and aliens. Executive producer: none other than ex-Monkee Michael Nesmith.
1983 (R) 93m/C Emilio Estevez, Harry Dean Stanton, Sy Richardson, Tracey Walter, Olivia Barash, Fox Harris, Jennifer Balgobin, Vonetta McGee, Angelique Pettyjohn; **D:** Alex Cox; **W:** Alex Cox. **VHS, Beta, LV** ★★★1/2

The Report on the Party and the Guests A controversial, widely banned political allegory, considered a masterpiece from the Czech new wave. A picnic/lawn party deteriorates into brutality, fascist intolerance and persecution. Many Czech film makers, some banned at the time, appear. Based on a story by Ester Krumbachova, who also co-wrote the screenplay. In Czech with English subtitles.
1966 71m/B *CZ* Jiri Nemec, Evald Schorm, Ivan Vyskocil, Jan Klusak, Zdena Skvorecka, Pavel Bosek; **D:** Jan Nemec; **W:** Jan Nemec. **VHS, Beta** ★★★★

Report to the Commissioner A rough, energetic crime-in-the-streets cop thriller. A young detective accidentally kills an attractive woman who turns out to have been an undercover cop, then is dragged into the

bureaucratic cover-up. *AKA:* Operation Undercover.
1974 (R) 112m/C Michael Moriarty, Yaphet Kotto, Susan Blakely, Hector Elizondo, Richard Gere, Tony King, Michael McGuire, Stephen Elliott; *D:* Milton Katselas; *W:* Abby Mann; *M:* Elmer Bernstein. **VHS, Beta** ★★★

Repulsion Character study of a young French girl who is repulsed and attracted by sex. Left alone when her sister goes on vacation, her facade of stability begins to crack, with violent and bizarre results. Polanski's first film in English and his first publicly accepted full-length feature. Suspenseful, disturbing and potent.
1965 105m/B *GB* Catherine Deneuve, Yvonne Furneaux, Ian Hendry, John Fraser, Patrick Wymark, James Villiers; *D:* Roman Polanski; *W:* Roman Polanski, Gerard Brach. **VHS, Beta, LV** ★★★1/2

Requiem for a Heavyweight The original television version of the story about an American Indian heavyweight boxer, played by Palance, who risks blindness in order to help his manager pay off bookies. Highly acclaimed teleplay written for "Playhouse 90."
1956 90m/B Jack Palance, Keenan Wynn, Ed Wynn, Kim Hunter, Ned Glass; *D:* Ralph Nelson; *W:* Rod Serling. **VHS, Beta** ★★★

Requiem for Dominic A Communist-bloc country in the midst of revolution accuses a man of terrorist activities. Can his friend, exiled for years, help him discover the truth? Interesting and timely premise matched with outstanding ensemble acting make for a superior thriller. Amnesty International receives partial proceeds from all sales of this video. In German with English subtitles. *AKA:* Requiem fur Dominic.
1991 (R) 88m/C *GE* Felix Mitterer, Viktoria Schubert, August Schmolzer, Angelica Schutz; *D:* Robert Dornhelm. **VHS, LV** ★★★1/2

The Rescuers Bernard and Miss Bianca, two mice who are members of the Rescue Aid Society, attempt to rescue an orphan named Penny from the evil Madame Medusa, who's after the world's biggest diamond. They are aided by comic sidekick, Orville the albatross, and a group of lovable swamp creatures. Very charming in the best Disney tradition. Based on the stories of Margery Sharp. Followed by "The Rescuers Down Under."
1977 (G) 76m/C *D:* Wolfgang Reitherman, John Lounsbery; *M:* Artie Butler; *V:* Bob Newhart, Eva Gabor, Geraldine Page, Jim Jordan, Joe Flynn, Jeanette Nolan, Pat

Buttram. Nominations: Academy Awards '77: Best Song ("Someone's Waiting for You"). **VHS, LV** ★★★

Reservoir Dogs Ultraviolent tale of honor among thieves. Six professional criminals known by code names to protect their identities (Misters Pink, White, Orange, Blonde, Blue, and Brown) are assembled by Tierney to pull off a diamond heist. But two of the gang are killed in a police ambush. The survivors regroup in an empty warehouse and try to discover the informer in their midst. In probably the most stomach-churning scene (there is some competition here), a policeman is tortured just for the heck of it to the tune of the Stealers Wheel "Stuck in the Middle with You." Unrelenting; auspicious debut for Tarantino with strong ensemble cast anchored by Keitel as the very professional Mr. White.
1992 (R) 100m/C Harvey Keitel, Tim Roth, Michael Madsen, Steve Buscemi, Christopher Penn, Lawrence Tierney, Kirk Baltz, Quentin Tarantino; *D:* Quentin Tarantino; *W:* Quentin Tarantino. Independent Spirit Awards '93: Best Supporting Actor (Buscemi). **VHS, LV** ★★★1/2

Resurrection After a near-fatal car accident, a woman finds she has the power to heal others by touch. She denies that God is responsible, much to her Bible Belt community's dismay. Acclaimed and well-acted.
1980 (PG) 103m/C Ellen Burstyn, Sam Shepard, Roberts Blossom, Eva LeGallienne, Clifford David, Richard Farnsworth, Pamela Payton-Wright; *D:* Daniel Petrie; *W:* Lewis John Carlino; *M:* Maurice Jarre. National Board of Review Awards '80: 10 Best Films of the Year, Best Supporting Actress (LeGallienne); Nominations: Academy Awards '80: Best Actress (Burstyn), Best Supporting Actress (LeGallienne). **VHS, Beta** ★★★1/2

The Return of Martin Guerre In this medieval tale, a dissolute village husband disappears soon after his marriage. Years later, someone who appears to be Martin Guerre returns, allegedly from war, and appears much kinder and more educated. Starring in a love story of second chances, Depardieu does not disappoint, nor does the rest of the cast. Based on an actual court case. Remade in 1993 as "Sommersby." In French with English subtitles. *AKA:* Le Retour de Martin Guerre.
1983 111m/C *FR* Gerard Depardieu, Roger Planchon, Maurice Jacquemont, Barnard Pierre Donnadieu, Nathalie Baye; *D:* Daniel

Vigne; **W:** Daniel Vigne, Jean-Claude Carriere. Cesar Awards '83: Best Writing, Best Score; National Society of Film Critics Awards '83: Best Actor (Depardieu); Nominations: Academy Awards '83: Best Costume Design. **VHS, Beta, LV ★★★★**

The Return of the Borrowers Sweet sequel to 1993's "The Borrowers" finds the six-inch Clock family—father Pod (Holm), mother Homily (Wilton), and teenaged daughter Arrietty (Callard)—having to find a new home. Lots of misadventures ensue as they must avoid nasty humans, a giant bee, a storm, and other dangers on their way to safety. Based on the novels by Mary Norton.
1996 165m/C GB Ian Holm, Penelope Wilton, Rebecca Callard, Sian Phillips, Tony Haygarth, Judy Parfitt, Ben Chaplin, Paul Cross, Pamela Cundell, Ross McCall, Richard Vernon, Danny Newman; **D:** John Henderson; **W:** Richard Carpenter; **M:** Howard Goodall. **VHS ★★★**

Return of the Jedi Third film in George Lucas' popular space saga. Against seemingly fearsome odds, Luke Skywalker battles such worthies as Jabba the Hut and heavy-breathing Darth Vader to save his comrades and triumph over the evil Galactic Empire. Han and Leia reaffirm their love and team with C3PO, R2-D2, Chewbacca, Calrissian, and a bunch of furry Ewoks to aid in the annihilation of the Dark Side. The special effects are still spectacular, even the third time around. Sequel to "Star Wars" (1977) and "The Empire Strikes Back" (1980).
1983 (PG) 132m/C Mark Hamill, Carrie Fisher, Harrison Ford, Billy Dee Williams, David Prowse, Kenny Baker, Denis Lawson, Anthony Daniels, Peter Mayhew; **D:** Richard Marquand; **W:** George Lucas, Lawrence Kasdan; **M:** John Williams; **V:** Alec Guinness, Frank Oz, James Earl Jones. Academy Awards '83: Best Visual Effects; People's Choice Awards '84: Best Film; Nominations: Academy Awards '83: Best Art Direction/Set Decoration, Best Sound, Best Original Score. **VHS, Beta, LV ★★★1/2**

Return of the Secaucus 7 Centers around a weekend reunion of seven friends who were activists during the Vietnam War in the turbulent '60s. Now turning 30, they evaluate their present lives and progress. Writer and director Sayles plays Howie in this excellent example of what a low-budget film can and should be. A less trendy predecessor of "The Big Chill" (1983) which, perhaps, was a few years ahead of its time.
1980 110m/C Mark Arnott, Gordon Clapp, Maggie Cousineau-Arndt, David Strathairn; **D:** John Sayles; **W:** John Sayles; **M:** Mason Daring. Los Angeles Film Critics Association Awards '80: Best Screenplay. **VHS, Beta ★★★1/2**

Reuben, Reuben Brilliant, but drunken poet Conti turns himself around when he falls in love with earthy college girl McGillis in her film debut. The student's dog Reuben unwittingly alters Conti's progress, however, in the film's startling conclusion. Based on the writings of Peter DeVries.
1983 (R) 100m/C Tom Conti, Kelly McGillis, Roberts Blossom, E. Katherine Kerr, Cynthia Harris, Joel Fabiani, Kara Wilson, Lois Smith; **D:** Robert Ellis Miller; **W:** Julius J. Epstein; **M:** Billy Goldenberg. National Board of Review Awards '83: Best Actor (Conti); Writers Guild of America '83: Best Adapted Screenplay; Nominations: Academy Awards '83: Best Actor (Conti), Best Adapted Screenplay. **VHS, Beta ★★★**

Reunion Robards stars as a Jewish businessman, living in the U.S., who returns to his boyhood home of Stuttgart, Germany, some 50 years after his leaving in 1933. He hopes to find out what happened to a boyhood school chum—the son of an artistocractic (and Aryan) German family. Film uses extensive flashbacks to show the rise of anti-Semitism and how it affects the friendship of both youths. Thoughtful and well-acted though occasionally plodding drama based on Fred Uhlman's novel.
1988 (PG-13) 120m/C FR GE GB Jason Robards Jr., Christien Anholt, Sam West, Francoise Fabian, Maureen Kerwin, Barbara Jefford, Alexander Trauner; **D:** Jerry Schatzberg; **W:** Harold Pinter. **VHS, Beta, LV ★★★**

Reversal of Fortune True tale of wealthy socialite Claus von Bulow (Irons) accused of deliberately giving his wife Sunny (Close) a near-lethal overdose of insulin. Comatose Close narrates history of the couple's courtship and married life, a saga of unhappiness and substance abuse, while Silver (as lawyer Dershowitz) et al prepare von Bulow's defense. An unflattering picture of the idle rich that never spells out what really happened. Irons is excellent as the eccentric and creepy defendant and richly deserved his Best Actor Oscar. From the novel by Dershowitz.
1990 (R) 112m/C Jeremy Irons, Glenn Close, Ron Silver, Annabella Sciorra, Uta

Hagen, Fisher Stevens, Julie Hagerty, Jack Gilpin, Christine Baranski; **D:** Barbet Schroeder; **W:** Nicholas Kazan. Academy Awards '90: Best Actor (Irons); Golden Globe Awards '91: Best Actor—Drama (Irons); Los Angeles Film Critics Association Awards '90: Best Actor (Irons), Best Screenplay; National Society of Film Critics Awards '90: Best Actor (Irons); Nominations: Academy Awards '90: Best Adapted Screenplay, Best Director (Schroeder). **VHS, Beta, LV, 8mm ★★★1/2**

Rhapsody in Blue Standard Hollywood biography of the great composer features whitewashed and nonexistent characters to deal with the spottier aspects of Gershwin's life. Still, the music is the main attraction and it doesn't disappoint. ♩ Rhapsody in Blue; Concerto in F; The Cuban Overture; Fascinatin' Rhythm; The Man I Love; Yankee Doodle Blues; Somebody Loves Me; Swanee; Mine.
1945 139m/B Robert Alda, Joan Leslie, Alexis Smith, Charles Coburn, Julie Bishop, Albert Basserman, Morris Carnovsky, Rosemary DeCamp, Herbert Rudley, Charles Halton, Robert Shayne, Johnny Downs, Al Jolson; **D:** Irving Rapper; **W:** Howard Koch; **M:** George Gershwin, Max Steiner, Ira Gershwin. Nominations: Academy Awards '45: Best Sound, Best Original Score. **VHS, LV ★★★**

Rich Man, Poor Man Classic television miniseries covers 20, sometimes bitter, years in the lives of the two Jordache brothers. It's 1945 in quiet Port Phillip, New York, with embittered German baker Axel (Asner), his unfulfilled wife Mary (McGuire), and sons Tom (Nolte) and Rudy (Strauss). Tom is wild and irresponsible, Rudy is ambitious and college-bound, and Julie Prescott (Blakely), Rudy's girl, overshadows both their lives. Based on the novel by Irwin Shaw. The first series contained 12 episodes. A second series, of 21 episodes, primarily followed the tribulations of the next generation, although Strauss returned as Rudy.
1976 720m/C Peter Strauss, Nick Nolte, Susan Blakely, Ed Asner, Dorothy McGuire, Bill Bixby, Robert Reed, Ray Milland, Kim Darby, Talia Shire, Lawrence Pressman, Kay Lenz; **M:** Alex North. **VHS ★★★**

Richard III This landmark film version of the Shakespeare play features an acclaimed performance by Laurence Olivier, who also directs. The plot follows the life of the mentally and physically twisted Richard of Gloucester and his schemes for the throne of England.
1955 138m/C GB Laurence Olivier, Cedric Hardwicke, Ralph Richardson, John Gielgud, Stanley Baker, Michael Gough, Claire Bloom; **D:** Laurence Olivier. British Academy Awards '55: Best Actor (Olivier), Best Director (Olivier), Best Film; Golden Globe Awards '57: Best Foreign Film; Nominations: Academy Awards '56: Best Actor (Olivier). **VHS, Beta, LV ★★★1/2**

Richard III The Brits once again bring the Bard's most notorious monarch to the screen, this time in a new setting. McKellen stars in the title role of the deformed and ruthless English king, now in an imagined 1930s London of swanky Art Deco, Black Shirt thugs and modern media. Purists may resent major dialogue cuts, but famous speeches (such as the "winter of our discontent" opener) are amusingly staged in this modern take. Gorgeously polished visuals are perfect foil for the slimy, evil goings-on. Based on both Shakespeare's play and Richard Eyre's stage adaptation (in which McKellen also starred).
1995 (R) 105m/C GB Ian McKellen, Annette Bening, Jim Broadbent, Robert Downey Jr., Nigel Hawthorne, Kristin Scott Thomas, Maggie Smith, John Wood; **D:** Richard Loncraine; **W:** Ian McKellen, Richard Loncraine; **M:** Trevor Jones. Nominations: Academy Awards '95: Best Art Direction/Set Decoration, Best Costume Design; Golden Globe Awards '96: Best Actor—Drama (McKellen). **VHS, LV ★★★1/2**

Ride the High Country The cult classic western about two old friends who have had careers on both sides of the law. One, Joel McCrea, is entrusted with a shipment of gold, and the other, Randolph Scott, rides along with him to steal the precious cargo. Although barely promoted by MGM, became a critics' favorite. Grimacing and long in the tooth, McCrea and Scott enact a fitting tribute and farewell to the myth of the grand ol' West. Wonderfully photographed by Lucien Ballard. The laserdisc edition carries the film in wide-screen format along with the original movie trailer. **AKA:** Guns in the Afternoon.
1962 93m/C Randolph Scott, Joel McCrea, Mariette Hartley, Edgar Buchanan, R.G. Armstrong, Ronald Starr, John Anderson, James Drury, L.Q. Jones, Warren Oates; **D:** Sam Peckinpah; **M:** George Bassman. **VHS, Beta, LV ★★★★**

Riff Raff Unsparing black comedy about the British working class by director Loach. Ex-con Stevie comes to London from Scotland to look for work and escape his thieving past.

He finds a nonunion job on a construction site, takes up squatter's rights in an abandoned apartment, and finds a girlfriend in equally struggling singer Susie, who turns out to be a junkie. Loach's characters deal with their unenviable lot in life through rough humor and honest sentiment. Regional accents are so thick that the film is subtitled.

1992 96m/C *GB* Robert Carlyle, Emer McCourt, Jimmy Coleman, George Moss, Ricky Tomlinson, David Finch, Bill Jesse; *D:* Ken Loach; *W:* Bill Jesse; *M:* Stewart Copeland. **VHS, LV** ★★★

Rififi Perhaps the greatest of all "heist" movies. Four jewel thieves pull off a daring caper, only to fall prey to mutual distrust. The long scene of the actual theft, completely in silence, will have your heart in your throat. In French with English subtitles. *AKA:* Du Rififi Chez les Hommes.

1954 115m/B *FR* Jean Servais, Carl Mohner, Robert Manuel, Jules Dassin; *D:* Jules Dassin; *W:* Jules Dassin. Cannes Film Festival '55: Best Director (Dassin); National Board of Review Awards '56: 5 Best Foreign Films of the Year. **VHS, Beta** ★★★½

The Right Stuff A rambunctious adaptation of Tom Wolfe's nonfiction book about the beginnings of the U.S. space program, from Chuck Yeager's breaking of the sound barrier to the last of the Mercury missions. Featuring an all-star cast and an ambitious script. Rowdy, imaginative, and thrilling, though broadly painted and oddly uninvolving. Former astronaut John Glenn was running for president when this was out.

1983 (PG) 193m/C Ed Harris, Dennis Quaid, Sam Shepard, Scott Glenn, Fred Ward, Charles Frank, William Russ, Kathy Baker, Barbara Hershey, Levon Helm, David Clennon, Kim Stanley, Mary Jo Deschanel, Veronica Cartwright, Pamela Reed, Jeff Goldblum, Harry Shearer, Donald Moffat, Scott Paulin, Lance Henriksen, Scott Wilson, John P. Ryan, Royal Dano; *D:* Philip Kaufman; *W:* Philip Kaufman; *M:* Bill Conti, Caleb Deschanel. Academy Awards '83: Best Film Editing, Best Sound, Best Original Score; Nominations: Academy Awards '83: Best Art Direction/Set Decoration, Best Cinematography, Best Picture, Best Supporting Actor (Shepard). **VHS, Beta, LV** ★★★

Ring of Bright Water Well done story of a pet otter from Gavin Maxwell's autobiography. The film stars the couple that made the delightful "Born Free." Beautiful Scottish Highlands photography adds to this captivating and endearing tale of a civil servant who purchases an otter from a pet store and moves to the country.

1969 (G) 107m/C *GB* Bill Travers, Virginia McKenna, Peter Jeffrey, Archie Duncan; *D:* Jack Couffer. **VHS, Beta** ★★★

The Rink Chaplin plays a waiter who spends his lunch hour on roller skates. Silent with musical soundtrack added.

1916 20m/B Charlie Chaplin; *D:* Charlie Chaplin. **VHS, Beta** ★★★

Rio Bravo The sheriff of a Texas border town (Wayne) takes a brutal murderer into custody and faces a blockade of hired gunmen determined to keep his prisoner from being brought to justice. Long, but continually entertaining. Generally regarded as an American film classic, with an all-star cast, didn't impress the critics at the time. Sequel: "El Dorado." Semi-remake was called "Assault on Precinct 13."

1959 140m/C John Wayne, Dean Martin, Angie Dickinson, Ricky Nelson, Walter Brennan, Ward Bond, Claude Akins, Bob Steele, John Russell; *D:* Howard Hawks. **VHS, Beta** ★★★½

Rio Grande The last entry in Ford's cavalry trilogy following "Fort Apache" and "She Wore a Yellow Ribbon." A U.S. cavalry unit on the Mexican border conducts an unsuccessful campaign against marauding Indians. The commander (Wayne) faces an unhappy wife and is estranged from his son, a new recruit. Featuring an excellent Victor Young score and several songs by the Sons of the Pioneers.

1950 105m/B John Wayne, Maureen O'Hara, Ben Johnson, Claude Jarman Jr., Harry Carey Jr., Victor McLaglen, Chill Wills, J. Carrol Naish; *D:* John Ford. **VHS, LV** ★★★

Riot in Cell Block 11 A convict leads four thousand prisoners in an uprising to improve prison conditions. Based on producer/ex-con Walter Wanger's own experience. Powerful and still timely. Filmed at Folsom Prison.

1954 80m/B Neville Brand, Leo Gordon, Emile Meyer, Frank Faylen; *D:* Donald Siegel. **VHS, Beta** ★★★

Riptide Shearer is a carefree American married to stuffy English lord Marshall. He goes off to America on a business trip, she's bored and goes to a costume party (everyone dresses as insects!) where she meets old flame Montgomery. He gets drunk, follows her home in an effort to rekindle their passion, and winds up in the hospital after a drunken fall. The returning Marshall is appalled by the scandalous press and instigates divorce proceedings. Eventually, they come to their senses and decide they do love each other. Quality production with an entertaining cast.

1934 90m/B Norma Shearer, Herbert Marshall, Robert Montgomery, Richard "Skeets" Gallagher, Ralph Forbes, Lilyan Tashman; **D:** Edmund Goulding; **W:** Edmund Goulding. **VHS** ★★★

Rising Son A family man who loves his job faces trauma when his factory closes at the same time his son informs him he's quitting medical school. Solid family drama and parable of economic hard times of the early '80s, sustained by top-drawer performances by Dennehy, Damon, and Laurie. Well directed by Coles. Made for cable.

1990 92m/C Brian Dennehy, Matt Damon, Piper Laurie, Graham Beckel, Ving Rhames, Jane Adams, Richard Jenkins, Emily Longstreth; **D:** John David Coles; **W:** Bill Phillips. **VHS, Beta** ★★★

Risky Business With his parents out of town and awaiting word from the college boards, a teenager becomes involved in unexpected ways with a quick-thinking prostitute, her pimp, and assorted others. Cruise is likeable, especially when dancing in his underwear. Funny, well-paced, stylish prototypical '80s teen flick reintroduced Ray-Bans as the sunglasses for the wannabe hip. What a party!

1983 (R) 99m/C Tom Cruise, Rebecca DeMornay, Curtis Armstrong, Bronson Pinchot, Joe Pantoliano, Kevin Anderson, Richard Masur, Raphael Sbarge, Nicholas Pryor, Janet Carroll; **D:** Paul Brickman; **W:** Paul Brickman; **M:** Tangerine Dream, Reynaldo Villalobos. **VHS, Beta, LV, 8mm** ★★★

The Ritz Weston tries to get away from his gangster brother-in-law by hiding out in a gay bathhouse in New York. Moreno plays a talentless singer Googie Gomez, who performs in the bathhouse while waiting for her big break. Moreno is great reprising her Tony-winning stage role, and Lester's direction is spiffy. Written by Terence McNally from his play.

1976 (R) 91m/C Rita Moreno, Jack Weston, Jerry Stiller, Kaye Ballard, Treat Williams, F. Murray Abraham; **D:** Richard Lester. **VHS, Beta, LV** ★★★

The River A massively lauded late film by Renoir about three British girls growing up in Bengal, India, all developing crushes on a one-legged American vet. Lyrical and heartwarming, with hailed cinematography by Claude Renoir. Rumer Godden wrote the novel, and co-scripted the screenplay with director Renoir. Satyajit Ray, one of India's greatest filmmakers, assisted Renoir.

1951 99m/C FR Patricia Walters, Adrienne Corri, Nora Swinburne, Radha, Arthur Shields, Thomas E. Breen, Esmond Knight; **D:** Jean Renoir; **W:** Jean Renoir. National Board of Review Awards '51: 5 Best Foreign Films of the Year. **VHS, Beta, LV** ★★★★

A River Runs Through It Contemplative exploration of family ties and coming of age with impact falling just short of the novel's; another well-crafted American tale directed by Redford. Set in Montana during the early part of the century, a Presbyterian minister teaches his two sons, one troubled and one on his way to success, about life and religion via fly-fishing. Based on the novel by Norman Maclean. The laserdisc version includes commentary by Redford.

1992 (PG) 123m/C Craig Sheffer, Brad Pitt, Tom Skerritt, Brenda Blethyn, Emily Lloyd, Edie McClurg, Stephen Shellan, Susan Taylor, Philippe Rousselot; **D:** Robert Redford; **W:** Richard Friedenberg; **M:** Mark Isham. Academy Awards '92: Best Cinematography; Nominations: Academy Awards '92: Best Adapted Screenplay, Best Original Score. **VHS, LV, 8mm** ★★★1/2

River's Edge Drug-addled high school student strangles his girlfriend and casually displays the corpse to his apathetic group of friends, who leave the murder unreported for days. Harrowing and gripping; based on a true story. Aging biker Hopper is splendid.

1987 (R) 99m/C Keanu Reeves, Crispin Glover, Daniel Roebuck, Joshua Miller, Dennis Hopper, Ione Skye, Roxana Zal, Tom Bower, Constance Forslund, Leo Rossi, Jim Metzler; **D:** Tim Hunter; **W:** Neal Jimenez; **M:** Jurgen Knieper. Independent Spirit Awards '88: Best Film, Best Screenplay; Sundance Film Festival '87: Special Jury Prize. **VHS, Beta, LV, 8mm** ★★★

The Road to Bali Sixth Bob-n-Bing road show, the only one in color, is a keeper. The boys are competing for the love of—that's right—Lamour. She must be some gal, cuz they chase her all the way to Bali, where they meet cannibals and other perils, including the actual Humphrey Bogart. Jones's debut, in a bit role. ♫ Moonflowers;

Chicago Style; Hoots Mon; To See You; The Merry-Go-Runaround; Chorale for Brass, Piano, and Bongo (instrumental).
1953 90m/C Bob Hope, Bing Crosby, Dorothy Lamour, Murvyn Vye, Ralph Moody, Jane Russell, Jerry Lewis, Dean Martin, Carolyn Jones; **D:** Hal Walker. **VHS, Beta ★★★**

The Road to Galveston Texas widow Jordan Roosevelt (Tyson) needs to pay her mortgage, so she turns her home into a residence for three Alzheimer patients. When her financial problems only worsen, Jordan decides to fulfill her lifetime goal and takes everyone on a trip to Galveston to see the ocean. Sentimental, fact-based TV movie cuts the saccharine through compelling performances.
1996 (PG-13) 93m/C Cicely Tyson, Piper Laurie, Tess Harper, Salle Ellis, Stephen Root, Starletta DuPois, James McDaniel, Penny Johnson, Clarence Williams, III; **D:** Michael Toshiyuki Uno; **W:** Tony Lee; **M:** Stanley Clarke. **VHS, Beta ★★★**

The Road to Morocco The third in the road movie series finds Hope and Crosby in Morocco, stranded and broke. To get some money, Crosby sells Hope into slavery to be the princess's (Lamour) personal plaything. Feeling guilty, Crosby returns to the palace to rescue Hope, only to find that he and the princess are getting married because the royal astrologer said it was in the stars. Crosby then tries to woo Lamour and, when the astrologer discovers the stars were mistaken, those two decide to marry. Quinn, however, also wants her and hilarious scenes ensue when the boys rescue Lamour from him. One of the funniest in the series. Watch for the camel at the end. ♪ Constantly; Moonlight Becomes You; Ain't Got a Dime to My Name; Road to Morocco.
1942 83m/C Bing Crosby, Bob Hope, Dorothy Lamour, Anthony Quinn, Dona Drake, Vladimir Sokoloff, Yvonne De Carlo; **D:** David Butler. Nominations: Academy Awards '42: Best Original Screenplay, Best Sound. **VHS, LV ★★★1/2**

The Road to Rio The wisecracking duo travel to Rio de Janeiro to prevent Spanish beauty Lamour (there she is again) from going through with an arranged marriage. Top-notch entry; fifth in the "Road" series. ♪ But Beautiful; You Don't Have To Know the Language; For What?; Experience; Apalachicola, Florida; Cavaquinho; Brazil.

1947 100m/B Bing Crosby, Bob Hope, Dorothy Lamour, Gale Sondergaard, Frank Faylen, The Andrews Sisters; **D:** Norman Z. McLeod; **W:** Jack Rose. Nominations: Academy Awards '47: Best Original Score. **VHS, Beta ★★★★**

The Road to Utopia Fourth of the "Road" films, wherein the boys wind up in Alaska posing as two famous escaped killers in order to locate a secret gold mine. One of the series' funniest and most spontaneous entries, abetted by Benchley's dry, upper-crust comments. ♪ Put It There, Pal; Welcome to My Dreams; Would You?; Personality; Sunday, Monday, or Always?; Goodtime Charlie; It's Anybody's Spring.
1946 90m/B Bing Crosby, Bob Hope, Dorothy Lamour, Jack LaRue, Robert Benchley, Douglass Dumbrille, Hillary Brooke; **D:** Hal Walker; **W:** Norman Panama. Nominations: Academy Awards '46: Best Original Screenplay. **VHS, Beta, LV ★★★**

The Road to Zanzibar After selling a fake diamond mine to a criminal, Crosby and Hope flee to Zanzibar, where they meet up with Lamour and Merkel. The guys put up the money for a safari, supposedly to look for Lamour's brother, but they soon discover that they too have been tricked. Deciding to head back to Zanzibar, Crosby and Hope find themselves surrounded by hungry cannibals. Will they survive, or will they be someone's dinner? Not as funny as the other road movies, but amusing nonetheless. ♪ It's Always You; You're Dangerous; On the Road to Zanzibar; You Lucky People You; Birds of a Feather; African Etude.
1941 92m/C Bing Crosby, Bob Hope, Dorothy Lamour, Una Merkel, Eric Blore, Iris Adrian, Lionel Royce; **D:** Victor Schertzinger. **VHS, LV ★★★**

The Road Warrior The first sequel to "Mad Max" takes place after nuclear war has destroyed Australia. Max helps a colony of oil-drilling survivors defend themselves from the roving murderous outback gangs and escape to the coast. The climactic chase scene is among the most exciting ever filmed; this film virtually created the "action-adventure" picture of the 1980s.
1982 (R) 95m/C Mel Gibson, Bruce Spence, Emil Minty, Vernon Wells; **D:** George Miller, Dean Semler; **W:** George Miller. Los Angeles Film Critics Association Awards '82: Best Foreign Film. **VHS, Beta, LV ★★★1/2**

The Roaring Twenties Three WWI buddies find their lives intersecting unexpectedly in Prohibition-era New York. Cagney becomes a bootlegger and vies with Bogart for status as crime boss. Lynn is the attorney working to prosecute them. Greatest of all gangster flicks. Cheesy script delivered with zest by top pros.
1939 106m/B James Cagney, Humphrey Bogart, Jeffrey Lynn, Priscilla Lane, Gladys George, Frank McHugh; **D:** Raoul Walsh. National Board of Review Awards '39: 10 Best Films of the Year. **VHS, Beta, LV** ★★★1/2

Rob Roy Kilt-raising though overlong tale of legendary Scot Robert Roy MacGregor mixes love and honor with bloodlust and revenge. Neeson's rugged clan leader fends off a band of dastardly nobles led by Cunningham (Roth), a foppish twit with an evil bent. Misty highland scenery and intense romantic interplay between Neeson and Lange as the spirited Mary MacGregor lend a passionate twist to an otherwise earthy, robust adventure of lore capped by one of the best sword fights in years. Both Neeson and Lange provide a gutsy substance to their characters: Neeson's Celtic hero is sexy and steadfast (and generally sports an Irish accent), while Lange inhabits a soulful and tenacious Mary. Roth's delightfully hammy performance as MacGregor's loathsome, bewigged nemesis delivers zip amid the high-minded speeches, plot lulls, and separated body parts. Visually stunning, with on-location shooting in the Scottish Highlands. More ambience is provided by Buswell's evocative score.
1995 (R) 144m/C Liam Neeson, Jessica Lange, Tim Roth, John Hurt, Eric Stoltz, Andrew Keir, Brian Cox, Brian McCardie, Gilbert Martin, Vicki Masson, David Hayman; **D:** Michael Caton-Jones; **W:** Alan Sharp, Karl Walter Lindenlaub. Nominations: Academy Awards '95: Best Supporting Actor (Roth); British Academy Awards '95: Best Supporting Actor (Roth); Golden Globe Awards '96: Best Supporting Actor (Roth). **VHS, LV** ★★★

Roberta A football player inherits his aunt's Parisian dress shop and finds himself at odds with an incognito Russian princess. Dumb plot aside, this is one of the best Astaire-Rogers efforts. A later remake was titled "Lovely to Look At." ♫ Let's Begin; Yesterdays; Smoke Gets in Your Eyes; I'll Be Hard to Handle; I Won't Dance; Lovely to Look At; Back Home Again in Indiana; The Touch of Your Hand; You're Devasting.

1935 85m/B Fred Astaire, Ginger Rogers, Irene Dunne, Lucille Ball, Randolph Scott; **D:** William A. Seiter; **M:** Max Steiner. Nominations: Academy Awards '35: Best Song ("Roberta"). **VHS, Beta** ★★★

Robin Hood Extravagant production casts Fairbanks as eponymous gymnastic swashbuckler who departs for Crusades as Earl of Huntington and returns as the hooded one to save King Richard's throne from the sinister Sheriff of Nottingham. Best ever silent swashbuckling.
1922 110m/B Douglas Fairbanks Sr., Wallace Beery, Sam DeGrasse, Enid Bennett, Paul Dickey, William E. Lowery, Roy Coulson, Bill Bennett, Merrill McCormick, Wilson Benge, Willard Louis, Alan Hale, Maine Geary, Lloyd Talman; **D:** Allan Dwan. **VHS, Beta** ★★★★

RoboCop A nearly dead Detroit cop is used as the brain for a crime-fighting robot in this bleak vision of the future. Humor, satire, action, and violence keep this moving in spite of its underlying sadness. Slick animation techniques from Phil Tippet. Verhoeven's first American film.
1987 (R) 103m/C Peter Weller, Nancy Allen, Ronny Cox, Kurtwood Smith, Ray Wise, Miguel Ferrer, Dan O'Herlihy, Robert DoQui, Felton Perry, Paul McCrane, Del Zamora; **D:** Paul Verhoeven; **W:** Michael Miner, Edward Neumeier; **M:** Basil Poledouris. Nominations: Academy Awards '87: Best Film Editing, Best Sound. **VHS, Beta, LV** ★★★

Rocco and His Brothers A modern classic from top director Visconti, about four brothers who move with their mother from the Italian countryside to Milan. Very long, sometimes ponderous, but engrossing, complex drama. Available shortened to 90 minutes, but the unedited version is much more rewarding. In Italian with English subtitles. **AKA:** Rocco et Ses Freres.
1960 175m/B *IT* Alain Delon, Renato Salvatori, Annie Girardot, Katina Paxinou, Claudia Cardinale, Roger Hanin; **D:** Luchino Visconti; **M:** Nino Rota. **VHS, LV** ★★★1/2

The Rock Cage follows up his Oscar win with a big-budget action hero turn, with great results. In an attempt to get benefits for the families of soldiers killed in various covert operations, a decorated general (Harris) and his commando squad occupy Alcatraz island, taking hostages and threatening to unleash a deadly gas bomb on San Francisco. Biochemical weapons expert Stanley Goodspeed (Cage) is called in to disarm the rockets, aided by John Patrick Mason (Connery), the only man to successfully escape from the island prison. Like most Simpson/Bruckheimer productions, credibility is stretched to the limit, but the action scenes and crisp pacing don't leave much time for pondering details, anyway. Connery, cool as ever, hasn't lost a step. Cage effectively plays up his character's inexperience at being the hero. Coproducer Don Simpson died of a drug overdose during production. **1996 (R) 136m/C** Nicolas Cage, Sean Connery, Ed Harris, Michael Biehn, William Forsythe, David Morse, John Spencer, John C. McGinley, Tony Todd, Bokeem Woodbine, Danny Nucci, Claire Forlani, Vanessa Marcil, Gregory Sporleder; **D:** Michael Bay; **W:** Jonathan Hensleigh; **M:** Nick Glennie-Smith. **VHS, LV ★★★**

Rock 'n' Roll High School The music of the Ramones highlights this non-stop high-energy cult classic about a high school out to thwart the principal at every turn. If it had been made in 1957, it would have been the ultimate rock 'n' roll teen movie. As it is, its 1970s milieu works against it, but the performances are perfect for the material and the Ramones are great. Songs include "Teenage Lobotomy," "Blitzkrieg Bop," "I Wanna Be Sedated" and the title track, among others. Followed less successfully by "Rock 'n' Roll High School Forever." **1979 (PG) 94m/C** The Ramones, P.J. Soles, Vincent Van Patten, Clint Howard, Dey Young, Mary Woronov, Alix Elias, Dick Miller, Paul Bartel; **D:** Allan Arkush, Dean Cundey. **VHS, Beta ★★★**

Rocky Box office smash about a young man from the slums of Philadelphia who dreams of becoming a boxing champion. Stallone plays Rocky, the underdog hoping to win fame and self-respect. Rags-to-riches story seems to parallel Stallone's life; he had been previously virtually unknown before this movie. Intense portrayal of the American Dream; loses strength in the subsequent (and numerous) sequels. **1976 (PG) 125m/C** Sylvester Stallone, Talia Shire, Burgess Meredith, Burt Young, Carl Weathers; **D:** John G. Avildsen; **W:** Sylvester Stallone; **M:** Bill Conti. Academy Awards '76: Best Director (Avildsen), Best Film Editing, Best Picture; Directors Guild of America Awards '76: Best Director (Avildsen); Golden Globe Awards '77: Best Film—Drama; Los Angeles Film Critics Association Awards '76: Best Film; National Board of Review Awards '76: 10 Best Films of the Year, Best Supporting

Actress (Shire); Nominations: Academy Awards '76: Best Actor (Stallone), Best Actress (Shire), Best Original Screenplay, Best Song ("Gonna Fly Now"), Best Sound, Best Supporting Actor (Meredith, Young). **VHS, Beta, LV, 8mm ★★★¹/2**

The Rocky Horror Picture Show When a young couple take refuge in a haunted castle, they find themselves the unwilling pawns in a warped scientist's experiment. Cult camp classic has been a midnight movie favorite for years and has developed an entire subculture built around audience participation. The tape includes a seven-minute short detailing the story behind the movie's popularity. May not be as much fun watching it on the little screen unless you bring the rice and squirt guns. ♪ The Time Warp; Science Fiction Double Feature; Wedding Song; Sweet Transvestite; The Sword of Damocles; Charles Atlas Song; Whatever Happened to Saturday Night; Touch-a Touch-a Touch-a Touch Me; Eddie's Teddy. **1975 (R) 105m/C** Tim Curry, Susan Sarandon, Barry Bostwick, Meat Loaf, Little Nell, Richard O'Brien; **D:** Jim Sharman; **M:** John Barry. **VHS, LV ★★★**

Roe vs. Wade Hunter is excellent as the single woman from Texas who successfully challenged the nation's prohibitive abortion laws in a landmark Supreme Court case. Television drama based on the actual 1973 case of Norma McCorvey. **1989 92m/C** Holly Hunter, Amy Madigan, Terry O'Quinn, Stephen Tobolowsky, Dion Anderson, Kathy Bates, James Gammon, Chris Mulkey; **D:** Gregory Hoblit. **VHS, Beta, LV ★★★**

Roger & Me Hilarious, controversial and atypical semi-documentary details Moore's protracted efforts to meet General Motors president Roger Smith and confront him with the poverty and despair afflicting Flint, Michigan, after GM closed its plants there. Includes some emotionally grabbing scenes: a Flint family is evicted just before Christmas; a woman makes a living by selling rabbits for food or pets; and a then soon-to-be Miss America addresses the socioeconomic impact of GM's decision. One of the highest-grossing non-fiction films ever released, and Moore's first. **1989 (R) 91m/C** Michael Moore, Bob Eubanks, Pat Boone, Anita Bryant; **D:** Michael Moore; **W:** Michael Moore. **VHS, Beta, LV ★★★¹/2**

Roman Holiday Hepburn's first starring role is a charmer as a princess bored with her official visit to Rome who slips away and plays at being an "average Jane." A reporter discovers her little charade and decides to cash in with an exclusive story. Before they know it, love calls. Blacklisted screenwriter Trumbo was "fronted" by Ian McLellan Hunter, who accepted screen credit and the Best Story Oscar in Trumbo's stead. The Academy voted to posthumously award Trumbo his own Oscar in 1993.

1953 118m/B Audrey Hepburn, Gregory Peck, Eddie Albert, Tullio Carminati; *D:* William Wyler; *W:* Dalton Trumbo. Academy Awards '53: Best Actress (Hepburn), Best Costume Design (B & W), Best Story; British Academy Awards '53: Best Actress (Hepburn); Golden Globe Awards '54: Best Actress—Drama (Hepburn); New York Film Critics Awards '53: Best Actress (Hepburn); Nominations: Academy Awards '53: Best Art Direction/Set Decoration (B & W), Best Black and White Cinematography, Best Director (Wyler), Best Film Editing, Best Picture, Best Screenplay, Best Supporting Actor (Albert). **VHS, Beta, LV, 8mm** ★★★1/2

Roman Spring of Mrs. Stone An aging actress determines to revive her career in Rome but finds romance with a gigolo instead in this adaptation of Tennessee Williams's novella. Leigh and Beatty are compelling, but Lenya nearly steals the show as Leigh's distinctly unappealing confidant. *AKA:* The Widow and the Gigolo.

1961 104m/C Warren Beatty, Vivien Leigh, Lotte Lenya, Bessie Love, Jill St. John; *D:* Jose Quintero; *W:* Gavin Lambert. Nominations: Academy Awards '61: Best Supporting Actress (Lenya). **VHS, Beta** ★★★

Romance on the High Seas A woman is scheduled to take a cruise vacation but skips the boat when she believes her husband is cheating on her. Her husband believes she is taking the cruise to cheat on him and hires a private detective to follow her. Pleasant comedy features the film debut of Doris Day. ♪ It's Magic; It's You or No One; The Tourist Trade; Put 'Em in a Box, Tie 'Em with a Ribbon, and Throw 'Em in the Deep Blue Sea; Two Lovers Met in the Night; Run, Run, Run; I'm in Love; Cuban Rhapsody.

1948 99m/C Jack Carson, Janis Paige, Don DeFore, Doris Day, Oscar Levant, S.Z. Sakall, Eric Blore, Franklin Pangborn, Leslie Brooks, William "Billy" Bakewell; *D:* Michael Curtiz; *W:* Julius J. Epstein. Nominations: Academy Awards '48: Best Song ("It's Magic"), Best Original Score. **VHS, LV** ★★★

Romancing the Stone Uptight romance novelist lives out her fantasies after she receives a mysterious map from her murdered brother-in-law and her sister is kidnapped in South America—the ransom being the map. Out to rescue her sister, she's helped and hindered by an American soldier of fortune (Douglas) whose main concern is himself and the hidden treasure described in the map. Great chemistry between the stars and loads of clever dialogue in this appealing adventure comedy. First outing with Turner, Douglas, and DeVito. Followed by "The Jewel of the Nile."

1984 (PG) 106m/C Michael Douglas, Kathleen Turner, Danny DeVito, Zack Norman, Alfonso Arau, Ron Silver; *D:* Robert Zemeckis; *M:* Alan Silvestri, Dean Cundey. Golden Globe Awards '85: Best Actress—Musical/Comedy (Turner), Best Film—Musical/Comedy; Los Angeles Film Critics Association Awards '84: Best Actress (Turner); Nominations: Academy Awards '84: Best Film Editing. **VHS, Beta, LV** ★★★1/2

Romeo and Juliet One of MGM producer Irving Thalberg's pet projects (and starring Thalberg's wife, Norma Shearer), this Shakespeare classic was given the spare-no-expense MGM treatment. Physically too old to portray teen-age lovers, both Howard and Shearer let their acting ability supply all necessary illusions. Also notable is Barrymore's over-the-top portrayal of Mercutio.

1936 126m/B Leslie Howard, Norma Shearer, John Barrymore, Basil Rathbone, Edna May Oliver; *D:* George Cukor. Nominations: Academy Awards '36: Best Actress (Shearer), Best Interior Decoration, Best Picture, Best Supporting Actor (Rathbone). **VHS, LV** ★★★★

Romeo and Juliet Young couple share love despite prohibitive conflict between their families in this adaptation of Shakespeare's classic play. Director Zeffirelli succeeds in casting relative novices Whiting and Hussey in the leads, but is somewhat less proficient in lending air of free-wheeling sixties appeal to entire enterprise. Kudos, however, to cinematographer Pasquale de Santis and composer Nino Rota. Also available in a 45-minute edited version.

1968 (PG) 138m/C *GB IT* Olivia Hussey, Leonard Whiting, Michael York, Milo O'Shea; *D:* Franco Zeffirelli; *M:* Nino Rota. Academy Awards '68: Best

Cinematography, Best Costume Design; Golden Globe Awards '69: Best Foreign Film; National Board of Review Awards '68: 10 Best Films of the Year, Best Director (Zeffirelli); Nominations: Academy Awards '68: Best Director (Zeffirelli), Best Picture. **VHS, Beta, LV ★★★1/2**

Room at the Top Ambitious factory man forsakes true love and marries boss's daughter instead in this grim drama set in industrial northern England. Cast excels, with Harvey and Sears as the worker and his wife. Signoret is also quite compelling as the abandoned woman. Adapted from John Braine's novel and followed by "Life at the Top" and "Man at the Top."
1959 118m/B *GB* Laurence Harvey, Simone Signoret, Heather Sears, Hermione Baddeley, Anthony Elgar, Donald Wolfit; *D:* Jack Clayton. Academy Awards '59: Best Actress (Signoret), Best Adapted Screenplay; British Academy Awards '59: Best Actress (Signoret), Best Film; Cannes Film Festival '59: Best Actress (Signoret); Nominations: Academy Awards '59: Best Actor (Harvey), Best Director (Clayton), Best Picture, Best Supporting Actress (Baddeley). **VHS ★★★1/2**

A Room with a View Engaging adaptation of E.M. Forster's novel of requited love. Carter stars as the feisty British idealist who rejects dashing Sands for supercilious Day- Lewis, then repents and finds (presumably) eternal passion. A multi-Oscar nominee, with great music (courtesy of Puccini), great scenery (courtesy of Florence), and great performances (courtesy of practically everybody, but supporters Smith, Dench, Callow, and Elliott must be particularly distinguished). Truly romantic, and there's much humor too.
1986 117m/C *GB* Helena Bonham Carter, Julian Sands, Denholm Elliott, Maggie Smith, Judi Dench, Simon Callow, Daniel Day-Lewis, Rupert Graves, Rosemary Leach, Tony Pierce-Roberts; *D:* James Ivory; *W:* Ruth Prawer Jhabvala. Academy Awards '86: Best Adapted Screenplay, Best Art Direction/Set Decoration, Best Costume Design; British Academy Awards '86: Best Actress (Smith), Best Film, Best Supporting Actress (Dench); Independent Spirit Awards '87: Best Foreign Film; National Board of Review Awards '86: 10 Best Films of the Year, Best Supporting Actor (Day-Lewis); Writers Guild of America '86: Best Adapted Screenplay; Nominations: Academy Awards '86: Best Cinematography, Best Director (Ivory), Best Picture, Best Supporting Actor (Elliott), Best Supporting Actress (Smith). **VHS, Beta, LV ★★★★**

Roots The complete version of Alex Haley's made-for-television saga following a black man's search for his heritage, revealing an epic panorama of America's past. Available on six tapes, complete at 570 minutes.
1977 90m/C Ed Asner, Lloyd Bridges, LeVar Burton, Chuck Connors, Lynda Day George, Lorne Greene, Burl Ives, O.J. Simpson, Cicely Tyson, Ben Vereen, Sandy Duncan; *D:* David Greene; *M:* Quincy Jones. **VHS, Beta ★★★★**

Roots: The Next Generation Sequel to the landmark television miniseries continuing the story of author Alex Haley's ancestors from the Reconstruction era of the 1880s to 1967, culminating with Haley's visit to West Africa where he is told the story of Kunta Kinte. On seven tapes.
1979 685m/C Georg Stanford Brown, Lynne Moody, Henry Fonda, Richard Thomas, Marc Singer, Olivia de Havilland, Paul Koslo, Beah Richards, Stan Shaw, Harry (Henry) Morgan, Irene Cara, Dorian Harewood, Ruby Dee, Paul Winfield, James Earl Jones, Debbie Allen; *Cameos:* Al Freeman Jr., Marlon Brando. **VHS ★★★**

Rope In New York City, two gay college students murder a friend for kicks and store the body in a living room trunk. They further insult the dead by using the trunk as the buffet table and inviting his parents to the dinner party in his honor. Very dark humor is the theme in Hitchcock's first color film, which he innovatively shot in uncut ten-minute takes, with the illusion of a continuous scene maintained with tricky camera work. Based on the Patrick Hamilton play and on the Leopold-Loeb murder case.
1948 (PG) 81m/C James Stewart, John Dall, Farley Granger, Cedric Hardwicke, Constance Collier; *D:* Alfred Hitchcock; *W:* Arthur Laurents. **VHS, Beta, LV ★★★1/2**

Rosalie Goes Shopping Satire about American consumerism hiding behind slapstick comedy, and it works, most of the time. Misplaced Bavarian (Sagebrecht) moves to Arkansas and begins spending wildly and acquiring "things." Twisty plot carried confidently by confident wackiness from Sagebrecht and supporters.
1989 (PG-13) 94m/C *GE* Marianne Sagebrecht, Brad Davis, Judge Reinhold, Willie Harlander, Alex Winter, Erika Blumberger, Patricia Zehentmayr; *D:* Percy Adlon; *W:* Eleonore Adlon, Percy Adlon; *M:* Bob Telson. **VHS, LV ★★★**

The Rose Modeled after the life of Janis Joplin, Midler plays a young, talented and self-destructive blues/

rock singer. Professional triumphs don't stop her lonely restlessness and confused love affairs. The best exhibition of the rock and roll world outside of documentaries. Electrifying film debut for Midler features an incredible collection of songs. ♪ Fire Down Below; I've Written A Letter to Daddy; Let Me Call You Sweetheart; The Rose; Stay With Me; Camellia; Sold My Soul To Rock 'n' Roll; Keep On Rockin'; When A Man Loves a Woman.

1979 (R) 134m/C Bette Midler, Alan Bates, Frederic Forrest, Harry Dean Stanton, David Keith; **D:** Mark Rydell, Vilmos Zsigmond. Golden Globe Awards '80: Best Actress—Musical/Comedy (Midler), Best Song ("The Rose"); Nominations: Academy Awards '79: Best Actress (Midler), Best Film Editing, Best Sound, Best Supporting Actor (Forrest). **VHS, Beta, LV ★★★**

Rose Marie An opera star falls in love with the mountie who captured her escaped convict brother. Hollywood legend has it that when a British singer was presented with the first line in "Indian Love Song," which is "When I'm calling you-oo-oo-oo-oo-oo-oo," the confused performer sang, "When I'm calling you, double oh, double oh, double oh . . ." Maybe true, maybe not, but funny anyway. Classic MacDonald-Eddy operetta. Remade in 1954. ♪ Indian Love Call; Pardon Me, Madame; The Mounties; Rose Marie; Totem Tom Tom; Just for You; Tex Yeux; St. Louis Blues; Dinah. **AKA:** Indian Love Call.

1936 112m/B Jeanette MacDonald, Nelson Eddy, James Stewart, Allan Jones, David Niven, Reginald Owen; **D:** Woodbridge S. Van Dyke; **M:** Rudolf Friml. **VHS, Beta, LV ★★★**

The Rose Tattoo Magnani, in her U.S. screen debut, is just right as a Southern widow who cherishes her husband's memory, but falls for virile trucker Lancaster. Williams wrote this play and screenplay specifically for Magnani, who was never as successful again. Interesting character studies, although Lancaster doesn't seem right as an Italian longshoreman.

1955 117m/B Anna Magnani, Burt Lancaster, Marisa Pavan, Ben Cooper, Virginia Grey, Jo Van Fleet; **D:** Daniel Mann; **W:** Tennessee Williams, Hal Kanter; **M:** Alex North. Academy Awards '55: Best Actress (Magnani), Best Art Direction/Set Decoration (B & W), Best Black and White Cinematography; British Academy Awards '56: Best Actress (Magnani); Golden Globe Awards '56: Best Actress—Drama (Magnani), Best Supporting Actress (Pavan); Nominations: Academy Awards

'55: Best Costume Design (B & W), Best Film Editing, Best Picture, Best Supporting Actress (Pavan). **VHS, Beta, LV ★★★1/2**

Rosemary's Baby A young woman, innocent and religious, and her husband, ambitious and agnostic, move into a new apartment. Soon the woman is pregnant, but she begins to realize that she has fallen into a coven of witches and warlocks, and that they claim the child as the antichrist. Gripping and powerful, subtle yet utterly horrifying, with luminous performances by all. Polanski's first American film; from Levin's best-seller.

1968 (R) 134m/C Mia Farrow, John Cassavetes, Ruth Gordon, Maurice Evans, Patsy Kelly, Elisha Cook Jr., Charles Grodin, Sidney Blackmer, William Castle, Ralph Bellamy; **D:** Roman Polanski; **W:** Roman Polanski; **M:** Krzysztof Komeda, William A. Fraker. Academy Awards '68: Best Supporting Actress (Gordon); Golden Globe Awards '69: Best Supporting Actress (Gordon); Nominations: Academy Awards '68: Best Adapted Screenplay. **VHS, Beta, LV ★★★★**

Rosencrantz & Guildenstern Are Dead Playwright Stoppard adapted his own absurdist play to film—which at first look makes as much sense as a "Swan Lake" ballet on radio. Patience is rewarded for those who stick with it. Two tragicomic minor characters in "Hamlet" squabble rhetorically and misperceive Shakespeare's plot tightening fatally around them. Uprooted from the stage environment, it's arcane but hilarious if you're paying attention. Roth and Oldman are superb as the doomed duo.

1990 (PG) 118m/C Gary Oldman, Tim Roth, Richard Dreyfuss, Iain Glen; **D:** Tom Stoppard; **W:** Tom Stoppard. Venice Film Festival '91: Best Picture. **VHS, Beta, LV ★★★**

Round Midnight An aging, alcoholic black American jazz saxophonist comes to Paris in the late 1950s seeking an escape from his self-destructive existence. A devoted young French fan spurs him to one last burst of creative brilliance. A moody, heartfelt homage to such expatriate bebop musicians as Bud Powell and Lester Young. In English and French with English subtitles. Available in a Spanish-subtitled version.

1986 (R) 132m/C FR Dexter Gordon, Lonette McKee, Francois Cluzet, Martin Scorsese, Herbie Hancock, Sandra Reaves-Phillips; **D:** Bertrand Tavernier; **W:** Bertrand Tavernier, David Rayfiel; **M:** Herbie Hancock. Academy Awards '86:

Best Original Score; Nominations: Academy Awards '86: Best Actor (Gordon). **VHS, Beta, LV** ★★★

Roxanne A modern comic retelling of "Cyrano de Bergerac." The romantic triangle between a big nosed, small town fire chief, a shy fireman and the lovely astronomer they both love. Martin gives his most sensitive and believable performance. Don't miss the bar scene where he gets back at a heckler. A wonderful adaptation for the modern age. **1987 (PG) 107m/C** Steve Martin, Daryl Hannah, Rick Rossovich, Shelley Duvall, Michael J. Pollard, Fred Willard, John Kapelos, Max Alexander, Damon Wayans, Matt Lattanzi, Kevin Nealon; **D:** Fred Schepisi; **W:** Steve Martin; **M:** Bruce Smeaton, Ian Baker. Los Angeles Film Critics Association Awards '87: Best Actor (Martin); National Society of Film Critics Awards '87: Best Actor (Martin); Writers Guild of America '87: Best Adapted Screenplay. **VHS, Beta, LV, 8mm** ★★★

Royal Wedding Astaire and Powell play a brother-and-sister dance team who go to London during the royal wedding of Princess Elizabeth, and find their own romances. Notable for the inspired songs and Astaire's incredible dancing on the ceiling and walls; Lerner's first screenplay. The idea came from Adele Astaire's recent marriage to a British lord. ♪ Too Late Now; Sunday Jumps; How Can You Believe Me When I Said I Love You When You Know I've Been A Liar All My Life?; You're All the World to Me; The Happiest Day of My Life; Open Your Eyes; Ev'ry Night at Seven; I Left My Hat in Haiti; What A Lovely Day For A Wedding. **AKA:** Wedding Bells. **1951 93m/C** Fred Astaire, Jane Powell, Peter Lawford, Keenan Wynn, Sarah Churchill; **D:** Stanley Donen; **W:** Alan Jay Lerner. Nominations: Academy Awards '51: Best Song ("Too Late Now"). **VHS, Beta, LV** ★★★

Ruby in Paradise Leaving her dead-end life in Tennessee, Ruby Gissing (Judd) moves to Panama City, Florida, and lands a job selling souvenirs for no-nonsense Mildred Chambers (Lyman). Although pursued by two very different men, Ruby concentrates more on self-exploration, recording her thoughts in a journal. A seemingly effortless portrayal of Ruby Lee by Judd (daughter of Naomi and sister of Wynonna Judd) makes for a pleasurable character study of a young woman on her own. **1993 (R) 115m/C** Ashley Judd, Todd Field,

Bentley Mitchum, Allison Dean, Dorothy Lyman, Betsy Dowds; **D:** Victor Nunez; **W:** Victor Nunez; **M:** Charles Engstrom. Independent Spirit Awards '94: Best Actress (Judd); Sundance Film Festival '93: Grand Jury Prize; Nominations: Independent Spirit Awards '94: Best Cinematography, Best Director (Nunez), Best Film, Best Screenplay, Best Supporting Actor (Field). **VHS, LV** ★★★

Ruggles of Red Gap Classic comedy about an uptight British butler who is "won" by a barbarous American rancher in a poker game. Laughton as the nonplussed manservant is hilarious; supporting cast excellent. Third and far superior filming of Harry Leon Wilson story. One of the all-time great comedies, the film was remade musically with Bob Hope and Lucille Ball as "Fancy Pants" (1950). **1935 90m/B** Charles Laughton, Mary Boland, Charlie Ruggles, ZaSu Pitts, Roland Young, Leila Hyams, James Burke, Maude Eburne; **D:** Leo McCarey; **W:** Walter DeLeon; **M:** Ralph Rainger. National Board of Review Awards '35: 10 Best Films of the Year; New York Film Critics Awards '35: Best Actor (Laughton); Nominations: Academy Awards '35: Best Picture. **VHS, Beta** ★★★★

The Rules of the Game Renoir's masterpiece, in which a group of French aristocrats, gathering for a weekend of decadence and self-indulgence just before WWII, becomes a metaphor for human folly under siege. The film was banned by the French government, pulled from distribution by the Nazis, and not restored to its original form until 1959, when it premiered at the Venice Film Festival. A great, subtle, ominous film landmark. In French with English subtitles. The laserdisc version includes a commentary by director Peter Bogdanovich. Heavily copied and poorly remade in 1989 as "Scenes from the Class Struggle in Beverly Hills." **AKA:** Le Regle du Jeu. **1939 110m/B** Marcel Dalio, Nora Gregor, Jean Renoir, Mila Parely, Julien Carette, Gaston Modot, Roland Toutain, Paulette Dubost, Odette Talazac; **D:** Jean Renoir; **W:** Jean Renoir. **VHS, Beta, LV, 8mm** ★★★★

The Ruling Class The classic cult satire features O'Toole as the unbalanced 14th Earl of Gurney, who believes that he is either Jesus Christ or Jack the Ripper. Tongue-in-cheek look, complete with dance and music, at eccentric upper-class Brits and their institutions. Uneven, chaotic, surreal and noteworthy.

1972 (PG) 154m/C *GB* Peter O'Toole, Alastair Sim, Arthur Lowe, Harry Andrews, Coral Browne, Nigel Green; **D:** Peter Medak. National Board of Review Awards '72: 10 Best Films of the Year, Best Actor (O'Toole); Nominations: Academy Awards '72: Best Actor (O'Toole); Cannes Film Festival '72: Best Film. **VHS, Beta, LV** ★★★1/2

Rumble Fish A young street punk worships his gang-leading older brother, the only role model he's known. Crafted by Coppola into an important story of growing up on the wrong side of town, from the novel by S.E. Hinton. Ambitious and experimental, with an atmospheric music score; in black and white.
1983 (R) 94m/B Matt Dillon, Mickey Rourke, Dennis Hopper, Diane Lane, Vincent Spano, Nicolas Cage, Diana Scarwid, Christopher Penn, Tom Waits; **D:** Francis Ford Coppola; **W:** Francis Ford Coppola; **M:** Stewart Copeland, Stephen Burum. **VHS, Beta, LV** ★★★

A Rumor of War The first big Vietnam drama for TV is a triumph, portraying the real-life experience of author Philip Caputo (based on his best-seller), from naive youth to seasoned soldier to bitter murder suspect at court martial. Succeeds where Stone's later, much-ballyhooed "Born on the Fourth of July" fails. Adapted by John Sacret Young.
1980 195m/C Brad Davis, Keith Carradine, Michael O'Keefe, Stacy Keach, Steve Forrest, Richard Bradford, Brian Dennehy, John Friedrich, Perry Lang, Chris Mitchum, Dan Shor, Jeff Daniels; **D:** Richard T. Heffron. **VHS, Beta** ★★★1/2

Rumpole of the Bailey: Rumpole's Return A feature-length film based on the popular British television series. A middle aged barrister refuses to settle for less than justice. Based on the character created by John Mortimer.
1990 106m/C *GB* Leo McKern. **VHS** ★★★

The Run of the Country Amid the scenic splendor of a small town south of the North Irish border in County Cavan, Danny (Keeslar) comes of age, sometimes the hard way. His relationship with his bullying dad (Finney), the local Garda officer, begins to crumble after the tragic death of his mum. So he runs away to live with the town malcontent Prunty (Brophy) and falls in love with the beautiful Annagh (Smurfit), who lives north of the border. Life gets even more complicated when Annagh learns she's pregnant. Director Yates, reunited with Finney for the first time since they won Oscars for the "The Dresser," sometimes digs too deeply into a big crock of standard Irish stew, occasionally delivering Celtic melodrama instead of poignant slice of life. The usual themes of family dysfunction, religious rebellion, and moral dilemma are augmented by the occasional appearance of the IRA. As the frustrated, violent father, Finney shines. In their debut, Keeslar and Smurfit are fine, but Brophy's Prunty is the one you'll remember. Adapted by Connaughton (who used similar geography for "The Playboys") from his novel.
1995 (R) 109m/C Albert Finney, Matt Keeslar, Victoria Smurfit, Anthony Brophy, David Kelly; **D:** Peter Yates; **W:** Shane Connaughton; **M:** Cynthia Millar. **VHS, LV** ★★★

Run Silent, Run Deep Submarine commander Gable battles his officers, especially the bitter Lancaster who vied for the same command, while stalking the Japanese destroyer that sunk his former command. Top-notch WWII sub action, scripted from Commander Edward L. Beach's novel.
1958 93m/B Burt Lancaster, Clark Gable, Jack Warden, Don Rickles, Brad Dexter; **D:** Robert Wise; **W:** John Gay. **VHS, Beta** ★★★

Runaway Train A tough jailbird and his sidekick break out of the hoosegow and find themselves trapped aboard a brakeless freight train heading for certain derailment in northwestern Canada. Harrowing existential action drama based on a screenplay by Akira Kurosawa. Voigt is superb.
1985 (R) 112m/C Jon Voight, Eric Roberts, Rebecca DeMornay, John P. Ryan, T.K. Carter, Kenneth McMillan; **D:** Andrei Konchalovsky; **W:** Andrei Konchalovsky, Djordje Milicevic, Edward Bunker; **M:** Trevor Jones. Golden Globe Awards '86: Best Actor—Drama (Voight); Nominations: Academy Awards '85: Best Actor (Voight), Best Film Editing, Best Supporting Actor (Roberts). **VHS, Beta, LV** ★★★

Running on Empty Two 1960s radicals are still on the run in 1988 for a politically motivated Vietnam War-era crime. Though they have managed to stay one step ahead of the law, their son wants a "normal" life, even if it means never seeing his family again. Well-performed, quiet, plausible drama.
1988 (PG-13) 116m/C Christine Lahti, River Phoenix, Judd Hirsch, Martha Plimpton, Jonas Arby, Ed Crowley, L.M. Kit Carson, Steven Hill, Augusta Dabney,

David Margulies, Sidney Lumet; **D:** Sidney Lumet; **W:** Naomi Foner; **M:** Tony Mottola. Golden Globe Awards '89: Best Screenplay; Los Angeles Film Critics Association Awards '88: Best Actress (Lahti); National Board of Review Awards '88: Best Supporting Actor (Phoenix); Nominations: Academy Awards '88: Best Original Screenplay, Best Supporting Actor (Phoenix). **VHS, Beta, LV, 8mm** ★★★

The Russians Are Coming! The Russians Are Coming! Based on the comic novel "The Off-Islanders" by Nathaniel Benchley, this is the story of a Russian sub which accidentally runs aground off the New England coast. The residents falsely believe that the nine-man crew is the beginning of a Soviet invasion, though the men are only looking for help. A memorable set of silly events follows the landing, engineered by a gung-ho police chief and a town filled with overactive imaginations.
1966 126m/C Alan Arkin, Carl Reiner, Theodore Bikel, Eva Marie Saint, Brian Keith, Paul Ford, Jonathan Winters, Ben Blue, Tessie O'Shea, Doro Merande, John Phillip Law; **D:** Norman Jewison. Golden Globe Awards '67: Best Actor—Musical/Comedy (Arkin), Best Film—Musical/Comedy; National Board of Review Awards '66: 10 Best Films of the Year; Nominations: Academy Awards '66: Best Actor (Arkin), Best Picture, Best Story & Screenplay. **VHS, Beta** ★★★

Ruthless People DeVito and his mistress spend a romantic evening plotting his obnoxious wife's untimely demise. Before he can put his plan into action, he's delighted to discover she's been kidnapped by some very desperate people—who don't stand a chance with Bette. High farcical entertainment is a variation on the story "The Ransom of Red Chief" by O. Henry.
1986 (R) 93m/C Bette Midler, Danny DeVito, Judge Reinhold, Helen Slater, Anita Morris, Bill Pullman; **D:** David Zucker, Jerry Zucker, Jim Abrahams; **W:** Dale Lanner; **M:** Michel Colombier. **VHS, Beta, LV** ★★★

Sabotage Early Hitchcock thriller based on Conrad's "The Secret Agent." A woman who works at a movie theater (Sidney) suspects her quiet husband (Homolka) might be the terrorist planting bombs around London. Numerous sly touches of the Master's signature humor. **AKA:** Woman Alone.
1936 81m/B Oscar Homolka, Sylvia Sidney, John Loder; **D:** Alfred Hitchcock; **W:** Charles Bennett. **VHS, Beta, LV, 8mm** ★★★

Saboteur A man wrongly accused of sabotaging an American munitions plant during WWII sets out to find the traitor who framed him. Hitchcock uses his locations, including Boulder Dam, Radio City Music Hall, and the Statue of Liberty, to greatly intensify the action. Stunning resolution.
1942 108m/B Priscilla Lane, Robert Cummings, Otto Kruger, Alan Baxter, Norman Lloyd, Charles Halton; **D:** Alfred Hitchcock; **W:** Alfred Hitchcock, Peter Viertel. **VHS, Beta, LV** ★★★

Sabrina Two wealthy brothers, one an aging businessman (Bogart) and the other a dissolute playboy (Holden), vie for the attention of their chauffeur's daughter (Hepburn), who has just returned from a French cooking school. Typically acerbic, in the Wilder manner, with Bogart and Holden cast interestingly against type (but it's Hepburn's picture anyway). Based on the play "Sabrina Fair" by Samuel Taylor. **AKA:** Sabrina Fair.
1954 113m/B Audrey Hepburn, Humphrey Bogart, William Holden, Walter Hampden, Francis X. Bushman, John Williams, Martha Hyer, Marcel Dalio; **D:** Billy Wilder; **W:** Billy Wilder, Ernest Lehman. Academy Awards '54: Best Costume Design (B & W); Directors Guild of America Awards '54: Best Director (Wilder); Golden Globe Awards '55: Best Screenplay; National Board of Review Awards '54: 10 Best Films of the Year, Best Supporting Actor (Williams); Nominations: Academy Awards '54: Best Actress (Hepburn), Best Art Direction/Set Decoration (B & W), Best Black and White Cinematography, Best Director (Wilder), Best Screenplay. **VHS, Beta, LV** ★★★

Sadie Thompson Swanson plays a harlot with a heart of gold, bawdy and good-natured, in the South Seas. A zealot missionary (Barrymore) arrives and falls in love with her. The last eight minutes of footage have been re-created by using stills and the original title cards, to replace the last reel which had decomposed. Remade as "Rain," "Dirty Gertie From Harlem," and "Miss Sadie Thompson." Based on W. Somerset Maugham's "Rain."
1928 97m/B Gloria Swanson, Lionel Barrymore, Raoul Walsh, Blanche Frederici, Charles Lane, James Marcus; **D:** Raoul Walsh. Nominations: Academy Awards '28: Best Actress (Swanson), Best Cinematography. **VHS, LV** ★★★

Safe Surburban California housewife Carol (Moore) literally becomes allergic to her environment and winds up seeking relief in a holistic center in Albuquerque, where director Haynes takes a shot at the New Age and finds a link to the AIDS crisis. Serious, stylistically detached look at a near future riddled with environmental toxins is led by Moore's performance as the sunny suburbanite undone by the unseen.

1995 (R) 119m/C Julianne Moore, Peter Friedman, Xander Berkeley, Susan Norman, James LeGros, Mary Carver, Kate McGregor Stewart; **D:** Todd Haynes; **W:** Todd Haynes, Alex Nepomniaschy; **M:** Ed Tomney. Nominations: Independent Spirit Awards '96: Best Actress (Moore), Best Director (Haynes), Best Film, Best Screenplay. **VHS, LV** ★★★

Sahara A British-American unit must fight the Germans for their survival in the Libyan desert during WWII. Plenty of action and suspense combined with good performances makes this one a step above the usual war movie.

1943 97m/B Humphrey Bogart, Dan Duryea, Bruce (Herman Brix) Bennett, Lloyd Bridges, Rex Ingram, J. Carrol Naish, Richard Nugent, Miklos Rozsa; **D:** Zoltan Korda. Nominations: Academy Awards '43: Best Black and White Cinematography, Best Sound, Best Supporting Actor (Naish). **VHS, Beta** ★★★

Saint Jack The story of a small-time pimp with big dreams working the pleasure palaces of late-night Singapore. Engrossing and pleasant. Based on Paul Theroux's novel.

1979 (R) 112m/C Ben Gazzara, Denholm Elliott, Joss Ackland, George Lazenby; **D:** Peter Bogdanovich; **W:** Peter Bogdanovich. **VHS, Beta** ★★★

Salt of the Earth Finally available in this country after being suppressed for 30 years, this controversial film was made by a group of blacklisted filmmakers during the McCarthy era. It was deemed anti-American, communist propaganda. The story deals with the anti-Hispanic racial strife that occurs in a New Mexico zinc mine when union workers organize a strike.

1954 94m/B Rosaura Revueltas, Will Geer, David Wolfe; **D:** Herbert Biberman. **VHS, Beta, LV, CD-I** ★★★1/2

Salvador Photo journalist Richard Boyle's unflinching and sordid adventures in war-torn El Salvador. Boyle (Woods) must face the realities of social injustice. Belushi and Woods are hard to like, but excellent. Early critical success for director Stone.

1986 (R) 123m/C James Woods, James Belushi, John Savage, Michael Murphy, Elpidia Carrillo, Cynthia Gibb; **D:** Oliver Stone; **W:** Oliver Stone, Richard Boyle, Robert Richardson; **M:** Georges Delerue. Independent Spirit Awards '87: Best Actor (Woods); Nominations: Academy Awards '86: Best Actor (Woods), Best Original Screenplay. **VHS, Beta, LV** ★★★1/2

Same Time, Next Year A chance meeting between an accountant and a housewife results in a sometimes tragic, always sentimental 25-year affair in which they meet only one weekend each year. Well-cast leads carry warm, touching story based on the Broadway play by Bernard Slade.

1978 119m/C Ellen Burstyn, Alan Alda; **D:** Robert Mulligan; **M:** Marvin Hamlisch. Golden Globe Awards '79: Best Actress—Musical/Comedy (Burstyn); Nominations: Academy Awards '78: Best Actress (Burstyn), Best Adapted Screenplay, Best Cinematography, Best Song ("The Last Time I Felt Like This"). **VHS, Beta, LV** ★★★

Sammy & Rosie Get Laid An unusual social satire about a sexually liberated couple living in London whose lives are thrown into turmoil by the arrival of the man's father - a controversial politician in India. Provides a confusing look at sexual and class collisions. From the makers of "My Beautiful Laundrette."

1987 97m/C *GB* Shashi Kapoor, Frances Barber, Claire Bloom, Ayub Khan Din, Roland Gift, Wendy Gazelle, Meera Syal; **D:** Stephen Frears; **W:** Hanif Kureishi; **M:** Stanley Myers. **VHS, Beta, LV** ★★★

Samson and Delilah The biblical story of the vindictive Delilah, who after being rejected by the mighty Samson, robbed him of his strength by shearing his curls. Delivered in signature DeMille style. Wonderfully fun and engrossing. Mature is excellent.

1950 128m/C Victor Mature, Hedy Lamarr, Angela Lansbury, George Sanders, Henry Wilcoxon, Olive Deering, Fay Holden; **D:** Cecil B. DeMille. Academy Awards '50: Best Art Direction/Set Decoration (Color), Best Costume Design (Color); Nominations: Academy Awards '50: Best Color Cinematography, Best Original Score. **VHS, Beta, LV** ★★★

Samurai 1: Musashi Miyamoto The first installment in the film version of Musashi Miyamoto's life, as he leaves his 17th-century village as a warrior in a local civil war only to return beaten and disillusioned. Justly award-winning. In Japanese with English subtitles.

1955 92m/C *JP* Toshiro Mifune; **D:** Hiroshi Inagaki. Academy Awards '55: Best Foreign Language Film. **VHS, Beta, LV** ★★★1/2

Samurai 2: Duel at Ichijoji Temple
Inagaki's second film depicting the life of Musashi Miyamoto, the 17th-century warrior, who wandered the disheveled landscape of feudal Japan looking for glory and love. In Japanese with English subtitles.
1955 102m/C *JP* Toshiro Mifune; *D:* Hiroshi Inagaki. **VHS, Beta, LV** ★★★1/2

Samurai 3: Duel at Ganryu Island
The final film of Inagaki's trilogy, in which Musashi Miyamoto confronts his lifelong enemy in a climactic battle. Depicts Miyamoto's spiritual awakening and realization that love and hatred exist in all of us. In Japanese with English subtitles.
1956 102m/C *JP* Toshiro Mifune, Koji Tsurata; *D:* Hiroshi Inagaki. **VHS, Beta, LV** ★★★1/2

San Francisco The San Francisco Earthquake of 1906 serves as the background for a romance between an opera singer and a Barbary Coast saloon owner. Somewhat overdone but gripping tale of passion and adventure in the West. Wonderful special effects. Finale consists of historic earthquake footage. Also available colorized. ♪ San Francisco; A Heart That's Free; Would You?; Air des Bijoux; Sempre Libera.
1936 116m/B Jeanette MacDonald, Clark Gable, Spencer Tracy, Jack Holt, Jessie Ralph, Al Shear; *D:* Woodbridge S. Van Dyke; *W:* Anita Loos. Academy Awards '36: Best Sound; Nominations: Academy Awards '36: Best Actor (Tracy), Best Director (Van Dyke), Best Picture, Best Story. **VHS, Beta, LV** ★★★1/2

The Sand Pebbles An American expatriate engineer, transferred to a gunboat on the Yangtze River in 1926, falls in love with a missionary teacher. As he becomes aware of the political climate of American imperialism, he finds himself at odds with his command structure; the treatment of this issue can be seen as commentary on the situation in Vietnam at the time of the film's release. Considered one of McQueen's best performances, blending action and romance.
1966 193m/C Steve McQueen, Richard Crenna, Richard Attenborough, Candice Bergen, Marayat Andriane, Gavin MacLeod, Larry Gates, Mako, Simon Oakland; *D:* Robert Wise; *W:* Robert Anderson; *M:* Jerry Goldsmith. Golden Globe Awards '67: Best Supporting Actor (Attenborough); Nominations: Academy Awards '66: Best Actor (McQueen), Best Art Direction/Set Decoration (Color), Best Color Cinematography, Best Film Editing,

Best Picture, Best Sound, Best Supporting Actor (Mako), Best Original Score. **VHS, Beta, LV** ★★★1/2

Sandakan No. 8 A Japanese woman working as a journalist befriends an old woman who was sold into prostitution in Borneo in the early 1900s. Justly acclaimed feminist story dramatizes the role of women in Japanese society. In Japanese with English subtitles. *AKA:* Brothel 8; Sandakan House 8.
1974 121m/C *JP* Kinuyo Tanaka, Yoko Takakashi, Komake Kurihara, Eitaro Ozawa; *D:* Kei Kumai. Berlin International Film Festival '75: Best Actress; Nominations: Academy Awards '75: Best Foreign Language Film. **VHS, Beta** ★★★

Sands of Iwo Jima Wayne earned his first Oscar nomination as a tough Marine sergeant, in one of his best roles. He trains a squad of rebellious recruits in New Zealand in 1943. Later they are responsible for the capture of Iwo Jima from the Japanese—one of the most difficult campaigns of the Pacific Theater. Includes striking real war footage.
1949 109m/B John Wayne, Forrest Tucker, John Agar, Richard Jaeckel; *D:* Allan Dwan. Nominations: Academy Awards '49: Best Sound, Best Actor (Wayne), Best Film Editing, Best Story. **VHS, LV** ★★★1/2

Sanjuro In this offbeat, satiric sequel to "Yojimbo," a talented but lazy samurai comes to the aid of a group of naive young warriors. The conventional ideas of good and evil are quickly tossed aside; much less earnest than other Kurosawa Samurai outings. In Japanese with English subtitles. *AKA:* Tsubaki Sanjuro.
1962 96m/B *JP* Toshiro Mifune, Tatsuya Nakadai; *D:* Akira Kurosawa. **VHS, Beta, LV** ★★★

Sansho the Bailiff A world masterpiece by Mizoguchi about feudal society in 11th-century Japan. A woman and her children are sold into prostitution and slavery. As an adult, the son seeks to right the ills of his society. Powerful and tragic, and often more highly esteemed than "Ugetsu." In Japanese with English subtitles. *AKA:* The Bailiff; Sansho Dayu.
1954 132m/B *JP* Kinuyo Tanaka, Yoshiaki Hanayagi, Kyoko Kagawa, Eitaro Shindo, Ichiro Sugai; *D:* Kenji Mizoguchi; *W:* Yoshikata Yoda; *M:* Fumio Hayasaka. **VHS, Beta, LV** ★★★★

Sarah, Plain and Tall New England school teacher (Close) travels to Kansas circa 1910 to care for the family of a widowed farmer who has

advertised for a wife. Superior entertainment for the whole family. Adapted for television from Patricia MacLachlan's novel of the same name by MacLachlan and Carol Sobieski. Nominated for nine Emmy Awards. A "Hallmark Hall of Fame" presentation.
1991 (G) 98m/C Glenn Close, Christopher Walken, Lexi Randall, Margaret Sophie Stein, Jon DeVries, Christopher Bell; **D:** Glenn Jordan. **VHS, LV** ★★★

Save the Tiger A basically honest middle-aged man sees no way out of his failing business except arson. The insurance settlement will let him pay off his creditors, and save face. David, as the arsonist, and Gilford, as Lemmon's business partner, are superb. Lemmon is also excellent throughout his performance.
1973 (R) 100m/C Jack Lemmon, Jack Gilford, Laurie Heineman, Patricia Smith, Norman Burton, Thayer David; **D:** John G. Avildsen; **M:** Marvin Hamlisch. Academy Awards '73: Best Actor (Lemmon); Writers Guild of America '73: Best Original Screenplay; Nominations: Academy Awards '73: Best Story & Screenplay, Best Supporting Actor (Gilford). **VHS, Beta, LV** ★★★

Say Anything A semi-mature, successful teen romance about an off-beat loner interested in the martial arts (Cusack, in a winning performance) who goes after the beautiful class brain of his high school. Things are complicated when her father is suspected of embezzling by the IRS. Joan Cusack, John's real-life sister, also plays his sister in the film. Works well on the romantic level without getting too sticky.
1989 (PG-13) 100m/C John Cusack, Ione Skye, John Mahoney, Joan Cusack, Lili Taylor, Richard Portnow, Pamela Segall, Jason Gould, Loren Dean, Bebe Neuwirth, Aimee Brooks, Eric Stoltz, Chynna Phillips, Joanna Frank; **D:** Cameron Crowe; **W:** Cameron Crowe; **M:** Anne Dudley, Richard Gibbs, Nancy Wilson. **VHS, Beta, LV** ★★★

Sayonara An Army major is assigned to a Japanese airbase during the Korean conflict at the behest of his future father-in-law. Dissatisfied with his impending marriage, he finds himself drawn to a Japanese dancer and becomes involved in the affairs of his buddy who, against official policy, marries a Japanese woman. Tragedy surrounds the themes of bigotry and interracial marriage. Based on the novel by James Michener.
1957 147m/C Marlon Brando, James Garner, Ricardo Montalban, Patricia Owens, Red Buttons, Miyoshi Umeki, Martha Scott; **D:** Joshua Logan, Ellsworth Fredericks. Academy Awards '57: Best Art Direction/Set Decoration, Best Sound, Best Supporting Actor (Buttons), Best Supporting Actress (Umeki); Nominations: Academy Awards '57: Best Actor (Brando), Best Adapted Screenplay, Best Cinematography, Best Director (Logan), Best Film Editing, Best Picture. **VHS, Beta** ★★★

Scandal A dramatization of Britain's Profumo government sex scandal of the 1960s. Hurt plays a society doctor who enjoys introducing pretty girls to his wealthy friends. One of the girls, Christine Keeler, takes as lovers both a Russian government official and a British Cabinet Minister. The resulting scandal eventually overturned an entire political party, and led to disgrace, prison, and death for some of those concerned. Also available in an unedited 115-minute version which contains more controversial language and nudity. Top-notch performances make either version well worth watching.
1989 (R) 105m/C GB John Hurt, Joanne Whalley-Kilmer, Ian McKellen, Bridget Fonda, Jeroen Krabbe, Britt Ekland, Roland Gift, Daniel Massey, Leslie Phillips; **D:** Michael Caton-Jones; **W:** Michael Thomas; **M:** Carl Davis. **VHS, Beta, LV** ★★★

Scaramouche Thrilling swashbuckler about a nobleman (Granger, very well cast) searching for his family during the French Revolution. To avenge the death of a friend, he joins a theater troupe where he learns swordplay and becomes the character "Scaramouche." Features a rousing six-and-a-half-minute sword battle.
1952 111m/C Stewart Granger, Eleanor Parker, Janet Leigh, Mel Ferrer, Henry Wilcoxon, Nina Foch, Richard Anderson, Robert Coote, Lewis Stone, Elisabeth Risdon, Howard Freeman; **D:** George Sidney. **VHS, LV** ★★★1/2

Scared Stiff Fleeing a murder charge, Martin and Lewis find gangsters and ghosts on a Caribbean island. Funny and scary, a good remake of "The Ghost Breakers," with cameos by Hope and Crosby. ♪ San Domingo; Song of the Enchilada Man; Mama Yo Quiero; You Hit the Spot; I Don't Care If the Sun Don't Shine; I'm Your Pal; When Somebody Thinks You're Wonderful.
1953 108m/B Dean Martin, Jerry Lewis, Lizabeth Scott, Carmen Miranda, Dorothy Malone; **Cameos:** Bob Hope, Bing Crosby; **D:** George Marshall. **VHS** ★★★

Scarface The violent rise and fall of a 1930s Chicago crime boss (based on the life of notorious gangster Al Capone). Release was held back by censors due to the amount of violence and its suggestion of incest between the title character and his sister. Producer Howard Hughes recut and filmed an alternate ending, without director Hawks' approval, to pacify the censors, and both versions of the film were released at the same time. Almost too violent and intense at the time. Remains brilliant and impressive. Remade in 1983. *AKA:* Scarface: The Shame of a Nation.
1931 93m/B Paul Muni, Ann Dvorak, Karen Morley, Osgood Perkins, George Raft, Boris Karloff; *D:* Howard Hawks. National Board of Review Awards '32: 10 Best Films of the Year. **VHS, Beta, LV** ★★★

Scarlet Claw Holmes and Watson solve the bloody murder of an old lady in the creepy Canadian village of Le Mort Rouge. The best and most authentic of the Sherlock Holmes series. *AKA:* Sherlock Holmes and the Scarlet Claw.
1944 74m/B Basil Rathbone, Nigel Bruce, Miles Mander, Gerald Hamer, Kay Harding; *D:* Roy William Neill. **VHS, Beta** ★★★

Scarlet Empress One of von Sternberg's greatest films tells the story of Catherine the Great and her rise to power. Dietrich stars as the beautiful royal wife who outwits her maniacal husband to become empress of Russia. Incredibly rich decor is a visual feast for the eye, as perfectionist von Sternberg fussed over every detail. Dietrich is excellent as Catherine, and von Sternberg's mastery of lighting and camerawork makes for a highly extravagant film. Based on the diary of Catherine the Great.
1934 110m/B Marlene Dietrich, John Lodge, Sam Jaffe, Louise Dresser, Maria Sieber, Sir C. Aubrey Smith, Ruthelma Stevens, Olive Tell; *D:* Josef von Sternberg; *W:* Manuel Komroff. **VHS** ★★★1/2

The Scarlet Pimpernel "The Scarlet Pimpernel," supposed dandy of the English court, assumes a dual identity to outwit the French Republicans and aid innocent aristocrats during the French Revolution. Classic rendering of Baroness Orczy's novel, full of exploits, 18th-century costumes, intrigue, damsels, etc. Produced by Alexander Korda, who fired the initial director, Rowland Brown. Remade for television in 1982. Available in colorized version.
1934 95m/B GB Leslie Howard, Joan

Gardner, Merle Oberon, Raymond Massey, Anthony Bushell; *D:* Harold Young. **VHS, Beta** ★★★1/2

The Scarlet Pimpernel Remake of the classic about a British dandy who saved French aristocrats from the Reign of Terror guillotines during the French Revolution. Made for British television version is almost as good as the original 1935 film, with beautiful costumes and sets and good performances from Seymour and Andrews.
1982 142m/C GB Anthony Andrews, Jane Seymour, Ian McKellen, James Villiers, Eleanor David; *D:* Clive Donner; *M:* Nick Bicat. **VHS, Beta, LV** ★★★

Scarlet Street A mild-mannered, middle-aged cashier becomes an embezzler when he gets involved with a predatory, manipulating woman. Lang remake of Jean Renoir's "La Chienne" (1931). Set apart from later attempts on the same theme by excellent direction by Lang and acting. Also available colorized.
1945 95m/B Edward G. Robinson, Joan Bennett, Dan Duryea, Samuel S. Hinds; *D:* Fritz Lang. **VHS, Beta** ★★★

Scenes from a Marriage Originally produced in six one-hour episodes for Swedish television, this bold and sensitive film excruciatingly portrays the painful, unpleasant, disintegration of a marriage. Ullman is superb. Realistic and disturbing. Dubbed.
1973 (PG) 168m/C SW Liv Ullmann, Erland Josephson, Bibi Andersson, Jan Malmsjo, Anita Wall, Sven Nykvist; *D:* Ingmar Bergman; *W:* Ingmar Bergman. Golden Globe Awards '75: Best Foreign Film; National Board of Review Awards '74: 5 Best Foreign Films of the Year; New York Film Critics Awards '74: Best Actress (Ullmann), Best Screenplay; National Society of Film Critics Awards '74: Best Actress (Ullmann), Best Film, Best Screenplay, Best Supporting Actress (Andersson). **VHS, Beta** ★★★★

Scent of a Woman Pacino is a powerhouse (verging on caricature) in a story that, with anyone else in the lead, would be your run-of-the-mill, overly sentimental coming of age/redemption flick. Blind, bitter, and semi-alcoholic Pacino is a retired army colonel under the care of his married niece. He's home alone over Thanksgiving, under the watchful eye of local prep school student Charlie (O'Donnell). Pacino's abrasive (though wonderfully intuitive and romantic) colonel makes an impact on viewers that lingers like a woman's scent long after the last tango.

S

▲

O'Donnell is competently understated in key supporting role, while the tango lesson between Pacino and Anwar dances to the tune of "classic." Box-office winner is a remake of 1975 Italian film "Profumo di Donna." The laserdisc version is available in letterbox format.

1992 (R) 157m/C Al Pacino, Chris O'Donnell, James Rebhorn, Gabrielle Anwar, Philip S. Hoffman, Richard Venture, Bradley Whitford, Rochelle Oliver, Margaret Eginton, Tom Riis Farrell, Frances Conroy, Donald E. Thorin; **D:** Martin Brest; **W:** Bo Goldman; **M:** Thomas Newman. Academy Awards '92: Best Actor (Pacino); Golden Globe Awards '93: Best Actor—Drama (Pacino), Best Film—Drama, Best Writing; Nominations: Academy Awards '92: Best Adapted Screenplay, Best Director (Brest), Best Picture; British Academy Awards '93: Best Adapted Screenplay. **VHS, LV** ★★★

The Scent of Green Papaya Tranquil film, set in 1951 Vietnam, follows 10-year-old peasant girl Mui as she spends the next 10 years as a servant in a troubled family, gracefully accommodating herself to the small changes in her life. At 20, she finds a fairy-tale romance with her next employer, a young pianist. Presents a romanticized view of the stoicism of Vietnamese women but is visually beautiful. Directorial debut of Hung is based on his childhood memories of Vietnam, which he re-created on a soundstage outside Paris. In Vietnamese with English subtitles.

1993 104m/C *VT* Tran Nu Yen-Khe, Lu Man San, Truong Thi Loc, Vuong Hoa Hoi; **D:** Tran Anh Hung; **W:** Tran Anh Hung, Patricia Petit. Nominations: Academy Awards '93: Best Foreign Language Film. **VHS, LV** ★★★

Schindler's List Spielberg's staggering evocation of the Holocaust finds its voice in Oscar Schindler (Neeson), womanizing German businessman and aspiring war profiteer, who cajoled, bribed, and bullied the Nazis into allowing him to employ Jews in his Polish factories during WWII. By doing so he saved over 1,000 lives. The atrocities are depicted matter of factly as a by-product of sheer Nazi evil. Shot in black and white and powered by splendid performances. Neeson uses his powerful physique as a protective buffer; Kingsley is watchful as his industrious Jewish accountant; and Fiennes personifies evil as Nazi Amon Goeth. Based on the novel by Thomas Keneally, which itself was based on survivor's memories. Filmed on location in Cracow, Poland; due to the sensitive nature of the story, sets of the Auschwitz concentration camp were reconstructed directly outside the camp after protests about filming on the actual site. A tour de force and labor of love for Spielberg, who finally garnered the attention and respect as a filmmaker he deserves.

1993 (R) 195m/B Liam Neeson, Ben Kingsley, Ralph Fiennes, Embeth Davidtz, Caroline Goodall, Jonathan Sagalle, Mark Ivanir, Janusz Kaminski; **D:** Steven Spielberg; **W:** Steven Zaillian; **M:** John Williams. Academy Awards '93: Best Adapted Screenplay, Best Art Direction/Set Decoration, Best Cinematography, Best Director (Spielberg), Best Film Editing, Best Picture, Best Original Score; British Academy Awards '93: Best Adapted Screenplay, Best Director (Spielberg), Best Film, Best Supporting Actor (Fiennes); Golden Globe Awards '94: Best Director (Spielberg), Best Film—Drama, Best Screenplay; Los Angeles Film Critics Association Awards '93: Best Cinematography, Best Film; National Board of Review Awards '93: Best Film; New York Film Critics Awards '93: Best Cinematography, Best Film, Best Supporting Actor (Fiennes); Writers Guild of America '93: Best Adapted Screenplay; Nominations: Academy Awards '93: Best Actor (Neeson), Best Costume Design, Best Makeup, Best Sound, Best Supporting Actor (Fiennes); Golden Globe Awards '94: Best Actor—Drama (Neeson), Best Supporting Actor (Fiennes), Best Original Score; MTV Movie Awards '94: Best Film, Breakthrough Performance (Fiennes). **VHS, LV** ★★★★

The Sea Hawk An English privateer learns the Spanish are going to invade England with their Armada. After numerous adventures, he is able to aid his queen and help save his country, finding romance along the way. One of Flynn's swashbuckling best. Available colorized.

1940 128m/B Errol Flynn, Claude Rains, Donald Crisp, Alan Hale, Flora Robson, Brenda Marshall, Henry Daniell, Gilbert Roland, James Stephenson, Una O'Connor; **D:** Michael Curtiz; **W:** Howard Koch. Nominations: Academy Awards '40: Best Interior Decoration, Best Sound, Best Score. **VHS, Beta, LV** ★★★1/2

Sea of Love A tough, tightly wound thriller about an alcoholic cop with a mid-life crisis. While following the track of a serial killer, he begins a torrid relationship with one of his suspects. Pacino doesn't stand a chance when Barkin heats up the screen.

1989 (R) 113m/C Al Pacino, Ellen Barkin, John Goodman, Michael Rooker, William Hickey, Richard Jenkins; **D:** Harold Becker;

W: Richard Price; **M:** Trevor Jones. VHS, Beta, LV ★★★1/2

The Sea Wolf Jack London's adventure novel about brutal, canny Captain Wolf Larsen (Robinson), his rebellious crew, and some unexpected passengers. Knox and Lupino are shipwreck survivors, picked up by Robinson and forced into working aboard his ship, the aptly named "Ghost." Crewman Garfield falls for Lupino and tries to rally his shipmates into resisting the meglomaniacal Robinson. Fine performances by all, especially Robinson as the personification of malevolent ego. Screen debut of Knox. Director Curtiz filmed entirely in studio tanks, sets, and pervasive fog machines. Previously filmed three times; later remade as "Barricade" and "Wolf Larsen."
1941 90m/C Edward G. Robinson, Alexander Knox, John Garfield, Ida Lupino, Gene Lockhart, Barry Fitzgerald, Stanley Ridges, Francis McDonald, David Bruce, Howard da Silva, Frank Lackteen, Ralf Harolde; **D:** Michael Curtiz; **W:** Robert Rossen. VHS ★★★★

The Seagull A pensive, sensitive adaptation of the famed Chekhov play about the depressed denizens of an isolated country estate. In Russian with English subtitles.
1971 99m/B Alla Demidova, Lyudmila Savelyeva, Yuri Yakovlev; **D:** Yuri Karasik. VHS, Beta ★★★

Seance on a Wet Afternoon Dark, thoughtful film about a crazed pseudo-psychic who coerces her husband into a kidnapping so she can gain recognition by divining the child's whereabouts. Directed splendidly by Forbes, and superb acting from Stanley and Attenborough, who co-produced with Forbes.
1964 111m/B GB Kim Stanley, Richard Attenborough, Margaret Lacey, Maria Kazan, Mark Eden, Patrick Magee; **D:** Bryan Forbes; **M:** John Barry. British Academy Awards '64: Best Actor (Attenborough); National Board of Review Awards '64: 10 Best Films of the Year, Best Actress (Stanley); Nominations: Academy Awards '64: Best Actress (Stanley). VHS, Beta ★★★1/2

The Search Clift, an American soldier stationed in post-WWII Berlin, befriends a homeless nine-year-old amnesiac boy (Jandl) and tries to find his family. Meanwhile, his mother has been searching the Displaced Persons camps for her son. Although Clift wants to adopt the boy, he steps aside, and mother and son are finally reunited. "The Search" was shot on location in the American Occupied Zone of Germany. Jandl won a special juvenile Oscar in his first (and only) film role. This was also Clift's first screen appearance, although this movie was actually filmed after his debut in "Red River," it was released first.
1948 105m/B Montgomery Clift, Aline MacMahon, Ivan Jandl, Jarmila Novotna, Wendell Corey; **D:** Fred Zinneman. Academy Awards '48: Best Original Screenplay; Golden Globe Awards '49: Best Screenplay; Nominations: Academy Awards '48: Best Actor (Clift), Best Director (Zinneman), Best Screenplay. VHS ★★★1/2

Search for Signs of Intelligent Life in the Universe Tomlin's brilliant one-woman show has been expanded into a wonderful film. As Tomlin's cast of 12 female and male characters meet and interact, they show every viewer his/her own humanity.
1991 (PG-13) 120m/C Lily Tomlin; **D:** John Bailey; **W:** Jane Wagner; **M:** Jerry Goodman. VHS ★★★

The Searchers The classic Ford western, starring John Wayne as a hard-hearted frontiersman who spends years doggedly pursuing his niece, who was kidnapped by Indians. A simple western structure supports Ford's most moving, mysterious, complex film. Many feel this is the best western of all time.
1956 119m/C John Wayne, Jeffrey Hunter, Vera Miles, Natalie Wood, Ward Bond, John Qualen, Harry Carey Jr., Olive Carey, Antonio Moreno, Henry Brandon, Hank Worden, Lana Wood, Dorothy Jordan, Patrick Wayne; **D:** John Ford; **W:** Frank Nugent; **M:** Max Steiner. VHS, Beta, LV ★★★★

Searching for Bobby Fischer Seven-year-old Josh Waitzkin (Pomeranc, in his debut) shows an amazing gift for chess, stunning his parents, who must try to strike the delicate balance of developing his abilities while also allowing him a "normal" childhood. Excellent cast features Mantegna and Allen as his parents, Kingsley as demanding chess teacher Pandolfini, and Fishburne as an adept speed-chess hustler. Pomeranc is great, and his knowledge of chess (he's a ranked player) brings authenticity to his role. Title comes from Pandolfini's belief that Josh may equal the abilities of chess whiz Bobby Fischer. Underrated little gem based on a true story and adapted from the book by Waitzkin's father.

1993 (PG) 111m/C Joe Mantegna, Max Pomeranc, Joan Allen, Ben Kingsley, Laurence "Larry" Fishburne, Robert Stephens, David Paymer, Robert Stephens, William H. Macy, Conrad Hall; **D:** Steven Zaillian; **W:** Steven Zaillian; **M:** James Horner. MTV Movie Awards '94: Best New Filmmaker Award (Zaillian); Nominations: Academy Awards '93: Best Cinematography. **VHS, Beta, LV** ★★★1/2

The Secret Agent Presumed dead, a British intelligence agent (Gielgud) reappears and receives a new assignment. Using his faked death to his advantage, he easily journeys to Switzerland where he is to eliminate an enemy agent. Strange Hitchcockian melange of comedy and intrigue; atypical, but worthy offering from the Master.
1936 83m/B *GB* Madeleine Carroll, Peter Lorre, Robert Young, John Gielgud, Lilli Palmer; **D:** Alfred Hitchcock; **W:** Charles Bennett. **VHS, Beta, LV** ★★★

The Secret Garden The well-loved Frances Hodgson Burnett story has been remade and even revamped as a Broadway musical, but this is considered the definitive version. An orphan girl arrives at her uncle's somber Victorian estate. She starts tending a long-forgotten garden, and with its resurrection joy returns to the household. O'Brien leads an outstanding cast in one of her final juvenile roles. In black and white, with Technicolor for later garden scenes.
1949 92m/B Margaret O'Brien, Herbert Marshall, Dean Stockwell, Gladys Cooper, Elsa Lanchester, Brian Roper; **D:** Fred M. Wilcox. **VHS, Beta, LV** ★★★

The Secret Garden Lonely orphan Mary Lennox is sent to live with her uncle in England after her parents' deaths. Mary, who has grown up in India, is selfish and unhappy until she discovers two secrets on her uncle's estate. Class production of the children's classic by Frances Hodgson Burnett with wonderful performances; added prologue and afterword showing Mary as an adult are unnecessary, but don't detract either. Made for television as a "Hallmark Hall of Fame" special.
1987 (PG) 100m/C Gennie James, Barret Oliver, Jadrien Steele, Michael Hordern, Derek Jacobi, Billie Whitelaw, Lucy Gutteridge, Julian Glover, Colin Firth, Alan Grint. **VHS, LV** ★★★

The Secret Life of Walter Mitty An entertaining adaptation of the James Thurber short story about a meek man (Kaye) who lives an unusual secret fantasy life. Henpecked by his fi-

ancee and mother, oppressed at his job, he imagines himself in the midst of various heroic fantasies. While Thurber always professed to hate Kaye's characterization and the movie, it scored at the box office and today stands as a comedic romp for Kaye. Available with digitally remastered stereo and original movie trailer.
1947 110m/C Danny Kaye, Virginia Mayo, Boris Karloff, Ann Rutherford, Fay Bainter, Florence Bates; **D:** Norman Z. McLeod. **VHS, Beta, LV** ★★★

The Secret of Roan Inish Irish myth comes to life in this fantasy about the importance of family and place, seen through the eyes of 10-year-old Fiona Coneelly (newcomer Courtney), who's sent to live with her grandparents in post-WWII County Donegal. Fiona's drawn to her grandfather's stories about the family's ancestral home on the island of Roan Inish and the loss of her baby brother Jamie, who was carried out to sea. Another family tale is about a Selkie—a beautiful seal/woman captured by a Coneelly fisherman who eventually returned to her ocean home. When Fiona visits Roan Inish she becomes convinced that Jamie is alive and being cared for by the island's seals. Director Sayles keeps a firm grip on the cuteness factor while cinematographer Wexler works his usual magic on the sea, sky, and land of Ireland. Based on the 1957 novel "Secret of the Ron Mor Skerry" by Rosalie K. Fry.
1994 (PG) 102m/C Jeni Courtney, Michael Lally, Eileen Colgan, John Lynch, Richard Sheridan, Susan Lynch, Cillian Byrne, Haskell Wexler; **D:** John Sayles; **W:** John Sayles; **M:** Mason Daring. Nominations: Independent Spirit Awards '96: Best Director (Sayles), Best Film, Best Screenplay. **VHS, LV** ★★★★

Secrets of Women A rare Bergman comedy about three sisters-in-law who tell about their affairs and marriages as they await their husbands at a lakeside resort. His first commercial success, though it waited nine years for release (1961). In Swedish with English subtitles. **AKA:** Kvinnors Vantan; Waiting Women.
1952 114m/B *SW* Anita Bjork, Karl Arne Homsten, Eva Dahlbeck, Maj-Britt Nilsson, Jarl Kulle; **D:** Ingmar Bergman; **W:** Ingmar Bergman. **VHS, Beta** ★★★

Seduced and Abandoned A lothario seduces his fiancee's young sister. When the girl becomes pregnant, he refuses to marry her. Family complications abound. A comic look at the Italian code of honor. In Italian with

English subtitles. *AKA:* Sedotta e Abbandonata.
1964 118m/B *IT* Saro Urzi, Stefania Sandrelli, Aldo Puglisi; *D:* Pietro Germi. Cannes Film Festival '64: Best Actor (Urzi); National Board of Review Awards '64: 5 Best Foreign Films of the Year. **VHS, Beta** ★★★

Seduction of Mimi Comic farce of politics and seduction about a Sicilian laborer's escapades with the Communists and the local Mafia. Giannini is wonderful as the stubborn immigrant to the big city who finds himself in trouble. One of the funniest love scenes on film. Basis for the later movie "Which Way is Up?"
1972 (R) 92m/C *IT* Giancarlo Giannini, Mariangela Melato; *D:* Lina Wertmuller; *W:* Lina Wertmuller. Nominations: Cannes Film Festival '72: Best Film. **VHS, Beta** ★★★

Seize the Day A man approaching middle age (Williams) feels that he is a failure. Brilliant performances by all, plus a number of equally fine actors in small roles. Based on the short novel by Saul Bellow.
1986 93m/C Robin Williams, Joseph Wiseman, Jerry Stiller, Glenne Headly, Tony Roberts; *D:* Fielder Cook. **VHS, Beta, LV** ★★★

The Senator Was Indiscreet A farcical comedy concerning a slightly loony senator with presidential aspirations. He thinks he can win the nomination because he keeps a diary that would prove embarrassing to numerous colleagues. The diary then falls into the hands of a journalist. Powell is wonderful as the daffy politician. Playwright Kaufman's only directorial effort. *AKA:* Mr. Ashton was Indiscreet.
1947 75m/B William Powell, Ella Raines, Hans Conried; *D:* George S. Kaufman. New York Film Critics Awards '47: Best Actor (Powell). **VHS** ★★★

Send Me No Flowers Vintage Hudson-Day comedy. Hudson plays a hypochondriac who thinks his death is imminent. He decides to provide for his family's future by finding his wife a rich husband. She thinks he's feeling guilty for having an affair.
1964 100m/C *R* Rock Hudson, Doris Day, Tony Randall, Paul Lynde; *D:* Norman Jewison; *W:* Julius J. Epstein, Philip C. Epstein. **VHS, Beta** ★★★

Sense and Sensibility Thanks to the machinations of greedy relatives, the impecunious Dashwood family is forced to move to a country cottage when father dies. Sensible Elinor (Thompson) looks after the house-hold while overly romantic Marianne (Winslet) pines for passion—ignoring the noble attentions of middle-aged neighbor Brandon (Rickman) for the far more dashing Willoughby (Wise). Elinor has her own hopes for marriage with boyishly ineffectual Edward Ferrars (Grant) and all three men have secrets to crush romantic dreams (at least temporarily). Somewhat slow-paced but witty adaptation (by Thompson) of Jane Austen's first novel, well-acted and beautifully photographed (oh, to be in the English countryside).
1995 (PG) 135m/C *GB* Emma Thompson, Kate Winslet, Hugh Grant, Alan Rickman, Greg Wise, Robert Hardy, Elizabeth Spriggs, Emile Francois, Gemma Jones, James Fleet, Harriet Walter, Imogen Stubbs, Imelda Staunton, Hugh Laurie, Richard Lumsden; *D:* Ang Lee; *W:* Emma Thompson; *M:* Patrick Doyle, Michael Coulter. Golden Globe Awards '96: Best Film—Drama, Best Screenplay; Los Angeles Film Critics Association Awards '95: Best Screenplay; National Board of Review Awards '95: Best Actress (Thompson), Best Director (Lee), Best Film; New York Film Critics Awards '95: Best Director (Lee); Screen Actors Guild Award '95: Best Supporting Actress (Winslet); Nominations: Academy Awards '95: Best Actress (Thompson), Best Adapted Screenplay, Best Cinematography, Best Costume Design, Best Supporting Actress (Winslet), Best Score, Best Picture; British Academy Awards '95: Best Actress (Thompson), Best Adapted Screenplay, Best Cinematography, Best Director (Lee), Best Film, Best Supporting Actor (Rickman), Best Supporting Actress (Winslet, Spriggs), Best Score; Directors Guild of America Awards '95: Best Director (Lee); Golden Globe Awards '96: Best Actress—Drama (Thompson), Best Director (Lee), Best Supporting Actress (Winslet), Best Score; Screen Actors Guild Award '95: Best Actress (Thompson), Cast; Writers Guild of America '95: Best Adapted Screenplay. **VHS** ★★★1/2

Separate But Equal One of TV's greatest history lessons, a powerful dramatization of the 1954 Brown vs. The Board of Education case that wrung a landmark civil rights decision from the Supreme Court. Great care is taken to humanize all the participants, from the humblest schoolchild to NAACP lawyer Thurgood Marshall (Poitier). On two cassettes.
1991 (PG) 194m/C Sidney Poitier, Burt Lancaster, Richard Kiley, Cleavon Little, John McMartin, Graham Beckel, Lynne Thigpen, Albert Hall; *D:* George Stevens; *W:* George Stevens. **VHS, LV** ★★★1/2

Separate Tables Adaptation of the Terence Rattigan play about a varied cast of characters involved in their personal dramas in a British seaside hotel. Guests include a matriarch and her shy daughter, a divorced couple, a spinster, and a presumed war hero. Their secrets and loves are examined in grand style. Fine acting all around.
1958 98m/B Burt Lancaster, David Niven, Rita Hayworth, Deborah Kerr, Wendy Hiller, Rod Taylor, Gladys Cooper, Felix Aylmer, Cathleen Nesbitt; **D:** Delbert Mann; **W:** John Gay. Academy Awards '58: Best Actor (Niven), Best Supporting Actress (Hiller); National Board of Review Awards '58: 10 Best Films of the Year; New York Film Critics Awards '58: Best Actor (Niven); Nominations: Academy Awards '58: Best Actress (Kerr), Best Adapted Screenplay, Best Black and White Cinematography, Best Picture, Best Original Score. **VHS, Beta ★★★1/2**

Sergeant Rutledge The story of a court-martial, told in flashback, about a black calvary officer on trial for rape and murder. A detailed look at overt and covert racism handled by master director Ford. It is always apparent Strode (as Rutledge) is a heroic, yet human, figure who refuses to be beaten down by circumstances. The courtroom setting is deliberately oppressive but does make the film somewhat static. Based on the novel "Captain Buffalo" by James Warner Bellah.
1960 112m/C Woody Strode, Jeffrey Hunter, Constance Towers, Billie Burke, Juano Hernandez, Carleton Young, Charles Seel, Jan Styne, Mae Marsh; **D:** John Ford; **W:** Willis Goldbeck, James Warner Bellah; **M:** Howard Jackson. **VHS ★★★**

Sergeant York Timely and enduring war movie based on the true story of Alvin York, the country boy from Tennessee drafted during WWI. At first a pacifist, Sergeant York (Cooper, well cast in an Oscar-winning role) finds justification for fighting and becomes one of the war's greatest heros. Gentle scenes of rural life contrast with horrific battlegrounds. York served as a consultant.
1941 134m/B Gary Cooper, Joan Leslie, Walter Brennan, Dickie Moore, Ward Bond, George Tobias, Noah Beery Jr., June Lockhart, Stanley Ridges, Margaret Wycherly; **D:** Howard Hawks; **W:** Abem Finkel, Harry Chandlee, Howard Koch, John Huston; **M:** Max Steiner. Academy Awards '41: Best Actor (Cooper), Best Film Editing; New York Film Critics Awards '41: Best Actor (Cooper); Nominations: Academy Awards '41: Best Black and White Cinematography, Best Director

(Hawks), Best Interior Decoration, Best Original Screenplay, Best Picture, Best Sound, Best Supporting Actor (Brennan), Best Supporting Actress (Wycherly), Best Original Score. **VHS, Beta ★★★★**

Serial Mom June Cleaver-like housewife Turner is nearly perfect, except when someone disrupts her orderly life. Didn't rewind your videotape? Chose the white shoes after Labor Day? Uh oh. Stardom reigns after she's caught and the murderer-as-celebrity phenomenon is exploited to the fullest. Darkly funny Waters satire tends toward the mainstream and isn't as perverse as earlier efforts, but still maintains a shocking edge (vital organs are good for an appearance or two). Turner's chameleonic performance as the perfect mom/crazed killer is right on target, recalling "The War of the Roses." Waterston, Lake, and Lillard are terrific as her generic suburban family.
1994 (R) 93m/C Kathleen Turner, Ricki Lake, Sam Waterston, Matthew Lillard, Mink Stole, Traci Lords; **Cameos:** Suzanne Somers, Joan Rivers, Patty Hearst; **D:** John Waters; **W:** John Waters; **M:** Basil Poledouris. **VHS, LV ★★★**

Serpico Based on Peter Maas's book about the true-life exploits of Frank Serpico, a New York undercover policeman who exposed corruption in the police department. Known as much for his nonconformism as for his honesty, the real Serpico eventually retired from the force and moved to Europe. South Bronx-raised Pacino gives the character reality and strength. Excellent New York location photography.
1973 (R) 130m/C Al Pacino, John Randolph, Jack Kehoe, Barbara Eda-Young, Cornelia Sharpe, F. Murray Abraham, Tony Roberts; **D:** Sidney Lumet. Golden Globe Awards '74: Best Actor—Drama (Pacino); National Board of Review Awards '73: Best Actor (Pacino); Writers Guild of America '73: Best Adapted Screenplay; Nominations: Academy Awards '73: Best Actor (Pacino), Best Adapted Screenplay. **VHS, Beta, LV ★★★**

The Servant A dark, intriguing examination of British class hypocrisy and the master-servant relationship. A rich, bored playboy is ruined by his socially inferior but crafty and ambitious manservant. Playwright Harold Pinter wrote the adaptation of Robin Maugham's novel in his first collaboration with director Losey. The best kind of British societal navel-gazing.
1963 112m/B *GB* Dirk Bogarde, James Fox, Sarah Miles, Wendy Craig; **D:** Joseph

Losey; **W:** Harold Pinter. British Academy Awards '63: Best Actor (Bogarde); New York Film Critics Awards '64: Best Screenplay. **VHS, Beta** ★★★1/2

The Set-Up Excellent, original if somewhat overwrought morality tale about integrity set in the world of boxing. Filmed as a continuous narrative covering only 72 minutes in the life of an aging fighter (Ryan). Told to throw a fight, he must battle gangsters when he refuses. Powerful, with fine performances, especially from Ryan in the lead. Inspired by Joseph Moncure March's narrative poem.
1949 72m/B Robert Ryan, Audrey Totter, George Tobias, Alan Baxter, James Edwards, Wallace Ford; **D:** Robert Wise. **VHS, Beta, LV** ★★★★

Seven If this grim thriller can't make you jump, you're dead, and you won't be the only one. Arrogant, ignorant detective David Mills (Pitt) is newly partnered with erudite old-timer William Somerset (Freeman) and they're stuck with the bizarre case of a morbidly obese man who was forced to eat himself to death. The weary Somerset is certain it's just the beginning and he's right—the non-buddy duo are on the trail of a serial killer who uses the seven deadly sins (gluttony, greed, sloth, pride, lust, envy, and wrath) as his modus operandi. Since most of the film is shot in dark, grimy, and unrelentingly rainy circumstances, much of the grotesqueness of the murders is left to the viewer's imagination—which will be in overdrive.
1995 (R) 127m/C Brad Pitt, Morgan Freeman, Gwyneth Paltrow, Kevin Spacey, R. Lee Ermey, Richard Roundtree, John C. McGinley, Julie Araskog, Reg E. Cathey, Peter Crombie; **D:** David Fincher; **W:** Andrew Kevin Walker; **M:** Howard Shore, Darius Khondji. National Board of Review Awards '95: Best Supporting Actor (Spacey); New York Film Critics Awards '95: Best Supporting Actor (Spacey); Nominations: Academy Awards '95: Best Film Editing; British Academy Awards '95: Best Original Screenplay. **VHS, LV** ★★★

Seven Beauties Very dark war comedy about a small-time Italian crook in Naples with seven ugly sisters to support. He survives a German prison camp and much else; unforgettably, he seduces the ugly commandant of his camp to save his own life. Good acting and tight direction. **AKA:** Pasqualino Settebellezze; Pasqualino: Seven Beauties.
1976 116m/C *IT* Giancarlo Giannini, Fernando Rey, Shirley Stoler, Elena Fiore, Enzo Vitale, Tonino Delli Colli; **D:** Lina Wertmuller; **W:** Lina Wertmuller. Nominations: Academy Awards '76: Best Actor (Giannini), Best Director (Wertmuller), Best Foreign Language Film, Best Original Screenplay. **VHS, Beta, LV** ★★★★

Seven Brides for Seven Brothers The eldest of seven fur-trapping brothers in the Oregon Territory brings home a wife. She begins to civilize the other six, who realize the merits of women and begin to look for romances of their own. Thrilling choreography by Michael Kidd—don't miss "The Barn Raising." Charming performances by Powell and Keel, both in lovely voice. Based on Stephen Vincent Benet's story. Thrills, chills, singin', dancin'—a classic Hollywood good time. ♪ When You're In Love; Spring, Spring, Spring; Sobbin' Women; Bless Your Beautiful Hide; Goin' Co'tin; Wonderful, Wonderful Day; June Bride; Lonesome Polecat Lament.
1954 103m/C Howard Keel, Jane Powell, Russ Tamblyn, Julie Newmar, Jeff Richards, Tommy Rall, Virginia Gibson; **D:** Stanley Donen. Academy Awards '54: Best Score; National Board of Review Awards '54: 10 Best Films of the Year; Nominations: Academy Awards '54: Best Color Cinematography, Best Film Editing, Best Picture, Best Screenplay. **VHS, Beta, LV, 8mm** ★★★1/2

Seven Chances Silent classic that Keaton almost didn't make, believing instead that it should go to Harold Lloyd. Lawyer Keaton finds that he can inherit $7 million if he marries by 7:00 p.m. After his girlfriend turns down his botched proposal, chaos breaks loose when he advertises for someone—anyone—to marry him and make him rich. Suddenly he finds what seems to be hundreds of women willing to make the sacrifice, setting up one of the great film pursuits. Memorable boulder sequence was added after preview audience indicated climax was lacking that certain something.
1925 60m/B Buster Keaton, T. Roy Barnes, Snitz Edwards, Ruth Dwyer, Frankie Raymond; **D:** Buster Keaton. **VHS** ★★★1/2

Seven Days in May Topical but still gripping Cold War nuclear-peril thriller. An American general plans a military takeover because he considers the president's pacifism traitorous. Highly suspenseful, with a breathtaking climax. Houseman's film debut in a small role.
1964 117m/B Burt Lancaster, Kirk Douglas, Edmond O'Brien, Fredric March,

Ava Gardner, John Houseman; **D:** John Frankenheimer; **W:** Rod Serling; **M:** Jerry Goldsmith. Golden Globe Awards '65: Best Supporting Actor (O'Brien); Nominations: Academy Awards '64: Best Art Direction/Set Decoration (B & W), Best Supporting Actor (O'Brien). **VHS, Beta, LV** ★★★1/2

Seven Faces of Dr. Lao Dr. Lao is the proprietor of a magical circus that changes the lives of the residents of a small western town. Marvelous special effects and makeup (Randall plays seven characters) highlight this charming family film in the Pal tradition. Charles Finney adapted from his novel.
1963 101m/C Tony Randall, Barbara Eden, Arthur O'Connell, Lee Patrick, Noah Beery Jr., John Qualen; **D:** George Pal. **VHS, Beta, LV** ★★★

The Seven Little Foys Enjoyable musical biography of Eddie Foy (played ebulliantly by Hope) and his famed vaudevillian troupe. Cagney's appearance as George M. Cohan is brief, but long enough for a memorable dance duet with Hope. ♪ Mary's a Grand Old Name; I'm a Yankee Doodle Dandy; I'm the Greatest Father of Them All; Nobody; Comedy Ballet; I'm Tired; Chinatown, My Chinatown.
1955 95m/C Bob Hope, Milly Vitale, George Tobias, Angela Clark, James Cagney; **D:** Melville Shavelson; **W:** Jack Rose, Melville Shavelson. Nominations: Academy Awards '55: Best Story & Screenplay. **VHS, Beta** ★★★

The Seven Percent Solution Dr. Watson persuades Sherlock Holmes to meet with Sigmund Freud to cure his cocaine addiction. Holmes and Freud then find themselves teaming up to solve a supposed kidnapping. Adapted by Nicholas Meyer from his own novel. One of the most charming Holmes films; well-cast, intriguing blend of mystery, drama, and fun.
1976 (PG) 113m/C Alan Arkin, Nicol Williamson, Laurence Olivier, Robert Duvall, Vanessa Redgrave, Joel Grey, Samantha Eggar, Jeremy Kemp, Charles Gray, Regine; **D:** Herbert Ross; **W:** Nicholas Meyer; **M:** John Addison. National Board of Review Awards '76: 10 Best Films of the Year; Nominations: Academy Awards '76: Best Adapted Screenplay, Best Costume Design. **VHS, Beta, LV** ★★★

Seven Samurai Kurosawa's masterpiece, set in 16th-century Japan. A small farming village, beset by marauding bandits, hires seven professional soldiers to rid itself of the scourge. Wanna watch a samurai movie? This is the one. Sweeping, complex human drama with all the ingredients: action, suspense, comedy. Available in several versions of varying length, all long—and all too short. Splendid acting. In Japanese with English subtitles. **AKA:** Shichinin No Samurai; The Magnificent Seven.
1954 204m/B JP Toshiro Mifune, Takashi Shimura, Yoshio Inaba, Kuninori Kodo, Ko Kimura, Seiji Miyaguchi, Minoru Chiaki; **D:** Akira Kurosawa; **W:** Akira Kurosawa; **M:** Fumio Hayasaka. Venice Film Festival '54: Silver Prize; Nominations: Academy Awards '56: Best Art Direction/Set Decoration (B & W), Best Costume Design (B & W). **VHS, Beta, LV** ★★★★

Seven Sinners A South Seas cabaret singer (Dietrich) attracts sailors like flies, resulting in bar brawls, romance, and intrigue. Manly sailor Wayne falls for her. A good-natured, standard Hollywood adventure. Well cast; performed and directed with gusto. **AKA:** Cafe of the Seven Sinners.
1940 83m/B Marlene Dietrich, John Wayne, Albert Dekker, Broderick Crawford, Mischa Auer, Billy Gilbert, Oscar Homolka; **D:** Tay Garnett. **VHS, Beta, LV** ★★★

Seven Thieves Charming performances and nice direction make this tale of the perfect crime especially watchable. Robinson, getting on in years, wants one last big heist. With the help of Collins and Steiger, he gets his chance. From the Max Catto novel "Lions at the Kill." Surprisingly witty and lighthearted for this subject matter, and good still comes out ahead of evil.
1960 102m/C Joan Collins, Edward G. Robinson, Eli Wallach, Rod Steiger; **D:** Henry Hathaway. Nominations: Academy Awards '60: Best Costume Design (B & W). **VHS** ★★★

The Seven Year Itch Classic, sexy Monroe comedy. Stunning blonde model (who else?) moves upstairs just as happily married guy Ewell's wife leaves for a long vacation. Understandably, he gets itchy. Monroe's famous blown skirt scene is here, as well as funny situations and appealing performances.
1955 105m/C Marilyn Monroe, Tom Ewell, Evelyn Keyes, Sonny Tufts, Victor Moore, Doro Merande, Robert Strauss, Oscar Homolka, Carolyn Jones; **D:** Billy Wilder; **W:** George Axelrod, Billy Wilder. Golden Globe Awards '56: Best Actor—Musical/Comedy (Ewell). **VHS, Beta, LV** ★★★

1776 A musical comedy about America's first Continental Congress. The delegates battle the English and each other trying to establish a set of laws and the Declaration of Independence. Adapted from the Broadway hit with many members of the original cast. Available in widescreen format on laserdisc. ♪ The Lees of Old Virginia; He Plays the Violin; But, Mr. Adams; Sit Down John; Till Then; Piddle, Twiddle and Resolve; Yours, Yours, Yours; Mama, Look Sharp; The Egg. **1972 (G) 141m/C** William Daniels, Howard da Silva, Ken Howard, Donald Madden, Blythe Danner, Ronald Holgate, Virginia Vestoff, Stephen Nathan, Ralston Hill; *D:* Peter H. Hunt. National Board of Review Awards '72: 10 Best Films of the Year; Nominations: Academy Awards '72: Best Cinematography. **VHS, Beta, LV ★★★**

The Seventh Cross Tracy stars as one of seven men who escape from a German concentration camp. When it is discovered they're gone, the commandant nails seven crosses to seven trees, intending them for the seven escapees. Watch for Tandy ("Driving Miss Daisy") in her first screen appearance. Effective wartime drama. From the novel by Anna Seghers. **1944 110m/B** Spencer Tracy, Signe Hasso, Hume Cronyn, Jessica Tandy, Agnes Moorehead, Herbert Rudley, Felix Bressart, Ray Collins, Alexander Granach, George Macready, Steve Geray, Karen Verne, George Zucco; *D:* Fred Zinneman. Nominations: Academy Awards '44: Best Supporting Actor (Cronyn). **VHS ★★★**

The Seventh Seal As the plague sweeps through Europe a weary knight convinces "death" to play one game of chess with him. If the knight wins, he and his wife will be spared. The game leads to a discussion of religion and the existence of God. Considered by some Bergman's masterpiece. Von Sydow is stunning as the knight. In Swedish with English subtitles. Also available on laserdisc with a filmography of Bergman's work and commentary by film historian Peter Cowie. *AKA:* Det Sjunde Inseglet. **1956 96m/B** SW Gunnar Bjornstrand, Max von Sydow, Bibi Andersson, Bengt Ekerot, Nils Poppe, Gunnel Lindblom; *D:* Ingmar Bergman; *W:* Ingmar Bergman; *M:* Erik Nordgren. Cannes Film Festival '57: Grand Jury Prize. **VHS, Beta, LV, 8mm ★★★★**

The Seventh Veil A concert pianist loses the use of her hands in a fire, and with it her desire to live. Through the help of her friends and a hypnotizing doctor, she regains her love for life. Superb, dark psycho-drama. Todd as the pianist and Mason as her guardian are both unforgettable. Wonderful music and staging. **1946 91m/B** GB James Mason, Ann Todd, Herbert Lom, Hugh McDermott, Albert Lieven; *D:* Compton Bennett. Academy Awards '46: Best Original Screenplay. **VHS, Beta ★★★1/2**

The Seventh Voyage of Sinbad Sinbad seeks to restore his fiancee from the midget size to which an evil magician (Thatcher) has reduced her. Ray Harryhausen works his animation magic around a well-developed plot and engaging performances by the real actors. Great score and fun, fast-moving plot. **1958 (G) 94m/C** Kerwin Mathews, Kathryn Grant, Torin Thatcher, Richard Eyer; *D:* Nathan (Hertz) Juran; *W:* Kenneth Kolb; *M:* Bernard Herrmann. **VHS, Beta, LV ★★★**

sex, lies and videotape Acclaimed, popular independent film by first-timer Soderbergh, detailing the complex relations among a childless married couple, the wife's adulterous sister, and a mysterious college friend of the husband's obsessed with videotaping women as they talk about their sex lives. Heavily awarded, including first prize at Cannes. Confidently uses much (too much?) dialogue and slow (too slow?) pace. Available on laserdisc with a deleted scene and interviews with the director; also includes two theatrical trailers and a short film by Soderbergh. **1989 (R) 101m/C** James Spader, Andie MacDowell, Peter Gallagher, Laura San Giacomo, Ron Vawter, Steven Brill; *D:* Steven Soderbergh; *W:* Steven Soderbergh; *M:* Cliff Martinez, Walt Lloyd. Cannes Film Festival '89: Best Actor (Spader), Best Film; Independent Spirit Awards '90: Best Actress (MacDowell), Best Director (Soderbergh), Best Film, Best Supporting Actress (San Giacomo); Sundance Film Festival '89: Audience Award; Nominations: Academy Awards '89: Best Original Screenplay. **VHS, Beta, LV, 8mm ★★★**

The Shadow Box Three terminally ill people at a California hospice confront their destinies. Pulitzer Prize-winning play by Michael Cristofer is actually improved by director Newman and a superb, well-chosen cast. Powerful. **1980 96m/C** Joanne Woodward, Christopher Plummer, Robert Urich, Valerie Harper, Sylvia Sidney, Melinda Dillon, Ben Masters, John Considine, James Broderick; *D:* Paul Newman; *M:* Henry Mancini. **VHS, Beta ★★★**

Shadow of a Doubt Uncle Charlie has come to visit his relatives in

Santa Rosa. Although he is handsome and charming, his young niece slowly comes to realize he is a wanted mass murderer—and he comes to recognize her suspicions. Hitchcock's personal favorite movie; a quietly creepy venture into Middle American menace. Good performances, especially by Cronyn. From the story by Gordon McConnell.
1943 108m/B Teresa Wright, Joseph Cotten, Hume Cronyn, MacDonald Carey, Henry Travers, Wallace Ford; **D:** Alfred Hitchcock; **W:** Thorton Wilder; **M:** Dimitri Tiomkin. Nominations: Academy Awards '43: Best Story. **VHS, Beta, LV ★★★1/2**

Shadow of the Thin Man In the fourth "Thin Man" film, following "Another Thin Man," Nick and Nora stumble onto a murder at the racetrack. The rapport between Powell and Loy is still going strong, providing us with some wonderful entertainment. Followed by "The Thin Man Goes Home."
1941 97m/B William Powell, Myrna Loy, Barry Nelson, Donna Reed, Sam Levene, Alan Baxter, Dickie Hall, Loring Smith, Joseph Anthony, Henry O'Neill; **D:** Woodbridge S. Van Dyke. **VHS, Beta ★★★**

Shadowlands Touching, tragic story of the late-in-life romance between celebrated author and Christian theologian C.S. Lewis (Hopkins) and brash New York divorcee Joy Gresham (Winger). Attenborough's direction is rather stately and sweeping and Winger is really too young for her role but Hopkins is excellent as (another) repressed man who finds more emotions than he can handle. Critically acclaimed adaptation of Nicholson's play will require lots of Kleenex.
1993 (PG) 130m/C GB Anthony Hopkins, Debra Winger, Edward Hardwicke, Joseph Mazzello, Michael Denison, John Wood, Peter Firth, Peter Howell; **D:** Richard Attenborough; **W:** William Nicholson; **M:** George Fenton. British Academy Awards '93: Best Film; Los Angeles Film Critics Association Awards '93: Best Actor (Hopkins); National Board of Review Awards '93: Best Actor (Hopkins); Nominations: Academy Awards '93: Best Actress (Winger), Best Adapted Screenplay; British Academy Awards '93: Best Actor (Hopkins), Best Actress (Winger), Best Adapted Screenplay, Best Director (Attenborough). **VHS, LV ★★★**

Shadows Director Cassavetes's first indie feature finds jazz player Hugh (Hurd) forced to play dives to support his brother Ben (Carruthers) and sister Lelia (Goldoni). Light-skinned enough to pass for white, Lelia takes on the uptown New York art crowd and gets involved with the white Tony (Ray), who leaves when he finds out her true heritage. Meanwhile, Ben drifts along with his friends who abandon him when trouble finds them. Script was improvised by cast.
1960 87m/B Hugh Hurd, Lelia Goldoni, Ben Carruthers, Anthony Ray, Rupert Crosse, Tom Allen; **D:** John Cassavetes; **M:** Charles Mingus, Shifi Hadi, Erich Kollmar. **VHS ★★★**

Shaft A black private eye is hired to find a Harlem gangster's kidnapped daughter. Lotsa sex and violence; suspenseful and well directed. Great ending. Academy Award winning theme song by Isaac Hayes, the first music award from the Academy to an African-American. Adapted from the novel by Ernest Tidyman. Followed by "Shaft's Big Score" and "Shaft in Africa." ♪ Theme From Shaft.
1971 (R) 98m/C Richard Roundtree, Moses Gunn, Charles Cioffi; **D:** Gordon Parks; **W:** John D.F. Black. Academy Awards '71: Best Song ("Theme from Shaft"); Golden Globe Awards '72: Best Score; Nominations: Academy Awards '71: Best Original Score. **VHS, Beta ★★★**

Shag: The Movie The time is 1963, the setting Myrtle Beach, South Carolina, the latest craze shaggin' when four friends hit the beach for one last weekend together. Carson (Cates) is getting ready to marry staid Harley (Power); Melaina (Fonda) wants to be discovered in Hollywood; and Pudge (Gish) and Luanne (Hannah) are off to college. They encounter lots of music, boys, and dancing in this delightful film. Not to be confused with other "teen" movies, this one boasts a good script and an above average cast.
1989 (PG) 96m/C Phoebe Cates, Annabeth Gish, Bridget Fonda, Page Hannah, Scott Coffey, Robert Rusler, Tyrone Power Jr., Jeff Yagher, Carrie Hamilton, Shirley Anne Field, Leilani Sarelle Ferrer; **D:** Zelda Barron; **W:** Robin Swicord, Lanier Laney, Terry Sweeney. **VHS, Beta, LV ★★★**

Shaka Zulu British miniseries depicting the career of Shaka, king of the Zulus (Cele). Set in the early 19th century during British ascendency in Africa. Good, absorbing cross-cultural action drama would have been better with more inspired directing by Faure.
1983 300m/C GB Edward Fox, Robert Powell, Trevor Howard, Christopher Lee, Fiona Fullerton, Henry Cele; **D:** William C. Faure. **VHS, Beta ★★★**

Shakespeare Wallah Tender, plausible drama of romance and postcolonial relations in India. A troupe of traveling Shakespeareans quixotically tours India trying to make enough money to return to England. Wonderfully acted and exquisitely and sensitively directed by Ivory.
1965 120m/B Laura Liddell, Geoffrey Kendal, Felicity Kendal, Shashi Kapoor, Madhur Jaffrey; **D:** James Ivory; **W:** Ruth Prawer Jhabvala, James Ivory. **VHS, Beta**
★★★1/2

Shall We Dance And shall we ever! Seventh Astaire-Rogers pairing has a famous ballet dancer and a musical-comedy star embark on a promotional romance and marriage to boost their careers, only to find themselves truly falling in love. Score by the Gershwins includes memorable songs. Thin, lame plot—but that's okay. For fans of good singing and dancing, and especially of this immortal pair. ♩ Slap That Bass; Beginner's Luck; Let's Call the Whole Thing Off; Walking the Dog; They All Laughed; They Can't Take That Away From Me; Shall We Dance.
1937 116m/B Fred Astaire, Ginger Rogers, Edward Everett Horton, Eric Blore; **D:** Mark Sandrich; **M:** George Gershwin, Ira Gershwin. Nominations: Academy Awards '37: Best Song ("They Can't Take That Away From Me"). **VHS, Beta, LV** ★★★

The Shame A Bergman masterpiece focusing on the struggle for dignity in the midst of war. Married concert musicians Ullmann and von Sydow flee a bloody civil war for a small island off their country's coast. Inevitably, the carnage reaches them and their lives become a struggle to endure and retain a small measure of civilized behavior as chaos overtakes them. Deeply despairing and brilliantly acted. In Swedish with English subtitles.
1968 (R) 103m/C SW Max von Sydow, Liv Ullmann, Gunnar Bjornstrand, Sigge Furst, Brigitta Valberg, Hans Alfredson, Ingvar Kjellson; **D:** Ingmar Bergman; **W:** Ingmar Bergman. National Society of Film Critics Awards '68: Best Actress (Ullmann), Best Director (Bergman), Best Film. **VHS**
★★★1/2

Shane A retired gunfighter, now a drifter, comes to the aid of a homestead family threatened by a land baron and his hired gun. Ladd is the mystery man who becomes the idol of the family's young son. Classic, flawless western. Pulitzer Prize-winning western novelist A.B. Guthrie Jr. adapted from the novel by Jack

Schaefer. Long and stately; worth savoring.
1953 117m/C Alan Ladd, Jean Arthur, Van Heflin, Brandon de Wilde, Jack Palance, Ben Johnson, Elisha Cook Jr., Edgar Buchanan, Emile Meyer; **D:** George Stevens; **W:** Jack Sher; **M:** Victor Young. Academy Awards '53: Best Color Cinematography; National Board of Review Awards '53: 10 Best Films of the Year, Best Director (Stevens); Nominations: Academy Awards '53: Best Director (Stevens), Best Picture, Best Screenplay, Best Supporting Actor (de Wilde, Palance). **VHS, Beta, LV**
★★★★

Shanghai Express Dietrich is at her most alluring in this mystical and exotic story that made legends out of both star and director. Dietrich plays Shanghai Lily, a woman of objectionable reputation, who has a reunion of sorts with ex-lover Brooks aboard a slow-moving train through China. Remade as "Peking Express." Based on a story by Harry Hervey.
1932 80m/B Marlene Dietrich, Clive Brook, Anna May Wong, Warner Oland, Eugene Pallette, Lawrence Grant, Louise Closser Hale; **D:** Josef von Sternberg; **W:** Jules Furthman. Academy Awards '32: Best Cinematography (Garmes). **VHS** ★★★1/2

Shanghai Triad Seventh collaboration of director Yimou and star Li takes place in a violent crime dynasty of 1930s Shanghai. Here, eight days are seen through the eyes of a young boy (Cuihua) initiated into the Triad to be the lackey of the mob boss's arrogant mistress (Li). The trio and some trusty associates flee to the country after things heat up with a rival mob. Yimou subtly distinguishes the dichotomy between the jaded criminals and the naive youth with the move from the city to the country and his use of color and tone while avoiding cliche. Plot twists are fresh and technical aspects impeccable.
1995 (R) 108m/C FR CH Gong Li, Li Bao-Tian, Li Xuejian, Shun Chun Shusheng, Wang Xiaoxiao Cuihua, Jiang Baoying; **D:** Zhang Yimou; **W:** Bi Feiyu, Lu Yue; **M:** Zhang Guangtain. Nominations: Academy Awards '95: Best Cinematography; Golden Globe Awards '96: Best Foreign Language Film. **VHS** ★★★1/2

The Shawshank Redemption Bank veep Andy (Robbins) is convicted of the murder of his wife and her lover and sentenced to the "toughest prison in the Northeast." While there he forms a friendship with lifer Red (Freeman), experiences the brutality of prison life, adapts, offers financial advice to the guards, and helps the

warden (Gunton) cook the prison books . . . all in a short 19 years. In his debut, director Darabont avoids belaboring most prison movie cliches while Robbins' talent for playing ambiguous characters is put to good use, and Freeman brings his usual grace to what could have been a thankless role. Adapted from the novella "Rita Hayworth and the Shawshank Redemption" by Stephen King.
1994 (R) 142m/C Tim Robbins, Morgan Freeman, Bob Gunton, William Sadler, Clancy Brown, Mark Rolston, Gil Bellows, James Whitmore; **D:** Frank Darabont, Roger Deakins; **W:** Frank Darabont. Nominations: Academy Awards '94: Best Actor (Freeman), Best Adapted Screenplay, Best Cinematography, Best Film Editing, Best Picture, Best Sound, Best Original Score; Directors Guild of America Awards '94: Best Director (Darabont); Golden Globe Awards '95: Best Actor—Drama (Freeman), Best Screenplay; Screen Actors Guild Award '94: Best Actor (Freeman), Best Actor (Robbins). **VHS, LV** ★★★1/2

She Done Him Wrong West stars as Lil, an 1890s saloon singer in the screen version of her Broadway hit "Diamond Lily," and imparts on the negligible plot her usual share of double entendres and racy comments. Grant is likeable as the hapless sap she beds. ♪ Silver Threads Among the Gold; Masie, My Pretty Daisy; Easy Rider; I Like a Guy What Takes His Time; Frankie and Johnny.
1933 65m/B Mae West, Cary Grant, Owen Moore, Noah Beery Sr., Gilbert Roland, Louise Beavers; **D:** Lowell Sherman. National Board of Review Awards '33: 10 Best Films of the Year; Nominations: Academy Awards '33: Best Picture. **VHS, Beta, LV** ★★★

She Wore a Yellow Ribbon An undermanned cavalry outpost makes a desperate attempt to repel invading Indians. Wayne shines as an officer who shuns retirement in order to help his comrades. Excellent color photography by Winston C. Hoch. Still fun and compelling. The second chapter in director Ford's noted cavalry trilogy, preceded by "Fort Apache" and followed by "Rio Grande."
1949 93m/C John Wayne, Joanne Dru, John Agar, Ben Johnson, Harry Carey Jr., Victor McLaglen, Mildred Natwick, George O'Brien; **D:** John Ford. Academy Awards '49: Best Color Cinematography. **VHS, Beta, LV** ★★★1/2

The Sheik High camp Valentino has English woman fall hopelessly under the romantic spell of Arab sheik who flares his nostrils. Followed by "Son of the Sheik."
1921 80m/B Agnes Ayres, Rudolph Valentino, Adolphe Menjou, Walter Long, Lucien Littlefield, George Waggner, Patsy Ruth Miller; **D:** George Melford. **VHS, Beta** ★★★

The Sheltering Sky American couple Winger and Malkovich flee the plasticity of their native land for a trip to the Sahara desert where they hope to renew their spirits and rekindle love. Accompanied by socialite acquaintance Scott with whom Winger soon has an affair, their personalities and belief systems deteriorate as they move through the grave poverty of North Africa in breathtaking heat. Based on the existential novel by American expatriate Paul Bowles who narrates and appears briefly in a bar scene. Overlong but visually stunning, with cinematography by Vittorio Storaro.
1990 (R) 139m/C Debra Winger, John Malkovich, Campbell Scott, Jill Bennett, Timothy Spall, Ben Vu-An, Sotigui Koyate, Amina Annabi, Paul Bowles; **D:** Bernardo Bertolucci; **W:** Mark Peploe, Bernardo Bertolucci, Vittorio Storaro; **M:** Ryuichi Sakamoto, Richard Horowitz. Golden Globe Awards '91: Best Score; New York Film Critics Awards '90: Best Cinematography. **VHS, Beta, LV** ★★★

Shenandoah A Virginia farmer (Stewart, in a top-notch performance) who has raised six sons and a daughter, tries to remain neutral during the Civil War. War takes its toll as the daughter marries a Confederate soldier and his sons become involved in the fighting. Screen debut for Ross.
1965 105m/C James Stewart, Doug McClure, Glenn Corbett, Patrick Wayne, Rosemary Forsyth, Katharine Ross, George Kennedy; **D:** Andrew V. McLaglen. Nominations: Academy Awards '65: Best Sound. **VHS, Beta, LV** ★★★

Sherlock Holmes and the Secret Weapon Based on "The Dancing Men" by Sir Arthur Conan Doyle. Holmes battles the evil Moriarty in an effort to save the British war effort. Good Holmes mystery with gripping wartime setting. Hoey is fun as bumbling Inspector Lestrade. Available colorized. **AKA:** Secret Weapon.
1942 68m/B Basil Rathbone, Nigel Bruce, Karen Verne, William Post Jr., Dennis Hoey, Holmes Herbert, Mary Gordon, Henry Victor, Philip Van Zandt, George Eldridge, Leslie Denison, James Craven, Paul Fix, Hugh Herbert, Lionel Atwill; **D:** Roy William Neill. **VHS, LV** ★★★

She's Gotta Have It Lee wrote, directed, edited, produced and starred in this romantic comedy about an independent-minded black girl in Brooklyn and the three men and one woman who compete for her attention. Full of rough edges, but vigorous, confident, and hip. Filmed entirely in black and white except for one memorable scene. Put Lee on the filmmaking map.
1986 (R) 84m/B Spike Lee, Tommy Redmond Hicks, Raye Dowell; *D:* Spike Lee. **VHS, Beta, LV ★★★**

Shin Heike Monogatari Mizoguchi's second to last film, in which a deposed Japanese emperor in 1137 endeavors to win back the throne from the current despot, who cannot handle the feudal lawlessness. Acclaimed; his second film in color. In Japanese with English subtitles. *AKA:* "New Tales of the Taira Clan."
1955 106m/C *JP* Raizo Ichikawa, Ichijiro Oya, Michiyo Kogure, Eijiro Yanagi, Tatsuya Ishiguro, Yoshiko Kuga; *D:* Kenji Mizoguchi. **VHS, Beta ★★★★**

Shine Astonishing true portrayal of musical genius and its cost. Teenaged pianist David Helfgott (Taylor) is a prodigy in his native Australia but is pushed to the limit by his authoritarian father Peter (Mueller-Stahl). Eventually defying his father's strictures, David accepts a scholarship to London's Royal College of Music, where he triumphs under the tutelage of professor Cecil Parkes (Gielgud), but then collapses from strain. For 15 years, he is confined to psychiatric hospitals, unable to play the piano, until the now-adult David (Rush) has a chance meeting with the loving Gillian (Redgrave), whose support enables him to resume his career. Helfgott himself plays piano for his screen counterparts.
1995 105m/C Geoffrey Rush, Noah Taylor, Armin Mueller-Stahl, Lynn Redgrave, John Gielgud, Googie Withers, Chris Haywood, Sonia Todd; *D:* Scott Hicks; *W:* Jan Sardi; *M:* David Hirschfelder. Australian Film Institute '95: Best Film, Best Director (Hicks), Best Screenplay, Best Actor (Rush), Best Supporting Actor (Mueller-Stahl), Best Cinematography, Best Film Editing, Best Score, Best Sound; Golden Globe Awards '97: Best Actor—Drama (Rush), Best Film—Drama; Los Angeles Film Critics Association Awards '96: Best Actor (Rush); National Board of Review Awards '96: Best Film; New York Film Critics Awards' 96: Best Actor (Rush); Nominations: Australian Film Institute '95: Best Actor (Taylor); Directors Guild of America Awards '96: Best Director (Hicks);

Golden Globe Awards '97: Best Screenplay, Best Score, Best Director (Hicks); Screen Actors Guild Award '96: Best Actor (Rush), Best Supporting Actor (Taylor), Cast. **VHS ★★★1/2**

Ship of Fools A group of passengers sailing to Germany in the '30s find mutual needs and concerns, struggle with early evidence of Nazi racism, and discover love on their voyage. Twisted story and fine acting maintain interest. Appropriate tunes written by Ernest Gold. Based on the Katherine Ann Porter novel. Leigh's last film role; she died two years later. Kramer grapples with civil rights issues in much of his work.
1965 149m/B Vivien Leigh, Simone Signoret, Jose Ferrer, Lee Marvin, Oskar Werner, Michael Dunn, Elizabeth Ashley, George Segal, Jose Greco, Charles Korvin, Heinz Ruehmann; *D:* Stanley Kramer; *W:* Abby Mann; *M:* Ernest Gold. Academy Awards '65: Best Art Direction/Set Decoration (B & W), Best Black and White Cinematography; National Board of Review Awards '65: 10 Best Films of the Year, Best Actor (Marvin); Nominations: Academy Awards '65: Best Actor (Werner), Best Actress (Signoret), Best Adapted Screenplay, Best Costume Design (B & W), Best Picture, Best Supporting Actor (Dunn). **VHS, Beta, LV ★★★**

Shirley Valentine A lively middle-aged English housewife gets a new lease on life when she travels to Greece without her husband. Collins reprises her London and Broadway stage triumph. The character frequently addresses the audience directly to explain her thoughts and feelings; her energy and spunk carry the day. Good script by Russell from his play. From the people who brought us "Educating Rita."
1989 108m/C *GB* Pauline Collins, Tom Conti, Alison Steadman, Julia McKenzie, Joanna Lumley, Bernard Hill, Sylvia Syms; *D:* Lewis Gilbert; *W:* George Hadjinassios, Willy Russell; *M:* Willy Russell. British Academy Awards '89: Best Actress (Collins); Nominations: Academy Awards '89: Best Actress (Collins), Best Song ("The Girl Who Used to Be Me"). **VHS, LV, 8mm ★★★**

Shock Corridor A reporter, dreaming of a Pulitzer Prize, fakes mental illness and gets admitted to an asylum, where he hopes to investigate a murder. He is subjected to disturbing experiences, including shock therapy, but does manage to solve the murder. However, he suffers a mental breakdown in the process and is admitted for real. Disturbing and lurid.

1963 101m/B Peter Breck, Constance Towers, Gene Evans, Hari Rhodes, James Best, Philip Ahn; **D:** Samuel Fuller; **W:** Samuel Fuller. **VHS, LV** ★★★

Shoeshine Two shoeshine boys struggling to survive in post-war Italy become involved in the black market and are eventually caught and imprisoned. Prison scenes detail the sense of abandonment and tragedy that destroys their friendship. A rich, sad achievement in neo-realistic drama. In Italian with English subtitles.
1947 90m/B *IT* Franco Interlenghi, Rinaldo Smordoni, Annielo Mele, Bruno Ortensi, Pacifico Astrologo; **D:** Vittorio De Sica; **W:** Cesare Zavattini, Sergio Amidei, Adolfo Franci, C.G. Viola. National Board of Review Awards '47: 10 Best Films of the Year; Nominations: Academy Awards '47: Best Original Screenplay. **VHS, Beta** ★★★★

Shogun Television miniseries chronicling the saga of a shipwrecked English navigator who becomes the first Shogun, or Samurai warrior chief, from the Western world. Colorfully adapted from the James Clavell bestseller. Also released in a two-hour version, but this full-length version is infinitely better. **AKA:** James Clavell's Shogun.
1980 550m/C Richard Chamberlain, Toshiro Mifune, Yoko Shimada, John Rhys-Davies, Damien Thomas; **D:** Jerry London; **M:** Maurice Jarre. **VHS, Beta, LV** ★★★1/2

Shoot the Piano Player Former concert pianist (Aznavour, spendidly cast) changes his name and plays piano at a low-class Paris cafe. A convoluted plot ensues; he becomes involved with gangsters, though his girlfriend wants him to try a comeback. Lots of atmosphere, character development, humor, and romance. A Truffaut masterpiece based on a pulp novel by David Goodis. In French with English subtitles. **AKA:** Tirez sur le Pianiste; Shoot the Pianist.
1962 92m/B *FR* Charles Aznavour, Marie DuBois, Nicole Berger, Michele Mercier, Albert Remy; **D:** Francois Truffaut; **W:** Marcel Moussey, Francois Truffaut; **M:** Georges Delerue. **VHS, Beta, LV** ★★★★

The Shooting Party A group of English aristocrats assemble at a nobleman's house for a bird shoot on the eve of WWI. Splendid cast crowned Mason, in his last role. Fascinating crucible class anxieties, rich wit social scheming, personality conflicts, and things left unsaid. Adapted from Isabel Colegate's novel.
1985 97m/C *GB* James Mason, Dorothy Tutin, Edward Fox, John Gielgud, Robert Hardy, Cheryl Campbell, Judi Bowker; **D:** Alan Bridges; **W:** Julian Bond. Los Angeles Film Critics Association Awards '85: Best Supporting Actor (Gielgud); National Society of Film Critics Awards '85: Best Supporting Actor (Gielgud). **VHS, Beta** ★★★★

The Shootist Wayne, in a supporting last role, plays a legendary gunslinger afflicted with cancer who seeks peace and solace in his final days. Town bad guys Boone and O'Brian aren't about to let him rest and are determined to gun him down to avenge past deeds. One of Wayne's best and most dignified performances about living up to a personal code of honor. Stewart and Bacall head excellent supporting cast. Based on Glendon Swarthout's novel.
1976 (PG) 100m/C John Wayne, Lauren Bacall, Ron Howard, James Stewart, Richard Boone, Hugh O'Brian, Bill McKinney, Harry (Henry) Morgan, John Carradine, Sheree North, Scatman Crothers; **D:** Donald Siegel; **M:** Elmer Bernstein. National Board of Review Awards '76: 10 Best Films of the Year; Nominations: Academy Awards '76: Best Art Direction/Set Decoration. **VHS, Beta, LV** ★★★★

The Shop Around the Corner A low-key romantic classic in which Stewart and Sullavan are feuding clerks in a small Budapest shop, who unknowingly fall in love via a lonely hearts club. Charming portrayal of ordinary people in ordinary situations. Adapted from the Nikolaus Laszlo's play "Parfumerie." Later made into a musical called "In the Good Old Summertime" and, on Broadway, "She Loves Me."
1940 99m/B Margaret Sullavan, James Stewart, Frank Morgan, Joseph Schildkraut, Sara Haden, Felix Bressart, Charles Halton; **D:** Ernst Lubitsch. **VHS, LV** ★★★1/2

The Shop on Main Street During WWII, a Slovak takes a job as an "Aryan comptroller" for a Jewish-owned button shop. The owner is an old deaf woman; they slowly build a friendship. Tragedy ensues when all of the town's Jews are to be deported. Sensitive and subtle. Surely among the most gutwrenching portrayals of human tragedy ever on screen. Exquisite plotting and direction. In Czech with English subtitles. **AKA:** The Shop on High Street; Obch Od Na Korze.
1965 111m/B *CZ* Ida Kaminska, Josef Kroner, Hana Slivkoua, Frantisek Holly, Martin Gregor; **D:** Jan Kadar, Elmar Klos.

Academy Awards '65: Best Foreign Language Film; New York Film Critics Awards '66: Best Foreign Film; Nominations: Academy Awards '65: Best Actress (Kaminska). **VHS, Beta, LV ★★★★**

Shopworn Angel Weepy melodrama about a sophisticated actress who leads on a naive Texas soldier who's in New York prior to being shipped out for WWI duty. Later, just before she goes on stage, she learns he's been killed at the front. She rallys to sing "Pack Up Your Troubles in Your Old Kit Bag and Smile, Smile, Smile." Lots of tears. Adapted from the story "Private Pettigrew's Girl" by Dana Burnet. This remake of the same-titled 1929 film considerably softened the characters. Remade again in 1959 as "That Kind of Woman."
1938 85m/B Margaret Sullavan, James Stewart, Walter Pidgeon, Nat Pendleton, Alan Curtis, Sam Levene, Hattie McDaniel, Charley Grapewin, Charles D. Brown; *D:* H.C. Potter; *W:* Waldo Salt. **VHS ★★★**

Short Cuts Multi-storied, fish-eyed look at American culture with some 22 characters intersecting—profoundly or fleetingly—through each other's lives. Running the emotional gamut from disturbing to humorous, Altman's portrait of the contemporary human condition is nevertheless fascinating. Based on nine stories and a prose poem by Raymond Carver. Available on laserdisc in a movie-only edition or a special edition.
1993 (R) 189m/C Annie Ross, Lori Singer, Jennifer Jason Leigh, Tim Robbins, Madeleine Stowe, Frances McDormand, Peter Gallagher, Lily Tomlin, Tom Waits, Bruce Davison, Andie MacDowell, Jack Lemmon, Lyle Lovett, Fred Ward, Buck Henry, Huey Lewis, Matthew Modine, Anne Archer, Julianne Moore, Lili Taylor, Christopher Penn, Robert Downey Jr., Jarrett Lennon, Zane Cassidy, Walt Lloyd; *D:* Robert Altman; *W:* Frank Barhydt, Robert Altman; *M:* Mark Isham. Independent Spirit Awards '94: Best Director (Altman), Best Film, Best Screenplay; National Society of Film Critics Awards '93: Best Supporting Actress (Stowe); Venice Film Festival '93: Best Film; Nominations: Academy Awards '93: Best Director (Altman); Golden Globe Awards '94: Best Screenplay; Independent Spirit Awards '94: Best Supporting Actress (Moore). **VHS, LV ★★★1/2**

Short Eyes When a child molester (Davison) enters prison, the inmates act out their own form of revenge against him. Filmed on location at New York City's Men's House of Detention, nicknamed "The Tombs."

Script by Miguel Pinero from his excellent play; he also acts in the film. Top-notch performances and respectful direction from Young bring unsparingly realistic prison drama to the screen. Title is prison jargon for child molester. *AKA:* The Slammer.
1979 (R) 100m/C Bruce Davison, Miguel Pinero, Nathan George, Donald Blakely, Curtis Mayfield, Jose Perez, Shawn Elliott; *D:* Robert M. Young. **VHS, Beta ★★★1/2**

A Shot in the Dark Second and possibly the best in the classic "Inspector Clouseau-Pink Panther" series of comedies. The bumbling Inspector Clouseau (Sellers, of course) investigates the case of a parlor maid (Sommer) accused of murdering her lover. Clouseau's libido convinces him she's innocent, even though all the clues point to her. Classic gags, wonderful music. After this film, Sellers as Clouseau disappears until 1975's "Return of the Pink Panther" (Alan Arkin played him in "Inspector Clouseau," made in 1968 by different folks).
1964 101m/C Peter Sellers, Elke Sommer, Herbert Lom, George Sanders, Bryan Forbes; *D:* Blake Edwards; *W:* William Peter Blatty, Blake Edwards; *M:* Henry Mancini. **VHS, Beta, LV ★★★1/2**

Show Boat The second of three film versions of the Jerome Kern/Oscar Hammerstein musical, filmed previously in 1929, about a Mississippi showboat and the life and loves of its denizens. Wonderful romance, unforgettable music. Director Whale also brought the world "Frankenstein." The laser edition includes a historical audio essay by Miles Kreuger, excerpts from the 1929 version, Ziegfeld's 1932 stage revival, "Life Aboard a Real Showboat" (a vintage short), radio broadcasts, and a 300-photo essay tracing the history of showboats. Remade 15 years later. ♪ Ol' Man River; Ah Still Suits Me; Bill; Can't Help Lovin' Dat Man; Only Make Believe; I Have the Room Above Her; You Are Love; Gallivantin' Around; Cotton Blossom.
1936 110m/B Irene Dunne, Allan Jones, Paul Robeson, Helen Morgan, Hattie McDaniel, Charles Winninger, Donald Cook, Bobby Watson; *D:* James Whale; *W:* Oscar Hammerstein; *M:* Oscar Hammerstein, Jerome Kern. **VHS, Beta, LV ★★★★**

Show Business Historically valuable film record of classic vaudeville acts, especially Cantor and Davis. A number of vaudevillians re-create their old acts for director Marin—unforgettable slapstick and songs. All this pegged on a plot that follows Cantor's rise to fame with the Ziegfield Follies. ♪ Alabamy Bound; I Want a Girl (Just Like the Girl Who Married Dear Old Dad); It Had to Be You; Makin' Whoopee; Why Am I Blue; They're Wearing 'Em Higher in Hawaii; The Curse of an Aching Heart; While Strolling in the Park One Day; You May Not Remember.

1944 92m/B Eddie Cantor, Joan Davis, George Murphy; **D:** Edwin L. Marin. **VHS, Beta, LV** ★★★

Shy People An urbanized New York journalist and her spoiled daughter journey the Louisiana bayou to visit long-lost relatives in order to produce an article for "Cosmopolitan." They find ignorance, madness, and ancestral secrets and are forced to examine their motives, their relationships, and issues brought to light in the watery, murky, fantastic land of the bayous. Well-acted melodrama with an outstanding performance by Hershey as the cajun matriarch. Music by Tangerine Dream; cinematography by Chris Menges.

1987 (R) 119m/C Jill Clayburgh, Barbara Hershey, Martha Plimpton, Mare Winningham, Merritt Butrick, John Philbin, Don Swayze, Pruitt Taylor Vince; **D:** Andrei Konchalovsky; **W:** Gerard Brach, Marjorie David; **M:** Tangerine Dream. Cannes Film Festival '87: Best Actress (Hershey). **VHS, Beta, LV** ★★★

Sid & Nancy The tragic, brutal, true love story of The Sex Pistols' Sid Vicious and American groupie Nancy Spungen, from the director of "Repo Man." Remarkable lead performances in a very dark story that manages to be funny at times. Depressing but engrossing; no appreciation of punk music or sympathy for the self-destructive way of life is required. Oldman and Webb are superb. Music by Joe Strummer, the Pogues, and Pray for Rain.

1986 (R) 111m/C Gary Oldman, Chloe Webb, Debbie Bishop, David Hayman; **D:** Alex Cox; **W:** Alex Cox. National Society of Film Critics Awards '86: Best Actress (Webb). **VHS, Beta, LV** ★★★1/2

Siegfried Half of Lang's epic masterpiece "Der Niebelungen," based on German mythology. Title hero bathes in the blood of a dragon he has slain. He marries a princess, but wicked Queen Brunnilde has him killed. Part two, in which Siegfried's widow marries Attila the Hun, is titled "Kriemheld's Revenge." These dark, brooding, archetypal tours de force were

patriotic tributes, and were loved by Hitler. Silent with music score. **AKA:** Siegfrieds Tod; Siegfried's Death.

1924 100m/B *GE* Paul Richter, Margareta Schoen; **D:** Fritz Lang. **VHS, LV** ★★★★

The Silence A brutal, enigmatic allegory about two sisters, one a nymphomaniac, the other a violently frustrated lesbian, traveling with the former's young son to an unnamed country beset by war. Fascinating and memorable but frustrating and unsatisfying: What is it about? What is it an allegory of? Where is the narrative? The third in Bergman's crisis-of-faith trilogy following "Through a Glass Darkly" and "Winter Light." In Swedish with English subtitles or dubbed. **AKA:** Tystnaden.

1963 95m/B *SW* Ingrid Thulin, Gunnel Lindstrom, Birger Malmsten; **D:** Ingmar Bergman; **W:** Ingmar Bergman. **VHS, Beta, LV** ★★★

Silence of the Heart Mother copes with aftermath of suicide of teenage son following her recent divorce. Hartley is captivating in this gripping drama.

1984 100m/C Mariette Hartley, Dana Hill, Howard Hesseman, Chad Lowe, Charlie Sheen; **D:** Richard Michaels; **W:** Phil Penningroth; **M:** Georges Delerue. **VHS** ★★★

The Silence of the Lambs Foster is FBI cadet Clarice Starling, a woman with ambition, a cum laude degree in psychology, and a traumatic childhood. When a serial killer begins his ugly rounds, the FBI wants psychological profiles from other serial killers and she's sent to collect a profile from one who's exceptionally clever—psychiatrist Hannibal Lector, a vicious killer prone to dining on his victims. Brilliant performances from Foster and Hopkins, finely detailed supporting characterizations, and elegant pacing from Demme. Some brutal visual effects. Excellent portrayals of women who refuse to be victims. Based on the Thomas Harris novel.

1991 (R) 118m/C Jodie Foster, Anthony Hopkins, Scott Glenn, Ted Levine, Brooke Smith, Charles Napier, Roger Corman, Anthony Heald, Diane Baker, Chris Isaak; **D:** Jonathan Demme; **W:** Ted Tally; **M:** Howard Shore, Tak Fujimoto. Academy Awards '91: Best Actor (Hopkins), Best Actress (Foster), Best Adapted Screenplay, Best Director (Demme), Best Picture; British Academy Awards '91: Best Actor (Hopkins), Best Actress (Foster); Directors Guild of America Awards '91: Best Director (Demme); Golden Globe Awards '92: Best Actress—Drama (Foster); National Board of

Review Awards '91: Best Director (Demme), Best Film, Best Supporting Actor (Hopkins); People's Choice Awards '92: Best Film—Drama; Writers Guild of America '91: Best Adapted Screenplay; Nominations: Academy Awards '91: Best Film Editing, Best Sound. **VHS, Beta, LV ★★★1/2**

Silent Running Members of a space station orbiting Saturn care for the last vegetation of a nuclear-devastated earth. When orders come to destroy the vegetation, Dern takes matters into his own hands. Speculative sci-fi at its best. Trumbull's directorial debut; he created special effects for "2001" and "Close Encounters." Strange music enhances the alien atmosphere.
1971 (G) 90m/C Bruce Dern, Cliff Potts, Ron Rifkin; **D:** Douglas Trumbull; **W:** Michael Cimino, Deric Washburn, Steven Bochco; **M:** Prof. Peter Schickele. **VHS, Beta, LV ★★★**

Silk Stockings Splendid musical comedy adaptation of "Ninotchka," with Astaire as a charming American movie man, and Charisse as the cold Soviet official whose commie heart he melts. Music and lyrics by Cole Porter highlight this film adapted from George S. Kaufman's hit Broadway play. Director Mamoulian's last film. ♪ Too Bad; Paris Loves Lovers; Fated to Be Mated; The Ritz Roll 'n' Rock; Silk Stockings; Red Blues; All of You; Stereophonic Sound; Josephine.
1957 117m/C Fred Astaire, Cyd Charisse, Janis Paige, Peter Lorre, George Tobias; **D:** Rouben Mamoulian; **M:** Andre Previn. **VHS, Beta, LV ★★★**

Silkwood The story of Karen Silkwood, who died in a 1974 car crash under suspicious circumstances. She was a nuclear plant worker and activist who was investigating shoddy practices at the plant. Streep acts up a storm, disappearing completely into her character. Cher surprises with her fine portrayal of a lesbian co-worker, and Russell is also good. Nichols has a tough time since we already know the ending, but he brings top-notch performances from his excellent cast.
1983 (R) 131m/C Meryl Streep, Kurt Russell, Cher, Diana Scarwid, Bruce McGill, Fred Ward, David Strathairn, Ron Silver, Josef Sommer, Craig T. Nelson; **D:** Mike Nichols; **W:** Nora Ephron, Alice Arlen; **M:** Georges Delerue. Golden Globe Awards '84: Best Supporting Actress (Cher); Nominations: Academy Awards '83: Best Actress (Streep), Best Director (Nichols), Best Film Editing, Best Original Screenplay,

Best Supporting Actress (Cher). **VHS, Beta, LV ★★★**

Silver Streak Pooped exec Wilder rides a train from L.A. to Chicago, planning to enjoy a leisurely, relaxing trip. Instead he becomes involved with murder, intrigue, and a beautiful woman. Energetic Hitchcock parody features successful first pairing of Wilder and Pryor.
1976 (PG) 113m/C Gene Wilder, Richard Pryor, Jill Clayburgh, Patrick McGoohan, Ned Beatty, Ray Walston, Richard Kiel, Scatman Crothers; **D:** Arthur Hiller; **W:** Colin Higgins; **M:** Henry Mancini. Nominations: Academy Awards '76: Best Sound. **VHS, Beta, LV ★★★**

Silverado Affectionate pastiche of western cliches has everything a viewer could ask for—except Indians. Straightforward plot has four virtuous cowboys rise up against a crooked lawman in a blaze of six guns. No subtlety from the first big western in quite a while, but plenty of fun and laughs. Laserdisc edition features a wide-screen film-to-tape transfer monitored by the photography director, set photos, release trailers, and other publicity hoohah as well as a special time-lapse sequence of the set construction, and interviews with the stars and director Kasdan. Letterboxed laserdisc version is available with Dolby Surround Sound.
1985 (PG-13) 132m/C Kevin Kline, Scott Glenn, Kevin Costner, Danny Glover, Brian Dennehy, Linda Hunt, John Cleese, Jeff Goldblum, Rosanna Arquette, Jeff Fahey; **D:** Lawrence Kasdan; **W:** Lawrence Kasdan; **M:** Bruce Broughton, John Bailey. Nominations: Academy Awards '85: Best Sound, Best Original Score. **VHS, Beta, LV ★★★**

Simon of the Desert Not Bunuel's very best, but worthy of the master satirist. An ascetic stands on a pillar in the desert for several decades—closer to God, farther from temptation. Pinal is a gorgeous devil that tempts Simon. Hilarious, irreverent, sophisticated. What's with the weird ending, though? In Spanish with English subtitles.
1966 46m/B Claudio Brook, Silvia Pinal; **D:** Luis Bunuel; **W:** Luis Bunuel. **VHS, Beta ★★★1/2**

A Simple Story A woman faces her 40th birthday with increasing uneasiness, though her life seems perfect from the outside. She evaluates her chances at love, child-bearing, and friendship, after having an abortion and breaking up with her lover. Schneider's performance is brilliant in this gentle, quiet drama. In French with English subtitles. *AKA:* Une Histoire Simple.

1979 110m/C *FR* Romy Schneider, Bruno Cremer, Claude Brasseur; *D:* Claude Sautet. Nominations: Academy Awards '79: Best Foreign Language Film; Cesar Awards '79: Best Actress (Schneider). **VHS, Beta ★★★**

The Sin of Madelon Claudet Hayes plays common thief who works her way into upper crust of Parisian society only to tumble back into the street, all in the name of making a better life for her illegitimate son. Very sudsy stuff, with an outstanding performance by Hayes. *AKA:* The Lullaby.

1931 74m/B Helen Hayes, Lewis Stone, Neil Hamilton, Robert Young, Cliff Edwards, Jean Hersholt, Marie Prevost, Karen Morley, Charles Winninger, Alan Hale; *D:* Edgar Selwyn. Academy Awards '32: Best Actress (Hayes). **VHS ★★★**

Sinbad the Sailor Fairbanks fits well in his luminent father's swashbuckling shoes, as he searches for the treasure of Alexander the Great. Self-mocking but hamhanded, and confusing if you seek the hidden plot. Still, it's all in fun, and it is fun.

1947 117m/C Douglas Fairbanks Jr., Maureen O'Hara, Anthony Quinn, Walter Slezak, George Tobias, Jane Greer, Mike Mazurki, Sheldon Leonard; *D:* Richard Wallace. **VHS, Beta, LV ★★★**

Since You Went Away An American family copes with the tragedy, heartache and shortages of wartime in classic mega-tribute to the home front. Be warned: very long and bring your hankies. Colbert is superb, as is the photography. John Derek unobtrusively made his film debut, as an extra.

1944 172m/B Claudette Colbert, Jennifer Jones, Shirley Temple, Joseph Cotten, Agnes Moorehead, Monty Woolley, Guy Madison, Lionel Barrymore, Robert Walker, Hattie McDaniel, Keenan Wynn, Craig Stevens, Albert Basserman, Alla Nazimova, Lloyd Corrigan, Terry Moore, Florence Bates, Ruth Roman, Andrew V. McLaglen, Dorothy Dandridge, Rhonda Fleming; *D:* John Cromwell; *W:* David O. Selznick; *M:* Max Steiner. Academy Awards '44: Best Score; Nominations: Academy Awards '44: Best Supporting Actress (Jones), Actress (Colbert), Best Black and White Cinematography, Best Film Editing, Best Interior Decoration, Best Picture, Best Supporting Actor (Woolley). **VHS, Beta, LV ★★★1/2**

Singin' in the Rain One of the all-time great movie musicals—an affec-

tionate spoof of the turmoil that afflicted the motion picture industry in the late 1920s during the changeover from silent films to sound. Co-director Kelly and Hagen lead a glorious cast. Music and lyrics by Arthur Freed and Nacio Herb Brown. Served as basis of story by Betty Comden and Adolph Green. Also available on laserdisc with the original trailer, outtakes, behind the scenes footage, and commentary by film historian Ronald Haver. Later a Broadway musical. ♪ All I Do is Dream of You; Should I?; Singin' in the Rain; Wedding of the Painted Doll; Broadway Melody; Would You; I've Got a Feelin' You're Foolin'; You Are My Lucky Star; Broadway Rhythm.

1952 103m/C Gene Kelly, Donald O'Connor, Jean Hagen, Debbie Reynolds, Rita Moreno, King Donovan, Millard Mitchell, Cyd Charisse, Douglas Fowley, Madge Blake, Joi Lansing; *D:* Gene Kelly, Stanley Donen; *W:* Adolph Green, Betty Comden. Golden Globe Awards '53: Best Actor—Musical/Comedy (O'Connor); National Board of Review Awards '52: 10 Best Films of the Year; Nominations: Academy Awards '52: Best Supporting Actress (Hagen), Best Original Score. **VHS, Beta, LV ★★★★**

Singles Seattle's music scene is the background for this lighthearted look at single twentysomethings in the '90s. Hits dead on thanks to Crowe's tight script and a talented cast, and speaks straight to its intended audience—the "Generation X" crowd. Real life band Pearl Jam plays alternative band Citizen Dick and sets the tone for a great soundtrack featuring the hot Seattle sounds of Alice in Chains, Soundgarden, and Mudhoney. The video contains six extra minutes of footage after the credits that was thankfully edited out of the final cut. Look for Horton, Stoltz (as a mime), Skerritt, and Burton in cameos.

1992 (PG-13) 100m/C Matt Dillon, Bridget Fonda, Campbell Scott, Kyra Sedgwick, Sheila Kelley, Jim True, Bill Pullman, James LeGros, Ally Walker, Devon Raymond, Camillo Gallardo, Jeremy Piven; *Cameos:* Tom Skerritt, Peter Horton, Eric Stoltz, Tim Burton; *D:* Cameron Crowe; *W:* Cameron Crowe; *M:* Paul Westerberg. **VHS, Beta, LV ★★★**

Sink the Bismarck British Navy sets out to locate and sink infamous German battleship during WWII. Good special effects with battle sequences in this drama based on real incidents. One of the better of the plethora of WWII movies, with stirring naval bat-

tles and stylish documentary-style direction.
1960 97m/B Kenneth More, Dana Wynter, Karel Stepanek, Carl Mohner, Laurence Naismith, Geoffrey Keen, Michael Hordern, Maurice Denham, Esmond Knight; **D:** Lewis Gilbert. **VHS, Beta ★★★**

Sister Kenny Follows the story of a legendary Australian nurse crusading for the treatment of infantile paralysis. Stirring, well-made screen biography. Based on Elizabeth Kenny's memoir, "And They Shall Walk."
1946 116m/B Rosalind Russell, Dean Jagger, Alexander Knox, Philip Merivale, Beulah Bondi, Charles Halton; **D:** Dudley Nichols. Golden Globe Awards '47: Best Actress—Drama (Russell); Nominations: Academy Awards '46: Best Actress (Russell). **VHS, Beta, LV ★★★**

Sisters Siamese twins are separated surgically, but one doesn't survive the operation. The remaining sister is scarred physically and mentally with her personality split into bad and good. The bad side commits a murder, witnessed (or was it?) by an investigative reporter. And then things really get crazy. De Palma's first ode to Hitchcock, with great music by Hitchcock's favorite composer, Bernard Herrmann. Scary and suspenseful.
1973 (R) 93m/C Margot Kidder, Charles Durning, Barnard Hughes; **D:** Brian De Palma; **W:** Brian De Palma; **M:** Bernard Herrmann. **VHS, Beta ★★★**

Sisters of Gion Mizoguchi's most famous and arguably best prewar film. Two geisha sisters in Tokyo's red-light district reflect the tension in Japanese culture by waging a quiet battle of tradition vs. progressiveness. Highly acclaimed. In Japanese with English subtitles.
1936 69m/B *JP* Isuzu Yamada, Yoko Umemura; **D:** Kenji Mizoguchi. **VHS, Beta ★★★1/2**

Six Wives of Henry VIII Michell has been called the definitive Henry VIII, and this BBC Classic Television Series (shown as part of "Masterpiece Theatre" on PBS) was perhaps the most praised series on British TV. Henry's wives were: Catherine of Aragon, Anne Boleyn, Jane Seymour, Anne of Cleves, Catherine Howard, and Catherine Parr. Each episode tells of their sometimes tragic fates as pawns in Henry's quest for an heir, and his changes from an eager young man to aged, bitter monarch. The 90-minute videos are available individually or as a boxed set.
1972? 540m/C *GB* Keith Michell, Annette Crosbie, Dorothy Tutin, Anne Stallybrass, Elvi Hale, Angela Pleasence, Rosalie Crutchley. **VHS ★★★**

Sixteen Candles Over a decade after hitting the theaters, "Sixteen Candles" is still popular — reaching near cult status among generation X-ers. Hilarious comedy of errors features the pouty Ringwald as an awkward teen who's been dreaming of her 16th birthday. But the rush of her sister's wedding causes everyone to forget, turning her birthday into her worst nightmare. Hughes may not be critically acclaimed, but his movies are so popular that they nearly take on a life of their own. Ringwald and Hall are especially charming as the angst-ridden teens, encountering one trauma after another. Great soundtrack includes the title song by The Stray Cats.
1984 (PG) 93m/C Molly Ringwald, Justin Henry, Michael Schoeffling, Haviland Morris, Gedde Watanabe, Anthony Michael Hall, Paul Dooley, Carlin Glynn, Blanche Baker, Edward Andrews, Carole Cook, Max Showalter, Liane Curtis, John Cusack, Joan Cusack, Brian Doyle-Murray, Jami Gertz, Cinnamon Idles, Zelda Rubinstein; **D:** John Hughes; **W:** John Hughes; **M:** Ira Newborn. **VHS, Beta, LV ★★★**

Slacker Defines a new generation: Overwhelmed by the world and it's demands, "Slackers" react by retreating into lives of minimal expectations. Filmed as a series of improvisational stories about people living on the fringes of the working world and their reactions (or lack thereof) to the life swirling around them. First feature for writer/director Linklater on a budget of $23,000; filmed on location in Austin, Texas with a cast of primarily non-professional actors.
1991 (R) 97m/C Richard Linklater; **D:** Richard Linklater; **W:** Richard Linklater. **VHS ★★★**

Slap Shot A profane satire of the world of professional hockey. Over-the-hill player-coach Newman gathers an odd-ball mixture of has-beens and young players and reluctantly initiates them, using violence on the ice to make his team win. The striptease on ice needs to be seen to be believed. Charming in its own bone-crunching way.
1977 (R) 123m/C Paul Newman, Michael Ontkean, Jennifer Warren, Lindsay Crouse, Jerry Houser, Melinda Dillon, Strother Martin; **D:** George Roy Hill; **M:** Elmer Bernstein. **VHS, Beta, LV ★★★**

Sleeper Hapless nerd Allen is revived 200 years after an operation gone bad. Keaton portrays Allen's love interest in a futuristic land of robots and giant vegetables. He learns of the hitherto unknown health benefits of hot fudge sundaes; discovers the truth about the nation's dictator, known as The Leader; and gets involved with revolutionaries seeking to overthrow the government. Hilarious, fast-moving comedy, full of slapstick and satire. Don't miss the "orgasmatron."

1973 (PG) 88m/C Woody Allen, Diane Keaton, John Beck, Howard Cosell; **D:** Woody Allen; **W:** Woody Allen, Marshall Brickman; **M:** Woody Allen. **VHS, Beta, LV ★★★1/2**

Sleeping Beauty Classic Walt Disney version of the famous fairy-tale is set to the music of Tchaikovsky's ballet. Lavishly produced. With the voices of Mary Costa and Bill Shirley.

1959 (G) 75m/C D: Clyde Geronomi, Eric Larson, Wolfgang Reitherman, Les Clark; **M:** George Bruns; **V:** Mary Costa, Bill Shirley, Barbara Luddy, Taylor Holmes, Verna Felton, Barbara Jo Allen, Pinto Colvig, Marvin Miller. Nominations: Academy Awards '59: Best Original Score. **VHS, Beta, LV ★★★**

Sleepless in Seattle Witty, sweet romantic comedy explores the differences between men and women when it comes to love and romance. When widower Hanks talks about his wife on a national talk show, recently engaged Ryan responds. Writer/director Ephron's humorous screenplay is brought to life by a perfectly cast ensemble; it also breathed new life into the classic weepie "An Affair to Remember," comparing it to "The Dirty Dozen" in an unforgettable scene. A movie full of fine detail, from Sven Nykvist's camera work to the graphic layout of the opening credits to the great score. Captured millions at the box office, coming in as the fourth highest grossing movie of 1993.

1993 (PG) 105m/C Tom Hanks, Meg Ryan, Bill Pullman, Ross Malinger, Rosie O'Donnell, Gaby Hoffman, Victor Garber, Rita Wilson, Barbara Garrick, Carey Lowell, Rob Reiner, Sarah Trigger; **D:** Nora Ephron; **W:** Jeffrey Arch, Larry Atlas, David S. Ward, Nora Ephron; **M:** Marc Shaiman. Nominations: Academy Awards '93: Best Original Screenplay, Best Song ("A Wink and a Smile"); Golden Globe Awards '94: Best Actor—Musical/Comedy (Hanks), Best Actress—Musical/Comedy (Ryan), Best Film—Musical/Comedy; MTV Movie Awards '94: Best Actress (Ryan), Breakthrough Performance (Malinger), Best On-Screen Duo (Tom Hanks/Meg Ryan),

Best Song ("When I Fall in Love"). **VHS, LV, 8mm ★★★1/2**

The Slender Thread Based on a true story, Poitier plays a college student who volunteers at a crisis center and must keep would-be suicide Bancroft on the phone until the police can find her. Filmed on location in Seattle. First film for director Pollack.

1965 98m/C Sidney Poitier, Anne Bancroft, Telly Savalas, Steven Hill; **D:** Sydney Pollack; **W:** Stirling Silliphant; **M:** Quincy Jones. Nominations: Academy Awards '65: Best Art Direction/Set Decoration (B & W), Best Costume Design (B & W). **VHS ★★★**

Sleuth A mystery novelist and his wife's lover face off in ever shifting, elaborate, and diabolical plots against each other, complete with red herrings, traps, and tricks. Playful, cerebral mystery thriller from top director Mankiewicz. Schaffer also scripted "Frenzy" for Hitchcock, from his play.

1972 (PG) 138m/C Laurence Olivier, Michael Caine; **D:** Joseph L. Mankiewicz; **W:** Anthony Shaffer; **M:** John Addison. Edgar Allan Poe Awards '72: Best Screenplay; New York Film Critics Awards '72: Best Actor (Olivier); Nominations: Academy Awards '72: Best Actor (Caine), Best Actor (Olivier), Best Director (Mankiewicz), Best Original Score. **VHS, Beta, LV ★★★1/2**

Slither Caan and Boyle become wrapped up in a scheme to recover $300,000 in cash, stolen seven years previously. Along the way they pick up speed freak Kellerman, who assists them in a variety of loony ways. Frantic chase scenes are the highlight.

1973 (PG) 97m/C James Caan, Peter Boyle, Sally Kellerman, Louise Lasser, Allen (Goorwitz) Garfield, Richard B. Shull, Alex Rocco; **D:** Howard Zieff; **W:** W.D. Richter. **VHS, Beta ★★★**

Small Change Pudgy, timid Desmouceaux and scruffy, neglected Goldman lead a whole pack of heartwarming tykes. A realistically and tenderly portrayed testament to the great director's belief in childhood as a "state of grace." Criticized for sentimentality, "Small Change" followed Truffaut's gloomy "The Story of Adele H." Steven Spielberg suggested the English translation of "L'Argent de Poche." In French with English subtitles.

1976 (PG) 104m/C *FR* Geory Desmouceaux, Philippe Goldman, Jean-Francois Stevenin, Chantal Mercier, Claudio Deluca, Frank Deluca, Richard Golfier, Laurent Devlaeminck, Francis

Devlaeminck; **D:** Francois Truffaut; **W:** Suzanne Schiffman. National Board of Review Awards '76: 5 Best Foreign Films of the Year. **VHS, Beta, LV** ★★★★

Smash-Up: The Story of a Woman A famous nightclub singer gives up her career for marriage and a family, only to become depressed when her husband's career soars. She turns to alcohol and her life falls apart. When her husband sues for divorce and custody of their child, she fights to recover from alcoholism. Hayward's first major role. **AKA:** A Woman Destroyed.

1947 103m/B Susan Hayward, Lee Bowman, Marsha Hunt, Eddie Albert; **D:** Stuart Heisler; **W:** John Howard Lawson. Nominations: Academy Awards '47: Best Actress (Hayward), Best Story. **VHS, Beta** ★★★

Smile Barbed, merciless send-up of small-town America, focusing on a group of naive California girls who compete for the "Young American Miss" crown amid rampant commercialism, exploitation, and pure middle-class idiocy. Hilarious neglected '70s-style satire. Early role for Griffith.

1975 (PG) 113m/C Bruce Dern, Barbara Feldon, Michael Kidd, Nicholas Pryor, Geoffrey Lewis, Colleen Camp, Joan Prather, Annette O'Toole, Melanie Griffith, Denise Nickerson; **D:** Michael Ritchie, Conrad Hall; **W:** Jerry Belson. **VHS, Beta, LV** ★★★

Smiles of a Summer Night The best known of Bergman's rare comedies; sharp satire about eight Swedish aristocrats who become romantically and comically intertwined over a single weekend. Inspired Sondheim's successful Broadway musical "A Little Night Music," and Woody Allen's "A Midsummer Night's Sex Comedy." In Swedish with English subtitles. **AKA:** Sommarnattens Leende.

1955 110m/B SW Gunnar Bjornstrand, Harriet Andersson, Ulla Jacobsson, Eva Dahlbeck, Jarl Kulle, Margit Carlquist; **D:** Ingmar Bergman; **W:** Ingmar Bergman. **VHS, Beta, LV** ★★★1/2

Smilin' Through First sound version of this melodrama/romance which Franklin had directed as a silent in 1922. Shearer is set to marry Howard when jealous rival March shows up armed at the wedding and accidentally kills the bride. March escapes and Howard spends his years as a recluse until his young niece, the image of his dead fiance (naturally, since she's also played by Shearer) arrives to live with him. She meets a young man who turns out to be March's son

(played again by March) and they fall in love. Pure sentiment done with high gloss. Remade in 1941.

1932 97m/B Norma Shearer, Fredric March, Leslie Howard, O.P. Heggie, Ralph Forbes, Beryl Mercer, Margaret Seddon; **D:** Sidney Franklin. **VHS** ★★★

Smooth Talk An innocent, flirtatious teenager catches the eye of a shady character, played by Williams. Disturbing and thought-provoking film that caused some controversy when it opened. Dern gives a brilliant performance as the shy, sheltered girl. Based on the Joyce Carol Oates story. Made for PBS' "American Playhouse" series.

1985 (PG-13) 92m/C Laura Dern, Treat Williams, Mary Kay Place, Levon Helm; **D:** Joyce Chopra; **W:** Tom Cole. Sundance Film Festival '86: Grand Jury Prize. **VHS, Beta, LV** ★★★

Smugglers' Cove Gorcey wrongly believes he has inherited a mansion. He and the Bowery Boys move in, only to stumble across a smuggling ring. Plenty of slapstick; the boys at their best.

1948 66m/B Leo Gorcey, Huntz Hall, Gabriel Dell; **D:** William Beaudine. **VHS** ★★★

The Snake Pit One of the first films to compassionately explore mental illness and its treatment. Following an emotional collapse de Havilland is placed in a mental institution by her husband. The severity of her depression causes her sympathetic doctor to try such treatments as electric shock, hydrotherapy, and drugs, along with the psychoanalysis which gradually allows her to accept her fears and make her recovery. Tour-de-force performance by de Havilland. Based on the novel by Mary Jane Ward.

1948 108m/B Olivia de Havilland, Mark Stevens, Leo Genn, Celeste Holm, Glenn Langan, Helen Craig, Leif Erickson, Beulah Bondi; **D:** Anatole Litvak; **W:** Frank Partos, Millen Brand; **M:** Alfred Newman. Academy Awards '48: Best Sound; New York Film Critics Awards '48: Best Actress (de Havilland); Nominations: Academy Awards '48: Best Actress (de Havilland), Best Picture, Best Director (Litvak), Best Screenplay, Best Original Score. **VHS** ★★★1/2

The Snapper Originally made for BBC television, Frears creates a small comic gem based on the second novel of Doyle's Barrytown trilogy. Set in Dublin, 20-year-old Sharon Curley (Kellegher) finds herself unexpectedly pregnant and refuses to name the fa-

ther. Family and friends are understanding—until they discover the man's identity. Affecting performances, particularly from Meany as Sharon's dad who takes a much greater interest in the birth of his grandchild than he ever did with his own children. Cheerful semi-sequel to "The Commitments" serves up domestic upheavals graced with humor and a strong sense of family loyalty.
1993 (R) 95m/C *IR* Tina Kellegher, Colm Meaney, Ruth McCabe, Colm O'Byrne, Pat Laffan, Eanna MacLiam, Ciara Duffy; *D:* Stephen Frears; *W:* Roddy Doyle. Nominations: Golden Globe Awards '94: Best Actor—Musical/Comedy (Meaney). **VHS, LV ★★★1/2**

Snoopy, Come Home Snoopy leaves Charlie Brown to visit his former owner Lila in the hospital and returns with her to her apartment house. From Charles Schultz's popular comic strip "Peanuts."
1972 (G) 80m/C *D:* Bill Melendez; *W:* Charles M. Schulz. **VHS, Beta, LV ★★★**

Snow White and the Seven Dwarfs Classic adaptation of the Grimm Brothers fairy-tale about the fairest of them all. Beautiful animation, memorable characters, and wonderful songs mark this as the definitive "Snow White." Set the stage for other animated features after Walt Disney took an unprecedented gamble by attempting the first animated feature-length film, a project which took over two years to create and $1.5 million to make, and made believers out of those who laughed at the concept. Lifelike animation was based on real stars; Margery Belcher (later Champion) posed for Snow, Louis Hightower was the Prince, and Lucille LaVerne gave the Queen her nasty look. ♪ Some Day My Prince Will Come; One Song; With a Smile and a Song; Whistle While You Work; Bluddle-Uddle-Um-Dum; The Dwarfs' Yodel Song; Heigh Ho; I'm Wishing; Isn't This a Silly Song?.
1937 (G) 83m/C *D:* David Hand; *W:* Ted Sears, Otto Englander, Earl Hurd, Dorothy Blank, Richard Creedon, Dick Richard, Merrill De Maris, Webb Smith; *M:* Frank Churchill, Paul Smith, Larry Morey, Leigh Harline; *V:* Adriana Caseloti, Harry Stockwell, Lucille LaVerne, Moroni Olsen, Billy Gilbert, Pinto Colvig, Otis Harlan, Scotty Matraw, Roy Atwell, Stuart Buchanan, Marion Darlington, Jim Macdonald. **VHS, LV ★★★★**

The Snows of Kilimanjaro Called by Hemingway "The Snows of Zanuck," in reference to the great producer, this film is actually an artful pastiche of several Hemingway short stories and novels. The main story, "The Snows of Kilimanjaro," acts as a framing device, in which the life of a successful writer is seen through his fevered flashbacks as he and his rich wife, while on safari, await a doctor to save his gangrenous leg.
1952 117m/C Gregory Peck, Susan Hayward, Ava Gardner, Hildegarde Neff, Leo G. Carroll, Torin Thatcher, Ava Norring, Helene Stanley, Marcel Dalio, Vincente Gomez, Richard Allen, Leonard Carey; *D:* Henry King; *W:* Casey Robinson. Nominations: Academy Awards '52: Best Art Direction/Set Decoration (Color), Best Color Cinematography. **Beta ★★★**

So Dear to My Heart A farm boy and his misfit black sheep wreak havoc at the county fair. Several sequences combine live action with animation. Heartwarming and charming; straightforward and likeable but never sentimental. Wonderful, vintage Disney. ♪ Sourwood Mountain; Billy Boy; So Dear To My Heart; County Fair; Stick-To-It-Ivity; Ol' Dan Patch; It's Whatcha Do With Watcha Got; Lavender Blue (Dilly Dilly).
1949 82m/C Bobby Driscoll, Burl Ives, Beulah Bondi, Harry Carey Sr., Luana Patten; *D:* Harold Schuster. Nominations: Academy Awards '49: Best Song ("Lavender Blue"). **VHS, Beta, LV ★★★1/2**

So Proudly We Hail True story of the lives of three war-front nurses and their heroism under fire during WWII. Colbert is Lt. Davidson in charge of nine Red Cross Army nurses serving in the Pacific. Lake and Goddard play the other leads. With the popularity of its stars and the patriotic spirit of the film, the picture hit box office gold. Critics praised its authenticity, as the film never fell victim to the usual standards of Hollywood glamour. Fans of Lake beware: she has short hair in this film because the government requested that she not appear as a servicewoman with her famous peek-a-boo hair style because female factory workers were getting their long Lake-inspired hair caught in the machinery.
1943 126m/B Claudette Colbert, Paulette Goddard, Veronica Lake, George Reeves, Barbara Britton, Walter Abel, Sonny Tufts; *D:* Mark Sandrich; *W:* Allan Scott; *M:* Miklos Rozsa. Nominations: Academy Awards '43: Best Cinematography, Best Original Screenplay (Scott), Best Special Effects, Best Supporting Actress (Goddard). **VHS ★★★**

So This Is Paris Roguish pre-Hays Code dancing duo seeks spice through alternative lovemates. Classic sophisticated Lubitsch, with outstanding camera work and a bit of jazz.

1926 68m/B Monte Blue, Patsy Ruth Miller, Lilyan Tashman, Andre de Beranger, Myrna Loy; *D:* Ernst Lubitsch. **VHS, Beta** ★★★

Soapdish A look at the backstage lives of the cast of a daytime soap opera. When the soap's ratings fall, a character written out of series via decapitation is brought back to give things a lift. While the writer struggles to make the reincarnation believable, the cast juggles old and new romances, and professional jealousies abound. Some genuinely funny moments as film actors spoof the genre that gave many of them a start.

1991 (PG-13) 97m/C Sally Field, Kevin Kline, Robert Downey Jr., Cathy Moriarty, Whoopi Goldberg, Elisabeth Shue, Carrie Fisher, Garry Marshall, Teri Hatcher, Paul Johansson, Costas Mandylor, Stephen Nichols, Kathy Najimy, Sheila Kelley; *Cameos:* Leeza Gibbons, John Tesh, Finola Hughes; *D:* Michael Hoffman; *W:* Andrew Bergman, Robert Harling; *M:* Alan Silvestri. **VHS, Beta, LV, 8mm** ★★★

The Soft Skin A classic portrayal of marital infidelity by the master director. A writer and lecturer has an affair with a stewardess. After the affair ends, his wife confronts him, with tragic results. Cliche plot is forgivable; acted and directed to perfection. Frequent Truffaut star Jean-Pierre Leaud served here as an apprentice director. In French with English subtitles. *AKA:* Le Peau Douce; Silken Skin.

1964 120m/B *FR* Jean Desailly, Nelly Benedetti, Francoise Dorleac; *D:* Francois Truffaut; *M:* Georges Delerue. **VHS, Beta, LV** ★★★

Soldier of Orange The lives of six Dutch students are forever changed by the WWII invasion of Holland by the Nazis. Based on the true-life exploits of Dutch resistance leader Erik Hazelhoff. Exciting and suspenseful; cerebral; carefully made and well acted. Made Rutger Hauer an international star.

1978 144m/C *NL* Rutger Hauer, Jeroen Krabbe, Edward Fox, Susan Penhaligon; *D:* Paul Verhoeven; *W:* Paul Verhoeven. Los Angeles Film Critics Association Awards '79: Best Foreign Film. **VHS, Beta, LV** ★★★

A Soldier's Story A black army attorney is sent to a Southern base to investigate the murder of an unpopular sergeant. Features WWII, Louisiana, jazz and blues, and racism in and outside the corps. From the Pulitzer Prize-winning play by Charles Fuller, with most of the Broadway cast. Fine performances from Washington and Caesar.

1984 (PG) 101m/C Howard E. Rollins Jr., Adolph Caesar, Denzel Washington, Patti LaBelle, Robert Townsend, Scott Paulin, Wings Hauser, Art Evans, Larry Riley, David Alan Grier; *D:* Norman Jewison; *M:* Herbie Hancock. Edgar Allan Poe Awards '84: Best Screenplay; Los Angeles Film Critics Association Awards '84: Best Supporting Actor (Caesar); Nominations: Academy Awards '84: Best Adapted Screenplay, Best Picture, Best Supporting Actor (Caesar). **VHS, Beta, LV** ★★★

Solid Gold Cadillac Holliday is a winning lead as Laura Patridge, an idealistic, small-time stockholder who discovers that the corporate board of directors are crooked. She makes waves at a stockholders meeting, gets noticed by the press, finds romance with former CEO Edward McKeever (Douglas), and works to oust the scalawags from power. The title comes from Laura's fervent desire to own a—you guessed it—solid gold Cadillac. Based on the Broadway play by George S. Kaufman and Howard Teichmann.

1956 99m/B Judy Holliday, Paul Douglas, Fred Clark, Neva Patterson, Arthur O'Connell, Ray Collins; *D:* Richard Quine; *W:* Abe Burrows; *M:* Cyril Mockridge. Academy Awards '56: Best Costume Design (B & W). **VHS** ★★★

Some Came Running James Jones' follow-up novel to "From Here to Eternity" does not translate nearly as well to the screen. Overlong and with little plot, the action centers around a would-be writer, his floozy girlfriend, and the holier-than-thou characters which populate the town in which he grew up and to which he has now returned. Strong performances by all.

1958 136m/C Frank Sinatra, Dean Martin, Shirley MacLaine, Martha Hyer, Arthur Kennedy, Nancy Gates; *D:* Vincente Minnelli; *M:* Elmer Bernstein. Nominations: Academy Awards '58: Best Actress (MacLaine), Best Costume Design, Best Song ("To Love and Be Loved"), Best Supporting Actor (Kennedy), Best Supporting Actress (Hyer). **VHS, Beta, LV** ★★★

Some Like It Hot Two unemployed musicians witness the St. Valentine's Day massacre in Chicago. They disguise themselves as women and join an all-girl band headed for Miami to escape the gangsters' retaliation.

Flawless cast includes a fetching Monroe at her best; hilarious script. Curtis does his Cary Grant impression. Classic scenes between Lemmon in drag and Joe E. Brown as a smitten suitor. Brown also has the film's famous closing punchline. Monroe sings "I Wanna Be Loved By You," "Running Wild," and "I'm Through With Love." One of the very funniest movies of all time.

1959 120m/B Marilyn Monroe, Tony Curtis, Jack Lemmon, George Raft, Pat O'Brien, Nehemiah Persoff, Joe E. Brown, Joan Shawlee, Mike Mazurki; *D:* Billy Wilder; *W:* Billy Wilder; *M:* Adolph Deutsch. Academy Awards '59: Best Costume Design (B & W); British Academy Awards '59: Best Actor (Lemmon); Golden Globe Awards '60: Best Actor—Musical/Comedy (Lemmon), Best Actress—Musical/Comedy (Monroe), Best Film—Musical/Comedy; National Board of Review Awards '59: 10 Best Films of the Year; Nominations: Academy Awards '59: Best Actor (Lemmon), Best Adapted Screenplay, Best Art Direction/Set Decoration (B & W), Best Black and White Cinematography, Best Director (Wilder). **VHS, Beta, LV** ★★★★

Somebody Up There Likes Me Story of Rocky Graziano's gritty battle from his poor, street-wise childhood to his prison term and his eventual success as the middleweight boxing champion of the world. Adapted from Graziano's autobiography. Superior performance by Newman (in his third screen role, after the miserable "The Silver Chalice" and forgettable "The Rack"); screen debuts for McQueen and Loggia.

1956 113m/B Paul Newman, Pier Angeli, Everett Sloane, Eileen Heckart, Sal Mineo, Robert Loggia, Steve McQueen; *D:* Robert Wise; *W:* Ernest Lehman. Academy Awards '56: Best Art Direction/Set Decoration (B & W), Best Black and White Cinematography; Nominations: Academy Awards '56: Best Film Editing. **VHS, Beta** ★★★

Someone to Watch Over Me After witnessing the murder of a close friend, a beautiful and very wealthy woman must be protected from the killer. The working-class New York detective assigned the duty is more than taken with her, despite the fact that he has both a wife and son at home. A highly watchable, stylish romantic crime thriller.

1987 (R) 106m/C Tom Berenger, Mimi Rogers, Lorraine Bracco, Jerry Orbach, Andreas Katsulas, Tony DiBenedetto, James Moriarty, John Rubinstein; *D:* Ridley Scott; *W:* Howard Franklin; *M:* Michael Kamen, Steven Poster. **VHS, Beta, LV** ★★★

Sometimes a Great Notion Trouble erupts in a small Oregon town when a family of loggers decides to honor a contract when the other loggers go on strike. Newman's second stint in the director's chair; Fonda's first role as an old man. Based on the novel by Ken Kesey. *AKA:* Never Give an Inch.

1971 (PG) 115m/C Paul Newman, Henry Fonda, Lee Remick, Richard Jaeckel, Michael Sarrazin; *D:* Paul Newman; *W:* John Gay; *M:* Henry Mancini. Nominations: Academy Awards '71: Best Song ("All His Children"), Best Supporting Actor (Jaeckel). **VHS, Beta** ★★★

Son of Dracula In this late-coming sequel to the Universal classic, a stranger named Alucard is invited to America by a Southern belle obsessed with eternal life. It is actually Dracula himself, not his son, who wreaks havoc in this spine-tingling chiller. *AKA:* Young Dracula.

1943 80m/B Lon Chaney Jr., Evelyn Ankers, Frank Craven, Robert Paige, Louise Allbritton, J. Edward Bromberg, Samuel S. Hinds; *D:* Robert Siodmak. **VHS, Beta, LV** ★★★

Son of Frankenstein The second sequel (after "The Bride of Frankenstein") to the 1931 version of the horror classic. The good doctor's skeptical son returns to the family manse and becomes obsessed with his father's work and with reviving the creature. Full of memorable characters and brooding ambience. Karloff's last appearance as the monster.

1939 99m/C Basil Rathbone, Bela Lugosi, Boris Karloff, Lionel Atwill, Josephine Hutchinson, Donnie Dunagan, Emma Dunn, Edgar Norton, Lawrence Grant; *D:* Rowland V. Lee. **VHS, Beta, LV** ★★★

Son of Paleface Hilarious sequel to the original Hope gag-fest, with the Harvard-educated son of the original character (again played by Hope) heading west to claim an inheritance. Hope runs away with every cowboy cliche and even manages to wind up with the girl. Songs include "Buttons and Bows" (reprised from the original), "There's a Cloud in My Valley of Sunshine," and "Four-legged Friend."

1952 95m/C Bob Hope, Jane Russell, Roy Rogers, Douglass Dumbrille, Iron Eyes Cody, Bill Williams, Harry von Zell; *D:* Frank Tashlin. Nominations: Academy Awards '52: Best Song ("Am I in Love"). **VHS, Beta, LV** ★★★1/2

Son of the Sheik A desert sheik abducts an unfaithful dancing girl. Valentino's well-done, slightly self-mocking last film. Silent. Sequel to "The Sheik" (1921).

1926 62m/B Rudolph Valentino, Vilma Banky, Agnes Ayres; *D:* George Fitzmaurice. **VHS, Beta, LV** ★★★

A Song Is Born A group of music professors try to trace the history of music. Kaye is in charge of a U.S. music foundation whose research has led him up to ragtime. He is soon, however, thrust into the sometimes seedy world of jazz joints and night spots, all in the name of research. Enter love interest Mayo, a woman on the run from her gangster boyfriend who hides out at the foundation. Not one of Kaye's funniest or best, but if you enjoy big band music, you'll love this. Includes music by Louis Armstrong and his orchestra, Tommy Dorsey and his orchestra, and Charlie Barnet and his orchestra. This was Kaye's last film for Goldwyn. ♪ A Song is Born; Bach Boogie; Anitra's Dance; I'm Getting Sentimental Over You; Blind Barnabas; Mockin' Bird; Redskin Rhumba; The Goldwyn Stomp; Daddy-O.
1948 113m/B Danny Kaye, Virginia Mayo, Benny Goodman, Hugh Herbert, Steve Cochran, J. Edward Bromberg, Felix Bressart; *D:* Howard Hawks. **VHS** ★★★

Song O' My Heart An early musical starring popular Irish tenor McCormack as a singer forced to abandon his career when he marries a woman he does not love. A tour de force for the lead in his movie debut. ♪ Little Boy Blue; Paddy Me Lad; I Hear You Calling Me; A Fair Story by the Fireside; Just For a Day; Kitty My Love; The Rose of Tralee; A Pair of Blue Eyes; I Feel You Near Me.
1929 91m/B John McCormack, Maureen O'Sullivan, John Garrick, J.M. Kerrigan, Tommy Clifford, Alice Joyce; *D:* Frank Borzage. **VHS, Beta** ★★★

The Song of Bernadette Depicts the true story of a peasant girl who sees a vision of the Virgin Mary in a grotto at Lourdes in 1858. The girl is directed to dig at the grotto for water that will heal those who believe in its powers, much to the astonishment and concern of the townspeople. Based on Franz Werfel's novel. Directed with tenderness and carefully cast, and appealing to religious and sentimental susceptibilities, it was a box-office smash.
1943 156m/B Charles Bickford, Lee J. Cobb, Jennifer Jones, Vincent Price, Anne Revere, Gladys Cooper; *D:* Henry King; *M:* Alfred Newman. Academy Awards '43: Best Actress (Jones), Best Black and White Cinematography, Best Interior Decoration, Best Score; Golden Globe Awards '44: Best Actress—Drama (Jones), Best Director (King), Best Film—Drama; Nominations: Academy Awards '43: Best Director (King), Best Film Editing, Best Picture, Best Screenplay, Best Sound, Best Supporting Actor (Bickford), Best Supporting Actress (Cooper). **VHS, Beta, LV** ★★★

A Song to Remember With music performed by Jose Iturbi, this film depicts the last years of the great pianist and composer Frederic Chopin, including his affair with famous author George Sand, the most renowned French woman of her day. Typically mangled film biography. ♪ Valse in D Flat (Minute Waltz); Mazurka In B Flat, Opus 7, No. 1; Fantasie Impromptu, Opus 66; Etude In A Flat, Opus 25, No. 1 (partial); Polonaise In A Flat, Opus 53 (partial); Scherzo In B Flat Minor; Etude In C Minor, Opus 10, No. 12; Nocturne In C Minor, Opus 48, No. 1; Nocturne In E Flat, Opus 9, No. 2.
1945 112m/C Cornel Wilde, Paul Muni, Merle Oberon, Nina Foch, George Coulouris; *D:* Charles Vidor; *M:* Miklos Rozsa. Nominations: Academy Awards '45: Best Actor (Wilde), Best Film Editing, Best Story. **VHS, Beta, LV** ★★★

Sons of Katie Elder After their mother's death, four brothers are reunited. Wayne is a gunman; Anderson is a college graduate; silent Holliman is a killer; and Martin is a gambler. When they learn that her death might have been murder, they come together to devise a way to seek revenge on the killer. The town bullies complicate matters; the sheriff tells them to lay off. Especially strong screen presence by Wayne, in his first role following cancer surgery. One of the Duke's most popular movies of the '60s.
1965 122m/C John Wayne, Dean Martin, Earl Holliman, Michael Anderson Jr., Martha Hyer; *D:* Henry Hathaway; *M:* Elmer Bernstein. **VHS, Beta, LV** ★★★

Sons of the Desert Laurel and Hardy in their best-written film. The boys try to fool their wives by pretending to go to Hawaii to cure Ollie of a bad cold when in fact, they are attending their lodge convention in Chicago. Also includes a 1935 Thelma Todd/Patsy Kelly short, "Top Flat." *AKA:* Sons of the Legion; Convention City; Fraternally Yours.
1933 73m/B Stan Laurel, Oliver Hardy, Mae Busch, Charley Chase, Dorothy Christy; *D:* William A. Seiter. **VHS, Beta** ★★★

Sophie's Choice A haunting modern tragedy about Sophie Zawistowska, a beautiful Polish Auschwitz survivor settled in Brooklyn after WWII. She has intense relationships with a schizophrenic genius and an aspiring Southern writer. An artful, immaculately performed and resonant drama, with an astonishing, commanding performance by the versatile Streep; a chilling portrayal of the banality of evil. From the best-selling, autobiographical novel by William Styron.
1982 (R) 157m/C Meryl Streep, Kevin Kline, Peter MacNicol, Rita Karin, Stephen D. Newman, Josh Mostel; **D:** Alan J. Pakula; **W:** Alan J. Pakula; **M:** Marvin Hamlisch. Academy Awards '82: Best Actress (Streep); Golden Globe Awards '83: Best Actress—Drama (Streep); Los Angeles Film Critics Association Awards '82: Best Actress (Streep); National Board of Review Awards '82: Best Actress (Streep); New York Film Critics Awards '82: Best Actress (Streep), Best Cinematography; National Society of Film Critics Awards '82: Best Actress (Streep); Nominations: Academy Awards '82: Best Adapted Screenplay, Best Cinematography, Best Costume Design, Best Original Score. **VHS, Beta, LV**
★★★½

The Sorrow and the Pity A classic documentary depicting the life of a small French town and its resistance during the Nazi occupation. Lengthy, but totally compelling. A great documentary that brings home the atrocities of war. In French with English narration.
1971 265m/B *FR* **D:** Marcel Ophuls. National Board of Review Awards '72: 5 Best Foreign Films of the Year. **VHS, Beta**
★★★½

Sorry, Wrong Number A wealthy, bedridden wife overhears two men plotting a murder on a crossed telephone line, and begins to suspect that one of the voices is her husband's. A classic tale of paranoia and suspense. Based on a radio drama by Louise Fletcher, who also wrote the screenplay. Remade for television in 1989.
1948 89m/B Barbara Stanwyck, Burt Lancaster, Ann Richards, Wendell Corey, Harold Vermilyea, Ed Begley Sr.; **D:** Anatole Litvak. Nominations: Academy Awards '48: Best Actress (Stanwyck). **VHS, Beta, LV**
★★★½

Soul of the Game TV movie follows the lives of three talented players in the Negro League during the 1945 season as they await the potential integration of baseball. Brooklyn Dodgers general manager Branch Rickey (Herrmann) has his scouts focusing on three men in particular; flashy, aging pitcher Satchel Paige (Lindo), mentally unstable catcher Josh Gibson (Williamson), and the young, college-educated Jackie Robinson (Underwood). Manages to resist melodrama through terrific performances.
1996 105m/C Delroy Lindo, Mykelti Williamson, Blair Underwood, Edward Herrmann, R. Lee Ermey, Gina Ravera, Salli Richardson, Obba Babatunde, Brent Jennings; **D:** Kevin Rodney Sullivan; **W:** David Himmelstein; **M:** Lee Holdridge. **VHS**
★★★

The Sound of Music The classic film version of the Rodgers and Hammerstein musical based on the true story of the singing von Trapp family of Austria and their escape from the Nazis just before WWII. Beautiful Salzburg, Austria location photography and an excellent cast. Andrews, fresh from her Oscar for "Mary Poppins," is effervescent, in beautiful voice, but occasionally too good to be true. Not Rodgers & Hammerstein's most innovative score, but lovely to hear and see. Plummer's singing was dubbed by Bill Lee. Marni Nixon, behind-the-scenes songstress for "West Side Story" and "My Fair Lady," makes her on-screen debut as one of the nuns. ♪ I Have Confidence In Me; Something Good; The Sound of Music; Preludium; Morning Hymn; Alleluia; How Do You Solve A Problem Like Maria?; Sixteen, Going on Seventeen; My Favorite Things.
1965 174m/C Julie Andrews, Christopher Plummer, Eleanor Parker, Peggy Wood, Charmian Carr, Heather Menzies, Marni Nixon, Richard Haydn, Anna Lee, Norma Varden, Nicholas Hammond, Angela Cartwright, Portia Nelson, Duane Chase, Debbie Turner, Kym Karath; **D:** Robert Wise; **W:** Ernest Lehman; **M:** Richard Rodgers, Oscar Hammerstein. Academy Awards '65: Best Adapted Score, Best Director (Wise), Best Film Editing, Best Picture, Best Sound; Directors Guild of America Awards '65: Best Director (Wise); Golden Globe Awards '66: Best Actress—Musical/Comedy (Andrews), Best Film—Musical/Comedy; National Board of Review Awards '65: 10 Best Films of the Year; Nominations: Academy Awards '65: Best Actress (Andrews), Best Art Direction/Set Decoration (Color), Best Color Cinematography (Color), Best Costume Design (Color), Best Supporting Actress (Wood). **VHS, Beta, LV** ★★★★

Sounder The struggles of a family of black sharecroppers in rural Louisiana during the Depression. When the father is sentenced to jail for stealing in order to feed his family, they must pull together even more, and one son finds education to be his way out of poverty. Tyson brings strength and style to her role, with fine help from Winfield. Moving and well made, with little sentimentality and superb acting from a great cast. Adapted from the novel by William Armstrong.

1972 (G) 105m/C Paul Winfield, Cicely Tyson, Kevin Hooks, Taj Mahal, Carmen Mathews, James Best, Janet MacLachlan; **D:** Martin Ritt, John A. Alonzo; **M:** Taj Mahal. National Board of Review Awards '72: 10 Best Films of the Year, Best Actress (Tyson); Nominations: Academy Awards '72: Best Actor (Winfield), Best Actress (Tyson), Best Adapted Screenplay, Best Picture. **VHS, Beta, LV ★★★★**

South Pacific A young American Navy nurse and a Frenchman fall in love during WWII. Expensive production included much location shooting in Hawaii. Based on Rodgers and Hammerstein's musical; not as good as the play, but pretty darn good still. The play in turn was based on James Michener's novel "Tales of the South Pacific." ♩ My Girl Back Home; Dites-Moi; Bali Ha'i; Happy Talk; A Cock-eyed Optimist; Soliloquies; Some Enchanted Evening; Bloody Mary; I'm Gonna Wash That Man Right Out of My Hair.

1958 167m/C Mitzi Gaynor, Rossano Brazzi, Ray Walston, France Nuyen, John Kerr, Juanita Hall, Tom Laughlin; **D:** Joshua Logan; **M:** Richard Rodgers, Oscar Hammerstein; **V:** Giorgio Tozzi. Academy Awards '58: Best Sound; Nominations: Academy Awards '58: Best Color Cinematography, Best Original Score. **VHS, Beta, LV ★★★1/2**

Southern Comfort A group of National Guardsmen are on weekend maneuvers in the swamps of Louisiana. They run afoul of some of the local Cajuns, and are marked for death in this exciting and disturbing thriller. Booth is excellent in a rare exploration of a little-understood way of life. Lots of blood. If you belong to the National Guard, this could make you queasy.

1981 (R) 106m/C Powers Boothe, Keith Carradine, Fred Ward, Franklyn Seales, Brion James, T.K. Carter, Peter Coyote; **D:** Walter Hill; **W:** Walter Hill, David Giler, Michael Kane; **M:** Ry Cooder. **VHS, Beta, LV ★★★**

The Southerner A man used to working for others is given some land by an uncle and decides to pack up his family and try farming for himself. They find hardships as they struggle to support themselves. A superb, naturalistic celebration of a family's fight to survive amid all the elements. From the story "Hold Autumn in Your Hand," by George Sessions Perry. Novelist Faulkner had an uncredited hand in the script. He thought Renoir the best contemporary director, and later said "The Southerner" gave him more pleasure than any of his other Hollywood work (though this is faint praise; Faulkner is said to have hated Hollywood).

1945 91m/B Zachary Scott, Betty Field, Beulah Bondi, Norman Lloyd, Bunny Sunshine, Jay Gilpin, Estelle Taylor, Blanche Yurka, Percy Kilbride, J. Carrol Naish; **D:** Jean Renoir; **W:** Hugo Butler, William Faulkner, Jean Renoir. National Board of Review Awards '45: Best Director (Renoir); Venice Film Festival '46: Best Film; Nominations: Academy Awards '45: Best Director (Renoir), Best Sound, Best Original Score. **VHS, Beta, 8mm ★★★★**

Spanking the Monkey "What'd ya do on your summer vacation?" Ray Aibelli (Davies) has an interesting answer in this dark comedy about family dysfunction, sexual politics, incest, and masturbation, topics which guarantee it a special place on the video shelf. Returning from his freshman year at MIT, Ray learns he must give up a prestigious internship to care for his bedridden mother (Watson) while Dad goes on an extended "business" trip. Much sexual and emotional confusion follows. Mom, it seems, is rather attractive, controlling, and in need of hands-on assistance. Black comedy is understated and sensitive, focusing attention on the story and characters rather than the delicate subject matter, but you'll be aware of the delicate subject matter nonetheless. Sharp directorial debut by Russell features fine performances by mostly unknown cast, elevating low-budget feel. See it with a relative.

1994 (R) 99m/C Jeremy Davies, Alberta Watson, Benjamin Hendrickson, Carla Gallo, Matthew Puckett; **D:** David O. Russell; **W:** David O. Russell. Independent Spirit Awards '95: Best First Feature; Sundance Film Festival '94: Audience Award; Nominations: Independent Spirit Awards '95: Best Supporting Actress (Gallo), Debut Performance (Davies). **VHS, LV ★★★**

Spartacus The true story of a gladiator who leads other slaves in a rebellion against the power of Rome in 73 B.C. The rebellion is put down and the rebels are crucified. Douglas, whose political leanings are amply on display herein, also served as executive producer, surrounding himself with the best talent available. Magnificent climactic battle scene features 8,000 real, live Spanish soldiers to stunning effect. A version featuring Kubrick's "director's cut" is also available, featuring a restored, controversial homoerotic bath scene with Olivier and Curtis. Anthony Mann is uncredited as co-director. A box-office triumph that gave Kubrick much-desired financial independence.

1960 (PG-13) 196m/C Kirk Douglas, Laurence Olivier, Jean Simmons, Tony Curtis, Charles Laughton, Herbert Lom, Nina Foch, Woody Strode, Peter Ustinov, John Gavin, John Ireland, Charles McGraw, Joanna Barnes; *D:* Stanley Kubrick; *W:* Dalton Trumbo; *M:* Alex North. Academy Awards '60: Best Art Direction/Set Decoration (Color), Best Color Cinematography, Best Costume Design (Color), Best Supporting Actor (Ustinov); Nominations: Academy Awards '60: Best Film Editing. **VHS, Beta, LV** ★★★★

A Special Day The day of a huge rally celebrating Hitler's visit to Rome in 1939 serves as the backdrop for an affair between weary housewife Loren and lonely, unhappy homosexual radio announcer Mastroianni. Good performances from two thorough pros make a depressing film well worth watching. In Italian with English subtitles or dubbed. *AKA:* Una Giornata Speciale; The Great Day.

1977 105m/C *IT* Sophia Loren, Marcello Mastroianni; *D:* Ettore Scola; *W:* Ettore Scola. Golden Globe Awards '78: Best Foreign Film; National Board of Review Awards '77: 5 Best Foreign Films of the Year; Nominations: Academy Awards '77: Best Actor (Mastroianni), Best Foreign Language Film. **VHS, Beta, LV** ★★★

Speed Excellent dude Reeves has grown up (and bulked up) as Los Angeles SWAT cop Jack Traven, up against bomb expert Howard Payne (Hopper, more maniacal than usual), who's after major ransom money. First it's a rigged elevator in a very tall building. Then it's a rigged bus—if it slows, it will blow, bad enough any day, but a nightmare in L.A. traffic. And that's still not the end. Terrific directorial debut for cinematographer De Bont, who certainly knows how to keep the adrenaline pumping. Fine

support work by Daniels, Bullock, and Morton and enough wit in Yost's script to keep you chuckling. Great nonstop actioner from the "Die Hard" school.

1994 (R) 115m/C Keanu Reeves, Dennis Hopper, Sandra Bullock, Joe Morton, Jeff Daniels, Alan Ruck, Glenn Plummer, Richard Lineback, Beth Grant, Hawthorne James, David Kriegel, Carlos Carrasco, Natsuko Ohama, Daniel Villarreal; *D:* Jan De Bont; *W:* Graham Yost; *M:* Mark Mancina. Academy Awards '94: Best Sound; MTV Movie Awards '94: Best Female Performance (Bullock), Most Desirable Female (Bullock), Best On-Screen Duo (Keanu Reeves/Sandra Bullock), Best Villain (Hopper), Best Action Sequence; Blockbuster Entertainment Awards '95: Movie, Video, Action Actress, Video (Bullock), Action Actress, Theatrical (Bullock); Nominations: Academy Awards '94: Best Film Editing; MTV Movie Awards '95: Best Film, Best Male Performance (Reeves), Most Desirable Male (Reeves), Best Kiss (Keanu Reeves/Sandra Bullock). **VHS, LV** ★★★1/2

Speedy Lloyd comes to the rescue when the last horse car in New York City, operated by his fiance's grandfather, is stolen by a gang. Thoroughly phoney, fun pursuit/action comedy shot on location. Look for a brief appearance by Babe Ruth.

1928 72m/B Harold Lloyd, Bert Woodruff, Ann Christy; *D:* Ted Wilde. Nominations: Academy Awards '28: Best Director (Wilde). **VHS, Beta** ★★★

Spellbound Peck plays an amnesia victim accused of murder. Bergman plays the psychiatrist who uncovers his past through Freudian analysis and ends up falling in love with him. One of Hitchcock's finest films of the 1940s, with a riveting dream sequence designed by Salvador Dali. Full of classic Hitchcock plot twists and Freudian imagery. Based on Francis Bleeding's novel "The House of Dr. Edwardes."

1945 111m/B Ingrid Bergman, Gregory Peck, Leo G. Carroll, Michael Chekhov, Wallace Ford, Rhonda Fleming, Regis Toomey; *D:* Alfred Hitchcock; *M:* Miklos Rozsa. Academy Awards '45: Best Score; New York Film Critics Awards '45: Best Actress (Bergman); Nominations: Academy Awards '45: Best Actor (Chekhov), Best Black and White Cinematography, Best Director (Hitchcock), Best Picture. **VHS, Beta, LV** ★★★1/2

Spider Woman A modernized Holmes and Watson adventure as the duo track down a woman responsible for a series of murders. His adversary

uses poisonous spiders to do her work. Zestful, superior Holmes. *AKA:* Sherlock Holmes and the Spider Woman.
1944 62m/B Basil Rathbone, Nigel Bruce, Gale Sondergaard, Dennis Hoey; *D:* Roy William Neill. VHS, Beta ★★★

Spiders One of the earliest surviving films by director Lang, and predates Indiana Jones by almost 60 years. In these first two chapters ("The Golden Lake" and "The Diamond Ship") of an unfinished four-part thriller, Carl de Vogt battles with the evil Spider cult for a mystically powerful Incan diamond. Restored version has original color-tinted scenes. Silent with organ score.
1918 137m/B *GE* Lil Dagover; *D:* Fritz Lang; *M:* Gaylord Carter. VHS, Beta, LV ★★★

The Spider's Stratagem Thirty years after his father's murder by the fascists, a young man returns to a small Italian town to learn why his father was killed. The locals resist his efforts, and he is trapped in a mysterious web where history and lies exert a stranglehold on the truth. Intriguing, highly literate thriller, outrageously lovely color photography. Based on a short story by Jorge Luis Borges. In Italian with English subtitles.
1970 97m/C *IT* Giulio Brogi, Alida Valli; *D:* Bernardo Bertolucci; *W:* Bernardo Bertolucci. VHS ★★★

Spies A sly criminal poses as a famous banker to steal government information and create chaos in the world in this silent Lang masterpiece. Excellent entertainment, tight plotting and pacing, fine performances. Absolutely relentless intrigue and tension. *AKA:* Spione.
1928 88m/B *GE* Rudolf Klein-Rogge, Lupu Pick, Fritz Rasp, Gerda Maurus, Willy Fritsch; *D:* Fritz Lang. VHS, Beta, LV ★★★1/2

The Spiral Staircase A mute servant, working in a creepy Gothic mansion, may be the next victim of a murderer preying on women afflicted with deformities, especially when the next murder occurs in the mansion itself. Great performance by McGuire as the terrified victim. Remade for television in 1975.
1946 83m/B Dorothy McGuire, George Brent, Ethel Barrymore, Kent Smith, Rhonda Fleming, Gordon Oliver, Elsa Lanchester, Sara Allgood; *D:* Robert Siodmak. Nominations: Academy Awards '46: Best Supporting Actress (Barrymore). VHS, LV ★★★

Spirit of St. Louis A lavish Hollywood biography of famous aviator Charles Lindbergh and his historic transatlantic flight from New York to Paris in 1927, based on his autobiography. Intelligent; Stewart shines as the intrepid airman. Inexplicably, it flopped at the box office.
1957 137m/C James Stewart, Patricia Smith, Murray Hamilton, Marc Connelly; *D:* Billy Wilder; *W:* Billy Wilder, Wendell Mayes; *M:* Franz Waxman. National Board of Review Awards '57: 10 Best Films of the Year. VHS, Beta ★★★

Spite Marriage When Sebastian's lover dumps her like yesterday's garbage, she marries Keaton out of spite. Much postnuptual levity follows. Keaton's final silent.
1929 82m/B Buster Keaton, Dorothy Sebastian, Edward Earle, Leila Hyams, William Bechtel, Hank Mann; *D:* Edward Sedgwick. VHS, Beta, LV ★★★

Spitfire True story of Reginald J. Mitchell, who designed "The Spitfire" fighter plane, which greatly assisted the Allies during WWII. Howard's last film. Heavily propagandist but enjoyable and uncomplicated biography, with a splendid score. *AKA:* The First of the Few.
1942 88m/B *GB* Leslie Howard, David Niven, Rosamund John, George King, Jon Stafford, Adrian Brunel, Patricia Medina; *D:* Leslie Howard; *M:* William Walton. VHS, Beta ★★★

Splendor in the Grass A drama set in rural Kansas in 1925, concerning a teenage couple who try to keep their love on a strictly intellectual plane and the sexual and family pressures that tear them apart. After suffering a mental breakdown and being institutionalized, the girl returns years later in order to settle her life. Film debuts of Beatty, Dennis, and Diller. Inge wrote the screenplay specifically with Beatty in mind, after the actor appeared in one of Inge's stage plays. Filmed not in Kansas, but on Staten Island and in upstate New York.
1961 124m/C Natalie Wood, Warren Beatty, Audrey Christie, Barbara Loden, Zohra Lampert, Phyllis Diller, Sandy Dennis; *D:* Elia Kazan; *W:* William Inge; *M:* David Amram. Academy Awards '61: Best Story & Screenplay; Nominations: Academy Awards '61: Best Actress (Wood). VHS, Beta, LV ★★★

Spy in Black A German submarine captain returns from duty at sea during WWI and is assigned to infiltrate one of the Orkney Islands and obtain confidential British information. Known in the U.S. as "U-Boat 29," this film is based on a J. Storer Clouston novel. This was the first teaming of director Powell and writer Pressburger, who followed with "Contraband" in 1940 .

1939 82m/B *GB* Conrad Veidt, Valerie Hobson, Sebastian Shaw, Marius Goring, June Duprez, Helen Haye, Cyril Raymond, Hay Petrie; *D:* Michael Powell; *M:* Miklos Rozsa. **VHS, Beta, LV ★★★**

The Spy Who Came in from the Cold The acclaimed adaptation of the John Le Carre novel about an aging British spy who attempts to infiltrate the East German agency. Prototypical Cold War thriller, with emphasis on de-glamorizing espionage. Gritty and superbly realistic with a documentary style which hampered it at the box office.

1965 110m/B Richard Burton, Oskar Werner, Claire Bloom, Sam Wanamaker, Peter Van Eyck, Cyril Cusack, Rupert Davies, Michael Hordern; *D:* Martin Ritt. British Academy Awards '66: Best Film; Edgar Allan Poe Awards '65: Best Screenplay; Golden Globe Awards '66: Best Supporting Actor (Werner); Nominations: Academy Awards '65: Best Actor (Burton). **VHS, Beta, LV ★★★1/2**

Stage Door An energetic ensemble peek at the women of the theater. A boarding house for potential actresses houses a wide variety of talents and dreams. Patrician Hepburn and wisecracking Rogers make a good team in a talent-packed ensemble. Realistic look at the sub-world of Broadway aspirations includes dialogue taken from idle chat among the actresses between takes. Based on the play by Edna Ferber and George S. Kaufman, who suggested in jest a title change to "Screen Door," since so much had been changed. Watch for young stars-to-be like Ball, Arden and Miller.

1937 92m/B Katharine Hepburn, Ginger Rogers, Lucille Ball, Eve Arden, Andrea Leeds, Jack Carson, Adolphe Menjou, Gail Patrick; *D:* Gregory La Cava. National Board of Review Awards '37: 10 Best Films of the Year; New York Film Critics Awards '37: Best Director (La Cava); Nominations: Academy Awards '37: Best Director (La Cava), Best Picture, Best Screenplay, Best Supporting Actress (Leeds). **VHS, Beta ★★★1/2**

Stage Fright Wyman will stop at nothing to clear her old boyfriend, who has been accused of murdering the husband of his mistress, an actress (Dietrich). Disguised as a maid, she falls in love with the investigating detective, and discovers her friend's guilt. Dietrich sings "The Laziest Gal in Town." The Master's last film made in England until "Frenzy" (1971).

1950 110m/B *GB* Jane Wyman, Marlene Dietrich, Alastair Sim, Sybil Thorndike, Michael Wilding, Kay Walsh; *D:* Alfred Hitchcock. National Board of Review Awards '50: 10 Best Films of the Year. **VHS, Beta, LV ★★★**

Stagecoach Varied group of characters with nothing in common are stuck together inside a coach besieged by bandits and Indians. Considered structurally perfect, with excellent direction by Ford, it's the film that made Wayne a star as the Ringo Kid, an outlaw looking to avenge the murder of his brother and father. The first pairing of Ford and Wayne changed the course of the modern western. Stunning photography by Bert Glennon and Ray Binger captured the mythical air of Monument Valley, a site that Ford was often to revisit. Based on the story "Stage to Lordsburg" by Ernest Haycox. Remade miserably in 1966 and again—why?—as a TV movie in 1986.

1939 100m/B John Wayne, Claire Trevor, Thomas Mitchell, George Bancroft, John Carradine, Andy Devine, Donald Meek, Louise Platt, Berton Churchill, Tim Holt, Tom Tyler, Chris-Pin Martin, Francis Ford, Jack Pennick; *D:* John Ford. Academy Awards '39: Best Supporting Actor (Mitchell), Best Score; National Board of Review Awards '39: 10 Best Films of the Year; New York Film Critics Awards '39: Best Director (Ford); Nominations: Academy Awards '39: Best Black and White Cinematography, Best Director (Ford), Best Film Editing, Best Interior Decoration, Best Picture. **VHS, Beta, LV ★★★★**

Stalag 17 A group of American G.I.s in a German POW camp during WWII suspects the opportunistic Holden of being the spy in their midst. One of the very best American movies of the 1950s, adapted from the play by Donald Bevan and Edmund Trzcinski. Wilder, so good at comedy, proved himself equally adept at drama, and brought a top-drawer performance out of Holden. Features superb photography from Ernest Laszlo, and a wonderful score.

1953 120m/B William Holden, Don Taylor, Peter Graves, Otto Preminger, Harvey Lembeck, Robert Strauss, Sig Rumann, Richard Erdman, Neville Brand; *D:* Billy Wilder; *W:* Billy Wilder, Edwin Blum; *M:* Franz Waxman. Academy Awards '53: Best Actor (Holden); National Board of Review Awards '53: 10 Best Films of the Year; Nominations: Academy Awards '53: Best

Director (Wilder), Best Supporting Actor (Strauss). **VHS, Beta, LV** ★★★★

Stalker A meteorite, crashing to Earth, has caused a wasteland area known as the Zone. The Zone is forbidden to anyone except three special guides called Stalkers. Three Stalkers enter the region searching for its center, which contains a room that supposedly reveals fantasies. From the Soviet team that made "Solaris." Filmed with both color and black-and-white sequences. Suspenseful atmosphere due to the director's use of long takes, movement, and color. In Russian with English subtitles.
1979 160m/C *RU* Alexander Kaidanovsky, Nikolai Grinko, Anatoli Solonitzin, Alice Freindlikh; **D:** Andrei Tarkovsky; **M:** Eduard Artemyev. **VHS** ★★★

Stand and Deliver A tough teacher inspires students in an East L.A. barrio to take the Advanced Placement Test in calculus. A superb, inspirational true story, with a wonderful performance from Olmos.
1988 (PG) 105m/C Edward James Olmos, Lou Diamond Phillips, Rosana De Soto, Andy Garcia, Will Gotay, Ingrid Oliu, Virginia Paris, Mark Eliot; **D:** Ramon Menendez; **W:** Tom Musca, Ramon Menendez; **M:** Craig Safan. Independent Spirit Awards '89: Best Actor (Olmos), Best Director (Menendez), Best Film, Best Screenplay, Best Supporting Actor (Phillips), Best Supporting Actress (De Soto); Nominations: Academy Awards '88: Best Actor (Olmos). **VHS, LV, 8mm** ★★★

Stand By Me A sentimental, observant adaptation of the Stephen King novella "The Body." Four 12-year-olds trek into the Oregon wilderness to find the body of a missing boy, learning about death and personal courage. Told as a reminiscence by narrator "author" Dreyfuss with solid performances from all four child actors. Too much gratuitous obscenity, but a very good, gratifying film from can't-miss director Reiner.
1986 (R) 87m/C River Phoenix, Wil Wheaton, Jerry O'Connell, Corey Feldman, Kiefer Sutherland, Richard Dreyfuss, Casey Siemaszko, John Cusack; **D:** Rob Reiner; **W:** Raynold Gideon; **M:** Jack Nitzsche. Nominations: Academy Awards '86: Best Adapted Screenplay. **VHS, Beta, LV, 8mm** ★★★

Stanley and Livingstone The classic Hollywood kitsch version of the Victorian legend-based-on-fact. American journalist Tracy sets out into darkest Africa to locate a long-lost British explorer. Lavish, dramatically solid fictionalized history. (The real Stanley did not become a missionary—but hey, this is the movies.) Tracy is excellent, as usual, and low-key.
1939 101m/B Spencer Tracy, Cedric Hardwicke, Nancy Kelly, Walter Brennan, Richard Greene, Charles Coburn, Henry Hull, Henry Travers, Miles Mander, Holmes Herbert, Paul Stanton, Brandon Hurst, Joseph Crehan, Russell Hicks; **D:** Henry King; **M:** Alfred Newman. **VHS, Beta** ★★★½

A Star Is Born A movie star declining in popularity marries a shy girl and helps her become a star. Her fame eclipses his and tragic consequences follow. Shows Hollywood-behind-the-scenes machinations. Stunning ending is based on the real-life tragedy of silent film star Wallace Reid, who died of a morphine overdose in 1923 at age 31. Remade twice, in 1954 and 1976.
1937 111m/C Janet Gaynor, Fredric March, Adolphe Menjou, May Robson, Andy Devine, Lionel Stander, Franklin Pangborn; **D:** William A. Wellman; **W:** William A. Wellman, David O. Selznick, Dorothy Parker; **M:** Max Steiner. Academy Awards '37: Best Story; National Board of Review Awards '37: 10 Best Films of the Year; Nominations: Academy Awards '37: Best Actor (March), Best Actress (Gaynor), Best Director (Wellman), Best Picture, Best Screenplay. **VHS, Beta, LV** ★★★½

A Star Is Born Aging actor helps a young actress to fame. She becomes his wife, but alcoholism and failure are too much for him. She honors his memory. Remake of the 1937 classic was Garland's triumph, a superb and varied performance. Newly restored version reinstates over 20 minutes of long-missing footage, including three Garland musical numbers. ♪ I'll Get By; You Took Advantage of Me; Black Bottom; Peanut Vendor; My Melancholy Baby; Swanee; It's A New World; Gotta Have Me Go With You; Somewhere There's Someone.
1954 (PG) 175m/C Judy Garland, James Mason, Jack Carson, Tommy Noonan, Charles Bickford, Emerson Treacy, Charles Halton; **D:** George Cukor. Golden Globe Awards '55: Best Actor—Musical/Comedy (Mason), Best Actress—Musical/Comedy (Garland); Nominations: Academy Awards '54: Best Actor (Mason), Best Actress (Garland), Best Art Direction/Set Decoration (Color), Best Costume Design (Color), Best Song ("The Man That Got Away"), Best Original Score. **VHS, Beta, LV** ★★★½

Star Spangled Rhythm Movie studio guard (Moore) has told his son (Bracken), a sailor, that he's actually the head of the studio in this WWII musical comedy. When he learns his son and his pals are coming for a visit, he enlists the aid of a friendly studio switchboard operator (Hutton) to pull a fast one. (Luckily, the real studio boss is out of town.) Plot doesn't matter anyway since it's just an excuse for a lot of studio stars to show up and perform. ♪ A Sweater, a Sarong and a Peek-a-Boo Bang; That Old Black Magic; Hit the Road to Dreamland; Old Glory; On the Swing Shift; Doing It for Defense; Sharp as a Tack; He Loved Me Till the All-Clear Came.

1942 99m/B Betty Hutton, Eddie Bracken, Victor Moore, Bing Crosby, Ray Milland, Bob Hope, Veronica Lake, Dorothy Lamour, Susan Hayward, Dick Powell, Mary Martin, Alan Ladd, Paulette Goddard, Cecil B. DeMille, Arthur Treacher, Preston Sturges, Eddie Anderson, William Bendix; **D:** George Marshall. **VHS** ★★★

Star Trek 2: The Wrath of Khan Picking up from the 1967 Star Trek episode "Space Seed," Admiral James T. Kirk and the crew of the Enterprise must battle Khan, an old foe out for revenge. Warm and comradely in the nostalgic mode of its successors. Introduced Kirk's former lover and unknown son to the series plot, as well as Mr. Spock's "death," which led to the next sequel (1984's "The Search for Spock"). Can be seen in wide-screen format on laserdisc.

1982 (PG) 113m/C William Shatner, Leonard Nimoy, Ricardo Montalban, DeForest Kelley, Nichelle Nichols, James Doohan, George Takei, Walter Koenig, Kirstie Alley, Merritt Butrick, Paul Winfield; **D:** Nicholas Meyer; **M:** James Horner. **VHS, Beta, LV, 8mm** ★★★

Star Trek 4: The Voyage Home Kirk and the gang go back in time (to the 1980s, conveniently) to save the Earth of the future from destruction. Filled with hilarious moments and exhilarating action; great special effects enhance the timely conservation theme. Watch for the stunning going-back-in-time sequence. Spock is particularly funny as he tries to fit in and learn the '80s lingo! Can be seen in widescreen format on laserdisc. Also available as part of Paramount's "director's series," in which Nimoy discusses various special effects aspects in the making of the film. The best in the six-part (so far) series.

1986 (PG) 119m/C William Shatner, DeForest Kelley, Catherine Hicks, James Doohan, Nichelle Nichols, George Takei, Walter Koenig, Mark Lenard, Leonard Nimoy; **D:** Leonard Nimoy; **W:** Nicholas

Meyer, Harve Bennett. Nominations: Academy Awards '86: Best Cinematography, Best Sound, Best Original Score. **VHS, Beta, LV, 8mm** ★★★

Star Trek Generations The sci-fi phenomena continues with the first film spin off from the recently departed "Star Trek: The Next Generation" TV series and the seventh following the adventures of the Enterprise crew. Captain Kirk is propelled into the future thanks to an explosion and manages to hook up with current starship captain, Picard. Of course, just in time to save the galaxy from the latest space loon, the villainous Dr. Soren (MacDowell), renegade Klingons, and your basic mysterious space entity. For comic relief, android Data gets an emotion chip. Terrific special effects (courtesy of Industrial Light and Magic) and yes, the heroic Kirk receives his mandatory grandiose death scene. Other original characters making a brief appearance are Scotty and Chekov. An entertaining romp through time and space.

1994 (PG) 117m/C William Shatner, Patrick Stewart, Malcolm McDowell, Whoopi Goldberg, Jonathon Frakes, Brent Spiner, LeVar Burton, Michael Dorn, Gates McFadden, Marina Sirtis, James Doohan, Walter Koenig, Alan Ruck; **D:** David Carson; **W:** Ronald D. Moore, Brannon Braga; **M:** Dennis McCarthy. **VHS, Beta** ★★★

Star Wars First entry of Lucas's "Star Wars" trilogy proved to be one of the biggest box-office hits of all time. A young hero, a captured princess, a hot-shot pilot, cute robots, a vile villain, and a heroic and mysterious Jedi knight blend together with marvelous special effects in a fantasy tale about rebel forces engaged in a life or death struggle with the tyrant leaders of the Galactic Empire. Set a new cinematic standard for realistic special effects, making many pre-"Star Wars" effects seem almost laughable in retrospect. Followed by "The Empire Strikes Back" (1980) and "Return of the Jedi" (1983).

1977 (PG) 121m/C Mark Hamill, Carrie Fisher, Harrison Ford, Alec Guinness, Peter Cushing, Kenny Baker, David Prowse, Anthony Daniels; **D:** George Lucas; **W:** George Lucas; **M:** John Williams; **V:** James Earl Jones. Academy Awards '77: Best Art Direction/Set Decoration, Best Costume Design, Best Film Editing, Best Sound, Best Visual Effects, Best Original Score; Golden Globe Awards '78: Best Score; Los Angeles Film Critics Association Awards '77: Best Film; National Board of Review

Awards '77: 10 Best Films of the Year; People's Choice Awards '78: Best Film; Nominations: Academy Awards '77: Best Director (Lucas), Best Original Screenplay, Best Picture, Best Supporting Actor (Guinness). **VHS, Beta, LV ★★★★**

Starman An alien from an advanced civilization lands in Wisconsin. He hides beneath the guise of a grieving young widow's recently deceased husband. He then makes her drive him across country to rendezvous with his spacecraft so he can return home. Well-acted, interesting twist on the "Stranger in a Strange Land" theme. Bridges is fun as the likeable starman; Allen is lovely and earthy in her worthy follow-up to "Raiders of the Lost Ark." Available in widescreen format on laserdisc.
1984 (PG) 115m/C Jeff Bridges, Karen Allen, Charles Martin Smith, Richard Jaeckel; **D:** John Carpenter; **W:** Bruce A. Evans, Raynold Gideon, Donald M. Morgan; **M:** Jack Nitzsche. Nominations: Academy Awards '84: Best Actor (Bridges). **VHS, Beta, LV ★★★**

Stars in My Crown McCrea provides a moving performance as the pistol-wielding preacher who helps the residents of a 19th-century small town battle a typhoid epidemic and KKK terrorism. Adapted from the novel by Joe David Brown.
1950 89m/B Joel McCrea, Ellen Drew, Dean Stockwell, Alan Hale, Lewis Stone, Amanda Blake, Juano Hernandez, Charles Kemper, Connie Gilchrist, Ed Begley Sr., James Arness, Jack Lambert, Arthur Hunnicutt; **D:** Jacques Tourneur; **W:** Margaret Fitts; **M:** Adolph Deutsch. **VHS ★★★**

The Stars Look Down A mine owner forces miners to work in unsafe conditions in a Welsh town and disaster strikes. Redgrave is a miner's son running for office, hoping to improve conditions, and to escape the hard life. Forceful, well-directed effort suffered at the box office, in competition with John Ford's similar classic "How Green Was My Valley." From the novel by A.J. Cronin.
1939 96m/B GB Michael Redgrave, Margaret Lockwood, Emlyn Williams, Cecil Parker; **D:** Carol Reed. National Board of Review Awards '41: 10 Best Films of the Year. **VHS, Beta ★★★**

Start the Revolution Without Me Hilarious, Moliere-esque farce about two sets of identical twins (Wilder and Sutherland) separated at birth, who meet 30 years later, just before the French Revolution. About as hammy as they come; Wilder is unforgettable.

Neglected when released, but now deservedly a cult favorite.
1970 (PG) 91m/C Gene Wilder, Donald Sutherland, Orson Welles, Hugh Griffith, Jack MacGowran, Billie Whitelaw, Victor Spinetti, Ewa Aulin; **D:** Bud Yorkin; **W:** Lawrence J. Cohen; **M:** John Addison. **VHS, Beta ★★★**

Starting Over His life racked by divorce, Phil Potter learns what it's like to be single, self-sufficient, and lonely once again. When a blind date grows into a serious affair, the romance is temporarily halted by his hang-up for his ex-wife. Enjoyable love-triangle comedy loses direction after a while, but Reynolds is subtle and charming, and Bergen good as his ex, a very bad songwriter. Based on a novel by Dan Wakefield.
1979 (R) 106m/C Burt Reynolds, Jill Clayburgh, Candice Bergen, Frances Sternhagen, Austin Pendleton, Mary Kay Place, Kevin Bacon, Daniel Stern; **D:** Alan J. Pakula; **W:** James L. Brooks; **M:** Marvin Hamlisch. Nominations: Academy Awards '79: Best Actress (Clayburgh), Best Supporting Actress (Bergen). **VHS, Beta, LV ★★★**

State Fair The second version of the glossy slice of Americana about a family at the Iowa State Fair, featuring plenty of great songs by Rodgers and Hammerstein. Adapted from the 1933 screen version of Phil Strong's novel. Remade again in 1962. ♪ It Might as Well Be Spring; It's a Grand Night for Singing; That's For Me; Isn't It Kinda Fun?; All I Owe Iowa; Our State Fair. **AKA:** It Happened One Summer.
1945 100m/C Charles Winninger, Jeanne Crain, Dana Andrews, Vivian Blaine, Dick Haymes, Fay Bainter, Frank McHugh, Percy Kilbride, Donald Meek, William Marshall, Harry (Henry) Morgan; **D:** Walter Lang; **W:** Oscar Hammerstein; **M:** Richard Rodgers, Oscar Hammerstein. Academy Awards '45: Best Song ("It Might as Well Be Spring"); Nominations: Academy Awards '45: Best Original Score. **VHS, Beta ★★★**

State of Grace Irish hood Penn returns to old NYC neighborhood as undercover cop and becomes involved with an Irish Westies mob in a fight for survival as urban renewal encroaches on their Hell's Kitchen turf. Shrinking client base for shakedown schemes and protection rackets forces them to become contract killers for the Italian mafia. Fine performances, with Penn tense but restrained, gang honcho Harris intense, and Oldham chewing up gritty urban scenery as psycho brother of Harris, but the story is long and meandering. Well-choreographed violence.

1990 (R) 134m/C Sean Penn, Ed Harris, Gary Oldman, Robin Wright, John Turturro, Burgess Meredith, John C. Reilly; *D:* Phil Joanou; *W:* Dennis McIntyre; *M:* Ennio Morricone. **VHS, LV** ★★★

State of Siege Third pairing of Montand and Costa-Gavras, about the real-life death of USAID employee Daniel Mitrione, suspected to be involved in torture and murder in Uruguay in the '60s. Quietly suspenseful, with snazzy editing; conspiracy-theory premise is similar to Stone's "JFK," and similarly disturbing, whether you believe it or not. Dubbed. *AKA:* Etat de Siege.

1973 119m/C *FR* Yves Montand, Renato Salvatori, O.E. Hasse, Jacques Perrin; *D:* Constantin Costa-Gavras. **VHS, Beta, LV** ★★★

State of the Union Liberal multimillionaire Tracy is seeking the Republican presidential nomination. His estranged wife (Hepburn) is asked to return so they can masquerade as a loving couple for the sake of his political career. Hepburn tries to help Tracy as the backstage political machinations erode his personal convictions. Adapted from a highly successful, topical Broadway play; the writers changed dialogue constantly to reflect the news. Capra and his partners at Liberty Pictures originally hoped to cast Gary Cooper and Claudette Colbert. Hepburn and Menjou were at odds politically (over communist witch hunts in Hollywood) but are fine together onscreen. *AKA:* The World and His Wife.

1948 124m/B Spencer Tracy, Katharine Hepburn, Angela Lansbury, Van Johnson, Adolphe Menjou, Lewis Stone, Howard Smith; *D:* Frank Capra. **VHS, Beta, LV** ★★★½

State of Things Ostensibly a mystery involving a film crew trying to remake a B-movie, "The Most Dangerous Man On Earth," but also an in-depth look at the process of filmmaking, a scathing look at nuclear warfare and an homage to Roger Corman and Hollywood at large. An enigmatic, complex film from Wenders prior to his American years. In German with English subtitles; some dialogue in English.

1982 120m/B *GE* Patrick Bauchau, Allen (Goorwitz) Garfield, Isabelle Weingarten, Viva, Samuel Fuller, Paul Getty III, Roger Corman; *D:* Wim Wenders. Venice Film Festival '82: Best Film. **VHS, Beta, LV** ★★★

Stavisky Sumptuously lensed story of Serge Stavisky, a con artist and bon vivant whose machinations almost brought down the French government when his corruption was exposed in 1934. Belmondo makes as charismatic an antihero as you could find. Excellent score complements the visuals. In French with English subtitles.

1974 117m/C Jean-Paul Belmondo, Anny Duperey, Charles Boyer, Francois Perier, Gerard Depardieu; *D:* Alain Resnais; *M:* Stephen Sondheim. New York Film Critics Awards '74: Best Supporting Actor (Boyer); Nominations: Cannes Film Festival '74: Best Film. **VHS** ★★★

Stay Hungry A wealthy southerner (Bridges) is involved in a real estate deal which depends on the sale of a gym where a number of body builders hang out. He becomes immersed in their world and finds himself in love with the working-class Field. Big Arnold's first speaking role in his own inimitable accent (his first role in "Hercules in New York" was dubbed). Offbeat and occasionally uneven comedy-drama based on a novel by Charles Gaines is a sleeper.

1976 (R) 102m/C Jeff Bridges, Sally Field, Arnold Schwarzenegger, Robert Englund, Scatman Crothers; *D:* Bob Rafelson; *W:* Bob Rafelson. **VHS, Beta, LV** ★★★

Steamboat Bill, Jr. City-educated student returns to his small hometown and his father's Mississippi riverboat, where he's an embarrassment to dad. But bond they do, to ward off the owner of a rival riverboat, whose daughter Keaton falls for. Engaging look at small-town life and the usual wonderful Keaton antics, including braving the big tornado.

1928 75m/B Buster Keaton, Ernest Torrence, Marion Byron, Tom Lewis; *D:* Charles Riesner. **VHS, Beta, LV** ★★★½

The Steel Helmet Hurriedly made Korean War drama stands as a top-notch war film. Brooding and dark, GIs don't save the world for democracy or rescue POWs; they simply do their best to survive a horrifying situation. Pointless death, confused loyalties and cynicism abound in writer-director Fuller's scathing comment on the madness of war.

1951 84m/B Gene Evans, Robert Hutton, Steve Brodie, William Chun, James Edwards, Richard Loo, Sid Melton; *D:* Samuel Fuller; *W:* Samuel Fuller. **VHS, Beta, LV** ★★★½

Steel Magnolias Julia Roberts plays a young woman stricken with severe diabetes who chooses to live her life to the fullest despite her bad health. Much of the action centers around a Louisiana beauty shop where the women get together to discuss the goings-on of their lives. Screenplay by R. Harling, based on his partially autobiographical play. Sweet, poignant, and often hilarious, yet just as often overwrought. MacLaine is funny as a bitter divorcee; Parton is sexy and fun as the hairdresser. But Field and Roberts go off the deep end and make it all entirely too weepy.

1989 (PG) 118m/C Sally Field, Dolly Parton, Shirley MacLaine, Daryl Hannah, Olympia Dukakis, Julia Roberts, Tom Skerritt, Sam Shepard, Dylan McDermott, Kevin J. O'Connor, Bil McCurcheon, Ann Wedgeworth, Janine Turner; **D:** Herbert Ross; **W:** Robert Harling; **M:** Georges Delerue, John A. Alonzo. Golden Globe Awards '90: Best Supporting Actress (Roberts); People's Choice Awards '90: Best Film—Drama; Nominations: Academy Awards '89: Best Supporting Actress (Roberts). **VHS, Beta, LV, 8mm ★★★**

Stella Dallas An uneducated woman lets go of the daughter she loves when she realizes her ex-husband can give the girl more advantages. What could be sentimental turns out believable and worthwhile under Vidor's steady hand. Stanwyck never makes a wrong step. From a novel by Olive Higgins Prouty. Remade in 1989 as "Stella," starring Bette Midler.

1937 106m/B Barbara Stanwyck, Anne Shirley, John Boles, Alan Hale, Marjorie Main; **D:** King Vidor. Nominations: Academy Awards '37: Best Actress (Stanwyck), Best Supporting Actress (Shirley). **VHS, Beta, LV ★★★**

The Sterile Cuckoo An aggressive coed pursues a shy freshman who seems to embody her romantic ideal. Minnelli's performance is outstanding; Burton as the naive young man is also fine. Pakula's splendid first directing job. **AKA:** Pookie.

1969 (PG) 108m/C Liza Minnelli, Wendell Burton, Tim McIntire; **D:** Alan J. Pakula; **W:** Alvin Sargent. Nominations: Academy Awards '69: Best Actor (Minnelli), Best Song ("Come Saturday Morning"). **VHS, Beta, LV ★★★**

The Stilts From modern Spanish cinema's preeminent director, this is a study of sexual dynamics revolving around a doomed love triangle. Aging professor Gomez wants young Del Sol to commit to him, but she won't; she has another, younger lover. Overwrought at times, but well acted. In Spanish with English subtitles.

1984 95m/C *SP* Laura Del Sol, Francesco Rabal, Fernando Gomez; **D:** Carlos Savrat. **VHS, Beta ★★★**

The Sting Newman and Redford together again in this sparkling story of a pair of con artists in 1930s Chicago. They set out to fleece a big-time racketeer, pitting brain against brawn and pistol. Very inventive, excellent acting, Scott Joplin's wonderful ragtime music is adapted by Marvin Hamlisch. The same directorial and acting team from "Butch Cassidy and the Sundance Kid" triumphs again.

1973 (PG) 129m/C Paul Newman, Robert Redford, Robert Shaw, Charles Durning, Eileen Brennan, Harold Gould, Ray Walston; **D:** George Roy Hill; **W:** David S. Ward; **M:** Marvin Hamlisch. Academy Awards '73: Best Adapted Score, Best Art Direction/Set Decoration, Best Costume Design, Best Director (Hill), Best Film Editing, Best Picture, Best Story & Screenplay; Directors Guild of America Awards '73: Best Director (Hill); People's Choice Awards '73: Best Film; Nominations: Academy Awards '73: Best Actor (Redford), Best Cinematography, Best Sound. **VHS, Beta, LV ★★★1/2**

The Stolen Children Highly acclaimed Italian neo-realist film that tells the story of a shy carabiniere and two children who have been placed in his care. They are an emotionally battered 11-year-old girl who was forced into prostitution by her mother and her sullen 9-year-old brother. As they journey from Milan to Sicily and gradually get to know each other, all three of the characters undergo a slight transformation. Gracefully executed, this haunting masterpiece explores the overriding themes of guilt and innocence and keeps you thinking about them long after the movie's over. In Italian with English subtitles. **AKA:** Il Ladro di Bambini.

1992 108m/C *IT* Enrico Lo Verso, Valentina Scalici, Giuseppe Ieracitano, Florence Darel, Marina Golovine, Fabio Alessandrini; **D:** Gianni Amelio; **W:** Gianni Amelio, Sandro Petraglia, Stefano Rulli; **M:** Franco Piersanti. Cannes Film Festival '92: Grand Jury Prize; Nominations: Cannes Film Festival '92: Best Film. **VHS ★★★1/2**

Stolen Kisses Sequel to "The 400 Blows," the story of Antoine Doinel: his unsuccessful career prospects as a detective in Paris, and his initially awkward but finally successful adventures with women. Made during Truffaut's involvement in a political crisis involving the sack of Cinematique Francais director Henri Langlois. Truffaut dedicated the film to Langlois and the Cinematique, but it

is a thoroughly apolitical, small-scale, charming (some say too charming) romantic comedy, Truffaut-style. Followed by "Bed and Board." *AKA:* Baisers Voles.
1968 90m/C *FR* Jean-Pierre Leaud, Delphine Seyrig; *D:* Francois Truffaut; *M:* Antoine Duhamel. National Board of Review Awards '69: 5 Best Foreign Films of the Year; National Society of Film Critics Awards '69: Best Director (Truffaut); Nominations: Academy Awards '68: Best Foreign Language Film. **VHS, Beta** ★★★1/2

The Stone Boy A boy accidentally kills his older brother on their family's Montana farm. The family is torn apart by sadness and guilt. Sensitive look at variety of reactions during a crisis, with an excellent cast led by Duvall's crystal-clear performance.
1984 (PG) 93m/C Glenn Close, Robert Duvall, Jason Presson, Frederic Forrest, Wilford Brimley, Linda Hamilton; *D:* Christopher Cain; *W:* Gina Berriault, Juan Ruiz-Anchia; *M:* James Horner, John Beal. **VHS, Beta** ★★★1/2

Stonewall Fictional account of the June 1969 police raid on Greenwich Village gay bar the Stonewall Inn, which is considered to have launched the modern gay rights movement. White-bread, Midwestern activist Matty Dean (Weller) arrives in New York and gets thrown in jail for defending streetwise drag queen LaMiranda (Diaz) from harassing cops. They become lovers, but Matty is also involved with conservative prepster Ethan (Corbalis), who thinks the flamboyant queens give the gay movement a bad name. Meanwhile, the drag queens at the mob-backed Stonewall are getting fed up with police raids and brutal treatment. Adapted from Martin Duberman's social history "Stonewall." Director Finch died during the final editing stages of the film.
1995 93m/C Frederick Weller, Guillermo Diaz, Brendan Corbalis, Bruce MacVittie, Duane Boutte, Peter Ratray, Luis Guzman; *D:* Nigel Finch; *W:* Rikki Beadle Blair; *M:* Michael Kamen. **VHS** ★★★

The Stooges Story "The Stooges Anthology" presents a history of the comedy team, from their vaudevillian beginnings to their television resurgence in the '60s. "Disorder in the Court" finds the trio making a mockery of the United States justice system, and in "Brideless Groom," Shemp must find a bride within forty-eight hours in order to collect an inheritance.

1990 90m/B Moe Howard, Larry Fine, Curly Howard, Shemp Howard. **VHS** ★★★

Stop Making Sense The Talking Heads perform 18 of their best songs in this concert filmed in Los Angeles. This is considered by many to be the best concert movie ever made. The band plays with incredible energy and imagination, and Demme's direction and camera work is appropriately frenzied and original. Features such Talking Heads songs as "Burning Down the House," "Psycho Killer," and "Once in a Lifetime." Band member Tina Weymouth's Tom Tom Club also performs for the audience.
1984 99m/C *D:* Jonathan Demme; *Performed by:* David Byrne, Tina Weymouth, Chris Franz, Jerry Harrison. **VHS, Beta, LV** ★★★1/2

Storm Over Asia A Mongolian trapper is discovered to be descended from Genghis Khan and is made puppet emperor of a Soviet province. Beautiful and evocative. Silent masterpiece. *AKA:* The Heir to Genghis Khan.
1928 70m/B *RU* I. Inkizhinov, Valeri Inkizhinov, A. Christiakov, A. Dedinstev, V. Tzoppi, Paulina Belinskaya; *D:* Vsevolod Pudovkin. National Board of Review Awards '30: 5 Best Foreign Films of the Year. **VHS, Beta** ★★★★

The Storm Within Based on Cocteau's play, many consider this domestic drama of a troubled family's tortured existence to be his finest work. De Bray plays the domineering mother, Marais plays the son, and Day is the woman he (and his father) love in this complex story of sexuality, parental rivalry and jealousy. With the film set in only two locations, Cocteau creates a claustrophobic intimacy within the walls of de Bray's family apartment and Day's apartment. An inferior remake, "Intimate Relations" was released in Britain in 1953. In French with English subtitles. *AKA:* Les Parents Terribles.
1948 98m/B *FR* Jean Marais, Yvonne de Bray, Gabrielle Dorziat, Marcel Andre, Josette Day; *D:* Jean Cocteau; *W:* Jean Cocteau. **VHS** ★★★1/2

The Story of a Cheat The hero of the film discovers at an early age that dishonesty is probably the best policy and he sets out to put his theory into use. Director/writer Guitry also turns in a great performance as the central character. Guitry was a major influence on such different directors as Welles, Resnais and Truffaut. Based on Guitry's novel "Memoires d'Un

Tricheur." In French with English subtitles.

1936 83m/B *FR* Sacha Guitry; **D:** Sacha Guitry; **W:** Sacha Guitry. **VHS** ★★★

Story of Adele H. The story of Adele Hugo, daughter of Victor Hugo, whose love for an English soldier leads to obsession and finally to madness after he rejects her. Sensitive and gentle unfolding of characters and story. Beautiful photography. In French with English subtitles. *AKA:* L'Histoire d'Adele H.

1975 (PG) 97m/C *FR* Isabelle Adjani, Bruce Robinson; **D:** Francois Truffaut; **W:** Suzanne Schiffman, Jean Gruault. National Board of Review Awards '75: 5 Best Foreign Films of the Year, Best Actress (Adjani); National Society of Film Critics Awards '75: Best Actress (Adjani); Nominations: Academy Awards '75: Best Actress (Adjani). **VHS, Beta, LV** ★★★

The Story of Louis Pasteur Formulaic Hollywood bio pic raised a notch or two by Muni's superb portrayal of the famous scientist and his career leading up to his most famous discoveries. Acclaimed in its time; excellent despite low budget.

1936 85m/B Paul Muni, Josephine Hutchinson, Anita Louise, Fritz Leiber, Donald Woods, Porter Hall, Akim Tamiroff, Walter Kingsford; **D:** William Dieterle. Academy Awards '36: Best Actor (Muni), Best Story & Screenplay; National Board of Review Awards '36: 10 Best Films of the Year; Nominations: Academy Awards '36: Best Picture. **VHS, Beta** ★★★

The Story of Qui Ju A simple story, beautifully directed and acted, about a peasant woman's search for justice. The pregnant Qui Ju's husband is assaulted and injured by the head of their village. Outraged, Qui Ju slowly climbs the Chinese administrative ladder from official to higher official as she insistently seeks redress. Presents a close observance of daily life and customs with a strong female lead. Adapted from the novel "The Wan Family's Lawsuit" by Chen Yuan Bin. In Mandarin Chinese with English subtitles.

1991 (PG) 100m/C *CH* Gong Li, Lei Lao Sheng, Liu Pei Qu, Ge Zhi Jun, Ye Jun, Yang Liu Xia; **D:** Zhang Yimou; **W:** Liu Heng. National Society of Film Critics Awards '93: Best Foreign Film; Venice Film Festival '92: Best Actress (Li), Best Film; Nominations: Independent Spirit Awards '94: Best Foreign Film. **VHS, LV** ★★★

The Story of the Late Chrysanthemum Classic drama about the son of a Kabuki actor who falls in love with a servant girl against his father's wishes. Their doomed affair is the center of the plot. Acclaimed and sensitive drama, in Japanese with English subtitles.

1939 115m/B *JP* Shotaro Hanayagi, Kakuo Mori, Kokichi Takada, Gonjuro Kawarazaki, Yoko Umemura; **D:** Kenji Mizoguchi. **VHS, Beta** ★★★1/2

The Story of Vernon and Irene Castle In this, their last film together for RKO, Astaire and Rogers portray the internationally successful ballroom dancers who achieved popularity in the early 1900s. Irene Castle served as technical advisor for the film and exasperated everyone on the set by insisting that Rogers be a brunette. Still fun, vintage Fred and Ginger. ♪ Only When You're In My Arms; Missouri Waltz; Oh, You Beautiful Doll; Nights of Gladness; By the Beautiful Sea; Glow, Little Glow Worm; Destiny Waltz; Row, Row, Row; The Yama Yama Man.

1939 93m/B Fred Astaire, Ginger Rogers, Edna May Oliver, Lew Fields, Jack Perrin, Walter Brennan; **D:** H.C. Potter. **VHS, Beta, LV** ★★★

The Story of Women Riveting factual account of a woman (Huppert) who was guillotined for performing abortions in Nazi-occupied France. In French with English subtitles. *AKA:* Une Affaire de Femmes.

1988 110m/C *FR* Isabelle Huppert, Francois Cluzet, Marie Trintignant, Nils Tavernier, Louis Ducreux; **D:** Claude Chabrol; **W:** Claude Chabrol, Colo Tavernier O'Hagan; **M:** Matthieu Chabrol. Los Angeles Film Critics Association Awards '89: Best Foreign Film; New York Film Critics Awards '89: Best Foreign Film; Venice Film Festival '88: Best Actress (Huppert). **VHS** ★★★

Strange Days It's 1999 in a volatile L.A. and vice cop-turned-street-hustler Lenny Nero (Fiennes) is plying his SQUID trade—discs that offer the wearer the chance to experience any vice. The seedily likeable Lenny draws the line at peddling snuff clips until one capturing the murder of his friend, hooker Iris (Bako), shows up. Lenny's in way over his head and turns to self-sufficient security agent Mace (Bassett) to save him. Also tied into this tangled web is Lenny's lost love, singer Faith (the annoying Lewis), who's now with dangerous junkie/promoter Philo (Wincott); murdered black activist/rapper Jeriko One (Plummer); dirty cops; and the biggest New Year's Eve party imaginable. The phenomenal Bassett heats up the screen (while kicking major butt) while the generally cerebral Fiennes shows why someone could care about this desperate lowlife. Bigelow's an action expert and struts on the film's dark visuals while offering some emotional impact with her society-on-the-eve-of-destruction saga.

1995 (R) 145m/C Ralph Fiennes, Angela Bassett, Juliette Lewis, Tom Sizemore, Michael Wincott, Brigitte Bako, Vincent D'Onofrio, William Fichtner, Richard Edson, Glenn Plummer, Josef Sommer; **D:** Kathryn Bigelow; **W:** James Cameron, Jay Cocks; **M:** Graeme Revell, Matthew F. Leonetti. **VHS ★★★**

Strange Interlude Shearer is at her best in screen adaptation of talky Eugene O'Neill play in which she portrays a young wife who wants a child, but discovers that insanity runs in her husband's family. Doing the only sensible thing, she decides to have a child by another man (Gable). Interesting because the characters' thoughts are revealed to the audience through voice-overs. **AKA:** Strange Interval.

1932 110m/B Norma Shearer, Clark Gable, May Robson, Ralph Morgan, Robert Young, Mary Alden, Maureen O'Sullivan, Henry B. Walthall; **D:** Robert Z. Leonard. **VHS ★★★**

The Strange Love of Martha Ivers Douglas is good in his screen debut as the wimpy spouse of unscrupulous Stanwyck. Stanwyck shines as the woman who must stay with Douglas because of a crime she committed long ago . . . Tough, dark melodrama; classic film noir.

1946 117m/B Barbara Stanwyck, Van Heflin, Kirk Douglas, Lizabeth Scott, Judith Anderson; **D:** Lewis Milestone; **M:** Miklos Rozsa. Nominations: Academy Awards '46: Best Story. **VHS, Beta, LV ★★★**

The Stranger Notably conventional for Welles, but swell entertainment nonetheless. War crimes tribunal sets Nazi thug Shayne free hoping he'll lead them to his superior, Welles. Robinson trails Shayne through Europe and South America to a small town in Connecticut. Tight suspense made on a tight budget saved Welles's directorial career.

1946 95m/B Edward G. Robinson, Loretta Young, Martha Wentworth, Konstantin Shayne, Richard Long, Orson Welles; **D:** Orson Welles. Nominations: Academy Awards '46: Best Story. **VHS, Beta ★★★1/2**

Stranger Than Paradise Regular guy, nerdy sidekick, and Hungarian girl cousin traipse around America being bored and having fun and adventure. New York, then on to Cleveland! The thinking person's mindless flick. Inventive, independent comedy made on quite a low budget was acclaimed at Cannes.

1984 (R) 90m/B GE Richard Edson, Eszter Balint, John Lurie; **D:** Jim Jarmusch; **W:** Jim Jarmusch; **M:** John Lurie. National Society of Film Critics Awards '84: Best Film. **VHS, Beta, LV ★★★**

Strangers on a Train Long before there was "Throw Momma from the Train," there was this Hitchcock super-thriller about two passengers who accidentally meet and plan to "trade" murders. Amoral Walker wants the exchange and the money he'll inherit for his father's death; Granger would love to end his stifling marriage and wed Roman, a senator's daughter, but finds the idea ultimately sickening. What happens is pure Hitchcock. Screenplay co-written by murder-mystery great Raymond Chandler. Patricia Hitchcock, the director's only child, plays Roman's sister. The concluding "carousel" scene is a masterpiece. From the novel by Patricia Highsmith.

1951 101m/B Farley Granger, Robert Walker, Ruth Roman, Leo G. Carroll, Patricia Hitchcock, Marion Lorne; **D:** Alfred Hitchcock; **W:** Raymond Chandler; **M:** Dimitri Tiomkin. National Board of Review Awards '51: 10 Best Films of the Year; Nominations: Academy Awards '51: Best Black and White Cinematography. **VHS, Beta, LV ★★★★**

Strangers: The Story of a Mother and Daughter Rowlands is the long-estranged daughter of Davis, who won an Emmy for her portrayal of the embittered widow. The great actress truly is at her recent best in this made-for-TV tearjerker, and Rowlands keeps pace.

1979 88m/C Bette Davis, Gena Rowlands, Ford Rainey, Donald Moffat; **D:** Milton Katselas. **VHS, Beta ★★★**

The Stratton Story Stewart and Allyson teamed up for the first of the three pictures they'd make together in this true story of Monty Stratton, the Chicago White Sox pitcher. A baseball phenom, Stratton suffers a devastating hunting accident which leads to the amputation of one leg. Learning to walk with an artificial limb, Stratton also struggles to resume his baseball career. Stewart's fine as always, with Allyson lending noble support as the loving wife. Chisox manager Jimmy Dykes played himself as did pitcher Gene Bearden, lending further authenticity to an excellent production.

1949 106m/B James Stewart, June Allyson, Frank Morgan, Agnes Moorehead, Bill Williams, Bruce Cowling; **D:** Sam Wood; **W:** Guy Trosper, Douglas S. Morrow. Academy Awards '49: Best Story. **VHS, Beta ★★★**

Straw Dogs An American mathematician, disturbed by the predominance of violence in American society, moves with his wife to an isolated Cornish village. He finds that primitive savagery exists beneath the most peaceful surface. After his wife is raped, Hoffman's character seeks revenge. Hoffman is good, a little too wimpy at times. A violent, frightening film reaction to the violence of the 1960s.

1971 (R) 118m/C *GB* Dustin Hoffman, Susan George, Peter Vaughan, T.P. McKenna, David Warner; **D:** Sam Peckinpah; **W:** David Zelag Goodman. Nominations: Academy Awards '71: Best Original Score. **VHS, Beta, LV ★★★**

Strawberry and Chocolate Sex, politics, and friendship set in 1979 Havana. University student David (Cruz) is sitting morosely in a cafe eating chocolate ice cream when he's spotted by older, educated, gay, strawberry-eating Diego (Perugorria), who manages to persuade David to visit him at his apartment. Resolutely hetero (and communist), David is appalled not only by Diego's sexuality but by his subversive politics. But gradually David's seduced by Diego's ideas and friendship into questioning the regime's harsh policies (and homophobia). Satiric and sympathetic—not only to the characters but to Cuba itself. Ill with cancer, Gutierrez Alea finished the film with the aid of Tabio. From the short story "The Wolf, the Forest and the New Man" by sceenwriter Paz. In Spanish with English subtitles. **AKA:** Fresa y Chocolate.

1993 (R) 110m/C *CU* Jorge Perugorria, Vladimir Cruz, Mirta Ibarra, Francisco Gattorno, Jorge Angelino, Marilyn Solaya; **D:** Thomas Gutierrez Alea, Juan Carlos Tabio; **W:** Thomas Gutierrez Alea, Senel Paz, Mario Garcia Joya; **M:** Jose Maria Vitier. Nominations: Academy Awards '94: Best Foreign Language Film. **VHS ★★★**

Strawberry Blonde A romantic comedy set in the 1890s, with Cagney as a would-be dentist infatuated with money-grubbing Hayworth (the strawberry blonde of the title), who wonders years later whether he married the right woman (chestnut

brunette de Havilland). Attractive period piece remade from 1933's "One Sunday Afternoon," and revived yet again in 1948 by Raoul Walsh.

1941 100m/B James Cagney, Olivia de Havilland, Rita Hayworth, Alan Hale, George Tobias, Jack Carson, Una O'Connor, George Reeves; **D:** Raoul Walsh; **W:** Julius J. Epstein, Philip C. Epstein. Nominations: Academy Awards '41: Best Original Score. **VHS, Beta ★★★**

Street of Shame A portrayal of the abused lives of six Tokyo prostitutes. Typically sensitive to the roles and needs of women and critical of the society that exploits them, Mizoguchi creates a quiet, inclusive coda to his life's work in world cinema. Kyo is splendid as a hardened hooker and has a memorable scene with her father. Kogure is also good. The great director's last finished work was instrumental in the outlawing of prostitution in Japan. In Japanese with English subtitles.

1956 88m/B *JP* Machiko Kyo, Michiko Kogure, Aiko Mimasu; **D:** Kenji Mizoguchi. **VHS, Beta ★★★1/2**

Street Scene Life in a grimy New York tenement district, circa 1930. Audiences nationwide ate it up when Elmer Rice adapted his own Pulitzer Prize-winning play and top helmsman Vidor gave it direction.

1931 80m/B Sylvia Sidney, William Collier Jr., Estelle Taylor, Beulah Bondi, David Landau; **D:** King Vidor; **M:** Alfred Newman. **VHS, Beta, 8mm ★★★**

A Streetcar Named Desire Powerful film version of Tennessee Williams' play about a neurotic southern belle with a hidden past who comes to visit her sister and is abused and driven mad by her brutal brother-in-law. Grim New Orleans setting for terrific performances by all, with Malden, Leigh, and Hunter winning Oscars, and Brando making highest impact on audiences. Brando disliked the role, despite the great impact it had on his career. Remade for television in 1984.

1951 (PG) 122m/B Vivien Leigh, Marlon Brando, Kim Hunter, Karl Malden; **D:** Elia Kazan; **W:** Tennessee Williams; **M:** Alex North. Academy Awards '51: Best Actress (Leigh), Best Art Direction/Set Decoration (B & W), Best Supporting Actor (Malden), Best Supporting Actress (Hunter); Golden Globe Awards '52: Best Supporting Actress (Hunter); National Board of Review Awards '51: 10 Best Films of the Year; New York Film Critics Awards '51: Best Actress (Leigh), Best Director (Kazan), Best Film; Nominations: Academy Awards '51: Best

Actor (Brando), Best Director (Kazan), Best Picture, Best Black and White Cinematography, Best Costume Design (B & W), Best Screenplay, Best Sound, Best Original Score. **VHS, Beta, LV** ★★★★

A Streetcar Named Desire Excellent made for television adaptation of the Tennessee Williams drama about fading southern belle Blanche du Bois (Ann-Margret in a terrific performance). D'Angelo is her plain sister Stella who lives with brutish husband Stanley (Williams) in the seamy French Quarter of New Orleans. Can't surpass the original but this version does have the advantage of not having to soft-pedal the drama for the fifties censors.
1984 94m/C Ann-Margret, Beverly D'Angelo, Treat Williams, Randy Quaid, Rafael Campos, Erica Yohn; **D:** John Erman; **M:** Marvin Hamlisch. **VHS** ★★★

Strictly Ballroom Offbeat, cheerfully tacky dance/romance amusingly turns every movie cliche slightly askew. Scott (Mercurio) has been in training for the Pan-Pacific ballroom championships since the age of six. While talented, he also refuses to follow convention and scandalizes the stuffy dance establishment with his new steps. When his longtime partner leaves him, Scott takes up with a love-struck beginner (Morice), with some surprises of her own. Ballet dancer Mercurio (in his film debut) is appropriately arrogant yet vulnerable, with Morice as the plain Jane turned steel butterfly. Wonderful supporting cast; great debut for director Luhrmann.
1992 (PG) 94m/C AU Paul Mercurio, Tara Morice, Bill Hunter, Pat Thomsen, Barry Otto, Gia Carides, Peter Whitford, John Hannan, Sonia Kruger-Tayler, Kris McQuade, Pip Mushin, Leonie Page, Antonio Vargas, Armonia Benedito; **D:** Baz Luhrmann; **W:** Craig Pearce, Baz Luhrmann; **M:** David Hirshfelder. Australian Film Institute '92: Best Costume Design, Best Director (Luhrmann), Best Film, Best Film Editing, Best Supporting Actor (Otto), Best Supporting Actress (Thomsen), Best Writing; Nominations: Golden Globe Awards '94: Best Film—Musical/Comedy. **VHS, LV** ★★★1/2

Strike Eisenstein's debut, and a silent classic. Stirring look at a 1912 clash between striking factory workers and Czarist troops.
1924 78m/B RU D: Sergei Eisenstein. **VHS, Beta** ★★★1/2

Strong Man A WWI veteran, passing himself off as an unlikely circus strongman, searches an American city for the girl whose letters gave him hope during the war. Perhaps Langdon's best full-length film..
1926 78m/B Harry Langdon, Gertrude Astor, Tay Garnett; **D:** Frank Capra. **VHS, Beta, LV** ★★★

Stroszek Three German misfits—a singer, a prostitute and an old man—tour the U.S. in search of their dreams. Touching, hilarious comedy-drama with a difference and an attitude. One of Herzog's easiest and also best films. In English and German with English subtitles.
1977 108m/C GE Eva Mattes, Bruno S, Clemens Scheitz; **D:** Werner Herzog; **M:** Chet Atkins. **VHS** ★★★

Student of Prague Early silent classic based on the German Faust legend: a student makes a pact with the devil to win a beautiful woman. Poor fellow. With either German or English title cards. Music track.
1913 60m/B GE Lothar Koemer, Grete Berger, Paul Wegener; **D:** Paul Wegener, Stellan Rye. **VHS, Beta** ★★★

The Stunt Man A marvelous and unique exercise in meta-cinematic manipulation. O'Toole, in one of his very best roles, is a power-crazed movie director; Railsback is a fugitive sheltered by him from sheriff Rocco. When a stunt man is killed in an accident, O'Toole prevails on Railsback to replace him, leading Railsback to wonder if O'Toole wants him dead. A labor of love for director-producer Rush, who spent nine years working on it, and waited two years to see it released, by Fox. Based on the novel by Paul Brodeur.
1980 (R) 129m/C Peter O'Toole, Steve Railsback, Barbara Hershey, Chuck Bail, Alex Rocco, Allen (Goorwitz) Garfield, Adam Roarke, Sharon Farrell, Philip Bruns; **D:** Richard Rush; **W:** Lawrence B. Marcus, Richard Rush; **M:** Dominic Frontiere. Golden Globe Awards '81: Best Score; Montreal World Film Festival '80: Best Film; National Board of Review Awards '80: 10 Best Films of the Year; National Society of Film Critics Awards '80: Best Actor (O'Toole); Nominations: Academy Awards '80: Best Actor (O'Toole), Best Adapted Screenplay, Best Director (Rush). **VHS, Beta, LV** ★★★★

Suddenly Crazed gunman Sinatra holds a family hostage in the hick town of Suddenly, California, as part of a plot to kill the president, who's passing through town. Tense thriller is a good display for Sinatra's acting talent. Unfortunately hard to find because Sinatra forced United Artists to take it out of distribution after hearing that Kennedy assassin Lee Harvey Oswald had watched "Suddenly" only days before November 22, 1963. Really, Ol' Blue Eyes should have stuck with making top-notch thrillers like this one, instead of degenerating into the world's greatest lounge singer.

1954 75m/B Frank Sinatra, Sterling Hayden, James Gleason, Nancy Gates, Paul Frees; **D:** Lewis Allen. **VHS, Beta** ★★★1/2

Suddenly, Last Summer Brain surgeon is summoned to the mansion of a rich New Orleans matron who wishes him to perform a lobotomy on her niece, supposedly suffering from a mental breakdown. Based on the play by Tennessee Williams. Softened for the censors, though the themes of homosexuality, insanity, murder, characterizations of evil, and unusual settings presage many movies of the next two decades. Extremely fine performances from Hepburn and Taylor. Clift never completely recovered from his auto accident two years before and does not come across with the strength of purpose really necessary in his character. Still, fine viewing.

1959 114m/B Elizabeth Taylor, Katharine Hepburn, Montgomery Clift, Mercedes McCambridge, Albert Dekker; **D:** Joseph L. Mankiewicz; **W:** Gore Vidal; **M:** Malcolm Arnold. Golden Globe Awards '60: Best Actress—Drama (Taylor); National Board of Review Awards '59: 10 Best Films of the Year; Nominations: Academy Awards '59: Best Actress (Hepburn), Best Actress (Taylor), Best Art Direction/Set Decoration (B & W). **VHS, Beta, LV** ★★★1/2

The Sugarland Express To save her son from adoption, a young woman helps her husband break out of prison. In their flight to freedom, they hijack a police car, holding the policeman hostage. Speilberg's first feature film is a moving portrait of a couple's desperation. Based on a true story, adapted by Hal Barwood and Matthew Robbins.

1974 (PG) 109m/C Goldie Hawn, Ben Johnson, Michael Sacks, William Atherton; **D:** Steven Spielberg; **W:** Steven Spielberg, Matthew Robbins, Hal Barwood, Vilmos Zsigmond; **M:** John Williams. Nominations: Cannes Film Festival '74: Best Film. **VHS, Beta, LV** ★★★

Sullivan's Travels Sturges' masterpiece is a sardonic, whip-quick romp about a Hollywood director tired of making comedies who decides to make a serious, socially responsible film and hits the road masquerading

as a hobo in order to know hardship and poverty. Beautifully sustained, inspired satire that mercilessly mocked the ambitions of Depression-era social cinema. Gets a little over-dark near the end before the happy ending; Sturges insisted on 20-year-old Lake as The Girl; her pregnancy forced him to rewrite scenes and design new costumes for her. As ever, she is stunning.

1941 90m/B Joel McCrea, Veronica Lake, William Demarest, Robert Warwick, Franklin Pangborn, Porter Hall, Eric Blore, Byron Foulger, Robert Greig, Torben Meyer, Jimmy Conlin, Margaret Hayes, Chester Conklin, Alan Bridge; **D:** Preston Sturges; **W:** Preston Sturges. National Board of Review Awards '42: 10 Best Films of the Year. **VHS, Beta, LV** ★★★★

The Sum of Us Sweet and faithful adaptation of David Stevens' stage play about a father and his gay son. Widowed Harry Mitchell (Thompson) shares his house with son Jeff (Crowe), who's never made a secret of his sexual orientation. Affable Harry only wants what's best for his boy, including his overenthusiastic welcome to Jeff's potential new boyfriend (Polson). Too bad Harry's not so lucky in love—his new woman friend Joyce (Kennedy) has problems with Jeff's sexuality. Well, she just has to adjust. Pervasive feel-good message may leave less well-adjusted viewers addled. Sensitive performances, though the film's antecedents as a play are highlighted by having the main characters talk directly to the camera. Aussie slang provides a challenge.

1994 (R) 99m/C *AU* Jack Thompson, Russell Crowe, John Polson, Deborah Kennedy, Mitch Mathews, Julie Herbert, Joss Moroney, Rebekah Elmaloglou; **D:** Kevin Dowling, Geoff Burton; **W:** David Stevens; **M:** Dave Faulkner. Australian Film Institute '94: Best Adapted Screenplay; Montreal World Film Festival '94: Best Screenplay; Nominations: Australian Film Institute '94: Best Film, Best Supporting Actor (Polson), Best Supporting Actress (Kennedy). **VHS** ★★★

Summer The fifth and among the best of Rohmer's "Comedies and Proverbs" series. A romantic but glum young French girl finds herself stuck in Paris during the tourist season searching for true romantic love. Takes time and patience to seize the viewer; moving ending makes it all worthwhile. In French with English subtitles. **AKA:** Le Rayon Vert; The Green Ray.

1986 (R) 90m/C *FR* Marie Riviere, Lisa

Heredia, Beatrice Romand, Eric Hamm, Rosette, Isabelle Riviere; **D:** Eric Rohmer; **W:** Eric Rohmer. VHS, Beta, LV ★★★★

Summer of '42 Touching if sentimental story about a 15-year-old boy's sexual coming of age during his summer vacation on an island off New England. While his friends are fumbling with girls their own age, he falls in love with a beautiful 22-year-old woman whose husband is off fighting in the war.
1971 (R) 102m/C Jennifer O'Neill, Gary Grimes, Jerry Houser, Oliver Conant; **D:** Robert Mulligan. Academy Awards '71: Best Original Score; Nominations: Academy Awards '71: Best Cinematography, Best Film Editing, Best Story & Screenplay. VHS, Beta, LV ★★★

Summer Stock Garland plays a farm owner whose sister arrives with a summer stock troupe, led by Kelly, to rehearse a show in the family barn. Garland agrees, if the troupe will help her with the farm's harvest. When her sister decamps for New York, leaving the leading lady role open, guess who steps into the breach. Slim plot papered over with many fun song-and-dance numbers. Also features Garland's first MGM short, "Every Sunday," made in 1936 with Deanna Durbin. ♩ Friendly Star; Mem'ry Island; Dig-Dig-Dig For Your Dinner; If You Feel Like Singing, Sing; Howdy Neighbor; Blue Jean Polka; Portland Fancy; You, Wonderful You; Get Happy. **AKA:** If You Feel Like Singing.
1950 109m/C Judy Garland, Gene Kelly, Gloria De Haven, Carleton Carpenter, Eddie Bracken, Phil Silvers, Hans Conried, Marjorie Main, Ray Collins, Deanna Durbin; **D:** Charles Walters. VHS, Beta, LV ★★★

Summertime Spinster Hepburn vacations in Venice and falls in love with Brazzi. She is hurt when inadvertently she learns he is married, but her life has been so bleak she is not about to end her one great romance. Moving, funny, richly photographed in a beautiful Old World city. From Arthur Laurents' play "The Time of the Cuckoo." **AKA:** Summer Madness.
1955 98m/C Katharine Hepburn, Rossano Brazzi; **D:** David Lean. National Board of Review Awards '55: 10 Best Films of the Year; New York Film Critics Awards '55: Best Director (Lean); Nominations: Academy Awards '55: Best Actress (Hepburn), Best Director (Lean). VHS, Beta, LV ★★★1/2

Sunday, Bloody Sunday Adult drama centers around the intertwined love affairs of the homosexual Finch, the heterosexual Jackson, and self-centered bisexual artist Head, desired by both. Fully-drawn characters brought to life by excellent acting make this difficult story well worth watching—though Head's central character is sadly rather dull. Day-Lewis makes his first (brief) screen appearance as a car vandalizing teenager. Powerful, sincere and sensitive.
1971 (R) 110m/C *GB* Glenda Jackson, Peter Finch, Murray Head, Daniel Day-Lewis; **D:** John Schlesinger. British Academy Awards '71: Best Actor (Finch), Best Actress (Jackson), Best Director (Schlesinger), Best Film; Golden Globe Awards '72: Best Foreign Film; New York Film Critics Awards '71: Best Screenplay; National Society of Film Critics Awards '71: Best Actor (Finch), Best Screenplay; Writers Guild of America '71: Best Original Screenplay; Nominations: Academy Awards '71: Best Actor (Finch), Best Actress (Jackson), Best Director (Schlesinger), Best Story & Screenplay. VHS, LV ★★★

A Sunday in the Country A lush, distinctively French affirmation of nature and family life. This character study with a minimal plot takes place during a single summer day in 1910 France. An elderly impressionist painter-patriarch is visited at his country home by his family. Highly acclaimed, though the pace may be too slow for some. Beautiful location photography. In French with English subtitles. **AKA:** Un Dimanche a la Campagne.
1984 (G) 94m/C *FR* Louis Ducreux, Sabine Azema, Michel Aumont; **D:** Bertrand Tavernier; **W:** Bertrand Tavernier, Colo Tavernier O'Hagan. Cannes Film Festival '84: Best Director (Tavernier); Cesar Awards '85: Best Actress (Azema), Best Cinematography, Best Writing; National Board of Review Awards '84: Best Supporting Actress (Azema); New York Film Critics Awards '84: Best Foreign Film. VHS, Beta ★★★1/2

Sundays & Cybele A ragged war veteran and an orphaned girl develop a strong emotional relationship, which is frowned upon by the townspeople. Warm and touching. In French with English subtitles. Also available in a letterboxed edition. **AKA:** Les Dimanches de Ville d'Arvay; Cybele.
1962 110m/B *FR* Hardy Kruger, Nicole Courcel; **D:** Serge Bourguignon; **M:** Maurice Jarre. Academy Awards '62: Best Foreign Language Film; National Board of Review Awards '62: 5 Best Foreign Films of the Year. VHS, Beta ★★★1/2

Sunday's Children Lyrical exploration of childhood continues trilogy

that includes "Fanny and Alexander" and "Best Intentions." Wistful childhood memoir takes up the story of Ingmar Bergman's family eight years after the director was born. Many of the same familial issues surface, but story soon narrows its focus to the relationship between little Ingmar, whom everyone calls Pu, and his stern father Henrik. Deeply emotional and intense, film represents the steps toward forgiveness that the elder Bergman is finally able to take regarding the painful relationship he had with his own father. Father-son theme made more poignant with Ingmar's son Daniel making his feature debut as director.
1994 118m/C *SW* Thommy Berggren, Lena Endre, Henrik Linnros, Jacob Leygraf, Maria Bolme, Bjorje Ahistedt, Per Myrberg; **D:** Daniel Bergman; **W:** Ingmar Bergman. **VHS ★★★1/2**

The Sundowners Slow, beautiful, and often moving epic drama about a family of Irish sheepherders in Australia during the 1920s who must continually uproot themselves and migrate. They struggle to save enough money to buy their own farm and wind up training a horse they hope will be a money-winner in racing. Well-acted by all, with Johns and Ustinov providing some humorous moments. Adapted from the novel by Jon Cleary. Filmed in Australia and London studios.
1960 133m/C Deborah Kerr, Robert Mitchum, Peter Ustinov, Glynis Johns, Dina Merrill, Chips Rafferty, Michael Anderson Jr., Lola Brooks, Wylie Watson; **D:** Fred Zinneman; **M:** Dimitri Tiomkin. National Board of Review Awards '60: 10 Best Films of the Year, Best Actor (Mitchum); Nominations: Academy Awards '60: Best Actress (Kerr), Best Adapted Screenplay, Best Director (Zinneman), Best Picture, Best Supporting Actress (Johns). **VHS, Beta, LV ★★★1/2**

Sunrise Magnificent silent story of a simple country boy who, prodded by an alluring city woman, tries to murder his wife. Production values wear their age well. Gaynor won an Oscar for her stunning performance. Remade in Germany as "The Journey to Tilsit." Based on a story by Hermann Suderman. *AKA:* Sunrise—A Song of Two Humans.
1927 110m/B George O'Brien, Janet Gaynor, Bodil Rosing, Margaret Livingston, J. Farrell MacDonald, Carl Mayer; **D:** F.W. Murnau. Academy Awards '28: Best Actress (Gaynor), Best Cinematography; Nominations: Academy Awards '28: Best Interior Decoration. **VHS ★★★★**

Sunrise at Campobello A successful adaptation (with Bellamy and Donehue repeating their roles) of the Tony Award-winning play that chronicles Franklin D. Roosevelt's battle to conquer polio and ultimately receive the Democratic presidential nomination in 1924. Garson gives an excellent performance as Eleanor Roosevelt. Screenplay by Schary, who adapted his own play, and also produced.
1960 143m/C Ralph Bellamy, Greer Garson, Hume Cronyn, Jean Hagen, Jack Perrin, Lyle Talbot; **D:** Vincent J. Donehue; **W:** Dore Schary. Golden Globe Awards '61: Best Actress—Drama (Garson); National Board of Review Awards '60: Best Actress (Garson); Nominations: Academy Awards '60: Best Actress (Garson), Best Art Direction/Set Decoration (Color), Best Costume Design (Color), Best Sound. **VHS, Beta ★★★**

The Sun's Burial Oshima's stylized and violent drama depicts life in Osaka's worst slum—a teeming underworld populated by teen gangs, prostitutes, and criminals. All want control of the area's most profitable business, an illegal blood-selling operation. In Japanese with English subtitles.
1960 87m/C *JP* Kayoko Honoo, Koji Nakahara, Masahiko Tsugawa, Fumio Watanabe; **D:** Nagisa Oshima. **VHS ★★★**

Sunset Boulevard Famed tale of Norma Desmond (Swanson), aging silent film queen, who refuses to accept that stardom has ended for her and hires a young down-on-his-luck screenwriter (Holden) to help engineer her movie comeback. The screenwriter, who becomes the actress' kept man, assumes he can manipulate her, but finds out otherwise. Reality was almost too close for comfort, as Swanson, von Stroheim (as her majordomo), and others very nearly play themselves. A darkly humorous look at the legacy and loss of fame with witty dialogue, stellar performances, and some now-classic scenes. Based on the story "A Can of Beans" by Brackett and Wilder.
1950 100m/B Gloria Swanson, William Holden, Erich von Stroheim, Nancy Olson, Buster Keaton, Jack Webb, Cecil B. DeMille, Fred Clark; **D:** Billy Wilder; **W:** Billy Wilder, Charles Brackett, D.M. Marshman Jr. Academy Awards '50: Best Art Direction/Set Decoration (B & W), Best Story & Screenplay, Best Score; Golden Globe Awards '51: Best Actress—Drama (Swanson), Best Director (Wilder), Best Film—Drama, Best Score; Nominations: Academy Awards '50: Best Actor (Holden), Best Actress (Swanson), Best Black and

White Cinematography, Best Director (Wilder), Best Film Editing, Best Picture, Best Supporting Actor (von Stroheim), Best Supporting Actress (Olson).**VHS, Beta, LV** ★★★1/2

The Sunshine Boys Two veteran vaudeville partners, who have shared a love-hate relationship for decades, reunite for a television special. Adapted by Neil Simon from his play. Matthau was a replacement for Jack Benny, who died before the start of filming. Burns, for his first starring role since "Honolulu" in 1939, won an Oscar.
1975 (PG) 111m/C George Burns, Walter Matthau, Richard Benjamin, Lee Meredith, F. Murray Abraham, Carol Arthur, Howard Hesseman; **D:** Herbert Ross; **W:** Neil Simon. Academy Awards '75: Best Supporting Actor (Burns); Golden Globe Awards '76: Best Actor—Musical/Comedy (Matthau), Best Film—Musical/Comedy, Best Supporting Actor (Benjamin); Nominations: Academy Awards '75: Best Actor (Matthau), Best Adapted Screenplay, Best Art Direction/Set Decoration. **VHS, Beta, LV** ★★★

Superman: The Movie The DC Comics legend comes alive in this wonderfully entertaining saga of Superman's life from a baby on the doomed planet Krypton to Earth's own Man of Steel. Hackman and Beatty pair marvelously as super criminal Lex Luthor and his bumbling sidekick. Award-winning special effects and a script that doesn't take itself too seriously make this great fun. Followed by three sequels.
1978 (PG) 144m/C Christopher Reeve, Margot Kidder, Marlon Brando, Gene Hackman, Glenn Ford, Susannah York, Ned Beatty, Valerie Perrine, Jackie Cooper, Marc McClure, Trevor Howard, Sarah Douglas, Terence Stamp, Jack O'Halloran, Phyllis Thaxter; **D:** Richard Donner; **W:** Mario Puzo, Robert Benton, David Newman; **M:** John Williams. Academy Awards '78: Best Visual Effects; National Board of Review Awards '78: 10 Best Films of the Year; Nominations: Academy Awards '78: Best Film Editing, Best Sound, Best Original Score. **VHS, Beta, LV** ★★★1/2

Superman 2 The sequel to "the movie" about the Man of Steel. This time, he has his hands full with three super-powered villains from his home planet of Krypton. The romance between reporter Lois Lane and our superhero is made believable and the storyline has more pace to it than the original. A sequel that often equals the first film—leave it to Superman to pull off the impossible.

1980 (PG) 127m/C Christopher Reeve, Margot Kidder, Gene Hackman, Ned Beatty, Jackie Cooper, Sarah Douglas, Jack O'Halloran, Susannah York, Marc McClure, Terence Stamp, Valerie Perrine, E.G. Marshall; **D:** Richard Lester; **W:** Mario Puzo, David Newman; **M:** John Williams. **VHS, Beta, LV** ★★★

Superstar: The Life and Times of Andy Warhol Even if you didn't grok Andy's 'pop' artwork and self-created celebrity persona, this ironic, kinetic, oft-rollicking documentary paints a vivid picture of the wild era he inspired and exploited. Interviewees range from Warhol cohorts like Dennis Hopper to proud executives at the Campbell Soup plant. One highlight: a Warhol guest shot on "The Love Boat."
1990 87m/C Tom Wolfe, Sylvia Miles, David Hockney, Taylor Mead, Dennis Hopper; **D:** Chuck Workman. **VHS** ★★★

Support Your Local Sheriff Amiable, irreverent western spoof with more than its fair share of laughs. When a stranger stumbles into a gold rush town, he winds up becoming sheriff. Garner is perfect as the deadpan sheriff, particularly in the scene where he convinces Dern to remain in jail, in spite of the lack of bars. Neatly subverts every western cliche it encounters, yet keeps respect for formula western. Followed by "Support Your Local Gunfighter."
1969 (G) 92m/C James Garner, Joan Hackett, Walter Brennan, Bruce Dern, Jack Elam, Harry (Henry) Morgan; **D:** Burt Kennedy; **W:** William Bowers. National Board of Review Awards '69: 10 Best Films of the Year. **VHS, Beta, LV** ★★★1/2

The Sure Thing College students who don't like each other end up travelling to California together, and of course, falling in love. Charming performances make up for predictability. Can't-miss director (and ex-Meathead) Reiner's second direct hit at the box office.
1985 (PG-13) 94m/C John Cusack, Daphne Zuniga, Anthony Edwards, Boyd Gaines, Lisa Jane Persky, Viveca Lindfors, Nicolette Sheridan, Tim Robbins; **D:** Rob Reiner; **W:** Jonathan Roberts, Steven L. Bloom. **VHS, Beta, LV, 8mm** ★★★

Susan and God A selfish socialite returns from Europe and starts practicing a new religion, much to the dismay of her friends and family. Despite her preaching, her own domestic life is falling apart and she realizes that her preoccupation and selfish ways have caused a strain on her marriage and her relationship with her daugh-

ter. An excellent script and a fine performance from Crawford make this a highly satisfying film. **AKA:** The Gay Mrs. Trexel.
1940 115m/B Joan Crawford, Fredric March, Ruth Hussey, John Carroll, Rita Hayworth, Nigel Bruce, Bruce Cabot, Rose Hobart, Rita Quigley, Marjorie Main, Gloria De Haven; **D:** George Cukor; **W:** Anita Loos. **VHS** ★★★

Suspicion Alfred Hitchcock's suspense thriller about a woman who gradually realizes she is married to a killer and may be next on his list. An excellent production unravels at the end due to RKO's insistence that Grant retain his "attractive" image. This forced the writers to leave his guilt or innocence undetermined. Available colorized.
1941 99m/B Cary Grant, Joan Fontaine, Cedric Hardwicke, Nigel Bruce, May Whitty, Leo G. Carroll, Heather Angel; **D:** Alfred Hitchcock. Academy Awards '41: Best Actress (Fontaine); New York Film Critics Awards '41: Best Actress (Fontaine); Nominations: Academy Awards '41: Best Picture. **VHS, Beta, LV** ★★★1/2

Suspiria An American dancer enters a weird European ballet academy and finds they teach more than movement as bodies begin piling up. Sometimes weak plot is aided by great-but-gory special effects, fine photography, good music, and a chilling opening sequence. Also available in unrated version.
1977 (R) 92m/C *IT* Jessica Harper, Joan Bennett, Alida Valli, Udo Kier; **D:** Dario Argento; **W:** Dario Argento. **VHS, Beta, LV** ★★★

Svengali A music teacher uses his hypnotic abilities to manipulate one of his singing students and make her a star. Soon the young woman is singing for sell-out crowds, but only if her teacher is present. Barrymore in a hypnotic performance. Adapted from "Trilby" by George Du Maurier. Remade in 1955 and 1983.
1931 76m/B John Barrymore, Marian Marsh, Donald Crisp; **D:** Archie Mayo. Nominations: Academy Awards '31: Best Cinematography, Best Interior Decoration. **VHS, Beta** ★★★

The Swan A twist on the Cinderella story with Kelly (in her last film before her marriage) as the charming beauty waiting for her prince. Both Guinness, as the crown prince, and Jourdan, as her poor tutor, want her hand (and the rest of her). Attractive cast, but story gets slow from time to time. Remake of a 1925 silent film. The laserdisc version also includes "Wedding in Monaco," the news short showing Kelly's wedding to Prince Rainier.
1956 112m/C Grace Kelly, Louis Jourdan, Alec Guinness, Jessie Royce Landis, Brian Aherne, Estelle Winwood; **D:** Charles Vidor. **VHS, LV** ★★★

Sweet Bird of Youth An acclaimed adaptation of the Tennessee Williams play about Chance Wayne, a handsome drifter who travels with an aging movie queen to his small Florida hometown, hoping she'll get him started in a movie career. However, coming home turns into a big mistake, as the town boss wants revenge on Chance for seducing his daughter, Heavenly. Williams' original stage ending was cleaned up, providing a conventional "happy" movie ending for the censors. Remade for television in 1989 with Elizabeth Taylor and Mark Harmon in the lead roles.
1962 120m/C Paul Newman, Geraldine Page, Ed Begley Sr., Mildred Dunnock, Rip Torn, Shirley Knight, Madeline Sherwood; **D:** Richard Brooks; **W:** Richard Brooks. Academy Awards '62: Best Supporting Actor (Begley); Golden Globe Awards '63: Best Actress—Drama (Page); Nominations: Academy Awards '62: Best Actress (Page), Best Supporting Actress (Knight). **VHS, Beta, LV** ★★★

Sweet Charity An ever-optimistic dime-a-dance girl has a hard time finding a classy guy to marry. MacLaine is appealing in this big-budget version of the popular Broadway musical by Neil Simon (derived from Fellini's "Notti di Cabiria"). Fosse's debut as film director. Watch for Cort as a flower child. ♪ My Personal Property; It's a Nice Face; Hey, Big Spender; Rich Man's Frug; If My Friends Could See Me Now; There's Gotta Be Something Better Than This; Rhythm of Life; Sweet Charity; I'm a Brass Band.
1969 148m/C Shirley MacLaine, Chita Rivera, John McMartin, Paula Kelly, Sammy Davis Jr., Ricardo Montalban, Bud Cort; **D:** Bob Fosse; **M:** Cy Coleman. Nominations: Academy Awards '69: Best Art Direction/Set Decoration, Best Costume Design, Best Original Score. **VHS, Beta, LV** ★★★

Sweet Lorraine A bittersweet, nostalgic comedy about the staff and clientele of a deteriorating Catskills hotel on the eve of its closing.
1987 (PG-13) 91m/C Maureen Stapleton, Lee Richardson, Trini Alvarado, Freddie Roman, John Bedford Lloyd, Giancarlo Esposito, Edie Falco, Todd Graff, Evan Handler; **D:** Steve Gomer; **W:** Michael

Zettler, Shelly Altman; **M:** Richard Robbins. VHS, Beta ★★★

Sweet Smell of Success Evil New York City gossip columnist J.J. Hunsecker (Lancaster) and sleazy press agent (Curtis) cook up smear campaign to ruin career of jazz musician in love with J.J.'s sister. Engrossing performances, great dialogue.
1957 96m/C Burt Lancaster, Tony Curtis, Martin Milner, Barbara Nichols, Sam Levene; **D:** Alexander MacKendrick; **W:** Ernest Lehman, Clifford Odets; **M:** Elmer Bernstein. VHS, LV ★★★1/2

Sweet Sweetback's Baadasssss Song A black pimp kills two policemen who beat up a black militant. He uses his street-wise survival skills to elude his pursuers and escape to Mexico. A thriller, but racist, sexist, and violent.
1971 97m/C Melvin Van Peebles, Simon Chuckster, John Amos; **D:** Melvin Van Peebles; **W:** Melvin Van Peebles. VHS, Beta ★★★

Sweethearts MacDonald and Eddy star as married stage actors trying to get some time off from their hectic schedule in this show-within-a-show. Trouble ensues when their conniving producer begs, pleads and tricks them into staying. Lots of well-staged musical numbers. ♪ Wooden Shoes; Every Lover Must Meet His Fate; Sweethearts; Pretty as a Picture; Summer Serenade; On Parade.
1938 114m/C Jeanette MacDonald, Nelson Eddy, Frank Morgan, Florence Rice, Ray Bolger, Mischa Auer; **D:** Woodbridge S. Van Dyke. Nominations: Academy Awards '38: Best Sound, Best Score. VHS, LV ★★★

Sweetie Bizarre, expressive Australian tragicomedy about a pair of sisters—one a withdrawn, paranoid Plain Jane, the other a dangerously extroverted, overweight sociopath who re-enters her family's life and turns it upside down. Campion's first feature.
1989 (R) 97m/C AU Genevieve Lemon, Karen Colston, Tom Lycos, Jon Darling, Dorothy Barry, Michael Lake, Andre Pataczek; **D:** Jane Campion; **W:** Gerard Lee, Jane Campion; **M:** Martin Armiger. Nominations: Academy Awards '91: Best Foreign Language Film. VHS, Beta, LV ★★★

Swept Away . . . A rich and beautiful Milanese woman is shipwrecked on a desolate island with a swarthy Sicilian deckhand, who also happens to be a dedicated communist. Isolated, the two switch roles, with the wealthy woman dominated by the crude proletarian. Sexy and provocative. **AKA:** Swept Away . . . By an Unusual Destiny in the Blue Sea of August.
1975 (R) 116m/C IT Giancarlo Giannini, Mariangela Melato; **D:** Lina Wertmuller; **W:** Lina Wertmuller. National Board of Review Awards '75: 5 Best Foreign Films of the Year. VHS, Beta, LV ★★★1/2

The Swimmer A lonely suburbanite swims an existential swath through the pools of his neighborhood landscape in an effort at self-discovery. A surreal, strangely compelling work based on a story by John Cheever.
1968 (PG) 94m/C Burt Lancaster, Janice Rule, Janet Landgard, Marge Champion, Kim Hunter, Rose Gregorio, John David Garfield; **D:** Frank Perry; **M:** Marvin Hamlisch. VHS, Beta, LV ★★★★

Swimming to Cambodia Gray tells the story of his bit part in "The Killing Fields," filmed in Cambodia, and makes ironic observations about modern life. It works.
1987 87m/C Spalding Gray; **D:** Jonathan Demme; **M:** Laurie Anderson, John Bailey. VHS, Beta, LV ★★★

Swing Time Astaire, a dancer who can't resist gambling, is engaged to marry another woman until he meets Ginger. One of the team's best efforts. Laserdisc version includes production photos and stills, commentary on Fred Astaire and musical films, and excerpts from "Hooray for Love" featuring Bill "Bojangles" Robinson and Fats Waller. ♪ The Way You Look Tonight; Waltz in Swing Time; Never Gonna Dance; Pick Yourself Up; A Fine Romance; Bojangles of Harlem.
1936 103m/B Fred Astaire, Ginger Rogers, Helen Broderick, Betty Furness, Eric Blore, Victor Moore; **D:** George Stevens; **M:** Jerome Kern, Dorothy Fields. Academy Awards '36: Best Song ("The Way You Look Tonight"). VHS, Beta, LV ★★★

The Swiss Family Robinson A family, seeking to escape Napoleon's war in Europe, sets sail for New Guinea, but shipwrecks on a deserted tropical island. There they build an idyllic life, only to be confronted by a band of pirates. Lots of adventure for family viewing. Filmed on location on the island of Tobago. Based on the novel by Johann Wyss.
1960 126m/C John Mills, Dorothy McGuire, James MacArthur, Tommy Kirk, Janet Munro, Sessue Hayakawa; **D:** Ken Annakin. VHS, Beta, LV ★★★

The Sword in the Stone The Disney version of the first volume of T.H. White's "The Once and Future King"

wherein King Arthur, as a boy, is instructed in the ways of the world by Merlin and Archimedes the owl. Although not in the Disney masterpiece fold, boasts the usual superior animation and a gripping mythological tale.
1963 (G) 79m/C D: Wolfgang Reitherman; **M:** George Bruns; **V:** Ricky Sorenson, Sebastian Cabot, Karl Swenson, Junius Matthews, Alan Napier, Norman Alden, Martha Wentworth, Barbara Jo Allen. Nominations: Academy Awards '63: Best Original Score. **VHS, Beta, LV** ★★★

Sybil Fact-based story of a woman who developed 16 distinct personalities, and the supportive psychiatrist who helped her put the pieces of her ego together. Excellent made-for-television production with Field's Emmy-winning performance.
1976 122m/C Sally Field, Joanne Woodward, Brad Davis, Martine Bartlett, Jane Hoffman; **D:** Daniel Petrie. **VHS, Beta** ★★★

T-Men Two agents of the Treasury Department infiltrate a counterfeiting gang. Filmed in semi-documentary style, exciting tale serves also as an effective commentary on the similarities between the agents and those they pursue. Mann and cinematographer John Alton do especially fine work here.
1947 96m/B Alfred Ryder, Dennis O'Keefe, June Lockhart, Mary Meade, Wallace Ford, Charles McGraw; **D:** Anthony Mann, John Alton. Nominations: Academy Awards '47: Best Sound. **VHS, Beta, LV** ★★★

Tabu: A Story of the South Seas Fascinating docudrama about a young pearl diver's ill-fated romance. The gods have declared the young woman he desires "taboo" to all men. Filmed on location in Tahiti. Authored and produced by Murnau and Flaherty. Flaherty left in mid-production due to artistic differences with Murnau, who was later killed in an auto accident one week before the premiere of film. Oscar-winning cinematography by Floyd Crosby.
1931 81m/B D: Robert Flaherty, F.W. Murnau. Academy Awards '31: Best Cinematography; National Board of Review Awards '31: 10 Best Films of the Year. **VHS, Beta** ★★★1/2

Take the Money and Run Allen's directing debut; he also co-wrote and starred. "Documentary" follows a timid, would-be bank robber who can't get his career off the ground and keeps landing in jail. Little plot, but who cares? Nonstop one-liners and slapstick.

1969 (PG) 85m/C Woody Allen, Janet Margolin, Marcel Hillaire, Louise Lasser; **D:** Woody Allen; **W:** Woody Allen; **M:** Marvin Hamlisch. **VHS, Beta, LV** ★★★

The Taking of Pelham One Two Three A hijack team, lead by the ruthless Shaw, seizes a New York City subway car and holds the 17 passengers for one million dollars ransom. Fine pacing keeps things on the edge. New cinematic techniques used by cameraman Owen Roizman defines shadowy areas like never before.
1974 (R) 105m/C Robert Shaw, Walter Matthau, Martin Balsam, Hector Elizondo, James Broderick, Earl Hindman, Dick O'Neill, Jerry Stiller, Tony Roberts, Doris Roberts, Kenneth McMillan, Julius W. Harris, Sal Viscuso; **D:** Joseph Sargent; **M:** David Shire, Owen Roizman. **VHS, Beta** ★★★

The Tale of the Frog Prince Superb edition of Shelley Duvall's "Faerie Tale Theatre" finds Williams the victim of an angry fairy godmother's spell. Garr to the rescue as the self-centered princess who saves him with a kiss. Directed and written by Idle of Monty Python fame.
1983 60m/C Robin Williams, Teri Garr; **D:** Eric Idle; **W:** Eric Idle. **VHS, Beta, LV** ★★★1/2

A Tale of Two Cities Lavish production of the Dickens' classic set during the French Revolution, about two men who bear a remarkable resemblance to each other, both in love with the same girl. Carefree lawyer Sydney Carton (Colman) roused to responsibility, makes the ultimate sacrifice. A memorable Madame DeFarge from stage star Yurka in her film debut, with assistance from other Dickens' film stars Rathbone, Oliver and Walthall.
1935 128m/B Ronald Colman, Elizabeth Allan, Edna May Oliver, Reginald Owen, Isabel Jewell, Walter Catlett, H.B. Warner, Donald Woods, Basil Rathbone, Blanche Yurka, Henry B. Walthall; **D:** Jack Conway; **W:** W.P. Lipscomb, S.N. Behrman; **M:** Herbert Stothart. Nominations: Academy Awards '36: Best Film Editing, Best Picture. **VHS, Beta** ★★★★

A Tale of Two Cities A well-done British version of the Dickens' classic about a lawyer who sacrifices himself to save another man from the guillotine during the French Reign of Terror. The sixth remake of the tale.
1958 117m/B *GB* Dirk Bogarde, Dorothy Tutin, Christopher Lee, Donald Pleasence, Ian Bannen, Cecil Parker; **D:** Ralph Thomas. **VHS, Beta** ★★★

Tales of Beatrix Potter The Royal Ballet Company of England performs in this adaptation of the adventures of Beatrix Potter's colorful and memorable creatures. Beautifully done. *AKA:* Peter Rabbit and Tales of Beatrix Potter.
1971 (G) 90m/C *GB D:* Reginald Mills. VHS ★★★1/2

Talk of the Town A brilliantly cast, strange mixture of screwball comedy and lynch-mob melodramatics. An accused arsonist, a Supreme Court judge and the girl they both love try to clear the former's name and evade the cops.
1942 118m/B Ronald Colman, Cary Grant, Jean Arthur, Edgar Buchanan, Glenda Farrell, Rex Ingram, Emma Dunn; *D:* George Stevens. Nominations: Academy Awards '42: Best Black and White Cinematography, Best Film Editing, Best Interior Decoration, Best Picture, Best Screenplay, Best Story, Best Original Score. VHS, Beta, LV ★★★

Talk Radio Riveting Stone adaptation of Bogosian's one-man play. An acidic talk radio host confronts America's evil side and his own past over the airwaves. The main character is loosely based on the life of Alan Berg, a Denver talk show host who was murdered by white supremacists.
1988 (R) 110m/C Eric Bogosian, Alec Baldwin, Ellen Greene, John Pankow, John C. McGinley, Michael Wincott, Leslie Hope; *D:* Oliver Stone, Robert Richardson; *W:* Eric Bogosian, Oliver Stone; *M:* Stewart Copeland. VHS, Beta, LV ★★★

The Tall Blond Man with One Black Shoe A violinist is completely unaware that rival spies mistakenly think he is also a spy, and that he is the center of a plot to booby-trap an overly ambitious agent at the French Secret Service. A sequel followed called "Return of the Tall Blond Man with One Black Shoe" which was followed by a disappointing American remake, "The Man with One Red Shoe." In French with English subtitles or dubbed. *AKA:* Le Grand Blond Avec Une Chassure Noire.
1972 (PG) 90m/C *FR* Pierre Richard, Bernard Blier, Jean Rochefort, Mireille Darc, Jean Carmet; *D:* Yves Robert; *W:* Francis Veber; *M:* Vladimir Cosma. VHS, Beta, 8mm ★★★

The Taming of the Shrew A lavish screen version of the classic Shakespeare comedy. Burton and Taylor are violently physical and perfectly cast as the battling Katherine and Petruchio. At the time the film was made, Burton and Taylor were having their own marital problems, which not only added an inner fire to their performances, but sent the interested moviegoers to the theaters in droves.
1967 122m/C *IT* Elizabeth Taylor, Richard Burton, Michael York, Michael Hordern, Cyril Cusack; *D:* Franco Zeffirelli; *W:* Franco Zeffirelli; *M:* Nino Rota. National Board of Review Awards '67: 10 Best Films of the Year; Nominations: Academy Awards '67: Best Art Direction/Set Decoration, Best Costume Design. VHS, Beta, LV ★★★★

Tampopo A hilarious, episodic Japanese comedy. A widowed noodle shop owner is coached by a ten-gallon-hatted stranger in how to make the perfect noodle. Popular, free-form hit that established Itami in the West. In Japanese with English subtitles.
1986 114m/C *JP* Ken Watanabe, Tsutomu Yamazaki, Nobuko Miyamoto, Koji Yakusho, Rikiya Yasuoka, Kinzo Sakura, Shoji Otake; *D:* Juzo Itami. VHS, LV ★★★

Targets Bogdanovich's suspenseful directorial debut. An aging horror film star plans his retirement, convinced that real life is too scary for his films to have an audience. A mad sniper at a drive-in movie seems to prove he's right. Some prints still have anti-gun prologue, which was added after Robert Kennedy's assassination.
1968 (PG) 90m/C Boris Karloff, James Brown, Tim O'Kelly; *D:* Peter Bogdanovich; *W:* Peter Bogdanovich. VHS, Beta ★★★

Tarnished Angels Reporter Burke Devlin (Hudson) is writing a story for the local New Orleans paper about a tormented trio of air circus barnstormers. A former WWI ace, Roger Shumann (Stack) cares more about flying than he does his sizzling wife Laverne (Malone), who's loved-from-afar by loyal mechanic Jiggs (Carson). When Roger's plane cracks up, he uses his wife to obtain use of an experimental aircraft in order to win a race—and brings disaster crashing around them all. Good action, fine cast. Based on William Faulkner's 1930 novel "Pylon."
1957 91m/B Rock Hudson, Robert Stack, Dorothy Malone, Jack Carson, Robert Middleton, Troy Donahue, Alan Reed, Robert J. Wilke, William Schallert; *D:* Douglas Sirk; *W:* George Zuckerman; *M:* Frank Skinner, Irving Glassberg. VHS ★★★

Tarzan and His Mate Second entry in the lavishly produced MGM Tarzan series. Weissmuller and O'Sullivan cohabit in unmarried bliss before the Hays Code moved them to a tree house with twin beds. Many angry elephants, nasty white hunters, and

hungry lions. Laserdisc includes the original trailer.
1934 93m/B Johnny Weissmuller, Maureen O'Sullivan, Neil Hamilton, Paul Cavanagh; *D:* Jack Conway. **VHS, LV** ★★★

Tarzan, the Ape Man The definitive Tarzan movie; the first Tarzan talkie; the original of the long series starring Weissmuller. Dubiously faithful to the Edgar Rice Burroughs story, but recent attempts to remake, update or improve it (notably the pretentious 1984 Greystoke) have failed to near the original's entertainment value or even its technical quality. O'Sullivan as Jane and Weissmuller bring style and wit to their classic roles.
1932 99m/B Johnny Weissmuller, Maureen O'Sullivan, Neil Hamilton; *D:* Woodbridge S. Van Dyke. **VHS, Beta, LV** ★★★

A Taste of Honey A plain working-class girl falls in love with a black sailor. When she becomes pregnant, a homosexual friend helps her out. A moving film with strong, powerful performances. Based on the London and Broadway hit play by Shelagh Delaney.
1961 100m/B *GB* Rita Tushingham, Robert Stephens, Dora Bryan, Murray Melvin, Paul Danquah; *D:* Tony Richardson; *W:* Tony Richardson, Shelagh Delaney; *M:* John Addison. British Academy Awards '61: Best Film, Best Supporting Actress (Bryan); Cannes Film Festival '62: Best Actor (Melvin), Best Actress (Tushingham). **VHS** ★★★

Tatie Danielle Pitch-black comedy from the director of "Life Is a Long Quiet River" sees a bitter, elderly widow moving in with her young nephew and making his life a hell. In French with yellow English subtitles.
1991 114m/C *FR* Tsilla Chelton, Catherine Jacob, Isabelle Nanty, Neige Dolsky, Eric Prat, Laurence Fevrier; *D:* Etienne Chatiliez; *W:* Etienne Chatiliez. **VHS, LV** ★★★

Taxi Blues A political allegory with the two protagonists representing the new and old Soviet Union. A hard-working, narrow-minded cabdriver keeps the saxophone of a westernized, Jewish, jazz-loving musician who doesn't have his fare. The two strike up a wary friendship as each tries to explain his view of life to the other. Good look at the street life of Moscow populated by drunks, punks, and black marketeers. Directorial debut of Lounguine. In Russian with English subtitles.
1990 110m/C *RU* Piotr Mamonov, Piotr Zaitchenko, Natalia Koliakanova, Vladimir Kachpour; *D:* Pavel Lounguine; *W:* Pavel

Lounguine. Cannes Film Festival '90: Best Director (Lounguine). **VHS** ★★★½

Taxi Driver A psychotic New York City taxi driver tries to save a child prostitute and becomes infatuated with an educated political campaigner. He goes on a violent rampage when his dreams don't work out. Repellant, frightening vision of alienation and urban catharsis. On-target performances from Foster and De Niro. The laserdisc version is slightly longer, with commentary by Scorsese and screenwriter Paul Schrader, storyboards, complete screenplay, and Scorsese's production photos.
1976 (R) 112m/C Robert De Niro, Jodie Foster, Harvey Keitel, Cybill Shepherd, Peter Boyle, Albert Brooks; *D:* Martin Scorsese, Michael Chapman; *W:* Paul Schrader. British Academy Awards '76: Best Supporting Actress (Foster); Cannes Film Festival '76: Best Film; Los Angeles Film Critics Association Awards '76: Best Actor (De Niro); New York Film Critics Awards '76: Best Actor (De Niro); National Society of Film Critics Awards '76: Best Actor (De Niro), Best Director (Scorsese), Best Supporting Actress (Foster); Nominations: Academy Awards '76: Best Actor (De Niro), Best Picture, Best Original Score. **VHS, Beta, LV, 8mm** ★★★

A Taxing Woman Satiric Japanese comedy about a woman tax collector in pursuit of a crafty millionaire tax cheater. Followed by the equally hilarious "A Taxing Woman's Return." In Japanese with English subtitles. *AKA:* Marusa No Onna.
1987 127m/C *JP* Nobuko Miyamoto, Tsutomu Yamazaki; *D:* Juzo Itami; *W:* Juzo Itami. **VHS, Beta, LV** ★★★½

A Taxing Woman's Return Funny, sophisticated, action-packed. Miyamoto returns as the dedicated tax investigator to fight industrialists, politicians, and other big swindlers, who have contrived to inflate Tokyo's real estate values. Sequel to "A Taxing Woman." In Japanese with English subtitles. *AKA:* Marusa No Onna II.
1988 127m/C *JP* Nobuko Miyamoto, Rentaro Mikuni, Masahiko Tsugawa, Tetsuro Tamba, Toru Masuoka, Takeya Nakamura, Hosei Komatsu, Mihoko Shibata; *D:* Juzo Itami; *W:* Juzo Itami. **VHS, LV** ★★★

Tea and Sympathy A young prep school student, confused about his sexuality, has an affair with an older woman, his teacher's wife. The three leads re-create their Broadway roles

in this tame adaption of the Robert Anderson play which dealt more openly with the story's homosexual elements.
1956 122m/C Deborah Kerr, John Kerr, Leif Erickson, Edward Andrews, Darryl Hickman, Norma Crane, Dean Jones; **D:** Vincente Minnelli; **W:** Robert Anderson, John Alton. **VHS, Beta, LV ★★★**

Teacher's Pet This charming comedy features a cynical newspaper editor who enrolls in a night college journalism course, believing that it won't teach anything of substance. He later becomes enamored of his instructor. Well written script and superb performance by Young as Gable's rival for Day.
1958 120m/B Clark Gable, Doris Day, Mamie Van Doren, Gig Young, Nick Adams; **D:** George Seaton; **W:** Fay Kanin, Michael Kanin. Nominations: Academy Awards '58: Best Story & Screenplay, Best Supporting Actor (Young). **VHS, Beta ★★★**

Tell Them Willie Boy Is Here Western drama set in 1909 California about a Paiute Indian named Willie Boy and his white bride. They become the objects of a manhunt (led by the reluctant local sheriff, Redford) after Willie kills his wife's father in self-defense. This was once-blacklisted Polonsky's first film in 21 years.
1969 (PG) 98m/C Robert Redford, Katharine Ross, Robert (Bobby) Blake, Susan Clark, Barry Sullivan, John Vernon, Charles McGraw; **D:** Abraham Polonsky; **W:** Abraham Polonsky; **M:** Dave Grusin, Conrad Hall. **VHS, Beta, LV ★★★**

The Ten Commandments DeMille's remake of his 1923 silent classic (and his last film) is a lavish biblical epic that tells the life story of Moses, who turned his back on a privileged life to lead his people to freedom outside of Egypt. Exceptional cast, with Fraser Heston (son of Charlton) as the baby Moses. Parting of Red Sea rivals any modern special effects. Available in wide-screen on laserdisc. A 35th Anniversary Collector's Edition is available at 245 minutes, in wide-screen format and Dolby Surround Sound, and 1,000 copies of an Autographed Limited Edition that includes an engraved bronze plaque and an imprinted card written and personally signed by Charlton Heston are also available.
1956 (G) 219m/C Charlton Heston, Yul Brynner, Anne Baxter, Yvonne De Carlo, Nina Foch, John Derek, H.B. Warner, Henry Wilcoxon, Judith Anderson, John Carradine, Douglass Dumbrille, Cedric Hardwicke, Martha Scott, Vincent Price, Debra Paget; **D:** Cecil B. DeMille; **M:** Elmer Bernstein. Academy Awards '56: Best Special Effects; Nominations: Academy Awards '56: Best Art Direction/Set Decoration (Color), Best Color Cinematography, Best Costume Design (Color), Best Film Editing, Best Picture, Best Sound. **VHS, Beta, LV ★★★**

Ten Days That Shook the World Silent masterpiece based on American author John Reed's book of the same name. Eisenstein, commissioned by the Soviet government, spared no expense to chronicle the Bolshevik Revolution of 1917 (in a flattering Communist light, of course). He was later forced to cut his portrayal of Leon Trotsky, who was then an enemy of the state. Includes rare footage of the Czar's Winter Palace in Leningrad. Haunting score, combined with some of Eisenstein's most striking work. See Warren Beatty's "Reds" for a fictional look at Reed and the Russian Revolution. **AKA:** October.
1927 104m/B *RU* Nikandrov, N. Popov, Boris Livanov; **D:** Grigori Alexandrov, Sergei Eisenstein; **M:** Dimitri Shostakovich. **VHS, Beta, LV ★★★1/2**

The Tenant Disturbing story of a hapless office worker who moves into a spooky Paris apartment house. Once lodged inside its walls, he becomes obsessed with the previous occupant, who committed suicide, and the belief that his neighbors are trying to kill him. Based on a novel by Roland Topor. **AKA:** Le Locataire.
1976 (R) 126m/C *FR* Roman Polanski, Isabelle Adjani, Melvyn Douglas, Jo Van Fleet, Bernard Fresson, Shelley Winters; **D:** Roman Polanski; **W:** Roman Polanski, Gerard Brach, Sven Nykvist. Nominations: Cannes Film Festival '76: Best Film. **VHS, Beta ★★★1/2**

Tender Mercies A down-and-out country western singer finds his life redeemed by the love of a good woman. Aided by Horton Foote's script, Duvall, Harper and Barkin keep this from being simplistic and sentimental. Duvall wrote as well as performed the songs in his Oscar-winning performance. Wonderful, life-affirming flick.
1983 (PG) 88m/C Robert Duvall, Tess Harper, Betty Buckley, Ellen Barkin, Wilford Brimley; **D:** Bruce Beresford; **W:** Horton Foote; **M:** George Dreyfus. Academy Awards '83: Best Actor (Duvall), Best Original Screenplay; Golden Globe Awards '83: Best Actor—Drama (Duvall); Los Angeles Film Critics Association Awards '83: Best Actor (Duvall); New York Film Critics Awards '83: Best Actor (Duvall);

Writers Guild of America '83: Best Original Screenplay; Nominations: Academy Awards '83: Best Director (Beresford), Best Picture, Best Song ("Over You"). **VHS, Beta, LV ★★★**

The Terminator Futuristic cyborg is sent to present-day Earth. His job: kill the woman who will conceive the child destined to become the great liberator and archenemy of the Earth's future rulers. The cyborg is also pursued by another futuristic visitor, who falls in love with the intended victim. Cameron's pacing is just right in this exhilarating, explosive thriller which displays Arnie as one cold-blooded villain who utters a now famous line: "I'll be back." Followed by "Terminator 2: Judgment Day."
1984 (R) 108m/C Arnold Schwarzenegger, Michael Biehn, Linda Hamilton, Paul Winfield, Lance Henriksen, Bill Paxton, Rick Rossovich, Dick Miller; **D:** James Cameron; **W:** James Cameron; **M:** Brad Fiedel. **VHS, Beta, LV ★★★**

Terminator 2: Judgment Day He said he'd be back and he is, programmed to protect the boy who will be mankind's post-nuke resistance leader. But the T-1000, a shape-changing, ultimate killing machine, is also on the boy's trail. Twice the mayhem, five times the special effects, ten times the budget of the first, but without Arnold it'd be half the movie. The word hasn't been invented to describe the special effects, particularly THE scariest nuclear holocaust scene yet. Worldwide megahit, but the $100 million budget nearly ruined the studio; Arnold accepted his $12 million in the form of a jet. Laserdisc features include pan and scan, widescreen and a "Making of T-2" short.
1991 (R) 139m/C Arnold Schwarzenegger, Linda Hamilton, Edward Furlong, Robert Patrick, Earl Boen, Joe Morton; **D:** James Cameron; **W:** James Cameron; **M:** Brad Fiedel. Academy Awards '91: Best Makeup, Best Sound, Best Sound Effects Editing, Best Visual Effects; MTV Movie Awards '92: Best Film, Best Male Performance (Schwarzenegger), Best Female Performance (Hamilton), Breakthrough Performance (Furlong), Most Desirable Female (Hamilton), Best Action Sequence; People's Choice Awards '92: Best Film; Nominations: Academy Awards '91: Best Cinematography, Best Sound. **VHS, LV, 8mm ★★★1/2**

Terms of Endearment A weeper following the changing relationship between a young woman and her mother, over a 30-year period. Begin-ning as a comedy, turning serious as the years go by, this was Brooks' debut as screenwriter and director. Superb supporting cast headed by Nicholson's slyly charming neighbor/astronaut, with stunning performances by Winger and MacLaine as the two women who often know and love each other too well. Adapted from Larry McMurtry's novel.
1983 (PG) 132m/C Shirley MacLaine, Jack Nicholson, Debra Winger, John Lithgow, Jeff Daniels, Danny DeVito; **D:** James L. Brooks; **W:** James L. Brooks; **M:** Michael Gore. Academy Awards '83: Best Actress (MacLaine), Best Adapted Screenplay, Best Director (Brooks), Best Picture, Best Supporting Actor (Nicholson); Golden Globe Awards '84: Best Actress—Drama (MacLaine), Best Film—Drama, Best Screenplay, Best Supporting Actor (Nicholson); National Board of Review Awards '83: Best Actress (MacLaine), Best Director (Brooks), Best Supporting Actor (Nicholson); National Society of Film Critics Awards '83: Best Actress (Winger), Best Supporting Actor (Nicholson); Nominations: Academy Awards '83: Best Actress (Winger), Best Art Direction/Set Decoration, Best Film Editing, Best Sound, Best Supporting Actor (Lithgow), Best Original Score. **VHS, Beta, LV ★★★**

Tess Sumptuous adaptation of the Thomas Hardy novel "Tess of the D'Ubervilles." Kinski is wonderful as an innocent farm girl who is seduced by the young aristocrat she works for and then finds marriage to a man of her own class only brings more grief. Polanski's direction is faithful and artful. Nearly three hours long, but worth every minute.
1980 (PG) 170m/C *GB FR* Nastassia Kinski, Peter Firth, Leigh Lawson, John Collin; **D:** Roman Polanski; **W:** Roman Polanski, Gerard Brach. Academy Awards '80: Best Art Direction/Set Decoration, Best Cinematography, Best Costume Design; Cesar Awards '80: Best Cinematography, Best Director (Polanski), Best Film; Golden Globe Awards '81: Best Foreign Film; Los Angeles Film Critics Association Awards '80: Best Cinematography, Best Director (Polanski); New York Film Critics Awards '80: Best Cinematography; Nominations: Academy Awards '80: Best Director (Polanski), Best Picture, Best Original Score. **VHS, Beta, LV ★★★**

Test Pilot Gable and Tracy star as daring test pilot and devoted mechanic respectively. When Gable has to land his experimental craft in a Kansas cornfield, he meets and falls in love with farm girl Loy. The two marry and raise a family, all the while she worries over his dangerous profession. When the Air Force asks him to test their new B-17 bomber, she refuses to watch, thinking the test will end in tragedy. Superb aviation drama featuring excellent cast.

1938 118m/B Clark Gable, Myrna Loy, Spencer Tracy, Lionel Barrymore, Samuel S. Hinds; **D:** Victor Fleming. Nominations: Academy Awards '38: Best Film Editing, Best Picture, Best Story. **VHS, Beta** ★★★½

Testament Well-made and thought-provoking story of the residents of a small California town struggling to survive after a nuclear bombing. Focuses on one family who tries to accept the reality of post-holocaust life. We see the devastation but it never sinks into sensationalism. An exceptional performance from Alexander.

1983 (PG) 90m/C Jane Alexander, William Devane, Ross Harris, Roxana Zal, Kevin Costner, Rebecca DeMornay; **D:** Lynne Littman; **W:** John Sacret Young; **M:** James Horner. Nominations: Academy Awards '83: Best Actress (Alexander). **VHS, Beta, LV** ★★★

The Testament of Orpheus Superb, personal surrealism; writer-director Cocteau's last film. Hallucinogenic, autobiographical dream-journey through time. Difficult to follow, but rewarding final installment in a trilogy including "The Blood of the Poet" and "Orpheus." In French with English subtitles.

1959 80m/B *FR* Jean Cocteau, Edouard Dermithe, Maria Casares, Francois Perier, Yul Brynner, Jean-Pierre Leaud, Daniel Gelin, Jean Marais, Pablo Picasso, Charles Aznavour; **D:** Jean Cocteau. **VHS, Beta** ★★★½

Thank Your Lucky Stars A lavish, slap-dash wartime musical that emptied out the Warner's lot for an array of uncharacteristic celebrity turns. Features Shore in her movie debut. ♪ They're Either Too Young or Too Old; Blues in the Night; Hotcha Cornia; Ridin' For A Fall; We're Staying Home Tonight; Goin' North; Love Isn't Born, It's Made; No You, No Me; Ice Cold Katie.

1943 127m/B Eddie Cantor, Dinah Shore, Joan Leslie, Errol Flynn, Bette Davis, Edward Everett Horton, Humphrey Bogart, John Garfield, Alan Hale, Ann Sheridan, Ida Lupino, Jack Carson, Dennis (Stanley Morner) Morgan, Olivia de Havilland; **D:** David Butler; **W:** Norman Panama. Nominations: Academy Awards '43: Best Song ("They're Either Too Young or Too Old"). **VHS, Beta, LV** ★★★

That Hamilton Woman Screen biography of the tragic 18th-century love affair between British naval hero Lord Nelson and Lady Hamilton. Korda exaggerated the film's historical distortions in order to pass the censor's production code about adultery. Winston Churchill's favorite film which paralleled Britain's heroic struggles in WWII. **AKA:** Lady Hamilton.

1941 125m/B Laurence Olivier, Vivien Leigh, Gladys Cooper, Alan Mowbray, Sara Allgood, Henry Wilcoxon; **D:** Alexander Korda; **M:** Miklos Rozsa. Academy Awards '41: Best Sound; Nominations: Academy Awards '41: Best Black and White Cinematography, Best Interior Decoration. **VHS, Beta, LV** ★★★

That Obscure Object of Desire Bunuel's last film, a comic nightmare of sexual frustration. A rich Spaniard obtains a beautiful girlfriend who, while changing physical identities, refuses to sleep with him. Based on a novel by Pierre Louys, which has been used as the premise for several other films, including "The Devil is a Woman," "La Femme et le Pantin," and "The Female." Available with subtitles or dubbed. **AKA:** Cet Obscur Objet Du Desir.

1977 (R) 100m/C *SP* Fernando Rey, Carole Bouquet, Angela Molina; **D:** Luis Bunuel; **W:** Luis Bunuel, Jean-Claude Carriere. Los Angeles Film Critics Association Awards '77: Best Foreign Film; National Board of Review Awards '77: 5 Best Foreign Films of the Year, Best Director (Bunuel); Nominations: Academy Awards '77: Best Adapted Screenplay, Best Foreign Language Film. **VHS, Beta, LV** ★★★½

That Thing You Do! The Wonders, a small-town foursome, hit the big time in 1964 after a substitute drummer (like that could ever happen) adds some kick to the band's new song and sets the local kids a-fruggin'. Developed by freshman director/screenwriter Hanks (who also plays the band's Svengali-like record exec) as a diversion from Oscar hype, it's nostalgic and uncomplicated to a fault, but engaging nonetheless. Hanks clone Scott puts the beat into the charmingly wholesome quartet, while the underused Tyler is disarming as the put-upon girlfriend. Look quick or you'll miss bosom buddy Scolari as a TV host. Can't-get-it-out-of-your-head title track (played 11 times in the film) was selected from over 300 submissions after Hanks put out the call to music publishers.

1996 110m/C Johnathon Schaech, Liv Tyler, Tom Everett Scott, Steve Zahn, Ethan

Embry, Tom Hanks, Obba Babatunde, Charlize Theron, Peter Scolari, Alex Rocco, Bill Cobbs, Rita Wilson, Chris Isaak, Kevin Pollak; **D:** Tom Hanks; **W:** Tom Hanks; **M:** Howard Shore. Nominations: Golden Globe Awards '97: Best Song ("That Thing You Do!"). **VHS, LV ★★★**

Theatre of Blood Critics are unkind to Shakespearian ham Price, and he eliminates them by various Bard-inspired methods with the assistance of his lovely daughter. Top-drawer comedy noir.
1973 (R) 104m/C *GB* Vincent Price, Diana Rigg, Ian Hendry, Robert Morley, Dennis Price, Diana Dors, Milo O'Shea; **D:** Douglas Hickox. **VHS, LV ★★★**

Thelma & Louise Hailed as the first "feminist-buddy" movie, Sarandon and Davis bust out as best friends who head directly into one of the better movies of the year. Davis is the ditzy Thelma, a housewife rebelling against her dominating, unfaithful, abusive husband (who, rather than being disturbing, provides some of the best comic relief in the film). Sarandon is Louise, a hardened and world-weary waitress in the midst of an unsatisfactory relationship. They hit the road for a respite from their mundane lives, only to find violence and a part of themselves they never knew existed. Outstanding performances from Davis and especially Sarandon, with Pitt notable as the stud who gets Davis' motor revved. Director Scott has a fine eye for set details.
1991 (R) 130m/C Susan Sarandon, Geena Davis, Harvey Keitel, Christopher McDonald, Michael Madsen, Brad Pitt, Timothy Carhart, Stephen Tobolowsky, Lucinda Jenney; **D:** Ridley Scott; **W:** Callie Khouri; **M:** Hans Zimmer. Academy Awards '91: Best Original Screenplay; National Board of Review Awards '91: 10 Best Films of the Year, Best Actress (Sarandon, Davis), Writers Guild of America '91: Best Original Screenplay; Nominations: Academy Awards '91: Best Actress (Davis), Best Actress (Sarandon), Best Cinematography, Best Director (Scott), Best Film Editing. **VHS, Beta, LV, 8mm ★★★**

Them! A group of mutated giant ants wreak havoc on a southwestern town. The first of the big-bug movies, and far surpassing the rest, this is a classic fun flick. See how many names you can spot among the supporting cast.
1954 93m/B James Whitmore, Edmund Gwenn, Fess Parker, James Arness, Onslow Stevens, Jack Perrin; **D:** Gordon Douglas. **VHS, Beta, LV ★★★**

There Was a Crooked Man An Arizona town gets some new ideas about law and order when an incorruptible and innovative warden takes over the town's prison. The warden finds he's got his hands full with one inmate determined to escape. Offbeat western black comedy supported by an excellent and entertaining production, with fine acting all around.
1970 (R) 123m/C Kirk Douglas, Henry Fonda, Warren Oates, Hume Cronyn, Burgess Meredith, John Randolph, Arthur O'Connell, Alan Hale Jr., Lee Grant; **D:** Joseph L. Mankiewicz; **W:** Robert Benton, David Newman. **VHS, Beta ★★★1/2**

There's No Business Like Show Business A top husband and wife vaudevillian act make it a family affair. Filmed in CinemaScope, allowing for full and lavish musical numbers. Good performances and Berlin's music make this an enjoyable film. ♪ When the Midnight Choo-Choo Leaves for Alabam; Let's Have Another Cup of Coffee; Play a Simple Melody; After You Get What You Want You Don't Want It; You'd Be Surprised; A Sailor's Not a Sailor; A Pretty Girl is Like a Melody; If You Believe Me; A Man Chases a Girl Until She Catches Him.
1954 117m/C Ethel Merman, Donald O'Connor, Marilyn Monroe, Dan Dailey, Johnny Ray, Mitzi Gaynor, Frank McHugh, Hugh O'Brian; **D:** Walter Lang. Nominations: Academy Awards '54: Best Costume Design (Color), Best Story, Best Original Score. **VHS, Beta, LV ★★★**

Theremin: An Electronic Odyssey Profiles the life of Russian scientist Leon Theremin (who died in 1993), founder of electronic music, and his revolutionary musical invention, the Theremin. Martin located the 95-year-old Theremin in Moscow in 1991, interviewed him on camera, then brought him back to the U.S. to film reunions with friends and colleagues he hadn't seen in 50 years. Martin's focus is on the impact of the Theremin on Hollywood movie scores heard in '50s sci-fi and thriller classics ("The Day the Earth Stood Still") and in popular music (The Beach Boys' "Good Vibrations" is commented on by Brian Wilson). Theremin's life proves as curious as his instrument, with his controversial interracial marriage to a ballet star, abduction by Russian agents, and imprisonment in a Soviet mental hospital. "Theremin" provides a fascinating and heartfelt tribute to the man's work and life.
1995 (PG) 84m/C **D:** Steven M. Martin; **W:**

Steven M. Martin; **M:** Hal Wilner. **VHS, LV**
★★★

Therese Stylish biography of a young French nun and her devotion to Christ bordering on romantic love. Explores convent life. Real-life Therese died of TB and was made a saint. A directorial tour de force for Cavalier. In French with English subtitles.
1986 90m/C *FR* Catherine Mouchet, Aurore Prieto, Sylvie Habault, Ghislaine Mona; **D:** Alain Cavalier; **W:** Alain Cavalier. Cannes Film Festival '86: Special Jury Prize; Cesar Awards '87: Best Cinematography, Best Director (Cavalier), Best Film, Best Writing. **VHS, Beta** ★★★

These Three A teenaged girl ruins the lives of two teachers by telling a malicious lie. Excellent cast. Script by Lillian Hellman, based on her play "The Children's Hour." Remade by the same director as "The Children's Hour" in 1961.
1936 92m/B Miriam Hopkins, Merle Oberon, Joel McCrea, Bonita Granville, Marcia Mae Jones, Walter Brennan, Margaret Hamilton; **D:** William Wyler. Nominations: Academy Awards '36: Best Supporting Actress (Granville). **VHS, Beta, LV** ★★★1/2

They Died with Their Boots On The Battle of Little Big Horn is re-created Hollywood style. Takes liberties with historical fact, but still an exciting portrayal of General Custer's last stand. The movie also marks the last time de Havilland worked with Flynn. Also available colorized.
1941 141m/B Errol Flynn, Sydney Greenstreet, Anthony Quinn, Hattie McDaniel, Arthur Kennedy, Gene Lockhart, Regis Toomey, Olivia de Havilland, Charley Grapewin; **D:** Raoul Walsh; **M:** Max Steiner. **VHS, Beta** ★★★

They Drive by Night Two truck-driving brothers break away from a large company and begin independent operations. After an accident to Bogart, Raft is forced to go back to the company where Lupino, the boss's wife, becomes obsessed with him and kills her husband to gain the company and win Raft. When he rejects her, she accuses him of the murder. Well-plotted film with great dialogue. Excellent cast gives it their all. *AKA:* The Road to Frisco.
1940 97m/B Humphrey Bogart, Ann Sheridan, George Raft, Ida Lupino, Alan Hale, Gale Page, Roscoe Karns, Charles Halton; **D:** Raoul Walsh. **VHS, Beta** ★★★1/2

They Knew What They Wanted A lonely San Francisco waitress begins a correspondence romance with a grape grower and agrees to marry him after he sends her a photo which shows him as being young and handsome. She arrives to discover Laughton had sent her a picture of another man. An accident, an affair, and a pregnancy provide further complications before a satisfactory ending is suggested. Flawed adaptation of Sidney Howard's play still has strong performances from Lombard and Laughton.
1940 96m/B Charles Laughton, Carole Lombard, Harry Carey Sr., Karl Malden, William Gargan; **D:** Garson Kanin. Nominations: Academy Awards '40: Best Supporting Actor (Gargan). **VHS, Beta** ★★★

They Live by Night A young fugitive sinks deeper into a life of crime thanks to his association with two hardened criminals. Classic film noir was Ray's first attempt at directing. Based on Edward Anderson's novel "Thieves Like Us," under which title it was remade in 1974. Compelling and suspenseful. *AKA:* The Twisted Road; Your Red Wagon.
1949 95m/B Cathy O'Donnell, Farley Granger, Howard da Silva, Jay C. Flippen, Helen Craig; **D:** Nicholas Ray. **VHS, Beta, LV** ★★★1/2

They Might Be Giants Woodward is a woman shrink named Watson who treats retired judge Scott for delusions that he is Sherlock Holmes. Scott's brother wants him committed so the family loot will come to him. Very funny in places; Woodward and Scott highlight a solid cast.
1971 (G) 98m/C George C. Scott, Joanne Woodward, Jack Gilford, Eugene Roche, Kitty Winn, F. Murray Abraham, M. Emmet Walsh; **D:** Anthony Harvey; **M:** John Barry. **VHS, Beta** ★★★

They Shoot Horses, Don't They? Powerful period piece depicting the desperation of the Depression Era. Contestants enter a dance marathon in the hopes of winning a cash prize, not realizing that they will be driven to exhaustion. Fascinating and tragic.
1969 (R) 121m/C Jane Fonda, Michael Sarrazin, Susannah York, Gig Young, Red Buttons, Bonnie Bedelia, Bruce Dern, Allyn Ann McLerie, Chaing I; **D:** Sydney Pollack. Academy Awards '69: Best Supporting Actor (Young); British Academy Awards '70: Best Supporting Actress (York); Golden Globe Awards '70: Best Supporting Actor (Young); New York Film Critics Awards '69: Best Actress (Fonda); Nominations: Academy Awards '69: Best Actress (Fonda), Best Adapted Screenplay,

Best Art Direction/Set Decoration, Best Costume Design, Best Director (Pollack), Best Film Editing, Best Supporting Actress (York), Best Original Score. **VHS, LV** ★★★1/2

They Were Expendable Two American captains pit their PT boats against the Japanese fleet. Based on the true story of a PT boat squadron based in the Philippines during the early days of WWII. One of the best (and most underrated) WWII films. Also available in a colorized version.
1945 135m/B Robert Montgomery, John Wayne, Donna Reed, Jack Holt, Ward Bond, Cameron Mitchell, Leon Ames, Marshall Thompson; **D:** John Ford. Nominations: Academy Awards '45: Best Sound. **VHS, Beta** ★★★1/2

They Won't Forget When a young girl is murdered in a southern town, personal interests take precedence over justice. Turner is excellent in her first billed role, as are the other actors. Superb script, and expert direction by LeRoy pulls it all together. Based on Ward Greene's "Death in the Deep South."
1937 95m/B Claude Rains, Otto Kruger, Lana Turner, Allyn Joslyn, Elisha Cook Jr., Edward Norris; **D:** Mervyn LeRoy; **W:** Robert Rossen, Aben Kandel. **VHS** ★★★1/2

Thief A big-time professional thief likes working solo, but decides to sign up with the mob in order to make one more big score and retire. He finds out it's not that easy. Taut and atmospheric thriller is director Mann's feature film debut. **AKA:** Violent Streets.
1981 (R) 126m/C James Caan, Tuesday Weld, Willie Nelson, James Belushi, Elizabeth Pena, Robert Prosky; **D:** Donald E. Thorin, Michael Mann; **W:** Michael Mann. Nominations: Cannes Film Festival '81: Best Film. **VHS, Beta, LV** ★★★

The Thief of Baghdad The classic silent crowd-pleaser, about a roguish thief who uses a genie's magic to outwit Baghdad's evil Caliph. With famous special effects in a newly struck print, and a new musical score by Davis based on Rimsky-Korsakov's "Scheerezade." Remade many times.
1924 153m/B Douglas Fairbanks Sr., Snitz Edwards, Charles Belcher, Anna May Wong, Etta Lee, Brandon Hurst, Sojin, Julanne Johnston; **D:** Raoul Walsh; **M:** Carl Davis. **VHS, Beta, LV** ★★★

Thief of Baghdad A wily young thief enlists the aid of a powerful genie to outwit the Grand Vizier of Baghdad. An Arabian Nights spectacular with lush photography, fine special effects, and striking score. Outstanding performance by Ingram as the genie.
1940 106m/C Sabu, Conrad Veidt, June Duprez, Rex Ingram; **D:** Tim Whelan, Michael Powell, Ludwig Berger; **M:** Miklos Rozsa. Nominations: Academy Awards '40: Best Color Cinematography, Best Original Score. **VHS, Beta, LV** ★★★1/2

Thieves Like Us Story of doomed lovers during the Depression is thoughtfully told by Altman. Older criminals Remsen and Schuck escape from jail with young killer Carradine. They only know one way to make a living—robbing banks—and it isn't long before they're once more working at their trade. They get a lot of press but they have a distinct problem. They're not really very good at what they do. With cops on their trail, the gang tries, unsuccessfully, to survive. Fletcher's film debut as Remsen's sister-in-law. Good period atmosphere and strong characters. Based on the novel by Edward Anderson and previously filmed as "They Live by Night."
1974 (R) 123m/C Keith Carradine, Shelley Duvall, Bert Remsen, John Schuck, Louise Fletcher, Anne Latham, Tom Skerritt; **D:** Robert Altman; **W:** Joan Tewkesbury, Calder Willingham, Robert Altman. **VHS** ★★★1/2

The Thin Blue Line The acclaimed docudrama about the 1977 shooting of a cop in Dallas County, and the incorrect conviction of Randall Adams for the crime. A riveting, spellbinding experience. Due to the film's impact and continued lobbying by Morris, Adams is now free.
1988 101m/C D: Errol Morris; **M:** Philip Glass. Edgar Allan Poe Awards '88: Best Screenplay. **VHS, Beta, LV** ★★★1/2

The Thin Man Married sleuths Nick and Nora Charles investigate the mysterious disappearance of a wealthy inventor. Charming and sophisticated, this was the model for all husband-and-wife detective teams that followed. Don't miss Asta, their wire-hair terrier. Based on the novel by Dashiell Hammett. Its enormous popularity triggered five sequels, starting with "After the Thin Man."
1934 90m/B William Powell, Myrna Loy, Maureen O'Sullivan, Cesar Romero, Porter Hall, Nat Pendleton, Minna Gombell, Natalie Moorhead, Edward Ellis; **D:** Woodbridge S. Van Dyke. Nominations: Academy Awards '34: Best Actor (Powell), Best Adapted Screenplay, Best Director (Van Dyke), Best Picture. **VHS, Beta, LV** ★★★1/2

The Thing One of the best of the Cold War allegories and a potent lesson to those who won't eat their vegetables. Sci-fi classic about an alien craft and creature (Arness in monster drag), discovered by an Arctic research team. The critter is accidentally thawed and then wreaks havoc, sucking the blood from sled dog and scientist alike. It's a giant seed-dispersing vegetable run amuck, unaffected by missing body parts, bullets, or cold. In other words, Big Trouble. Excellent direction, assisted substantially by producer Hawks, and supported by strong performances. Available colorized; remade in 1982. Loosely based on "Who Goes There?" by John Campbell. *AKA:* The Thing From Another World.
1951 87m/B James Arness, Kenneth Tobey, Margaret Sheridan, Dewey Martin; *D:* Christian Nyby, Howard Hawks; *W:* Charles Lederer; *M:* Dimitri Tiomkin. **VHS, Beta, LV** ★★★1/2

Things to Come Using technology, scientists aim to rebuild the world after a lengthy war, followed by a plague and other unfortunate events. Massey and Scott each play two roles, in different generations. Startling picture of the world to come, with fine sets and good acting. Based on an H.G. Wells story, "The Shape of Things to Come."
1936 92m/B *GB* Raymond Massey, Ralph Richardson, Cedric Hardwicke, Derrick DeMarney; *D:* William Cameron Menzies. **VHS, Beta** ★★★1/2

Things to Do in Denver When You're Dead Jimmy the Saint (Garcia) is an ex-mobster gone straight who is called upon by his former boss, the Man With the Plan (Walken), to do one last easy-money job. Jimmy agrees and rounds up his old gang, a colorfully off-color group which includes Pieces (Lloyd), a porn movie projectionist and Critical Bill (Williams), a hair-trigger psycho who works in a funeral parlor. The job goes awry and the group becomes a target of hitman Mr. Shhh (Buscemi). Hipster dialogue, crime-gone-wrong formula, and the presence of Buscemi instantly scream Tarantino rip-off, but the performances make it a worthwhile genre entry.
1995 (R) 115m/C *AND* Andy Garcia, Christopher Lloyd, William Forsythe, Bill Nunn, Treat Williams, Jack Warden, Steve Buscemi, Fairuza Balk, Gabrielle Anwar, Christopher Walken; *D:* Gary Fleder; *W:* Scott Rosenberg; *M:* Michael Convertino. **VHS, LV** ★★★

The Third Man An American writer of pulp westerns (Cotten) arrives in post-war Vienna to take a job with an old friend, but discovers he has been murdered. Or has he? Based on Graham Greene's mystery, this classic film noir thriller plays on national loyalties during the Cold War. Welles is top-notch as the manipulative Harry Lime, blackmarket drugdealer extraordinare. The underground sewer sequence is not to be missed. With a haunting (sometimes irritating) theme by Anton Karas on unaccompanied zither. Special edition features trailer.
1949 104m/B Joseph Cotten, Orson Welles, Alida Valli, Trevor Howard, Bernard Lee, Wilfrid Hyde-White; *D:* Carol Reed; *W:* Graham Greene. Academy Awards '50: Best Black and White Cinematography; British Academy Awards '49: Best Film; Cannes Film Festival '49: Best Film; Directors Guild of America Awards '49: Best Director (Reed); National Board of Review Awards '50: 5 Best Foreign Films of the Year; Nominations: Academy Awards '50: Best Director (Reed), Best Film Editing. **VHS, Beta, LV, 8mm** ★★★★

13 Rue Madeleine Cagney plays a WWII spy who infiltrates Gestapo headquarters in Paris in order to find the location of a German missile site. Actual OSS footage is used in this fast-paced early postwar espionage propaganda piece. Rex Harrison rejected the part taken by Cagney.
1946 95m/B James Cagney, Annabella, Richard Conte, Frank Latimore, Walter Abel, Sam Jaffe, Melville Cooper, E.G. Marshall, Karl Malden, Red Buttons; *D:* Henry Hathaway. **VHS, Beta** ★★★

Thirty Seconds Over Tokyo Dated but still interesting classic wartime flagwaver details the conception and execution of the first bombing raids on Tokyo by Lt. Col. James Doolittle and his men. Look for Blake Edwards, as well as Steve Brodie in his first screen appearance. Based on a true story.
1944 138m/B Spencer Tracy, Van Johnson, Robert Walker, Robert Mitchum, Phyllis Thaxter, Scott McKay, Stephen McNally, Louis Jean Heydt, Leon Ames, Paul Langton; *D:* Mervyn LeRoy; *W:* Dalton Trumbo. Academy Awards '44: Best Special Effects; Nominations: Academy Awards '44: Best Black and White Cinematography. **VHS, Beta** ★★★

32 Short Films about Glenn Gould Perceptive docudrama about the iconoclastic Canadian classical pianist who secluded himself in the studio, forsaking live performances for much of his career. A combination of dramatic re-creation, archival material, and interviews depict the biographical details of the driven artist who died at the age of 50. Feore is memorable in the title role, especially since he's never actually shown playing the piano. Title and film structure refer to Bach's "Goldberg" Variations, a recording which made Gould's reputation.

1993 94m/C *CA* Colm Feore, Gale Garnett, David Hughes; *D:* Francois Girard; *W:* Don McKellar, Francois Girard. Genie Awards '93: Best Cinematography, Best Director (Girard), Best Film, Best Film Editing; Nominations: Independent Spirit Awards '95: Best Foreign Language Film. **VHS, LV** ★★★

36 Fillete Lili, an intellectually precocious 14-year-old French girl who's literally bursting out of her children's dress size 36 fillete, discovers her sexuality. So while on vacation with her family she becomes determined to see if she can seduce a middle-aged playboy. In French with English subtitles.

1988 88m/C *FR* Delphine Zentout, Etienne Chicot, Oliver Parniere, Jean-Pierre Leaud; *D:* Catherine Breillat. **VHS** ★★★

The 39 Steps The classic Hitchcock mistaken-man-caught-in-intrigue thriller, featuring some of his most often copied set-pieces and the surest visual flair of his pre-war British period. The laserdisc version includes a 20-minute documentary tracing the director's British period. Remade twice, in 1959 and 1979.

1935 81m/B *GB* Robert Donat, Madeleine Carroll, Godfrey Tearle, Lucie Mannheim, Peggy Ashcroft, John Laurie, Wylie Watson; *D:* Alfred Hitchcock; *W:* Charles Bennett, Alma Reville; *M:* Louis Levy. **VHS, Beta, LV, 8mm** ★★★★

This Boy's Life Carolyn and her teenage son are in search of a new life, far from her abusive ex-boyfriend. In the town of Concrete, just outside Seattle, she meets ex-military man Dwight (De Niro), a slick but none too suave mechanic who might be the answer to her dreams, but then again, he might not. Nicely crafted performances from all, but keep your eye on DiCaprio (great in his first major role) as the confused and abused teen divided between dreams of prep school and the allure of the going-nowhere crowd. Based on the memoirs of Tobias Wolff; director Caton-Jones sensitively illustrates the skewed understanding of masculinity in the 1950s. Vintage soundtrack takes you back.

1993 (R) 115m/C Robert De Niro, Ellen Barkin, Leonardo DiCaprio, Jonah Blechman, Eliza Dushku, Chris Cooper, Carla Gugino, Zachary Ansley, Tracey Ellis, Kathy Kinney, Gerrit Graham; *D:* Michael Caton-Jones; *W:* Robert Getchell; *M:* Carter Burwell. **VHS, Beta, LV** ★★★

This Gun for Hire In his first major film role, Ladd plays a hired gun seeking retribution from a client who betrays him. Preston is the cop pursuing him and hostage Lake. Ladd's performance as the cold-blooded killer with a soft spot for cats is stunning; his train-yard scene is an emotional powerhouse. Based on Graham Greene's novel "A Gun for Sale." Remade as "Short Cut to Hell." The first of several films using the Ladd-Lake team, but the only one in which Ladd played a villain.

1942 81m/B Alan Ladd, Veronica Lake, Robert Preston, Laird Cregar; *D:* Frank Tuttle; *W:* Albert Maltz, W.R. Burnett. **VHS, Beta, LV** ★★★1/2

This Happy Breed A celebrated film version of Noel Coward's classic play depicts the changing fortunes of a large family in England between the world wars. Happiness, hardships, triumph and tragedy mix a series of memorable episodes, including some of the most cherished moments in popular British cinema, though its appeal is universal. Narrated by Laurence Olivier.

1947 114m/C *GB* Robert Newton, Celia Johnson, John Mills, Kay Walsh, Stanley Holloway; *D:* David Lean; *W:* David Lean. **VHS** ★★★1/2

This Is Spinal Tap Pseudo-rockumentary about heavy-metal band Spinal Tap, profiling their career from "England's loudest band" to an entry in the "where are they now file." Hilarious satire, featuring music performed by Guest, McKean, Shearer, and others. Included are Spinal Tap's music video "Hell Hole," and an ad for their greatest hits album, "Heavy Metal Memories." Features great cameos, particularly David Letterman's Paul Schaffer as a record promoter and Billy Crystal as a surly mime. First feature for Reiner (Meathead on "All in the Family"). Followed by "The Return of Spinal Tap." *AKA:* Spinal Tap.

1984 (R) 82m/C Michael McKean, Christopher Guest, Harry Shearer, Tony Hendra, Bruno Kirby, Rob Reiner, June Chadwick, Howard Hesseman, Dana Carvey, Ed Begley Jr., Patrick Macnee, Fran Drescher; *Cameos:* Billy Crystal, Paul Schaffer, Anjelica Huston; *D:* Rob Reiner;

W: Christopher Guest. **VHS, Beta, LV, 8mm** ★★★1/2

This Land Is Mine A timid French schoolteacher gathers enough courage to defy the Nazis when they attempt to occupy his town. Laughton's characterization is effective as the meek fellow who discovers the hero within himself in this patriotic wartime flick.
1943 103m/B Charles Laughton, Maureen O'Hara, George Sanders, Walter Slezak, George Couloulis, Una O'Connor; **D:** Jean Renoir. Academy Awards '43: Best Sound. **VHS, Beta, LV** ★★★

This Man Must Die A man searches relentlessly for the driver who killed his young son in a hit-and-run. When found, the driver engages him in a complex cat-and-mouse chase. Another stunning crime and punishment tale from Chabrol. **AKA:** Que La Bete Meure; Uccidero Un Uomo.
1970 (PG) 112m/C FR Michael Duchaussoy, Caroline Cellier, Jean Yanne; **D:** Claude Chabrol. National Board of Review Awards '70: 5 Best Foreign Films of the Year. **VHS, Beta** ★★★1/2

This Sporting Life A gritty, depressing portrait of a former coal miner who breaks into the violent world of professional rugby, and whose inability to handle social differences causes problems. He begins an affair with the widow from whom he rents a room but finds they are capable of only a physical attachment. One of the best of the British early '60s working-class angry young man melodramas.
1963 134m/B GB Richard Harris, Rachel Roberts, Alan Badel, William Hartnell, Colin Blakely, Vanda Godsell, Arthur Lowe; **D:** Lindsay Anderson; **W:** David Storey. British Academy Awards '63: Best Actress (Roberts); Cannes Film Festival '63: Best Actor (Harris); National Board of Review Awards '63: 10 Best Films of the Year; Nominations: Academy Awards '63: Best Actor (Harris), Best Actress (Roberts). **VHS, Beta** ★★★

The Thomas Crown Affair A multimillionaire (McQueen) decides to plot and execute the perfect theft, a daring daylight robbery of a bank. Dunaway is the gorgeous and efficient insurance investigator determined to nab him. One of the best visual scenes is the chess match between the two as they begin to fall in love. Strong production with Oscar-winning theme "The Windmills of Your Mind." ♪ The Windmills of Your Mind. **AKA:** Thomas Crown and Company; The Crown Caper.

1968 (R) 102m/C Steve McQueen, Faye Dunaway, Jack Weston, Yaphet Kotto; **D:** Norman Jewison; **W:** Alan R. Trustman, Haskell Wexler. Academy Awards '68: Best Song ("The Windmills of Your Mind"); Golden Globe Awards '69: Best Song ("The Windmills of Your Mind"). **VHS, Beta** ★★★

The Thorn Birds Pioneers find danger and romance in the Australian outback as they struggle to begin a dynasty. Charismatic priest sometimes hurts, sometimes helps them. One of Stanwyck's last performances; Ward's American television debut. Originally a ten-hour television epic based on Colleen McCullough novel. Emmy nominations for Actor Chamberlain, Supporting Actor(s) Brown and Plummer, Supporting Actress Laurie, direction, photography, music, costume design, and editing. On four cassettes.
1983 486m/C Rachel Ward, Richard Chamberlain, Jean Simmons, Ken Howard, Mare Winningham, Richard Kiley, Piper Laurie, Bryan Brown, Christopher Plummer, Barbara Stanwyck; **D:** Daryl Duke; **M:** Henry Mancini. **VHS, Beta** ★★★

Those Magnificent Men in Their Flying Machines In 1910, a wealthy British newspaper publisher is persuaded to sponsor an air race from London to Paris. Contestants come from all over the world and shenanigans, hijinks, double-crosses, and romance are found along the route. Skelton has fun in prologue, while Terry-Thomas is great as the villain. Fun from start to finish.
1965 138m/C GB Stuart Whitman, Sarah Miles, Robert Morley, Alberto Sordi, James Fox, Gert Frobe, Jean-Pierre Cassel, Flora Robson, Sam Wanamaker, Terry-Thomas, Irina Demick, Benny Hill, Gordon Jackson, Millicent Martin, Red Skelton; **D:** Ken Annakin; **W:** Ken Annakin, Jack Davies. Nominations: Academy Awards '65: Best Story & Screenplay. **VHS, Beta, LV** ★★★

A Thousand Clowns A nonconformist has resigned from his job as chief writer for an obnoxious kiddie show in order to enjoy life. But his independence comes under fire when he becomes guardian for his young nephew and social workers take a dim view of his lifestyle. Balsam won an Oscar for his role as Robard's agent brother. Adapted from Herb Gardner's Broadway comedy.
1965 118m/B Jason Robards Jr., Barry Gordon, William Daniels, Barbara Harris, Gene Saks, Martin Balsam; **D:** Fred Coe; **W:** Herb Gardner. Academy Awards '65: Best Supporting Actor (Balsam); National Board of Review Awards '65: 10 Best Films

of the Year; Nominations: Academy Awards '65: Best Adapted Screenplay, Best Picture, Best Original Score. **VHS, Beta** ★★★

Three Broadway Girls Three gold-diggers go husband-hunting. Well-paced, very funny telling of this old story. Remade many times, including "How to Marry a Millionaire," "Three Blind Mice," "Moon Over Miami," and "Three Little Girls in Blue." **AKA:** The Greeks Had a Word for Them.
1932 78m/B Joan Blondell, Ina Claire, Madge Evans, David Manners, Lowell Sherman; **D:** Lowell Sherman. **VHS, Beta** ★★★

Three Brothers An acclaimed Italian film by veteran Rosi about three brothers summoned to their small Italian village by a telegram saying their mother is dead. Sensitive and compassionate. In Italian with English subtitles. Adapted from Platonov's story "The Third Son."
1980 (PG) 113m/C *IT* Philippe Noiret, Charles Vanel, Michele Placido, Vittorio Mezzogiorno, Andrea Ferreol; **D:** Francesco Rosi; **W:** Francesco Rosi. Nominations: Academy Awards '81: Best Foreign Language Film. **VHS, Beta** ★★★

Three Came Home Colbert is an American married to a British administrator in the Far East during WWII. Conquering Japanese throw the whole family into a brutal POW concentration camp, and their confinement is recounted in harrowing and unsparing detail. Superior drama, also laudable for a fairly even-handed portrayal of the enemy captors. Based on an autobiographical book by Agnes Newton-Keith.
1950 106m/B Claudette Colbert, Patric Knowles, Sessue Hayakawa; **D:** Jean Negulesco. **VHS** ★★★

Three Comrades Taylor, Tone, and Young are three friends, reunited in bleak, post-WWI Germany, who meet and befriend Sullavan, a tubercular beauty. Reluctant to marry because of her health, she's finally persuaded to wed Taylor, amidst the country's increasing unrest. Tragedy strikes Sullavan and the politicized Young, and the two remaining comrades face an uncertain future. Bleak but forceful and passionate drama. Sullavan's performance is superb. Based on the novel by Erich Maria Remarque. Fitzgerald's script was heavily re-written because both Sullavan and producer Mankiewicz found his approach too literary with unspeakable dialogue.
1938 99m/B Robert Taylor, Margaret

Sullavan, Robert Young, Franchot Tone, Lionel Atwill, Guy Kibbee, Henry Hull, George Zucco, Monty Woolley, Charley Grapewin, Spencer Charters, Sarah Padden; **D:** Frank Borzage; **W:** F. Scott Fitzgerald, Edward Paramore; **M:** Franz Waxman. New York Film Critics Awards '38: Best Actress (Sullavan); Nominations: Academy Awards '38: Best Actress (Sullavan). **VHS** ★★★

Three Days of the Condor CIA researcher Redford finds himself on the run from unknown killers when he is left the only survivor of the mass murder of his office staff. Good performance by Dunaway as the photographer who shelters him. Excellent suspense tale. Based on "Six Days of the Condor" by James Grady.
1975 (R) 118m/C Robert Redford, Faye Dunaway, Cliff Robertson, Max von Sydow, John Houseman; **D:** Sydney Pollack; **W:** David Rayfiel; **M:** Dave Grusin, Owen Roizman. Edgar Allan Poe Awards '75: Best Screenplay; Nominations: Academy Awards '75: Best Film Editing. **VHS, Beta, LV** ★★★

The Three Faces of Eve An emotionally disturbed woman seeks the help of a psychiatrist, who discovers she has three distinct personalities. Powerful performances highlight this fascinating study based on a true story.
1957 91m/B Joanne Woodward, David Wayne, Lee J. Cobb, Nancy Kulp, Vince Edwards; **D:** Nunnally Johnson. Academy Awards '57: Best Actress (Woodward); Golden Globe Awards '58: Best Actress—Drama (Woodward). **VHS, LV** ★★★1/2

Three Godfathers A sweet and sentimental western has three half-hearted outlaws on the run, taking with them an infant they find in the desert. Dedicated to western star and Ford alumni Harry Carey, Sr. (whose son is one of the outlaws in the film), who died of cancer the year before. Ford had first filmed the tale with Carey Sr. as "Marked Men" in 1919.
1948 82m/C John Wayne, Pedro Armendariz Sr., Harry Carey Jr., Ward Bond, Mae Marsh, Jane Darwell, Ben Johnson, Mildred Natwick, Guy Kibbee; **D:** John Ford. **VHS, Beta** ★★★

The 317th Platoon An emotionally gripping war drama of the French-Vietnamese War in which the 317th Platoon of the French Army, consisting of 4 French commanders and 41 Laotians, is ordered to retreat to camp Dien Bien Phu. The men begin their march and slowly succumb to the elements and ambushes. Days later, when what is left of the platoon finally reaches Dien Bien Phu, the

▲

camp is in enemy hands and the remnants of the 317th Platoon are killed in cold blood. Director Shoendoerffer portrays this struggle, conflict, and the quiet haunting tension of war with great skill. In French with English subtitles.
1965 100m/B FR Jacques Perrin, Bruno Cremer, Pierre Fabre, Manuel Zarzo; **D:** Pierre Schoendoerffer; **W:** Pierre Schoendoerffer. **VHS, LV ★★★**

Three Men and a Baby The arrival of a young baby forever changes the lives of three sworn bachelors living in New York. Well-paced, charming and fun, with good acting from all. A remake of the French movie "Three Men and a Cradle."
1987 (PG) 102m/C Tom Selleck, Steve Guttenberg, Ted Danson, Margaret Colin, Nancy Travis, Philip Bosco, Celeste Holm, Derek De Lint, Cynthia Harris, Lisa Blair, Michelle Blair; **D:** Leonard Nimoy; **W:** James Orr, Jim Cruickshank; **M:** Marvin Hamlisch. People's Choice Awards '88: Best Film—Musical/Comedy. **VHS, Beta, LV, 8mm ★★★**

Three Men and a Cradle Remade in the U.S. in 1987 as "Three Men and a Baby," this French film is about three bachelors living together who suddenly find themselves the guardians of a baby girl. After the initial shock of learning how to take care of a child, they fall in love with her and won't let her go. Fans of the American version may find themselves liking the original even more. In French with English subtitles. **AKA:** Trois Hommes et un Couffin.
1985 (PG-13) 100m/C FR Roland Giraud, Michel Boujenah, Andre Dussollier; **D:** Coline Serreau; **W:** Coline Serreau. Cesar Awards '86: Best Film, Best Supporting Actor (Boujenah), Best Writing; Nominations: Academy Awards '85: Best Foreign Language Film. **VHS, LV ★★★1/2**

Three Men on a Horse Comedy classic about mild-mannered McHugh's ability to predict horse races and the bettors that try to take advantage of him. Blondell is great as the Brooklynese girlfriend of one of the bettors. Lots of laughs, but don't watch for the horse-racing scenes, because there aren't many.
1936 88m/B Frank McHugh, Joan Blondell, Carol Hughes, Allen Jenkins, Guy Kibbee, Sam Levene; **D:** Mervyn LeRoy. **VHS ★★★**

The Three Musketeers D'Artagnan swashbuckles silently amid stylish sets, scores of extras and exquisite costumes. Relatively faithful adaptation of Alexandre Dumas novel, slightly altered in favor of D'Artagnan's lover. Classic Fairbanks, who also produced.
1921 120m/B Douglas Fairbanks Sr., Leon Barry, George Siegmann, Eugene Pallette, Boyd Irwin, Thomas Holding, Sidney Franklin, Charles Stevens, Nigel de Brulier, Willis Robards; **D:** Fred Niblo. **VHS, Beta, LV ★★★1/2**

The Three Musketeers Extravagant and funny version of the Dumas classic. Three swashbucklers and their country cohort, who wishes to join the Musketeers, set out to save the honor of the French Queen. To do so they must oppose the evil cardinal who has his eyes on the power behind the throne. A strong cast leads this winning combination of slapstick and high adventure. Followed by "The Four Musketeers" and "The Return of the Musketeers."
1974 (PG) 105m/C Richard Chamberlain, Oliver Reed, Michael York, Raquel Welch, Frank Finlay, Christopher Lee, Faye Dunaway, Charlton Heston, Geraldine Chaplin, Simon Ward, Jean-Pierre Cassel; **D:** Richard Lester. Golden Globe Awards '75: Best Actress—Musical/Comedy (Welch). **VHS, Beta ★★★1/2**

Three on a Match An actress, a stenographer, and a society woman get together for a tenth year reunion. They become embroiled in a world of crime when Blondell's gangster boyfriend takes a liking to Dvorak. She leaves her husband and takes up with the crook. The results are tragic. Bogart's first gangster role.
1932 64m/B Joan Blondell, Warren William, Ann Dvorak, Bette Davis, Lyle Talbot, Humphrey Bogart, Patricia Ellis, Grant Mitchell; **D:** Mervyn LeRoy. **VHS, Beta ★★★**

The Three Penny Opera Mack the Knife presides over an exciting world of thieves, murderers, beggars, prostitutes, and corrupt officials in a seedy section of London. Based on the opera by Kurt Weill and Bertolt Brecht, which was based on "The Beggar's Opera" by John Gay. Remake of "The Threepenny Opera" (1931). **AKA:** Die Dreigroschenoper.
1962 124m/C GE Curt Jurgens, Hildegarde Neff, Gert Frobe, June Ritchie, Lino Ventura, Sammy Davis Jr. **VHS, Beta, LV ★★★**

Three Smart Girls Fast-moving musical features three high-spirited sisters who attempt to bring their divorced parents back together. Their plan is thwarted when they learn of their father's plan to marry a gold digger. 15-year-old singing sensation

Durbin made her debut in this film. Based on a story by Commandini. Followed by "Three Smart Girls Grow Up." ♪ My Heart is Singing; Someone to Care for Me.
1936 84m/B Deanna Durbin, Binnie Barnes, Alice Brady, Ray Milland, Charles Winninger, Mischa Auer, Nan Grey, Barbara Read; **D:** Henry Koster; **W:** Adele Commandini, Austin Parker. **VHS ★★★1/2**

3:10 to Yuma In order to collect $200 he desperately needs, a poor farmer has to hold a dangerous killer at bay while waiting to turn the outlaw over to the authorities arriving on the 3:10 train to Yuma. Stuck in a hotel room with the outlaw's gang gathering outside, the question arises as to who is the prisoner. Farmer Heflin is continually worked on by the outlaw Ford, in a movie with more than its share of great dialogue. Suspenseful, well-made action western adapted from an Elmore Leonard story.
1957 92m/B Glenn Ford, Van Heflin, Felicia Farr, Richard Jaeckel; **D:** Delmer Daves; **M:** George Duning. **VHS, Beta, LV ★★★1/2**

Throne of Blood Kurosawa's masterful adaptation of "Macbeth" transports the story to medieval Japan and the world of the samurai. Mifune and Chiaki are warriors who have put down a rebellion and are to be rewarded by their overlord. On their way to his castle they meet a mysterious old woman who prophesizes that Mifune will soon rule—but his reign will be short. She is dismissed as crazy but her prophesies come to pass. So steeped in Japanese style that it bears little resemblance to the Shakespearean original, this film is an incredibly detailed vision in its own right. In Japanese with English subtitles. **AKA:** Kumonosujo, Kumonosu-djo; Cobweb Castle; The Castle of the Spider's Web.
1957 105m/B *JP* Toshiro Mifune, Isuzu Yamada, Takashi Shimura, Minoru Chiaki, Akira Kubo; **D:** Akira Kurosawa; **W:** Hideo Oguni, Shinobu Hashimoto, Riyuzo Kikushima, Akira Kurosawa; **M:** Masaru Sato. **VHS, Beta, LV ★★★★**

Through a Glass Darkly Oppressive interactions within a family sharing a holiday on a secluded island: a woman recovering from schizophrenia, her husband, younger brother, and her psychologist father. One of Bergman's most mysterious, upsetting and powerful films. In Swedish with English subtitles. Part of Bergman's Silence-of-God trilogy followed by "Winter Light" and "The Silence."

1961 91m/B *SW* Harriet Andersson, Max von Sydow, Gunnar Bjornstrand, Lars Passgard; **D:** Ingmar Bergman; **W:** Ingmar Bergman, Sven Nykvist. Academy Awards '61: Best Foreign Language Film; National Board of Review Awards '62: 5 Best Foreign Films of the Year; Nominations: Academy Awards '62: Best Story & Screenplay. **VHS, Beta ★★★**

Throw Momma from the Train DeVito plays a man, henpecked by his horrific mother, who tries to persuade his writing professor (Crystal) to exchange murders. DeVito will kill Crystal's ex-wife and Crystal will kill DeVito's mother. Only mama isn't going to be that easy to get rid of. Fast-paced and entertaining black comedy. Ramsey steals the film. Inspired by Hitchcock's "Strangers on a Train."
1987 (PG-13) 88m/C Danny DeVito, Billy Crystal, Anne Ramsey, Kate Mulgrew, Kim Greist, Branford Marsalis, Rob Reiner, Bruce Kirby; **D:** Danny DeVito; **W:** Stu Silver; **M:** David Newman. Nominations: Academy Awards '87: Best Supporting Actress (Ramsey). **VHS, Beta, LV ★★★**

Thunder Bay Stewart and Duryea are a pair of Louisiana wildcat oil drillers who believe there is oil at the bottom of the Gulf of Mexico off the coast of the town of Port Felicity. They decide to construct an oil platform which the shrimp fisherman of the town believe will interfere with their livelihoods. Tensions rise between the two groups and violence seems likely. Action packed, with timely storyline as modern oil drillers fight to drill in waters that have historically been off-limits.
1953 82m/C James Stewart, Joanne Dru, Dan Duryea, Gilbert Roland, Marcia Henderson; **D:** Anthony Mann; **W:** John Michael Hayes. **VHS, Beta ★★★**

Thunder Road Mitchum comes home to Tennessee from Korea and takes over the family moonshine business, fighting both mobsters and federal agents. An exciting chase between Mitchum and the feds ends the movie with the appropriate bang. Robert Mitchum not only produced, wrote and starred in this best of the moonshine-running films, but also wrote the theme song "Whippoorwill" (which later became a radio hit). Mitchum's son, James, made his film debut, and later starred in a similar movie, "Moonrunners." A cult favorite, still shown in many drive-ins around the country.
1958 (PG) 92m/B Robert Mitchum, Jacques Aubuchon, Gene Barry, Keely Smith, Trevor Bardette, Sandra Knight, Jim Mitchum, Betsy Holt, Frances Koon; **D:**

T

Arthur Ripley; **W:** Robert Mitchum. **VHS, Beta ★★★**

Thunderbolt & Lightfoot Eastwood is an ex-thief on the run from his former partners (Kennedy and Lewis) who believe he's made off with the loot from their last job, the robbery of a government vault. He joins up with drifter Bridges, who helps him to escape. Later, Eastwood manages to convince Kennedy he doesn't know where the money is. Bridges then persuades the men that they should plan the same heist and rob the same government vault all over again, which they do. But their getaway doesn't go exactly as planned. All-around fine acting; notable is Bridges' scene dressed in drag. First film for director Cimino.
1974 (R) 115m/C Clint Eastwood, Jeff Bridges, George Kennedy, Geoffrey Lewis, Gary Busey; **D:** Michael Cimino; **W:** Michael Cimino; **M:** Dee Barton. Nominations: Academy Awards '74: Best Supporting Actor (Bridges). **VHS, Beta, LV ★★★**

THX 1138 In the dehumanized world of the future, people live in underground cities run by computer, are force-fed drugs to keep them passive, and no longer have names—just letter/number combinations (Duvall is THX 1138). Emotion is also outlawed and when the computer-matched couple THX 1138 and LUH 3417 discover love, they must battle the computer system to escape. George Lucas' first film, which was inspired by a student film he did at USC. The laser-disc format carries the film in widescreen.
1971 (PG) 88m/C Robert Duvall, Donald Pleasence, Maggie McOmie; **D:** George Lucas; **W:** George Lucas; **M:** Lalo Schifrin. **VHS, Beta, LV ★★★**

Tiger Bay A young Polish sailor, on leave in Cardiff, murders his unfaithful girlfriend. Lonely ten-year-old Gillie sees the crime and takes the murder weapon, thinking it will make her more popular with her peers. Confronted by a police detective, she convincingly lies but eventually the sailor finds Gillie and kidnaps her, hoping to keep her quiet until he can get aboard his ship. A delicate relationship evolves between the child and the killer as she tries to help him escape and the police close in. Marks Hayley Mills' first major role and one of her finest performances.
1959 107m/B *GB* John Mills, Horst Buchholz, Hayley Mills, Yvonne Mitchell; **D:** J. Lee Thompson. **VHS, Beta ★★★**

Tightrope Police inspector Wes Block pursues a killer of prostitutes in New Orleans' French Quarter. The film is notable both as a thriller and as a fascinating vehicle for Eastwood, who experiments with a disturbing portrait of a cop with some peculiarities of his own.
1984 (R) 115m/C Clint Eastwood, Genevieve Bujold, Dan Hedaya, Jennifer Beck, Alison Eastwood, Randi Brooks, Regina Richardson, Jamie Rose; **D:** Richard Tuggle; **M:** Lennie Niehaus. **VHS, Beta, LV ★★★**

Till the Clouds Roll By/A Star Is Born Ostensibly concerns the life and career of songwriter Jerome Kern. Highlighted by stellar performances from a number of musical stars of the day. Maudlin and unconcerned with factual accuracy, the film nonetheless is an exuberant celebration of Kern's talent.
1946 249m/C Judy Garland, Frank Sinatra, Robert Walker, Fredric March, Janet Gaynor, Andy Devine, Lionel Stander, Franklin Pangborn, Van Heflin, Lucille Bremer, Kathryn Grayson, Lena Horne, Tony Martin, Angela Lansbury, Dinah Shore, Virginia O'Brien, Cyd Charisse, Adolphe Menjou; **D:** William A. Wellman, Richard Whorf. **VHS, Beta ★★★**

Time After Time In Victorian London, circa 1893, H.G. Wells is experimenting with his time machine. He discovers the machine has been used by an associate, who turns out to be Jack the Ripper, to travel to San Francisco in 1979. Wells follows to stop any further murders and the ensuing battle of wits is both entertaining and imaginative. McDowell is charming as Wells and Steenburgen is equally fine as Wells's modern American love interest.
1979 (PG) 112m/C Malcolm McDowell, David Warner, Mary Steenburgen, Patti D'Arbanville, Charles Cioffi; **D:** Nicholas Meyer; **W:** Nicholas Meyer; **M:** Miklos Rozsa. National Board of Review Awards '79: 10 Best Films of the Year. **VHS, Beta, LV ★★★**

The Time Machine English scientist living near the end of the 19th century invents time travel machine and uses it to travel into various periods of the future. Rollicking version of H.G. Wells' classic cautionary tale boasts Oscar-winning special effects. Remade in 1978.
1960 103m/C Rod Taylor, Yvette Mimieux, Whit Bissell, Sebastian Cabot, Alan Young; **D:** George Pal. Academy Awards '60: Best Special Effects. **VHS, Beta, LV ★★★**

Time of the Gypsies Acclaimed Yugoslavian saga about a homely, unlucky Gypsy boy who sets out to steal his way to a dowry large enough to marry the girl of his dreams. Beautifully filmed, magical, and very long. In the Gypsy language, Romany, it's the first feature film made in the Gypsy tongue. *AKA:* Dom Za Vesanje.
1990 (R) 136m/C *YU* Davor Dujmovic, Sinolicka Trpkova, Ljubica Adzovic, Hunsija Hasimovic, Bora Todorovic; *D:* Emir Kusturica. Cannes Film Festival '90: Best Director (Kusturica). **VHS, Beta, LV ★★★**

The Time of Your Life The only Cagney film that ever lost money. A simple but engaging story of people trying to live their dreams. Cagney is delightful as a barroom philosopher who controls the world around him from his seat in the tavern. Although it was not very popular with audiences at the time, the critics hailed it as an artistic achievement. Based on William Saroyan's play.
1948 109m/B James Cagney, William Bendix, Jeanne Cagney, Broderick Crawford, Ward Bond, James Barton, Paul Draper, Natalie Schafer; *D:* H.C. Potter. **VHS ★★★★**

A Time to Kill Powerful story of revenge, racism, and the question of justice in the "new south." John Grisham had a lot of clout when he finally sold his first and favorite novel to the movies, including veto power over the leading man—director Schumacher was for Woody Harrelson; Grisham was opposed, but both finally agreed on newcomer McConaughey. He's outstanding as idealistic smalltown Mississippi lawyer Jake Brigance, called to defend an anguished father Carl Lee Hailey (Jackson), who's accused of killing the rednecks who raped his young daughter. Jake's assisted by former mentor Lucien Wilbanks (Sutherland) and ambitious northern law student Ellen Roark (Bullock) against ruthless prosecutor Rufus Buckley (Spacey). Is it emotionally manipulative? You betcha. But Grisham's done well on screen, and Schumacher (who also did "The Client") knows how to get the most from his cast and script.
1996 (R) 150m/C Matthew McConaughey, Samuel L. Jackson, Sandra Bullock, Kevin Spacey, Donald Sutherland, Brenda Fricker, Oliver Platt, Charles S. Dutton, Ashley Judd, Patrick McGoohan, Kiefer Sutherland, Chris Cooper, Rae'ven Kelly, John Diehl, Tonea Stewart, M. Emmet Walsh, Anthony Heald, Kurtwood Smith; *D:* Joel Schumacher; *W:* Akiva Goldsman; *M:* Elliot Goldenthal. Nominations: Golden Globe Awards '97: Best Supporting Actor (Jackson). **VHS, LV ★★★1/2**

Tin Cup You've got your romantic triangle, you got your sports, you've got Costner reteamed with Shelton— "Bull Durham" on a golf course? Can lightening strike twice? Ron "Tin Cup" McAvoy (Costner) is a West Texas golf hustler who had the ability but not the steadiness to be on the pro tour. When McAvoy decides on a last-ditch effort to qualify for the U.S. Open, he turns to psychologist Dr. Molly Griswold (Russo) to get his game together. And the fact that Molly is the girlfriend of McAvoy's longtime rival—and successful PGA player—Don Simms (Johnson), well Tin Cup isn't adverse to playing for the lady's affections either. The U.S. Open scenes were filmed at Houston's Kingwood Country Club, and the actors do hit their own shots.
1996 (R) 133m/C Kevin Costner, Rene Russo, Don Johnson, Richard "Cheech" Marin, Linda Hart, Dennis Burkley, Rex Linn, Lou Myers, Richard Lineback, Mickey Jones; *D:* Ron Shelton; *W:* Ron Shelton, John Norville; *M:* William Ross. Nominations: Golden Globe Awards '97: Best Actor—Musical/Comedy (Costner). **VHS, LV ★★★**

The Tin Drum German child in the 1920s wills himself to stop growing in response to the increasing Nazi presence in Germany. He communicates his anger and fear by pounding on a tin drum. Memorable scenes, excellent cast. In German with English subtitles. Adapted from the novel by Gunter Grass. *AKA:* Die Blechtrommel
1979 (R) 141m/C *GE* David Bennet, Mario Adorf, Angela Winkler, Daniel Olbrychski, Katharina Thalbach, Heinz Bennet, Andrea Ferreol, Charles Aznavour; *D:* Rainer Werner Fassbinder, Volker Schlondorff; *M:* Maurice Jarre. Academy Awards '79: Best Foreign Language Film; Cannes Film Festival '79:Best Film; Los Angeles Film Critics Association Awards '80: Best Foreign Film; National Board of Review Awards '80: 5 Best Foreign Films of the Year. **VHS, Beta ★★★1/2**

The Tin Star Perkins is the young sheriff who persuades veteran bounty hunter Fonda to help him rid the town of outlaws. Excellent Mann western balances humor and suspense.
1957 93m/B Henry Fonda, Anthony Perkins, Betsy Palmer, Neville Brand, Lee Van Cleef, John McIntire, Michel Ray; *D:* Anthony Mann; *M:* Elmer Bernstein. Nominations: Academy Awards '57: Best Story & Screenplay. **VHS, Beta ★★★**

Titanic Hollywoodized version of the 1912 sinking of the famous luxury liner sets the scene for the personal drama of a mother (Stanwyck) who wants to flee her husband (Webb) for a new life in America. Story gets a little too melodramatic, but it's not a bad retelling of the sea tragedy. Film is quite effective in conveying the panic and the calm of the actual sinking. A 20-foot-long model of the ship was built for the re-creation of that fateful moment when the "Titanic" hit the inevitable iceberg.
1953 98m/B Clifton Webb, Barbara Stanwyck, Robert Wagner, Richard Basehart, Audrey Dalton, Thelma Ritter, Brian Aherne; **D:** Jean Negulesco; **W:** Charles Brackett, Walter Reisch, Richard L. Breen. Academy Awards '53: Best Screenplay, Best Story. **VHS ★★★**

To Be or Not to Be Sophisticated black comedy set in wartime Poland. Lombard and Benny are Maria and Josef Tura, the Barrymores of the Polish stage, who use the talents of their acting troupe against the invading Nazis. The opening sequence is regarded as a cinema classic. One of Benny's finest film performances, the movie marks Lombard's final screen appearance. Classic Lubitsch. Remade in 1983.
1942 102m/B Carole Lombard, Jack Benny, Robert Stack, Sig Rumann, Lionel Atwill, Felix Bressart, Helmut Dantine, Tom Dugan, Charles Halton; **D:** Ernst Lubitsch. Nominations: Academy Awards '42: Best Original Score. **VHS, Beta ★★★1/2**

To Catch a Thief On the French Riviera, a reformed jewel thief falls for a wealthy American woman, who suspects he's up to his old tricks when a rash of jewel thefts occur. Oscar-winning photography by Robert Burks, a notable fireworks scene, and snappy dialogue. A change of pace for Hitchcock, this charming comedy-thriller proved to be as popular as his other efforts. Kelly met future husband Prince Rainier during shooting in Monaco. Based on the novel by David Dodge.
1955 103m/C Cary Grant, Grace Kelly, Jessie Royce Landis, John Williams, Charles Vanel, Brigitte Auber; **D:** Alfred Hitchcock; **W:** John Michael Hayes. Academy Awards '55: Best Color Cinematography; Nominations: Academy Awards '55: Best Art Direction/Set Decoration (Color), Best Costume Design (Color). **VHS, Beta, LV ★★★**

To Dance with the White Dog Robert Samuel Peek (Cronyn) is a pecan-tree grower from rural Georgia who has been married to Cora (Tandy) for 57 years. Then she dies and their fussing daughters (Baranski and Wright) wonder how their father will survive. But Sam's increasing loneliness is checked when he befriends a stray white dog that it seems no one else can see. Based on the novel by Terry Kay. Made for television.
1993 (PG) 98m/C Hume Cronyn, Jessica Tandy, Christine Baranski, Amy Wright, Esther Rolle, Harley Cross, Frank Whaley, Terry Beaver, Dan Albright, David Dwyer; **D:** Glenn Jordan; **W:** Susan Cooper, Neil Roach. **VHS ★★★**

To Die For Beauteous, manipulative Suzanne Stone (Kidman) wants to be somebody—preferably a big TV personality—and nothing will stop her. She recruits a scruffy threesome to help her ice sweet-but-dim hubby, Larry (Dillon), even going so far as to seduce aimless teenager Jimmy (Phoenix). Satiric comedy, loosely based on the Pamela Smart murder case and adapted from the novel by Joyce Maynard. Van Sant retains his fresh and hip storytelling, backed by Henry's zesty script. All the actors shine—with standout performances from Kidman as the monstrous Suzanne and Phoenix (River's younger brother) as the lost/horny Jimmy.
1995 (R) 103m/C Nicole Kidman, Matt Dillon, Joaquin Rafael (Leaf) Phoenix, Casey Affleck, Alison Folland, Illeana Douglas, Dan Hedaya, Wayne Knight, Kurtwood Smith, Holland Taylor, Maria Tucci, Susan Traylor; *Cameos:* George Segal, Buck Henry; **D:** Gus Van Sant; **W:** Buck Henry, Johnny Burne; **M:** Danny Elfman, Eric Alan Edwards. Golden Globe Awards '96: Best Actress—Musical/Comedy (Kidman); Nominations: British Academy Awards '95: Best Actress (Kidman). **VHS, LV, 8mm ★★★**

To Have & Have Not Martinique charter boat operator gets mixed up with beautiful woman and French resistance fighters during WWII. Top-notch production in every respect. Classic dialogue and fiery romantic bouts between Bogart and Bacall. Bacall's first film. Based on a story by Ernest Hemingway. Remade in 1950 as "The Breaking Point" and in 1958 as "The Gun Runners."
1944 100m/B Humphrey Bogart, Lauren Bacall, Walter Brennan, Hoagy Carmichael, Marcel Dalio, Dolores Moran, Sheldon Leonard, Dan Seymour; **D:** Howard Hawks. **VHS, Beta, LV ★★★1/2**

To Kill a Mockingbird Faithful adaptation of powerful Harper Lee novel, both an evocative portrayal of childhood innocence and a denunciation of bigotry. Peck's performance as southern lawyer defending a black man accused of raping a white woman is flawless. Duvall debuted as the dim-witted Boo Radley. Lee based her characterization of "Dill" on Truman Capote, a childhood friend. **1962 129m/B** Gregory Peck, Brock Peters, Phillip Alford, Mary Badham, Robert Duvall, Rosemary Murphy, William Windom, Alice Ghostley, John Megna, Frank Overton, Paul Fix, Collin Wilcox; *D:* Robert Mulligan; *W:* Horton Foote; *M:* Elmer Bernstein. Academy Awards '62: Best Actor (Peck), Best Adapted Screenplay, Best Art Direction/Set Decoration (B & W); Golden Globe Awards '63: Best Actor—Drama (Peck), Best Score; Nominations: Academy Awards '62: Best Black and White Cinematography, Best Director (Mulligan), Best Picture, Best Supporting Actress (Badham), Best Original Score. **VHS, Beta, LV ★★★★**

To Live Superb drama follows the lives of one family—weak but adaptable Fugui (You), his strong-willed wife Jiazhen (Li), and their young daughter and son—from prerevolutionary China in the 1940s through the '60s Cultural Revolution. Fugui loses the family fortune in the gambling houses, actually a blessing when the Communists come to power, and the family must struggle to survive financial and increasingly difficult political changes, where fate can change on a whim. Subtle saga about ordinary human lives reacting to terrifying conditions boasts extraordinary performances and evocative imagery. Adapted from the novel "Lifetimes" by Yu Hua. In Chinese with English subtitles. *AKA:* Huozhe.
1994 130m/C *CH* Ge You, Gong Li, Niu Ben, Guo Tao, Jiang Wu; *D:* Zhang Yimou; *W:* Lu Wei, Yu Hua; *M:* Zhao Jiping. British Academy Awards '94: Best Foreign Film; Cannes Film Festival '94: Best Actor (You), Grand Jury Prize; Nominations: Golden Globe Awards '95: Best Foreign Language Film. **VHS, LV ★★★★**

To Sleep with Anger At first a comic, introspective look at a black middle-class family going about their business in the heart of Los Angeles. Sly charmer Glover shows up and enthralls the entire family with his slightly sinister storytelling and a gnawing doom gradually permeates the household. Insightful look into the conflicting values of Black America. Glover's best performance.
1990 (PG) 105m/C Danny Glover, Mary

Alice, Paul Butler, Richard Brooks, Carl Lumbly, Vonetta McGee, Sheryl Lee Ralph; *D:* Charles Burnett; *W:* Charles Burnett, Walt Lloyd. Independent Spirit Awards '91: Best Actor (Glover), Best Director (Burnett), Best Screenplay, Best Supporting Actress (Ralph); Sundance Film Festival '90: Special Jury Prize. **VHS, Beta ★★★1/2**

Toast of New York Arnold plays Jim Fisk, a New England peddler who rises to become one of the first Wall Street giants of industry. Atypical Grant performance.
1937 109m/B Edward Arnold, Cary Grant, Frances Farmer, Jack Oakie, Donald Meek, Billy Gilbert; *D:* Rowland V. Lee. **VHS, Beta, LV ★★★**

Tokyo-Ga Impelled by his love for the films of Yasujiro Ozu, Wenders traveled to Tokyo and fashioned a caring document of both the city and of Ozu's career, using images that recall and comment on Ozu's visual motifs.
1985 92m/C *D:* Wim Wenders; *W:* Wim Wenders. **VHS, Beta ★★★★**

Tokyo Story Poignant story of elderly couple's journey to Tokyo where they receive little time and less respect from their grown children. Masterful cinematography, and sensitive treatment of universally appealing story. In Japanese with English subtitles.
1953 134m/B *JP* Chishu Ryu, Chieko Higashiyama, So Yamamura, Haruko Sugimura, Setsuko Hara; *D:* Yasujiro Ozu; *W:* Yasujiro Ozu. **VHS ★★★1/2**

Tom and Huck Tom Sawyer and pal Huck Finn are the only witnesses to a murder. Tom's friend Muff is framed for the crime, and the boys are being tracked by the real killer, Injun Joe. They must decide to come forward, expose the true fiend, and risk their own hides or run away and let an innocent man hang. True to the Twain story, Thomas plays a mischievous Tom to Renfro's troublemaking Huck. Film was shot in Mooresville, Alabama, population 69, just down the road a piece from the Hannibal, Missouri of Twain fame.
1995 (PG) 91m/C Jonathan Taylor Thomas, Brad Renfro, Eric Schweig, Charles Rocket, Amy Wright, Micheal McShane, Marian Seldes, Rachel Leigh Cook, Lanny Flaherty, Courtland Mead, Peter M. MacKenzie, Heath Lamberts; *D:* Pete Hewitt; *W:* Stephen Sommers, David Loughery; *M:* Stephen Endelman. **VHS ★★★**

Tom & Viv American T.S. Eliot (Dafoe) is an Oxford student in 1914 when he meets the moody, monied Vivien Haigh-Wood (Richardson). After a

T

whirlwind courtship, they marry—disastrously. Eliot begins to establish himself as a poet, while Vivien serves as muse/typist and unsuccessfully battles her misdiagnosed illnesses with too much drinking and drugs, as well as embarrassing public scenes. As Eliot gains success, he increasingly distances himself from the unhappy Viv, until finally committing her to an asylum. Dafoe is fine as the chilly, withdrawn poet but Richardson steals the film as his flamboyant, lost wife. Based on the play by Michael Hastings, who co-wrote the screenplay.
1994 (PG-13) 115m/C *GB* Willem Dafoe, Miranda Richardson, Rosemary Harris, Tim Dutton, Nickolas Grace, Philip Locke, Clare Holman, Joanna McCallum; **D:** Brian Gilbert; **W:** Michael Hastings, Adrian Hodges; **M:** Debbie Wiseman. National Board of Review Awards '94: Best Actress (Richardson), Best Supporting Actress (Harris); Nominations: Academy Awards '94: Best Actress (Richardson), Best Supporting Actress (Harris); Golden Globe Awards '95: Best Actress—Drama (Richardson). **VHS, LV ★★★**

Tom Jones Bawdy comedy based on Henry Fielding's novel about a rustic playboy's wild life in 18th-century England. Hilarious and clever with a grand performance by Finney. One of the sexiest eating scenes ever. Redgrave's debut. Theatrically released at 129 minutes, the film was recut by the director, who decided it needed tightening before its 1992 re-release on video.
1963 121m/C *GB* Albert Finney, Susannah York, Hugh Griffith, Edith Evans, Joan Greenwood, Diane Cilento, George Devine, David Tomlinson, Joyce Redman, Lynn Redgrave, Julian Glover, Peter Bull, David Warner; **D:** Tony Richardson; **W:** John Osborne; **M:** John Addison. Academy Awards '63: Best Adapted Screenplay, Best Director (Richardson), Best Picture, Best Original Score; British Academy Awards '63: Best Film, Best Screenplay; Directors Guild of America Awards '63: Best Director (Richardson); Golden Globe Awards '64: Best Film—Musical/Comedy, Best Foreign Film; National Board of Review Awards '63: Best Director (Richardson); New York Film Critics Awards '63: Best Actor (Finney), Best Director (Richardson), Best Film; Nominations: Academy Awards '63: Best Actor (Finney), Best Art Direction/Set Decoration (Color), Best Supporting Actor (Griffith), Best Supporting Actress (Cilento, Evans, Redman). **VHS, Beta, LV ★★★★**

Tom Sawyer Winning adaptation of Mark Twain's oft told tale of boyhood in Hannibal, Missouri. Cast reprised their roles the following year in "Huckleberry Finn."
1930 86m/B Jackie Coogan, Mitzie Green, Lucien Littlefield, Tully Marshall; **D:** John Cromwell. **VHS, Beta ★★★**

Tom Thumb Diminutive boy saves village treasury from bad guys. Adapted from classic Grimm fairytale. Special effects combine live actors, animation, and puppets.
1958 92m/C *GB* Russ Tamblyn, Peter Sellers, Terry-Thomas; **D:** George Pal. Academy Awards '58: Best Special Effects. **VHS, Beta, LV ★★★**

Tomb of Ligeia The ghost of a man's first wife expresses her displeasure when groom and new little missus return to manor. One of the better Corman adaptations of Poe. Also available with "The Conqueror Worm" on laserdisc. **AKA:** Tomb of the Cat.
1964 82m/C *GB* Vincent Price, Elizabeth Shepherd, John Westbrook, Oliver Johnston, Richard Johnson; **D:** Roger Corman; **W:** Robert Towne. **VHS, Beta, LV ★★★**

Toni An Italian worker falls for his landlady and they make plans to marry. A grim turn of events, however, brings tragic consequences. Based on the lives of several townsfolk in the village of Les Martiques, the film was shot in the town and members of the local populace were used as characters. In French with English subtitles.
1934 90m/B *FR* Charles Blavette, Jenny Helia, Edouard Delmont, Celia Montalvan; **D:** Jean Renoir. **VHS, Beta ★★★1/2**

Too Far to Go Terrific TV adaptation of a series of John Updike stories focusing on the rocky longtime marriage of not-so-proper New Englanders Danner and Moriarty.
1979 98m/C Blythe Danner, Michael Moriarty, Glenn Close, Ken Kercheval; **W:** William Hanley. **VHS ★★★**

Too Hot to Handle Two rival photographers searching for a beautiful lady pilot's missing brother wind up in Brazil, where they encounter a dangerous tribe of voodoo types. Amusing, if exaggerated, picture of the lengths to which reporters will go to for a story. Classic Gable.
1938 105m/B Clark Gable, Myrna Loy, Walter Pidgeon, Walter Connolly, Leo Carrillo, Virginia Weidler; **D:** Jack Conway. **VHS ★★★**

Tootsie A stubborn, unemployed actor disguises himself as a woman to secure a part on a soap opera. As his popularity on television mounts, his

love life becomes increasingly soap operatic. Hoffman is delightful, as is the rest of the stellar cast. Debut of Davis; Murray's performance unbilled. Laserdisc version features audio commentary by director Sidney Pollack, behind the scenes footage and photographs, and complete coverage of Tootsie's production.
1982 (PG) 110m/C Dustin Hoffman, Jessica Lange, Teri Garr, Dabney Coleman, Bill Murray, Charles Durning, Geena Davis, George Gaynes, Estelle Getty, Christine Ebersole, Sydney Pollack; *D:* Sydney Pollack; *W:* Larry Gelbart, Murray Schisgal, Don McGuire, Owen Roizman; *M:* Dave Grusin. Academy Awards '82: Best Supporting Actress (Lange); British Academy Awards '83: Best Actor (Hoffman); Golden Globe Awards '83: Best Actor—Musical/Comedy (Hoffman), Best Film—Musical/Comedy, Best Supporting Actress (Lange); New York Film Critics Awards '82: Best Director (Pollack), Best Screenplay, Best Supporting Actress (Lange); Writers Guild of America '82: Best Original Screenplay; Nominations: Academy Awards '82: Best Actor (Hoffman), Best Cinematography, Best Director (Pollack), Best Film Editing, Best Original Screenplay, Best Picture, Best Song ("It Might Be You"), Best Sound, Best Supporting Actress (Garr). **VHS, Beta, LV ★★★★**

Top Hat Ginger isn't impressed by Fred's amorous attentions since she's mistaken him for a friend's other half. Many believe it to be the duo's best film together. Choreography by Astaire and score by Berlin makes this one a classic Hollywood musical. Look for a young Lucille Ball as a clerk in a flower shop. ♪ Cheek to Cheek; Top Hat, White Tie and Tails; Isn't This A Lovely Day; The Piccolino; No Strings.
1935 97m/B Fred Astaire, Ginger Rogers, Erik Rhodes, Helen Broderick, Edward Everett Horton, Eric Blore, Lucille Ball; *D:* Mark Sandrich; *W:* Dwight Taylor, Allan Scott; *M:* Irving Berlin, Max Steiner. Nominations: Academy Awards '35: Best Interior Decoration, Best Picture, Best Song ("Cheek to Cheek"). **VHS, Beta, LV, 8mm ★★★★**

Topaze A shy, depressed teacher is fired from his job at a private school and takes a new job, unaware that his boss is using him in a business scam. From the French play by Marcel Pagnol. An American version was also filmed in 1933; Pagnol produced his own version in '51. In French with English subtitles.
1933 92m/B *FR* Louis Jouvet, Edwige Feuillere, Marcel Vallee; *D:* Louis Gasnier;

W: Marcel Pagnol; *M:* Max Steiner. **VHS, Beta ★★★**

Topaze After losing his job, a pathetic school teacher gets involved with the mob and winds up a powerful businessman. Remake of two earlier versions, one French and one American. Based on the play by director Pagnol. In French with English subtitles.
1951 95m/B *FR* Fernandel, Helen Perdriere, Pierre Larquey; *D:* Marcel Pagnol. **VHS ★★★1/2**

Topkapi An international bevy of thieves can't resist the treasures of the famed Topkapi Palace Museum, an impregnable fortress filled with wealth and splendor. Comic thriller based on Erie Ambler's "The Light of Day."
1964 122m/C Melina Mercouri, Maximilian Schell, Peter Ustinov, Robert Morley, Akim Tamiroff; *D:* Jules Dassin; *M:* Manos Hadjidakis. Academy Awards '64: Best Supporting Actor (Ustinov); National Board of Review Awards '64: 10 Best Films of the Year. **VHS, Beta ★★★**

Topper George and Marion Kerby return as ghosts after a fatal car accident, determined to assist their pal Cosmo Topper. Immensely popular at the box office, followed by "Topper Takes a Trip" and "Topper Returns." The series uses trick photography and special effects to complement the comedic scripts. Inspired a television series and remade in 1979 as television movie. Also available colorized.
1937 97m/B Cary Grant, Roland Young, Constance Bennett, Billie Burke, Eugene Pallette, Hoagy Carmichael; *D:* Norman Z. McLeod. Nominations: Academy Awards '37: Best Sound, Best Sound, Best Supporting Actor (Young). **VHS, Beta ★★★1/2**

Topper Returns Cosmo Topper helps ghost find the man who mistakenly murdered her and warns her friend, the intended victim. Humorous conclusion to the trilogy preceded by "Topper" and "Topper Takes a Trip." Followed by a television series. Also available colorized.
1941 87m/B Roland Young, Joan Blondell, Dennis O'Keefe, Carole Landis, Eddie Anderson, H.B. Warner, Billie Burke; *D:* Roy Del Ruth. Nominations: Academy Awards '41: Best Sound. **VHS, Beta, LV ★★★**

Topper Takes a Trip Cosmo Topper and his wife have a falling out and ghosts Kerby help them get back together. The special effects sequences are especially funny. Followed by

"Topper Returns." Also available colorized.

1939 85m/B Constance Bennett, Roland Young, Billie Burke, Franklin Pangborn, Alan Mowbray; **D:** Norman Z. McLeod. Nominations: Academy Awards '39: Best Special Effects. **VHS, Beta ★★★**

Torment Tragic triangle has young woman in love with fellow student and murdered by sadistic teacher. Atmospheric tale hailed by many as Sjoberg's finest film. Ingmar Bergman's first filmed script. In Swedish with English subtitles. **AKA:** Hets; Frenzy.

1944 90m/B SW **D:** Alf Sjoberg; **W:** Ingmar Bergman. **VHS, Beta ★★★**

Tortilla Flat Based on the John Steinbeck novel of the same name, two buddies, Tracy and Garfield, struggle to make their way on the wrong side of the tracks in California. Garfield gets a break by inheriting a couple of houses, Tracy schemes to rip-off a rich, but eccentric, dog owner. In the meantime, both fall for the same girl, Lamarr, in perhaps the finest role of her career. Great performances from all, especially Morgan.

1942 105m/B Spencer Tracy, Hedy Lamarr, John Garfield, Frank Morgan, Akim Tamiroff, Sheldon Leonard, John Qualen, Donald Meek, Connie Gilchrist; **D:** Victor Fleming. Nominations: Academy Awards '42: Best Supporting Actor (Morgan). **VHS ★★★**

Total Recall Mind-bending sci-fi movie set in the 21st century. Construction worker Quaid (Schwarzenegger) dreams every night about the colonization of Mars, so he decides to visit a travel service that specializes in implanting vacation memories into its clients' brains and buy a memory trip to the planet. Only during the implant, Quaid discovers his memories have been artificially altered and he must find out just what's real and what's not. Intriguing plot and spectacular special effects. Laced with graphic violence. Based on Phillip K. Dick's "We Can Remember It For You Wholesale."

1990 (R) 113m/C Arnold Schwarzenegger, Rachel Ticotin, Sharon Stone, Michael Ironside, Ronny Cox, Roy Brocksmith, Marshall Bell, Mel Johnson Jr.; **D:** Paul Verhoeven; **W:** Gary Goldman, Dan O'Bannon; **M:** Jerry Goldsmith. Academy Awards '90: Best Visual Effects; Nominations: Academy Awards '90: Best Sound. **VHS, Beta, LV, 8mm ★★★**

A Touch of Class Married American insurance adjustor working in London plans quick and uncommitted affair but finds his heart doesn't obey the rules. Jackson and Segal create sparkling record of a growing relationship.

1973 (PG) 105m/C George Segal, Glenda Jackson, Paul Sorvino, Hildegarde Neil, K. Callan, Mary Barclay, Cec Linder; **D:** Melvin Frank; **W:** Jack Rose. Academy Awards '73: Best Actress (Jackson); Golden Globe Awards '74: Best Actor—Musical/Comedy (Segal), Best Actress—Musical/Comedy (Jackson); Nominations: Academy Awards '73: Best Picture, Best Song ("All That Love Went to Waste"), Best Story & Screenplay, Best Original Score. **VHS, Beta ★★★**

Touch of Evil Stark, perverse story of murder, kidnapping and police corruption in Mexican border town. Welles portrays a police chief who invents evidence to convict the guilty. Filled with innovative photography reminiscent of "Citizen Kane," as filmed by Russell Metty.

1958 108m/B Charlton Heston, Orson Welles, Janet Leigh, Joseph Calleia, Akim Tamiroff, Marlene Dietrich, Valentin de Vargas, Dennis Weaver, Zsa Zsa Gabor, Mort Mills, Victor Milian, Joanna Moore, Joi Lansing; **Cameos:** Ray Collins, Mercedes McCambridge, Joseph Cotten; **D:** Orson Welles; **W:** Orson Welles; **M:** Henry Mancini. **VHS, Beta, LV ★★★★**

Tous les Matins du Monde Haunting tale of two 17th-century French baroque composers and their relationship with each other and their music. Gerard Depardieu plays Marin Marais, who eventually becomes a court composer at Versailles. As a young man, he studies under Sainte Colombe, a private and soulful musician, about whom little is known even today. Depardieu's son Guillaume (in his film debut) plays the young Marais, who startles the quiet Sainte Colombe home and has an affair with one of his daughters (Brochet). Filmmaker Corneau lends a quiet austere tone which parallels the life and music of Sainte Colombe. In French with English subtitles. **AKA:** All the Mornings of the World.

1992 114m/C FR Gerard Depardieu, Guillaume Depardieu, Jean-Pierre Marielle, Anne Brochet, Caroline Sihol, Carole Richert, Violaine Lacroix, Nadege Teron, Miriam Boyer, Michel Bouquet; **D:** Alain Corneau; **W:** Pascal Quignard, Alain Corneau; **M:** Jordi Savall, Yves Angelo. Cesar Awards '92: Best Cinematography, Best Director (Corneau), Best Film, Best Supporting Actress (Brochet), Best Score. **VHS, LV ★★★**

Toute Une Nuit Assorted people stumble melodramatically in and out of one another's lives on steamy summer night in Brussels. Fine combination of avant-garde technique and narrative. In French with English subtitles. *AKA:* All Night Long.
1982 90m/C *BE FR* Aurore Clement, Tcheky Karyo, Veronique Silver, Angelo Abazoglou, Natalia Ackerman; *D:* Chantal Akerman; *W:* Andra Akers. **VHS** ★★★

Toy Story First feature length, wholly computer animated film confirms what we suspected all along—toys do have lives of their own when we're not around. Pull-string cowboy Woody (Hanks), as favorite toy, presides over his fellow playthings in Andy's room. Enter new toy on the block, Buzz Lightyear (Allen), a space ranger action figure who thinks he's real. Jealous Woody and his delusional, high-tech companion soon find themselves in the outside world, where they must join forces to survive. Funny, intelligent script and voice characterizations that rival many live-action movies in depth and emotion. All this, and Don Rickles berating an actual hockey puck.
1995 (G) 80m/C *D:* John Lasseter; *W:* Joss Whedon, Joel Cohen, Alec Sokolow; *M:* Randy Newman; *V:* Tom Hanks, Tim Allen, Annie Potts, John Ratzenberger, Wallace Shawn, Jim Varney, Don Rickles, John Morris, R. Lee Ermey, Laurie Metcalf, Erik von Detten. Nominations: Academy Awards '95: Best Screenplay, Best Song ("You've Got a Friend in Me"), Best Score; Golden Globe Awards '96: Best Film—Musical/Comedy, Best Song ("You Got a Friend in Me"). **VHS** ★★★★

The Train During the German occupation of Paris in 1944, a German general (Scofield) is ordered to ransack the city of its art treasures and put them on a train bound for Germany. Word gets to the French Resistance who then persuade the train inspector (Lancaster) to sabotage the train. A battle of wills ensues between Scofield and Lancaster as each becomes increasingly obsessed in outwitting the other—though the cost to all turns out to be as irreplaceable as the art itself. Filmed on location in France. Frankenheimer used real locomotives, rather than models, throughout the film, even in the spectacular crash sequences. *AKA:* Le Train; Il Treno.
1965 133m/C Burt Lancaster, Paul Scofield, Jeanne Moreau, Michel Simon, Suzanne Flon, Wolfgang Preiss, Albert Remy; *D:* John Frankenheimer; *W:* Frank Davis, Walter Bernstein; *M:* Maurice Jarre. Nominations: Academy Awards '65: Best Story & Screenplay. **VHS, LV** ★★★★

Trainspotting From the same team who offered the violently comedic "Shallow Grave," comes an equally destructive look at a group of Edinburgh junkies and losers. Heroin-user Mark Renton (McGregor) once again decides to get off junk but to do so he has to get away from his friends: knife-wielding psycho Begbie (Carlyle), Sick Boy (Miller), Spud (Bremner), and Tommy (McKidd). He heads for a semi-respectable life in London, but Begbie and Spud wind up involving him in a serious money drug deal that spells trouble. Strong fantasy visuals depict drug highs and lows, while heavy Scottish accents (and humor) may prove difficult. Based on the 1993 cult novel by Irvine Welsh. Film drew much controversy for supposedly being pro-heroin but the junkie's life is hardly portrayed as being attractive in any way.
1995 (R) 94m/C *GB* Ewan McGregor, Ewen Bremner, Jonny Lee Miller, Robert Carlyle, Kevin McKidd, Kelly Macdonald, Shirley Henderson, Pauline Lynch; *D:* Danny Boyle; *W:* John Hodge. British Academy Awards '95: Best Adapted Screenplay; Nominations: Australian Film Institute '96: Best Foreign Film; British Academy Awards '95: Best Film; Independent Spirit Awards '97: Best Foreign Film. **VHS, LV** ★★★

Trapeze Lancaster is a former trapeze artist, now lame from a triple somersault accident. Curtis, the son of an old friend, wants Lancaster to teach him the routine. Lollobrigida, an aerial acrobat, is interested in both men. Exquisite European locations, fine camera work. The actors perform their own stunts.
1956 105m/C Burt Lancaster, Tony Curtis, Gina Lollobrigida, Katy Jurado, Thomas Gomez; *D:* Carol Reed; *M:* Malcolm Arnold. **VHS, Beta, LV** ★★★

Treasure Island Fleming's adaptation of Robert Louis Stevenson's eighteenth century English pirate tale of Long John Silver is a classic. Beery is great as the pirate; Cooper has trouble playing the boy. Also available colorized. Multitudinous remakes.
1934 102m/B Wallace Beery, Jackie Cooper, Lionel Barrymore, Lewis Stone, Otto Kruger, Douglass Dumbrille, Chic Sale, Nigel Bruce; *D:* Victor Fleming. **VHS, Beta, LV** ★★★½

Treasure Island Spine-tingling Robert Louis Stevenson tale of pirates and buried treasure, in which young cabin boy Jim Hawkins matches wits with Long John Silver. Some editions excise extra violence. Stevenson's ending is revised. Full Disney treatment, excellent casting.

1950 (PG) 96m/C Bobby Driscoll, Robert Newton, Basil Sydney, Walter Fitzgerald, Denis O'Dea, Ralph Truman, Finlay Currie; **D:** Byron Haskin, Frederick A. (Freddie) Young. **VHS, Beta, LV** ★★★★

Treasure of the Sierra Madre Three prospectors in search of gold in Mexico find suspicion, treachery and greed. Bogart is superbly believable as the paranoid, and ultimately homicidal, Fred C. Dobbs. Huston directed his father and wrote the screenplay, based on a B. Traven story.

1948 126m/B Humphrey Bogart, Walter Huston, Tim Holt, Bruce (Herman Brix) Bennett, Barton MacLane, Robert (Bobby) Blake, Alfonso Bedoya; **D:** John Huston; **W:** John Huston; **M:** Max Steiner. Academy Awards '48: Best Director (Huston), Best Screenplay, Best Supporting Actor (Huston); National Board of Review Awards '48: 10 Best Films of the Year, Best Actor (Huston); Nominations: Academy Awards '48: Best Picture. **VHS, Beta, LV** ★★★★

A Tree Grows in Brooklyn Sensitive young Irish lass growing up in turn-of-the-century Brooklyn tries to rise above her tenement existence. Based on the novel by Betty Smith. Kazan's directorial debut.

1945 (PG) 128m/B Peggy Ann Garner, James Dunn, Dorothy McGuire, Joan Blondell, Lloyd Nolan, Ted Donaldson, James Gleason, John Alexander, Charles Halton; **D:** Elia Kazan; **M:** Alfred Newman. Academy Awards '45: Best Supporting Actor (Dunn); National Board of Review Awards '45: 10 Best Films of the Year; Nominations: Academy Awards '45: Best Screenplay. **VHS, Beta, LV** ★★★1/2

The Tree of Wooden Clogs Epic view of the lives of four peasant families working on an estate in turn of the century Northern Italy. The title comes from the shoes the peasants wear. When a young boy breaks a shoe, his father risks punishment by cutting down one of his landlord's trees to make a new pair of clogs. Slow moving and beautiful, from former industrial filmmaker Olmi. In Italian with English subtitles. **AKA:** L'Albero Degli Zoccoli.

1978 185m/C *IT* Luigi Ornaghi, Francesca Moriggi, Omar Brignoli, Antonio Ferrari; **D:** Ermanno Olmi; **W:** Ermanno Olmi. Cannes Film Festival '78: Best Film; New York Film Critics Awards '79: Best Foreign Film. **VHS, Beta, LV** ★★★★

The Trial Expressionistic Welles adaptation of classic Kafka novella about an innocent man accused, tried, and convicted of an unknown crime in an unnamed exaggeratedly bureaucratic country. Another Welles project that met with constant disaster in production, with many lapses in continuity. **AKA:** Le Proces; Der Prozess; Il Processo.

1963 118m/B *FR* Anthony Perkins, Jeanne Moreau, Orson Welles, Romy Schneider, Akim Tamiroff, Elsa Martinelli; **D:** Orson Welles. **VHS, Beta** ★★★1/2

Tribute to a Bad Man Hard-nosed rancher Cagney will stop at nothing to retain his worldly possessions in this 1870s Colorado territory western. His ruthless behavior drives girlfriend Papas into the arms of hired hand Dubbins. Spencer Tracy and Grace Kelly were originally cast for the roles of Jeremy Rodock and Jocasta Constantine, but Kelly backed out and Tracy was fired due to differences with director Wise. Based on the short story by Jack Schaefer.

1956 95m/C James Cagney, Don Dubbins, Stephen McNally, Irene Papas, Vic Morrow, Royal Dano, Lee Van Cleef, James Griffith, Onslow Stevens, James Bell, Jeanette Nolan, Bud Osborne, Tom London, Dennis Moore, Buddy Roosevelt, Carl Pitti; **D:** Robert Wise; **W:** Michael Blankfort; **M:** Miklos Rozsa. **VHS** ★★★

The Trip to Bountiful An elderly widow, unhappy living in her son's fancy modern home, makes a pilgrimage back to her childhood home in Bountiful, Texas. Based on the Horton Foote play. Fine acting with Oscar-winning performance from Page.

1985 (PG) 102m/C Geraldine Page, Rebecca DeMornay, John Heard, Carlin Glynn, Richard Bradford; **D:** Peter Masterson; **W:** Horton Foote, Fred Murphy. Academy Awards '85: Best Actress (Page); Independent Spirit Awards '86: Best Actress (Page), Best Screenplay; National Media Owl Awards '87: First Prize; Nominations: Academy Awards '85: Best Adapted Screenplay. **VHS, Beta, LV, 8mm** ★★★

Tristana Allegorical tale of a beautiful girl (Deneuve) who moves in with a hypocritical benefactor following the death of her mother. She is quickly exploited and seduced by the one who would protect her, but runs away with an artist in pursuit of love. Searing in its commentary on Catholicism, death, lust, and the woebegone place of humanity in the world, the movie is also widely seen as a depiction of fascist Spain's attempt to find its place in the twentieth century. Based on the novel by Benito Perez Galdos. In Spanish with English subtitles.

1970 (PG) 98m/C *SP IT FR* Catherine Deneuve, Fernando Rey, Franco Nero, Lola Gaos, Antonio Casas, Jesus Fernandez, Vincent Solder; *D:* Luis Bunuel; *W:* Luis Bunuel. **VHS** ★★★★

Trois Couleurs: Blanc Bittersweet comedic rags-to-riches tale spiced with revenge and lasting love. "White" focuses on equality and begins when a bewildered Polish hairdresser is divorced by his disdainful French wife, who takes him for everything he has. Returning to his family in Poland, Karol doggedly works his way into wealth. Then he decides to fake his death and leave his fortune to the ex he still loves—or does he? In Polish and French with English subtitles. Part 2 of Kieslowski's trilogy, following "Trois Couleurs: Bleu" and followed by "Trois Couleurs: Rouge." *AKA:* White; Three Colors: White. **1994 (R) 92m/C** *FR SI PL* Zbigniew Zamachowski, Julie Delpy, Janusz Gajos, Jerzy Stuhr; *Cameos:* Juliette Binoche, Florence Pernel; *D:* Krzysztof Kieslowski; *W:* Krzysztof Piesiewicz. Berlin International Film Festival '94: Best Director (Kieslowski). **VHS** ★★★

Trois Couleurs: Bleu First installment of director Kieslowski's trilogy inspired by the French tricolor flag. "Blue" stands for liberty—here freedom is based on tragedy as Julie (Binoche) reshapes her life after surviving an accident which killed her famous composer husband and their young daughter. Excellent performance by Binoche, which relies on the internalized grief and brief emotion which flits across her face rather than overwhelming displays for expression. In French with English subtitles. *AKA:* Three Colors: Blue; Blue. **1993 (R) 98m/C** *FR* Juliette Binoche, Benoit Regent, Florence Pernel, Charlotte Very; *Cameos:* Emmanuelle Riva; *D:* Krzysztof Kieslowski; *W:* Krzysztof Piesiewicz, Krzysztof Kieslowski, Slawomir Idziak. Cesar Awards '94: Best Actress (Binoche), Best Film Editing, Best Sound; Los Angeles Film Critics Association Awards '93: Best Score; Venice Film Festival '93: Best Actress (Binoche), Best Film; Nominations: Golden Globe Awards '94: Best Actress—Drama (Binoche), Best Foreign Language Film, Best Original Score. **VHS, LV** ★★★

Trois Couleurs: Rouge "Red" is for fraternity in the French tricolor flag and, in director Kieslowski's last film in his trilogy, emotional connections are made between unlikely couples. There's law student Auguste and his girlfriend Karin, young fashion model Valentine, and a nameless retired judge, brought together by circumstance and destined to change each other's lives. Subtle details make for careful viewing but it's a rewarding watch and a visual treat (keep an eye on cinematographer Sobocinski's use of the color red). Binoche and Delpy, who starred in the earlier films, also make an appearance, as Kieslowski uses the finale to tie up loose ends. In French with English subtitles. *AKA:* Three Colors: Red; Red. **1994 (R) 99m/C** *FR PL SI* Irene Jacob, Jean-Louis Trintignant, Frederique Feder, Jean-Pierre Lorit; *Cameos:* Juliette Binoche, Julie Delpy, Benoit Regent, Zbigniew Zamachowski; *D:* Krzysztof Kieslowski; *W:* Krzysztof Kieslowski, Krzysztof Piesiewicz; *M:* Zbigniew Preisner, Piotr Sobocinski. Cesar Awards '94: Best Score; Independent Spirit Awards '95: Best Foreign Film; Los Angeles Film Critics Association Awards '94: Best Foreign Film; New York Film Critics Awards '94: Best Foreign Film; National Society of Film Critics Awards '94: Best Foreign Film; Nominations: Academy Awards '94: Best Cinematography, Best Director (Kieslowski), Best Original Screenplay; Cesar Awards '94: Best Actor (Trintignant), Best Actress (Jacob), Best Director (Kieslowski), Best Film; Golden Globe Awards '95: Best Foreign Language Film. **VHS, LV** ★★★½

Tropic of Cancer Based on Henry Miller's once-banned, now classic novel, this film portrays the sexual escapades of the expatriate author living in 1920s Paris. Torn stars as the carefree, loose-living writer and Burstyn plays his disgusted wife. **1970 (NC-17) 87m/C** Rip Torn, James Callahan, Ellen Burstyn, David Bauer, Phil Brown; *D:* Joseph Strick. **VHS** ★★★

Trouble in Mind Stylized romance is set in the near future in a run-down diner. Kristofferson is an ex-cop who gets involved in the lives of a young couple looking for a better life. Look for Divine in one of her/his rare appearances outside of John Waters' works. **1986 (R) 111m/C** Kris Kristofferson, Keith Carradine, Genevieve Bujold, Lori Singer, Divine, Joe Morton, George Kirby, John Considine; *D:* Alan Rudolph; *W:* Alan Rudolph. Independent Spirit Awards '86: Best Cinematography. **VHS, Beta, LV, 8mm** ★★★

The Trouble with Harry When a little boy finds a dead body in a Vermont town, it causes all kinds of problems for the community. No one is sure who killed Harry and what to do with

the body. MacLaine's film debut and Herrmann's first musical score for Hitchcock.
1955 (PG) 90m/C John Forsythe, Shirley MacLaine, Edmund Gwenn, Jerry Mathers, Mildred Dunnock, Mildred Natwick, Royal Dano; **D:** Alfred Hitchcock; **W:** John Michael Hayes; **M:** Bernard Herrmann. **VHS, Beta, LV** ★★★

True Confessions Tale of corruption pits two brothers, one a priest and the other a detective, against each other. Nice 1940s period look, with excellent performances from De Niro and Duvall. Based on a true case from the John Gregory Dunne novel.
1981 (R) 110m/C Robert De Niro, Robert Duvall, Kenneth McMillan, Charles Durning, Cyril Cusack, Ed Flanders, Burgess Meredith, Louisa Moritz; **D:** Ulu Grosbard; **W:** John Gregory Dunne, Joan Didion; **M:** Georges Delerue, Owen Roizman. **VHS, Beta, LV** ★★★

True Grit Hard-drinking U.S. Marshal Rooster Cogburn (Wayne) is hired by a young girl (Darby) to find her father's killer. Won Wayne his only Oscar. Based on the Charles Portis novel. Prompted sequel, "Rooster Cogburn."
1969 (G) 128m/C John Wayne, Glen Campbell, Kim Darby, Robert Duvall; **D:** Henry Hathaway; **M:** Elmer Bernstein. Academy Awards '69: Best Actor (Wayne); Golden Globe Awards '70: Best Actor—Drama (Wayne); National Board of Review Awards '69: 10 Best Films of the Year; Nominations: Academy Awards '69: Best Song ("True Grit"). **VHS, Beta, LV** ★★★

True Love Low-budget, savagely observed comedy follows the family and community events leading up to a Bronx Italian wedding. Authentic slice-of-life about two young people with very different ideas about what marriage and commitment mean. Acclaimed script and performances.
1989 (R) 104m/C Annabella Sciorra, Ron Eldard, Aida Turturro, Roger Rignack, Michael J. Wolfe, Star Jasper, Kelly Cinnante, Rick Shapiro, Suzanne Costallos, Vinny Pastore; **D:** Nancy Savoca; **W:** Nancy Savoca, Richard Guay. Sundance Film Festival '89: Grand Jury Prize. **VHS, Beta, LV** ★★★

True Stories Quirky, amusing look at the eccentric denizens of a fictional, off-center Texas town celebrating its 150th anniversary. Notable are Kurtz as the Laziest Woman in America and Goodman as a blushing suitor. Directorial debut of Byrne. Worth a look.
1986 (PG) 89m/C David Byrne, John Goodman, Swoosie Kurtz, Spalding Gray, Annie McEnroe, Pops Staples, Tito Larriva;

D: David Byrne; **W:** David Byrne, Beth Henley; **M:** David Byrne. **VHS, Beta, LV** ★★★1/2

Truly, Madly, Deeply The recent death of her lover drives a young woman into despair and anger, until he turns up at her apartment one day. Tender and well-written tale of love and the supernatural, with believable characters and plotline. Playwright Minghella's directorial debut.
1991 (PG) 107m/C Juliet Stevenson, Alan Rickman, Bill Paterson, Michael Maloney, Christopher Rozycki, Keith Bartlett, David Ryall, Stella Maris; **D:** Anthony Minghella; **W:** Anthony Minghella. Australian Film Institute '92: Best Foreign Film; British Academy Awards '91: Best Original Screenplay. **VHS** ★★★

The Truth About Cats and Dogs Funny, intelligent Abby (Garofalo) hosts a popular radio call-in show for pet lovers. When a handsome Brit photographer (Chaplin) phones in with a Great Dane problem, he becomes intrigued by her voice and asks for a date. Insecure about her looks, Abby asks her beautiful-but-dim girlfriend Noelle (Thurman) to fill in. Naturally, both women fall for the shy Englishman. Charming, updated version of "Cyrano de Bergerac" theme works because of strong lead performances, especially Garofalo, who steals the show with her dry, self-effacing wit. Entertaining romantic comedy features some nice scenes of Santa Monica too.
1996 (PG-13) 97m/C Janeane Garofalo, Uma Thurman, Ben Chaplin, Jamie Foxx, Richard Coca, Stanley DeSantis; **D:** Michael Lehmann. **VHS, LV** ★★★

Tucker: The Man and His Dream Portrait of Preston Tucker, entrepreneur and industrial idealist, who in 1946 tried to build the car of the future and was effectively run out of business by the powers-that-were. Ravishing, ultra-nostalgic lullaby to the American Dream. Watch for Jeff's dad, Lloyd, in a bit role.
1988 (PG) 111m/C Jeff Bridges, Martin Landau, Dean Stockwell, Frederic Forrest, Mako, Joan Allen, Christian Slater, Lloyd Bridges, Elias Koteas, Nina Siemaszko, Corin "Corky" Nemec, Marshall Bell, Don Novello, Peter Donat, Dean Goodman, Patti Austin; **D:** Francis Ford Coppola; **W:** Arnold Schulman, David Seidler; **M:** Joe Jackson, Carmine Coppola. Golden Globe Awards '89: Best Supporting Actor (Landau); New York Film Critics Awards '88: Best Supporting Actor (Stockwell); Nominations: Academy Awards '88: Best Art Direction/Set Decoration, Best

Costume Design, Best Supporting Actor (Landau). **VHS, Beta, LV, 8mm ★★★**

Tumbleweeds William S. Hart's last western. Portrays the last great land rush in America, the opening of the Cherokee Strip in the Oklahoma Territory to homesteaders. Preceded by a sound prologue, made in 1939, in which Hart speaks for the only time on screen, to introduce the story. Silent, with musical score.
1925 114m/B William S. Hart, Lucien Littlefield, Barbara Bedford; **D:** King Baggott. **VHS, Beta, LV ★★★**

Tunes of Glory Guinness and Mills are wonderful in this well made film about a brutal, sometimes lazy colonel and a disciplined and educated man moving up through the ranks of the British military. York's film debut. From the novel by James Kennaway, who adapted it for the screen. Laserdisc version contains interview with director Neame.
1960 107m/C GB Alec Guinness, John Mills, Dennis Price, Kay Walsh, Susannah York; **D:** Ronald Neame; **M:** Malcolm Arnold. Nominations: Academy Awards '60: Best Adapted Screenplay. **VHS, Beta, LV ★★★1/2**

Turtle Diary Two lonely Londoners collaborate to free giant turtles from the city aquarium with the aid of a zookeeper, and the turtles' freedom somehow frees them as well. Jackson and Kingsley are stunning. Adapted by Harold Pinter from the Russell Hoban book.
1986 (PG) 90m/C GB Ben Kingsley, Glenda Jackson, Richard Johnson, Michael Gambon, Rosemary Leach, Jeroen Krabbe, Eleanor Bron; **D:** John Irvin; **W:** Harold Pinter; **M:** Geoffrey Burgon. **VHS, Beta, LV ★★★**

The Tuskegee Airmen Cable drama based on the formation and WWII achievements of the U.S. Army Air Corps' first squadron of black combat fighter pilots, the "Fighting 99th" of the 332nd Fighter Group. They were nicknamed after the segregated military outpost where they trained in Tuskegee, Alabama, and distinguished themselves in combat, never losing a single bomber, and receiving more than 800 medals. Cast all do a fine job in what turns out to essentially be a standard action/war movie. Based on a story by former Tuskegee airman, Robert W. Williams.
1995 (PG-13) 107m/C Laurence "Larry" Fishburne, Cuba Gooding Jr., Allen Payne, Malcolm Jamal Warner, Courtney B. Vance, Andre Braugher, John Lithgow, Rosemary Murphy, Christopher McDonald; **D:** Robert Markowitz; **W:** Paris Qualles, Ron Hutchinson, Trey Ellis; **M:** Lee Holdridge. **VHS ★★★**

Twelve Angry Men Fonda sounds the voice of reason as a jury inclines toward a quick-and-dirty verdict against a boy on trial. Excellent ensemble work. Lumet's feature film debut, based on a television play by Reginald Rose.
1957 95m/B Henry Fonda, Martin Balsam, Lee J. Cobb, E.G. Marshall, Jack Klugman, Robert Webber, Ed Begley Sr., John Fiedler, Jack Warden, George Voskovec, Edward Binns, Joseph Sweeney; **D:** Sidney Lumet; **W:** Reginald Rose. Berlin International Film Festival '57: Golden Berlin Bear; British Academy Awards '57: Best Actor (Fonda); Edgar Allan Poe Awards '57: Best Screenplay; National Board of Review Awards '57: 10 Best Films of the Year; Nominations: Academy Awards '57: Best Adapted Screenplay, Best Director (Lumet), Best Picture. **VHS, Beta, LV ★★★★**

Twelve Chairs Take-off on Russian folktale first filmed in Yugoslavia in 1927. A rich matron admits on her deathbed that she has hidden her jewels in the upholstery of one of twelve chairs that are no longer in her home. A Brooksian treasure hunt ensues.
1970 (PG) 94m/C Mel Brooks, Dom DeLuise, Frank Langella, Ron Moody, Bridget Brice; **D:** Mel Brooks; **W:** Mel Brooks. **VHS, Beta, LV ★★★**

12 Monkeys Forty years after a plague wipes out 99 percent of the human population and sends the survivors underground, scientists send prisoner James Cole (Willis) to the 1990s to investigate the connection between the virus and seriously deranged fanatic Jeffrey Goines (Pitt), whose father happens to be a renowned virologist. Director Gilliam's demented vision is a bit tougher and less capricious than usual, and the convoluted plot and accumulated detail require a keen attention span, but as each piece of the puzzle falls into place the story becomes a fascinating sci-fi spectacle. Pitt drops the pretty-boy image with a nutzoid performance that'll make revelers stop swooning in a heartbeat. Inspired by the 1962 French short "La Jetee."
1995 (R) 131m/C Bruce Willis, Madeleine Stowe, Brad Pitt, Christopher Plummer, David Morse, Frank Gorshin, John Seda; **D:** Terry Gilliam; **W:** David Peoples, Janet Peoples; **M:** Paul Buckmaster. Golden Globe Awards '96: Best Supporting Actor (Pitt); Nominations: Academy Awards '95:

Best Supporting Actor (Pitt), Best Costume Design; MTV Movie Awards '96: Best Male Performance (Pitt). **VHS, LV ★★★**

Twelve O'Clock High Epic drama about the heroic 8th Air Force, with Peck as bomber-group commander sent to shape up a hard-luck group, forced to drive himself and his men to the breaking point. Compelling dramatization of the strain of military command. Includes impressive footage of actual WWII battles. Best-ever flying fortress movie.
1949 132m/B Gregory Peck, Hugh Marlowe, Gary Merrill, Millard Mitchell, Dean Jagger, Paul Stewart; **D:** Henry King. Academy Awards '49: Best Sound, Best Supporting Actor (Jagger); Nominations: Academy Awards '49: Best Actor (Peck), Best Picture; New York Film Critics Awards '50: Best Actor (Peck). **VHS, Beta, LV ★★★1/2**

Twentieth Century Maniacal Broadway director Barrymore transforms shop girl Lombard into a smashing success adored by public and press. Tired of Barrymore's manic-excessive ways, she heads for the Hollywood hills, pursued by the Profile in fine form.
1934 91m/B Carole Lombard, John Barrymore, Walter Connolly, Roscoe Karns, Edgar Kennedy, Ralph Forbes, Charles Lane, Etienne Girardot, Snow Flake; **D:** Howard Hawks; **W:** Charles MacArthur, Ben Hecht. **Beta ★★★★**

20,000 Leagues Under the Sea From a futuristic submarine, Captain Nemo wages war on the surface world. A shipwrecked scientist and sailor do their best to thwart Nemo's dastardly schemes. Buoyant Disney version of the Jules Verne fantasy.
1954 127m/C Kirk Douglas, James Mason, Peter Lorre, Paul Lukas, Robert J. Wilke, Carleton Young; **D:** Richard Fleischer. Academy Awards '54: Best Art Direction/Set Decoration (Color), Best Special Effects; National Board of Review Awards '54: 10 Best Films of the Year; Nominations: Academy Awards '54: Best Film Editing. **VHS, Beta, LV ★★★1/2**

21 Hours at Munich Made-for-TV treatment of the massacre of Israeli athletes by Arab terrorists at the 1972 Olympics. Well-done. The film was produced using the actual Munich locations.
1976 100m/C William Holden, Shirley Knight, William Knight, Franco Nero, Anthony Quayle, Noel Willman; **D:** William A. Graham. **VHS ★★★**

25 Fireman's Street An evocative drama about the residents of an old

house in Hungary which is about to be torn down, and their evening of remembrances of life before, during and after WWII. In Hungarian with English subtitles.
1973 97m/C Rita Bekes, Peter Muller, Lucyna Winnicka; **D:** Istvan Szabo. **VHS, Beta ★★★**

Twice in a Lifetime Middle-aged man takes stock of his life when he's attracted to Ann-Margret. Realizing he's married in name only, he moves in with his new love while his former wife and children struggle with shock, disbelief, and anger. Well-acted, realistic, and unsentimental.
1985 (R) 117m/C Gene Hackman, Ellen Burstyn, Amy Madigan, Ann-Margret, Brian Dennehy, Ally Sheedy; **D:** Bud Yorkin; **W:** Colin Welland. **VHS, Beta, LV ★★★**

Twist & Shout Sequel to the popular Danish import "Zappa," in which two teenage lovers discover sex and rock and roll. Transcends the teens discovering sex genre. In Danish with English subtitles. Profanity, nudity, and sex. **AKA:** Hab Og Karlighed.
1984 (R) 107m/C DK Lars Simonsen, Adam Tonsberg, Ulrikke Juul Bondo, Camilla Soeberg; **D:** Bille August; **W:** Bille August. **VHS, Beta ★★★**

Two Daughters Director Ray wrote the scripts for two stories based on the writings of Nobel Prize—winner Rabindranath Tagore, one about the relationship between an orphan and a postman, the other about a young man who declines to marry the girl arranged to be his intended. In Hindi with English subtitles. **AKA:** Teen Kanya.
1961 114m/B IN **D:** Satyajit Ray; **W:** Satyajit Ray. **VHS, Beta ★★★**

Two English Girls A pre-WWI French lad, with a possessive mother, loves two English sisters, one an impassioned, reckless artist, the other a repressed spinster. Tenderly delineates the triangle's interrelating love and friendship over seven years. Based on the novel "Les Deux Anglaises et le Continent" by Henri-Pierre Roche. In French with English subtitles. **AKA:** Les Deux Anglaises et le Continent.
1972 (R) 108m/C FR Jean-Pierre Leaud, Kika Markham, Stacey Tendeter, Sylvia Marriott, Marie Mansert, Philippe Leotard; **D:** Francois Truffaut; **M:** Georges Delerue. **VHS, Beta, LV ★★★1/2**

Two-Faced Woman Garbo, in her last film, attempts a ruse when she finds her husband may be interested in an old flame. Pretending to be her twin sister in an attempt to lure Dou-

glas away from the other woman, she's fooled a little herself. Romantic comedy unfortunately miscasts Garbo as an Americanized ski bunny.
1941 90m/B Greta Garbo, Melvyn Douglas, Constance Bennett, Roland Young, Ruth Gordon, Robert Sterling, George Cleveland, Frances Carson; **D:** George Cukor. **VHS, Beta ★★★**

Two for the Road After over a decade of marriage, Finney and Hepburn look back and find only fragments of their relationship. Mancini score adds poignancy to the couple's reflections on their stormy life. Touching and well-acted.
1967 112m/C Audrey Hepburn, Albert Finney, Eleanor Bron, William Daniels, Claude Dauphin, Nadia Gray, Jacqueline Bisset; **D:** Stanley Donen; **W:** Frederic Raphael; **M:** Henry Mancini. Nominations: Academy Awards '67: Best Story & Screenplay. **VHS, LV ★★★1/2**

Two for the Seesaw Mitchum stars as a Nebraska attorney who comes to New York and gets involved with MacLaine. Humorous and touching comedy-drama worked better on stage, because the large screen magnified the talkiness of Gibson's play. Unusual casting of Mitchum as a Midwest lawyer and MacLaine as a New York Jewish bohemian.
1962 119m/B Robert Mitchum, Shirley MacLaine, Edmond Ryan, Elisabeth Fraser, Eddie Firestone, Billy Gray, Vic Lundin; **D:** Robert Wise; **W:** Isobel Lennart; **M:** Andre Previn. Nominations: Academy Awards '62: Best Black and White Cinematography, Best Song ("Song from Two for the Seesaw (Second Chance)"). **VHS, LV ★★★**

Two Mules for Sister Sara American mercenary in 19th-century Mexico gets mixed up with a cigar-smoking nun and the two make plans to capture a French garrison. MacLaine and Eastwood are great together. Based on a Boetticher story.
1970 (PG) 105m/C Clint Eastwood, Shirley MacLaine; **D:** Donald Siegel; **W:** Albert Maltz; **M:** Ennio Morricone. **VHS, Beta ★★★**

2001: A Space Odyssey Space voyage to Jupiter turns chaotic when a computer, HAL 9000, takes over. Seen by some as a mirror of man's historical use of machinery and by others as a grim vision of the future, the special effects and music are still stunning. Critically acclaimed and well accepted by some, simply confusing to others. Martin Balsam originally recorded the voice of HAL, but was replaced by Rain. From Arthur C. Clarke's novel "The Sen-

tinel." Followed by a sequel, "2010: The Year We Make Contact." Laserdisc edition is presented in letterbox format and features a special supplementary section on the making of "2001," a montage of images from the film, production documents, memos, and photos. Also included on the disc is a NASA film entitled "Art and Reality," which offers footage from the Voyager I and II flybys of Jupiter.
1968 139m/C *GB* Keir Dullea, Gary Lockwood, William Sylvester, Dan Richter; **D:** Stanley Kubrick; **W:** Arthur C. Clarke, Stanley Kubrick; **V:** Douglas Rain. Academy Awards '68: Best Visual Effects; National Board of Review Awards '68: 10 Best Films of the Year; Nominations: Academy Awards '68: Best Art Direction/Set Decoration, Best Director (Kubrick), Best Story & Screenplay. **VHS, Beta, LV ★★★★**

Two Women A mother and her 13-year-old daughter travel war-torn Italy during WWII and must survive lack of food, crazed monks and brutal soldiers. Tragic, moving, well-directed. Loren received well-deserved Oscar. In Italian with English subtitles or dubbed. **AKA:** La Ciociara.
1961 99m/B *IT* Sophia Loren, Raf Vallone, Eleonora Brown, Jean-Paul Belmondo; **D:** Vittorio De Sica; **W:** Cesare Zavattini, Vittorio De Sica; **M:** Armando Trovajoli. Academy Awards '61: Best Actress (Loren); British Academy Awards '61: Best Actress (Loren); Cannes Film Festival '61: Best Actress (Loren); Golden Globe Awards '62: Best Foreign Film; National Board of Review Awards '61: 5 Best Foreign Films of the Year; New York Film Critics Awards '61: Best Actress (Loren). **VHS, Beta ★★★★**

Ugetsu The classic film that established Mizoguchi's reputation outside of Japan. Two 16th-century Japanese peasants venture from their homes in pursuit of dreams, and encounter little more than their own hapless folly and a bit of the supernatural. A wonderful mix of comedy and action with nifty camera movement. Based on the stories of Akinara Ueda. In Japanese with English subtitles. **AKA:** Ugetsu Monogatari.
1953 96m/B *JP* Machiko Kyo, Masayuki Mori, Kinuyo Tanaka, Sakae Ozawa; **D:** Kenji Mizoguchi. Venice Film Festival '53: Silver Prize; Nominations: Academy Awards '55: Best Costume Design (B & W). **VHS, Beta, LV, 8mm ★★★1/2**

Ulzana's Raid An aging scout and an idealistic cavalry lieutenant lock horns on their way to battling a vicious Apache chieftain. A violent, gritty western that enjoyed critical reevaluation years after its first release.

1972 (R) 103m/C Burt Lancaster, Bruce Davison, Richard Jaeckel, Lloyd Bochner, Jorge Luke; **D:** Robert Aldrich. **VHS, Beta, LV** ★★★

Umberto D A government pensioner, living alone with his beloved dog, struggles to keep up a semblance of dignity on his inadequate pension. De Sica considered this his masterpiece. A sincere, tender treatment of the struggles involved with the inevitability of aging. In Italian with English subtitles. Laser edition features letterboxed print.

1955 89m/B *IT* Carlo Battista, Maria Pia Casilio, Lina Gennari; **D:** Vittorio De Sica; **W:** Cesare Zavattini, Vittorio De Sica. New York Film Critics Awards '55: Best Foreign Film; Nominations: Academy Awards '56: Best Story. **VHS, Beta, LV, 8mm** ★★★★

Umbrellas of Cherbourg A bittersweet film operetta with no spoken dialogue. Deneuve is the teenage daughter of a widow who owns an umbrella shop. She and her equally young boyfriend are separated by his military duty in Algeria. Finding she is pregnant, the girl marries a wealthy man, and her former lover returns, he too marries someone else. But when they meet once again will their love be rekindled? Lovely photography and an evocative score enhance the story. In French with English subtitles; also available dubbed in English (not with the same effectiveness). Oscar nominee for cinematography and story. **AKA:** Les Parapluies De Cherbourg; Die Regenschirme Von Cherbourg.

1964 90m/C *FR* Catherine Deneuve, Nino Castelnuovo, Anne Vernon, Ellen Farner, Marc Michel, Mireille Perrey, Jean Champion, Alfred Wolff, Dorothee Blanck; **D:** Jacques Demy; **W:** Jacques Demy; **M:** Michel Legrand. Cannes Film Festival '64: Best Film; Nominations: Academy Awards '65: Best Foreign Language Film, Best Song ("I Will Wait for You"), Best Story & Screenplay, Best Original Score. **VHS, Beta** ★★★½

Un Chien Andalou Masterful surrealist short features a host of classic sequences, including a razor across an eye, a severed hand lying in the street, ants crawling from a hole in a man's hand, priests, dead horses, and a piano dragged across a room. A classic. Score features both Wagner and tango.

1928 20m/B *FR* Pierre Batcheff, Simone Marevil, Jaime Miravilles; **D:** Luis Bunuel, Salvador Dali. **VHS, Beta** ★★★★

The Unbearable Lightness of Being Tomas (Day-Lewis), a young Czech doctor in the late 1960s, leads a sexually and emotionally carefree existence with a number of women, including provocative artist Olin. When he meets the fragile Binoche, he may be falling in love for the first time. On the eve of the 1968 Russian invasion of Czechoslovakia the two flee to Switzerland, but Binoche can't reconcile herself to exile and returns, followed by the reluctant Tomas who has lost his position because of his new-found political idealism. They lead an increasingly simple life, drawn ever closer together. The haunting ending caps off superb performances. Based on the novel by Milan Kundera.

1988 (R) 172m/C Daniel Day-Lewis, Juliette Binoche, Lena Olin, Derek De Lint, Erland Josephson, Pavel Landovsky, Donald Moffat, Daniel Olbrychski, Stellan Skarsgard; **D:** Philip Kaufman; **W:** Jean-Claude Carriere, Philip Kaufman. British Academy Awards '88: Best Adapted Screenplay; Independent Spirit Awards '89: Best Cinematography; National Society of Film Critics Awards '88: Best Director (Kaufman), Best Film; Nominations: Academy Awards '88: Best Adapted Screenplay, Best Cinematography. **VHS, Beta, LV** ★★★½

Uncle Buck When Mom and Dad have to go away suddenly, the only babysitter they can find is good ol' Uncle Buck, a lovable lout who spends much of his time smoking cigars, trying to make up with his girlfriend, and enforcing the teenage daughter's chastity. More intelligent than the average slob/teen comedy with a heart, due in large part to Candy's dandy performance. Memorable pancake scene.

1989 (PG) 100m/C John Candy, Amy Madigan, Jean Kelly, Macaulay Culkin, Jay Underwood, Gaby Hoffman, Laurie Metcalf, Elaine Bromka, Garrett M. Brown; **D:** John Hughes; **W:** John Hughes; **M:** Ira Newborn, Ralf Bode. **VHS, Beta, LV** ★★★

Under Fire Three foreign correspondents, old friends from the past working together, find themselves in Managua, witnessing the 1979 Nicaraguan revolution. In a job requiring objectivity, but a situation requiring taking sides, they battle with their ethics to do the job right. Fine performances, including Camp as a mercenary. Interesting view of American media and its political necessities.

1983 (R) 128m/C Gene Hackman, Nick Nolte, Joanna Cassidy, Ed Harris, Richard Masur, Hamilton Camp, Jean-Louis Trintignant; *D:* Roger Spottiswoode; *W:* Ron Shelton, Clayton Frohman; *M:* Jerry Goldsmith. Nominations: Academy Awards '83: Best Original Score. **VHS, Beta, LV** ★★★1/2

Under Satan's Sun A rural priest is tortured by what he sees as his sins and failings to his parishioners. He is further tempted from the straight path by a beautiful murderess, a worldly priest, and, perhaps by Satan in disguise. Stylized film is not easily accessible, but Depardieu's performance is worth the effort. Based on the Georges Bernanos book "Diary of a Country Priest." In French with English subtitles. *AKA:* Under the Sun of Satan; Sous le Soleil de Satan.

1987 97m/C *FR* Gerard Depardieu, Sandrine Bonnaire, Yann Dedet, Alain Artur, Maurice Pialat; *D:* Maurice Pialat; *W:* Maurice Pialat. Cannes Film Festival '87: Best Film. **VHS** ★★★

Under the Roofs of Paris An early French sound film about the lives of young Parisian lovers. A gentle, highly acclaimed melodrama. In French with English subtitles. *AKA:* Sous les Toits de Paris.

1929 95m/B *FR* Albert Prejean, Pola Illery, Gaston Modot; *D:* Rene Clair. National Board of Review Awards '31: 5 Best Foreign Films of the Year. **VHS, Beta** ★★★1/2

Under the Volcano An alcoholic British ex-consul finds his life further deteriorating during the Mexican Day of the Dead in 1939. His half-brother and ex-wife try to save him from himself, but their affair sends him ever-deeper into his personal hell. Finney's performance is pathetic and haunting. Adapted from the novel by Malcolm Lowry.

1984 112m/C Albert Finney, Jacqueline Bisset, Anthony Andrews, Katy Jurado; *D:* John Huston; *M:* John Beal, Alex North. Los Angeles Film Critics Association Awards '84: Best Actor (Finney); Nominations: Academy Awards '84: Best Actor (Finney), Best Original Score; Cannes Film Festival '84: Best Film. **VHS, Beta, LV** ★★★

Underground Exhausting black comedy, set in Yugoslavia from 1941 to 1992, follows the adventures of Marko (Manojlovic) and his best friend Blacky (Ristovski). They run a black-market operation and lead Communist Party meetings while trying to avoid the Gestapo in WWII Belgrade. Hiding out in a cellar, where refugees have put together a munitions factory, the treacherous Marko manages to convince everyone that the war is still going on—20 years later in fact—until the truth unexpectedly comes out (thanks to a pet monkey). The final section sees Marko unscrupulously dealing arms and drugs amidst the breakup of Yugoslavia in a civil war and the violence on all sides. *AKA:* Once Upon a Time There Was a Country.

1995 192m/C *YU* Miki Manojlovic, Lazar Ristovski, Mirjana Jokovic, Slavko Stimac, Ernst Stotzner, Srdan Todorovic, Mirjana Karanovic; Cameos: Emir Kusturica; *D:* Emir Kusturica; *W:* Emir Kusturica, Dusan Kovacevic; *M:* Goran Bregovic. Cannes Film Festival '95: Best Film. **VHS** ★★★

The Underneath Recovering gambling addict Michael Chambers (Peter Gallagher) returns home after skipping out on his debts and his wife Rachel (sultry newcomer Elliott) several years before. Old passions ignite in more ways than one, and Michael's lust for his ex, now married to a hot-tempered hoodlum, leads him to risk it all for a final big score. Moody and tense study of the complexities of emotion is capped by smart lead performances but style wins out over substance and the finale definitely leaves more questions than answers. Remake of the 1949 film noir classic "Criss Cross," based on Don Tracy's novel of the same name.

1995 (R) 99m/C Peter Gallagher, Alison Elliott, William Fichtner, Elisabeth Shue, Adam Trese, Paul Dooley; *D:* Steven Soderbergh; *W:* Sam Lowry, Daniel Fuchs; *M:* Cliff Martinez. Nominations: Independent Spirit Awards '96: Best Cinematography. **VHS** ★★★

Underworld Inspired gangster saga finds bank robber Bull Weed (Bancroft) befriending a genteel bum, known as Rolls Royce (Brook), and taking him into his gang. The bum has brains and soon makes Weed king of the underworld but there's jealousy when Weed's moll Feathers (Brent) falls for Royce. Climactic shoot-out set a standard for the genre.

1927 85m/B George Bancroft, Clive Brook, Evelyn Brent, Larry Semon, Fred Kohler Sr.; *D:* Josef von Sternberg. **VHS** ★★★

Underworld, U.S.A. A man infiltrates a tough crime syndicate to avenge his father's murder, which winds up with him caught between the mob and the feds. A well-acted and directed look at the criminal underworld.

1960 99m/B Cliff Robertson, Dolores Dorn, Beatrice Kay, Robert Emhardt, Larry

Gates, Paul Dubov; *D:* Samuel Fuller; *W:* Samuel Fuller. **VHS, Beta ★★★**

Unfaithfully Yours A conductor suspects his wife is cheating on him and considers his course of action. He imagines punishment scenarios while directing three classical works. Well-acted by all, but particularly by Harrison as the egotistical and jealous husband. Another of Sturges' comedic gems. Remade in 1984.
1948 105m/B Rex Harrison, Linda Darnell, Kurt Kreuger, Rudy Vallee, Lionel Stander, Edgar Kennedy; *D:* Preston Sturges. **VHS, Beta, LV ★★★1/2**

The Unforgiven A western family is torn asunder when it is suspected that the eldest daughter is of Indian birth. Film takes place in 1850s Texas. One of Huston's weakest ventures, but viewed in terms of 1950s prejudices it has more resonance. Fine acting from all the cast, especially Gish. Watch for the stunning Indian attack scene.
1960 123m/C Burt Lancaster, Audrey Hepburn, Lillian Gish, Audie Murphy, John Saxon, Charles Bickford, Doug McClure, Joseph Wiseman, Albert Salmi; *D:* John Huston. **VHS, Beta, LV ★★★**

Unforgiven Will Munny (Eastwood) lives a quiet life with his stepchildren on his failing pig farm, but his desperado past catches up with him when the Schofield Kid invites him to a bounty hunt. Munny reluctantly agrees, mistakenly believing that once the killing is through he can take up his peaceful ways again. Enter sadistic sheriff Little Bill Daggett (Hackman), who doesn't want any gunmen messing up his town. Eastwood uses his own status as a screen legend to full advantage as the aging gunman who realizes too late that his past can never be forgotten. Director Eastwood is also in top form with his well-seasoned cast and myth-defying Old West realism. Surprising critical and box office hit. The laserdisc version is available in letterbox format.
1992 (R) 131m/C Clint Eastwood, Gene Hackman, Morgan Freeman, Richard Harris, Jaimz Woolvett, Saul Rubinek, Frances Fisher, Anna Thomson, David Mucci, Rob Campbell, Anthony James; *D:* Clint Eastwood; *W:* David Peoples; *M:* Lennie Niehaus, Jack N. Green. Academy Awards '92: Best Director (Eastwood), Best Film Editing, Best Picture, Best Supporting Actor (Hackman); Directors Guild of America Awards '92: Best Director (Eastwood); Golden Globe Awards '93: Best Director (Eastwood), Best Supporting Actor (Hackman); New York Film Critics Awards '92: Best Supporting Actor (Hackman); National Society of Film Critics Awards '92: Best Director (Eastwood), Best Film, Best Screenplay, Best Supporting Actor (Hackman); Nominations: Academy Awards '92: Best Actor (Eastwood), Best Art Direction/Set Decoration, Best Cinematography, Best Original Screenplay, Best Sound. **VHS, Beta, LV, 8mm ★★★1/2**

The Unholy Three Ventriloquist Chaney, working with other carnival cohorts, uses his talent to gain entrance to homes which he later robs. Things go awry when two of the gang strike out on their own and the victim is killed. When the wrong man is accused, his girl, one of Chaney's gang, begs Chaney to get him free, which he does by using his vocal talents. Chaney decides being a criminal is just too hard and goes back to his ventriloquism.
1925 70m/B Lon Chaney Sr., Harry Earles, Victor McLaglen, Mae Busch, Matt Moore, Matthew Betz, William Humphreys; *D:* Tod Browning. **VHS ★★★1/2**

The Unholy Three Chaney remade his silent hit of 1925 for his first and only talking picture (he died before the film was released). The story is essentially the same. Chaney is a ventriloquist who, with his circus friends, work as scam artists and thieves. When an innocent man is accused of their crimes Chaney tries his ventriloquist tricks to come to his aid, only in this version Chaney is exposed as a fraud and is sent to prison. Rumors that Chaney was a mute had him agreeing to appear in a "talkie" and he actually used five different voices for his various roles.
1930 75m/B Lon Chaney Sr., Lila Lee, Elliott Nugent, Harry Earles, John Miljan; *D:* Jack Conway. **VHS, LV ★★★**

The Uninvited A brother and sister buy a house in England, only to find it is haunted. Doors open and close by themselves, strange scents fill the air, and they hear sobbing during the night. Soon they are visited by a woman with an odd link to the house —her mother is the spirit who haunts the house. Chilling and unforgettable, this is one of the first films to deal seriously with ghosts.
1944 99m/B Ray Milland, Ruth Hussey, Donald Crisp, Cornelia Otis Skinner, Gail Russell; *D:* Lewis Allen. Nominations: Academy Awards '44: Best Black and White Cinematography. **VHS, LV ★★★**

Union Pacific Full DeMille treatment highlights this saga about the building of America's first transcontinental

railroad. Jeff Butler (McCrea) is the construction overseer who must battle saboteurs and Indians (although the U.S. Calvary does arrive to save the day). He also gets to fall for self-sufficient postmistress Mollie Monahan (Stanwyck). DeMille borrowed the actual golden spike used to drive in the last rail in 1869 for his reenactment of the completion celebration. Based on the book "Trouble Shooters" by Ernest Haycox.
1939 136m/B Joel McCrea, Barbara Stanwyck, Robert Preston, Brian Donlevy, Akim Tamiroff, Lynne Overman, Robert Barrat, Anthony Quinn, Stanley Ridges, Henry Kolker, Evelyn Keyes, Regis Toomey; **D:** Cecil B. DeMille; **W:** Walter DeLeon, Jesse Lasky Jr., C. Gardner Sullivan. **VHS** ★★★

The Unknown Typically morbid Chaney fare has him working as a circus freak while trying to win the heart of his assistant. After drastic romancing he's still rejected by her, so he plots to kill the object of her intentions. Ghoulish as it is, the picture is really top-notch.
1927 60m/B Lon Chaney Sr., Norman Kerry, Joan Crawford, Nick De Ruiz, Frank Lanning, John St. Polis; **D:** Tod Browning. **VHS** ★★★1/2

An Unmarried Woman Suddenly divorced by her husband of 17 years, a woman deals with change. She enters the singles scene, copes with her daughter's growing sexuality, and encounters a new self-awareness. Mazursky puts real people on screen from start to finish.
1978 (R) 124m/C Jill Clayburgh, Alan Bates, Cliff Gorman, Michael Murphy; **D:** Paul Mazursky; **W:** Paul Mazursky; **M:** Bill Conti. Cannes Film Festival '78: Best Actress (Clayburgh); Los Angeles Film Critics Association Awards '78: Best Screenplay; National Board of Review Awards '78: 10 Best Films of the Year; New York Film Critics Awards '78: Best Screenplay; National Society of Film Critics Awards '78: Best Screenplay; Nominations: Academy Awards '78: Best Actress (Clayburgh), Best Original Screenplay, Best Picture; Cannes Film Festival '78: Best Film. **VHS, Beta** ★★★

The Unsinkable Molly Brown A spunky backwoods girl is determined to break into the upper crust of Denver's high society and along the way survives the sinking of the Titanic. This energetic version of the Broadway musical contains many Meredith Willson (Music Man) songs and lots of hokey, good-natured fun. ♪ Colorado Is My Home; Leadville Johnny Brown (Soliloquy); I Ain't Down Yet; Belly Up to the Bar, Boys; He's My Friend; I've Already Started; The Beautiful People of Denver; I May Never Fall in Love with You; Up Where the People Are.
1964 128m/C Debbie Reynolds, Harve Presnell, Ed Begley Sr., Martita Hunt, Hermione Baddeley; **D:** Charles Walters; **M:** Meredith Willson. Nominations: Academy Awards '64: Best Actress (Reynolds), Best Art Direction/Set Decoration (Color), Best Color Cinematography, Best Costume Design (Color), Best Sound, Best Original Score. **VHS, Beta, LV** ★★★

The Untouchables Big-budget, fast-paced and exciting re-evaluation of the popular TV series about the real-life battle between Treasury officer Eliot Ness and crime boss Al Capone in 1920s Chicago. History sometimes takes a back seat to Hollywood's imagination in the screenplay, but it doesn't really matter since there are splendid performances by De Niro as Capone and Connery as Ness' mentor to help it look realistic. Costner does a fine job showing the change in Ness from naive idealism to steely conviction. Beautifully filmed with excellent special effects.
1987 (R) 119m/C Kevin Costner, Sean Connery, Robert De Niro, Andy Garcia, Charles Martin Smith, Billy Drago, Richard Bradford, Jack Kehoe; **D:** Brian DePalma; **W:** David Mamet, Stephen Burum; **M:** Ennio Morricone. Academy Awards '87: Best Supporting Actor (Connery); Golden Globe Awards '88: Best Supporting Actor (Connery); National Board of Review Awards '87: 10 Best Films of the Year, Best Supporting Actor (Connery); Nominations: Academy Awards '87: Best Art Direction/Set Decoration, Best Costume Design, Best Original Score. **VHS, Beta, LV, 8mm** ★★★1/2

Unzipped Witty, behind-the-scenes look at whiz-kid fashion designer Isaac Mizrahi as he prepares for the showing of his 1994 collection. Alternately filmed in black-and-white and color in a variety of film stocks, Keeve captures Mizrahi's varying moods, from his creative struggles to his unique sense of humor and gift for mimicry. Highlights include scenes with Mizrahi's doting mother. Fashionphiles will love every minute, and strictly off-the-rack viewers can enjoy the supermodels on parade.
1994 (R) 76m/C D: Douglas Keeve. Sundance Film Festival '95: Audience Award. **VHS, LV** ★★★

Up Close and Personal Ambitious Reno card dealer Tally Atwater (Pfeif-

fer) wants to get into broadcasting and finds her chance at a Miami TV station where she's mentored by successful veteran-reporter-turned-producer Warren Justice (Redford). They fall in love but find their careers clashing as Tally climbs the media success ladder. Originally inspired by the tragic life of NBC reporter Jessica Savitch, whose problems with drugs and abusive relationships lead to a sad ending, film turned into a star-powered romance with media trappings and another variation of "A Star is Born." It's now "suggested" by Alanna Nash's book "Golden Girl."
1996 (PG-13) 124m/C Michelle Pfeiffer, Robert Redford, Kate Nelligan, Stockard Channing, Joe Mantegna, Glenn Plummer, James Rebhorn, Noble Willingham, Scott Bryce, Raymond Cruz, Dedee Pfeiffer, Miguel Sandoval, James Karen, Karl Walter Lindenlaub; **D:** Jon Avnet; **W:** Joan Didion, John Gregory Dunne; **M:** Thomas Newman. **VHS** ★★★

Up the Down Staircase A naive, newly trained New York public school teacher is determined to teach the finer points of English literature to a group of poor students. She almost gives up until one student actually begins to learn. Good production and acting. Based on Bel Kaufman's novel.
1967 124m/C Sandy Dennis, Patrick Bedford, Eileen Heckart, Ruth White, Jean Stapleton, Sorrell Booke; **D:** Robert Mulligan. **VHS** ★★★

Used Cars A car dealer is desperate to put his jalopy shop competitors out of business. The owners go to great lengths to stay afloat. Sometimes too obnoxious, but often funny.
1980 (R) 113m/C Kurt Russell, Jack Warden, Deborah Harmon, Gerrit Graham, Joe Flaherty, Michael McKean; **D:** Robert Zemeckis; **W:** Robert Zemeckis. **VHS, Beta, LV, 8mm** ★★★

The Usual Suspects Twisted noir-thriller about some crooks, a 91-million-dollar heist, and mysterious crime lord Keyser Soze. Customs agent Kujan (Palminteri) tries to get a straight story out of small-time con man "Verbal" Kint (Spacey) about a burning tanker in the San Pedro harbor, 27 dead bodies, and the other four temperamental criminals involved: ex-cop-turned thief Keaton (Byrne), explosives expert Hockney (Pollak), and hot-headed partners McManus (Baldwin) and Fenster (Del Toro). Nothing is as it seems, and the ending keeps everyone guessing, right up to the final credits. Terrific

performances from all complement the intelligent, humorous script. And yes, the title does come from the famous line in "Casablanca."
1995 (R) 105m/C Kevin Spacey, Gabriel Byrne, Chazz Palminteri, Kevin Pollak, Stephen Baldwin, Benicio Del Toro, Giancarlo Esposito, Peter Postlethwaite, Dan Hedaya, Suzy Amis, Paul Bartel; **D:** Bryan Singer; **W:** Christopher McQuarrie, Newton Thomas Sigel; **M:** John Ottman. National Board of Review Awards '95: Best Supporting Actor (Spacey); New York Film Critics Awards '95: Best Supporting Actor (Spacey); Nominations: Academy Awards '95: Best Screenplay, Best Supporting Actor (Spacey); Golden Globe Awards '96: Best Supporting Actor (Spacey); Independent Spirit Awards '96: Best Cinematography, Best Screenplay, Best Supporting Actor (Del Toro). **VHS, LV** ★★★1/2

Vagabond Bleak, emotionally shattering, powerful and compelling, this film traces the peripatetic life of an amoral and selfish young French woman who has no regard for social rules and tremendous fear of responsibility in her drifting yet inexorable journey into death. Told via flashbacks from the moment when she is found dead, alone, and unaccounted for by the roadside, this film will not leave you unscathed. Written by New Wave director Varda. In French with English subtitles. **AKA:** Sans Toit Ni Loi.
1985 105m/C FR Sandrine Bonnaire, Macha Meril, Stephane Freiss, Elaine Cortadellas, Marthe Jarnias, Yolanda Moreau; **D:** Agnes Varda; **W:** Agnes Varda. Cesar Awards '86: Best Actress (Bonnaire); Los Angeles Film Critics Association Awards '86: Best Actress (Bonnaire), Best Foreign Film. **VHS, Beta, LV** ★★★1/2

The Valley of Decision Entertaining poor-girl-meets-rich-boy story with Peck as a wealthy mill owner who falls in love with beautiful housemaid Garson (the Queen of MGM at the time). Set in 1870 Pittsburgh; based on Marcia Davenport's novel.
1945 111m/B Gregory Peck, Greer Garson, Donald Crisp, Lionel Barrymore, Preston Foster, Gladys Cooper, Marsha Hunt, Reginald Owen, Dan Duryea, Jessica Tandy, Barbara Everest; **D:** Tay Garnett; **W:** John Meehan, Sonya Levien. **VHS** ★★★

The Valley of Gwangi One of the best prehistoric-monster-westerns out there. Cowboys discover a lost valley of dinosaurs and try to capture a vicious, carnivorous allosaurus. Bad move, kemosabe! The creatures move via the stop-motion model ani-

mation by f/x maestro Ray Harryhausen, here at his finest.
1969 (G) 95m/C James Franciscus, Gila Golan, Richard Carlson, Laurence Naismith, Freda Jackson; **D:** James O'Connolly; **W:** William Bast. **VHS, Beta, LV** ★★★

Valmont Another adaptation of the Choderlos de Laclos novel "Les Liaisons Dangereuses." Various members of the French aristocracy in 1782 mercilessly play each other for fools in a complex game of lust and deception. Firth and Bening are at first playfully sensual, then the stakes get too high. They share an interesting bathtub scene. Well-acted, the 1988 Frears version, "Dangerous Liaisons," is edgier. Seeing the two films together makes for interesting comparisons of characters and styles.
1989 (R) 137m/C Colin Firth, Meg Tilly, Annette Bening, Fairuza Balk, Sian Phillips, Jeffrey Jones, Fabia Drake, Henry Thomas, Vincent Schiavelli, T.P. McKenna, Ian McNeice; **D:** Milos Forman; **W:** Jean-Claude Carriere; **M:** Christopher Palmer. Cesar Awards '90: Best Art Direction/Set Decoration, Best Costume Design; Nominations: Academy Awards '89: Best Costume Design. **VHS, Beta, LV** ★★★

Vampyr Dreyer's classic portrays a hazy, dreamlike world full of chilling visions from the point of view of a young man who believes himself surrounded by vampires and who dreams of his own burial in a most disturbing way. Evil lurks around every corner as camera angles, light and shadow sometimes overwhelm plot. A high point in horror films based on a collection of horror stories by Sheridan le Fanu. In German with English subtitles. **AKA:** Vampyr, Ou L'Etrang e Aventure De David Gray; Vampyr, Der Traum Des David Gray; Not Against the Flesh; Castle of Doom; The Strange Adventure of David Gray; The Vampire.
1931 75m/B GE Julien West, Sybille Schmitz, Harriet Gerard, Maurice Schutz; **D:** Carl Theodor Dreyer; **W:** Carl Theodor Dreyer; **M:** Wolfgang Zeller. **VHS, Beta** ★★★★

The Van The last of writer Roddy Doyle's Barrytown trilogy (following "The Commitments" and "The Snapper") is set in 1989–90, in Dublin, where baker Bimbo (O'Kelly) has just lost his job. Tired of sitting around the pub, he takes his redundancy money and buys a filthy, dilapidated fish 'n' chips van, which he decides to run with best friend Larry (Meaney), with

their families helping out. The months pass quickly, and their venture turns out to be a big success, but the close quarters puts a strain on the men's friendship until Bimbo has another idea.
1995 (R) 105m/C IR Donal O'Kelly, Colm Meaney, Ger Ryan, Caroline Rotwell, Neili Conroy, Ruaidhri Conroy; **D:** Stephen Frears; **W:** Roddy Doyle; **M:** Eric Clapton, Richard Hartley. **VHS** ★★★

Vanina Vanini An acclaimed Rossellini historical drama about the daughter of an Italian aristocrat in 1824 who nurses and falls in love with a wounded patriot hiding in her house. Based on a Stendhal short story. In Italian with English subtitles.
1961 113m/B IT Sandra Milo, Laurent Terzieff; **D:** Roberto Rossellini. **VHS, Beta** ★★★1/2

Vanishing Prairie This documentary examines the wonders of nature that abound in the American prairie. From the "True-Life Adventures" series.
1954 60m/C D: James Algar. Academy Awards '54: Best Feature Documentary. **VHS, Beta** ★★★

Vanya on 42nd Street A group of actors in street clothes rehearse a workshop production of Chekhov's play, "Uncle Vanya" in New York's dilapidated New Amsterdam Theater. Theatrical director Gregory first gets his group together in 1989, with Mamet's contemporary adaptation, and they continue to work in private until Malle films their production some four years later before a small, select audience. Shawn, best known for "My Dinner with Andre," portrays Vanya with depth and complexity. The other actors shine as well, often against type, in this complex Russian drama of desperation.
1994 (PG) 119m/C Wallace Shawn, Julianne Moore, Brooke Smith, Larry Pine, George Gaynes, Lynn Cohen, Madhur Jaffrey, Phoebe Brand, Jerry Mayer, Andre Gregory; **D:** Louis Malle; **W:** David Mamet; **M:** Joshua Redman, Declan Quinn. Nominations: Independent Spirit Awards '95: Best Supporting Actor (Pine), Best Supporting Actress (Smith). **VHS, LV** ★★★1/2

Variety Simple and tragic tale of a scheming young girl and the two men of whom she takes advantage. The European circus in all its beautiful sadness is the setting. Extraordinary cast and superb cinematography. Silent.
1925 104m/B GE Emil Jannings, Lya de Putti, Warwick Ward, Werner Krauss; **D:** E.A. Dupont. **VHS, Beta** ★★★★

Variety Lights Fellini's first (albeit joint) directorial effort, wherein a young girl runs away with a traveling vaudeville troupe and soon becomes its main attraction as a dancer. Filled with Fellini's now-familiar delight in the bizarre and sawdust/tinsel entertainment. In Italian with English subtitles. *AKA:* Luci Del Varieta; Lights of Variety.
1951 93m/B *IT* Giulietta Masina, Peppino de Filippo, Carla Del Poggio, Folco Lulli; *D:* Federico Fellini, Alberto Lattuada; *W:* Federico Fellini, Tullio Pinelli, Ennio Flaiano, Alberto Lattuada. **VHS, Beta** ★★★1/2

The Verdict Newman plays an alcoholic failed attorney reduced to ambulance chasing. A friend gives him a supposedly easy malpractice case which turns out to be a last chance at redeeming himself and his career. Adapted from the novel by Barry Reed. One of Newman's finest performances.
1982 (R) 122m/C Paul Newman, James Mason, Charlotte Rampling, Jack Warden, Milo O'Shea, Lindsay Crouse; *D:* Sidney Lumet; *W:* David Mamet. National Board of Review Awards '82: Best Director (Lumet); Nominations: Academy Awards '82: Best Actor (Newman), Best Adapted Screenplay, Best Director (Lumet), Best Picture, Best Supporting Actor (Mason). **VHS, Beta, LV** ★★★

Veronika Voss Highlights the real life of fallen film star Sybille Schmitz who finally took her own life out of despair. Played by Zech, Voss is exploited by her physician to turn over all of her personal belongings for morphine. A lover discovers the corruption and reveals it to the authorities. This causes great upheaval resulting in Voss' suicide. Highly metaphoric and experimental in its treatment of its subject. In German with English subtitles. *AKA:* Die Sehns Ucht Der Veronika Voss.
1982 (R) 105m/C *GE* Rosel Zech, Hilmar Thate, Conny Froboess, Anna Marie Duringer, Volker Spengler; *D:* Rainer Werner Fassbinder; *M:* Peer Raben. **VHS** ★★★

Vertigo Hitchcock's romantic story of obsession, manipulation and fear. Stewart plays a detective forced to retire after his fear of heights causes the death of a fellow policeman and, perhaps, the death of a woman he'd been hired to follow. The appearance of her double (Novak), whom he compulsively transforms into the dead girl's image, leads to a mesmerizing cycle of madness and lies. Features Herrmann's haunting music.
1958 (PG) 126m/C James Stewart, Kim Novak, Barbara Bel Geddes, Tom Helmore, Ellen Corby, Henry Jones, Raymond Bailey, Lee Patrick; *D:* Alfred Hitchcock; *W:* Sam Taylor; *M:* Bernard Herrmann. Nominations: Academy Awards '58: Best Art Direction/Set Decoration, Best Sound. **VHS, Beta, LV** ★★★★

Victim A successful married English barrister (Bogarde) with a hidden history of homosexuality is threatened by blackmail after the death of his ex-lover. When the blackmailers, who are responsible for his lover's suicide, are caught, Bogarde decides to prosecute them himself, even though it means revealing his hidden past. One of the first films to deal straightforwardly with homosexuality. Fine performances.
1962 100m/C *GB* Dirk Bogarde, Sylvia Syms, Dennis Price, Peter McEnery; *D:* Basil Dearden. **VHS, Beta** ★★★1/2

Victor/Victoria An unsuccessful actress in Depression-era Paris impersonates a man impersonating a woman and becomes a star. Luscious music and sets. Warren as femme fatale and Preston as Andrews' gay mentor are right on target; Garner is charming as the gangster who falls for the woman he thinks she is. ♪ You and Me; The Shady Dame from Seville; Le Jazz Hot; Crazy World; Chicago Illinois; Gay Peree.
1982 (PG) 133m/C Julie Andrews, James Garner, Robert Preston, Lesley Ann Warren, Alex Karras, John Rhys-Davies; *D:* Blake Edwards; *W:* Blake Edwards; *M:* Henry Mancini. Academy Awards '82: Best Score; Cesar Awards '83: Best Foreign Film; Golden Globe Awards '83: Best Actress—Musical/Comedy (Andrews); National Board of Review Awards '82: Best Supporting Actor (Preston); Writers Guild of America '82: Best Adapted Screenplay; Nominations: Academy Awards '82: Best Actress (Andrews), Best Adapted Screenplay, Best Art Direction/Set Decoration, Best Costume Design, Best Supporting Actor (Preston), Best Supporting Actress (Warren). **VHS, Beta, LV** ★★★

Village of the Damned A group of unusual children are born in a small English village. They avoid their fathers and other men, except for the one who is their teacher. He discovers they are the vanguard of an alien invasion and leads the counterattack. Exciting and bone-chilling low-budget thriller. From the novel, "The Midwich Cuckoos," by John Wyndham. The sequel, "The Children of the Damned" (1964) is even better.

1960 78m/B *GB* George Sanders, Barbara Shelley, Martin Stephens, Laurence Naismith, Michael C. Goetz; *D:* Wolf Rilla; *W:* Stirling Silliphant. **VHS, Beta, LV ★★★**

Vincent & Theo The story of Impressionist painter Vincent Van Gogh and his brother Theo, a gallery owner who loved his brother's work, yet could not get the public to buy it. Increasing despair and mental illness traps both men, as each struggles to create beauty in a world where it has no value. Altman has created a stunning portrait of "the artist" and his needs. The exquisite cinematography will make you feel as if you stepped into Van Gogh's work.
1990 (PG-13) 138m/C Tim Roth, Paul Rhys, Johanna Ter Steege, Wladimir Yordanoff; *D:* Robert Altman. **VHS, Beta, LV ★★★**1/2

Violence at Noon Highly disturbing film in which two women protect a brutal sex murderer from the law. Living among a quiet community of intellectuals, this conspiracy ends in a shocking finale in Oshima's stylized masterpiece. In Japanese with English subtitles.
1966 99m/B *JP* Saeda Kawaguchi, Akiko Koyama; *D:* Nagisa Oshima. **VHS ★★★**

Violette Fascinating true-life account of a 19-year-old French girl in the 1930s who, bored with her life and wanting to be with her lover, decides to poison her parents so she can receive her inheritance. Her mother survives but her father dies, and the girl is sent to prison for murder. Extraordinary performance by Huppert and the film is visually stunning. *AKA:* Violette Noziere.
1978 (R) 122m/C *FR* Isabelle Huppert, Stephane Audran, Jean Carmet, Jean Francoise, Bernadette LaFont; *D:* Claude Chabrol. Cannes Film Festival '78: Best Actress (Huppert); Cesar Awards '79: Best Supporting Actress (Audran); Nominations: Cannes Film Festival '78: Best Film. **VHS ★★★**

The V.I.P.'s Slick, sophisticated drama set in the V.I.P. lounge of a British airport. Trapped by fog, several of the passengers get acquainted and are forced to face their problems as they spend the night in the airport lounge. Taylor stars as Frances Andros, a wealthy young woman leaving her husband (Burton) for life in the U.S. with her lover, Jourdan. A movie tycoon, an Australian entrepreneur, his secretary, and a duchess are among the other passengers grounded by the fog. Both Rutherford and Smith give excellent performances and it was a tossup as to which actress would be nominated for the Oscar.
1963 119m/C *GB* Elizabeth Taylor, Richard Burton, Louis Jourdan, Elsa Martinelli, Margaret Rutherford, Maggie Smith, Rod Taylor, Orson Welles, Linda Christian, Dennis Price; *D:* Anthony Asquith; *M:* Terence Rattigan; *M:* Miklos Rozsa. Academy Awards '63: Best Supporting Actress (Rutherford); Golden Globe Awards '64: Best Supporting Actress (Rutherford); National Board of Review Awards '63: Best Supporting Actress (Rutherford). **VHS ★★★**

The Virgin Queen Davis stars in this historical drama, which focuses on the stormy relationship between the aging Queen and Sir Walter Raleigh. Collins is the lady-in-waiting who is the secret object of Raleigh's true affections. Previously, Davis played Queen Elizabeth I in "Elizabeth and Essex." Davis holds things together.
1955 92m/C Bette Davis, Richard Todd, Joan Collins, Herbert Marshall, Dan O'Herlihy, Jay Robinson, Romney Brent; *D:* Henry Koster. Nominations: Academy Awards '55: Best Costume Design (Color). **VHS, Beta ★★★**

The Virgin Spring Based on a medieval ballad and set in 14th-century Sweden. The rape and murder of a young innocent spurs her father to vengeance and he kills her attackers. Over the girl's dead body, the father questions how God could have let any of it happen, but he comes to find solace and forgiveness. Stunning Bergman compositions. In Swedish with English subtitles; also available in dubbed version. *AKA:* Jungfrukallan.
1959 88m/B *SW* Max von Sydow, Brigitta Valberg, Gunnel Lindblom, Brigitta Pattersson, Axel Duborg; *D:* Ingmar Bergman. Academy Awards '60: Best Foreign Language Film; Golden Globe Awards '61: Best Foreign Film; Nominations: Academy Awards '60: Best Costume Design (B & W). **VHS, Beta ★★★**1/2

The Virginian A classic early-talkie western about a ranch-hand defeating the local bad guys. One line of dialogue has become, with modification, a standard western cliche: "If you want to call me that, smile." Based on the novel by Owen Wister. With this starring role, Cooper broke away from the juvenile lovers he had been playing to the laconic, rugged male leads he would be known for. Huston is perfectly cast as the outlaw leader.

1929 95m/B Gary Cooper, Walter Huston, Richard Arlen, Chester Conklin, Eugene Pallette; **D:** Victor Fleming. **VHS, Beta** ★★★

Viridiana Innocent girl, with strong ideas about goodness, visits her worldly uncle's home before she takes her vows as a nun. He has developed a sick obsession for her, but after drugging the girl he finds he cannot violate her purity. He tells her, however, since he is no longer chaste so she will not join the church. After her uncle's suicide, Viridiana learns she and his illegitimate son Jorge have inherited her uncle's rundown estate. Viridiana opens the house to all sorts of beggars, who take shameless advantage, while Jorge works slowly to restore the estate and improve the lives of those around him. Considered to be one of Bunuel's masterpieces and a bitter allegory of Spanish idealism versus pragmatism and the state of the world. In Spanish with English subtitles.
1961 90m/B *SP MX* Silvia Pinal, Francesco Rabal, Fernando Rey, Margarita Lozano, Victoria Zinny; **D:** Luis Bunuel; **W:** Luis Bunuel. Cannes Film Festival '61: Best Film. **VHS, Beta** ★★★★

Visions of Light: The Art of Cinematography Excellent documentary on the way films look and how the art of photographing movies can contribute as much, if not more, than cast, director, and script. Scenes from 125 films, from "Birth of a Nation" to "Goodfellas" are shown, with commentary from a number of cinematographers, including Gordon Willis, William A. Fraker, Conrad Hall, Ernest Dickerson, Vilmos Zsigmond, and Michael Chapman, on how they achieved certain effects and their collaborations with the director of the film.
1993 95m/C **D:** Arnold Glassman, Stuart Samuels, Todd McCarthy; **W:** Todd McCarthy. New York Film Critics Awards '93: Best Feature Documentary; National Society of Film Critics Awards '93: Best Feature Documentary. **VHS, LV** ★★★

Viva Villa! Exciting action biography of Mexican revolutionary Pancho Villa, well-portrayed by the exuberant Beery. The film follows the early Robin Hood-like exploits of Villa and his men who soon join Walthall and his peasant army in overthrowing the government. But Villa's bandito instincts and ego cause problems and a power struggle ensues. Director Howard Hawks went uncredited for his work on the film, being fired by the studio after an incident while on location in Mexico.
1934 115m/B Wallace Beery, Fay Wray, Stuart Erwin, Leo Carrillo, Donald Cook, George E. Stone, Joseph Schildkraut, Henry B. Walthall, Katherine DeMille, David Durand, Frank Puglia; **D:** Jack Conway; **W:** Ben Hecht. Nominations: Academy Awards '34: Best Adapted Screenplay, Best Picture, Best Sound. **VHS, LV** ★★★

Viva Zapata! Chronicles the life of Mexican revolutionary Emiliano Zapata. Brando is powerful as he leads the peasant revolt in the early 1900s, only to be corrupted by power and greed. Quinn well deserved his Best Supporting Actor Oscar for his performance as Zapata's brother. Based on the novel "Zapata the Unconquered" by Edgcumb Pinchon.
1952 112m/B Marlon Brando, Anthony Quinn, Jean Peters, Margo, Arnold Moss, Joseph Wiseman, Mildred Dunnock; **D:** Elia Kazan; **W:** John Steinbeck; **M:** Alex North. Academy Awards '52: Best Supporting Actor (Quinn); British Academy Awards '52: Best Actor (Brando); Cannes Film Festival '52: Best Actor (Brando); Nominations: Academy Awards '52: Best Actor (Brando), Best Art Direction/Set Decoration (B & W), Best Story & Screenplay, Best Original Score. **VHS, Beta, LV** ★★★★

Vivacious Lady Romantic comedy about a mild-mannered college professor who marries a chorus girl. Problems arise when he must let his conservative family and his former fiancee in on the marriage news. Good performances. Appealing.
1938 90m/B Ginger Rogers, James Stewart, James Ellison, Beulah Bondi, Charles Coburn, Jack Carson, Franklin Pangborn; **D:** George Stevens. Nominations: Academy Awards '38: Best Cinematography, Best Sound. **VHS, Beta** ★★★

Von Ryan's Express An American Air Force colonel leads a group of prisoners of war in taking control of a freight train in order to make their exciting escape from a WWII POW camp in Italy. Strong cast.
1965 117m/C Frank Sinatra, Trevor Howard, Brad Dexter, Raffaella Carra, Sergio Fantoni, John Leyton, Vito Scotti, Edward Mulhare, Adolfo Celi, James Brolin, James B. Sikking; **D:** Mark Robson; **W:** Wendell Mayes; **M:** Jerry Goldsmith. **VHS, Beta, LV** ★★★

Voyage of the Damned The story of one of the most tragic incidents of WWII. In 1939, 1,937 German-Jewish refugees fleeing Nazi Germany are bound for Cuba aboard the Hamburg-America liner S.S. St. Louis.

They are refused permission to land in Cuba (and everywhere else) and must sail back to Germany and certain death. Based on the novel by Gordon Thomas and Max Morgan-Witts.

1976 (G) 134m/C Faye Dunaway, Max von Sydow, Oskar Werner, Malcolm McDowell, Orson Welles, James Mason, Lee Grant, Katharine Ross, Ben Gazzara, Lynne Frederick, Wendy Hiller, Jose Ferrer, Luther Adler, Sam Wanamaker, Denholm Elliott, Nehemiah Persoff, Julie Harris, Maria Schell, Janet Suzman; **D:** Stuart Rosenberg; **M:** Lalo Schifrin. Golden Globe Awards '77: Best Supporting Actress (Ross); Nominations: Academy Awards '76: Best Adapted Screenplay, Best Supporting Actress (Grant), Best Original Score. **VHS, Beta** ★★★

Voyage to the Bottom of the Sea The crew of an atomic submarine must destroy a deadly radiation belt which has set the polar ice cap ablaze. Fun stuff, with good special effects and photography. Later became a television show.

1961 106m/C Walter Pidgeon, Joan Fontaine, Barbara Eden, Peter Lorre, Robert Sterling, Michael Ansara, Frankie Avalon; **D:** Irwin Allen; **W:** Irwin Allen, Charles Bennett. **VHS, Beta, LV** ★★★

Wages of Fear American oil company controls a desolate Central American town whose citizens desperately want out—so desperately that four are willing to try a suicide mission to deliver nitroglycerine to put out a well-fire raging 300 miles away. The company's cynical head has offered $2,000 to each man, enough to finance escape from the hell-hole they live in. Complex, multidimensional drama concentrates on character development for the first half—crucial to the film's greatness. This is the restored version. Remade by William Friedkin as "Sorcerer" in 1977. Based on a novel by Georges Arnaud. In French with English subtitles. **AKA:** Le Salaire De La Peur.

1953 138m/B *FR* Yves Montand, Charles Vanel, Peter Van Eyck, Vera Clouzot, Folco Lulli, William Tubbs; **D:** Henri-Georges Clouzot; **W:** Henri-Georges Clouzot; **M:** Georges Auric. British Academy Awards '54: Best Film; Cannes Film Festival '53: Best Actor (Vanel), Best Film. **VHS, Beta, LV** ★★★★

Wagon Master Two cowboys are persuaded to guide a group of Mormons, led by Bond, in their trek across the western frontier. They run into a variety of troubles, including a band of killers who joins the wagon train to escape a posse. Sensitively directed, realistic and worthwhile. Inspired the TV series "Wagon Train." Also available colorized.

1950 85m/B Ben Johnson, Joanne Dru, Harry Carey Jr., Ward Bond, Jane Darwell, James Arness; **D:** John Ford. **VHS, Beta, LV** ★★★

Waikiki Wedding Enjoyable musical about a scheming pineapple promoter (Crosby) who meets the woman of his dreams in a contest he concocted. Contest winner Ross dislikes Hawaii and wants to go home and Crosby must keep her from going . . . first for business reasons and later, for love. Supporting cast includes Hawaiian Prince Leilani and a pig. Lots of song and dance and Hawaiian sunsets, along with Burns and Raye, the other couple destined for love on the islands, keep the story moving. ♪ Sweet Leilani; Sweet Is the Word for You; In a Little Hula Heaven; Blue Hawaii; Okolehao; Nani Ona Pua.

1937 89m/B Bing Crosby, Bob Burns, Martha Raye, Shirley Ross, George Barbier, Leif Erickson, Grady Sutton, Granville Bates, Anthony Quinn; **D:** Frank Tuttle; **W:** Frank Butler, Don Hartman, Walter DeLeon, Francis Martin; **M:** Leo Robin, Ralph Rainger, Karl Struss. Academy Awards '37: Best Song ("Sweet Leilani"). **VHS** ★★★

Wait Until Dark A photographer unwittingly smuggles a drug-filled doll into New York, and his blind wife, alone in their apartment, is terrorized by murderous crooks in search of it. A compelling thriller based on the Broadway hit by Frederick Knott, who also wrote "Dial M for Murder." The individual actors' performances were universally acclaimed in this spine-tingler.

1967 105m/C Audrey Hepburn, Alan Arkin, Richard Crenna, Efrem Zimbalist Jr., Jack Weston; **D:** Terence Young; **W:** Robert B. Carrington; **M:** Henry Mancini. Nominations: Academy Awards '67: Best Actress (Hepburn). **VHS, Beta, LV** ★★★

Waiting to Exhale Adaptation of Terry McMillan's novel about four African-American women hoping to reach the point in their love lives when they can relax and stop waiting for the right man. After the string of dogs and users they choose, you want to tell them not to hold their breath. The women are supposed to be close friends, but all of their stories are broken up into vignettes. This erodes the ensemble feeling of the movie, but performances are strong all around. Retaining the book's feel of just-between-friends girl talk, it may be a little harsh for those who are, shall we say, estrogen-challenged. A lush R&B soundtrack is the perfect backdrop for the ladies' soulful yearning for real love. **1995 (R) 120m/C** Whitney Houston, Angela Bassett, Loretta Devine, Lela Rochon, Gregory Hines, Dennis Haysbert, Mykelti Williamson, Michael Beach, Leon, Wendell Pierce, Donald A. Faison, Jeffrey D. Sams; Cameos: Wesley Snipes; **D:** Forest Whitaker; **M:** Ronald Bass; **M:** Babyface. MTV Movie Awards '96: Best Song ("Sittin' Up in My Room"), Breakthrough Performance (Rochon); Nominations: MTV Movie Awards '96: Best Song ("Exhale [Shoop Shoop]") **VHS ★★★**

Wake Island After Pearl Harbor, a small group of Marines face the onslaught of the Japanese fleet on a small Pacific Island. Although doomed, they hold their ground for 16 days. Exciting, realistic, and moving. The first film to capitalize on early "last stands" of WWII; also among the most popular war movies. Shown to soldiers in training camps with great morale-raising success. **1942 88m/B** Robert Preston, Brian Donlevy, William Bendix, MacDonald Carey, Albert Dekker, Walter Abel, Rod Cameron, Barbara Britton; **D:** John Farrow. New York Film Critics Awards '42: Best Director (Farrow); Nominations: Academy Awards '42: Best Director (Farrow), Best Original Screenplay, Best Picture, Best Supporting Actor (Bendix). **VHS, Beta ★★★**

A Walk in the Sun The trials of a group of infantrymen in WWII from the time they land in Italy to the time they capture their objective, a farmhouse occupied by the Germans. Excellent ensemble acting shows well the variety of civilians who make up any fighting force and explores their fears, motivations, and weaknesses. Producer and director Milestone also made "All Quiet on the Western Front" and the Korean War masterpiece "Pork Chop Hill." Released in the final days of the war, almost concurrently with two other WWII films of the first echelon, "The Story of G.I. Joe" and "They Were Expendable." **AKA:** Salerno Beachhead. **1946 117m/B** Dana Andrews, Richard Conte, John Ireland, Lloyd Bridges, Sterling Holloway; **D:** Lewis Milestone; **W:** Robert Rossen. **VHS, Beta, LV, 8mm ★★★1/2**

The Wall The last film by Guney, author of "Yol," about orphaned boys in prison in the Turkish capital of Ankara trying to escape and/or rebel after ceaseless rapings, beatings, and injustice. An acclaimed, disturbing film made from Guney's own experience. He died in 1984, three years after escaping from prison. Brutal and horrifying. In Turkish with English subtitles. **AKA:** Guney's The Wall; Le Mur; Duvar. **1983 117m/C** *TU* Ayse Emel Mesci, Saban, Sisko; **D:** Yilmaz Guney; **W:** Yilmaz Guney. Nominations: Cannes Film Festival '83: Best Film. **VHS, Beta ★★★1/2**

Wall Street Stone's energetic, high-minded big-business treatise in which naive, neophyte stockbroker Sheen is seduced into insider trading by sleek entrepreneur Douglas, much to his blue-collar father's chagrin. A fast-moving drama of '80s-style materialism with a mesmerizing, award-winning performance by Douglas as greed personified. Expert direction by Stone, who co-wrote the not-very-subtle script. His father, to whom this film is dedicated, was a broker. Look for Stone in a cameo. **1987 (R) 126m/C** Michael Douglas, Charlie Sheen, Martin Sheen, Daryl Hannah, Sean Young, James Spader, Hal Holbrook, Terence Stamp, Richard Dysart, John C. McGinley, Saul Rubinek, James Karen, Josh Mostel, Millie Perkins, Cecilia Peck, Grant Shaud, Franklin Cover; **Cameos:** Oliver Stone; **D:** Oliver Stone; **W:** Oliver Stone, Stanley Weiser, Robert Richardson; **M:** Stewart Copeland. Academy Awards '87: Best Actor (Douglas); Golden Globe Awards '88: Best Actor—Drama (Douglas); National Board of Review Awards '87: Best Actor (Douglas); Golden Raspberry Awards '87: Worst Supporting Actress (Hannah). **VHS, Beta, LV ★★★**

The Wanderers Richard Price's acclaimed novel about youth gangs coming of age in the Bronx in 1963. The "Wanderers," named after the Dion song, are a gang of Italian-American teenagers about to graduate high school, who prowl the Bronx with the feeling that something is slipping away from them. Fascinating, funny, and touching. Manz is unforgettable as a scrappy gal. A wonderful '60s soundtrack (Dion, the Four Seasons) colors this coming-of-age-the-hard-way film. **1979 (R) 113m/C** Ken Wahl, John Friedrich, Karen Allen, Linda Manz; **Cameos:** Richard Price, Michael Chapman; **D:** Philip Kaufman; **W:** Philip Kaufman. **VHS, Beta ★★★1/2**

The Wannsee Conference A startling, important film depicting, in real time, the conference held at the

Wannsee on January 20, 1942, during which 14 members of the Nazi hierarchy decided in 85 minutes the means and logistics of effecting the Final Solution. Re-created from the original secretary's notes. Horrifying and chilling. Along with "Shoah," a must-see for understanding the Holocaust and the psychology of genocide. In German with English subtitles. *AKA:* Wannseekonferenz.
1984 87m/C *GE* Dietrich Mattausch, Gerd Brockmann, Friedrich Beckhaus; *D:* Heinz Schirk. **VHS, Beta, LV ★★★1/2**

War and Peace The massive Russian production of Leo Tolstoy's masterpiece, adapting the classic tome practically scene by scene. All of the production took place in the Soviet Union. So painstaking that it took more than five years to finish, no other adaptation can touch it. Hugely expensive ($100 million, claimed the Russians), wildly uneven production. Great scenes of battle and aristocratic life. Though this version is far from perfect, one asks: Is it humanly possible to do screen justice to such a novel? In Russian with English subtitles. On four tapes. (Beware the two-part, poorly dubbed version that was also released.)
1968 373m/C *RU* Lyudmila Savelyeva, Sergei Bondarchuk, Vyacheslav Tihonor, Hira Ivanov-Golarko, Irina Gubanova, Antonina Shuranova; *D:* Sergei Bondarchuk. Academy Awards '68: Best Foreign Language Film; Golden Globe Awards '69: Best Foreign Film; National Board of Review Awards '68: 5 Best Foreign Films of the Year; New York Film Critics Awards '68: Best Foreign Film; Nominations: Academy Awards '68: Best Art Direction/Set Decoration. **VHS, Beta, LV ★★★**

War in the Sky Director William Wyler's documentary account of the Army Air Corps in action. Extraordinary footage of the Thunderbolt, the P47 Fighter, and the B17 Bomber.
1982 90m/C *D:* William Wyler. **VHS, Beta ★★★**

The War Lord Set in the 11th century, Heston stars as Chrysagon, a Norman knight and war lord who commands a peasant village. While battling his enemies, he becomes enamored of a peasant girl named Bronwyn (Forsyth), who is unfortunately engaged to someone else. Pulling rank, Chrysagon uses an ancient law that allows noblemen the first night with a bride and the two fall in love. The two vow to never part, but that sets the stage for even more bloody

battles. Fine acting and great production values make this a well-adapted version of the play "The Lovers" by Leslie Stevens.
1965 121m/C Charlton Heston, Richard Boone, Rosemary Forsyth, Guy Stockwell, Niall MacGinnis, Henry Wilcoxon, James Farentino, Maurice Evans, Michael Conrad; *D:* Franklin J. Schaffner; *W:* John Collier, Millard Kaufman. **VHS, Beta, LV ★★★**

The War of the Roses Acidic black comedy about a well-to-do suburban couple who can't agree on a property settlement in their divorce so they wage unreserved and ever-escalating combat on each other, using their palatial home as a battleground. Expertly and lovingly (if that's the word) directed by DeVito, who plays the lawyer. Turner and Douglas are splendid. Adapted from the novel by Warren Adler. Laserdisc version includes previously deleted scenes and commentary from DeVito.
1989 (R) 116m/C Michael Douglas, Kathleen Turner, Danny DeVito, Marianne Sagebrecht, Sean Astin, G.D. Spradlin, Peter Donat, Heather Fairfield, Dan Castellaneta, Danitra Vance; *D:* Danny DeVito; *W:* Michael Leeson; *M:* David Newman, Stephen Burum. **VHS, Beta, LV ★★★**

The War of the Worlds H.G. Wells's classic novel of the invasion of Earth by Martians, updated to 1950s California, with spectacular special effects of destruction caused by the Martian war machines. Pretty scary and tense; based more on Orson Welles's radio broadcast than on the book. Still very popular; hit the top 20 in sales when released on video. Classic thriller later made into a TV series. Produced by George Pal, who brought the world much sci-fi, including "The Time Machine," "Destination Moon," and "When Worlds Collide," and who appears here as a street person.
1953 85m/C Gene Barry, Ann Robinson, Les Tremayne, Lewis Martin, Robert Cornthwaite, Sandro Giglio; *D:* Byron Haskin. Academy Awards '53: Best Special Effects; Nominations: Academy Awards '53: Best Film Editing, Best Sound. **VHS, Beta, LV ★★★1/2**

The War Room Eye opening, sometimes disturbing documentary presents a behind the scenes peek at what really goes on during a Presidential campaign. When filming began in June '92 Bill Clinton was an unknown political quantity and advisors George Stephanopoulous and James Carville were masterminding

his campaign. The "War Room" refers to the building in Little Rock where they struggled to organize a small army of volunteers into a winning team. Highlights include the Democratic National Convention, the North Carolina leg of Clinton's campaign bus tour, three Presidential debates, and the week leading up to election night.
1993 (PG) 93m/C D: Chris Hegedus, D.A. Pennebaker. National Board of Review Awards '93: Best Feature Documentary; Nominations: Academy Awards '93: Best Feature Documentary. **VHS, LV** ★★★

The War Wagon The Duke plans revenge on Cabot, the greedy mine owner who stole his gold claim and framed him for murder for which he spent years in prison. He assembles a gang to aid him, including a wise-cracking Indian (Keel) and the man sent by Cabot to kill him (Douglas). Wayne's plan is to steal the gold being shipped in Cabot's armor-plated stagecoach, the "war wagon." Well-written, good performances, lots of action. Based on the book "Badman" by Clair Huffaker. The laserdisc version is available in letterbox format.
1967 101m/C John Wayne, Kirk Douglas, Howard Keel, Robert Walker Jr., Keenan Wynn, Bruce Dern, Bruce Cabot, Joanna Barnes; **D:** Burt Kennedy. **VHS, Beta, LV** ★★★

Warlock Claustrophic, resonant town-bound tale of a marshal (Fonda) and his adoring sidekick (Quinn) who clean up a town which then turns against him. Unusual story, fine performances carry this well beyond the run-of-the-mill cow flick. Fonda reestablished himself at the box office as a western star, after "Stage Struck" and "Twelve Angry Men." From the novel by Oakley Hall. Look for "Bones" McCoy from "Star Trek" in a bit part.
1959 122m/C Henry Fonda, Anthony Quinn, Richard Widmark, Dorothy Malone, Wallace Ford, Richard Arlen, Regis Toomey, DeForest Kelley; **D:** Edward Dmytryk; **W:** Robert Alan Aurthur. **VHS, Beta** ★★★

Watch on the Rhine Couple involved with the anti-Nazi underground has escaped the country, but is pursued and harassed by Nazi agents. Adapted by Hammett and Hellman from her play. Performed on stage before the U.S. entered the war, it was the first American play and movie to portray the ugliness of fascism as an ideology, as opposed to the more devious evil of its practical

side. The Production Code at the time required that a killer always be punished; the murderer (whose screen motives had been noble) refused to film the offending scene, which explains the tacked-on ending. Superb drama from a pair of highly gifted writers and a great cast. Shumlin also directed the play.
1943 114m/B Bette Davis, Paul Lukas, Lucile Watson, Donald Woods, Beulah Bondi, Geraldine Fitzgerald, George Coulouris, Henry Daniell, Helmut Dantine; **D:** Herman Shumlin; **W:** Lillian Hellman, Dashiell Hammett; **M:** Max Steiner. Academy Awards '43: Best Actor (Lukas); Golden Globe Awards '44: Best Actor—Drama (Lukas); National Board of Review Awards '43: 10 Best Films of the Year; New York Film Critics Awards '43: Best Actor (Lukas), Best Film; Nominations: Academy Awards '43: Best Picture, Best Screenplay, Best Supporting Actress (Watson). **VHS, Beta** ★★★1/2

The Waterdance Autobiographical film based on the experiences of writer/co-director Jimenez. When writer Joel Garcia (Stolz) is paralyzed in a hiking accident he finds himself dealing with not only the rehab process itself but his feelings, the feelings of his married lover, and those of his fellow patients. Deals unsentimentally with all the physical adjustments, including the sexual ones. Resolutions may be predictable but the performances rise above any script weaknesses. The title refers to Hill's dream of dancing on water—and the fear of drowning if he stops.
1991 (R) 106m/C Eric Stoltz, Wesley Snipes, William Forsythe, Helen Hunt, Elizabeth Pena, Grace Zabriskie; **D:** Neal Jimenez, Michael Steinberg; **W:** Neal Jimenez; **M:** Michael Convertino. Independent Spirit Awards '93: Best First Feature, Best Screenplay; Sundance Film Festival '92: Best Screenplay, Audience Award. **VHS, LV** ★★★

Waterloo Bridge In London during WWI, a soldier from an aristocratic family and a ballet dancer begin a tragic romance when they meet by chance on the foggy Waterloo Bridge. When he's listed as dead, her despair turns her to prostitution. But then he returns from POW camp, they once again meet by accident on Waterloo Bridge, and their romance resumes. Four-hanky drama with fine performances by Leigh (her first after "Gone with the Wind") and Taylor.
1940 109m/B Vivien Leigh, Robert Taylor, Lucile Watson, Sir C. Aubrey Smith, Maria Ouspenskaya, Virginia Field; **D:** Mervyn LeRoy. Nominations: Academy Awards '40:

Best Black and White Cinematography, Best Original Score. **VHS, Beta, LV** ★★★

Waxworks A major achievement in German Expressionism, in which a poet imagines scenarios in a wax museum fairground that involve Jack the Ripper, Ivan the Terrible and Haroun al-Rashid. Influential and considered ahead of its time. Silent.
1924 63m/B GE William Dieterle, Emil Jannings, Conrad Veidt, Werner Krauss, Jon Gottowt, Olga Belajeff; **D:** Paul Leni; **W:** Henrik Galeen. **VHS, Beta** ★★★

Way Down East Melodramatic silent drama of a country girl who is tricked into a fake marriage by a scheming playboy. The famous final scene of Gish adrift on the ice floes is in color. One of Griffith's last critical and popular successes. This tape includes the original Griffith-approved musical score. Remade in 1935 with Henry Fonda.
1920 107m/B Lillian Gish, Richard Barthelmess, Lowell Sherman, Creighton Hale; **D:** D.W. Griffith. **VHS, Beta, LV** ★★★

Way Out West The classic twosome journey way out west to deliver the deed to a gold mine to the daughter of their late prospector pal. The obligatory romance is missing, but you'll be laughing so hard you won't notice. One of Stan and Ollie's best. Score includes the song "Trail of the Lonesome Pine." Also included on this tape is a 1932 Todd and Pitts short, "Red Noses." Available colorized.
1937 86m/B Stan Laurel, Oliver Hardy, Rosina Lawrence, James Finlayson, Sharon Lynne, ZaSu Pitts, Thelma Todd, William Haines; **D:** James W. Horne. Nominations: Academy Awards '37: Best Original Score. **VHS, Beta** ★★★

The Way We Were Big box-office hit follows a love story between opposites from the 1930s to the 1950s. Streisand is a Jewish political radical who meets the handsome WASP Redford at college. They're immediately attracted to one another, but it takes years before they act on it and eventually marry. They move to Hollywood where Redford is a screenwriter and left-wing Streisand becomes involved in the Red scare and the blacklist, much to Redford's dismay. Though always in love, their differences are too great to keep them together. An old-fashioned and sweet romance, with much gloss. Hit title song sung by Streisand. Adapted by Arthur Laurents from his novel. ♪ The Way We Were.
1973 (PG) 118m/C Barbra Streisand, Robert Redford, Bradford Dillman, Viveca Lindfors, Herb Edelman, Murray Hamilton, Patrick O'Neal, James Woods, Sally Kirkland; **D:** Sydney Pollack; **W:** Arthur Laurents; **M:** Marvin Hamlisch. Academy Awards '73: Best Song ("The Way We Were"), Best Original Score; Golden Globe Awards '74: Best Song ("The Way We Were"); National Board of Review Awards '73: 10 Best Films of the Year; Nominations: Academy Awards '73: Best Actress (Streisand), Best Art Direction/Set Decoration, Best Cinematography; Academy Awards '73: Best Costume Design. **VHS, Beta, LV, 8mm** ★★★

Wayne's World Destined to become one of the top movies of all time— Not! This "Saturday Night Live" skit proved to be so popular that it got its own movie, not unlike the plot, which has slimy producer Lowe take the public access "Wayne's World" into the world of commercial television. The zany duo of Wayne and Garth are as much fun on the big screen as they are on SNL and there are many funny moments, several of which are destined to become comedy classics. A huge box office hit that spawned a sequel.
1992 (PG-13) 93m/C Mike Myers, Dana Carvey, Rob Lowe, Tia Carrere, Brian Doyle-Murray, Lara Flynn Boyle, Kurt Fuller, Colleen Camp, Donna Dixon, Ed O'Neill; **Cameos:** Alice Cooper, Meat Loaf; **D:** Penelope Spheeris; **W:** Mike Myers, Bonnie Turner, Terry Turner; **M:** J. Peter Robinson. MTV Movie Awards '92: Best On-Screen Duo (Mike Myers/Dana Carvey). **VHS, LV** ★★★

We All Loved Each Other So Much Sensitive comedy follows three friends over 30 years, beginning at the end of WWII. All three have loved the same woman, an actress. Homage to friendship and to postwar Italian cinema. Includes a full-scale re-creation of the fountain scene in "La Dolce Vita." In Italian with English subtitles.
1977 124m/C IT Vittorio Gassman, Nino Manfredi, Stefano Satta Flores, Stefania Sandrelli, Marcello Mastroianni, Federico Fellini; **D:** Ettore Scola. **VHS, Beta, LV** ★★★½

We Dive at Dawn Interesting, tense British submarine drama. The "Sea Tiger" attempts to sink the German battleship "Brandenburg" off Denmark. Good cast. Mills prepared for the role by riding an actual submarine, turning "a pale shade of pea-green" when it crash-dived.
1943 98m/B GB Eric Portman, John Mills; **D:** Anthony Asquith. **VHS, Beta** ★★★

We Think the World of You
When bisexual Oldman goes to prison, his lover Bates, whose feelings are unresolved and complex, finds friendship with Oldman's dog. Odd, oft-bitter comedy-drama of love and loyalty characterized by excellent acting and respectful, gentle direction. From the novel by Joseph R. Ackerly.
1988 (PG) 94m/C *GB* Alan Bates, Gary Oldman, Frances Barber, Liz Smith, Max Wall, Kerry Wise; *D:* Colin Gregg. **VHS, Beta, LV ★★★**

The Wedding Banquet Charming story about a clash of customs and secrets. Naturalized American Wai Tung (Chao, in his debut) lives comfortably with his lover Simon (Lichtenstein) while hiding the fact that he's gay from his Chinese parents. To appease his parents and get his "wife" a green card, he marries for convenience and watches as the deception snowballs. Comedy of errors was shot on a small budget ($750,000) and examines small details with as much care as the larger ones. A fine effort from director Lee that's solidly humorous, but also poignant. In English and Chinese with English subtitles. **AKA:** Xiyan.
1993 (R) 111m/C *TW* Winston Chao, May Chin, Mitchell Lichtenstein, Sihung Lung, Ah-Leh Gua; *D:* Ang Lee; *W:* Ang Lee, Neil Peng, James Schamus. Nominations: Academy Awards '93: Best Foreign Language Film; Golden Globe Awards '94: Best Foreign Language Film; Independent Spirit Awards '94: Best Actor (Lichtenstein), Best Actress (Chin), Best Director (Lee), Best Film, Best Screenplay, Best Supporting Actress (Gua). **VHS, LV ★★★**

Wedding in Blood Two French lovers plot to kill their respective spouses, and proceed to do so amid calamity and much table-turning. Sharp social satire and suspenseful mystery. Based on a true story. In French with English subtitles.
1974 (PG) 98m/C *FR IT* Claude Pieplu, Stephane Audran, Michel Piccoli; *D:* Claude Chabrol. **VHS, Beta ★★★**

The Wedding March Von Stroheim's famous silent film about romantic couplings in pre-WWI Vienna. The director also stars as a prince preparing to marry for money, who falls in love with a beautiful, but poor, woman. Romance and irony, with a memorable finale. Like many of his other great films, it was taken from him and reedited. Initially the first of two halves; the second, "The Honeymoon," has been lost. Next to "Greed," his most successful film.
1928 113m/B Erich von Stroheim, Fay Wray, ZaSu Pitts, George Fawcett, Maude George, Matthew Betz, George Nicholls, Cesare Gravina; *D:* Erich von Stroheim; *M:* Gaylord Carter. **VHS, Beta ★★★★**

Wee Willie Winkie A precocious little girl is taken in by a British regiment in India. Sugar-coated. If you're a cinematic diabetic, be warned. If you're a Temple fan, you've probably already seen it. If not, you're in for a treat. Inspired by the Rudyard Kipling story.
1937 (PG) 99m/B Shirley Temple, Victor McLaglen, Sir C. Aubrey Smith, June Lang, Michael Whalen, Cesar Romero, Constance Collier; *D:* John Ford. Nominations: Academy Awards '37: Best Interior Decoration. **VHS, Beta ★★★**

Weekend A Parisian couple embark on a drive to the country. On the way they witness and are involved in horrifying highway wrecks. Leaving the road they find a different, equally grotesque kind of carnage. Godard's brilliant, surreal, hyper-paranoiac view of modern life was greatly influenced by the fact that his mother was killed in an auto accident in 1954 (he himself suffered a serious motorcycle mishap in 1975). In French with English subtitles.
1967 105m/C *FR IT* Mireille Darc, Jean Yanne, Jean-Pierre Kalfon, Valerie Lagrange, Jean-Pierre Leaud, Yves Beneyton; *D:* Jean-Luc Godard; *W:* Jean-Luc Godard; *M:* Antoine Duhamel. **VHS ★★★**

We're Not Dressing Loose musical adaptation of J.M. Barrie's "The Admirable Crichton" with the butler transformed into singing sailor Crosby. Fabulously wealthy heiress Lombard invites her pals for a South Seas yachting adventure. Only the ship gets wrecked and everyone winds up on a small island where the practical Crosby whips everyone into shape (and romances Lombard). Burns and Allen supply additional comedy as a pair of botanists who just happen to be studying the local fauna. ♪ Good Night Lovely Little Lady; I'll Sing About the Birds and the Bees; It's Just a New Spanish Custom; Let's Play House; Love Thy Neighbor; May I?; Once in a Blue Moon; She Reminds Me of You.
1934 74m/B Bing Crosby, Carole Lombard, George Burns, Gracie Allen, Ethel Merman, Leon Errol, Ray Milland; *D:* Norman Taurog; *W:* Horace Jackson, Francis Martin; *M:* Harry Revel, Mack Gordon. **VHS, LV ★★★**

Wes Craven's New Nightmare
Seems the six previous conjurings of
Freddy's tortured but fictional soul
have inadvertently created a real supernatural force bent on tormenting
the lives of retired scream queen Langenkamp, her son (Hughes), writer-
director Craven, and surprisingly mild
alter-ego Englund. Craven's solution
is to write a script that reunites series
principals for a final showdown with
the slashmaster in Hell. Clever and
original in a genre known for neither
trait, this movie-in-a-movie-about-a-
movie is equal parts playful gimmick
and inspired terror that will give even
the most seasoned Kruegerphile the
heebie-jeebies.
1994 (R) 112m/C Robert Englund, Heather
Langenkamp, Miko Hughes, David
Newsom, Tracy Middendorf, Fran Bennett,
John Saxon, Wes Craven, Robert Shaye,
Sara Risher, Marianne Maddalena; **D:** Wes
Craven; **W:** Wes Craven; **M:** J. Peter
Robinson. Nominations: Independent Spirit
Awards '95: Best Film. **VHS, LV ★★★**

West Side Story Gang rivalry and
ethnic tension on New York's West
Side erupts in a ground-breaking musical. Loosely based on Shakespeare's "Romeo and Juliet," the
story follows the Jets and the Sharks
as they fight for their turf while Tony
and Maria fight for love. Features frenetic and brilliant choreography by
co-director Robbins, who also directed the original Broadway show,
and a high-caliber score by Bernstein
and Sondheim. Wood's voice was
dubbed by Marni Nixon and Jimmy
Bryant dubbed Beymer's. The laserdisc version includes the complete
storyboards, production sketches, reissue trailer, and an interview with
Wise in a letterbox format with digital
stereo surround sound. ♪ Prologue;
Jet Song; Something's Coming;
Dance at the Gym; Maria; America;
Tonight; One Hand, One Heart; Gee,
Officer Krupke.
1961 151m/C Natalie Wood, Richard
Beymer, Russ Tamblyn, Rita Moreno,
George Chakiris, Simon Oakland, Ned
Glass; **D:** Robert Wise, Jerome Robbins;
W: Ernest Lehman; **M:** Leonard Bernstein,
Stephen Sondheim. Academy Awards '61:
Best Art Direction/Set Decoration (Color),
Best Color Cinematography, Best Costume
Design (Color), Best Director (Wise), Best
Film Editing, Best Picture, Best Sound,
Best Supporting Actor (Chakiris), Best
Supporting Actress (Moreno), Best Score;
Directors Guild of America Awards '61:
Best Director (Wise), Best Director
(Robbins); New York Film Critics Awards
'61: Best Film; Nominations: Academy

Awards '61: Best Adapted Screenplay.
VHS, Beta, LV ★★★1/2

Western Union A lavish, vintage epic
romantically detailing the political
machinations, Indian warfare, and
frontier adventure that accompanied
the construction of the Western
Union telegraph line from Omaha,
Nebraska, to Salt Lake City, Utah,
during the Civil War. A thoroughly entertaining film in rich Technicolor. This
was Lang's second western, following his personal favorite, "The Return
of Frank James." Writer Carson uti-
lized the title, but not the storyline, of
a Zane Grey book. The German Lang
showed himself a master of the most
American of genres, yet made only
one more western, "Rancho Notorious" (1952), another masterpiece.
1941 94m/C Randolph Scott, Robert
Young, Dean Jagger, Slim Summerville,
Virginia Gilmore, John Carradine, Chill
Wills, Barton MacLane, Minor Watson,
Charles Middleton, Irving Bacon; **D:** Fritz
Lang; **W:** Robert Carson. **VHS, Beta
★★★1/2**

The Westerner A sly, soft-spoken
drifter champions Texas border
homesteaders in a land war with the
legendary Judge Roy Bean. "The Law
West of the Pecos" sentences drifter
Cooper to hang, but Cooper breaks
out of jail. He falls for damsel Davenport and stays in the area, advocating
the rights of homesteaders to Brennan. Brennan's Bean is unforgettable
and steals the show from Cooper.
Film debuts of actors Tucker and Andrews. Amazing cinematography;
Brennan's Oscar was his third, making him the first performer to pull a
hat trick.
1940 100m/B Gary Cooper, Walter
Brennan, Doris Davenport, Dana Andrews,
Forrest Tucker, Charles Halton; **D:** William
Wyler. Academy Awards '40: Best
Supporting Actor (Brennan); Nominations:
Academy Awards '40: Best Interior
Decoration, Best Story. **VHS, Beta, LV
★★★1/2**

Westward the Women Taylor is Buck
Wyatt, a scout hired to wagon-train
150 mail-order brides from Chicago
to California. When his lustful hired
hands turn out to be all hands, Taylor
and the ladies must fight off attacking
Indians on their own. Notable film allowing women to be as tough as men
is not your typical western. Based on
the Frank Capra story.
1951 116m/C Robert Taylor, Denise
Darcel, Hope Emerson, John McIntire,
Beverly Dennis, Lenore Lonergan, Marilyn
Erskine, Julie Bishop, Renata Vanni,

Frankie Darro, George Chandler; **D:** William A. Wellman; **W:** Charles Schnee; **M:** Jeff Alexander. **VHS** ★★★

Wetherby Playwright David Hare's first directorial effort, which he also wrote, about a Yorkshire schoolteacher whose life is shattered when a young, brooding stranger comes uninvited to a dinner party, and then shoots himself in her living room. Compelling but oh, so dark. Richardson, who plays a young Redgrave, is actually Redgrave's daughter.
1985 (R) 97m/C GB Vanessa Redgrave, Ian Holm, Judi Dench, Joely Richardson, Tim McInnery, Suzanna Hamilton; **D:** David Hare; **W:** David Hare; **M:** Nick Bicat. Berlin International Film Festival '85: Golden Berlin Bear; National Society of Film Critics Awards '85: Best Actress (Redgrave). **VHS, Beta** ★★★

The Whales of August Based on the David Berry play, the story of two elderly sisters—one caring, the other cantankerous, blind, and possibly senile—who decide during a summer in Maine whether or not they should give up their ancestral house and enter a nursing home. Gish and Davis are exquisite to watch, and the all-star supporting cast is superb—especially Price as a suave Russian. Lovingly directed by Anderson in his first US outing.
1987 91m/C Lillian Gish, Bette Davis, Vincent Price, Ann Sothern, Mary Steenburgen, Harry Carey Jr.; **D:** Lindsay Anderson; **W:** David Berry. National Board of Review Awards '87: Best Actress (Gish); National Media Owl Awards '88: First Prize; Nominations: Academy Awards '87: Best Supporting Actress (Sothern). **VHS, Beta, LV, 8mm** ★★★1/2

What Ever Happened to Baby Jane? Davis and Crawford portray aging sisters and former child stars living together in a decaying mansion. When the demented Jane (Davis) learns of her now-crippled sister's (Crawford) plan to institutionalize her, she tortures the wheelchair-bound sis. Davis plays her part to the hilt, unafraid of Aldrich's unsympathetic camera, and the viciousness of her character. She received her tenth Oscar nomination for the role.
1962 132m/B Bette Davis, Joan Crawford, Victor Buono, Anna Lee, B.D. Merrill; **D:** Robert Aldrich. Nominations: Academy Awards '62: Best Actress (Davis), Best Black and White Cinematography, Best Sound, Best Supporting Actor (Buono). **VHS, Beta, LV** ★★★1/2

What Happened to Rosa? This early Goldwyn release, a whimsical Cin-derella story, casts Normand as an endearing shop girl duped by a gypsy's bogus predictions. Believing herself to be the reincarnation of a Castillian noblewoman she dons a fancy gown, attends a fancy ship-board ball and captures the heart of the fancy doctor of her dreams. But fearing his rejection of her true identity, she slips away during the chaos of a brawl, leading the good doctor to believe that she is dead. A comedy of errors unfolds before they meet again and live happily ever after. No doubt it jerked a few tears in its day.
1921 42m/B Mabel Normand, Hugh Thompson, Doris Pawn, Tully Marshall, Eugenie Besserer, Buster Trow; **D:** Victor Schertzinger. **VHS** ★★★

What Price Glory? Remake of the 1926 silent classic about a pair of comradely rivals for the affections of women in WWI France. Strange to have Ford directing an offbeat comedy, but it works: masterful direction, good acting. Demarest broke both legs in a motorcycle accident during shooting.
1952 111m/C James Cagney, Dan Dailey, Corinne Calvet, William Demarest, James Gleason, Robert Wagner, Casey Adams, Craig Hill, Marisa Pavan; **D:** John Ford. **VHS, Beta** ★★★

What Price Hollywood? Aspiring young starlet decides to crash film world by using an alcoholic director as her stepping stone. Bennett is lovely; Sherman is superb as an aging, dissolute man who watches his potential slip away. From a story by Adela Rogers St. John. Remade three times as "A Star is Born."
1932 88m/B Constance Bennett, Lowell Sherman, Neil Hamilton; **D:** George Cukor; **M:** Max Steiner. Nominations: Academy Awards '32: Best Original Screenplay. **VHS, Beta, LV** ★★★

What's Eating Gilbert Grape Offbeat is mildly descriptive. Depp stars as Gilbert Grape, the titular head of a very dysfunctional family living in a big house in a small Iowa town. His Momma (Cates) weighs more than 500 pounds and hasn't left the house in seven years, he has two squabbling teenage sisters, and 17-year-old brother Arnie (DiCaprio) is mentally retarded and requires constant supervision. What's a good-hearted grocery clerk to do? Well, when free-spirited Becky (Lewis) is momentarily marooned in town, Gilbert may have found a true soulmate. Performances, especially DiCaprio's, save this from the oddball/cute factor although flick would have benefitted from streamlining, particularly the scenes involving Depp and bad-haircut Lewis. Based on the novel by Hedges. *AKA:* Gilbert Grape.

1993 (PG-13) 118m/C Johnny Depp, Leonardo DiCaprio, Juliette Lewis, Mary Steenburgen, Darlene Cates, Laura Harrington, Mary Kate Schellhardt, Kevin Tighe, John C. Reilly, Crispin Glover, Penelope Branning; *D:* Lasse Hallstrom; *W:* Peter Hedges; *M:* Alan Parker, Bjorn Isfalt. National Board of Review Awards '93: Best Supporting Actor (DiCaprio); Nominations: Academy Awards '93: Best Supporting Actor (DiCaprio); Golden Globe Awards '94: Best Supporting Actor (DiCaprio). **VHS, Beta, LV** ★★★

What's New Pussycat? A young engaged man, reluctant to give up the girls who love him, seeks the aid of a married psychiatrist who turns out to have problems of his own. Allen's first feature as both actor and screenwriter. Oscar-nominated title song sung by Tom Jones. *AKA:* Quoi De Neuf, Pussycat?.

1965 108m/C Peter Sellers, Peter O'Toole, Romy Schneider, Paula Prentiss, Woody Allen, Ursula Andress, Capucine; *D:* Clive Donner; *W:* Woody Allen; *M:* Burt Bacharach, Hal David. Nominations: Academy Awards '65: Best Song ("What's New Pussycat?"). **VHS, Beta, LV** ★★★

What's Up, Doc? A shy musicologist from Iowa (O'Neal) travels to San Francisco with his fiance (Kahn) for a convention. He meets the eccentric Streisand at his hotel and becomes involved in a chase to recover four identical flight bags containing top secret documents, a wealthy woman's jewels, the professor's musical rocks, and Streisand's clothing. Bogdanovich's homage to the screwball comedies of the '30s. Kahn's feature film debut.

1972 (G) 94m/C Barbra Streisand, Ryan O'Neal, Madeline Kahn, Kenneth Mars, Austin Pendleton, Randy Quaid; *D:* Peter Bogdanovich; *W:* David Newman, Buck Henry, Robert Benton; *M:* Artie Butler. Writers Guild of America '72: Best Original Screenplay. **VHS, Beta** ★★★

What's Up, Tiger Lily? This legitimate Japanese spy movie—"Kagi No Kag" (Key of Keys), a 1964 Bond imitation—was re-edited by Woody Allen, who added a new dialogue track, with hysterical results. Characters Terri and Suki Yaki are involved in an international plot to secure egg salad recipes; Allen's brand of Hollywood parody and clever wit sustain

the joke. Music by the Lovin' Spoonful, who make a brief appearance.

1966 90m/C *JP* Woody Allen, Tatsuya Mihashi, Mie Hama, Akiko Wakabayashi; *D:* Woody Allen, Senkichi Taniguhi; *M:* Jack Lewis. **VHS, Beta, LV** ★★★

When Father Was Away on Business Set in 1950s Yugoslavia. A family must take care of itself when the father is sent to jail for philandering with a woman desired by a Communist Party offical. The moving story of the family's day-to-day survival is seen largely through the eyes of the father's six-year-old son, who believes dad is "away on business." In Yugoslavian with English subtitles.

1985 (R) 144m/C *YU* Moreno D'E Bartolli, Miki Manojlovic, Mirjana Karanovic; *D:* Emir Kusturica. Cannes Film Festival '85: Best Film; Nominations: Academy Awards '85: Best Foreign Language Film. **VHS** ★★★1/2

When Harry Met Sally Romantic comedy follows the long relationship between two adults who try throughout the changes in their lives (and their mates) to remain platonic friends—and what happens when they don't. Wry and enjoyable script is enhanced by wonderful performances. Another directional direct hit for "Meathead" Reiner, and a tour de force of comic screenwriting for Ephron, with improvisational help from Crystal. Great songs by Sinatra sound-alike Connick.

1989 (R) 96m/C Billy Crystal, Meg Ryan, Carrie Fisher, Bruno Kirby, Steven Ford, Lisa Jane Persky, Michelle Nicastro, Harley Jane Kozak; *D:* Rob Reiner; *W:* Nora Ephron; *M:* Harry Connick Jr., Marc Shaiman. British Academy Awards '89: Best Original Screenplay; Nominations: Academy Awards '89: Best Original Screenplay. **VHS, Beta, LV, 8mm** ★★★

When Hell Was in Session In more than seven years as a prisoner of the Viet Cong, Holbrook is subjected to torture, starvation, and psychological warfare to break his will. Based on the true story of Navy Commander Jeremiah Denton. Painful and violent. Made for TV.

1982 98m/C Hal Holbrook, Eva Marie Saint, Ronny Cox; *D:* Paul Krasny. **VHS, Beta** ★★★

When the Clouds Roll By Psychosatire pits demented doctor against Fairbanks in experiment to make him suicidal basket case. Fairbanks seems to contract ferocious nightmares, passionate superstitions, a spurning lover, and a warrant for his

arrest, none of which suppresses his penchant for acrobatics.
1919 77m/B Douglas Fairbanks Sr., Herbert Grimwood, Kathleen Clifford, Frank Campeau, Ralph Lewis, Daisy Robinson, Albert MacQuarrie; **D:** Victor Fleming. **VHS, Beta** ★★★1/2

When Night Is Falling Camille (Bussieres) is a professor of mythology at a Calvinist college in Toronto and engaged to theologian Martin (Czerny). Vaguely unsatisfied, Camille meets Petra (Crawford), a trapeze artist in a traveling circus, gets drawn into her world, falls in love, and must decide what she wants from her life. Lots of yearning, romance, and fantasy. Lesbian lovemaking scenes caused a ratings problem (the MPAA originally deemed them worthy of NC-17).
1995 (R) 96m/C *CA* Pascale Bussieres, Rachael Crawford, Henry Czerny, David Fox, Don McKellar, Tracy Wright; **D:** Patricia Rozema; **W:** Patricia Rozema; **M:** Lesley Barber. VHS ★★★

When the Wind Blows An animated feature about a retired British couple whose peaceful—and naive—life in the country is destroyed by nuclear war. Poignant, sad, and thought-provoking, and just a little scary. Features the voices of Ashcroft and Mills; Roger Waters, David Bowie, Squeeze, Genesis, Hugh Cornell, and Paul Hardcastle all contribute to the soundtrack. Based on the novel by Raymond Briggs.
1986 80m/C *GB* **D:** Jimmy T. Murakami; **V:** Peggy Ashcroft, John Mills. **VHS, Beta, LV** ★★★

Where Angels Fear to Tread Another turn-of-the-century tale of the English in Italy from the pen of E.M. Forster. Widowed, fortyish Lilia (Mirren) is urged by her stuffy in-laws to spend some time in Italy. Much to everyone's dismay she impulsively marries a 21-year-old Italian—with disastrous consequences. Based on Forster's first novel, the characters are more stereotypical and the story less defined than his later works and the movies made from them. Impressive performances and beautiful settings make up for a somewhat lackluster direction that isn't up to the standards set by the team of Merchant Ivory, responsible for the Forster films "A Room with a View" and "Howard's End."
1991 (PG) 112m/C *GB* Rupert Graves, Helena Bonham Carter, Judy Davis, Helen Mirren, Giovanni Guidelli, Barbara Jefford, Thomas Wheatley, Sophie Kullman; **D:**

Charles Sturridge; **M:** Rachel Portman. **VHS, LV** ★★★

Where Eagles Dare During WWII, a small group of Allied commandos must rescue an American general held by the Nazis in a castle in the Bavarian Alps. Relentless plot twists and action keep you breathless. Well-made suspense/adventure. Alistair MacLean adapted his original screenplay into a successful novel.
1968 (PG) 158m/C Clint Eastwood, Richard Burton, Mary Ure, Michael Hordern, Anton Diffring, Ingrid Pitt, Patrick Wymark, Robert Beatty; **D:** Brian G. Hutton. VHS, Beta, LV ★★★

Where's Poppa? A Jewish lawyer's senile mother constantly ruins his love life, and he considers various means of getting rid of her, including dressing up as an ape to scare her to death. Filled with outlandish and often tasteless humor, befitting its reign as a black comedy cult classic. Adapted by Robert Klane from his novel. *AKA:* Going Ape.
1970 84m/C George Segal, Ruth Gordon, Ron Leibman, Vincent Gardenia, Rob Reiner, Trish Van Devere; **D:** Carl Reiner, Jack Priestley. VHS, Beta, LV ★★★

While the City Sleeps Three newspaper reporters vie to crack the case of a sex murderer known as "The Lipstick Killer" with the editorship of their paper the prize. Good thriller-plus with the emphasis on the reporters' ruthless methods of gaining information rather than on the killer's motivations. Lang's last big success. Based on "The Bloody Spur" by Charles Einstein.
1956 100m/B Dana Andrews, Rhonda Fleming, George Sanders, Howard Duff, Thomas Mitchell, Ida Lupino, Vincent Price, Mae Marsh; **D:** Fritz Lang. VHS, Beta, LV ★★★

While You Were Sleeping Feel-good romantic comedy finds lonely Lucy Moderatz (Bullock) collecting tokens for the Chicago train system and admiring yuppie lawyer Peter Callaghan (Gallagher) as he commutes to and fro. Fate conspires to throw them together when Lucy rescues Peter after a mugging. Trouble is, he's not conscious so Lucy goes to the hospital with him, where she's mistaken for his fiancee. She continues the charade and is warmly welcomed by the Callaghan family, with the exception of Peter's brother, Jack (Pullman), who smells a rat even as he falls under the token collector's spell. Meanwhile, Peter remains in a coma, allowing Jack and Lucy to supply romantic comedy. Gallagher brings a serenity to his role as the unconscious Peter, while Bullock and Pullman take the predictable plot and deliver performances that earn them another notch on the climb to stardom.

1995 (PG) 103m/C Sandra Bullock, Bill Pullman, Peter Gallagher, Jack Warden, Peter Boyle, Glynis Johns, Micole Mercurio, Jason Bernard, Michael Rispoli, Ally Walker, Monica Keena; **D:** Jon Turteltaub; **W:** Fred Lebow, Daniel G. Sullivan; **M:** Randy Edelman, Phedon Papamichael. Blockbuster Entertainment Awards '96: Comedy Actress, Video (Bullock), Comedy Actress, Theatrical (Bullock); Nominations: Golden Globe Awards '96: Best Actress— Musical/Comedy (Bullock). **VHS, LV ★★★**

Whiskey Galore During WWII, a whiskey-less Scottish island gets a lift when a ship, carrying 50,000 cases of spirits, wrecks off the coast. A full-scale rescue operation and the evasion of both local and British government authorities ensue. The classic Ealing studio comedy is based on the actual wreck of a cargo ship off the Isle of Eriskay in 1941. **AKA:** Tight Little Island.

1948 81m/B *GB* Basil Radford, Joan Greenwood, Gordon Jackson, James Robertson Justice; **D:** Alexander MacKendrick. **VHS, Beta ★★★1/2**

The Whistle Blower A young government worker in England with a high-security position mysteriously dies. His father, a former intelligence agent, begins investigating his son's death and discovers sinister Soviet-related conspiracies. A lucid, complex British espionage thriller. Adapted from the John Hale novel by Julian Bond.

1987 98m/C *GB* Michael Caine, Nigel Havers, John Gielgud, James Fox, Felicity Dean, Gordon Jackson, Barry Foster; **D:** Simon Langton; **W:** Julian Bond; **M:** John Scott. **VHS, Beta, LV ★★★**

Whistle Down the Wind Three children of strict religious upbringing find a murderer hiding in their family's barn and believe him to be Jesus Christ. A well done and hardly grim or dull allegory of childhood innocence based on a novel by Mills's mother, Mary Hayley Bell. For a film relying heavily on child characters, it's important to portray childhood well and realistically. That is done here, as in "To Kill a Mockingbird." Mills is perfect. The film is Forbes's directorial debut and Richard Attenborough's second production.

1962 98m/B *GB* Hayley Mills, Bernard Lee, Alan Bates; **D:** Bryan Forbes; **M:**

Malcolm Arnold. National Board of Review Awards '62: 10 Best Films of the Year. **VHS, Beta ★★★1/2**

The White Balloon Beautifully told story from the viewpoint of determined seven-year-old Tehranian Reziah (Mohammadkhani), who wants to properly celebrate the Islamic New Year by buying a particularly plump goldfish (a symbol of harmony) from the pet shop. She manages to beg the money from her mother and sets off but, distracted by the street sights, Reziah loses the banknote, which falls into a street grate. Various characters seek to help her but it's Reziah's resourceful brother Ali (Kalifi) who gets a balloon seller to finally retrieve the money. Farsi with subtitles. **AKA:** Badkonake Sefid.

1995 85m/C *IN* Aida Mohammadkhani, Mohsen Kalifi, Fereshteh Sadr Ofrani, Anna Bourkowska, Mohammad Shahani, Mohammad Bahktiari; **D:** Jafar Panahi; **W:** Abbas Kiarostami. New York Film Critics Awards '96: Best Foreign Film. **VHS ★★★1/2**

White Christmas Two ex-army buddies become a popular comedy team and play at a financially unstable Vermont inn at Christmas for charity's sake. Many swell Irving Berlin songs rendered with zest. Paramount's first Vista Vision film. Presented in widescreen on laserdisc. ♪ The Best Things Happen While You're Dancing; Love, You Didn't Do Right By Me; Choreography; Count Your Blessings Instead of Sheep; What Can You Do With a General; Mandy; The Minstrel Show; Sisters; Heat Wave.

1954 120m/C Bing Crosby, Danny Kaye, Rosemary Clooney, Vera-Ellen, Dean Jagger; **D:** Michael Curtiz; **W:** Norman Panama. Nominations: Academy Awards '54: Best Song ("Count Your Blessings Instead of Sheep"). **VHS, Beta, LV, 8mm, CD-I ★★★**

The White Cliffs of Dover Prime example of a successful '40s "women's weepie." American Dunne goes to England in 1914, falls in love, and marries the British Marshal. He joins the WWI troops and is killed, without knowing he had a son. Dunne raises the boy in England as a new threat looms with the rise of Hitler. Now grown, he goes off to do his duty and she joins the Red Cross, where she sees him again among the wounded, another victim of the ravages of war. Dunne is fine in her noble, sacrificing role. McDowall is the young son with Taylor (with whom he'd already worked in "Lassie Come Home") as a childhood friend. Based on the poem by Alice Duer Miller. Bring the hankies.

1944 126m/B Irene Dunne, Alan Marshal, Frank Morgan, Peter Lawford, Gladys Cooper, May Whitty, Sir C. Aubrey Smith, Roddy McDowall, Van Johnson, Elizabeth Taylor, June Lockhart, John Warburton, Jill Esmond, Norma Varden, Tom Drake, Arthur Shields; *D:* Clarence Brown. Nominations: Academy Awards '44: Best Black and White Cinematography. **VHS ★★★**

White Heat A classic gangster film with one of Cagney's best roles as a psychopathic robber/killer with a mother complex. The famous finale —perhaps Cagney's best-known scene—has Cagney trapped on top of a burning oil tank shouting "Made it, Ma! Top of the world!" before the tank explodes. Cagney's character is allegedly based on Arthur "Doc" Barker and his "Ma," and his portrayal is breathtaking. Also available colorized.

1949 114m/B James Cagney, Virginia Mayo, Edmond O'Brien, Margaret Wycherly, Steve Cochran; *D:* Raoul Walsh; *M:* Max Steiner. Nominations: Academy Awards '49: Best Story. **VHS, Beta, LV ★★★1/2**

White Hunter, Black Heart Eastwood casts himself against type as Huston-esque director who is more interested in hunting large tusked creatures than shooting the film he came to Africa to produce. Based on Peter Viertel's 1953 account of his experiences working on James Agee's script for Huston's "African Queen." Eastwood's Huston impression is a highlight, though the story occasionally wanders off with the elephants.

1990 (PG) 112m/C Clint Eastwood, Marisa Berenson, George Dzundza, Jeff Fahey, Timothy Spall, Charlotte Cornwell, Mel Martin, Alun Armstrong, Richard Vanstone; *D:* Clint Eastwood; *W:* Peter Viertel, James Bridges, Burt Kennedy, Jack N. Green; *M:* Lennie Niehaus. **VHS, Beta, LV, 8mm ★★★**

White Mama A poor widow (Davis, in a splendid role) takes in a street-wise black kid (Harden) in return for protection from the neighborhood's dangers, and they discover friendship. Poignant drama, capably directed by Cooper, featuring sterling performances all around Made-for-TV drama at its best.

1980 96m/C Bette Davis, Ernest Harden, Eileen Heckart, Virginia Capers, Lurene Tuttle, Anne Ramsey; *D:* Jackie Cooper. **VHS, Beta ★★★**

White Mischief An alternately ghastly and hilarious indictment of the English upper class between the World Wars, and the decadence the British colonists perpetrated in Kenya, which came to world attention with the murder of the philandering Earl of Errol in 1941. Exquisitely directed and photographed. Acclaimed and grandly acted, especially by Scacchi; Howard's last appearance.

1988 (R) 108m/C Greta Scacchi, Charles Dance, Joss Ackland, Sarah Miles, John Hurt, Hugh Grant, Geraldine Chaplin, Trevor Howard, Murray Head, Susan Fleetwood, Alan Dobie, Jacqueline Pearce; *D:* Michael Radford; *M:* George Fenton, Roger Deakins. **VHS, Beta, LV, 8mm ★★★**

White Nights Based on a love story by Dostoyevski. A young woman pines for the return of her sailor while a mild-mannered clerk is smitten by her. Both of their romantic fantasies are explored. The dance-hall cadence is mixed with dreamy, fantastic flashbacks. In Italian with English subtitles. Equally good Soviet version made in 1959.

1957 107m/C *IT* Maria Schell, Jean Marais, Marcello Mastroianni; *D:* Luchino Visconti; *M:* Nino Rota. **VHS ★★★**

The White Rose An aspiring minister travels to see the world he intends to save, and winds up falling from grace. Complicated menage a trois is finally sorted out at the end. Silent.

1923 120m/B Mae Marsh, Carol Dempster, Ivor Novello, Neil Hamilton, Lucille LaVerne; *D:* D.W. Griffith. **VHS, Beta ★★★**

The White Sheik Fellini's first solo effort. A newlywed bride meets her idol from the comic pages (made with photos, not cartoons; called fumetti) and runs off with him. She soon finds he's as ordinary as her husband. Brilliant satire in charming garb. Remade as "The World's Greatest Lover." Woody Allen's "The Purple Rose of Cairo" is in a similar spirit. In Italian with English subtitles. *AKA:* Lo Sceicco Bianco.

1952 86m/B *IT* Alberto Sordi, Giulietta Masina, Brunella Bova, Leopoldo Trieste; *D:* Federico Fellini; *W:* Federico Fellini, Tullio Pinelli, Ennio Flaiano; *M:* Nino Rota. **VHS ★★★**

The White Zombie Lugosi followed his success in "Dracula" with the title role in this low-budget horror classic about the leader of a band of zombies who wants to steal a beautiful young woman from her new husband. Set in Haiti; the first zombie movie. Rich and dark, though ludicrous. Based on the novel "The Magic Island" by William Seabrook.

1932 73m/B Bela Lugosi, Madge Bellamy, John Harron; *D:* Victor Halperin; *M:* Xavier Cugat. **VHS, Beta ★★★**

Who Framed Roger Rabbit?
Technically marvelous, cinematically hilarious, eye-popping combination of cartoon and live action creates a Hollywood of the 1940s where cartoon characters are real and a repressed minority working in films. A 'toon-hating detective is hired to uncover the unfaithful wife of 2-D star Roger, and instead uncovers a conspiracy to wipe out all 'toons. Special appearances by many cartoon characters from the past. Coproduced by Touchstone (Disney) and Amblin (Spielberg). Adapted from "Who Censored Roger Rabbit?" by Gary K. Wold.

1988 (PG) 104m/C Bob Hoskins, Christopher Lloyd, Joanna Cassidy, Alan Tilvern, Stubby Kaye; *D:* Robert Zemeckis; *W:* Jeffrey Price, Peter S. Seaman; *M:* Alan Silvestri, Dean Cundey; *V:* Charles Fleischer, Mae Questel, Kathleen Turner, Amy Irving, Mel Blanc, June Foray, Frank Sinatra. Academy Awards '88: Best Film Editing, Best Visual Effects; National Board of Review Awards '88: 10 Best Films of the Year; Nominations: Academy Awards '88: Best Art Direction/Set Decoration, Best Cinematography, Best Sound. **VHS, Beta, LV ★★★★**

Who Is Killing the Great Chefs of Europe?
A fast-paced, lightly handled black comedy. When a gourmand, well-played by Morley, learns he must lose weight to live, a number of Europe's best chefs are murdered according to their cooking specialty. A witty, crisp, international mystery based on Ivan and Nan Lyon's novel. *AKA:* Too Many Chefs; Someone is Killing the Great Chefs of Europe.

1978 (PG) 112m/C George Segal, Jacqueline Bisset, Robert Morley, Jean-Pierre Cassel, Philippe Noiret, Jean Rochefort, Joss Ackland, Nigel Havers; *D:* Ted Kotcheff; *M:* Henry Mancini. Los Angeles Film Critics Association Awards '78: Best Supporting Actor (Morley). **VHS ★★★**

Who'll Stop the Rain?
A temperamental Vietnam vet (Nolte) is enlisted in a smuggling scheme to transport a large amount of heroin into California. An excellent blend of drama, comedy, action, suspense, and tragedy. Based on Robert Stone's novel "Dog Soldiers." Outstanding period soundtrack by Creedence Clearwater Revival, including title song. Violent and compelling tale of late-'60s disillusionment. *AKA:* Dog Soldiers.

1978 (R) 126m/C Nick Nolte, Tuesday Weld, Michael Moriarty, Anthony Zerbe, Richard Masur, Ray Sharkey, David Opatoshu, Charles Haid, Gail Strickland; *D:* Karel Reisz; *W:* Judith Rascoe. Nominations: Cannes Film Festival '78: Best Film. **VHS, Beta, LV ★★★1/2**

Who's Afraid of Virginia Woolf?
Nichols debuts as a director in this biting Edward Albee play. A teacher and his wife (Segal and Dennis) are invited to the home of a burned-out professor and his foul-mouthed, bitter, yet seductive wife (Burton and Taylor). The guests get more than dinner, as the evening deteriorates into brutal verbal battles between the hosts. Taylor and Dennis won Oscars; Burton's Oscar-nominated portrait of the tortured husband is magnificent. Richard and Liz's best film together.

1966 127m/B Richard Burton, Elizabeth Taylor, George Segal, Sandy Dennis; *D:* Mike Nichols; *W:* Ernest Lehman; *M:* Alex North, Haskell Wexler. Academy Awards '66: Best Actress (Taylor), Best Art Direction/Set Decoration (B & W), Best Black and White Cinematography, Best Costume Design (B & W), Best Supporting Actress (Dennis); National Board of Review Awards '66: 10 Best Films of the Year, Best Actress (Taylor); Nominations: Academy Awards '66: Best Actor (Burton), Best Adapted Screenplay, Best Director (Nichols), Best Film Editing, Best Picture, Best Sound, Best Supporting Actor (Segal), Best Original Score. **VHS, Beta, LV ★★★★**

Who's Minding the Mint?
A money checker at the U.S. Mint must replace $50,000 he accidentally destroyed. He enlists a retired money printer and an inept gang to infiltrate the mint and replace the lost cash, with predictable chaos resulting. Non-stop zaniness in this wonderful comedy that never got its due when released. Thieves who befriend Hutton include Denver of "Gilligan's Island" and Farr, later of "M*A*S*H."

1967 97m/C Jim Hutton, Dorothy Provine, Milton Berle, Joey Bishop, Bob Denver, Walter Brennan, Jamie Farr; *D:* Howard Morris. **VHS, Beta ★★★**

Who's That Knocking at My Door?
Interesting debut for Scorsese, in which he exercises many of the themes and techniques that he polished for later films. An autobiographical drama about an Italian-American youth growing up in New York City, focusing on street life, Catholicism and adolescent bonding. Begun as a student film called "I Call First"; later

developed into a feature. Keitel's film debut. **AKA:** J.R.; I Call First.
1968 90m/B Harvey Keitel, Zena Bethune; **D:** Martin Scorsese. **VHS, Beta** ★★★

Whose Life Is It Anyway? Black humor abounds. Sculptor Dreyfuss is paralyzed from the neck down in an auto accident. What follows is his struggle to persuade the hospital authorities to let him die. Excellent cast headed impressively by Dreyfuss; Lahti as his doctor and hospital head Cassavetes also are superb. From Brian Clark's successful Broadway play.
1981 (R) 118m/C Richard Dreyfuss, John Cassavetes, Christine Lahti, Bob Balaban, Kenneth McMillan, Kaki Hunter, Thomas Carter; **D:** John Badham; **W:** Reginald Rose, Brian Clark. **VHS, Beta** ★★★★

The Wicker Man The disappearance of a young girl leads a devoutly religious Scottish policeman to an island whose denizens practice bizarre pagan sexual rituals. An example of occult horror that achieves its mounting terror without gratuitous gore. The first original screenplay by playwright Shaffer. Beware shortened versions that may still lurk out there; the 103-minute restored director's cut is definitive.
1975 103m/C Edward Woodward, Christopher Lee, Britt Ekland, Diane Cilento, Ingrid Pitt; **D:** Robin Hardy; **W:** Anthony Shaffer. **VHS, Beta** ★★★½

Wife Versus Secretary Excellent acting against type creates a near-perfect picture of romantic relationships. Harlow and Gable play a secretary and her boss who have a wonderful professional relationship, but Loy worries something else is afoot. Could have been a heavy-handed soap opera, but the witty dialogue and Brown's fine pacing make it much more. Stewart later claimed that he purposely messed up his romantic scenes with Harlow in order to spend more time in her arms.
1936 89m/B Clark Gable, Jean Harlow, Myrna Loy, May Robson, Hobart Cavanaugh, James Stewart, George Barbier, Gilbert Emery; **D:** Clarence Brown. **VHS** ★★★½

Wild at Heart Dern and Cage are on the lam, going across country to escape her mother, his parole officer, and life. Humorous and frightening, sensual and evocative as only Lynch can be. Sweet love story of Sailor and Lula is juxtaposed with the violent and bizarre, obsessive brand of love of the people they encounter. Unmistakable Wizard of Oz imagery sprin-

kled throughout, as are some scenes of graphic violence. Ladd is unnerving as Dern's onscreen mother (she also has the role offscreen). Based on the novel by Barry Gifford.
1990 (R) 125m/C Nicolas Cage, Laura Dern, Diane Ladd, Willem Dafoe, Isabella Rossellini, Harry Dean Stanton, Crispin Glover, Grace Zabriskie, J.E. Freeman, Freddie Jones, Sherilyn Fenn, Sheryl Lee; **D:** David Lynch; **W:** David Lynch; **M:** Angelo Badalamenti. Cannes Film Festival '90: Best Film; Independent Spirit Awards '91: Best Cinematography; Nominations: Academy Awards '90: Best Supporting Actress (Ladd). **VHS, Beta, LV** ★★★½

The Wild Bunch Acclaimed western about a group of aging outlaws on their final rampage, realizing time is passing them by. Highly influential in dialogue, editing style, and lyrical slow-motion photography of violence; Peckinpah's main claim to posterity. Holden and Ryan create especially memorable characters. Arguably the greatest western and one of the greatest American films of all times. Beware of shortened versions; after a pre-release showing to the East Coast critics, producer Feldman cut key scenes without Peckinpah's knowledge or consent.
1969 (R) 145m/C William Holden, Ernest Borgnine, Robert Ryan, Warren Oates, Strother Martin, L.Q. Jones, Albert Dekker, Bo Hopkins, Edmond O'Brien, Ben Johnson, Jaime Sanchez, Emilio Fernandez, Dub Taylor; **D:** Sam Peckinpah; **W:** Walon Green, Sam Peckinpah. National Society of Film Critics Awards '69: Best Cinematography; Nominations: Academy Awards '69: Best Story & Screenplay, Best Original Score. **VHS, Beta, LV** ★★★★

The Wild Child The brilliant film based on the journal of a 19th-century physician who attempts to educate and civilize a young boy who has been found living in the wilderness, without any comprehension of human life. Tenderly told coming-of-age tale, with surprising sensitivity for its subject. In French with English subtitles. **AKA:** L'Enfant Sauvage.
1970 (G) 85m/B FR **D:** Francois Truffaut; **W:** Jean Gruault; **M:** Antoine Duhamel. National Board of Review Awards '70: Best Director (Truffaut); National Society of Film Critics Awards '70: Best Cinematography. **VHS** ★★★½

Wild Hearts Can't Be Broken Depicts the true-life story of Sonora Webster, a small town Georgia girl who runs away from a foster home to join a carnival in the early 1930s, hoping to become a stunt rider. She be-

comes a horse-diver (a Depression-era sideshow phenomena) and is blinded in a diving accident, but returns to find romance and ride again. Storyline has little screen tension, but it doesn't detract from this fresh family film with a feisty heroine, a sweet romance, and horses. Nice U.S. screen debut for British actress Anwar.
1991 (G) 89m/C Gabrielle Anwar, Cliff Robertson, Dylan Kussman, Michael Schoeffling, Kathleen York, Frank Renzulli; **D:** Steve Miner; **W:** Oley Sassone; **M:** Mason Daring. **VHS, Beta** ★★★

The Wild One The original biker flick: two motorcycle gangs descend upon a quiet midwestern town and each other. Brando is the leader of one, struggling against social prejudices and his own gang's lawlessness to find love and a normal life. The classic tribute to 1950s rebelliousness. Based vaguely on a real incident in California. Quaint after nearly 40 years, but still the touchstone for much that has come since, and still a central role in Brando's now-long career. Brando himself believes it failed to explore motivations for youth gangs and violence, only depicting them. Banked in Britain until 1967.
1954 79m/B Marlon Brando, Lee Marvin, Mary Murphy, Robert Keith, Jerry Paris, Alvy Moore, Jay C. Flippen; **D:** Laslo Benedek. **VHS, Beta, LV** ★★★1/2

Wild Reeds Emotional coming-of-age tale set in 1962 (at the end of the French war in Algeria) and focusing on three classmates at a French boarding school. Sensitive Francois (Morel) is just coming to the realization that he likes boys, particularly working-class Serge (Rideau) who's attracted to Francois' confidante Maite (Bouchez). The provocateur is Algerian-born Henri (Gorny), a bitter political militant who enjoys his battles with classmates and teachers alike. Politics and youthful passions are forced into crises. French historical/political context may prove a barrier. In French with English subtitles. **AKA:** Les Roseaux Sauvages.
1994 110m/C *FR* Gael Morel, Stephane Rideau, Elodie Bouchez, Frederic Gorny, Michele Moretti; **D:** Andre Techine; **W:** Gilles Taurand, Olivier Massart, Jeanne Lapoirie, Andre Techine. Cesar Awards '95: Best Director (Techine), Best Film, Best Screenplay; Los Angeles Film Critics Association Awards '95: Best Foreign Film; National Board of Film Critics Awards '95: Best Foreign Film. **VHS** ★★★

Wild Strawberries Bergman's landmark film of fantasy, dreams and nightmares. An aging professor, on the road to accept an award, must come to terms with his anxieties and guilt. Brilliant performance by Sjostrom, Sweden's first film director and star. Excellent use of flashbacks and film editing. An intellectual and emotional masterpiece. In Swedish with English subtitles. **AKA:** Smultron-Stallet.
1957 90m/B *SW* Victor Sjostrom, Bibi Andersson, Max von Sydow, Ingrid Thulin, Gunnar Bjornstrand, Folke Sundquist, Bjorn Bjelvenstam; **D:** Ingmar Bergman; **W:** Ingmar Bergman. Golden Globe Awards '60: Best Foreign Film; National Board of Review Awards '59: 5 Best Foreign Films of the Year; Nominations: Academy Awards '59: Best Story & Screenplay. **VHS, Beta, LV, 8mm** ★★★★

Will Penny Just back from a cattle drive, a range-wandering loner looks for work in the wrong place and offends a family of outlaws who come after him. His escape from them leads to another kind of trap—one set by a love-hungry woman (Hackett, in a strong performance). Heston considers this film his personal best, and he's probably right. Superbly directed western, with excellent cinematography and professional, realistic portrayals, flopped in theaters, moviegoers preferring simultaneous Heston outing "Planet of the Apes." Photography by Lucien Ballard.
1967 109m/C Charlton Heston, Joan Hackett, Donald Pleasence, Lee Majors, Bruce Dern, Anthony Zerbe, Ben Johnson, Clifton James; **D:** Tom Gries; **M:** Elmer Bernstein. **VHS, Beta, LV** ★★★1/2

William Shakespeare's Romeo and Juliet Bright and loud update on Shakespeare's tragedy of feuding families and first love with a contemporary fantasy setting, Verona Beach, and attitude (the Montagues and the Capulets are high-tech industry rivals). However, the 16th-century Elizabethan language is intact, although Luhrmann's said to have cut at least half the text. Hot-blooded Romeo (DiCaprio) takes one look at angelic Juliet (Danes) and falls instantaneously in love/lust. This doesn't please Juliet's family, including quick-tempered cousin Tybalt (Leguizamo) who goes after Romeo with far-reaching consequences. Filmed in Mexico City. **AKA:** Romeo and Juliet.
1996 120m/C Leonardo DiCaprio, Claire Danes, John Leguizamo, Brian Dennehy, Diane Venora, Paul Sorvino, Pete Postlethwaite, Paul Rudd, Harold Perrineau Jr., Jesse Bradford, Miriam Margolyes, Vondie Curtis-Hall, Christina Pickles, M. Emmet

W

▲

Walsh; **D:** Baz Luhrmann; **W:** Baz Luhrmann, Craig Pearce; **M:** Nellee Hooper. **VHS** ★★★

Willy Wonka & the Chocolate Factory When the last of five coveted "golden tickets" falls into the hands of sweet but very poor Charlie, he and his Grandpa Joe get a tour of the most wonderfully strange chocolate factory in the world. The owner is the most curious hermit ever to hit the big screen. He leads the five young "winners" on a thrilling and often dangerous tour of his fabulous factory. Adapted from Roald Dahl's "Charlie and the Chocolate Factory." Without a doubt one of the best "kid's" movies ever made; a family classic worth watching again and again. ♪ Willy Wonka, the Candy Man; Cheer Up, Charlie; I've Got a Golden Ticket; Oompa-Loompa-Doompa-Dee-Doo; Pure Imagination. **1971 (G) 100m/C** Gene Wilder, Jack Albertson, Denise Nickerson, Peter Ostrum, Roy Kinnear, Aubrey Woods, Michael Bollner, Ursula Reit, Leonard Stone, Dodo Denney; **D:** Mel Stuart; **M:** Leslie Bricusse. Nominations: Academy Awards '71: Best Original Score. **VHS, Beta, LV** ★★★1/2

Wilson Biography of Woodrow Wilson from his days as the head of Princeton University, to the governorship of New York, and as U.S. President during WWI. After the war, Wilson conceives of the League of Nations but is unable to sell it to a U.S. still bent on isolationism. This lavish film won critical plaudits but was a major money-loser. **1944 154m/C** Alexander Knox, Charles Coburn, Geraldine Fitzgerald, Thomas Mitchell, Ruth Nelson, Cedric Hardwicke, Vincent Price, William Eythe, Mary Anderson, Sidney Blackmer, Stanley Ridges, Eddie Foy Jr., Charles Halton; **D:** Henry King; **W:** Lamar Trotti; **M:** Alfred Newman. Academy Awards '44: Best Color Cinematography, Best Film Editing, Best Interior Decoration, Best Original Screenplay, Best Sound; Golden Globe Awards '45: Best Actor—Drama (Knox); Nominations: Academy Awards '44: Best Actor (Knox), Best Director (King), Best Picture, Best Original Score. **VHS** ★★★

Winchester '73 Superb acting and photography characterize this classic, landmark western. Simple plot—cowboy Stewart pursues his stolen state-of-the-art rifle as it changes hands—speeds along and carries the viewer with it, ending with an engrossing and unforgettable shootout. Almost single-handedly breathed

new life into the whole genre. Laserdisc version contains a special narration track provided by Stewart. Mann's and Stewart's first teaming. **1950 82m/C** James Stewart, Shelley Winters, Stephen McNally, Dan Duryea, Millard Mitchell, John McIntire, Will Geer, Jay C. Flippen, Rock Hudson, Tony Curtis, Charles Drake; **D:** Anthony Mann. **VHS, Beta, LV** ★★★1/2

The Wind One of the last great silents still stands as a magnificent entertainment. Gish, in possibly her best role, is an innocent Easterner who finds herself married to a rough cowpoke and raped by a married man in a bleak frontier town. Director Sjostrom has a splendid feel for landscape, and the drama—climaxing with a tumultuous desert storm—is intense yet fully believable. Based on the novel by Dorothy Scarborough. **1928 74m/B** Lillian Gish, Lars Hanson, Montagu Love, Dorothy Cumming, Edward Earle, William Orlamond; **D:** Victor Sjostrom; **W:** Frances Marion. **VHS, Beta** ★★★★

The Wind and the Lion In turn-of-the-century Morocco, a sheik (Connery) kidnaps a feisty American woman (Bergen) and her children and holds her as a political hostage. President Teddy Roosevelt (Keith) sends in the Marines to free the captives, who are eventually released by their captor. Directed with style by Milius. Highly entertaining, if heavily fictionalized. Based very loosely on a historical incident. **1975 (PG) 120m/C** Sean Connery, Candice Bergen, Brian Keith, John Huston, Geoffrey Lewis; **D:** John Milius; **W:** John Milius; **M:** Jerry Goldsmith. Nominations: Academy Awards '75: Best Sound, Best Original Score. **VHS, Beta, LV** ★★★

The Window A little boy (Disney star Driscoll, intriguingly cast by director Tetzlaff) has a reputation for telling lies, so no one believes him when he says he witnessed a murder . . . except the killers. Almost unbearably tense, claustrophobic thriller about the helplessness of childhood. Tetzlaff clearly learned more than a thing or two from the master, Hitchcock, for whom he photographed "Notorious." Based on the novella "The Boy Who Cried Murder" by Cornell Woolrich. Driscoll was awarded a special miniature Oscar as Outstanding Juvenile for his performance. **1949 73m/B** Bobby Driscoll, Barbara Hale, Arthur Kennedy, Ruth Roman; **D:** Ted Tetzlaff. Edgar Allan Poe Awards '49: Best Screenplay; Nominations: Academy

Awards '49: Best Film Editing. **VHS, Beta, LV ★★★1/2**

A Wing and a Prayer Better-than-average WWII Air Force action flick. Battles rage throughout the Pacific theater and the men aboard the aircraft carrier struggle to do their part to save the world for freedom. Fine cast receives Hathaway's excellent unsentimental direction.
1944 97m/B Don Ameche, Dana Andrews, William Eythe, Charles Bickford, Cedric Hardwicke, Kevin O'Shea, Richard Jaeckel, Harry (Henry) Morgan; **D:** Henry Hathaway. Nominations: Academy Awards '44: Best Original Screenplay. **VHS ★★★**

Wings of Desire An ethereal, haunting modern fable about one of many angels observing human life in and above the broken existence of Berlin, and how he begins to long to experience life as humans do. A moving, unequivocable masterpiece, with as many beautiful things to say about spiritual need as about the schizophrenic emptiness of contemporary Germany; Wenders' magnum opus. In German with English subtitles, and with black-and-white sequences. Magnificent cinematography by Henri Alekan. **AKA:** Der Himmel Uber Berlin.
1988 (PG-13) 130m/C GE Bruno Ganz, Peter Falk, Solveig Dommartin, Otto Sander, Curt Bois; **D:** Wim Wenders; **W:** Wim Wenders, Peter Handke. Independent Spirit Awards '89: Best Foreign Film; Los Angeles Film Critics Association Awards '88: Best Cinematography, Best Foreign Film; New York Film Critics Awards '88: Best Cinematography; National Society of Film Critics Awards '88: Best Cinematography. **VHS, Beta, LV ★★★1/2**

Winning A race car driver (Newman) will let nothing, including his new wife (Woodward), keep him from winning the Indianapolis 500. Newman does his own driving. Thomas' film debut.
1969 (PG) 123m/C Paul Newman, Joanne Woodward, Robert Wagner, Richard Thomas, Clu Gulager; **D:** James Goldstone; **M:** Dave Grusin. **VHS, Beta, LV ★★★**

The Winslow Boy A cadet at the Royal Naval College is wrongly accused of theft and expelled. Donat as the boy's lawyer leads a splendid cast. Despite consequences for his family, the boy's father (Hardwicke) sues the government and fights his son's battle, as the case makes the papers and he approaches bankruptcy. Plot would seem far-fetched if it weren't based on fact. Absorbing. Based on a play by Rattigan, who co-wrote the script.
1948 112m/B GB Robert Donat, Cedric Hardwicke, Margaret Leighton, Frank Lawton, Kathleen Harrison, Basil Radford; **D:** Anthony Asquith; **W:** Terence Rattigan, Frederick A. (Freddie) Young. **VHS, Beta ★★★1/2**

The Winter Light The second film in Bergman's famous trilogy on the silence of God, preceded by "Through a Glass Darkly" and followed by "The Silence." Bleak and disturbing view of a tortured priest who searches for the faith and guidance he is unable to give his congregation. Hard to swallow for neophyte Bergmanites, but challenging, deeply serious and rewarding for those accustomed to the Swede's angst. Polished and personal. In Swedish with English subtitles. **AKA:** Nattvardsgaesterna.
1962 80m/B SW Gunnar Bjornstrand, Ingrid Thulin, Max von Sydow; **D:** Ingmar Bergman; **W:** Ingmar Bergman. National Board of Review Awards '63: 5 Best Foreign Films of the Year. **VHS, Beta, LV ★★★1/2**

Wise Blood Gothic drama about a drifter who searches for sin and becomes a preacher for a new religion, The Church Without Christ. Excellent cast in achingly realistic portrayal of ersatz religion, southern style. Many laughs are more painful than funny. Superb, very dark comedy from Huston. Adapted from the Flannery O'Connor novel.
1979 (PG) 106m/C Brad Dourif, John Huston, Ned Beatty, Amy Wright, Harry Dean Stanton; **D:** John Huston; **M:** Alex North. **VHS, Beta ★★★1/2**

Wish You Were Here Poignant yet funny slice of British postwar life roughly based on the childhood memoirs of famous madame, Cynthia Payne. A troubled and freedom-loving teenager expresses her rebellion in sexual experimentation. Mum is dead and Dad just doesn't understand, so what's a girl to do, but get the boys excited? Lloyd, in her first film, plays the main character with exceptional strength and feistiness. Payne's later life was dramatized in the Leland-scripted "Personal Services."
1987 92m/C GB Emily Lloyd, Tom Bell, Clare Clifford, Barbara Durkin, Geoffrey Hutchings, Charlotte Barker, Chloe Leland, Trudy Cavanagh, Jesse Birdsall, Geoffrey Durham, Pat Heywood; **D:** David Leland; **W:** David Leland; **M:** Stanley Myers. British Academy Awards '87: Best Original Screenplay; National Society of Film Critics Awards '87: Best Actress (Lloyd). **VHS, Beta, LV ★★★**

The Witches Nine-year-old boy on vacation finds himself in the midst of a witch convention, and grand high witch Huston plans to turn all children into furry little creatures. The boy, with the help of his good witch grandmother, attempts to prevent the mass transmutation of children into mice. Top-notch fantasy probably too spooky for the training wheel set. Wonderful special effects; the final project of executive producer Jim Henson. Based on Roald Dahl's story. **1990 (PG) 92m/C** Anjelica Huston, Mai Zetterling, Jasen Fisher, Rowan Atkinson, Charlie Potter, Bill Paterson, Brenda Blethyn, Jane Horrocks; *D:* Nicolas Roeg; *W:* Allan Scott; *M:* Stanley Myers. Los Angeles Film Critics Association Awards '90: Best Actress (Huston); National Society of Film Critics Awards '90: Best Actress (Huston). **VHS, Beta, LV, 8mm** ★★★1/2

Withnail and I A biting and original black comedy about a pair of unemployed, nearly starving English actors during the late 1960s. They decide to retreat to a country house owned by Withnail's uncle for a vacation and are beset by comic misadventures, particularly when the uncle, who is gay, starts to hit on his nephew's friend. Robinson, who scripted "The Killing Fields," makes his successful directorial debut, in addition to drafting the screenplay from his own novel. Coproduced by George Harrison and Richard Starkey (Ringo Starr). **1987 (R) 108m/C** *GB* Richard E. Grant, Paul McGann, Richard Griffiths; *D:* Bruce Robinson; *M:* David Dundas. **VHS, Beta, LV** ★★★1/2

Without Warning: The James Brady Story White House Press Secretary Brady took a bullet in the brain during the 1981 shooting of President Reagan, and made a slow, grueling recovery. This fine made for cable TV film spares none of it, concentrating on the stricken man and his family, and opting out of disease-of-the-week cliches (though the pic's politics won't please the gun-adorers). Based on Mollie Dickinson's biography "Thumbs Up." **1991 (R) 120m/C** Beau Bridges, Joan Allen, David Strathairn, Christopher Bell, Gary Grubbs, Bryan Clark, Steve Flynn, Christine Healy, Susan Brown; *D:* Michael Toshiyuki Uno; *W:* Robert Bolt. **VHS** ★★★

Witness A young Amish boy traveling from his father's funeral witnesses a murder in a Philadelphia bus station. The investigating detective (Ford, in one of his best roles) soon discovers the killing is part of a conspiracy involving corruption in his department. He follows the child and his young widowed mother to their home in the country. A thriller with a difference, about the encounter of alien worlds, with a poignant love story. McGillis, in her first major role, is luminous as the Amish mother, while Ford is believable as both a cop and a sensitive man. An artfully crafted drama, richly focusing on the often misunderstood Amish lifestyle. **1985 (R) 112m/C** Harrison Ford, Kelly McGillis, Alexander Godunov, Lukas Haas, Josef Sommer, Danny Glover, Patti LuPone; *D:* Peter Weir; *M:* Maurice Jarre, John Seale. Academy Awards '85: Best Film Editing, Best Original Screenplay; Edgar Allan Poe Awards '85: Best Screenplay; Writers Guild of America '85: Best Original Screenplay; Nominations: Academy Awards '85: Best Actor (Ford), Best Art Direction/Set Decoration, Best Cinematography, Best Director (Weir), Best Picture, Best Original Score. **VHS, Beta, LV, 8mm** ★★★1/2

Witness for the Prosecution An unemployed man is accused of murdering a wealthy widow whom he befriended. Ailing defense attorney Laughton can't resist taking an intriguing murder case, and a straitforward court case becomes increasingly complicated in this energetic adaptation of an Agatha Christie story and stage play. Outstanding performances by Laughton, with excellent support by real life wife, Lanchester, as his patient nurse. Power, as the alleged killer, and Dietrich as a tragic woman are top-notch (see if you can detect Dietrich in an unbilled second role). **1957 116m/B** Charles Laughton, Tyrone Power, Marlene Dietrich, Elsa Lanchester, John Williams, Henry Daniell, Una O'Connor; *D:* Billy Wilder; *W:* Harry Kurnitz, Billy Wilder. Golden Globe Awards '58: Best Supporting Actress (Lanchester); Nominations: Academy Awards '57: Best Actor (Laughton), Best Director (Wilder), Best Film Editing, Best Picture, Best Sound, Best Supporting Actress (Lanchester). **VHS, Beta, LV** ★★★1/2

The Wizard of Oz From the book by L. Frank Baum. Fantasy about a Kansas farm girl (Garland, in her immortal role) who rides a tornado to a brightly colored world over the rainbow, full of talking scarecrows, munchkins and a wizard who bears a strange resemblance to a Kansas fortune-teller. She must outwit the Wicked Witch if she is ever to go home. Delightful performances from

Lahr, Bolger, and Hamilton; King Vidor is uncredited as co-director. Director Fleming originally wanted Deanna Durbin or Shirley Temple for the role of Dorothy, but settled for Garland who made the song "Over the Rainbow" her own. She received a special Academy Award for her performance. For the 50th anniversary of its release, "The Wizard of Oz" was restored and includes rare film clips of Bolger's "Scarecrow Dance" and the cut "Jitterbug" number, and shots by Buddy Ebsen as the Tin Man before he became ill and left the production. Laserdisc edition includes digital sound, commentary by film historian Ronald Haver, and test footage, trailers and stills, as well as Jerry Maren talking about his experiences as a Munchkin. Yet another special release of the film, "The Ultimate Oz," contains a documentary on the making of the film, a reproduction of the original script, still photos, and liner notes. ♪ Munchkinland; Ding Dong the Witch is Dead; Follow the Yellow Brick Road; If I Only Had a Brain/a Heart/the Nerve; If I Were the King of the Forest; The Merry Old Land of Oz; Threatening Witch; Into the Forest of the Wild Beast; The City Gates are Open.
1939 101m/C Judy Garland, Margaret Hamilton, Ray Bolger, Jack Haley, Bert Lahr, Frank Morgan, Charley Grapewin, Clara Blandick, Mitchell Lewis, Billie Burke; **D:** Victor Fleming; **W:** Noel Langley; **M:** Herbert Stothart. Academy Awards '39: Best Song ("Over the Rainbow"), Best Original Score; Nominations: Academy Awards '39: Best Color Cinematography, Best Interior Decoration, Best Picture, Best Special Effects. **VHS, Beta, LV ★★★★**

The Wolf Man Fun, absorbing classic horror with Chaney as a man bitten by werewolf Lugosi. His dad thinks he's gone nuts, his screaming gal pal just doesn't understand, and plants on the Universal lot have no roots. Ouspenskaya's finest hour as the prophetic gypsy woman. Ow-oo! Chilling and thrilling.
1941 70m/B Lon Chaney Jr., Claude Rains, Maria Ouspenskaya, Ralph Bellamy, Bela Lugosi, Warren William, Patric Knowles, Evelyn Ankers; **D:** George Waggner. **VHS, Beta, LV ★★★½**

A Woman Called Golda Political drama following the life and career of Golda Meir, the Israeli Prime Minister and one of the most powerful political figures of the 20th century. Davis portrays the young Golda, Bergman taking over as she ages. Superior made-for-television bio-pic.
1982 192m/C Ingrid Bergman, Leonard Nimoy, Anne Jackson, Ned Beatty, Robert Loggia, Judy Davis; **D:** Alan Gibson; **W:** Steven Gethers, Howard Gast. **VHS, Beta ★★★**

Woman in the Dunes Splendid, resonant allegorical drama. A scientist studying insects in the Japanese sand dunes finds himself trapped with a woman in a hut at the bottom of a pit. Superbly directed and photographed (by Hiroshi Segawa). Scripted by Kobo Abe from his acclaimed novel. In Japanese with English subtitles. **AKA:** Suna No Onna; Woman of the Dunes.
1964 123m/B *JP* Eiji Okada, Kyoko Kishida, Koji Mitsui, Hiroko Ito, Sen Yano; **D:** Hiroshi Teshigahara; **M:** Toru Takemitsu. Cannes Film Festival '64: Grand Jury Prize; Nominations: Academy Awards '64: Best Director (Teshigahara), Best Foreign Language Film. **VHS, Beta ★★★★**

A Woman Is a Woman Godard's affectionate sendup of Hollywood musicals is a hilarious comedy about a nightclub dancer (Karina) who desperately wants a baby. When boyfriend Belmondo balks, she asks his best friend Brialy. Much ado is had, with the three leads all splendid. Godard's first film shot in color and Cinemascope, with great music. In French with English subtitles. **AKA:** Une Femme Est Une Femme; La Donna E Donna.
1960 88m/C *FR* Jean-Claude Brialy, Jean-Paul Belmondo, Anna Karina, Marie DuBois; **D:** Jean-Luc Godard; **M:** Michel Legrand. **VHS ★★★**

The Woman Next Door One of Truffaut's last films before his sudden death in 1984. The domestic drama involves a suburban husband who resumes an affair with a tempestuous now-married woman after she moves next door, with domestic complications all around. An insightful, humanistic paean to passion and fidelity by the great artist, though one of his lesser works. Supported by strong outings from the two leads. In French with English subtitles. **AKA:** La Femme d'a Cote.
1981 (R) 106m/C *FR* Gerard Depardieu, Fanny Ardant, Michele Baumgartner, Veronique Silver, Roger Van Hool; **D:** Francois Truffaut; **W:** Suzanne Schiffman; **M:** Georges Delerue. **VHS, Beta, LV ★★★**

Woman of Paris/Sunnyside This double feature highlights the talents of Charlie Chaplin. "A Woman of Paris" is the tragic story of a French country girl who winds up a kept woman. Chaplin's only dramatic di-

rectional outing; he makes only a cameo appearance. Straightforward but hip story of sex and society. In "Sunnyside," an example of high Chaplin hijinks, the comic plays a hotel handyman who can't win.
1923 111m/B Adolphe Menjou, Edna Purviance, Carl Miller, Lydia Knott; *Cameos:* Charlie Chaplin; *D:* Charlie Chaplin. **VHS, Beta ★★★1/2**

Woman of the Year First classic Tracy/Hepburn pairing concerns the rocky marriage of a renowned political columnist and a lowly sportswriter. Baseball scene with Hepburn at her first game is delightful. Hilarious, rich entertainment that tries to answer the question "What really matters in life?" Tracy and Hepburn began a close friendship that paralleled their quarter-century celluloid partnership. Hepburn shepherded Kamin and Lardner's Oscar-winning script past studio chief Louis B. Mayer, wearing four-inch heels to press her demands. Mayer caved in, Tracy was freed from making "The Yearling," and the rest is history.
1942 114m/B Spencer Tracy, Katharine Hepburn, Fay Bainter, Dan Tobin, Reginald Owen, Roscoe Karns, William Bendix, Minor Watson; *D:* George Stevens; *W:* Ring Lardner Jr., Michael Kanin; *M:* Franz Waxman. Academy Awards '42: Best Original Screenplay; Nominations: Academy Awards '42: Best Actress (Hepburn). **VHS, Beta, LV ★★★★**

A Woman Under the Influence Strong performances highlight this overlong drama about a family's disintegration. Rowlands is the lonely, middle-aged housewife who's having a breakdown and Falk is her blue-collar husband who can't handle what's going on.
1974 (R) 147m/C Gena Rowlands, Peter Falk, Matthew Cassel, Matthew Laborteaux, Christina Grisanti; *D:* John Cassavetes; *W:* John Cassavetes. Golden Globe Awards '75: Best Actress—Drama (Rowlands); National Board of Review Awards '74: Best Actress (Rowlands); Nominations: Academy Awards '74: Best Actress (Rowlands), Best Director (Cassavetes). **VHS, Beta ★★★**

A Woman's Face An unpleasant, bitter woman with a hideous scar on her face blackmails illicit lovers as a form of revenge for a happiness she doesn't know. She even plots to murder a child for his inheritance. But after plastic surgery, she becomes a nicer person and doubts her plan. Lean, tight suspense with a bang-up finale. In Swedish with English subti-

tles. Remade in Hollywood in 1941. *AKA:* En Kvinnas Ansikte.
1938 100m/B SW Ingrid Bergman, Anders Henrikson, Karin Carlsson, Georg Rydeberg, Goran Bernhard, Tore Svennberg; *D:* Gustaf Molander. **VHS, Beta ★★★**

A Woman's Face A physically and emotionally scarred woman becomes part of a blackmail ring. Plastic surgery restores her looks and her attitude. Begins with a murder trial and told in flashbacks; tight, suspenseful remake of the 1938 Swedish Ingrid Bergman vehicle. Climax will knock you out of your chair.
1941 107m/B Joan Crawford, Conrad Veidt, Melvyn Douglas, Osa Massen, Reginald Owen, Albert Basserman, Marjorie Main, Donald Meek, Charles Quigley, Henry Daniell, George Zucco, Robert Warwick; *D:* George Cukor. **VHS, Beta ★★★**

A Woman's World Slick, sophisticated look at big business in the '50s, with Webb as the boss who chooses his next general manager based on the suitability of the executive's wives. Beautiful costumes, witty dialogue, and good acting make this worthwhile viewing. Plus, film offers a nostalgic look at New York in the '50s, with several shots of Fifth Avenue, Macy's, Park Avenue, and the long-gone Stork Club. Based on a story by Mona Williams.
1954 94m/C Clifton Webb, June Allyson, Van Heflin, Lauren Bacall, Fred MacMurray, Arlene Dahl, Cornel Wilde, Elliott Reid, Margalo Gillmore, Alan Reed, David Hoffman, George Melford; *D:* Jean Negulesco; *W:* Claude Binyon, Richard Sale, Mary Loos, Howard Lindsay, Russel Crouse. **VHS ★★★**

The Women A brilliant adaptation of the Clare Boothe Luce stage comedy about a group of women who destroy their best friends' reputations at various social gatherings. Crawford's portrayal of the nasty husband-stealer is classic, and the fashion-show scene in Technicolor is one not to miss. Hilarious bitchiness all around. Remade semi-musically as "The Opposite Sex." Another in that long list of stellar 1939 pics.
1939 133m/B Norma Shearer, Joan Crawford, Rosalind Russell, Joan Fontaine, Mary Boland, Lucile Watson, Margaret Dumont, Paulette Goddard, Ruth Hussey, Marjorie Main; *D:* George Cukor; *W:* Anita Loos. **VHS, Beta, LV ★★★1/2**

Women in Love Drama of two steamy affairs, based on D.H. Lawrence's classic novel. Deservedly Oscar-winning performance by Jackson; controversial nude wrestling scene with Bates and Reed is hard to forget. Plot is dumped on in favor of atmosphere. Followed nearly two decades later (1989) by a "prequel": "The Rainbow," also from Lawrence, also directed by Russell and starring Jackson.

1970 (R) 129m/C *GB* Glenda Jackson, Jennie Linden, Alan Bates, Oliver Reed, Michael Gough, Eleanor Bron; *D:* Ken Russell; *M:* Georges Delerue. Academy Awards '70: Best Actress (Jackson); Golden Globe Awards '71: Best Foreign Film; National Board of Review Awards '70: 10 Best Films of the Year, Best Actress (Jackson); National Society of Film Critics Awards '70: Best Actress (Jackson); Nominations: Academy Awards '70: Best Adapted Screenplay, Best Cinematography, Best Director (Russell). **VHS, Beta** ★★★

The Women of Brewster Place Seven black women living in a tenement fight to gain control of their lives. (Men in general don't come out too well.) Excellent, complex script gives each actress in a fine ensemble headed by Winfrey (in her TV dramatic debut) time in the limelight. Pilot for the series "Brewster Place." Based on the novel by Gloria Naylor. Winfrey was executive producer.

1989 180m/C Oprah Winfrey, Mary Alice, Olivia Cole, Robin Givens, Moses Gunn, Jackee, Paula Kelly, Lonette McKee, Paul Winfield, Cicely Tyson; *D:* Donna Deitch; *W:* Karen Hall; *M:* David Shire. **VHS, Beta** ★★★

Women on the Verge of a Nervous Breakdown Surreal and hilarious romp through the lives of film dubber Maura, her ex-lover, his crazed ex-mistress, his new lover, his son, and his son's girlfriend. There's also Maura's friend Barranco, who inadvertently lent her apartment to Shiite terrorists and now believes the police are after her as an accomplice in an airline hijacking. They meet in a comedy of errors, missed phone calls, and rental notices, while discovering the truth and necessity of love. Fast-paced and full of black humor, with loaded gazpacho serving as a key element. Introduced Almodovar to American audiences. In Spanish with English subtitles. *AKA:* Mujeres al Borde de un Ataque de Nervios.

1988 (R) 88m/C *SP* Carmen Maura, Fernando Guillen, Julieta Serrano, Maria Barranco, Rossy de Palma, Antonio Banderas; *D:* Pedro Almodovar; *W:* Pedro Almodovar; *M:* Bernardo Bonazzi. National Board of Review Awards '88: 5 Best Foreign Films of the Year; New York Film Critics Awards '88: Best Foreign Film; Nominations: Academy Awards '88: Best Foreign Language Film. **VHS, Beta, LV** ★★★1/2

Woodstock Step into the way-back machine and return to the times of luv, peace, and understanding. Powerful chronicle of the great 1969 Woodstock rock concert celebrates the music and lifestyle of the late '60s. More than 400,000 spectators withstood lack of privacy, bathrooms, parking, and food while wallowing in the mud for four days to catch classic performances by a number of popular performers and groups. Martin Scorsese helped edit the documentary, trail-blazing in its use of split-screen montage. A director's cut is available at 225 minutes.

1970 (R) 180m/C *D:* Michael Wadleigh. Academy Awards '70: Best Feature Documentary; Nominations: Academy Awards '70: Best Film Editing, Best Sound. **VHS, Beta, LV** ★★★★

Work/Police Two Chaplin two-reelers. In "Work (The Paper Hanger)" (1915), a family hires Charlie and cohorts Armstrong and Purviance to repaper a house. Little did they know! In "Police" (1916), Charlie plays an ex-con released into the cruel world. Unremittingly hilarious. Silent with music score.

1916 54m/B Charlie Chaplin, Billy Armstrong, Charles Insley, Marta Golden, Edna Purviance; *D:* Charlie Chaplin. **VHS, Beta** ★★★1/2

Working Girl Romantic comedy set in the Big Apple has secretary Griffith working her way to the top in spite of her manipulative boss (Weaver in a powerful parody). Griffith gets her chance to shine when Weaver breaks a leg. She meets Ford for business that turns to romance. A 1980s Cinderella story that's sexy, funny, and sharply written and directed. Nice work by Ford, but this is definitely Griffith's movie. And keep an eye on gal pal Cusack.

1988 (R) 115m/C Melanie Griffith, Harrison Ford, Sigourney Weaver, Joan Cusack, Alec Baldwin, Philip Bosco, Ricki Lake, Nora Dunn, Olympia Dukakis, Oliver Platt, James Lally, Kevin Spacey, Robert Easton; *D:* Mike Nichols; *W:* Kevin Wade; *M:* Carly Simon, Rob Mounsey, Michael Ballhaus. Academy Awards '88: Best Song ("Let the River Run"); Golden Globe Awards '89: Best Actress—Musical/Comedy (Griffith), Best Actress—Musical/Comedy, Best Song ("Let the River Run"), Best Supporting Actress (Weaver); Nominations: Academy

Awards '88: Best Actress (Griffith), Best Director (Nichols), Best Picture, Best Supporting Actress (Cusack, Weaver). **VHS, Beta, LV** ★★★

Working Girls An acclaimed, controversial look by independent filmmaker Borden into lives of modern brothel prostitutes over the period of one day. The sex is realistically candid and perfunctory; the docudrama centers on a prostitute who is a Yale graduate and aspiring photographer living with a female lover. Compelling, touching, and lasting, with sexually candid language and scenery.
1987 93m/C Amanda Goodwin, Louise Smith, Ellen McElduff, Maurisia Zach, Janne Peters, Helen Nicholas; **D:** Lizzie Borden; **W:** Lizzie Borden, Sandra Kay; **M:** David Van Tiegham. **VHS, Beta** ★★★

The World According to Garp Comedy turns to tragedy in this relatively faithful version of John Irving's popular (and highly symbolic) novel, adapted by Steve Tesich. Chronicles the life of T.S. Garp, a struggling everyman beset by the destructive forces of modern society. Nevertheless, Garp maintains his optimism even as his life unravels around him. At the core of the film is a subplot involving a group of extreme feminists inspired in part by Garp's mother, the author of "A Sexual Suspect." Close and Lithgow (as a giant transsexual) are spectacular, while Williams is low-key and tender as the beleagured Garp. Ultimately pointless, perhaps, but effectively and intelligently so.
1982 (R) 136m/C Robin Williams, Mary Beth Hurt, John Lithgow, Glenn Close, Hume Cronyn, Jessica Tandy, Swoosie Kurtz, Amanda Plummer, Warren Berlinger, Brandon Maggart; **Cameos:** George Roy Hill; **D:** George Roy Hill; **W:** Steve Tesich; **M:** David Shire. Los Angeles Film Critics Association Awards '82: Best Supporting Actor (Lithgow), Best Supporting Actress (Close); New York Film Critics Awards '82: Best Supporting Actor (Lithgow); Nominations: Academy Awards '82: Best Supporting Actor (Lithgow), Best Supporting Actress (Close). **VHS, Beta, LV** ★★★

A World Apart Cinematographer Menges' first directoral effort is a blistering, insightful drama told from the point of view of a 13-year-old white girl living in South Africa, oblivious to apartheid until her crusading journalist mother is arrested under the 90-Day Detention Act, under which she might remain in prison permanently. Political morality tale is also a look at the family-vs-cause choices activists

must make. Heavily lauded, with good reason; the autobiographical script is based on Slovo's parents, persecuted South African journalists Joe Slovo and Ruth First.
1988 (PG) 114m/C GB Barbara Hershey, Jodhi May, Linda Mvusi, David Suchet, Jeroen Krabbe, Paul Freeman, Tim Roth; **D:** Chris Menges; **W:** Shawn Slovo; **M:** Hans Zimmer. British Academy Awards '88: Best Original Screenplay; Cannes Film Festival '88: Best Actress (Hershey), Best Actress (May, Mvusi), Grand Jury Prize; New York Film Critics Awards '88: Best Director (Menges). **VHS, Beta, LV** ★★★1/2

The World of Apu Finale of director Ray's acclaimed Apu trilogy (following "Pather Panchali" and "Aparajito"). Aspiring writer Apu drops out of the university for want of money and takes up with an old chum. An odd circumstance leads him to marry his friend's cousin, whom he comes to love. She dies in childbirth (though her baby boy lives); Apu is deeply distraught, destroys the novel he was working on, and becomes a wanderer. His friend finds him five years later and helps him begin again with his young son. Wonderfully human, hopeful story told by a world-class director. From the novel "Aparajito" by B. Bandopadhaya. In Bengali with English subtitles. **AKA:** Apu Sansat; Apur Sansar.
1959 103m/B IN Soumitra Chatterjee, Sharmila Tagore, Alok Charkravarty, Swapan Makerji; **D:** Satyajit Ray; **W:** Satyajit Ray; **M:** Ravi Shankar. National Board of Review Awards '60: 5 Best Foreign Films of the Year. **VHS, Beta** ★★★★

The World of Henry Orient Charming, eccentric comedy about two 15-year-old girls who, madly in love with an egotistical concert pianist, pursue him all around New York City. Sellers is hilarious, Walker and Spaeth are adorable as his teen groupies; Bosley and Lansbury are great as Walker's indulgent parents. For anyone who has ever been uncontrollably infatuated. Screenplay by the father/daughter team, Nora and Nunnally Johnson, based on Nora Johnson's novel.
1964 106m/C Peter Sellers, Tippy Walker, Merrie Spaeth, Tom Bosley, Angela Lansbury, Paula Prentiss; **D:** George Roy Hill; **W:** Nunnally Johnson, Nora Johnson; **M:** Elmer Bernstein. National Board of Review Awards '64: 10 Best Films of the Year. **VHS, Beta, LV** ★★★1/2

Woyzeck Chilling portrayal of a man plunging into insanity. Mired in the

ranks of the German Army, Woyzeck is harassed by his superiors and tortured in scientific experiments, gradually devolving into homicidal maniac. Based on Georg Buchner play. In German with English subtitles.
1978 82m/C GE Klaus Kinski, Eva Mattes, Wolfgang Reichmann, Josef Bierbichler; **D:** Werner Herzog; **W:** Werner Herzog. Nominations: Cannes Film Festival '79: Best Film. **VHS** ★★★

WR: Mysteries of the Organism Makavejev's breakthrough film, a surreal, essayist exploration of the conflict/union between sexuality and politics—namely, Wilheim Reich and Stalin. A raunchy, bitterly satiric nonnarrative that established the rulebreaking Yugoslav internationally. In Serbian with English subtitles.
1971 84m/C Milena Dravic, Jagoda Kaloper, Tuli Kupferberg, Jackie Curtis; **D:** Dusan Makavejev; **W:** Dusan Makavejev. **VHS, Beta** ★★★

Written on the Wind Sirk's frenzied, melodrama-as-high-art dissection of both the American Dream and American movies follows a Texas oil family's self-destruction through wealth, greed and unbridled lust. Exaggerated depiction of and comment on American ambition and pretension, adapted from Robert Wilder's novel.
1956 99m/C Lauren Bacall, Rock Hudson, Dorothy Malone, Robert Stack, Robert Keith, Grant Williams, Edward Platt, Harry Shannon; **D:** Douglas Sirk; **W:** George Zuckerman. Academy Awards '56: Best Supporting Actress (Malone); Nominations: Academy Awards '56: Best Song ("Written on the Wind"), Best Supporting Actor (Stack). **VHS, Beta** ★★★1/2

Wuthering Heights The first screen adaptation of Emily Bronte's romantic novel about the doomed love between Heathcliff and Cathy on the Yorkshire moors. This film dynamically captures the madness and ferocity of the classic novel, remaining possibly the greatest romance ever filmed. Excellent performances from Wyler's sure direction, particularly Olivier's, which made him a star, and Oberon in her finest hour as the exquisite but selfish Cathy. Remade twice, in 1953 (by Luis Bunuel) and in 1970.
1939 104m/B Laurence Olivier, Merle Oberon, David Niven, Geraldine Fitzgerald, Flora Robson, Donald Crisp, Cecil Kellaway, Leo G. Carroll, Miles Mander, Hugh Williams; **D:** William Wyler; **W:** Ben Hecht, Charles MacArthur; **M:** Alfred Newman. Academy Awards '39: Best Black and White Cinematography; National Board of Review Awards '39: 10 Best Films of the Year; New York Film Critics Awards '39: Best Film; Nominations: Academy Awards '39: Best Actor (Olivier), Best Director (Wyler), Best Interior Decoration, Best Picture, Best Screenplay, Best Supporting Actress (Fitzgerald), Best Original Score. **VHS, Beta, LV** ★★★★

X: The Man with X-Ray Eyes First-rate Corman has Milland gain power to see through solid materials. Predates Little Caesars campaign. *AKA:* The Man With the X-Ray Eyes; X.
1963 79m/C Ray Milland, Diana Van Der Vlis, Harold J. Stone, John Hoyt, Don Rickles, Dick Miller, Jonathan Haze; **D:** Roger Corman; **W:** Ray Russell, Robert Dillon; **M:** Les Baxter. **VHS, Beta, LV** ★★★

Yankee Doodle Dandy Nostalgic view of the Golden Era of show business and the man who made it glitter—George M. Cohan. His early days, triumphs, songs, musicals and romances are brought to life by the inexhaustible Cagney in a rare and wonderful song-and-dance performance. Told in flashback, covering the Irishman's struggling days as a young song writer and performer to his salad days as the toast of Broadway. Cagney, never more charismatic, dances up a storm, reportedly inventing most of the steps on the spot. ♪ Give My Regards to Broadway; Yankee Doodle Dandy; You're a Grand Old Flag; Over There; I Was Born in Virginia; Off the Record; You're a Wonderful Girl; Blue Skies, Grey Skies; Oh You Wonderful Girl.
1942 126m/B James Cagney, Joan Leslie, Walter Huston, Richard Whorf, Irene Manning, Rosemary DeCamp, Jeanne Cagney, S.Z. Sakall, Walter Catlett, Frances Langford, Eddie Foy Jr., George Tobias, Michael Curtiz; **D:** Michael Curtiz; **W:** Robert Buckner. Academy Awards '42: Best Actor (Cagney), Best Sound, Best Score; New York Film Critics Awards '42: Best Actor (Cagney); Nominations: Academy Awards '42: Best Director (Curtiz), Best Picture, Best Story, Best Supporting Actor (Huston). **VHS, Beta, LV** ★★★★

The Year of Living Dangerously Political thriller features Gibson as an Australian journalist covering a political story in Indonesia, circa 1965. During the coup against President Sukarno, he becomes involved with a British attache (Weaver) at the height of the bloody fighting and rioting in Jakarta. Hunt is excellent as male photographer Billy Swan, central to the action as the moral center. Rumored to be based on the activities of CNN's Peter Arnett, although the original source is a novel by C.J. Koch, who reportedly collaborated/battled with Weir on the screenplay. Fascinating, suspenseful film, set up brilliantly by Weir. Shot on location in the Philippines (then moved to Sydney after cast and crew were threatened). First Australian movie financed by a U.S. studio.

1982 (PG) 114m/C *AU* Mel Gibson, Sigourney Weaver, Linda Hunt, Michael Murphy; **D:** Peter Weir; **W:** Peter Weir, David Williamson; **M:** Maurice Jarre, John Seale. Academy Awards '83: Best Supporting Actress (Hunt); Los Angeles Film Critics Association Awards '83: Best Supporting Actress (Hunt); National Board of Review Awards '83: Best Supporting Actress (Hunt); New York Film Critics Awards '83: Best Supporting Actress (Hunt); Nominations: Cannes Film Festival '83: Best Film. **VHS, Beta, LV ★★★1/2**

Year of the Quiet Sun A poignant, acclaimed love story about a Polish widow and an American soldier who find each other in the war-torn landscape of 1946 Europe. Beautifully rendered, with a confident sense of time and place, making this much more than a simple love story. In Polish with English subtitles.

1984 (PG) 106m/C *PL GE* Scott Wilson, Maja Komorowska; **D:** Krzysztof Zanussi. Venice Film Festival '84: Best Film. **VHS, Beta, LV ★★★1/2**

The Yearling This family classic is a tear-jerking adaptation of the Marjorie Kinnan Rawlings novel about a young boy's love for a yearling fawn during the post civil-war era. His father's encouragement and his mother's bitterness play against the story of unqualified love amid poverty and the boy's coming of age. Wonderful footage of Florida. Jarman was awarded a special Oscar as outstanding child actor.

1946 128m/C Gregory Peck, Jane Wyman, Claude Jarman Jr., Chill Wills, Henry Travers, Jeff York, Forrest Tucker, June Lockhart, Margaret Wycherly; **D:** Clarence Brown. Academy Awards '46: Best Color Cinematography, Best Interior Decoration; Golden Globe Awards '47: Best Actor—Drama (Peck); Nominations: Academy Awards '46: Best Actor (Peck), Best Actress (Wyman), Best Director (Brown), Best Film Editing, Best Picture. **VHS, Beta, LV ★★★1/2**

Yellow Submarine The acclaimed animated fantasy based on a plethora of mid-career Beatles songs, sees the Fab Four battle the Blue Meanies for the sake of Sgt. Pepper, the Nowhere Man, Strawberry Fields, and Pepperland. The first full-length British animated feature in 14 years features a host of talented cartoonists. Fascinating LSD-esque animation and imagery. Speaking voices provided by John Clive (John), Geoff Hughes (Paul), Peter Batten (George), and Paul Angelis (Ringo). The Beatles themselves do appear in a short scene at the end of the film. Martin fills in as music director, and Segal of "Love Story" fame co-scripts. ♪ Yellow Submarine; All You Need is Love; Hey, Bulldog; When I'm Sixty-Four; Nowhere Man; Lucy in the Sky With Diamonds; Sgt. Pepper's Lonely Hearts Club Band; A Day in the Life; All Together Now.

1968 (G) 87m/C *GB* **D:** George Duning, Dick Emery; **W:** Erich Segal; **M:** George Martin. **VHS, Beta, LV ★★★1/2**

Yesterday, Today and Tomorrow Trilogy of comic sexual vignettes featuring Loren and her many charms. She plays a black marketeer, a wealthy matron, and a prostitute. Funny, and still rather racy. Loren at her best, in all senses; includes her famous striptease for Mastroianni. **AKA:** Ieri, Oggi E Domani; She Got What She Asked For.

1964 119m/C *IT FR* Sophia Loren, Marcello Mastroianni, Tony Pica, Giovanni Ridolfi; **D:** Vittorio De Sica. Academy Awards '64: Best Foreign Language Film; British Academy Awards '64: Best Actor (Mastroianni). **VHS ★★★1/2**

Yojimbo Two clans vying for political power bid on the services of a samurai (Mifune) who comes to town. The samurai sells his services to both parties, with devastating results for all. In Japanese with English subtitles or dubbed. Re-made by Sergio Leone as the western "A Fist Full of Dollars."

1961 110m/B *JP* Toshiro Mifune, Eijiro Tono, Suuzu Yamda, Seizaburo Kawazu, Isuzu Yamada; **D:** Akira Kurosawa; **W:** Hideo Oguni, Shinobu Hashimoto, Akira Kurosawa; **M:** Masaru Sato. Nominations: Academy Awards '61: Best Costume Design (B & W). **VHS, Beta, LV, 8mm ★★★★**

You Can't Cheat an Honest Man The owner of a misfit circus suffers a variety of headaches including the wisecracks of Charlie McCarthy. Contains Field's classic Ping-Pong battle and some of his other best work.

1939 79m/B W.C. Fields, Edgar Bergen, Constance Moore, Eddie Anderson, Mary Forbes, Thurston Hall; **D:** George Marshall. **VHS, Beta ★★★**

You Can't Take It with You The Capra version of the Kaufman-Hart play about an eccentric New York family and their nonconformist houseguests. Alice Sycamore (Arthur), the stable family member of an offbeat clan of free spirits, falls for Tony Kirby (Stewart), the down-to-earth son of a snooty, wealthy, and not always quite honest family. Amidst the confusion over this love affair, the two families rediscover the simple joys of life.
1938 127m/B James Stewart, Jean Arthur, Lionel Barrymore, Spring Byington, Edward Arnold, Mischa Auer, Donald Meek, Samuel S. Hinds, Ann Miller, H.B. Warner, Halliwell Hobbes, Dub Taylor, Mary Forbes, Eddie Anderson, Harry Davenport, Lillian Yarbo; *D:* Frank Capra; *W:* Robert Riskin. Academy Awards '38: Best Director (Capra), Best Picture; Nominations: Academy Awards '38: Best Cinematography, Best Film Editing, Best Screenplay, Best Sound, Best Supporting Actress (Byington). **VHS, Beta, LV ★★★1/2**

You Can't Take It with You Taped performance of the Kaufman and Hart comedy about the strange pastimes of the Sycamore family who must behave themselves to impress their daughter's boyfriend's stuffy family.
1984 116m/C Colleen Dewhurst, James Coco, Jason Robards Jr., Elizabeth Wilson, George Rose; *D:* Ellis Raab. **VHS, Beta, LV ★★★**

You Were Never Lovelier Charming tale of a father who creates a phony Romeo to try to interest his daughter in marriage. Astaire appears and woos Hayworth in the flesh. The dancing, of course, is superb, and Hayworth is stunning. ♪ Dearly Beloved; I'm Old Fashioned; Shorty George; Wedding in the Spring; You Were Never Lovelier.
1942 98m/B Fred Astaire, Rita Hayworth, Leslie Brooks, Xavier Cugat, Adolphe Menjou, Larry Parks; *D:* William A. Seiter; *M:* Jerome Kern, Johnny Mercer. Nominations: Academy Awards '42: Best Song ("Dearly Beloved"), Best Sound, Best Original Score. **VHS, Beta, LV ★★★1/2**

You'll Never Get Rich A Broadway dance director is drafted into the Army, where his romantic troubles cause him to wind up in the guardhouse more than once. He of course gets the girl. Exquisitely funny. ♪ Since I Kissed My Baby Goodbye; The A-stairable Rag; Shootin' the Works for Uncle Sam; Wedding Cake Walk; Dream Danc-

ing; Boogie Barcarolle; So Near and Yet So Far.
1941 88m/B Fred Astaire, Rita Hayworth, Robert Benchley; *D:* Sidney Lanfield. Nominations: Academy Awards '41: Best Song ("Since I Kissed My Baby Goodbye"), Best Original Score, Best Original Score. **VHS, Beta, LV ★★★**

Young and Innocent Somewhat uneven thriller about a police constable's daughter who helps a fugitive prove he didn't strangle a film star. *AKA:* The Girl Was Young.
1937 80m/B *GB* Derrick DeMarney, Nova Pilbeam, Percy Marmont; *D:* Alfred Hitchcock. **VHS, Beta, LV ★★★**

Young Bess Simmons and real-life husband Granger star in this splashy costume drama about 16th-century England's young Queen. Features outstanding performances by Simmons as Elizabeth I and Laughton (repeating his most famous role) as Henry VIII. Based on the novel by Margaret Irwin.
1953 112m/C Jean Simmons, Stewart Granger, Deborah Kerr, Charles Laughton, Kay Walsh, Guy Rolfe, Kathleen Byron, Cecil Kellaway, Rex Thompson; *D:* George Sidney; *W:* Jan Lustig, Arthur Wimperis; *M:* Miklos Rozsa. **VHS ★★★1/2**

Young Frankenstein Young Dr. Frankenstein (Wilder), a brain surgeon, inherits the family castle back in Transylvania. He's skittish about the family business, but when he learns his grandfather's secrets, he becomes obsessed with making his own monster. Wilder and monster Boyle make a memorable song-and-dance team to Irving Berlin's "Puttin' on the Ritz," and Hackman's cameo as a blind man is inspired. Garr ("What knockers!" "Oh, sank you!") is adorable as a fraulein, and Leachman ("He's vass my—boyfriend!") is wonderfully scary. Wilder saves the creature with a switcheroo, in which the doctor ends up with a certain monster-sized body part. Hilarious parody.
1974 (PG) 108m/B Peter Boyle, Gene Wilder, Marty Feldman, Madeline Kahn, Cloris Leachman, Teri Garr, Kenneth Mars, Richard Haydn; *Cameos:* Gene Hackman; *D:* Mel Brooks; *W:* Gene Wilder, Mel Brooks; *M:* John Morris. Nominations: Academy Awards '74: Best Adapted Screenplay, Best Sound. **VHS, Beta, LV ★★★★**

The Young in Heart A lonely, old woman allows a family of con-artists into her life for companionship. Impressed by her sweet nature, the parasitic brood reforms. The cute com-

edy was a real crowd-pleaser in its day, especially after the bittersweet ending was replaced with a happier variety. Based on the novel "The Gay Banditti" by I.A.R. Wylie.
1938 90m/C Janet Gaynor, Douglas Fairbanks Jr., Paulette Goddard, Roland Young, Billie Burke, Minnie Dupree, Richard Carlson, Charles Halton; **D:** Richard Wallace; **W:** Charles Bennett, Paul Osborn. Nominations: Academy Awards '38: Best Cinematography, Best Score. **VHS** ★★★

The Young Lions A cynical WWII epic following the experiences of a young American officer and a disillusioned Nazi in the war's last days. Martin does fine in his first dramatic role. As the Nazi, Brando sensitively considers the belief that Hitler would save Germany. A realistic anti-war film.
1958 167m/B Marlon Brando, Montgomery Clift, Dean Martin, Hope Lange, Barbara Rush, Lee Van Cleef, Maximilian Schell; **D:** Edward Dmytryk; **W:** Edward Anhalt. Nominations: Academy Awards '58: Best Black and White Cinematography, Best Sound, Best Original Score. **VHS, Beta, LV** ★★★

Young Man with a Horn Dorothy Baker's novel, which was loosely based on the life of jazz immortal Bix Beiderbecke, was even more loosely adapted for this film, featuring Kirk as an angst-ridden trumpeter who can't seem to hit that mystical "high note." ♪ The Very Thought of You; I May be Wrong; The Man I Love; Too Marvelous for Words; With a Song in My Heart; Pretty Baby; I Only Have Eyes for You; Limehouse Blues; Melancholy Rhapsody.
1950 112m/B Kirk Douglas, Doris Day, Lauren Bacall, Hoagy Carmichael; **D:** Michael Curtiz. **VHS, Beta, LV** ★★★

Young Mr. Lincoln A classy Hollywood biography of Lincoln in his younger years from log-cabin country boy to idealistic Springfield lawyer. A splendid drama, and one endlessly explicated as an American masterpiece by the French auteur critics in "Cahiers du Cinema."
1939 100m/B Henry Fonda, Alice Brady, Marjorie Weaver, Arleen Whelan, Eddie Collins, Ward Bond, Donald Meek, Richard Cromwell, Eddie Quillan, Charles Halton; **D:** John Ford; **W:** Lamar Trotti. National Board of Review Awards '39: 10 Best Films of the Year; Nominations: Academy Awards '39: Best Story. **VHS, Beta, LV** ★★★1/2

The Young Philadelphians Ambitious young lawyer Newman works hard at making an impression on the snobbish Philadelphia upper crust. As he schemes and scrambles, he woos debutante Rush and defends buddy Vaughn on a murder charge. Long, but worth it. Part of the "A Night at the Movies" series, this package simulates a 1959 movie evening with a Bugs Bunny cartoon, "People Are Bunny," a newsreel and coming attractions for "The Nun's Story" and "The Hanging Tree." **AKA:** The City Jungle.
1959 136m/B Paul Newman, Barbara Rush, Alexis Smith, Billie Burke, Brian Keith, John Williams, Otto Kruger, Robert Vaughn; **D:** Vincent Sherman; **M:** Ernest Gold. Nominations: Academy Awards '59: Best Black and White Cinematography, Best Costume Design (B & W), Best Supporting Actor (Vaughn). **VHS, Beta** ★★★

Young Winston Based on Sir Winston Churchill's autobiography "My Early Life: A Roving Commission." Follows him through his school days, journalistic career in Africa, early military career, and his election to Parliament at the age of 26. Ward is tremendous as the prime minister-to-be.
1972 (PG) 145m/C *GB* Simon Ward, Robert Shaw, Anne Bancroft, John Mills, Jack Hawkins, Ian Holm, Anthony Hopkins, Patrick Magee, Edward Woodward, Jane Seymour; **D:** Richard Attenborough. Golden Globe Awards '73: Best Foreign Film; Nominations: Academy Awards '72: Best Art Direction/Set Decoration, Best Costume Design, Best Story & Screenplay. **VHS, Beta** ★★★

You're a Big Boy Now Kastner, a virginal young man working in the New York Public Library, is told by his father to move out of his house and grow up. On his own, he soon becomes involved with man-hating actress Hartman and a discotheque dancer. A wild and weird comedy. Coppola's commercial directorial debut.
1966 96m/C Elizabeth Hartman, Geraldine Page, Peter Kastner, Julie Harris, Rip Torn, Michael Dunn, Tony Bill, Karen Black; **D:** Francis Ford Coppola; **W:** Francis Ford Coppola. Nominations: Academy Awards '66: Best Supporting Actress (Page). **VHS, Beta** ★★★

Z The assassination of a Greek nationalist in the 1960s and its aftermath are portrayed by the notorious political director as a gripping detective thriller. Excellent performances, adequate cinematic techniques, and important politics in this highly acclaimed film.

1969 128m/C *FR* Yves Montand, Jean-Louis Trintignant, Irene Papas, Charles Denner, Georges Geret, Jacques Perrin, Francois Perier, Marcel Bozzuffi; *D:* Constantin Costa-Gavras; *W:* Constantin Costa-Gavras. Academy Awards '69: Best Film Editing, Best Foreign Language Film; Cannes Film Festival '69: Special Jury Prize, Best Actor (Trintignant); Golden Globe Awards '70: Best Foreign Film; New York Film Critics Awards '69: Best Director (Costa-Gavras), Best Film; National Society of Film Critics Awards '69: Best Film; Nominations: Academy Awards '69: Best Adapted Screenplay, Best Director (Costa-Gavras), Best Picture; Cannes Film Festival '69: Best Film. **VHS, Beta, LV ★★★★**

Zabriskie Point Antonioni's first U.S. feature. A desultory, surreal examination of the American way of life. Worthy but difficult. Climaxes with a stylized orgy in Death Valley.
1970 (R) 112m/C Mark Frechette, Daria Halprin, Paul Fix, Rod Taylor, Harrison Ford, G.D. Spradlin; *D:* Michelangelo Antonioni; *W:* Michelangelo Antonioni, Sam Shepard, Fred Gardner, Tonino Guerra, Clare Peploe. **VHS, Beta, LV ★★★**

Zazie dans le Metro One of Malle's early movies, this is one of the best of the French New Wave comedies. A young girl, wise beyond her years, visits her drag queen uncle in Paris. She wants to ride the subway, but the ensuing hilarious adventures keep her from her goal. In French with English subtitles. *AKA:* Zazie in the Underground; Zazie in the Subway.
1961 92m/C *FR* Catherine Demonget, Philippe Noiret, Carla Marlier; *W:* Louis Malle. **VHS ★★★1/2**

Zebrahead Zack and Nikki are two high schoolers in love—which would be okay except Zack's white and Nikki's black. Will their romance succumb to the pressures of society, family, and friends? Writer/director Drazan's expressive debut features one of last appearances by Sharkey as Zack's dad. Outstanding performances by the young and largely unknown cast, particularly Rapaport and Wright, and a great musical score enrich the action. Filmed on location in Detroit, with plenty of authentic Motown scenery to chew on, including Cody High School and a shootout at the eastside Skateland. Developed with assistance by the Sundance Institute.
1992 (R) 102m/C Michael Rapaport, N'Bushe Wright, Ray Sharkey, DeShonn Castle, Ron Johnson, Marsha Florence, Paul Butler, Abdul Hassan Sharif, Dan Ziskie, Candy Ann Brown, Helen Shaver,

Luke Reilly, Martin Priest; *D:* Tony Drazan; *W:* Tony Drazan; *M:* Taj Mahal. Sundance Film Festival '92: Filmmakers Trophy. **VHS, LV, 8mm ★★★**

Zelig Documentary spoof stars Allen as Leonard Zelig, the famous "Chameleon Man" of the 1920s, whose personality was so vague he would assume the characteristics of those with whom he came into contact, and who had a habit of showing up among celebrities and at historic events. Filmed in black-and-white; intersperses bits of newsreel and photographs with live action. Allen-style clever filmmaking at its best.
1983 (PG) 79m/B Woody Allen, Mia Farrow, Susan Sontag, Saul Bellow, Irving Howe, Gordon Willis; *D:* Woody Allen; *W:* Woody Allen. New York Film Critics Awards '83: Best Cinematography; Nominations: Academy Awards '83: Best Cinematography, Best Costume Design.
VHS, Beta, LV, 8mm ★★★1/2

Zelly & Me A strange little drama about a young orphan living with her maniacally possessive grandmother, who forces the child into her own interior life through humiliation and isolation from anyone she cares for. Well-acted and interesting film that suffers from an overly introspective plot and confusing gaps in the narrative. Look for director Lynch on the other side of the camera. *AKA:* Phoebe.
1988 (PG) 87m/C Isabella Rossellini, Alexandra Johnes, David Lynch, Glynis Johns, Kaiulani Lee, Joe Morton; *D:* Tina Rathborne; *W:* Tina Rathborne; *M:* Pino Donaggio, Mikael Salomon. **VHS, Beta, LV ★★★**

Zero for Conduct Vigo's classic French fantasy about an outrageous rebellion of schoolboys against bureaucratic adults. More of a visual poem than a drama, it inspired Lindsay Anderson's "If. . . ." One of only four films created by Vigo before his early death. Banned across Europe at release. In French with English subtitles. *AKA:* Zero de Conduit.
1933 49m/B *FR* Jean Daste, Robert Le Flon, Louis Lef'evre, Constantin Kelber, Gerard de Bedarieux; *D:* Jean Vigo; *W:* Jean Vigo. **VHS, Beta ★★★★**

Ziegfeld Girl Three star-struck girls are chosen for the Ziegfeld follies and move on to success and heartbreak. Lavish costumes and production numbers in the MGM style. ♪ You Stepped Out of a Dream; I'm Always Chasing Rainbows; Minnie from Trinidad; Mr. Gallagher & Mr. Shean; You Never Looked So Beautiful.

1941 131m/B James Stewart, Judy Garland, Hedy Lamarr, Lana Turner, Tony Martin, Jackie Cooper, Ian Hunter, Charles Winninger, Al Shear, Edward Everett Horton, Philip Dorn, Paul Kelly, Eve Arden, Dan Dailey, Fay Holden, Felix Bressart, Mae Busch, Reed Hadley; **D:** Robert Z. Leonard. **VHS, Beta, LV** ★★★

Zooman Hard-hitting message on violence and responsibility. Gang member Zooman (Kain) spots members of a rival gang in a Brooklyn neighborhood, whips out his gun, and begins firing. When the shooting stops, a little girl sitting on her stoop is dead—what's even worse for her estranged parents is the fact that obvious witnesses refuse to identify the gunman for fear of their own safety. So father Reuben (Gossett Jr.) puts up a sign about their plight, attracting lots of media attention, and neighborhood hostility. Based on Fuller's 1978 play "Zooman and the Sign." Made for cable TV.
1995 (R) 95m/C Louis Gossett Jr., Charles S. Dutton, Khalil Kain, Cynthia Martells, CCH Pounder, Vondie Curtis-Hall, Hill Harper; **D:** Leon Ichaso; **W:** Charles Fuller. **VHS** ★★★

Zorba the Greek A young British writer (Bates) comes to Crete to find himself by working his father's mine. He meets Zorba, an itinerant Greek laborer (Quinn), and they take lodgings together with an aging courtesan, who Zorba soon romances. The writer, on the other hand, is attracted to a lovely young widow. When she responds to him, the townsmen jealously attack her. Zorba teaches the young man the necessary response to life and its tragedies. Based on a novel by Nicolai Kazantzakis. Masterpiece performance from Quinn. Beautifully photographed, somewhat overlong. Film later written for stage production. **AKA:** Zormba.
1964 142m/B Anthony Quinn, Alan Bates, Irene Papas, Lila Kedrova; **D:** Michael Cacoyannis. Academy Awards '64: Best Art Direction/Set Decoration (B & W), Best Black and White Cinematography, Best Supporting Actress (Kedrova); Nominations: Academy Awards '64: Best Actor (Quinn), Best Adapted Screenplay, Best Director (Cacoyannis), Best Picture. **VHS, Beta, LV** ★★★1/2

Zulu Dawn An historical epic about British troops fighting the Zulus at Ulandi in 1878. Shows the increasing tensions between the British colonial government and the Zulus. Stunning landscapes unfortunately don't translate to the small screen. Good but unoriginal colonial-style battle drama.
1979 (PG) 117m/C Burt Lancaster, Peter O'Toole, Denholm Elliott, Nigel Davenport, John Mills, Simon Ward, Bob Hoskins, Freddie Jones; **D:** Douglas Hickox; **M:** Elmer Bernstein. **VHS, Beta, LV** ★★★

Zvenigora Dovzhenko's first major film, and a lyrical revelation in the face of Soviet formality: a passionate, funny fantasy tableaux of 1,000 years of Ukrainian history, encompassing wild folk myths, poetic drama, propaganda and social satire. Silent.
1928 73m/B *RU* Mikola Nademsy, Alexander Podorozhny, Semyon Svashenko; **D:** Alexander Dovzhenko. **VHS, Beta** ★★★★

CATEGORY INDEX

The Category Index contains over 325 genre, sub-genre, thematic, or significant scene classifications, ranging from the general (such as comedy) to the particular (such as killer beasts). A list of categories precedes the index.

Big
The Big Chill
The Bishop's Wife
Blume in Love
Borsalino
The Breakfast Club
Breaking Away
Broadcast News
Butterflies Are Free
Carnal Knowledge
Carnival in Flanders
Cesar
Chimes at Midnight
Chloe in the Afternoon
Choose Me
Chungking Express
City Lights
Claire's Knee
Cleo from 5 to 7
Come to the Stable
The Courtship of Eddie's Father
Cousin, Cousine
Crazy from the Heart
Crimes & Misdemeanors
The Decameron
The Decline of the American
   Empire
The Devil & Daniel Webster
Diary of a Chambermaid
Diary of a Mad Housewife
Different for Girls
Dim Sum: A Little Bit of Heart
Dinner at Eight
Do the Right Thing
Don Quixote
Down by Law
Drugstore Cowboy
Eat a Bowl of Tea
Eat Drink Man Woman
Educating Rita
Enemies, a Love Story
The Fabulous Baker Boys
First Name: Carmen
The Fisher King
Five Corners
The Flamingo Kid
Flesh
Forrest Gump
The Four Musketeers
Fried Green Tomatoes
Georgy Girl
Get Shorty
Gin Game
Ginger & Fred
Girlfriends
Good Morning, Vietnam
Goodbye Columbus
The Graduate
The Great McGinty
A Great Wall
Gregory's Girl
Grumpy Old Men
Guess Who's Coming to Dinner
Hangin' with the Homeboys
Hannah and Her Sisters
The Heartbreak Kid
Hold Your Man
Household Saints
Housekeeping
I Vitelloni
Insignificance
It Started in Naples

It's a Wonderful Life
Joshua Then and Now
Judge Priest
Kicking and Screaming
The Kid
The Kid/Idle Class
Kotch
La Dolce Vita
La Ronde
Lady for a Day
Larks on a String
The Last Detail
The Last of Mrs. Cheyney
Last Summer in the Hamptons
Le Beau Serge
Le Petit Amour
A League of Their Own
Letters from My Windmill
Like Water for Chocolate
The Little Theatre of Jean
   Renoir
The Little Thief
Local Hero
Love Finds Andy Hardy
Lovers and Other Strangers
Loves of a Blonde
Madame Sousatzka
Made for Each Other
Marius
The Marriage of Maria Braun
M*A*S*H
M*A*S*H: Goodbye, Farewell &
   Amen
May Fools
Mediterraneo
Metropolitan
The Milagro Beanfield War
Mr. Deeds Goes to Town
Mr. Mom
Moscow on the Hudson
Murmur of the Heart
My Beautiful Laundrette
My Dinner with Andre
My Life as a Dog
Mystic Pizza
The Nasty Girl
Next Stop, Greenwich Village
Next Summer
Night on Earth
Nobody's Fool
North Dallas Forty
The Object of Beauty
Oblomov
One Arabian Night
One Flew Over the Cuckoo's
   Nest
The Paper Chase
Parenthood
People Will Talk
Peppermint Soda
The Philadelphia Story
Pocketful of Miracles
Pollyanna
Postcards from the Edge
The Prime of Miss Jean Brodie
Prizzi's Honor
Queen of Hearts
Return of the Secaucus 7
The Rules of the Game
Say Anything
Secrets of Women
Seduced and Abandoned

The Seven Percent Solution
Seven Thieves
Shag: The Movie
Shirley Valentine
Short Cuts
Slap Shot
Smugglers' Cove
The Snapper
Snoopy, Come Home
Stage Door
Starting Over
Steamboat Bill, Jr.
Stranger Than Paradise
Strawberry Blonde
Strong Man
Stroszek
The Sugarland Express
The Sunshine Boys
Sweet Lorraine
Sweetie
Swept Away . . .
Taxi Blues
A Taxing Woman
Teacher's Pet
That Thing You Do!
They Might Be Giants
A Thousand Clowns
Three Men and a Baby
Three Men and a Cradle
The Time of Your Life
To Sleep with Anger
Tom Sawyer
Tootsie
True Love
Truly, Madly, Deeply
Two for the Road
Two for the Seesaw
Ugetsu
Up the Down Staircase
We Think the World of You
Whose Life Is It Anyway?
Wise Blood
Wish You Were Here
The Women
The World According to Garp
The World of Henry Orient
WR: Mysteries of the Organism
Yesterday, Today and Tomorrow
You're a Big Boy Now

Comedy Performance
see Concert Films

Comic Adventure
*see also Action Adventure;
   Comedy*
The Absent-Minded Professor
Back to the Future
Back to the Future, Part 3
Bagdad Cafe
Cartouche
Chan Is Missing
Crocodile Dundee
Flipper
Flirting with Fate
48 Hrs.
Foul Play
Ghostbusters
Lust in the Dust
Midnight Run
Romancing the Stone
Silver Streak
Slither
Speedy

Death Becomes Her
Defending Your Life
D.O.A.
Dona Flor and Her Two
  Husbands
Donovan's Brain
The Duellists
The English Patient
The Entertainer
Executive Suite
Fearless
Friendly Fire
The Funeral
Ghost
The Ghost and Mrs. Muir
Heaven Can Wait
Here Comes Mr. Jordan
Hold That Ghost
I Married a Witch
I Walked with a Zombie
It's a Wonderful Life
Liliom
The Loved One
Macbeth
Night of the Living Dead
Poltergeist
Portrait of Jennie
Scared Stiff
Scrooge
The Seventh Seal
Stand By Me
Things to Do in Denver When
  You're Dead
To Dance with the White Dog
Topper
Topper Returns
Topper Takes a Trip
Truly, Madly, Deeply

Dedicated Teachers
see also Hell High School;
  Blackboard Jungle
Born Yesterday
A Child Is Waiting
Children of a Lesser God
The Corn Is Green
Dead Poets Society
Educating Rita
Madame Sousatzka
Matilda
The Miracle Worker
Mr. Holland's Opus
The Paper Chase
The Prime of Miss Jean Brodie
Stand and Deliver
Up the Down Staircase

Dental Mayhem
see also Doctors & Nurses
Brazil
The Dentist
Little Shop of Horrors
Marathon Man
The Paleface
Reuben, Reuben
Serial Mom
Strawberry Blonde
12 Monkeys

Deserts
The Adventures of Priscilla,
  Queen of the Desert
Beau Geste
Desert Hearts
The Desert Rats

The English Patient
Fatal Attraction
The Flying Deuces
Gallipoli
Gunga Din
Indiana Jones and the Last
  Crusade
Lawrence of Arabia
Mad Max
Morocco
The Passenger
Patriot Games
The Road to Morocco
The Road Warrior
Sahara
The Sheik
The Sheltering Sky
Son of the Sheik
Star Wars
The Wind and the Lion

Detective Spoofs
see also Detectives
The Adventures of Sherlock
  Holmes' Smarter Brother
The Naked Gun: From the Files
  of Police Squad
The Pink Panther
The Pink Panther Strikes Again
A Shot in the Dark

Detectives
see also Cops; Detective
  Spoofs; Feds
The Adventures of Sherlock
  Holmes' Smarter Brother
After the Thin Man
Alphaville
The Big Sleep
Blackmail
Bullitt
Cat and Mouse
Charlie Chan at the Opera
Chinatown
Dead Again
The Detective Story
Devil in a Blue Dress
Dick Tracy
Dick Tracy: The Original Serial,
  Vol. 1
Farewell, My Lovely
The Glass Key
Heat
The Hound of the Baskervilles
Kiss Me Deadly
The Late Show
Laura
The Long Goodbye
The Maltese Falcon
Manhattan Murder Mystery
Mr. Arkadin
Murder at the Gallop
Murder, My Sweet
Murder on the Orient Express
The Naked Gun: From the Files
  of Police Squad
Night Moves
No Way to Treat a Lady
On Dangerous Ground
Out of the Past
The Pink Panther
The Pink Panther Strikes Again
Prime Suspect: The Scent of
  Darkness

The Private Life of Sherlock
  Holmes
Scarlet Claw
Sea of Love
The Seven Percent Solution
Shadow of the Thin Man
Sherlock Holmes and the
  Secret Weapon
A Shot in the Dark
Someone to Watch Over Me
Spider Woman
Stolen Kisses
They Might Be Giants
The Thin Man
Vertigo
Who Framed Roger Rabbit?
Witness

Disasters
see also Action Adventure;
  Meltdown
Airport
Apollo 13
The Buddy Holly Story
The China Syndrome
Das Boot
Die Hard 2: Die Harder
Fearless
Get Shorty
Hurricane
In Old Chicago
Independence Day
A Night to Remember
Titanic
The Unsinkable Molly Brown

Disease of the Week
see also AIDS
Beaches
The Best Little Girl in the
  World
Brian's Song
Camille
Cleo from 5 to 7
Cries and Whispers
An Early Frost
Interrupted Melody
Lorenzo's Oil
Love Story
On Her Majesty's Secret
  Service
Philadelphia
The Pride of the Yankees
The Shadow Box
Shadowlands
Terms of Endearment

Disorganized Crime
see also Crime & Criminals;
  Organized Crime
Fargo
Get Shorty
Home Alone
The League of Gentlemen
Reservoir Dogs
Ruthless People
Things to Do in Denver When
  You're Dead

Divorce
see also Marriage
The Accidental Tourist
The Awful Truth
California Suite
Desert Hearts
Divorce—Italian Style

▲ 483 • CATEGORY INDEX

Big Combo
The Big Easy
The Big Heat
The Big Sleep
Blade Runner
Blood Simple
The Blue Dahlia
Blue Velvet
Bob le Flambeur
Body Double
Body Heat
Bulletproof Heart
Cape Fear
Chinatown
Choose Me
Criss Cross
Crossfire
Dance with a Stranger
Dark Mirror
Dead Again
Detour
D.O.A.
Double Indemnity
Fallen Angels 1
Farewell, My Lovely
Fatal Attraction
Force of Evil
Frantic
Gilda
The Glass Key
The Grifters
Gun Crazy
High & Low
High Sierra
The Hitch-Hiker
In a Lonely Place
Johnny Angel
Key Largo
The Killing
Kiss Me Deadly
Kiss of Death
The Lady from Shanghai
The Last Seduction
Laura
Le Doulos
Leave Her to Heaven
The Long Goodbye
Macao
The Maltese Falcon
The Manchurian Candidate
Manhunter
Mildred Pierce
Murder, My Sweet
The Naked City
The Narrow Margin
Night Moves
Nightfall
No Way Out
On Dangerous Ground
One False Move
Out of the Past
Panic in the Streets
Performance
Pickup on South Street
The Postman Always Rings
   Twice
The Public Eye
Pulp Fiction
The Red House
Red Rock West
Reservoir Dogs
Rope

Scarlet Street
The Set-Up
sex, lies and videotape
The Silence of the Lambs
Sorry, Wrong Number
The Strange Love of Martha
   Ivers
Sunset Boulevard
Sweet Smell of Success
Taxi Driver
They Live by Night
The Third Man
This Gun for Hire
Touch of Evil
Trouble in Mind
True Confessions
The Underneath
The Usual Suspects
While the City Sleeps
White Heat
Who'll Stop the Rain?
Wild at Heart
The Window
Film Stars
Bombshell
Bruce Lee: Curse of the
   Dragon
Chaplin
Ed Wood
Frances
The Josephine Baker Story
The King of Kings
Man of a Thousand Faces
My Favorite Year
Play It Again, Sam
The Player
The Purple Rose of Cairo
Superstar: The Life and Times
   of Andy Warhol
Targets
Veronika Voss
What Ever Happened to Baby
   Jane?
Work/Police
Filmmaking
*see also At the Movies/Behind
   the Scenes*
Barton Fink
Day for Night
Ed Wood
84 Charlie Mopic
Get Shorty
Hearts of Darkness: A
   Filmmaker's Apocalypse
Hi, Mom!
The Player
The Stunt Man
Sullivan's Travels
Visions of Light: The Art of
   Cinematography
Wes Craven's New Nightmare
White Hunter, Black Heart
Fires & Firemen
see also Boom!; Disasters
Fahrenheit 451
The Firemen's Ball
Frankenstein
In Old Chicago
Pretty Poison
Quest for Fire
Roxanne
Save the Tiger

Fish & Fishing
see Go Fish
Flight
see Airborne
Flower Children
The Big Chill
Born on the Fourth of July
Conspiracy: The Trial of the
   Chicago Eight
Easy Rider
Fritz the Cat
Hair
High Hopes
The Return of the Secaucus 7
Who'll Stop the Rain?
Woodstock
Yellow Submarine
Folklore & Mythology
Black Orpheus
Darby O'Gill & the Little People
Faust
Iphigenia
Jason and the Argonauts
Kismet
Kriemhilde's Revenge
Monty Python and the Holy
   Grail
Pathfinder
The Secret of Roan Inish
Siegfried
Zvenigora
Food
see Edibles
Foreign Intrigue
see also Spies & Espionage
Above Suspicion
Crimson Tide
The Day of the Jackal
Diamonds Are Forever
Dr. No
An Englishman Abroad
Foreign Correspondent
The Hunt for Red October
License to Kill
The Little Drummer Girl
The Man Who Knew Too Much
Marathon Man
Reilly: Ace of Spies
The Spy Who Came in from the
   Cold
The Third Man
Topaz
Frame-Ups
City Hall
F/X
The Fugitive
The Life of Emile Zola
Murder
My Cousin Vinny
North by Northwest
Presumed Innocent
France
see also Paris
An American in Paris
Borsalino
Breathless
Buffet Froid
Carnival in Flanders
Cesar
Charade
Danton
Dirty Rotten Scoundrels

Oceans
*see Disasters; Go Fish; Sail
  Away; Submarines*
Oedipal Allegories
see also Family Ties
The Brothers Karamazov
Hamlet
The Manchurian Candidate
Murmur of the Heart
New York Stories
Oedipus Rex
Psycho
White Heat
Oldest Profession
Accatone!
Anna Christie
Arthur
Band of Gold
Belle de Jour
Butterfield 8
Caravaggio
Casino
Christiane F.
Cinderella Liberty
Crimes of Passion
Cry, the Beloved Country
Diary of a Lost Girl
Diva
Elmer Gantry
Flesh
Gigi
Hustling
I Want to Live!
Klute
La Chienne
The Last Temptation of
  Christ
Leaving Las Vegas
Life of Oharu
Lola Montes
Madame Rosa
Mamma Roma
Marriage Italian Style
McCabe & Mrs. Miller
Midnight Cowboy
Miss Sadie Thompson
Mona Lisa
My Life to Live
My Own Private Idaho
Nana
Never on Sunday
Night of the Generals
Nights of Cabiria
The Owl and the Pussycat
Pandora's Box
Panic in Needle Park
Pennies from Heaven
Pretty Baby
Pretty Woman
Prime Suspect 3
Queen Kelly
Risky Business
Saint Jack
Sandakan No. 8
Sansho the Bailiff
Sisters of Gion
Street of Shame
The Sun's Burial
Sweet Charity
Sweet Sweetback's
  Baadasssss Song
Taxi Driver

Things to Do in Denver When
  You're Dead
Tightrope
Waterloo Bridge
Working Girls
On the Rocks
see also Pill Poppin'
Barfly
Casino
Clean and Sober
Come Back, Little Sheba
Country Girl
Days of Wine and Roses
Desert Bloom
Dona Flor and Her Two
  Husbands
Drunken Angel
Educating Rita
El Dorado
The Entertainer
Fat City
Frances
Georgia
I'll Cry Tomorrow
The Informer
Ironweed
Le Beau Serge
Leaving Las Vegas
Long Day's Journey into Night
The Lost Weekend
My Favorite Year
Papa's Delicate Condition
Reuben, Reuben
Scent of a Woman
Smash-Up: The Story of a
  Woman
A Star Is Born
Under the Volcano
The Verdict
What Price Hollywood?
Whiskey Galore
Only the Lonely
An Autumn Afternoon
Birdman of Alcatraz
The Browning Version
Choose Me
Citizen Kane
Cyrano de Bergerac
A Day in the Docks of New
  York
Eat Drink Man Woman
The Eclipse
E.T.: The Extra-Terrestrial
Every Man for Himself & God
  Against All
Harold and Maude
The Heart Is a Lonely Hunter
Hiroshima, Mon Amour
The Hunchback of Notre Dame
Husbands and Wives
The Lonely Passion of Judith
  Hearne
Marty
Mouchette
Ninotchka
None But the Lonely Heart
The Passion of Anna
Persona
The Prime of Miss Jean Brodie
Queen of the Stardust Ballroom
Rachel, Rachel
The Red Desert

Samurai 2: Duel at Ichijoji
  Temple
The Seagull
Seize the Day
Separate Tables
Sleepless in Seattle
Summer
Turtle Diary
Vagabond
While You Were Sleeping
Opera
see also Musicals
Cosi
Interrupted Melody
A Night at the Opera
Order in the Court
*see also Justice Prevails . . . ?;
  Law & Lawyers*
The Accused
Adam's Rib
Anatomy of a Murder
The Andersonville Trial
Breaker Morant
Carrington, V.C.
Compulsion
Conspiracy: The Trial of the
  Chicago Eight
The Court Martial of Billy
  Mitchell
A Cry in the Dark
The Devil & Daniel Webster
A Dry White Season
A Few Good Men
I Want to Live!
In the Name of the Father
Indictment: The McMartin Trial
Inherit the Wind
The Judge and the Assassin
Judgment at Nuremberg
A Killing in a Small Town
L.A. Law
The Last Wave
Murder
Perry Mason Returns
Philadelphia
Presumed Innocent
Remember the Night
Reversal of Fortune
Roe vs. Wade
Rumpole of the Bailey:
  Rumpole's Return
Separate But Equal
Sergeant Rutledge
To Kill a Mockingbird
Tom and Huck
The Trial
Twelve Angry Men
The Verdict
The Winslow Boy
Witness for the Prosecution
A Woman's Face
Organized Crime
*see also Crime & Criminals;
  Disorganized Crime; Gangs*
Angels with Dirty Faces
Atlantic City
Ball of Fire
Big Combo
Brighton Rock
A Bronx Tale
Bugsy
Bullets Over Broadway

The Unsinkable Molly Brown
What Price Hollywood?
Working Girl
Ziegfeld Girl
Rape
The Accused
Bad Lieutenant
Casualties of War
Dead Man Walking
Death and the Maiden
Diary of a Lost Girl
From the Life of the
    Marionettes
It's Alive
Ms. 45
Open Doors
A Passage to India
Rashomon
Rob Roy
Straw Dogs
A Time to Kill
To Kill a Mockingbird
The Wind
Rebel With a Cause
see also Rebel Without a
    Cause; The Resistance
The Accused
The Adventures of Robin Hood
Blue Collar
Boyz N the Hood
Braveheart
The Burmese Harp
The China Syndrome
Dead Poets Society
Die Hard
Die Hard 2: Die Harder
East of Eden
The Fugitive
Gandhi
Gorillas in the Mist
Guess Who's Coming to Dinner
Hair
In the Name of the Father
La Marseillaise
Lawrence of Arabia
The Loneliness of the Long
    Distance Runner
Lust for Life
Man of Marble
Mr. Smith Goes to Washington
Network
Norma Rae
Odd Man Out
One-Eyed Jacks
Outbreak
Paths of Glory
A Raisin in the Sun
Rob Roy
The Rock
Roe vs. Wade
The Sand Pebbles
Sansho the Bailiff
The Scarlet Pimpernel
Serpico
Silkwood
This Land Is Mine
The Tin Star
The Westerner
Rebel Without a Cause
see also Rebel With a Cause
All Night Long
Badlands

Breathless
A Clockwork Orange
Easy Rider
Ferris Bueller's Day Off
Five Easy Pieces
Going Places
Hud
If . . .
Rebel Without a Cause
sex, lies and videotape
Thunder Road
West Side Story
The Wild One
Red Scare
see also Russia/USSR
Baltic Deputy
Commissar
Death of a Bureaucrat
Earth
Indochine
The Inner Circle
Man of Iron
Man of Marble
Mandela
Mother Kusters Goes to Heaven
Open Doors
Reds
Requiem for Dominic
Strike
When Father Was Away on
    Business
Religion
see also Judaism; Nuns &
    Priests; Religious Epics;
    Saints
Breaking the Waves
Catholics
Chariots of Fire
Come to the Stable
Crimes of Passion
Dead Man Walking
Devi
El Cid
El: This Strange Passion
Friendly Persuasion
The Godfather, Part 3
Green Pastures
Hallelujah!
The Hoodlum Priest
Household Saints
Inherit the Wind
Jesus of Nazareth
The Last Temptation of Christ
Major Barbara
A Man Called Peter
The Milky Way
The Miracle
Monty Python's Life of Brian
The Night of the Iguana
Ordet
The Passion of Joan of Arc
Queen Margot
Quo Vadis
Resurrection
Shadowlands
The Song of Bernadette
Susan and God
Therese
Through a Glass Darkly
When Night Is Falling
Whistle Down the Wind
The Winter Light

Wise Blood
Witness
Religious Epics
see also Religion
Ben-Hur
David and Bathsheba
El Cid
The Gospel According to St.
    Matthew
Judith of Bethulia
A Man for All Seasons
The Song of Bernadette
The Ten Commandments
Rescue Missions
Apollo 13
The City of Lost Children
Die Hard
Die Hard 2: Die Harder
The Inn of the Sixth Happiness
The Magnificent Seven
Outbreak
Raid on Entebbe
The Rock
The Searchers
Seven Samurai
The Slender Thread
Toy Story
Waikiki Wedding
The Resistance
see also World War II
Casablanca
Holocaust
The Last Metro
Passage to Marseilles
Soldier of Orange
The Train
Revenge
Angel and the Badman
Ballad of Cable Hogue
The Beguiled
Black Sunday
The Blue Lamp
Cape Fear
Cartouche
Chan Is Missing
The Count of Monte Cristo
The Cowboys
Daddy's Gone A-Hunting
Darkman
Death and the Maiden
Desperado
Dirty Harry
The Empire of Passion
The Fall of the House of Usher
Far Country
Fiorile
For Your Eyes Only
The Four Musketeers
Freaks
"G" Men
The Godfather
The Godfather 1902-1959: The
    Complete Epic
The Godfather, Part 2
Halloween
Hamlet
He Who Gets Slapped
High Noon
House of Strangers
I Married a Witch
Johnny Handsome
The Late Show

License to Kill
Macbeth
Mad Max
The Man from Laramie
The Man in the Iron Mask
Manon of the Spring
Marathon Man
The Mask
Men . . .
Ms. 45
The Mummy
Oklahoma Kid
On Dangerous Ground
One Arabian Night
One-Eyed Jacks
The Outlaw Josey Wales
Pathfinder
Patriot Games
The Raven
Reservoir Dogs
Short Eyes
Sons of Katie Elder
Star Trek 2: The Wrath of Khan
Straw Dogs
Theatre of Blood
This Gun for Hire
This Man Must Die
A Time to Kill
Trois Couleurs: Blanc
Underworld, U.S.A.
Unfaithfully Yours
Valmont
The Virgin Spring
The War Wagon
The White Sheik
The Women

Road Trip
see also Bikers; Chases; Fast Cars
The Adventures of Milo & Otis
The Adventures of Priscilla, Queen of the Desert
Around the World in 80 Days
Bad Company
Bound for Glory
Breathing Lessons
Butch Cassidy and the Sundance Kid
A Canterbury Tale
Citizens Band
Detour
The Doom Generation
Down by Law
Duel
Easy Rider
Flirting with Disaster
The Grapes of Wrath
Harry and Tonto
Homeward Bound: The Incredible Journey
The Journey of Natty Gann
Kings of the Road—In the Course of Time
La Strada
Lamerica
Lost in America
Midnight Run
The Muppet Movie
My Own Private Idaho
Night on Earth
Paper Moon
Pee Wee's Big Adventure

Pierrot le Fou
Rain Man
The Rain People
The Road to Bali
The Road to Morocco
The Road to Rio
The Road to Utopia
The Road to Zanzibar
The Road Warrior
Slither
Starman
The Sure Thing
Thelma & Louise
They Drive by Night
Those Magnificent Men in Their Flying Machines
Twentieth Century
Two for the Road
Wages of Fear
Weekend
Wild at Heart
The Wizard of Oz

Roaring '20s
Bullets Over Broadway
The Cotton Club
Eight Men Out
The Roaring Twenties
Underworld
The Untouchables

Robots & Androids
see also Technology-Rampant
Alien
Aliens
Blade Runner
The Day the Earth Stood Still
Edward Scissorhands
The Empire Strikes Back
Forbidden Planet
Return of the Jedi
RoboCop
Silent Running
Star Wars
The Terminator
Terminator 2: Judgment Day

Rock Stars on Film
see also Concert Films
Backbeat
Blow-Up
Chuck Berry: Hail! Hail! Rock 'n' Roll
Coal Miner's Daughter
Flaming Star
A Hard Day's Night
Heat
Help!
Jailhouse Rock
La Bamba
The Last Temptation of Christ
The Man Who Fell to Earth
Merry Christmas, Mr. Lawrence
Pat Garrett & Billy the Kid
Performance
Quadrophenia
Rock 'n' Roll High School
Woodstock
Yellow Submarine

Role Reversal
see also Gender Bending; Identity
Anastasia
Angel on My Shoulder
Babe

The Bank Dick
Big
Christmas in Connecticut
Coming to America
Dave
Dr. Jekyll and Mr. Hyde
48 Hrs.
Gentleman's Agreement
Johnny Guitar
Kagemusha
Kim
La Femme Nikita
La Ronde
The Lady Vanishes
Male and Female
Monkey Business
My Fair Lady
Now, Voyager
Performance
Persona
Pocketful of Miracles
The Prince and the Pauper
Prisoner of Zenda
Psycho
Roman Holiday
The Scarlet Pimpernel
A Tale of Two Cities
Tootsie
Victor/Victoria

Romance
see Late Bloomin' Love; Lovers on the Lam; Romantic Adventures; Romantic Comedy; Romantic Drama; Romantic Triangles

Romantic Adventures
The African Queen
Gun Crazy
Mogambo
Pocahontas
Red Dust
Romancing the Stone

Romantic Comedy
Adam's Rib
All Night Long
The American President
Anna Karenina
Annie Hall
The Apartment
Arthur
Ball of Fire
Barefoot in the Park
Belle Epoque
Bells Are Ringing
Bombshell
Born Yesterday
Breakfast at Tiffany's
Bull Durham
California Suite
The Cameraman
Christmas in Connecticut
The Clock
Closely Watched Trains
Clueless
Come Blow Your Horn
Coming to America
Crocodile Dundee
Crossing Delancey
Defending Your Life
Designing Woman
Desk Set
The Devil & Miss Jones

China Seas
Crimson Tide
Damn the Defiant
Das Boot
The Fighting Sullivans
Flipper
History Is Made at Night
The Hunt for Red October
In Which We Serve
Jaws
Knife in the Water
Le Crabe Tambour
Lifeboat
The Long Voyage Home
Lord Jim
Love Affair
Mister Roberts
Monkey Business
Mutiny on the Bounty
A Night to Remember
Old Ironsides
Operation Petticoat
Pueblo Affair
Romancing the Stone
Run Silent, Run Deep
The Sand Pebbles
The Sea Wolf
Ship of Fools
Sinbad the Sailor
Sink the Bismarck
Steamboat Bill, Jr.
They Were Expendable
Titanic
To Have & Have Not
The Unsinkable Molly Brown
Voyage of the Damned
We're Not Dressing

San Francisco
Barbary Coast
Chan Is Missing
Dim Sum: A Little Bit of Heart
Dirty Harry
48 Hrs.
Foul Play
I Remember Mama
Invasion of the Body Snatchers
Pacific Heights
The Rock
San Francisco
Time After Time
What's Up, Doc?

Sanity Check
see also Doctors & Nurses;
   Hospitals & Medicine;
   Shrinks
Aguirre, the Wrath of God
An Angel at My Table
Arsenic and Old Lace
Bedlam
Camille Claudel
The Collector
A Day at the Races
Dead of Night
Despair
Deutschland im Jahre Null
Devi
Diary of a Mad Housewife
Dr. Jekyll and Mr. Hyde
Dr. Mabuse, Parts 1 & 2
Dr. Strangelove, or: How I
   Learned to Stop Worrying
   and Love the Bomb

Dog Day Afternoon
Don't Look Now
A Double Life
Easy Rider
El: This Strange Passion
The Fall of the House of
   Usher
Fear Strikes Out
The Fisher King
Frances
From the Life of the
   Marionettes
The Goalie's Anxiety at the
   Penalty Kick
Hamlet
Harvey
The Haunting
Heavenly Creatures
The Horror Chamber of Dr.
   Faustus
The Hospital
How to Get Ahead in
   Advertising
Hush, Hush, Sweet Charlotte
I Never Promised You a Rose
   Garden
Interiors
The King of Hearts
The Last Seduction
Leave Her to Heaven
Lethal Weapon
Lethal Weapon 2
Lilith
Mad Love
Man Facing Southeast
Manhunter
Marat/Sade
Mother Kusters Goes to Heaven
Network
One Flew Over the Cuckoo's
   Nest
The Onion Field
Peeping Tom
Performance
The Pink Panther Strikes Again
The Pit and the Pendulum
Play Misty for Me
Poison
The President's Analyst
Psycho
Richard III
The Ruling Class
Scarlet Empress
Seance on a Wet Afternoon
Seven Days in May
Shock Corridor
The Silence of the Lambs
Sisters
Sophie's Choice
Spellbound
Story of Adele H.
Strangers on a Train
A Streetcar Named Desire
Sybil
The Tenant
They Might Be Giants
The Three Faces of Eve
12 Monkeys
What Ever Happened to Baby
   Jane?
White Heat
A Woman Under the Influence

Satanism
see also Occult
The Black Cat
Black Sunday
The Devil & Daniel Webster
The Devils
The Exorcist
Rosemary's Baby
Satire & Parody
see also Black Comedy;
   Comedy; Genre Spoofs
The Adventures of Sherlock
   Holmes' Smarter Brother
Airplane!
All Through the Night
The Apartment
Auntie Mame
Bananas
Being There
The Best Man
Big Deal on Madonna Street
Black and White in Color
Bob Roberts
Boy Meets Girl
The Brady Bunch Movie
Bread and Chocolate
The Candidate
Champagne for Caesar
A Clockwork Orange
The Coca-Cola Kid
Cold Turkey
Dark Star
Death of a Bureaucrat
Diary of a Chambermaid
The Discreet Charm of the
   Bourgeoisie
Down & Dirty
11 Harrowhouse
The Fortune Cookie
The Front
Genevieve
Gentlemen Prefer Blondes
Get Shorty
Going Places
The Great Dictator
Hail the Conquering Hero
Hairspray
Heaven Can Wait
High Hopes
The Hospital
Hot Shots!
I'm All Right Jack
I'm Gonna Git You Sucka
The King of Hearts
L'Age D'Or
The Last Polka
Love and Death
The Man in the White Suit
The Man Who Came to Dinner
Men . . .
The Milky Way
Modern Times
Monty Python and the Holy
   Grail
Monty Python's Life of Brian
The Mouse That Roared
The Naked Gun: From the Files
   of Police Squad
National Lampoon's Animal
   House
The Nutty Professor
On the Avenue

Vampyr

CAST INDEX

The Cast Index contains listings for every actor appearing in at least three three- and four-star video creations selected for this book. This list includes hundreds of celebrities and a host of some very obscure performers. The actors are listed alphabetically by last name, and their corresponding three- and four-star movies immediately follow.

Caroline Aaron
Alice '90
Crimes & Misdemeanors '89
Edward Scissorhands '90
John Abbott
Anna and the King of Siam '46
Deception '46
Humoresque '46
Walter Abel
Fury '36
Holiday Inn '42
The Indian Fighter '55
Mr. Skeffington '44
So Proudly We Hail '43
13 Rue Madeleine '46
Wake Island '42
F. Murray Abraham
All the President's Men '76
Amadeus '84
Looking for Richard '96
The Ritz '76
Serpico '73
The Sunshine Boys '75
They Might Be Giants '71
Joss Ackland
Citizen X '95
The Hunt for Red October '90
Lady Jane '85
Lethal Weapon 2 '89
The Object of Beauty '91
Saint Jack '79
White Mischief '88
Who Is Killing the Great Chefs of Europe? '78
Brooke Adams
Days of Heaven '78
Dead Zone '83
Gas Food Lodging '92
Invasion of the Body Snatchers '78
Edie Adams
The Apartment '60
The Best Man '64

Love with the Proper Stranger '63
Nick Adams
The FBI Story '59
Hell Is for Heroes '62
Mister Roberts '55
No Time for Sergeants '58
Picnic '55
Pillow Talk '59
Rebel Without a Cause '55
Teacher's Pet '58
Wesley Addy
The Big Knife '55
The Europeans '79
The Grissom Gang '71
Hiroshima '95
Kiss Me Deadly '55
Network '76
Isabelle Adjani
Camille Claudel '89
Quartet '81
Queen Margot '94
Story of Adele H. '75
The Tenant '76
Luther Adler
D.O.A. '49
House of Strangers '49
The Last Angry Man '59
Voyage of the Damned '76
John Agar
Fort Apache '48
Sands of Iwo Jima '49
She Wore a Yellow Ribbon '49
Jenny Agutter
An American Werewolf in London '81
Darkman '90
The Railway Children '70
Brian Aherne
The Best of Everything '59
Forever and a Day '43
A Night to Remember '42
The Swan '56
Titanic '53

Danny Aiello
Bang the Drum Slowly '73
City Hall '95
Do the Right Thing '89
Fort Apache, the Bronx '81
The Front '76
The Godfather, Part 2 '74
Hide in Plain Sight '80
Moonstruck '87
Once Upon a Time in America '84
The Purple Rose of Cairo '85
Radio Days '87
Anouk Aimee
8 1/2 '63
La Dolce Vita '60
Lola '61
A Man and a Woman '66
Claude Akins
The Caine Mutiny '54
From Here to Eternity '53
Rio Bravo '59
Eddie Albert
Carrie '52
The Heartbreak Kid '72
I'll Cry Tomorrow '55
The Longest Day '62
Oklahoma! '55
Roman Holiday '53
Smash-Up: The Story of a Woman '47
Frank Albertson
Ah, Wilderness! '35
Fury '36
It's a Wonderful Life '46
Nightfall '56
Psycho '60
Jack Albertson
Days of Wine and Roses '62
Miracle on 34th Street '47
Willy Wonka & the Chocolate Factory '71
Alan Alda
And the Band Played On '93

Kathy Bates
Come Back to the Five &
 Dime Jimmy Dean, Jimmy
 Dean '82
Dick Tracy '90
Dolores Claiborne '94
Fried Green Tomatoes '91
Misery '90
Roe vs. Wade '89
Michael Bates
Bedazzled '68
A Clockwork Orange '71
Patton '70
Alan Baxter
Abe Lincoln in Illinois '40
Saboteur '42
The Set-Up '49
Shadow of the Thin Man '41
Anne Baxter
All About Eve '50
Angel on My Shoulder '46
The Fighting Sullivans '42
The Magnificent Ambersons
 '42
The North Star '43
The Razor's Edge '46
The Ten Commandments '56
Nathalie Baye
And the Band Played On '93
Day for Night '73
La Balance '82
The Return of Martin Guerre
 '83
John Beal
Double Wedding '37
Edge of Darkness '43
The Firm '93
Les Miserables '35
Little Minister '34
Sean Bean
Caravaggio '86
The Field '90
Goldeneye '95
Patriot Games '92
Emmanuelle Beart
La Belle Noiseuse '90
Manon of the Spring '87
Mission: Impossible '96
Nelly et Monsieur Arnaud '95
Ned Beatty
The Big Easy '87
Crazy Horse '96
Deliverance '72
The Execution of Private
 Slovik '74
Friendly Fire '79
Hear My Song '90
Larry McMurtry's Streets of
 Laredo '95
Nashville '75
Network '76
A Question of Love '78
Silver Streak '76
Superman: The Movie '78
Superman 2 '80
Wise Blood '79
A Woman Called Golda '82
Warren Beatty
Bonnie & Clyde '67
Bugsy '91
Dick Tracy '90
Heaven Can Wait '78

Lilith '64
McCabe & Mrs. Miller '71
The Parallax View '74
Reds '81
Roman Spring of Mrs. Stone
 '61
Splendor in the Grass '61
Louise Beavers
Bullets or Ballots '38
The Jackie Robinson Story
 '50
Mr. Blandings Builds His
 Dream House '48
She Done Him Wrong '33
Graham Beckel
The Paper Chase '73
Rising Son '90
Separate But Equal '91
Scotty Beckett
Battleground '49
The Charge of the Light
 Brigade '36
Conquest '37
Heaven Can Wait '43
The Jolson Story '46
Kings Row '41
Love Affair '39
My Favorite Wife '40
Don Beddoe
Golden Boy '39
The Narrow Margin '52
The Night of the Hunter '55
Bonnie Bedelia
The Boy Who Could Fly '86
Die Hard '88
Die Hard 2: Die Harder '90
Lovers and Other Strangers
 '70
Presumed Innocent '90
They Shoot Horses, Don't
 They? '69
Noah Beery, Jr.
Of Mice and Men '39
Only Angels Have Wings '39
Red River '48
Sergeant York '41
Seven Faces of Dr. Lao '63
Wallace Beery
Ah, Wilderness! '35
The Big House '30
The Champ '31
China Seas '35
Dinner at Eight '33
The Four Horsemen of the
 Apocalypse '21
Grand Hotel '32
The Last of the Mohicans '20
Old Ironsides '26
Robin Hood '22
Treasure Island '34
Viva Villa! '34
Ed Begley, Jr.
The Accidental Tourist '88
Blue Collar '78
Citizens Band '77
Eating Raoul '82
Running Mates '92
This Is Spinal Tap '84
Ed Begley, Sr.
It Happens Every Spring '49
On Dangerous Ground '51
Patterns '56

Road to Salina '68
Sorry, Wrong Number '48
Stars in My Crown '50
Sweet Bird of Youth '62
Twelve Angry Men '57
The Unsinkable Molly Brown
 '64
Barbara Bel Geddes
Caught '49
I Remember Mama '48
Panic in the Streets '50
Vertigo '58
Harry Belafonte
Carmen Jones '54
Kansas City '95
The Player '92
Marshall Bell
No Way Out '87
Total Recall '90
Tucker: The Man and His
 Dream '88
Tom Bell
Let Him Have It '91
Prime Suspect '92
Prime Suspect 3 '93
Prospero's Books '91
Wish You Were Here '87
Ralph Bellamy
The Awful Truth '37
Boy Meets Girl '38
Brother Orchid '40
Carefree '38
The Court Martial of Billy
 Mitchell '55
Dive Bomber '41
His Girl Friday '40
Missiles of October '74
Pretty Woman '90
The Professionals '66
Rosemary's Baby '68
Sunrise at Campobello '60
The Wolf Man '41
Jean-Paul Belmondo
Borsalino '70
Breathless '59
Cartouche '62
Is Paris Burning? '68
Le Doulos '61
Mississippi Mermaid '69
Pierrot le Fou '65
Stavisky '74
Two Women '61
A Woman Is a Woman '60
James Belushi
Little Shop of Horrors '86
Salvador '86
Thief '81
Robert Benchley
China Seas '35
Foreign Correspondent '40
The Road to Utopia '46
You'll Never Get Rich '41
William Bendix
The Blue Dahlia '46
The Detective Story '51
The Glass Key '42
Lifeboat '44
Macao '52
Star Spangled Rhythm '42
The Time of Your Life '48
Wake Island '42
Woman of the Year '42

State of Things '82
Yvonne Furneaux
La Dolce Vita '60
The Mummy '59
Repulsion '65
Jean Gabin
French Can-Can '55
Grand Illusion '37
La Bete Humaine '38
Le Chat '71
Le Jour Se Leve '39
The Lower Depths '36
Pepe Le Moko '37
Christopher Gable
The Boy Friend '71
The Lair of the White Worm '88
The Rainbow '89
Clark Gable
China Seas '35
Dance Fools Dance '31
Gone with the Wind '39
Hold Your Man '33
Honky Tonk '41
Idiot's Delight '39
It Happened One Night '34
It Started in Naples '60
Manhattan Melodrama '34
The Misfits '61
Mogambo '53
Mutiny on the Bounty '35
Red Dust '32
Run Silent, Run Deep '58
San Francisco '36
Strange Interlude '32
Teacher's Pet '58
Test Pilot '38
Too Hot to Handle '38
Wife Versus Secretary '36
Zsa Zsa Gabor
Boy's Night Out '62
Lili '53
Lovely to Look At '52
Moulin Rouge '52
Touch of Evil '58
Charlotte Gainsbourg
Jane Eyre '96
Le Petit Amour '87
The Little Thief '89
Michel Galabru
Belle Epoque '92
The Judge and the Assassin '75
La Cage aux Folles '78
Peter Gallagher
Fallen Angels 1 '93
The Hudsucker Proxy '93
The Murder of Mary Phagan '87
The Player '92
sex, lies and videotape '89
Short Cuts '93
The Underneath '95
While You Were Sleeping '95
James Gammon
Ironweed '87
Larry McMurtry's Streets of Laredo '95
The Milagro Beanfield War '88
Roe vs. Wade '89
Greta Garbo
Anna Karenina '35

As You Desire Me '32
Camille '36
Conquest '37
The Flesh and the Devil '27
Grand Hotel '32
Joyless Street '25
The Kiss '29
Mata Hari '32
Ninotchka '39
Queen Christina '33
Two-Faced Woman '41
Andy Garcia
Dead Again '91
The Godfather, Part 3 '90
Stand and Deliver '88
Things to Do in Denver When You're Dead '95
The Untouchables '87
Vincent Gardenia
Bang the Drum Slowly '73
Cold Turkey '71
The Hustler '61
Little Shop of Horrors '86
Moonstruck '87
Where's Poppa? '70
Reginald Gardiner
Christmas in Connecticut '45
A Damsel in Distress '37
The Flying Deuces '39
The Great Dictator '40
The Horn Blows at Midnight '45
The Man Who Came to Dinner '41
Mr. Hobbs Takes a Vacation '62
Ava Gardner
Around the World in 80 Days '56
The Barefoot Contessa '54
55 Days at Peking '63
The Long, Hot Summer '86
Mogambo '53
The Night of the Iguana '64
On the Beach '59
Seven Days in May '64
The Snows of Kilimanjaro '52
Allen (Goorwitz) Garfield
Bananas '71
The Candidate '72
The Conversation '74
The Cotton Club '84
Desert Bloom '86
Hi, Mom! '70
Nashville '75
The Owl and the Pussycat '70
Slither '73
State of Things '82
The Stunt Man '80
John Garfield
Air Force '43
Body and Soul '47
Force of Evil '49
Four Daughters '38
Gentleman's Agreement '47
Hollywood Canteen '44
Humoresque '46
The Postman Always Rings Twice '46
The Sea Wolf '41
Thank Your Lucky Stars '43
Tortilla Flat '42

Judy Garland
A Child Is Waiting '63
The Clock '45
Easter Parade '48
Girl Crazy '43
The Harvey Girls '46
In the Good Old Summertime '49
Judgment at Nuremberg '61
Life Begins for Andy Hardy '41
Love Finds Andy Hardy '38
Meet Me in St. Louis '44
The Pirate '48
A Star Is Born '54
Summer Stock '50
Till the Clouds Roll By/A Star Is Born '46
The Wizard of Oz '39
Ziegfeld Girl '41
James Garner
The Americanization of Emily '64
Barbarians at the Gate '93
Boy's Night Out '62
Breathing Lessons '94
Decoration Day '90
Duel at Diablo '66
The Great Escape '63
Larry McMurtry's Streets of Laredo '95
Sayonara '57
Support Your Local Sheriff '69
Victor/Victoria '82
The Wheeler Dealers '63
Peggy Ann Garner
Jane Eyre '44
The Keys of the Kingdom '44
A Tree Grows in Brooklyn '45
Teri Garr
After Hours '85
The Black Stallion '79
Close Encounters of the Third Kind '77
The Conversation '74
Mr. Mom '83
The Player '92
The Tale of the Frog Prince '83
Tootsie '82
Young Frankenstein '74
Greer Garson
Goodbye, Mr. Chips '39
Julia Misbehaves '48
Julius Caesar '53
Madame Curie '43
Mrs. Miniver '42
Pride and Prejudice '40
Random Harvest '42
Sunrise at Campobello '60
The Valley of Decision '45
Vittorio Gassman
Big Deal on Madonna Street '58
The Family '87
We All Loved Each Other So Much '77
Larry Gates
Above and Beyond '53
The Hoodlum Priest '61
The Sand Pebbles '66
Underworld, U.S.A. '60

Radio Days '87
Seize the Day '86
Serpico '73
The Taking of Pelham One
Two Three '74
Cliff Robertson
The Best Man '64
Charly '68
Picnic '55
Three Days of the Condor '75
Underworld, U.S.A. '60
Wild Hearts Can't Be Broken
'91
Andrew (Andy) Robinson
Charley Varrick '73
Dirty Harry '71
Mask '85
Edward G. Robinson
Barbary Coast '35
Brother Orchid '40
Bullets or Ballots '38
Double Indemnity '44
House of Strangers '49
Key Largo '48
Kid Galahad '37
Little Caesar '30
Our Vines Have Tender Grapes
'45
The Prize '63
Scarlet Street '45
The Sea Wolf '41
Seven Thieves '60
The Stranger '46
Flora Robson
Black Narcissus '47
55 Days at Peking '63
Fire Over England '37
Les Miserables '78
Murder at the Gallop '63
The Sea Hawk '40
Those Magnificent Men in
Their Flying Machines '65
Wuthering Heights '39
May Robson
The Adventures of Tom
Sawyer '38
Anna Karenina '35
Bringing Up Baby '38
Dinner at Eight '33
Four Daughters '38
Joan of Paris '42
Lady for a Day '33
Red Headed Woman '32
A Star Is Born '37
Strange Interlude '32
Wife Versus Secretary '36
Alex Rocco
The Godfather '72
The Godfather 1902-1959:
The Complete Epic '81
Hustling '75
Slither '73
The Stunt Man '80
That Thing You Do! '96
Eugene Roche
Cotton Comes to Harlem '70
Foul Play '78
The Late Show '77
They Might Be Giants '71
Jean Rochefort
The Clockmaker '76
Le Crabe Tambour '77

Pardon Mon Affaire '76
The Tall Blond Man with One
Black Shoe '72
Who Is Killing the Great Chefs
of Europe? '78
Ginger Rogers
Bachelor Mother '39
The Barkleys of Broadway
'49
Carefree '38
Follow the Fleet '36
42nd Street '33
The Gay Divorcee '34
Gold Diggers of 1933 '33
Kitty Foyle '40
Monkey Business '52
Roberta '35
Shall We Dance '37
Stage Door '37
The Story of Vernon and Irene
Castle '39
Swing Time '36
Top Hat '35
Vivacious Lady '38
Mimi Rogers
Bulletproof Heart '95
The Player '92
Someone to Watch Over Me
'87
Gilbert Roland
Around the World in 80 Days
'56
The Bad and the Beautiful '52
The Sea Hawk '40
She Done Him Wrong '33
Thunder Bay '53
Esther Rolle
Driving Miss Daisy '89
I Know Why the Caged Bird
Sings '79
To Dance with the White Dog
'93
Howard E. Rollins, Jr.
King '78
Ragtime '81
A Soldier's Story '84
Ruth Roman
Champion '49
Far Country '55
Since You Went Away '44
Strangers on a Train '51
The Window '49
Beatrice Romand
Claire's Knee '71
Le Beau Mariage '82
Summer '86
Cesar Romero
Around the World in 80 Days
'56
Donovan's Reef '63
Julia Misbehaves '48
The Little Princess '39
Lust in the Dust '85
Orchestra Wives '42
The Thin Man '34
Wee Willie Winkie '37
Michael Rooker
Cliffhanger '93
Eight Men Out '88
Henry: Portrait of a Serial
Killer '90
JFK '91

Mississippi Burning '88
Sea of Love '89
Mickey Rooney
The Adventures of
Huckleberry Finn '39
Ah, Wilderness! '35
Bill '81
Bill: On His Own '83
The Black Stallion '79
Boys Town '38
Breakfast at Tiffany's '61
The Bridges at Toko-Ri '55
Captains Courageous '37
Girl Crazy '43
The Human Comedy '43
Life Begins for Andy Hardy
'41
Little Lord Fauntleroy '36
Love Finds Andy Hardy '38
Manhattan Melodrama '34
A Midsummer Night's Dream
'35
National Velvet '44
Francoise Rosay
Bizarre Bizarre '39
Carnival in Flanders '35
The Pedestrian '73
Katharine Ross
Butch Cassidy and the
Sundance Kid '69
The Graduate '67
Shenandoah '65
Tell Them Willie Boy Is Here
'69
Voyage of the Damned '76
Isabella Rossellini
Blue Velvet '86
Death Becomes Her '92
Fallen Angels 1 '93
Fearless '93
The Funeral '96
Wild at Heart '90
Tim Roth
The Cook, the Thief, His Wife
& Her Lover '90
Pulp Fiction '94
Reservoir Dogs '92
Rob Roy '95
Rosencrantz & Guildenstern
Are Dead '90
Vincent & Theo '90
A World Apart '88
Richard Roundtree
Once Upon a Time . . . When
We Were Colored '95
Seven '95
Shaft '71
Mickey Rourke
Barfly '87
Body Heat '81
Diner '82
Johnny Handsome '89
Rumble Fish '83
Gena Rowlands
Another Woman '88
A Child Is Waiting '63
An Early Frost '85
Faces '68
Lonely Are the Brave '62
Night on Earth '91
Strangers: The Story of a
Mother and Daughter '79

599 • CAST INDEX ▲

Diane Venora
Bird '88
The Cotton Club '84
F/X '86
Heat '95
Ironweed '87
William Shakespeare's Romeo and Juliet '96
Richard Venture
The Effect of Gamma Rays on Man-in-the-Moon Marigolds '73
Missing '82
Scent of a Woman '92
Gwen Verdon
Alice '90
Cocoon '85
The Cotton Club '84
Damn Yankees '58
Oldest Confederate Widow Tells All '95
Karen Verne
All Through the Night '42
Kings Row '41
The Seventh Cross '44
Sherlock Holmes and the Secret Weapon '42
John Vernon
Charley Varrick '73
Dirty Harry '71
I'm Gonna Git You Sucka '88
National Lampoon's Animal House '78
The Outlaw Josey Wales '76
Tell Them Willie Boy Is Here '69
Abe Vigoda
The Godfather '72
The Godfather 1902-1959: The Complete Epic '81
The Godfather, Part 2 '74
Look Who's Talking '89
James Villiers
Mountains of the Moon '90
Repulsion '65
The Scarlet Pimpernel '82
Pruitt Taylor Vince
Mississippi Burning '88
Nobody's Fool '94
Shy People '87
Frank Vincent
Goodfellas '90
Jungle Fever '91
Raging Bull '80
Monica Vitti
The Eclipse '66
L'Avventura '60
Phantom of Liberty '74
The Red Desert '64
Ruediger Vogler
Alice in the Cities '74
Kings of the Road—In the Course of Time '76
Marianne and Juliane '82
Jon Voight
Catch-22 '70
Coming Home '78
Deliverance '72
Desert Bloom '86
Heat '95
Midnight Cowboy '69
Mission: Impossible '96

Runaway Train '85
Gian Marie Volonte
Christ Stopped at Eboli '79
A Fistful of Dollars '64
Open Doors '89
Erich von Stroheim
As You Desire Me '32
The Birth of a Nation '15
Blind Husbands '19
Foolish Wives '22
Grand Illusion '37
Hearts of the World '18
Intolerance '16
The North Star '43
Sunset Boulevard '50
The Wedding March '28
Max von Sydow
Awakenings '90
The Best Intentions '92
Citizen X '95
Conan the Barbarian '82
The Emigrants '72
The Exorcist '73
Hannah and Her Sisters '86
Hiroshima: Out of the Ashes '90
Hour of the Wolf '68
The Magician '58
The Passion of Anna '70
Pelle the Conqueror '88
The Quiller Memorandum '66
The Seventh Seal '56
The Shame '68
Three Days of the Condor '75
Through a Glass Darkly '61
The Virgin Spring '59
Voyage of the Damned '76
Wild Strawberries '57
The Winter Light '62
Robert Wagner
Broken Lance '54
Dragon: The Bruce Lee Story '93
Harper '66
The Longest Day '62
The Pink Panther '64
The Player '92
The Streets of San Francisco '72
Titanic '53
What Price Glory? '52
Winning '69
Ralph Waite
Cliffhanger '93
Cool Hand Luke '67
Five Easy Pieces '70
The Grissom Gang '71
Tom Waits
The Cotton Club '84
Down by Law '86
Ironweed '87
Rumble Fish '83
Short Cuts '93
Anton Walbrook
The Forty-Ninth Parallel '41
Gaslight '39
La Ronde '51
The Life and Death of Colonel Blimp '43
Lola Montes '55
The Red Shoes '48

Raymond Walburn
Christmas in July '40
The Count of Monte Cristo '34
Hail the Conquering Hero '44
Mr. Deeds Goes to Town '36
Christopher Walken
Annie Hall '77
At Close Range '86
Basquiat '96
The Comfort of Strangers '91
Dead Zone '83
The Deer Hunter '78
The Funeral '96
King of New York '90
The Milagro Beanfield War '88
Next Stop, Greenwich Village '76
Pennies from Heaven '81
Pulp Fiction '94
Sarah, Plain and Tall '91
Things to Do in Denver When You're Dead '95
Robert Walker
The Clock '45
Madame Curie '43
Since You Went Away '44
Strangers on a Train '51
Thirty Seconds Over Tokyo '44
Till the Clouds Roll By/A Star Is Born '46
Max Wall
Little Dorrit, Film 1: Nobody's Fault '88
Little Dorrit, Film 2: Little Dorrit's Story '88
We Think the World of You '88
George Wallace
Defending Your Life '91
Forbidden Planet '56
A Rage in Harlem '91
Eli Wallach
Baby Doll '56
Cinderella Liberty '73
Girlfriends '78
The Godfather, Part 3 '90
The Good, the Bad and the Ugly '67
How the West Was Won '63
How to Steal a Million '66
Lord Jim '65
The Magnificent Seven '60
The Misfits '61
Night and the City '92
Seven Thieves '60
J.T. Walsh
A Few Good Men '92
Good Morning, Vietnam '87
The Grifters '90
Hoffa '92
The Last Seduction '94
Nixon '95
Red Rock West '93
Kay Walsh
The Horse's Mouth '58
In Which We Serve '42
Oliver Twist '48
Stage Fright '50
This Happy Breed '47
Tunes of Glory '60
Young Bess '53

M. Emmet Walsh
Blade Runner '82
Blood Simple '85
Clean and Sober '88
The Deliberate Stranger '86
The Milagro Beanfield War '88
Ordinary People '80
Raising Arizona '87
Reds '81
They Might Be Giants '71
A Time to Kill '96
William Shakespeare's Romeo and Juliet '96
Ray Walston
The Apartment '60
Damn Yankees '58
Fast Times at Ridgemont High '82
Of Mice and Men '92
Silver Streak '76
South Pacific '58
The Sting '73
Tracey Walter
At Close Range '86
Batman '89
City Slickers '91
Married to the Mob '88
Matilda '96
Philadelphia '93
Repo Man '83
Julie Walters
Educating Rita '83
Prick Up Your Ears '87
The Wedding Gift '93
Henry B. Walthall
The Birth of a Nation '15
Judge Priest '34
Judith of Bethulia '14
Strange Interlude '32
A Tale of Two Cities '35
Viva Villa! '34
Sam Wanamaker
The Spy Who Came in from the Cold '65
Those Magnificent Men in Their Flying Machines '65
Voyage of the Damned '76
Fred Ward
Bob Roberts '92
Escape from Alcatraz '79
Henry & June '90
The Player '92
The Right Stuff '83
Short Cuts '93
Silkwood '83
Southern Comfort '81
Simon Ward
The Four Musketeers '75
If... '69
The Three Musketeers '74
Young Winston '72
Zulu Dawn '79
Jack Warden
The Apprenticeship of Duddy Kravitz '74
Being There '79
Brian's Song '71
Bullets Over Broadway '94
Donovan's Reef '63
From Here to Eternity '53
The Great Muppet Caper '81
Heaven Can Wait '78

Night and the City '92
Raid on Entebbe '77
Run Silent, Run Deep '58
Things to Do in Denver When You're Dead '95
Twelve Angry Men '57
Used Cars '80
The Verdict '82
While You Were Sleeping '95
David Warner
Ballad of Cable Hogue '70
The Company of Wolves '85
Holocaust '78
Masada '81
Providence '77
Rasputin: Dark Servant of Destiny '96
Straw Dogs '72
Time After Time '79
Tom Jones '63
H.B. Warner
The Devil & Daniel Webster '41
Hitler's Children '43
It's a Wonderful Life '46
Lost Horizon '37
Mr. Deeds Goes to Town '36
Mr. Smith Goes to Washington '39
A Tale of Two Cities '35
The Ten Commandments '56
Topper Returns '41
You Can't Take It with You '38
Jack Warner
The Blue Lamp '49
A Christmas Carol '51
The Quatermass Experiment '56
Robert Warwick
The Awful Truth '37
Hopalong Cassidy '35
Sullivan's Travels '41
A Woman's Face '41
Mona Washbourne
Brideshead Revisited '81
The Collector '65
If... '69
My Fair Lady '64
O Lucky Man! '73
Denzel Washington
Courage Under Fire '96
Crimson Tide '95
Devil in a Blue Dress '95
Glory '89
Malcolm X '92
Much Ado about Nothing '93
Philadelphia '93
A Soldier's Story '84
Craig Wasson
Body Double '84
Go Tell the Spartans '78
Malcolm X '92
Ethel Waters
Cabin in the Sky '43
The Member of the Wedding '52
Pinky '49
Sam Waterston
Crimes & Misdemeanors '89
Friendly Fire '79
Hannah and Her Sisters '86
Interiors '78

The Killing Fields '84
The Man in the Moon '91
Serial Mom '94
Bobby Watson
The Band Wagon '53
Captains Courageous '37
Show Boat '36
Lucile Watson
The Great Lie '41
Julia Misbehaves '48
Made for Each Other '39
Mr. & Mrs. Smith '41
Waterloo Bridge '40
The Women '39
Minor Watson
Abe Lincoln in Illinois '40
The Jackie Robinson Story '50
Western Union '41
Woman of the Year '42
Wylie Watson
Brighton Rock '47
The Sundowners '60
The 39 Steps '35
David Wayne
Adam's Rib '50
The Last Angry Man '59
Portrait of Jennie '48
The Three Faces of Eve '57
John Wayne
The Alamo '60
Angel and the Badman '47
Big Trail '30
The Comancheros '61
The Cowboys '72
Dark Command '40
Donovan's Reef '63
El Dorado '67
Flying Leathernecks '51
Fort Apache '48
Hondo '53
How the West Was Won '63
The Long Voyage Home '40
The Longest Day '62
The Man Who Shot Liberty Valance '62
The Quiet Man '52
Red River '48
Rio Bravo '59
Rio Grande '50
Sands of Iwo Jima '49
The Searchers '56
Seven Sinners '40
She Wore a Yellow Ribbon '49
The Shootist '76
Sons of Katie Elder '65
Stagecoach '39
They Were Expendable '45
Three Godfathers '48
True Grit '69
The War Wagon '67
Patrick Wayne
Mister Roberts '55
The Searchers '56
Shenandoah '65
Dennis Weaver
Duel '71
Duel at Diablo '66
The Gallant Hours '60
Touch of Evil '58
Fritz Weaver
Demon Seed '77

DIRECTOR INDEX

The Director Index contains listings for every director making at least three three- and four-star video creations selected for this book. The directors are listed alphabetically by last names; each director is followed by the corresponding three- and four-star movie and year of production.

Jim Abrahams
Airplane! '80
Hot Shots! '91
Ruthless People '86
Robert Aldrich
The Big Knife '55
The Dirty Dozen '67
The Flight of the Phoenix '65
The Grissom Gang '71
Hush, Hush, Sweet Charlotte '64
Kiss Me Deadly '55
Ulzana's Raid '72
What Ever Happened to Baby Jane? '62
Woody Allen
Alice '90
Annie Hall '77
Another Woman '88
Bananas '71
Broadway Danny Rose '84
Bullets Over Broadway '94
Crimes & Misdemeanors '89
Everything You Always Wanted to Know about Sex (But Were Afraid to Ask) '72
Hannah and Her Sisters '86
Husbands and Wives '92
Interiors '78
Love and Death '75
Manhattan '79
Manhattan Murder Mystery '93
A Midsummer Night's Sex Comedy '82
New York Stories '89
The Purple Rose of Cairo '85
Radio Days '87
Sleeper '73
Take the Money and Run '69
What's Up, Tiger Lily? '66
Zelig '83
Pedro Almodovar
The Flower of My Secret '95
High Heels '91

Law of Desire '86
Women on the Verge of a Nervous Breakdown '88
Robert Altman
Brewster McCloud '70
Buffalo Bill & the Indians '76
Come Back to the Five & Dime Jimmy Dean, Jimmy Dean '82
Kansas City '95
The Long Goodbye '73
M*A*S*H '70
McCabe & Mrs. Miller '71
Nashville '75
The Player '92
Short Cuts '93
Thieves Like Us '74
Vincent & Theo '90
Gianni Amelio
Lamerica '95
Open Doors '89
The Stolen Children '92
Lindsay Anderson
If . . . '69
O Lucky Man! '73
This Sporting Life '63
The Whales of August '87
Ken Annakin
The Longest Day '62
The Swiss Family Robinson '60
Those Magnificent Men in Their Flying Machines '65
Jean-Jacques Annaud
The Bear '89
Black and White in Color '76
Quest for Fire '82
Michelangelo Antonioni
Blow-Up '66
The Eclipse '66
L'Avventura '60
The Passenger '75
The Red Desert '64
Zabriskie Point '70

Michael Apted
Coal Miner's Daughter '80
Gorillas in the Mist '88
Incident at Oglala: The Leonard Peltier Story '92
Gillian Armstrong
High Tide '87
Little Women '94
My Brilliant Career '79
Jack Arnold
Creature from the Black Lagoon '54
The Incredible Shrinking Man '57
It Came from Outer Space '53
Marilyn: The Untold Story '80
The Mouse That Roared '59
Hal Ashby
Being There '79
Bound for Glory '76
Coming Home '78
Harold and Maude '71
The Last Detail '73
Anthony Asquith
The Browning Version '51
Carrington, V.C. '54
Importance of Being Earnest '52
Pygmalion '38
The V.I.P.'s '63
We Dive at Dawn '43
The Winslow Boy '48
Richard Attenborough
Chaplin '92
Gandhi '82
Shadowlands '93
Young Winston '72
Bille August
The Best Intentions '92
Pelle the Conqueror '88
Twist & Shout '84
John G. Avildsen
The Karate Kid '84
Rocky '76
Save the Tiger '73

You Can't Cheat an Honest Man '39
Penny Marshall
Awakenings '90
Big '88
A League of Their Own '92
Archie Mayo
Angel on My Shoulder '46
Orchestra Wives '42
Petrified Forest '36
Svengali '31
Paul Mazursky
Blume in Love '73
Enemies, a Love Story '89
Harry and Tonto '74
Next Stop, Greenwich Village '76
An Unmarried Woman '78
Leo McCarey
The Awful Truth '37
The Bells of St. Mary's '45
Duck Soup '33
Going My Way '44
Love Affair '39
Ruggles of Red Gap '35
Norman Z. McLeod
Horse Feathers '32
It's a Gift '34
Monkey Business '31
The Paleface '48
The Road to Rio '47
The Secret Life of Walter Mitty '47
Topper '37
Topper Takes a Trip '39
Peter Medak
The Krays '90
Let Him Have It '91
The Ruling Class '72
Bill Melendez
Bon Voyage, Charlie Brown '80
A Boy Named Charlie Brown '70
Snoopy, Come Home '72
Jean-Pierre Melville
Bob le Flambeur '55
Le Doulos '61
Les Enfants Terrible '50
Nicholas Meyer
The Day After '83
Star Trek 2: The Wrath of Khan '82
Time After Time '79
Nikita Mikhalkov
Burnt by the Sun '94
Dark Eyes '87
Oblomov '81
Lewis Milestone
All Quiet on the Western Front '30
Edge of Darkness '43
The Front Page '31
The General Died at Dawn '36
The North Star '43
Of Mice and Men '39
Pork Chop Hill '59
The Red Pony '49
The Strange Love of Martha Ivers '46
A Walk in the Sun '46

George Miller
Lorenzo's Oil '92
Mad Max '80
The Road Warrior '82
Vincente Minnelli
An American in Paris '51
The Bad and the Beautiful '52
The Band Wagon '53
Bells Are Ringing '60
Brigadoon '54
Cabin in the Sky '43
The Clock '45
The Courtship of Eddie's Father '62
Designing Woman '57
Father of the Bride '50
Father's Little Dividend '51
Gigi '58
Home from the Hill '60
Lust for Life '56
Madame Bovary '49
Meet Me in St. Louis '44
The Pirate '48
The Reluctant Debutante '58
Some Came Running '58
Tea and Sympathy '56
Kenji Mizoguchi
The Crucified Lovers '54
47 Ronin, Part 1 '42
47 Ronin, Part 2 '42
Life of Oharu '52
Princess Yang Kwei Fei '55
Sansho the Bailiff '54
Shin Heike Monogatari '55
Sisters of Gion '36
The Story of the Late Chrysanthemum '39
Street of Shame '56
Ugetsu '53
Robert Mulligan
Fear Strikes Out '57
Love with the Proper Stranger '63
The Man in the Moon '91
The Rat Race '60
Same Time, Next Year '78
Summer of '42 '71
To Kill a Mockingbird '62
Up the Down Staircase '67
F.W. Murnau
Faust '26
The Haunted Castle '21
The Last Laugh '24
Nosferatu '22
Sunrise '27
Tabu: A Story of the South Seas '31
Ronald Neame
The Chalk Garden '64
The Horse's Mouth '58
The Prime of Miss Jean Brodie '69
Tunes of Glory '60
Jean Negulesco
The Best of Everything '59
Daddy Long Legs '55
Humoresque '46
Johnny Belinda '48
Three Came Home '50
Titanic '53
A Woman's World '54

Roy William Neill
The Black Room '35
Scarlet Claw '44
Sherlock Holmes and the Secret Weapon '42
Spider Woman '44
Ralph Nelson
Charly '68
Duel at Diablo '66
Lilies of the Field '63
Requiem for a Heavyweight '56
Paul Newman
The Effect of Gamma Rays on Man-in-the-Moon Marigolds '73
The Glass Menagerie '87
Rachel, Rachel '68
The Shadow Box '80
Sometimes a Great Notion '71
Fred Niblo
Ben-Hur '26
Mark of Zorro '20
The Three Musketeers '21
Mike Nichols
The Birdcage '95
Carnal Knowledge '71
Catch-22 '70
Gin Game '84
The Graduate '67
Postcards from the Edge '90
Silkwood '83
Who's Afraid of Virginia Woolf? '66
Working Girl '88
Laurence Olivier
Hamlet '48
Henry V '44
Richard III '55
Max Ophuls
Caught '49
The Earrings of Madame De . . . '54
La Ronde '51
La Signora di Tutti '34
Letter from an Unknown Woman '48
Lola Montes '55
Reckless Moment '49
Nagisa Oshima
The Empire of Passion '76
In the Realm of the Senses '76
Merry Christmas, Mr. Lawrence '83
The Sun's Burial '60
Violence at Noon '66
Frank Oz
Dirty Rotten Scoundrels '88
Little Shop of Horrors '86
The Muppets Take Manhattan '84
Yasujiro Ozu
An Autumn Afternoon '62
Drifting Weeds '59
Early Summer '51
Late Spring '49
Tokyo Story '53
G.W. Pabst
Diary of a Lost Girl '29
Don Quixote '35

IF YOU LIKED THE *VIDEOHOUND'S GUIDE TO THREE- AND FOUR-STAR MOVIES 1998*, YOU'LL ALSO ENJOY THE ALL-INCLUSIVE *VIDEOHOUND'S GOLDEN MOVIE RETRIEVER 1998*.

1,700 pages • 1001 Categories • 13 Indexes

"The best thing to come out of Detroit since the Supremes. Leonard Maltin, watch your behind."
— *New York Post*

"You get the most for your money... plus plenty of chutzpah."
— *USA Today*

"If one can't find a video film in this book, it probably isn't worth finding."
— *The Ottawa Citizen*

"Worth its weight in rental fees."
— *Staten Island Advance*

"Highly recommended."
— *Video Store*

AVAILABLE IN BOOKSTORES NOW.